JOHN DEERE'S COMPANY

A HISTORY OF DEERE & COMPANY AND ITS TIMES

WAYNE G. BROEHL, JR.

DOUBLEDAY & COMPANY, INC.

The author is grateful to the following for kind permission to reprint material as noted below.

Two cartoons and photograph from *Farm Implement News* (August 4, 1910; September 23, 1920; November 21, 1929). Copyright © Intertec Publishing Corporation, Overland Park, Kansas, reprinted by permission.

Two line drawings from Percy W. Bidwell and John I. Falconer, *History of Agriculture in the Northern United States: 1620–1860.* Copyright © Carnegie Institution of Washington, reprinted by permission.

Two tables from Fred Shannon, *The Farmer's Last Frontier.* Copyright © Estate of Fred Shannon, reprinted by permission.

Table from Lester Larson, *Farm Tractors: 1950–1975.* Copyright © American Society of Agricultural Engineers, reprinted by permission.

Library of Congress Cataloging in Publication Data

Broehl, Wayne G.
   John Deere's Company.

   Bibliography
   Includes index.
1. Deere & company—History.   2. Deere, John, 1804–1886.   3. Industrialists—United States—Biography.   4. Agricultural machinery industry—United States—History.   I. Title.
   D94 6.U6D39   1984   338.7'681763'0973
ISBN 0-385-196641-14 (Doubleday)

Library of Congress Catalog Card Number 84-6023

ACKNOWLEDGEMENTS

Any study as complex as this book involves major debts to others. A host of them is owed here, and I wish to directly acknowledge a few, recognizing that there were many other significant contributions.

A business history typically involves a single firm, in this case Deere & Company. Cooperation of living executives, line employees, and retirees can be fundamentally useful in preparation of such a book. Deere & Company recognized from the start the wisdom of engaging an outside scholar and allowing him to view the company at arm's length, for only with such independence can an objective study be accomplished. Deere management exhibited a keen sense of this requirement, their single caveat being that, given the highly competitive nature of the agricultural machinery industry, no future product information prematurely be made available. In order to retain this arm's length relationship, it was agreed that there would be no financial relationship between me and the company. Instead, Deere made a grant to Dartmouth College, and the research and writing of this study was a formal project of the Research Program at the Amos Tuck School of Business Administration at the college. For their perception of, and enthusiasm for, this basic principle of a sound independent business history, I owe particular thanks to the three members of the Deere chairman's office at that time—William Hewitt, chairman and chief executive officer, Ellwood Curtis, vice chairman, and Robert Hanson, president. All three were profoundly helpful in my research; the objectivity of the manuscript would not have been the same without their unstinting cooperation.

A number of other Deere personnel read the entire manuscript, in the process helping to ensure that it was as free of factual errors as possible. Two people were particularly helpful in this regard: Dr. Leslie Stegh, the archivist, and Elizabeth Denkhoff, corporate secretary for the company. Walter Vogel, Boyd Bartlett, Robert Boeke, Robert Weeks, Curtis Tarr, and Joseph K. Hanson, Jr., also reviewed the entire manuscript. Commenting on key sections were James Davis, Thomas Gildehaus, Gordon Millar, Neel Hall, Joseph Dain, Clifford Peterson, George Neiley, and Roy Harrington. A number of retirees of the company provided valuable insights; particularly to be mentioned are George French, the late Edmond Cook, and William Bennett. Ruth Moll, curator for the William Butterworth Foundation, contributed important insights from her personal relations with William Butterworth and his family, and Kay Vogel, curator of the Deere-Wiman House was also helpful. Dr. Herbert Morton and Barbara A. Standley ably edited the manuscript, and the transition from manuscript to book was aided measurably by Kenneth McCormick, Chester Lasell and Wayne Burkart. The entire staff of the archives department of the company was involved importantly in the project; the contributions of Vicki Eller, Ann Lee, and Nancy Swanson were particularly helpful. A number of executives in other companies in the industry, as well as in the industry association, the Farm and Industrial Equipment Institute, contributed valuable insights; I particularly want to recognize the help of Greg Lennes at the International Harvester Company Archives, and David Crippen at the Greenfield Village & Henry Ford Museum. Pat Greathouse, international vice president at the United Automobile, Aircraft and Machine Workers (AFL-CIO) was invaluable to my gaining perspective on the labor relations of the farm equipment industry.

The list of research librarians who have helped me at one stage or another of this project is very long indeed. I especially wish to thank those at the Vermont Historical Society, the Sheldon Museum in Middlebury, Vermont, the University of Vermont, the Illinois State Historical Society, the Chicago Historical Society, the State Historical Society of Iowa, the Minnesota Historical Society, the State Historical Society of Missouri, and the F. Hal Higgins Library of Agricultural Technology at the University of California, Davis. Significant research materials were also studied at the Worcester Polytechnic Institute. Finally, my debts to the Baker Library of Harvard Business School and to my own colleagues in the Baker Library of Dartmouth College and the Amos Tuck School of Business Administration Library are important.

A number of my academic colleagues read significant sections of this book. Prof. Alfred D. Chandler, Jr., of Harvard Business School, reviewed a number of chapters, and his perceptive suggestions aided the manuscript at an important point. Dr. Glenn Leggett, president emeritus of Grinnell College, was most influential at the early stages of the book. Prof. Fred Carstensen of the University of Connecticut also made significant contributions. My own Tuck School colleague, Dr. David Bradley, likewise helped at a critical point in the manuscript. My research assistant, Barbara Morin, was indispensable to me throughout the project. I would also like to thank Mrs. William Hewitt for her insights about her father, Charles Deere Wiman, and for aiding my understanding of the Deere family relationship to the business.

Finally, a profound thanks for those people who loyally aided the preparation of the many drafts of the manuscript: Eleanor Lackey, Joan Adams, Frances Moffitt, and Suzanne Sweet.

CONTENTS

PART I
OPENING THE PRAIRIE
THE JOHN DEERE YEARS
(1837–59)

PART II
MARKETING AND MANUFACTURING
IN AN EXPANSIONIST AGE:
THE CHARLES DEERE YEARS
(1860–1907)

PART III
CONSOLIDATION AND CONTROL:
THE WILLIAM BUTTERWORTH YEARS
(1908–27)

PART V
WORLDWIDE CORPORATION:
THE WILLIAM HEWITT YEARS
(1955–82)

CONCLUSION

INTRODUCTION

John Deere is an authentic American folk hero, whose legend began in his own lifetime when, in 1837, he developed a steel plow that cut without sticking through the rich prairie soil of the Midwest. Today he is remembered as the person "who gave to the world the steel plow." One of his first three plows now stands on exhibit at the Smithsonian Institution. For more than 145 years, Deere & Company has provided agricultural machinery for the farmers of North America and, since about the turn of the century, for much of the rest of the globe, too. Since the early 1960s, it has been the largest agricultural machinery manufacturer in the world. For many years the relationship between the farmer and the distinctive green Deere tractor in his field has been uniquely symbiotic.

Only a small number of American businesses today have had a life extending back to a period before the Civil War. Those that do, in the main, are successful businesses. Those that did not survive—weakened by recurring business cycles, changing tastes, or inept leadership—were taken over, liquidated, or forced into bankruptcy. Many more famous names of yesteryear were obliterated in mergers and other corporate vicissitudes.

This book chronicles the history of one of America's oldest business firms. John Deere's company did not begin or grow in isolation, and its story can be told and understood only within the changing historical setting in which it struggled. The Deere chronicle is played out within the context of a century and a half of social, economic, and technological change—the emigration of New Englanders to the prairie states, widespread economic destabilizations beginning with the Panic of 1857, the onrush of the Westward Movement, and the burgeoning of the commercial centers, towns, and villages of the breadbasket of the nation. The Grangers interacted with the manufacturers in a convoluted relationship; Charles Deere, the founder's son, stepped into the middle of a controversy there. The trust movement deeply affected the company just before the turn of the century; a giant combination was formed by the industry leader, and Deere was pushed to stay competitive. After prosperous days during World War I, the company and the industry again suffered severely in the post-war depression. The "farm problem" of the 1930s provided another setback. World War II and the three decades that followed were upbeat, but the worldwide depression of the early 1980s brought renewed trauma and fierce international competition, with "the Japanese challenge" in the forefront.

Deere & Company has been a family concern for most of its existence. In its early years it was a partnership and later, from 1868, a corporation; both were owned throughout the nineteenth century almost entirely by the Deere family. In the twentieth century—as the company's stock first began to be dispersed into the hands of various descendants, and later to others through public offerings—the family relinquished its voting control of the corporation. Nevertheless, for its key management, the company was led until 1982 by members of the Deere family. Remarkably, during the entire 145-year period of family control, there were only five chief executive officers.

A successful corporate life of such duration teaches many lessons. There had to have been a number of correct decisions—this seems self-evident—but there were setbacks, too. Agriculture itself has had a recurring pattern of ups and downs; the capital goods industries serving it have been forced to innovate and adapt in order to serve the agriculturalist over the years of both prosperity and depression. Deere's decision-making process in the face of this complexity is well documented by the words and actions of the participants, and the story of its development should prove not only valuable to analysts of management practice but also interesting to the general reader.

This book begins with the mature years of John Deere, who emigrated from Vermont in 1837 to found a small blacksmith shop in the tiny village of Grand Detour, on the northern prairie of Illinois. He had had a similar operation for a number of years in Vermont, but the Panic of 1837 had forced him to run out on debts and try his fortune, along with thousands of other emigrating Vermonters, in the great Westward Movement of the early nineteenth century. This was a period of rapid growth for farming in the Midwest and of an expanding role for the agricultural implement manufacturers. Those that had good products and the marketing skills to make their products known made great progress. Deere's own version of the steel plow—in truth, his was only one of many—was produced and marketed with such flair that he soon was one of the best-known plow producers of the area. After moving from the tiny town to Moline, a larger city on the Mississippi River, he widened his operation into a major plow and harrow establishment, operating under several different partnerships with several different people over a decade or so. Another panic in 1857 forced many, including John Deere, to the brink of bankruptcy, but Deere was saved by the help of friends and the financial acumen of his young son, Charles.

Charles Deere dominates the scene from just before the Civil War to after the turn of the century. During his tenure, the partnership was changed to a corporate form, and product development, scheduling, pricing, and warranties all were regularized as the firm expanded its operations throughout the Midwest, the South, the Plains States, and the Far West. New endeavors—wagons, buggies, corn planters—entered the product line in this period to complement the plows and harrows. But it was in marketing, particularly, that Charles Deere's business judgment shone most brilliantly. He instituted new concepts for older, traditional distribution mechanisms. Especially important were the semiautonomous branch houses, which gave the firm the fast growth and customer acceptance that soon made Deere the largest plow manufacturer in the world. The late nineteenth century was also a period of "big business" developments, with new forms of combinations and trusts; in turn, public outcry triggered the passage of antitrust laws and other constraints. Charles Deere assiduously pursued a major "plow trust"; failing in this, he drew together and centralized a larger Deere & Company, shortly after the turn of the century.

William Butterworth, a young lawyer, took over the company after the death of his father-in-law, Charles Deere, in 1907. The firm first was expanded into what came to be known as "the modern company," with the addition of several other agricultural machinery manufacturers. These brought to Deere hay tools, grain drills, chilled plows, and a number of other related products. Deere's arch-competitor during this period was the newly formed combination of several companies in the field of harvesting equipment, the International Harvester Company. At one point early in Butterworth's tenure as chief executive officer, discussions were held between Deere and International Harvester about merging the two organizations. This fell through, and Butterworth and his colleagues turned to developing Deere's own harvesting equipment. New, strong personalities came into the business at this time and the operation flourished throughout World War I. Perhaps the most important policy move of the time was the decision, taken after much argument and tension among management, to begin manufacturing a tractor with an internal combustion engine. A small company making a tractor called the "Waterloo Boy" was purchased, and Deere began making its own tractors.

The postwar period was difficult in several respects. First, the Federal Trade Commission launched an extensive investigation of the agricultural machinery industry. Although the principal target was International Harvester, then the giant of its kind, the effects of the investigation were felt throughout the industry. A second difficult problem came with the acute business downturn in 1920–21. Butterworth and his colleagues were forced to revamp the company's management structure and take many stringent actions to avert a debacle.

Charles Deere's grandson (William Butterworth's nephew), Charles Wiman, came to the company at the beginning of World War I. After being seasoned in the business through the 1920s, Wiman was appointed president of the company in 1928, while Butterworth kept the role of chairman and elder statesman for the organization. A trained engineer, Wiman led the company through a deep depression in the early and mid-1930s. Deere's relations with its customers during this period were stronger than ever; the company made a key policy decision to allow a great many farmer receivables to stay in place, held in abeyance when the customers could not pay. This belief in the farmers' integrity succeeded in heightening an already fabled farmer loyalty to Deere.

New farm legislation later in the 1930s, coupled with brightening prospects in agriculture, soon put the industry back on its feet. At this time, Deere and the Caterpillar Tractor Company made common cause by marketing some of the Deere equipment through joint dealerships (a practice that continued well into the 1950s). With World War II, Deere was called upon for a wide range of war products, Wiman himself serving as a colonel in the Ordnance Department of the United States Army. (His close confidant and company counsel, Burton Peek, acted as company president in the interim.) Because of Wiman's abiding interest in product development—evidenced all through the 1930s, when such interests were difficult to afford—the company came through the wartime period with a set of products that were outstanding in the field. Deere's tractors at that time, though, were still powered by two-cylinder engines, while the other companies in the industry were increasingly selling four- and six-cylinder versions. The familiar Deere two-cylinder "Poppin' Johnnies" were very simple and rugged and were great favorites with the farmers, but Wiman came to believe that a shift to a larger-cylinder tractor was inevitable. The decision was made late in his tenure, in 1953, to carry through the necessary product development for this change. Wiman also had experience once again with the government, when the United States Department of Justice decided to prosecute three companies in the industry for antitrust violations. The government's attorneys picked the J.I. Case Company to try first, with Deere to be the next defendant. The government lost the first case in the courts, however, and the whole antitrust campaign was dropped.

In the mid-1950s, Charles Wiman learned that he had a terminal illness, and he decided to bring his son-in-law, William Hewitt, into senior management in the newly created post of executive vice president. Hewitt had worked in the company for a number of years, but he had been with the central organization only a short time. Upon Wiman's death, Hewitt was appointed president and chief executive officer.

It was a fortuitous choice, for in the Hewitt period, from 1955 to 1982, the company experienced impressive growth and financial success. Hewitt managed the process of bringing the new four- and six-cylinder tractors into the Deere line. Seven years of development culminated in a spectacular introduction of the models—called "the New Generation of Power"—at a noteworthy dealer show in Dallas in 1960.

Hewitt also made an early decision to carry the company much more widely into the international sphere. An old-line German tractor manufacturer, Heinrich Lanz, was purchased, and Deere began to "learn the ropes" of doing business abroad. The company experienced more than a decade of difficulties and losses, which led it to consider the feasibility of merging its international operations with those of a stronger foreign company. There were particularly extended negotiations with Fiat, the Italian company, in 1970–71, but just about this time Deere's own operations turned the corner, and a merger was no longer attractive.

Indeed, Deere's international operations became major contributors to company revenues. In the 1970s, the company expanded widely around the world, enlarging its early endeavors in Mexico and Argentina, extending its efforts throughout Western Europe (with a particularly important manufacturing operation in France, and another in Spain), and also expanding around the rest of the globe. A small South African operation became an excellent success; a joint effort with an Australian company has been mutually beneficial. The company carried initiatives to the People's Republic of China and to Middle Eastern countries, and it also attempted, with little success, to sell from time to time to the Soviet bloc. An important bond was made with a Japanese concern, the Yanmar Diesel Engine Company, in the late 1970s. A joint venture was organized to develop a set of Japanese-built small tractors to be marketed under the John Deere name, these to complement the larger tractors that the company already was making in North America and in Europe.

Product diversification was encouraged, too, first with an industrial equipment division (light and medium earthmoving, forestry, and construction machines), then with a consumer products division, carrying the Deere logo (lawn and garden tractors, snow blowers, and similar products). Insurance and financial services divisions also contributed to their diversification.

Many challenges emerged in the early 1980s. A worldwide recession brought renewed threats to the industry, serious enough to almost bankrupt several other competitors, including the old arch-rival, International Harvester. Deere itself had to retrench, but not before the company had refurbished its capital equipment and physical plant in the late 1970s.

Deere & Company's history is notable for providing insights into the management process, particularly regarding organizational structure and the role of decentralized operations in building individuality and independence among management personnel. The firm has been characterized throughout most of its existence by a bent toward entrepreneurship and innovation. Yet this commitment to individuality has always been framed within overall corporate goals and an abiding concern for quality. The firm's continuity of operation in the face of difficulty, aided by a keen sense of the longer run, has given it a stability and steadiness critical in an industry that has been inherently cyclical—and in a world of unpredictable challenges.

This story of a durable family-oriented organization exemplifies the values of a closely held operation, as well as the disabilities and difficulties of such an approach. The company has recently turned outside the family for its senior management. No longer a "family-led" operation, it entered a new era under the leadership of Robert A. Hanson with a firm focus on the virtues of close cooperation and a family orientation among its employees.

PART I

OPENING THE PRAIRIE:
THE
JOHN DEERE YEARS
(1837–59)

CHAPTER 1

VERMONTERS' WAY WEST

My Deare Son
I am now in expectation to of embarking for England the first fair wind . . .
be Dutifull to your mother Kind to your Sister & Brothers
have the fear of god before you implore his protection & you will obtain it
and likewise the good will of all mankind.

WR Deere

◁*Owl's Head landing, Lake Memphremagog, Vt., (Bettmann Archive)*

Blacksmith John Deere faced a troubling decision in November 1836. Five years earlier, at the small Vermont crossroads village of Leicester Four Corners, he had opened a blacksmith shop with the support of a silent partner, Jay Wright. Ill fortune dogged the venture. Shortly after the shop opened, it burned to the ground. Deere, undaunted, decided to rebuild. Within months, disaster struck again when the second shop was destroyed by another fire. Again Deere rebuilt, once more apparently obtaining additional capital from Wright. But times were bad, and Deere finally had to give up the struggling venture to take employment in Royalton, Vermont, at regular wages, maintaining and repairing the iron parts of stagecoaches.

Within months, Deere's instinct for individual proprietorship carried him back into business as a blacksmith, this time in the small out-of-the-way Vermont hamlet of Hancock, near the home of the Lambs, his wife's parents. The debts to Wright remained unpaid; worse, Wright now was insisting on immediate repayment and had carried his claims to a Leicester Four Corners justice of the peace. A writ had been served on Deere in October 1836 "by the arresting of the defendant and by taking of bail of him for his appearance according to the exigence of said writ by the Deputy Sheriff of Addison County." On November 7 Deere was to appear before the justice, either to satisfy Wright's claim or to have "any Sheriff or Constable—to attach chattels or estate the goods of the defendant . . .or for the want thereof take his body if he and him safely keep."[1]

Thus the dilemma: pay the debts or have his property attached, perhaps even he himself threatened with imprisonment (for although the ugly practice of incarceration for debt had not been enforced in Vermont for several years, it still existed on the books of Vermont statutes—this "relic of barbarism," to quote one of the local newspapers in 1830). Economic conditions in Vermont had much worsened in the 1830s; the little village of Hancock had not proven to be a good choice for a blacksmith shop. Faced with a demand that he could not meet, John Deere left Hancock and Vermont in November 1836 and headed west, leaving his family behind. His destination was Grand Detour, Illinois.

It is not easy to trace John Deere's roots. He came from a family of modest means (his father a tailor, his mother a seamstress); few family records have been preserved. Even John Deere's birth, which the family Bible tells us was on February 7, 1804, at Rutland, Vermont, was not recorded officially at the time (a not uncommon lapse in those days). His father was William Rinold Deere; he was probably a Welshman, for both that middle name and the last name appear in records of Glamorgan County in Wales. It is a family-held belief that William Deere arrived in the New World about 1790, perhaps by way of Canada, working his way down to Rutland, Vermont; again we cannot be certain, for formal records of migration from Canada into the United States were not kept. (Even the passenger lists into Canada were spottily maintained, and no William

Rinold Deere appears there.) The first hard source for William is the United States census of 1800, which lists him, along with a wife and three children: two sons and one daughter, all under ten years of age.

William's wife—John's mother—was born Sarah Yates; again, it simply is not possible to definitely trace her lineage. A family belief holds that she was born to Capt. James Yates, a Revolutionary War soldier serving in Portsmouth, New Hampshire, who moved to Connecticut, married, and produced Sarah and two sons. Connecticut records do not record her birth, although they do chronicle the birth of two sons to Capt. James Yates. There also are other leads placing her in Connecticut before she married William. (Still, John Deere himself contradicted part of the story. In the census of 1880, he stated that both his mother and father were born in England!)[2]

What we do know is that William and Sarah were married and living in Rutland in the 1790s and that the family was growing. William, Jr., arrived sometime between 1794 and 1796, Francis in 1799, Jane sometime after that, Elizabeth in 1803, and John on February 7, 1804. There is no record of the vocation or status of William, Sr., until 1806, when we find the family residing in Middlebury, Vermont, and the father pursuing his vocation as a "merchant tailor." In April of that year the following advertisement appeared in the *Middlebury Mercury*:

The subscriber respectfully informs the inhabitants of Middlebury and the vicinity, that he has comenced [sic] the tailoring Business, in the village over M. Henshaw's Store, at the west end of the Bridge. He hopes to please those who will favor him with their custom.

Wm. Deere

Middlebury Ap. 14, 1806

Middlebury, a town of about 1,263 at that time, had become an important commercial and stagecoach center, boasting of sawmills, cider and grist mills, a carriage factory, and edgetool, scythe, and carding machine manufactories. Calvin Elmer advertised "fashionable mahogany and cherry sideboards, circular, swelled and plain bureaus, desks, tables, stands, . . . bedsteads made on shortest notice"; Epaphras Miller had set up a tannery "a few rods east of the bridge" with leather "of the first quality to be sold for cash or exchanged for rawhides at the Tan Works." A dyer had built a small smelter; blacksmith shops were springing up, developing forges and furnaces, paying cash for "bloomery"and taking in "refined iron"for pots and pans; and Eben Judd had established a factory for cutting marble in 1806. The main shopping center was burgconing with all kinds of retail stores, while a new department store advertised more than 250 items for sale, from bedpans to shawls.

This accelerating commercial growth was likely the main reason for the senior Deere's move to Middlebury, where he hoped his services would be needed by the many new mill owners, shopkeepers, and especially those in the learned professions. Rutland had no "grammar" school, offering secondary instruction, nor a college. Middlebury, on the other hand, dissatisfied with the prevailing common schools, had established a grammar school in 1797; hardly had the latter opened its doors when the town, prodded by the peripatetic Yale president, Timothy Dwight, "prayed" to the legislature to establish a college or university within the grammar school buildings. After considerable pressure, the legislators acquiesed and in 1800 Middlebury College took its place among the institutions of higher learning in New England.

Not to be outdone, the proponents of education for young ladies sent to Connecticut for a Miss Ida Strong to come and start a ladies' academy in the town courthouse. With a new building erected in the following year, the academy attracted young women from remote towns and villages of Vermont and New York, keeping pace with the flood of young men coming into Middlebury to reap the benefits offered by the grammar school and college. It was indeed a heyday for Middlebury.[3]

Expansion of educational opportunities in the town meant a greater number of salaried professionals to purchase tailor-made clothing, a matter of particular importance to William Deere. His fortunes turned upward almost immediately. By July 1806 he was advertising for help: "A Journeyman Tailor, will find employ by applying to Wm. Deere." His search continued throughout the summer, but apparently with little success. By November 5, there was a hint of increased urgency in the advertisement: "Wanted immediately, A Journeyman Tailor. One who is a good workman will find encouragement." The same notice appeared up into the winter, stopping abruptly after January 21, 1807, with what results we do not know.

Silence descends on the history of the family for more than a year. Only the family Bible, with entries written much later, reveals the birth of another son, George, in August 1807.

The year 1808 was to be cruel and crucial for the Deere family. Although there were now four sons, all were still too young to help in the tailoring business. Perhaps the father, rushed in his work, could find no spare time to take on the twelve-year-old William, Jr., as an apprentice. What he needed was trained help. Consequently, that year found the elder son apprenticed to and living with Maj. Hastings Warren, who offered in the *Middlebury Mercury* "Sideboards of all kinds, Commodes, Secretaries and Bookcases . . . Washstands . . . Bedsteads, Sofas, . . . Chairs," the products of his cabinetmaking business. In the only extant letter from William, Sr., the latter admonishes his son to "be faithful to your master and to his interest; be obedient to him and Mrs. Warren."

Of greater moment, however, is that the letter, written from Boston on June 26, 1808, reveals that William, Sr., was about to embark on a voyage to England; that, in spite of evidence that he was busy at his trade, he had amassed debts which he could not pay; and that he had hopes, though now diminished, of inheriting some assets in England which would put him on a firmer financial footing. The letter reads as follows:

Boston June 26th 1808

My Deare Son

I am now in expectation to of embarking for England the first fair wind. I have received here accounts from home, some Different to what we heard; my Cousin that was Supposed to Die at Sea is returned home to England. Consequently it will make a great alteration in my affairs but I hope to obtain the means of paying my Debts & making our family Comfortable My Dear Child as I am to be absent from you many months I wish you to attend to a few kinds of instruction from [one] who has your welfare at [heart] be faithful to your master and to his interest be obedient to him & Mrs. Warren be friendly and kind to all the family. Let Truth & Honesty be your guide & on no pretense Deviate from it.

be Dutifull to your mother Kind to your Sister & Brothers have the fear of god before you implore his protection & you will obtain it and likewise the good will of all mankind

may God bless you & all the family will be the constant prayer of your father & friend

W R Deere

my respects to Major Warren
and his family
PS Wrote by last post to your mother & enclosed twenty Dollars have sent a Triffle in this for you.[4]

These words portray a loving and kind father, respectful of God and of his fellow man, who was hoping to return in better financial circumstances that would make life easier for his family. Sadly, it was the last anyone ever heard of him. Family legend subscribes to the belief that William Deere arrived safely in England but was lost at sea on the return trip. The year 1808 was an inauspicious year for an Atlantic crossing, and there is a real possibility that his ship might have been sunk or captured. The Napoleonic Wars were winding down, with the warring nations, England and France, each determined to prevent vital materials from reaching the enemy's ports. The Imperial Decrees of Napoleon and the British Orders in Council made American disobedience dangerous for its neutral ships, and their cargoes and passengers as well. Jefferson, with his retaliatory embargo on such shipping out of America, enacted in December 1807, added the specter of seizure by the United States as well.

In addition, sinkings occurred on a regular basis from natural hazards. In 1807, four ships were lost just off of Salem harbor and in a nine-year period at this time forty vessels foundered on reefs off the Cohasset, Massachusetts, shore. If William Deere was a passenger on one such vessel the historian will never know, for the Boston customs records of ship clearances for this period were destroyed.

The confirmation of Deere's absence came with the Vermont census of 1810, in which "Sally" Deere is listed as head of household, with two boys under ten years of age (John and George) and a daughter under ten (Elizabeth). Of the second son, Francis, there is no information. About eleven years old, he, too, may have been apprenticed out; his life, however, was to be a short one, for a headstone in the Middlebury cemetery testifies that he died in 1822, at age twenty-three. There is no record at this time (or later) of the other daughter, Jane; William Deere's letter of 1808 implies only one daughter, Elizabeth.

Records of the year 1810 add other information about the family. A religious revival swept through the Middlebury region, as it did all over Vermont in that year, and it recorded that Sarah Deere became a communicant of the Congregational Church. She appears, as Sally Deere, in the *Catalogue of Members* for 1810 as a new member.[5]

William, Jr., in spite of his apprenticeship with Major Warren, did not become a cabinetmaker, but apparently returned home to help his mother in the tailoring business (so reports the *Middlebury Directory*). There is no mention of son William, though, in her advertisement in the Middlebury *National Standard* in May 1816: "Mrs. Deere has removed to the house of Mr. S. Hopkins opposite Mr. Schuyler's house where she will be happy to serve her old customers and the public in various branches of the tailoring business on short notices." Since she speaks of her "old customers," it appears that she had been tailoring ("habit making," as she called it in one of her advertisements) throughout the preceding years. Indeed, it likely would have been her only source of income for the three children living at home.

It seems improbable that Mrs. Deere, eking out a meager living, could have afforded to send the younger children to any but the district schools. But an interesting advertisement appeared in the *National Standard* in 1821 which seems to suggest that William had at some time acquired more than the minimal tools of learning: he now proposed to open his own school for "Young Ladies and Gentlemen." Although he already had taught for eighteen months in the common schools (so his advertisement trumpeted), his curriculum did not include the classics required for admission to colleges like Middlebury. The chances are that he himself did not go to college. By 1823 he had expanded his advertisement—and his offerings; there was now a "ladies school" upstairs, a "small scholar's" downstairs, and another room for "young gentlemen" across the street. Many of these self-styled pedagogues failed, however, because of

Exhibit 1–1. John Deere's brother, William, advertises for students (Middlebury National Standard, *March 25, 1823)*

Ladies and Gentlemen's School.

THE subscriber, being employed as a teacher in the new Brick School House in the western school district in this village, has obtained the consent of the trustees thereof to receive into the school, young ladies and gentlemen from abroad.

In consequence of this arrangement, the upper part of the school house will be set apart for the exclusive accommodation of young ladies, under the instruction of Miss F. Weeks.

The small scholars of the district, whose parents or friends, are not particularly solicitous to give them the advantages of a ladies school, will be taught in the lower room.

For the accommodation of young gentlemen, he has provided a room in Mr. J. Hagar's brick building, opposite the school house, where they will receive proper attention.

In addition to the Latin and Greek Languages, which will be taught by a competent Instructor, the French Language will be taught by Monsieur J. B. Meilleur, whose Method and capacity in teaching his native language, has gained him the approbation of the connoisseurs therein.

The several branches of useful and polite literature such as Orthography, Elocution, Penmanship, Grammar, Rhetoric, Arithmetic and higher branches of Mathematics, (paying particular attention to the practice of surveying) Book-keeping, Geography, History, Natural and Moral Philosophy, Chemistry, Minerology, Botany, Logic, Perspective and ornamental drawing and Painting both in water and oil colours, will be taught in this school by competent Instructors. Lessons will likewise be given on the Piano Forte and the principles of Music will be taught by Mr. S. Woodman.

Lectures on Chemistry and Botany will be given by J. A. Allen, M. D.

Lectures on Natural Philosophy will also be given.

Recitations or instructions, which can in any manner interrupt other studies, will be attended to in a separate room. Particular attention will at all times be given to the decent and moral deportment of the scholars.

The Spring Term will commence on the second Monday in April.

WM. DEERE.

N. B. The public are respectively referred to Messrs. J. Hagar, J. Satterlee, S. S. Phelps, Esqrs. Trustees of said school and to Rev. J. Hough, for further satisfaction.

Middlebury, March 22, 1823.

competition and hard times, and among these apparently was William Deere, for he left Vermont with his wife and child sometime in the early 1820s. Family beliefs hold that he moved permanently to Ireland; at any rate, he passed from the central Deere story.[6]

LEARNING A TRADE

From John's extant letters it is patent that his education was rudimentary, with limitations even in ordinary spelling and grammar, not to mention those in the classics. Some have assumed that he also had attended the academy, but there is no evidence of this. What rings more true is that sometime during his early teens he did take employment, likely with Epaphras Miller, the tanner. It was in this period that John and his mother made a momentous decision. Perhaps she saw that there was little hope for the future unless a young man had a special skill; perhaps it was necessary to find a more secure position for this next son, with a promise of immediate housing, training, and some remuneration. What-

---

Exhibit 1–2. *"The Blacksmith" (Edward Hazen,* The Panorama of Professions and Trades; or Every Man's Book, *1837)*

---

ever the reason, it was decided that young John would apprentice himself
to a well-known blacksmith, Capt. Benjamin Lawrence, and learn a trade.
It was 1821 and John was seventeen years old. Under the conditions of the
contract, he was to receive a yearly stipend, amounting to thirty dollars
the first year, with a yearly increment of five dollars, bringing his wages
to forty dollars in his last year. This seems a modest sum by modern
standards but was consistent with those of the time. In addition, of
course, he was to receive his board and room, probably his clothes, and
possibly some instruction in reading, writing, and arithmetic.

The blacksmith in those days was indispensable to a community,
rendering all kinds of services, from shoeing horses and producing pots,
pans, and skillets, to manufacturing farm implements such as hay rakes,
forks, scythes, and plows. Among the most demanded services was the
furnishing of the ironwork for the stagecoaches, as well as for mills,
which abounded in this time. So busy was Middlebury that the services of
seven blacksmiths were required and the shop of Captain Lawrence
undoubtedly bustled with activity, to the benefit of the new apprentice,
who would learn all aspects of his trade.

Yet it was not all hard work. As a member of Lawrence's household,
John lived in comfortable conditions in a home that was still standing as
late as the 1930s on a knoll above Frog Hollow. On the banks of the river
in the Hollow stood the blacksmith shop itself, now merely an excavation
site on which some desultory archaeological digging has taken place. It
was not far to descend to work each day and return in the evening to a
pleasant household where also lived a young daughter, Melissa, who
must have caught the eye of the prospective blacksmith. (It is told, within
the family, that many years later, after the death of his first wife, John
Deere returned to Middlebury, hoping to make Melissa his second wife.
He found that she had been widowed earlier and had already married for a
second time.)[7]

It was at this time that Deere met and began to court a young lady from
Hancock, Vermont, by the name of Demarius Lamb. Her parents, William
and Mary Lamb, had arrived in Vermont and settled in Hancock at just
about the time that William and Sarah Deere made their home in
Rutland. The Lambs would eventually confer on the world six daughters,
all destined to play a role in the history of the Deere company. The third
of these daughters was Demarius. She was well educated, family legend
holding that she probably attended Mrs. Emma Willard's School for
Young Ladies in Middlebury. Emma Willard, after the retirement of Miss
Strong, had become headmistress of the school and conducted it in her
own home from 1814 to 1819, after her marriage to the local Dr. Willard.
Only after this date was her name associated with Russell Sage College in
Troy, New York. It would seem quite plausible that John's acquaintance
with Demarius may have begun while she boarded at Middlebury, prior
to, or during, his apprenticeship under Captain Lawrence. It was a

common practice for parents to send offspring to academies to board, where they could receive a better and higher education than the district schools offered; she may have lived with her elder brother, Charles Lamb, then residing in Middlebury.

For John Deere, the 1820s laid the foundation on which his future life was to be built; his apprenticeship ended, he was able to hire out as a journeyman in 1825 to two different blacksmiths, David Wells and Ira Allen, whose homes and shops stood on adjoining lots on Court Street, in Middlebury. His mother died the next year, leaving behind the three youngest children. Little is known of the circumstances of George's and Elizabeth's lives at this time. George, according to family history, left home at an early age "to fend for himself"; he became a seaman, then later an engraver. His son, George, was ordained a Universalist minister and many years after had a number of contacts with John Deere in the latter's old age. Elizabeth turned up years later (1837) in a Shaker community in Ohio, after she had been shipwrecked enroute to visit her brother, John, in Grand Detour. Presumably she, too, might have had to hire out to support herself in the ten years after her mother's death.

Running between the Wells and Allen shops, John would have been kept busy "ironing" wagons, buggies, and stagecoaches, for Wells specialized in ironing and Allen had set up a shop for carriage making. John must have established a reputation as a hard worker, for a year later Col. Ozias Buel came to him and asked him to come to Colchester Falls (now Winooski), above Burlington Village, where extensive ironwork was required. Buel had purchased thirty acres and was building a sawmill and a linseed-oil mill, for which the young Deere did all the ironwork. Now launched on his own, the new blacksmith could think of establishing a family of his own. In 1827 John and Demarius were married.

Immediately following the wedding, John and Demarius took up residence in Vergennes, north of Middlebury, where he worked with the local blacksmith, John McVene. But the year 1828 found Deere and his wife in Salisbury, Vermont, where a son, Francis Albert, was born (again according to the family Bible, for there is no official record of his birth). This was to be the first of many moves by John Deere and his young family, and the explanation must lie within the economic conditions of northern New England at the time. The agricultural economy of Vermont especially was in a crippled state, with the urban markets for its products not yet established in New England, and with adequate transportation for marketing farther away. A farmer throughout the 1820s and '30s relied less upon the specialist for his needs than upon himself. Since money was scarce, he either bartered for his goods and services or, in many cases, was forced to become a "jack of all trades," making his own implements of husbandry and his own household goods. Income for the blacksmiths must have been slim indeed, and competition was keen. In Middlebury there were seven blacksmiths in 1822; in Vergennes, McVene was already established. According to a history of Salisbury, there were two black-smith shops in the early nineteenth century, where parts for wagons, sleighs, hinges, and latches were made. John Deere may have worked in one of these, but the Salisbury historian guessed that he was most likely employed at the Briggs shovel factory since "Deere specialized in making tools."[8]

Whatever his work, Deere apparently sought a new opportunity, for two years later, in the census of 1830, he is listed as a head of household in Leicester, Vermont (population in 1820, 543). That census poses a puzzle, for it lists, besides his wife and baby son, another male and another female between the ages of twenty and thirty as residents of his household. These could be the elusive brother George and sister Elizabeth. Despite small resources, Deere had decided to set up his own business at the "Four Corners." Likely he chose this place because it was the crossroads for the main stagecoach lines that started in Vergennes, ran through Middlebury, Leicester, and Brandon, and finally eastward to New Hampshire and Boston. It was not the agricultural community so much as the stage lines that attracted the "iron monger," for the coaches running over very rough roads were in constant need of repair. Such work would supplement the income earned in the manufacture and sale of farmers' tools.

With high hopes, Deere used what little capital he had to buy a piece of land in 1829 from a Stephen Sparks and built his first blacksmith shop. Then, three months later, another deed shows that he sold this land to Darius Holman. The reason can only be surmised: he may have made a business "merger" for the purpose of raising more capital for equipping his shop. Fortune, however, did not treat him kindly. Two disastrous fires put him deeply in debt at the same time that the family was enlarged once again with the birth of daughter Jeannette. Deere's first attempt at proprietorship had not succeeded, and with growing responsibilities he was forced once more to make a move and take employment that would pay him regular wages.

This time the destination was Royalton, Vermont, where he acquired work once again as an ironer of stagecoaches. It was a significant move because there he met and worked for a man, Amos Bosworth, who may have been instrumental later in encouraging him to move to Illinois. Bosworth, a second-generation resident of Royalton, was half owner of the leading hotel in town, later known as the Cascadnac, and was also involved in the stagecoach business. He hired Deere to do the ironwork for his line, as well as for the itinerant wagons, coaches, and carriages that stopped at his tavern. A man of property, with more than one house in his name, it is possible that he loaned the Deere family a home in which to live. There another Deere daughter, Ellen Sarah, was born in the year 1832.

Royalton seemed a flourishing town at this time, with numerous new

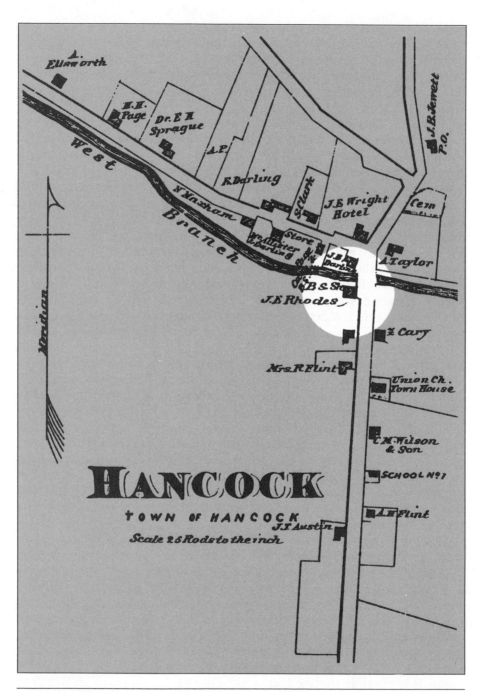

Exhibit 1–3. *The town of Hancock, Vt., ca. 1870s, showing the location of the J.E. Rhodes blacksmith shop, believed to be the site of John Deere's blacksmith shop in 1836 (F.W. Beers,* Atlas of Addison Co., Vermont, 1871)

mills erected on its streams and agriculture improving with the use of metal shares on plows. Despite appearances, migration out of Royalton had been continuous since the beginning of the century, and "it was so commonplace to have relatives in the vast West, lost or long unheard of, as to be hardly worth recording." In Royalton, John Deere must have listened to many a tale of the fortunes both farmers and mechanics could make by migrating. Certainly he must have heard Amos Bosworth extoll the prospects of leaving home for a new life on the prairies. Likely, he also was privy to the tales of woe contained in many letters from homesick settlers who complained of agues, debts, extreme cold and heat, and the difficulty of tilling the prairie sod.

Royalton afforded Deere a breathing spell in which to accumulate a little cash, but the lure of individual proprietorship soon brought another move, this time to Hancock, the former home of the Lambs. Deere had not yet paid off his Leicester debts, but he was able to induce Dr. Josiah Brooks to sell him a piece of land in the village on April 19, 1833. Evidence of his penury, however, lies in a second deed in which Deere soon mortgaged the property back to Dr. Brooks. Deere's home was on this land. The location of the Deere blacksmith shop has not been as easily placed; several locations in the village are suggested as possible sites. Wherever situated, it became the venue for another effort at "common blacksmithing." One Hancock resident recalled that John Deere had made a log chain for his father from discarded scythes, and while not a thing of beauty, "no two links being of a length or the same size—it had been a joy to its owners, for after more than fifty years' use it had never broken!"

Another story, without documentation but accepted as part of family lore, relates that John Deere's tined pitchforks had become so renowned throughout the area that Mr. Fairbanks of the famous St. Johnsbury Fairbanks Scales Company tried to induce Deere to work for him. Legend also has it that Deere was too painstaking and meticulous a craftsman, polishing the tines of his forks "until they slipped in and out of the hay like needles" and his shovels and hoes "like no others that could be bought—scoured themselves of the soil by reason of their smooth, satiny surface," and therefore there was no possibility of "quick money-getting." Indeed, it was a family-held belief that John Deere was "no business man," that he was "too easy" in making his collections. This may have been true. But it was a poor time for all persons to collect debts—including Deere's own![9]

THE EMIGRANT WAVE

Times were bad in Vermont generally in the 1830s. Land was no longer at a premium; indeed, some was actually going begging. Luther Goodhue, one of John Deere's Hancock neighbors, hoped to rent a neighbor's land that he had been seeking for several years. Now, in 1833, he wanted a bargain: "You probably have been informed that other land in Hancock has been reduced one-half within two years and no lands this side of the mountain will rent as high now as formerly. . . . I should not be willing to give more than seven dollars a year. . . . " The Middlebury paper reported a few months later that "the general distress is daily widening and the deep and subtle alarm which was for a period confined to the large cities is spreading itself throughout the country and beginning to be felt by all classes of the community."

Part of the unease in Vermont reflected national problems—the speculative mania of land sales, the abrupt cutting of land sale speculation on

TO THE PUBLIC.

INFORMATION having arrived that all the Banks in New-York and Boston have suspended specie payment for the Bills of their respective issues, and that the same course has been adopted by many of the New-England country Banks; and it is believed that *all* the Banks must adopt the same measure for the present.

In consequence of which, the Directors of the Bank of Caledonia are compelled to suspend the payment of their Bills in specie for the present.

The Bank has sustained no loss, and its assets are abundantly sufficient to cover all its liabilities. Its bills will be received in payment of all debts; and holders of the Bills are respectfully cautioned not to sacrifice them, for every Bill will be eventually redeemed.

SAM'L SIAS.
JOSIAH SHEDD.
SAM'L B. MATTOCKS.
IRA BRAINERD.

Danville, May 15th, 1837.

Exhibit 1–4. *The Panic of 1837 reaches Vermont (courtesy of Wilbur collection, Bailey\ Howe Library, University of Vermont)*

CALEDONIA CATTLE FAIR.

Exhibition of Manufactures, and Ploughing Match.

The Executive Officers and Committee of Management of the Caledonia Cattle Fair met at Lyndon Corner on the 25th inst., and have made the necessary arrangements for a Cattle Show, and exhibition of Manufactures, at St. Johnsbury Plain, on Thursday the 12th day of October next, at nine o'clock in the forenoon.

That the expectations of the Society may be realized, the Committee solicit from the Farmers, Mechanics, and Manufacturers of the County their co-operation in endeavoring to render the Show more interesting than last year. The Society was indebted for much of the interest of the exhibition last year to the attention extended towards them by the Ladies. They would solicit from their fair friends the favor, that they would permit the Hall to be adorned the present year with the evidences of their beautiful handy work.

The Committee will cause every care to be taken that the articles offered for exhibition are preserved from injury.

The Executive Officers and Committee of Arrangements have, as provided by the Constitution of said Society, appointed the following gentlemen on the different Committees, who are requested to attend and report.

COMMITTEES:

ON OXEN,
TIMO. P. FULLER,
LEONARD HARRINGTON
REUBEN C. BENTON

ON STEERS,
OTIS EVANS,
SEWELL BRADLEY,
THEOPHILUS DREW.

ON MILCH COWS,
WELCOME BEMIS,
CLOUD HARVEY,
THOMAS PIERCE.

ON HEIFERS,
ABEL BUTLER,
HIAL BRADLEY,
EZRA C. CHAMBERLAIN.

ON BULLS,
ELISHA DAVIS,
SYLVESTER HALL,
JOHN ARMINGTON.

ON SWINE,
JOHN HILL,
JOEL ROBERTS,
JOHN MORRILL, (of Danville)

ON SHEEP,
ISRAEL P. DANA,
JAMES WORKS,
ABEL EDGEL.

ON BUTTER,
CALVIN MORRILL,
EPHRAIM CHAMBERLAIN,
LEVI P. PARKS.

ON CHEESE,
LUTHER CLARKE,
SALMA DAVIS,
WM. GILKERSON.

ON WOLLEY MANUFACTURES,
ROBERT HARVEY,
WM. H. PALMER,
LUCIUS KIMBALL.

ON HOUSEHOLD MANUFACTURES,
MOSES KITTREDGE
JOHN KELSEY,
LUCIUS DENISON

ON PLOUGHS,
ABEL PIERCE,
WM. SHEARER,
CHARLES HOSMER.

ON IRON MANUFACTURES
HUXHAM PADDOCK,
JAMES KNAPP,
COTTON G. DICKINSON.

On the Ploughing match

JOHN MATTOCKS,
ISRAEL P. DANA,
SYLVANUS HEMINGWAY.

Dinner will be in readiness at 2 o'clock, at Ide's Hotel. Tickets to be had at the Bar.

Welcome Bemis,
Thomas Pierce,
Timothy Fisher,
Jacob Blake,   } *Com. of Arrangements.*
Clarke Cushman,
Sewell Bradley,

EPHRAIM CHAMBERLAIN, Secretary.

Lyndon, Sept. 25, 1837.   [CALEDONIAN PRESS.]

Exhibit 1–5. The Caledonia, Vt., cattle fair and "ploughing match," 1837 (courtesy of Wilbur collection, Bailey|Howe Library, University of Vermont) credit by the Specie Act in 1836, and, finally, the beginnings of an economic downturn that came to be known as the "Panic of 1837." Most of Vermont's problems, though, were indigenous to and exacerbated by Vermonters themselves. At the root of this was the "sheep craze."

Vermont was multiplying its sheep flocks on an unprecedented scale; the state flocks in 1840 stood at 1,500,000 animals, almost six sheep per capita. A revealing little book, *Statistical View of the Number of Sheep in the Several Towns and Counties* . . . , published in 1837, captured the mosaic of sheep herds, town by town. The state was literally dotted with these animals. Except for a few hamlets in remote mountain districts in the Green Mountain range, just about every town had more than 1,000 sheep, a fair amount more than 5,000, and a few along the two great river valleys upwards of 10,000 per town. Prices for wool held reasonably well until 1837, so the sheepmen themselves only became pinched after 1840. The broader problem lay in the fact that Vermont had truly become a monoculture. As the governor put it in 1842: "Our citizens have become so dependent upon the growing of wool that this article may be said to be the staple of the state." Since sheepherding could be done more profitably on a large scale, the state witnessed a Vermont adaptation of the old English enclosure. "Beware of the 'Western fever' and above all, sell not your farms to your rich neighbors for sheep pastures," a Windsor, Vermont, newspaper cautioned in 1834.

In this rush to monoculture, practically all other aspects of Vermont agriculture atrophied. Though dairying remained important, the total number of cows had actually declined. Likewise, field crops had stabilized at a level primarily to maintain local consumption, with little attempt toward commercial agriculture. Sheep raising required only modest amounts of labor and capital input, other than the animals themselves and the large acreage of pasture land. Thus men on the Vermont farms and in the little villages had worsening outlooks for productive employment.

This narrowing of agricultural complexity brought about by the onrush of monoculture had effects, often detrimental ones, on agriculture-related businesses. Blacksmith-based farm operations, for example, tended to shrink. Wagons still needed to be built and repaired, horses were still the universal method of transportation, but a blacksmith's forge is best utilized in a flourishing agricultural economy with ever-widening horizons of crop and animal culture. Vermont just did not fit this image. Thus national economic tensions, compounded by some peculiarly Vermont complications, darkened the outlook for John Deere's blacksmith operation in Hancock. In 1830, even before the Deeres had returned there, Hancock's population had peaked at only 470 people. By 1840 its population had declined to 455, and it continued downward until 1910. It must have become obvious to the blacksmith in 1836 that his prospects were not good if he remained in an economically declining community.

VALUABLE LANDS

AT AUCTION.

The undersigned, as the sole acting Executor of DANIEL BOARDMAN, late of the City and State of New-York, deceased, will sell at PUBLIC AUCTION

On Thursday, Oct. 20th, 1836,

AT 12 O'CLOCK, NOON, AT THE SALES ROOM OF

MESSRS. FRANKLIN & JENKINS

No. 15 Broad-street, in the City of New-York, the following LANDS, viz:

IN VERMONT.

In Addison County, 1370 Acres, viz: In Hancock, 780 acres; Kingston, 450 acres; Bristol, 40 acres; Starksboro', 100 acres.
In Caledonia County, 1926 Acres, viz: In Goshen, 258 acres; Goshen Gore, by Walden, 505 acres; Goshen Gore, by Plainfield, 87 acres: Groton, 482 acres: Peacham, 100 acres: Sheffield, 290 acres: Walden, 231 acres.
In Chittenden County, 4077 Acres, viz: Bolton, 300 acres; Huntington, 125 acres; Mansfield, 2696 acres; Underhill, 856 acres; Westford, 170 acres.
In Essex County, 9860 Acres, viz: Brunswick, 1237 acres; Canaan, 645 acres; Averill, 4478 acres in 14 whole rights; Guildhall, 1447 acres: Lewis, 331 acres: Lunenburg, 50 acres: Minehead, now Bloomfield, 1242 acres: Wenlock, 424 acres.
In Franklin County, 5196 Acres, viz: In Bakersfield, 510 acres, Berkshire, 100 acres; Montgomery, 776 acres; Sterling, 3770 acres: Newbury, 540 acres.
In Orleans County, 806 Acres, viz: In Eden, 312 acres; Wolcott, 134 acres; Westfield, 360 acres.
In Rutland County, 4814 Acres, viz: In Chittenden, 2674 acres; Pittsfield, 980 acres; Mount Tabor, 212 acres; Pittsford, 144 acres: Shrewsbury, 106 acres.
In Washington County, 6997 Acres, viz: In Duxbury, 5619 acres; Elmore, 300 acres; Fayston, 230 acres; Middlesex, 607 acres: Marshfield, 640 acres: Moretown, 50 acres, 60 acres: Waterbury, 185 acres: Waitsfield, 30 acres.
In Windham County, 980 Acres, viz: Somerset, 720 acres; Stratton, 260 acres. Windsor County—Barnard, 25 acres.

STATE OF NEW-YORK.

In Hamilton County.—One third of the southern half of Township No. 22, Totten & Crossfield's Purchase, surveyed into Lots and numbered from 1 to 30, and containing in the whole, as per survey, 3775 50-100 Acres.

STATE OF VIRGINIA.

Greenbrier County—3464 Acres, being part of a Patent of 5000 acres granted to John Brynside, June 8th, 1798. Said Land is situated on Man's & Beecher's Creeks, branches of the Great Kenhawa and Meadow Rivers.
"   "   also, 1634 Acres, part of a patent of 3000 acres granted to the said John Byrnside. Sept. 19, 1797, situated on
"   "   also, 2500 Acres, patented Sept. 19, 1797, situated between Anthony and Little Creeks. 25 miles from Lewisburg.
"   "   also, 1000 Acres, patented Sept. 20, 1797, situated on the South branches of Howard's Creek, about 12 miles from Lewisburg, and 2 miles from the WHITE SULPHUR SPRINGS.
Monroe County—4980 Acres, residue of a patent for 9800 acres, granted Sept. 27, 1797, situated near the junction of the Greenbrier and Kenhawa Rivers. All the above patents are on record, and also regular conveyances from the Patentees.

STATE OF OHIO.

Ashtabula County—150 Acres, viz: Town of Morgan, No. 10, Range 4, half of Lot No. 71, 50 acres, and Lot No. 83, 100 acres, lying on both sides of Grand River.

For all of which Lands the usual Executor's Deeds will be given. Terms made known at the time of sale. For further particulars enquire of the subscriber at his Office, No. 43 Liberty-street, New-York.

F. W. BOARDMAN,

Executor of Daniel Boardman, deceased.

New-York, August, 1836.

J. W. BELL, PRINTER, 17 ANN-STREET, NEW-YORK.

Exhibit 1–6. Vermont land auction, 1836 (courtesy of Vermont Historical Society)

Emigration became increasingly attractive, and after 1830 the exodus from Vermont rose precipitously—"from a steady stream to a freshet, not to say a flood," observed Lewis Stilwell, one of the authorities on migration from Vermont. Lucy Hurlburt wrote her friend, Charity Bryant,

Exhibit 1–7. *Vermont village road, ca. early 1870s (courtesy of Vermont Historical Society)*

from the little village of Waybridge, Vermont, in 1832 that "quite a number of the inhabitants of this town have moved to the states of Ohio and Illinois." A Fair Haven resident wrote in 1838 to a friend in the Wisconsin Territory: "The Spring has been very cold and backward here . . . crops just beginning to start a little . . . there is a great many emigrating to the Far West this Spring. People here generally complain of hard times, tho our burden not as poor as it was a few years ago. . . .I am fully determined to leave this before a great while . . . write me the best chance you know of, for I think that I shall go West in the course of this season. . . ."[10]

It was not just the wish to get away; the pull of new lands tugged very hard indeed. The signposts almost always pointed west, first to the areas immediately beyond the eastern shores, then through the Cumberland Gap into the Ohio Valley, and, closer to the time of John Deere, to fan out over the vast prairies of the Midwest, finally to reach later into the Great Plains and the Oregon Territory. Each of these waves of American migration trumpeted its own set of hyperbole. The 1820s and '30s were marked by a "hard-sell" promotion of emigration, aided materially by the ease of land purchase from the federal government. As one Illinois settler in 1838 frankly put it, "Uncle Sam deals in abundance with us as yet." As land sales multiplied, so did land speculation.

Emigrants' letters were full of high promise and excitement. Effusively extolling the flora and fauna and the virtues of agriculture, they flowed back to the East in larger and larger volume in the 1830s. To be sure, the emigrants also wrote of the privations of the frontier, the difficulties in breaking the prairie and bringing it under cultivation, and other obstacles to settling a virgin area. Oft mentioned was an allegedly higher incidence of sickness in the Midwest. According to an immigrant settling in Randolph County, Illinois, in 1830: "The country from the eastern part of Ohio to the Mississippi has undoubtedly a billious tendency. It is manifest in the countenances of the inhabitants. As soon as I entered Ohio/and so ever since, I saw less of the rose on the cheek/more of a sallow appearance than what prevails in the East . . . and almost everywhere in this widely extended region, the chill/fever are occasionally felt." But even here the writer muted his criticism with an optimistic view of the problem: "But it is a poor country for Doctors. The fevers have a remarkable similarity . . . may be treated with a good deal of safety in a very uniform way. This is so well understood that the inhabitants are generally their own physicians . . . and in this they succeed well."

The stalwarts among the town fathers and other loyal boosters in the New Hampshire and Vermont villages found themselves threatened by the "Western craze." The official gazeteer of New Hampshire centered its attack on the health question, but in the process it almost gave away the game by inadvertently stressing all of the other virtues: "Although labor is comparatively high, land cheap, and Winters lose much of their rigor and length . . . fever and ague sap the constitution and send back the adventurer a lean, sallow invalid for life, or lay him prematurely in the grave." A Vermont newspaper editor went even further in castigating "Westernism": "We trust the Executive will notice this conspiracy and take efficient measures to suppress it. It is high time an example should be made."

The critics of emigration also received support from several famous visitors to the West, none of whom had any intention of settling there. Charles Dickens, who was in Illinois in 1842, commented about the prairie: "Great as the picture was, its very flatness and extent, which left nothing to the imagination, tamed it down and cramped its interest. I felt little of that sense of freedom and exhilaration which a Scottish heath inspires, or even our English Downs awaken." William Cullen Bryant visited his brother in southern Illinois in 1832 and found the prairies to be "the most salubrious, and I am sure it is the most fertile, country I ever saw; at the same time I do not think it beautiful." The sense of vastness and isolation seemed particularly to trouble many of the visitors from abroad. Harriet Martineau, the English writer, visited Illinois and the prairie in 1836 and evocatively described a trip to the outlying prairie areas in the northern part of the state: "I never saw insulation, (not desolation) to compare with the situation of a settler on a wide prairie. A single house in the middle of Salisbury Plain would be desolate. A single house on a prairie has clumps of trees near it, rich fields about it; and flowers, strawberries, and running water at hand. But when I saw a settler's child tripping out of home-bounds, I had a feeling that it would never get back again. It looked like putting out to Lake Michigan in a canoe."

A number of other English visitors to Illinois during the first three decades of the century came with intentions to settle. These English emigrants drew bitter comments from those back in England. The *London Quarterly Review* commented in 1822: "There are thousands of our poor countrymen who have been seduced from their homes by . . .artificers of fraud; have embarked their little all in their journey to these gloomy wilds, that are at this moment pining in despair, and hastening to a strange grave with broken hearts. They cannot return, and the land of their birth will know them no more. Happily, their sufferings are not greatly protracted, for the climate is not congenial to their constitutions and they perish before the moth ."

Illinois itself appeared to have a special effect on visitors during this period, for many people traveled all through the Midwest looking for the most propitious spot to settle. "Why, my dear friend Robert, it's the Nile of America," wrote Cornelius Swartout to his brother in 1837. "I saw corn that the ears on the stalks were higher than I could reach . . .fifteen and half high. You will think it a fish story, but it is a fact which I have proof." Another settler added his vision: "This is the land that flows with milk and honey." Chimed in another, "I have raised as much as I did for ten years in Maine farming." Finally, perhaps the most enthusiastic: "There is some new comers but some in our Grove say they would not be back near Buffalo, York state, and be compeled to stay there for no sum under $1000. They call our Grove a Paradise."

There had been substantial immigration into southern Illinois in the first two decades of the nineteenth century, a pattern of migration that brought the hunter-trader of West Virginia, southern Ohio, Tennessee, and Kentucky into the state. It is a striking fact, though, that virtually no settlement had occurred in many parts of the great prairie of northern Illinois in these first two decades. There was a startling lack of foresight about the potentials of the prairies; even James Monroe, later the architect of the Louisiana Purchase, sweepingly dismissed the area in a letter to Thomas Jefferson in 1786: "A great part of the territory is miserably poor, especially that near lakes Michigan & Erie & that upon the Mississippi & the Illinois consists of extensive plains wh. have not had from appearances & will not have a single bush on them, for ages. The districts therefore within wh. these fall will perhaps never contain a sufficient number of Inhabitants to entitle them to membership in the confederacy. . . . "

How this great prairie came to be there is a matter of some conjecture. The theorists of the early nineteenth century favored the hypothesis that it was the result of fires—a combination of those started spontaneously by lightning and those set by the Indians in their annual hunts. (It was a common Indian device to burn the dry grass to stampede the game.) It stretches one's beliefs more than a little to accept this as the sole explanation, however. True, man-initiated burnings in the spring were also widely practiced, "to destroy the weeds, long grass, snakes, bugs and worm's nests," as one settler wrote to his uncle, but today's soil scientists believe that the prairies more likely resulted from a buildup of a dense root network in the perennial grass, so impenetrable as to choke out seedling trees. Other factors—temperature, wind, humidity, rainfall, and topography—also influenced the forest-prairie equation.[11]

If northern Illinois had this vast agricultural potential so lyrically espoused by so many writers, who then would be its settlers? There were ready candidates. New England had a pattern of agriculturally based small holdings and cultivating practices quite suited to prairie farming. (It is hard to imagine, seeing the heavily forested New Hampshire and Vermont of today, that these two states had a great many of their hills cleared and in agriculture by the late 1700s.) The great prairie in the upper part of Illinois particularly captured the imaginations of the restless agriculturalists of upper New England. The Vermont farmers with their small hill farms and rough pieces of land still coughing up new rocks every plowing season, with a short, sometimes too-short growing season, listened to these tales of the "inexhaustible depth" of the rich Midwestern soils and began laying plans to go. In the process, they let their own properties deteriorate: "Men . . . who intend as soon as possible to emigrate . . . will not take much interest in improving their lands, fences or buildings, and as for the work of public utility, such as better roads, bridges and schoolhouses and churches, they are ready to say, 'of what use will these things be to us? We are expecting to remove and must provide for ourselves elsewhere'."

Often the Vermonters emigrated as a community, a number of them settling in Illinois. Citizens of Benson, Vermont, moved en masse to Du Page County, Illinois, in 1832 to form a "Christian Colony," pledged to establish both church and school in the undeveloped West. There is a town called Vermont in Illinois and another called Vermontville in Michigan, the latter a famous group colonization effort from Poultney, Vermont. Stilwell reports that Wheatland, Greengarden, Tremont, and Vergennes in Illinois were established as "sterling, simon-pure Vermont settlements—where Vermont qualities were accentuated and Vermont solidarity maintained."

New England's role should not be exaggerated, however. The national census of 1850 puts its contribution into perspective. It asked for the first time the place of origin of each person. Of the ten states that contributed most heavily to the Illinois population of some 850,000, only two New England states were included—Vermont at the ninth position, with 11,381, and Massachusetts at the tenth, with 9,230. (Vermont was the second-smallest of the six New England states, however, and so it felt the effects of migration more severely.) The figures become more striking when northern Illinois is analyzed separately. Alan Bogue, the well-known historian of the Midwest, made a detailed calculation of the farmers in Bureau County, just south of Dixon, for the year 1850. There New England accounted for almost one-quarter of the population (263 of 1,161), with Massachusetts and Vermont making up the largest totals (87 and 66, respectively). The average age of these New Englanders was more than forty years; these particular pioneers were mostly mature men. Bogue comments: "The boy settler and his child wife were rarities."

Lewis Stilwell cautioned against stereotyping the Vermont farmer as just a simple agriculturalist:

These farmer-emigrants would hardly have been Vermonters if they had not, vaguely or deliberately, regarded farming as a point of departure and as a means to a better end. They began by breaking prairie and building their log barns and shake-roofed shanties, as if agriculture were their permanent calling. But it was not long before they jumped at the first chance to start a mill or a general store or a crossroads tavern in order to emancipate themselves from the soil and join the ranks of businessmen and specialists. To be a persistent and enthusiastic devotee of old-fashioned farming demanded more of the peasant type of soul than most Vermonters possessed. To be ambitious meant to want to leave the plow, and ambitiousness was one of the most dominant of Yankee qualities.

Remember, too, that not everyone would have seen the Vermonter as that honest salt of the earth that most of them held as their own self-image. A writer in the 1850s stated succinctly the view from southern Illinois: "They had never seen the genuine Yankee. They had seen a skinning, trafficking, and tricky race of peddlers from New England, who much infested the West and South with tin ware, small assortments of merchandise, and wooden clocks; and they supposed that the whole of the New England people were like these specimens. They formed the opinion that a genuine Yankee was a close, miserly, dishonest, selfish getter of money, void of generosity, hospitality, or any of the kindlier feelings of human nature." And it was tit for tat. The northern people formed an equally unfavorable opinion of their southern neighbors. The northern man believed that southerner to be a "long, lank, lean, lazy, and ignorant animal, but little in advance of the savage state; one who was content to squat in a logcabin, with a large family of ill-fed and ill-clothed, idle, ignorant children." Stereotypes die hard![12]

SETTLING THE PRAIRIE

The way West was particularly influenced in this period by the canal boom; the importance of the opening of the Erie Canal in 1825 can hardly be overemphasized. Traffic on it became enormous almost instantly; the debt on it was paid off completely within just a few years. Road building proceeded apace with canal building; often the two were side by side.

Other forms of travel also grew, forming a connecting system. By stagecoach or by wagons pulled by their own teams, families converged on the Erie Canal all along its route. Buffalo, New York, was the staging point for the steamer packets on Lake Erie. Some families would disembark at Erie, Pennsylvania, or at Cleveland, Ohio, and travel by canal boat down to the Ohio River. Others would stay on the packet boat to Detroit, Michigan, leave the boat there, and go by wagon or stagecoach overland either to a port on the eastern shore of Lake Michigan, whence they could cross by boat to Chicago, or to the Kankakee River, down which they could float to the great Illinois River, the major water route north and south through the state of Illinois. Yet others arriving at Detroit would opt to take the Great Lakes route up through Lakes Huron and Superior and down Michigan to Chicago (though it was generally agreed that this was a somewhat less advantageous route). In general, the lake steamers were favored by most emigrants. One Chicago newspaper gushed: "It is difficult to conceive of their superiors whether we regard swiftness or beauty of model. They float upon the water like swans; they move through it like its own finny inhabitants. Travellers from the South and East are in raptures with them and they may well be so."

William Pooley analyzed the costs of transportation along these routes. From Albany, New York, to Buffalo in the mid-1830s the fare was $15.62 by packet. Within just a few years it had dropped to $14.50 and later, when the railroads began to compete, the cost fell to $11.00. The trip from Buffalo to Chicago by steamboat cost about $20.00 at the end of the 1830s, falling to only $10.00 by 1850. Steerage passage on the same boats was about one-half of these costs: "You can now come from Buffalo to Chicago in a Steam boat deck passage and board yourself for six to eight dollars," wrote on Illinois settler back to his brother in Vermont in 1838.

The freight rates, too, began high but fell sharply within a few years; in the early 1840s the rates from Buffalo to Chicago were quoted at $.50 per hundredweight on heavy materials and $.875 on lighter-weight goods. Clearly, rate classifiers were more concerned with space than they were with weight.

One could bring his own wagon and team, but this, of course, raised the expense. There was a lively debate by travelers and others as to whether the emigrant should take his horses, cattle, hogs, and wagons. Some authorities felt the costs were too high, others advised it, one of the latter noting that the masters of boats seemed "to take great interest in the shipment of choice stock to the West."

Once the settlers arrived, land speculation became the game of the day. "It is utterly beyond me," wrote a Canton, Illinois, settler in 1836, "to describe the numbers of men from all parts of the globe buying land. . . . I would willingly lay out all I have. . . . I only regret that my attention was not sooner turned to this subject." Sarah Aiken, only fifteen years old, wrote her teenage friend in New York that her family had given $900 in late 1834 for a farm in central Illinois and was offered $2,500 for it the following spring. An English minister on the Illinois frontier wrote back to his superior on Harley Street, London, of the great proselytizing opportunities for the church: "Precious souls every day go wanting, like the choice wheat bending down with success with no one to put in the sickle to bind them to the covenant of redeeming love." In the same breath, the minister also eulogized Mammon's opportunities for profit: "While you are doing your duty as a faithful minister of Christ in gathering the lambs . . .the means for the maintenance of 'your household' of your children and grandchildren, etc. will be graciously 'provided'. . . . Lands which may be purchased at one crown per acre will in a few years be worth ten . . . a few hundred laid out this way will soon be thousands."

Daniel Webster, as did many other public figures in Washington, bought properties all over the Midwest; one of the largest was in northern Illinois. Webster had visited there himself in June 1837 and purchased 1,000 acres, which he named "Marshfield." He sent his son, Daniel Fletcher Webster, a lawyer like his father, to oversee the enterprise, but Fletcher had neither the temperament nor the capacity for farming. The operation soon ran into all sorts of difficulties: "I have planted about 25 acres of corn, but the *draught* [sic] the *worms* and the *birds* have made such sad havoc that I hardly hope to raise two hundred bushels off the whole yet. . . .Such crops as have not been destroyed for the causes above are not doing well. *Hail* fell yesterday that were *nine* inches in circumference by actual *measurement*." By 1840 Fletcher had had enough, and he returned East, "weaned . . . of my Western fever." Speculation was one thing, serious farming something else.

Thus a vast, virgin area—the great prairie—became peopled with a large number of generally optimistic emigrants, significant numbers of them New Englanders. The reasons are not difficult to understand, yet it is surprising how rapidly it all came about after 1825. By the first half of the 1830s, the ethos of the prairies seemed to be put in place. Pooley concluded: "In this period just described (1833–37) the character of the settlement of northern Illinois was fixed once for all—the prairie man who was primarily a pioneer of the agricultural class or the third type in the succession as followed heretofore, had now jumped into first place to the exclusion of the hunter and the small farmer. Events had operated for this and the result was inevitable." Still, one of the more striking manifestations of the story of the westward movement in the United States of the nineteenth century is this peopling of the great breadbasket of the world, our present-day Middle West, carried through over a very short period of time in the 1830s and influenced by a particular group of people from a particular part of the country, the Yankees of New England.[13]

JOHN DEERE MOVES WEST

Emigration must have held a special attraction for John Deere in the mid-1830s. Not only was his business situation in Hancock precarious, he had the frightening complication of a debtor's disgrace unless the debt owed to Wright in Leicester could be repaid. Bankruptcy not only stared him in the face, but also the appellation of a public debtor. Better to make a new start, pay the debt later.

Prospects for blacksmithing in the new West seemed promising, too. One emigrant to central Illinois wrote in 1836: "As yet there is but little manufacturing done in the County, the supplies necessary are brought from the East, but still a mechanic has a fair field open for his enterprise. All kinds of trade do well, such as are adapted to a new country. Especially carpenters, blacksmiths, shoemakers, tanners, cabinetmakers, turners, wheel-wrights, masons, tinners, etc. The finer kinds of trades are much carried on at present, but still there is room for them and for enterprising young men in particular." Given the circumstances, for a restless man like John Deere, the attractions of the West must have been very persuasive. Sometime in November 1836 (no records today precisely pin down the exact day) John Deere packed a few tools and a bit of money and left Hancock for the great prairie. This was not just a "fishing expedition," for John Deere had a single destination—Grand Detour, Illinois

Already drawn to Grand Detour was another Vermonter, Leonard Andrus, who played a major role in one of John Deere's early business ventures in Illinois. Andrus was the original settler of the village in 1835. Its location was on the Rock River, about 100 miles west of Chicago, at a point where the river makes a sweeping "U." (The Indian legend is more romantic—the Rock River believed itself so beautiful that it just had to circle back to look at itself!) The river's unique configuration there seemed ideally suited for harnessing its water power. Andrus, along with his two cousins, Willis T. and Willard A. House, soon had a sawmill and a gristmill in operation and had built crude log cabins for their own living quarters. According to one of the House descendants: "Their kitchen was located outdoors and culinary operations were often watched by lounging Indians. For their dressing room, a patch of tall grass near the river bank was cut down, and there they made their toilet, using the water of Rock River for a mirror."

Remembrances and extant documents do not tell us how John Deere heard of Grand Detour—Deere himself left only the statement that he "came to Grand Detour by canal boat and stage." The best clue comes from an Ogle County history, which states that "Amos Bosworth

Exhibit 1–8. *Two views of blacksmith shop, Hancock, Vt., ca. 1927, believed to be the building that housed John Deere's blacksmith shop in 1836 (Deere Archives)*

[Deere's employer in Royalton] also arrived with Emery T. Gates and his team and 11 other passengers including the parents of Mr. Bosworth.'' The surmise is that Bosworth himself had been in Grand Detour as early as 1836 and had returned to get the others within a year or so. (Andrus, incidentally, married Bosworth's daughter, Sarah, in 1839.) At any rate, once having placed Amos Bosworth in Grand Detour, it is not difficult to imagine that in some fashion—personally, through a third party, or by mail—Bosworth extolled Grand Detour to Deere, and Deere had his destination.[14]

He came without his family. Eight-year-old Francis and the three younger sisters—six-year-old Jeannette, four-year-old Ellen, and two-year-old Frances—together with his wife Demarius, six months pregnant when he left her, all remained in Hancock. No wagon or team or animals or other capital stock accompanied the blacksmith, other than his own tools of the trade from the Hancock shop. At age thirty-two, John Deere started over.

CHAPTER 2

JOHN DEERE'S STEEL PLOW

When Mr. Deere came West, money was not hanging on the bushes or floating in the streams. Mr. Deere told me he had near $1100 on his arrival in Grand Detour, and when he moved to Moline he had nearly $10,000, which he had produced from his eleven years' labor in Grand Detour, including the money he had when he came to Illinois, which amount would scarcely build a wire fence around a John Deere works of today.

J.T. Hamilton

◁*"At the anvil," photo mural, John Deere historic site, Grand Detour, Ill.*

John Deere brought to Grand Detour, Illinois, an indispensable trade—blacksmithing. Before his arrival, the nearest blacksmiths were miles away from the little village, over a primitive track. Almost before Deere could catch his breath in his new community, his skills were in demand. The sawmill of Leonard Andrus and his colleagues was standing idle, its pitman shaft broken. There was no forge in readiness, so Deere set to work and, with stone from a neighboring hill and mortar from the clay soil of the riverbed, built a crude forge, fired it, and began repairing the shaft. Within a couple of days, he had the sawmill back in operation.

Deere's next order of business was to get his shop under roof, a substantial undertaking. Just how much money did he bring with him to finance such immediate needs? Legends about John Deere often repeat the same story, that he came with the sum of $73.73. Sometimes the storyteller vows that he left Hancock with that amount, sometimes that he arrived in Grand Detour with exactly the same amount. There also is another version, attributed to John Deere by J.T. Hamilton, who first met Deere in 1848 and worked for him after the Civil War. In a set of remembrances penned very much later, in 1916, Hamilton recounted: "When Mr. Deere came West, money was not hanging on the bushes or floating in the streams. Mr. Deere told me he had near $1,100 on his arrival in Grand Detour, and when he moved to Moline he had nearly $10,000, which he had produced from his eleven years' labor in Grand Detour, including the money he had when he came to Illinois, which amount would scarcely build a wire fence around a John Deere works of today."

Still, even though Hamilton states that Deere told him this in person, other scraps of information suggest a figure closer to the legendary $73.73. Fragmentary evidence indicates that Deere probably was quite impecunious at the time he left Hancock—his assets likely coming mostly from his shop, which he had just sold to his father-in-law for $200. It is probable that he left something less than half of that with Demarius and took something more than half with him. The smaller figure seems confirmed, too, by the fact that he apparently did not buy any land in Grand Detour in the period 1837–41, although the land boom was in full force at the time he arrived and his neighbors were speculating in property all over the town and surrounding area.

GETTING STARTED

John Deere constructed a small blacksmith shop building during the first summer on rented land. Typically, blacksmith buildings were short-lived. If the constant intense heat did not succeed in burning them down, the dirt and tailings and leavings of the shops would make them undesirable for alternative occupancy, and sooner or later the buildings would probably be razed. Most Grand Detour old-timers remembered John Deere's little shop as rising out back of his home, but few traces remained of the shop by the 1960s, even though the home has stood through time.

In the 1960s, Deere & Company decided to resurrect the entire Deere property as a historical site (it was later designated by the National Parks Service as a Registered Historical Landmark). The search for the location of the original blacksmith shop was an ideal project for the industrial archaeologist, and a group of professionals from the University of Illinois was commissioned for the task. In a matter of days they had identified the exact site, and by a process of inference and analysis they were able to determine how the little building probably had been constructed and how it was laid out inside for the work that was to be done there.

First, a magnetometer picked up the general location of the forge. Test excavations soon revealed a great deal of scrap iron, burned bricks, slag, broken pottery—all kinds of debris suggesting that this had once been an intensively used site. As the archaeologists dug farther, a number of post holes came into view, some still with the decayed mold of the original post. The holes outlined a rectangular building about twenty-six feet wide and about thirty-one feet long.

The team speculated about the posts and how they were utilized. Charred fragments of some of the timbers of the building were dispatched to the Forest Products Laboratory of the U.S. Department of Agriculture in Madison, Wisconsin; the report back was that some of the material used in the building was slippery American elm and silver maple. "This is a little bit unusual," commented the team's leader, "because with the abundance of walnut and oak at the time, buildings were very often constructed of what we consider to be those better woods. However, walnut and oak are two of the hardest woods to deal with; it takes a lot more work to make a dressed timber out of an oak or walnut log than it does out of elm or pine. . . . "

How was the structure erected? One possibility was that, once inserted in the ground, the posts were then extended up to the eave line to a plate at the top, which could then hang curtaining or surface material such as siding, horizontal boards, and so on. But the team thought otherwise: "This really doesn't make a very satisfactory building. Considering where Mr. Deere came from, New England, we might assume that what he did was to put posts in the ground, level the tops of these posts and then upon these posts put a sill, a dressed timber sill, and upon the sills of this building erect a braced frame structure. This would be the kind of construction technique that Deere would be familiar with from New England."

Within the original shop area was quickly found the base of the forge, a large piece of local dolomite rock. Though only the base was left, it was possible, by utilizing records of the contemporary technology for a blacksmith's forge of the 1830s, for the archaeologists to reconstruct the forge in a drawing. A base of brick just a few feet away from the forge puzzled them. "At first, this was rather a mystery, but around this square base of brick we began finding a great deal of slag, molding sand, and other indications of some kind of a casting operation. In order to cast, iron has to be melted, so we presume that here on the frontier, very early in his career at Grand Detour, Mr. Deere must have put in a small cupola or iron melting furnace. Working again from our knowledge of the technology of the time and what could be done with local materials, we know that Deere could very well have built a small cupola of brick and that within it, using pig iron, limestone and coke, he could have melted sufficient iron for any kind of casting operation he wanted in the shop. Once having standardized his plow, it was quicker to cast certain of the parts of that plow than to forge them all by hand."

As one faced the forge, with the furnace to the right, there was a large, shallow depression, a cross-shaped area in the ground directly to the left. In excavating this, the team found fine reddish dust mixed in with the clay that formed the floor of the shop. Upon analysis, this red dust was found to be the residue from a grinding operation. The team commented: "Knowing that perhaps the most important process in the production of the plow was to grind the plow bottom to make it absolutely smooth, we reconstruct a large grinding wheel for the shop, and in order to support that grinding wheel, there would have been necessary a large, timber-supporting framework.'' Looking at it from above, this frame is cross-shaped. To keep the framework from shifting on the floor of the shop, as the wheel turned, the frame had to be sunk several inches in the ground and clay had to be tamped tight around it. Then, when the wheel was turning, the framework would not shake so badly.

Another mystery puzzled the team: Why, in a shop twenty-six feet by thirty-one feet devoted to plow production, would Deere have fitted things in so tightly? The grinding wheel was on one side of the forge and on the other side was the furnace. All three pieces were built cheek to jowl, so close as to almost preclude ready movement.

Why so close together? The solving of yet another question soon brought an answer to this one, too. Just behind the forge, where Deere had built a small addition to the shop, there was an odd coffin-shaped pit. Outside of the addition, to the north, strange circular marks in the ground were found, not very definite, but enough to indicate that there had been something very large and circular outside of the north wall of the shop.

Again an understanding of the technology of the time, and a further clue from the legend that Mr. Deere had installed horsepower in his first plow factory, led to the inference that the outside area was a horse-driven treadmill, about twenty-five feet in diameter. The horse walked, fixed in place in a pen over the treadmill, and as the horse walked, the large wooden treadmill turned below him. On the underside of the circumference of the treadmill were wooden teeth. These engaged a lantern gear, which was at the end of a long shaft that extended into the shop addition. The strange, coffin-shaped pit was in perfect placement for the great counter wheel that would have had to be on the main driveshaft. From this counter wheel, belts would have been attached to an overhead shaft running behind the furnace, the forge, and the grindstone. From that overhead drive shaft, belts would have come down to turn the grindstone, to operate the large bellows necessary for the furnace air blast, and to operate the smaller bellows for the forge. Thus the reason for the compact arrangement of the shop was clear: Deere wanted to operate the shop off one drive shaft. To be operated this way, the machines all needed to be fairly close together. (Each time power is belted from one shaft to another, a great deal of power is lost; better to try to get the maximum possible off one drive shaft.)

With this set of inferences in place, the team was able to complete the plat of the full building. "In order to accommodate all this equipment, an addition to the original blacksmith shop was made by a 22-foot extension at the forge end, and so Mr. Deere ended up with a little plow factory that measured 26 feet wide by 53 feet long. The treadmill for the horse would have been located outside of this.... Usually in such situations some kind of a shed roof was provided to protect the whole treadmill structure."

It was indeed an innovative physical layout, and John Deere manifestly had the blacksmithing prowess to go with it. Soon people residing in the town and those out on the farms around it piled upon the floor of his little shop their broken trace chains and clevises, their worn-out Bull-tongues and other cracked or worn plowshares. The young blacksmith was kept busy seven days a week hammering, welding, drawing out, laying, casting, assembling. Deere's special skill at manufacturing farm implements also quickly surfaced; his old Vermont trick of sharpening and polishing the tines on the hayforks and polishing the shovels and other sharp implements soon made a reputation for him among the residents of Grand Detour.

One of the early histories of the county relates an anecdote that rings true. An old merchant in Oregon, the next town north, tells the story of Deere coming into his store with a lot of pitchforks. Placing them on the floor, Deere stepped on the tines, bending them to the floor. When he then stepped off, the tines sprang back to their original configuration. The merchant confessed at the time he suspected a trick and asked Mr. Deere if he would permit him to step on them. He was given permission. "But," said the merchant, "suppose they break?" "I will bear the loss," was the essence of Deere's reply. The merchant stepped on the forks, found there was no deception, and took the entire consignment for subsequent sale.

The exact date of this story is not given, but it likely occurred early in Deere's Grand Detour days. As the story was related, Deere himself had come to Oregon and was acting straightforwardly as a peddler or field man for a manufacturing organization. Of course, he was also the manufacturer. In effect, he was acting the part of the very common "one man band" typical of small villages all over the Midwest and West during that period. There were many builders of good machinery, and so what really counted was persuading the farmer to adopt certain practices and buy the equipment. Deere's reputation in these early years rested on his manufactured product, but it was largely his ability to dramatize these products and get them into the hands of his customers, scattered out over the wide prairies, that made him a business success.

In that first year in Grand Detour, Deere also began hewing out a small wood-framed home for his family. Since this home was still intact in the early 1980s, we can readily reconstruct, with the help of the industrial archaeology team of the University of Illinois, how he built that first section of it.

The house, as most in those days, began as a small structure, to be added to later. The central part, built first, was a simple story-and-a-half cottage, with two rooms below, a stairway to the upper story, and one large open sleeping space above. The total size was approximately eighteen feet by twenty-four feet; though not a large home by nineteenth-century Midwestern standards, it was only the second frame house in the little village. (The first, called the "red house," had been built by Willard House for his family; the rest of the settlers were living in log cabins.) Later that year, a third frame building was built for a store; it was first occupied by a Mr. Palmer, and sold the next year to one of early Grand Detour's most substantial citizens, Solon Cumins.

The town itself grew quickly. In the following year, five more frame buildings were erected: a modest hotel built by the Rock River Mill Company (the sawmill enterprise), with Robert McKenny as its proprietor; a frame house built by E.H. Shaw that was later converted to a bar; homes for Calvin Turner and a Mr. Martin; and a storehouse for the mill company. Thus the enterprising village of Grand Detour had by 1838 a half dozen frame buildings with tenants, in addition to several dozen less imposing log cabins. Some time in this period, probably almost at the start, a tavern was built, to be run by Irad Hill. With a sawmill, a gristmill, John Deere's blacksmith shop, and a country store, the town's business base was well grounded by the end of 1838.

That year, too, brought great personal satisfaction to John Deere, for Demarius and their children arrived. The four offspring had increased to five a few months after John had left Hancock, with the birth in March of Charles Henry Deere. Mrs. Deere came West by wagon (perhaps part of the way it was loaded aboard a barge or a steamer), accompanied not only by her three daughters and two sons, but also by her brother-in-law, John Peek, and his family. It was an arduous trip at best. The wagon was piled high with household goods; the break with Vermont was complete. Stories of the reunion abound, too, the favorite being that Demarius walked the last few miles into Grand Detour with baby Charles in her arms and, when John Deere ran to meet them, handed him the baby saying, "Here, John, I carried him all the way from Vermont." We do not need much imagination to picture the joy of that reunion—the family together once again, John Deere seeing his infant son for the first time. John and Demarius Deere and their five young children were now Illinoisans and would remain so for the rest of their lives.[1]

The New Englanders came to Illinois to farm the land. They had read of the unparalleled richness of the soil of the great prairies; now they were on hand to take advantage of it. But they made a curious misjudgment at the start. It was almost as if they had decided to give a party on the prairies, but had forgotten to come! Instead of tilling the prairie soil, the farmers who came to Illinois in the 1820s and '30s avoided the open prairie and instead began to clear the timbered areas, as their ancestors had done in the East. For almost two centuries pioneering had taken place in the forest, and clearing woodlands had come to be a national way of life. Many farmers shared two hypotheses that were later to prove to be painfully wrong. "If this prairie land is unable to supply nourishment for timber, then it cannot be 'strong' enough for field crops. For another thing, this prairie country seems singularly lacking in streams and springs. There must not be much water underneath those open lands. Let's go where the oaks are tallest. That's where the soil is richest." Both of these premises were false; indeed, they were quite the reverse of reality. The fibrous roots of the wild prairie grasses had been producing humus of great natural fertility for centuries. The matted prairie sod itself helped to check the leeching of calcium and other minerals, so needed for plant nutrition. The patches of wooded areas scattered over the prairies— the "groves," as they came to be known, a word that appears in so many Illinois place names—however, contained much less organic matter than did the brown silt loam in the undulating prairies and the black gumbo of the flatlands. The great primeval glaciers had treated all of this land to their eroding, enriching heritage, but the oaks and the willows in the groves had done little to add to the inherited fertility.

There were other, more valid, reasons for preferring the timbered groves for initial settlement. Timber meant wood, both for burning and for home building. One can sympathize with the pioneer as he weighed the prospect of settling out on the prairie. Not only would he be isolated, but the logs for the cabin and for the fires that would need to be built within it would have to be teamed over the land from the nearest wood lot. Those who settled among the trees saw their prairie neighbors pull way ahead of them in yields a few years later. As one put it: "Breaking the turf is, to the prairie agriculturalist, what clearing the ground is to those of wooded countries; the difference being that one man with a good team and plow will break three acres of the former in a day while the same force employed in the forest would scarcely prepare a like area for cultivation in a year."

By the late 1830s, about the time of John Deere's arrival, the pronounced advantages of the prairie soil became widely known. Soil analysis, for example, began to be utilized, and prairie agriculture began in earnest. John Deere's Ogle County had a scarcity of timber, and this did check the flow of immigration for a while, but as one of Deere's farmer-neighbors put it: "The economy together with the arts and sciences have removed further notions and objections and the tide [of immigration] is again setting back in most parts of the county."

Another obstacle to farming on the prairies was more formidable. The prairie was covered with a thick mat of grasses, often shoulder high. If this impenetrable covering indeed snuffed out seedlings of trees, it also presented a major task for the settlers' first cultivation. In sum, there needed to be a "prairie breaking."

There is a wonderfully evocative imagery about this word "breaking." It seems to capture the very essence of the pioneer story. The term "breaking" of land was not born with the settlement of the West, of course. Not only had there been breaking plows in New England—Daniel Webster himself had commissioned the building of a great monolith of a breaker reputed then to be the "largest plow ever built on this continent" —but also far back in English agricultural history, long before the settlement of New England. Still, "prairie breaking" captures the essence of the arduous, physically demanding fight with nature that was demanded of the settlers.

Agricultural advice, soon found in great volume in various Midwestern newspapers and journals, concentrated on this critically important first step. The types of equipment to be used, the depth of the plowing, the width of the cut, the best time of the year for breaking—all were argued at great length by the farmers, the editors, and others. The heart of the matter was cutting and turning that thick mat of prairie grasses. If there was hazel or redroot, or if there was willowroot, the farmer knew he faced a herculean task. One correspondent of the *Prairie Farmer* graphically discussed the depth at which to cut: "Cutting off a plant at the neck is always the most fatal to it; shallow plowing will cut the weeds and grass off at or near the neck of the plants and they may consequently soon die." If this description seems a bit macabre—the writer almost endows the grasses with human qualities—there was a compelling need to cut the roots at a place that would allow the turned sod to dry and decompose in the most efficient manner. The farmers coined the term "fire fanged" for improperly cut sod; as one anonymous cultivator put it, "instead of being rotted . . . the strong wiry roots of which the sod is mainly composed remain nearly as strong as when first turned over." He advocated more or less a "skinning" slice, no more than about two inches.[2]

The typical pattern was to use the great prairie-breaking plow, an enormous, heavy instrument perhaps weighing upwards of 125 pounds to be pulled by four, six, or even eight pair of oxen. There was soon a lively debate among the farmers, editors, and others about whether these juggernauts really were wise; Solon Robinson, a widely quoted authority,

Exhibit 2–1. *"Plowing on the Prairies Beyond the Mississippi," sketched by Theodore R. Davis* (Harper's Weekly, *May 9, 1868*)

was skeptical. "Fancy upon a level smooth piece of ground, free from sticks, stumps and stones, a team of four, five or even six yoke of oxen, hitched to a pair of cartwheels, and to them hitched a plow with a beam fourteen feet long, and the share, & c. of which weight from sixty to one hundred and twenty-five pounds of wrought iron steel, in which cuts the furrow from sixteen to twenty-four inches wide, and you will figure the appearance of a "breaking team' in operation." Robinson let his sarcasm hang out boldly: "If you ask me if this is necessary, I can only tell you that I suppose it is, for it is *fashionable.*" Robinson's preference was for a smaller plow, with less team. The large multipaired rigs were usually hired by the farmer as custom work; he would generally pay from two to four dollars per acre for the service (the lower price being more characteristic of the 1830s and '40s). But many farmers, progressive ones among them, chose to do their own breaking. All sorts of combinations were used; smaller numbers of oxen, teams of horses, or even an individual horse, with commensurately sized plows. An Illinois farmer maintained that as long as the land had very little hazel or redroot, he could do a good plowing with a cut of twelve inches with his pair of good horses. Still, tradition dies slowly in agriculture, and one reporter found that as late as 1857 most prairie breaking was still being done with four to six oxen and the heavy plow.

DEERE'S BREAKTHROUGH

Although prairie breaking has been highly dramatized, it was actually less important than the next step, the cultivation that had to be done the next season. Over the history of American agriculture, tillage and cultivation practices have loomed large in determining just how productive a given piece of land would be. One Indiana farmer in 1845 told a story that is an apt illustration of this point. Two brothers had settled together on the Indiana prairie, one of them on a rich bottomland farm and the other on a "cold, ugly, clay soil, covered with Black-jack oak." The latter kept getting more than seventy bushels to the acre, the former only about fifty. One brother was steadily growing rich on poor land and the other steadily growing poor on rich land. The farmer telling the story continues his homily: "One day the bottom-land brother came down to see the Black-jack oak farmer, and they began to talk about their crops and farms, as farmers are very apt to do. 'How is it,' said the first, 'that you manage on this poor soil to beat me in crops.' The reply was 'I *work* my land.' That was it, exactly. Some men rely on the soil, not on labor or skill, or care. *Some men expect their Lands to work, and some men expect to WORK THEIR LAND*—and that is just about the difference between a good and a bad farmer." Solon Robinson made much the same point: "Although it is easy to bring dry prairie land into cultivation, it requires a persevering industry on the part of the settler, sometimes accompanied with great privation and hardships for himself and family; and in this case, 'a bad beginning' does not 'make a good ending'."

Now, in trying to carry out subsequent cultivation, farmers encountered an intriguing problem. The rich black gumbo soil characteristic of the prairies was surely one of its bountiful blessings; rumor was that one could stick a crowbar down into it at night and it would sprout ten-penny nails before morning. But this very quality of sticky humus was also a curse to the early pioneer farmers. The soil was simply so adhesive when it contained any moisture that it stuck to everything—especially the plows. Sticking was especially troublesome in that first plowing after the breaking had been done, for this was an early-spring effort, at a time when the soil was often water-laden. Over and over in the literature this problem is reiterated. Farmers had to carry paddles with them and stop every few yards to scrape off the sticky soil from the parts of the plow. As this fresh soil was not only to be cut but also to be turned, there would have to be one or another form of moldboard, the extensive surface of which provided many square inches of area subject to soil adhesion.[3]

It is here that John Deere enters agricultural history. Sometime very early in his residence in Grand Detour, likely in that first year of 1837, he happened to be in the little sawmill owned by Andrus where he had repaired the pitman shaft a few days after arriving in town. On the floor was a broken steel mill saw. Precise details of this saw have long since disappeared into history; Edward C. Kendall, the curator of agriculture at the Smithsonian Institution's United States National Museum, studied the problem and concluded: "The circular saw, especially of the larger size, was probably not very common in America in the 1830s. . . . In a small, new, pioneering community it seems unlikely that the local sawmill would have been equipped with the newer circular saw rather than the familiar up and down saw which remained in use throughout the nineteenth century, and in places, well into the twentieth century. The up and down saw was a broad strip of iron or steel with large teeth in one edge. Driven by water power it slowly cut large logs into boards."

John Deere asked to have the broken saw blade and took it back to his blacksmith shop, for he had an idea for its use, relating directly to the need for a "plow that would scour." Deere might well have heard even back in Vermont of plows that did not scour and that picked up sticky soil, although the soil there was not especially noted for this difficulty except in the wet season of early spring. In Illinois it had to be high in his consciousness almost from the instant he began talking with farmers in the blacksmith's shop, for the area around Grand Detour abounded in this gumbo soil. Deere's idea was an ingenious one—to use the smooth steel of the saw blade, itself polished many times over by the thousands of strokes backward and forward through the logs of Ogle County, to form a smooth surface for the parts of a plow. John Deere recounted the next events many years later to a friend:

I cut the teeth off with a hand chisel, with the help of a striker and sledge, then laid them on the fire of the forge and heated what little I could at a time and shaped them as best I could with the hand hammer. After making the upright standard out of bar iron, I was ready for the wood parts. I went out to the timber, dug up a sapling and made the crooks of the roots for handles, shaped the beam out of a stick of timber with an ax and drawing-knife, and finally succeeded in constructing a very rough plow. I set it on a dry-goods box by the side of the shop-door. A few days after, a farmer from across the river drove up. Seeing the plow, he asked:

"Who made that plow?"

"I did, such as it is, wood work and all."

"Well," said the farmer, "that looks as though it would work. Let me take it home and try it, and if it works all right, I will keep it and pay you for it. If not I will return it."

"Take it," said I, "and give it a thorough trial."

About two weeks later, the farmer drove up to the shop, without the plow, and paid for it, and said: "Now get a move on you, and make me two more plows just like the other one."

There is another version of this story that involves the Lewis Crandall farm, just across the Rock River from the blacksmith shop. The essential story, often recounted with many variations, goes something like this: Having finished the plow with a piece of sawblade steel that was going to scour, Deere looked around for a field of *gumbo suprema*. Crandall's land lay in the Rock River bottom and was just this kind of sticky, humus soil. Deere himself took the plow over to the field, hitched it to Crandall's team, and personally plowed the first long furrow. The result was the same; the plow did indeed scour beautifully.

But this bare story has not satisfied inveterate storytellers. A well-embroidered variation was told by a Chicago newspaperman in 1926:

Farmer Crandall's field, across the Rock River from Grand Detour, was filled with neighbors from all over the countryside. They had been arriving since dawn—men, women and children, in ox-drawn carts and wagons, a-horseback and a-foot.

They stood about in groups, some in earnest discussion, some stolidly silent, all tense with excitement. The day of days had come. The young blacksmith from Rutland, Vermont, who claimed he could accomplish the impossible, was about to demonstrate his claim.

The newfangled plow he had fashioned from a discarded steel jig-saw blade and brought across the river in a rowboat, was even now being hitched to the horse he had borrowed from Farmer Crandall.

"Giddap," he said, gripping the plow handles.

Down the field they moved, followed by the entire countryside. Down the field they moved and in their wake—ah, miracle of miracles!—a clean cut furrow; a clean cut furrow slice of black, greasy soil. The impossible had been accomplished. A plow had been found that would work—that would cleave, without carrying, the rich alluvial earth of the Mississippi valley; that would, as the farmers say, scour itself.

No wonder, on that summer day in 1837, men tossed their hats high in air, huzzaed and slapped one another on the back; no wonder women cheered and children danced for joy. An empire had been won.

It really matters not which version is closer to the actual events. The important message was that a piece of polished steel had been incorporated by John Deere into a plow, and this plow had been able to scour the most sticky of Illinois soils.

Our knowledge of these first plows is greatly enhanced by an event that occurred in 1901—the discovery of one of John Deere's first three plows, one of two made in 1838. This plow had been owned by the Brierton family, just south of Grand Detour, continuously through all of the intervening years and as Joseph Brierton's son described it to Charles Deere in 1901, it seemed unassailable that the plow had been purchased in 1838 from John Deere. The company kept the plow at its Moline headquarters for a number of years, finally presenting it to the Smithsonian Institution in 1938, where it has been on display ever since.

Photographs of the plow immediately make clear the unconventional construction of the moldboard. It is essentially a parallelogram, curved in a concave fashion. Deere must have given a great deal of thought to the shape, to the special curve of his moldboard, for its exact contours would determine just how well the soil would be turned over after the share had made the cut. The width of the moldboard for this plow was just twelve inches; it was a light plow, a small plow that could be pulled by one horse.

Its unconventional look might have been dictated, thought Smithsonian curator Kendall, by the constraints of that saw blade; the width of saw blades at that time was generally ten to twelve inches, their thickness just about that of the moldboard (the latter was about .228 to .238 inch). Kendall even sketched in a Smithsonian bulletin how Deere might have cut and bent a saw blade to gain the particular concave configuration. Yet, when Kendall had the 1838 plow subjected to a spark test, the results seemed to show that the share and landside were steel, but the moldboard itself was wrought iron.

Clearly, the available supply of broken saw blades soon would have been exhausted, and manufacturers such as John Deere would have been forced to search around for what steel they could lay their hands on and finish the remainder of the plows with wrought iron. Steel was already available in modest quantities in the Midwest at that time; as early as 1841 steel was being shipped to Illinois and Mississippi River ports on consignment to local merchants. This advertisement appeared in a Galena, Illinois, newspaper in mid-1841: "STEEL—2000 lbs. of cast, English, blister, American do., also plates 5" wide for plows, for sale by June 24, John Dowling." By 1844, Deere was ordering steel directly from

Exhibit 2–2. *John Deere's 1838 Plow, Smithsonian Institution (Deere Archives)*

the St. Louis office of the well-known Pittsburgh organization, Lyon Shorb & Co. One bill of lading for 1844 has been preserved, an order for "plow steel" (probably cast steel), "bars iron" (probably wrought iron), and "springsteel" (which would either be blister steel or carburized cast steel).

The mixture, in this Pittsburgh order, of wrought iron and the various steels is a clue that Deere's plows came out in some mixed combination. When the blacksmith shop itself was rediscovered by the University of Illinois industrial archaeological team in 1962, metal leavings were found that would have had to have been used in the shop prior to Deere's removal to a new location in the early 1840s. The team's technical engineers identified much of this scrap as trimmings of blister steel, a form of carburized steel in common usage in the colonial period and up to approximately 1860.

The Smithsonian's Kendall guessed that most of Deere's early plows had wrought-iron moldboards, with steel shares; the earliest extant John Deere advertisement, from April 1843, mentions this combination. Yet it is conceivable that both shares and moldboards for many of his early plows were steel, while other parts—landsides and standards—were wrought iron. By the latter part of the 1840s, Deere's advertisements emphasized steel moldboards. The first plow could well have had both a steel share and a steel moldboard; John Deere's own description of how it was made implies as much.

Generally, when better quality steel was desired, it was imported from England. The Pittsburgh company probably obtained its steel from England, directly or through the firm of Naylor & Co. in New York City, a major importer of iron and steel. Later, Deere also dealt directly with Naylor.

By the mid-1840s cast steel of adequate quality was being made in the United States. James Swank, author of a definitive history of iron and steel making up to 1885, noted John Deere's role. "The first slab of cast plow steel ever rolled in the United States was rolled by William Woods, at the steel works of Jones & Quigg, [in Pittsburgh] in 1846, and shipped to John Deere, of Moline, Illinois." Dates here do not quite match—Deere was not in Moline at that time—and we have no further record of how this purchase occurred. It was not until the 1850s, though, that the quality of cast steel in the grades used for saws and agricultural machinery came up to the English standard; even then, said Swank, the American steel manufacturers "did not make tool steel of the best quality as a regular product."

Often the steel purchased by Deere was corroded or dented, having traveled great distances, and would need to be polished. If the moldboard was wrought iron, an extensive grinding and polishing operation was required to bring it to full "self-polishing" status, with a surface similar to that of steel. It was this quality of smoothness, dominant in John Deere's thinking since his Vermont days, that apparently set his plows apart from those of his competitors—they did indeed go through the soil with ease, and with enough speed to emit a slight whine, earning them the sobriquet, "the singing plows."

Sometimes the shop's polishing apparatus broke down, and when it did, the quality of the plows deteriorated. One farmer from the little village of Inlet Grove, a few miles south of Grand Detour, had been furnishing John Deere the charcoal for his blacksmith forges. He charged from fifty cents to one dollar a load, and took the remainder of his compensation in needed repairs on his wagon and other farm equipment. One day he asked John Deere if he would trade charcoal for a plow; when he took the plow for a practice run it did not scour very well, because it had not been polished, and John Deere came along to personally inspect the problem. Presumably, as soon as the polisher was back in operation, the plow was repolished for the still unsatisfied customer.[4]

History has credited John Deere with being "the inventor of the steel plow"; as one writer on the subject put it in a flight of fancy, "he gave to the world the steel plow." This overstates the case, as historians are so often guilty of doing, and at this point it must be stated unequivocally that John Deere was not the first person to use steel in a plow. New ideas for plow technology were burgeoning in this period—the first half of the nineteenth century turned out to be one of the most innovative in the history of agricultural machinery. Cast-iron plows had been made in Scotland as early as 1763; an American patent was taken out by Charles Newbold in 1797. At that time the American farmer was skeptical of

JOHN DEERE'S COMPANY

A PICTORIAL HISTORY OF DEERE & COMPANY AND ITS TIMES

John Deere lived in Grand Detour from 1836 to 1848 in the house shown on these pages. Above is the home as depicted in Combination Atlas of Ogle County *(1872), 24 years after Deere left.*

*A*t left are two views of
the house after restoration
by Deere & Company. It
is now part of the John Deere
Historic Site, a registered
National Historic Landmark
(National Park Service), and
is a Historic Landmark
of Agricultural Engineering
(American Society of
Agricultural Engineers).

*T*he Grand Detour area had an abundance of natural resources, including water power and water borne transportation. Its location is illustrated by the map (left, from Combination Atlas of Ogle County, 1872) and the recent photography (above). The town's name came from the unusual bend of the river. Ferry service was established early; one of the ferry boats is shown at top, left.

*S*urrounded by rich farm
land, John Deere immediately
saw a need for plows that
would scour in the prairie
soil. He quickly abandoned
the more mundane chores of
a local blacksmith and
became a plow manufacturer.
His restored blacksmith
shop is shown (opposite page
and below). The top left
view is an artist's depiction,
in the archaeological
exhibition building at the
John Deere Historic Site, of
activity in the shop.

*P*lowing midwestern soils was a difficult job, as illustrated in "The Last Furrow," by Herbert Dicksee (1899). John Deere's plows made the task easier and helped to open vast new territories to agriculture and settlement. Above are two drawings of Deere's first plow as scholars believe it appeared.

JOHN DEERE'S PLOW WORKS. 1847.

*I*n the late 1840s John Deere relocated to Moline, a site more suitable for his growing plow business. By then Moline was an established community on the Mississippi River. Top, left, is Moline in 1857 and above is a view courtesy of the Rock Island County Historical Society. The area included Fort Armstrong on an island in the river, top, and riverfront industries like John Deere's plow works, bottom left.

MOLINE
PLOW FACTORY!

DEERE, TATE & GOULD,
MANUFACTURERS OF
PLOWS, GRAIN DRILLS, &c.,
MOLINE, ROCK ISLAND COUNTY, ILLINOIS.

The subscribers, situated at the foot of the "Upper Rapids," on the Mississippi River, are manufacturing all kinds of STEEL PLOWS, known as the

"MOLINE CENTRE-DRAFT PLOW."

As we have unlimited water power—are in the immediate vicinity of inexhaustible beds of bituminous Coal, and in continual receipt of the best Lumber of the upper regions of Iowa and Wisconsin, (three very important considerations,) we are enabled to execute all branches of our business, in the most durable and substantial manner, and CHEAPER than the same quality of work can be executed in any other locality in the country.

We claim for our PLOWS superiority over any other now in use, for the following properties, viz:

First. Lighter, or easier draft.

Second. Put together with bolts and nuts, instead of rivets, so that they are more readily repaired.

Third. Much better painted and finished, and warranted to be as represented.

We have also a large supply of CAST STEEL MOLD BOARDS, made expressly for us, by Messrs. Naylor & Co., Sheffield, England, which are unrivalled for scouring and durability.

Mr. DEERE commenced the manufacture of these Plows about ten years ago, known as the "Grand de Tour Plow," upon which our Plows are a great improvement.

We would return our sincere thanks to the community for the liberal patronage heretofore received, and hope, by attention and care, in selecting the best materials, and employing superior workmen, to merit a continuance of the same. An *impartial trial* is all we ask, feeling sure of success, if that is granted.

DEERE, TATE & GOULD.

FOR SALE BY

MISSOURI REPUBLICAN PRINT.

John Deere soon expanded his business by taking on partners who had special abilities and needed capital. This allowed him to develop his innate skills of product improvement and market development. Shown below are John Deere (left) and John Gould, his key partner.

The Grand de Tour Plow. About ten years ago, a Mr. Deere commenced the making of a plow with the above name, which soon became celebrated in all the Rock River region, and for a considerable distance up and down the Mississippi. This plow, with improvements, is still manufactured by the original inventor, or one of the firm of Deere, Sate, & Gould, at Moline, the call for it having been greatly extended. Cast-steel mould-boards, made by Noyes & Co., of Sheffield, England, are now used. The implement is now named the "Moline Center Draft Plow."

Above is an article from the Prairie Farmer, *March 1851, illustrating the wide recognition of Deere's product. Left is an advertisement showing product diversification, early emphasis on superior quality, and expanding market areas.*

*D*eere enterprises were a key factor in the growth of Moline (shown in 1877), especially under the leadership of Charles H. Deere, John's son (left). Workers from Europe and the eastern states were attracted to Moline in large numbers, and some Deere factory workers are pictured at right.

By the 1880s Deere & Company had about 800 employees (some are shown at left) and supported cultural activities like the Deere Coronet Band (bottom) for its growing force of skilled workers. Moline had other important manufacturers. Below is an advertising item of the Moline Wagon Company. It was later acquired by Deere & Company.

MOLINE PLOW WORKS

ESTABLISHED 1847.

Compliments of DEERE & COMPANY January 1st 1882.

The Gilpin Sulky Plow was an extremely successful Deere & Company product. It is shown on the opposite page with John Deere at left. The much expanded factory is shown just to the right of the plow and in a close-up illustration at top of page. The Gilpin Sulky plow helped continue Deere's leadership, which led to a greatly diversified product line and expanded marketing network, as illustrated by the advertising piece above.

*D*espite two world wars and a major depression, Deere & Company grew into one of the nation's leading corporations. A centennial was observed. Products were diversified and improved in function and design as Deere advanced the mechanization of farming.

*S*ince the mid-1960s, Deere & Company's three main
lines have been agricultural, industrial and consumer
products; with the subsequent addition of the insurance
and financial services operations, these remain the focus
of the Company into the 1980s.

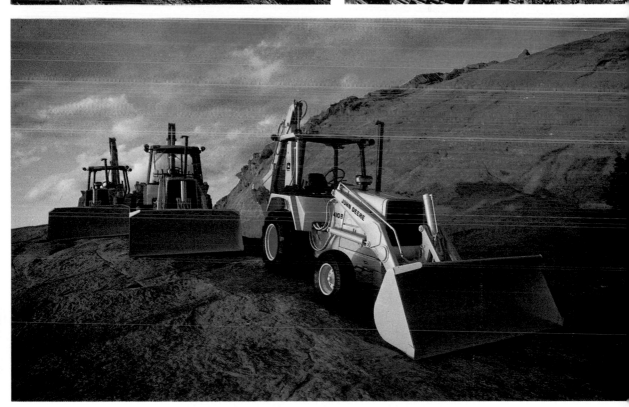

*S*eventeen John Deere combines at work on a ranch in Texas testify to the contribution of modern agricultural machinery in feeding the world's population (Overleaf).

using something other than wood, many feeling that it "poisoned the land, injured its fertility, and promoted the growth of weeds." Opposition faded, however, with the development of an "improved" cast-iron plow by Jethro Wood, first patented by him in 1814 and put into manufacturing on a considerable commercial scale by 1817. By the time Wood brought out a second version in 1819, he was selling almost 4,000 per year.

The cast-iron plow had an enormous advantage over the old wooden or wrought-iron varieties: it could be replicated time after time by the manufacturer. Each of the earlier wood or wrought iron plows was an individualized version done by the artisan's own hands. By casting, the exact piece could be duplicated again and again. Jethro Wood carried the process one step further by breaking his plow into component parts and making these interchangeable, thus enabling the farmer to replace a worn-out or broken part with a new one from the factory. The Wood plow could be built more cheaply and kept in service more readily and at less expense.

The cast-iron plow worked very well on the sandy soils of the East, but in heavier soils it could not hold its smooth surface. The cast-iron surfaces abounded in small cavities known as blowholes; in addition, cast iron cannot take a high polish. By the early 1830s, blacksmiths and other artisans of the Midwest were searching around for ways to incorporate steel in the plow. Clearly, the first person to do this was not John Deere.

R.L. Ardrey, in his classic book on American agricultural implements, gives credit to John Lane of Lockport, Illinois, as the first to successfully incorporate steel in the plow. Lane, too, was a blacksmith and in 1831 had taken another old saw and, by cutting it into three links, had made a moldboard of the requisite length, another piece forming the share, and an anchor wing of iron. Lane never made a commercial success of his plow; his granddaughter remembered many years later: "As it would bend, he never put it on the market." Lane did take second prize at the Third Annual Cattle Show and Fair at Ottawa, Illinois, in September 1843, but he was handily beaten by the Elgin plow, another plow incorporating steel. In 1846, the Elgin manufacturer recounted his successful day at the fair and how he had been forced to use a piece of saw blade because his steel shipment from Pittsburgh had not arrived, and then commented on the invention of the steel plow itself. "Indeed, among some half dozen of our prominent plough manufacturers within the bounds of the Union Agricultural Society, who have, with such commendable spirit and perseverance, aided in the bringing out the invaluable implement which now blesses many of our farmers, it is hard to make distinction. Each is entitled to honor greater than the conqueror of armies. Mr. Lane of Will County, Messrs. Pierce, and Scovill & Gates of Cook, Jones of Dupage, the lamented Bristol, with Guptil & Renwick of Kane, and among the rest your humble servant would claim a small portion. The first plow made with steel moldboard I believe was made by

Mr. Lane." These were all Chicago-area manufacturers and it appears that
John Deere's version of the plow was not even known in that area at that
time.

EARLY RIVALRIES

Deere had enough of an entrepreneurial bent to see the possibilities in
1837 of his first plow, and he made two more the next year. He was not
much of a recordkeeper and no written accounts of this first half dozen
years are extant; it seems clear, though, that Deere shifted into plow
manufacturing in a substantial way by the third year, 1839, when he
made ten plows. His remembrances later were that he made forty in the
year 1840, seventy-five in the year 1841, and 100 in the year 1842. This
would certainly qualify him as the premier manufacturer for his small
area (say, in a twenty-five-mile radius), but these 228 plows built over the
first half dozen years of Deere's life in Grand Detour would hardly
nominate him as a major manufacturer. The census of 1860, noting the
explosion of plow manufacturing over the previous thirty years, told of
one plow-making establishment in Pittsburgh, Pennsylvania, that was
building 100 plows daily in 1836, most of them of patterns adapted largely
for the Midwest. When its production was combined together with that of
another well-known Pittsburgh company, almost 34,000 plows yearly
were coming out of this one city alone. Many of these Eastern plows
incorporated steel in at least the plowshare itself. The Pittsburgh plows
found their way readily to southern Illinois and one of the issues of the
Sangamon Journal of Springfield, Illinois, in 1836 carried an advertisement
for a plow that "never loads with earth, runs steady, requires only
one-half or two-thirds the strength of a team requisite to carry any
other—and does the work far better." John Lyman, the merchant selling
the plow in Springfield, displayed some real salesmanship, too: "Farmers!
Will you try it? Do so then, and if you do not find my plow equal to the
above description, you may return it and take your money paid for it."
The following year Lyman had obtained some improved versions of the
Pittsburgh plow, "made in the best style, polished and laid in steel."

What often happened was that a small hometown Western artisan
would decide to manufacture at least part of the plow under an arrangement to pay royalties to the original manufacturer. Patent protection was
more or less rudimentary in the 1840s, leading Edmund Burke, the
commissioner of patents, to decry in his annual report to Congress in
1846 the "wanton aggression upon the rights of the meritorious inventor." Burke was even more judgmental, almost messianic, in his report of
1848 in his castigation of "the wilfull infringer of the rights of the
inventor" as being "base and corrupt morally . . . as common thieves.
His offense is committed from the same depraved and wicked motive . . .
and [he] should be hunted from society with the same inexorable

perseverance." The patenter, of course, wanted as narrow and restrictive a definition as possible for his new idea. Oftentimes, though, the royalty was deliberately "forgotten"—the design just pirated and adapted to the new manufacturer's ideas.

One of the best-known plow manufacturers in Illinois was the firm of Jewett & Hitchcock, purchased by these two men in 1841 from H.E. Bridge, a foundryman in Springfield. Soon Jewett and Hitchcock were advertising the "Jewett's Improved Patent Cary Plow," all over the state. "The moldboard of this so well and so favorably known plow is made of wrought iron, 5/16 of an inch thick, and the share of steel which carries a fine edge, the whole face of the moldboard and share is ground smooth, so that it scours perfectly bright in any soil and will not choke in the foulest ground." The Cary (also called Dagen) plow was originally made in Connecticut, and its rather standardized form soon had manufacturers copying it throughout the East. The Jewett improvement introduced the use of rivets for attaching the moldboard and sheath. We do not know whether Jewett ever paid any royalties back to the Connecticut originators. This plow, though, became a well-known one in Illinois all through this period. Other manufacturers and merchants also sold the Jewett-Hitchcock version, just substituting their names in exactly the same advertisement.

One of these was John Deere. We learn of this from his advertisement in the *Rock River Register* in early 1843. This little newspaper had started out in Mt. Morris, a few miles north of Grand Detour, in 1842, but its young editor, D.C. Dunbar, died and the paper had been purchased and moved to Grand Detour in 1843. By this time, the effects of a depression were being felt everywhere and John Deere was compelled to add at the bottom of the advertisement (calling attention to it by a small hand with a pointing finger): "The Price of Plows, in consequence of hard times, will be reduced from last year's prices."

This Deere advertisement is worth analysis. First, Deere clearly was selling Jewett plows the previous year, as the prices were reduced "from last year's prices." A likely inference would be that Deere had contracted with Benjamin Jewett in the previous year, when Jewett first began selling his "improved" version. The production figures cited above for the early 1840s came directly from John Deere, but at a much later period, at the end of his life. How clearly would he have remembered the numbers of Jewett plows sold as contrasted to the number of plows he manufactured himself? John Deere had said that he "made" 100 plows in 1842; perhaps he sold an additional set of Jewett plows, too. There is no way at present to determine the exact combination of manufactured and jobbed plows that came out of John Deere's shop in the first half dozen years.

A puzzling story of the relationship between the Deere plow and the H.H. May plow from Galesburg, Illinois, gives a glimmer of the push-and-tug among plow manufacturers in this early period. May had come to

PATENT CARY PLOUGH.

JOHN DEERE respectfully informs his friends and customers, the agricultural community, of this and the adjoining counties, and dealers in Ploughs, that he is now prepared to fill orders for the same on presentation.

The mould board of this well, and so favorably known PLOUGH, is made of wrought iron, and the share of steel, 5-16th of an inch thick, which carries a fine sharp edge. The whole face of the mould board and share is ground smooth, so that it scours perfectly bright in any soil, and will not choke in the foulest of ground. It will do more work in a day, and do it much better and with much less labor, to both team and holder, than the ordinary ploughs that do not scour, and in consequence of the ground being better prepared the agriculturalist obtains a much heavier crop.

☞The price of Ploughs, in consequence of hard times, will be reduced from last year's prices.

Grand Detour, Feb. 3, 1843.   2tf

Galesburg in 1837 from New England, where, alleged his biographer, he had pioneered the reaper a half dozen years before Cyrus McCormick. There, according to a local Galesburg historian, he had "invented" the steel plow. The historian even had the precise date for the event: "But after five years of discouraging experiments, on May 6, 1842, Mr. May noticed that the cavities in fine steel were many times less than in cast or wrought iron, and concluded at once to try fine steel for plows, and within two days he had a plow running, made of one of Wm. Nowland's best saw-mill saw plates, and it would scour bright in any soil, which made that day one of great rejoicing in Galesburg."

This claim could be dismissed as just another example of local pride were it not for a chain of events that happened to John Deere twenty-five years later. By the mid-1860s, to anticipate our story, Deere had become a major plow manufacturer, operating by this time in the town of Moline, a name that had become synonymous with superior plows. John Deere was the largest manufacturer in the town and called his product "the Moline Plow." About this time, in the mid-1860s, another firm, Candee, Swan & Co., began using the name "Moline Plow" in its advertisements, and Deere brought suit for trademark infringement. In the course of the trial, a good deal of information surfaced, including some revealing tidbits about the May plow. Three of Deere's former partners— Luke E. Hemenway, Robert N. Tate, and John M. Gould—and his former shop foreman, Andrew Friberg, testified in the case. By this time, Friberg had left the Deere organization to become one of the partners in the rival Moline firm. All had been involved with Deere either as associates or as fellow townsmen back in the Grand Detour days, and they were quizzed by both complainant and defense lawyers. Memories had dimmed a bit, for most of the key events had happened more than twenty years earlier. Still, some remarkably pungent comments ensued.

Hemenway had the earliest association; he had been a partner with John Deere for about nine months in 1841–42. How much business was he doing at that time? "He carried on general blacksmithing, not extensively. I knew him as blacksmith of the village; I think he did not have more than one forge at that time, and worked that himself. The business of the country did not demand more." He was a good mechanic, Hemenway agreed. Tate seemed less certain: "I don't presume that John Deere has any pretensions to be a machinist. He may be a good judge of a plow and not know anything of it; as an original he does not possess the element of faculty. John Deere may be and is a good judge of plows; as to the fundamental structure of the plow, he is deficient, never having applied himself practically while I have known him." Gould framed his view of Deere slightly differently: "In the first place, when he made a plow he tried it himself in different soils; if he could add an improvement to it he did so, and would then turn it over to a farmer to be tried by him also. If any improvements were suggested they were made. If he came across anything new which he regarded as an improvement, he adopted it, and tried that before offering it for sale to the public. His improvements were thus made by copying, reflection, and constant experiments. Making plows was his hobby since I have known him. . . . " Gould was then asked a key question, "Would you call him a man of inventive ability?" Gould replied, "I should not call him a man of general inventive ability. The improvements he would make would be by practice or experimenting, more than creative or inventive."

The thrust of this questioning had more purpose than titillating the court with some personal views about John Deere. One of the important threads of the trademark case was to establish whether John Deere had indeed made important inventions relating to the plow. It was at this point that the May plow intruded into the case. Tate was the first to mention it. When asked to identify the inventor of the various plows that had been made, or were then being made, in Moline, Illinois, under the name of J. Deere, or John Deere, Plows, Tate replied: "The plow history goes back to 1841. A person by the name of Hitchcock commenced what he called the Diamond Plow, in Princeton, Ill. Afterwards, May, of Galesburg, manufactured a plow in shape nearly the form that is manufactured now. This is the earliest I recollect of seeing a steel moldboard. The share and moldboard were combined at that time, and May was the first man that laid any claim to the improved steel plow. There is no improvement on the May steel plow, as made in 1843, or later, perhaps up to this time. . . . While at Grand Detour we borrowed the May Plow, and copied its improvements in 1847. I essentially consider May the sole constructor, in form, of the western steel plow."

Friberg had a more colorful way of telling the same story: "He [John Deere] told me once, when he commenced making plows, there was a plow made in the country around Galesburg, or in Galesburg, I can't tell which, that they called the Diamond Plow. . . . He said he heard this plow gave good satisfaction, so he went and got one for a pattern; then he went and bought stock for fifty of them . . . then he made out a bill of sale of that stock to one of his workmen; so he went to work to help in making the plows, and they sold them. He done that so that the patentee could not come at Mr. Deere for the use of his patent."

It seems clear that both Tate and Friberg are remembering a real incident relating to the May plow. Their facts, however, are a bit off. May had twice attempted to have his plow patented; in 1842 his application was rejected "for want of novelty," and in 1844, after May refiled, it was turned down for exactly the same reason. So John Deere, to whatever degree he borrowed some plow part configuration from May, was not afraid of a patent suit as such. He would not have had to pay a licensing fee, such as he had done for the Hitchcock plow; nevertheless the subterfuge described by Friberg easily could have happened. The dates that Tate and Friberg ascribe to these events also seem slightly off. If the

May plow had really been built precisely on that magical date of May 6, 1824, given by the Galesburg historian, this would have been at least four years after John Deere had made his first plow in Grand Detour. Indeed, Deere's plow of 1838, now in the Smithsonian Institution, almost had to be earlier than May's.

How, then, to explain the Friberg-Tate allegations of pirating? The best inference is that Deere, at a later point, did indeed pirate ideas from the May plow in order to improve his own—as likely he did with many other plows. So, too, did the other manufacturers. Now, adding Gould's comments, a mind's-eye picture of John Deere begins to emerge. He was an excellent smith, he worked at the forge himself, and he possessed a "Vermont tinkerer's" mechanical ability. He was not an engineer, nor even a master mechanic, but he did possess, as Gould so succinctly pointed out, the ability to make adaptations from a variety of sources and put them together in a well designed piece of equipment that would find ready customer acceptability. He pirated ideas from many other people, as they undoubtedly did from him. If pirating seems a harsh word, it is clear nonetheless that plow manufacturers all through the Midwest in the 1830s and '40s were blatantly exploiting each other's ideas and innovations.

Certainly from the standpoint of the users—the farmers all through the Midwest—the results of this rivalry were extremely beneficial. As one Plainfield, Illinois, farmer put it, addressing his "annual cattle show" in 1844: "But a few years ago the man who would have agreed to produce a plow which would scour itself on our prairie soil would easily have commanded $50 for the implement. Yet we have them now, by a dozen manufacturers, which do that perfectly. And how has it been done? Not certainly by giving the matter up, and calling it an impossibility—nor, by selling out and going back East in disgust—declaring that the prairies can never be plowed. It has been done by setting ourselves about it—and I confess in a manner too that I never expected to see."

The Illinois Supreme Court justice who finally ruled on the trademark case—incidentally, against the Deere claim of infringement—summed up John Deere's unique position in history very well: "The testimony . . . tends to show that Deere was not the inventor of any material part of his plow, and that his great recommendation and praise is, that he had the sagacity to discern to what profitable use the inventions of others could be applied, and by a well directed judgment he has constructed a plow not inferior to any in use in our widespread agricultural community, all of which entitles him to as much credit as if an original inventor."[5]

LIFE AND BUSINESS IN GRAND DETOUR

Although for its first half dozen years Grand Detour lay in the shadow of a depression, it grew briskly. The panic of 1837 had been severe enough to sharply depress business conditions, and the index of wholesale commodity prices, which had stood at 131 in February 1837, by December 1842 had fallen to 69. Yet all through this period Grand Detour was a bustling frontier community full of new people and new ideas. Earnest Calkins, describing Galesburg (south and west of Grand Detour) in this same period, commented on the same incongruity: "A country-wide panic affected this little self-contained isolated community suprisingly little. It was not yet hitched up to the national economic machinery, and its problems were peculiarly its own. There was no unemployment. Everyone was busy with his own construction job, which could still go on without check. They did not miss money; they had little in any case. There was no bank, no circulating medium, most of what they needed was produced among themselves, and an ingenious system of barter took care of exchange of goods for services. They reverted for the time being to an even more primitive state of society, such as must have existed before money was invented."

Many of the new settlers in the 1837–42 period brought substantial capital. Solon Cumins, for example, bought controlling interest in the Grand Detour Hydraulic Company in 1838 (changing its name to the Rock River Mill Company) and then set up a substantial country store that by 1840 was doing, by Cumins' own account, a $40,000 business. George Cushing was the town's first carpenter, Ebenezer Day the millwright. Wagons were made by S.E. Hathaway; he soon married Sophronia Weatherby, who had been the town's first maiden lady back in 1836. The cabinetmaker was Mr. Henry; George L. Herrick was the journeyman tinker, working in the shop of G. Clements. O.F. Palmer was shoemaker; O. Eddy worked with him. First settler Willard House became postmaster and also in 1838 obtained the rights to open a ferry across the Rock River, to connect with Dixon and points south and west. A celebrated sign was nailed to the ferry boat sometime during this period either by House or one of his successors: "Since man to man is so unjust, I do not know what man to trust. I've trusted many to my sorrow, pay today and I'll trust tomorrow." Leonard Andrus had established a mail stage line in 1838 from Dixon to Rockford by way of Grand Detour, obtaining rights for the United States mail service. The town's complement of public servants included Erastus Hubbell as justice of the peace, Calvin Turner as constable, and Mr. Goodrich as schoolteacher in his own home. (In 1839 a brick schoolhouse was constructed and Sophronia Weatherby became the first full-time schoolteacher; the little building was also used for church services, elections, etc.) Three churches were organized—Congregational, Episcopal, and Methodist-Episcopal denominations—all operating out of parishioners' homes in the first few years. Irad Hill operated a flourishing tavern, undoubtedly furnishing some grist for the sermons at the churches. (The temperance movement was active in the early days of Grand Detour, and in February 1839 a temperance society was organized, with just about everyone in town—it had seventy-two members.)

The tavern and the church were the two chief centers for socializing, for there was not much else in the way of entertainment. A Rock River resident in 1837 wrote his friend in Buffalo, New York: "You have musick and dancing too. The only musick that I have heard for three months is Dick's tin horn—what I shall do this winter, I don't know—no books, no musick, no theatre, no nothing."

Sarah Margaret Fuller, later the literary critic for Horace Greeley's *New York Tribune*, on a visit about this time, described the Grand Detour area with verve: "Passing through one of the fine, park-like woods, almost clear from underbrush, carpeted with thick grasses and flowers, we met, (for it was Sunday) a little congregation just returning from their service, which had been performed in a rude house in its midst. It had a sweet and peaceful air, as if such words and thoughts were very dear to them. The parents had with them all their little children; but we saw no old people; that charm was wanting, which exists in such scenes in older settlements, of seeing the silver bent in reverence beside the flaxen head." But Miss Fuller was no Pollyanna about this pioneer country. "So many dwellings of the new settlers . . . showed plainly that they had no thought beyond satisfying the grossest material wants. Sometimes they look attractive, the little brown houses, the natural architecture of the country in the edge of the timber but almost always when you came near, the slovenliness of the dwelling and the rude way in which objects around it were treated, when so little care would have presented a charming whole, were very repulsive . . . their progress is Gothic, not Roman. . . ."

One is often tempted to idealize the past, particularly the village of yesteryear. The image is often of a bucolic, friendly, slow-paced life in which everyone is "a friend to man." How might Grand Detour have fitted this description? Another traveler described a short stay in the village in his diary, the year being 1839:

[One-quarter] an hour brought me in midst of some fifteen or twenty houses—widely scattered over a low & to appearances swampy prairie—& as I enquired for Tavern things looked really dismal—McKinney Kept Store—Bar—grog shop—Tavern & store houses all in one building—the scene around was so gloomy—& dull—did not see any one stirring—in course of short time Landlord said supper ready—followed—but when saw table was struck mute—face chair—a long table some 20 ft extended in the middle—covd with an oil cloth—on about 4 ft of this table at one end were arranged in an order in unison with all around—a large white Dish was fast spreading a ps. of pork—3 inch cubic—a broken plate of rather dingy bread—about 2 in square of Molasses Cake—a plate of questionable Butter—a bottle of Lapis[?]—a few peeld Onions—& this our supper with additon of a cup of Herb Tea—with black sugar and milkless—as expect no cows in country—But I was hungry or else I could not have swallowed a mouthful [--] butter strong & Bread sour—another traveller myself & Landlord sat down—Ye Gods save me from likes again—a dirty Tallow Candle illumined the way to our mouths—I soon made my meal I assure you—then repaired to Barr room which Kept in Store—where were some half dozen young men smoking—drinking & bargaining about rifles—almost suffacated—ask'd to be shown to my room —Ye Nymphs of all odd places—the smell of tar fish—whisky struck my olfactory nerves—& such a room—beggars description [—] broken windows—with tattered rags for curtains—a rickety floor without a rag of carpet—a bedstead in corner as if tumbling down—with bed & bedding that long were strangers to water—at the other extremity were placed without order—whiskey—pork—fish & Tar Barrells —in rich profusion & ill ask did I sleep in such a 12 x 15—true I did—but after a restless night from smells & unheard of yelping of Prairie Wolves during night.

Oct 14 I was up so soon as dim twilight appeared [—] glad to get rid of such accomodations—going to door could scarce see, such a heavy frost & fog—but any thing better—than the howling of Wolves, Knawing of rats—barking of dogs—& tinckling of cow bells—with the minutia to make up an infernal concerto—7 a.m. stage coming to door—asked if going to have breakf before starting [—] Oh yes says Landlord & lead me into self same room as night before & then the same table etc—well says I, if this is not a little too much—it was so bad that a drunken coot in Barr room would not sit down to it & let out some of his vituperations— saying it was not fit for hogs—etc—8 a.m. Jumpd into stage with a light heart & belly too, in hopes to find a spot where they live—shall long remember Grand De Tour—shall hold it up in warning to all travellers.

The anonymous traveler's warnings about the Grand Detour area were rooted in reality, for this was a rough and ready period for frontier life and frontier justice. With so few law enforcement officers, the settlers sometimes resorted to cruder ways to preserve law and order. Grand Detour had a notorious case in this particular period. A "banditti" gang was operating through the area, allegedly led by a giant man called John Driscoll, three of his sons, and a number of other locals. Seven members of the gang had been jailed in Oregon, Illinois, in early 1841. Next door was a two-story brick courthouse, built to be ready for occupancy and the subsequent trial of the seven. The night before the courthouse was to open, other members of the gang set the building on fire. Their goal, to burn the records of the case, was not achieved, however, and the seven were found guilty and sentenced to a year in prison. They served a short time, then escaped.

This was too much for the outraged citizenry and a group of them decided to rid the county of the gang of criminals, one way or another. They entered into a compact, calling themselves by the well-known vigilante name of "Regulators" (many of them preferred the sobriquet "lynching club"). On first blush it may seem startling that the New Englanders fell in with this idea so readily. Thomas Ford disagreed in his famous history of Illinois, written in 1854 after his governorship (1842– 46). "The old peaceful, staid, puritan Yankee, walked into a fight in defence of his claim, or that of his neighbor, just as if he had received a regular backwoods education in the olden times. It was curious to witness this change of character with the change of position, in emerging from a government of strict law to one of comparative anarchy. The readiness with which our Puritan population from the East adopted the mobocratic spirit, is evidence that men are the same everywhere under the same circumstances."

At first the Regulators agreed to a plan that allowed suspects to be notified to leave the area "under pain of whipping if the order was not obeyed." Lamentably, one excess soon led to another. The first captain of the Regulators had supervised a severe beating of one of the suspected banditti; his sawmill was burned down soon after. The second captain resigned forthwith after receiving a letter signed with a skull and crossbones. The third captain, John Campbell, exacerbated the situation by forming a large posse to "run the Driscolls out of the area." A few days later he was shot from ambush and died within a few minutes; Mrs. Campbell, catching a glimpse of the three assassins, thought she recognized two of the sons of John Driscoll.

The Regulators now lost all reason and turned themselves into full-blown vigilantes. An unruly mob of 500 or more men seized John Driscoll and one of his sons, William; neither was alleged to have been present at the shooting, but both were assumed to be "accomplices before the fact." Out of the group, 111 men were selected to be the jury, and a "drumhead" trial was rushed through to the inevitable verdict of guilty. The 111 men, each equipped with a musket, were divided into two groups. First, approximately half of the group was lined up and John Driscoll was brought out; blindfolded, with his arms pinioned behind his back, he was made to kneel. At a signal, all the guns were fired at him in a single volley. The son, William, was next, and the other half of the group carried through the second execution. The macabre ritual over, the crowd split into two sections, one going past John Driscoll's home and burning it to the ground, the other doing the same to the home of David Driscoll, one of the sons assumed to have been involved in the shooting.

There was an immediate reaction to the vigilantes' outburst, and within two months a grand jury indictment came forward, presenting a true bill against all the 111 men, each and every one named. Several citizens of Grand Detour were on the jury, Leonard Andrus among them. The defendants pleaded not guilty; the trial went through a few desultory motions, with a few witnesses being called, but with no direct evidence presented. Without leaving their seats in the jury boxes, the jury returned a verdict of not guilty.[6]

Glimpses of the more prosaic aspect of life in Grand Detour itself appear in the few issues of the *Rock River Register* that have been preserved. The paper was published in Grand Detour for only the two years of 1842 and 1843, and there are only a few issues extant. These issues are marked by a thread of moralistic piety, coupled with an equal eye for titillating stories. An article on "flirts and flirting" warns: "No girl ever made a happy union by flirtation; because no man capable of making a woman permanently happy was ever attracted by that which is disgusting to rational and refined minds.... Flirtation in a woman is equivalent to libertinism in a man; it is the manifestation of the same loose principles, . . . let the young, the lovely, and the gifted, therefore, adhere to that nature which has made them what they are.... " One wonders whether the editor had recently been burned in a love affair, for one column over he comments: "Say what you will of old maids, their love is generally more strong and sincere than that of the young inconsiderate creatures whose hearts vibrate between the joys of wedlock and the dissipations of the ballroom.... Her love is like a May shower, which makes rainbows but fills no cisterns."

The paper included a smattering of Illinois news and very sketchy news of the nation and the world (several articles, incidentally, telling of the maiden voyage of the famous steamship, the Great Western, that year). Interestingly, Vermont news found a prominent place in the paper. Evidence of the depression was noted here and there; the editors were forced to drop the price of the paper from $2.50 a year to $2.00 a year. By August 1843, the national political campaign and its local variations came into larger focus and the editors developed a special rate for the insertion of candidates' names for one dollar, "invarably [sic] in advance." Foreclosures and bankruptcy notices were found in every issue. Wheat prices were sagging in the country; the grain was selling at $.375 per bushel in Chicago, only $.30 in Peoria. Two farms were offered for rent by W.G. Dana in September 1842; they were still going begging in the paper well into the spring of 1843. Commented the editors in the same issue, "The entire assets of a recent bankrupt were 'nine small children!' We presume the creditors acted magnanimously and let him keep them."

The dominant subject of the paper was business. The advertisements scattered throughout each issue gave a panoply of trading interactions, thrusts and parries of competition, successes and failures. Solon Cumins was obviously the town Rockefeller—his ads for his famous "Brick Store" were the largest, his assortment of goods amazing. In November 1842 he announced, "New goods—cheaper than the cheapest!!!" Many of his goods were received "direct from NEW YORK, the largest, cheapest, best selected stock of Goods ever before offered West of Chicago." The stock embraced "every article usually kept in a Country Store," and included "Broad Cloths, Cassineres, Sattinnette, Sheeps-Grey Cloth, Kentucky Jeans, Merinoes, Muslin de Laines of every quality, Moleskins, Ginghams, Prints, Velvets, Silks, Shawls, Fancy Handkerchiefs. . . . Also a large and splendid assortment of Ready made Clothing, cheap as dirt." The ad went on to elaborate many other items of clothing, as well as crockery, glassware, hardware, groceries, nails, glass, paints, oils, drugs and medicines, iron and steel, "in fact, everything that is wanted in the Country." Cumins and his partners—both House brothers now were associated with him—made a straight-out pledge "to sell goods at lower prices than any other Store within one hundred miles of us." To make certain that there was no misunderstanding about how these goods were to be purchased, large type noted at the bottom: "No credit will be given, NONE NEED INQUIRE." Cumins' was not to be the only store, though, for M.T.D. Greely opened a new store, "Directly north, and next adjoining the Brick Store." Apparently believing that he needed to make a large splash to compete with Cumins, Greely listed many dozens of additional products (probably all carried by Cumins) and even included a "choice lot of LIQUORS." Greely tried to carve out his price niche: "Without pretending to sell 'cheaper than the cheapest' the subscriber pledges himself to sell at the best cash prices, his neighbors to the contrary notwithstanding."

Other tradesmen also advertised, although on a lower profile than the two competing country stores. In addition to being prepared to manufacture tin, copper, steel, and iron goods "on short notice," George Herrick, the tinsmith, also advertised a new cistern pump. "No one will fail to purchase who has a cistern," he confidently vowed. O.F. Palmer, the shoemaker, had just taken in a partner, O. Eddy, and opened a new shop on Water Street, next to the tin shop. Like the proprietors of the country stores and many other shops, Palmer and Eddy would take wheat, the universal "coin of the realm," as well as hides in exchange. Another firm was put together at this time, the partnership of Wright and Pomeroy, for a cabinet manufactory; they preferred lumber in exchange for cabinet work, but would also accept wheat as payment. W.G. Dana needed black and white walnut and basswood saw logs for his mill. H.J. Hathaway had "constantly on hand, and is constantly manufacturing Segars of the best quality at his residence." Business must have been better for Hathaway than most of the other firms, for he also needed two experienced hands. Even the professionals of the town advertised occasionally. E.W. Evans, the local barrister, offered to take cases anywhere in Ogle County, as well as in Lee and Whiteside counties. An advertisement for Dr. William M. Bass, the town's physician and surgeon, carried a small insertion that included a woodcut of a mortar and pestle; his office was at his residence, "where he may be found at all times ready to attend to calls, except when absent on professional business."

John Deere also placed an advertisement in the paper, and its first appearance, in the issue of November 11, 1842, points to a little known aspect of John Deere's life in Grand Detour. In this issue, John Deere took a small half-inch ad as follows: "NOTICE. All persons indebted to the undersigned will save costs by making immediate payment. John Deere, Grand Detour, November 4, 1842." A clue to the reason for this notice is found on the same page of the paper—a large advertisement taken out by William Prentiss, United States marshall of the district for the purpose of announcing a marshall's sale under auspices of the United States Circuit Court. The sale—sixty-eight acres of land—was to satisfy a claim of plaintiffs D.M. Wilson and D.M. Brown against John Deere and George Cushing, impleaded with John Peck, William Stickney, Charles Lamb, and L. Andrews.

Sadly, the full story of the case is lost. The records of both the United States circuit and United States district courts for this district were destroyed in the great Chicago fire in October 1871 (as were so many other archival treasures of those days). We do know that it was not John Deere's land, for at that time he owned no such land in his own name, but everything else is conjecture. Perhaps it was Cushing's land. Inclusion of the other four men, being sued in conjunction with Cushing and Deere, would seem to imply a joint endeavor that might have involved six different people not connected to each other directly by business links. The debt could have been for construction materials—home building was often done by sharing labor and material.

The property in this advertisement sold at auction in July 1842, bringing $667 toward the total judgment of $787 (the successful bidder for the land one James H. Collins). Here the matter rests; we have no further information.

As if this were not trouble enough for John Deere, the next year, 1843, brought an even more serious court case. This time he was the sole defendant. It was the Vermont case involving his debt at Leicester, following him, twelve years later, to Illinois. This was the case that stemmed from a set of notes signed back in 1831, after his Leicester blacksmith shop had been twice gutted by fire. One of these debts, a note for the sum of $78.76, had been brought by the plaintiff, Jay Wright, to the justice of the peace at Leicester, Marshal I. Doty, and the latter had rendered a judgment against Deere and issued a summons in November 1836. It was this summons that had led Deere to leave Vermont because of his inability at that time to pay this debt. Now the payment of this note and others signed by Deere at that time totaling (with interest and court costs) a tidy sum of $1,000 was being sought by Wright in the Ogle County Circuit Court. Fortunately, these records remain intact in the Ogle County circuit courthouse in Oregon, Illinois. The final result appears in the court record in a brief paragraph: the case was dismissed per agreement of the parties, with the defendant paying the court costs. We do not know how much John Deere paid to Wright. Probably it was enough to put a considerable dent in Deere's fortunes at that particular moment. Whatever it demanded of him, the important thing was that John Deere had now satisfied his obligations in Vermont, and he could turn to his new life in Illinois free of this earlier burden.

Partial records of cases that were heard by the justice of the peace for Grand Detour also survive. Most of the time these are merely the dockets themselves—names of plaintiff and defendant, amount of the suit, costs assessed by the court. In a few cases, backup documentation is attached. One of the very early cases—a suit brought in October 1839 before James

G. Hagans by John Deere against Levi Dorth (or Dort) asking for $14.56—contains a ledger of Dorth's debts:

1839   Dorth to John Deere

April 10.	Sharpening 3 wedges.	.37
	Shoeing 2 horses.	2.75
	Cash paid to House	1.00
19.	Cash paid same	15.00
	Repairing shoe	.62
May 24.	One plow	24.00
July 10.	Shoeing horse.	1.25
21.	Shoeing horses	3.50

$48.49

Paid

April-May	By 10 lb. horse nails	3.75	
	By 10 lb. horse nails	3.75	
	By 4½ lb. horse nails.	1.68	
	By 10 lb. horse nails	3.75	

12.93

35.56

Paid 21.00

Owed. . . . $14.56

One other Deere billing of this early period has been preserved (in this case paid promptly) and reads as follows:

Jan. 26, 1839   Esq. Cotton Dr. to John Deere

Pitch Fork	.92
Repairing brass kettle.	1.00
Casing mill bucket.	1.75
One new shoe	1.13
Repairing two shoes.	.62
Repairing of yoke and staple.	.50
Pin to wheel to plow	.25

6.17

These two bills tell a good deal about John Deere's work and pricing practices in that third year of his shop in Grand Detour. There were, for example, various prices for shoeing horses. For Dorth, Deere repaired one shoe for $.62, but for Cotton, two shoes at the same price. It is hard to compare entries that say "shoeing horse" with those that say "shoeing horses"; we just do not know how many shoes were put on, etc. While there does appear some rhyme to Deere's pricing policy, it apparently had different applications to different people.

The most striking single entry is the plow sold to Dorth on May 24. The price, twenty-four dollars, seems high compared to the going price of plows in that period of ten to twelve dollars. As Deere moved more substantially into plow production, his own prices came down closer to the latter figures. Only three plows had been built by this date, and only a total of ten in the year 1839; the Dorth plow would have been one of the earliest of John Deere's plows. The total of sixteen dollars "paid to House," appearing on the Dorth bill is puzzling. The implication is that John Deere paid cash to one of the House brothers in a substantial amount, with a debit to Dorth, perhaps settling other, unrelated debts in one of those complicated trilateral arrangements so common in those days. Whatever the reason for this particular debit, it was clear that Dorth had total debts of forty-eight dollars and paid $12.93 on this debt by using "in kind" exchange of horse nails, and a further twenty-one dollars, the source not indicated. Dorth apparently refused to pay the remaining $14.56. Deere carried the case to the justice of the peace, and Dorth again declined payment. Finally, Deere took the case to the Ogle County Circuit Court, where in February 1841 he was finally recompensed.

The full docket of Salmon C. Cotton, the justice of the peace for Grand Detour in the early 1840s, remains intact and through it a sense of the early business relationships of Grand Detour emerges. In the docket for the period April 10, 1841, through May 25, 1844, Deere appears as plaintiff twenty-eight different times in a docket of approximately 165 cases. The amounts in the Deere cases are generally quite small—John Frye is sued for $3.25 (the constable here "levied on one old wagon," which he sold, but "found no more property"). The amount David Cable owed was $3.50, but the constable could not find any Cable real goods as "the defendant secrets his property." By March 1842, the price of plows from the Deere shop had apparently dropped to ten dollars, for Amos Rice owed that amount on account for "one diamond plow." In this instance Rice "made an amicable settlement." One of the suits was not for cash but for delivery of "good merchandisable winter wheat" (the debtor, by name of Parting Plain, apparently failed to deliver). Another suit was brought in April 1844 before Cotton's court by Deere against William G. Dana, one of the hydraulic company partners, regarding a note dating back to 1838. Amos Bosworth was also on the note, but he had died in 1840 (surely a blow to John Deere to lose so close a friend), and Dana apparently had let the debt slide. When it was brought before Cotton, Dana insisted that he would not have an impartial trial before the court and obtained its transfer to the nearest justice, Thomas McKinney. Unfortunately, we do not have McKinney's docket and do not know how it was settled (in this case it was a substantial amount—more than thirty dollars).

The large number of cases pursued by John Deere points out the collection problem of a tradesman who was selling services. A farmer would come in to John Deere with a horse in want of a shoe, and with a plowing or a harvesting to be accomplished before any sort of cash came to him to pay the blacksmith. Credit had to be part of an operation like John Deere's. The amounts were small and the service obtainable in other places (particularly so in the later years, when several other blacksmiths became available within the nearby area). It was tempting sometimes for a farmer to shift to a new shop, "forgetting" the debt owed. Mutual trust had to be the cement of the frontier, but its adhesive power sometimes weakened and resort to the courts became a necessary next step. Collection was a bugaboo to Deere and other small businessmen all through this period.[7]

PARTNERSHIPS

If each of these court law cases was minor, another Deere legal document in March 1843 was major, and it carried positive implications. By articles of agreement dated March 20, 1843, John Deere and Leonard Andrus agreed to become "co-partners in the art and trade of blacksmithing, plow-making and all things thereto belonging at the said Grand Detour, and all other business that said partners may hereafter be necessary for their mutual interest and benefit." The agreement was to last for three years and the new firm was to operate under the name of "Leonard Andrus." John Deere was to furnish as his capital "what stock he has now on hand and other materials at a fair valuation and also a sufficient amount of cash capital to make up the same amount including the stock as furnished by said Andrus." Deere agreed to employ his whole time in the business, not to follow any other trade or business for his own private advantage or benefit, "but [to] at all times faithfully exercise his best skill and ability to promote the *interest of the copartnership.*" In turn, Andrus also agreed to employ his whole time in the business. (It is not clear what happened to the existing Andrus stage line.) The remaining copy of this significant document is a puzzling one. It is in the handwriting of Leonard Andrus but is not signed by either party and there are significant blank sections in the document, particularly those relating to annual rents to be paid to Deere for furnishing the shop and outbuildings. The final document consummating the relationship has long since disappeared.

No financial statements or other account books remain of this first partnership, so the amount of capital each brought to the firm cannot be

Exhibit 2–3. *Plow factory of Leonard Andrus and John Deere, Grand Detour, Ill., ca. 1843 (Deere Archives)*

determined. In 1842 Deere acquired 160 acres of farm land by filing a claim, "letters patent," at the Dixon Land Office, paying $200. Later that same year he sold this land, in four separate parcels, for a total of $1,000. The net profit from his plow sales for that year likely would have been less than $500 (100 plows, selling for $10, might have made him $200 to $300). When these land sales, plow sales, blacksmith services, and prior capital were all summed, Deere's capital probably came to something under $1,500. Nevertheless, there was enough capital between the two partners to finance construction of a large two-story factory building. Its location, on the Rock River at a point where water power could be harnessed readily, was about a block from John Deere's blacksmith shop; at this point he gave up the latter and moved across to the new factory.

The informal business relationships between Deere and Andrus prior to the agreement of March 1843 remain shrouded in the mists of early Grand Detour legends. They probably had many business dealings—it would be natural to have such interactions between a blacksmith and a stage (mail-route) proprietor. There are stories that Andrus helped Deere to make the plows. The belief was that Andrus might have collaborated with Deere in obtaining his first grinding wheel and might have actually done some of the grinding, or have participated in the selling of the plows. We have no way of knowing now, and one would have thought it mattered little—except for a "tempest in a teapot" in 1937 exactly 100 years after

1837, the year that John Deere "gave to the world the steel plow."

We have already established the fact that the Deere plow was not the first plow, nor was it a breakthrough invention. But John Deere did make a plow in 1837, and this resourceful and innovative man subsequently became one of the great contributors to American agriculture. What could be more logical than for Deere & Company to celebrate this 100th anniversary at some appropriate date in 1937? One small problem. Andrus and Deere had finally split apart in 1847 (to anticipate our story for a moment), and Andrus continued as a separate plow company under the name of the Grand Detour Plow Company (first in the home town, then, later, at Dixon, Illinois). In 1919 it was acquired by a predecessor company of the J.I. Case Company. With Andrus involved with Deere, in some fashion or other, probably right from the start in 1837, it seemed eminently logical to the J.I. Case Company to celebrate its 100th anniversary in 1937, too. As the complementary, or conflicting, anniversaries (whichever view one chose to take) approached, a fevered set of argumentative counterclaims flew back and forth between and among all of the individuals and companies involved—Deere, Case, the descendants of the two families, the town of Grand Detour (for there was to be put in place one, or maybe more than one, plaque to the event). Even the state of Illinois and the United States Congress were drawn in as authenticators of the event. Finally, each company went ahead with its own celebration, each commemorating the anniversary with its own plaque at Grand Detour.[8]

In 1844, when Andrus and Deere rewrote the articles of agreement to bring Horace Paine into the partnership, enough information was provided to reconstruct a surrogate balance sheet. In this new agreement, Paine agreed to bring $1,000 to the firm. Andrus and Deere agreed to contribute all of their stock at hand in the blacksmith shop—castings, patterns, flasks, tools, iron, etc.—and also the town lot on which the furnace stood, together with the buildings and machinery on this land. Deere and Andrus were to receive a credit of $300 for blacksmith work already done, and the balance of the invoiced capital amount of $1,566.65 was the amount Andrus and Deere were to furnish as capital stock to match the $1,000 of Paine. Further, to bring the account closer to one-third each, Andrus and Deere were to furnish an additional $833.45 by the following May. At this point, Deere and Andrus would have company notes payable for $1,200 each, Paine $1,000. Paine was to be allowed to continue his business (by now he was part owner of the firm of W.A. House and Company), but he had to devote his full personal time to the partnership. There was a proviso at the end of the agreement that if George Andrus, a relative of Leonard from the state of New York, wished to become a co-partner and could furnish an additional amount of capital in the sum of $1,000, he, too, could become a partner. (He never took the opportunity.) The total capital at the time of the second (Paine) agreement came to approximately $3,600, a not inconsequential amount at that time.

We have no record of how much Andrus and Deere were taking out from the firm in wages, partnership drawings, etc., nor a record of production in those first years. After-the-fact remembrances put the output in 1843 at 400 plows, up from 75 in 1841, 100 in 1842. This would average about two plows per working day. How many people would be needed to accomplish this and the related blacksmithing that continued to form a significant part of the business? The answer depends in part on the level of equipment available. From the remembrances only twenty or so years later in the trademark case, there were three forges, one of which was worked by Deere himself. During this period of the Andrus partnership agreement, the new, larger factory building soon had steam power. John Gould, who had come to Grand Detour in August 1844 to work with the firm, recounted more about this:

> When at Grand Detour they had steam power for their works, but did not have room, steam power, etc., enough to melt their metal for castings. They built a cupola detached from their works and arranged with horse power to melt their metal. They did not own horses enough themselves, so they borrowed of their neighbors. They would cast about twice a week and it took about two and a half hours, with horse power, to melt the metal, which was quite a curiosity to the people there, as it was the only foundry in the country nearer than Galena. In those days, when they were going to melt, people would come in from quite a distance to see them melt the iron. At that time, during their early experiences, I recall that Mr. Deere needed some iron that they did not have—I forgot now what it was—and he drove with a one horse spring wagon to Springfield, Illinois, the nearest place where he could obtain what he wanted.

The number of people engaged in the Deere operation at that time was probably no more than eight or ten. Apparently both Deere and Andrus from time to time also did some selling, taking a load of plows out into the countryside to peddle them individually to farmers. Plows may also have been left on consignment in nearby country stores, just as in the case of the Oregon pitchforks.

Deere had a helper on the selling side, his young nephew, Samuel Charters (Charter) Peek, whose mother, Lucretia, was another of the William Lamb daughters from Granville, Vermont. Charter Peek not only sold when necessary, but was Deere's bookkeeper before the Andrus association. It seems abundantly clear from all available evidence that John Deere had only a rudimentary understanding of finance and accounting and did little personal writing or bookkeeping. H.C. Peek, Charter Peek's brother, was fond of retelling a story about Charter Peek's efforts to understand the John Deere bookkeeping mind: "One day he came to a queer entry in the day book that he could make nothing of and called Mr. Deere to explain. He said, 'You have an education and can read writing can't you?' Charter said, 'Yes, it looks like Red house over the river, $1.50 to me.' 'That's what it is. One day a man came to have some work done, I did not know his name, but he lived in a red house across the river so I put it down.,'" H.C. Peek also described Deere as a "great driver at his work" and a hard taskmaster for his employees: "Kept everybody who worked for him busy . . . no lazy man need apply for a job with him." Charter Peek recounted another story that Deere, preceded by one of the workmen at the factory, was carrying plows down a stairs in the factory. The man did not go fast enough to suit Deere, so he gave him a push. The man fell and was hurt. He was so angry that he started for Deere, who ran and hid. After awhile Deere hunted up Charter and said, "I did not mean to hurt that man, go find him and smooth it over. He is a damned good man. I don't want to lose him."

There are also many vignettes of Deere's concentration and perseverance in those earlier years. John Gould mentioned "his hammering in the morning, when I was in the store in bed at four o'clock, and at ten o'clock at night; he had such indomitable determination to do and work out what he had in his mind." Another acquaintance remembered him as "a real Yankee," with little time for words. "When a customer came in to Deere's shop," the man recounted, "the blacksmith would look up and ask what he wanted. Deere would listen, never saying another word, and go immediately to work on the job." Robert Tate remembered Deere's relations with the employees during the period of the Deere-Tate partnership in the early 1850s. This testimony occurred in the trademark case: "Interrogatory 1: What was the nature of the instructions given by John Deere while superintending the work at the forges? Answer: I considered the interference of Mr. Deere might have been avoided by informing me in what manner the error could be remedied. Very frequently he would take the hammer from a man and use it for a few minutes in order to show him wherein he was wrong. Interrogatory 2: Did he usually succeed in this manner in convincing them of their error? Answer: Sometimes he would; but conveying his instructions not very agreeably, would fail in doing so."

One Grand Detour descendant implied that the Deeres were not at that time at the top of the social ladder of Grand Detour, such as it was. "Mrs. House came from a very good family and rather looked down upon the Deeres. John Deere was of ordinary birth, although a very good mechanic." In truth, the very egalitarianism so characteristic of the frontier would have made Mrs. House's alleged slur laughable to most. Even an English settler, perhaps more used to a class society, wrote to his friend in Aberdeen, Scotland, in 1836: "Although it may appear egotistical and vain, I must inform you that I assume a rank in society here far above any I hoped for. I now feel the benefit of public respect and it is my utmost ambition now to merit it." H.C. Peek probably captured the essence of Deere more fairly: "He was always well dressed, better than the average, and made a good appearance everywhere. . . . He was a 'good liver,' 'great meat eater'—hale and hearty."[9]

The partnership with Horace Paine as the third party under the firm name L. Andrus & Company lasted for only two years and terminated for what reason we do not know. On October 20, 1846, Andrus and Deere drew up yet another partnership agreement, this time including a new third party, Oramil C. Lathrop, with the firm now to be called Andrus, Deere & Lathrop. Lathrop was to furnish $1,500, $1,000 in cash and the balance in a note payable in one year. In turn, Andrus and Deere agreed to furnish $1,500 each toward the capital, to be made up of the stock on hand in the blacksmith shop and furnace ("Flashes, Patterns, Castings, Tools, Iron, Coal, Plow beams, Handles, Lumber, etc., etc.), together with their shop buildings, the steam engine, and an extra lot of land belonging to Andrus and Deere known as Moon Island. There was a protective clause that said in essence that if all of this totaled more than the Andrus and Deere proportions of the capital stock, then the company would give Andrus and Deere notes "for the overplus."

The agreement was duly signed by the three parties and witnessed in the presence of a new person in the firm—F. A. Deere. John Deere's eldest child and first son was then a young man of eighteen years. Albert (he was called by his middle name) had graduated from Rock River Seminary at Mt. Morris, Illinois, and had come with his father as the new bookkeeper. Deere apparently had become increasingly uneasy about the way Andrus was keeping the books. John Gould commented on this preoccupation: "Mr. Andrus was the financial man of the concern, but Mr. Deere was always quite inquisitive about the financial matters as to how the business was growing, while Mr. Andrus was rather reticent about such matters. Mr. Deere felt as though there might be something wrong, which he did not understand in the financial matters, and not being satisfied with the management, and felt as though he should have someone more interested on his side of the question." It must have been a satisfying day to John Deere to have his own son, well schooled, keeping track of the figures. "Then Mr. Deere felt as though he had someone more on his side of the question," Gould reported.

Tragically, Francis Albert Deere had no chance to fulfill his father's proud hopes, for on January 13, 1848, he was taken violently ill and died within hours, "being unconscious from the start." No record remains documenting the cause. Gould, there in person, recognized how devastating the loss was: "A very severe and lamentable affair for Mr. Deere."

The Lathrop partnership also was short lived, for on June 22, 1847, Andrus and Deere dissolved it (we do not know what happened to Lathrop's share) and made a new partnership agreement "under the name & stile of Andrus & Deere." This also turned out to be only a temporary expedient. The loss of his trusted son and his growing unease about the Andrus bookkeeping soon led Deere to ask for a total dissolution of the partnership. By this time Robert N. Tate had moved to Grand Detour; he had been hired by Deere and Andrus, first to put up a new steam engine for the firm, then to institute a remodeling of the plow-making tools, presses, grindstones, etc., and to build a new power lathe. He also was making hoes "and sent a lot via plow peddlers." Tate reported the chain of events that ensued in 1848: "Deere took it into his head to dissolve partnership.... Andrus offered $1200 for Deere's interest and he would take $1200 and let Deere have the concern ... so Deere came to the conclusion to take $1200 and leave early in June."

At this point John Deere made a critically important decision—to move away from Grand Detour. It must have approached in difficulty the earlier decision to leave Vermont, for his ties to Grand Detour were strong; not only was there the business, but three children had been born there, too—Emma Charlotte in 1840, Hiram Alvin in 1842 (he died in 1844), and Alice Marie in 1844.

It seemed almost certain by 1848 that the new railroad being planned for the area would bypass Grand Detour. One had only to look at the topography and the likely routes to know that the railroad was not destined to come through the town. Too many bridges and too many grades would be required. There was a popularly held story that the citizenry of Grand Detour deliberately chose not to have a railroad come near; one variation of the story alleged that the House brothers had observed what iniquities railroads had visited upon Constantine, Michigan, and carried this hostility all the way to Grand Detour. In truth, Grand Detour was bypassed by the railroad precisely because it lay on the great bend of the river, a beautiful situation geographically but a poor one for hardheaded railroad men. John Deere must have sensed the future transportation difficulties of Grand Detour; he had been teaming plows all through the area too many times, and he knew that rail and water routes were going to be far the more effective means of distribution for manufacturing enterprises.

The people in Peru, Illinois, were interested in Deere's projected move and made offers to the two men, but a lack of timber, reports Tate, "was a sad stumbling block ... although a merchant named Bruister, a man of means, the principal merchant in Peru, would have given us two lots if we would locate there."[10] Deere and Tate then turned West, traveling to the great water route, the Mississippi. A site at the mouth of the Rock River looked promising, but the owner of the local hydraulic company would not give them a firm quote on the price of power, and they left that day for Rock Island, just a few miles away. Not deterred by a pair of caged bear cubs fighting that night outside the Rock Island House (so reports Tate), they soon made connections with a key person in the area, Col. John Buford, who had an interest in the hydraulic operation at nearby Moline. In May 1848 the firm of Andrus & Deere was terminated and the new firm of Deere and Tate began the manufacturing of plows in Moline, Illinois.

CHAPTER 3

THE MOVE TO MOLINE

*I will never from this seventh day of February,
eighteen hundred sixty A.D. put my name to a paper that
I do not expect to pay—so help me God.*

Charles Deere

John Deere's partnerships in Grand Detour had seemed almost star-crossed, with not only a full measure of business problems but also of acrimonious personal difficulties. Yet, rather than going it alone, Deere chose again to commit himself to a partnership, this time with the Englishman Robert N. Tate. They signed an agreement on June 19, 1848, shortly after returning together from a trip to Moline, where they had arranged for water rights from the Fergus and Buford foundry waterwheel and the use of a small plot of land just below the latter's foundry and machine shop.

The new community, while still only a village, nevertheless was larger than Grand Detour. It was one of three adjacent towns that later came to be called "the Tri Cities" (and eventually, in the mid-twentieth century, the "Quad Cities," when East Moline became large enough to claim its right). Moline and Rock Island, on the Illinois side of the Mississippi River, were then a couple of miles apart (later their mutual growth made them completely contiguous). Across the Mississippi River, by ferry at that time, was Davenport, Iowa. The Mississippi makes an abrupt bend just above Moline and heads west for about twenty miles. Thus, Moline, upriver of Rock Island, was also east of it, and was south of Davenport (somewhat confusing for the chroniclers of the "Westward Movement"; one would expect that going to the Iowa territory would carry one farther west). The Rock River, flowing from its headwaters in central Wisconsin and on past Grand Detour, enters the Mississippi just below Rock Island. Think of the water-based transportation routes commanded by the confluence of these two rivers, both running through very fertile land!

To add to the attraction of this area, a rocky island about 2½ miles long and ¾ mile wide bifurcates the Mississippi at this point. The wider channel was the northern one; the lower, generally called "the Slough," was much narrower—ideal for water power.

The Rock Island area—the Illinois mainland, not the island—historically had been the territory of the Sauk (or Sac) Indians, and there they had built a great village under the tribe's venerable chief, Black Hawk. Though there had been treaties with the white men, beginning in 1804, that seemed to guarantee security of tenure to the Indians, the area was extraordinarily attractive to settlers, who poured into Illinois in large numbers by the 1820s. Fort Armstrong was founded on the island in 1816. Permanent settlements followed by 1828, squarely on land occupied by Black Hawk. The settlers gave short shrift to the chief's claims, acrimony escalated, and the outraged Sauk leader set in motion one of the most dramatic events in the settling of the West, the Black Hawk War (1832). The hostilities began with the settlers chasing the tribe through northern Illinois and southern Wisconsin. Finally, a battle took place at the mouth of the Bad Axe River in Wisconsin; the Sauk warriors were almost annihilated, Black Hawk was captured, and Indian influence in the whole area came to an end. Though the "war" was more in the nature of an incident, it created a national sensation, and with elimination of the Indian threat, settlers flocked anew into the area. A newspaper editor in 1848 estimated that the valley of the Mississippi had doubled its population in each of the two preceding decades, and that it would reach 10 million by 1850. Rock Island itself quickly became a famous river town; by the census of 1850 it had 1,711 inhabitants.

At the same time, the settlers were swept by an "improvement fever." For John Deere, the most important was the construction in 1841 of a dam across the head of the Slough, the precise site of the new village of Moline. Factories mushroomed along the river bank just below the dam, and it was there that Deere and Tate purchased water rights and land for their proposed factory.[1]

STARTING THE NEW FACTORY

Deere's choice of Tate as a partner is a puzzling one in several ways. Tate brought no substantial capital to the firm; indeed, Deere probably had enough financial wherewithal with the sale of the Grand Detour business to make a start on his own. Tate was essentially a manufacturing man, adept at remodeling tools, presses, grindstones, polishing wheels, power lathes, etc., and he was also willing and able to be a working shop superintendent. These were significant assets; still, they were essentially the strengths of Deere himself. Further, John Deere was a gruff, strong-willed man—any joint sharing of shop management would always present a threat of a blowup.

Tate moved to Moline immediately after the consummation of the water-rights agreement; wasting little time, he contracted for a small shop building from Jacob Bell as a staging point for the new building, giving Bell one month's rent of $2.50 in cash on the spot. By the middle of July Tate and his small cadre of new employees—"old man Hibbard," Pomeroy, Wallace, Jones, Philander, and a contracted outside mason—had begun the sixty-foot by twenty-four-foot blacksmith shop. The rafters were raised by July 28 and within a few weeks Tate had the building finished. They must have been an excellent working team, for on August 31 Tate reported in his diary: "Started our big belt and our machinery moved for the first time!" They rented another building for storage of the finished stock and had the new plow manufactory in full production by mid-September. "September 26—finished the *first ten plows!*"

By today's standards, such a rapid startup seems astounding. Yet we must remember that the manufacturing process itself was a simple state of the art, already well known. Foundries, mills, and manufacturing establishments sprang up all over the frontier during this period, most all of them carbon copies of each other. The later post-Civil War period would witness a shakeout of such small businesses, where the more

innovative, development-minded companies would overpower the weaker, tradition-limited companies. In this period, though, the real difficulties were not those of manufacturing, but of finance and marketing.

A THIRD PARTNER

Finance had never been Deere's strength, nor was it Tate's. Then who
could be trusted with this unfathomable task? A felicitous answer came
in the person of John M. Gould, close friend of John Deere since Gould
had moved to Grand Detour in 1844. The department store of Dana and
Troop had employed Gould as a clerk and his abilities soon garnered him
a partnership with the other two at a full one-third interest in the firm.
Deere continued to maintain residence in Grand Detour during the
summer and fall of 1848, traveling back and forth to Moline to consult
with Tate but returning to his family often. After the first trip to Moline,
Deere and Tate decided to offer Gould a partnership in the new plow
business.

Gould at first demurred, but Deere was persistent. John Gould tells the
story in his own words: "Every time he came to Grand Detour he urged
me to do this, saying that he and Tate could make plows, but could not
attend to the other part of buying and selling and looking after financial
matters." Gould laid the matter before his two partners, William G. Dana
and Charles H. Troop, and they responded in a frank way that Gould later
recalled almost verbatim: "While they did not wish to have me leave,
they were satisfied that manufacturing was the principal thing for this
country; that we were raising oats and corn at a market price then of
about eight and ten cents a bushel and wheat at from 49 to fifty-cents a
bushel, which were shipped to the New England states to feed employees
and manufacturers of implements, which ought to be made here in this
country. . . . " Gould, impressed by the rationale of Messrs. Dana and
Troop, finally made the decision to go to Moline.

The level of trust among Dana, Troop, and Gould was considerably
better grounded than that of Deere and Andrus, for the three department
store partners agreed on a lump-sum value for Gould's interest, all this
without taking a formal inventory. There was one condition: Gould
should take as part payment a horse and buggy that the firm owned. Dana
and Troop promised to pay the remainder in cash as fast as they could
obtain the money. So, while the partnership agreement drawn up that fall
of 1848 among Deere, Tate, and Gould provided for a full one-third
interest for Gould, he brought little actual capital. Deere himself solved
the problem by loaning Gould the money for his share at the rate of six
percent per annum, about half the going interest rate at that time.

These two new Moline partnership agreements, the first with Tate
alone and the superseding agreement with Gould, were John Deere's fifth
and sixth partnership agreements in a period of less than half a dozen

years. Partnerships were a popular form of organization in the first half of
the nineteenth century, both in frontier country and all through the East,
the advantages of the limited-liability corporate form being only incompletely appreciated at that time. A partnership was particularly valuable
as an accumulator of capital, and this feature dominated the earlier
partnership agreements among Deere, Andrus, Lathrop, and Paine. The
precise contributions of capital from each person were delineated, each
partner was expected to devote full-time energies to the firm, and, if the
partnership was to be terminated, all company debts would be paid first
and the balance then divided according to agreed shares.

In point of fact, the legal liability of each of the partners for all the
others' actions in regard to the firm was essentially unlimited. Indeed,
this was one of the great advantages of the partnership form, as Henry
Carey (one of the legal authorities on partnerships in the early nineteenth
century) noted: "It strengthens their credit in the mercantile world,
enables them to carry on a more extensive trade, and, as it were, to be
personally present for the furtherance of their interests in separate parts
of the world." Thus, for a plow company, one partner could be in St. Louis
making firm commitments for purchase of iron and steel, another partner
could be in rural Iowa making binding sales arrangements with a dealer
whose credit he was assessing on the spot, and a third partner could be
back at the manufacturing location committing the firm to hiring new
employees or making irrevocable purchases of local goods and services to
be used in the shop.

But the unspoken corollary was that each, too, was responsible to the
others for every one of his binding actions in relation to the firm. Thus
the great strength of the partnership form was also one of its potential
disabilities; as Carey warned, "It is necessary that a person who enters
into a partnership should be thoroughly satisfied of the probity and
integrity of those with whom he thus connects himself." In the new
Moline firm, the three partners knew each other well, their level of trust
was high—deservedly so, it turned out, for none of the three ever indulged
a moral slip in regard to the others.

With both Tate and Gould aboard, John Deere's role now shifted, and in
a way that had a profound effect on the future of the firm. In Deere's
blacksmith shop of the early Grand Detour days, he was a sole proprietor,
in charge of the entire shop. In the five years with Leonard Andrus, he
remained devoted principally to the construction of the plow (a function
that apparently included at least some design responsibilities). Now Tate
was to be shop superintendent—and John Deere turned his attention to
sales and marketing.

Tate was asked about this in the Candee-Swan patent case of 1868 and
responded: "From the year 1848, in June, until March, 1852, I consider
[Deere's] principal efforts were alone directed to the proper distribution of
the plow and management of the teams and the persons who had [the

teams] in charge." Asked if John Deere had worked at the forge during those four years with Tate, the latter replied, "I never knew him engaged in the manufacture of anything pertaining to the plow, except at short intervals, where his attention was drawn to any one at the forges of which the smiths were engaged, for the purpose of instructing them." Thus the three men in the firm made an explicit (and logical) functional splitting of the firm's basic tasks—Tate as superintendent, Deere as marketing and sales manager, and Gould as manager of finance.[2]

TRANSITION PROBLEMS

A first order of business was to clean up the leftovers of the old partnership in Grand Detour. A plow manufactory, by its very nature, cannot be rapidly terminated. Andrus & Deere plows had been let on consignment (under all sorts of terms and conditions of credit and financing) to outlets scattered all through Illinois, Iowa, and Wisconsin. Thus, while Andrus & Deere was terminated "precisely on May 13, 1848" (Tate's words), the business of winding up the affairs of the firm extended over many months.

Just how much capital John Deere extracted from the defunct firm to bring to Moline is not clear—the termination agreement between Andrus and Deere has long since been lost. Tate's diary gives a clue—Andrus had offered Deere a "buy-sell," $1,200 either way, "so Deere came to the conclusion to take $1,200 and leave early in June," Tate reports. Clearly, this $1,200, presumably paid in cash, was not the entire worth of Deere's share; in the earlier agreement in 1846 among Andrus, Deere, and Oramil Lathrop each party had contributed $1,500, and later Deere and Andrus "bought out the interest" of Lathrop. Logically, Deere's share was much above the initial $1,500. Why, then would he have been willing to take $1,200?

Some clues to this question are found in a fascinating little notebook retrieved from this period—what is called on its cover "John Deere's Book," for the period 1848–55. The first section of the document contains a list in alphabetical order of some 260 accounts, by name and town. A few of these were individual farmers, but the bulk were Andrus and Deere "agents," some located in the larger towns, but most in smaller hamlets and villages scattered throughout the agricultural areas. A few of the larger houses had become somewhat specialized, but even they would have been something like "general hardware"; such a firm would sell thousands of items, farm machinery only a part of its business. (The more specialized "agricultural warehouses" of the East had not yet found their way to the Illinois and Iowa frontier). These smaller emporiums were almost always the ubiquitous general store, where the country merchant would be buying and selling provisions, cloth, garments, household needs, agricultural equipment, and "what have you." The latter often included whiskey, sold out of a barrel and hardly ever consumed on the premises, but taken back to the farm for "medicinal purposes." Most of the store's trade was barter, in a complex kaleidoscope of transactions that almost always included the buying and selling of agricultural produce.

Some of the amounts in the Deere accounts were quite small—Steven Adams of Pine Creek, Illinois, owed only $.76; R.A. Morris of "Iowa" only $.37. Others were substantial—S. Burlison of Springfield, Iowa, had the highest total—$319—and five more accounts owed more than $200 each. The total of all of the 260 accounts cumulated to $8,265. The page following the alphabetical list contained twenty-one "doubtful demands," the largest one fortunately being only $32. Finally, at the end of this section a note in John Deere's unmistakable hand, "All the foregoing notes and accounts are payable to Mr. Peek/his Sect. Webb [also] good— John." This personal confirmation by John Deere is dated October 11, 1848, on what apparently was a listing as of that date of just what was owed Deere from a set of accounts receivable of the firm Andrus & Deere.

A plotting of the 100 or more towns involved, scattered over western Illinois and eastern Iowa, confirms the statement of Gould that "at the dissolution between Andrus and Deere it was understood that Mr. Deere was to have the territory contiguous to the river and nearby and on the western side of the river, Wisconsin, Missouri and Iowa and they were not to interfere with each other's territory." This would have given Andrus eastern and central Illinois and presumably Indiana, Michigan, Ohio, and on east (Andrus was to continue his operation under the name Grand Detour Plow Company). John Deere, in turn, picked up the rights to the territory for what turned out to be the heart of the Midwestern corn belt. Incidentally, it is not clear just how long the two parties honored this territorial split. No accounts-receivable ledgers remain for either firm for the early 1850s; when we again pick up clues as to precise accounts payable of the Deere operation, the firm is selling all over the area, overlapping old Andrus ground.

The total of more than $8,200 owed Andrus & Deere seems surprisingly high, given what we know of the production levels of the terminated Grand Detour firm. Figures here are sketchy indeed; one authority gives the total plow production of 1848 as 700, another 1,000. If we give the firm all of the benefit of doubt and extrapolate a 1,000-production figure for the last year of production of Andrus & Deere, and price these at the then-going figure of approximately $8 per plow, we would have only a total of $8,000 sales for the year. Probably the receivables were those at the beginning of the crop season of 1848—say, June 1848, the result of the so-called "spring trade." At this date, the various agents scattered over northern Illinois and eastern Iowa, comprising the bulk of the approximately 260 separate accounts, had each taken a consignment of plows to peddle to farmers in their own areas. As Gould described it: "Business was done entirely then . . . by leaving plows to be sold on commission, taking a receipt for the number of plows and the price, to be paid for when sold." The likelihood was that few, if any, of these farmers would have paid for the plows in cash. Only after the harvest was in would the farmer pay the agent and the agent in turn pay the plow company.

We do not know whether Deere was given all of these accounts receivable to collect for his own use or whether some (perhaps one-half) was to go back to Andrus. There is no record in the little memorandum book of any payment to Andrus, though there are payments to employee Charter Peek, John Deere's nephew, for the many weeks of traveling to collect the amounts. In strictly financial terms, the combination of Deere's $1,200 and the as yet uncollected accounts receivable might have just about balanced out the Andrus side, inasmuch as the latter took all of the buildings and most of the equipment.

In terms of future opportunity, though, Deere came out very much the better, for he had managed to garner the active role of dealing with all of these accounts—not only for collection purposes but for the promotion of future business. Charter Peek recorded all sorts of bits and scraps of specific business leads resulting from these collection trips: "J.C. Hallock of Boston's Grove will com and get a lod of ploughs to pedle out. . . . Loon has eight on hand. . . . C.B. Mufford will write if he wants anymore—has eight on hand. . . . G.A.D. Andrus near Marion will be a good place to sele ploughs, from 20 to 50. N. Donahoo, Yankee Grove, has 8 on hand, will want nine or ten more in the spring. . . . Thomas Wragg will not want anymore but Hans Carter will sele on his place—will want 10, 12. . . . George Martin has 16 on hand—wants some brakers & som left hand ploughs in place of Wright. . . . McBeere, Quarkkrtown [sic] will be a good place to sele ploughs. . . . " Thus, detailed commercial intelligence found its way into the little notebook, not organized very well, to be sure, but nevertheless an invaluable hands-on feeling for what was going on "out in the field." Deere's new territory, combined with this ongoing collections relationship with all of these accounts, gave the new firm a special marketing advantage at a critical juncture in the growth of this soon-rich agricultural territory.

The receipts from Charter Peek's assiduous work in collection were not spectacular— by the following spring only about $2,400 had been reported in the book as having been received. Few of the accounts were fully cleared—J.H. Olds of Princeton had paid $194 on his $217 receivable, but A. Keator of Union Grove had paid only $50.35 on his $221 debt (and this in five separate small payments). The Burlison account in Springfield, Iowa, the largest in the memorandum book at $313, had been brought down to an even $200 by the following spring. Still, less than one-third of the total amount due had been collared by the end of the last entry in the memorandum book. These accounts surely were shifted in some way to the books of Deere, Tate & Gould, for continuing business would undoubtedly be done with most, if not all, of these customers.

While Deere and Peek were pushing the fieldwork of collection, it was Gould who was to bring rationality into the chaotic termination process. The first order of business, one that cried for attention, was to straighten out the books of both the new firm and of Deere and Andrus. Gould movingly recounted his dismay at their disarray: "There are accounts, or what might be called accounts, where a sort of diary was kept by a young man; no regular books were kept; if anything was sold, they said they had sold such a man, such a thing and there was no regular order of business at all."

Gould was well trained, and he set about at once to interpret and record the vast array of random scraps of information. "I opened immediately a set of books by the double entry system, which was the first set kept in this county, nor were there any in Scott County. It was well known that Deere & Tate had a system of double entry book-keeping, which seemed to be a curiosity to the other merchants and businessmen; they did not know what it was like. They frequently came into the office to see the system."

The little memorandum book ceased being used as a company account book by early 1849 (Gould built up his own set of books as the senior secretary and financial accountant), but entries continue through the mid-1850s on various aspects of John Deere's own personal affairs. Some of the entries apparently are in Charter Peek's handwriting, including some joyous doodlings: "Tomorrow, Tomorrow, Tomorrow, to Miss Alice Deere, Deere . . . in all the sounds of it, it is—it is—is—it is a great. . . . " (Not likely a romantic allusion by Peek, for Alice was just a six-year-old girl in 1850!) Other entries in 1850 and 1851 are in John Gould's strong and unmistakable handwriting, all of them relating to "John Deere's Private Accounts." Most of the items were prosaic—charges for cordwood, carpet, curtains, washstands, etc. In a private account for Ellen Deere, John Deere's own handwriting records in 1855 the purchase of a "pianah fort" for $350, apparently a gift to the 23-year-old daughter. On the next two pages, in yet another handwriting, are recipes for "Lemon Cake, Delicate Cake, Coconut Cake, Cocunut Pie, and Queen's Cake." The handwriting for the five recipes is all from one person, most likely Charter Peek. (Coconut pie called for an interesting ingredient: "To your taste a glass of wine.") There the book ends, and this fascinating glimpse of the early company leaves us tantalized but unfulfilled in terms of both the company and the family.[3]

YET ANOTHER PARTNER?

Tate's diary helps to fill in some of the gaps of those first years in Moline. The comings and goings of the principals in the company are recorded, together with weddings and deaths, scraps of information about the manufacturing back at the shop, and a whole range of miscellaneous comments about the early Moline days.

Labor and personnel problems dominated the first months in the fall of 1848. Pomeroy and his wife came to Moline in early August, boarding with Tate at three dollars a week. A few days later Kinsey, the blacksmith, commenced working, but the next day Davis quit. "August 23d. Pomeroy took sick Wednesday afternoon. . . . Sepember 4th Pomeroy sick of a boil!!!! . . . September 10 Pomeroy and I gathering nuts. *Bad.*" On September 26 Pomeroy moved out of Tate's house; on the same date "William Moore taken sick . . . Corey, Moore, Osborn and Beery all sick." The work at the shop moved along during those first months; on September 14, 142 shears were on hand, "nearly all ground." And by mid-September Isaac Thomas was shaving wood beams. By October, eighteen finished plows were moving out of the shop to be sold ("Johnson took 16 plows off this morning—October 18"). The pace of the shop was settling to a routine; by October 27, Tate reported, "Plows manufactured this week Tuesday 10, Wednesday 6, Thursday 9, Friday 7." Still, the labor difficulties continued: "October 23d—Fergus building castles in the air, Corey sick, apples and raw cabbage, Corey vom."

On November 4 John Deere's family arrived from Grand Detour and moved in with Tate. These quarters must have been cramped, remembering that the Deere family itself was now eight (the six living children in 1848 were Jeannette, eighteen years of age; Ellen, sixteen; Frances, fourteen; Charles, eleven; Emma, eight; and Alice, four). Charles particularly lamented his share of the discomfort—to occupy a bed upon a trunk in the hall. That pervasive winter malady, "cabin fever," infiltrated the crowded house, and tempers rose from time to time—unfortunately, a portent.

The travails of sickness that were plaguing the members of the firm and their families continued: "January 26 Mrs. Deere taken sick very suddenly." Shop absenteeism, too, was up: "February 3d—John Pirin and Shafer absent all week. The young German filling up and Detlif in their places." By mid-February Tate was attempting to get better control over the marketing side: "On the 15th Negus's peddler (Conger) took his second load of plows. Made an addition to his contract, to wit: that one half all notes received for plows by him shall be due prior to October 1849." That bitter winter also saw many deaths, of both adults and children. Cholera was a constant threat, an implacable scourge that could decimate whole towns before it abated. The somber epidemic of 1833–35 had burned out, but it rose again in 1848 and 1849. In the latter year, it was said that every steamboat on the river was affected. Tate, always willing to judge, commented about one death: "Old Mr. Briggs, the painter, . . . died about a week ago. Rather intemperate, half his time drunk. . . . Briggs practiced painting but was a poor hand."

On February 14 came the first hint of overt tension between Tate and

Deere: "On the 14th went to spend the evening at Mr. Cass's. Pomeroy, Gould and Perkins present!!! *Deere came to try to break it up. Rude, rude.*" A few weeks later another caustic comment: "Deere kicks up another rumpus about money—Money!!!" Tate seemed irritated by a number of Deere's comments, "April 5th—speaking of Charter Peek, Deere called him Granny Peek."

By mid-May 1849, business was picking up: "Great call for breakers, breakers, breakers, and one-horse plows." Tate recorded the plows produced in those first months—255 in January, 215 in February, 194 in March, 301 in April, and 235 in May. This early success led the firm at this point to take two new steps, each linked to the other. The first was the decision to add a substantial addition to the building on a lot below the old shop—eighty feet by thirty feet, two stories in height, and built massively with oak floors to accommodate heavier machinery. The second decision buttressed the first—Deere and his two partners decided to take a fourth partner. Tate first reported it in a strangely worded entry in his diary, dated June 23: "Saturday night, twenty minutes past eleven, decided on taking Mr. Atkinson as a partner in the firm, Deere, Tate & Gould."

Charles Atkinson was a close friend of the Deeres, who later was linked with the family by the marriage of his niece, Mary Little Dickinson, to Charles Deere. Atkinson was one of the original proprietors of the town of Moline; in the company of D.B. Sears and others, he platted the town in 1843 and became, according to one of his biographers, "a conspicuous promoter." By 1849 he was an elected official of the town of Moline, the assessor, and also the landlord for the home occupied by the Tate and Deere families during the winter of 1848.

Tate explained the reason for Atkinson's involvement as "the seeing to the peddling, seeing to the collecting of our outstanding debts, and a proper distribution of our stock." This does not make much sense, though, since Deere and Gould were together doing precisely these things. The most crying need was additional capital to finance the new building, and Atkinson's affluence made him an attractive partner.

Tate left shortly after that June 23, Saturday-night decision, for a trip to the East, to purchase new machinery for the firm. While Tate was away, John Deere publicly announced a change in the name of the firm itself. A *Davenport Gazette* article on the company in the September 20, 1849, issue put it ever so ungraciously by recounting a visit to the "Plow Manufactury of Messrs. Deere, Atkinson & Co. (formerly Deere, Tate & Gould)." This must not have been a legal fait accompli, however, as there presumably was still a partnership agreement between Deere, Tate, and Gould. Tate arrived back from the East at just about this time. In his own words: "On my return I found matters changed. Mr. John Gould told me that the firm had altered from Deere, Tate & Gould to Deere, Atkinson & Co. I was confounded. Atkinson, when I first saw him, I accosted him at this change and told him they might take my name from these books as soon as they pleased. Charles posted to Deere, very indignant. Soon Deere caught me alone and said, 'Well, hold on Tate, let us talk this thing over. Now keep quiet, don't get wrathy. I intend to straighten that up.' Shortly after this he got unreasonably cross with Mr. Atkinson, and he never let him rest until he got rid of him." Tate's memory of this event may be a bit cloudy (this section of his diary appears to have been rewritten at a later date), for he continued: "I think he drew from the business $23,000 and that near settled, and Deere, Tate & Gould got in lumber from C. Atkinson through Chamberlain & Dean to pay an old debt that Chamberlain owed Atkinson. Atkinson had taken lumber from Chamberlain to square up a former partnership account that had long existed, having run a sawmill located in the middle of the dam. I never knew how much Chamberlain owed Atkinson—someway about $500. This put up the shell of the building."

Tate's syntax here is less than exact, so we will attempt an interpretation. Chamberlain and Dean had built a sawmill in 1843, half way out on the Mississippi slough dam. Tate implies that Atkinson was paid $23,000 as a settlement in order to back out of the new partnership agreement, and that Atkinson gave the lumber owed him by Chamberlain and Dean for an earlier debt to the Deere, Tate & Gould partnership. This lumber, worth according to Tate about $500, was then used to put up the shell of the new factory building. Most aspects of this story make sense—the trading of previous debts for in-kind materials was widespread in the quasi-barter economies of the frontier towns. The one incongruous note in Tate's story is the amount of $23,000—this is just too high a figure for what was presumably at the maximum a one-quarter interest in the firm. Could Tate have meant $2,300? This would make more sense, and complete the vignette for us.

Tate explains away the Atkinson affair with an interesting rationalization that may or may not be true. "He [Atkinson] had been crippled in one of his hands by the premature discharge of a powder flask, suffered the horses he drove to get the mastery of them and had a bad runaway. This fatal change in usefulness, and my objecting to my name being struck out of the firm, put an end to Atkinson being one of our firm. All that had been done in my absence was broken up and matters moved on a little longer in the old way."

The Atkinson matter did not prevent Tate and Deere from resuming friendly relations; the families continued to see each other often. At about this time Tate reported that "Anny lost Ellen Deere's gold ring, and on Sunday I traversed the distance between the Deere house and ours every half hour thinking that if I kept exactly the same track to and fro, I should catch a gleam from the bright ring. The distance was over 100 yards. At last the bright speck appeared and I found the ring."

On the last day of August the firm received its first machinery ordered by Tate on his Eastern trip—"the cornering, tennanting, and boring machines," Tate recorded. Written permission for extending the power lines to the new building was granted on September 11 and Tate immediately set about putting up the new shop, meticulously enscribing all of the particulars: "The spread of waterwheel 70, the upright shaft in new building 113, line shaft 182." On October 2, "Removed our traps from Spencer White's shop into new building. First plow wooded by Sudlow Tuesday, October 2d in new shop."

This same day's entry recorded one more personal misfortune to the Deere family: "Howard's two brothers here from the East. They state their brother died Sept. 13th of dysentery. The deceased was engaged to be married to Jeannette Deere. He was said to be worth $800." The Deere family had already lost a two-year-old son, Hiram, in 1844, and an unnamed child who died at birth in 1845, as well as the twenty-year-old son Francis, who had died in 1848. A happy event occurred in April 1851 when Jeannette married James Chapman, a budding lawyer of Moline. But just a week later Tate reported: "Deere people nearly all sick. Poor Frances not expected to live. . . . " And then, in the same entry, "She died tonight, April 15th, of congestion of the lungs." Mrs. Deere was eight months pregnant during that terrible week of sickness; on June 17 a new daughter, Mary, was born, but she lived only until April of the next year. Later, in December 1851, the family had its second son-in-law—Ellen married Christopher Columbus Webber. Webber, originally a New Yorker, had come to Geneseo, Illinois, in 1836, where he and his older brother established a small dry goods business. Christopher came to Rock Island in 1849, first opening another store and then joining the manager of the Union Foundry. He was thirty-two at the time of the marriage, Ellen was nineteen.

The new machinery had been put successfully in place, but not without incident—on October 29, 1849, "the tall Irishman came near killing himself" in the process of putting up an intermediate shaft to drive the hewing machine. Thereafter the plowmaking process took a sharp upward turn. The total number of plows made in the year 1849 was 2,136; by February 1850, 347 were being produced per month, and 391 came off the lines in March of that year. The work force itself was approximately sixteen through this period. Tate reminds himself in the diary all through this period of some of the cost implications: "Sixteen men at $1.25 per day equals $20, or $120 per six days, producing 67 plows at a cost for labor of $1.80 each. . . . Supposing that 16 men can turn out 67 plows per 6 days, the interest on $3219.42 invested in machinery and buildings for shop at 10 percent equals 472 or 6 ½ per plow. The above includes $150 per annum for rent of power." Tate made an estimate in July 1850 of the cost of some of the more popular plow models: "Steel landside cost $5.30; common c standard, 4.85, wrought iron standard 4.64. . . . This included team and keep." The sophistication of the machinery in the plant had been deepened measurably; the planing machine that arrived from Worcester, Massachusetts, in December 1849 itself cost $1,800. Manufacturing innovations were coming more rapidly by the late 1840s, and Deere was in the forefront in taking advantage of them.

These plows had not only to be made but sold, and at this point the critical importance of marketing made itself evident to the partners. Gould himself became involved: "Almost the first thing I had to do, after I had gotten the books straightened up and got a young clerk to take care of them, was to go over into Iowa (the Legislature being in session then in Iowa City) and ascertain from the members of the Legislature, the best men in the business towns in the state with whom we could arrange to do business. . . . We had at that time a member of the Legislature who was a resident of Dewitt in Clesson County, Iowa, a merchant, and through his assistance I got an introduction to the businessmen in different parts of the state with whom we corresponded to establish the agencies to sell our plows. I then went to the different points and was gone about two weeks, with a span of horses and a sleigh, making quite a number of agencies by person interview. Then upon my return I commenced to correspond with the different parties, whose names I had obtained in the above manner, for the spring trade."

There was no such thing as an exclusive dealership in those days, but already certain brand loyalties were being espoused by farmers. This fact gave Deere a formidable challenge, for there already were a number of respected plows in the new territory, and much of that territory knew little of the Deere product. George W. Vinton (yet another Lamb link, his mother being one more of the William Lamb daughters) joined the firm in the 1850s as a field man and described this problem. "The difficulties are great to succeed in introducing a new plow without reputation. That reputation has to be made by coming in contact with the farmers and having them actually tried. It requires time and expense to get it introduced . . . there being so many good plows introduced, from long experience with the farmers who have used them it is only with great inducement you can induce them to try a new brand of plows that have heretofore been unknown to the trade. Dealers who have good plows refuse to take them generally, for the reason they already have something that suits and supplies the market, and they do not wish to take the risk and have the annoyance of introducing a new make or a new brand of plows when they have a plow that has been introduced and gives satisfaction to the trade."

Often field representatives like Vinton were away from the home office for extended periods. One traveler at this time, C.C. Alvord, told of starting from Moline in January of one year: "I went to St. Louis, and went up the Missouri, crossing and recrossing, and visiting various towns in it. I think I was in all the river towns on each side of the river as high up as Savannah, except Harman. . . . I got back in May, I think."

Oliver Lester, testifying in the Candee-Swan patent case in 1868, told of his traveling days for Deere in the early 1850s, of how he visited twice a year throughout Illinois, parts of Iowa, Minnesota, Wisconsin, Indiana, Missouri, and Kansas. Asked by the prosecutor, "What sort of points, as to size, did you visit throughout the extent of the country mentioned by you—that is to say, the larger, or the smaller?" he answered: "I visited both. I took the towns clean. Stopped at all of them pretty much." This assiduousness in visiting every possible outlet helps to explain Lester's description of himself at the start of the trial as a "traveling agent or guerrilla." The marketers seemed even then to garner colorful monikers —the counterparts of the Vintons, Alvords, and Lesters in the Eastern wholesale centers at that time, the men who prowled the hotels to collar the visiting Western buyers, were "drummers" or "borers." "Guerrilla" must have sounded too combative, for the word "traveler" became the favored term for that restless band of farm implement men out in the field visiting those skeptical, conservative agents.

The dominance of credit continued. "There was but one agent in our whole clientage," Gould lamented, "that would pay us the money for what plows he sold and that was Lyton & Allan of Des Moines, Iowa, called at that time Fort Des Moines, 180 miles from here. Whenever we sent there and counted up the plows they had sold, they never asked us to wait until they collected, but paid us for as many as were sold. They were the only exception among all our agents who would pay us the money for the plows that were sold—others said 'We cannot afford to advance the money. We have sold them to the farmers and got notes. You can have the notes, but we cannot cash these notes and you can wait until we collect,' so it was impossible for us to finance our business and know what we could do in the way of receiving funds for our sales. Many nights, I have gotten out of bed and walked the floor, knowing that I had some money to pay in a few days and did not know where I could get it. My brain felt as though I had a swarm of bees in it."

Credit terms always need to be carefully recorded, and by the early 1850s, the firm had a small printed receipt form, worded as follows: "RECEIVED OF JOHN DEERE, Plows to Sell at $_____ each and account for said Plows, when sold at the above prices, deducting commissions as specified below, and freight and drayage (if any) or return said Plows when demanded, in good order and condition, free of charges, commission on ____ Plows, ____ each, Signed _____." (The earliest of these contract forms still extant is one with a dealer in Hampton, Illinois, just north of Moline in the spring season of 1854 for four plows at eight dollars each, with a commission due of $.75 each.) This early form must not have been fully satisfactory, for in 1855 Deere changed its wording to have a printed caveat: "And pay for said Plows by the first June 1856," with no mention of any return privileges. Putting rules into print did not guarantee payment, however; the same Hampton dealer filled out such a form in 1855 for six plows at seven dollars each and wrote in longhand "when sold."[4]

TRANSPORTATION TRAVAILS

The logistics of getting the plows into the hands of these agents was no small task in those days. The quality of the roads in both western Illinois and eastern Iowa was not very good, and most shipments had to be teamed out to the farming towns by way of these roads. (At the time John Deere started in Moline, the railroad was not yet a significant factor in marketing and distribution.) "Our business, of course, was all on the river," Gould noted, "otherwise, we had to use wagons to haul the plows to the country. We would ship plows to Galena, Dubuque, Burlington, Muscatine and Keokuk and then send teams to distribute from these points." Roads in these agricultural hinterlands were generally mud-deep in spring, dust-deep in summer and fall (the plank road was not yet common in this area).

The marketing abilities of the teamster himself should not be underestimated. The typical pattern was for the teamster, usually an independent contractor, to pick up a load of plows at one of the river transshipment points and deliver them inland to the various merchants previously contacted by the traveling man. (At this early date, the merchant probably could not be considered a "dealer" in the sense that this term was used at later stages of marketing development, when the retail merchants had formal links with the company.) Some teamsters themselves became traveling salesmen and marketeers. James First, one of the early pioneers of Moline and an employee in the Deere enterprise in the mid-1850s, remembered his role this way: "At regular intervals the salesmen would back up their wagons at the factory door, load on plows to capacity, generally not more than two dozen, and start out over routes through the country to sell direct to the farmers. There generally was no advance announcement of the John Deere sales outfit. The teamster would stop at the farms along the way and if the farmer was in need of a plow the deal would be closed on the spot, the goods delivered, and the collection made. Then the teamster-salesman would move on to the next place. If he had any plows left at the end of the route—none of them at that time extended further west than Iowa City—it was generally easy to arrange with some storekeeper to keep them in stock and sell them on commission. None of the goods was supposed to be brought back to the factory." This was the way the teamster saw it; how did it look from the storekeeper's perspective? It must have bred frequent tensions between teamster and storekeeper—the latter would likely be unenthusiastic about the teamster already preempting the best customers. If the teamster had to sell for hard cash on the spot, however, it was not likely that too many sales were made on this basis. The home office would have to vest considerable trust in a teamster's judgment if any credit was to be extended.

It was the great river system—the Mississippi and its tributaries—that acted as the nexus for the whole system, a transshipment mechanism of incalculable economic value. Up until the early 1850s the steamboat was undisputed king in the Deere territories, and the genesis of a vast lore of legends and stories. By early 1851 the firm was claiming an immense territory as its domain; an advertisement in March of that year pointed up the tremendous influence of the river system itself in this expansion: "We are now furnishing agents in all the important points on the Missouri and the Mississippi River from St. Louis to St. Anthonys, on the Wisconsin River to Fort Winnebago, in almost all the counties in Iowa, and in all the river counties and second tier from the river in Illinois north of Adams and Schuyler."

But river transportation suffered from one serious disability in these colder climes—its water could (and would) freeze. Sometimes the steamers from St. Louis and the South were not able to make their way up to Rock Island until perilously late in the "spring trade" agricultural season. The *Rock Island Advertiser*, commenting on the first boat's arrival on March 10, 1852, became a bit extravagant in its prose: "This year Miss Isippi has been as coquetish as others of her sex are wont to be, and has retained her crystal jewels far beyond her wonted time. She seems to have taken a sincere liking to Jack Frost, and appears unwilling to exchange his iron embrace to romp with the beautiful Queen of Spring."

Railroads felt no such subservience to Jack Frost, and by 1854 the first train had arrived in Rock Island via the just-completed Chicago and Rock Island Railroad. "Passengers can go from Rock Island to Chicago in six hours, to Toledo in 14 hours, to New York in 42 hours," trumpeted the railroad's president. Probably the greatest transportation coup of this decade for the West, though, was the next one mile of this line—the railroad bridge across the Mississippi River, linking Rock Island with Davenport, Iowa, in 1856. Everyone knew this extension was more than just to Davenport, or even to the rest of the state of Iowa. At stake was the vast territory beyond; as the *Advertiser* put it, this would "connect the Atlantic with the Missouri River, and ultimately with the Pacific Ocean."

This very first bridge across the mighty river was the harbinger of many more soon to come. But the steamboaters looked on them with undisguised antipathy as both navigation hazards and economic rivals. Their remonstrances on the former seemed prophetic, for just two weeks after the Rock Island bridge opened, it was hit by the steamboat *Effie Afton*, which promptly caught fire and incinerated both the boat and a span of the bridge. A massive, messy lawsuit followed, with the railroaders (aided by Abraham Lincoln, their lawyer) finally besting the steamboaters. The bridge was put back into commission later that year and soon torn down and rebuilt. Once the railroaders won the case—and the right to span the river—many more bridges were constructed; by 1886, fifteen railroads had bridged the upper river alone.[5]

Tate is our only source for much of the company figures for this period. Fortunately, he kept monthly production statistics for each of the years 1849–51, and we can see the early manifestation of the seasonal cycle so pronounced in the farm equipment industry, with the build-up of inventory in the fall and early winter for the "spring trade" (exhibit 3-1).

Exhibit 3–1   **Deere, Tate & Gould Plow Production
1849-51**

The *Prairie Farmer* correspondent visited Moline in early 1851 and came away duly impressed. "These enterprising and go-a-head men give constant employment to some twenty or thirty men, and turn out some of the very best kind of plows. . . . They will find it difficult to meet the demand that will be made for others."

Sandwiched in between all of Tate's bits and scraps about the company were additional nuggets of gossip about the town: "March 29th 1850 Samuel Meek's wagon and four yoke of cattle passed through Moline today on their way to St. Jo where Keys and Martin will join them. They have gone to St. Joseph's by steamboat (this man Martin killed his boss Edwards. Before they got through they shot him. Keys knows all about it)." May 29th: "Ellen and Charles Deere got the measles. Emma has just got well of same complaint. Frances has them." Partner John Gould's activities were noted: "August 25th. Rain, rain, from 16th to 25th. This date John Gould married to Miss Hannah Dimock." The year 1850 ended amicably, "Mr. Deere, Mr. Gould and Mr. Dimock took dinner with us Christmas Day."

FINANCIAL INTRICACIES

This same year, 1850, marked the appearance of an important new source of information about the firm, for credit reports from the Mercantile Agency were initiated for the Moline-Rock Island area. (The Mercantile Agency was founded in 1841 by Lewis Tappan, became R.G. Dun & Co. in 1859, and Dun & Bradstreet, Inc., in 1933. The John M. Bradstreet firm itself dated to 1849.) Their correspondent, in the cryptic, terse language of the credit agency, gives us only two sentences (exhibit 3-2)—but they contain within them some new information that does not show up in the Tate or Gould reminiscences. According to the report, the firm is honest and responsible for any amount of debt agreed to and its habits good. Though the firm is "exclusively" engaged in the manufacturing of plows, it also has a store with stock worth $2,000 to $3,000, housed in real estate worth $2,000.

It is this last observation that is startling, for we now find that Deere,

Exhibit 3–2. First credit report on Deere, Tate & Gould by The Merchantile Agency, August 19, 1850 (courtesy of R.G. Dun & Company Collection, Baker Library, Harvard Business School)

Tate & Gould is also a store with a "stock of goods." Gould talked of some of the firm's early local retail trade: "After a little, we got the business systematized and running pretty well.... We had no pay-day for the employes. We traded our plows to the merchants in Davenport and Rock Island, Muscatine and other towns nearby and then gave orders to our men on the stores for what they needed, and we had a boardinghouse where the present lumber sheds of the Plow Company now is, west of the post office, in which we had our men board at $1.75 per week. We paid our good blacksmiths $20.00 a month and boarded them and managed in that way, by trading with the merchants to pay the employes until such time as they had to leave, or we had to discharge them and then we had to raise a little money to pay them." In other words, most of the wages were paid in kind—a barter arrangement involving a number of merchants around the town. In turn, those emporia could draw on Deere, presumably not only for plows but for other goods handled by the company.

Money was extremely scarce in Illinois in those days—at least, good money. The paper money was very often worth less than its face value and was all too frequently worthless. In 1836 the second Bank of the United States ceased to exist, and state and local banks sprang up all over the country, ill conceived in most cases, undercapitalized, and with a paucity of specie to back up the burgeoning variety of notes being issued on an almost indiscriminate basis. "Wild-cat" banks many of them were, for their home offices could be found just about as easily as a wild cat's lair. "Shin plasters," "saddlebags," "red-dogs"—the terms of derision springing up all over the country mirrored the antagonisms and contempt that so many people felt at being hoodwinked by weak, often venal, banking and currency practices. Specie—hard money of gold or silver— was in terribly short supply, so much prized that often farmers and businessmen would sell their products at a much lower price if they could have the surety of the hard money in return.

John Gould remembered these days all too well. "The matter of financing was a very troublesome affair, there being no bank nearer than Galena and Burlington, at that time. Cook & Sargent, a firm in Davenport of law and land agents, Mr. Cook being a lawyer and Mr. Sargent a land agent, they could occasionally sell us exchange on St. Louis and New York...." In a bankless state like Iowa, it was quite common for a land agent to evolve into a private bank. "The currency or money that we used was mostly foreign money; we had Mexican, French, and English coins and very few bank notes, there being some from Missouri, Ohio, and Indiana, but mostly a hard money—what we call specie. When I wanted some exchange to send to St. Louis or New York—especially in the winter time when there were not steamboats running, I would go over to Cook and Sargent's office and occasionally there would be a time when they couldn't draw and I would have to bring my bag of money home again. In the summer time our trade with St. Louis of that kind was sent by the clerks on the steamboats. It is almost impossible for a person now to conceive of the inconveniences of doing business without banks."

Anyone with hard currency in his pockets was likely to be hounded by those desperate for specie. John Deere's firm, faced with one of its periodic, indeed frequent, shortfalls in hard currency, desperately needed $200. It was mid-winter, and no payments were going to be coming in for a good many weeks or months. Deere was chatting with Lemuel Andreas, one of the town merchants, and was told that the latter had borrowed $2,000 from a young Swedish immigrant fresh in town from the old country. Gould recounted the ensuing story: "Mr. Deere probably came home in as quick time as he possible could, came into the office in a great hurry and said to me, 'Tailor Johnson over here has an acquaintance who has some money—you hunt him up as quick as you can and see what you can do.' I went to Mr. Johnson's shop and told him what I wanted. He said 'Yes, that man has got some money,' and told me where I could find him, but the man couldn't speak English, so I had to get Mr. Johnson to go with me. Johnson told him what I wanted and he said I could have the money so I borrowed $200.00 from him in gold for one year at 10 percent interest. That relieved us of the great strain that was upon us for that amount of money."[6]

The problem of money itself was exacerbated by the slowness and undependability of the communication system, especially the mails. The way of handling the post office in Moline particularly exasperated Gould. "The post office at that time was on 17th Street between what is now First and Second Avenue, facing west. The postmaster was then Dr. Wells. The office was open perhaps three or four hours during the day. The office had some 26 or 30 boxes and our box was so situated that we could look in at the window and see if there was anything in it. If there was, I would try and find the postmaster to get the mail. The stage arrived here every night just a little before dark and left early in the morning. To send mail out, we had to take it to the doctor's private room, which was in the old Moline House, in the evening. He would make up his mail there. The mail business was very inconvenient and everybody was dissatisfied, but we couldn't help ourselves. The doctor had a pull and held the office. When I found there was some mail in the box, I hunted around until I found the doctor in a store, sitting on the counter, telling stories. I said there was some mail in the box and he replied, 'Very well, I will go down and open the office after awhile.'"

Communications were aided considerably in the early 1850s by telegraph links under the aegis of the Illinois and Mississippi Telegraph Co. By 1853 there were direct lines from Chicago, through Rock Island and there were direct lines from Chicago, through Rock Island and Moline, to St. Louis. The railroad right of way was generally the easiest route for telegraph construction, so many communities at one moment gained two superb new instruments of communication.

The panoply of all of these financial intricacies of the firm comes alive for us via the first consequential corporate record book extant on John Deere's partnerships—the "Deere, Tate & Gould Journal Blotter C—1850–51." This is a chronological daybook journal, showing debit-credit notations for all the transactions of each day, prior to posting to the ledger books (the latter, unfortunately, long ago destroyed). This particular journal covers the period November 21, 1850, to April 26, 1851, and chronicles literally hundreds of transactions. A substantial portion is for the "store" accounts, some for other employees, but most for the three partners themselves. All three of the men made purchases for their entire families through the books of the business. These accounts were priced at the going retail rate for the good or service, with periodic reconciliations, each partner being charged for the sum total of all of his purchases, the firm having already paid for them with the company's cash or goods. For example, the reconciling journal entry for February 1, 1851, is: "John Deere—$724.15, R.N. Tate—$367.24, J.M. Gould—$612.66." Think of the profound legal implications of using a partnership in this way—in effect, each family stood ready to pay any debt related to any family expenditure of the others!

These hundreds of transactions, large and small, give us not only an excellent window into the lives of the families, but a fascinating panorama of prices from which we can build nearly a full price list for every activity in the village. Tate bought on November 23, 1850, for the account of his wife, Hannah, twenty yards of "Delain," for a total of $5.00, three additional yards of calico at $.32, another swatch of calico at $.21, one pair of worsted hose at $.42, and two pair of shoes at $1.00 each. Candles were $.11, a lamp $.29, 2¼ pounds of soap came to $.18, a fur cap went for $2.25, buck gloves $1.40, a half pound of tobacco $.25, two bushels of turnips were $.40, ten pounds of salt was $.18, two pounds of rice $.16. John Deere paid $5.00 in 1850 for a buffalo robe, and bought his son Charles a pocket-knife for $.21. Just before Christmas in 1850, he purchased a coat at the substantial price of $6.25 and added to it a "crevat" at $1.46. Thomas Hodkinson, one of the Deere employees, also charged a tie at just about the same time—perhaps the fact that it was a "fancy silk crevat" made his price $.04 higher, at $1.50.

In addition to merchandise itself, the account book captures a number of other interests of the partners. John Deere was preoccupied with the schoolhouse at that time, attending himself to even the small details. In November 1850, he bought eight lights of 8½x11 glass at $.34 to "put in schoolhouse," and a grand total of $.13 worth of school candles was purchased the next month. Likewise, Deere's subscription to the Sunday school went through the books—a $.50 charge each time, about once a month. Tuition was also being paid to "Denison," and in a substantial amount, for the balance of the account still due was itself $20. It is not clear who or what "Denison" was, but the charge was more than likely connected with Charles Deere's education. Gould was a stickler for detail in the account book—a full journal entry was made charging John Deere $.05 for postage. Deere's penchant for small arithmetic errors also shows up in Gould's accounts. "Pd girl for error in making change at the house," a debit to John Deere of $.35. About the same time, a counterfeit $10 bill from the "State Bank of Ohio" had to be written off.

The firm itself also recorded its trades through these pages; for example, one box of garden seed "on commision, to be sold at 5 cts. per paper and a commission of 33⅓% allowed on all sold. 200 papers @ 3⅓—$6.67." Other merchandise was purchased in larger volume and sold in quantity to outsiders. The store must have dealt substantially in yard goods and other sewing needs—one account, for example, noted a write-down on some wool received from Isaac Williams; "Wool was left to be sold at 20¢ but was too poor." The sum total of all of this "store" selling still remained a minor element in the total operation of the partnership—there was no doubt that the plow business was the central focus. Still, it is surprising that the firm was so involved in so many activities, surely some drain on the energies and concentration of the partners. Yet this was typical of the businessmen of that time. The "general merchants" of the frontier were very general indeed!

The plow business itself dominates the journal, and through these entries we gain our first precise figures on sales prices, accounts receivable, notes payable, and other aspects of the business side of the firm. Familiar names of old retail clients and suppliers of the firm jump out at us all through these pages. Naturally, there are many more dealers than before, and the amounts of their accounts are larger. In just one day's entry, for Saturday, March 15, 1851, thirty-nine separate accounts have items recorded (presumably for sales over the preceding month or so), with totals ranging upward to some accounts at more than $500. B.H. and T.B. Wallace of Lexington, Missouri, for example, took six 10-inch plows at $42 each, six 11-inch plows at $42, twelve 12-inch plows at $96, twelve 9-inch plows at $72, and thirty 14-inch plows at $270, for a sum total of $522. Thus we can begin to develop a price structure for the firm at this time, the plows ranging in price from $6 to $9. A 16-inch "breaker," sold to McIlwaine and Nappur of Comanche (no state noted), carried a price of $15. The breaker also came in an 18-inch model for $17, a 21-inch breaker for $20, and a 23-inch breaker for $23. An unexplained exception gave E.B. Scott of Wapello, Iowa, his plows at a discount—$8.25 instead of $9, etc. One important client, Burrows and Prettyman of Davenport, bought one plow "with coulter" for $13—a clue that tells us that some of the plows had detachable coulters. Burrows and Prettyman also ordered five "one-horse" plows at $7.25 each. Other journal entries note the amount of regular dealer discounts to be charged against the plow account. Hauling charges from the teamsters were paid from time to time and river transportation levies also are scattered throughout the journal. For example, on March 27, 1851, $110.25 went to Beatman, Pittman &

Company, the river transport organization, for shipping 439 plows, "to be forwarded up the Mo River & fret not collected of the Mo. boats—see their letter on file." Many of these plows making the long trip up the Missouri River were destined for Indian territory. (Tate reports in April 1851, for example: "Finished 29 B plows to go up the Missouri to the Osage Indians.") And occasional unfortunate vicissitudes connected with this river shipping intruded; Tate reports on May 7, 1851, of a whole lot of plows being lost when a barge sank.[7]

A GRAIN DRILL, BEFORE ITS TIME

One account, with William A. Ayres, reports the sale to him of a single grain drill at eighty dollars. It is not clear how much of this machine was actually manufactured by Deere, Tate & Gould. (Already other purchased agricultural equipment such as scythes, hay forks, manure forks, "Lamson's snaths," etc., was being jobbed through the store.) A Deere advertisement in the August 1851 issue of the *Prairie Farmer* called it "Seymour's grain drill" (a well-known Eastern machine). "This machine is the invention of a practical man, a good mechanic, and the result of several years' travel and experience." The drill had nine tubes, sowing a six-foot width. "It possesses one advantage that we think makes it so superior to any other, and is very important in a seed sower," continued the advertisement, "*i.e.*: the readiness with which the person tending it can see whether any of the droppers (or tubes) failed to deliver the grain regularly, as they are all in plain sight and under the eye of the driver. From its peculiar construction, therefore, a failure to deliver the seed constantly cannot occur." The grain drill had taken premiums at five fairs, though in the advertisement Deere was not willing to list the exact awards.

Seed drills were not new to the agriculturalist. Indeed, back in 1731 the English agricultural writer, Jethro Tull, in his famous book, *Horse-Hoeing Husbandry*, espoused the argument that seeds should not be sown broadcast, but planted in rows by drills in order to more readily allow hoeing by horsepower with proper implements. R.L. Ardrey reports primitive Assyrian grain drills as far back as 680 B.C. Grain drills did not get much of a start in the United States until the 1840s, but in that decade and in the early 1850s they became quite popular in the East.

Leo Rogin points out in his classic study of nineteenth-century farm machinery, however: "The implement, as then made, did not lend itself to the superficial methods of preparing the soil characteristic of the prairie regions, and there is little evidence that it made much headway during the fifties." Prior to the Civil War, the hand rotation sower was common in the territory served by John Deere, a broadcast sower instrument worn around the neck of the farmer, who walked through the fields. ("Will sow Six Acres per hour, at a common walking gait," said an advertisement for Cahoon's planter, an instrument patented in the late 1850s.) Such instruments were often ineffectual, especially on windy days, with the seed tending to be scattered very unevenly. Another alternative was the so-called seed-box seeder, generally used with a cultivator attachment, or sometimes with other tillage implements such as the plow, the cultivator, or the roller. Most of these more sophisticated machines did not gain acceptance until the 1860s. Though grain drills were established technology in the East, they certainly were not in the Midwest during the 1850s.

Thus it is not surprising that the sale of the grain drill by Deere, Tate & Gould to William A. Ayres on March 22, 1851, was apparently the only one in the years 1850 and 1851 (though at least seven had been in stock). No advertisements after 1853 mention grain drills, no notations in ledger or journal books can be found. It seems obvious that the Seymour gambit was an abortive one.

Yet its importance should not be underestimated, for John Deere had now carried product development into a completely new field of agricultural machinery. It is a pity that no documentation remains of how he happened to take this excursion on the drill. Clearly, it was not intended to be just a peripheral line—the size of the advertisements and their focus was not inconsequential. Was the Seymour drill one that Tate might have purchased on his Eastern trip? Or was it an idea that John Deere had picked up along the way? A small enterprise known as the Keystone Manufacturing Company at Sterling, Illinois, owned by a Mr. Gault, began making a similar product beginning about 1857. But Gault, too, failed to achieve much market penetration until after 1860. Gault and Deere were "pioneers before their time" with the seeder; both would come back in later decades to this field, each with considerable success.[8]

AN ACCOUNTS-PAYABLE CRISIS

Gould kept meticulous books for the firm in his tall and elegant handwriting. On December 21, 1850, he caught a ten-cent error in a John Deere merchandise account, made back on September 5. If there was any sloppiness in the backup for the ledger, Gould straightforwardly stated it. For example, on December 11, 1850, he noted one plow returned from H. McNeal, "so Deere says—was forgotten." An eleven-dollar payment on a note of Jonathan Perry is put not to the Perry account, but to "suspense." "We entered this to suspense account because the note is in the hands of someone in that vicinity for collection and Thompson has the receipt."

It is in the accounts-payable and notes-payable general entries that we begin to see the tense financial dealings that reinforced Gould's memory of "having gotten out of bed and walked the floor, knowing I had some money to pay in a few days and did not know where I could get it." Large machinery bills were due—a $3,091 bill with S.H. Morse and Company was to be paid in $500 amounts in June, October, and November 1851, followed by a $1,000 payment in December and the remaining $591 in January 1852. Interest on the Morse account was charged at 10 percent, and the resulting $311 had to be added to the cost. There were also large amounts due Naylor & Co., the longstanding iron and steel supplier in New York. Another supplier well known to John Deere (he had begun dealing with them back in the early 1840s in Grand Detour) was Lyon, Shorb & Co. of St. Louis. The amounts here were not as large as those with Naylor or Morse—in April 1861, for example, the account stood at $2,359. But the Lyon, Shorb relationship turned out to be the thorniest of all for the partnership. Gould tells the story: "Sometime during the second winter that I was here, in the middle of the Winter, the credit man of Lyon, Shorb & Co. came up by stage and came into the office in the morning and said, 'Mr. Gould, I would like to see your last balance sheet.' I showed it to him and after he had examined it, he turned to me and said, 'Mr. Gould, I don't see why you cannot pay your debts.' It frightened me a little, for I could see what his object was in coming here in the winter by stage. 'Well,' I replied, 'if we have time, we certainly can, we are all right.' 'Well,' he said, 'Mr. Vinton has sent me here to get security.'" Inasmuch as Albert Vinton was the St. Louis manager of Lyon, Shorb, Gould felt he had no alternative but to share the private balance sheet with the creditor.

Gould did not have long to wait for a reply: "It was probably not more than 10 or 12 days from that time, upon the very first boat after the river was open, sometime in February, he returned and came in to the office. And when I met him I concluded that he came for what he was sent for in the first place. He told me at once that Mr. Vinton said absolutely that we must give security for that debt. I could not understand why he had such orders and did not know for a long time the cause, but afterwards learned that Mr. Vinton had stock in Mr. Andrus' factory in Grand Detour and the probability was that they were determined to break us up and get us out of the way in their territory. After considerable deliberation among Mr. Deere, Mr. Tate and I, we finally concluded that we would make an effort to give him a real estate and chattel mortgage, upon condition that we could have 6 – 11 – 18 and 24 months time, with 6% interest to pay the debt. He said he would have to submit that to Mr. Vinton by mail—that he would not go back again. Not long after he received the reply, 'You are on the ground—do what you think is best,' and so he accepted our offer. We gave him our notes and mortgages."

But Gould felt he had outsmarted Lyon, Shorb: "Then I could see that we would possibly have trouble getting stock to continue our business and I went right to St. Louis, to another firm, Runyan, Hillman & Co., a Tennessee iron house and reported to Mr. Hillman exactly what we had done with Lyon, Shorb & Co. and that we had really got a capital of $1800 that we didn't expect to have, by having this deal with Lyon, Shorb & Co.

and that the trade released us from paying them anything on our old bills and that the prospects were that we could pay and pay promptly for stock after that and the reply was, 'You can have all the stock of us that you want,' so we were then in shape to go on with the business."

John Deere himself also made a trip to St. Louis in conjunction with the Lyon, Shorb debt, taking his son Charles with him. "I remember my first ride on the steamboat when I accompanied my father to St. Louis," reminisced Charles Deere later. "We visited one of his chief creditors and supply mills, and I got very angry at the going over my father submitted to because he was behind in his payments."

In the narrower sense, Gould was quite correct that the arrangement freed working capital for the firm, but it also increased the long-term debt, and a mortgage on fixed capital, at that. The Mercantile Agency respondent was quick to pick this up, reporting in April 1852: "I was surprised to find on the record the following mtgage—'On May 6/51' d. t. & g. 'executed a mtgage to William A. Lyon, John Lyon and Daniel C. Stewart,' all of St. Louis to secure the payt of the 2 notes, one for 2790/$ on or before the 1st of July 52, the other for 2816/$ due 1 Jan 53. The mortgage covers the Moline prop/other lands." The respondent continued, "It is almost if not quite impossible to estimate his pecuniary standing, as the bus which he is now, and has been engaged is scattered over such an extent of Territory. His cr. is regarded good in this vici."

Five months later, though, in September 1852, the assiduous Mercantile Agency reporter had an unsettling single-line report: "Has some val. prop but is embarrassed." Apparently the Gould optimism about the Lyon, Shorb notes freeing up working capital did not work that way during this particular summer (though we have no balance sheet to verify the precise situation). The crisis was apparently short-lived, for in August 1853 the credit agency reporter gave a more optimistic message: "In response, is now relieved of the mortgage above & apprs. to be unincumbd."[9]

THE PARTNERSHIP FALLS APART

Despite the long friendships of the three men in the partnership, the course of the business relationships of Deere, Tate & Gould was rocky and all too often abrasive. Tate wrote his brother an optimistic letter in September 1851: "We are making at present 75 plows a week. We owe a great deal, and there is a great deal owing us. Our books show over $30,000 in notes of over $10 to $100 over an area of 1,000 square miles. Our business, however, is lucrative, our factory one of the largest if not quite the largest in the state. In short, our name is up, and I don't know why we should not do well." Privately to his diary, though, he began reporting more and more tensions. October 30, 1851—"John Deere fugeling about buying John Gould's interest in the firm"; November

5—"Deere told me he had agreed to give John Gould $2,600 for his interest." January 31, 1852—"I have come to no agreement yet with Deere"; February 7—"No agreement with Cain yet. Juggle, juggle"; February 13—"Told Deere I had concluded not to go into business with him but he pretended not to hear a word of it. I have seen enough of his one-sided moves, so I put an end to it, and so left the control of it all to John Deere. Settled up with him, charged him with the time I spent on manufacturing his stock, 24½ days at $2.50, $60.00, and so brought his fugeling to an end, and sold out to him, agreeing to take for my interest the amount he had allowed Gould, $2,600."

What really had happened? John Gould had his own version:

> After awhile, in the transaction of business, Mr. Deere and Mr. Tate did not agree upon the manner of making plows. Mr. Deere wanted to make improvements all the time, while Mr. Tate did not believe in that; he thought that what was made was good enough. Mr. Deere would say to Mr. Tate, "We have got to change this or that about the plow and make an improvement," and Mr. Tate would inevitably reply, "Damn the odds, they have got to take what we make." Mr. Deere would say, "They haven't got to take what we make and somebody else will beat us, and we will lose our trade." These little bickerings lasted quite a long time between them, both being honest and sincere in their convictions. Mr. Tate was one of the kind that would carry his grist in one end of the bag and a stone in the other, if he was going to market.
>
> Finally the trouble between Mr. Deere and Mr. Tate was getting so intense that Mr. Deere proposed to me that we have a dissolution, that he wanted to be rid of Mr. Tate and he said, "Now suppose you close up the business of Deere, Tate & Gould, take your time for it and I will go alone, with Mr. Chapman, who had married Miss Deere and he could take my place in the business and then when I got the thing straightened out, if I wanted to come back, we could make a new trade." I took the year 1852, from the first of April until November in traveling over the country and closing out the business and collecting.

What was the truth? Tate and Deere did indeed have a very complex personal relationship. They were close friends in those early days in Moline and the Tate diary abounds with allusions to personal links bringing the two families together. Deere and Tate took trips together, meals were shared. Special events brought them together: "On the 27th had a sleigh ride to Rock Island, a party . . . our company consisted of Major Downing, Thos. Merriman, Doctor Chamberlin, James Chapman, John Deere, his daughter Jeannette and I." Even after the split they continued this pattern of closeness. A number of times over the next year or so they dined together, and Tate continues his diary entries on all of the Deere family. In mid-1854 Tate and Deere took a trip to Chicago together. "Got there Friday morning at half after four a.m.," Tate reports. "Cold, cold. The ground covered with hoar frost. A real winter morning. Cold, bleak, low wet Chicago!" The next day they split up to do their separate business activities, then "Deere and I went to hear the Black Swan sing. I got lost and while we were separated I heard a match of two drummers from the street. Found Deere." Yet Tate also could not resist a dig at Deere: "While here Deere mistook coconuts for pineapples!" Tate seemed often to find John Deere irritating and disparaged him in the diary time and time again.

John Gould's relationships with Deere seemed much more amicable and, indeed, Gould himself appeared more stable in his views toward many of the partnership and family interactions. Still, it is a bit dangerous to generalize about motives and values from Tate's very extensive, fascinating, and revealing diary; Gould's very well written, analytical reminiscence, done a number of years after the fact; and nothing in the actual hand of Deere, the third person involved. The last stands mute on all these matters, for there is very little remaining directly in the words or handwriting of John Deere.

Gould's version that Tate wanted to peddle a standardized product as long as the consumer would accept it, and that Deere was constantly wanting to change and improve, fits consistently with a number of other bits of evidence about the two men. Tate and Gould both testified in the Candee-Swan patent case in the late 1860s, and in the process talked a great deal about John Deere's innovativeness and concern for marketing and product innovations. Probably one of many reasons for the splitting of the partnership was the fundamental difference in business philosophy between two of the partners.

Predictably, the process of dissolution of the partnership again was complicated. The Deere plow inventory had to be separated from the Deere, Tate & Gould plow stock, and proper accounting made for the two lots of equipment. (Tate himself was going to go into the plow business, so this made it more difficult.) The spring trade accounts out in the field for that year were still owed—the amount on June 22, reported Tate, was more than $7,000. Surprisingly, with all this high finance going on, John Deere went East during that month (for what reason we do not know); on this same day's entry Tate received a letter from Deere "in the South of Maine." In March 1853, Gould paid Tate seventy-eight dollars, the first Deere, Tate & Gould dividend. Another $674 came in June. By the end of the season the major portion of the former partnership accounts were at least reconciled among the three partners, if not fully paid off by the debtor farmers and merchants. Also, in the process, the store part of the business was sold outright; the obituary of George D. Bromley in the newspapers in February 1870 reported that he had "in 1852 purchased the Dry Goods Business of Deere, Tate & Gould in Moline."

Which of the two partners, Tate or Gould, first had the idea of jettisoning the partnership? Subsequent events confirmed that both men had other plans. Gould's decision fit well with his conservative nature: "During the time I was closing out the business of Deere, Tate & Gould, I had been thinking of a factory for making wooden ware, tubs, pails, churns, wash-boards, etc., as the pine logs were floating right past here and everything was convenient to make them and I concluded that if I could get into that business, I would like it better than to go back to the plow business, as the product of a factory of that kind could be sold entirely to merchants who could pay money, instead of having to wait for the plows to be sold." The pail factory, called Dimock and Gould, was built on the island side of the Mississippi slough, just upriver from the dam; not a very complicated process, it was soon in successful operation, advertising tubs, pails, bedstands, and "all kinds of turned stuff."

Tate's split was not nearly as cleancut—he chose to make his own plows, in competition, at least in part, with John Deere. By May 1853, he reports in his diary, "25 plows up and painted. 21 more primed and 4 more to wood yet. 2 wooded and not painted. . . . " On June 1, "Packing plows. Nearly already!" There are some fragmentary indications in the diary that Deere and Tate had split their territories in some fashion. A considerable portion of Tate's production in his own shop, both in 1853 and 1854, went to California. Charles Atkinson, in the Candee-Swan patent case in 1868, when asked about Tate's new operation, recalled: "As near as I recollect, his business was making or getting up plows for the California market, more in nature of an adventure than a permanent business." Tate himself testified in the case: "From 1851 to 1855 I manufactured plows alone for the California market." Still, John Deere also sold there; one large order of 100 plows was dispatched in May 1853, together with twenty more for Oregon.

Just who acquired the rights to the seeder is not clear. John Deere ran a small advertisement in March 1852 under his own name, "successor to Deere, Tate & Gould," calling attention to his plows and "also a Superior article of Seed Drill." Tate also purported to sell the Seymour drill in his advertisement of March 1854: "Moline!! Tate has now on hand and ready to deliver a lot of Seymour's matchless Grain Drills. This is truly one of the best Farming Implements of the Age." Tate does not say that he himself made the drill in his own shop—just that he had "a lot" for sale.

Tate also began to make wagons, and this business turned out to be much larger than plows. On November 21, 1853, just a few months after he had begun operating as a separate entity, he already had sold twenty-five wagons, some of them "one-horse" at fifty-five dollars and others "two-horse," selling from sixty-two to seventy-five dollars. Tate's record keeping left a good deal to be desired. Two of the wagons he sold to "self," another to "the Wallace boy, Iowa," one to "a Geneseo farmer," and another to "a German." Not a very effective customer list for follow-ups!

Later, in January 1856, Tate opted for open competition with Deere, forming a full-line plow company with Charles Buford and the latter's son, Bassett, doing business as Buford & Tate. Despite this, during these first years after the break in the partnership Tate and Deere remained close friends and seemed to have worked out some kind of agreement on plow territories that reasonably satisfied both.[10]

A SON IN THE BUSINESS

Personal reasons, lying deep in the personality and psyche of John Deere, intruded into the picture at this point. The loss of son Francis in that last, bitter year in Grand Detour must have been traumatic beyond measure, for it happened just at that precious irreplaceable moment in a father's life when his son first reaches maturity and can take his place as an equal. In the case of Francis, the loss was especially severe, for the son was to join his father in the business—and to keep straight those accounts his father so incompletely understood.

Now, once again John Deere had a member of the family he could trust—James Chapman, Jeannette's new husband. Though he was a practicing lawyer and was not to join the firm full time, his perspective was particularly needed at that moment. Chapman was closely linked to the firm, newspaper articles during this mid-1850s period often refer to the company as Deere & Chapman. It was apparently not a formal partnership agreement, however, and in all of the advertisements of the firm the name was "John Deere."

Within a year, too, another member of the family—sixteen-year old Charles, John Deere's oldest living son—joined the firm, to remain with it for fifty-four years, until his death in 1907. For a great many of the later years he was the company's chief executive officer, an inestimable influence on the firm, and so his early life is important.

John Deere had evidenced real concern about Moline's primitive educational climate in the early 1850s, threatening more than once "to move his folks over to Davenport to get them schooling" (Tate's diary entry in August 1850). The first public school did not come to Moline until 1853, though there were already 3,307 "common schools" in the state by 1851. Charles attended several of the small local private schools, conducted in homes. The first was at the Cass residence, a small house that was later torn down to build the town's Carnegie library. "Later there was school at the old engine house under the two Chapmans," recounted Charles, "and still later I was taught at Anson Hubbard's house in a school which was taught by Mrs. Hasbrook, an English lady, sister of Mrs. Joseph Huntoon." Despite his father's insistence, Charles had much ambivalence toward formal schooling. "I know I made progress at the Hasbrook School . . . but I can hardly say as much for the time spent at the two Chapmans' school during the previous winter. There were frequent clashes between the teachers and the boys and my part in the excitement usually resulted in being relegated to the shop to work off my enthusiasm at running a drill. This penalty usually gave me an excellent lesson in application, though otherwise it was not all to my taste."

Apparently he was often in trouble with his stern father for such mischief. "I had a boy's usual troubles with his father, and there were tight arguments sometimes. There was usually a hickory stick at home after every fight that was reported to father. School had not many attractions in those days, and mother's protecting wing was anxiously sought when reports of lapses of attendance reached home." By his own admission, he was not too assiduous in his schoolwork in those earlier days. He enthusiastically hunted, and at the Grand Detour house used to trap quail at the river-side corner of their lot. Perhaps we should not take him literally on another feature of the chase. He reported (in his own words): "The Indians would come in to spend the Winter on their reservation which was just beyond the boundaries of our place. We used to hunt the Indian boys, who ventured beyond their boundaries; a guard was constantly kept, and woe to the poor Indian boy who was caught alone."

He loved to go with his father on business trips, when the elder Deere traveled around neighboring farms to experiment and try the plows he had built. "I used to follow in the furrow during the test," Charles remembered, "but there was always an unpleasant side of those trips in the study of the multiplication table, spelling and the like."

From the home schools Charles went across the river to Davenport's Iowa College, from there to a year at Knox College in Galesburg, and then to Bell's Commercial College in Chicago for business education. Bell's had been instituted in the early 1850s and by the time Charles Deere matriculated, young men were coming to it from all over the Midwest. The college's advertisements in the mid-1850s were expectedly self-congratulatory: "The extraordinary patronage bestowed upon this popular institution affords gratifying evidence that the superior advantages and facilities it offers for the acquisition of a thorough Commercial Education are favorably appreciated." The central focus was on bookkeeping in a simulated office environment. Business mathematics was also taught, as well as "Commercial Law" and the "art of detecting counterfeit Bank Notes." The college had a library of more than 1,000 volumes, not an inconsequential number in that day. In 1853, Charles Deere was graduated from Bell's and "reported at my father's office modestly contending that I was a full-fledged bookkeeper," in effect, having completed the mid-nineteenth-century equivalent of today's M.B.A. from a graduate business school.

Charles Deere joined his father sometime in early 1854, working with Reuben Wells, until then the only bookkeeper. "We were a rather easygoing force," admitted Charles, "and with the social facilities of nearby towns, I enjoyed the usual experiences of the average boy, sometimes greatly at the expense of my business." The young man was a quick learner, though, and soon broadened the reach of his responsibilities to the marketing side of the business. "I advanced to head salesman, in charge of dealers and salesmen, and often took to the road on initial trips into any territory to introduce our plows. We reached out and added the territory of Eastern Illinois, which was then controlled by Springfield and Peoria factories." The younger Deere also inherited his father's enthusiasm for moving out into the field and driving the equipment himself. "I used to accompany our wagons in delivering plows through the country and learned to be quite proficient in hitching to and running a plow. Driving horses came naturally to me whether a plow team or a trotter, and this has always been one of my most pleasant recreations."

In 1851 John Deere had hired Andrew Friberg, a young Swedish immigrant, in the country for less than a year. (He was one of the first from that country; large numbers followed, as well as a great many from Germany.) When Tate left and the partnership was dissolved, Deere asked Friberg to assume command of the shop. The young Swede did not speak English very well and, as he reported later in the Candee-Swan case, "I did not like to take the responsibility and I asked Mr. Deere to have another the responsibility and I asked Mr. Deere to have another man do that; I could make more money to work at the fire and work piecework. Mr. Deere got another man to take charge, and I went to work at my fire again, welding shares, and continued about a year. The person who took charge was named Charles Richardson, who on and off acted as foreman about one year. I had to expend a good deal of time in showing Richardson, as well as the men, what to do. After Richardson left, I assumed the whole charge of the shop. . . . "

With the orbit of the business extending ever wider, the work at the home office—bookkeeping, finance, etc.—also mushroomed, and Deere persuaded Luke Hemenway, who had been with Deere for a couple of years in the early Grand Detour days, to join him in Moline. Hemenway reported in August 1855 and assumed the role of head bookkeeper.[11]

HOW INNOVATIVE WAS JOHN DEERE?

The first five years of the new firm of "John Deere"—1853–57—were halcyon ones. Approximately 4,000 plows were produced in 1852, 3,959 in 1853. We have no exact figures for 1854, but the 1855 amount had jumped to more than 8,000 and the 1856 figures were reported by various outside sources as being from 13,400 to 15,000. Unfortunately, no balance sheets or profit-and-loss statements for these years survived, but extant leaves of journal books, cash books, and employee time records give us considerable related scraps with which to reconstruct at least part of the business activity. Shop employment during this five-year period tripled; there had been about twenty employees at the time the partnership split, and there were sixty-eight employees reported in early 1856. Most men were on a day rate. Each had a monthly salary established for him, and these monthly salaries were divided by an arbitrary twenty-six days, irrespective of month, giving some strange day rates. For example, according to the "Mechanics and Laborers' Timebook" for 1852–55, "$6 per mo. is 23⅓¢ per day; $7 per mo. is 26¹²⁄₁₈¢ per day." For most of the active employees, the day rates ranged from $.57 $\%_{13}$ ($19.00 per month) to some at $1.50 per day ($39.00 per month). A few employees were on piece rates. In July 1855, for example, E. Peterson ground sixty-six plows at $.09 each for a total weekly wage of $5.94; A. Gordon in that same week was paid an amazing sum of $18.00—180 plows painted at $.10 each. There were also piece rates for clevises ($.14 for each), for moldboards ($.05 for each, presumably assembly only), bolts at $.02 each. The total number of employees was fairly steady all through the twenty-seven months, but the total number of hours worked over the various weeks of this period again evidenced substantial seasonal swings—a buildup during the winter months, slow times in the summer months.

No internal records remain on sales, but outside sources occasionally give some clues; a Rock Island newspaper reported in March 1853 that the sales the previous twelve months came to $88,000. Thus the sales all through this period were a rough multiple of ten over the physical plow production—congruent with the price structure that was in effect during that time. One of the remaining memorandum books of that period, for the years 1853–54, notes the following price schedule:

Wholesale prices, plows at shop		
2-horse steel landslide	cash	$8.00
Same due October 1		$8.75
2-horse iron landslide	cash	$7.25
Same due October 1		$8.00
"B" or 12-in. plow	cash	$6.50
Same due October 1		$7.00
"C" or 10-in. plow	cash	$6.00
Same due October 1		$6.75
Breakers	cash	$2 ½ less than retail
Same due October 1		$1.75 less than retail
Retail prices		
2-horse steel landside	cash	$11.00
Same due October 1		10 pct. added
2-horse iron landside	cash	$10.00
Same due October 1		10 pct. added
"B" or 12-in. plow		$9.00
Same due October 1		10 pct. added
"C" or 10-in. plow	cash	$8.00
Same due October 1		10 pct. added
Breakers	*cash only*	$1 p. in.
Breakers under 15 in.	*cash only*	$15.00
Extra rigging for breakers full		$10.00
Single wheels		$1.00 p. wheel

MOLINE PLOWS!

MANUFACTURED BY

JOHN DEERE,

MOLINE, ROCK ISLAND CO., ILLS.

◆·◆·◆

An experience of twenty years in the manufacture of Plows for use in Alluvial Soils, warrants me in saying that these Plows have been brought the nearest to perfection of any one offered to the Western Farmers. I have the statement of hundreds of our best farmers, that for ease of draft, and perfect plowing, no implement has ever been introduced that will compete with them. They are all made of superior material as represented, and the excellence of workmanship employed in their manufacture is apparent to every one who examines them; they have taken precedence in every market to which they have been introduced. I would invite the attention to a list of some of the styles manufactured; saying, that any kind of Plows not in my list, will be made to order. Persons wishing to purchase anything in my line, will do well to call and examine my stock, before purchasing elsewhere.

A. No. 1, IMPROVED CLIPPER.—Mold board Cast Steel, Share of best German Steel, *with high steel land side.* This Plow is well suited to all kinds of old ground plowing, is of very easy draft, and turns the furrow completely over without breaking. Cuts 14 inches.

No. 1. IMPROVED CLIPPER.—Of the same material and shape, and used for the same kind of work as the A No. 1, but has low steel land side. Cuts 14 inches.

X No. 1, IMPROVED CLIPPER.—Of same material as A No. 1 and No. 1, but differs somewhat in shape, lapping the furrows more than the others. This Plow is universally esteemed for plowing in heavy stubble. Cuts 14 inches.

B No. 1 IMPROVED CLIPPER.—Of the same material and style of the other clippers, but smaller. Cuts 12 inches. It was got up to meet the objection sometimes made, that the 14 inch clippers were too large for an ordinary team; but I will guarantee the 14 inch Moline Clipper Plow to draw no harder in the same work, than an ordinary 12 inch Plow of other make.

No. 2. IMPROVED CLIPPER.—German Steel Mold Board and Share, with Iron land side, same pattern, and suited to the same work of the X No. 1, differs only in material. Cuts 14 inches.

No. 4. CAST STEEL PLOW.—Cast Steel Mold board, German Steel Share, Steel land side. This Plow is particularly adapted for plowing *bottom lands* where other Plows scour with difficulty or not at all. *They are warranted to scour in any soil.* Cuts 14 inches.

No. 5. STEEL PLOW.—American Steel Mold board, German Steel Share, with steel land side. same shape as No. 4. Cuts 14 inches.

No. 6. Same as No. 5, except has Iron land side, and more nearly resembles the Plows generally made in the West, than any Plow I make: they will be found of superior strength and finish, and well suited for general use. Cuts 14 inches.

No. 7. Same as No. 6, except it is smaller. Cuts 12 inches.

Exhibit 3–3. Advertisement for Deere's "Clipper" line of plows, ca. 1857

Around 1857 Deere gave up his byline, "Centre-draft," and adopted the word "Clipper" for his stubble (stirring) plow line (exhibit 3-3.) These were the heavy sellers in the product line, but the company continued to make breakers in a number of sizes, as well as double plows, shovel plows, cultivators, harrows, etc. Though the contract outfits, independents who traveled through the agricultural areas with their own equipment, often continued to use the large 24-inch iron breakers (or even larger), the steel breakers greatly reduced the draft because of superior design and quality of materials. So Deere and others also made a large number of small steel breakers for the farmers who preferred to do their own breaking with a relatively small power unit, usually their own horses (thus the term "horse breaker"). "These Plows are so constructed that the draft on them is reduced nearly one-third," said a Deere ad in 1856 for its "Rod and Mold-board Easy Draft Breaking Plows."

We have only one breakdown of the product mix in this period, in the newspaper article covering the production of 1857—the oft-cited 13,400 plows. "Of these," said *The Cultivator*, "800 were large breakers, cutting 18–24 inches—1,300 small breakers cutting 12–16 inches—9,000 stubble plows, cutting 12 to 14 inches—1,000 corn plows—300 Michigan double plows and 100 double and single shovel plows and cultivators." (The editor failed to account for the remaining 900.)

How improved were these plows over those made in the first year of the Moline operation? The Gould story of the Deere-Tate split implied that John Deere was constantly striving for product improvement and change,

Exhibit 3–4. *Deere's "Rod and Mold-Board Easy Draft Breaking Plows," as illustrated in* (Country Gentleman, *August 20, 1857)*

a view corroborated in a number of other first-hand testimonials of that period. There appears, however, to be no evidence of any massive Deere-based plow innovation during this period. The kinds of improvements occurring at this point were smaller ones, some of them involving new production methods, others fine tuning on the plow itself. Deere's advertisements of the period stressed not only the wide variety of styles available but also warranted their materials and construction. An advertisement in early 1857 noted: "I am putting into my plows this year a better quality of steel than is used in any other plow in this state; and although I use Gibbs' Patent Dry Grinder, (having the exclusive right to do so in this country from the proprietor) in the finish of my plows, still, I will warrant the TEMPER of my steel to be unimpaired and of even and desirable hardness and *free from flaws.*"

"Midnight requisitioning" of other plow makers' ideas continued unabated, and John Deere was apparently among the borrowers. This was a widespread activity all through the 1840s and '50s. People were purloining each other's ideas on a wholesale basis all over the Midwest (probably more so than in the East, inasmuch as the presence of large, national firms and more stable, longstanding relationships back there made it more difficult to pilfer). Andrew Friberg, testifying in the later court case, was cross-examined about the copying of other plows. At one point, he was asked a question about a two-horse breaking plow, allegedly made a few miles north of Moline: "There was a plow brought to the shop marked 'Made in Galena.' Mr. Deere wanted to get up a plow similar to that—a two-horse plow—and he wanted me to do it. There was another man had charge of the shop at that time and I told Mr. Deere you better let him do it. He failed to get one up to suit Mr. Deere, so Mr. Deere came to me and told me to get one up, and I done so."

The lawyers bored in further on Friberg, querying him on some of the production methods themselves. An especially innovative plow concept had been developed in the late 1840s by a Connecticut manufacturer, F.F. Smith. He called it the "Double Michigan Plow," also known as the "Sod and Subsoil Plow." Made first as a cast-iron plow and later as a steel-bottom plow, it is not to be confused with the so-called "double," *i.e.,* two-bottom, gang plow. For the Michigan plow, there was a smaller forward plow on the beam that pared off the sod to a depth of three to six inches, separating the roots of the grass or vegetable matter and laying its slice surface down on the bottom of the previous furrow. A few inches back of this smaller plow was a larger one that would plow deeper and raise and deposit its slice on top of the forward one. As an *American Farmer* writer put it in 1853: "In being raised and turned, the subsoil is broken and mellowed, and spread loose and evenly over the sward or vegetable matter and manures, and in such depth as admits of plowing and harrowing the grain without disturbing them." The Smith patent was not based on the concept itself of the two different-sized plow bottoms, but on a much narrower focus, relating to the construction of the coulter. Thus the "Michigan Plow" was widely copied by other manufacturers to their own special variations.

Deere began advertising his own Michigan plow, stating in his advertisements that he had "the sole right to make the Michigan Double Plow in this county." It is not clear whether John Deere actually had purchased this right from Smith; Friberg, when grilled about this, said he did not believe that Deere had. Smith also held a patent on a way of pouring iron into a dry sand mold and the subsequent hardening of it—and Deere was using this process, too. Apparently John Deere had obtained rights for one of these two patents, but not the other.

Smith for some reason had scheduled a visit to the Deere factory. Friberg was asked about this: "Did or did not Mr. Deere have any right from Mr. Smith to use that patent process of which you have spoken about?" He replied: "I believe not. Mr. Deere told me, the day before Mr. Smith came out here, to remove all suspicious things in regard to the cast iron mould and the hardening, and be careful what I said to him when he came to the shop. . . . The principal thing I got out of the way at the time was the case mould in which we poured the metal. I don't remember what there was aside from this about the hardening process to remove." Smith was apparently satisfied with whatever royalty he was obtaining for whichever of the two patents were involved, for no further difficulties occurred because of this, and Deere continued to advertise his "rights" to the Michigan plow.

Cases like the Michigan double plow incident and the earlier May controversy tend to make the headlines, both then and now, and overshadow the smaller, indigenous improvements and changes instituted by each manufacturer. There seems no doubt that the Deere products were being constantly upgraded and improved, both in design and in quality, and what started as a small, strictly local shop in the small river town of Moline in 1848 was, by 1857, one of the major agricultural machinery manufacturers in the Midwest. Farmers were being deluged with new ideas and new products, and the canny caution of the agriculturist sorted out the good from the not-so-good. As Clarence Danhoff pointed out in an admirable book on agricultural innovation in the mid-1800s: "Change in the techniques of farming, in terms of implements, was a highly complex process, to which the inventor, the manufacturer, the innovating farmer, and his imitators, each made indispensable contributions. . . . The interaction between innovator and manufacturer was of great significance, with the innovator supplying leadership to those who shared his faith in the possibility of improvement upon the familiar." It was just this kind of farmer, "snug" rather than "slack," to use the euphemism of that period, that the Deere agents constantly sought for the kind of interactions that they knew would lead to better implements. The more than tripling of production by John Deere in a period of five years is eloquent testimony to the fact that farmers agreed with the rather immodest Deere statement often used in his promotions of "the wide spread notoriety of these plows."[12]

NEW ADVERTISING DEVICES

Two factors especially heightened this "notoriety"—the Deere advertising and the Deere involvement in agricultural fairs. The firm had exhibited a keen sense of advertising and public relations right from the start of the Deere, Tate & Gould partnership. The half-column advertisement placed in a number of newspapers in 1849 had an attention-getting headline (exhibit 3-5) and the copy stressed what the partners felt were the firm's key assets. "Our skill and long experience . . . enabled [us] to furnish Plows of all kinds and complete order . . . always on hand and made in the same thorough manner and warranted." The advertisement stressed the fact that cast steel was being manufactured "expressly for us" at the Naylor Company Works in Sheffield, England. To assuage the farmer's possible concern at the cost of such imported steel the partners immediately noted that this would be "at a trifling increase of cost over the common articles generally in use." Lyon, Shorb's steel was also mentioned. The machinery used in the manufacturing process was touted: "Heavy cast iron presses for bending and shaping the Mould-board, Share and Landside." Finally mentioned was the key point, the interchangeability of the material, "which makes them uniform in shape and size, so that either part broken or worn out can be replaced without the trouble of carrying the plow to the shop. By knowing the size of the Plow which may need any such part or parts we can send them whenever ordered, and always warranted to fit." The concept itself of interchangeable component parts for the plow could be traced back to Jethro Wood

Exhibit 3–5. Headline from a Deere advertisement, ca. 1849 (Deere Archives)

PLOWS! PLOWS!!
DEERE, TATE & GOULD'S
IMPROVED CENTRE DRAUGHT
POLISHED CAST-STEEL
PLOWS.

(1819) and even before. But it took a self-confident manufacturer, sure of his shop methods and quality control, to be willing to promise "always warranted to fit."

The spelling of the star of the Deere product line is interesting—in this advertisement of 1849 it is called a "centre draught" plow, adopting the British spelling of both words. By 1851, the second word had become "draft," though the first remained the same. (Predictably, the *Prairie Farmer* adopted the Americanized version for both words whenever it discussed the plow in its editors' column.) In an advertisement in the Moline *Directory* in 1856, the firm called it "center-draft," but the advertisements continued the half-British name until it was dropped in the late 1850s.

Block advertising was accepted by the *Prairie Farmer* after January 1851 and by March of that year Deere, Tate & Gould had their first advertisement there. It was a wordier version, and it indulged in considerable "boosterism" for the town of Moline and the region: "The subscribers being permanently located in this place which is at the foot of the Upper Rapids on the Mississippi River, in the immediate vicinity of inexhaustible beds of bituminous coal, and in continued receipt of a selection from the best lumber of the upper regions of Iowa and Wisconsin (sections which produce by far the best timber in the West) and in possession of an unlimited water power for propelling the numerous kinds of machinery necessary to perform our work. . . . " The advertisement went on to stress again the quality of the materials, the lightness of the plow draft, the ease of repair, and, for the first time, the paint and finish. The sales message continued: "We will send plows to agents by waggon [*sic*] into every neighborhood where twenty can be sold in a season within 175 miles of the factory. We are now manufacturing about 4,000 plows yearly and can increase to 10,000 if necessary." The continuing, abiding concern of Deere for the feelings and views of the farmer-consumer was stressed again: "Our particular attention is devoted to improvement in all agricultural implements, and with the patronage proportioned to our merits we will 'keep posted up' and not be behind hand in giving the farmers the best tools of the times, by which means we will not only realize a profit ourselves but conduce to the general wealth of the country."

John Deere's first advertisement as a single proprietor in 1852 was not quite as long, dropping out all of the pretentious statements about the town and the area (exhibit 3-6). Again there was special stress on product improvement: "Particular attention will always be paid to every improvement in farming utensils, calculated to benefit the agriculturist. . . . " In 1854 a woodcut of three plows appeared in the advertisement for the first time. (exhibit 3-7) The drawing is rather primitive, and we cannot tell whether these plows were actually drawn by sight from John Deere products or were composites culled from some other place. In late 1855

Moline Centre Draft Plow.

THE Subscriber, (successor to Deere, Tate & Gould,) is preparecd to furnish Plows to all who may see fit to favor him with their orders—on reasonable notice, and at rates to suit the times.

The Moline Plows claim superiority over all others now in use, for being made of the best quality of materials, lighter and easier draft, put together with bolts and nuts instead of rivets, consequently more readily repaired, and much better finished.— Warranted to be as represented.

Particular attention will always be paid to every improvement in farming utensils, calculated to benefit the Agriculturist, and the subscriber believes that his customers will find the Moline Plows, hereafter, not only equal, but superior to any heretofore manufactured at this place, and would therefore respectfully solicit, not only a continuance, but an increase of his former patronage.

With the facilities for manufacturing which are had at this place, I can increase from 4,000 (the number now manufactured) to 10,000, yearly if necessary. Always on hand and for sale, Wholesale or Retail, every variety of one and two horse Plows; all sizes of Breakers. Also a superior article of Seed Drill. JOHN DEERE.
Moline, Ill., April 1, '52.

Exhibit 3–6. *John Deere, on his own again, advertises his plow line, 1852 (Deere Archives)*

---

the company stationery appeared with a large representation of a single plow (exhibit 3-7). Again, we cannot assume that this was a lifelike representation of the Deere, for at the bottom of the logo was the name of the artist, "W. Davis N.Y."

The Candee-Swan testimony revealed an interesting vignette on this process of preparing illustrations. At some point in the mid-1850s, Deere had apparently used some plow cuts for advertisements that appeared to have come from the catalog of a competitor, Ruggles, Nourse & Mason. This was the famous Eastern manufacturer (from Worcester, Massachusetts) who had won so many premiums at the National Plowing Match in 1851 with the celebrated Eagle and Deep Tiller plows. Friberg, when asked about this, admitted: "I saw Mr. Deere have their catalog in his hand, cut out the cut of a plow, which, I think, was sent to Chicago and engraved. The same cut afterwards appeared in Mr. Deere's catalogue." In

Exhibit 3–7. Top,*woodcut from a Deere advertisement, 1854; bottom, logo from Deere & Company stationery, 1855*

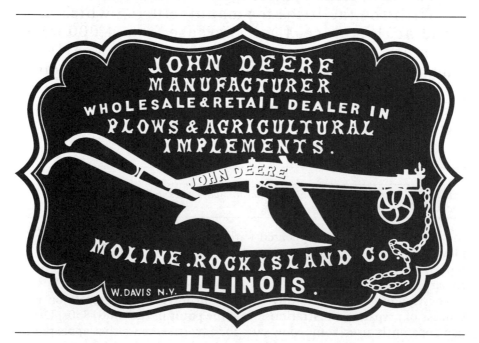

1857 the first drawing of the Deere "Improved Clipper" appeared in *Country Gentleman*, and this time there was no doubt that it was a Deere machine, not a copy of some other plow. A few months later this was redrawn (with a different moldboard and without the rolling coulter) for use in the advertisements of the late 1850s (exhibits 3-8 and 3-9).

Exhibit 3–8. *Deere's "Improved Clipper" with rolling coulter. (Country Gentleman, August 20, 1857)*

Artists also made a number of pictorial representations of the factory buildings themselves during this period, but could not make up their minds about some spellings and other features. The earliest version of the first Moline factory, a woodcut in *Montague's Illinois and Missouri Directory, 1854–1855*, published in St. Louis in 1854, shows the small three-story building with lettering on the front and side—"John Deere" and "Plough Factory" (exhibit 3-10). This woodcut was later redrawn, with different horses and wagons outside, the words "Plow Works," and a date on the side of the building for the year 1847 (exhibit 3-10).

How could this be? Wasn't the date of founding really 1848? The originator of this error was none other than John Deere himself! John Gould later recounted the story: "Under the supervision of C.O. Nason some white bricks were inserted in the building, indicating the birth of the plant as being in 1847. When I noted the error I called Mr. Deere's attention to it and while he admitted the fact of the error he said it was then too late to correct it, since it would not very well be changed." All the way into the twentieth century the byline, "Established 1847," remained. Apparently John Gould was never able to persuade John Deere to rectify his grudgingly admitted mistake!

In the 1856–57 period, the advertisements stressed anew the "ease of draft," with the breaking plows held out as having "the draft on them

NEW ADVERTISEMENTS.

☞ APPROPRIATE ADVERTISEMENTS inserted at TEN
CENTS per line each insertion.

MOLINE PLOWS.—The subscribers would call the attention of Farmers and others interested to the MOLINE
PLOWS for 1859. In many respects they will be superior to
any ever before offered to the public. We shall be prepared
at all times to fill orders for Stirring or Old Plows of every desirable style, but especially the IMPROVED CAST STEEL
CLIPPER PLOW of three different styles, which is acknowledged by Farmers and others, who have seen them used, to
be the very best plow in use. *We challenge the world to produce a better one!* Also, the MICHIGAN DOUBLE SOD AND
SUBSOIL PLOW, two sizes; BREAKERS of every size and
description made to order, including "Stenton's Patent Double Prairie Plow. His "Patent Landside Cutter" will be attached to any Breaker if desired. Double and single Shovel
Plows, Cultivators, Harrows, Ox Yokes and Bows, Rolling Cutters and Clasps, &c. Repairing done Promptly and in the best
manner. Thankful for the very liberal patronage already received by this establishment, its continuance is most respectfully solicited by   DEERE & CO,
    v3n3-12   Successors to John Deere, Moline, Ill.

Exhibit 3–9. *Another rendition of the "Improved Clipper," without coulter, ca. 1858 (Deere
Archives)*

Exhibit 3–10. *Artists' conceptions of the Deere factory, showing confusion about the name of the firm and its date of founding (Deere Archives)*

reduced nearly one-third." The center-draft, two-horse plow "turns its furrows entirely over," continued the advertisement, "leaving it flat, and in such a manner that the farmer can sow his seed upon the clean and freshly upturned soil, instead of the old way of sowing them on weeds and grass roots." The advertisement appeared to be adopting again Jethro Tull's old watchword, for one of the cultivators of the firm was now called "the horse-hoe." It also stressed particularly that the various plows of the company had "met with *merited approbation* from Agricultural Associations and have in *every instance* where they have been offered, received premiums from the State and county fairs, as being superior to anything ever offered to the *Western Farmer.*"

A letterhead from the company in 1857, coming out under the heading "Moline Plow Manufactory," noted another new product: "Manufacturer of all kinds of Stirring Plows, Rod and Mould Board Breakers, Corn Plows. Also the Mich. Double Plow, Cultivators, Harrows, Ox Yokes, & c., & c." The ox yoke was a departure from cultivating machinery for the firm. While volume of sales was not great, many compliments redounded from the farmers and the agricultural journal editors. It was always nice when the prestigious *Prairie Farmer* gave kudos, as it did in September 1859: "Mr. Deere also exhibits Ox Yokes—fine specimens, and so far as we are able to judge, correctly made. This is an important matter—the making of Ox Yokes. There are some who are professionals that know nothing of the art of making a yoke in which oxen will work with ease."[13]

Another extremely potent source of advertising came from the agricultural fairs. The agricultural exhibition or fair has to be one of the truly unique features of the profession of agriculture. For years farmers everywhere have gathered together to exchange information and compare results. It is a two-way process, too, for the suppliers and manufacturers are there, both to teach about and to sell their products and also to learn from their farmer-peers. The exhibition/fair has served as the ideal vehicle— sometimes the area it draws from is just the village or town and its immediate environs, sometimes a larger sweep is cast to encompass the very boundaries of the personal links of the farmer (say, a county-wide organization). The largest of these events might be at a state or even a national level, the latter being more common in England, Germany, and France, the former the preeminent venue in the United States, both in the nineteenth century and later, the ubiquitous "State Fair."

Probably John Deere could not have submitted his plows to competition in the Grand Detour days, for the first Ogle County Fair was not until 1853. There were local fairs in northern Illinois in that period—the Ottawa Fair in October 1846 had a plow competition with a number of northern Illinois manufacturers competing. Deere, though, was not among them. The "First Annual Fair of the Rock Island County Society for the Promotion of Agriculture and the Mechanic Arts" was held in October 1853 and the Deere firm won two dollars for the best "Center

Draft Plow'' (John Deere himself was one of the judges). In the next
month he exhibited in the first annual fair of Henry County and, though
no specific awards were made, the local correspondent of the paper
gushed, ''Mr. John Deere had some splendid articles in the line of Plows
on exhibition, and I may venture the assertion that at very few fairs in
Yankeedom will a more beautiful, or better article be exhibited. The
Committee on Manufactured Articles awarded a Diploma to Mr. Deere,
on his breaking, stirring, and corn plow.'' The annual fair of the Illinois
State Agricultural Society also began in that year, 1853, and by 1855 had a
whole variety of plow categories.

Plows

Plow for Old Ground Prairie

John Deere, Moline, Rock Island County, first premium . . . . Diploma
Wm. Parlin & Co., Canton, Fulton County, second premium $10

Discretionary

E. & C. H. Dawson, Jacksonville, for steel clipper . . . . Medal and Transactions
Gauble & French, Kankakee, Kankakee County, for three double sod and stubble plows . . . . Transactions
First & Bradley, Chicago, for one plow . . . . Transactions

Plow for Clay Soil

John Lane, jr. Lockport, Will County, first premium . . . . Diploma
S. O. Vaughan, Naperville, second premium $10

Plow for Two Horses

Augustus Guibor, Peoria, first premium . . . . Diploma
Roderick Owen, Tiskilwa, Bureau County, second premium $10

Timothy and Blue Grass Sward Plow

S.O. Vaughan, first premium. . . . . Diploma
Jones & Cagwin, Joliet, second premium $10

Subsoil Plow

First & Bradley, first premium . . . . Diploma

Discretionary

James P. Skinner, Rockford. . . . . Medal and Transactions
Solomon & Co., Carrington (?) one plow. . . . . Transactions

Over in Iowa, the county and state fairs also burgeoned. The Iowa State
Fair began in 1854, and by 1855 John Deere had begun competing. That
year at Fairfield, Iowa, he won both a first and a second place for his
cultivators but did not win any of the plow contests. In the next year at
Muscatine, Deere took a plow award as such—for the best subsoil plow.
At these fairs the products were not only put on display in the tents for
comparison, but were also subjected to field tests. Competition plowing

was the basis upon which most awards were made and all sorts of agricultural equipment were tried out side by side with their competitors, all of this played out before a multitude of skeptical farmers walking right alongside the experimenter. John Deere's plows were favorites, and they often won. One of these victories was at the Illinois State Fair of 1858. Deere, ever the marketeer, gave the driver a present, "a splendid 'Deere Plow' of the value of *twenty dollars!*" The reporter from the *Prairie Farmer* continued: "Facts like this ought to be known among farmers." And indeed these farmers would know, if John Deere had anything to say about it!

John Deere's fame at these agricultural fairs spread rapidly, and after he won the first prize at the Illinois State Fair in 1855, the local Rock Island paper ran a special editorial, noting that the *Chicago Tribune* writer had said that Deere's subsoil plow was "the finest that he ever saw." The Rock Island paper was so moved by this new renown for one of its native citizens that it congratulated the whole town: "Mr. Deere not only deserves a premium for it from the State Fair, but some kind of suitable memorial from his fellow citizens of this vicinity. He is the best, the largest, the most liberal, and studiously honest manufacturer of plows in the whole North-west."[14]

The state fair competitions also provided the place for another John Deere foray into a new and untested product. As with the seed drill, it turned out that he was just a bit ahead of his time. The innovation was the steam plow.

JOHN DEERE AND THE FAWKES STEAM PLOW

The late 1850s witnessed one of the most exciting events in American agriculture up to that time—the adaptation of the iron horse to the plow. Indeed, with that Brobdingnagian name, it seemed only natural that the locomotive should get off the steel rail and move right down through the farmer's field! Steam power had come to the farm in the early part of the nineteenth century, first in stationary power units for milling, straw cutting, crushing, threshing, and those many other agricultural tasks that required point-of-application horsepower. It seemed only a natural extension of the stationary engine to put it on wheels as a portable steam engine that could be pulled by animal power right to the spot where something as place-changing as threshing could be done.

The giant step, though, was the next one—development of a self-propelled agricultural steam engine that could pull implements through a field. The British had already been experimenting; their most popular idea was the stationary steam engine placed at the edge of a field, applying its power to cables attached to independent gang plows. A windlass on the engine boiler would coil the steel cable, at the same time pulling the plow through the field. Either the cable was anchored by a pulley on the far side of the field or two engines could be used, each one stationed at opposite sides of the area to be plowed. By the 1860s some 8,000 of these large, complicated units were in operation, with exports even as far away as Egypt. A few of these monsters were brought to the United States, but the cable system was not popular in this country. What everyone wanted was the self-propelled steam engine actually pulling the plow through the field. So exciting was this idea that agricultural societies and individuals all over the East, South, and Midwest were offering prizes for the first person who could successfully bring this dream to reality.

Several steam plowing vehicles were built in the late 1850s. As with the steel plow, it is virtually impossible, or at least irrelevant, to ascertain "who was first." Obed Hussey, the famous reaper manufacturer, was one; he had exhibited a steam plow at the Indiana State Fair in 1856. But it was another machine, built by Joseph W. Fawkes, an unknown Pennsylvanian, that captured the nation's fancy and did more to dramatize the potentials of this type of power for farming than probably any other to that time. And in this case, John Deere was directly involved.

Fawkes first demonstrated his new contraption at the state fair in Centralia, Illinois, in 1858. It was an awkward, strange-looking, 30-horsepower engine with an upright boiler, the "Lancaster." The acclaim was instant. "The excitement of the crowd," said a *Chicago Press* reporter, "was beyond control . . . their shouts and loud huzzas echoed far over the prairie. . . . The goal was won, steam had conquered the face of nature and the steam plow had become a fact." Echoed the *Wisconsin Farmer,* "Fawkes is immortal."

John Deere, his imagination stirred by the steam plow, that year began assembling the type of gang plow needed as the necessary accoutrement to its gigantic partner. He wrote a Chicago friend: "It will be a great day when Illinois can show a steam engine taking along a breaking plow, turning over a furrow ten or twelve feet in width as it goes. I think we shall be able to see it before June passes away." Deere continued with a surprising piece of information: "There's also a steam engine being built at my shop to haul it, and do other farming work. The person who is getting it up is sanguine of success. He is certainly one of the best practical mechanics in our state."

Only scraps of evidence confirm the Deere efforts to build a steam plow. But the important fact was that Deere and Fawkes had made connections, and the "famous plow manufacturer of Moline," as the *Chicago Press* reporter covering the story called him, agreed to make the gang plow for the next Fawkes assault on the Illinois prairie, scheduled for the Illinois State Fair of 1859. The results there were mixed but were immediately followed just weeks later with a spectacular success at the famous U.S. Agricultural Society contest in Chicago. There the grand gold medal of honor was to be given "for that machine which shall supersede the plow, as now used, and accomplished the most thorough disintegration of the soil, with the greatest economy of labor, power, time and money." Careful reading of this notice implied that any kind of machine might win. So, of the five entrants submitting implements, three were variations on the plow itself—and one of these was John Deere's! His candidate was the double Michigan plow. The committee, though, discarded it as "nothing but an ordinary plow, double it is true, but still a plow to be drawn by horses or oxen in the usual way." Likewise, the other two plow variations were also disqualified. This left two steam engines— the Fawkes version and one competitor, built by James Waters of Detroit, Michigan. Fawkes bested Waters handily, taking the grand gold medal of honor and vicariously bringing with him John Deere, for eight Deere plows, welded together, had been pulled by Fawkes to the championship.

The Fawkes steam plow, for all its fame, turned out to be a false start. Abraham Lincoln made one of his infrequent agricultural speeches just a few weeks after the Fawkes victory and chose the steam plow as his focus. He first showed his ignorance by suggesting an alternative—a preposterous mechanical device as a plow attachment with a revolving chain that would run transversely to tear up the ground at right angles to the steam engine. Then he raised the question as to how enough water could be brought to the fields to keep a steam engine running and ended lamely: "I have not pointed out difficulties in order to discourage, but in order that, being seen, they may be the more readily overcome."

Lincoln's pessimism about the steam plow was well founded. The Fawkes engine was just too unwieldy. While there were other attempts at steam plowing and a few desultory successes, it was not until almost twenty years later that the steam traction engine really became an effective instrument and began to be used widely on the eastern prairie. The brief moments of glory for Fawkes were also moments of acclaim for John Deere—an exciting way to cap the decade.

It would be tedious to list in detail all of the premiums that John Deere's plows accumulated in these years. Suffice it to say that at state fairs and the smaller county and town fairs the inherently good products of the firm were assiduously and cleverly marketed in a way that increased the reputation of the company in a very significant way. Indeed, one of John Deere's plows showed up at the Vermont State Fair in 1856 and took the "First Premium." The *Moline Workman* commented: "This triumph is all the greater from the fact that it occurred in the neighborhood of the plow shop of Ruggles, Nourse & Mason, the largest Eastern manufactory, where, of course, their plows are as plenty as the rocks which do so abound in those regions." In the process, the *Workman* editor could not resist a cut at New England: "The only thing which will prevent Deere's plows from becoming popular among the hills of New England is the fact that there is so little land worth cultivation."[15]

THE MID-1850s:
GOOD TIMES FOR MANY . . . BUT?

During the first decade of John Deere's tenure in Moline, from 1848 to 1857, the upswing in business in the country was so massive as to be called by many the "Golden Age." There was a large amount of investment, an expansion in the money supply, a rise in the price level. The California gold rush combined with a major inflow of money from abroad to give a boost to a strengthened banking system. There was burgeoning railroad expansion all through the Midwest and West, and the westward movement was accentuated in the process, John Deere's Midwestern territory being particularly favored. Illinois doubled its population between 1850 and 1860 (from just over 851,000 to more than 1.7 million), Wisconsin's population more than doubled in the same period, Missouri's almost doubled, and Iowa's population grew from 43,112 in 1840 to 192,214 in 1850, and then almost tripled in the next six years to 517,875 by 1856.

The agriculturalist fared relatively well in this environment; the wholesale price index for farm products rose to 98 in 1855 (1910–14=100), still below "all commodities" (at 110) but relatively much higher than the indices of the 1830s and '40s. Again the Midwest was most favored; by 1860 the top-ranking wheat states were Illinois, Indiana, and Wisconsin, and corn production in the north central states doubled from 1850 to 1860, in the latter year about 50 percent of the total crop.

By the late 1850s the Midwest began to dominate agricultural machinery production—startlingly so, as the census of 1860 showed. There were only thirty plow manufacturers left in New England by this date, doing just over $500,000 in annual sales with just two of these in Worcester, Massachusetts, doing $367,000 of the total. Even the Middle Atlantic states, with New York and once-dominant Pennsylvania, now had just 126 plow manufacturers, with $674,000 of business. But the "Western" states—what we now call the Midwestern states—had 248 plow establishments, with annual sales of more than $1.6 million. Illinois was far and away the largest; its 121 plow manufacturers did more than $800,000 of business, almost 30 percent of the plow business of the entire country. These 121 Illinois plow establishments were scattered over fifty of the ninety-five counties making returns in the agricultural census. There are no census figures on the actual number of plows produced in the United States in 1860, but if we could make a rough approximation that the average plow sold for about ten dollars, then perhaps something around 285,000 plows were produced in that census year. How prophetic had been Messrs. Dana and Troop when they had released John Gould from the dry goods firm. Remember their words? "We were raising oats and corn . . . which were shipped to the New England states to feed employees and manufacturers of implements, which ought to be made here in this country. . . . " Now they were!

In just about a decade, John Deere had cajoled and bullied his company into the forefront of these Illinois firms. His skills were not those of an inventor; though he was one of the first to use steel on the plow, it was his clever and dramatic presentation of this feature, reiterated over and over in his advertising and marketing, that made his name. His products were excellent right from the start, even though some of the technology had been "borrowed." He had a keen sense of what the farmer was thinking and adapted his products to the demands of the most progressive cultivators. He was even ahead of the latter in regard to both the seed drill and the steam plow—he was willing to take risks, commit capital for the kind of expansion he saw coming. By 1856, the firm's annual sales were in the neighborhood of $140,000 and annual production was approximately 14,000 plows, making the company one of the half dozen largest plow manufacturers of about 420 in the entire United States—quite a feat considering the embryonic organization put together only nine years before by John Deere and Robert Tate. In the process, it had graduated from a narrowly local company to a regional manufacturer serving a clientele over many states. The conceptual leap in business thinking required by this growth cannot be overemphasized; the firm was now a complex, major business. The local newspaper's hyperbolic description of John Deere as "the Napoleon plow maker" seemed perfectly in order.

Even the always cautious Mercantile Agency respondent appeared satisfied—indeed, almost lyrical. "March 54—Is w from 15 to 20 m $. Excelt bus. ref. Is persevering + of go habs. July 54—same. December 21/54—thk him perfly safe and respons. July 17/55—Safe and respons. January 24/56—gd for 20000/$, safe + reliable. August 11/56—perf safe. January 13/57—pfly safe for all contracts."

But even the prescience of the credit expert could not forecast what was ahead. Another impending business crisis loomed just over the horizon, called in retrospect "the Panic of 1857." Though there were some portents, the trigger was the failure of the New York City branch of the Ohio Life Insurance and Trust Company in August of that year. This precipitated a sharp financial panic, fueled by the decade-long speculation in railroad securities and real estate. Though the panic was short-lived, its severity confined to about eighteen months, it succeeded in bankrupting a number of businesses and institutions already overextended during the expansionary period. It was a time of ruthless competition, which swiftly eliminated marginal firms. Only the few strong firms managed to survive until the Civil War boom brought prosperity.

DISASTER STALKS JOHN DEERE

John Deere was one of the threatened. As the firm headed into the

"Spring Trade" selling of the early months of 1857, all looked good on the surface. The Mercantile Agency report of January 13, 1857, corroborated this public view—"Pfly safe for all contracts." But the truth was that the firm was not "perfectly safe." Cash flow problems had always plagued the agricultural equipment business, and over the crop season of 1857 the flow of payments began running slower and slower, finally drying up as the full effects of the downturn became more evident. A Wisconsin farm equipment dealer put his own situation poignantly: "It is the hardest times here to raise Money that I ever saw. Nothing fetches it. I do not know what we are going to do. We are owing some and have got some owing to us—but we cannot collect a dollar. Farmers will not sell there [sic] produce to pay debts while it is so low. I cannot blame them much. Wheat is worth only 40 cents per bushel and hard to get cash at that price, corn 20 to 25, oats 20, potatos 20, beef 3 to 5 per lb, pork 4½ to 5, butter 12½ to 15, lard 12½, eggs 10 cts per dozen." The dealer's problem thus automatically became the manufacturer's problem—no one had any cash. Any poor credit risk—for example, a merchant who did not pay over the full crop season—would quickly exacerbate the cash flow problem.

This is what happened to John Deere. Some very substantial bills for raw materials had been accumulating; the two biggest accounts were with a Pittsburgh steel company—Singer, Hartman—and with the English house of Naylor & Co. As collections slowed, the creditors became more insistent.

The situation soon looked serious enough to warrant emergency action. James Chapman, Deere's lawyer son-in-law, quickly made the decision to change the legal form of the organization, effective July 1, 1857. A partnership was once again formed, this time with four partners—John Deere, Charles Deere, Luke Hemenway, and David H. Bugbee. The name of the firm was to be "John Deere & Company," with a capital stock of $32,000, "each partner paying an equal part of the capital stock and sharing equally in the profits or losses of the business." For the first time, new provisions were added relating to both the account system and the limits of liability. Books were to be kept by double entry, open at all times to the inspection of any member of the firm. A further provision attempted to constrain unlimited liability: "Neither of the said co-partners shall sign or endorse any note or bond or assume any pecuniary liability either personally or in the name of the firm, where the name of the firm may be involved or endangered, otherwise than for the uses and purposes of the firm." It is clear from the wording of the agreement that Hemenway and Bugbee were junior partners, for there were provisions for payment of the two of them on salary "for services." The agreement even made explicit the relationship of the partners' family needs—"each partner shall have the privilege of drawing out $800 per annum for family expenses." Hemenway apparently paid no cash, but Bugbee at the same time took a mortgage on some of John Deere's property in the sum of

$6,178, probably paying a like amount of cash into the business.

At the same moment of the signing of the partnership agreement, John Deere and his wife, a co-owner, deeded to Charles Deere a quarter of the plow shop for a consideration of $10,000. On the same date, July 1, 1857, John and Charles Deere jointly sold to John Deere & Company the real estate on which the factory was built (together with two other lots nearby). In turn, the company was to pay John Deere and Charles Deere a total of $35,000 for the property, by way of one-, three-, four-, and five-year notes dated July 1, 1857. (Our documentation here is not complete. While the partnership agreement itself is extant in its original form, the only documentation for the private arrangement between father and son is in some handwritten notes of Charles Deere about the transaction. The actual agreement itself is no longer in existence.)

The total effect of the arrangement remains a bit murky today, as, indeed, it did to the Mercantile Agency respondent. After having given the enthusiastic assurance in January 1857 (which noted above), he now was quite disconcerted by the new developments: "July 15/57 (tel. in answer to ? if he had suspended). No, J.D. is all right." Not until a few months later did the credit agency analyst find out the full situation. "Jan 19/58 reps 'JD/Co' comp of J. Dr his son Chas D. who was just of age but not w any cap. JD is a man of quite a la. estate. Has ppy on this that in ordinary times w. bring 30m/$. He is hon + v. energetic man. Was las bus some 70 or 80m/$ in a year. Is now consd good + prompt, yet is some behind because he cannot collect. Maybe he will have a run, yet we do not thk he will fail. We thk him good for 30m/$."

As we sift the scraps of information in company and private documents, it seems clear that this shift to the new partnership was more than just a legal arrangement. The essence of all of this was to take out of the firm itself certain monies that would then go to John and Charles Deere for their own personal accounts (although this was only to be paid over time as the notes came due). There were at least two reasons for these moves. First, Chapman probably wanted to forestall a personal John Deere bankruptcy by building a new legal entity. The arrangements between family and partnership put some of the family assets in the family name, rather than that of the proprietorship. The second reason seems more dominant—to remove John Deere from the management, at least temporarily, and substitute Charles Deere. Again, the reasons for this were probably complex. Partly it was to shift some legal responsibility, but another goal was to substitute Charles Deere's judgment for that of his father's. There are several versions we need to hear to appreciate the full import of this change.

First, John Gould himself was brought back into the picture. By this time Gould was not only a successful manufacturer but had been elected a judge for the town of Moline. More important even than this, though, was the establishment by Gould and his partner of a new banking house,

Gould, Dimock & Co. (they reversed the names used for the pail factory). This was fortuitous beyond all expectations for John Deere, as Gould describes: "Just about that time Mr. Deere became embarrassed to some extent and had to make a partial suspension. . . . They were somewhat embarrassed and had not paid Naylor & Co. for their steel. I had then organized the bank of Gould, Dimock & Co., composed of D.C. Dimock, Charles P. Ryder and myself, doing business on Second Avenue, exactly north of the present Peoples Savings Bank & Trust Company. We had a very small capital, but Deere & Co., had not the means to pay Naylor & Co. and had really no security they wanted to give, and they proposed that they would arrange to pay certain amounts at different times, dividing it up into about four different payments and asked the agent if he would take acceptances of Gould, Dimock & Co., which, for some reason unknown to me, he accepted. Charles Deere came to me and told me what he had proposed and asked me, if they would give me their regular commercial notes which they had, for a certain commercial amount, which was about double what they owed Naylor & Co., if I would accept and also wanted the privilege of exchanging them as they matured and they wanted to use them by substituting other notes, which I accepted. At the time, it seemed very strange to me, as Deere & Co. were then worth ten or twenty times as much as Gould, Dimock & Co., but it satisfied their creditors and, as they matured, they paid their debt."

In essence, the fact that Gould, Dimock & Co. was a banking house seemed to assure Naylor & Co. of credit strength. In reality, as Gould honestly points out, the Deere organization was worth considerably more than the bank. If we read Gould correctly, Charles Deere had used his own commercial accounts receivable as collateral—roughly double that which was needed for the Naylor notes. Gould, incidentally, mentions only the one creditor company, but a substantial amount was also owed to Singer, Hartman; Tate reported in his diary on November 18, 1857, that this amount was "over $10,000." The situation began to sound more ominous with Tate's next sentence: "Mr. Jennings, one of the partners of Snyder & Hartman [sic] . . . has been around Deere ever since Saturday."

The problem with Naylor & Co. was compounded by the fact that a new shipment of steel from them in late 1857 was alleged by Deere to be faulty. Apparently part of that same lot went to Tate, too, and he reports on January 17, 1858: "Went to Moline for Deere to pass sentence on the quality of steel got by Naylor & Company [sic]. Deere refuses the bill. The scrap here that I was referred to, rendered it much too difficult for me to decide. We had the same steel and no serious trouble, and that was all I could say about it." The Deere firm already had "Bills Payable" to Naylor & Co. for about $16,000, and either John Deere or Charles Deere was now trying to send some of the purchased steel back as faulty.

George Vinton, who had joined the firm by this time, later elaborated on the quality problem of the Naylor steel: "About this time, John Deere imported a large bill of steel from England as he thought it superior to the American steel. This steel was received and made into plows. The plows came back and the steel was soft and they would not scour. The steel was not better than puter [*sic*]. In due time the payments became due for this steel. John Deere's capital was limited for his business and he could not make the payment of the steel that proved worthless. They threatened to close up the factory. Mr. Webber took the matter in charge and made John Deere put his property out of his hands to avoid an attachment from shutting up the business. The factory was deeded to Charles H. Deere, other real estate was deeded to me and to other parties so as to effect a compromise. It was a busy time, you bet. Mr. Webber finally got a compromise of 40¢ on the dollar by giving as security Dimock, Gould & Co. bankers, and placed in their hands collateral for security." Vinton makes son-in-law Christopher C. Webber the go-between rather than Gould, but this is unlikely for Webber was not in the firm at that time. Vinton was writing to Webber's son, and may have wanted to make the Webber family more central to the story!

The legal maneuverings were not yet finished. On March 13, 1858, the partnership of John Deere & Company was dissolved and the firm reverted to a single proprietorship: "It is agreed by the partners that John Deere shall take all the stock on hand, & property of every kind as his own; & shall pay all the debts of the Company. He alone shall have the powr to collect the debts of the Company, and hereby has full powr to recover the same, or any partner in the name of the firm. . . . " The provisions of the original partnership agreement allowing Hemenway and Bugbee a salary for the time under the partnership if it were dissolved now came into effect. In essence, the entire entity was essentially back where it was on July 1, 1857; Charles Deere noted: "The business fell back into jno Deere's hands."

The Mercantile Agency respondent chronicled the better times. "March 17/58—Diss'd. J. Deer goes on—G'd but hard up. . . . May 18/58—Carries on a very extensive bus. & is g. A year ago if he had closed up his bus he would hv. ben. w. 100m/$ over and above paying his debts—but the past year has been a hard one for him. He has lost a gd. deal by bad debts, having to pay heavy interest. Decrease of R.E. Besides we do not think that his bus. is financed as closely as it was formerly, or as it should be, but we think, if he was to close today, he wd come out w. about $65 or $70,000 clear. The most of this is in R.E. say at any rate 40m/$ so that we consider 'D' perfectly safe, still owing to the hard times, difficulty of collecting $, he is hard up. He is now cutting down his business and using every exertion to collect and, I think that if his creditors are lenient, inside of six months he will pay all his debts. . . . June 30/58—Hard up but will come out alright, with $80,000 over and above liabilities."

In reality, though, the managerial responsibility for the firm had shifted—as it turned out, permanently—to Charles Deere. In a second deed made later that year (October 5, 1858) John Deere apparently turned over the remainder of his interest to Charles. The deed itself is missing; we have only Charles Deere's telegraphic scribblings on this. Charles Deere gave his father a series of notes totaling $15,000, to be paid over an eleven-year period in six staggered amounts of $2,142 each, with a seventh at the end of the balance. At the bottom of the "memorandum of trade," Charles Deere noted "part of the notes for stock in shop were paid by my assuming indebtedness which was a lein [*sic*] upon the shop" (a judgment against the property had been obtained by the Singer, Hartman firm).

Key documents are no longer in existence, so we cannot be certain of all the details. The essence of the arrangement comes through quite clearly though. The temporary legal gambit of the new partnership became no longer necessary in March 1858, when the combination of the Gould, Dimock & Co. banking arrangements and the acceptance of debts by Charles Deere had tided the firm over its acute financial crisis. Tate, ever the gossip, had noted in April: "There is a report that Deere has collapsed the firm of Deere & Son." His choice of words was not quite correct. The firm had been reconstituted back to its original structure. The October 1858 deed, though, is ample corroborative evidence that John Deere was no longer to be the chief executive officer of the organization—his ownership had in effect been transferred, within the family, to be sure, but nevertheless now firmly resting in the hands of Charles Deere. John Deere continued his personal involvement in the work of the organization; as John Gould later put it, "So far as I know he was [out] financially, but he has always given his personal attention to the establishment, and has been about the works." Stephen H. Velie, a John Deere son-in-law, commenting many years later on the occasion of John Deere's eightieth birthday, put it more bluntly: "The commercial convulsion of 1857 came very near bankrupting him and the management of the business was in 1858 turned over to his son Chas. H. Deere, then 21 years old, who has ever since been acknowledged head of the concern."[16]

BEYOND THE FIRM:
JOHN DEERE'S MOLINE

John Deere's public life and involvement in the community continued unabated through these years. Early in the 1850s he had become interested in politics and had taken the post as chairman of the Whig county convention. When the Republican Party was formed he rapidly became active in it and was a strong abolitionist. Feelings ran very high about politics in this period, particularly as they related to the slavery issue. Deere even had a split with his own family, for James Chapman was a Democrat (as also was John Gould). By 1858 tempers were very hot and each party not only castigated the other in vitriolic prose but sometimes resorted to more physical approaches. In September 1858 the Democrats held a mass meeting with an outside speaker from Peoria. As the speaker was spewing out some purple prose relating to the "Black Republicans," the latter (also in attendance) "attempted to break up the meeting by yelling, hooting and bellowing, in a manner that would disgrace the lowest brothel in existence. It was a concerted action, led so, we understand, by John Deere, a man who would like to be considered a gentleman. We have never before in any community, witnessed so mean, dirty and disgraceful an affair." Before we believe this judgment implicitly, though, let's remind ourselves that the newspaper was unabashedly Democratic!

Deere was also active in another organization, one with only a brief existence, dedicated also to strong action. There had begun to be considerable local crime, most of it of a petty nature but some more serious, especially involving the theft of horses. This seemed of such consequence that a group of citizens gathered in June 1854 to form a new organization called the Moline Property Protection Society. It had an eminent group of sponsors—A.F. Perkins was president and Charles Atkinson vice president, and the treasurer and member of the executive committee was John Deere. The newspaper reported: "J. Deere stated the object of the meeting to be to form a society to protect ourselves from the depredations of thieves." The newspaper added its own comment, "Now fully organized, equipped and well supplied with 'sinews of war' notice is give to the horse thieves in particular and the light fingered gentry in general, that a warm reception awaits them." Apparently nothing ever came of this incipient vigilante movement, for a year later a letter to the editor, signed "one of the losers by the thieves," lamented that the organization, which the writer remembered as being "the Horse Thief Association," had never gotten off the ground and asked for a new meeting. Again, though, there was not enough interest to arouse action and the law and order of the town was left to the police.

Two years later in September 1857, John Deere himself might have wished for a bit more "order" from the law. Tate reported on September 5: "Mr. Deere's house has been robbed. Several articles taken, a silver watch belonging to Charlie worth $100 and several dollars in change and quite a lot of choice cake. The father's pants were overhauled, rifled and thrown back to his bedside again." The *Rock Island Argus* took note of the burglary, too, and affixed an addendum: "Mr. Deere had a counterfeit bill in his pocket, which the ruffians left."

Most of John Deere's involvements in the town were more prosaic. In 1855 he ran for trustee of the town, running ninth in a slate of fourteen. He must not have felt too badly about this, as his twenty-eight votes just matched Tate's twenty-eight—and John Gould had only one vote! Deere was a stockholder and active in the Moline Fire Engine Company and was one of the three trustees of the Congregational Church (he was also a contributor in a substantial way to the Chicago Theological Seminary). There was an occasional bit of personal excitement. In October 1857 Deere's horse and buggy ran away, turning over the buggy and completely destroying it (fortunately, without John Deere in it). In March 1859 he and a Mr. Tompson from Quincy, riding across the railroad bridge, discovered it to be on fire, spreading rapidly in a great wind. The two of them gave alarm and helped to hold the flames down until the fire department could arrive. "Had it not been for two barrels of water standing on the platform nothing would be left of the Great Rock Island bridge but a mass of smouldering ruins." Deere continued his abiding interest in the agricultural scene, being elected in November 1860 as president of the Rock Island County Agricultural Society. Certainly as an eminent public citizen of Moline, John Deere came into his own during the decade of the 1850s.

Moline and Rock Island themselves had changed enormously during this decade, too. The deepening of the economic base of the two towns had proceeded apace all through the early and middle years of the decade; the temporary setback of the Panic of 1857 curbed a bit of excessive optimism. The boosterism of the *Rock Island Advertiser* in 1853—"The facilities of Moline for business are unsurpassed and unsurpassable"— had to be modified in light of several bankruptcies during this unpleasant business downturn. Still, the two towns—indeed, small cities—ended the decade on an economic upbeat, confident and hopeful about the future.

The decade was crammed full of human events, no one of which was catastrophic or earth-shaking, but the sum total added to the lore of local history that provides the values of the people involved. The educational systems of the two towns had markedly improved during the decade, as had their social and cultural lives. There were concerts, with artists not only from the East but from Europe, and the Rock Island Lecture Association sponsored visiting lecturers from all over the country. In 1855, for example, Ralph Waldo Emerson was one of seven lecturers for "the season"; in 1858, though, the town refused to welcome the controversial lecturer on free love, "a certain Dr. Barrows, a sort of perambulating lecturer on one thing and another." The two towns had their share of disastrous fires, just as countless other towns and cities did all through the nineteenth century. (There was more than occasional antagonism between Rock Islanders and Moliners, and with an extraordinarily large number of Moline fires in 1858, some Rock Islanders alleged that they were set on purpose.) The two towns, being on the great river, had their share of floods in this decade, repeated, unfortunately, many more times over the following years. But the river was a superb asset for the two towns as well, not only economically but for its recreational value (the papers full of reports of "moonlight excursions," etc.). Politics crammed the decade, inevitably as the great war over slavery approached. Perhaps only the temperance issue could compete with the political for the attention of the citizenry of the two towns. In every sense, the decade was a time of increasing activity for the two small cities and the area around them.[17]

CHARLES DEERE'S VOW

Back at the company itself, meanwhile, some additional shifts had occurred. On December 24, 1858, the Mercantile Agency correspondent noted a new change: "J. has sold out to C.C. Webber. Deer's [sic] debts want attention." At this point, Charles Deere had apparently been willing to bring Christopher Webber into the firm. Webber, Charles Deere's brother-in-law, had experienced difficulties in his Union Foundry in the Panic of 1857 and, to use the euphemism of a later biographer, "withdrew from the Company." In March 1859 the credit correspondent reported: "John Deer [sic] has a good reputation as a plough maker and has done a good bus. As a busman he has always been prompt & reliable. He has recently retired from the bus. for the purpose of closing out his outside matters & the firm of Deer & Co. is composed of Chas. D his son and C.C. Webber his son-in-law."

The correspondent apparently was uneasy about this new alignment: "Chas. D. has but little experience in the bus . . . Webber has some considerable ppty . . . his reputation as a bus. man is decidely bad, for tho he may be responsible, he is not prompt to pay—but prompt to collect. The general impression here is that he has worked himself into the Plow Factory for the purpose of mkg money, even at the sacrifice not only of Deer's reputation but of Deer himself."

Charles Deere's first three years as the chief executive of the organization were indeed trying ones. Luke Hemenway put it succinctly in a letter to Charles Deere many years later: "The wild and stormy financial years of 1857 and 58, those were years that tried men—we never knew whether they were of 'hay & stubble' and would burn, or could stand the trial of those fiery years." Charles was a young man in those difficult years of 1858–60, twenty-one when he took over in 1858. The responsibility of the tottering business was squarely on his shoulders and he took this burden seriously—no longer was it "a rather-easy going force." The business judgment and, indeed, the very character of Charles Deere must have been forged in this trying time. We have a unique entree to this period of Charles Deere's life in the fortunate preservation of one of the most valuable of all of the company documents—a small private memorandum book of Charles Deere's for the years 1858–69. The predominant number of entries refer to the first three-year period, and they are evocatively revealing of Deere's traumas in regard to the firm. Two dimensions of Charles Deere's responses stand out—his sense of purpose and order, and his frustration and panic.

A number of items in the private memorandum relate to accounts, and we see both order and frustration in his description of them. A note to himself early in the memorandum book, probably in 1858, states: "I agree on my return home look up the memorandum of plows. I made them over with Simonds & Leadbetter, with Garnett & Co. subject to our order. *Be sure to do it thoroughly.*" The expenses of a long trip through western Illinois in late 1859 were denominated—his supper usually $.25, sometimes $.50, in Plymouth $.75. On the same trip, precise entries were made, with full firm name, for all payments. A bill to F.G. Schmieling & Co. of St. Louis for twenty-four plows and two small corn shellers read: "To be sent on the opening of navigation in Spring." There were also judgments on the financial stability of dealers: "Thos. J. Beard, Macomb is good. . . . J. F. Cowgill, Bardollph,—price list left, *don't know him.* . . . Kinnie & Carling, Augusta—not good." Blunt comments about backsliders were included: "The notes of Hinkley are worthless except one against Pennington is sound and a prospect of getting the amount. Chandler & Co. have the matter in their hands. . . . Hall is not of much account. Would not trust him, his partner F is his brother-in-law & considered good for a reasonable amt. Chandler & Co. say Hall is a 'fly up the crick'. . . . Townsend of Avon is good & I think we had better close up with Marsh—as fast as possible & sell him. If Marsh does not pay his note, due in 30 days, you had better look after him. . . . George Marsh is a good businessman. Will buy of us next season. His notes will be paid at maturity—if they are not, we had better look up after him, as he is hard up, but honest. I think will pay us. He is owing a man in Galesburg by name of Bugbee (call & see him)."

This was not a stable period for many of the dealers, and significant numbers of them were picking up stakes, walking out on debts, and either returning East or moving farther West. One particular debtor dealer worried Deere: "D.C. Marshall says Parsons is going to leave soon, break up housekeeping & Williams is only waiting to get his money. . . . Wells told me that Parsons was going East soon with his family. . . . Mapes asked Parsons what he was going to do with the store—said Williams would take it into Iowa with him. . . . G.B. Shaw says Parsons is going East next week." On one page, still in his own hand as an apparent reminder to himself, is a detailed set of strategies in regard to selling to one dealer: "First say that we cannot let them have plows on concession . . . are not able to carry over the season . . . will sell them plows on hand at 30% off less 50¢ pr. plow, furnish them at 30% off payable 1st July for Spring and 1st December for Fall purchases. . . . If you have to carry them don't give over 25% off and all over a stock of $300, they pay us for, or $500 at the outside. . . . If you cannot make satisfactory arrangements with them look out for other parties who want the plows . . . they have not been adverse to sign over plows to me."

Reminders about future product lines are interspersed throughout:

"See the Corn Sheller that is made in Chicago. It is an apple grinder too. . . . Whittemore & Belcher & Co. Chicopee Falls, Massachusetts, makes a good Corn Sheller—No. 10 is best size. . . . See Morrison, Pittsburgh, about mould castings. . . . we sent them a pattern by ex. of small clevis." Also throughout are small notes to himself about his own personal life: "Got a red dog pup W.H. Towner, Augusta, Illinois . . . dog was recommended by J. Hall, station agt. at Augusta . . . dog was about two mos. old when I got him." A few months later: "Inquire of Jno. Park—wants to train my pup in June . . . Jno. Porter who lives near him is a good trainer." Some personal expenditures are noted here and there: "Get measured for shirts—J.P. James under Fremont in Lake Street . . . shirts for all weather." Another page lists books that Deere wants to read: "Write Griggs & Co., Chicago, for Landers, *Analysis of English Words* . . . book—get it—*Self Help* by Samuel Smiles, *Gold Foil* by Timothy Titcomb, *Homes in the New World*, Frederick Bauer [sic] get books: *The Genuine Woman*, by Mitch Det [sic] *The Habits of Good Society*."

The most revealing of all the sections of the memorandum book, however, are those dealing with the financial arrangements between Charles Deere and his partners. There are extensive entries relating to the agreements with his father, including a listing of the notes that Charles Deere owed John Deere for the business. At one point near this notation is an enigmatic passage: "The reason that C. Deere notes were not entered in Jno. Deere's books was that J.D. did not want Bugbee & Hemenway to find out how much he gave for it & how he bought." In the back of the book Deere itemizes what he apparently owed at a particular time (probably around 1860); it includes a $4,284 note to Naylor & Co., a $5,500 note to the bank (presumably Gould's), and additional amounts for the grand total of $14,684.

There are also detailed notations relating to C.C. Webber & Co. With no further documentation, it is almost impossible to decipher their meaning; apparently Webber had been through a forced sale of some of his properties, for one of the notes states: "I paid C.C. Webber & made no a/c for the above $500. You hold the U.S. Marshall's receipt to apply on judgment against Webber & Drury. . . . " In May 1860 the Mercantile Agency correspondent reported that Charles Deere "had purchased the interest of Webber so that he is alone in the business."

A month later the correspondent chronicled further trouble in John Deere's own accounts: "Is abt. to assign. . . . August 1/60—We are not aware that he has assigned. . . . September 13/60—He has an assignment alry. prepared to execute, held in abeyance yet. He is in very bad condition. Can't pay more than 35 to 45¢ on the $. Has a large amt. of assets, but they are almost valueless. Has some 60m w. of bills receivable that not give 10¢ on the $ for. Can't pay what he owes at all, much less can he buy anything." The entry for December 27, 1860, was even more ominous. "Ans. upon question will his endorst. on 25¢/$ add to the value of the paper?—We do not think that it will, as, D, is closing up his old bus. and has mv. to space outsid."

Probably the most disturbing note of all those in the Charles Deere memorandum book was a Mercantile Agency report, copied by Charles Deere in his own hand. "Jno. Deere—Deere & Co. his successors. J.D. sold out to them to close up his business. C.C. Webber, the Co., swore that he was worth $80,000 some time ago. Is a man of no business character. Allows his notes to go to protest & Co. will make money even at the expense of Jno. Deere. There is a long story about it. Not much said about Chas. H. Deere. Think on the whole that we could get our pay for a reasonable amount of them sometime."

Interpretation of this harsh, anonymous missive is complicated. The "man of no business character" who lets his notes go to protest can be read to mean either John Deere or C.C. Webber. Given the facts we already know, this pejorative indictment could well have been made about either man by an outsider viewing the company in its darkest hours of the panic. The credit correspondent made essentially the same point in August 1860 (speaking of Charles Deere): "D docs not allow himself to get entangled in his father's and 'Webbers' bus. We consd him sf., vy careful young man." Later in that year, the correspondent noted, "I have examined the record & do not find that 'John Deere' has ever made an assignment. . . . Even if he had assigned, it would not affect Deere & Co. as he has not . . . any interest in that firm. In conversation with our Bankers here they tell me that 'D & Co' have promptly met their engagements during the whole of the hard times . . . we consider the concern good & reliable. 'D' is hons., indus., & attent."

So Charles Deere had weathered the difficult times, and in the process had established his own reputation as "honest, industrious, attentive, safe—a very careful young man." His father's debts had been overcome without the embarassment of an assignment.[18]

At no place in the memorandum book—nor, indeed, in any other place where Charles Deere's original words are found—does Charles Deere ever hint at irritation or condemnation of his father. In the little memorandum book, though, on its own separate page—and personally signed by him—he writes: "I will never from this seventh day of February, eighteen hundred sixty A.D. put my name to a paper that I do not expect to pay—so help me God."

PART II

MARKETING
AND MANUFACTURING
IN AN EXPANSIONIST AGE:

THE
CHARLES DEERE YEARS
(1860–1907)

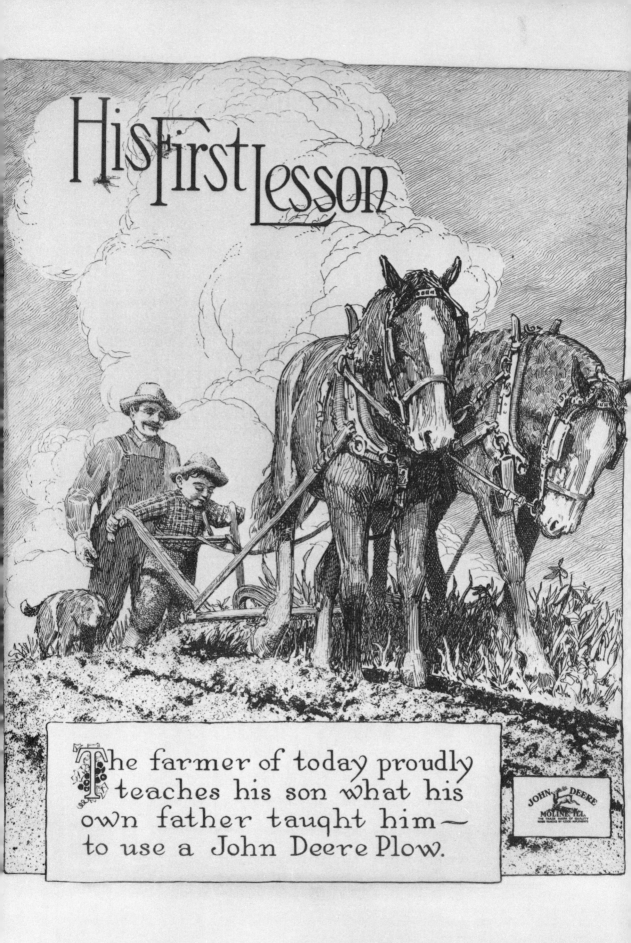

His First Lesson

The farmer of today proudly teaches his son what his own father taught him— to use a John Deere Plow.

JOHN DEERE
MOLINE, ILL.
THE TRADE MARK OF QUALITY
MADE FAMOUS BY GOOD IMPLEMENTS

CHAPTER 4

AFTER THE CIVIL WAR

*He asked me if I was dealing in Moline Plows, and
who I got them of . . . I answered that we got them from Pope &
Baldwin, of Quincy, on commission. He said he wanted to
take my order; that he was right from the shop; that he could
get them shipped to Hannibal for less than half
what we paid on them to Quincy . . . In glancing over his
shoulder, I saw the name Candee, Swan & Co., and I
asked him if John Deere was not in the shop yet. He told me
that he represented another shop, but made the
plow the same, used the same names, numbers, and all; that
they had Deere's foreman and a good many
of his hands, and were finishing the plows up much better.*

Shelbina, Missouri, hardware dealer, 1866

The turbulence of the late 1850s subsided as the new decade began. In the countryside around Moline, conditions improved considerably by the year 1860, helped by better weather and a good crop; the population continued to expand with the arrival of new immigrants. The *Davenport Democrat* trumpeted the lands of Scott County and other contiguous Iowa hinterlands: "Eastern men still retain the idea that we are all pioneering under the most disadvantageous circumstances, that the red man, the buffalo and the wild beasts of the forest actually come about our dwellings, and through the crevices between the logs, take cognizance of the internal economy of our household affairs." Not true, wrote the editor, "so bring your families and settle in the land of promise." The Moline *Independent*, touting the Illinois side of the river, bragged of "the general belief that Moline is destined to be the greatest manufacturing town in the West."

The *Democrat* also crusaded during this period for a "mechanics' institute," where the evenings of the "hundreds of vigorous, intelligent and ambitious young men employed as laborers and mechanics" could be taken up with reading, socializing, and "other social union which operates to stimulate high and honorable purposes." The *Democrat* was worried that many of these young men would "wander into the billiard rooms, beer rooms, and other questionable places of resort, where their money is foolishly expended, and their morals seriously infected with vulgar instincts." Across the river the *Rock Island Argus* also viewed the situation with alarm. "Bad boys and girls in this city are greatly on the increase, and unless they change their habits they will be in danger of passing a night in jail. . . . They create disturbances at singing schools and evening meetings, and the boys render night hideous by their yells on the streets—removing signs, boxes from stores, & c. . . . " The *Argus* suggested a more vigorous remedy: "Any person has a right to arrest them and take them to jail, and few examples of this sort might be beneficial."

Despite these aberrations, the general mood had turned positive. Charles Deere, too, was infected by this new optimism and, as he plotted his strategy for the 1860 "season," he boldly expanded the company's catalog and price list from the twenty-four pages of the previous year to thirty, including for the first time a handsome woodcut of the factory building itself.

The catalog contained other clues to Charles Deere's outlook on the new decade. Illustrations included facsimiles of two of the cups won by the company at previous fairs and another of the two sides of the "Grand Gold Medal of Honor" given to the company at the St. Louis Agricultural and Mechanical Exhibition in 1858 for "the best plow for all uses." His appeal was cast widely to all of the farmers in Illinois, Iowa, and Wisconsin, and he reminded them of the "over 50 first premiums at the different County Fairs last season." The catalog concluded with his father's oft-repeated thesis: "The determination of the proprietors to improve rather than deteriorate on their already acknowledged superiority of manufacturing will be a sufficient guarantee to all that every exertion will be made to furnish promptly a superior article at a low figure."[1]

A momentous conflict was about to engulf the country, however. The Civil War was to be fought on American soil, over agricultural lands and across traditional trading routes. Obviously, it was going to deeply affect the country's agriculture, among its other manifold dislocations.

THE NORTH-SOUTH CONFLICT

As the war opened, the first concerns centered on potential disruption to food supplies; even the British press worried of diminution in the supply of wheat and cotton. Trade routes with the South indeed were cut, and much of the produce of Illinois farms lost significant markets. For the early months of the war, the farmers of the Midwest were again in severe straits (the Illinois Central Railroad, concerned about the debt-laden farmers on the railroad's own land, even provided less-than-cost transportation to Chicago markets).

The unease about the farmer's plight proved unfounded. Though they initially were distressed in 1861 and 1862 by sagging commodity prices, the wartime years were marked by good agricultural weather in the United States, coupled with crop failures in Great Britain from 1860 to 1863 and a general shortage of food in continental Europe for most of that time. The army needed vast quantities, too, and the combination made for prosperity for the farmers—and, too, their suppliers.

An important development in farm structure in the Midwest occurred along the way—for the first time in Illinois, and to a lesser degree in Iowa and Indiana, there was truly large-scale farming. The conventional view of the Midwestern pioneer farmer characterized him as cultivating perhaps forty to sixty acres of land. But in this Civil War period, both the government and private entrepreneurs (particularly abetted by the Illinois Central Railroad) encouraged much larger plots, typically more than twice as large and ranging upward to thousands of acres. Michael Sullivant's farm in east central Illinois was an 80,000-acre holding. Sullivant was cultivating and pasturing 23,000 acres in one single block in Champaign County; employing a force of 100 to 200 men, 200 horses and mules, and a large number of oxen; and using a great amount of agricultural machinery. He became financially embarrassed and lost that particular piece of land but then turned to a larger tract of some 40,000 acres near Paxton, where he soon had planted some 18,000 acres in corn and 5,000 acres in other crops. In one year during the mid-1860s he was reported to have harvested 450,000 bushels of corn.

Such a gargantuan operation needed farm equipment on a large scale. Paul Wallace Gates, historian of the Illinois Central Railroad, commented on the Sullivant machine sheds: "The amount of farm machinery necessary to perform work on this large scale is almost staggering. One hundred fifty steel plows, 75 breaking plows, 142 cultivators, 45 corn planters, 25 gang-harrows, a ditching plow operated by 68 oxen and 8 men, an upright mower to clip the hedges and numerous power shellers were employed."

Even the smaller farms now took advantage of the rapidly improving machinery of this period. William H. Osborn, president of the Illinois Central Railroad in this period and a thoroughgoing advocate of mechanization, noted in 1864 that whereas a few years previously a small farmer generally chose not to plant more than forty acres, with improved machines a man could take care of sixty to seventy acres of land in crops. Osborn was especially complimentary about the new wheat and corn planters and cultivators brought onto the market in 1863 and 1864.

It did appear in the process that the "frontier" thesis of Frederick Jackson Turner—that an Eastern laborer could go West and readily start a farm if he were out of work or dissatisfied with his existing situation— was no longer true. Clarence Danhof suggests that it might have taken as much as $1,000 (in money of those days) to get a Western prairie farm under way. The agricultural and geographic records from the census of 1860 show that the average-sized farm was 91 improved acres (146 in total), with a farm value of some $2,854 and a value in equipment of $120. For the smaller farms under fifty acres, the average was twenty-five improved acres out of a total of thirty acres, a farm value of $598, and an equipment sum of $55. Perhaps $500 would be a more reasonable estimate of the amount of capital a man might need to start one of these under-fifty-acre farms.

We must be cautious not to overgeneralize the pace of the "agricultural revolution" of the 1850s and '60s. Many small farmers continued to get by on limited capital and less-than-adequate equipment. The extent of the use of machinery in the Civil War has been exaggerated by some analysts. The Midwest had experienced a boom and the Great Plains and Pacific coast had experimented widely with large, heavy equipment such as gang plows, etc. The East was slower, emphasizing lighter, simpler models, and the South lagged further behind in just about everything except rice-production machinery.

Still, the tremendous agricultural growth in the West during the Civil War period is clearly illustrated by the success of A.C. Fulton, a farmer from Davenport, Iowa, who wrote the *Prairie Farmer* in December 1863 about the experience on his sixty-two-acre farm. He had broken the farm originally in July 1862 at a cost of $2.50 per acre. Twenty acres were put in wheat and corn, the balance in onions, potatoes, sorghum, and some vegetables for home consumption. The total gross receipts for the year 1863 amounted to $10,111 and the net profits—after deducting three dollars per acre for interest and all the cost for seed, labor, transportation, commission, and other expenses—was $7,905, a large $127-per-acre net profit. Fulton concluded: "I am now enlarging the above sixty-two-acre farm, adding and enclosing six hundred acres more." The farm papers, such as *Prairie Farmer*, were full of such success stories during the later war years.[2]

THE DEERE FAMILY IN THE WAR PERIOD

James Chapman, John Deere's son-in-law, was the only member of the immediate family to serve in the army during the war. A Rock Island County regiment of volunteers was formed in 1862, and Chapman was instrumental in recruiting one of the companies, being elected its first lieutenant. The company joined the 129th Illinois Volunteers, seeing action in Kentucky. Chapman and a number of other officers became embroiled in a bitter controversy in 1863 between Republican abolitionists and the Democrats. In October 1863 a number of these officers, including Chapman, were dismissed from the service "for disloyalty." The *Rock Island Argus* alleged that the disloyalty of Chapman and the others so dismissed was "for being Democrats." The *Argus* continued: "The crime of Lieut. Chapman consisted in not wishing to serve with negro soldiers, and for saying so, in a letter published in the *Argus*." Race relations were very tense in that third year of the war, and the *Argus* carried a strongly racist line at that time. In December 1862, for example, the newspaper exhorted: "White Men! Remember that the Abolitionists have boasted that they would control the mass convention tomorrow afternoon. Let everyone who wants Illinois preserved to white men turn out and get their neighbors to turn out and fill the court house. . . . Mechanics! unless you want a negro to work at the same bench with you, turn out and remonstrate against their coming here."

John Deere was a vigorous Republican—according to the strongly Democratic *Argus*, "a raging abolitionist"—but he argued vehemently with the authorities about the inequity of the decision in the Chapman case. A month later Chapman was reinstated as first lieutenant in the 129th, the general order noting that "the charges against him having been satisfactorily explained."

Feelings about the great conflict were extremely strong in the mid-war period, and tensions and frustrations were often played out via the political arena. The *Argus*, vitriolically partisan to the Democrats, constantly castigated the "abolitionists," with particular focus on John Deere. In the April 1863 primary election, John Deere took an active role in his party, and the *Argus*, always willing to lambaste him, alleged that he had called a young war-veteran opponent "a worthless coote." A few months later, in July, Andrew Friberg, the Deere superintendent, got into a political argument and struck his opponent a fierce blow. Brought before a Moline justice, he was fined four dollars, but the political adversary demanded a change of venue to Rock Island and again brought the case before a jury. The latter agreed with the earlier Moline decision and dismissed the suit. The *Argus* had a field day with the case, though, calling Friberg "the abolition black guard and fighter" and a "bully" and ridiculed the dismissal by the jury as "a piece of private hugger-mugger to screen a guilty man from just punishment." James Chapman resigned from the service in March 1864 and came back to Moline to again take up the cudgel of the Democrats, particularly in the bitter political campaign in November of that year.

The John Deere family added a son-in-law and a daughter-in-law during the early 1860s. Daughter Emma married Stephen H. Velie in May 1860; she was twenty, he was thirty at the time of the marriage. Velie was a New Yorker and had come to Rock Island in 1853 to work with C.C. Webber. He was briefly in the grocery business in Princeton, Illinois, returning to Rock Island in 1861 to open an office in the courthouse for "the purpose of furnishing abstracts of land titles, etc." The *Rock Island Argus* commented at the time, "Mr. Velie is well known in this city as a very competent and correct businessman." The daugher-in-law was added two years later. In September 1862, Charles Deere married Mary Little Dickinson, a twenty-one-year-old Chicagoan, whose mother was related to Charles Atkinson, the close friend of the Deeres in Moline.

In 1863 Velie joined his brother-in-law Charles Deere in the plow business, remaining with the firm through the rest of his life as company secretary and confidant of Charles Deere. The two worked closely together for thirty-two years, in an intimate colleague relationship of trust, confidentiality, and complete frankness. When Velie joined the firm in 1863, it was still a small, regional operation; by 1895, when he died, the company was a prominent national enterprise.

We have a unique window to Velie's thinking, as we did with the Charles Deere diary, in a set of his letters written in the mid-1880s to his second son, Charles, who was then beginning his own business life with the company as a bill clerk in the Minneapolis office. These letters tell a good deal about both the man and his times. This was the "Gilded Age" of American business, a hurly-burly period of rugged individualism, often expressed through a primitive "survival of the fittest" mentality. Success itself was the prime virtue, with that very success often taken as the single measure of virtue. Indeed, Velie himself often articulated just such thoughts, for example, once telling Charles "success in business is almost always a sure indication of merit."

But Velie took a far more professional view of business life than such simplistic descriptors implied, and in the process inculcated these in his son. Velie valued learning highly, though not of the formal variety, for "dealing and associating with men is the best school and educates better than books." Thus, what was needed was on-the-job education, for "active business pursuits develop the mind more rapidly than the

schools, especially if one sets apart a portion of each day for reading."
Velie mailed his son copies of the prestigious *North American Review*,
for "these sober reviews and scientific periodicals afford the businessman
an opportunity to keep abreast of the best ethical thought and latest
scientific discoveries in the little time he has for reading." On another
occasion a copy of the portentous *Princeton Review* came forward, and
Charles was cautioned: "You will notice some comments in the margins,
as I always read speculative subjects, controversially arguing as I read
against unsound propositions or unfair conditions." Yet Velie was always
a bit skeptical of formal education: "The events recorded in books and the
experience of writers is suggestive only.... Dealing and associating with
men is the best school and educates faster than books in the practical
affairs of life, especially if you regard every man you meet as competent to
instruct you in something. There is a great deal of worldly wisdom in the
common people."

Charles was to pay particularly close attention to the business itself.
"How are you getting along in your plow machinery and business
education? Learn all you can and as fast as you can and take every
occasion to get an insight into accounts and settlements, the manner of
keeping books, etc." The job of bill clerk was not a terribly exciting
assignment, so his father warned him: "Your position will familiarize you
with prices and addresses of customers. Thoroughness of work and
keeping everything up in good shape is what tells. 'Act well your part,
there all the honor lies.' That is what shows the superiority of one man
over another." One's own work habits were of supreme importance.
"Plod on, keeping your eyes and ears and mind open to a comprehension
of everything that is for the best interest of the business. Make it a point
to do even the smallest things with thoughtful, painstaking care, for it is
perfection in little things that stamp the character.... Pick up all the
knowledge you can find lying around loose in all departments of the
business," he continued, "which can be done by offering to assist
whenever you have a spare moment. Keep your eyes and ears open and be
of all benefit you can to the business."

Velie's own meticulous financial instincts guided his own life. "A
judicious care of money is a secret of pecuniary success," he importuned
Charles, "and the financing of a private individual in his personal affairs
requires the same thoughtful care as for an empire." Charles had
overspent on his small salary at one point and his father attacked the
problem directly: "How are you getting along working out of your
embarrassment of last year? Bear in mind that keeping expenditures
within income means self-respect, independence and a competency while
the reverse, expenditures beyond income leads to mortification and
ultimate failure." He admonished: "The force of habit is so strong and
controlling in its influence that we should always be on the watch to
check a tendency to hurtful habits and cherish only those that tend to our

Exhibit 4–1. *List of subscribers, including John and Charles Deere, for a Moline company of volunteers during the Civil War (courtesy of Rock Island County Historical Society)*

present and future well being. . . . Industrious habits are of prime importance and when once acquired employment is a pleasure."

Soon Charles had a promotion, to traveler, and Velie was pleased: "I believe it to be the best mercantile school in the world, for in order to succeed a man has to make a thorough, thoughtful study of the merits of his own line of goods and both the merits and demerits of his competitors. He must become a student of human nature and learn the peculiarities of his customers, their idiosyncrasies in order to avoid treading on their toes." His philosophy of selling continued in another letter: "To do this one must learn to give his whole mind to the case in hand, keep his customer diverted and interested without ever divulging costs, make him feel that your goods are worth what you ask for them and that no goods of same quality can be afforded at less. The asking price of an article is always taken as an index to its quality and every seller is anxious to get all that his goods are worth in the market. A 'cut' in price as a rule savors of inferiority and makes the purchaser wary." Further subtle psychological advice was forthcoming on how to handle the customer. "It is natural for the buyer to manifest indifference and requires the closest watching by the seller to determine the right time to commit him. It is dangerous to let a fish go when you once have had him on the hook. It is a good accomplishment to be a good salesman, requiring as much patience as to be a good fisherman, and an entirely different knowledge as well."

The pervading ethic of family ownership by now was firmly entrenched, and Velie frequently conjured up the image of founder John Deere, grandfather of the Velie sons: "It is a great source of pride and gratification to John Deere to know that some of his grandsons have grown up to be active, energetic men with an ambition for active, burning careers; feeling as he does that when he is gone and when those now managing the factory will retire by reason of the infirmity of age there are those directly interested by ties of kindred acquiring experience and ability to take their places and perpetuate the good name and fame of the establishment."

The other two executives in the firm, George Vinton and Charles Nason, were also related to the Deeres by marriage (both were sons-in-law of William Lamb; John Deere was their uncle). Thus all the management with the exception of Andrew Friberg had familial links.

In 1864 Friberg developed respiratory problems and left Deere to go West to the mountains for his health. At this point a new individual joined the company, a man destined to have a profound influence on the Deere product line. He was Gilpin Moore, a thirty-three-year-old Rock Island machinist and shop superintendent. Moore had taken his apprenticeship in Christopher Webber's foundry in the early 1850s and had been superintendent of that firm's machine shop in the mid-1850s. Moore was not just a machinist and shop leader, for he possessed an innovative ability that soon was to mean much to the Deere operation.

As to brother-in-law Christopher Webber, it is not clear just what his relation was to the firm during the Civil War. Several of Webber's biographers said that he joined the Deere firm in 1862 (none of them mentioning an earlier, abortive partnership of the late 1850s), but there is no evidence that he was taking any operative role in the company. In 1864 he was elected an alderman in Rock Island; he died in March 1865, leaving his widow, Ellen, with five small children. Webber clearly was held in high regard in Rock Island; Robert Tate commented, "A steamboat blew her whistle and fired a gun—the boat Hawkeye." His six-year-old son, Charles C., later became a major company figure.

Another sad event for the family had occurred just a few weeks before Christopher Webber died. Demarius Lamb Deere, John Deere's wife and the mother of his nine children, passed away at age sixty. Later, in the summer of that year, John Deere returned to the Lamb homestead in Vermont, reacquainting himself with Lucenia, the maiden sister of Demarius. In May 1866 John Deere and Lucenia Lamb were married.[3]

THE COMPANY'S WARTIME RECORD

The company did very well indeed during the Civil War (though we must depend only on outside documentation for the story). In November 1860, the firm of Deere & Company was dissolved and Charles Deere continued as the "Moline Plow Manufactory," signing all advertising and promotional literature with his own name. This signalled Christopher Webber's exit from the firm; the R.G. Dun & Company correspondent noted again Webber's difficulties with his own debts and commented: "Since then the business had been carried on by 'C.H.D.' alone, who by the consent of 'W' still uses the name 'D & Co.'" Apparently the usually perceptive credit analyst failed to pick up the formal dissolution of the partnership.

The credit correspondent continued to chronicle the firm's increasing good fortune as the war wore on. "Jany 5, 63—Has lar amt. of ppy in his name, say 20 m/$, R.E. & 10 m pers. This was all at one time his father's & in my opinion is so yet but if it is 'Chas. H.' he has a sufficiency to have a good cr.... . Aug 5, 63— Ag. a fine bus. & consid perfectly good.... Fby 5, 64—Good. worth 25 m.... Dec 29, 64— Deere & Co. good.... Dec 29, 64— Deere & Co. good.... Dec 29, 64—Worthy of credit for any reasonable amt.... Aug 15, 66—r.e. 50 m/$—cap 50 m/$,—worth 150 m/$, cr. unlimited, made 100 m/$ last year, assessed 40 m/$ per ppy.... Dec 66—First class. Rich." What a difference those six years made. In September 1860 John Deere had $60,000 of receivables "that not give 10¢ on the $ for." In December 1866, Charles Deere was "Rich"!

The company remained Charles Deere's alone until late in the Civil War; in July 1864 the firm was again reconstituted as Deere & Company, with John and Charles sharing equally in the partnership. Each of the parties "contributed the sum of $70,000 in stock, buildings and machinery and outstanding debts as per books of C.H. Deere." It was a simple, one-page partnership agreement and the realities of the operating situation were little changed from that of the 1858 takeover by the son.

In truth, John Deere was never very far away from his beloved plow shop. With Charles handling the financial end of the business with exemplary aplomb, and with Andrew Friberg and then Gilpin Moore managing the shop itself, Deere could turn to his first love, the tinkering with products that had produced so many advances in the earlier years. In early January 1864, John Deere obtained the first actual patent by a member of the firm, one relating to molds for casting steel plows, an ingenious concept of coating the inner surface of the dry sand mold with black lead (plumbago) and then tempering this with fire-clay water. A second patent, a few months later, made this concept more explicit, particularly concerning the mixing of the ingredients (they were to be mixed "to about the consistence of cream with a solution of fire-clay in water, to which may be added a little beer or molasses to increase the adhesiveness of the sand when necessary"). A year later, in 1865, John Deere obtained his third patent, a much more complex one relating to securing together the landside, moldboard, and share so that they would all be held together in a firmer way and more readily detached "at pleasure."

The product line had stayed essentially the same for the first two years of the war, though prices rose on a number of the plows, "owing to the great advance in Iron and Steel, and all materials used in the manufacture," noted Deere in the catalog of 1862. It was a sellers market, and the company was able to demand cash payment, rather than credit. (As the catalog euphemistically put it, "We are also obliged to *hold our Plows for cash*, or as near that as practicable, owing to the shortening of credit by all Iron and Steel Manufacturers and Importers to four months' time.") The price rise ranged from $.75 on the corn plows to two dollars on the Clippers. Breaking-plow prices increased only minimally, and the cultivators and harrows stayed the same. Ox yokes had dropped out of the catalog altogether—there was no further mention of them anywhere, so we can assume that the product line itself was dropped.

In 1863 the company took on the manufacture of a riding cultivator, the "Hawkeye," made under patent arrangement with its inventor, W. Furnas. This was the first Deere implement adapted to riding—a signal step forward for the cultivator and a forerunner of the famous Deere product of the 1870s, the Gilpin sulky plow. The concept of a sulky—a machine upon which one rode—had been experimented with by many people in the earlier years, but the sulky cultivator really came into its own in the 1860s (followed right away by the sulky plow). Deere's version of this was one of many. The Hawkeye won the first premium at the Iowa State Fair in 1863 and rapidly achieved acclaim throughout the Deere territory as a major innovation. One of the farmer's testimonials—those eulogistic "fan letters" all manufacturers were so enthusiastic to solicit —called the Hawkeye a "patriotic machine." The farmer recommended it to "the farming fraternity" as a machine having many superiorities, "not the least among which is its capabilities of furnishing substitutes for half the hands in the corn field, thus allowing a larger force to seek their line of duty upon 'the tented field'." Deere sold about 500 of these in 1864, the first year it was marketed, and more than quadrupled that figure the following year. The catalog of 1865 featured a full-page picture of the cultivator with two fine horses pulling it, and the text devoted two full pages to praising the Hawkeye's virtues. The lavish description emphasized its ease of operation and described how all of the shovels could be raised to clear the ground by pressing one's feet on a pair of treadles, "thus leaving the hands free to guide the team." The paragraph ended on a seemingly macabre note: "A one-arm or one-legged man can manage it." In truth, this was an important comment to make, for many hundreds of agriculturalists had lost arms or legs in the war and in the frequent farm accidents from the often dangerous rudimentary machinery of those early days. (A Cass County plow manufacturer featured in this period a sulky plow "especially adapted for small boys, old men and cripples.")[4]

THE BEGINNINGS OF PRICE COLLABORATION

A profoundly important event for the plow manufacturers of the West occurred during the course of the war, in early 1864. In January of that year, fourteen plow manufacturers from Illinois and one from Wisconsin gathered together in Chicago and formed a "plow makers' society." George Vinton represented Deere as its general agent. The fifteen companies were among the largest in the industry, a dominant group of manufacturers.

The subject of the meeting was prices. Evidence was presented at the meeting that steel prices were again to be pushed up. In three months, iron had been advanced $.01 per pound and steel $.015, while paints, varnish, and other necessary articles for the plow makers' use had also advanced significantly. Only labor had remained stable during this three-month period. "In fact," noted the *Prairie Farmer* reporter, "it costs $1 more now to make the plows more generally in use than it did on the first day of October last." Having assimilated this disturbing news, the plow makers resolved that the price of all plows quoted in the present manufacturers' lists at eleven to sixteen dollars should be advanced $1.50 over the list price (with plows quoted under eleven and over sixteen dollars proportionally advanced). Shovel plows and coulters were raised similarly, as well as "patent" cultivators. In substance, each plow maker could price his plows separately, but all agreed to raise their own existing prices by a standard figure. If there were further increases in iron and steel, a formula would then put plow prices up by a proportionate amount.

On June 30, 1864, the group held their second meeting and formed a permanent organization under the name Northwestern Plow Makers' Association. Col. John Dement of Dixon, Illinois, was elected president and Charles Deere secretary. By the following December iron and steel prices had risen and there was considerable discussion about just how much to again advance plow prices. "The only difference was in the amount being necessary; some taking a moderate stand while others were for a large rise putting the profits of the manufacturer beyond contingency," noted the *Prairie Farmer* reporter. The moderates prevailed; "the result was a medium advance." These two meetings were the first of a great many over the next several decades. The Northwestern Plow Manufacturers Association (its amended name) placed itself centrally into the pricing process, with vigorously debated price lists developed for each season.

The importance of this price-making function was critical to the industry, and the issues revolving around it are discussed in later chapters. Meanwhile, though, Deere was experiencing not cooperation, but trouble from one of the members of the association.[5]

THE TRADEMARK IMBROGLIO

Robert K. Swan had come to Moline in 1857, "penniless, having spent all of his money for medical treatment in St. Louis," said his 1877 biographer. Forty-one years of age at the time, he found a job with Alonzo Nourse, who made fanning mills, chain pumps, and hay rakes. Nourse appointed him as a traveler, to sell in the summer and collect in the winter. Henry W. Candee had originally come to Rock Island in 1845, moved to Moline in 1850, and also began working with Nourse; shortly after Swan came to the firm, Candee and Swan bought the business and continued in the manufacture of the line under their own name, Candee, Swan & Co.

Across town in Moline, another personnel change was taking place. Andrew Friberg had come back from the mountains of the West in 1865, recovered from his illness, and Charles Deere put him back on the job in the plow factory. But it was clear that Gilpin Moore had supplanted Friberg as shop superintendent and head of engineering. Friberg was probably disgruntled by his rival's ascendancy, and in July 1865 he persuaded Robert Tate to let him run the blacksmith shop at Buford & Tate, "for $5 per day," according to Tate. Tate was embroiled in an enormous controversy with Basil Buford about their partnership, and just about this time the two split up. Though the firm continued, it was not a very congenial place to work; somehow, Friberg, Candee, and Swan made connections and the latter two persuaded Friberg to join them. The reason was soon apparent—Candee, Swan & Co. had decided to go into the plow business.

One more plow manufacturer should not have troubled any of the existing manufacturers, certainly not Charles Deere. The firm was in extraordinarily good shape at that particular moment. Competitors there always were, but one stayed ahead of them by building a superior line under a superior name.

It was this latter—the name—that was the rub. The Deeres were the only plow manufacturers in Moline, ever since John Deere had come to the town in 1848 and hired the two blacksmith-plow makers, Cyrus Kinsey and D.P. Beery. Buford and Tate were substantial manufacturers in the area, but they were Rock Islanders, not Moliners. In Charles Deere's mind—and especially in his customers' minds—his firm made *the* Moline plow.

Candee, Swan brought out its first catalog in mid-1866. In it were a number of shocks for Charles Deere. In the first place, it was almost identical to the existing Deere price list. Obviously, Candee and Swan intended to closely duplicate Deere's product line, exactly duplicate the price structure for all similar models, and even adopt precisely the Deere numbering system for all of the plows. There were some differences in the two brochures— Deere held patents for the Hawkeye cultivator and for Black's gang plow; Candee, Swan sold the Hoosier cultivator and Weir's corn plow. Still, if the two brochures were laid side by side, it would be clear that the Moline *Republican* printers had used the same typesettings for most of the pages. Deere's brochure had three illustrations, that of Candee, Swan only one—and, if one looked closely, there was only a subtle difference in the two pictures. Anyone picking up the two brochures would be hard pressed to know which was which, unless looking to the front cover and the name. Even the names of the factories themselves added confusion, as Deere had called his factory the "Moline Plow Works," and Candee and Swan now chose to call theirs the "Moline Union Agricultural Works."

As if this were not enough, the single most disturbing feature of the new Candee, Swan operation was their trademark. They had constructed theirs to look almost exactly like that of Deere & Company (exhibit 4-2).

Charles Deere watched the actions of the new firm in that summer and fall of 1866 for any overt misrepresentation. Their traveling salesman was none other than Robert K. Swan himself, and soon Deere thought that he had adduced evidence that Swan was deliberately misrepresenting his company as Deere & Company. In the subsequent court case brought by Deere for trademark infringement, a Shelbina, Missouri, hardware and agricultural implement dealer testified: "He asked me if I was dealing in Moline Plows, and who I got them of. . . . I answered that we got them from Pope & Baldwin, of Quincy, on commission. He said he wanted to take my order; that he was right from the shop; that he could get them shipped to Hannibal for less than half what we paid on them to Quincy. . . . In glancing over his shoulder, I saw the name Candee, Swan & Co., and I asked him if John Deere was not in the shop yet. He told me that he represented another shop, but made the plow the same, used the same names, numbers and all; that they had Deere's foreman and a good

Exhibit 4–2. *Similar logos involved in the Deere-Candee, Swan trademark lawsuit, 1867*

many of his hands, and were finishing the plows up much better.... He told me to say nothing about the transaction to Mr. Pope, that is, the conversation as to terms and figures he had offered me plows at. He left me a price list card."

Candee and Swan told the court: "No injury was intended to the plaintiffs, but honest competition was invited." Another complainant witness, a second Missouri dealer, told how this competitive argument ran. "I asked him what Moline Plow he was selling; if it was John Deere's Plow he was selling, he said no, it was not John Deere's Plow, but a plow just as good as John Deere's, made in the same place, and the same brand on, 'Moline, Ills.' He also told me that they had Mr. Deere's foreman employed, and that the plow was just exactly like Mr. Deere's, and he said that it would sell just as good on account of having 'Moline, Ills.' on ... that it don't make any difference about the name, so long as the brand 'Moline, Ills.' is on; the plow will sell just as well as Mr. John Deere's; he told me he sold it most everyway as The Moline Plow, and had no trouble in selling it as The Moline Plow. He told me the farmers would not know the difference if Moline, Ills. was on. It did not make any difference about the manufacturer's name."

Was the Swan sales pitch unfair and misleading? Even before the suit Charles Deere had taken steps to counteract it. In July 1866 he announced in a broadside the formal association of Stephen Velie and George Vinton with the firm, and he took the occasion to assure the farmers that "the 'Deere Plow' shall not only maintain its well-known reputation, but the knowledge and skill attained by long experience will be applied to enhance it." In retrospect, this phraseology was unwise—almost emphasizing the name Deere at the expense of the name Moline. This first salvo in Deere's attack on Candee and Swan was followed by another broadside, even more combative: "Another evidence of superiority is found in the fact plow makers in different parts of the country are changing their styles and shapes to imitate ours, while others go still farther and assert that they have a mechanic from our shop (discharged years ago for incompetency) and are making the 'Moline Plow,' advertising them as such, and *seeking to get them introduced* on the reputation our plows have acquired. . . . These things are calculated to mislead the public and we allude to them that our friends may be prepared to expose the attempted deceptions." A later advertisement went further, alleging that "unscrupulous manufacturers have recently appropriated this name for the purpose of palming off a confessedly inferior imitation, *using all the numbers, letter, names* peculiar to our plows." Finally, Charles Deere became almost messianic in castigating the opposition: "We really believe that no man can live an exemplary Christian life and use a poor plow. We therefore think that every farmer should spare no pains to get what he knows to be reliable and not allow himself to be deceived by flaming advertisements, claims of scientific principles, red stripes, etc. which are nearly always used to cover up bungling, awkward, inferior and useless implements." Deere's own dealers, by this time loyal, undying allies, also placed their own advertisements, often even more ad hominem. A Peoria, Illinois, agricultural house cautioned against other dealers "palming off a counterfeit" and a Newton, Iowa, dealer voiced: "I sell the genuine John Deere Moline Plow, & Hawkeye Cultivator—these plows are too well known to need any puffing" (exhibit 4-3).

By early 1867 Deere decided that exhortations by advertising would not be enough, and he took Candee, Swan & Co. to court. Deere asked for an injunction but could not persuade the judge to issue a temporary restraining order. Candee and Swan breathed a collective sigh of relief and immediately put out their own broadside: "As many of our customers and others, too, have formed the impression that we are to discontinue the manufacture of plows, we beg to inform you to the contrary. . . . Our Mr. Swan will be pleased to call upon you during the present month, to make all necessary arrangements for fall trade. . . . "

Despite the surface cooperation of the plow makers in their new association, pirating of key personnel continued. In late February 1867 Charles Deere wrote in his diary, "A man named Wm. M. Miller tried to get in our shop through misrepresentation . . . he got in and saw our southern plows. . . . " The truth came out the next day, for "Miller proves

JOHN DEERE'S
MOLINE PLOWS.

The great increasing demand consequent upon the high reputation attained for this Plow, have led dealers in **other** Plows, for the purpose of making sales, **claim that theirs are the Deere Plows, or Moline,** (a name by which our Plow is known,) not having sufficient confidence in their own Plow to offer them upon their own merits.

We therefore wish to
CAUTION

The Farmers against such impositions and deceptions practised by such dealers, seeking in in this way to deceive them, and palming off a counterfeit upon them.

TAKE NOTICE.

All of John Deere's Plows are branded on the beam with the trade mark.

Which other dealers or manufacture not and dare not us. The only place where the farmers can buy the above Plows is at the

PEORIA AGRICULTURAL HOUSE,
51 S. Washington St.,

Opposite Toby & Anderson's Plow Factory, **PEORIA, ILLINOIS.**
CHAS. TAYLOR.

Peoria National Democrat Print.

Exhibit 4–3. A retailer's advertisement, warning of "counterfeit" Deere plows, ca. 1867, an exhibit in the Deere-Candee, Swan trademark lawsuit

to be from St. Louis trying to hire plowmakers . . . in Burman Bros. employ, also has letters from Wm. Markham & Co. . . . He had Estes and three or four others call on him at the Moline House. . . . Buford Bros. and James Norton got after him in Rock Island, made him show his hand and frightened him considerably."

This must have been the final straw for Charles Deere, and he decided to press the Candee-Swan case. Deere felt particularly hostile toward Friberg, who, he thought, had taken with him to the new firm the know-how and the product engineering he had learned both with John Deere and later with Charles Deere. Candee and Swan had exploited this association blatantly. In their first catalog they trumpeted: "Our Andrew Friberg, who has charge of the Iron Department, is the oldest and most experienced *practical Plowmaker* in the North-West." The price list for 1868 went even further. "Our Mr. Friberg for twelve years had charge of the Iron Department of Mr. Deere's shop, and to his skill as a Mechanic they in great measure owe their justly merited popularity."

The case was soon on the docket of the Rock Island Circuit Court, scheduled for its term of May 1867. Candee and Swan apparently decided that the best defense was an attack on the opposition, and they initiated a hypothesis that Friberg and Tate were the inventive geniuses, not John Deere. As to the success of Deere & Company, their brief noted: "Much less is it true through the large, experienced, rare skill and ingenuity and untiring energy and industry of said John Deere. . . . It is true that Deere & Co. make good plows . . . and it is also true that Deere is a man of untiring energy and industry, but the experience, ingenuity and skill which has given a reputation to his plows is due to Robert Tate and Andrew Friberg. . . . "

To Charles Deere, Friberg's relocation was a defection, a clear case of "pirating," and he reacted bitterly. In a Deere broadside of December 1866, he implied that a mechanic from their shop had been "discharged years ago for incompetency," the wording patently pointing the finger at Friberg. This was a petulant statement, manifestly untrue, and the defense demolished any implication of Friberg having been discharged by a set of questions concerning Friberg's re-entry into the Deere firm in 1866. The Candee deposition bluntly concluded: "If this statement, as to the plow maker and workman applied to these defendants and Andrew Friberg, it was a deliberate falsehood." Still, given the provocation of an employee leaving with all the trade "secrets," it is not surprising that Charles Deere reacted the way he did.

Tensions among the participants mounted after the formal court case was instituted. Vinton had been the company representative at the Illinois State Fair at Quincy in September 1867. On the last day, the *Quincy Daily Whig and Republican* published a long article on the results of the fair, stating in the process: "Prominent among the extensive displays in this line stand Messrs. Candee, Swan & Co., of Moline.

The Moline Plows have ever held the highest reputation among our farmers, and the display by the above firm cannot be enlarged upon too highly.... They have passed through the fire of innumerable lawsuits and come out of the flames unscathed and untouched." Vinton was incensed about what he thought was a planted story, and he confronted Swan right on the fairgrounds. Thomas Pope, an agricultural implement dealer in Quincy (selling Deere's plows), happened to be present and reported the incident. "Mr. Vinton asked Mr. Swan whether he wrote the article, or authorized it; I am not positive which. The reply was either in the affirmative or evasive, not a negative. Mr. Vinton then asked if he paid for it. The reply was: 'That is my business.'"

By this time, the differences were rubbing friendships raw. Swan became the special nemesis of the Deere people, despite the fact that he and John Deere were good friends. Charles Atkinson became increasingly concerned and decided to talk with John, rather than Charles—"I expressed to him my regrets that such a controversy existed, and hoped that it might be settled." He talked also to Swan and was asked about this in court: "Mr. Swan stated in a conversation with me, in substance, that he had learned something which he was not aware of before, as to the use of the letter, numbers, figures or combinations, in marking plows. He said, in substance, that he was satisfied that it was wrong to use said numbers, letters, & c., on their plows, and that they would discontinue the use of them." Atkinson then allowed that Swan was not completely contrite. "In the same conversation he said they would continue the use of the word Moline on their plows, because he thought they had a right to do so, by reason of the plows being made in Moline." Atkinson urged Swan to talk to Charles Deere—but Swan apparently never did so. The case ran its course without any further efforts at compromise, and with further eroding of long-time friendships.

The case itself had precedent-setting implications in regard to the law of trademarks. First was the question of whether Deere & Company could preempt the name "Moline." Could a company, by constant usage of the name of its town in its advertising, actually have that name become so closely associated with its product that no other similar product could incorporate it? There was substance to the Deere claim that not only had they often used the term "the Moline Plow" in their literature, but that also farmers had come to think of it as such. The defense was quick to point out, though, that more frequently Deere had used terminology such as "John Deere's Celebrated Plows," and "The Deere Plow." Several Deere advertisements and broadsides in the late 1850s and early '60s were headlined, "Moline Plows," and one in the early 1860s actually said "the Moline Plow." Still, evidence of widespread usage was not that clear, and the defendants' lawyers cleverly brought this out in their cross-examinations. Witnesses were always asked, when queried about the trademark itself, whether the abbreviation "Ill." was added to the word

"Moline." The witnesses uniformly said that it was. In essence, the defendants were making the case that the town was a geographical description—a generic term—rather than a trademark. They introduced into the evidence advertisements from other Moline firms using Moline in their title— Moline Iron Works, Moline Mills, Moline Paper Mill— none of whom claimed Moline as a trademark per se.

The actual drawing of the logo itself involved a more difficult defense for the Candee-Swan lawyers. Their clients had indeed almost precisely duplicated the configuration of the Deere trademark, substituting their own name in the semi-circular section. The Candee-Swan lawyers had a two-pronged attack. First, they were able to show that at certain times— for example, with Deere's case steel plow—the latter firm had used a horizontal configuration, rather than the half circle. The second half of the argument held that other manufacturers had also used the same configuration—the half circle for the name and the town of manufacture on the horizontal. Here the critical testimony turned out to come from none other than Robert Tate, John Deere's old partner.

Tate had been subpoenaed by the defendants, and he testified at considerable length about his early relationship with the John Deere shop. It was his testimony regarding the May plow from Galesburg, Illinois, that was reported at length in an earlier chapter. Tate also had much to say about the numbering system and John Deere's personal innovative ability, and he made a number of other miscellaneous and sometimes gratuitous comments about the whole situation. Tate told himself in his diary: "Hawley, lawyer for Deere, questioned me very closely as to how and what manner I constructed the first plows made by Buford & Tate so as to be able to get the exact shape of what is called the no. 6 old ground, and other plows we were manufacturing. . . . Mr. Conly, whose duty it was to write down all I said . . . had got so befogged that he begged Mr. Hawley to stop me. 'Mr. Tate, cannot you give us a more plain and homely description of your "Modus Operandi" so that we can make sense of your description?'; 'No, sir, but I can abbreviate it by using more geometric terms if that will mend or help to make this court all plow makers.' 'Oh, no, you have said enough.' So I sat down."

Tate was asked about his trip in 1849 as a Deere partner to the East, visiting the Ruggles, Nourse & Mason manufacturing plant in Massachusetts. Quizzed by the lawyers as to whether there was anything original about the way John Deere had made his own trademark, Tate replied: "I consider there is nothing original in it. . . . I was East in 1849, and plows were branded so by Ruggles, Nourse & Mason." This was a rather devastating comment, particularly because Tate went on to describe how Deere had also adapted the Ruggles numbering system, too. This more or less demolished the Deere claim that Candee, Swan had preempted Deere's number system. It was obvious that manufacturers everywhere were copying each others' nomenclature.

Thus the various allegations by Deere all seemed to be on shaky ground. At one critical point, the question came up as to whether the Candee-Swan plow itself was an exact duplicate of the Deere plow. Friberg himself provided the key testimony. He described in detail the differences between the two plows—the Candee-Swan old ground plows did not have as high a landside, there were differences in the thicknesses of some of the parts, etc. Friberg continued: "The block is raised on these plows of our make, so as to give a truer shape to the plow. When we commenced making plows we made a long point on them. Mr. Deere, at that time, was making a short point to his plows. When Deere & Co. saw our plows, they commenced making their plows with a longer point so as to correspond with ours." Friberg's testimony was never contradicted by Deere, and a careful look at the drawings of the plows in the two brochures of mid-1866 mentioned above shows this difference. Charles Atkinson had said in his earlier testimony that Deere had brought his plow to its present perfection not by imitating other plows but by "improving on the imperfections of other plows." Now it appeared that Deere was also improving his share points by adopting the more effective Candee-Swan version.

The most potent of the Deere arguments in the case related to the issue of deception. The most telling single witness in this regard for the Deere side was J.E. Winzer, a clerk for the Chicago office of J.N. Bradstreet & Son. To appreciate fully the import of this, we need one additional fact. By mid-1868 Candee Swan & Co. was having severe financial difficulties. At this point, Stillman W. Wheelock, the owner of the Moline Paper Mill and a founding stockholder of the Moline Water Power Company, bought into the firm as partner, infusing some $75,000 of capital into the tottering business. The firm was renamed the Moline Plow Company at that time—before the court case had been settled. In October of that year, the credit company received a request from the "Moline Plow Company" for information about a particular dealer in Eddyville, Iowa. Winzer, the clerk receiving the request, duly filled out information about the dealer ("not recommended for credit") and then mailed the report to the "Moline Plow Works— Moline, Illinois." The letter was promptly delivered by the United States mail to Charles Deere's plow works! Deere, sensing the import of the mistake, wrote the Bradstreet office and asked for the return of the original request. It was obvious by the wording of the return letter—"We enclose a *copy* of the ticket which you sent us"—that even at this point the Bradstreet correspondent did not know that there were two companies, and that the request had come from one, the answer given to the other. Winzer was queried about this in the trial: "It probably occurred on account of the type of the firms being nearly alike, and because I hadn't become accustomed to sending letters to the Moline Plow Company, but had always sent them to the Moline Plow Works. . . . " If as sophisticated a concern as the Bradstreet organization could make such a mistake, it seemed likely that many others would fall into the same error. This reinforced the Deere arguments stressing the confusion in the minds of farmers and dealers.

The case was finally concluded in November 1869; the result was a sweeping victory for Deere & Company. The defendants were "forever restrained and enjoined" from calling themselves "the Moline Plow Co." Further, they were not to be allowed to put any terminology such as "The Moline Plow" or " Moline Plow" or "Moline Plows" on any trademark or "in any way or manner using the word 'Moline,' either upon their plows or in advertising the same." They were further enjoined from imitating Deere in any advertising or selling, including the numbering system itself. To cap the decision, the judge precluded the defendants from using the words "Candee, Swan & Co." or other words in a semi-circular form if to do so would in any way imitate the Deere brand. The case seemed on its face to be an overwhelming, indeed unconditional, victory for Charles Deere.

But circuit court cases often have a way of not standing up under appeal—and this is exactly what happened. The defendants immediately took the case to the next higher court, the Illinois State Supreme Court. Its decision was rendered in October 1871. In contrast to the circuit court judge's short, two-page judgment, the chief justice wrote a comprehensive twenty-four page opinion. He observed that "Deere and his associates . . . have enjoyed for more than twenty years the monopoly in this manufacture at this favored locality." The justice gave prominent feature to Robert Tate's testimony, particularly that relating to the early relationship with John Deere. He reiterated the May "Galesburg plow story," and concluded about John Deere: "The machine so indispensable to our prosperity has been greatly improved by him—not perhaps, by applying original conceptions of his own mind to any part of it, but by careful study of the labors of others, and, with unerring judgments, adapting them to his own."

The justice then turned to the legal underpinning for the trademark. He, too, used the word "pirating," and discussed in detail some of the past legal precedent for trademarks, quoting both American and British cases. He rejected the notion that Deere could preempt the term "Moline Plow," for, as the justice put it: "This portion of the claim set up by appellees must fall to the ground. . . . As that is only a generic term, it is seen, they can claim no exclusive right to the use of that name by which to designate their manufacture." Similarly, he rejected the lower court's view that the trademark itself was unique enough to be able to be claimed as exclusive by Deere. According to the justice: "It is not such as to amount to a false representation." His concluding paragraph, truly a devastating one, continued: "There was no pretension by appellees, of a trade mark, until appellants commenced to manufacture, and that successfully, plows at Moline, and which they published far and wide as the 'Moline Plow,' and thus interfered with the monopoly appellees had created. For their audacity, in so interfering, the sternest decrees of the law are invoked, but, in this court, the invocation will be in vain, on such facts as are presented by this record." The injunction was dissolved, the bill dismissed, the decree reversed.

It was a stunning setback for Deere—one that everyone knew was final. The chief justice had confined himself to the trademark issue; at no point did he explicitly treat the issue of misrepresentation. If there indeed had been fraudulent intent by Candee, Swan to pass its goods off as those of Deere & Company, this was not ruled upon by the court. The principle has been well established in later cases—both in law and in ethics—that no man has the right to sell his own goods as the goods of another. Courts now hold that injury is not just to the seller who lost the sale, but to the buyer who was induced to purchase something he did not desire (whether or not the goods turned out to be better than those intended to be bought). But it was not so at this time.

The case was a temporary setback for Deere and a great boost for the Moline Plow Company, which went on to become a major plow manufacturer in the country. The case has long since been forgotten, its antagonisms buried. The epitaph for the case was probably best stated by the *Davenport Daily Democrat* back in 1871: "It has been a very long and expensive suit, in which both parties have manifested a good deal of pluck."[6]

FROM PARTNERSHIP TO CORPORATION

After thirty-one years of operation as either a partnership or a single proprietorship, John and Charles Deere took an important legal step, incorporating the firm on August 15, 1868, to be named "Deere & Company" (not the abbreviated version, Deere & Co., that had been used from time to time). The capital stock specified on that date was $150,000, with four shareholders—the two Deeres, Stephen Velie, and George Vinton. A year later, Charles V. Nason and Gilpin Moore were given small shareholdings. The composition of ownership was: Charles Deere, 40 percent; John Deere, 25 percent; Velie, 14 percent; Vinton, 10 percent; Moore, 6 percent; and Nason 5 percent. We have few clues as to how these percentages among the six were determined, or even why Charles Deere and his associates decided at this particular moment to incorporate.

A great deal of information about the firm was disclosed in the papers of incorporation, however. A detailed appraisal was made of all the physical property; its total was $105,000 in buildings and $45,265 in machinery and equipment. Each of these physical assets was listed and described, and we gain a complete picture for the first time of just exactly what composed "the Plow Works" of the company. Also included in that first year's corporate record book was an official balance sheet, signed by

Exhibit 4–4. *One of the earliest uses of the "leaping Deere" trademark, 1875 (Deere Archives)*

Stephen Velie as secretary of the company (John Deere was elected president, Charles Deere became vice president). The total business done in that first year of incorporation, 1868–69, was $646,563; this had been accomplished by selling 41,133 plows, harrows, and cultivators. The net gain for that year was $198,437; a $25,000 dividend was declared and the actual capital left in the firm after this was $423,237. The net gain of this particular year was especially large; the firm did not reach a higher level until a dozen years later, in 1880–81.

Nevertheless, overall company growth continued strongly upward. Even the Panic of 1873, a serious downturn for the country as a whole, was only a brief setback, far less painful for the company and for Charles Deere than the bitterly remembered depression of 1857.[7]

THE GRANGERS TAKE ON THE MANUFACTURERS

A new organization destined to send sharp reverberations through the agricultural equipment industry was formed in December 1867. The Order of Patrons of Husbandry soon became known as the "Grange," its members as "Grangers." At the start, its leaders articulated a self-consciously low-profile purpose, the "social improvement and enlightenment of the agricultural classes," and they espoused mainly pious rubrics of cooperation and mutual aid. The cooperative notion itself was deeply embedded in the group; this powerful psychological tool played on the farmer's deepest urges, incorporating those frontier linkages among people that had meant so much to the original settlement of the farming territory. The Grangers thus exploited a post-Civil War version of a populist thread that had its progenitors back in the Jeffersonian and Jacksonian periods.

But farmers were also stubbornly independent, many times being unwilling to join together in anything. As one Granger admitted: "Farmers, as a general rule, are or have been the most bigoted, the most conceited, and the most prejudiced of any of the classes or professions in this country . . . as much from their isolation as anything else." There was an exclusivity in the Grangers that troubled many non-member farmers. For example, the Wisconsin organization specifically stated "mutual support in case of sickness, death or distress shall only apply . . . to bonafide members of such corporation." Worse, the national Grange was set up as a secret society by its constitution, and farmers seemed inclined to distrust it right from the start.

After 1870, though, depression settled on the farm. An already serious threat to agriculture from the Panic of 1873 was further exacerbated for the farmers by traumatic grasshopper attacks all through the Midwestern and Plains states in 1874. Lesser scourges also occurred in 1875 and 1876. Faced with these new conditions, the Grange leaders pragmatically turned the organization to a set of more aggressive, indeed, militant goals, and upon this the farmers performed a surprising flip-flop, flocking to form orders throughout the farming states. Featured was a campaign against the middleman in business and the "monopolist" in manufacturing. The Grangers assiduously lambasted the railroads and the "coal ring," but centered some of their most virulent attacks on what they came to believe was their most important target, the agricultural machinery dealer (and the manufacturer that served him).

Already there was general discontent about the low price of farm products and the high price of farm implements. The years after the Civil War had seen the farmer's plight exacerbated by money stringencies, overextended credit purchasing, and a paucity of returns. The Grange's growth kited after the Panic of 1873, which had reinforced the farmer's feelings about the conspiracy of all of those above him—the bankers, the railroaders, and, especially, the machinery manufacturers. Books and pamphlets in great volume poured out to the farmer, and letters to the editors in the newspapers of the country were planted, all decrying high prices and berating the "insatiable greed" of the implement makers and agents. "Nothing but an 'armed neutrality'—that is, the ability to meet combinations by combinations and votes—will enable farmers to treat with either manufacturers or railroad men . . . *power* is always respected; inefficiency or cowardice never," wrote one correspondent to the *Prairie*

Farmer in early 1873. Incidentally, that respected farmer paper seemed itself to lose objectivity at this time, plumping for the Granger movement in unequivocable terms. The culprits, said the *Prairie Farmer* editor, were "a horde of speculators and monopolists, who purchase at their own agreed price what is for sale, and to another horde of monopolists, who sell what the farmer needs at prices fixed by an equally potent organization." The magazine was not above personal attacks on the officers of the Eastern corporations; the "broad margins" of profit were such that "men like Fisk may waste not their own but others substance upon harlots and riotous living . . . that Vanderbilt and Scott may roll in lordly state in palace cars through provinces subdued by watered stocks. . . . " When Victoria Woodhull, the notorious advocate of "free love," showed up in the Davenport, Iowa, area as a lecturer in support of the Grangers, the local paper was thrust into a considerable moral dilemma. The editor did report that one Granger wife had no such ambivalence about Ms. Woodhull: "She got out of a sick bed to wait for her farmer at the door of Woodhull's grange, and then she raked all the hayseed out of his head with a broomhandle." The *Prairie Farmer* warned that the Grange's opponents "through narrow mindedness, or selfishness, or spite, are saying hard things about it, throwing distrust upon it, and insinuating all manner of dishonesty of purpose," and advised the order's proponents to defend it "by a strict living up to the truly noble and generous principles and objects enunciated in its constitution, and so beautifully and feelingly taught in its ritual."

The specially chosen devil to be exorcised was the middleman, in this case the implement agent out in the field, who was selling plows, harvesting machinery, cultivators, and all the other agricultural needs at retail "list" prices. The rhetoric of the Grangers was (indeed, is) ageless— it was "petty tyranny" to be forced to pay these "parasites" their "unnecessary and always extravagant exactions." The middleman "was a dead weight upon Society, adding nothing to the value of the goods and acting as a leech on the purse of the producer." "The smooth-tongued gentleman who calls on us with his matched grays and fine carriage, and persuades us that we need a reaper . . . must be paid for his visit," railed a Wisconsin newspaper in 1874. "His fancy rig and handsome salary are rung from our hard earnings." Between the cost of manufacturing and the price paid by the farmer there was believed to be an enormous markup that "goes to pay a host of useless and expensive servants, who men of any other calling would have had the economy and good sense to have discharged long ago." The Wisconsin editor then moved from rhetoric to specific figures: "Instead of buying of the manufacturer, we buy of the county agent, who gets from 20 to 50 percent; the state agent, say, 10 percent; and the general agent, 5 percent. So there is from 35 to 65 percent of what we pay swallowed up before it reaches the manufacturer." The farmer was overawed by these agents, said one of the Grange officers. "In his guileless innocence he supposed they were little below the angels in oral truth and purity, and even now it is almost enough to make one ashamed of the class he belongs to, to go downtown and see the gapeing mullet-heads that belong to our own class, standing with mouths wide open and listening to whatever dapper clerks, counter-hoppers and men who live by their wits, see proper to tell them."

Simplistic diagnosis often leads to simplistic solutions. The answer to this dilemma seemed patently clear to the agriculturalists—buy directly from the manufacturers or, to use the Granger terminology, from "first hands." Further, the farmer wanted to know just what these manufacturers' costs were, so that he could make his own judgment about what would be a "fair" profit. "The farmer does not understand this manufacturing business," the *Prairie Farmer* editor observed. "He wants light. . . . Farmers believe the prices of machinery are far too high. Will manufacturers make a clean breast of it, and tell them why they are not so?"

The manufacturer with the highest profit was Cyrus W. McCormick. The reaper was a major piece of equipment, costing at that time more than $200. Incredible tales were floated about McCormick and his company—about his supposedly intractable opposition to the Grange and particularly about the alleged large markup from the cost of manufacture of the reaper. From coast to coast, rumors that McCormick had bragged that he could manufacture the reaper for forty-five dollars (sometimes the figure quoted was thirty-seven, sometimes fifty dollars) led the naive farmer to accept some figure in this range as gospel truth and vow to fight the "reaper monopoly."

McCormick adroitly answered the Grange attacks with a conciliatory offer: "When we are approached by the Patrons' agents . . . with propositions for the purchase of our machines for cash on delivery, and in considerable numbers, we shall, of course, be pleased to meet them . . . to deal directly at our city office, or indirectly through our agents, with farmers or their agents on time. . . . " As the farmers looked at his words more closely though, they realized that McCormick had put two conditions on such sales—that they be for cash, and that they be in significant lot sizes for the orders. Even if purchases were made by the Grangers directly with Chicago, they still were given the same one price that would have been quoted by the agents themselves. "Mr. McCormick would rather lose a sale than vary the price. . . . The demand for the McCormick machinery, generally recognized as superior in service and quality, was a big factor, possibly a major factor in holding McCormick to a one-price-to-all policy," noted one historian.

But McCormick was not the only person, nor was the reaper the only machine to attract the vitriol of the farmer. The plow cost the farmer considerably less money than the reaper, but it was critically important to the farming function. It was inevitable that venom would be directed toward the plow manufacturer.[8]

CHARLES DEERE FACES THE GRANGE

The Northwestern Plow Manufacturers Association met in November 1873 to decide collectively how to respond to the demand for direct sales. After a vehement argument, a large majority of the companies in attendance resolved "that we will sell no plows to Farmers' Clubs or Granges, except at retail prices, but we recommend our agents in all localities to sell to parties wishing to buy largely for cash, at rates as much reduced as the expenses incidental to doing business will permit." In essence, all dealings had to be conducted only with the agents. Nineteen of the companies agreed without reservation, two others went along "conditionally," and seven of the members refused to sign.

The reaction was immediate. The "Plow Ring," as it quickly was dubbed, was lambasted by the Grangers for its stand, and efforts immediately began to encourage defections from among the nineteen signers. "Four of these manufacturers have agents here, and they have sold single plows for cash-in-hand to the Clubs at less than the retail cash price, and in lots at wholesale," reported one respondent to the *Chicago Tribune*. At this critical point, Charles Deere joined Cyrus McCormick in the eye of the storm. On January 17, 1874, the *Chicago Tribune* published a remarkable interview with Deere, a verbatim question-and-answer piece that was prominently featured in a major, headlined article in the influential newspaper. "Mr. Deere was quite free in communicating his views," noted the paper, and indeed he was. Deere approved of the Grange movement itself, for "rightly directed, much good will grow out of it." The agriculturalist was largely the cause of his own problem by his constant tendency toward overproduction of grain, "keeping under cultivation an immense area of land with a comparatively sparse population." In this frenzy for production, the single greatest evil of the system, Deere felt, grew out of the credit system, "the abuse of which has involved not only farmers, but others, beyond their present ability to extricate themselves."

Earlier, the prosperity of the Civil War had provided manufacturers the opening to get off the "credit treadmill," and many had seized the opportunity with alacrity. But competition in the post-war period brought back demands for "terms," and by the time of the *Tribune* interview, many farm machinery firms were again overextended on credit.

Deere elaborated on this point: "In the long period of prosperity which we have lately passed through, manufacturing, as well as farming, has been stimulated beyond legitimate demand, and the great competition and anxiety to sell have led to lengthened credits, by which the farmer has been involved in debt for much that he could more profitably have got along without." The answer, according to Deere, was the adoption of the "cash system," which he felt would lower prices. Deere seemed always to have a keen sense of balance between offering the necessary inducements for a sale and the excess of that same policy—overextending credit. As he put it in a letter to A.F. Vinton in late 1872: "While we want to do a large business and intend to do all we can to make ours so, we cannot do it by loose manner of trading or a long credit system. . . . You know well the necessity of selling to good houses, and while we do not want to miss any of them where it is desirable for us to sell, we cannot give them the old line of credit and continue in the business. We had a long letter from A. Perry & Co. a few days ago. They do not seem to think that plow and cultivator manufacturers pay for their material. . . . "

Exhibit 4–5. *"The farmers' movement in the West—meeting of the Grangers in the woods near Winchester, Scott County Illinois," sketched by Jos. B. Beale (*Frank Leslie's Illustrated Newspaper, *August 30, 1873)*

At one point in the interview, Deere seemed to depart from his traditional role as a thoroughgoing marketeer to advocate a more conservative buying posture for the farmer: "Greater care will be taken, and instead of the damage to farm machinery by exposure when not in actual use—which is now estimated to be greater than the wear, entailing an annual loss to Western farmers of millions yearly—we shall see these articles kept in good order and properly housed."

The *Tribune* reporter then questioned Deere about the agents, opening with a rather loaded allegation: "The Grangers seem to think there are too many non-producers fattening upon their substance." Deere's response was that there were too many dealers in agricultural implements in a particular place, with "undue efforts . . . to overload the purchasers, involving an unhealthy and unsafe credit-system. This is not an evil of monopoly, but of competition. . . . The present factories are all that are required to furnish the West with plows for many years." Then, asked the reporter, should not the manufacturers reduce the number of agents by "agreeing upon a fair division of territory." "That would be monopoly instead of competition," Deere replied, "and monopoly in its most offensive form. It would be an attempt to make a farmer buy one brand of plows in one county and another brand in another county." Asked by the reporter whether the farmers would be able to "dispense with the services of the middleman," Deere bluntly replied, "They cannot succeed."

He continued: "They cannot improve upon the Natural Laws of Trade. All the leading plow manufacturers . . . have frankly expressed it in their resolution to continue to do business in the old and only safe way. . . . Middlemen appear to have been the outgrowth of necessity, and have taken their position, if not on the invitation, certainly with the encouragement of farmers . . . who prefer to make their selections from stocks kept on hand for their accommodation, just when they have need of a particular implement, and who find it very handy, in case of breakage, to go to the same middleman and get the necessary repairs. . . . When the poor emigrant has secured a homestead, and, with the last vestige of his means, has put up a little shanty, he finds that he needs implements to till the soil. He goes to the middleman, tells him he has nothing left, and asks to be trusted for the things which are indispensable to his success. The middleman has confidence in his honesty, and gives him credit and, with it, a substantial start in life."

Why, queried the reporter, did Deere insist that he could not sell to purchasing agents of clubs or Granges? Deere's response focused on their lack of organization. "One of the most prominent Patrons in Iowa told us quite recently that his organization was yet in its infancy, and that it would be years before the officers could say to manufacturers: 'We will take the product of your shops and distribute them to the farmers more to their satisfaction than is now done by dealers.'" There was a need to ship in carload lots, Deere maintained, and the Granges could not gather enough orders ahead of the season to be able to make up such a lot. "A car contains 150 plows or 100 cultivators," continued Deere. "There are twenty-five principal plow shops engaged in supplying the West, and, with so many different makes of implements, it would be impossible to find in the territory of any one purchasing agent the requisite number of farmers who would unite at once upon an order for any single make of plows and even if it were possible, these Grange agents could not obtain their orders and notify us in time to get the goods into their hands for the current season's use." The reporter countered: "What objection would there be to declaring virtual free trade in plows—selling to any and every merchant who would pay for his order?" Here Deere made an ingenious comparison between the plow makers and the *Tribune*, "which by means of extended patronage in the best facilities which a large capital commands can furnish an amount of reading matter in each issue which would bankrupt a country publisher to attempt at double the subscription price." Deere thus left no doubts about the plow makers' intent to maintain the agency system.

The reporter next questioned the fixed-price system. Deere responded with a surprising view: "We have a list price, which is the maximum dealers are allowed to charge. It affords them a fair compensation . . . and allows them to deduct a percentage when they think it is to their advantage to do so. No restraint is placed upon them in this respect. They are at liberty to sell plows as cheaply as they desire or can afford to. If there were no middleman limit, extortionate charges might be made in isolated localities." The reporter probed further: "You asserted, I believe, that you could place plows in the hands of farmers through your agents . . . at lower rates than small local Granges can supply them. Have you any evidence to offer on this point?" Deere apparently felt that this question was potentially damaging, and answered with a rather general assertion: "The very fact that we send plows to regular agents in the most distant parts of the country is sufficient evidence. Our business has increased from year to year, while the small local shops, without the advantages of the accumulated capital, perfecting machinery, skilled workmen and experience can scarcely maintain an existence. If plow manufacturing on a small scale were a profitable business, would not all present shops thrive and new ones spring up in every town? The truth is, that were it not for the large factories, plows would be 20 percent higher than they are at present and the large increases are only possible through this agency system."

Citing McCormick's earlier (apparent) concessions to the Grange, the reporter asked: "Can you offer no particular inducements to Clubs or Granges desiring to buy in quantities?" Deere agreed that the company would sell to farmers who "will club together and order large lots for cash" but added that these would always be handled through his local agents, and "at rates that will compete with any establishment in the country, small or large—in other words, at the existing rates of the dealers." Some wholesale houses apparently did buy directly from Deere at the regular Deere prices, but turned around and sold to Grange members at cut-rate prices. The firm of Beach and Morse, of Chicago, for example, billed itself in 1876 as the "General Implement Supply Depot for Patrons of Husbandry," and sold the Gilpin sulky plow of Deere at fifty-six dollars (the quoted retail price was sixty-eight dollars). But these outside sales of Deere equipment were definitely the exception.

At this point the interview ended, and the reporter summed up his own views in his last sentence: "This conversation shows that the plow makers have not assumed their present position without due reflection

and thus, in their estimation, any other course would have been suicidal."

The response to the interview was prompt—and critical. One reporter
drew invidious comparisons between McCormick and Deere, noting that
"McCormick's reaper establishment has accepted the overtures of the
Granges, and will sell implements directly to the Grange agent at factory
prices for cash. The plow factories at Rock Island and Moline and
elsewhere have refused to sell except through their own agents." The
Prairie Farmer added fuel to the controversy by alleging that there was a
"company engaged in making plows and cultivators at Moline, Illinois"
that was manufacturing and selling a gang plow under its own trademark,
to be subsequently sold at list price by the company's agent, while at the
same time making exactly the same plow but without putting a trademark on it, and in turn selling the latter direct to the Granges under
another trademark. "It is . . . alleged, (we cannot vouch for the fact,
though we believe it), that the company will sell any and all patterns of
its plows, unvarnished and unstenciled, at agents' rate, allowing the
purchaser to brand them with any name he likes, so that that of the
maker is not used." The editor piously continued: "We do not relate these
cases for the purpose of making reflections upon this way of doing
business, as every reader can make his own; but to show that the
combination, the strongest of the kind ever known in this country, is
feeble, nigh unto dissolution."

Deere was stung by this last reproof, and he drafted a lengthy response
for the *Prairie Farmer's* pages. "We have not the present season, nor any
previous season, made any plows and put them out without our brand on
them as manufacturers. The shape and style of our plows are well-known
throughout the West and can be identified as well without the brand, and
we do not believe any farmer would buy them as readily without the
brand as with it, the name of the manufacturer usually being a sort of
guarantee of quality. The allusion in the article referred to is so pointed
that we cannot let it pass without this explicit denial."

Letters began pouring into the *Tribune* about both Deere's original
article and the subsequent controversy about it. At this point, dealers and
agents also wrote in, defending their own role, stressing especially their
function in providing credit to the farmer. One anonymous writer, calling
himself "middleman," added some further dimensions. "It is very seldom
that you can get a farmer to order an implement of any kind during the
winter, or until about the time he wishes to use it. In many cases he does
not know himself what new implements he will have occasion to buy,
until he is in the midst of his season's business. He often flatters himself
that he can make the old plow, or the old planter, or the old reaper, do for
another year, until a day's experience with the old implement undeceives
him. . . . There are also large numbers of farmers who make it a point not
to purchase an implement until the dealers are all well stocked up, and

they can have an opportunity to go through their warehouses and ascertain what improvements have been made, who is selling at the lowest prices, who will give the longest time, who gives the largest discount from regular price, & c. & c. & c."

This same dealer also articulately stated the agent's case against the manufacturer's perennial efforts to press the dealer to handle only his line. "Deere & Company probably makes not less than forty to fifty varieties of plows, including the different sizes, right and left hand, stirring and breaking plows, and c. & c. Twelve to twenty of these varieties are required to make up a fair allotment for a dealer doing any considerable business in most localities in Illinois. But there is no one locality that uses Deere's plow, or any other plow, exclusively. We have a mixed population, and the dealer who aspires to doing a leading business must keep the plows of two or three factories. If there is anything about which men are whimsical or capricious, it is in regard to the comparative merits of agricultural implements."

In the same issue, a farmer from Kansas—writing about "Mr. John Deere's reasons" for not selling farm implements to farmers except at retail prices—judged the Deere argument to be "a very lame affair." He was particularly exercised about some of the letters of the agents in the paper. The farmer "supposes the machine ready, wheat ripe, weather first-rate, hands all there, a few rounds, then a smashup. That is correct. Then, when the hands are all idle we trot off to town to see Mr. Middleman to get an extra to replace the broken piece. Mr. Middleman cooly informs us that the manufacturers haven't sent any, but he will order us one! We feel very much like choking the wind out of him, and the maker of it too, if we could get at him. Then we hurry off to the blacksmith's, and sometimes we get what we want by waiting our turn. If we succeed in using the machine one season without repairs, we think we are doing well; but the next harvest the machine wants more or less repairing, and we go to Mr. Middleman for some extras, when he tells us he is not selling the machine this year, and has no extras for the machine we bought of him last year, he will sell us a better thing than that ever was! Then we feel like choking him three or four times. Now, Mr. Middleman, this is not the exception, but as near to the rule as the exception."

The Illinois Grangers met in convention in December 1873, denounced the action taken by the Northwestern Plow Association, and decided on a boycott. Over the succeeding weeks, the *Prairie Farmer* reported a growing list of organizations that had agreed "to have no dealings with those plow manufacturers." By March 1874 the list was becoming very long, and the editor seemed to be a bit bored, reporting "the passage of the usual resolutions concerning the Plow Makers' Ring." (This particular list included the Fidelity Grange and the Wide Awake Grange.)

The die seemed cast for a no-holds-barred confrontation between the

Grangers and the manufacturers. Granges joined together in several states in attempts to manufacture their own implements. In Iowa, the State Grange purchased a small harvester factory and was able in 1874 to sell about 250 machines at considerably below the previous list price. In addition, several plow factories and other implement works were started, particularly after the National Grange began to support such endeavors with its own resources.

The experiment was a resounding failure. F.A. Shannon's analysis sums up the problems: "The independent competitors were not always fair in their practices, and the management of the Granges was slow in developing efficiency. Furthermore, the policy of price cutting proved a bad one. It provoked price wars in which the older and stronger companies were the better able to endure. Selling too close to cost, the cooperatives had no funds left for improvements, expansion, bad seasons, or law suits." The proprietor granges, threatened by mounting debt, disbanded rather than being sued, and the grand experiment in manufacturing faded away completely. The agency system itself survived the intense but brief Grange attack with hardly a chink in the armor of the major manufacturers. Charles Deere's thesis that the large, strong manufacturer was also the most efficient and lowest-cost producer probably had considerable merit. Defections to direct Grange selling and to price concessions to the Grange came largely from the smaller, peripheral manufacturer. The Northwestern Plow Association held firm during the period of attack—and came through it almost unscathed.[9]

WHAT DID PLOWS COST TO MANUFACTURE?

A closer look at Charles Deere's propositions in the *Chicago Tribune* article is nevertheless in order. Fortunately for our analysis, a few records on costs for the company in the nineteenth century are extant for precisely this period. Detailed costs of manufacturing for the year 1869 are available for the full plow line. Time estimates had been made for each of the operations, and a standard cost for each segment listed. In addition, the major steel components were each billed by the weight of the component in the particular plow, charged at the applicable price for that particular quality of steel. For example, Appendix exhibit 1, reproduced just as it was compiled—breaks down the construction and finishing costs for one of the company's most widely sold products, the 14-inch cast steel plow, with wooden beam.

A price list for the company in 1869 has also been preserved, allowing direct comparisons between the costs and retail "list" prices. The agents received discounts from these list prices, at figures often bargained back and forth between company and dealer. Apparently the most common dealer discount practice at that time was the 25 percent discount upon billing to the agent, with a 20 percent additional discount on the already discounted price at settlement. Another dealer discount pattern used at least some of the time was 30 percent plus 10 percent. Thus, for each of the products there was a manufacturing cost, a dealer price, and a retail list price. Three of the several dozen products sold in the year 1869, with the applicable figures, are shown in Appendix exhibit 2.

The markups of the retail list prices over manufacturing clearly vary by the type of product—the widely sold Clipper plow having a much smaller markup than the lower-volume breakers. The two alternate dealer discount patterns gave somewhat varying dealer cost, though not too wide a spread. There is evidence in these cost records that some time in the early 1870s the company considered several other dealer discount patterns. The computations shown in Appendix exhibit 3 were made, for example, for a walking cultivator, one that carried a list price of $28.50.

The Granger reasoning about price was quite unsophisticated, and one can sympathize with Charles Deere as he turned away the *Chicago Tribune* reporter's question about the price-making function in the company. What the farmers would have liked to have done was to take the "manufacturing cost" of $10.25 for the Clipper plow in 1869 (Appendix exhibit 2) and add to it only those costs directly attributable to the process of getting the plow into their hands. When the company charged the dealer $16.60 for the plow (at the discount of 25 percent plus 20 percent), this left a margin of $6.45. The company then had to subtract from this margin the administrative and selling costs for the home office, the insurance and interest costs for the period, the amortization of the physical assets (both buildings and machinery), and the costs incidental to getting the product from the factory to all of the various locations around the system. This latter freight charge was built in by Moline in order to be able to make the plows available at any point in the system at the standard retail list price (and provide the dealers all through the system a standard discount figure).

No detailed profit and loss statements or other expense accounts remain for any year of the late 1860s and the 1870s, though we do have some scraps of information about salaries paid, at least to officers. In 1871, all were to receive a salary of $1,500 each "in case the profits as shown by the balance sheet should be less than $75,000." If more than $75,000, the salaries were to be $1,750 and, if exceeding $100,000, they were to be upped to $2,000. The following year, salaries for all officers were set at a flat rate of $2,000, save for John Deere, who received a salary of $500. In 1873 James S. McKenzie, the bookkeeper, received $1,800 a year; William T. Ball, the order and shipping correspondent, received $1,500; A.L. Vinton received $2,000 as a traveling salesman in Iowa (but J. N. Leeper, who traveled Texas and Missouri, received only $1,500). J. Manwell was to receive $1,600 or $1,800 for the year, "conditional upon his success and ability." George Waters, the "copyist" (letter writer), received $1.50 per day.

The profit and loss statements included in the year-end figures are too sketchy to really understand the details of the business. To get some feeling of profitability per machine, we are driven back to using the aggregate figures of total revenues, earnings, and total "plows sold" for these years. Two cautions are in order. First, the earnings figures may be slightly understated, due to rather high arbitrary depreciation charges. Second, the "plows sold" aggregate number is just that—a total of all the machines of all kinds made during those years. Thus in this number are cast steel plows, breaker plows, cultivators, etc. No breakdown by product line is available until the year 1892. Still, these aggregate figures provide some interesting information, as shown in Appendix exhibit 4.

The year 1874–75 was the year of the height of Grange membership. Its abortive efforts at manufacturing, coupled with ineffectual internal management in many Granges and lack of external clout against its presumed antagonists soon led to a precipitous decline in membership. The *Prairie Farmer* tried to gloss over these erosions in strength, alleging in early 1877 that "the apparent shrinkage is in reality healthful." But by the late 1870s, the Grange was a shadow of itself. Other farmer organizations came along to take its place, and other Grange-influenced institutions, such as the new mail-order houses (especially Montgomery Ward), continued to flourish.[10] But the implacable antagonism of many farmers toward the railroads and the large agricultural machinery manufacturers continued to fester.

REVOLUTION IN MARKETING

The Grangers' attacks did succeed in putting renewed focus on the channels of marketing, where major innovations were occurring. "In the 1840s," Alfred D. Chandler, Jr., pointed out in *The Visible Hand*, "the traditional mercantile firm, operating much as it had for half a millenium, still marketed and distributed the nation's goods. Within a generation it was replaced in the sale of agricultural commodities and consumer goods by modern forms of marketing enterprises." The modern commodity dealer evolved in the 1850s and '60s; at the same time, the full-line, full-service wholesaler began to market most of the nation's consumer goods. Fundamentally aided by the new speed, dependability, and regularity of transportation and communication, the wholesaler could now more readily become a jobber, actually taking title to the manufacturers' goods. Midwest and Far West business burgeoned as the "Westward Movement" gathered speed after the Civil War, and many of these jobbers now located in the mushrooming cities of Chicago, St. Louis, Kansas City, Minneapolis, and Dallas.

A few manufacturers did bypass the wholesale jobber, keeping this function within the firm itself. These were likely to be organizations with technologically complex products—relatively costly and requiring demonstration, complicated servicing, and ongoing followup. The traditional middlemen, used to a generic product of simplicity, were generally unable to make the needed adjustments to meet these demands.

The machinery industries were prominent examples. Chandler cited the sewing machine industry as the first instance of this practice and the business machine industry as another pioneer. Both were producers of a complex product requiring extensive interaction between the maker and the user. I.M. Singer Company, the leader in sewing machines, moved aggressively to set up a network of company-owned branch stores, manned by full-time, salaried regional agents. The scale company, E&T Fairbanks, also followed this pattern, as later did the larger typewriter firms.

So, too, did Cyrus McCormick in selling his harvesters. Indeed, agricultural machinery fit well the rubric of Singer—that for relatively costly, complex equipment it was best to hold the jobbing function within the firm. McCormick did start out using some independent distributors outside of the Midwest and the Plains states, but by the mid-1880s had converted almost all to salaried managers and staff, selling to franchise agents, or "dealers," in the modern sense.

Charles Deere recognized this need at an early point, just after the Civil War. Indeed, he was a pioneer in an innovative variant of the manager-operated branch house. Deere's approach to the branch house was considerably more complex than McCormick's, with subtle interactions between the central organization and the branch heads that carried important implications for later management policy in regard to decentralization.[11]

DEERE'S INNOVATION IN
THE BRANCH HOUSE

Marketing and distribution functions stand out prominently in the first thirty-odd years of Deere's existence. Throughout this period the basic way of doing business had been essentially the same, though, of course, the intensity and geographical sweep did change markedly over this time. The company had sent its own sales personnel—the "travelers"—throughout the territory to visit agricultural implement dealers. These retail outlets, which ranged from hardware dealers to provision houses and a wide range of other local emporia, at first had very little link to, or loyalty to, the company. As relations expanded over the years, the alliances became more and more interdependent, and there finally grew up a very substantial retail-house bond with the company. Still, the dealer of this period was an independent, tied to the company only by his daily business relationships, trust, and loyalty built up by a series of mutually beneficial transactions in selling Deere products.

Exhibit 4–6. *George Vinton, the company's first general agent, demonstrating Deere equipment, June 12, 1870 (Deere Archives)*

In interacting with the group, which by 1869 included several thousand dealers, the company kept its marketing organization centralized, operating out of Moline. Travelers might be based in a town considerably distant from Moline, in effect working out of their own "offices." Still, the organizational pyramid peaked directly up to Moline, with George Vinton as the company's "general agent" (the title officially established by the bylaws of incorporation in 1868).

Deere & Company thus was a highly centralized organization throughout its first thirty years of business life. The territory was the nation itself, but the reins were always held by the small group in Moline. Charles Deere had the title of vice president; his father was titular president until his death in 1886, but there was little doubt in anyone's mind, inside the company or outside, that Charles was chief executive officer. Stephen Velie, with the title of secretary, was the chief financial officer, as well as the arbiter of all major purchasing. Velie was Charles Deere's closest confidant, a complement to the latter by personality and training—Deere the entrepreneurial marketer and organization builder, Velie the judicious, cautious numbers-oriented financier, lending stability to the wide-ranging CEO. In the factory, Gilpin Moore was superintendent of iron works, and also an inventor of note; Charles Nason was superintendent of wood work and the paint shop, doubling also as the expert in water and steam power. With George Vinton as general agent,

these five people (excluding John Deere) made up the central management of the firm for most of the second half of the nineteenth century.
Only Moore, of the five, was not linked to the John Deere family by birth
or marriage.

In the earlier years, a full-scale centralization of authority and responsibility made eminent sense. Though Deere & Company was in the process
of becoming one of the largest plow manufacturers in the country, it was
still a relatively small firm as contrasted, for example, with the railroads.
The span of control for Charles Deere, as chief executive officer, was
narrow, the affiliations with financial institutions, etc., relatively simple
for Velie. But the numbers of people out in the field, in the marketing
organization, had grown quite large, taxing Vinton's control. In 1869
Charles Deere made a critically important decision—to set up a separate,
distinct branch house in Kansas City. Four more sales branches followed
in the period 1869–89. These five cities—Kansas City, St. Louis, Minneapolis, Council Bluffs/Omaha, and San Francisco—mirror significantly
the agricultural growth of the post-Civil War period for the country.
Further, they bring into the Deere story some important characters in the
panoply of players—strong-willed, independent men of the likes of Alvah
Mansur from St. Louis, Charles C. Webber from Minneapolis, Lucius
Wells from Council Bluffs, the Hawley brothers from San Francisco, and
others.

The entrepreneurs for the first branch, organized in Kansas City in 1869,
were Charles Deere and Alvah Mansur; the new company was to be called
Deere, Mansur & Co. The organizational vehicle was a "co-partnership,"
with the parties of the first part being John and Charles Deere, Stephen
Velie, George Vinton, Gilpin Moore, and Charles Nason (in other words, the
directors of the parent company in toto). The party of the second part was
Mansur.

Alvah Mansur was born in Lowell, Massachusetts, in 1833 and had
come to Moline prior to the Civil War. After first working for awhile in
the hardware business, he joined John and Charles Deere in the plow
company in 1859. During the Civil War he had been a first lieutenant
with the 19th Illinois Volunteer Infantry Regiment and after the war had
gone to the Colorado Territory for "mining interests" in Central City.
Just how he and Charles Deere came back together in 1869, and why it
was decided at that time to enter into the co-partnership for a branch, is
not clear as no correspondence remains of this particular period. The R.G.
Dun & Co. correspondent in Kansas City did report the formation
approvingly, commenting on Mansur: "Age 40–45, married. Hab., Char.
& capac. good—attent. & hons. Prosp. good." The next line might give us
momentary pause, for it said "branch of the firm at Mobile, Ala." (The
correspondent later caught his error, crossed it out, and substituted
"Moline, Ill.")

The partnership agreement provided for a capital of $20,000, to be

Exhibit 4–7. Left, *Charles C. Webber, a grandson of John Deere, manager of the Minneapolis branch and a Deere & Company director from 1886 to 1944, ca. 1890; right, Alvah Mansur, Charles Deere's partner in the first two Deere branches at Kansas City and St. Louis and in Deere & Mansur, the planter company, ca. late 1880s. (Deere Archives)*

shared equally by the two parties (though only $12,000 was paid in, with the amount carried on the Deere & Company books being $5,750). The term of the partnership was to be five years, but in fact it continued until October 1, 1875, when the company was reorganized under the same name. In this reorganization, the capital was reduced to $10,000 and Charles S. Wheeler became the resident manager. Wheeler was to share one-quarter of the profits, but to furnish no capital. At this point the parties of the first part became only Charles and John Deere and Velie, taking one-third of the $10,000 in capital and one-quarter of the profits; Mansur furnished the remaining two-thirds of the capital and took half the profit.

With Wheeler now assuming day-to-day oversight, Mansur decided to move to St. Louis in 1875 to set up a second co-partnership with Deere & Company—the firm's second sales branch. Here Mansur contributed $10,000 of the $15,000 total capital, John and Charles Deere and Velie providing the remaining $5,000. The two co-partners then hired L.B. Tebbetts as manager; Mansur was to take five-twelfths of the profits, Deere & Company four-twelfths, and Tebbetts the remaining three-twelfths. The R.G. Dun & Co. correspondent in St. Louis was, if anything, even more positive about Mansur and his new venture: "M is an active, shrewd man of undoubted integ. & is in good circums. The house will take a prominent position, has command of all the resources required for success & will doubtless do a lar. bus."

St. Louis was a longstanding Deere territory; the Mississippi River conduit between Moline and the downriver hub made this so right from the start. For about ten years prior to the agreement of 1875 the company had a close relationship with William Koenig & Co., a hardware and agricultural equipment jobbing firm in that city. At some point during this relationship, Deere actually had invested $10,000 in Koenig. This interest ceased when Mansur and Tebbetts began their operation in 1876.

On-the-spot operating management differed between the two new houses, in ways that were not always immediately apparent. Wheeler in Kansas City and Tebbetts in St. Louis were the full-time managers and were given some ownership interest in the business. Mansur, being physically located in St. Louis, tended to exercise more authority there at the start. He also owned the largest bloc of stock in Kansas City; at first, with Wheeler in charge, he left most of the daily decision-making to him. But Wheeler's interests were bought out in 1882 (equally by Alvah Mansur and Deere & Company) and G.W. Fuller was brought in as manager with no ownership interest. Mansur at this point took a more active role in Kansas City, too, and clearly now was the chief officer in both places.

Mansur was a combative, intensely competitive man, particularly in his battles with other firms in the trade. A vignette will illustrate. In 1877 a major industrial exposition was held in Kansas City, and Mansur entered the "Cortland Platform Spring Wagon," a two-horse spring wagon he was selling out of the Kansas City branch. Smith & Keating, a Kansas City competitor, sold the "Bain" wagon, and entered it in not only the two-horse spring competition, but also the one-horse spring and the two-horse farm wagon contests. Smith & Keating won in the last two judgings, but lost to Mansur in the two-horse spring. Flush with its double victory, the Kansas City firm put out a circular to the trade claiming the Bain had won "the first and only premium on wagons." Mansur was outraged and immediately wrote Smith & Keating, demanding a printed circular retraction, "proof of such circular to be submitted to us *for our approval by tomorrow.*" Predictably, Smith & Keating refused, but in their return letter obliquely admitted their deception. "Your insulting letter received. By re-reading our card we see that it might be misconstrued if a party desired to do so." Calling the Mansur claim a "technicality," they threatened retaliation. "If you provoke it, expect to hear very unpleasant truths. We do not like to put in print such matters as your St. Louis experience with Joliet people, or refer to Moline failure. We intend, however, if attacked, to teach you to behave yourself. . . ."

By now Mansur was angry, and he immediately put out a circular recording the actual judges' votes on the two-horse spring wagon, in the process castigating Smith & Keating by name. "We dislike personalities, and have requested Messrs. Smith & Keating to 'correct' their statement themselves, but they have not complied. . . . Honorable dealers may form their opinion of a firm, who, apparently lacking confidence in their goods . . . endeavor to do so by trickery and deception."

Not to be outdone, the Kansas City people put out a monster circular, printing their own original claim, Mansur's first letter, their reply, and Mansur's circular. Last, they quoted their own judges' words and an affidavit from the secretary of the exposition to the effect that "the Bain was given the FIRST and only Premium given on *both* Farm and Spring Wagons." It would have taken more of a grammarian than the usual equipment dealer to catch the nuances of the emphasis of the word "both." At this point Mansur wrote Deere that he felt it best to "drop the matter"—he apparently concluded that any further communications to the trade would increase the stature of the double-winner Bain over Mansur's single prize. But Mansur was unbowed, adding a note to Deere admitting that "while we were about it, we made it as strong as we thought the circumstances warranted."

After the Civil War, agriculture in the northern Plains states burgeoned, and they became a major agricultural region. Deere's links there had been with individual dealers until 1880, when Charles Deere himself entered into a partnership in that year with W.J. Dean, who ran an agricultural implement house in Minneapolis under the name Christian & Dean. The new partnership was an equal one, with each man putting $10,000 in the business. A year later, on January 1, 1881, Dean was joined by Charles C. Webber, son of Christopher C. Webber, Charles Deere's brother-in-law and some-time partner in the 1850s. There was some confusion between the two names, even after the father died in 1865. Charles felt so, signing a letter to his mother in 1876, just before he graduated from Lake Forest Academy, "from your aff'ct son, Charles— C C Webber which is the C C Webber best" (subsequently, he was known throughout his adult life as "C.C."). Charles began working for grandfather John Deere as mail boy in 1877 and soon was sent to the field as a traveling man. Then came the assignment in 1881 to Minneapolis. A new agreement was made with Dean at this point; the document is missing, so we depend on the manuscript notes of P.C. Simmon, the company's secretary during the early 1900s. "Deere & Company took over the business, furnishing $20,000 capital. Mr. Dean was made Manager, and under his contract, deposited $10,000 with Deere & Company as a guarantee fund for the success of the business to the extent of being chargeable with one-half of any net loss. He was to receive one-half of the net profits."

Lacking any further explanation, this seems a rather draconian arrangement for Dean—his capital contributed was presumably $20,000, but half of it was to be treated as a drawing account, in effect. This arrangement only lasted for two years, however, and in December 1883 the capital of the branch house was increased to $60,000, with a more permanent arrangement in terms of ownership and management. There were three

Exhibit 4–8. *"The grasshopper plague in Iowa—farmers of Wright County driving away the pest by burning straw covered with green grass," sketched by Howard Purcell* (Frank Leslie's Illustrated Newspaper, *August 22, 1874*)

parties to the arrangement—Charles Deere and Stephen Velie took one-third of the business, Dean and C. C. Webber each another one-third.

Simmon tried to be diplomatic in picturing this new basis: "The management was divided between Mr. Dean and Mr. Webber." In truth, Webber took over from this point and remained the operating head of the Minneapolis branch for more than sixty years. During most of this period, from 1886 until his death in 1944, he was also a director of the parent company—a man of tremendous influence on the whole organization, with more than half a century of major management involvement. His influence on the Twin Cities was also notable over these years, with his particular interest the navigational development of the upper Mississippi River. (His mother, though, felt Minneapolis to be a wicked big city. She cautioned Charles in 1893, at the point when Dean left the firm and it was reincorporated as Deere & Webber Co.: "I cannot keep the thought down that your temptations will be increased in a measure C.V. [Charles Velie] is when in Minneapolis. The wine bottle circulates freely, and they think nothing of it. . . . It is my prayer that you be delivered from temptation." She needed no such caveats, though, for C.C. Webber was always the exemplary paragon in his business and personal life, a great influence on all his associates and friends.

The trade in the Plains states west of the Missouri River noticeably picked up in the 1870s, and dealers in this area were given the advantage of carload rates to Council Bluffs by January 1881. In that same year, a co-partnership was established for a branch house there, with a total capitalization of $45,000. The first one-third was taken by the three Moline Deere executives, Charles and John Deere and Stephen Velie. The second one-third was taken by another Moline company, the Moline Wagon Company (Morris Rosenfield was its president, and C.A. Benser was also involved). The remaining one-third was taken by the man who was to become the local manager, Lucius Wells. The company adopted the name Deere, Wells & Company. Wells remained as its operating head until 1899, whereupon the branch was moved across the Missouri River to Omaha.

The "California trade" had always been rather unusual, even back in the days when John Deere had split up with Robert Tate, and the latter had taken the California business of the firm. Sales there began to be substantial at about the midpoint of the Civil War, and by the end of the conflict the Deere name was widely known throughout the great agricultural fields of the state. Marcus C. Hawley & Co., a large San Francisco hardware and agricultural house, was the Deere link to California. In a large advertisement in the *California Farmer* just at the end of the war, Hawley featured the company: "Plows! Plows! We have for sale the celebrated Deer's [sic] Moline Plows." (Several years of working with the company hadn't improved their spelling!)

The Hawley jobbing link continued apace, to the mutual advantage of both parties, until 1889. At that point Charles Deere and his associates decided to make San Francisco the location of the next branch of the company. The Deere Implement Company was incorporated under the laws of California, with a capital of $200,000—Deere taking $80,000, Hawley $100,000, and Fredrick W. Vaughan (the manager) the remaining $20,000. Half of the existing Hawley building on Market Street was to be devoted to the branch.

Thus, by 1889, Deere & Company had its five key branches in place—the original one at Kansas City, followed by St. Louis, Minneapolis, Council Bluffs/Omaha, and San Francisco. The distances from Moline varied, the territories certainly were wide ranging, the personnel involved gave each individual entity its own special character. Nevertheless, the essential concepts of the branch houses were the same among all five. An appreciation of the underlying philosophy behind this branch house development is critical to an understanding of the company.[12]

DECENTRALIZED OPERATION, COORDINATED CONTROL

Tension between management centralization and management decentralization has widely characterized American corporations. A company's strength often is determined by its ability to develop the aggressiveness, independence, and autonomy of a decentralized operation—each decisionmaker feeling like he is running his own show—while at the same time retaining the kind of centralized coordination and control that allows the whole to be the strongest entity. In recent years, patterns of decentralization have given profound emphasis to individual initiative and intra-organizational competitiveness. But nineteenth-century management was most often characterized by centralization; not until the concepts of structure developed by Alfred P. Sloan and Donaldson Brown at General Motors Corporation in the early 1920s (when they coined the terms "decentralized operation and coordinated control") did the philosophy of decentralization truly come into its own.

Deere & Company's history of grappling with these concepts has been instructive. In the very early branch-house years, the late 1870s to the early 1890s, the company haltingly introduced incipient decentralization. All of these five early branches were hybrids. Each had shared ownership, with Charles Deere and Stephen Velie taking central roles for the company side, and with strong local owner-managers owning the addition segments. Four of the five branches began as co-partnerships; only San Francisco was a corporation from the start. There were various ownership and capital changes over these early years in all five, but their essential hybridized character was present for all. They owed allegiance to the company, taking orders and directions from Moline, yet at the same time they were individual, indeed entrepreneurial, businesses, taking an additional set of orders and directions from a manifestly independent local manager who considered himself in every respect the "chief executive officer."

The R.G. Dun & Co. correspondents, as perceptive as they usually were, could not quite fathom the relationship. Over and over, in their reports on all of the branch houses, they reiterated the theme of home office dominance. "Resp. rests with the main house," noted the Kansas City man, time and again. The St. Louis correspondent agreed: "The respon. of the concern rests upon Deere & Co. (a corporation) of Moline, Ills. . . . being respons. for all the debts of this concern." The St. Louis man expanded on this in a subsequent report: "In some respects their bus. is in some aspects similar to Com^n agents—they have no special time to pay for the goods they acquire . . . they do not require any loc. capt. . . . "

The Dun reporters were accurate in a narrow sense—the Moline parent would stand behind its branches financially and, being itself of impeccable credit stature, the credit rating of the branch was confirmed in the process. In the final analysis, this was the "bottom line" for a credit correspondent. But the credit company obviously had only an incomplete understanding of how this financial accountability would be sorted out when it came to the four branches that were co-partnerships. In the event of a forced liquidation (an unlikely event, to be sure), all the partners were liable for the debts—and a creditor would have to look to all partners in some (probably messy) combination for restitution.[13]

BRANCH INFLUENCE ON
PRODUCT DEVELOPMENT

A useful place to start understanding branch-home office interactions is with the product itself. Here the company's approach had been highly centralized, for the product line itself was conceived, engineered, and manufactured at the Moline factory. Gilpin Moore and his manufacturing and engineering associates were the prime innovators. Moore himself was the company's inventor par excellence in the nineteenth century. By the time of his retirement in the 1890s, he held thirty-one patents in his own name, together with four others jointly held. Most of these were significant, commercially viable new ideas; in particular, his famous Gilpin sulky plow, first built in 1875, was nationally renowned. It was not the first successful sulky (riding) plow in the country (despite apocryphal stories by Deere historical buffs), for others had come from different companies in the 1860s. Because of its practical design and excellent construction, however, the Gilpin sulky plow had an instantaneous success; by the late 1870s it was one of the largest-selling sulky plows in the country. The sulky made Gilpin Moore's name, though a number of his other patents were just as innovative.

In the early 1880s, Moore became unhappy about royalties from one of his earlier patents, and he decided to leave Deere & Company. The first inkling was the sudden appearance of a printed handbill from a newly formed "Rock Island Plow Co., successors to B.D. Buford & Co." Listed prominently as a member was Gilpin Moore, "who, for the past twenty years, has been superintendent of Deere & Co.'s Moline Plow Works." A colleague of Charles Deere, upset, sent the handbill to him with Moore's name underlined, and asked: "How is this?" When, a few days later, the *Davenport Daily Democrat* obliquely mentioned that "a gentleman from Moline who has had ten years' experience in the Deere Plow Company has been engaged to take the general superintendence of the works," Charles Deere went into action. Terribly upset by the thought of losing one of his key colleagues, he persuaded Moore to return, but not before personally purchasing those shares in the Davenport company which Moore had already contracted to buy.

Despite the centralized control of innovation, there was a natural synergy between home office and field regarding product development. The branch managers and their respective travelers knew the operations of their own territories and could readily sense both the strengths and weaknesses of the existing line and the need for a new product. Field tests were often arranged by branch managers, who knew the right farmers to use. Webber was especially keen for new product development, often sending pointed, explicit letters forward to "Uncle Charles," his usual salutation, and to the others at the Moline office. In 1893, for example, the home office decided to make the Gazelle gang plow with only 12-inch bottoms. Webber fired back a letter: "Our trade is on the 14-inch gang, that is the size of bottom that people want. . . . Crucible cast steel shares can be used in less than half of our territory only. We only send soft gangs, so to speak, to a few places in Minnesota, and the territory where we can send them in Dakota seems to be growing less every year. . . . Why do you set the beams 13 inches apart on a 12 inch plow? That is just what we used to try to avoid by setting the beams 12 inches apart, and putting on a 13-inch bottom, and we did not find that experiment to work very well." Webber then continued in his typically pungent way: "We feel that you are rather ignoring our territory in getting up this gang plow. We repeat that we doubt the advisability of putting these bottoms closer together, and our traveling men who have had a good deal of experience in the field with gang plows are of the opinion that it would be rather a dangerous experiment."

Such letters and admonitions from the field did influence product development, but it is clear from this correspondence that the main thrust for the product was centered strongly in Moline. First, Moore and his associates were an able team, both innovative in regard to new ideas and practical in respect to implementation. The dominant role of the Moline group in product development was widely recognized around the system. Webber himself put it succinctly in the late 1880s: "We all look to the factory as having more or less claim on us for the future."

Moore and his associates were, in turn, kept on their toes not so much by the branch managers and the rest of the field as by Charles Deere and Stephen Velie. By the heyday of the branch houses in the 1880s and '90s, Deere and Velie had been operating top management men for a number of years, and they had garnered a remarkable amount of technical knowledge about the product. Indeed, both Deere and Velie, though never trained in engineering, were able to describe explicitly to patent attorneys, to Gilpin Moore, to outsiders the more technical aspects of the products. In 1889, a new patent was being sought, and Charles Deere took exception to the way the patent attorney was handling the case. "We want the patent strong enough to keep others from imitating and using the construction. . . . While this is not a great order of invention, it is an economical and simple device," Deere wrote. He went on to describe precisely the way he wanted the patent attorney to change the wording.

Velie was a stickler for product quality. For example: "I have noticed that whenever we have departed from the principle or practice of using the best stock of its kind to save money on first cost, it has been at the cost of reparations and annoyances that are not fully compensated for by the money saved. It is hardly safe to say that because we have saved $3,000 or $4,000 in the cost of cultivator shovels by buying a cheaper steel this year and at a cost of less than $1,000 in additional breakages that therefore we are $2,000/$3,000 better off than we otherwise would have been. The value of a reparation is commensurate with the extent of the savings, and the money that is saved at its expense is by no means clear gain but on the contrary may be more than absorbed in contingent disadvantages."

Both Velie and Deere did a great deal of traveling (thanks to the excellent railroad networks in their territories), and their on-the-spot investigations in regard to quality and other features of the product were invaluable. On one of Velie's trips to Minneapolis, he found some poorly made plows. "The firm here will ship you today by express two moldboards that are very imperfectly hardened, as you will see on arrival. These are about as bad as any we have ever sent out and though there have not been many other complaints, it looks as if we ought to make such tests as will prevent *any* such going out."

Deere was in the field often, and his evident delight in selling the product gave him a natural rapport with the travelers and the branch managers. Stephen Velie was a fortunate counterpoint for him here. Velie's caution made him a watchdog on expenses, inventories, and the other specifics inherent in a centralized control system. His close personal relationship with Deere allowed them to talk through differences in a frank and open way, resulting in a melding of their philosophies. "I sometimes take advantage of your absence to give my views more in detail than I can at any other time," wrote Velie on one of Charles Deere's frequent absences, "and consider it good to you and to me that you have them."

Velie continued with an issue that was on his mind: "Sometimes a good deal of money is made by taking great risks but it seldom happens that any honor or profit comes to a manufacturer in bringing a new departure or anything not proven comparatively profitable.... It scares me—my living depends upon the success of this Company—yours does not, and that is why I evince the most timidity. We have always been cautious of too radical changes and of new implements but always put out too many of the new article rather than too few." He continued his concern about what he felt was an excessively large product list in another letter to Deere: "In the conduct of our business in the past we have, I believe, been more disposed to cater to the wishes of our customers as made known to us through our own travelling men and those of the branch-house than perhaps any of our competitors, and the result is that our list of plows is far more numerous in proportion than that of any of our competitors.... Perhaps by reason of this catering to customers wishes we have been enabled to take a larger volume of business than we otherwise would have done, with the drawback however of having to carry a larger stock, but on the whole we have thought that our course has been the correct one; possibly carried to excess in some direction." Velie was practical enough to realize how difficult it was to cut the product list. He wrote in the late 1880s: "In order to decrease our list numerically it is necessary that the new series *have all the merits* and *all the talking points of the old*. Otherwise we doubtless find our list increased instead of diminished."[14]

SCHEDULING AND PRICING: COMPANY VS. BRANCH

If the branches accepted the product line more or less as planned by Moline, they had a great deal to say about the number of plows and other equipment to be sent to them. The inevitable push-and-tug between factory and field about quantity was present even in early branch-house days. The branch managers were thoroughgoing marketeers, and they wanted as much equipment in their hands as might remotely be demanded by the customers in that period. No good marketing man ever wants to be caught short. A letter from Mansur to Charles Deere in the mid-1880s was typical: "I hope you won't fail to push work on those 100 Columbias as we need every one of them *now* and we are *holding some plow shipments* for them to make up. You should also *start* another 100 Columbias." Wells was blunt to Charles Deere on the home-office factory schedules (in a letter in the early 1890s): "We are not getting the goods as our trade requires them. . . . Every day or two we get a letter from your office advising that you cannot fill orders because we already have these articles on hand. . . . We haven't anything of this kind. . . . Your office seems to have the idea that we are not sending out goods from here. . . . We think we are judges of the requirements of this trade. . . . "

The branches not only wanted a full stock on hand, they wanted it on their own terms. For pricing policy, the branch houses were in an ambivalent position. The marketeer tends to stress volume, and therefore wants a "competitive" price—that is, the lowest one possible. Central management, on the other hand, is more concerned about factory costs and the need to maintain margins. Both groups are, of course, aware of break-evens, overall profitability, etc. Nevertheless, tensions over price between field and home office are inevitable—and healthy, if managed properly.

The company, as one of the founding and leading members of the Northwestern Plow Association, was committed to the goal of "price discipline"—in effect, an industry-wide price structure. This cartelization of the price-making function was not an easy thing to maintain—the manufacturers themselves more than occasionally allowed (or even abetted) surreptitious shaving of posted prices. By the early 1870s the manufacturers were coming under increasing fire from Grangers for a whole set of alleged wrongs, centralized price making being one.

Managing branch-house pricing turned out to be quite difficult. Moline did establish each year a common price list for all products—printed and distributed widely—presumably to be applied uniformly throughout the system. The company also printed a standard contract for the branches to use with their own dealers. The wording left no doubt about the home-office intention, as this example from 1879 shows: "In consideration of the exclusive sale of the DEERE CULTIVATOR in our place for the coming season's trade, and your efforts to establish a uniform retail price on them among dealers, we hereby promise and agree to hold the retail price uniformly at $25.00 and in no case to sell for less than $23.00 spot cash." There were constant pressures from the field, however, and the posted price was always eroding at one place or another. Dealers would often shave prices in the face of local competitive pressures. Deere's popular Gilpin sulky plow was being purchased so widely that it was hard for the factory to keep up with orders, and in 1876 the company felt the need to put out this circular to dealers: "Occasional complaints reach us from various localities regarding the cutting of prices of the Gilpin, and in view of this we would suggest a propriety of holding to our retail list as near as possible, as our present orders are much in excess of our most sanguine expectations. . . . This leads us to the conclusion that our customers need not fear the carrying over of any of the Gilpins." George Fuller, the branch manager in Kansas City beginning in 1882, put the situation there succinctly (in a letter to Charles Deere in 1889): "I am willing to co-operate in anything that would have any tendency to stiffen prices. . . . Goods are sold in this market lower than they should be . . . too many houses located here and too many kinds of goods upon the market for sale . . . no confidence between the dealers, each being afraid of each other. Then again, we have a line of cheaper goods on sale here, which the dealers use as a club and a leverage for the forcing down of prices. . . . I have no doubt but what if the Bradley people, Parlin & Orendorff, Moline Plow Co., Rock Island Plow Co., Eagle Plow Co., Standard Implement Co. and ourselves took a firm stand with reference to prices, we would sell as many goods as we are now selling, and at quite a little better prices than we are now getting. But there seems to be no friendly co-operation among the dealers here, as to prices; each is afraid of the others."

Sometimes the competition among local dealers became cutthroat. In 1893, for example, which was another depression year, Lucius Wells was so frustrated with the "implement street walkers," as he called them, that he cried to Moline for help. "The only way they can be managed is to bring a pressure, or some influence on their principals—the eastern manufacturers." This would have been a hard thing to effect, though, for each of Deere's peers in the Northwestern Plow Association was faced with deteriorating business and had to balance "statesmanship" at the association level with self-protection in the field.

Charles Deere often was called as final arbiter, and of course had the authority himself to modify arrangements. S.W. Ganz, one of the travel-

ers in the 1870s and '80s, finally wrote Deere: "He positively says that he
will not handle Plows next season if he has to pay Association prices.
Should you make any arrangements with him, I would suggest that you
compel him to hold the retail prices up, as we have a man at Yorkville
who will stand no cutting."

Price relations with the branch houses themselves were also complicated. Since Deere owned significant segments of all five of the branch
houses, Moline presumably could dictate the pricing policy at the branch
level. But, of course, the branch houses were not company houses. They
were, in fact, set up so as to deal at arm's length with Moline on orders,
which once made were carried on the branch's accounting sheets. Thus a
branch was a separate, semi-autonomous entity, buying product from
Moline and selling it to the dealers in its own territory. The managers
were individualists who owned significant pieces of their businesses and
did not take kindly to dictation by central management.

Mansur was prickly about almost all company-branch relationships.
There had been a history of acrimony dating back to the renewal of the
Kansas City co-partnership in 1879. Charles Deere and Stephen Velie had
proposed to Mansur that Wheeler be given some ownership interest.
Mansur balked and wrote them, complaining about his own profit share
(after Wheeler had been promised a quarter share of profits): "As I told
you, I think he will accept a smaller interest or may consent to a salary
and percentage." Velie chose to interpret Mansur's letter as a threatened
break in the partnership and sent a hard-bargaining letter in return:
"While we have no doubt that personal friendship and confidence will
continue to have with us its due weight in all our business transactions,
we cannot see it to our own interests to accept your proposition. I have
inferred that nothing but an apprehension of the future in the plow trade
would lead you to propose so radical a change in our business relations.
Our faith—and your lack of it—is doubtless the principle [*sic*] cause of
this difference in our propositions."

Mansur, shocked at this, wrote back immediately: "I take it that your
letter of 19th inst. has not been written without some care and fore-
thought, nor without the full knowledge and approval of the majority of
your Company, so that it may be taken as the matured view of Deere &
Co. Premising this, I have to say in answer that much as I regret this new
revelation, I am of course glad to be warned of your true position and
feelings relative to our future connection. Stripped of its generalities,
what you say is that if you can see a larger profit by discontinuing your
connection with us, you will do so. I do not for a moment complain of
this, for as you say, 'tis purely business. I had not, however . . . arrived at
this purely business standpoint . . . of my own volition. But now I am
forced by your action to take this same position and to stand henceforth
squarely upon your own platform." Mansur was forced to back down,
though. Hearing rumors that Wheeler was contemplating the formation

of his own plow house if not allowed some ownership, he finally agreed to the new capital arrangement.

By 1883 competition was becoming heavy in Mansur's territory and he complained, "We have already been compelled to sell *below cost* to meet our *competitors.*" When the 1882–83 price list was submitted to him by Moline, he rejected several list prices out-of-hand: "We leave *blank* the price for Queen cult³—we need lower prices." The next year, 1884, Moline proposed to make the discount 45 percent, 9 percent at settlement, and 5 percent additional if cash was paid by July 1. Mansur countered with a proposal for 45, 9, and 5 percent on most of the line, and an additional 5 percent over and above for the Texas plow and breakers (as well as an extra 5 percent for cash payment by July 1). He added, almost threateningly, "Anything short of this, I do not think under all the circumstances we would be willing to accept and even then *there will be many trades which we cannot reach*. There is need for dispatch in this matter so we can post our travelers at once."

Perhaps because of the belligerency of this letter, Moline decided to grant these new terms, writing Mansur: "This is a 5% better disc. all around than last year and 5% + 5% better than on breakers." Thus the Gilpin sulky plow, which carried an approximately sixty-five-dollar retail price tag (depending on the numbers of extra shares), was billed to Deere, Mansur at just over thirty-two dollars, subject to 9 percent and 5 percent at settlement.

The next year feelings were still ruffled. Mansur wrote Moline: "In reply to your 17th, if the 'items of difference' you refer to are those occurring in the St. Louis ofc., we are glad to learn that you are willing to discuss them at all—something that you have heretofore throughout the entire year persistently declined to do in any spirit. The same is very nearly true in reference to the list of prices, terms & c. which you sent up and have since insisted as being a contract, notwithstanding we have repeatedly declined to agree to it. Do you think it any fairer to assume that *you* are all right and *we* all wrong?" By 1888 prices had softened further. Mansur wrote Deere in May of that year: "The plow order from Colorado Springs was taken by one of our travellers at 40% disct., which we refused, and was taken by Parlin & Orendorff at same disct. & filled by them." The situation worsened over the remainder of the year and Mansur penned a discouraged note in December: "Trade is dull here and collections harder than hard—never knew them as bad since the grasshopper year '73. . . . Prices are lower & terms are longer than ever and there will be no money in the biz. this year."

When one branch house was able to negotiate special arrangements on these prices and terms, the other branch houses would learn about them via the grapevine—and then demand equal treatment. Lucius Wells wrote Charles Deere in early 1888: "After your departure from the Wagon Co.'s office, when I was there a few days since, I had some talk with Messrs.

Good and Atkinson regarding prices, and asked them to make us the same figures that had been made Deere, Mansur & Co. They gave no satisfaction, and rather refused to make an answer, but I thought they would give the matter a consideration and would advise us, but we have heard nothing from them at all regarding the matter. Isn't there some way that this matter can be fixed?" Webber apparently enjoyed more discretion than the others in regard to pricing, reporting, for example, on January 1889, "We are holding about the same as other standard concerns on plows and cut to meet outside competition where necessary."[15]

WARRANTIES AND REPAIRS

If prices could be softened by a branch manager through pressure on the home office, the same process could be applied to more discretionary issues—warranties, repairs, and other policies involving a large amount of judgment in application. A striking example, embodying the essence of the nineteenth-century issues of decentralization, came in a letter from Mansur to Moline in 1885. On the letter itself are handwritten replies by the Moline executives. Each of these is repeated in full here. Mansur wrote on August 4, 1885:

Deere & Co, Moline, Il

Dear Sirs,

The attitude which you take on question of repairs is one which does not fit our case at all.

There must be some lea-way [sic] allowed a jobbing house in their question of repairs, and they must have some independence of action, no matter how closely they may confine themselves to the letter of the warranty. In other words, there are cases where we must settle with a customer, and must settle then and there, allowing for repairs, where it is utterly impossible to obtain the broken parts claimed to be defective.

What we claim is, in such cases as this, we must be the absolute judge in the matter and not compelled to communicate with you before we can decide.

There must be some change in the methods now employed by you on this question with us.

Think this matter over, and try to put yourselves in our place; and see if we cannot arrive at some arrangement that will be equitable and satisfactory to both parties.

Yours truly,
Deere, Mansur Co.

James T. Francis, the office manager in Moline, penned on the letter a proposed reply, sending it on to Charles Deere:

In these exceptional cases where you deem it policy to make an allowance, where defective parts can't be produced or in other cases where you make a "policy" allowance, since you share the benefit in holding the customers, etc., suppose you share the expense and we go halvers on such allowances. How does this strike you?

Mr. Deere, What do you think of the above? If it costs *them* money to make these allowances it puts them on their guard.

                                                                                                          Francis

Charles Deere's instincts seemed always to lie in part with the field; Francis reported his reply in a further note to Velie, "Mr. Deere says okay and to refer to you." Four days later the answer came back from Velie, again written right on the original Mansur letter:

We must insist on some such check. We must insist on a proper voucher for a repair under warranty and where a new price is supplied *no allowance made unless the old one is produced.*

The dealer who objects to this is too sensitive to be honest. Some dealers are too liberal when it comes to giving away other people's goods. We have a right to see the defective part in order to trace the fault and remedy it—this position is a finality, with any other discussion closed.

                                                                                                          SHV

Encapsulated in this one set of responses are the differing perspectives of the four principals. Mansur wanted independence and personal discretion on warranties—to be able to cater to a demanding customer at his own discretion. Most of all, he wanted speed—to be able to make the decision on the spot, without having to refer it by mail back to Moline. Mansur put his argument bluntly: "We must be the absolute judge." The compromise proposal of Francis appeals to the vested interest of both parties, and phrases the proposal as a question—how does it "strike you" to go "halvers?" Deere saw the quid pro quo, and readily agreed. Velie, always conscious of the need for effective central corporate control mechanisms, insisted on documentation. The rather gratuitous comment about "too liberal" dealers is followed by a closing sentence that makes no bones about who had the final word.

Another showdown between Mansur and the home office occurred in this same period, again related to repairs. The St. Louis branch had earlier requested that the Moline factory develop a special adaptation of the Taber double shovel plow. St. Louis furnished Moline a sample, and the latter proceeded to build the new product. The new shovels were tried out in the field, and though C.H. Pope, the St. Louis office manager, reported that the customers said the shovels were "the best implements of the kind ever sent into the market," a few of them did break. Pope duly forwarded a request to Moline for repayment for the faulty plows. The Moline people alleged that the fault lay with the St. Louis branch, that they had put excessively heavy special attachments on the shovels and thus had overloaded them. Further, asserted Moline, the St. Louis branch had asked for the plow to be made "at their risk, except for defective material." They therefore refused the "Memoranda of Debit." Pope sent an outraged letter in return: "We take the position that if these shovels were made at our risk of breakage except for defective material, you should have so notified us when you took our order.... We do not question your care in selecting material, but seems to us very peculiar that if the material in these shovels, which were undoubtedly manufactured by you, was as good as it should be, these shovels should have given way when other shovels made by different concerns and according to the same specifications did like service without giving way.... Referring now to Mr. Deere's letter, ... we should like to have his authority for the statement that the breakage of Taber Shovels results from the special attachments which we put on to this shovel. We have written our customers on this subject, and they advise us that they do not personally know of a single instance where the breakage took place with anything except the ordinary Double Shovel Blade attached to the standard. It is not impossible that some of the breakages did take place when other attachments were used.... It is absolutely certain that *most* of the breakages did not so take place."

When Pope's letter arrived in the Moline office, Velie immediately wrote Charles Deere: "They are still harping on the effect of your letter to Blount, making as I think a mountain out of a mole hill and also keep ringing the changes on the few blocks that were broken. You want to stiffen them up on these points, and give them to understand that it is out of the question...." At this point Mansur himself became incensed, and penned a long letter back to Charles Deere. He reiterated their feeling that the material was defective, and went on: "You seem to conclude that because we did not *insist* upon the allowance claimed, that we were wrong and you were right. This is not a fair inference. If it were, then there would be very many cases in which we are wrong and you right. Whereas we are constantly giving way in similar cases where we feel we are right. The fact is we *never* make a claim of this character or so near *never* that I am safe in saying that not once in ten times that Deere & Co. do not, at first, say they cannot allow it and as a rule they sit down on it just that way. There is no concern with whom we do business that holds us up so tight to the bull ring in this respect, giving us so little latitude for the exercise of our own judgment and paying so little heed to our statements concerning these claims as do Messrs. Deere & Co.... We fight with our customers in every way possible to protect you agst. unjust claims and very often agst. what seem to be just ones, yet it does not seem to weigh. If we could do with you what our customers very frequently do with us, flatly refuse to pay their bills until we make the allowance claimed, you would perhaps realize our position and see our side of the case." The correspondence on this particular matter ends here, and we have no way of knowing who won the battle. It was an omen, though, of a subsequent near-break between Mansur and Deere, occurring in late 1889, when the co-partnership agreements were to be renewed.[16]

INTER-BRANCH CONFLICT

There were many troublesome inter-branch tensions; by far the most sensitive was the delineation of respective territories. The territories of these five key branches were contiguous and never precisely defined. There was always an overlap at the edges, a necessary complication, inasmuch as the branches dealt with dealers who were in business before the branches were established—and who had natural trade relations in directions that did not always correspond exactly with the branch boundary lines. Some dealers insisted on dealing directly with Moline, even though they were situated right in the middle of one of the branch territories. George Fuller, who was manager in Kansas City after Charles Wheeler's interest had been bought out in 1882, was upset that a Princeton, Missouri, dealer wanted to buy direct. He wrote Moline (in the curious third-party way that some correspondents used at this time): "We did not understand that our Mr. Fuller agreed with your Mr. Deere to relinquish Mercer County. While at St. Louis Mr. Deere told the writer that Mr. Spear of Spear Bros., Princeton, Mo., preferred buying their goods direct. . . . We told him, all right, go ahead, but do not remember of having agreed to the relinquishing of Mercer County."

More troublesome were cases in which one branch usurped another's customer. A Yuma, Colorado, dealer had ordered from Wells at Council Bluffs, but Deere, Mansur at Kansas City felt it should have had the order. Wells coveted the Colorado area, as he felt it was not being served well from Kansas City. He wrote: "It is not our purpose to annoy you further regarding the matter of territory, but for your information, we enclose herewith report from our traveling agent of the town of Sterling, Colorado, and other points in that vicinity. You will observe that there are none of your goods to amount to anything being sold there now. Had the territory been ours, we should have placed at least two car loads of your goods there this year. Please do not understand this that we are arguing the point, we merely call your attention to it for your information."

Four years later, Wells used almost the same opening sentence in a dispute between his branch and the Moline factory sales personnel. "We have no disposition to annoy you when unnecessary, but matters are in such shape that there seems to be no other course for us to pursue." The Wells traveling man had done the missionary work with a group of beet-sugar growers in Nebraska, but when the actual product was developed by the Moline factory, the Moliners wrote the contract in Moline without giving credit to Council Bluffs. "They are not acting in good faith in the matter at all," alleged Wells, "and we are not satisfied with it and thought we would present the case to you. Now, if we cannot depend upon [the factory] at all, we will simply take other steps to get the machinery elsewhere."

Webber had somewhat the same problem with the Moline factory personnel when he wanted to move further west in Minnesota. Webber was more temperate in his wording: "The dealers in that territory buy most of their goods in this market, and if you will look into the matter you will find that most of the goods which you have sold there have been shipped by us—we think the territory can be worked from here to your advantage, otherwise we would not want it." Sometimes Moline would be caught in the middle on these arguments—Webber had aggressively moved into Montana in the early 1880s and encroached upon the territory of an independent dealer who had dealt directly with the company in prior years. The independent dealer, according to a Deere traveling man, "stated rather forcibly that they could not and would not handle anybody's goods unless the territorial restrictions were removed and unless they could be assured of absolute protection in the territory assigned."

An interesting jurisdictional quarrel among branches occurred in an actual "territory"—the Oklahoma area. The St. Louis branch had insisted that the Oklahoma Territory was its private domain, but Velie thought otherwise. He had visited Texas in 1888 and written Charles Deere at that time: "Within the next five years the Indian territory will be opened up to settlement and the tide of emigration will set strongly into the Southwest ere long. . . . Emigration associations have been formed this season in Texas to which large amounts of money have been subscribed." He noted that the St. Louis branch had been selling about half of its equipment to the state of Texas, but that with the new railroads into the area, Kansas City would be a more logical headquarters for Texas.[17]

The trend line for Deere & Company was strongly upward after the Civil War, with only occasional brief and modest setbacks—in 1873, for example. Indeed, within just a year of the Panic of 1873, the company reached $1 million in sales and sold 50,000 plows. Appendix exhibit 5 shows the financial results for the company's first two decades as a corporation. On cumulative sales of $20,800,000 in these twenty years,

Exhibit 4-9   **United States agricultural growth 1870–90**

	1870	**1880**	**1890**
Number of farms (000)	2,660	4,009	4,565
Acreage in farms (000)	407,723	536,064	623,207
Value of farmland and buildings ($000,000)	$7,441,000	$10,193,000	$13,273,000
Value of farm machinery ($000,000)	$271,000	$406,000	$494,000

Source: U.S. Department of Commerce, Historical Statistics of the United States: Colonial Times to 1957, (1960), pp. 278, 285.

the firm had earned more than $3,200,000, a healthy 15.3 percent profitability. Cash dividends of $1,407,000 had been paid out; thus, more than 56 percent of the earnings had been retained in the business. In the process, the company had produced and sold more than 1,300,000 plows.

The company's rapid growth mirrored that of the agricultural economy as a whole. Deere's special way of marketing was proving effective, exploiting a well-engineered, well-made product. How did the manufacturing arm of the business itself adjust to these rapid changes of the post-Civil War era?

WE SELL THE
JOHN DEERE

MOLINE, ILLINOIS.

PLOWS

DEERE WALKING CULTIVATOR

CHAPTER 5

PRODUCTS, PRICES, AND PEOPLE

The team of the French plow balked for a little while,
and the man with the team on the American plow ran ahead
of his horses for fear the French plow might be beaten.
They also managed to smuggle both the whips to the French
side, and sliced away, while Mr. [Charles] Deere had
only his umbrella to poke up the four horses on his plow.

"Paris Exhibition of 1878,"
Scientific American

◁*Late nineteenth-century dealer sign (Deere Archives)*

D uring the last half of the nine-
teenth century, "the revolution in production came more slowly than did
the revolution in distribution," noted Alfred D. Chandler, Jr., in *The
Visible Hand*. Yet this period did witness the ascendancy of mass
production. New machinery and processes were developed, and the
quality of raw materials was improved. Perhaps most important, innovations were made in synchronizing the flows of materials through the
factory and in supervising the work force. In the metalworking industries, better materials—particularly steel from the Bessemer process—
required new types of machines and machine tools. The process of
fabricating a substantial number of parts—most to be interchangeable—
became more exacting, and these challenges put demands on shop
management. It was not just a coincidence that the "scientific management" movement got its early start in metalworking factories.

The driving force of expansion was most often the market. New
products were being demanded all through American industry, and they
were bought in large volume as the economy grew over the second half of
the nineteenth century. In agricultural machinery, the innovations were
product variations, rather than basic inventions, though there were a few
of the latter. One noteworthy step was James Oliver's patenting of the
"chilled" plow. (It was made by a special method of cooling iron or steel
by passing a stream of warm water over the metal, together with an
annealing process that made the metal tougher and produced a mirror-
like finish that was rust-resistant). A new type of planter, the "check
row" planter, appeared; Deere contributed to its early development. In
the main, though, developments in agricultural machinery during the
1860–1900 period were extensions of previous ideas—improvements in
gang plows, refinements in harrows (the springtooth and disk harrows),
and, in general, the substitution of riding machinery for walk-behind. The
steam traction engine came back into the picture, too, making new
demands for heavier equipment to be pulled behind it. These changes
took place in an era characterized by intense competition within the
industry, serious recessions, and an outcropping of disruptive labor
unrest.[1]

THE DEERE POSTWAR PRODUCT LINE

The Deere products in the second half of the nineteenth century fell
into five basic product families: (1) walking and wheeled plows, both
single-bottom and gang; (2) cultivators, walking and wheeled; (3) harrows;
(4) drills and planters; and (5) wagons and buggies (and, in the 1890s,
bicycles). When Deere & Company put out its catalog and price list in
1866—and found it duplicated almost to a machine by the firm of
Candee, Swan & Co.—the total product line, all product families included, was just thirty-one implements. By the time that "Catalogue 27" was

issued in late 1900, the company had a total of 287 separate, distinct models of single-blade walking plows. There were also several dozen gang plows, some 164 cultivators, and several dozen harrows.

Certain of these products became so prominent and well known that they fundamentally influenced company growth. First in importance was the Gilpin sulky plow. A single-lever sulky, it was strong and durable, constructed of an iron beam, iron frame, and iron-bound wood (all iron after 1879) made for long-lasting usage.

The Gilpin, though not the first of its kind, must be considered one of the most outstanding nineteenth-century sulky plows. First developed in 1875, it was immediately patented—probably the company's most important nineteenth-century patent. An Osage, Iowa, implement dealer wrote directly to Charles Deere in 1876 eulogizing its ease of handling. "I took it to our county fair, and put it into a trial with the Crosley. We selected a piece of ground, one end of which was good smooth prairie, while the other end was very rough, and a low piece of breaking ground that had gone back and was thickly covered with weeds so high as a man's shoulders. To satisfy the many spectators present that the plow was easy to handle, I got a lady who had never run a plow before to mount the Gilpin, while a man of a good deal of experience run the Crosley. The Gilpin was run all depths from 4 to 11 inches deep, as persons would call for it, and in every instance it done its work splendidly. Much better than any man could do with any hand plow. The difference in the work performed by the two plows was so great that anyone could tell the difference nearly as far off as they could see the field. The Gilpin burried [*sic*] the tall weeds entirely out of sight, while the Crosley left them sticking out of the ground, & did not do as good work anywhere."

The Gilpin's features had to be tested by more formal trials—and here the Gilpin had instantaneous success. The company first put the implement into competition in 1875, and it won so many "firsts" that it seemed to take every contest in sight. In Brussels, Illinois, and Portage des Sioux, Missouri, in August 1875; in Atlanta, Illinois, in September of that year; in October at Cunningham, Missouri; and in March 1876 at three different towns in central Missouri, the Gilpin was, as the company circular of early 1876 proclaimed, "victorious in all points!"

Just a year before the single-bottom Gilpin had been brought out, the company had begun marketing its own gang plow. The Black's gang plow of the 1860s was manufactured by the company under license, with only "Deere's imprint," as the catalog of 1866 admitted. This new gang plow, the Deere gang, came in both double-bottom and triple-bottom models (exhibit 5-1). (The plow shares on the latter model could not be swung clear of the ground and came to be used chiefly on the larger ranches in California and the Northwest, where the light nature of the soil and the superficial character of the seedbed preparation allowed the larger units).

The double-bottom Deere gang was equally a resounding success in the

Exhibit 5–1. *"Scene on the Grandin Farm, Dakota—twenty Deere gang plows in operation,"* ca. 1879 (Deere Archives)

field trials of the mid-1870s. Because the Gilpin and the Deere gang had done so well in the Illinois and Iowa competitions, Charles Deere decided to enter them both in a much grander contest, the famous Paris Exhibition of 1878 at Petit-Bourg, France.

Other Deere plows had won honors at a Paris exhibition in 1867, in Vienna in 1873, and in Philadelphia at the Centennial Exhibition in 1876. This time, though, there was to be a head-to-head field contest, and even the prestigious *Scientific American* was to be there.

Deere brought along the Gilpin, the Deere gang, and a walking plow. The *Scientific American* editors featured the three in a multi-page story of the plow trials. "The greatest interest of the day," said the writer, "was shown in the competitor trials of Deere's Illinois Gang Plow and the *bisoc* of Meixmoron de Dombasle, of Nancy, France." The French gang plow was not a sulky—the Deere plow was, and the reporter noted that "the riding feature was very curious to most of the spectators."

During the day of the trial, the French plow was worked with six horses and the Deere with four until the point when they started on the competitive trial, when both were limited to the four horses. The teams were changed when half of the ground allotted had been plowed; this did not work out quite as planned, though, for "the teamsters in each case whipped up so cruelly that in mercy to the brutes—no, not the brutes, but the horses—the trial was concluded rather sooner than was intended." The reporter chronicled the ensuing argument: "The team of the French plow balked for a little while, and the man with the team on the American plow ran ahead of his horses for fear the French plow might be beaten. They also managed to smuggle both the whips to the French side,

Exhibit 5–2. *Portion of Deere advertisement, noting the company's first prize at the Vienna Exposition, 1873 (Deere Archives)*

and sliced away, while Mr. Deere had only his umbrella to poke up the four horses on his plow." The reporter, apparently not wanting to make an international incident of it, diplomatically added: "This was only some bi-play of the French teamsters and was soon stopped. There are no fairer people in the world than the French judges, but the workmen could not forbear trying to take advantage of this."

The results of the trial quickly assuaged Charles Deere's ire, for the Deere gang won the contest handily. The *Scientific American* included the complete details in its issue of September 21, 1878 (exhibit 5-3). Only seven "special prizes" were given for the field trials of agricultural machinery, and one of these was for the Deere gang—a "Sevres Vase, valued at one thousand francs," trumpeted the Deere catalog the following year. All in all, the Paris Exhibition was a major boost not only to the morale of Charles Deere and his associates but to the reputation of two of the most important products of the company—the Gilpin sulky and the Deere gang.[2]

In 1881 the Gilpin was improved in a major way by the development of a "power-lift," a device that allowed a simple pressure from the hand on a catch to throw the plow blade out of the ground after one revolution of the wheel. The company at this point offered to modify the older plows to incorporate the power lift, and the Gilpin continued to be made in essentially this form for the rest of the century (and in modest quantities well beyond World War I). "The King of the Riding Plows," said the company, and few would question its claim. An advertisement of 1898 published a letter from a Galesburg farmer, who had two twenty-year-old

Exhibit 5–3. *The Deere gang takes first place in the plowing match at the Paris Exhibition in 1878* (Scientific American, *September 21, 1878*)

Dynamometric Trials of Gang Plows at Petit-Bourg (Seine et Oise), France, August 6th, 1878. Reported for the SCIENTIFIC AMERICAN, by Dr. Edward H. Knight, U. S. Commissioner, etc.

NAMES OF EXHIBITORS.		Meixmoron de Dombasle, Nancy (Meurthe et Moselle), France.		Deere & Company, Moline, Illinois, United States.	
		TRIALS. (1)			
		1. Going.	2. Returning.	1. Going.	2. Returning.
Surface Measure by Planimeter	Square Millimeters	115,160	112,735	120,870	125,970
Length of trace (2)	Meters	2.430	2.365	2.512	2.377
Mean ordinate (3)	Millimeters	49.39	47.67	48.12	52.995
Corresponding effort	Kilogram-Meters	497.31	500.25	504.97	556.13
Mean depth of furrow	Millimeters	151.1	161.3	163.0	167.3
Mean width of furrow slice of the gang plow	Millimeters	678.1	626.0	695.6	709.0
Section of land turned	Square meter	0.102664	0.100974	0.113383	0.118616
Power necessary to displace one metric cube of earth (4)	Kilogram-Meters	4844.1	4956.2	4453.7	4680.0
Mean of two trials	Kilogram-Meters	4899.2		4566.9	
Length of furrow	Meters	160	160	160	160
Time of travel	min./sec.	4 8	4 42	4 12	4 22
Weight of Plow	Kilos	247		260	

(1) The ground was slightly inclined.
(2) The base line on the paper ribbon of the dynamometer.
(3) Mean distance between the base and profile lines on paper ribbon.
(4) Kilogram-Meter, the French dynamic unit. The power required to line 1 kilogram to a height of one meter. One cheval-vapeur (horse power) is the power required to lift 75 kilos. a distance of 1 meter (i.e. 75 kilogram-Meters) in a second. 1 kilogram equals 2.2046 pounds avoirdupois. 1 meter equals 39.37079 inches.

Gilpins "doing good work yet," and continued: "The old war cry of the Gilpin, 'keep the share sharp and the point set well down' needs only to be heeded to demonstrate that no riding plow manufactured today can accomplish more work . . . with less draft than the Gilpin."

Despite the success of the various manufacturers' sulkies, they were not universally preferred, some farmers still insisting on the proven walking plow. Leo Rogin, in his definitive book on nineteenth-century farm machinery, noted a temporary downturn in interest in the sulky and riding plows in the early 1880s. In 1882 the *Nebraska Farmer* observed "a general disposition among farmers to abandon what at one time seemed to be coming into general use; the riding or sulky plow. . . . There was never a machine so popular that was so short lived." Two new concepts provided renewed impetus to the sulkies, however. The first involved the tilt of the sulky wheel.

The Gilpin and its counterparts were all two-wheeled plows. The share was attached to a landside, just as with the walking plow, and the experienced agriculturist would keep the Gilpin, or any similarly well-built, two-wheeled plow, running straight by keeping the right pressure on the share as it met the new cut. Still, one needed considerable practice to sense the proper amount of pressure. In the mid-1870s the innovative "W.L. Casaday's Patent plow" was developed by the Oliver Chilled Plow Works, a strange-looking variation that had one of its wheels set at an angle such that if it was driven in the furrow, with the wheel pressed down into the angle of the previous cut, the plow share itself would be pressed into just the right position for the next cut (exhibit 5-4). In effect, the tilted wheel replaced the landside. Then, three years later, in 1884, the Moline Plow Company brought out its famous Flying Dutchman, a three-wheeled plow that soon brought most manufacturers to this new concept. Deere adopted the three-wheeled approach in the mid-1880s

Exhibit 5–4. *Two renditions of "W.L. Casaday's Patent plow" (Robert L. Ardrey,* American Agricultural Implements*)*

W. L. CASADAY'S PATENT, MAY 2, 1876.   W. L. CASADAY'S PATENT, SEPT. 6, 1881.

with its New Deal gang. The company's Gazelle, brought out in the early 1890s, was the first of the staggered wheel models of the company, and the same principle was carried over in the Ranger single-bottom plow in the mid-1890s, as well as other models of the late 1890s and early 1900s.

The Deere gang plow was substantially improved in 1884 and again in 1885 by the addition of an auxiliary lever that allowed the farmer to vary the depth of the plow while the plow was running. Essentially this same model of the Deere gang was manufactured on into the 1890s.

Along with the old, a new set of walking and riding gangs were brought out by the company in the late 1880s and early 1890s that themselves became much more substantial sellers. These were the so-called "New Deal" lines, made both as single-bottom walking or riding plows and as gang versions—from two-gang up to a monster six-gang, in 8-, 10-, 12-, and 14-inch versions. With the two-bottom generally drawn by four or six horses, it was obvious that the draft for a six-bottom would require great motive power.

The answer to this need gives us the second installment of a story told in a previous chapter—for steam plowing once again seemed destined to come into its own. The company published a brochure on steam plowing in 1889, touting the New Deal gangs and the concept of steam plowing as it was practiced in its "second generation." Deere itself had experimented with its gangs using a borrowed steam tractor and developed its larger versions of the New Deal just for this purpose. Exhibit 5-5, pictures a page from the catalog of 1889, including the enumeration of special needs for steam plowing—the ground had to be level to keep the steam safely in the boiler, two men were necessary to run the operation (one for the engine and one to manage the gang plow), and long furrows and large fields were required for turning areas at the ends of the fields. The "special circular" in the advertisement elaborated on these points and included a simplified cost analysis that seemed to imply that a gang plow of five 14-inch bottoms could plow 1.75 acres in one hour, utilizing an engine speed of 2.5 miles per hour. The brochure's author estimated that upward of twenty acres per day could be plowed and that the engine "will not consume to exceed one ton of coal." Based upon this, the author estimated the total cost at ten dollars, giving a per-acre cost of only $.50. Ideal conditions were assumed for these extrapolations, but given that the steam plow was most often used in large-scale plowing on the "bonanza" farms in California and the Northwest, the assumptions were realistic. At any rate, the company stood ready to serve the steam-plowing fraternity for its new "day" in the agricultural sun.

The steam plow enjoyed only a brief success in agricultural history, however. Rogin put it succinctly: "The publicity which attended the employment of steam tractors for plowing in California has created the impression that this came to be the characteristic mode of plowing in those regions. Steam-tractor plowing, however, like harvesting with the

New Deal Gang with Traction Engine.

Thus far no other manufacturer has produced a make-shift even for steam plowing which is capable of general or extended introduction. We were the first to construct a large gang of plows, and have to-day in the New Deal four, five and six-furrow gangs, the only plows of the kind that can successfully be used with an engine as motive power. By this addition to a steam equipment the latter can be employed in plowing two seasons, and yield with much larger profits and far less work for the operators than during the threshing season.

The necessary conditions are that the ground must be firm enough to stand the weight of the engine and fairly level so that steam may be safely kept in the boiler. The better the shape the ground is in for plowing the more satisfactory of course will be the results.

In operating, two men are necessary — one to run the engine and guide it so as to keep an even width of furrow, and one to manage the plow gang. No outfit of this kind is handy to handle at the ends of rows, or in turning corners, so that long furrows and large fields are desirable.

In hitching to an engine several links of heavy chain are necessary between the engine and the gang, so as to give slack enough to lift the plows out of the ground. An ordinary traction engine, either eight or ten horse, such as is to be found in every farming locality, will run a four, five or six-furrow New Deal Gang Plow with ease.

We guarantee the New Deals to do good work, but will of course give no warranty on the engine or power.

Send for special circular.

Exhibit 5–5. *Steam plowing with a New Deal gang plow (Deere & Company catalog, 1889)* steam-drawn harvester-thresher, represented at its peak but a minor element in the wheat-growing of the Sacramento and San Joaquin valleys and the other extensive sub-humid regions of the Pacific area.''

Deere soon made more complex versions of the gang plow, beginning in the 1890s. The first new models at that time were the Poole and Kid sulkies and the Gazelle gang. In turn, these were superseded by the Stag sulky and the Stag gang, with the New Deere sulky and New Deere gang providing the top of the line. Another successful model in the 1890s was the Secretary, based on a patent issued to the company in 1895 (exhibit

5-6). This was the company's first disk plow (other companies had made these for many years) and came in single- and double-disk versions. Another model, the Deere disk plow, was made from single- up through quadruple-disk versions. By this time, many special models were customized for particular soils in particular parts of the country; the catalog of Mansur & Tebbetts (the St. Louis-Dallas branch house) in 1895 featured a number of plows specially for the South—the Rice King pony gang for Arkansas and Louisiana, the Deere sulky lister for Kansas and Nebraska, the Yazoo lister for the deep South, the Texas Ranger for its namesake. Occasionally single plows were made on special order, generally oversized versions for railroad ditching, etc. A railroad plow made by the company in 1879 for the Iron Mountain and Southern Railroad was used for track ditching in southern Missouri (exhibit 5-7). This Gargantua

Exhibit 5–6. *Two popular products of the 1890s:* left, *the Secretary plow;* right, *the Gazelle gang plow. (Deere Archives)*

Exhibit 5–7. *1879 Deere railroad plow, made for the Iron Mountain and Southern Railroad, used for track ditching in southern Missouri (Deere Archives)*

weighed 1,800 pounds and its moldboard was 36 inches high. In operation, it was rigged to a flat car behind two steam locomotives and, when pulled alongside, could ditch and throw the residue dirt six to ten feet away from the track.[3]

Cultivators were also improved during the decades after the Civil War. The company's mainstay in the early 1860s, the Hawkeye sulky corn cultivator, was improved in 1866 with one of the company's early postwar patent purchases (from George Perry of Muscatine, Iowa). Then, in 1867, Gilpin Moore patented a new walking cultivator, first pictured in the company's catalog of 1868 (exhibit 5-8).

The Hawkeye was dropped out of the product line about 1876 and replaced by the Peerless and Deere Riding cultivators. Later there were other more sophisticated versions of riding cultivators, including the Princess in the early 1880s; the Columbia, which stayed in the line from the mid-1880s until well into the 1900s; and the New Matchless, also in the 1880s. The bulk of the trade, however, was concentrated in the walking cultivators (several of the riding cultivators, for example, the Princess, were also adaptable to walking-cultivator use). The tongueless principle was widely adapted to the cultivator around 1877, and the company began making its version as a sled runner model, appropriately calling it the Arctic. The later Queen and the Junior were also tongueless, but with wheels (the sled variation not turning out to be particularly successful). The Antelope, Reindeer, and Fawn cultivators had especially long lives in the product line.

Harrows were not made in as many models. In the catalog of 1876 only one was shown, the Scotch harrow, a forty-tooth model. By the mid-1880s

Exhibit 5–8. *Line drawings of Deere cultivators in the 1860s, from company catalogs (Deere Archives)*

several variations had been introduced—the Vibrating harrow, the Glidden, and the Deere Smoothing harrow. When the Eclipse harrow was brought out in 1885 (in 71-, 83-, 95-, 107-, and 155-tooth models) the company advertising man trumpeted "total Eclipse" at the top of his advertisement, hoping that the farmer understood that the competitor harrows were the ones in eclipse! Additional varieties of all the harrows were available by the late 1880s, and by 1900 not only had these been improved and expanded, but new clod crushers and pulverizers were on the market.

Product-line breakdowns were kept as permanent records only from 1892. Fortunately, an earlier fragment of a record remains for individual models manufactured in the period 1879–83. The best sellers were these five:

Year (ending June 30)	Walking Plows	Gilpin Sulkies	Deere Spring Cultivators	Shovel Plows	Harrows
1879	40,544	5,497	4,862	5,328	6,727
1880	39,464	5,964	10,067	5,659	5,938
1881	45,171	5,773	15,464	9,018	6,326
1882	50,025	7,704	16,777	9,645	7,393
1883	48,858	7,841	13,818	9,198	14,604

Clearly the walking plows were dominant, accounting for more unit sales than the other four combined.[4]

DEERE'S CORN PLANTER

Although Deere & Company kept its same product line all through this period, Alvah Mansur and Charles Deere joined together in 1877 to form a separate corporation in Moline to manufacture corn planters. It was called Deere & Mansur Company, the name close enough to the co-partnership name in Kansas City (Deere, Mansur & Company) to cause some confusion from time to time. This new corporation was not a co-partnership, to be shown on the parent company's books, but a wholly independent entity, with the predominant number of shares owned by the two entrepreneurs. The R.G. Dun correspondent put it frankly in his first report on the new company: "Composed of wealthy men."

The Deere corn planter—which employed an innovative rotary planting mechanism—was a success right from the start. The company made a profit of more than $10,000 in its first full year, 1879, and $48,000 in 1882. The Dun correspondent nodded approvingly: "Close corporation composed of very wealthy men, making money."

By far the most common way of planting corn in the earlier years of the nineteenth century, and before, was in hills—a practice adopted from the ancient way of the Eastern Indians. The usual method was to draw a shovel plow across a previously plowed field at intervals of three to four feet, followed by another pass at right angles. The corn was then hand-dropped at each furrow intersection and hand-covered with a hoe. Sometimes the checked double-pass approach was shortcut by a farmer who would make a single pass and drop the corn in the desired check pattern by sight. Other variations were also common; in "listing," for example, two furrows were thrown against each other, the corn being planted in the ridge (the rows being about three feet apart).

Hand corn-planting and hand hoeing were generally considered "boys work," a very slow process. The burgeoning of the corn market and, especially, the labor shortages of the Civil War, soon demanded a more efficient method. After all, a man or boy could only plant about an acre a day and there were only twenty days or so of good planting weather each spring. Hand planting severely limited the total acreage that could be planted.

A planter is one of the most interesting of all agricultural machines, inasmuch as its product is not immediately seen upon operation. The plow throws up a furrow, the harvester separates the grain right before one's eyes—but the planter puts a seed down under the ground and not until the new plant comes up are the results revealed. As George W. Crampton wrote in Deere's respected farmer publication, *The Furrow*: "The loss in yield due to use of an inferior planter is so well known . . . even the slightest inaccuracy is of such great importance that it will more than pay a farmer to discard immediately an inferior planter and purchase an accurate machine."

The first truly successful mechanical corn planter came through the innovations of George W. Brown in the 1850s and '60s (although a patent for a mechanical planter had been obtained by Eliakim Spooner in 1799). Brown did his manufacturing at Galesburg, Illinois, and by the end of the Civil War was the preeminent corn-planter manufacturer in the country. Brown's machine was a two-row version, a rather crude affair with boxed-in wheels and a slide drop. The first step, before actually using the planter, was to mark off the ground in crisscross rows, using a sled marker. Then, as the machine itself was drawn across the field by the driver, a second person sitting on the front of the seeder—in the "dropper seat"—operated the planter mechanism. The dropper lever was jerked when the forward movement crossed the mark made by the sled marker (exhibit 5-9). "It was a rigid test of the accuracy of eye and rapidity of action," wrote Crampton, "and every man who operated one of them in his youth seems to have a vivid recollection of it."

George Brown was an assiduous seeker of patent protection, and he was able in the 1850s and early 1860s to obtain separate patents on individual segments of his machine. The wide acceptance of corn planters during the Civil War (and his own particular success) soon brought many

Exhibit 5–9. Top, *Two-row hand planter made by Randall & Jones, 1850s; bottom, George Brown corn planter, showing "dropper seat," ca. 1870s. (Percy Wells Bidwell and John I. Falconer*, History of Agriculture in the Northern United States*)*

competitors. One of Brown's biographers reported the results (rather self-righteously, to be sure): "Other men in different parts of the country without saying 'by your leave,' or even 'thank you,' helped themselves to Mr. Brown's patents and commercial manufacturing and selling corn-planters. Of course after all his trouble and expense Mr. Brown could not quietly permit the fruits of his labors to go into the hands of others. He protested in vain, asked them to either desist, or pay him for his invention. They refused to do either, and he commenced proceedings in the federal courts."

Brown eventually won most of his patent suits. They all covered the original machine, though in the slide-drop version. Brown had experimented with a rotary mechanism but had never used it in his products. The Deere machine did, however. The first Deere & Mansur advertisements featured this "latest and most valuable improvement," headlined under a large banner as the "Deere Rotary Drop."

Brown sued and the case was tried in January 1881. The circuit court judge agreed with Deere that Brown had never used the rotary concept. "The plaintiff seemingly attached very little value to his patent until the defendants and their associates introduced and popularized it. Still," the judge continued, "the plaintiff's rights exist and must be protected." The judge held that there was nothing new in the individual segments of the rotary concept, but that the particular combination of these was new: "Here is an introduction into old machinery of a new and peculiar wheel and forked transverse bar, whereby, in combinations with well-known devices, the desired result could be produced—a new combination." Deere had infringed on this patent, the judge ruled, as "the combinations are the same, and the devices used are the same, with merely colorable change as to form."

Brown was not prepared to fill any orders for a rotary-drop machine. So, after the decision had gone against them, Deere & Mansur came back to the court, requesting that they be allowed to fill the hundreds of orders they had for their planters for the spring of 1881. The judge said no, that they must settle with Brown first.

Brown immediately put out a circular to the trade that appeared to threaten all dealers with reprisals if they sold the Deere & Mansur planters, and even seemed to imply legal moves against farmer-users. "The result of this suit is very important to all parties manufacturing, selling and using rotary-drop corn planters, as it makes each party having no authority from Mr. Brown, liable for damages. . . . Now, settlement must be made or their sales must cease."

This put Charles Deere's and Alvah Mansur's danders up and they sent out their own flyer, repeating Brown's words, noting that Brown "has had ample and varied experience in *enlarging* old, worthless, dead patents," and concluding, "Our reply to his closing remark is, 'now settlement' will not 'be made,' neither will 'their sales cease.' We shall continue to supply the trade with rotary drop planters, greatly improved, differing wholly from, and therefore not infringing this old, abandoned and worthless device contained in Mr. Brown's reissued patent No. 6384, and continue as heretofore, to fully guarantee all parties who have bought or may buy, not only corn planters but any other implement from us, against all loss or damage, by reason of any claims or threats of Mr. Brown or any other man.''

As a matter of fact, Brown's threat was not idle rhetoric. Farmers at this time had been pressured to either pay royalties or cease using products ranging from farmhouse and barnyard instruments such as sliding gates, milk cans, clover hullers, sewing machines, barbed wire, and drivewalls to actual agricultural machinery such as plows and grain binders. Historian Earl W. Hayter quoted one lamenting Western writer of that period: "How is a farmer to know to whom to pay the royalty, even if it was legal, with three or four applicants swarming around him, all claiming to be the legal patentees. . . . "

Whether Deere & Mansur ever paid Brown anything, or whether any farmer was harassed, does not appear to be known. From this time forward, the rotary concept became almost universally adopted, for it had the requisite speed to be used with a new collateral device, the "check-rower." This was an ingenious attachment for the planter that utilized a wire or rope, anchored at the end of the field, that was pulled through the planter as it moved toward the anchor. Knots were located at the regularly spaced points where the seed was to be dropped, and as each knot reached the planter, it triggered the rotary drop. In combinaton, a good rotary-drop planter and a workable check-rower could successfully plant the fields in that square, check-rowed pattern that would allow cross-cultivation.

The check-rower eliminated the "dropper boy," though the earliest versions still required two people—the driver, who operated the elevating-depressing lever of the planter itself, and the assistant, who wound up the wire or rope on a reel attached to the side of the planter. Soon, though, the check-rower was built right into the machine itself, so that the takeup of the reel would be automatically done as the machine moved down the field. This truly made the planter a one-person machine.

C.W. Mansur, Alvah's nephew, remembered the problems with the use of the rope in the early days. "When this rope was left out overnight and it became damp there was great shrinkage, so when you started in the morning to plant it was too short and when you finished at night you had rope to spare, consequently, out of check. To overcome this difficulty manufacturers used a tarred rope and when this was left out overnight, while it no longer would shrink and expand, it was food for field mice with the result that you frequently had a large number of sections the next morning."

Deere & Mansur brought out its Deere and Moline planters in 1881. "Either of these machines will work perfectly on any of the standard

Exhibit 5 10. *Early truck used by Deere & Mansur, undated photograph (Deere Archives)*

check-rowers, a warrant of the manufacturer being given to that effect," noted a farm-paper reporter. The machine worked very effectively—each of the six chambers in the rotary disc would always drop a kernel when the opening appeared, and there was apparently very little cutting of the corn kernel, which, if it happened, destroyed the kernel and caused a skip in the planting. Additional plates could be ordered to plant other types of small seeds—broom corn, sorghum, cucumbers, navy beans, castor beans, etc. By the early 1880s, there was also an attachment for planting pumpkin or squash seed in every other hill in every other row. A simple fertilizer attachment could also be ordered. "They undeniably increase the crop and prevent insects from disturbing the corn when small," noted a company advertisement of 1883.

Beginning with the 1879 season the company also made a stalk cutter and by 1885 had added a sulky hay rake. Alvah Mansur sold the latter at the branch but apparently was not particularly partial to it. While he touted it in his catalog of 1886 as "so satisfactory, wherever introduced that we have added it to our regular line," in the same catalog he offered the Coates lock-lever springseat rake, the New Gleaner sulky rake, the Albion sulky rake, the Greensburg revolving rake, and the Tiffin revolving rake, all competitor models!

Most check-row planting was still done as hill culture, the holes in the planter's plate being large enough so that each drop allowed enough grains for a hill. The plate could be taken out and a thin plate put in to use for drilling. Still, the accuracy of single-kernel planting in these earlier models was not as dependable as the farmer demanded. The goal was always to have the same number of kernels in each hill—usually three—and experiments had shown that productivity was ten to fifteen bushels higher per acre when the same number of seeds was put in each hill, rather than two in one hill, five in another, etc. In the mid-1890s, Deere & Mansur developed a new concept, an accumulative single-kernel drill planter, that increased the accuracy from 65–70 percent to about 80–85 percent. This was followed almost immediately by the development of the "edge drop," a major innovation. Grains of corn are generally more uniform in thickness or edgewise measurement than in length or breadth. By the use of this edge-measuring device, great accuracy could be obtained in the number of kernels to be dropped.

It was a nuisance, though, to contend with the check-row, and there were countless efforts through all these years to perfect a wireless way of planting. Yet even up into the 1930s, the wire check-row system was the most widely used way of planting corn. As Crampton put it in his *Furrow* article of 1929, "The so-called wireless planter, a machine designed to space off the ground without the use of the wire . . . has been worked upon for years with unvarying failures so far as the production of commercially successful machines. . . . Probably more patents have been granted and more money has been wasted in experiments upon them than on any other single farm tool." Crampton concluded his article by recounting the great fear of the farmer: "If a single mistake is made with the wireless planter it will spoil an entire field, as it would be impossible to follow an error once made without stopping and adjusting for it each time in going across the field."

Deere & Mansur sold its planters under the Deere label through Deere branch houses, even though it was a completely separate venture not showing on Deere & Company books, even for dividends. This concept of a free-standing, separate manufacturing entity for a new agricultural implement is important as a harbinger of other, later Deere manufacturing-plant decisions. The documentation about the initiation of the idea is slim, and we cannot be certain just what was running through Charles Deere's mind as he once again joined with Alvah Mansur in a separate endeavor. After-the-fact analyses by later company personnel have stressed that this was a self-conscious decision, made for organizational reasons. A company historian put it: "It was determined that the policy should be to have only one leading implement manufactured by any one plant, in order that it might be made and marketed by specialists." It is true that later this concept did become a hallmark of company organizational policy. Here, though, one could probably build an equally good hypothesis that Charles Deere welcomed Alvah Mansur's capital but did not want it shoehorned into the parent company at this point. The end result was clear; from 1877 to 1909, Deere & Mansur was a wholly separate company.[5]

DEERE'S WAGONS AND BUGGIES

The company began selling wagons in the 1880s, but the story itself goes back to 1853. At that time James First, a recent immigrant from Germany, had come to Moline. He worked briefly with John Deere in the blacksmith shop but left after a few months in a dispute with Deere over his salary. He soon turned to his own employment, opening a blacksmith shop in which he began to construct wagons on a small job-shop scale. In 1869 Morris Rosenfield and Charles Benser joined with First to form the Moline Wagon Company, a co-partnership of the three. First kept his holdings only a few years, selling out to the others sometime in the 1870s.

Rosenfield was the president and chief executive officer until 1896. In 1881 the company bought a one-third interest in the Deere co-partnership in Council Bluffs, Iowa —Deere, Wells & Company—and began selling wagons through that outlet. By the mid-1880s the firm, now a substantial manufacturer of wagons, began building other links with the Deere organization that soon became very close (and finally led to its purchase by Deere in the early 1900s).

Alvah Mansur was also carrying wagons (and buggies) by the early 1880s, but he had chosen to go his own way. The St. Louis branch catalog of 1886 featured Mitchell wagons, purchased from the Racine, Wisconsin, manufacturer of the same name and Old Hickory wagons from the Kentucky Wagon Manufacturing Company of Louisville, Kentucky. In 1888 Mansur's catalog was a mammoth one, its 495 pages jammed full of all sorts of agricultural products. By this time, in addition to the Mitchell and Old Hickory wagons, the company devoted 143 pages of the catalog to a whole set of lines of buggies—the Derby, the Red Star, the Victoria, the Goldsmith, and the Sterling. In 1889, Mansur and L.B. Tebbetts formed a new subsidiary, the Mansur & Tebbetts Carriage Co., to assemble and market buggies under the Mansur & Tebbetts name; the St. Louis branch also continued to sell a number of outside buggy lines. For the wagons, though, the firm began to handle only those from the Moline Wagon Company.

Thus, by the 1880s, Deere had direct organizational links into this new industry. It was a fascinating business, putting the company in touch with two more of the agriculturist's favorites—his farm wagon and his farm-to-town buggy (exhibit 5-11).

Not all of the branch managers were as enthusiastic about wagons and buggies as Mansur; though C.C. Webber sold them in his Minneapolis

REPRODUCTION OF A BRIGHT-COLORED POSTER
SHOWING, IN A SCENE OF PROSPERITY, TAKEN FROM LIFE,
AS AN IMPORTANT FEATURE,

The New Moline
LIGHT RUNNING AND DURABLE.

SUCCESS AND THE NEW MOLINE WAGON GO HAND IN HAND.

Gives Satisfaction to the Dealer and Farmer.
Makes Money for Both.

——————— GENERAL AGENTS : ———————

John Deere Plow Co.,
KANSAS CITY, MO. and DENVER, COLO.

Deere, Wells & Co.,
COUNCIL BLUFFS, IOWA.

Mansur & Tebbetts Imp. Co.,
ST. LOUIS, MO. and DALLAS, TEXAS.

Deere & Webber Co.,
MINNEAPOLIS, MINN.

Exhibit 5–11. *Deere wagon and buggy advertisements, 1895–90 (Deere Archives)*

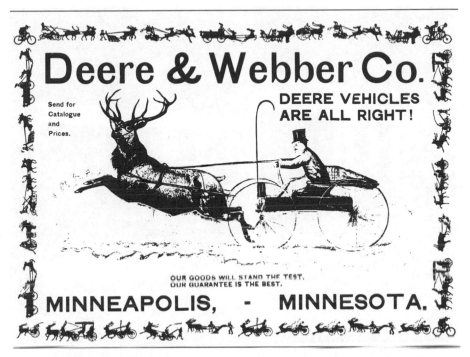

branch, he was vocal about his concern that the company not spread itself too thin. His reasoning was put well in a letter to a new San Francisco branch manager: "There is one thing that you should not allow your travelers to forget . . . that is, that their first duty is to get the plow trade, that that is their main business as long as they are connected with a Deere house, and that if they have not got the best plow trade in every town in their territory, it is their business to tell you so and give the reasons, that you may assist them in properly handling the matter to get the trade that they seem to be unable to land. . . . In the hustle for wagon trade, buggy trade and trade in general, none of us want to overlook the fact that plow trade is our principal mission."

Webber's single-minded concentration on agricultural machinery made itself felt throughout the company, for he never was backward about cautioning others with the shoemakers' adage, "stick to the last." The branch manager at Kansas City had become quite excited about the harness business and came up to Minneapolis to talk to Webber about the prospects. In a letter to Charles Deere, Webber inveighed against the move: "We took the position from the start that while this harness business was a good business, and showed a nice profit, and could be run without very much additional effort on the part of management, that it was not a line that would help materially their implement business; that is, the management would have to be largely separate, under a salaried manager, the goods would have to be sold on the road by special

Exhibit 5–12. *John Deere Plow Company exhibit, Palace of Transportation, St. Louis World's Fair, 1904 (Deere Archives)*

salesmen, and we could not see where there was very much in it for the John Deere Plow Co. at Kansas City, excepting as a means of making more money, and their balance sheets down there show that they were quite well off on the money-making proposition as they were." Webber once again reiterated his abiding philosophy: "We felt that what we wanted them to do was to concentrate their efforts more on their implement business and enlarge that rather than to take on a new line that might divide their attention."

Webber's spritely views, expressed so often, make all the more surprising the "bicycle caper" at the Minneapolis branch. In the mid-1890s, there occurred in the country one of those "herd mentality" upsurges in consumer purchasing that so delight the marketing fraternity. *American Heritage* called this one "the great bicycle craze." The fad lasted less than five years, reaching its peak around 1896 and starting to taper off by 1897. But while it lasted it was an all-pervading advertising subject and a delightful new device for the public to desport upon—in bicycle races, bicycle excursions, bicycle fairs, etc. The bicycle seemed veritably to free people, to make them more mobile and at the same time more personally in control of their lives.

Bicycles themselves were, of course, not a new product—what was new came through the development of the "modern safety." This version was first perfected in the late 1880s and was at the start called a "lowdown," with its two pneumatic-tired wheels of equal size. Made in both men's and women's versions, it could be quickly mastered by just about anyone, young or old. It was this particular version of the bicycle—the safety—that triggered the bicycle craze.

We do not know whether C.C. Webber himself became personally enamored with riding the bicycle, but there was no doubt about the business interest of the Minneapolis branch in this newfangled machine. Charles Velie seemed to be the branch-house specialist for the bicycle, though the original impetus clearly came from Webber himself. The latter wrote the San Francisco branch manager in 1893, for example, that "if there is anything in this bicycle business, any money to be made, we want to take hold of it." And take hold they did. By 1894 *Farm Implement News* reported that Deere & Webber had ordered 1,000 bicycles for the season and by 1895 the sales of bicycles and buggies alone accounted for more than $150,000 of sales and a tidy profit. By that year, Deere & Webber Company was selling not only two outside makes—the Tribune and the Peerless—but it was having manufactured under the company's name three of its own bicycles—the Deere Leader, the Deere Roadster, and the Moline Special. In August 1895 the branch held the "Deere Road Race" over a twenty-mile course at Lake Harriet, outside of Minneapolis. There were 127 people entered in the race, 119 of them showed up and 90 actually finished the race. A St. Paul cyclist, an "amateur," won the race in the tidy time of fifty-four minutes and seventeen seconds. All this occurred before an immense crowd, with Charles Velie prominently in charge as referee.

In 1896 there were major cycle shows in Minneapolis and Kansas City, and the company was a prominent exhibitor at both, bicycles now also being sold in the Kansas City and Omaha branches. Velie even developed a special bicycle trademark (exhibit 5-13), with a deer on a company bicycle as a rider, "to show," said *Farm Implement News*, "that even the deer is left behind in the race unless he mounts one of this particular build of bicycles." By 1897, though, the trade was falling off and soon the issues of *Farm Implement News* downplayed the bicycle as a subject of any interest to readers of a farm implement publication. At the company, too, the fall of the bicycle as a major product was as precipitous as its rise. By 1898 there is no further mention in *Farm Implement News* of Deere and Webber's bicycle business, and sometime shortly after 1900 the company was more or less out of the trade altogether (though Deere & Company did come back briefly to the bicycle business in the 1970s). It was, indeed, a craze for both company and industry, and a short-lived one at that. Arthur S. Dewing, in chronicling the rise and fall of the American Bicycle Company, also poignantly described the fate of Deere & Webber: "Public taste, fickle at all times, and especially fickle regarding its

Exhibit 5–13. *The Deere bicycle trademark, 1890s (Deere Archives)*

amusements, became suddenly weary of the plaything, and threw it aside. Millions of dollars worth of property invested in the manufacture of bicycles consequently became worthless."[6]

AGRICULTURAL MACHINERY PRICES, 1870–1900

The prices of Deere products, and those of the company's competitors, declined during the 1870s, '80s, and '90s, mirroring the strong secular decline in prices generally. (The Warren-Pearson wholesale price index of commodities, which had stood at 185 in 1865, had dropped to 90 in 1879 and 81 by 1889 [1910–14 = 100]). A widely read report published by the United States Department of Agriculture in 1901 stated "conspicuously the fact that from 1860 to 1895 the retail prices of agricultural machinery and implements have declined to an enormous extent, and this in spite of the fact that these implements and machines have in the meantime increased in efficiency, in durability, in workability, in lightness of weight, and in strength of materials. There has been a progress from wood to iron and from iron to steel; and from large patterns to small ones; and during the same time there has been an increased utilization of applied power."

George K. Holmes, the author of the report, had queried hundreds of manufacturers about their price patterns from 1860 to 1900, and he was able to document individual manufacturer prices for comparable equipment over these years (unfortunately for historians, he gave all of these an anonymous number, and the key to this was lost sometime over the ensuing years). This was a challenging analytical task for Holmes, for, as one of the plow manufacturers wrote him: "Our list prices have changed constantly. They run up and down, and our discounts vary also. . . . Our list prices will probably vary up or down twice a year, and our discounts vary considerably. The size of the order controls the price. The terms of payment control the price to a considerable degree, so it is utterly impossible for us to make this up on our line of goods in a manner that will be at all satisfactory." As long as we are forewarned by such caveats, we can accept the Holmes data as documenting a wide-ranging pattern of falling prices in agricultural implements and machinery. The prices of carriages and buggies had fallen very sharply, "the decline often being from 25 to 50%," said Holmes. Mowers had fallen markedly; he reported one establishment with prices declining from $100 in 1860 to $40 in 1900, another from $160 to $40 in the same period. Reaper prices, too, had also dipped substantially—one firm in the Holmes report had a price in 1860 of $150, down to $60 by 1900; another had fallen from $125 to $40 in this same period. Holmes had a detailed listing of some 110 separate plow prices, and he concluded that "the price of good walking plows diminished very largely from 1860 to 1900. . . . In all cases reported, the diminutions are very perceptible." (He noted one plow establishment with a drop from $16.50 to $4.50, another from $6.50 to $3.00, a third from $10.50 to $8.50.)

The Holmes study was one of the first really substantial efforts to analyze agricultural machinery prices, product by product, model by model. By the standards of 1900, it was a solid research effort and documented beyond question the significant drop in agricultural machinery costs to the farmer. Holmes also attempted a comparison, as he put it, "between the old-time methods of production, in which hand labor was assisted only by the comparatively rude and inefficient implements of the day, and the present time, when hand labor has not only the assistance of highly efficient and perfected implements and machinery but has been considerably displaced by them." For the crop year of 1899 he made some aggregate estimates of the savings for seven crops and the figures were striking. For corn alone, Holmes estimated that the new methods saved $523 million; the total for the seven crops was $681 million.

For these figures, Holmes drew mainly from a monumental study done two years earlier under the direction of Carroll D. Wright, the United States commissioner of labor. It was a 1,600-page tome titled *Hand and*

Machine Labor that analyzed twenty-seven different farm crops, revealing not only the savings in man-hours of labor but also the changes in labor cost per unit of production (including a very useful distinction between wages and the costs attributable to draft animals). Fred A. Shannon, a respected agricultural historian, summarized this mass of information with two evocative tables, covering ten crops (Appendix exhibit 6). Shannon was more cautious than Holmes and Wright about the purported $681 million savings but did corroborate that the amounts were indeed startling: "Though the actual economy was much less, the Census of 1900 showed a lowering in cost of all items of production of the leading crops, amounting to 46.37 per cent."

Wright also computed the labor time and cost for the production of the plow itself; here his figures were even more surprising. The comparisons were for two landside plows of unspecified size, the earlier with wooden moldboard and plated point, and the later a cast-iron plow. Wright did not know the date the wooden-moldboard version was built—it was probably about 1850, when the wage rate was $.60 per day. The iron-moldboard version was built in 1896, when wage rates ranged from $1.50 to $2.25 per day. It took 118 hours of time to build the earlier plow, 3 hours and 45 minutes for the 1896 model—a 31½ to 1 ratio. The labor cost of the former was $5.44, the latter $.79—a 7 to 1 ratio. Wright summarized this: "It will be seen that very much more has been gained in reducing the time needed . . . than in lessening its money cost, yet the latter is seen to be now only one-seventh of what it was formerly. . . . The explanation of this, without doubt, lies on the one hand in the wonderful inventiveness of the age in which we live, and on the other in the fact that the reward which now comes to labor is much larger than before." Though we must be properly skeptical about the precision of calculation of both of those turn-of-the-century government analysts, the basic thesis—that agricultural machinery of far superior quality was available to the farmer at substantially lessened cost—was unassailable.

We face the same methodological difficulties expressed by Holmes when we attempt to develop a pattern of price trends for Deere & Company, for its products were tinkered with, changed, and improved over all of these years. The plow of 1866 was not the same as the plow of 1898. Still, trends are discernible. For example, the list price of a 14-inch cast-steel plow with wooden beam was $26.00 in 1869, had fallen to $21.50 by 1875, to $19.00 in 1881, and to $17.25 in 1898. The 12-inch breaker, listed at $35.00, had dropped to $24.50 by 1875; it was improved in 1881, however, and the price rose to $26.50 (this then falling to $20.50 by 1898). The Gilpin sulky plow had first carried a price tag of $70.00; this was reduced only modestly to $65.00 by 1881 and to $57.00 by 1898. The company's average earnings per plow, however, stayed quite steady through these three decades. Perhaps a clearer way to show the pattern of Deere prices over these decades is by aggregate figures. The average gross revenue per plow in the period 1874–75 was at its all-time high at $22.40; this figure declined over the next twenty-five years in a significant way (exhibit 5-14). The fact that Deere & Company could maintain its average earnings per machine in the face of a pronounced secular decline in prices is a testimony particularly to the heightened productivity of the manufacturing process.[7]

The secular decline in prices of plows and other manufactured goods was paralleled by a pervasive decline in raw material prices. New techniques of processing and production in the iron and steel industry, in the paint and varnish industry—in a great many of the basic industries throughout the country—had markedly lowered their costs of production and therefore the subsequent prices to the intermediate manufacturers. Deere & Company purchases of raw materials were recorded after 1869; Appendix exhibit 7 shows several of these, for the last year of each of the decades.

Exhibit 5–14   **Average Gross Revenue and Earnings per Plow**
1870–1899

Source: P.C. Simmon, "History of Deere & Company" (ca. 1921), Corporate Minutes, 1870–1900.

Not all of the company's components were so reduced, however; the cost of wood rose higher over these four decades, as shown in Appendix exhibit 8. But since wood was relatively less important than metals and paint as a component of cost, the average cost of raw materials for Deere implements declined substantially.

IMPROVEMENTS IN MANUFACTURING

Manufacturing methods were still rudimentary in the early 1870s, with only small, incremental changes from the first days of the company. John Kiel, a long-service Deere employee, told of his early days in the shop in 1874:

There was no whistle at this time, so a bell was rung when it was time to start work. In some parts of the shop we had gas lighting, which was manufactured in the Company's own plant. In the blacksmith shop they used torches when it got dark, and everyone had a hand kerosene lamp. . . . In those days, everything was handwork, so iron and steel was transported from the Steel Storage to the shearers, etc., on shoulders and wheel barrows, as we had no trucks at that time in which to haul this material around. There were 35 to 40 blacksmiths who worked at forges, most of them having a helper. For this work, they used regular blacksmith coal. There were four drops—two real old-timers and two more up-to-date ones—on which they did some welding on landsides, as at that time all plow bottoms were built up on the little frog which was welded on the landside. One drop was kept busy welding shares. For heating the shares and landsides for these drops, they used Hard Coal. At that time we made many full-bar plows and those shares had to be welded by hand to the bar or landside. There was one share-plating hammer, which sometimes could not work fast enough and had to be worked overtime—sometimes even working at night, when it could be heard all over town. We had three soring [sic] hammers, one of which was all iron; one hammer was used for drawing cultivator beams and the other one was for general work. The fellow that was drawing the beams would throw them in a rough pile instead of piling them up as we do now-a-days; then, in the morning, he had to get them out of the way before he could go to work. There was one Alligator Shearing Machine which did all the heavy cutting, as we got very little cut-to-length stock from the rolling mills. We had three punches, two with shears, where we cut the lighter stock. There were also two planers, as all shares and moldboards had the joint-edge planed. We had two bolt machines, which, when compared with our present machines, worked very slowly.

When the work in the blacksmith shop was completed, the stock was hauled to the fitting shop or the cultivator department. The parts used on the plows were made of iron and had no cutting edge, so such things as hanging and standing cutters had a steel edge welded on. At that time we were building a wheel plow—the Deere Gang—and we made about four a day. A year later, they were made at the rate of ten per day. Mr. Gilpin Moore was working on the Gilpin Sulky about this time, and when it was perfected, I helped to build them. There were about twenty-five plow fitters at this time. At that time we also made many Breaker Plows and all were fitted with extra shares; thus, the plow was built first and then the share was removed and another share was fitted to the plow, after which both shares and the plow were stamped with a number. On other plows, we did not guarantee extras to fit.

Kiel was describing here a reasonably sophisticated system of inter-changeability. Deere had been guaranteeing the uniformity of parts for some of its plows since the late 1850s, its catalogs trumpeting: "This advantage is appreciated when we reflect that one well-hardened mold-board will wear out two or three shares, and when Plows are furnished for distant markets where it is almost impossible to get a Plow properly repaired, the value of duplicate shares is still further enhanced."

But, as Kiel admitted, interchangeability was promised only for some of the products. Part of the problem lay in the particular uses to which agricultural machinery was put, as a special study of interchangeability in the census of manufacturing of 1880 pointed out: "Agricultural machines have, as a rule, comparatively few fitting points, partly because the action of these implements is not mainly between the parts of the implement itself, but upon the soil or crops, so that interchangeability is not as important a feature. This is really a prime distinction between agricultur-al implements and the other forms of interchangeable mechanism. . . . Watches, clocks, and fire-arms have practically no exterior action so far as the functions of the mechanical parts are concerned, such action in the locomotive being confined to a few rolling surfaces, and in the sewing-machine to the point of a needle. But in the plow, cultivator,

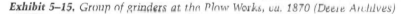

Exhibit 5–15. *Group of grinders at the Plow Works, ca. 1870 (Deere Archives)*

seed-drill, mower, etc., the principal acting parts work against extraneous bodies, whether clods of soil or gavels of grain, with which fitting and interchangeability are out of the question."

The rest of the plow was important, too, noted Kiel:

At this early date most of the plows had wooden beams. These beams were purchased rough and it was quite a job to finish them, as the machinery was very crude. Making the plow handles was also quite a job, and we had a lot of handle dressers. The beaming of the plows was a very particular job and we had quite a crew of beamers, each having a boy helper. All holes in the beams had to be bored by hand, by the beamers themselves, but later on we got a flexible boring machine. We also made a lot of cultivators— many with wooden rigs. At that time we made all the wheels, which had cast hubs, wooden spokes and rim. The iron tire was shrunk on cold by a machine. The wheels for the Deere Gang were of the cast hubs, iron spokes in cast rim and iron tire. The wheels for the Gilpin Sulky were also made of wood, but later of iron. The plows would go from the Fitting Shop to the Grind Shop. There they had a lot of sandstones with water running on them, as they were afraid of ruining the plows. From the grinders, the plows would go to the polishers, where they were gone over with four or more wheels. In those days, everything was painted by hand in the following procedures: 1st: A priming coat; 2nd: Second coat; 3rd: Striped; 4th: Varnished. It certainly required a lot of painters. After the tools were finished, they were shipped on flat cars. It took about 120 Walking Cultivators to make a carload. I do not remember how many walking plows it took to make a load, but they were piled in in fine shape. The cars were switched with oxen.

In the next two decades, however, methods of manufacturing did change radically—new, improved machinery became available through-out the manufacturing process—and along with this physical equipment, human productivity—the employees' efforts—also improved markedly. Company records do not document many of these changes, for most of the new ideas and better ways were again "small steps," each advancing efficiency one more notch. At certain times, however, quantum jumps were made in productivity, with these often linked to "belt tightening" in times of business downturn. After the Panic of 1893 there was great concern all through the country about labor productivity and widespread efforts were made to cut costs in the face of a sagging market. The board of directors of the company finally resolved in 1895 to make a detailed study of labor productivity. The blacksmith department was chosen for an intensive analysis, and a rudimentary version of a time study was taken from July 1, 1897, to July 1, 1898. The results chronicled a complex pattern of the handling of parts, with 8,387,927 different pieces being handled in 28,603,410 operations at a rate of 28,437 per day.

This calculation clearly startled the management, for a major work simplification program was immediately begun. The manager of the project soon reported back to the board: "By making a careful comparison of the tonnage with other seasons you find that we are handling more stock per man than has ever been accomplished before in this depart-

Exhibit 5–16. *Carload of plows, 1882 (Deere Archives)*

ment." All through the plant other significant improvements had occurred. "The change in dipping wheel plows over brushing is now saving
us at a conservative estimate $20.00 to $25.00 per day; the value of room
saved we are unable to estimate, but it is 50% or more. In connection
with the dipping, an over-head track system, connected directly with our
warehouse, is reducing the cost of loading cars of wheel plows 50 to 75%.
With less men and no teams we now load a car in two hours. Usually a
shippers' gang of ten men with two teams will load but two cars per day
or ten hours, or five hours to each car. The Foundry has also been a factor
the past twelve months in reducing cost of products, as a great many
patterns have been grated up and size of flasks reduced thereby, making
reduction on piece-work prices. . . . The cultivator department (Pete
Linn's) has seen changes the past year by the re-arranging of our machines
and benches, which has facilitated in getting goods out quickly. Also the
same can be said of the steel lever harrow department. As regards
improvements contemplated at an early date, we mention the dipping of
walking plows (Beam and Bottom), drilling all sulky and gang frames on
gang drills; boring harrow bars on compound boring machines; and doing
away with hand dressing on all tongues, neck yokes, singletrees and
eveners."[8]

By this time, the "scientific management" movement was taking hold
in American industry, and the rather rudimentary efforts of Deere in this
turn-of-the-century effort at work simplification were soon followed by
much more sophisticated approaches. Frederick Winslow Taylor, the

"father of scientific management," worked with Deere briefly in this period, mostly on the company's cost accounting system. Soon, too, the company itself was to have new, well-trained managers infused with these new concepts. It is also important to understand how these managerial efforts related to the employees with which they interfaced. The company's labor relations in the second half of the nineteenth century now went through some unsettling developments.

Exhibit 5–17. Top, *Plant transportation, utilizing a crawler "tractor," ca. 1910s;* bottom, *Fritz Kohl, car-loader with the company from 1868, undated photograph (Deere Archives)*

1847.

1856.

1876.

1880.

1884.

1888.

1894.

1897.

Exhibit 5–18. *"Fifty years of factory growth," depicting the expansion of the Moline Plow Works (Deere Archives)*

THE LABOR MOVEMENT

The period of 1865–1900 was an important one in employee relations for the country. The birth of a national labor movement came during these decades, and industrial relations patterns moved haltingly toward the more professional approach of later years.

Wages comprised a significant part of the total cost of manufacture. In the face of declining prices over the period 1868–1900, wage rates around the country had remained relatively stable, and, as a result, real earnings had appreciated significantly. (Stanley Lebergott, in his important study of manpower, reported that the average annual earnings of nonfarm employees in 1865 was $512, falling to $386 in 1880 and standing at only $470 in 1899, but for the same three years the real earnings were, respectively, $328, $395, and $563.) Nevertheless, there was much turbulence in employer-employee relations at many places and in many periods through these years; hours of work, unemployment, and unions were particularly important issues.

The Moline area was not immune. There had been some labor conflict in the vicinity as far back as the early 1860s, largely confined to the coal industry in and around Coal Valley. A confrontation there in December 1863 had resulted in the replacement of a number of recalcitrant employees by new workers. Right after the Civil War there was agitation for the eight-hour day, and the state of Illinois even passed legislation to that effect in 1867, albeit of such limited scope that it did not affect the Moline companies. There were some unruly incidents in the Chicago area over the length of the work day, but "happily, this latter action has been entirely confined to the lowest class of laborers," commented the *Davenport Democrat*, "men who to their own loss are ignorant and unthinking. These have been going about the city in gangs intimidating the more respectable classes. . . . "

Labor tensions around the country simmered just under the surface all through the years of the Grange attacks on business and ignited into major conflagration in 1876 and 1877. Ugly violence broke out in connection with the railroad strikes in Pittsburgh and other eastern cities, and labor disputes soon infiltrated Moline industries. There was a strike at one of the Moline sawmills in April 1876, and then in August of that year the molders at Deere struck over a piece-rate change that the company had made. Three days later, the *Davenport Democrat* reported a rather decisive turn of events: "The strike . . . is at an end. That is, new men have been employed in place of those who refused to work at the reduced prices."

A few months later, though, the national railroad strike spilled over to Moline's railroad employees. At the same time, the employees of Deere and the other shops and mills threatened a general strike. The issue was a 10 percent wage cut that the company had just announced. The *Democrat* noted the company's reason: "They claimed that other factories were making implements cheaper, paying less wages, and that, in order to compete with rival concerns they should take such action in the matter as should seem for their best interests." The company issued a statement the next day, noting sagging business prospects and the skyrocketing bad debts of the company, and continued: "In regard to wages for the future, we can say that we will not ask them to work for us for less money than like establishments are paying throughout the country. We are not willing now and cannot fix wages for the year and agree to run our works. We kindly and earnestly counsel all who are identified with these works to a calm and rational consideration of the question in all its bearings, assuring them that they shall be met with like consideration on our part."

The men responded by holding a secret meeting that evening and ended up forming a labor organization, commenting that "they were not to blame and ought not to suffer because Deere & Co. had a good many bad debts during the past season." They abjured any violence, though, "unless Deere & Co. should attempt to ship or receive freight, in which case they will not be responsible for the consequences." The company was upset a few days later to find out that "some agents of other Moline factories, now on the road, are circulating the report that Deere & Co. have shut down for a year." The Moline paper editorialized: "This is calculated to injure Deere & Co . . . and is a disreputable advantage to take." A week later the strike was settled, essentially on the company's terms, "relying upon the Company's sense of fairness and justice," as the newspaper put it. An aggregate 10 percent cut was instituted, though the lower-paying jobs were not themselves reduced. A few weeks later the *Moline Review*, commenting on rumors that a "Labor Party" was to be formed, disputed a *Rock Island Argus* allegation relating to the Deere employees' involvement: "The *Argus* charges that the workmen of Deere & Co. have always voted as Mr. Deere and Mr. Velie dictated at the polls. We have a better opinion of the manly independence and intelligence of their workmen than to believe this and believe that both Mr. Deere and Mr. Velie are too true gentlemen to endeavor to dictate to their men how they shall vote." A national "Workingmen's" movement did happen to be formed at this time—the so-called Greenback Party—but it did not make much headway in Moline.

The company's wage structure was indeed competitive with others in the farm-equipment industry at this time. Sharing of wage information was common among members of the Northwestern Plow Association, and a few of the confidential reports remain. One study, conducted in 1878 by Ralph Emerson of the Emerson, Talcott firm in Rockford, Illinois, compared wage rates for both highly skilled and "ordinary" employees in a number of wage classifications. There is no way of ascertaining how many companies were involved in each of the towns he reported on; Moline presumably might have included others besides

Deere. The results, seen in Appendix exhibit 9, confirmed that as early as the 1870s Moline was one of the highest paying manufacturing cities in the farm equipment industry. In six of seven occupations, its wage rates were as high as those in other cities surveyed, or higher.

If the Greenbackers achieved only modest acceptance around the country, another soon-famous labor organization—the Knights of Labor —was much more successful. By 1886 the Knights, under their charismatic leader, Terrence Powderly, had captured headlines all over the country. The Knights were advocates of "one big union," and when their organizers showed up in the Moline area in 1885, they pushed the notion of "organizing all workingmen of the three cities, of whatever trade or calling." But the employees of the area were much more trades-conscious than this required, and all through this early period the craft union was preferred over any industrial union concepts, Knights or otherwise.

National tensions fueled by the Knights soon stirred up the local caldron, and in April 1886 the grinders at Deere & Company went on strike. This was disconcerting to the company, for it had just completed an expensive air-filtering system for their shop. ("The grinding shop is so freed from dust that there is little or no danger of contracting grinders' consumption," a *Davenport Democrat* writer had just reported.) The grinders wanted a wage cut of 1884 restored, but, as the *Davenport Democrat* put it: "The Company claims that grinding cannot be called skilled labor, as a laboring man with no knowledge of the work can become proficient at it in three or four weeks."

The strike dragged on for a few days, in tandem with a national Knights plan for a show of strength all over the country on May 1. Charles Deere was in Salt Lake City at the time, and Stephen Velie wrote to him: "The status of the grinders strike remains about the same. The polishers were ordered out by the Knights to uphold the grinders. We are putting new men on as fast as obtainable, but no polishing this week. Many of them show a disposition to come back, but are deterred by the Ex. Committee. . . . It looks as if the troubles might culminate on 1st May, and if all Knights of Labor are ordered out on that day, it will close us down with the rest." To everyone's surprise, May Day came and went with no concerted effort by the Knights, locally or nationally, and Velie wrote Deere on May 3: "I think the labor troubles culminated on Saturday, and from now boycotts and other demands of labor organizations will simmer down. They have been 'sent on the ground' by the anarchists and communists, who control them. . . . When the laborers find they are being led to their extinction, they will desert the organization."

For once, though, Velie was dead wrong. The following day, May 4, 1886, there occurred one of the ugliest incidents in all of American labor history—the Haymarket Riot in Chicago. As the Chicago police met a group of paraders, a bomb exploded and seven policemen were killed. The shock to the nation was profound—this was surely the most severe labor confrontation the country had ever experienced. Velie correctly sensed that this would give the national organization a fatal setback. He wrote Deere the next day: "The culmination of the labor troubles in Chicago resulted in more serious loss of life than at St. Louis, but think the career of those Anarchists, Schwab, Spies, Fielding, Parsons, is at an end. They have had full sway there, and for the last two or three years in their incendiary harangues on the lake front Sunday have been educating the rabble up to disregard of law and deeds of violence." The following day the grinders' strike was settled amicably, with a compromise wage settlement worked out by Gilpin Moore.[9]

Exhibit 5–19. *Deere & Company's Moline office force, 1889:* seated, left to right: *S.H. Velie, Sr., Gilpin Moore, Charles Deere, Charles Pope. (Deere Archives)*

TOO MUCH BRANCH INDEPENDENCE

The period of the late 1880s also witnessed increased tensions between the central company and the branches. The strong personalities out in the field seemed ever more maverick. Alvah Mansur and L.B. Tebbetts now owned more than 83 percent of the St. Louis branch-house partnership, and they had gone into farm implements of all sorts in a large way. Their mammoth catalog included not only Deere machinery but also many other agricultural machinery products—shellers, feed mills, fanning mills, field rollers, fence machines, road scrapers, windmills, and even school bells. The catalog itself did not show it, but Mansur & Tebbetts also stocked competitor plows.

This blatant conflict of interest greatly troubled Velie, who wrote Charles Deere: "The door has been opened for the distribution of steel plows and cultivators of other than our make, up to one third of the product of our shops, in effect turning our own guns against us. Our name endorsing goods of rivals—our goods held or sold in some instances at exorbitant profits. The difference in price often inducing the trade to take rival makes, especially such as are endorsed by Deere, Mansur & Co., 'branch of Deere & Co.,' we in effect also becoming endorsers. . . . The interests of ours in the product of the present establishment have become secondary or substitute to that of the branch and our facilities for distribution employed to distribute rival goods. . . . " Velie was particularly upset about Mansur's manipulation of profit margins and concluded, "We should either hold them to exclusive sale or *have a voice in fixing the margin of profit.* . . . My own preference is strongly for the former—exclusive sale; for 'you cannot serve two masters' nor 'a house divided against itself.' "

Deere, never backward about pressing a point, chose now to act on Velie's advice by broaching with Mansur the possibility of a formal split. This greatly upset Mansur, for he wrote back immediately: "Before a connection of twenty years standing and one which has been uniformly profitable to both is broken off, the steps should be very thoroughly & seriously considered. . . . I am willing to sacrifice something rather than sever the ties of so long standing and so interwoven with both of our lives that it seems to me like taking away a part of mine."

George Fuller, Mansur's local manager at Kansas City, felt personally threatened by the split (he owned none of the branch), and he warned Deere that Mansur fully intended to remain in business in Kansas City as a separate, competitor company. Fuller wanted a new corporation, with Deere & Company as majority holder. But Velie wrote: "We have concluded to take the decisive step—a complete break, both in St. Louis and Kansas City." Mansur finally agreed, and the relationship that had been so close was severed.

Mansur now changed the St. Louis firm's name to Mansur & Tebbetts Implement Company and began to handle Deere & Company's goods straightforwardly as a jobber; despite Fuller's alarmism, Mansur chose not to contest Deere in Kansas City. The tension could not be fully resolved, though, until the respective territories for St. Louis and Kansas City could be ironed out, and this issue became a substantial irritant. Tebbetts wrote Deere in October: "We are confident K. City has been too grasping in the matter of territory and the factory will suffer." Finally, each agreed to stay out of the other's way, and Mansur sent Deere and

Velie cigars for Christmas. (He failed to put his name with them and had to write: "Forgot to enclose my card and don't want you to be guessing over it too long.")

Despite the apparently amicable resolution of the tension, Mansur continued to be sharp with Deere on his demands, writing about discounts in January 1892: "I cannot state the case to you any more clearly or strongly than was done in the letter which I showed you. You should make our discount 40 and 17. This is a slight concession on your part in price, and will barely enable us to meet some of the lesser and general competition from other jobbers and manufacturers. . . . I wish you would take this matter up at once and trust you will see it to your interest to give us a favorable reply." Deere, ever willing to give tit for tat, wrote back immediately: "I did not give the matter of increasing discounts any further thought or report to anyone of our Company as I can see no way for them to set a greater disc. than has been agreed upon. There is no room, you know, on price of material: labor prices were never stronger than they are now & demand was never better. . . . I do not see any grounds on which it could be justified."

Yet, amazingly, Alvah Mansur and Charles Deere remained abiding friends, often embarking together on entrepreneurial ventures. The correspondence between the two in the late 1880s and early 1890s is filled with shared information on good investments—new land available, new stocks to buy, etc. Mansur had more modest means and sometimes begged off on his own investment, but he passed along the information to Deere. In May 1892 he wrote (in regard to a mining speculation in which the two of them were interested): "I cannot myself go into it, haven't got the money to spare, and am so loaded up with schemes that do not want anything more at present."

At the time of the split, the Kansas City branch house was incorporated under the laws of Missouri as the John Deere Plow Company; S.H. Velie's son, S.H. Velie, Jr., was given a minority position in this new corporation and served under the managership of Fuller until the latter left the firm in 1904. The two Stephen Velies led to the same confusion of names that the two C.C. Webbers, father and son, caused. Fuller plaintively wrote Charles Deere in 1892: "Do you mean this, for S. H. V. Jr. to do this, or your Mr. Velie at Moline?"

Thus, for several years in the early 1890s, Deere & Company did not have any ownership in the St. Louis branch. Finally, in 1893, the company began negotiations with Mansur to buy back some of the lost proprietorship. Velie, Sr., wrote Charles Deere, advocating either "a slice of their stock, or a jobbers profit out of some of the territory they are now handling." Mansur countered with an offer to buy back into Kansas City. Webber vehemently opposed this: "You would be getting back to where you were five years ago. . . . You do not want the St. Louis people for their capital, and Mr. Mansur will give the Kansas City business no attention. Rather than do it, it would be advisable to break entirely with St. Louis."

Finally a compromise was worked out—Deere & Company bought a one-fifth interest, but sold none of Kansas City to Mansur. Webber, always the stickler on branch relations, immediately wrote Moline: "Now that St. Louis is fairly established as a branch, they should send you monthly abbreviated trial balances and itemized report of sales, same as is furnished by the other houses. The sooner they get in line on these things, the better." The minority ownership was once again unsatisfactory; when Mansur died in 1898 the company purchased the remaining holdings.[10]

As if the acrimony with Mansur were not enough, Deere and Velie, Sr., now became unhappy about their San Francisco branch. Remember that the Hawleys had been Deere's "branch house" for more than three decades, from before the Civil War until 1889, but only as a jobber, not a formal branch. The Hawley enterprise was already a substantial hardware house, doing more than half a million dollars of business by the early 1870s, only one-third of which was in agricultural implements. But it had some substantial internal problems. An R.G. Dun & Co. correspondent commented in 1872 about "the fear that they were too widespread to be entirely desirable for a very large amount . . . the a/c should be closely watched." He added, more gratuitously than the usually antiseptic credit prose, "They are notorious for selling for little or no profit." The correspondent explained this apparent incongruity: "They collect closely, wh. they do from necessity as a bus. they do is out of proportion to their means & are constantly closely run & pinched & not infrequently 'spout' Bills of Lading at high rates before goods arrive." The correspondent also had pungent views about Fredrick Vaughn, Deere's new branch manager after 1889: "Is steady and indefatigable worker, but is essentially a boaster & gd. judges have as little confidence in the ultimate success of its mode of do. bus. as they have in his statements."

The new arrangement in 1889 was a corporation, the Deere Implement Company. The Hawleys took $80,000 of the stock, Deere & Company $100,000, with the remaining $20,000 given to Vaughn. Half of the existing Hawley building on Market Street was to be devoted to the Deere branch.

Such an arrangement would be a fragile one, even under the best of circumstances. Enormous good will would be demanded of both parties in allowing an existing business to continue, yet with a segment of it sliced out, with the latter owned in part by an outside party. The strain was too great in this case. Within months, Vaughn was complaining to Charles Deere of alleged intransigence on the part of the local partners. He had wanted to hire a new assistant, "but as usual got 'sit down on' by the powers. Mr. Hawley says that he does not want to go further into the future than Jany. 1st. . . . Hawleys are 'economical' and do not want to spend any money. I find myself hampered at every step and do not know where it will all end."

The enmity between the Hawleys and Vaughn stemmed particularly from pricing the stock of goods that would be in the Deere Implement Company, and how sales of various pieces of equipment would be credited—in other words, what should be the full line, and under which house would a particular product be sold. Vaughn's complaints finally motivated Stephen Velie, Sr., to propose a stringent solution to Charles Deere: "Get Mr. Vaughn placed in such a position as manager as that he will not be hampered or annoyed by frivolous opposition or unreasonable restrictions. Rather than have it continue as disagreeable as it has seemed to have been during the past five months, we are in a position to start an independent house to a good deal better advantage than we could have done on the first of August." Velie's notion of splitting completely away from Hawley appealed to Deere, so the latter made a personal trip to San Francisco a month later, still willing to negotiate a continuing arrangement with the Hawleys, but also prepared to sever it if necessary.

The negotiations were protracted, full of irritations. Deere poured out his frustrations in confidential letters to Velie, warning him: "Keep pretty close watch of our mail, it won't do to leave it entirely to a new man." After more than a week of fruitless negotiations, Deere wrote: "We are in trouble here; I fear we have struck a deadlock and have got a hard set to buck." The Hawley side had the trump card, inasmuch as they held four out of the five directorships in the California corporation. Deere was in the classic position of the minority shareholder, outvoted by the majority. Deere commented to Velie: "I am sorry to see disposition on part of HBH Co. to make the most of it."

Days passed, and the extended time in San Francisco began to play on the nerves of Charles Deere; he penned a poignant plea to Velie: "Please look after my family a little." But the next day his old combative business instincts surfaced again and he told Velie: "I am not going to run away from it as long as anything remains to be done or without precipitating settlement in one way or another." Still, Deere's heightening frustration with the situation caused him to add a startling postscript: "I want no more Branch Houses."

Negotiations proceeded haltingly for several more days, but finally it seemed that the Hawleys had decided to sell all their shares in Deere Implement Company to Deere & Company. Deere immediately wrote Velie to come right out. By that afternoon, though, Deere countermanded the instructions—the deal had fallen through. "The letter I wrote you this morning is all no good. . . . HBH & Co. did not submit their proposition to sell out to us, which they promised at last interview." Deere finally had to admit to Velie that probably the only course left was to sue the Deere Implement Company for an accounting of the various parties' interests.

Exhibit 5–20. *Branch house office and display floor scenes:* top, *Lansing,* center *and* bottom, *San Francisco, ca. 1912–13. (Deere Archives)*

Deere was bitter about the Hawley change of heart. "I am satisfied Hawleys thought from the start to fix us so we would have to buy them out at their price. . . . The Hawleys are sharpers of the highest die." After all the bad news, Deere could at least manage a final positive comment to Velie: "Of course disasters look larger and worse at a distance. . . . " But he confided to Mansur a day later: "Am getting enough of this country and want to go home."

The Hawleys let Deere anguish for four more days; on February 19, they finally agreed to sell, albeit on their own terms. Deere capitulated, writing Velie: "For the day, we have dropped the weapons of war and talked peace."

Now came the issue of valuing the inventory of Deere equipment that Hawley still held. Deere continued: "I have set no time, of course, for leaving here yet, we have got to make the D.I. Co. pay for their plows and allow them *no discounts*." Deere warned Velie again about secrecy at home: "Only keep quiet at home, for the Hawley Boys are the devil, as you know by this time." Deere must have been depressed by the protracted push-and-tug, for he added another postscript: "Can't write any more tonight. Tell my wife you heard from me as I haven't written her for a day or two."

The Hawley group countered with an offer to sell the Deere inventory at "60 cents on the dollar" and added "if this Proposition is not acceptable or any of our previous ones we must respectfully but politely say, we have no other one to submit." The Hawleys won this battle, too; their compromise proposal became the basis for the final settlement, and the weeks of tense negotiations came to an end. The Hawleys still were arguing among themselves about their own sharing, and Vaughn disparagingly remarked that they were "having a monkey and parrot time."

The Deere Implement Company did stay in the same building with the Hawleys, however, and this later led to one further argument. As part of the settlement, the Deere Implement Company had agreed to pay $5,000 a year for "good will" for each of the four following years. In turn, Hawley was to turn over to the Deere Implement Company every order they received for agricultural implements. Shortly after the first $5,000 payment had been made, Vaughn reported his feeling that the Hawleys were not living up to their side of the agreement—that they were taking orders and shipping agricultural implements to customers. Matters again became tense, Vaughn reporting in December 1892: "Instead of marking the goods on the sidewalk where we could see them, as before, the goods were loaded upon the dray, the drayman carrying the tags in his pocket, to be put on either between the store and the freight house, or at the freight house. When this became known to us, we had our warehouse man (opposite the freight house) get pointers on these shipments. After keeping this account for nearly a year, and at about the time the next payment would be due, we, upon the advice of our attorney, notified them that we should withhold the $5,000.00 payment for good-will."

Business turned downward all through the country over the next year or two, particularly because of the Panic of 1893. Deere & Company decided to retrench in San Francisco by cutting back on the number of lines handled there, by asking Vaughn and others for salary reductions, and by moving the operations to a new location on the outskirts of the city. This precipitated the resignation of Vaughn, who wrote Charles Deere in July 1896: "I consider this a suicidal policy if you expect to continue in the California trade, as in my estimation such changes will cause losses much greater than the saving made."

This time Charles Deere asked C.C. Webber to handle the on-the-spot negotiations—and Webber experienced the same multi-week negotiation process; Webber first wanted to settle with Vaughn, then form a new branch house, with a new manager (John D. Sibley). In his usual frank way, Webber exhorted Deere to make a rapid settlement with Vaughn. As Webber reminded Deere, "Do not forget that Vaughn's interest in this concern is just one tenth. That your interest lies largely now in getting rid of him and getting yourself into condition to attempt at least to pull out of the rut that the house has fallen into and to get your money out of your assets here."

The negotiations bogged down as they had in the Hawley situation, and Webber wrote on August 28: "Dear Uncle: Our settlement moves slowly—don't dare to try and hurry matters too much for fear Vaughn will jump the track." Finally, after almost three weeks of negotiations, Webber concluded the agreement with Vaughn and hired Sibley as his replacement. Webber penned a note to Deere: "I assure you that this has not been a pleasant task nor would I stay here another week with this thing still hanging fire for the $500 difference that we have finally agreed to give him."

Webber had been able to accomplish the negotiations without leaving ill feelings and wrote Deere, as he was leaving town: "Believe Mr. Vaughn friendly to all of us, and he will do what he can to help Sibley." Sibley had obviously been impressed by Webber in the negotiations and asked that Webber send him an assistant. Webber wrote Deere: "Sibley would prefer that we send someone from here, someone that has been educated in the implement line in this part of the world, rather than to take a Californian, and try to educate him all over again."[11]

Thus Deere & Company prepared to move into the new century with five key branches in St. Louis, Kansas City, Minneapolis, Council Bluffs, and San Francisco (exhibits 5-20 and 5-21). A smaller branch was opened in Indianapolis in the 1890s; there were also sub-branches at Dallas and Nashville, and close links with four key jobbers, called at that time "associate houses." The latter were Spencer & Lehman of Decatur, Illinois (from 1883), in central Illinois; H.H. Sickels & Co. of Des Moines, Iowa (from 1877), in central and northern Iowa; Lourie Implement Co. of

Keokuk, Iowa (from 1891), in eastern Iowa; and C.H. Dodd & Co. of Portland, Oregon (from 1891), in Oregon and Washington.

Were one to view simplistically the experiment with the close-to-autonomous branches at St. Louis and San Francisco, the conclusion would likely be negative. Much lost motion and many missed opportunities for Deere & Company had ensued. Yet the principle itself was highly innovative, a precursor of widespread industry patterns a few decades later. Charles Deere, a thoroughgoing entrepreneur, was reaching for a new device that would allow him to be entrepreneurial with a partner who was separated from him by many physical miles and by less-than-perfect communications. The semi-autonomous profit center was just

Exhibit 5–21. *The five major Deere branch houses, ca. 1894 (Deere Archives)*

such a mechanism. Its lack of lasting success with Mansur and the Hawleys stemmed not from its inapplicability, or even, for that matter, wholly from the prickliness of Mansur and the intransigence of the Hawleys. New ideas need time to develop and come to fruition. Charles Deere learned a great deal from this experience, and his successors would later profit from this ground-breaking managerial initiative.

JOHN DEERE'S LATER YEARS

John Deere kept the titular post of president of Deere·& Company even though his role in the firm was minimal after the Civil War. His one-quarter ownership gave him ample funds to indulge himself in other activities.

First, there was farming. He purchased a large tract east of Moline in the early 1860s and raised registered Jersey cattle and Berkshire hogs. He was just as strong-willed and opinionated about his farm as he was about his business. H.C. Peek recounted one trip to the farm: "He prided himself on running all its operations. A man was cutting grass with a mower. He called him to stop, asked him where the horse rake was, and ordered him to go raking the hay. The man started to obey when I said, 'Uncle, in Ogle County we let our hay dry before we rake it.' 'Oh thunder,' he said, 'I never thought of that.' then he called to the man 'Go on with your mowing, what are you stopping there for?' The man grinned and started his team."

Secondly, John Deere renewed his interest in Vermont. After he returned there in 1866 to marry Demarius Lamb's sister, Lucenia, fresh associations with his Vermont friends brought him back frequently for long visits.

In Moline itself, John Deere took his rightful place as an important, influential senior resident. He was chairman of Decoration Day services one year, made a speech to the St. Louis Board of Trade in another, was host to a group of Cincinnati businessmen in a third year ("at their head as the procession made the rounds of the Deere Plow Works, was hearty old John Deere himself"). There were episodes of personal excitement here and there; for example, in 1868 he chanced upon a "shameless sinner," who had come by an overturned hay wagon and, seeing no one there, had begun to sell the goods from the broken wagon. Deere ran after the man, caught him, and forced him to give up his loot—not an inconsequential act for a man of sixty-four years! In 1871 he was thrown from a sleigh in West Davenport "and was made senseless for several minutes by the fall." Fortunately, he rapidly recovered.

Probably the most important event was his entry into politics and his subsequent election as mayor of Moline on April 16, 1873. He served during the depression following the Panic of 1873, when the dominant concern was temperance, a burning issue all over the country. Drinking in saloons had always been popular in Moline, the Germans wanting their beer gardens, the Irish their pubs, etc. Now an extension of a liquor license faced the town council. The ensuing debate resulted in a tie vote. "Mayor Deere decided that he would not untie them by his casting a vote," reported the *Davenport Democrat*, "preferring that it go to the people for settlement." Over the next several weeks the Prohibitionists and the anti-temperance forces campaigned vigorously for an anticipated referendum, exchanging insults: "While the crusaders were engaged in recording the names of Schrader's visitors, a load of beer was brought up in a beer wagon from Rock Island and drinking in the street commenced. A large crowd assembled, anti-temperance speeches were made, stones thrown and cheers, howls, and groans rent the air. Mayor Deere ordered Marshal Follett to disperse the crowd. . . . It was a disgraceful affair." A week later the council capitulated to the anti-temperance faction without the referendum, passing a special ordinance allowing additional licenses for a group of four individuals to open wine- and beer-selling emporiums. The *Democrat* sermonized: "Oh, Moline! What has become of thy moral atmosphere?" John Deere rose to this bait and refused to sign the licenses. Later in the same year, another licensee was put in jail for twenty days for having sold liquor to a minor, and an unruly crowd of anti-temperance advocates then marched through the streets, yelling epithets at Mayor Deere. John Deere's year as mayor of the town was rather unpleasant.

John Deere used his own personal resources generously, contributing to a wide range of local educational, religious, and charitable organizations. He put not just money but also time and interest into these ventures. He sometimes invested in new, struggling enterprises and agonized over their successes and failures as if he were the chief executive. For example, after investing in a small jewelry and crockery concern, he wrote William Ball (his nephew by marriage, and his personal business manager): "You did just right in the B and J affair. I don't want them to fail if you can help them with any means and be safe. They wanted 15 hundred or 2 thousand and said they could pay cash. . . . If they paid cash, they could buy enough cheaper to nearly pay the interest. . . . I don't want that crockery store to fail if I can help it."

John Deere had reached the age of eighty, two years earlier, in 1884. Burton F. Peek recounted an evocative story about him at this age. "About 1884 or 1885 John Deere came to Ogle County to attend a meeting of the Old Settlers' Association. He stayed at our house. There were also present one of his contemporaries, John Gale. They had lived at or near Grand Detour at the same time. They were reminiscing on the early days and . . . having a little party at a 'tavern.' They became rather boisterous, so much so that the landlord protested. The argument became rather violent and the landlord was finally forced to take refuge in the corner behind a barrel of salt fish. The two Johns, each with a salt fish, stood over him, and every time he raised his head they smacked him."

In his later years, Deere's well-known generosity sometimes made him the target of charlatans and fortune-seekers. Near the end of his life there was consternation in the family when they learned that a group of "spiritualists" had insinuated themselves into the old man's life, hoping to persuade him to endow their cause. Fortunately, nothing came of it.

On May 17, 1886, John Deere died at the age of eighty-two. "Probably no other funeral in Moline was ever attended by so many people or drew forth the public evidence of mourning," recounted Nellie Ball Rosborough many years later. "I remember going with my parents to the private funeral service in his home and to the service in the church. On the altar was a sheaf of garnered grain and there was a large floral plow with the name, 'John Deere' on the beam." As the cortege wound its way through the city, a crowd of some 2–3,000 people surrounded the grave, awaiting the burial of the plow pioneer.[12]

In retrospect, John Deere's contribution to his company and to the agricultural equipment industry all over the world emerges clearly. He was energetic and purposeful, moving forward despite ownership squabbles, business ups and downs, marketing battles, and countless other problems. He was not himself a major inventor; on the other hand, there is ample documentation of his highly productive role as an adapter and marketing innovator. He was not a financier; indeed, his lack of knowledge and judgment about money matters almost lost him the company more than once. Nor was he always the diplomatic leader; often his temper exploded over small slips by others. But he did have a knack for organization, an abiding concern for quality, and a feeling for the role of the agricultural equipment industry in America's growth that made him a preeminent producer and distributor of agricultural machinery.

Above all, he was a charismatic leader, a man of great bearing, commanding attention and respect wherever he went. He personified company integrity and loyalty, and he must have instilled more than a modicum of leadership qualities in his successor-son, Charles Deere.

THE FAMILY IN TRANSITION

The provisions in John Deere's will were reported in detail by the press. The bulk of his stock went to his four daughters; a small block was willed to his widow, Lucenia. No stock was left directly to Charles Deere; according to one newspaper: "The will sets forth as to the testator's son, C.H. Deere, that assistance was given him while living, including an advantageous position in business, but he is now above want and has a good share of this world's goods, and therefore the testator thought it just that the bulk of the property be divided among his other children." Charles Deere remained far and away the major stockholder, with 49.8 percent. Only Stephen Velie, Sr., and his wife held a truly significant additional shareholding (2,050 shares, just over 20 percent of the company's outstanding shares).

Charles Deere had become one of the leading citizens of the state of Illinois in the decades after the Civil War. His business investments ranged widely, and he took an active management role in many of the companies. He was particularly interested in the Hennepin Canal project to link the Illinois River to the Mississippi at Moline. As far back as the 1850s he fought fires as an active member and secretary of the Moline fire fighting enterprise (and fell from a ladder in June 1855, running a large hook deep into his leg); in the late 1870s he was instrumental in the founding of the Deere Hose Company. He was one of the founders of the water company and was involved with his father in the Moline National Bank. His position as a business leader of the town and state soon was widely recognized and he gained a reputation for rectitude that was sullied apparently only once; he was given a one-week suspension from the Union League Club in Chicago in 1888 for "introducing into the Club on the 18th of June, without consent of the Board, a person residing in or within fifty miles of this City."

Local politics fascinated Charles Deere as much as it did his father. Charles was a strong supporter of the local Republican Party, particularly when his father was mayor, though he found himself at political odds with Stillman Wheelock, who was mayor in the late 1870s and early 1880s. Wheelock, by this time, was president of the Moline Plow Company, the old antagonist of Deere & Company in the famous trademark case of the late 1860s. In 1881, when Wheelock decided to seek a second term as mayor, Charles Deere opposed him in the Republican caucus. The vote was extremely close. Wheelock had twenty-three votes,

Deere twenty-two. At about this same time, in 1880, the Moline manufacturers were accused by several letter writers in the local papers of forcing their employees to vote a "party line." The twelve major companies in the town joined together in a public statement and issued an "emphatic denial and denunciation of the charge." They continued: "However anxious as we are to have the present prosperous administration of public affairs continue, and would use all honorable means to convince everyone engaged in manufactories, either as an employer or employee, that our interests are mutual, and that the prosperity of one is the prosperity of the other, yet we would scorn to promote even so desirable an end by questionable means."

There was an implication of paternalism in these accusations, and it might well have been leveled particularly against Deere & Company. The company had shown a strong sense of responsibility toward its employees, developing a benefit program unique for its time. The John Deere picnics each summer were major social events for the town; when industrial accidents occurred, as they did frequently in the nineteenth century, the company was assiduous in concern and generous in compensation, long before it was required by workmen's compensation laws. In sum, the company sought to be a benevolent employer, though some construed its actions as paternalism.

Charles Deere enjoyed a happy family and social life during these decades. There was genuine affection among the four members of his family—himself, his wife, Mary, and his two daughters, Anna and Katherine. In 1872 he constructed a beautiful home on the hill overlooking the Moline shops, described by the local paper as a "Swiss Villa style," which he named Overlook. There many glittering social events were held over the years, and the large home and its grounds have remained a landmark of the city to the present. Letters found among Charles Deere's papers—from his wife, his children, and other relatives and friends—chronicle deep personal attachments. The notes from his wife express a particularly affectionate and warm feeling. The children, who were educated in private Eastern schools, traveled abroad with their parents. Charles Deere's many business trips took him away from home a great deal, and the letters from his wife over and over record her dislike of being apart.

Both girls were married in the early 1890s, Anna to William Dwight Wiman in 1890 and Katherine to William Butterworth in 1892. William Wiman was the scion of a well-known Eastern industrialist, Erastus Wiman, who had been the mainspring in the development of Staten Island, as well as an executive in the Canadian organization linked to R.G. Dun and Co. and president of both the Great Northern Telegraph Company of Canada and the Staten Island Railroad Company. William Butterworth was the descendant of a long line of Virginians; his father had been United States representative from the First District of Ohio in the late 1870s and early 1880s. Butterworth had graduated from Lehigh University and obtained his law degree at the National University Law School in Washington. After his marriage to Katherine Deere, he began working with the company. It was still customary in those days to ask in writing for the hand of a daughter in marriage, and stylized, respectful letters from both Wiman and Butterworth to Charles Deere remain in the latter's files. Both of the weddings were major social events in Moline, and both young families began with considerable financial underpinnings.

At one point in this period, Charles Deere had a near-tragic accident, reminiscent of his father's. The *Davenport Democrat* chronicled it:

> SEVERE ACCIDENT—While sitting in his office yesterday morning Chas. Deere Esq., of the Deere Plow Co. observed that his horse, a spirited animal, hitched in the yard, had become frightened, and went out to quiet him. The horse had broken the hitching strap, and was plunging about when Mr. Deere caught him by the bit, and in a sharp scuffle to gain mastery, he was thrown violently upon the ground, his head striking against the brick walls. He was picked up rigid and insensible, and so remained for eight or ten minutes. It was feared that life was extinct. He finally rallied, and was taken home, and at last account the doctors were of the opinion that though severely injured, the accident would not prove fatal. It was a very narrow escape.

It was a narrow escape for the firm as well as for Deere himself. No other member of the family was ready in that year to step into his position, and there would have been a leadership crisis of some moment had Charles Deere died from this accident.[13]

Now this very leadership was to be put at issue in a startling bid from a British syndicate put forth in 1889.

FARM IMPLEMENT NEWS

Vol. XXXII. No. 4   CHICAGO, ILL., OCTOBER 19, 1911. $2.00 Per Year.

Better Stay in the Frying Pan.

CHAPTER 6

CHALLENGES TO INDEPENDENCE

*You know I have regarded the scheme with much
apprehension of its ultimate consequences—feeling as I do
that the welfare of all present stockholders and of all
connected with the plow business in any way is
intimately interwoven with the ability and fidelity and
integrity with which the Deere & Co. establishment is
managed . . . I somehow cannot divest myself of the
apprehension that in turning it over to alien management
and control it will become the football of stock
speculation and 'wreckless' manipulating.*

Stephen Velie, Sr., 1890

◁*Cover cartoon from trade press (*Farm Implement News, *October 19, 1911)*

Sometime in the late 1880s Charles Deere was contacted by a private party. Would he and the other shareholders of Deere & Company consider selling the firm to an outside group? From the start, it was made clear that the group wanted full control. Yet the substance of the proposal looked attractive enough to persuade Deere to pursue the matter.

Why would Charles Deere and his associates consider giving up the company they regarded so highly? The answer lay partly in pressures for growth. The 1880s had been a lively decade for business combination. The great Standard Oil trust had been put in place in 1882, and other agglomerations had occurred throughout American industry—the American cotton oil trust, the national lead trust, the whiskey and sugar trusts, and others. By 1890 there had been so much reaction against the excesses of this combination movement that one of the country's most important pieces of business regulation, the Sherman Anti-Trust Act, was passed.

But the consolidation movement continued, utilizing other legal forms of organization, the holding company in particular. At the same time, British investors invaded American capital markets, making multimillion-dollar purchases of companies throughout American industry. Chicago newspapers were full of stories about the trend. In one month in mid-1889, *Chicago Tribune* readers were regaled with numerous stories about proposed takeovers in several industries: July 14, a milling syndicate ("Millions of English money said to be back of it"); July 17, the Milwaukee flour mills ("A representative of English capitalists now in the Cream City"); July 20, the grain elevators ("Forty big wheat bins bought up by the Englishmen"); July 24, the steel works ("English capitalists would buy all the plants in Pittsburgh"); August 4, cotton ("Foreign capital seeking to get all the American factories"); August 5, a celluloid trust ("English capitalists propose to get control"); August 7, iron mines ("Foreign capital operating largely . . . "); August 9, sugar ("Stupendous scheme of an English-German syndicate").

Finally, on September 29, a front-page story appeared under the ominous headline, "IN FOREIGN HANDS—Gigantic Transfer of Prominent American Properties. SOLD TO ENGLISH SYNDICATES." So important did this article appear that it was carefully clipped and circulated among the Deere management. Deere's reason for the absorbing interest in the newspaper story was that a British syndicate was the company's suitor.

The syndicate made no bones about its intent to buy a full-scale plow combination. It was already negotiating with other plow manufacturers. There did seem ample reason for such a combination, if alone just for defensive purposes. The suppliers with whom the plow companies all had to deal had been able to hold themselves together remarkably well. By the late 1880s, a group of steel suppliers had banded together as a self-styled "Steel Trust" and had demanded the signing of an agreement between it and the Northwestern Plow Association.

The plow association did have the potential for being a full-fledged combination—voluntary agreements had been made all through these years by the member plow makers about prices, warranties, and a wide range of other business matters. Yet the organization never had effective sanctions; instead, it relied on moral suasion and reciprocal relationships to maintain agreements. More often the leadership of the association had to plead with the backsliders. As C.W. Mitchell, the secretary of the association in this period, wrote: "If we could only have a little confidence in each other, and when a buyer asks for these very low prices, pass him by for the present, insisting upon good paying prices, it does seem to me that we would be able to get all the business that we could. . . . Let us have faith in each other to that extent of believing that others are sticking for good prices."

The very notion of all the plow manufacturers banding together with all the steel suppliers smacked too much of price collusion to satisfy many of the plow group. Stephen Velie, Sr., wrote one of the other plow-company executives: "I do not like the idea of the members of the steel syndicate taking it upon themselves to make any explanation of the cause for the increased price of steel that links the Plow Association with it, and I trust they have been advised . . . not to make any reference to the N.W.P.A. in making quotations to outsiders for steel." Velie also wrote to Alvah Mansur about the power of the steel trust: "The combination of Syndicate steel holds strong and they claim that there is no object in anybody's breaking it, as this kind of steel should not be made at a price less than the present." Charles Deere was also pessimistic about the ability of the plow makers to stand up to the steel syndicate, writing another plow-company president: "Presume we are not now in position to act on a combination, and must say that we have very little faith in effecting anything with the Steel syndicate." The truth of the matter was that the Northwestern Plow Association was just that, an association, not a trust or combination with its own discipline and sanction system.

The proposition to sell Deere & Company to the Englishmen was tempting also because it would bring a large amount of cash to Charles Deere and his associates. Still, control would be lost. Even if the British syndicate retained most of the current management, it probably would not keep the chief executive officer. Key decisions would be made four thousand miles away in London. The reputation of the company would change—and profoundly so. Already the farmers were hostile to intrusion by the British. Land grabbing by aliens had been decried all through the 1880s, and the British flow of capital exacerbated these feelings. Farmers contemptuously spat the words "British Gold" as a mark of deepest opprobrium. How much of this fallout would Deere & Company inherit if it sold to the British?[1]

The final factor allowing Charles Deere to consider the British offer was that John Deere was no longer there. His death in 1886 had altered the family's perspective in planning for the future.

THE BRITISH SYNDICATE'S BID

When F.L. Underwood, a Kansas City broker and promoter, approached Charles Deere in the summer of 1889 on behalf of the British group, he made it clear that his clients wanted three companies in an all-or-nothing package—Deere & Company, Deere & Mansur, and the Moline Plow Company. Charles Deere himself, as negotiator on the plowmen's side, faced a formidable task. Each of the companies had its own set of shareholders to be apprised of every detail and persuaded to go along. At Deere & Company, Charles Deere was the largest shareholder but was not so dominant that he felt he could act unilaterally. His four sisters each held significant blocks; Stephen Velie, Sr., and his wife owned a major holding and there were other smaller holdings to be reckoned with, especially that of nephew C.C. Webber, always an independent voice. Although Charles Deere owned sizable stock in Deere & Mansur, the other owners—Alvah Mansur, John Good, and several additional people— were all outside the direct Deere orbit.

The third company, the Moline Plow Company, had been Deere's protagonist in the Candee-Swan trademark case. Charles Deere had no ownership in it. He was dealing almost at arms-length with Stillman Wheelock, John Stephens, Andrew Friberg, and the other Moline Plow Company shareholders (which included holdings by an Eastern share-holder, wholly independent of local management). Apparently Charles Deere felt that he could not negotiate from a strong enough position without at least majority control in Deere & Company, so he purchased enough shares from the holdings of E.B. Atkinson to attain majority ownership of the corporation. By the time the negotiations with Under-wood actually got underway, he held 50.2 percent of the stock in Deere.

Pricing the potential transaction was going to be a complicated matter. Each of the three companies had its own recent past performance and profit potentials—and they were not at all comparable. Deere & Company at that time was capitalized for $1 million; at the end of the fiscal year 1888–89, the surplus account was just over $1 million and assets totaled just under $2.3 million.

Deere and Stephen Velie, Sr., feeling that the high depreciation charge of previous years understated the assets, wrote the assets up by $335,000; a further calculation also was made for undivided profits of the branch houses, adding another $200,000. The total asset figure then became $2.8 million. A second step was taken a few months later, with the issuance of an additional $500,000 in stock and the declaration of a $370,000 cash dividend. (This was only the second time in company history that dividend payments had exceeded earnings for a particular year; the

Exhibit 6–1. *John Deere, 1804–86 (Deere Archives)*

company had earned $217,000 in 1889, down from $240,000 in 1888). These changes gave a more realistic appearance to the balance sheet and—important for the Deere shareholders—they took some of the earnings out of the company prior to the potential sale.

Deere & Mansur had had a bad year in 1884, and since that year its earnings picture had not been as imposing as the group might have

wanted. Mansur seemed willing to leave the bargaining basis to Deere: "I
told Underwood I would agree to anything you would on the Planter Shop
and he said the price you fixed was $250 [the per-share price, or $250,000
for the whole]. But I took this to be a cash price." Mansur was in
negotiations with Deere already, in relation to the St. Louis and Kansas
City branches, and told Deere in this letter: "Would like to have it soon,
as I need money." John Good, on the other hand, kept holding out for a
larger figure and admonished Deere: "We went over our figures again and
now make the lowest price of which we will sell $400,000. . . . With the
shape the business is now in, and the prospects ahead we do not care to
sell for less than the price named above."

The Moline Plow Company was not in as good shape as the other two
companies, having had a bad year in 1888 and serious losses in several
earlier years that had been written off. Underwood told Wheelock,
"While these losses can undoubtedly be obviated, yet it will be difficult
for us to convince our friends of the fact in view of the record which we
are compelled to show them." Underwood initially priced the Moline
Plow Company at $650,000, with $200,000 of this amount to be taken in
debentures of the new British holding company. Indeed, as Deere and
Underwood warily circled each other in these price negotiations, it soon
became more evident that not all of the deal with the syndicate would be
cash, that some securities of a yet-to-be-determined form would need to
be accepted in the new British company (with majority control vested in
the British group).

Up to this moment everyone had presumed the negotiations to be
private and confidential—there had been no mention in the Moline or
Rock Island press, nor in the trade publications. But the news leaked out
to the financial community and the "fraternity" of promoters ranging
about the country. Another promoter soon appeared on the scene, and
Deere and Underwood learned that this man, Thomas S. Nickerson, a
Boston investment-bond broker, had already made a tender offer to
Stillman Wheelock for part of the Moline Plow Company stock. Underwood wrote Deere: "If they have already entered into a contract with Mr.
Nickerson, it would be useless waiting because they would be carried
along from month to month with specious promises and false hopes."
Underwood still believed that the Moline Plow Company could not sell
its own shares to advantage if acting alone, but he became upset when he
learned that Nickerson was also evidencing interest in the stock of Deere
& Company and Deere & Mansur.

Letters from other promoters, most of them representing other British
syndicates, now reached Charles Deere, including one from A.M.
DaCosta, a Kansas City manufacturer's agent who held himself out to be
"associated with one of the greatest, if not the greatest, of the buying
syndicates." DeCosta put forth a logical reason as to why so many of the
syndicates were using Kansas City agents: "Paradoxical as it may seem,

Kansas City or Omaha are far better points to start these negotiations in than either New York or Boston, because in far western towns with direct cable communications to London, the news is withheld from the great home centers, and hence publicity is avoided therein."

March 1890 came, and Wheelock had failed to negotiate a separate sale of the Moline Plow Company, so he resumed talks with Underwood. A.L. Bryant, Wheelock's colleague, admitted to difficulties with their own minority holders: "During this time the stockholders of the company have become inflated. . . . A year ago the option on this plant could have been had for very reasonable money and at very low figure, but today all are wild and have visions of enormous wealth, all to be derived from English Syndicates whom, some of our stockholders seem to think, have nothing to do but squander large bricks of gold." Bryant then instituted what was to be the first of many efforts by the Moline Plow Company to persuade Underwood to make a separate deal, but Underwood replied: "I do not do that kind of business." Underwood could not resist a side remark about the way the Moline Plow Company was handling its finances: "I note what you say about making dividends on your stock. In my judgment, it would be folly to make a dividend on your stock in the present condition of your Company. You have to cut down your liabilities, and get closer to shore. This is gratuitous advice but it is sound."

Velie, Sr., meanwhile, was becoming increasingly uneasy about the apparent Moline Plow Company disloyalty, and he wrote Deere from Paris, France: "I am prepared to see a black eye given to these ponderous financial schemes at most any time, and great caution is necessary to prevent serious complications during pendancy and before completion of the transaction." He continued with a more personal concern: "You know my feeling is that we ought to transmit this business in a sound condition to those who come after us and that it will add more to our name and fame and perhaps to our purses to do so than it will to turn it over to alien hands."

Velie, Sr., was still in Europe when the board of directors of Deere & Company met on July 16, 1890. No record of the discussion itself remains, but at the end of the meeting a resolution was passed, recommending to the shareholders that the company be sold for a price of $3 million, at least $2 million of which was to be in cash. The other two companies were to be part of the deal, with Deere & Mansur valued at $300,000 and the Moline Plow Company at $800,000. The new holding company was to be valued at not more than $4,850,000. The minutes also recorded Velie's vote, by letter, "in which he agreed with reluctance to a sale of the plant under certain conditions as to payment and management for a term of years."

The question was, which of the consortia, if any, would take up the offer. Underwood still seemed reluctant at this price. Nickerson appeared back on the scene, apparently having expanded the scope of his own

Exhibit 6–2. Left, *Charles H. Deere and Mary Little Deere, undated photograph;* right, *"Overlook," the Charles Deere home in Moline, as it looked in the late nineteenth century. (Deere Archives)*

combination by approaching Martin Kingman, president of an important Peoria, Illinois, farm machinery company (who also just happened to own a block of the Moline Plow Company stock.)

Webber had meanwhile mulled over the board meeting, and he startled Deere with a fresh proposal—the company itself should be the promoter. "The more I think of the plan of consolidating the three plants on our own account or by our own efforts the better it looks to be.... Unless I am very much mistaken, the bonds and preferred stock could largely be sold at home, that is, in the vicinity of Moline. . . . A pool could be formed for a term of five or ten years of a certain part of the stock, so as to keep the management in our own hands. . . . The brokers get too much in the Underwood deal and I would not until you have looked into this matter with care let Mr. Underwood know that the stockholders have signed. It does not seem to me that it is necessary to go so far away from home to market so good a property." Webber soon had some misgivings about his own thoughts, for he wrote Deere a few days later, "I would not want to take it upon myself to say that it would be best to allow the Underwood proposition to pass, since the price is good and the stockholders mostly favor it."

Velie, Sr., too, had the same misgivings about the board meeting, and he wrote a letter in his usual pungent style to C.C. Webber on August 30, 1890. A major portion of the letter was devoted to the Underwood proposition:

You know I have regarded the scheme with much apprehension of its ultimate consequences—feeling as I do that the welfare of all present stockholders and of all connected with the plow business in any way is intimately interwoven with the ability and fidelity and integrity with which the Deere & Co. establishment is managed. It has given honor and profit to all who have been connected with it in the past and will continue to do so for time to come so long as its managers shall continue true to their trust. Its character and reputation are firmly established and universally acknowledged. Although a purely industrial institution, it has its moral and politico-economic aspects and an influence commensurate with its varied and wide spread connections and associations, and I cannot help but regard its managers whoever they are for the time being as trustees charged with the duty and under obligations to so manage its affairs as to transmit its standing and character unimpaired to posterity. And I fully believe that in so doing they will also conserve their own best interests. I somehow cannot divest myself of the apprehension that in turning it over to alien management and control it will become the football of stock speculation and "wreckless" manipulating.

It was as clear a statement as had been put in writing about the underlying Deere values. Webber sent the Velie letter directly on to Charles Deere in Moline.

As the year 1890 progressed, the business situation deteriorated around the world, and especially in London. Underwood wrote Deere in mid-November: "Nothing can be done with the business before the 1st of December because of the terrible depression existing in London as well as in this country.... No one could float a company of any kind at the present time." Nickerson had meanwhile followed through on one of his options for Moline Plow Company stock, and he wrote Deere at the end of November: "As my Corporation in London wishes to proceed immediately with the prospectus for the reorganization of the Moline Plow Company it is very desirable that we should have your figures and terms early next week so that we may decide promptly whether the two concerns can be amalgamated." Nickerson then dropped a none-too-subtle threat: "It is certainly desirable for all concerned, as well as for the city of Moline, that the proposed consolidation should be made now, instead of increasing the plant and capital of the Plow Co. in opposition to your business."

The situation became further complicated in the same month by the entry of yet another international promotional consortium, a group with a London address calling itself the American Exploration and Development Corporation. Charles Deere asked his new son-in-law, William Wiman, to do some discreet inquiries about it (Wiman and his bride were in Europe at the time). Wiman, in turn, enlisted the aid of his father, Erastus Wiman, who himself instituted an investigation of the company and wrote Deere: "I send you herewith a list of the stockholders in the Exploration Company about which you wrote Will. You will see what a strong body of men they are, including one of the Rothschilds, and a number of other prominent names."

Erastus Wiman was a man of national reputation not only as a financier but also as a "political economist," a sobriquet bestowed upon him by the press not for his formal training in the field but because of his peripatetic speaking and writing on economic matters. He had come to Moline in October 1890 for the wedding of his son and Charles Deere's daughter, Anna. With Deere enmeshed in the London negotiations, it seems quite likely that the two industrialists discussed the combination movement; the wording of later Deere memoranda on consolidation is remarkably similar to some of Wiman's public pronouncements on the matter.

Wiman was an unabashed apologist for monopoly; as early as 1888, he was praising the railroad consolidations of Cornelius Vanderbilt, and he was quoted in the *Boston Herald* in September of that year: "There is a great deal said in these days about monopoly, and the ends that result from it. But we hear little as to the loss which needless competition causes; of the fortunes that are lost in the senseless bidding for business that is not big enough to yield a profit, and of the cutting of prices. . . . " His views soon commanded an international forum. In a controversial article, "British Capital and American Industries," published in 1890 in the prestigious *North American Review*, he plumped unequivocally for the British takeover of American businesses. Central to his argument was his belief that the British would hasten consolidation and thus reduce "the waste of expensive competition." Wiman felt no concern about the British being absentee owners; it was true, he admitted, that often "men perfectly unfamiliar with the business are placed in its practical control" and that "the average London director [was] chosen in many instances because he has a handle to his name, and not a few of them are denominated 'Guinea-pigs,' because they get a guinea for attending every directors' meeting." Nevertheless, the "sense of control" protected against "a reckless and unauthorized departure from conservative business principles." Wiman held little brief for the owner-manager, for "the impersonal character of a corporation rids it of the pride of possession inherent in personal proprietorship, and the impediments toward a union of interests, in rivalry, jealousy, and false or unjust estimates of value, are all removed." Convinced of the efficacy of outright British control, Wiman looked forward to as much as one-half of American industry being owned abroad. Economic historian Roger V. Clement commented on this: "With curious wrongheadedness, Wiman recalled the Boston Tea Party, and yet was able to conclude, after commenting on the desirability of amity between the two nations, that 'nothing will contribute more certainly to this harmony than the mutuality of interests which is certain to be created by the investment of British capital in American industrial enterprises.'"

Despite the Wiman enthusiasm for this new group that included a Rothschild (a magic name, always), nothing came of it. Nickerson, though, was still in the picture and seemed willing to up the ante. Velie, Sr., suspected stock watering, and wrote Nickerson: "The estimate you make of the probable sum the Moline Plow Company will be stocked for ($1,250,000) by the new Company does not bear out your statement that your 'friends in London do not intend to put large promotion fees on any of the properties'. . . . In discussing this subject heretofore at various times with other so-called 'promoters,' the outside limit of commissions and promoter's fees was considered to be 20%, and it was never settled that we would take stock at par at this advance; and I for one, would not feel like taking, or recommending my friends to take, one-third pay in stock if loaded down to a greater extent." Velie was blunt with Nickerson at the end of the letter: "Our pride in the name and interest in the prosperity of Moline and its manufacturing establishments should, and doubtless will, preclude the possibility of our becoming a party to loading down the three under consideration with conditions calculated to prove their ultimate ruin. Consolidation even under American names and management are not popular with the public. Under a foreign directory and name the prejudices and disadvantages would multiply."

At this point Deere backed off from the Nickerson negotiation. Nickerson penned a petulant reply: "I can only conclude that you have not at any time met me in the frank and sincere manner in which my Corporation have approached you. I did not expect such treatment from the *President of Deere & Company.*"

But when Deere went back to Underwood, he was informed that the British proposition was "dead." Ever the promoter, though, Underwood now turned up with a new purchasing consortium, a group of Boston financiers, who came forward with a proposal to consolidate the three companies and to issue new securities for a new American company, to be capitalized at $5 million. Deere wrote Webber about it and the latter responded immediately: "I think some such plan much better than the old one which was under consideration. Such an arrangement would do a concern good rather than harm."

Wheelock at the Moline Plow Company was again the stumbling block. He still wanted to sell his shares separately to Underwood on his own terms. Meanwhile, as Wheelock was playing his "cat-and-mouse" game with Underwood, one of his minority shareholders from the East was surreptitiously trying to persuade Andrew Friberg and other minority shareholders to sell their shares in a block privately to Underwood. The latter turned them aside, though. Deere and Velie, sick of the twists and turns of the Moline Plow Company, now decided to go ahead without them. Everyone at Deere seemed pleased: Charles Nason vowed that "he was not sure but that the M.P. Co. hurt us less as a competitor than it would in a consolidation," and Velie, Sr., added, "the M.P. Co. might prove an elephant." Velie even felt that "in the natural course of events it won't be long before a majority of the stock can be bought at perhaps less than par and then opportunity would be afforded to investigate for ourselves its condition & that of its branch houses."

Underwood demurred, however, for he still wanted the Moline Plow Company in the combination: "In the present condition of things there can be no question but that it will be a much easier matter to float the company if a consolidation is made. . . . People will go into an enterprise made up of the consolidation of several concerns, when they would not look at an investment in the stock of a single one of them." Further, Underwood's tactics seemed to be working. Wheelock told Underwood that he was ready to close "on the old terms" and the Eastern shareholder also anxiously sought out Underwood. Deere and Velie, Sr., relented and agreed to include the Moline Plow Company. Velie wrote Stephens with an offer, the combined firm to have a total capitalization of $5,250,000. Velie told Webber: "It is now proposed to take in the 3 under the name Deere & Company . . . running the other two under their present names but consolidating all their certificates of stock . . . the heads of departments in them may be denominated managing director." The New York investment house Lee Higginson & Co. was to be the principal underwriter; Col. Thomas Lee Higginson of the firm came to Moline and pronounced the Deere arrangements sound. Still, one of the lawyers noted that one stockholder could defeat the entire arrangement.

This is just what happened. The foot-dragger was once more Stillman Wheelock. Velie, Sr., wrote Deere on May 20: "Wheelock still held out in his unreasonable demand and all the other stockholders were disgusted with him, for he really is as anxious to sell as any of them." Underwood was quite upset, and wrote Wheelock: "I am obliged to withdraw all offers made to you and ask you to take notice to that effect, as it is now exceedingly doubtful if anything can be done in the line of our plans."

Underwood's agenda still contemplated the three companies as a package, though, and he proposed to Deere that the latter purchase the Wheelock shares, on his own, for Deere's account. Deere was willing, but he and his associates did not believe the Moline Plow Company to be worth as much as Underwood did, particularly because Velie, Sr., had learned that there was fresh financial trouble at their Kansas City branch. At this point there appeared to be an impasse—Underwood and the underwriters insisting on the combination, Deere and his associates not wishing to pay the Stillman Wheelock price. Throughout the fall desultory negotiations continued, without success.

Fate itself finally took a hand. On January 8, 1892, Stillman Wheelock suddenly died. This unexpected event profoundly changed the negotiations for the Moline Plow Company stock. Underwood anxiously wrote Charles Deere a few days later, urging him to purchase the block of Moline Plow Company stock held by Martin Kingman: You need then have no apprehension of him as a competitor in any direction. Kingman himself wrote Charles Deere in February about the Moline Plow Company, but nothing came of it. By March it became apparent that Kingman had in mind an alternative scheme—he himself purchasing the Moline Plow Company! S.H. Velie, Jr., was aghast: "I consider that such an event would be a catastrophe to the Deere business." Underwood urged Deere to move more rapidly: "Can't we hurry things a little, I don't want to make another fiasco."

Deere did actually begin buying some stock in the Moline Plow Company, but the large bulk of Wheelock's stock remained in the hands of the Wheelock executors. Friberg and Stephens were also willing to sell their shares to Deere, rather than to Kingman. ("Stephens says he wants to beat Kingman at any cost," said an Underwood associate.) The small block of Deere stock in the Moline Plow Company did have the advantage of allowing Deere and his associates to examine the books of the company, a point that Stephen Velie, Sr., earlier had emphasized. Velie, still skeptical about bringing the third company in, expressed his reservations again to Deere in mid-April: "It is impossible for anybody to say what course would be best for the stockholders of Deere & Co. I am not disposed to stand out alone against the consummation of the present scheme if our examination of the M.P.Co. discloses no rottenness that is not already developed."

By early May, Stephens and Friberg (and some members of their families) changed their minds about selling and decided to continue managing the company. Once again, efforts toward consolidation of the three companies soured. Underwood and his associates were quite unhappy about this turn of events, and Velie wrote Charles Deere that they "have it in for me—are terribly let down." One of the minority shareholders in the Moline Plow Company, who had sold his own stock, told Velie that the company was better off without the addition—that "Deere & Co. need have no regrets, for the concern will be purchasable at half the price in less than two years."

Finally, after all of these labyrinthine negotiations, all deals fell through. There was some acrimony about the sale of the small blocks of stock that Charles Deere and Underwood had held in the Moline Plow Company in these final days of negotiations, but these were finally settled to everyone's satisfaction. After one of the most protracted and frustrating negotiations Charles Deere had ever entered, the company remained a family firm. Though a trying experience, it was an instructive one, for it gave Deere, Velie, Sr., and others an increased appreciation of the quality of their own management, a reaffirmation of the efficacy of family ownership, and a renewed spirit of closeness.[2]

THE CHALLENGE OF UNIONISM

There was another country-wide business collapse in the 1890s, and it was a severe one for Deere & Company. A sag in 1891 was followed in late 1893 by a precipitous downslide that *Bradstreet's* periodical lamented as the worst in eighty years. As early as 1892, *Farm Implement News* exhorted the machinery companies to demand cash and "exercise great care in giving credit." By early 1895 L.B. Tebbetts, the St. Louis Deere executive, was noting "unexpectedly discouraging features.... Dealers do not propose to buy for possible, let alone probable, sales . . . now only buying the tools actually needed in preparing the ground for the seed." Business was so dead, said the paper's Moline correspondent, "that the mourners have not even the heart to hold a wake."[3]

One of the spillovers of the worsening times was an increase in labor tensions. In 1892, Charles Deere became worried enough about unionism to employ a private detective firm, the Pinkerton National Detective Agency, to conduct an undercover surveillance of organizing activities in the plant. The Pinkerton agency had aroused considerable acclaim among businessmen—and antagonism from labor—in the early and mid-1870s for searching out, on behalf of the Philadelphia and Reading Railroad, an embryonic labor organization in the Pennsylvania coal fields that called itself the Molly Maguires. The only remaining private reports of the Pinkerton operative at Deere are for the year 1892, and it is clear that he was concentrating on the grinders. Operative "W.H.B." came to town in January 1892, reporting on January 10: "At 7:30 a.m. I went to the restaurant and had breakfast and remained there for an hour, and as it was snowing no one was on the streets so I went to my room and remained there most of the day." After breakfast on the following Thursday, the operative stopped at a saloon on Third Avenue: "The bartender and I played two games of dice and during the time he said that the grinders and polishers have been on strike twice. . . . He further said all the men ought to strike together, then they would win their point." Later that day, he went to the Plow Works and reported to Gilpin Moore: "I told him I could not get in with the men in the grinding room as they all talk Swedish. Mr. Moore said he knew it would be impossible for a man who did not talk Swedish to get in with the men in the grinding department, and as this was the only department where trouble was expected, and he thought that I had done all I could, that I might return to Chicago and said that if he required another man he would write to the agency."

No records exist of any follow-up activities. The tenor of this report suggests that this was Deere's first use of the Pinkertons—and probably its last for several years. The detective agency received a black eye for its role in a steel employees' strike at Homestead, Pennsylvania, later that year (seven Pinkerton detectives there acting as strikebreakers were shot and killed by the strikers). In an incident a few months later the company seemed willing to leave detective work to public authorities. The company had shut down for a number of weeks because of slow orders, and William Butterworth, the young lawyer who was Charles Deere's son-in-law, reported to Deere, then away on a business trip: "Some bloody anarchist has threatened in an anonamous [*sic*] letter to us that unless we start up soon he will blow up the place with dynamite. Nothing has been done in the matter except that the fact was told to Marshal Kittelsen, who seems to know who most of the anarchists are around town and where they congregate." The only other records of Pinkerton billings are for further services in 1898, though there may have been other instances in the 1890s.

As business conditions worsened, competition for the declining orders of the farmers led to cutthroat competition among equipment dealers. Deere & Company saw its sales of machines drop from more than

146,000 in 1892 to just less than 109,000 in 1894. Profitability sank, too, and the board of directors in their meeting of September 25, 1894, decided to take aim directly at wage rates. The company had just concluded a comparative wage survey, and Stephen Velie, Sr., reported: "The fact [is] that this Company were paying considerably higher rates per day for common and partially skilled labor than some of our competitors, so much higher that we could not compete with them on equal terms in selling goods." Velie put on the record for his colleagues the labor wage rates over the years, and he then introduced the results of the survey (Appendix exhibit 10). It corroborated the longstanding belief that the company's wage rates were quite competitive with the industry, particularly in the more skilled job classifications. The board decided to make a $.10 cut in daily wage rates for the common labor jobs, but to maintain the better-than-average rates in the skilled classifications.

The grinders, meanwhile, were looking for an excuse to flex their muscles, and in September 1895 again went on strike. This time the issue was not wages, but work assignments. The *Moline Dispatch* laid the issues out: "Two months or more ago Deere & Co. introduced in the grinding shop a contrivance for 'trueing' the grindstones, especially designed for saving the stone from chipping or wearing away, as was the case with the use of the plow-shares formerly handled in trueing the stones. This device, the men declare, is too heavy for them to wield, claiming that it requires two men to manage one of them. Formerly they had been accustomed to fasten a piece of plow-share on a bar, giving it considerable play on the end of the bar, which the employers say was of necessity difficult to control, requiring more grinding, as well as chipping the stone. This morning, just after starting up, the foreman approached Superintendent Moore, and stated that the new machine was too heavy, and asked that they have the old plan back. Mr. Moore promised them a lighter machine for some of the work, and the old plow-shares for the kind of work where practicable. The men, however, did not consider this a sufficient concession, and they walked out."

At the bottom of the article, though, the *Dispatch* reporter admitted the real reason for the walkout: "It is the intention of the grinders to organize a union." When the company agreed the next day to "allow their men to use their choice of the old or new way of trueing," the grinders responded with the demand that the wage levels before the wage cut of 1894 be restored. Gilpin Moore argued "that if they would show him any better paid grinders in the country than the Company's shops he would grant their request." The following day the *Dispatch* reporter commented about the grinders: "Each day they hold secret meetings and studiously avoid interviewing." In the next column, the newspaper reported a disturbing happening, possibly linked to the strike: "Toby, C.H. Deere's pet fox terrier, has passed into the unknown realm. His death was due to poisoning by persons maliciously inclined. Toby was a dog whose remarkable intelligence made him a great favorite."

After about a week of the strike, the grinders appealed to the newly formed Illinois Board of Labor Arbitration, which had been set up by Gov. John P. Altgeld in 1895, but a week later one of the grinders' leaders stated to the paper, "I do not consider them necessary to the settlement. Chances are too largely in our favor," and the state board was not brought into the matter. The company, meanwhile, had been hiring fresh employees—"green hands," said the *Dispatch*—to replace the strikers. The situation became tense a few weeks later, after the strike had dragged on for a while. In mid-October the company imported a group of about twenty skilled grinders from South Bend, Indiana—"a gang of Belgians and Hungarians," said the *Dispatch*. The local grinders immediately accused the company of importing "scabs," and the *Dispatch* reported the consequences in the next day's paper: "At 3 o'clock the nine Hungarians went to Deere & Co.'s office and explained that they were afraid to go to work; that they had been told they were to be 'talked nice to' this one time, but if they went to work they would have to look out for consequences. The nine also told Deere & Co. that the six Belgians had been badly abused during last night, in evidence of which one of them has a black eye." Marshal Kittelsen that night "arrested a striker giving his name as Nels Johnson, but whose last name is in reality Wida. Wida stepped in the Company's grind shop carrying a spike, which was deemed sufficiently suspicious to warrant an arrest." Finally, late in the month, after seven weeks of striking, the grinders returned, under a promise from Gilpin Moore that "he would look into the matter of a scale of wages, renewing his promise to pay as much as any other shop is paying." Several of the South Bend men were subsequently employed at the company in other departments.

The year 1897 witnessed more labor unrest. First the molders struck in July over a proposed wage cut by the company. This was followed a few days later by a strike in the drilling department, where the company proposed to use a uniform common-labor scale of $1.30. The *Dispatch* elaborated: "Mr. Moore says that the drillers have heretofore received from $1.80 down to $1.30. Boys as young as the law will allow are taken in this department and kept till they can do or wish to do other work. Drilling, he says, is boy's work, and boy's wages are paid for it. When work is plenty none but boys are kept at work and when they get old enough to become mechanics they should quit it. He has ordered the pay to be made from $1.60 down." This issue of "boy's work" was a complicated one; on the one hand, employees wanted to have their youngsters given such an opportunity, yet on the other hand they did not want to be replaced by such labor. Indeed, at the Deere & Mansur plant, where there was also considerable labor unrest in 1897, the company there had proposed to replace some of their striking core makers with women. (The *Dispatch* commented on this: "The boys are already laughing in their sleeves at the idea of a kindergarten of girls under the tutorship of Foreman Kirkhove.")

The arguments with the drillers and the molders were soon settled by a compromise, but the labor tensions of that year continued at other companies. The Moline Plow Company had a strike of its core makers, the Union Malleable Iron Works a similar strike with both its molders and core makers, and Deere & Mansur a long strike with its molders. This was the year, too, that the molders in the Moline area linked themselves with the National Iron Molders Union, with M.J. Keough, the second vice-president of the national organization, doing a considerable amount of the organizing.

Probably the most unusual labor settlement of this period was in late 1897, when the painters struck at Deere & Mansur. They were demanding a wage increase, and the company was standing firm. The employees raised the issue of the possibility of arbitration by the state board and to their surprise the company agreed. The matter went before the Illinois Board of Labor Arbitration in early December 1897, and when the board made their decision public a week later, Deere & Mansur had won. The *Dispatch* reported the reasoning: "In its decision the Arbitration Board says that the only reason set forth for the demand for increased wages was the alleged fact that higher wages were being paid for the same kind of work by competing companies. The Board finds that the employees were misinformed as to the wages paid by other companies. The day wages paid by the Deere & Mansur company are higher than the wages paid by most of its competitors, while the prices for piece work average quite as much as the prices paid by the other companies. The Board finds, therefore, that the demanded increase of wages is without sufficient justification." The *Dispatch* reporter talked to the president of the Federal Union, the organization representing the painters: "He said that it did not surprise him any, he expected just such a decision. The story that the witnesses told the Board when it sat here was altogether milder and less convincing than their talk in advance of the state of affairs and what they would testify to."

Samuel Gompers, the renowned president of the American Federation of Labor, came to Moline in April 1898, exhorting a large assemblage of 250 or so "union laboring men" to "a persistent, day-to-day fight for the union labor cause." Gompers also "urged above all things truthfulness and cool judgment," and this seemed to be the watchword for that year's labor relations. The *Moline Dispatch* of July 16, 1898, enumerated a list of all of the unions in the town, together with their officers and places and times of meetings. By then, there were unions for barbers, core makers, bricklayers, machinists, typographers, iron molders, pattern makers, grinders, polishers, blacksmiths, plow fitters, retail clerks, stonemasons, stonecutters, and wheel makers. Deere had some further discussions with the molders that year, but the two sides jointly reached an amicable agreement, the newspaper commenting on "the fair-minded conduct of the men."

Peace did not last, however. The following year, on July 21, 1899, Deere's grinders and polishers walked out "over details of shop management," and three days later the blacksmiths had a separate strike over "wash up time." The plow fitters put forth their demands on July 31, fifty of them turning out that day. The drillers, not to be outdone, struck the following day. The strikes were ostensibly settled by August 4, but unrest surfaced again in October when the drillers walked out, refusing to handle castings from a carload shipped into Moline from a non-union foundry in another town. The molders were also unhappy over outside contracting. Earlier, in the face of the molders' strike, the company had contracted for about one thousand tons of castings from an out-of-town foundry. When the first of the castings arrived, the drillers checked with Gompers (the drillers union was now affiliated with the American Federation of Labor) and Gompers charged them not to handle the castings. The plow fitters also refused to handle the castings in sympathy with the molders and drillers. The issue was finally resolved when the company agreed not to contract further for castings during the remainder of the production year, and the unions agreed that the material already contracted for from the outside would be handled by their members.[4]

THE MANUFACTURERS FIGHT BACK

Up to this point, labor relations in the Moline area had been essentially local. To be sure, national unions were active at the local level; national labor officials traveled into the Moline area for consultation, exhortation, and actual leadership. In May 1901, however, a new dimension was added. The National Association of Machinists sent out an order all through its locals in the United States, Canada, and northern Mexico for a national strike to further its demands for a nine-hour work day at ten hours pay. The strike affected just about every major employer in the Moline-Rock Island-Davenport area. At this point, several Moline firms (including Deere & Company) attended the National Metal Trades Association meetings in New York and came away, to quote the *Farm Implement News*, "firm in their determination to stand by the Metal Trades Association, in which none was a member before the convention, but with which several are now affiliated."

The National Metal Trades Association had been founded two years earlier, in August 1899, after a series of machinists strikes had been called in shops in Chicago, Cleveland, Detroit, and elsewhere. After protracted negotiations, it reached a settlement with the union, but the fragile peace lasted only a year—until the national walkout in May 1901. This time the association unilaterally cancelled its contract with the union (on June 10) and eight days later announced a new "open shop" policy. *Farm Implement News* commented: "The Declaration of Principles, or as some delight to call it, their 'Declaration of Independence,' has been adopted by the local manufacturers and they are to be a unit in demanding the right to run their shops as they see fit. They will brook no intervention of any union dictating the length of day or the wages to be paid for any class of work. As one manufacturer said, so long as they furnish the capital, their shops, the machinery and brains, or at least part of them, they reserve the right to direct them."

Charles Deere allowed himself to be quoted on the issue in a major article in the *Moline Dispatch* on August 3, 1901: "Until the last few years, this wage scale has been regarded as fixed for the next year, and has resulted in steady employment for our men, at a wage considerably in advance of that paid by our competitors at other points. Of late, however, this annual adjustment has been seriously disturbed by monthly, almost weekly, demands for increases and readjustments; demands in many cases instigated by those only indirectly interested in the results. The consequence has been a condition of unrest and discontent among the men, sometimes accompanied by a loss of profitable employment, for we have been forced in many instances to give up the manufacture of certain lines which went to our competitors paying lower wages. So serious have these troubles become that we have decided to adopt a written agreement, instead of relying upon this annual fixing of prices. These agreements are identical with those used by our competitors at many places, and have been in use at the Rock Island Plow Co.'s for several years." Privately, however, Deere was considerably less militant in regard to his employees, confiding to his diary: "Met a committee of our Blacksmith's at 3 P.M.—gentlemen, all of them . . . good men who have made a mistake."

The "written agreement" referred to by Deere was an individual contract with each employee. The printed form was developed by the Tri-City Manufacturers Association (the newly formed local manufacturers group, affiliated with the National Metal Trades Association) and followed verbatim the association's "Declaration of Principles." The form included a blank for entering the wage per hour and stated further: "I promise, during such season, to make no demand upon them for an increase of wages or shorter day than 10 hours, nor to participate in any strike, nor to unite with other employees in any concerted action with a view to securing greater compensation." The employee, in signing, also agreed to the full set of "principles," which were enumerated on the reverse side of the form (exhibit 6-3).

Clearly, the labor relations picture for the Tri-City Manufacturers Association had taken a harsh turn. The local unions allowed national issues, in part, to determine their local strategy; likewise, the local manufacturers were depending, in part, on attitudes and policies laid down by a national association. "The National Metal Trades Association," according to labor historian Philip Taft, "became a leading propo-

DECLARATION OF PRINCIPLES

Adopted by the Metal Trades Association.

Endorsed by Tri-City Manufacturers Association.

WE, the members of the National Metal Trades Association, declare the following to be our principles, which shall govern us in our relation with our employees:

1. Since we, as employers, are responsible for the work turned out by our workmen, we must, therefore, have full discretion to designate the men we consider competent to perform the work and to determine the conditions under which that work shall be prosecuted. The question of the competency of the men being determined solely by us, and while disavowing any intention to interfere with the proper functions of labor organizations, we will not admit of any interference with the management of our business.

2. Disapproving absolutely of strikes and lockouts, the members of this Association will not arbitrate any question with men on strike. Neither will this Association countenance a lockout on any arbitrable question unless arbitration has failed.

3. *Employment.*—No discrimination will be made against any man because of his membership in any society or organization. Every workman who elects to work in a shop will be required to work peaceably and harmoniously with his fellow employees.

4. *Apprentices, Helpers and Handymen.*—The number of apprentices, helpers and handymen to be employed will be determined solely by the employer.

5. *Methods and Wages.*—Employers shall be free to employ their work people at wages mutually satisfactory. We will not permit employees to place any restriction on the management, methods or production of our shop, and will require a fair day's work for a fair day's pay.

Employees will be paid by the hourly rate, by premium system, piece work or contract, as the employer may elect.

6. It is the privilege of the employee to leave our employ whenever he sees fit, and it is the privilege of the employer to discharge any workman when he sees fit.

7. The above principles being absolutely essential to the successful conduct of our business, they are not subject to arbitration.

In case of disagreement concerning matters not covered by the foregoing declaration, we advise our members to meet their employees, either individually or collectively, and endeavor to adjust the difficulty on a fair and equitable basis. In case of inability to reach a satisfactory adjustment we advise that they submit the question to arbitration by a board composed of six persons, three to be chosen by the employer and three to be chosen by the employee or employees. In order to receive the benefits of arbitration, the employee or employees must continue in the service and under the orders of employer pending a decision.

In case any member refuses to comply with this recommendation, he shall be denied the support of this Association unless it shall approve the action of said member.

8. *Hours and Wages.*—Hours and wages being governed by local conditions, shall be arranged by the local Association in each district.

In the operation of piece work, premium plan or contract system now in force or to be extended or established in the future, this Association will not countenance any conditions of wage which are not just, or which will not allow a workman of average efficiency to earn at least a fair wage.

MOLINE, ILL., June 29, 1901.

DEERE & COMPANY,
Members of the Association.

Exhibit 6–3.

nent of the anti-union forces in the country. It cooperated closely with other belligerent employers' associations, and sought to prevent the expansion of unions on the industrial plane and to reduce its influence in the halls of Congress and state legislatures." Clarence Bonnett, in his study of employers' associations, noted the sharp change of course of the National Metal Trades Association, "which began its career as a negotiatory association, became distinctly belligerent in 1901." The association was vehemently against strikes and lockouts and would not allow its members to negotiate with unions. In case of strikes the association intruded, providing strike-breaking services and undercover activity. The turn of the century thus saw Deere & Company caught up in the changing character of labor management relations across the country.[5]

RECOVERY

Economic prospects for agriculture and its suppliers turned upward in 1897, when the crops in Kansas and the Southwest were "enormous." *Farm Implement News* reported the "Northwest wading in clover . . . up to the chin," and Tebbetts vowed that "we can hear the roar of the approaching wave of prosperity." By 1898, "all is bustle and hope in Implement Row" and the farmers and implement men began to look forward to what was to be one of agriculture's golden eras.

But it had been a trying period, and many important machinery companies had gone bankrupt. In July 1896, *Farm Implement News* reported three buggy-company failures; the Keystone Manufacturing Company went under in January 1897. While Deere executives worried incessantly during the 1890s, the financial soundness and marketing position of the company were firmly maintained. Financial and production figures amply demonstrated its ability to survive hard times (Appendix exhibit 11).

Meanwhile, the structure of the implement industry was continuing to change. The census figures of 1900 confirmed a trend that had been steadily evolving since 1860, an increase in size and a decrease in number of firms. (By 1900 there were only a third as many as in 1860, the numbers dropping from 2,116 in 1860, to 1,943 in 1880, 910 in 1890, and 715 in 1900.) In 1900 the industry had sold more than $101 million worth of goods, with Illinois now a solid first. "The preeminence of Illinois in the manufacture of agricultural implements," said the census analysts, "is strikingly shown by a comparison of its output of certain selected implements and machines"—170,069 of 295,799 wheeled cultivators, 194,375 of 477,520 harrows, 182,782 of 261,957 harvesters. Plow manufacture was more widely distributed than that of any other agricultural implement, yet even so Illinois produced 283,050 of the United States total of 1,074,999. (Interestingly, the census statisticians compiled a table of the agricultural machinery production of all cities with a population of more than 20,000; there were twenty-five, and they accounted for $60 million of the $101 million total. Moline was not among them, not because of its production, but because of its small population. The census of manufactures in 1905 had to make an exception and put Moline on the list, despite the fact it was still well under 20,000 population—after all, it was the second city in the entire industry in value of products!)[6]

THE "PLOW TRUST"

As the country recovered from the depression of the mid-1890s, a second and much larger wave of mergers began, reflecting the ebullience of the nation's financial markets and responses to the Sherman Act. The act had made illegal all agreements to fix prices through cartels or trade associations. Lawyers, as a result, began to urge their corporate clients to combine via single, legally defined enterprises. For the year 1899 alone, there were some 105 of these legal consolidations, almost equaling the total number for the entire period 1890–98. It was also the year of consolidation activity in agricultural machinery. Industry trade papers recounted the proposed "Thresher Trust," and similar efforts were underfoot in agriculture (including, according to the *New York Times* in August of that year, a "Skunk Trust"—a purported combination of skunk raisers, breeding the "odoriferous animals" for their pelts).

In March 1899, a major story broke in the implement trade magazines about a "Plow Trust." It was a startlingly ambitious proposal, a combination of "great extent," so the *New York Times* said. "Unlimited New York capital was reported to be behind it," said *Farm Implement News*, with "Chicago men engineering the deal." The *Times* story headlined the fact that total capitalization for the trust was to be some $60 million, with the plans "upon which options have been secured . . . situated at Syracuse, N.Y., Moline, Rock Island, Canton and Springfield, Ill., Racine, Wisc., South Bend, Ind. and Louisville, Ky." The New York capitalists were not identified by name, nor were the companies themselves disclosed in the early publicity.

By early May the *New York Times* became more specific. It reported that a meeting had taken place in Chicago to discuss the new "American Plow Company," and the proposed capital had ballooned to $65 million. Options allegedly had already been taken on the Oliver Chilled Plow Works. Another article by the *Times* mentioned Deering, McCormick, David Bradley & Co., and Walter A. Wood, as well as J.I. Case, but it did not mention Deere. *Farm Implement News* a few days later disclosed for the first time the attorney who was representing the Eastern interests— Judge William A. Vincent of a prominent Chicago legal firm. When the Northwestern Plow Association met for its regular meeting early in May, eighteen manufacturers stayed after the meeting to discuss the venture (a dangerous step legally, if it could be shown that the association was involved). *Implement Age* a few days later alleged that Vincent had options on "80 percent of the plow business in the country," adding that he was backed by the United States Mortgage and Trust Company of New York.

Manifestly, something very large indeed was being contemplated, and it understandably raised considerable interest in the press. Why was such a trust needed? The *New York Times* said it was due to "the increase in the price of steel and the consolidation of large steel and iron industries" —in other words, a trust to combat another trust. *Implement Age* was more skeptical. "It may be that the object is to increase prices of goods.... We predict that the trust will have to appropriate a large sum to keep down opposition.... To pay dividends on capital and watered stock will necessarily compel any such trust that may be formed to sell plows at a higher price than they can be made and sold by others." *Implement Age* editorialized that "the 'trusts' seem to be beyond all laws." It continued with a surprisingly simplistic reasoning: "Now, a 'trust' is either right or it is wrong. There can be no half-way place between right and wrong. If right, they should be encouraged, but if wrong they should be rigidly suppressed by law." The editor made no bones about which side he felt the issue lay: "They have become so bold as to defy the courts.... Whenever that stage is reached there is danger to law and order." Both *Implement Age* and *Farm Implement News* encouraged machinery retailers to write in their opinions about the proposed plow trust, and in general the response was rather negative. "There is a great deal of skepticism expressed with reference to the successful formation of the various trusts contemplated in the implement business," noted *Implement Age* a few weeks later. "A majority of the jobbers are opposed first, last, and all the time to the combination idea.... "

When the Northwestern Plow Association met a few days later, it decided to broaden its membership to include related implement manufacturers, but it explicitly eschewed a stronger organizational structure. "No attempt was made to form a 'trust,'" noted *Implement Age*. "The object was to consult in regard to increasing the price of goods necessitated by the great advance of raw materials." Apparently the association, or as the *New York Times* called it the "small trust," held together well enough in the following months to succeed in cooling off the "big trust" idea. A general 25 percent rise in prices was announced by the association in September; commented the *Moline Dispatch*: "Plow Price Soars." By the time the Illinois governor, John R. Tanner, convened a major conference on trusts in early September (to which Charles Deere was the Moline representative), the notion of a trust seemed undesirable, if not detrimental. Nothing more was heard of the plow trust through the rest of that fall, nor indeed through the following year.

But the *New York Times* was right—the Northwestern Plow Association was still just a "little trust"—and could not discipline its membership to provide the kind of agreement on prices, credit, and other fundamentals that many implement manufacturers felt was needed. By April 1901 the papers were again full of reports of a trust. The idea moved quickly this time—so much groundwork had been done in the previous eighteen months—and within a few days *Farm Implement News* was reporting: "Plow Combination Practically Assured." The capital was reported this time to be in the neighborhood of $50 million, with an unnamed group of twenty companies involved. Now, though, one of the manufacturers took a major public role, being quoted at length in the trade papers and general newspapers. It was Charles Deere. He was in the chair as the presiding officer in the several-day meeting held in mid-April 1901 that relaunched the project. The *Moline Dispatch* added, "His name is mentioned in connection with the presidency of the organization [the proposed combination]."

Charles Deere went into these key negotiations more alone than he had been in the 1889–91 efforts, for his longtime colleague, friend, and confidant, Stephen Velie, Sr., had died in 1895. No longer having the painfully honest comments of his closest associate to help him hone and refine his own views, Deere probably entered the sensitive new negotiation with some trepidation. His personal motivations must have been mixed. On the one hand, he was not to lose control this time—indeed, he would be the head of a vastly larger entity, however the final deal evolved. A private memorandum to the Deere management made this clear: "Such a consolidation would be the pioneer and the parent implement combine, and might, from this fact, control or absorb the principal makers of vehicles and farm tools, thus making it the nucleus of one of the largest combinations in existence."

On the other hand, a very unsettling issue had intruded—Charles Deere's health. By this time pernicious anemia was plaguing Deere, draining his energies and making his future uncertain. It was not a condition that was widely discussed, although one implement journal did publicly comment: "That Charles H. Deere will ever serve as the President is most doubtful, because of the same ill health which has kept him from active duty at his own works for the six years past. . . . It was only Mr. Deere's ill health and desire to retire from active business that made him consent to the Trust proposition at all."

In the May 2 issue of *Farm Implement News*, Charles Deere finally made a major public statement concerning the combination. "A large number of plow manufacturers have given a New York bank an option on their plants, for the purpose of consolidation and forming a public company," Deere began. "The object, the usual one in such movements —minimizing the waste of competition, and consequent abuse in the trade (a great tax on the industry), centralization of manufacture, and making a marketable investment stock in which operatives and the public will acquire interest." Deere anticipated hostility toward the proposal: "The organization of the company is not to be accomplished through the straight sell-out of all the companies. The options cover any part of the stock of the companies up to ½ of the capital stock, but the decision to sell lies with the individual stockholders, and each has the privilege of determining how much he shall sell or whether he will dispose of any. By another stipulation the managers of the companies retain their present position for at least five years." Deere's words gave some people pause, though, for he admitted that "the probable result of the new company will be to abandon the smaller plants and increase the capacity and manufacture of the larger ones." Deere alluded to Moline in his statement: "The prominence of this locality, as a plow making center, would, in my view, be enhanced and general good insured."

Deere would not disclose the names of the twenty companies, however, and the reporter admitted: "No one seems to know just what companies are in the score which are thought to have given options." The well-known Canton, Illinois, company, Parlin & Orendorff, immediately stated publicly that they were not in the consortium, and within a few days J.I. Case also disavowed involvement. The twenty for which options were held by the Eastern group were finally named in mid-May, and *Farm Implement News* enumerated them in a major headline:

TRADE NEWS

PROGRESS OF PROPOSED PLOW COMBINATION.

FATE OF PROJECT RESTS WITH NEW YORK BANK FROM WHOM DECISION IS EXPECTED JUNE 1.

CONCERNS WHICH HAVE GIVEN OPTIONS— PLAN OF ORGANIZATION—PROBABLE CAPITALIZATION.

DEERE & CO., Moline, Ill.
DEERE & MANSUR COMPANY, Moline, Ill.
MOLINE PLOW COMPANY, Moline, Ill.
GRAND DETOUR PLOW COMPANY, Dixon, Ill.
ROCK ISLAND PLOW COMPANY, Rock Island, Ill.
MORRISON MANUFACTURING COMPANY, Fort Madison, Ia.
DAVID BRADLEY MANUFACTURING COMPANY, Bradley, Ill.
B. F. AVERY & SONS, Louisville, Ky.
BUCHER & GIBBS PLOW COMPANY, Canton, O.
SYRACUSE CHILLED PLOW COMPANY, Syracuse, N. Y.
SOUTH BEND CHILLED PLOW COMPANY, South Bend, Ind.
FULLER & JOHNSON MANUFACTURING COMPANY, Madison, Wis.
KINGMAN PLOW COMPANY, Peoria, Ill.
PEKIN PLOW COMPANY, Pekin, Ill.
PERU PLOW & WHEEL COMPANY, Peru, Ill.
SATTLEY MANUFACTURING COMPANY, Springfield, Ill.
J. THOMPSON & SONS MANUFACTURING COMPANY, Beloit, Wis.
MINNEAPOLIS PLOW WORKS, Minneapolis, Minn.
UNION MALLEABLE IRON COMPANY, Moline, Ill.
BETTENDORF METAL WHEEL COMPANY, Davenport, Ia.

It took everyone only a moment to notice several other significant omissions—for example, the Oliver Chilled Plow Company was not among the twenty. For the time being, the Oliver group would not discuss their view of the trust, but the J.I. Case organization wrote *Farm Implement News*: "While we have at various times during the past two years been approached with a view to getting us to join in such a deal, we have constantly refused to join in any deal looking toward a consolidation of the plow interests."

The role of the old backslider, the Moline Plow Company, now became more and more ambiguous. G.P. Stephens, the vice president, now told *Farm Implement News*: "All we want is to be let alone and allowed to run our own business. We do not want to go into a trust, but we will sell out. What we want is to be allowed to run our factory as we have been, independent of our rivals. Rather than get into a long fight, we will dispose of our plant if we are offered our price." Stephens then muddied the waters for the others by advocating that "in these times of organization of combines of capital there should also be a combination of the employees of these combinations." Stephens continued: "I believe more than ever that the labor problem is the most serious with which the trust will have to deal. As long as there are big combinations of capital, it is but natural to expect that the employee will also join in hands for mutual protection. I would be in favor of an open recognition of the union."

This seemed almost a heresy for a manufacturer, so the *Moline Dispatch* queried Charles Deere about the Stephens view. Deere's view was quite different. "When a factory is so harassed by competition and the profits are cut down to nothing, you know the first thought of the manufacturer is to cut down on the cost of manufacture and the working men are the first to feel it. When that competition is removed, there is not the same necessity for reducing expenses to meet competition and the employees do not suffer."

Deere obviously was trying to allay the employees' fears, but at the same time his words were bound to rekindle the smouldering wrath of the farmers. *Farm Implement News* commented about this: "The anti-trust sentiment, according to popular belief, has its greatest development among farmers. . . . The opposition is based upon the prevailing belief that all trust products are sold at exorbitant prices, unreasonable profits being necessary to provide for dividends on heavily watered stock. . . . The only industrial combination whose product was used exclusively by farmers, that has heretofore been organized, was the late lamented Twine Trust. The intense antagonism of the agricultural class to this trust, the wave of vigorous opposition that swept over the country and the disastrous failure of the concern are still fresh in the minds of implement men." Stephen Velie, Sr., had recognized this threat at the time of the negotiations with the British syndicate, telling Deere "the prospectus would be demoralizing in the extreme if published in Granger papers, which it undoubtedly would be."

Charles Deere's profile rose even higher in the public press when a controversy developed between the New York promoters and the Midwestern manufacturers. Deere continued to be mentioned as the probable new president of the consolidated company, but the New Yorkers wanted to know where the company would be located. The *Moline Dispatch* reported: "A fight now seems to be waging over the location of the central offices. There is a general desire that these offices be located in Moline, but some of the New Yorkers want them in Chicago, where there is a greater variety of interests in the line of amusements and accommodations, though it is recognized from a business standpoint the combination would be no better situated in Chicago than in Moline."

Rumors now began to fly in all directions. One of the manufacturers in the proposed combination told the papers that all kinds of farm implements were going to be brought into the group. Charles Deere immediately denied this and expressed concern about how the story had arisen. It did appear that the syndicate was attempting to bring in some smaller plow concerns. *Farm Implement News* speculated on this: "It is surmised that the failure of the promoters to interest some of the largest concerns has inspired the attempt to gather in some of the smaller manufacturers. . . . What resulted from the visits of those who came to Chicago after the principal conference is not known, but it is reported on good authority that one of the arguments used to swing them into line related to a certain important material used in steel plow construction—soft center steel—and to the prospect which independent concerns might be compelled to face—inability to procure this essential line of material. One manufacturer who has thus far repelled all advances and did not come to Chicago either during or after the conference, declared that the matter has been presented to him in that light, and he frankly admitted that it caused him some uneasiness."

As the spring of 1901 wore on, the press reiterated the imminence of the trust. The *Moline Dispatch* reported on May 24: "Big Plow Trust is Now a Certainty." Judge Vincent was quoted: "I see no reason for further concealment of the fact that a consolidation of a large majority of the best plow manufacturing concerns has been made. . . . The different concerns invited to join are now being operated by the old companies as the agents of a new company." Vincent stated that all of the factories involved would be closed on July 1 for a five- to six-week period, during which the United States Mortgage and Trust Company would audit each one. "A corps of experts will be sent to each plant to count, weigh and value each article, manufactured or unmanufactured and check up or pass upon every item of bills receivable and accounts receivable. From present indications it will require till Sept. 1 to complete the organization of the big company. There are millions of pieces of merchandise to be handled and hundreds of thousands of items to value." The *Dispatch* also reported the settlement of the headquarters issue: "It is believed that Chicago has won in the struggle for the headquarters."

Late in May, *Farm Implement News* was able to obtain from the various manufacturers enough information to lay out in detail the proposed arrangements. The total capital of the new organization, to be called the American Plow Company, was to be about $75 million, of which $35 million would be preferred stock and $40 million common stock. The audit company would provide a net value, and from this the stockholders of each company could receive up to 50 percent of this net value in cash. *Farm Implement News* commented: "Only a few, however, will take so large a proportion of cash. Many of the manufacturers have such faith in the stock of the new company that they prefer large stock holdings to cash payment, particularly on account of the large premium of common stock to be apportioned." The consolidation was to be accomplished by "capitalists identified with two great New York insurance companies, the Equitable and the Mutual Life." The cash payments were estimated to be approximately $13 million; an additional $5 million would be furnished as working capital so that "the combination will begin business with $5 million of cash capital, besides all of the bills receivable and accounts receivable of the various concerns." The reporter caught the euphoria of the promoters: "The leading spirits of the movement are confident that the cash resources will be so ample that there will never be any occasion whatever for the company to borrow money."

The article also spelled out who was going to be in control managerially: "The New York money men modestly disclaim any intention of interfering in the management of the company. They are financiers and not plow or implement manufacturers. They propose to let the plow men themselves, who built up the industry . . . run the business and work out their own salvation." If this could be taken at face value, it was a profound difference from the demand by the British consortium that they have unequivocable control.

The options expired on June 1, and at this point the arrangements were still not complete. Charles Deere was quoted by *Farm Implement News*: "If the deal has not already been complete, it will be in a short time." The reporter commented: "In this case extensions will be asked on all options and they will be granted without any dissent upon the part of the owners of them. Now that the project is so sure none will draw back because of the little reason that the options were not closed exactly within the limits set." Over the remainder of June optimistic statements emanated from all of the participants that could be reached for comment; Martin Kingman of Kingman Plow Company was quoted with a positive statement, and all of the participants met in New York City in late June, where the articles of incorporation were taken out (the legal entity was to be a New Jersey company).

Privately, though, there were serious misgivings in the Deere group, particularly relating to the branch houses. Webber wrote Deere on

June 20: "Nothing definite has ever been decided as to how the outside branch houses were to be treated. Both Mr. Pope and yourself know the basis that has been planned as to these interests, and while you have always said that you purposed to protect these interests, nothing definite has been arranged." Fuller wrote on the same day from Kansas City, but with a different perspective, much more at arm's length: "As we are a separate corporation, we might be left out of the trust in an independent way. If this could be done we of course would like to continue to buy Deere & Co. and Deere & Mansur Co. goods, but as Deere & Co. and Deere & Mansur Co.'s product is a little less than 30 percent of our volume we would like if it could be done to be left out in an independent way." The issue seemed to trouble Webber enough for him to pen a separate, handwritten letter: "As you know, I have not been in favor of this big trust, as my letters to you will show. What I wanted, and what most of us wanted that were active in the business, was our own combination, that we might continue at work in our own business. . . . I cannot conceive why any stockholder of Deere & Co. would want to exchange his stock or 50% of it for the stock of a plow trust that omitted such large interests as Oliver, P.&O., LaCrosse, etc. and yet included so many of the small companies that cannot be compared in any way. . . . *Don't let it go that way—it will be a great mistake.*"

Was Charles Deere "going it alone" by this point, acting without consultation with his peers? Likely he was so prominently associated with the project that he could not have bailed out, had he wished. The implied criticism in Webber's comments must have disturbed Deere, though.

On July 2, a disconcerting development surfaced. The syndicate that held an option on the Moline Plow Company was required to make a deposit of $500,000 on July 1. When the day arrived, the holders of the option failed to meet the requirements. Charles Deere was immediately interviewed and the *Dispatch* reported on July 3: "C.H. Deere returned last evening from a trust meeting in New York but he has avoided his office today. The tenor of the talk of those who were at New York, is that the deal will go through by October 1, but advices are now at hand that the promotion of the combination fell through with the failure to take up the Moline Plow Co. option." Two days later the *Dispatch* had a headline article, with the banner reading: "Deere Agrees Plow Combine has Failed." Deere told the paper that "the plow trust will not materialize now" because the prices asked by the individual concerns turned out to be too discouraging to the promoters. Privately, in his diary, Deere confided another perspective: "The labor situation at the present time is not conducive to plow trust building."

It seemed unbelievable that a deal so close to completion could sour so fast, but there were clear indications that agreements were coming apart. There was a brief flurry of excitement in August, when Charles Deere and several others of the manufacturers involved in the previous proposal met with members of the Oliver Chilled Plow Company. But the *Dispatch* of September 10 headlined: "Deere Sees Failure of Move for a Trust." Deere was quoted in *Farm Implement News* in the middle of the same month: "I do not believe the new organization of plow manufacturers will be a success. There are too many manufacturers ready to enter the field and their interests are important enough to prevent the forming of the consolidation." Further overtures were made in October to renew the option on the Moline Plow Company, and Charles Deere spent many days in Chicago attempting to hold the consortium intact. When rumors were reported in the press of organized opposition by some small manufacturers, that seemed to be the swan song. The country's financial markets had deteriorated in the latter half of the year, and Charles Deere was quoted in the *Farm Implement News* issue of December 12 that the plan was probably not feasible at that particular time. Martin Kingman formally withdrew from the consortium of manufacturers on December 19, and the American Plow Company proposal collapsed. Vincent attempted to resurrect it in late 1902, but nothing came of it. That was the year that the great consolidation took place in the reaper-thresher segment of the industry, with the birth of the International Harvester organization. But the plow makers were not destined to so consolidate. Never again was there a concerted move to form a "plow trust."[7]

THE ERA OF PROSPERITY

The first years of the new century were thriving ones for agriculture. As economist Harold F. Williamson put it: "The period from about 1898 to the World War I era has generally been regarded as one of exceptional stability and relative well-being for the American farmer." Farm productivity was rapidly increased by new farm machinery. Farm markets kept pace with the growth of population and expansion of industry; the devices for getting farm products through marketing channels to the customers were themselves made much more efficient and economical. Even though export markets had declined somewhat after 1900 as Europe's agriculture gained its own strength (abetted by European duties and embargoes against American farm products), domestic demand had moved steadily upward. Growth of the U.S. market more than compensated for the international losses. Wheat and corn acreage expanded throughout the period; cotton, tobacco, and citrus-fruit production grew at even more significant rates. In the South, though cotton was still "King," considerable diversification of cropping was achieved. Prices for farm products rose fairly steadily during the early part of the decade and sharply at the end, ahead of the composite "all commodities" indices.

The number of farms rose from about 5.7 million to about 6.4 million, and the farmers' income moved almost steadily upward from 1900 until 1910.

Not all was rosy, of course. Credit was not always available, soil erosion and depletion had not yet been realistically addressed, the ever-present menace of disease and pest had seemed to be intensified by the high degree of cultivation and animal breeding, the state of the art for insecticides and pesticides was primitive, and farm tenancy had risen, exacerbating some of the social tensions of the rural areas. Still, the decade was markedly good for the farmer and for the agricultural machinery producers.

A number of breakthroughs in farm equipment technology had already occurred. Effective harvesters, hay loaders, disk harrows, and wheeled plows and a great variety of other machinery had been perfected in the second half of the nineteenth century. In infancy during this first decade were the internal combustion engine adaptations to the tractor and the motor vehicle; important developments also came for manure spreaders. Still, the decade 1900–10 was marked not so much by technological developoment as by production and marketing expansion. Census figures for 1899 and 1909 provide clues to this progress, though the government analysis did point out that both these years were somewhat "exceptional" on the higher side. The number of establishments in the agricultural implement industry had dropped in those ten years from 715 to 640, continuing the trend of a half century; the total number of wage earners had risen from 46,582 to 50,551. The total value of the product, which was just over $100 million in 1899, exceeded $146 million in 1909. Growth in the numbers of individual products varied widely; indeed, some—for example, harvesters—had actually declined. The production of tillage equipment, Deere's main products at that time, showed substantial increases over the ten-year period and only the number of wheeled plows declined, as shown below:[8]

Product	1899	1909
Small cultivators	207,171	469,696
Wheeled cultivators	295,799	435,429
Disk harrows	97,261	193,000
Other harrows	380,259	507,820
Disk plows	17,345	22,132
Shovel plows	103,320	254,737
Steam plows	207	2,355
Wheel (sulky) plows	135,102	134,936
Walking plows	819,022	1,116,000

CONFLICTS IN ST. LOUIS

The prosperity of the first decade of the new century was marked by aggressive marketing and rapid changes in field offices. Some of the Deere branches and their branch managers were up to the challenge, others were not. C.C. Webber, the "dean" of the branch managers, assumed a key role both by length of service and by sheer knowledge, drive, and expertise. His exhortations to the field personnel became classics. To a Brookings, South Dakota, dealer he wrote: "Keep hammering away and get all you can, and find out just who the farmers are who are going to want spring goods . . . do not let up a minute simply because you are not actually booking very many orders. Keep working all the harder to get business." To a Grafton, North Dakota, dealer: "I am not satisfied with the manner in which the J.S. Bresnahan & Co. paper is being pushed—in fact, Mr. Jones has the idea that you are not pushing it, that you are afraid of offending somebody. Now, that is an old fashioned way of doing business . . . see that some actual hustling is done on this paper, without fear or favor." To a Hutchinson, Minnesota, dealer: "I think the reason the boys may be a little worried is because we have been going for them pretty strong for money; not but what we consider the debt a safe debt, but rather to urge them to force their collections. They have been inclined to be too easy with this, we think. They have not realized the necessity of crowding collections up in this new country. . . . "

Webber soon stepped into the biggest Deere & Company controversy of the decade over branch policy. St. Louis began the decade as the largest of the branches in both sales and profit. In truth, from a practical marketing standpoint it was too large. There were two reasons why largeness in St. Louis had become an anomaly. First, the burgeoning trade of the Southwest had become increasingly engrossing, apparently somewhat to the detriment of the regular, longstanding trade around St. Louis itself. There were numbers of products for the "Texas trade" and other Southwest markets that required special adaptations, special knowledge, special marketing expertise. Often these were not readily consistent with the trade in the central states. There were serious logistical problems, too. Should St. Louis warehouse material for the Southwest? Should St. Louis begin assembly operations or even some basic manufacturing, if it was to serve such special markets? Some manufacturing already was being performed in St. Louis—the old Mansur & Tebbetts operation included a separate factory for manufacturing buggies, housed in a separate building of more than fifty thousand square feet; carriages were manufactured at the rate of about ten thousand vehicles per year. The problem came to a head in the early 1900s, when Dallas exhorted central management to split St. Louis and Dallas cleanly, making the latter a full branch. There was a sharp difference of opinion on the board about how to accomplish this. The St. Louis physical facilities were overtaxed, and some addition was necessary in either the warehouse or the carriage factory, or both. C.H. Pope was given the assignment to work out plans for a new building addition, while the other executives began discussing how the branch business might be split. Pope came back with an ambitious plan for a large structure that would house both expanded warehousing and expanded carriage manufacturing. Webber took up the cudgel against the plan, arguing that such a large expansion would tie Dallas to St. Louis for warehousing—when the key to the whole change was to establish Dallas on its own feet. "Pope's plan at St. Louis scares me. . . . [It will be] an investment counting buildings and land of $500,000 before we get through with it, and will require as much ability to run it pretty nearly as it does to run the plant at Moline. We should cut Dallas absolutely loose from St. Louis, all with the view of curtailing this great big investment at St. Louis." Webber could not resist a few jibes at Mansur and his organization: "Let St. Louis hustle around in their own territory, and show a profit in that territory."

An interesting complexity was the question of interbranch profit center accounting. When vehicles were shipped to other branches, the St. Louis carriage factory set the transfer prices under general guidelines set forth by Moline. But other branch managers felt they were being double-charged and that by juggling costs St. Louis was making a greater profit on the vehicles than it had been instructed to do by Moline. Webber often had assumed the role of mediator in these flaps.

As might be expected, St. Louis supported the Pope plan—it was certainly attractive to a branch manager. The issue was complicated by the fact that George Tebbetts, Alvah Mansur's old partner, now proposed to buy a piece of the business, and on terms that immediately raised the hackles of some of the Deere board members. Webber, for one, was unalterably opposed. He wrote Charles Deere: "I am not in sympathy with your ideas in connection with Mr. George Tebbetts. His proposition is altogether one-sided, and is so one-sided that I doubt that he expects anything to come of it. . . . He would make a lot of money and make it pretty easily. If we are going to pay anybody a big salary to take charge of that vehicle business, I would pick out McCrea. . . . I do not see how we can have harmony at St. Louis with Mr. Tebbetts and Mr. [Charles] Mansur both in the concern. Mr. Mansur is the manager, he is the man that we have got to look to, and as long as he is in that position, we have got to give him support. We cannot expect him to make a success of it if we keep pulling the other way all the time."

The Tebbetts proposal was dropped, but the Pope building proposal remained before the board. Webber dashed off a hurried letter to Charles Deere: "Mr. Pope . . . proposes to let the excavating contract next Monday morning, and speaks about pushing with vigor work upon the entire structure. If you have not given him authority to let that excavating contract, I would call him off. What I mean especially is that I would not start the building and dig the cellar for it until I knew just how much that building was going to call for.... Now I am not writing this letter to criticize anyone, but solely in the interest of the Company. We had better keep the brakes on that St. Louis building, or it will get away from us." Webber prevailed, and the building plans were cut back to a more modest size.

Exhibit 6–4. *"We walked 300 miles"—William Hoyt pulls his wife and child in a Deere sulky cultivator from Moline to the St. Louis World's Fair, June 1904 (courtesy of Deere-Wiman House)*

This still left the question of how to make the split between St. Louis and Dallas. J.C. Duke, who had worked with Charles Mansur for several years in St. Louis, was to be made the new head of the Dallas entity. But was he to be a branch manager, and was Dallas to be a new branch? At first, it was a compromise. Webber reported it to Deere: "Mr. Duke was rather in favor of an entire separation, but the plan finally decided upon [is] of a partial separation, making Mr. Duke associate manager, giving him full charge of the Texas business, making him his own price and cutting him loose, practically, from St. Louis except in the way of book-keeping and the shipping of goods." Then, in August 1904, Dallas was given the status of a full-fledged branch house with the formation of a co-partnership by Charles Deere, William Butterworth, and Schiller

Hosford (the latter, related to the Deeres by marriage, was now secretary of the company).

The peregrinating Webber continued to involve himself in the other branches, too. At Omaha, George Peek had been given the branch managership (he was related back to Samuel Charter Peek, the Lamb descendant who had worked with John Deere). Peek had taken hold very well, to the satisfaction of all concerned. He had worked for Webber in Minneapolis just before the promotion, and Webber had repeatedly urged central management to increase Peek's salary. When Peek was unclear about a branch policy, he would often write C.C. Webber, who would whip off his director's hat and put on his branch cap. In 1904 Peek was confused about Deere policy on allocation of inventory costs to the branch accounts, and queried Webber. The latter replied: "I have never thought that clause in our contract about compelling us to settle for goods when the inventory ran above a certain price could be kept straight, or that it was a fair proposition.... They always want us to load up and fill our warehouses with goods, and they cannot ask us to do that if they are going to enforce this settlement clause." Of course the "they" Webber was referring to also included himself!

Webber reserved his most pointed darts for the Kansas City branch. He began to feel that George Fuller was no longer up to the job of branch manager, writing Charles Deere in August 1904: "In my judgment Mr. Fuller has let down a good deal in the last two or three years and has not nearly the same energy or ability that he used to have.... We would not suffer at Kansas City but probably be better off if a change was made there." Always alert to organizational interrelations, Webber continued: "Mr. Fuller has shown a narrowness in wanting to be the whole thing at Kansas City, and if he stays we should have a clearer understanding as to the division of authority. The shaking up that has been brought at Kansas City the last year or two and the reaching out for more business has been done by Mr. Velie, who, to my mind, is a whole lot more important in the business." Webber had been exhorting Stephen Velie, Jr., for months to exert more influence at Kansas City; one letter particularly exemplified Webber's own vision of the branch house: "We should not forget that these branch houses are established primarily for the purpose of marketing Deere & Company's goods. I think he [Fuller] has, up to this time, had the wrong idea of it.... It has occurred to me that he did not have sufficient respect for the quality of the line, and have looked upon the proposition of the branch house being rather superior to the factory, that money was to be made out of the branch house, even if the factory did not make much money." Webber had an abiding belief in a high-volume, low-margin approach, and he criticized Fuller for his high prices: "What you must have is a better representation and a larger volume on Deere & Company's line.... You must spend the necessary money in the expense account to get this increased volume.... You will not make any more money than you are making now, but you will get a much larger volume of plow business.... We have to have a plow trade, and that was the first thing to consider.... We have spent all the money in traveling force that was necessary to help us get that trade—rather extravagant in that direction."

Fuller was persuaded soon after to retire and S.H. Velie, Jr., became manager on November 1, 1904. Webber continued to coach Velie, and when Charles Deere voiced some misgivings about the new manager a year or so later, Webber ringingly came to his defense: "Now, you complain about Steve some, think he is hasty and don't keep the brakes on enough, and things of that kind. You want to talk that way to him yourself if you think so and let him make his own defense. If you think he is making mistakes, talk it over with him. He will listen to you as attentively as anyone I know of, and will be influenced greatly by your advice...." Velie stayed, testimony once again to Webber's influence. There were limits to how far Charles Deere could be pushed, however, as Webber ruefully learned in the issue of the advisory board.[9]

AN EXPERIMENT IN MANAGEMENT

Overshadowing the problems with the branches was evidence of tension and dissension among top management. Charles Deere had been the driving force behind the 1901–02 consolidation effort—and no one had any misapprehensions about who would have been in charge of the greater company had it come to fruition. Major changes in management would have followed, too. Indeed, the apparent weaknesses in the branch-house system, with its divided ownership and loyalties, would had to have been faced and solved; a single management structure would probably have been used for all the Deere entities. There were mixed loyalties, no doubt about it. They came up constantly in relations between Deere & Company and Deere & Mansur Company. Such problems would have been resolved in favor of a clear-cut, single line of authority and responsibility.

This did not happen. In the vacuum that was left by the shattered consolidation plans, the existing management structure continued in place. Webber, for one, had been willing to go along with the consolidation, even though he and other branch-oriented members of the company had felt that the branch-house interests were being sublimated to those of the central company. In April 1902 Webber had written a shareholder: "I feel rather than to prevent the consolidation by declining to sign it on account of my branch-house interests not realizing as much as it seems to me they should, that for the sake of harmony, and as this proposed deal seems to be as good as can be had, to go ahead with it."

If the consolidation did go through, however, Webber wanted some changes in management practices. He was joined in these feelings by

Willard L. Velie, the third son of Stephen H. Velie, Sr. The two older brothers already in the business, Charles and Stephen, Jr., had kept low profiles. Not so Willard. He had been a company employee from 1890 to 1900 and had briefly assumed the role of secretary before leaving Deere to form the Velie Carriage Company in 1900. He had been elected a director upon his father's death (his two older brothers were not), and he had kept this post after leaving the employ of the company. Willard Velie was a vocal board member, most often siding with Webber.

Just before the "plow trust" fell through, Webber wrote Velie: "I should take it from your letter that one of your main objections is that there is no definite promise of a radical change in the controlling interest of management. . . . I have placed some faith in our ability to make the new company one to be run by the Board of Directors, but . . . if the Board of Directors were controlled by one interest, that might not count for much just at present." Webber reiterated these same feelings a few days later to W.A. Rosenfield of the Moline Wagon Company: "Under the one company it would be a public corporation, in which no one would . . . absolutely control it. The stock would be in such shape that a stockholder might increase or diminish his interest according to his liking at most any time. It is fair to presume that in such a large company, management would rest on merit, and when the management was not right the stockholders would likely look for a change." This was a surprisingly blunt letter sent to an outsider, with its hardly veiled criticism of the existing top management of the company. And this really meant Charles Deere himself.

Although Charles Deere was still the chief executive officer of the organization, he now turned over more responsibilities to his son-in-law, William Butterworth. The latter was treasurer of the company and had expanded his purview to more than just the financial side of the business. In effect, Butterworth had become general manager.

Webber and Velie still decried the centralization of management in Moline and in July 1903 Webber propounded a striking new proposal to Charles Deere. At that time the sales department was being reorganized and Webber took the occasion to propose to Deere the formation of an "Advisory Board." In his meticulous way, Webber spelled out his thinking, leaving no doubt as to how it might operate: "Our business has reached the stage in size and varied interests where we should have an Advisory Board, the managers or officers to report to this Board, and the actual management of the business to rest with this Board. . . . Their acts would at all times be subject to the Board of Directors." He suggested that the board meet as often as twice a month during some months, at the minimum once a month. As for its composition, Webber proposed a heretical suggestion: "The members of this Board need not be Directors, but can be made up of any of the stockholders desired." Webber proposed that the board would be made up of Deere, Butterworth, S.H. Velie, Jr.,

Schiller Hosford, W.L. Velie, himself, and one of the three more junior officers, C.H. Pope, George Mixter, or George Peek. Webber ended: "Vice Chairman, anyone you might name."

Over the succeeding days a number of letters were exchanged. Charles Deere immediately raised questions about non-directors being on the advisory board and Webber responded: "The reason for going outside is in the line of efficiency as well as harmony. In other words, we want to get into this Advisory Board the best material that we have to make it valuable." Webber was diplomatic, soft-pedaling the mutiny: "It is not necessary to outline here the matter that should be brought before this Board. All this will develop as the Board gets a going, but all matters that are weighty and important should come before this Board and the Board feel responsibility about them." In this letter Webber chose to mince no words about Butterworth's role: "I would want Mr. Butterworth to know all about it and have him not only sanction these meetings but be anxious for them. That is, none of us want to journey to Moline once a month for the purpose of a visit. We want to go there for business, and while we are there on this Advisory Board business our business would be at Deere & Company's office and shop until those duties were attended to." Webber was alluding to the increasingly haphazard board meetings, which were less frequent than earlier and often riddled with absenteeism. Webber ended with his central goal: "It is simply a proposition to divide responsibility and to get the best there is out of the rest of us."

When the directors met on the matter with Deere, Butterworth, W.L. Velie, and Hosford in attendance, the advisory board was voted into existence. Its scope was startlingly wide: "Any important matter relative to the policy to be pursued by said Company or to the conduct or management of its business, or the business of any of its branch houses may be submitted to the consideration and judgment of said Advisory Board by any member of said Board, or by any officer or Director of Deere & Company, or by the manager of any of its branch houses. . . . " The membership of the board varied somewhat from Webber's suggestion. Deere headed it, Webber was its vice chairman, and the other members were S.H. Velie, Jr., Butterworth, W.L. Velie, Hosford, and W.E. McCrea (a non-director who had come to the company from the Moline Wagon Company just the previous month, with an assignment of sales manager of branch houses and export trade).

The new advisory board met for the first time in October 1903 and took up a wide range of company issues; one of these was the resolution to split the St. Louis and Dallas offices into two separate branch houses. A second meeting was scheduled, but Schiller Hosford telegraphed a postponement to Webber—Charles Deere and Butterworth were not in the office. Webber responded with a sharp letter: "I do not believe that it is proper to handle the matter in this way. If so, our meetings are likely not to be thought of as occurring with any regularity." He also enlisted his sometime ally, W.L. Velie: "I think it would simplify this matter very much if someone else was appointed as vice chairman—someone at Moline. That would be very satisfactory to me." Webber's ruffled feathers were smoothed, though, and he remained as vice chairman. But the point was well made that the advisory board should be a regularized feature, not subject to the whims of individual travel schedules.

The advisory board seemed to function reasonably well over the following months, meeting as scheduled and taking up matters that heretofore had not come before the board of directors itself. Early in 1905, though, an issue surfaced that threatened the continued existence of the advisory board. St. Louis branch-house business had continued to expand, and in late December the branch-house manager put before the advisory board a proposal for a new warehouse. The board appointed a subcommittee to look into the matter, composed of W.L. Velie, Butterworth, and McCrea. When their report was submitted, there was a split opinion— Velie believed that a six-story warehouse was adequate, Butterworth (and, presumably, the St. Louis branch people) plumped for a seven-story structure. In his report, Velie compared the amount of warehouse space at Kansas City, Minneapolis, and Omaha with that of the St. Louis branch and maintained that the six-story version, which he estimated would have 180,000 square feet, "would meet all the requirements of the business at St. Louis." Butterworth disputed the available floor space— the six-floor version contained only 103,000 square feet of usable space, he vowed. Six stories "would be found inadequate for the economic handling of the business . . . and each of the branch houses used for comparisons, that it was not fair to assume warehouse space by comparison of sales only." The advisory board argued the matter at length and finally recommended the six-story version proposed by Velie. The minutes do not recount the individual votes, but we know that Charles Deere concurred in the decision, at least at that moment.

On February 21, the board of directors met, with Deere, Butterworth, Schiller Hosford, and C.H. Pope present. This group promptly countermanded the advisory board proposal and voted a seven-story structure. Webber was quite disconcerted and immediately wrote Charles Deere: "I was rather surprised at the turn that the St. Louis improvement took at the last meeting. At the previous meeting you were with the majority in standing fast for a six-story building, and I never quite understood the desire expressed at the last meeting to add on the other story, excepting that it came through Mansur's solicitation, and his ideas and his wishes we have all of us been familiar with a long time, and were at the time he made it six stories. I have given the St. Louis proposition as much attention as anyone, and I am strong for making that building only six stories." Webber then went on to the issue that really concerned him most: "Aside from that, it was passed upon and definitely decided, and if the Board is going to be a useful factor, its resolutions must be complied with. Harmony and good feeling in the Board is probably more important than the point as to whether the St. Louis building is either six or seven stories."

When the advisory board held its next meeting, Deere was not there. The minutes were terse and noncommittal, but apparently at that meeting a statement was made by one of the directors bluntly noting that the advisory board was not the controlling entity. Webber sat down a day later and penned an outraged letter to Moline: "The purpose seemingly manifested at the February and March meetings to overrule the Advisory Board's instructions as to the St. Louis warehouse, and the opinion expressed at the March meeting that the Board was without authority would seem to end the usefulness of the Board. . . . To be a useful factor in the business the officers must work in harmony with the Board, which exists by their approval, and abide by the decisions of its majority, carefully given for the good of the business. If this is not to be, I can see no good reason for continuing the Board. . . . It should be respected or done away with." Webber could not resist moralizing about the St. Louis situation itself: "Going on as you are now headed means a failure to fully profit by the separation of Dallas and St. Louis but rather a St. Louis rent account equal to the old one practically, with our own money invested at that."

There was an instant response to Webber's provocative challenge. The advisory board was dismantled, ceasing to function in any way from that date. Butterworth was clearly the victor in the argument over the warehouse, and in the process he had established his own authority over matters in a way that was unmistakable to those around him. Charles Deere, having sided with the advisory board in the initial report on the St. Louis warehouse, had finally supported the Butterworth view. No written notes survive of the board meeting in which the advisory board was given its coup de grâce. The decision must have had Charles Deere's blessing; he chaired the meeting and his view would have prevailed in any case, given his commanding position of ownership. It must have been a difficult decision for Deere, for he had to make a choice not only on a critical management concept—whether there should be an advisory board—but also on a personal preference for his son-in-law's views versus his nephew's. Uneasy rests the mantle of leadership in a family corporation; even if one owns a commanding position in the stock, those minority interests represent not only company but family linkages, with all of the interpersonal baggage this typically involves.

Webber expected too much of the advisory board, given its curious composition. The concept of an executive committee had been adopted by a number of companies—a segment of a board constituted in such a way that it could act authoritatively between board meetings. Railroads had used such a device, as had United States Steel and Dupont. But Deere's advisory board was not a true executive committee, given clear executive authority to make decisions. Rather, it was a hybrid, its authority limited as advisory. In actual practice a number of "resolutions" were passed in its meetings, all presumably only recommendations to the full board, but by practice becoming faits accompli at the moment the advisory board voted. Yet when the confrontation between two factions came, the board of directors of the company reasserted its ultimate authority and refused to accept the recommendation of the advisory board. Webber took this as repudiation, for he apparently felt that the advisory board was really an executive committee, with final authority. Today, this is the reality—decisions of an executive committee involving basic policymaking of the firm are generally ratified in an official way at the next board of directors' meeting. Had Webber not confused the concepts involved here, the advisory board might well have stayed in place and grown into a more viable entity within the company. As it was, the leadership tilt at this time was back toward the Moliners— especially Charles Deere and William Butterworth. And they were now girding themselves for the biggest challenge of the era—competition from the new manufacturing giant, International Harvester.[10]

CONFRONTING INTERNATIONAL HARVESTER

One of the most remarkable consolidations in the entire history of the farm equipment industry occurred in August 1902, a bellwether event with implications far beyond the industry itself. The International Harvester Company was created from an amalgam of principal manufacturers of harvesting machines in the United States—the McCormick Harvesting Machine Co., the Deering Harvester Co., and the Milwaukee Harvester Co. At consolidation, the firm had about 90 percent of the total production of grain binders in the United States and about 80 percent of the total production of mowers. International Harvester immediately proceeded to acquire several of the remaining competing manufacturers —it secretly gained control of D.M. Osborne & Co. in 1903, and then added the Minnie Harvester Co., the Aultman-Miller Co., and the Keystone Co. Soon the new firm extended itself into numerous other lines, sometimes by converting part of its harvester facilities and in other cases purchasing established concerns. Tillage implements, manure spreaders, farm wagons, gasoline engines, tractors, and cream separators found their way into the International Harvester line. By 1911, it had more than 50 percent of the business in manure spreaders and about 37 percent of the business in disk harrows. Cyrus H. McCormick, the president of the company and son of the inventor of the reaper, testified in later judicial proceedings that the reasons for combination lay in "fierce competition" and his desire to remove "unbusinesslike methods." McCormick's worries were echoed by other executives in the consolidated company. McCormick argued that many of his sales were made below cost in the hurly-burly period before the consolidation. His views were challenged, however, by independent analyses which pointed out that the profits of the five combining concerns during the five preceding years, 1898–1902, aggregated nearly $43 million.

McCormick was not alone in his preoccupation with "cutthroat" competition. All through American industry in this period, there was a recurrent fear of unbridled competition. Firms worried that price structures would erode, drop below costs, and turn profitability into loss. Charles Deere's abiding concern for countering what he felt were detrimental competitive practices in the industry—his constant search for consolidation—was rooted in a belief also held by a great many of the top management spokesmen for American industry.

Still, consolidation did not halt overly aggressive competitive practices. International Harvester was a case in point. Once this new firm emerged, it engaged in tactics that were subsequently found by the courts to be objectionable (in the famous International Harvester antitrust case of 1918). William Z. Ripley, in his seminal book *Trusts, Pools and Corporations*, noted six of these practices:

1. Maintenance of bogus independent companies in the early years of the company's operation

2. Attempts to force dealers carrying its harvesting machines to stock additional lines or certain International Harvester lines exclusively

3. Efforts to secure an undue proportion of desirable dealers in a given town by giving only one of its several brands of harvesting machines to a dealer, thus tending to restrict the outlet for competitive goods

4. Use of "suggested price" lists, tending to influence the final retail price; earlier the contracts themselves provided for fixing of retail prices by the company

5. Discrimination in prices and terms

6. Misrepresentations by salesmen regarding competitors

Charles Deere and his associates worried about this awesome new giant of the industry. At first the company took a self-effacing hands-off posture, stressing—especially to dealers and farmers—that the product lines of the two companies were mutually exclusive, that International Harvester made harvesters and Deere made plows and cultivators. International Harvester was particularly strong in the wheat areas of the Middle West and Plains states, so it generally fell to C.C. Webber to respond and adapt to the International Harvester threat. Shortly after the consolidated International Harvester began operation, in early 1903, rumors spread throughout Minnesota that Deere was going to take on Harvester. Webber had developed company links with a number of dealers in the area who also sold harvesters; sometimes these were International Harvester machines, sometimes competing equipment. One of Webber's dealers had dropped the International Harvester line in 1903 and taken up a competing brand. To the International Harvester field men, this looked like a deliberate retaliatory thrust into the harvesting business by Deere. Webber immediately wrote his dealer: "I simply wish to mention it to you so you will be careful not to drag us into the proposition. Our basis with non-competing manufacturers in our line is that of non-interference with their business, and we do not want them to interfere with ours." Webber was not content to leave the matter there, and a few days later wrote James Deering at International Harvester, assuring him of Deere's policy of nonintervention. "Mr. George G. Mill at Litchfield, Minnesota, who has hithertofore sold the McCormick binder, has changed this year to the Minneapolis binder, and Mr. Mill is doing his best to make the Minneapolis binder popular, which you will undoubtedly agree with me he has a right to do," Webber wrote Deering. Webber continued in a conciliatory tone: "I have never attempted to control in any way the contracts that Mr. Mill or other local partners might make for these outside goods, and told Mr. Mill at that time that he should do as he thought best.... All of the local partners of the concerns mentioned in which I am interested must depend upon their own energy and. ability to make money, and I have never attempted to interfere in any way with contracts for outside goods—that is, goods other than our own goods." Webber then explicitly disavowed any Deere interest in harvesters: "We are not in the binder business in any way, do not intend to go into it, and our travelers have not made the statements that they are charged with. Our policy in the past so far as the binder trade is concerned has been to keep hands off the binder business, and that will be our policy in the future, viz;—not to take sides in a controversy at all in which we are not interested." In retrospect, this statement looks overly timid, almost tying the hands of the company forever. At the time, though, it mirrored the longstanding Deere philosophy of keeping out of others' pastures.

Interestingly, many of the International Harvester executives seemed to have been equally cautious when they worked for separate companies before the consolidation. For example, in 1896, the Deering Harvester Company was considering an acquisition, and J. Deering wrote William Deering: "I told Mr. French that the Acme Co. of Pekin, who make the Hodges header, were making a binder and mower. He said, 'Yes, and they are foolish.' I asked him why. He said, 'Just as you would be foolish to take up the manufacture of plows.' I asked him why we could not take up the manufacture of plows if Mr. Thomas is right as to the ability that the harvester manufacturers have for pushing in that line of business. He replied: The harvester business has been made a success by firms who have confined themselves to the harvester business and to the making of those things which they can make in large numbers all of the same kind. Plows, on the other hand, are made by the dozen and by the hundred, the manufacturers taking special orders from different individuals with modifications of the regular type, so that they often make but a few of each kind, and so that variety made by them runs up into the hundreds, in some cases many hundreds.'" In the same letter, Deering also reported a rather gratuitous comment made by the Acme president about the Deere organization and Charles Deere himself: "He stated, by the way, that the Deere Co. employs 700 men and is old-fogish and behind the times, but not so old-fogish and behind the times as their chief competitor, the Oliver Co. Deere, he said, is worth from 3 to 5 million dollars, which has come to him so easily and with so little trouble on his part that he has no occasion and little disposition to work hard or push hard."

By 1902, the tune had changed. Cyrus McCormick and his colleagues were then taking a much more pragmatic and opportunistic view of acquisitions. Even with their strength, the Harvester executives were acutely aware that moving into a new field might provoke retaliation. McCormick, in discussing the Osborne negotiations with George W. Perkins in late 1902, commented: "Another objection is the spring tool features.... If we buy into this trade, we might thereby provoke an invasion of our field by new competitors without securing any compensating advantages for the International." "Nevertheless," he continued, "the question whether it is good business policy for us to embark in the spring tool business deserves more serious consideration by the International than it has yet received."

McCormick here exhibited a good deal more tactical and strategic perception than did Webber, for the latter's view seemed to be based on caution, even fear. And it soon became apparent that Harvester was having less and less hesitation about moving into new product lines that competed head-on with Deere and others. Demand was falling for harvesters, freeing up plant capacity for manufacturing other implements. First, the company moved into cultivating equipment, cream separators, and other agricultural machinery. Then, in October 1903, a rumor circulated that particularly disconcerted Deere—that the hay-tool operations of the Dain Manufacturing Company in Ottumwa, Iowa, were being sought by Harvester. Deere and Dain had had a longstanding relationship, with the Dain equipment sold in most of the Deere branches. Webber was so provoked by the rumor that he wrote Joseph Dain, the company president, and posed the question bluntly: "We have heard it rumored that your Company was negotiating for the sale of their plant to the International Harvester Co. It has come from several sources, and the rumor has been quite persistent. Now, I do not know whether there is anything in it or not, but should rather think not, as I have always thought that you were the kind of a fellow that wanted to run your own business pretty much in your own way. However, I want an expression from you about this, as if you have any such intentions, naturally we should know about it, so that we may prepare for the change which will take place in our line a year from this time."

Dain immediately assured Webber of his strong loyalty to his old Deere friends. But Harvester immediately effected an alternate plan: to go into haying machinery on its own. Now it was Joseph Dain who needed support, and early in 1905 Charles Deere sent a team of Deere executives, headed by Webber, to Ottumwa to reassure him. Out of this meeting came a five-year exclusive selling contract for Dain equipment, to be marketed through all of the Deere branch houses. Joseph Dain extracted an agreement from the Deere team that his Dain rake bar loader would be handled on an exclusive basis by Deere, a not unimportant concession by Deere, since it required jettisoning a similar machine made by Deere & Mansur. Deere & Mansur found itself on the outside, almost as an unwanted cousin, not explicitly within the structure of the Deere organization, its links stemming only through Charles Deere's personal ownership. "Mr. Deere arranged that matter for us, and authorized us to go ahead with the deal," Webber wrote one of the branch managers a few days after the meeting. In other words, Charles Deere took out of his personal left pocket (Deere & Mansur) in order to strengthen his larger right pocket (Deere & Company). How well this set with the other Deere & Mansur shareholders was not recorded.

Arrangements like the Dain long-term contract assured Deere of obtaining equipment, but it did not guarantee that the supplier itself would not be sold during the period. A few months after the Dain contract was signed, the company initiated discussions about a similar contract with a small company making seed drills, the American Seeding Machine Co. Webber wrote Charles Mansur: "We have been talking it over, Mr. Velie and myself, since my return this morning. We can see some objections to a straight 5 year term contract with the Seeding Machine Co. For instance, suppose they should sell out to the International, if you please, and we should have this 5 year contract on our hands, and the contract should be a valid one, we would be tied up to buy our drills from the International people for a term of years. . . . They might make it very unpleasant for us and do us a great deal of harm." Webber's suggestion was a contract including a one-year termination clause, and that was what was done.

One of the most unsettling of the International Harvester tactics during this 1903–04 period was its practice of secretly buying a company without disclosing the real ownership, continuing the firm under the old name as an ostensible "competitor" of International Harvester. Webber had picked up rumors in October 1903 of just such a maneuver and immediately wrote Charles Deere: "I learned from the leading spirit in the American Seeding Machine Co. that the International Harvester Co. owned, and had owned for some months, D.M. Osborne & Co. and

Adriance, Platt & Co. . . . had bought both of these concerns out some months ago but were not letting it be generally known and that they proposed to continue to run them as separate and independent concerns." Webber then mentioned the name of a third company, one that soon became central to the Deere people: "These gentlemen also told me that the International were negotiating with the Acme Harvester Co. at Pekin, Illinois, and that it was likely they would buy that concern out also."

It was now dawning on Deere that International Harvester intended to be aggressive and that timidity would be viewed as a sign of weakness. The Deere board met on December 13, 1904, to discuss both Acme and International Harvester. Schiller Hosford was blunt in recording the minutes: "Considerable consideration was given to the growing corruption and aggressive methods adopted by the International Harvester Company with a view of our interests being on the alert constantly for new developments." At this point, a far-reaching decision was made: the Deere leaders decided to reverse their earlier decision to stay out of the harvesting machinery business and to consider buying the Acme organization as a first step.

The Acme proposition was a mixed one at best. It had not been a successful company, being run at that time by its creditors. Webber nosed around among various dealers, asking them their opinion of the product lines of the company, and he wrote Charles Deere about his findings: "The old Acme concern had a very poor selling organization. . . . The products themselves were satisfactory and the crisis financial situation in the firm made it an attractive time to get involved." Any effort to buy Acme had to be made delicately, for already rumors were flying that International Harvester was stepping up its bidding for Acme. Webber warned Charles Deere of his fear that "perhaps we were being used to make the International bid go up." It was not clear to Webber just what International Harvester's intentions really were; he continued in his letter to Charles Deere: "I learned something about the International's methods. It seems that several concerns they have strung along and made them think they were going to buy them out, and in this way got the inside facts in connection with their business and got all the information they wanted, and then either made them a ridiculously low offer or made none at all."

Webber, deputed to approach Acme, proceeded very gingerly. In his first talk with the creditors, Webber disclaimed any interest in taking over Acme. Rather, he said, Deere would be willing to help Acme remain an independent concern, free from the control of the International Harvester Company: "We were not looking for a chance to get into the binder business, or a place to invest money in outside enterprises. . . . We were interested in the matter to the extent only of keeping the plant going."

This was not entrepreneurial enough for Charles Deere's taste. He wanted to pursue the matter further and dispatched C.H. Pope to Pekin to investigate the physical condition of the plant. Webber responded: "I note that you have decided to send Mr. Pope over to Peoria . . . allright, he should be able to make an intelligent report. I am not very anxious to get into the harvester business nor do I believe that it is necessary for us to get into it now. I feel that I would rather attend to our own business and keep sawing wood in that to the best of our ability. . . . " Webber admitted that there would probably never be another opportunity quite so promising "to get into the harvester and binder business in as easy a way, or with so small an investment as is presented by this Acme proposition." But his inherent conservatism urged Deere and the others away from the proposition: "I rather believe from the way International is moving that they intend to take up the general line, and to be active competitors of ours in the general jobbing business at least. . . . We do not want to drive them into the plow business, and neither do we want them to drive us out of it, nor do we want them to become, without a good show of resistance, competitors of ours in the general jobbing business."

Webber's view finally prevailed, and the company backed off from the proposition. The Acme creditors made a brave showing, vowing to continue as an independent concern. So Deere & Company decided to stay out of harvesters—and International Harvester chose to stay out of plows. But it was only "for the moment," for both companies moved frontally into each other's product lines in just a few years.

Though there was no direct confrontation on plows and harvesters, competition developed over other products. International Harvester's offerings soon cut deeply into Deere product lines. In 1904, it was wagon manufacturing; by 1906, C.C. Webber penned a plaintive letter to Charles Deere (who was vacationing in Santa Barbara, California): "They are making a hard canvass now on the new lines they have taken on, viz: wagons, manure spreaders, gas engines, hay tools such as Dain makes for us, and things of that kind. . . . They are this year making an aggressive campaign for business on these lines, and naturally with more or less success." Webber was especially fearful of further inroads: "You will notice what Mr. Mansur says about Grain Drills and Riding Cultivators. We have not much doubt about the correctness of this information. In addition to the lines that I have mentioned above, they are putting a cream separator on the market. . . . When they get that launched, we presume a gang and sulky will be the next thing that they will pick up, and the question occurs to us naturally as to what we are going to do about it."

There was no doubt that International Harvester was a well-organized, aggressive, and thorough marketeer. Webber described their strategy: "The International have 3 block men in the territory of some of our travelers, 4 in the territory in some of them, and as high as 5, and it is probably safe to say that they average 4 block men to each traveler or block man of our own. . . . The most important thing for us to do is to hold our own against the International, to thoroughly work the trade with travelers, giving travelers less territory all the time, so that they can visit a dealer oftener and keep in close touch with him. . . . " Webber constantly worried that his own travelers were viewing their competitor Harvester counterparts with too much alarm; in a letter to S.H. Velie, Jr., as to whether the company should get into the manufacture of manure spreaders, a field that International Harvester had preempted, he said: "We rather believe it is not the best policy to allow our travelers to throw the scare into us, so to speak, on this International proposition."

Webber soon changed his adamant stance against competition with International Harvester: "Are we going to sit still and let them get into the trade first with one of our tools and then with another, and finally land with a pretty complete line of plows on the market, with a strong hold on the trade? . . . Are we going to wait for them to do all this unmolested? . . . Are we going to give them some competition in their own special line—harvesters and mowers?" Webber answered his rhetorical questions with a surprising about-face—get into harvesters. There were various ways to do this, Webber suggested. One was to pick up the Acme Co., still fighting to keep alive in the market. But this did not seem to be in the cards, for, as Webber put it, Acme was more likely to "land in the lap of the International whenever they wanted." Alternatively Deere could either start up its own harvester operation—"get the right man or the right men to take off their coats and go to work at it, and to make up their minds to make a life job of it and make it go"—or perhaps join together with some other plow companies, wagon companies, or manure-spreader companies in a joint operation. Another way, Webber noted, was to get Dain involved: "They are rather half inclined to do it anyway."

Nothing came of any of these proposals. The directors temporized and finally decided against any such audacious move. But the outside pressure continued to build, and not many months later Webber, now very much the bold activist, pressed Charles Deere about alternatives involving combination. Webber now embraced the "plow trust" idea, applied this time to harvesters. He discarded the Dain possibility ("Mr. Dain would move with too much slowness in the matter"), and instead he pushed Charles Deere to take the lead in a much larger effort: "The proper thing to do was to interest the implement and wagon manufacturers generally, all manufacturers that have been affected by International competition, have them all contribute to the formation of a concern for the manufacture of binders. In this way the financial drain would not be heavy on any single manufacturer, and the results would be better, because the new concern would have the friendship of all the independent manufacturers in the country . . . a formidable blow to the International."

But Deere did not have the stomach for yet a third effort toward combination, and nothing came of Webber's aggressive suggestion.

END OF AN ERA

By 1905 Deere was quite ill; the malaise in top management was becoming more pronounced. Yet there were flashes of the old Charles Deere spark; at one point in 1905, Webber wrote Deere (on the issue of the new St. Louis expenditures) that "the mania for spending money has struck them again at Moline." Charles Deere had supported Butterworth in the St. Louis warehouse decision, but now, too, seemed quite uneasy about the escalating expenditures in the company. Deere then penned a blunt memo to Butterworth: "We have to have *everything* and too expensive outfits. Stop it, and get along with such outfits as you have or such as will do for the time. There seems to be no end to outlay of money. Stop it!" Later in the year, Webber himself demonstrated anxiety about Butterworth in a letter to Deere: "There is going to be a tremendous business all over the middle west in 1906 . . . I think Mr. Butterworth is alive to the situation. He seems to be, and assured me that he was watching it closely, and was confident of his ability to get material. But it will not do any harm to check him up occasionally on it, and not let him be over-confident."

Exhibit 6–5. *Charles H. Deere demonstrating a walking plow, 1905 (Deere Archives)*

The next year, 1906, marked Charles Deere's sixty-ninth year of age and his forty-ninth year of leadership of the company. Now it became evident to all that Charles Deere was seriously ill. In June 1906 Deere's daughter, Anna, died at age forty-two, after a long illness. This sad event, according to his friends, further weakened him. He continued his active direction of the business, chairing all the board meetings for the remainder of that year and on through to the summer of 1907. Doctors later were quoted as saying that his worsening physical condition had been brought on at least in part by "the close application during the forty years of his vigorous manhood that he devoted to building up the plow industry." George Vinton (Deere's sales manager in the early 1870s who had sold his stock in the company in a dispute over dividend payouts at that time) was with Deere off and on during this period, and he told C.C. Webber about it in a letter written in 1908: "I told him that he ought to unload some of the responsibility of his business, more than what he was, that his health would be impaired by constantly thinking and anxiety and I had suggested a year before his death to bring you to the factory, that he had implicit confidence in your ability and integrity and that you were identified financially and otherwise with the family. His reply was that you could not be taken away from your present business or he would gladly do so." Vinton was also with Charles Deere in the summer of 1907, when his health was noticeably deteriorating. "While he was sick he was on his boat on Campbell's Island and sent for me to come up," wrote Vinton. "I went up and found him alone. Dr. Taylor had just left. He was very weak and nervous. We talked for some time. The weather had just changed and this was about four o'clock in the afternoon and he wanted me to stay all night with him. He took me back in the boat and said he didn't have clothes enough on his bed. I said to him, 'Charlie, you're pretty sick.' He replied in his way, 'George, I'm sick forever.... I ought to have quit business twelve years ago.'... He left that night for Chicago and I never saw him alive again." Deere's condition steadily worsened during the fall, and on October 29, 1907, he died. An era had passed in Deere & Company.[11]

PART III

CONSOLIDATION
AND CONTROL:

THE
WILLIAM BUTTERWORTH YEARS
(1908–27)

CHAPTER 7

EMERGENCE OF THE MODERN COMPANY

*For some years our traveling men and our agents had been
pressing us very strongly to go into the plow business, but we had
up to the present time strongly declined such a policy . . .
while it was true we have bought some small threshers as an
accommodation to our trade, we had more than once declined to go into
the thresher business, even though urged to do so by our agents . . .
The same line of reasoning had thus far kept us away from
taking up plows, but of course if the plow people went into the harvester
business we might find ourselves drawn into the plow business.*

Cyrus McCormick 1909

◁*Anniversary calendar art (Deere Archives)*

Important decisions had to be made when the board of directors met on November 26, 1907—its first meeting without the presence of Charles Deere, who had so dominated it over the years. The first decision was ceremonial—the formal eulogy, by resolution, always appended to the board minutes at the death of an important member of the firm. In this case it conveyed particular affection and admiration, for the directors had worked closely with Charles Deere over a great many years. Charles Pope prepared the tribute; he first called attention to Deere's integral role in the plow world and his great influence on his own community. He then put particular focus on Deere's entrepreneurial drive: "Although his was a dominant and aggressive personality, he was ever approachable and a patient, interested listener to any cause earnestly presented.... He appreciated to the fullest the persistence that produces results, and once embarked in adventure, he enjoyed the fight and the pluck that was set aside with nothing short of successful accomplishment." Pope concluded: "We who were his associates for many years thus record our regard and testify to his simple, strong and manly character, and to his sterling worth."

Local eulogies emphasized the loss to the town, paid tribute to Deere's friendliness, and emphasized his modesty. The obituaries in the national press focused on his important role in state and national Republican politics. Much attention was paid to his great personal wealth (*e.g.,* the *Chicago American* headlined its article: "Millionaire Deere Dies in Chicago"). Charles Deere had not been a "public" personage, was not known for personal or corporate philanthropies or for non-business involvements. He was preeminently a businessman, widely active as a board member of other firms, past president of the Illinois Manufacturers' Association, a pillar in the agricultural machinery industry. Charles Deere legitimately had taken his place in the forefront of successful American businessmen.

Charles Deere's private diaries, covering the first years of his business life, reflected the thoughts of an eager young businessman keenly aware of all the facets of his then-faltering business and knowledgeable about the industry and the world around him. Further, his early writings give evidence of his emerging leadership qualities—the ability to initiate management decisions and make them stick, even when it came to reining in his father. The abiding Deere family integrity also showed through.

These same qualities were abundantly in evidence over the remaining fifty-odd years of Deere's management life. He stressed innovation and the importance of effective marketing. His entrepreneurial drive carried him into new businesses; even in his last few years, gravely ill, he remained enthusiastic about business life. Yet, in his last years there was also unsettling evidence of a caution and unwillingness to act decisively that was uncharacteristic of his earlier years. Sick and tired, he seemed unable to make the hard decisions about succession that finally would have solidified his longstanding quest to balance the needs of the central organization in Moline with the initiative and independence of the branches and factories. It was almost as if he could not let go at the last minute. He had brought along William Butterworth, his son-in-law, as the next-in-command, yet he left Butterworth with a legacy of tensions among top management and unresolved problems about people. Perhaps the loss of his alter ego, Stephen Velie, Sr., took away the leaven that had proved to be effective over a thirty-year period. In evaluating the Charles Deere period, this pattern of two strong management persons at the very top of the organization, each with expertise in his own field but complementary in total skills, seemed an effective model for leadership in a complex organization. Velie was painfully honest, blunt in his reactions to some of Charles Deere's ideas, yet thoroughly supportive and positive in total. There was indeed a sterling quality about their relationship.

Charles Deere's management style in the company was consistent. He himself evolved the early concepts of decentralization that became a hallmark for the company in the second half of the nineteenth century. In this, he surely differed from his father, who had been unable to delegate, often not trusting his colleagues. He had a keen sense of organization structure and coupled this with an inherently conservative financial posture. He seemed to have a particular prescience about longer-run issues; he thought globally, and in terms of long-run maximization of the business. While he was a good tactician, he sometimes became overly impatient in situations that seemed too convoluted or drawn out. But it was in the strategic realm that his perception was greatest. His skill in seeing the rapidly evolving marketing demands of the hurly-burly agricultural machinery world of the 1870–1900 period gave the firm a tremendous jump on the field by the turn of the century (just in time to face a new giant of a competitor, the International Harvester Company).

After adoption of the eulogy, the board turned to important practical considerations. First was the choice of a new chief executive officer. There was little doubt, from the pattern of the previous few years, that William Butterworth was heir apparent, and he was promptly elected president. Butterworth had been a central figure in Moline management since before the turn of the century; in his role as treasurer, he had always presented the operational statistics at the board meetings, comprehensive analyses of the entire operation. In effect, Butterworth had been given the role, clearly by Charles Deere himself, of informal second-in-command. His assumption of the chief executive's post was preordained.

Yet there had been persistent tensions among shareholder groups in the last decade of Charles Deere's life—between Moline and the branches, and, particularly, among the three strong personalities in the family at that particular time of Butterworth, C.C. Webber, and W.L. Velie. The demise of the advisory board had brought these out in the open.

A report by the United States Bureau of Corporation in 1910 comment-ed briefly about Deere & Company and Butterworth in the process of a massive study of International Harvester—and it was not very compli-mentary to the new president. "It appears that the organization is somewhat unfortunate in that the present president of Deere & Co., William Butterworth, is new to the business. Mr. Butterworth, who is by profession a lawyer, was elected president on the death of Charles Deere about a year ago, because of his relation to the latter's estate as his son-in-law. Competent outside authority considers that the Deere organi-zation is much weakened by Mr. Butterworth's lack of experience." It was evident "that the looseness of organization" made Deere a "less efficient competitor" of International Harvester; however, "loyalty to the Deere tradition . . . still seems to be strong." Nevertheless, "there is more or less dissension between those stockholders whose special interest [was] the plow business" and those more directly concerned with other lines of manufacture.

The board members had tried to ameliorate some of these tensions by changing certain key features of organization structure at the time of Butterworth's election. The bylaws were amended to provide for two vice presidents; Willard Velie was elected to the second post, joining C.C. Webber. Willard Velie had emerged as the spokesman for his side of the family (neither of his two older brothers, Stephen, Jr., nor Charles, had become a major force in top management; neither was on the board). Webber was the link between generations, a close associate of Charles Deere for decades, long a potent force in the top echelon of the firm.

The board, in this first meeting without Charles Deere, also attempted to regularize its own behavior, the minutes unintentionally catching some of its members' ambivalence. "In future, the business affairs of the Company should be so far as possible carried on by the Directors, who would hold meetings regularly and so be thoroughly advised and in-formed of all of its operations." An enigmatic sentence was then appended: "It was recommended that all mail of a business character should be addressed to Deere & Company and not to individual officers." The intimation that there had been incipient cronyism and personal cliques was unmistakable. Though the minutes do not record who made these particular statements, it seems likely that Velie and Webber were the originators of both of these statements, interested as they were in bringing about more balance and representation in the affairs at Moline.

There were other organizational steps taken at the meeting. Burton F. Peek was elected treasurer and given Charles Deere's board post. Schiller Hosford continued as secretary; a few months later, Pope was elected as assistant treasurer. The opening of a New York City office to handle export business was voted; at the same time, the board members agonized over worsening business conditions and exhorted each other that "great effort should be made in Moline and among all the branch houses to reduce stocks of all sorts to the lowest possible point before the end of the present fiscal year."

The country was experiencing a serious business downturn—a number of banks had failed in October and November, unemployment had risen, and food prices had soared. What we now call the Panic of 1907 was short-lived, saved by the intervention at a critical moment of J. Pierpont Morgan and other financial leaders, who restored confidence by massive loans at critical junctures. The performance of the company was down in the fiscal year ending July 1, 1908, but not seriously. The firm was still able to pay a dividend of $600,000, the same as the previous year, and the surplus account at the end of the year had risen from $2.5 million to more than $3.6 million.[1]

THE FACTORIES GET A NEW LEADER

George Mixter, for one, was optimistic enough about the coming year, 1909, that he agreed to an incentive basis for his salary, based upon company profitability. (The record shows no such arrangement for any of the other executives at this time.) Mixter was already a major new figure in Deere management. A great-grandson of John Deere, he had graduated from the Sheffield Scientific School at Yale University (where his father was a professor of chemistry) and had done some post-graduate work at Johns Hopkins University before entering Deere & Company in 1896 at age of twenty. He began his career as a clerk for Deere & Webber in Minneapolis, but within a year came to Moline, becoming a master mechanic at the John Deere Plow Works. In 1900 he made a long business trip for the company, traveling first to France, Sweden, and Germany, then on to South America to establish a John Deere outlet in Chile and to visit for a number of months the already existing agencies in Buenos Aires and rural Argentina. Upon his return to Moline a year later, he became assistant superintendent in the Plow Works. When his superior, John J. Courtney, died in 1904, Mixter became superintendent of all manufacturing in the company. He held this position for many years and became, in the process, the unchallenged spokesman for the factories, as his uncle, C.C. Webber, had become for the branches.

The ability of the Deere workmen to put out a solid, well-built product was unquestioned. Market acceptance of the Deere line left no doubt about this. But the internal management of production was in a rather chaotic state by about 1900, and Mixter had been given the fortuitous assignment when he had first come to Moline in 1897 to straighten out the confusion. He later described conditions: "In those days no specifications were available, no complete set of piece rate prices were available . . . all detail information as to the cost of any given article had to be gathered from every corner of the shop. The process consisted of getting

Exhibit 7–1. *Group portrait of several male members of the Deere family.* Front, *Timothy A. Murphy, Charles Skinner, Willard L. Velie, Stephen H. Velie, Jr., Stuart Harper;* rear, *John Deere Cady, Charles Velie, William Butterworth, William Wiman, undated photograph, ca. 1900. (Deere Archives)*

the shippers to deliver what they called a complete implement. It was then necessary to write up the specification and chase all over the shop to find the direct labor cost of the various items.... At that time we were given flat percentages to add for heat, power, light, and selling expenses. After about a year's work on details of direct costs, it seemed to me that very little was known about overhead percentages." Mixter obtained a pamphlet from the Stove Manufacturing Association, and from this he improvised new general ledger accounts; these became the basis of the company's modern cost accounting system. Mixter commented on his experience: "This gave me a very unusual opportunity to learn each detail of both product and manufacturing operations in the plow shop . . . [and] gave me the basis of my knowledge of cost accounting, which I have always considered my greatest asset."

Mixter's next assignment in Moline was to straighten out the loosely constructed piece-rate system. "I became convinced of the mutual injustice of the then existing piece rate price," Mixter later recounted. "We were paying over half of our pay-roll on the basis of these prices. I became interested in Taylor's analysis of unit time of doing work and at that time initiated what is the present piece rate system at the Deere plants. The result was a radical reduction in labor costs, and by tying the piece rate prices with individual contracts initiated in 1901, the men were to a large extent induced to cut loose, and their earnings rapidly increased." Mixter considered this realignment of great importance to his later efforts: "It is my belief, looking back over the years, that the greatest accomplishment of my period as Assistant Superintendent was in the establishment of an honest piece rate system, which . . . re-established the confidence of the men with Deere & Company which had been sadly destroyed during the period after Mr. Gilpin Moore's practical withdrawal and before Mr. Courtney became Superintendent."

The superintendent's report of July 1903, a remarkably comprehensive document throughout, added further comments about the wage rate system: "[In the blacksmith shop] strong effort has been made to get action in this department. Conditions which were rotten to the core are somewhat improved . . . our plans are now in shape to get this shop going on a decent basis. . . . [We have] cut piece prices for next season without changing method . . . discharged five prominent loafers . . . made a large number of new dies, which have wiped out one-half of the handwork . . . urged men to step out and do all they were able. . . . We believe that no scheme of shop management is right that does not in the long run give satisfaction to both employer and employee, which does not make it apparent that their best interests are mutual, and which does not bring about such thorough and hearty cooperation that they can pull together instead of apart. The interest of both parties can only be well cared for on a basis of GOOD WAGES AND LOW LABOR COSTS, brought about by the gradual selection and development of a body of picked men who will work extra hard and receive extra high wages and be dealt with individually instead of in masses." Mixter was frankly anti-union, and he continued: "After considering carefully the ways and means for making the interest of employer and employee mutual, it must not be forgotten that ability to shut down is a winning trump. To surely handle labor WE NEED A WAREHOUSE [to store stock in case of such a strike]."

Mixter seemed to have hit the happy medium in employee relations of being humane and thoughtful on one hand, yet tough and demanding on the other, always pushing the men for high standards, high quality, and a fast pace. In 1903 he persuaded the officers of the company to install extensive environmental controls in the grinding room, careful to impress his fellow executives with their cost-saving features. At the same time Mixter plumped for incentive concepts as the underpinning for all compensation plans. He felt quite negative about day-rate wages—"These are fixed charges which even the most skillful foreman cannot avoid"— and pressed hard for bringing as many employees as possible under some form of incentive. Mixter sensed the need for clear authority and the importance of a manager carrying sufficient practical clout to make his ideas stick. Only a few weeks after he became superintendent he wrote William Butterworth: "Since Mr. Courtney's resignation I have had no instructions as to what extent you wish me to assume Mr. Courtney's work. In questions of the day and hour I have assumed full authority. But I feel that plans for future development should be based on a clear understanding on my part of the Company's desires for the future."

Mixter, incidentally, had sought Webber's views on whether this letter should be sent, and his uncle had been his usual cautious self: "It would not be my judgment to take this matter up at this time in such a formal way as this letter would do. It is all right for you to talk to Mr. Butterworth along these lines, but I doubt the advisability of sending this letter. . . . " Webber concluded with one of his choicer aphorisms: "Briefly my idea is this—show now that you can run the shop and run it right, and that you are alive in the situation, and competent to handle it in every way." Webber still realized that Mixter would "do as you think best," and Mixter did just that by sending the letter anyway, in the process establishing a pattern of independence that allowed him to stand up for his own beliefs with all of top management right from the start.

Most of Mixter's relations during this earlier period were with William Butterworth and the other executives at Moline—there was not much direct correspondence with his uncle for many months. But he was sensitive to Webber, and diplomatic when necessary. Webber had a particular peeve, the color and quality of Deere's now well-known green paint, and had earlier written Charles Deere a surprisingly authoritarian letter: "You get hold of this letter, and get some energetic and thorough action on this proposition. We believe you ought to get a fine expert to help you. . . . I regard it as of very great importance. . . . You can afford to spend some money to find out how you can stop this, and get your goods back under the class of well painted implements." Mixter replied promptly, and apologetically: "John Deere goods are no longer the best finished goods on the market. . . . In the dipping process ample time has not been given each coat to dry . . . the 'Apple Green' color has deteriorated . . . our 'Apple Green' even of the best quality is too delicate a color to carry sufficiently heavy varnish. . . . We suggest that the 'Apple Green' be restored to its original bright green and darkened as much as possible and yet remain the same to the eye of the trade." One wonders how a color can simultaneously brighten and darken—but never mind, the paint did change, and quickly.

But, when he thought he was right, Mixter was outspoken. For example, he became embroiled with Webber in 1904 about whether some of the rear wheels on New Deere gangs sent to Minneapolis had been located properly, or whether they had inadvertently been built with the wheel out of line a few inches. Mixter wrote a caustic letter to Butterworth: "I have repeatedly told Mr. Browne [Webber's assembly man in Minneapolis] that if he ever found a plow with a rear wheel 2½" inside the landside to express it to Moline at my expense. . . . Now if Mr. Webber wishes his New Deere Gangs built with the rear wheel on a line with the landside or anywhere within 2 feet of the back of the plow, we will build them so. I do not think the present location of the rear wheel can be improved, but if it will please Mr. Webber's feelings or cheer up Mr. Browne by permitting him to say 'I told you so' it would be easy to build Minneapolis plows this way. . . . I am just as tired of hearing this broad statement of Mr. Browne's."

Webber was also equally pointed in his letters to the factory; a couple of

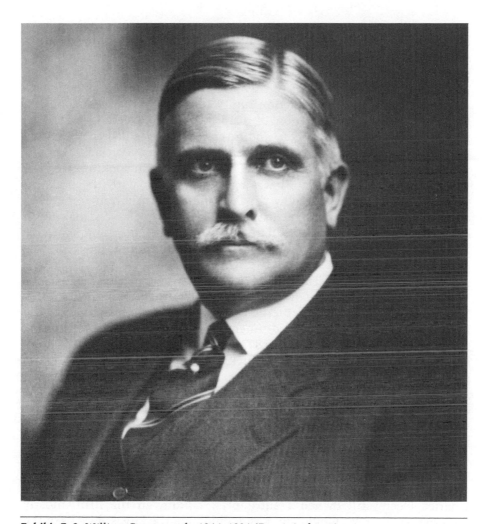

Exhibit 7–2. *William Butterworth, 1864–1936 (Deere Archives)*

years later Webber was again on his high horse about the gangs, and he wrote Mixter: "I am not in very good humor over gang plow construction today, and have written a couple of letters to the factory, because I wanted to give it to them strong down there. I don't know who is at the bottom to blame for this inclination to run in cheap material, but we don't want any more of it in our plows. . . . In starting Poole out here, you had better let him understand that we are not in a very happy frame of mind, and he wants to come up here with the idea of keeping his eyes and ears open and accomplishing something."

One of the perplexing questions in multiproduct shops like Deere was the determination of economic lot sizes—whether particular models could be built in enough quantity to warrant the initial cost of development and the subsequent special tooling costs. Fortunately, the company had several very popular models during this period that achieved very substantial per-year sales. There were a few, though, that limped along on small sales volume, and Mixter was always after the sales and marketing personnel to agree to eliminate them (the production bias was always toward the long, stable production run). Early in his superintendency he vetoed Charles Deere's notion of adapting one of Deere's Australian plows to the California market, and he constantly needled the branches he felt were too compliant on special adaptations. Portland was his particular target. He wrote Butterworth in 1907: "In looking over the various shop troubles today, I was again impressed with the hopeless variety of small lots required by the Portland house. You remember that after Mr. Payton's trip up there last fall, there was some talk of making an effort to educate the Portland institution along the lines of *John Deere Plows*. Are we expected to furnish any men from the shop for this campaign?"

One of Mixter's most frustrating problems during his early years in the superintendency stemmed from the company's relations with its key foundry supplier, a Moline firm, the Union Malleable Iron Company. The foundry had its roots in the mid-nineteenth century in Moline, carrying the Union Malleable name after 1872. In the 1880s William T. Ball, John Deere's personal secretary, had bought into the company and was its secretary and treasurer during this period; A.F. Vinton, another former Deere employee, had also been in management during this period. The company had had spotty profitability over many years, a problem not unknown to the foundry business. In 1888 Charles Deere loaned the firm the sum of thirteen thousand dollars, a very substantial amount in those days. In 1894, Stephen Velie, Sr., and John Gould took over the ownership of the company. At one point in the mid-1890s William D. Wiman was made president and treasurer, but his tenure was brief. By the early 1900s Charles Deere still owned a substantial holding in the firm, mostly preferred stock; F.W. Gould and J.M. Gould held the largest blocks of the common.

Deere & Company naturally had used Union Malleable as one of its prime suppliers throughout this period, but often with exasperating results. Malleable was also serving other customers, and the Deere people more than once felt that Malleable was taking Deere for granted, and preferentially serving the outsiders. At one point in 1902 the Charles Deere consolidation plans included bringing Malleable directly into the expanded Deere & Company, but several of the executives took exception to this (Webber being particularly outspoken) and Deere dropped the notion.

Mixter made no bones about his belief concerning Malleable recalcitrance, and in 1905 he began attacking Malleable frontally. He wrote Butterworth: "I understand our contract is for 3,500 tons from Union or

½ their capacity—they do not give us half their molders. I believe you personally can bring pressure on Union to get that work. The backing the factory is getting today on Malleable will not enable us to meet the situation. Can you not see your way clear to make Union give us 65 molders tomorrow? Not next month—not when Mr. Gould wakes up and our orders are cancelled.... " This seemed not to nudge them, for by the following July Mixter was again exhorting Butterworth: "I mean to make it perfectly clear that I consider the product of Union a dangerous thing for this Company. I do not think their present organization and management is such as to ensure good malleable, and that I consider their treatment of Deere & Company, during the past season, as a cash loss to this company."

Butterworth apparently was not able to remonstrate strongly enough, for Mixter wrote in January 1907: "What I desire to especially point out is that Union is slighting us at present. They are not holding 60 men on our work and today the malleable situation is not nearly as favorable as on December 1st. There is no need of my repeating my personal opinions of Mr. Gould's attitude toward Deere interests. I believe it is a subject of very worthy consideration, with a view of some very radical remedy." (In this same letter he also castigated the quality of steel coming from the Crucible Steel Company: "I feel sure that the stock shipped us by the Crucible Company and marked *crucible cast steel* appears to be a poor grade of soft center steel, and I suspicion they are pawning off some other scrap on us . . . it costs us money and reputation when they send us rubbish.") Still the situation with Malleable did not improve, leaving a residual of acrimony that was only to be removed a few years later by the full-scale acquisition of Malleable by Deere & Company.

Mixter's personality was vigorous and charismatic. His extensive academic training had honed his mind incisively; his face-to-face relationships were blunt but quite effective. His memoranda and letters were models both of meticulousness and directness. No one could fail to know where he or she stood after receiving a Mixter missive. By the time of Charles Deere's death and William Butterworth's ascension to the presidency, Mixter had bulled his way to a powerful position in top management, a unique addition to the team that was to become a new generation of Deere family managers.[2]

MIXTER'S RUSSIAN DIGRESSION

The export market that beckoned the agricultural machinery manufacturers more than any other in the period just before World War I was Russia. This vast country, underdeveloped and primitive as much of it was, still produced more than 20 percent of the world's grain, second only to the United States. The International Harvester Company had been particularly adept at exploiting this market; before the turn of the century, its predecessor companies had sold harvesting equipment there in large amounts. By 1909 Harvester not only had several major agents in the country but was also opening its own factory, the Lubertzy Works, near Moscow.

George Mixter took an extensive trip to Russia in the summer of 1909. The Germans were the competitors on plows for Russia, Mixter reported, though he also found substantial numbers of plows from the Canton, Illinois, firm of Parlin & Orendorff. Mixter's report to the board carefully analyzed the geography of the country, its agricultural potential, and the reach of all of the competitors. Mixter felt that dealing through agents would not work in Russia, that the company would need to open its own branches there to be effective.

Even this was pictured by Mixter as only a halfway house. Mixter concluded his report with a startling recommendation—that the company open its own manufacturing plant in Russia. "I think this Russian factory would be possible. . . . The progress of Russia and Siberia in the past few years indicates that the time is right for such a move." Material was relatively inexpensive and available, wages per day were "less than half of those at Moline." These potential employees were excellent, Mixter thought: "The men work fast and with proper machinery would produce work at a very low direct labor cost. Deere would need only to send a manager, a Russian-speaking superintendent and probably six skilled men for a year or so; after that, the factory could run on its own." The limited purchasing power of the Russian agriculturist was an offsetting negative factor, Mixter admitted, but he concluded, "I feel that the large expenditure necessary to create a plow trade in Russia should not be undertaken unless it be coupled with the determination to ultimately manufacture in Russia."

Everywhere Mixter went, he ran into International Harvester agents. Several of them suggested that they would like to sell Deere plows along with the International products. Mixter, ever wary of the great competitor, wrote: "This idea has evident faults and I would not suggest it except possibly at Omsk." The board rejected any and all relations with Harvester (but did reverse itself later, in 1915).

The board also did not act on Mixter's suggestion of a Russian plant, being preoccupied by that time with the harvester project and related matters. Perhaps it was just as well, too. International Harvester reported in its annual report of 1918 that an additional $10.4 million was to be charged off against losses at the Lubertzy Works, bringing the total as of that date to some $24.2 million of losses in the Russian manufacturing operation. In 1924 the Soviet government nationalized the International Harvester plant, with no compensation, and the remaining depreciated book value of the investment (by this time down to about $2.3 million) was charged off against the earnings of that year. Deere did obtain a large Russian order in 1910 for some 900 plows, to be delivered in

Vladivostok, but Russia never materialized as a major market before World War I.[3]

THE CASE MERGER TALKS

Despite the success of the company in weathering the downturn in 1908, the company executives seemed to fear that threatening events were just around the corner. The board minutes in July 1909 were frank: "A discussion of trade conditions throughout the world followed, it appearing that in the rapid growth and encroachment of competition, together with the menace of monopolizing manufacturing tendencies in the various lines of goods used upon the farm, suggested a wise provision for contingencies on the part of the Company at a time when its financial situation rendered it convenient." The directors decided upon a "Contingent Reserve Fund," setting aside $100,000 at the start and an additional 10 percent of factory earnings each year, all of which "shall be invested in high class listed bonds."

What to do? Charles Deere's response to threats from the marketplace had been to consolidate—to strengthen one's own market power by increased size. Butterworth, Webber, Velie, and the others now turned in the same direction. Shortly after the board meeting in July 1909, the company made a new overture to an outsider, in private. This time it was an important name in the field of agricultural machinery—the J.I. Case Threshing Machine Company.

Case in many ways appeared to be an ideal partner. It was about the same size as Deere; Burton Peek's memorandum on the proposal noted Case's assets to be approximately $13 million, with average earnings over the five-year period ending in 1906 about $887,000 per year. (Peek also noted one issue of debt, a set of mortgage bonds, of which $2.9 million were outstanding.) Case was an acknowledged leader in its two fields—farm steam engines and threshing machines. There was a workable dealer organization in place, with thirty-five branch houses scattered around the country, and the production facilities at Racine seemed excellent.

But there was one rub. Deere still was preoccupied with harvesters and the perceived threat from its arch-competitor, the super-sized International Harvester Company. Harvester had dominated company thinking for more than a half dozen years, and the vacillation and indecision about what to do about it continued to sap the executives' energies. Just a few weeks before, Deere finally had aborted the negotiations looking toward the purchase of Frost & Wood Company of Brockville, Ontario, thus failing in another effort to get into harvesting machinery. Burton Peek and Mixter were the bargainers with the Case group, and they lost no time in admitting that their true reason for the proposed consolidation was their desire to produce harvesters. The deal almost immediately fell through, in part because of differences of opinion over the amount of common and preferred stock that each company's owners would receive, and in part because of Case's skepticism about turning their successful formula for manufacturing threshers into harvester manufacture.[4]

INTERNATIONAL HARVESTER DRAWS CLOSER

In the J.I. Case negotiations Deere was the hunter, Case the prey. Now Butterworth found that at the very moment he was pursuing Case he became the hunted—by none other than International Harvester!

In early December 1909 the general manager of Harvester, Alexander Legge, suggested to Harvester management that they approach Butterworth about supplying Deere with a line of grain binders. Deere was not the only one that feared a competitor; it was clear that the Harvester people were discussing this matter as a defensive measure. "If an arrangement of this kind could be worked out," Legge wrote in a private memorandum to Harvester management, "the chances are there would be less price demoralization than would be the case if they were bringing out a new machine of their own design." Legge noted that Harvester had excess capacity that could probably save Deere a large investment in capital facilities. "I think it is safe to say," continued Legge, "we could sell the machines and make a fair profit at a price that would be attractive to them." Harvester had heard that Deere was planning for a harvester in Canada—the news had leaked out to the public—so Legge suggested that International Harvester might buy plows from Deere for the Canadian trade in exchange for a Deere promise of staying out of harvesters. "I think we can well afford to make some overtures along this line before going into the fight that is sure to follow their entering the harvesting machine field." Butterworth came to the Wisconsin Steel Company offices from time to time (it was a subsidiary of International Harvester, but also sold to Deere) and Legge proposed that "we could easily bring this matter up for discussion without appearing to have gone to them with any definite position."

On the same day that Legge wrote this letter, someone higher up in his own organization took matters in his own hands. Cyrus McCormick himself, the Harvester president, had learned that Butterworth was trying to persuade one of his own employees, a harvester expert, to leave International Harvester and come with Deere & Company. McCormick knew Butterworth personally and immediately rang him on the telephone, proposing that the two get together. An unusual meeting followed, documented fully by McCormick (though, surprisingly, Butterworth left nothing in writing about the confrontation).

McCormick spoke first: "The case of McAllister had come to my attention and I thought it was rather a mistake for two companies like the Deere and the I.H. Co. to get their wires crossed in a matter of this kind, which was really a minor question. . . . I suggested that not speaking as the President of our Company but as an acquaintance of his . . . he should look at the matter in a broad way and realize that the young man had made a mistake which he was now anxious to rectify."

McCormick continued, more aggressively. The alleged pirating of McAllister seemed to indicate Deere's intention to invade the harvester business; would Butterworth confirm this? "While I did not care to ask any information which was of a private nature, I would be glad to have such direct information as I was equally able to give him about our Company in case he should wish information of the same kind. . . . We were not doing things the success of which depended upon keeping them quiet because we found that it did not take long for any policy we might be thinking of adopting to become known quite generally."

At this point, McCormick chose to broach what appeared to be his real agenda: "For some years our traveling men and our agents had been pressing us very strongly to go into the plow business, but we had up to the present time strongly declined such a policy. . . . Our need for expansion moved along the direction of taking on new lines such as engines, cream separators, manure spreaders, etc. where we did not have to invade the territory of our friends and allies in the implement business. . . . While it was true we have bought some small threshers as an accommodation to our trade, we had more than once declined to go into the thresher business, even though urged to do so by our agents. . . . The same line of reasoning had thus far kept us away from taking up plows, but of course if the plow people went into the harvester business we might find ourselves drawn into the plow business."

With this not-too-veiled threat laid on the table, McCormick turned to his underlying proposal. If Deere needed a binder, "it might be possible for them to get it from us and thus save a large investment in plant and save going into the business with which, as yet, they had very little experience." As if to underline the import of his earlier words, McCormick repeated: "For Western Canada we had been obliged by the competition of Massey-Harris & Co. to get some plows for Western Canada but that fact was the extent of what we were doing in the plow line."

Butterworth replied and McCormick captured his words: "He had several times thought it would be important if the interests of the two companies could have some conference. . . . It was not too much egotism to say that the Deere plows stood in the same relation to the general business that the McCormick harvesters did and he was very glad indeed to explain to me quite frankly any matters of policy which might affect the interests of the two companies. . . . It was quite true that for a long time their entire organization had been bringing strong pressure to bear upon them to go into the harvester business because of the position in the trade which was being taken by the I.H. Co. and because of the trend of the trade in general." There was a special problem in Canada, Butterworth noted, where the high duty level had persuaded Deere to build its own manufacturing facilities for its plows. Inasmuch as Deere had found that the agents in Canada also wanted a harvester line, Butterworth continued: "They are just now preparing to arrange for a harvester line of binders, reapers and mowers, but this was only for Canada. . . . That was the object they had in engaging a man from our Company, as they did not know where to go to get a better man." McCormick could not swallow this, and expostulated: "If the companies were in cordial relations with each other, I thought it was not impossible that we might point him to where he could get a man without necessarily taking one from our Company. I had in mind the getting of a man from one of the other companies such as Wood, Johnson, Acme, etc." Butterworth admitted that Deere "knew nothing about the harvester business and had no wish to enter into it. . . . Their plow business was full of sufficient complications to give them all they wanted to think about."

Nevertheless, Butterworth continued: "As a trustee of the Deere interests, which own the majority of the John Deere Plow Company, it was up to him and his co-trustees to make the business so secure that there could be no question as to its permanency and looking ahead they could not just see where the outcome of the business would lie, unless they were able to furnish as long a line to their agents as their competitors did." What manifestly would be an entrepreneurial venture —to become more a full-line company by a move into harvesters—was being couched by Butterworth here as a defensive, protective act. Further, he was defending not the company as a whole, but "the Deere interests," for which he was "co-trustee." This was the Charles Deere estate, for which he and Burton Peek were, indeed, trustees. There was potential conflict of interest in the dual roles of chief executive officer and trustee; how Butterworth would handle this with his fellow stockholders remained to be seen.

Finally, the moment came for Butterworth to respond to McCormick's carrot about consolidation: "He personally would welcome any arrangement by which they could get harvesters from us and give us plows if their organization required them and he was also very glad to have this opportunity of coming together for any general conference which might be beneficial. . . . He would be glad to think matters over and see me again, and asked me whether the McA. matter could be allowed to stand over for one or two weeks while they were digesting some of these things that had been referred to by me and by him."

McCormick, ever sensitive to his company's precarious legal position, ended with a warning: "Bear in mind that it was only possible for a certain line of conferences to be held between his company and ours, and we could not and would not do anything which was contrary to the law of arranging anything as competitors." McCormick felt they were on safe ground, however, for he continued: "There was so little in which his company were really competitors of ours at the present time that any general conference between us was entirely feasible. . . . On any matter of large policy like this he would always find us ready to tell him what we thought about the matter or to say that we could not discuss this, and I assumed their attitude was the same."

McCormick appended a postscript to himself in his minutes of this long meeting: "I forgot to mention that in talking, Mr. Butterworth said they took quite seriously our arrangement with Parlin & Orendorff as being an indication that we might possibly make an alliance with P.&O. for this country as well as for Canada." Butterworth obviously was sensitive about International Harvester's already close links with the Canton plow manufacturer, even though the Parlin & Orendorff plows were only in the Canadian trade. Butterworth was prescient here—International Harvester did buy Parlin & Orendorff in 1919.

About three weeks elapsed between this first McCormick-Butterworth encounter and an equally revealing second meeting, in early January 1910. The two industrialists chose to lunch at the Chicago Club, and this time they viewed each other with more caution. McCormick opened with a blunt caveat: Because of the tariff situation in Canada, business relationships in that country were "entirely" different from those in the United States, "so that any suggestion with regard to the mutual interests on one side of the line would not necessarily imply the same treatment on the other side." Butterworth countered with a proposal startling in its scope: "He asked me whether I thought it would be feasible for Deere & Co. to sell the product of the I.H. Co. in the U.S.A. if the I.H. Co. sold all their products in foreign countries where they did not have such an organization." McCormick flatly rejected this: "I replied that although I felt the value of Deere & Co.'s selling organization in the U.S.A. I did not suppose their selling organization was nearly as strong as that of the I.H. Co. with its 100 general agencies and its large force of men, that I could think of no plan which would change or diminish the activity of the I.H. Co. selling organization in the U.S.A."

McCormick then returned to the question of International Harvester's overtures in plows. "We were still reluctant to go into the plow business in the U.S.A. unless we should be forced to such a move. . . . Would it not be feasible for the I.H. Co. to keep out of the plow line in this country and for the D. Co. to keep out of the harvester line for a certain term of years." Butterworth seemed at this point to back off, admitting that "the more they thought of it, the more they were disinclined to go forward with the harvester business." Still, Butterworth cautioned, some of the product lines of the two companies overlapped quite substantially; he noted four—peg tooth harrows, disk harrows, corn planters, and stalk cutters ("in this the competition is direct, so far as disk harrows are concerned, but the I.H. Co. does not do so much on corn planters or stalk cutters").

McCormick hammered away at keeping Deere out of harvesters, even implying that they together might forestall other efforts, too: "I assumed that if the D. Co. decided to keep out of the harvester line it would not be difficult for them to procure the same agreement from the other interests such as Moline, Oliver and Rock Island Companies." Butterworth did agree that "he was quite sure that it would not be to the interest of any of those companies named to go into the harvester line, especially if there was any arrangement made between the D. Co. and the I.H. Company."

McCormick then pursued the Canadian situation: "I assumed it would be necessary for them to manufacture plows in Canada and Mr. B. said it would, but it was not material to them as to how their goods were sold in Canada, provided a sufficient quantity of J.D. goods were sold through a proper organization." McCormick countered: "I told him . . . that I assumed they would have to manufacture plows in Canada, but even on this basis, it might be feasible for the factory to be operated by joint action." McCormick was encouraged that Butterworth was receptive to this proposal: "He seemed quite favorable to an alliance in Canada for any reasonable basis between the I.H. Co. and J.D. and repeated the statement . . . that what he, as a trustee of the Deere estate, was seeking to do was to make more secure the D. interests rather than to undertake the erection of more manufactories." On this upbeat note, the noteworthy luncheon ended.

But no joint relationship whatsoever was to be. Neither Deere nor International Harvester records tell us why the proposal fell through, but it was obvious by the actions of Deere over the next few days that no serious deal with International Harvester was going to occur. With fractured relations with J.I. Case, with no harvester project with Foster & Wood, and with no consummated arrangements with International Harvester, the executive committee finally realized that they must take initiative into their own hands and find a strong corporate vehicle that could resist pressures from such aggressive competitors as International Harvester. There was no longer any room for vacillation or temporizing. Events now required a decisive step.[5]

THE MODERN COMPANY

If one had to pick a single day in the history of Deere & Company as a "watershed," a likely candidate would be January 6, 1910. The directors of the company met that day and unanimously passed a critically important resolution. It began: "The Directors and Stockholders of Deere & Company view with much concern the aggressions of competitors and feel that for the conservation of their investments and interests a unification of their allied factories and distributing houses should be perfected. . . . " Reiterated again were the defensive, protective rationales for consolidation—the fear of competitor "aggression" and the deep concern for any possible deterioration of Deere assets due to market weakness. A second important clue to the future appeared in the next sentence, for the resolution was promulgated "with a view, also, of acquiring the business of such other companies as it may be deemed expedient to acquire under such terms as may be agreed upon." No longer was the proposed consolidation only to include Deere & Mansur and the branches, there were other outsiders already in mind. The final sentence left little doubt as to the urgency felt by the board: "We request the appointment by the President of Deere & Company, within 5 days from this date, of a Committee of five, which shall formulate a plan of re-organization . . . and its plan, when formulated, shall be submitted to the undersigned and the other parties in interest at the earliest practicable day."

Thus was put in motion, with surprising speed (contrary to the past), actions that were to lead to the birth, in less than two years, of "the modern company" (the euphemism used in Deere lore to separate ante- and post-1911 company forms). What seemed to the Deere board to be a monumental reorganization was certainly miniscule in comparison to the creation of the giants, International Harvester in 1901 and United States Steel in 1902. This time consolidation "took."

Hundreds of questions about finances, capital accounts, valuation of physical properties, and shareholder interests had to be faced. After these were settled, even more complex and subtle managerial issues would surface—operating relationships among the entities, marketing and public relations strategies, and a whole set of human interplays that finally gave flesh and blood to the arrangement. The overall goal was clear to everyone—a new, consolidated company, established in such a manner that it would legally control all its parts, operating them under a single management (*i.e.,* the Deere board of directors). This new company would be so capitalized that it could compensate the holders of all the shares of all the entities with some combination of shares—on an equitable basis—in the new company. A series of critical steps would be needed:

1. Consolidate all branches and eliminate all individual, "outside" ownership blocs

2. Bring in Deere & Mansur, to become wholly owned by the company under the same formula, thereby eliminating product overlaps, such as had occurred with Dain

3. Gain complete control of Union Malleable and make certain that its management always assumed that its "first" customer is the company

4. Find and bring into the orbit of the company several other agricultural machinery manufacturers, complementary to the company, which would then result in an organization closer to a "full line" company

5. Broaden the capital structure and make it large enough to allow the purchase

of all branches and other companies, using some combination of capital instruments (common and preferred stock, perhaps some bonds), and leaving enough residual capitalization to purchase other companies later

6. Tightly control these capital instruments through some voting trust arrangement whereby present management made the decisions, precluding outsiders gaining control of any of these capital instruments; at the same time, make available a small amount of these capital instruments to certain employees

7. Emphasize the name Deere throughout the organization, by re-naming the company itself Deere & Company and by using the name "John Deere" or "Deere" widely through the various entities of this new company

8. Consolidate all the managements under the guidance of a management team that is also the board of directors of the new company; in accomplishing this, maintain a balance among the entities (e.g., between branches and Moline), but guarantee the centrality of Moline control

9. Extend the "reach" of the new company throughout the United States, with stepped-up marketing efforts, etc., that will emphasize the national character of the company; make only modest thrusts abroad into international markets

10. Keep the corporate headquarters physically located in Moline—and make Moline the psychological center of the company's universe

11. In some way, out of all of this, get the company into harvesting equipment

The first stage, carried out over the first four months of 1911, accomplished most of these objectives. A new holding company, carrying the identical name of the historic parent, Deere & Company, was formed.

The Committee on Reorganization—which included the two lawyer-executives, Butterworth and Burton Peek, and C.C. Webber, W.L. Velie, and Schiller Hosford—then folded into the new Deere & Company the parent, the branch houses, Union Malleable, and Deere & Mansur, all new holdings to be based on a complicated formula developed by the committee. The Ft. Smith Wagon Company (Ft. Smith, Arkansas) had been taken over by Deere & Company in May 1907 but had been run as a separate organization; now it, too, was brought under the new holding company.

Next, two new companies were added. The first was the Marseilles Manufacturing Company, which had been in business since 1870 in Marseilles, Illinois, making corn shellers and portable elevators. Its sheller was one of the best known on the market. Earlier, Deere & Mansur had also manufactured shellers, but got out after the turn of the century and in 1908 contracted with Marseilles to keep the shellers in the Deere line of products. In 1910 Deere & Company took over full control of Marseilles and moved the plant to East Moline, changing the name of the company to the Marseilles Company.

The second company, Kemp & Burpee, had been founded in 1877 at Magog, Quebec, and manufactured one of the first practical manure

spreaders in North America. In 1880 the company had moved to Syracuse, New York, and around 1902 the John Deere sales organization had
begun selling the Kemp & Burpee Success spreader. In late 1910 Deere &
Company took over the property, plant, and equipment; the operation
was also moved to East Moline. Both Marseilles and Kemp & Burpee were
brought into the new holding company, using the formula of the
committee on reorganization.

When the Haskins & Sells representative, T.F. Wharton, presented his
figures, the net assets of Deere & Company were valued at about $22.7
million and the net average earnings for the previous five years at $3.1
million. At first, the committee on reorganization proposed a figure of
$22.7 million for the preferred stock and $18.7 million for common stock,
but after considering the plans for further acquisitions, it leaned toward a
proposed capitalization at $50 million—$30 million in preferred stock
and $20 million in common stock. W.L. Velie argued that this was too
high; when the final vote was taken in early April, the preferred was set at
$22.1 million and the common at $16.8 million. Shareholders in each
company were then allocated their proper share of both preferred and
common stock, based on Wharton's formula.

In Wharton's list of the common stock holdings—a critically important
set, inasmuch as these were the voting shares—the total number of
shares was 169,248. Of this, the Deere estate (with William Butterworth
and Burton Peek as trustees) held 43,653 shares. Butterworth himself held
just over 5,000 shares, and, as trustee for his wife, Katherine, another
11,000. When the 13,218 shares of Anna Deere Wiman (also with
Butterworth as trustee) were added, the total of the Butterworth-Peek
trusteeship and personal holdings came to about 74,000—in other words,
not a majority of the total shares. This was likewise the case for the other
two large holdings. W.L. Velie, S.H. Velie, and C.D. Velie held in total
some 29,000 shares; C.C. Webber held just over 7,000 shares. If one added
together this group of closely related family holdings—the Butterworth-
Deere estate interests combined with the Velie-Webber interests, the
total was about 110,000 shares, a clear majority. There were several dozen
other holdings of common stock; some other members of the family also
owned stock in Deere & Company, and there were important holders
from Deere & Mansur (John Good and others) and smaller ones from
Marseilles, Union Malleable, Ft. Smith Wagon Company, etc.

Picturing these common-stock holdings by blocs was really an idle
exercise, however, given the presence of an ingenious plan put into effect
in April 1911 for pooling the common stock. Subscribers to all of the
common stock were invited to put their shares into a voting trust, headed
by Butterworth, Webber, W.L. Velie, Schiller Hosford, George Mixter,
George Peek, and Burton Peek. The agreement was to be in effect for three
years until June 1914. The trust agreement not only gave full voting
powers to the trustees, but committed the "subscribers" (as they were

called in the document) not to assign the certificate or any interest therein to someone else. Almost all of the holders immediately agreed to the pooling arrangement, and the trustees were thereby given complete control over the new holding company for the three-year period, irrespective of additions that might ensue from further acquisitions.[6]

DAIN JOINS

A separate, almost simultaneous action brought another company into the fold in late 1910, when the company's old friend, Joseph Dain at the Dain Manufacturing Company, also sold to Deere. Dain agreed to remain with the new organization as its president and the Dain Manufacturing Company would retain its separate identity even though it was now wholly owned by Deere.

Joseph Dain had left his small retail furniture business in Meadville, Missouri, in 1881 to form a new company to manufacture his own inventions—sweep rakes and hay stackers. In a few years he had moved to Springfield, Missouri, then to Armourdale, Kansas, then back to Missouri (to Carrolltown, where the company was first incorporated in 1890). Having outgrown the Carrolltown facilities by 1900, Dain moved the company to Ottumwa, Iowa. The sales of the company had averaged about $870,000 per year during the five years immediately preceding the consolidation into Deere; the profits during that same five-year period had averaged about $82,000. A small subsidiary of Dain had been opened in Canada at Welland, Ontario, in 1908, and this company, too, was made a part of the Deere settlement. Dain and his fellow shareholders accepted a formula that produced preferred stock in the sum of $868,100 and common stock in the amount of $242,000.

Though the Dain firm was a small one in the constellation of interests of the new company, it was critically important in one regard, for the kind of research and product development done by Joseph Dain had clear applications to harvesting equipment. Dain was immediately persuaded to head the harvester department, though he continued to reside in Ottumwa to supervise the hay tool company; he also became a vice president and had supervision of the patent and experimental department. Though the company management pressed Dain to come to Moline and actually take hands-on charge of the harvester department, Dain demurred and the job was assumed by W.R. Morgan, a former International Harvester sales manager. Dain finally did move to Moline in 1913, but he continued his leadership in the Dain Company over the next several years; he achieved national recognition in 1916 with his election to the presidency of the National Implement and Vehicle Association.

Two other negotiations loomed ahead, both so large that Butterworth, Peek, Webber, and the others felt it wise to consummate all of the previous deals before seriously coping with these last two, and to immediately announce the consolidation to the public. The consolidation already had surfaced in the Moline newspapers and the farm-equipment trade journals in late March 1911, well in advance of Deere's formal meeting of April 7 that ratified all of it. *Farm Implement News* devoted a full page to what they considered a major story, detailing all of the companies that were joining and noting the increase in the capitalization of the new company to $50 million. Its reporter put particular emphasis on the Dain acquisition, for it "causes the Deere dream of a complete line to blossom into flower." The reporter, ever anxious to gain a scoop, queried the Deere spokesman about plans in Canada, for rumor had it that a major new plant addition was to be made at the Dain property in Welland, Ontario, supposedly for "a harvester for the Canadian trade." But the company, ever fearful of International Harvester retaliation, was uncommunicative on this matter.

The other point that intrigued the press in the complete Deere announcement was the proposal to sell stock to the employees. The *Farm Implement News* reporter speculated: "Naturally the majority of the employees who take advantage of the opportunity afforded will be Moline residents." But the reporter did not cover one point of concern to the Deere people, and a news story in the next issue, probably planted by Deere, cleared it up: "It should be distinctly understood that this merger does not embrace a 'trust,' as the smaller concerns are consenting to a complete merger, for which they are being paid with stock in the new Deere & Company."

THE SYRACUSE CHILLED PLOW COMPANY

The legal details settled and the official announcement in place, the company turned to its last two negotiations. Talks with the Syracuse Chilled Plow Company had been initiated several months earlier but had been put aside in order to complete the first stage. The chilled plow company had been in existence since 1876, having first been called the Robinson Chilled Plow Co., and at the time of Deere's acquisition was headed by a third-generation descendant of the well-known early-nineteenth-century plow maker, Thomas Wiard. In 1879 the company's name was changed to the Syracuse Chilled Plow Company, for the town where Robinson had begun its business (and where it was then located). By the time of the negotiations with Deere, fourth-generation W.W. Wiard was the company's head. By 1900 the firm had flowered, and the quality of its chilled plow was well respected throughout the East. Its sales over the previous five years had averaged about $1.25 million, and profits during this same period about $185,000 per year.

The Syracuse company was eager to join Deere, and the negotiations went amazingly quickly. George Mixter later recounted the story. "I went to Syracuse, telephoned Mr. Chase from the hotel. Mr. Chase and Mr. Wiard immediately came to my room. I stated the general conditions of the implement trade and asked if they would care to be associated with Deere & Company. They immediately telephoned for their private ledger and spread before me the facts. I was particularly impressed with the reliability of their figures and the character of the men. After some talk they retired to an adjoining room and in a short time returned and stated in a general way what kind of a deal they were willing to make with Deere & Company. I returned to Moline, stated the facts to the Executive Committee of Deere & Company, and immediately returned to Syracuse to consummate the deal. Accompanied by Mr. Wharton, we arrived at Syracuse on Saturday noon. During Saturday afternoon and Sunday and most of two nights, Mr. Wharton devoted himself to examining the books while I made a tentative appraisal of the property. And on Monday noon we handed Mr. Chase a draft of the National Park Bank for $400,000 as an initial payment on the deal. These details . . . show how possible it is to do things rapidly under the right conditions."

Deere had had a chilled plow in its line since the late nineteenth century, but it was not a popular product, probably because it was a copy of competitor plows (an "exact imitation of the Oliver," S.H. Velie, Sr., admitted) and it did not have Deere's own design in it. The arrangements for the Syracuse purchase were similar to the earlier ones, though in this case a substantial amount was paid in cash. (The Syracuse shareholders received $400,000 in preferred stock, just $10,000 in common stock, and $940,000 in cash; C.A. Chase and W.W. Wiard also received personally some $28,000 each of Deere common stock.) The management of the Syracuse operation remained in the hands of Wiard and Chase, and the manufacturing operations were left in Syracuse. The only change from previous Syracuse operations was the selling through Deere branch houses instead of directly to the trade.

THE VAN BRUNT ACQUISITION

The last purchase to complete the modern company was that of the Van Brunt Manufacturing Company of Horicon, Wisconsin (alternatively called Van Brunt & Wilkins Manufacturing Company and Van Brunt & Davis Company in the 1880s). Two brothers, Daniel C. and George W. Van Brunt, had originally brought the firm to Horicon in 1861, after a year of operation in Mayville, Wisconsin. George left the business soon after, but Daniel C. Van Brunt continued to control the business until his death in 1901. The company's product was the result of a critical need of the mid-nineteenth century—some way of getting small grains seeded into the ground with enough cover to prevent the hoards of passenger pigeons from eating them almost instantaneously. There were millions of these birds in the Midwest and the Northwest during that period—a real menace to frontier agriculture, though by about 1910 their flocks had diminished somewhat. Daniel Van Brunt invented a series of grain drills and held several tightly drawn patents. During the first decade of the new century the Van Brunt organization had marketed directly to dealers and had handily outsold Deere & Company.

Van Brunt had been wooed off and on during the half dozen years preceding the Deere negotiations by the International Harvester Company. Willard Van Brunt had repeatedly refused to consider a sale to them for reasons not disclosed.

Van Brunt's major business was in the upper Middle West and Plains states, and inevitably the Van Brunt competition made C.C. Webber not only knowledgeable about the company but finally "itching" to gain control of it. Just as soon as the first stage was in hand, Webber went to Horicon, accompanied by Butterworth, Burton Peek, and George Mixter, to negotiate with Daniel Van Brunt's son, Willard A. Van Brunt, then the chief executive. In June 1911, the two parties agreed to consolidate. Deere & Company acquired all the capital stock of Van Brunt as of August 1, 1910, paying a total of $1,517,600 in Deere preferred stock, an additional $1,246,746 in common stock, and a cash payment of just under $500,000. The factory was to be continued at Horicon and the existing management left precisely in place. The only major procedural change was the assumption of marketing by the various Deere branch houses. Thus the last brick was put in place for the enlarged house of Deere (exhibit 7-3).[7]

CHANGES IN MANAGEMENT PHILOSOPHY

It was now up to the Deere top management to organize and manage the new consolidation so that the results would justify the complicated planning and negotiation just completed. New companies had been brought on board, each with its own management and its own operating philosophy, and they varied widely. The company now had preferred stock, its holders with not only first claim on profits each year, but cumulative rights if a dividend was passed. Outsiders also now held stock; initially these shareholders were from the constituent companies, but within a year Deere made its first public offering of preferred stock. Some stock was also sold to employees, an interesting complexity for management.

Finally, there were critical management issues to be faced. Could the longstanding differences of opinion among the top management group be reconciled? How should the balance between centralization and decentralization be resolved? Some branches had been in the Deere orbit for many years, but others were just coming into the organization after years

Deere & Company owns about 84.91 acres of land situated in and near the City of Moline, Illinois, as follows:

Ground occupied by Factories..................	21.50 acres
Ground occupied by Lumber Yard..............	20.67 acres
Ground occupied by Experimental Farm........	42.74 acres
Total...............................	84.91 acres

The factories are devoted principally to the manufacture of plows, cultivators and harrows. The buildings have been almost entirely rebuilt during the recent years, and are of the most modern mill construction, steel and concrete, with a floor area of over 2,500,000 square feet, or about 58 acres. The Company also owns ten acres of real estate in the City of East Moline, Illinois, on which additional factory buildings are being erected.

All of the properties of the Company are protected against fire loss by the most modern equipment. Practically the entire properties are provided with automatic sprinklers, together with other protection, making the risks acceptable to the Mutual Companies. .

The business and properties of the Subsidiary Companies are:

Deere & Mansur Company (manufacturers of corn planters, disc harrows, hay rakes and hay loaders), owns 12.75 acres of real estate situate in the City of Moline, and occupied by its factory. The buildings are of brick and concrete, and have a floor area of 543,450 square feet.

Moline Wagon Company (manufacturers of farm wagons) owns 8.37 acres of real estate situate in the City of Moline and occupied by its factory. The buildings are of brick and have a floor area of 417,132 square feet.

The Marseilles Company (manufacturers of manure spreaders, grain elevators and corn shellers) owns 27.97 acres of real estate situate in the City of East Moline. The buildings are of brick and have a floor area of 388,496 square feet.

Van Brunt Manufacturing Company (manufacturers of grain drills and other seeding machinery) owns 15.80 acres of real estate situate in the City of Horicon, Wisconsin. The buildings are of brick and have a floor area of 291,661 square feet.

Syracuse Chilled Plow Company (manufacturers of chilled plows and other implements for the Eastern trade) owns 5.10 acres of real estate situate in the City of Syracuse, New York. The buildings are of brick and have a floor area of 570,671 square feet.

Union Malleable Iron Company (manufacturers of malleable iron castings for all purposes) owns 9.68 acres of real estate in East Moline. The buildings are of brick and have a floor area of 237,744 square feet.

The Davenport Wagon Company (manufacturers of metal running gear farm wagons) owns 1.10 acres of real estate situate in the City of Davenport, Iowa. The buildings are of concrete and have a floor area of 80,000 square feet.

Dain Manufacturing Company of Iowa (manufacturers of hay-making machinery) owns 43.63 acres of real estate situate in the City of Ottumwa, Iowa. The buildings are of brick and have a floor area of 184,984 square feet.

Dain Manufacturing Company, Limited (manufacturers of hay tools and other implements for the Canadian trade) owns 167.63 acres of real estate situate in the City of Welland, Ontario. The buildings are of brick and concrete and have a floor area of 95,944 square feet.

Fort Smith Wagon Company (manufacturers of wooden farm wagons for the Southern and Southwestern trade) owns 15.98 acres of real estate situate in the City of Fort Smith, Arkansas. The buildings are of brick and have a floor area of 167,110 square feet.

The John Deere Plow Company of St. Louis (manufacturers of buggies) owns .82 acres of real estate situate in the City of St. Louis, Missouri. The buildings are of brick and have a floor area of 126,180 square feet.

The Moline Lumber Company owns a modern saw and planing mill at Malvern, Arkansas, together with the real estate occupied by them.

The Moline Timber Company owns valuable timber lands in Arkansas, aggregating approximately 25,718 acres, and containing approximately 161,800,000 feet of hardwood lumber.

The Fort Smith Wagon Company owns valuable timber lands in Sevier County, Arkansas, aggregating 7,920 acres, and containing approximately 39,077,000 feet of hardwood lumber.

The Moline Wagon Company is the owner of timber lands in Franklin Parish, Louisiana, aggregating 8,093 acres and containing approximately 46,680,000 feet of hardwood lumber.

The Company also has sales organizations at Minneapolis, Omaha, Sioux Falls, Moline, Bloomington, Des Moines, Kansas City, Denver, Oklahoma City, Indianapolis, St. Louis, Dallas, New Orleans, Atlanta, Baltimore, Syracuse, Spokane, Portland, San Francisco, Welland (Ontario), Winnipeg, Saskatoon, Regina and Calgary, and an Export Department at Moline.

The capital stock of all of these Companies (except a relatively small proportion of the Fort Smith Wagon Company Stock) is owned by Deere & Company.

Exhibit 7–3. *The "Modern Company"—Deere & Company, as pictured in the annual report of 1912* of independent operation; too tight control by the center might not set well.

Willard Velie, Burton Peek, and George Mixter had been delegated by the board to draw up the new articles of incorporation and bylaws. These were read line for line at the meeting of January 4, 1911, and among a number of important codicils was one that would later become quite controversial—a provision establishing an executive committee. In a curious aberration, Willard Velie was chosen chairman of the committee; Butterworth, though president and chief executive officer, was only a member (the others were C.C. Webber, George Mixter, Burton and George Peek, and Floyd Todd). The discussion about the committee was not wholly amicable. Willard Velie wrote Burton Peek a long letter just two days later, a document full of innuendoes about Butterworth: "One of the advantages which it was thought would accrue from the consolidation was that the largest interest could not and would not attempt to dominate, but on the contrary there would be a diffusion of authority and a distribution of discretion on important matters among those Directors whose judgment and experience were competent. . . . The creation of an Executive Committee has tended to clarify the situation, but the atmosphere is still murky, principally I assume because there has been an intimation that I am unwarrantably seeking prominence in the new organization. . . . I do not consider this a defection, for I have worn the 'stripes' for something over twenty years, and I believe a just board of pardons would recognize my demand for a parole, especially since some portion of the chastisement administered was endured for others. Like many of us, I am seeking a chance to grow old less fast, and I cannot in justice to myself consent to be a wheel horse to be lashed at pleasure by a thoughtless driver."

Velie must have felt that this was not blunt enough, for in May 1911, he penned another letter to the executive committee: "I desire to say a word regarding the possible disadvantage . . . which may accrue through a wrong conception of the duties and responsibilities of the Executive Committee, and of those of the individual members thereof. The primary object in selecting from the directors seven members who, through accidents of residence, experience and fitness, qualify for the job, was to secure a less unwieldy medium for the quick transaction of the vitally important business of the organization whose ramifications and complexities positively preclude centralization of authority in an individual. . . . I do not wish to convey the thought that there has been an arrogation of authority by any one whose province has been specialized, but merely to sound a warning note against such a possible and natural contingency."

Velie then brought up again the seemingly trivial matter that had become so symbolic of control and power—who should "open the mail." "To insure to the Executive Committee the opportunity to discuss

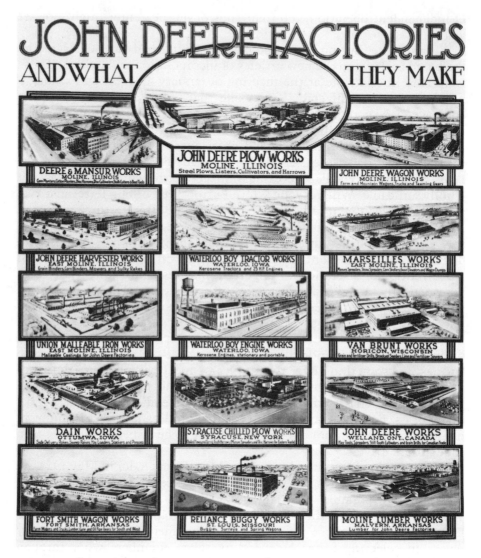

matters of gravity and importance," Velie wrote, "I think a consistent effort should be made to cause everyone who has new ideas, or who wants a ruling, to write his well-considered views, rather than to talk them desultorily to individuals, and to insist that communications be addressed to the Executive Committee who shall alone be privileged to open or to peruse them."

Velie by this point had become the spokesman—indeed, the advocate—of a shared management. Charles Deere's colleagues had had great admiration for Deere's management but mixed feelings about how he had concentrated authority into his hands as the chief executive officer. C.C. Webber and W.L. Velie (joined later by George Peek) had represented the "loyal opposition" in the years from about the turn of the century—particulary after S.H. Velie, Sr., had died. Now it seemed clear that Velie was taking up the cudgel against William Butterworth. To be sure, Butterworth remained the chief executive officer, but the establishment of the executive committee, chaired by the leading proponent of shared management, mirrored the board's desire for a different management philosophy.

There was a further problem. On the one hand, the board agreed that a centralization of finance and the development of a unified accounting system under a single financial officer was critically needed to consolidate the many financial policies of the constituent companies. At the same time, many of the board felt that the financial officer should come from outside the existing management group. Expectedly, this was threatening to Butterworth, who had been treasurer under Charles Deere and had continued to dominate financial planning after he himself became president. Now there was a much expanded scope with all the new companies, and Butterworth realized that a strong financial executive was imperative. Such talent had not been developed internally, and it was inevitable that an outsider be sought.

A search committee was appointed to find this special person, tentatively to be called the comptroller. A month later, in June, the committee reported back that they had persuaded T.F. Wharton, the able Haskins & Sells officer who had effected the consolidation, to come with the company. There was no question but that he was coming in at a high level, for his salary was well above many of the other executives' on the board, and he was also to be given the opportunity to purchase $25,000 of common stock. Wharton's entry upon the scene gave the company a powerful accounting and finance expert, a person with unimpeachable personal qualities of integrity and frankness, and standing independent of any faction in the organization.

The coordination of territories and marketing personnel for the combined companies did not present many problems. The company had already marketed Dain products, and the Eastern geographical location of the Syracuse Chilled Plow operation made the transition relatively simple for it. The Van Brunt group, too, was not a difficult one to assimilate. There were some minor complications with the company trademark.

The regular trademark, "John Deere, Moline, Illinois" and the "leaping deer," the trademark of the plow company, were also now to be used by Deere & Mansur, Marseilles, and the Davenport Wagon Company. The Moline Wagon Company was also to adopt the trademark, omitting its old trademark of the "running dog." Contrariwise, Dain had a most effective trademark, the "Great Dain Dog"; here Dain was to use "John Deere, Moline, Illinois" but to continue the use of the dog. Incidentally, at this time George Peek also persuaded the board to make a formal

Exhibit 7–4. *Dain Manufacturing Company's "Great Dain" trademark, ca. 1908, which was retained after the company's purchase by Deere in 1910*

resolution changing the caption in the trademark from "Inventor of the steel plow" to "He gave to the world the steel plow"—thus clearing up an inaccuracy that had persisted since the 1840s!

Problems connected with centralized purchasing proved more difficult. Inventory control had been a persistent headache, seemingly one of the potential drawbacks of a decentralized management style. A motion passed by the executive committee in May 1911 advocated "collective buying of all materials for the constituent companies," but asked in the process that "this matter be taken up personally with the factories." The latter were outspokenly unwilling to turn over their individual purchasing authority to someone more centralized in the Moline hierarchy, and the issue of authorization for purchase of materials continued to plague the company over many more years.[8]

CONTROVERSY OVER THE HARVESTER

The divisiveness within the board continued to simmer during late 1911 and 1912, erupting eventually in arguments regarding the desirability of manufacturing harvesters. The story is linked closely to the offering of $10 million of preferred stock to the general public in 1912. The capitalization of the combined company authorized such stock, and most of the board felt that the company needed more working capital for its expansion. Earlier, the board had always felt leery of outside financing, except for short-term working capital needs met by hometown and nearby Chicago banks. As Willard Velie put it: "Our policy is to depend upon local and other banks . . . and thanks to the prestige acquired through sixty odd years of successful, honest endeavor . . . we have been cheerfully and indulgently served even in periods of depression and of panics." Velie had almost a pathological fear of the New York financial community: "Bankers . . . are often, tentatively at least, our enemies and actually our bitterest competitors. Because of their holdings of stock in various large merged companies, New York capitalists who are furnishing the money and the inspiration to the International Harvester Co. and others, view our aggressions with unrest, especially since 'We have carried the war [the Deere harvester efforts] to Africa.'" Velie concluded: "Large capitalists in the present-day definition are proverbially and admittedly conscienceless." Velie's belief was that a preferred stock offering was least dangerous, and it was this vehicle that the board chose.

To no one's surprise, given the excellent record of the company, the underwriting firm of White, Weld & Co. had no difficulty whatsoever in marketing the shares. Deere's board then had the pleasant task of deciding how to utilize these proceeds.

The executive committee met in July and enunciated a conservative policy: the new funds were first to be applied to the short-term indebtedness of the company (not the bonds, debentures, and five-year notes, though; these were to be retired from earnings). Expenditures for expansion and improvement in any given year were to be limited to one-half the net profits of the preceding year after deducting the dividends for preferred stock and all other fixed charges, and additionally limited to the sum of $1 million, unless the net profits for the preceding year exceeded $4 million. The board thus reaffirmed the conservatism that had been the watchword of the company for so many years.

The early results of consolidation seemed ample justification for the board's optimism about the future. The profit of the combined companies was reported at $4 million in the year ending October 31, 1911. In the following year—the first complete one for the "modern company"—the results were reported for the first time in a publicly printed and distributed annual report, and the profits were listed at more than $4.3 million. (After World War I, the net profit for 1911 was revised to $3.3 million, and for 1912 to $3.6 million.) This report also disclosed a total of $37.8 million of preferred stock issued, of an authorized $40 million, and just over $20 million of common stock, of the authorized $25 million. In addition to the $10 million of preferred stock publicly sold, the company had issued $16,300 in preferred stock to employees "on completion of monthly payments." (The company had made available 5,000 shares—and this already had been oversubscribed; some $136,000 had been contracted for by October 31, 1912.) William Butterworth signed the annual report as president and his last sentence in the brochure noted, with fine understatement, "The business of the Company for the past year has been satisfactory, and the prospects for the coming year are very good."

Thus, there was no financial constraint to hold back a new-product effort and harvesters were on everyone's mind. When it came to deciding what to do, opinions differed sharply. The company had already committed itself to the manufacture of a harvester for the Canadian trade, to be made at Dain's Welland plant in Ontario. The Canadian tariff duties on agricultural machinery made this a necessary competitive move. Without this step, the Canadian trade would be absorbed by others, particularly International Harvester. Seven or eight machines were field-tested in Canada in the summer of 1910 under the direction of Harry J. Podlesak, and Butterworth advocated staying in Canada for the following year. Velie felt otherwise: "The binder situation in the United States was much more serious than Canada today. . . . The experimental work should be done in Moline, where our best talent could render assistance in every detail." Velie's view prevailed. Rented quarters were obtained and manufacturing was begun in East Moline.

The inevitable next question was whether to redirect this experimental work and develop a harvester for the United States—in other words, whether to challenge International Harvester with a domestically produced harvester for U.S. farm markets. Butterworth opposed any U.S. manufacture and wrote the executive committee before the key meeting in July 1912: "I do not think that we should enter or undertake to enter the harvester business in this country at this time. . . . For the next few years, we can well devote our entire efforts and our best thoughts to securing further betterments and more nearly perfecting our own organization . . . introducing new methods . . . raising our standard of manufacture . . . increasing the efficiency of our men . . . at the same time prosecuting our harvester business in Canada and proceeding experimentally with that business in this country." Butterworth drove his point home further with a six-page "Statement of the Deere Interests in Reference to the Future Policy of Deere & Company." He argued strongly for a conservative posture relating to any debt, and against taking on the International Harvester Company: "It would be the height of unwisdom to attack the International Harvester Company, which has at least $7.00 to our $1.00 in working capital, and can command $10.00 to our $1.00, and which can possibly shut out from us the avenues of credit. A serious fight with them will mean a serious depletion of our profits, maybe their absolute curtailment, thus endangering our dividends, the passing of one of which would very seriously affect its market price and do great damage to our credit." Butterworth even raised the bogeyman of loss of control by the board: "This could possibly lead to putting other forces into our Board of Directors." He concluded: "The theory that because the Harvester Company may go into the plow business, we should go into che harvester business and so start a fight with them, seems to me to be most unwise. I would avoid a fight with them as long as possible."

Willard Velie took the opposite position. After reminding the board of the impending antitrust suit against the International Harvester Company, Velie opined: "In the disintegration of the International Harvesting [*sic*] Machine Co. which the government will doubtless accomplish, it is inevitable that the organization be split up into two or more separate, ostensibly independent companies. Whether there shall be two or six does not impeach the logic of the contention that each constituent offering a full line, including plows, will be a real competitor of ours, and that their competition in the aggregate will be more menacing and intense than is that of the present more or less unwieldy consolidation." Velie argued against the Butterworth version of conservation as being too static: "There is no such thing as equilibrium in business; the movement is either progressive or retrogressive. My opinion, carefully considered, is that to conserve what we have we must aspire to get more."

Velie quickly garnered support from others on the executive committee, particularly George Mixter and George Peek, the latter just having been brought to Moline as the general sales manager of the company. When the issue came to the board, Velie and Peek jointly offered a resolution that some of the proceeds of the preferred stock issue be used to construct a harvester plant in Moline, "that we may supply the trade of this country and abroad with a line of harvesting machinery . . . as soon as our binders shall have been carefully weighed in the balance of experience and found *not* wanting." Mixter followed with a resolution that the company should authorize enough material to build four thousand binders for the coming season. It was too united a front for Butterworth to fight, so he swallowed his misgivings, and both resolutions were voted unanimously.

Ground was broken for the new plant in East Moline, just a few weeks after the July 12, 1912, meeting. A move of this moment could not be kept secret for long, and soon the industry press was trumpeting stories of "the newcomer" (exhibit 7-5). This caused consternation at International Harvester: a revealing set of handwritten notes made at a private meeting of key Harvester executives on January 1, 1913, chronicled wide disagreement about just what retaliatory strategy to adopt. Present were Cyrus and Harold McCormick; John Wilson, the general counsel; A.E. Mayer, the vice president for sales; and Alexander Legge, the general manager. Four options were elaborated: "(1) make exchange trade with Deere; (2) buy out Deere or other Co.; (3) form new company subsidiary to IH Company for plows; (4) make agreement as to each keeping out of the other's business (make a truce for 3 or 5 years)." Legge opted for a truce but went on: "Let them make move, then we make best purchase we can quickly & go into plows." Harold McCormick also favored a truce, but he, too, wanted a "financial arrangement to get into plow business by buying or building plows."

Exhibit 7–5. *Deere joins its competitors in harvesting equipment (*Farm Implement News, *August 4, 1910)*

Vol. XXXI.   No. 31.   CHICAGO, ILL., AUGUST 4, 1910. $2.00 Per Year.

The Newcomer in the Harvest Field.

There is no evidence in either company's records of any further contact. The "truce," if indeed there was one, was quite tenuous. It was not long after this that Harvester signed an exclusive agreement for obtaining plows from Parlin & Orendorff, and within half a dozen years had purchased both that company and the Chattanooga Plow Co.[9]

EARLY SHERMAN ANTI-TRUST PROSECUTIONS

Deere's sensitivity at the time of the consolidation that the press not consider the new company a "trust" was rooted in reality. By the turn of the century, assaults by various state governments on the trusts had gained considerable momentum; more importantly, the federal government by then was vigorously using the Sherman Anti-Trust Act to bring antitrust cases against a number of the giants of American industry. First was the Northern Securities Co. case of 1904, early in Theodore Roosevelt's administration, which outlawed that railroad holding company. Then came the two famous cases of 1911, American Tobacco Co. and Standard Oil Co. of New Jersey, each resulting in dissolution of the company involved. By this latter date, the International Harvester Co. case was making its ponderous way through the courts toward a final decision in 1918. The first two decades of the twentieth century thus became noteworthy in the saga of trustbusting efforts by the federal government.

Once Charles Deere's hopes about the "plow trust" had gone glimmering, it seemed Deere had little to fear from the Sherman Act. As the oil and tobacco cases and the International Harvester suit moved through the courts, Deere executives had watched warily, giving testimony to government investigators when asked, but otherwise trying to keep a low profile. In 1911, the company was pressed to give information to government field investigators for the International Harvester case and agonized over how much to say about its arch rival. Finally, after four separate board meetings dominated by the issue, the directors suggested to Burton Peek to reply to the Department of Justice that "we feel their practices are unfair in a number of instances, but extremely fair in others." A year later, Harvester asked Deere for copies of the latter's agents' contracts for the years 1902 through 1912 and, after considerable additional discussion, Deere's board decided to comply—but with trepidation. William Butterworth himself finally was called to testify in the Harvester antitrust suit in 1912, and he was queried mostly about the Dain mowers and how they measured up to International Harvester competition. The Butterworth testimony merely confirmed what was already known—that Deere was a remote, insignificant competitor to Harvester.

When the government attorneys asked why Deere itself had gone into harvesters, Butterworth's answer centered on the tactics of the full line.

"The companies with which we were competing were taking on full lines; that is, they were selling both plows and binders. . . . We had been selling plows with our other lines. . . . Our competitors took on the plow line, which gave them what you might term a full line, and we were obliged to take on the binder, in order to compete."

But it was clear from both Butterworth's testimony and the data introduced in the International Harvester case that Deere had no overwhelming marketing share in any of its lines. In plows there never had been a single dominant plow company—even as late as that time, many dozens of plow manufacturers still were in the picture. In mowers, rakes, etc., Deere was only a second-level power. At the time the company acquired the Syracuse Chilled Plow Company, Burton Peek was asked by the Deere board whether this acquisition, and the attempted acquisition of the Chattanooga Plow Company, constituted an antitrust threat. Peek's answer was unequivocal—Deere had nothing to fear from the Sherman Act. The "rule of reason" doctrine had just evolved out of the Standard Oil case; though the acquiring of the Syracuse company would result in, indeed, an "actually competing company" (to use Peek's words), neither restraint of trade nor the establishment of a monopoly would be intended or affected. Peek reasoned that "there would be no shutting down of plants, and none of the unfair competition which characterized the Standard Oil and American Tobacco cases," and this would ameliorate any dangers.[10]

So, despite its prominence in the industry, Deere seemed remarkably free of concerns with antitrust accusations of "conspiracies in restraint of trade."

GEORGE PEEK'S MANUALS

Prior to Deere's consolidations in 1911, sales practices in the field had been the creatures of individual branch managers, varying widely as these highly independent executives each put his mark on "his own" branch. It produced a remarkably variegated pattern. Now, though, these policies were to go through an interesting metamorphosis.

The catalyst for change was George Peek. When Peek came to Moline in 1911 to head the sales organization, one of his first moves was a trip to all of the branch houses. He had come from a branch, so he expected to find a strong pattern of decentralization all over. But Peek was startled by what he found—the methods used were just too diffuse. Individual branches had conflicting ways of handling their travelers, their dealers, their relations with Moline.

Such inexplicable differences violated Peek's sense of organization and order. He returned to Moline determined to put together a central policy, written down in a manual that would apply uniformly to all branch house managers. The document he developed was a tour de force. It came before the board in December 1911 and was greeted with great enthusiasm: "The Manual . . . which was compiled, edited and written by Mr. George N. Peek, crystalizes the best intelligence of himself and of others who have been adjudged, by reason of experience and conscientious devotion to the larger affairs of Deere & Company, unusually competent advisors, collaborators and contributors." The board realized that it was treading on dangerous ground in attempting to corral the branch managers. It left no doubt, though, of its resolve to carry out new, centralized policy making; the members gave their "utter endowment" of the manual and requested that "the policies enunciated therein be rigidly adhered to, and that in a spirit of hearty cooperation they be inaugurated at once and carried out literally."

The manual covered just about every facet of branch-house operation—advertising; publicity; pricing and pricing concessions; estimation of demand and orders back to Moline; treatment of both the branch-house travelers and the factory field men; training, assignment, and monitoring of the branch sales managers; and even special instructions on how to develop sales campaigns "in a poor crop year." Included also was a standard "memorandum of agreement," to be used between the branch and the dealer; the contract generally would be drawn for several years, with an annual covenant specifying the prices for the crop year. A standard termination clause was also to be included, whereby either party could cancel after twelve months notice. The retail dealer was to be given an exclusive territory, and this was to be described explicitly in the contract. A price list developed by Deere was to be appended, guaranteeing to the dealer that the Deere prices would stand for the time period and that these would be set high enough to enable the dealer "to successfully compete with the leading manufacturers of like goods and still preserve a fair margin of profit."

Peek devoted an extensive section in the manual to the setting of retail prices, and he gave the branch houses a set of arguments that would serve them in persuading the dealers to maintain prices. Peek made clear, though, that while "we have a right to make prices that we will charge for our goods . . . we have no right to regulate the prices at which dealers should sell them, and do not desire to do so." Peek did reserve the right for the company to put out its own retail price list, "providing the price list is gotten up for the benefit and guidance of our own salesmen, and for our own use in quoting prices to farmers who come into our place of business to buy goods."

Peek called all the branch house managers together in February 1912 to explain these new policies. At the end of the meeting, he suggested that his own condensation of these policies might be sent out in booklet form to all of the salesmen. Some of the branch managers objected and took issue with several of Peek's caveats, particularly with the concept of the full line and the closely related notion of an exclusive dealership. Some of the more aggressive branch managers felt that the Peek statements on these two subjects were too "diplomatic" and might constrain them somewhat in pressing dealers to sell exclusively Deere products— typically the dream of the manufacturer.

How does one accomplish such a highly desired eventuality? One way was to suggest that the dealer limit himself voluntarily to one producer's goods. Another way was to persuade the dealer to do so, with one or another persuasive techniques. The most serious club was the manufacturer's threat to terminate his relationship with the dealer. The nuances of this relationship between dealer and manufacturer are complex indeed, and in a great many cases it would be difficult to determine exactly just what the manufacturer was telling the dealer in relation to the question of exclusivity.

In some Deere branches, the pressures on dealers to take a full line had been substantial. In 1910, for example, the Kansas City branch manager, Michael J. Healey, gave some advice to the Minneapolis branch sales managers about how their salesmen should handle recalcitrant dealers: "Occasionally they will run across a dealer who has handled our full line for a number of years, excepting, say, wagons and drills. This dealer may be unfair because he has not given us an opportunity to put in our wagons and drills, and he does not know whether they will sell better than the other fellow's or not. They will find this kind of dealer a hard man to handle, and in a general way the best thing to do with him is to try to induce him to put in a sample of the goods which he does not handle. If they cannot induce him to put in a sample, and if he is within a radius of 200 or 300 miles of the office, they should take him into the office and let the managers work on him. Then, if they can induce him to put in a sample order, after he has received the goods, go to his place of business and try to effect a sale to a farmer and follow the tool into the field and see that it works satisfactorily. This kind of work very often brings about good results." Healey's words danced down the tightrope between persuasion and pressure: "They should know that in our fight for business, we do not countenance the use of *coercion, dictatorial,* or *bulldozing methods;* also that we are opposed to having our men approach dealers in a wobbly-kneed manner, with a voice which sounds as if they had left two-thirds of it at home. *They should know that there is a difference between coercion and a firm stand for what is right.* They should know that while we do not countenance coercion, we do expect our men to make a firm stand for a reasonable amount of business, and that in making this stand they must use some diplomacy."

Peek's manual, on the other hand, did state frankly the company reasons why the full line benefited the dealer and included the words: "It is manifestly to the dealer's advantage to handle one line of goods." But there was clearly no evidence of pressure. Peek wrote Butterworth a few days later, disagreeing with the branch managers: "There was an objection raised to having that part of our full-line argument put in booklet form, but we are of the opinion that the disadvantages of doing so are overestimated." Still, Peek did finally decide to put his statement out only as a company bulletin, rather than a printed booklet for wide distribution. The board felt uneasy enough about even this to pass a resolution, exhorting the branch managers to "treat all the matter contained therein as confidential and to so guard them that they may not pass into competitive or unfriendly hands."

With the branch managers now accepting the new policies—perhaps a bit grudgingly—Peek then developed a salesman's manual, to be used by the branches for their traveling men and also to be given to each dealer. These were comprehensive books containing full data on all of the product lines, together with collateral information about the soil-culture department, suggestions for approaching a customer, pricing formulas, and extensive information on plow-share technology. The same set of central policies was reiterated in the front of the book, in briefer form. The salesmen were exhorted to "acquire the work habit" and to put in a full week of effort: "On the sixth day, if you cannot get direct results for us, at least get some indirect ones, by putting in the day in some of the towns where we do not have the desired representation. . . . We do not consider it fair to draw six days' wages for five days' work."

Peek's ideas often clashed with more traditional views of marketing. For example, C.C. Webber opposed the use of automobiles by travelers in 1914. The Deere & Webber branch-house directors unanimously backed him, their board resolution noting that "the nature of our business is such that our travelers cannot use automobiles to the same advantage as the jobber of groceries, drugs, etc., and that in furnishing automobiles for the use of travelers we would be encouraging the defeat of the object for which we have been striving for a long time, namely, the spending of more time by the traveler with the dealers. . . . " Peek, on the other hand, was enthusiastic about the automobile, and he soon had them widely adopted around the system.

George Peek himself was an eloquent persuader, a hustler, even a huckster—though probably not as high-pressured as men like Healey. Still, Peek soon appointed Healey as his branch manager in Kansas City; he was willing to accept some bull-ahead types in his sales force! Peek's influence on the organization was profound, coming as it did at a time when the total organization was in a considerable state of flux. The issue of the tractor was a case in point.[11]

ARRIVAL OF THE TRACTOR

While the steam tractor had been a modest influence on the farmer in the nineteenth century, the horse, mule, and ox continued as the mainstays of the agriculturalist right up to the beginning of the twentieth century. Gasoline-engine tractors had begun appearing in the 1890s, but not until 1910 were enough made to show up in the census statistics of total horsepower available in the country (exhibit 7-6).

Exhibit 7–6

**Power Units and Power Available on
American Farms, (000) 1910**

	Number	Horsepower
Oxen.	640	640
Mules	3,787	3,017
Horses	17,430	17,474
Windmills.	900	297
Steam engines.	72	3,600
Gas engines	600	1,800
Gas tractors	10	500

Source: Federal Trade Commission, Report on the Agricultural Implement and Machinery Industry, (1938), *p. 99.*

By 1930 the number of tractors was up to 920,000, and they furnished more than 22 million horsepower. Even then the horse was still an important factor, the 12.8 million animals furnishing more than 13 million horsepower. (The census takers seem to be giving us an anomaly here, but "horsepower" was an engineering standard, not a head count.) In those two decades—from 1910 to 1930—the realities of American agriculture had irrevocably changed. The gasoline tractor had supplanted not only the horse but the steam tractor, just as the trade magazine *Gas Review* had predicted in its issue of December 1910: "The steam tractor people are making a tremendous effort to stay the tide that is setting in in favor of the gas tractor, but there is no use. The men in the field who have had trouble with leaky flues, with foaming boilers, and the other evil effects of alkali water, are mighty glad to get rid of the steam engines."

To arrive at this exalted position, the gasoline tractor had to compete head-on with that other gasoline vehicle, the automobile, for the farmer's funds. Barton W. Currie, one of the editors of *The Country Gentleman*, put it bluntly in a classic early book on the tractor (published in 1916): "The farm-implement people at first watched the automobile begin its rural inroads with small apprehension. They were not prepared for the wave of buying that suddenly set in. It didn't seem possible or at all likely that the farmer could or would pay cash for automobiles when he wouldn't for his harvesting machinery or even his tillage tools. But he did. He had to or go without. He dug up the cash somehow. He overcame his natural reluctance to borrow rather than owe. He went even farther than that—he laid by money with the distinct object of purchasing an automobile. He saved by purchasing fewer farm implements or by making those he had go further than was his custom. The implement manufacturers complain that he has carried this skimping to excess, with

the result that his farm is not nearly so efficiently equipped as it was before he began buying automobiles. It is estimated that in the year 1915 American farmers bought almost $200,000,000 worth of automobiles. Iowa farmers alone bought 68,000 cars. The carless Kansas farm is almost a freak. This means that farmers are paying practically as much cash for automobiles as they are owing for implements."[12]

Thus the farm-equipment manufacturers dilemma: Was the tractor a significant piece of agricultural machinery? Was it destined to be a major new innovation that would be adopted widely? Should an agricultural machinery manufacturer concentrate on supplying the implements that would be pulled by another's tractor, or should he jump into tractor manufacturing, considering it an integral part of the long line?

EASING INTO THE TRACTOR MARKET

As one might guess, given all the other tensions within Deere & Company management, there were acerbic disagreements about just what to do with the tractor. The International Harvester Company had begun making its own tractors by 1906 and was leading the industry by 1911. Other long-line companies had also taken the plunge—the J.I. Case Threshing Machine Company began making tractors as far back as 1892; its counterpart name in Racine, the J.I. Case Plow Works, joined with the Wallis Tractor Company to bring out a popular gasoline tractor around 1912. Other long-liners, for example, Massey-Harris Company, had stayed out in this early period, but even the smaller competitors in the Rock Island-Moline area built tractors in quantity at early dates: the Rock Island Plow Company began making its Heider tractor in 1914, the Moline Plow Co. entered the field a year later with the Universal.

In 1908 the first of the soon-famous Winnipeg Agricultural Motor Competitions was held, with both steam and gasoline tractors of various sizes vying in hauling and plowing competition. At the contest of 1908, all of the tractors pulled one company's plows—the Cockshutt, built in Canada. The following year and thereafter the competing tractor companies chose their own make of plow. Deere and Cockshutt were the overwhelming choices in 1909, *Farm Implement News* commenting: "The largest plow in the field was the John Deere plow, which was fitted with fourteen 14 inch bottoms, coupled in pairs and raised and lowered by means of seven hand levers." International Harvester stood out alone by picking a Parlin & Orendorff plow, thus anticipating its own eventual purchase of the Canton, Illinois, plow company. In the Winnipeg meet of 1910, the seven-bottom, 14-inch Deere gang plow was chosen by the Gas Traction Company of Minnesota for the "over 30 horsepower" gasoline engine competition, and the combination won the gold medal. The Gas Traction Company made a unique tractor called the Big Four, which stood out not only because of its great weight (19,000 pounds) and the

enormous size of its rear drive wheel (96 inches in diameter), but also for its unique automatic plowing guide. The guide extended out in front of the tractor some dozen feet—a small wheel with a vertical rod about seven feet high with an arrow at the top, positioned in such a way that the wheel dropped into the last furrow, thus allowing the tractor to be kept in proper relation to the furrows with less difficulty for the operator. It developed 30 horsepower at the drawbar, and probably sold for about $3,000 (exact price lists for many of these early tractors are today almost nonexistent; we do know the Big Four sold for $2,800 in 1916).

Deere's assocation with Gas Traction's Big Four became even closer in 1912, when both the St. Louis and Atlanta branches offered the Big Four as a Deere product in their catalogs. (The practice of selling outside makes was common among the branches all through this period; the St. Louis branch will be remembered for its undiscriminating sale of outside, competitor buggies back in the 1890s.) One of the catalog pictures was in four colors, with the dominate red and green colors standing out, the green almost exactly the shade that Deere itself came to use over the following years (exhibit 7-7). One page of the catalog chronicled a plow trial in Sunnyside, Arkansas, using a Deere engine gang along with "Our Big Four '30' Gas Tractor"—a pointed implication that the Big Four "30" was a Deere-recommended product. In this sense, at least, the Big Four "30" could be considered as Deere & Company's first tractor.

Still, the tractor was not actually manufactured by the company, so in March 1912, the board of directors decided to investigate the possibilities of purchasing the Gas Traction Company and to make the Big Four by Deere & Company employees. But the Gas Traction executives had not been terribly pleased with the Deere relationship, as Burton Peek wrote: "The ground for their complaint was that we were making too much money too easily out of the deal." As sales of the Big Four had been moving along well, Peek continued, "We did not see how they could afford to turn us down." Much to Deere's surprise, the Gas Traction group did turn Deere down and sold instead to Emerson-Brantingham Implement Company of Rockford, Illinois. The latter continued to make improved versions of the Big Four in succeeding years, but there was no further Deere relationship.[13]

The company's international involvement in tractors began in 1912, in an out-of-the-way place. An export department had been established in Moline in 1911 (there had been a separate organization, the John Deere Export Company, from 1908 to 1911, with offices in New York). It sold not only Deere equipment but also that of other manufacturers; one such item was the well-known Minneapolis tractor, the Twin City, manufactured by the Minneapolis Steel and Machinery Company. Deere's sales were in Argentina and Uruguay. The Minneapolis Steel catalog for 1912 (exhibit 7-8) carried a number of pictures of the big Twin City tractor pulling a Deere engine gang plow (though the catalog failed to note the

The Big Four "30"

The Big Four "30" Gas Tractor

Exhibit 7–7. *Two views of the Big Four "30," from the catalog of 1912, Deere's St. Louis branch (Deere Archives)*

Deere name). The Twin City was noteworthy for the fact that it also had a plowing guide, similar to that of the Big Four, called the "Cuddy Steering Device." The front-mounted plowing guides did not catch on, though, and both the Cuddy and the Big Four mechanisms disappeared into limbo soon after.

Deere also flirted with International Harvester at this time. In 1911, a query had come forward to the Deere executive committee from the Kansas City branch, asking whether the branch could be allowed by Moline to approach International about promoting Deere engine gangs. Somehow, any kind of relationship with International was different than any with another company. George Peek opposed it, and his resolution "that we refrain from forming sales connections with the International Harvester Company on engine gangs or other important lines, either at home or abroad" was carried unanimously. (Not every branch listened to the board; the San Francisco branch sold Deering mowers and reapers in this period!)

W.L. Velie was uneasy about the position the company was left in, inasmuch as the only tractor company "with which we were at the present connected" was a lesser company in the industry, Hart-Parr, and this mostly involved some joint exhibits at a few fairs. Burton Peek then pushed through a second resolution that the company "consider this proposition of identifying ourselves with some tractor company" and this also carried unanimously.[14]

THE EXPERIMENTAL TRACTOR

Still unresolved was the question of whether Deere itself should consider manufacturing its own tractor. One faction in Deere management strongly advocated this notion, and in the directors' meeting of March 5, 1912, Willard Velie surfaced as its leader. He offered a resolution that was startlingly wide in its scope: "In view of the inevitable future use by farmers for diverse purposes of gasoline and kerosene tractors . . . a movement to produce a tractor plow should be started at once, having in view constantly that the success of the same would be enhanced if not assured, were it possible to divorce the tractor from the plow and to thus make it available for general purposes." Though there were rumblings under the surface, the resolution passed unanimously. By July of that year, C.H. Melvin had been transferred from the experimental department and given the special assignment of designing and building a prototype tractor.

The evidence seemed to point to the conclusion that Deere was irrevocably launched on a strategy of building its own tractor. But the unanimous vote cloaked the real opposition in other quarters of management. One person who was strongly opposed was William Butterworth. In a set of private notes to himself, written sometime in 1912, Butter-

Exhibit 7–8. *Deere & Company, "sole export agents" for the Twin City gas tractor, sells machines in Uruguay, ca. 1912, top, Bullock plowing in Uruguay; bottom, Twin City 40 pulling a ten-bottom plow in Uruguay at a demonstration before students and government officials. (Deere Archives)*

Exhibit 7–9. *Two Deere experimental motorized cultivators: top, Silver two-row motor cultivator, 1916–18; bottom, One-row Tractivator, 1917. (Deere Archives)*

worth laid out four tightly packed pages of handwritten thoughts concerning management problems and possible cost-cutting efforts within the company. The last page concluded with a set of comments on over-all "economic policy" (he followed these two words with a dash and added the word "conservative"). He then spelled out how this cautious policy might be effected:

Buy carefully

Manufacture under slow bill

Reduce our large inventory by converting into cash

Reduce our bank loan as much as possible

Spend no money for any kind of expansion beyond our present Harvester addition and the Foundry

Finally, he appended one more line—the last line in the entire memorandum: "Drop all tractor expenditures."

Butterworth's adamancy about tractors stemmed in considerable part from his uneasiness about the reaction of the banking community to loans to agricultural machinery companies. He seemed particularly worried about the fallout from the difficulties that the Advance-Rumely Thresher Company had had as a result of a bad crop failure in Canada in 1914. Rumely had sold a large number of its Oil Pulls in Canada and in the process had overextended credit to the farmers. The latter's impecuniosity at the end of the season left Rumely holding huge amounts of bad paper. The company already was indebted to bankers for an unsettlingly large amount, and the latter threw the company into receivership in January 1915. While the company was reformed again later that year and had a successful year following, the fact that the Rumely family had lost its hold on the company in the process must have heightened Butterworth's fears that the same thing could happen to Deere & Company.

Butterworth seemed particularly fearful of letting outsiders know too much of company finances. Once the public offering of preferred stock was consummated, Butterworth found to his dismay that the underwriters now had a proprietary interest in the firm, which they were never reluctant to exercise. Apparently the company was not attentive enough to them in early 1914, for White, Weld & Company, the underwriters, sent a peremptory telegram: "We shall be gravely dissatisfied if your Executive Committee at meeting this week does not take action to furnish us with full information in regular monthly statements, which we have been requesting steadily, covering current assets, current liabilities and trade situation." The board was upset by this and only reluctantly agreed to give out the information, provided "they should be gone over in person with a White, Weld & Company representative, to the end that proper understanding of the conditions . . . might be secured." The latter

Exhibit 7–10. Top left, *Avery steam tractor, pulling a Deere gang plow, ca. 1900–10;* bottom left, *Huber tractor, pulling a Deere gang plow, undated photograph;* top right, *Melvin experimental tractor, pulling a Deere manure spreader, 1912;* bottom right, *John Deere instructional camp for sales personnel, Campbell's Island, near East Moline, ca. 1910. (Deere Archives)*

immediately dispatched a man to Moline, who bluntly made it clear that they "had sold our stock through a large number of brokers who were continually asking them for information as to our progress, particularly since our recent statement showed such largely increased liabilities . . . and they should be in a position to give correct information."

At least in the case of the Melvin tractor, Butterworth's conservative posture on tractors did not need to be put to the test. The experimental tractor was not a success. Only one model was built and its efficacy in field trials was disappointing, both as to performance and durability. By the spring of 1914 all further work was halted. But it was only a matter of time before the tractor issue would come up again.[15]

WARNING SIGNALS—
THE PROFIT EROSION OF 1914

Perhaps internal tensions would have died away over time if the organization had continued to expand sales and, especially, profits. Though both were up in 1912 and 1913, the next year, 1914, was a shocker for management. Sales fell about 11 percent and profits dropped by more than 50 percent. The final total was only $2 million, well below the $2.6 million that was scheduled to be paid out in preferred dividends. The board finally decided not to pass the dividend, and the surplus, which at the beginning of the year had been $5.9 million, now was down to $5.3 million.

What had happened? A small part of the difficulty could be attributed to the effects of drought in late 1913, though it was not really severe. Dislocations following the outbreak of war in Europe in August 1914 could have begun to have an effect, but even a cursory look at the situation intimated problems within the company itself, though it was hard to identify them precisely.

There was another small loss in harvesters. During the start-up mode of the new harvester department in East Moline, the deficit in the three years through 1913 had accumulated to more than $600,000. The new harvesters were selling reasonably well, despite the heavy physical weight of the machine. It weighed in at 2,032 pounds in 1913, but further design tinkering took off another thirty-two pounds the following year. But these were well over International Harvester's two models, the Deering (at 1,700) and the New McCormick (at 1,864). Still, George Peek and George Mixter as sales and production heads, respectively, pushed for expansion, and the following year, with sales doubled, the losses were down to just $55,000. By 1915, the harvester business of the company showed a profit. Clearly the major source of difficulty lay elsewhere.

A look at the whole organization disclosed evidence of numerous factors driving up internal costs. In the softening market of late 1913, the company had an inordinately high inventory, both of finished goods and of raw materials and work-in-process. A resolution of the executive committee meeting of October 28, 1913, exhorted the factory managers to avoid additions to plants, to give "the most drastic and minute attention" to expense items, and to conservatively estimate sales volume in their proposed manufacturing budgets for the upcoming year. Raw material prices were beginning to fall around the country, and the company was stuck with high-cost inventory in large quantities. "There should be the closest kind of contact between the buyer, the factory superintendent and the sales manager. Often meetings between them are infrequent and desultory. Again, there is not a proper cooperation. Harmony in daily conferences will assuredly bring timely revisions of estimates, and permit the facilities of the shop to be properly employed."

The plow department, which was always at center stage in the company's plans, seemed to be one of the prime offenders, and as early as 1913 it was under criticism for having allowed its inventory to balloon. When the executive committee took the matter up, an acrimonious discussion ensued. George Mixter and George Peek were particularly frustrated about their own divided authority in relation to the department —as they put it, "the impossibility of actively managing the current business of the Plow Department through the efforts of the Committee." They advocated giving increased authority to the head of the plow department and also exhorted the executive committee itself to get more involved.

This oblique reference to executive committee performance opened Pandora's box, for a number of the top management group opined that the slippage around the system was due in considerable part—perhaps fundamentally—to a malaise in top management itself. As the months passed, veiled allusions appeared about this underlying malady, and finally in late 1913 George Peek addressed a memorandum to "the Voting Trustees." (He stated that he had chosen to address the letter this way because "they are the actual holders of the stock of Deere & Company and have a grave responsibility.") He first quoted verbatim from the bylaws of the company about the stated responsibilities of the executive committee and finance committee and the duties of the various officers. He then recalled the fact that there should have been ninety-five meetings of the executive committee from November 1, 1912, to October 1, 1913, but that only twenty had actually been held, with just two of these having the full group present. Peek noted that the order of business for the executive committee meetings had "not been closely followed." In regard to the purchasing department, "on only a few occasions has the Executive Committee been given any information regarding the purchase of materials, either as to prices, quality or quantity purchased." He had equally pointed comments about the patent department, Wharton's new job as secretary-treasurer-comptroller, and even the two jobs of vice president of manufacturing and vice president of sales (the latter his own). As to the job of president: "Mr. Butterworth, on account of his time being so fully taken up with estate and other matters, and for other reasons, is unable to advise him [Wharton] on many important phases of such a complicated business." It was quite true that Butterworth was spending considerable time on Deere estate matters, as was Burton Peek, the other trustee; George Peek's remarks now openly articulated what many of management had been privately saying.

The executive committee came in for particularly harsh treatment by Peek: "There are many matters of general importance decided by the Executive Committee and Board of Directors, and there are many duties following the acts of these two organizations which are not looked at by anybody in particular. . . . The Executive Committee is the supreme authority in the organization, but no well-defined plan has ever been laid out and adhered to for putting into effect all of its rules and regulations."

Peek ended what must have been a shocker of a memorandum with a series of eight separate suggestions. Most dealt straightforwardly with regularizing procedures, but there was one that was quite startling: Peek proposed the establishment of the position of executive vice president— one person through whom the business of the company could be funneled to the executive committee. Peek's wording was carefully chosen: "I believe we should have a man in charge of the business of the General Company, subject to the Executive Committee, who is so situated that he can be on the job at anytime, and who shall, except as specifically provided for otherwise by the rules of procedure of the Executive Committee, be the point of contact between the Executive Committee and the public; the Executive Committee and the officers of the Company; and the Executive Committee and subsidiary companies." In effect, this person would be the general manager of the company.

This position would not have been controversial in most companies, but it certainly was here. In effect, Peek was not too subtly criticizing the performance of both Butterworth as president and Velie as chairman of the executive committee. Each was being faulted for lack of attention to duty—Butterworth for divided loyalties between the company and the Deere family trusteeship, Velie for his part-time role while also running his own two large companies (a carriage firm and, later, a major U.S. automobile firm, maker of the Velie). Both Butterworth and Velie were being chastised for their mutual ill will and their failure to coordinate their activities.

The records of the next few months give ample evidence that William Butterworth responded to the needling of Peek and others, for there was a noticeable increase in Butterworth memoranda and other actions in the company (particularly in regard to the executive committee). These memoranda are extant, some of them in Butterworth's handwritten drafts that reveal much about his private concerns. Inventory control was a dominant theme. Echoing Velie's comments six months earlier, in March 1914, Butterworth sent a comprehensive memorandum to the executive committee on this problem, meticulously enumerating the whole-good needs and exhorting the branches to cease ordering additional product from the factories until they could bring their branch inventories down to manageable figures. Butterworth advocated that the inventory balance could be facilitated by an interchange of branch inventories, physically moving product from one branch to another. In turn, said Butterworth, "our Factories must slow down at once to the lowest point of production which will not bring about harmful disorganization." Butterworth's conclusions mirrored his sense of urgency: "We know it will mean very radical and drastic action. Something must be done and done quickly or we shall be in a very embarrassing situation, from which it will be almost impossible to extricate ourselves before the end of the fiscal year, if at all." This was certainly a far cry from Butterworth's optimistic statement at the end of the annual report of 1912!

The agricultural situation itself brightened over the summer of 1914 and the company's inventory soon declined to manageable proportions. Butterworth was honestly able to say in the printed annual report that came out on December 31, 1914, that "these excess inventories are now disposed of and all stocks are on a normal basis, so that the factories during the coming year should make a more favorable showing." Still, the damage had been done. It had been a very unsettling experience for the Deere management group.

Although such matters as inventories, purchasing commitments, and manufacturing costs were now better in hand, it seemed likely that improvement had occurred mostly because of exhortations and specific, small cost-cutting steps, rather than from an attack on the underlying disabilities of the management structure itself. On the last day of the year, December 31, 1914, George Mixter and George Peek joined together to write a two-page memorandum to the executive committee that addressed this concern. They first called attention again to the fact that earnings were $560,000 less than the preferred dividend requirement. Though efforts were being made to reduce expenses, "we believe . . . that we must go deeper to eliminate basic conditions that are unprofitable to the stockholders, to whom, primarily, we are obligated." The failure of the management of the "General Company" was obvious, Peek and Mixter stated, and the executive committee "has absolute control" over this. When the executive committee had been formed it was presumed to provide "for prompt harmonious, forceful, decisive action." But the recent failures were due in considerable part to "lack of power to initiate and carry out promptly broad business strategy throughout the organization" and "lack of constructive work by the Executive Committee." Permeating this were "attempts to substitute the impersonal Executive Committee for the personal responsibility between man and man."

The memorandum reiterated Peek's earlier demand for an executive vice president and also pointedly noted that this person should be "an active working executive for the business." They concluded the memorandum with a short paragraph urging the appointment of such a person and ended: "Neither one of us will permit himself to stand in the way of the success of this plan."

This time there was a quick, very public rejoinder by Willard Velie, who was most affected by the proposal. He was obviously nettled by the Mixter-Peek attack. In separate, individually typed letters to each member of the executive committee, Velie wrote stingingly. He began with feigned self-effacement: "This communication is written from a stockholder's viewpoint, is ingenuous, is free from politics, does not contemplate personal advancement or increased prestige, and takes carefully and considerably into account the warm personal friendship which has existed between those whose conclusions are so radically disagreed with, and myself." He noted the Peek-Mixter letter and commented on it: "I submit that it is dangerous to record a criticism so generic and so misleading, that in the minds of the lay recipients (the Directors) there may be matured a conclusion, which however, innocently erroneous, might result in a miscarriage of justice; the accessories in other words might be punished with undue severity, and the culprits escape with eclat." Velie felt that Peek and Mixter had given rather short shrift to the issue of the ballooning of expenses: "Would it be impertinent to enquire by whose authority and under whose constant scrutiny from day to day and from hour to hour, have the expenses been increased to a distressing maximum? In general, excessive expenditures which may be eliminated presuppose past management. . . . " Velie made quite clear that he felt that Peek and Mixter had a large hand in this: "The proponents have been vested with nearly absolute discretion with respect to the manufacturing and selling, by the Executive Committee, and have never within the writer's knowledge been interfered with or estopped, unless after discussion it was clearly shown that hobbles should be used." Later in the letter he did say he "still had confidence in the men . . . both of whom have assuredly gained much wisdom from experience, and with their natural ability, probity and industry are still the logical spokesmen . . . in their respective branches, manufacturing and selling."

Velie was unalterably opposed to the concept of the general manager. "We have no one in our organization whose experience is so varied and whose judgment is so infallible," Velie stated, "that he looms large above the mental horizon of the Directors and Executive Committee. . . . I would prefer as a Stockholder in this Company, to take the sober, disinterested, composite opinion of the Executive Committee, in preference to the arrogant opinion of any member thereof." It was clear that Velie was satisfied with the structural relationships between the executive committee and the board of directors and wanted no changes (despite his earlier criticisms that Butterworth was arrogating too much power in his own hands). Rather, Velie suggested, the remedies for the sagging fortunes of the company lay with smaller, step-by-step cost-cutting measures within the organization: "I suggest that when the Directors are really acquainted with the internal disorders, it should be their pleasure and duty to apply corrective measures of an unsentimental, impartial and non-partisan character, that their collective conscience may be stilled." Velie's pique came through as he closed his letter: "While I think it was injudicious to air the unfortunate incompatibility which has long existed, to the marked disadvantage of the Company's advance, between the proponents and which is specifically called 'the lack of harmony' within, perhaps after all it was well that the Directors should know everything. . . . It is my sincere hope that the hatchet has been permanently and deeply interred." The last line of his letter was blunt and unequivocal: "I firmly believe that the present structure should be preserved, until the results of the initiated and to be initiated reforms and economies are known and measured."

Attached to the Velie letter was a comprehensive report that Velie had requested of Wharton, analyzing, company by company, the sales and profit picture, as well as expenditures for plant and equipment. The "excessive" inventories came in for particular scrutiny by Wharton; he estimated that they stood at $5 million in excess of requirements. Wharton noted the loss in interest payments that this meant to the company, as well as the increased expense in taxes and insurance. Clearly, there was ample room for the kind of cost and inventory slashing that Velie wanted to emphasize.

As chief executive officer, William Butterworth also sent a memorandum to the executive committee, a crucial one that stated a number of remedial suggestions not only for internal cost cutting but for the overall management structure itself. Buttterworth's memorandum came directly to the central point: "We should return to the old way of running our business. This means that the Moline Board of Directors should be the Board of the Deere & Company Factory, only, and be responsible only for the Factory showing. . . . The Board of Directors of each subsidiary Company should be solely responsible for the business of its Company, with no interference from Moline in the way of instructions." In other words, Butterworth at this point seemed willing to carry the policy of decentralization almost to its ultimate—to have a set of separate companies, each autonomous, each with its own board of directors and each able to take independent, final decisions, almost without recourse by the central company. Butterworth did envision linkages, for "each subsidiary Company should, of course, have the privilege of getting advice at all times from Moline." This advice would be purveyed by "a Committee known as the ADVISORY COMMITTEE who, in the interim between meetings, could decide questions of policy and act as a sort of 'Court of Last Resort' on questions placed before them by subsidiary Companies. . . . " As if to make the point explicitly clear, Butterworth added: "The Manager of each subsidiary Company should be responsible to the Directors of his own Company only." To be sure, the boards of the individual companies were made up predominantly from the Moline board, but also they had significant parochial membership.

Butterworth's specific suggestions centered mostly on the "Plow Factory." In the process, he seemed to place himself in the role of speaking only for this single entity within the company. All in all, it was a curious memorandum for a chief executive officer of a large holding company to write. The original handwritten notes that Butterworth used show a number of ideas crossed out before the final draft. One particularly revealing assessment that was omitted from the memorandum reflects Butterworth's private misgivings: "Everybody seems to be hiding behind the Executive Committee and throwing the blame, but no credit on it. Managers of the subsidiary Companies do not want to take the responsibility of the conduct of the business unless they can have full authority to do what they think best, and they ought to be left alone." In essence, Butterworth's true feelings were for highly autonomous segments of the business "to be left alone."

Some members of the executive committee felt that the salaries paid to some of top management were excessive. C.C. Webber wrote Velie in early December 1914 (after he had received a detailed analysis of administrative costs from Wharton): "When we have failed, as we have this year, to make our preferred dividend, it is time we hunted for extravagance and waste.... We should set a good example by commencing at home.... I am impressed with the fact that the big item of expense that he reports on, comes under the heading of 'Executive and General,' and in said expenses there is practically no savings proposed for 1915. And the big item of salaries under this heading is that [of] the Executive Committee and the General Administrative, representing together about $58,000 with no saving of consequence proposed for 1915." Webber then continued in a startlingly pointed way: "My own salary, I am today writing Mr. Wharton to discontinue, and I believe it would be appropriate for the President and the Chairman to themselves recommend a reduction in their own salaries." Webber then made the same point that Peek had made a few months earlier about the role of the president and the chairman of the executive committee, only in this case framed even more bluntly: "For, like myself, they give but a portion of their time to the General Company, have other interests that take a good deal of their time, are very largely interested in the stock of the Company, and I do not know where we can show our determination for sensible economy all along the line any better than in a revision of said salaries."

THE JANUARY SHOWDOWN

A meeting of the board of directors as a whole to discuss all of these issues that had come to a head in 1914 was finally scheduled for January 5, 1915. The meeting, one of the most important that the company had had in its history, lasted two days. Butterworth, as chairman, opened the meeting with a statement of what he felt were three points each member needed to keep in mind—"that we should return to the old way of running our business," that "the Moline Board of Directors should be the Board of Deere & Company's factory only and be responsible only for the factory showing," and that "the Board of Directors of each subsidiary company should be solely responsible for the business of its company with no interference from Moline in the way of instructions." He then asked each member of the board for his own comments about management structure and policy.

Joseph Dain, who was sitting next to Butterworth, opened: "I thought the management from here was having a little too much to say about the Dain Manufacturing Company's business," though the situation had eased in the recent period. Still, Dain noted, the branches did have enormous independence. "I told St. Louis at one time that we would take our goods away from them if we did not get better results but I could not do that now with the present arrangement. . . . I do not see that we would get much relief under your resolution, Mr. President."

Ralph Lourie, the Moline branch manager, allowed as there had been "a disposition on the part of the Branch House Managers and on the part of a good many Factory Managers to hide under the Executive Committee." He continued: "I believe if we had a General Manager here it might be better. . . . I would rather be responsible to some one in the General Organization that I knew had authority than to make my peace with fourteen rather than one. . . . If you want to have a thing *not* done, refer it to a committee. . . . " Frank Silloway, who worked in sales with George Peek, echoed Lourie's view: "I believe we should have somewhere a sort of a head place that acts as a rudder to the ship to guide us to the places that we wish to go. I think it is a good thing to have an organization that can act as a sort of judge."

George Mixter spoke at length. "It seems to me that a Board of nineteen directors, scattered over such a distance as our Board is, is entirely too large to be an operating, current managing unit and it is absolutely necessary to have an Executive Committee of some kind. . . . I do feel that the various interests of the members of the Executive Committee make it rather difficult for the Committee to continuously consider from day to day the details of the business. . . . " Mixter ended with a strong plea for a general manager, repeating his earlier arguments.

Burton Peek took exception to Mixter. "I do not agree with Mr. Mixter that the boards are too large." Peek continued with a flat comment that in the matters of purchases of machinery, equipment, etc., "these items I think should be absolutely left to the subsidiary companies." Several others reiterated the view of the impotence of the executive committee.

Then it was C.C. Webber's turn, and he spoke movingly: "I do not think we can get along without an Advisory Board at Moline. I think with the number of corporations we have got, it is going to be more and more necessary to give them help from Moline and to often guide them. Perhaps we have made mistakes . . . certainly, we will not remedy it by letting thirty or thirty-five companies run themselves. . . . " Yet Webber was uneasy about the concept of a general manager: "It would be disastrous to this business to place it in the hands of one man. When Mr. Deere was here, that was different, but to go back to the plan of having one man decide off-hand all those big questions and do away with this

Advisory Board would be absolutely disastrous to this business, in my judgment." Webber had a much more limited version for a general manager. The post should be "not for the purpose of taking power away from the Executive Committee but rather as a go-between: perhaps also to relieve the Executive Committee of a lot of trifling things." Webber's old two-hat problem of being both a branch manager and a central-office executive pointed up his ambivalence on the balance between centralization and decentralization. At this moment, he plumped for centralization: "You cannot get on here with thirty-five or forty corporations and turn them loose and forget them. The Executive Committee have said to each fellow that you are responsible and you are on the job and we certainly have no desire to take away that responsibility. We must not do that. I believe that as time goes on you have got to recognize more and more that you are largely responsible here in Moline." C.A. Chase spoke immediately after Webber and came on much more strongly: "I believe in the idea of a central organization. . . . The larger and more important matters which affect the whole organization must be controlled and dictated absolutely from Moline." When Willard Velie's turn came, Velie apparently decided not to carry his earlier, vehement rejoinders any further and said only: "I believe I have no comments, Mr. President."

The tenor of the discussion seemed to favor, if not more centralization, at least greater intervention by the executive committee; many of the advocates of this latter view also supported the appointment of a strong general manager. Charles Mansur wanted "a stiff governing body," Frank Silloway "a central man." At the end of the board meeting, Butterworth made a short summary statement noting, first, that there did not seem to be "much difference of opinion between those who have spoken" (perhaps a bit of an understatement!) and then reiterating that he himself felt that it "should be brought out . . . that the subsidiary companies should be made to realize and should assume the responsibility for making a showing."

At that point Butterworth adjourned the meeting, to be reconvened on the afternoon of the same day. When the members reassembled at 2 P.M., Webber immediately took the floor. "Inasmuch as there seemed to be so much interest in this matter of management and policy," he opened, he did not think "we ought to dismiss it entirely or take hasty action either." Then Webber put his personal view bluntly: it should not be just put up to the Executive Committee, but rather, "we should have the best judgment of all the Board." A formal resolution was immediately introduced "that this Board looks with favor on the recommendation for the appointment of a General Manager . . . " and, surprisingly, it passed by unanimous vote.

The matter was then sent to the executive committee for the latter's recommendation at the next board meeting. When the committee members met on January 27, they adopted a resolution directing Butterworth and Floyd Todd to formulate a plan and come back to a second meeting of the executive committee that day with their suggestions. When the adjourned meeting reopened that afternoon, Butterworth presented their report: "After due consideration, we have concluded that the present by-laws and rules of procedure of the Executive Committee provide adequately both as to officials and their duties, for the proper transaction of the business of the Company.... We believe that much of the difficulty of the past has occurred because of the failure to hold more frequent conferences between the officials of the General Company at Moline.... We recommend that matters of importance should be discussed daily between those members of the Executive Committee in Deere & Company's office and such other members as they may desire to consult." They continued, in regard to specific job assignments, "that such day to day business and other matters, the responsibility for the discharge of which are now delegated to the President, shall, during his absence, be delegated to the Vice President in Charge of Sales or in his absence the Vice President in Charge of Manufacturing." Yet, at the same time, Butterworth and Todd also handed more autonomy outward: "We also wish to strongly impress on this Board, the importance of Subsidiary Managers, fully realizing they are responsible for their respective businesses and that they, and not the Executive Committee, will be held to account for the results of the operation thereof." Butterworth ended with a single-line resolution that seemed to close the issue: "*Resolved*, that the present methods of handling the business be continued and that such modification be made in the by-laws and rules of procedure as may be necessary to carry out this recommendation."

When the recommendation came forward to the board at its next meeting on February 13, the executive committee resolution was unanimously approved. In a less-than-oblique reference to Velie's role, the board did recommend a change in the bylaws that "in the absence or inability of the President, his duties shall be performed by the Vice-President in charge of Sales, or in his absence the Vice-President in charge of factories."[16]

There the matter rested. The message had come through loud and clear—there was to be no executive vice president or general manager at this time. Further, no additional authority was to be vested in the central company for the operation of the various subsidiaries and branches. Indeed, if anything, autonomy was increased. To be sure, strong representations were made about accountability for this independent, semi-autonomous authority. Yet, one could read between the lines that the company was to remain decentralized, and on a basis not at all clear to all of the individuals involved. The pointed queries that had been made by Peek, Webber, and some of the others about the roles of Butterworth and Velie were laid on the record, out in the open. In a sense, they were probably efficacious; Butterworth, in particular, once again seemed to be more directly engaged in the detailed financial and operational analysis that he had done so well in the years before Charles Deere's death. Velie's role as chairman of the executive committee continued intact. There were salary cuts for top management that year, but the rapidly improving economic conditions of 1915 soon made the controversy seem academic. As a matter of fact, the cost cutting, belt tightening, and other ameliorative steps taken in late 1914 and early 1915 raised profits in fiscal 1915 to $3.4 million, well over the $2.6 million needed for the preferred dividend. The management of the company, which took hold after Charles Deere's half century of leadership, had brought about a great consolidation, challenged International Harvester's domination of harvesting equipment, and survived two business downturns over a period of eight years. It had done so despite its inability to resolve the conflicts over the philosophy of management that would guide the new "Modern Company."

BUYING POWER
OF FARM PRODUCTS GREATEST IN YEARS

Government statistics show that the purchasing power of farm products, at the present time, is greater than it has been for years. It requires fewer bushels of corn, wheat and oats, fewer pounds of hay, pork and beef to buy farm machinery today than it has for years.

Figures below show the amount of farm produce required to purchase farm machinery at the present time, as compared with five and ten years ago. Comparisons given below cover only corn and wheat, but any of the staple farm products can be used as an example, equally well with any implement. Prices of farm products based on government statistics.

 CORN REQUIRED TO BUY A JOHN DEERE SULKY PLOW

1907-80 Bu. **1912-86 Bu.** **1918-56 Bu.**

New Deere Light Draft Sulky

WHEAT REQUIRED TO BUY A JOHN DEERE GRAIN BINDER

1907-149 Bu. **1912-175 Bu.** **1918-101 Bu.**

John Deere Light Draft Grain Binder

 HAY REQUIRED TO BUY A JOHN DEERE-DAIN SYSTEM RAKE

1907-5¹⁄₅ Tons. **1912-5¹⁄₃ Tons.** **1918-3¹⁄₃ Tons.**

John Deere-Dain System Rake

NOTE—1907 prices based on December 1st, average farm prices. 1912 prices based on yearly average farm prices. Present price on corn based on No. 5 Grade, December 4th, 1917, Chicago cash sales. Price of wheat for 1918 based on minimum price of $2.20, established by the government. Present price of hay based on December 4th, 1917, Chicago cash sales.

GOOD IMPLEMENTS OVERCOME THE LABOR SHORTAGE
Increase the Yield and Decrease the Cost of Crop Production

CHAPTER 8

WORLD WAR I
AND ITS AFTERMATH

*There is one thing I want to ask you to look out for and that
is any further action by the Directors relating to the
building of a tractor. I am opposed to any step being taken
towards the manufacture by any of our factories of a tractor.
I have acquiesced in the experimental work which has
been done, but I am beginning to feel that we are wasting our
stockholders' money in going any further with it.*

William Butterworth, 1916

By the end of 1915, the war in Europe had raged for a year and a half. Although business activity in the United States declined at the start and agriculture had continued flat, it was not too many months before the country's production began to respond to the increase in demand from Europe for food and materials. When the United States finally entered the conflict in 1917, the pace of American industry had been stepped up enormously, both for war production and non-war efforts. Agriculture, in particular, experienced an explosion. The popular slogan, "Food Will Win the War," pushed the farmers to production levels for certain crops that were unprecedented. Wheat production hit one billion bushels in 1915, a level not reached again until World War II. Corn production stayed rather stable during the war years, and the market for some crops, notably cotton, even declined. Prices for farm products rose rapidly with general price inflation, and wholesale farm prices outpaced the "all commodity" index in four of the five years of 1914 through 1918. Price inflation increased the farmers' cost of production, and the unprecedented demands for wheat introduced dislocations. Still, the wartime boom in business and agriculture pushed aside long-range concerns. Economic historian Harold F. Williamson commented, "These danger signals were little heeded amid the seeming, if wholly spurious, evidences of continuing post-war prosperity."

In the early days of the war, Deere management had been very cautious as it tried to adapt its plans to the greatly changed situation. But as the months of the war wore on, it was obvious that American business, Deere included, was going to be greatly challenged by the insistent demands put upon it. Profits were up in 1915, despite a decline in sales, and in 1916 both profits and sales rose. By the end of the war, the company had experienced four successful years, with sales and profits for 1918 ($39.9 million and $5.6 million) both all-time records for the company (Appendix exhibit 12).

For those who went through the Great War, on or off the battlefield, these five years were remembered as traumatic and difficult ones; the matter-of-fact sales and profit figures belied the demands put on everyone in the company. The organization stayed essentially the same as at the formation of the modern company, and the product lines stayed stable. The Plow Works, Deere & Mansur, Marseilles, and Dain operated at excellent efficiency and profitability throughout this period; Van Brunt had a more difficult period at the start, but by 1917 was also well up in contribution. The wagon companies did very well; a number of government orders for military escort wagons and parts came early in the war and, though Fort Smith Wagon Company had the only company strike during the period (in 1916), both wagon companies were solidly in the black. Buggies were not so fortunate—the automobile was already writing their obituaries. By 1921, the company was making plans to phase out Reliance Buggy. Another acquisition, the Syracuse Chilled Plow Company, did poorly in those first years, but picked up in 1917 and 1918. Surprisingly, given its spotty record in the past, Union Malleable did quite well, attributable especially to its top management (for labor difficulties in the wartime period were especially felt in this organization). The harvester department, so much on the minds of Deere management in the several years just before the war, began making a substantial profit in 1915 and repeated this performance again in 1916. In 1917 a very serious inventory discrepancy was discovered, and it brought a loss for that year of some $208,000. (A physical inventory had been taken and was some $450,000 below book value, "indicating a lack of precise methods of handling materials and records," said the "Manufacturing report.") By 1918, though, the group had turned itself around to register a $283,000 profit. Nevertheless the outlook for the harvester business in general and the Deere harvester in particular remained somewhat doubtful; competition was still extremely strong, and the Deere harvester was not yet widely accepted.

The advent of the war itself also markedly changed the character of export sales. The company soon dealt directly with the governments of the Allies for war materiel—the French government bought commissary and hospital equipment (ambulances, wagons, carts, etc.), and there was also an order for shrapnel and wheels from Russia. When the United States entered the war, the company turned to making combat and escort wagons and other war materiel for the United States War Department. Ocean transport was frequently tenuous; at one point, in September 1917, a shipment of plows to Argentina was sent by sailing ship, presumably less of a target for the U-boats. Orders for conventional agricultural machinery for export customers also continued during the war, though at a reduced scale from the already modest amounts of the pre-war period. [1]

EMPLOYEE RELATIONS

The company entered the World War I period with optimism about, and satisfaction with, the quality of its employee relations. A noteworthy series of meetings for all of the factory managers and the Moline top management group had been held in late 1911 and early 1912, shortly after the modern company was put together, and at these, Deere's employment and labor relations policies were formally codified and put together in the equivalent of a company policy manual. George Mixter and George Peek set the tone for the discussions. All aspects of the factory organization were analyzed, and the thoroughgoing concern of Deere for retention of loyal, long-service employees, for identifying and training future leaders, and for preempting union issues permeated the two meetings. The individual contract remained a cornerstone of the personnel policy of the company, reflecting vestiges of paternalism; a copy of the agreement, appended to the meeting minutes, contained the statement that the "employee agrees . . . not to join in any concerted action to change hours, wages or working conditions." To make this even clearer, G.K. Wilson, the director of personnel, later stated that "undesirable men (through sympathy with labor organization or irregular habits) can be excluded."

While it was obvious that the company desired to maintain an open shop, the rhetoric was not militant. In the meeting of 1912, Mixter was asked bluntly by one of the superintendents: "Do you recommend a non-union plant?" Mixter replied, "No, not exactly. We have had success without them, but there are some good organizations, especially those established on the railroads."

By this time, the Industrial Workers of the World had gained considerable headway in the country. Formed in 1905 from segments of the Western Federation of Miners (1893) and the American Labor Union (1898), the IWW was devoted to a restructuring of the wage system, and the concept of "one big union"—a nineteenth-century version of industrial unionism—was the central organizing theme. Mixter was unalterably opposed to the IWW: "The most radical organization of labor. . . . While they are comparatively small now, it is essential for the welfare of our employees for us to watch this 'IWW.'" Yet, Mixter was most sympathetic to workers as individuals: "Most strikes are brought about by some unfair treatment and it is our duty to treat the men fairly. . . . We should endeavor to find out the state of their minds—whether or not they are satisfied. This is a matter that should be thought of by all and you cannot give it too much attention."

For the United States, the decade beginning in 1905 had been one of heavy immigration; in each of six of these ten years more than one million people had entered the United States (the only such years in the history of the country). Most of the immigrants came from central, eastern, and southern Europe. These patterns were reflected in the changing makeup of Deere's Moline work force of nearly 2,500, and a breakdown was given at the factory managers' meeting of 1912:

National Origin	Number of Workers	Percent of Work Force
Swedes and Norwegians	891	36
Americans	527	21.5
Belgians	456	18.6
Russians and Jews.	281	10.5
Germans.	101	4.1
Bohemians	50	2
Italians	49	2
Greeks	44	1.9
Hungarians.	42	1.8
French, Finns, and Danes	17	0.7

When they arrived *IN THE QUAD-CITIES*

1840 — Germans (1st wave), Belgians, English, Scots, Welsh
1850 — Irish
1860 — Swedes
Blacks (1st wave)
Germans (2nd wave)
1870
1880 — Germans (3rd wave)
1890
Belgians, Poles, Greeks, Italians, Serbs, Croatians, Eastern Europeans — 1900
1910
Blacks (2nd wave)
Mexican immigration begins — 1920
1930
1940
Blacks (3rd wave)
1950
1960
Chinese
1970
American Indians
Asian Indians
Laotians, Cambodians, Vietnamese
1980

***Exhibit 8–1.** Immigration to the Moline area over the years (Moline Dispatch, March 7, 1982)*

These periodic ethnic breakdowns of the work force were never conducted with census-like accuracy; for example, it is not clear whether the "Americans" above were native-born, or were American citizens, a potentially larger group. But it was obvious that a significant shift had taken place since the turn of the century; another such survey (with similar limitations) had been made in 1901, and then the Swedish had really dominated—717 of the 1,151 employees were Swedish natives or of Swedish descent (there were 203 Americans, but only 3 Bohemians and just 1 Russian).

A.H. Head, the superintendent of the plow department, addressed himself to the special personnel policies inherent with foreign-born labor, including clannishness in departments having large numbers of one nationality working together: *"We must depend upon him* to handle the larger part of our rough manufacturing work and for all general roust-abouting. This means that we must re-adjust our ideas to some extent. . . . The foreigner must be given credit for possessing a *brain*, and our aim should be to find the right key to manipulate it. The cause of our failure to secure success from this class of help is more frequently our own fault than it is that of the man employed. . . . He is anxious to learn, but usually is unable to understand our language and does not secure a real comprehension of what is required of him. Special efforts must be made to have him thoroughly understand what is wanted and to impress upon him the quality and quantity of the work required. He will respond to attention and considerate treatment more readily than his American brother, and appreciates a pleasant word of good fellowship more than we realize. If properly instructed, he takes pride in his labor and will strive to produce the best quality possible. . . . The fact must not be overlooked that foreigners are quite as apt to vary in their fitness for a job as our American workman. Many failures in the handling of foreign labor in the factories are due to lack of consideration being given to the training these men have had in their own country. . . . Remember, that the Southern European is human and must be so treated."

Head continued with a frank expression of his attitudes—and prejudices—toward nationalties:

The Swedes and Norwegians have in earlier years constituted the larger portion of the force. . . . The Swede possesses many very desirable characteristics, among these is his native training to work, which usually develops accuracy and energy. . . . He can always be depended upon to instruct and break in any green man of his own nationality but is very slow to assist other nationalities. . . . There has been a very noticable change in the type of Swedish emigrants during the past year due to the socialistic unrest in the Old Country. The younger Swedish element coming over are not inclined to work. They prefer a "white collar" job and don't care to hold that for any length of time. A large number of young boys go wrong due primarily to their belief that they should not be expected to work for their living. . . . The first and probably the most dependable of other nationalities have been the Belgians. . . . They are found desirous of making good money and willing to return its equivalent in amount of work performed.... Poles, Lithuanians, Russians, Slavs have worked to good advantage on grinding and polishing operations.... They have proved more adaptable than any other nationality and it has been a task to secure sufficient other labor to keep proper division of nationality in these departments.... These nationalities are best fitted for work which might be termed more or less repetitious and where the element of monotony is strong.... About two years ago the introduction of Bohemians was taken up and at this time there are quite a large number of them employed. They are proving very satisfactory from every standpoint.... Those from rural Bohemia make good laborers.... In the Plow Plant the Greeks have never proven desirable or adapted to the work.... They are clannish and inclined to quit in a bunch.... Austrians and Hungarians are not available in sufficient quantities to permit of securing the best men of these nationalities. The majority of them are of a roving disposition which precludes their remaining on the job for sufficient length of time to permit of their handling of it to good advantage. The better Hungarians are excellent men when located with their family . . . hardy, rugged, and full of spirit . . . in fact rather hard to handle on that account.... The Germans, when available, are exceptionally good shop help, but this nationality seems to remain largely in the East and cannot be secured in this locality.... The Italians have proved exceptionally well adapted to bench work, export boxing and labor of a similar nature.... Special care must be exercised to avoid the employment of those from Southern Italy as they are not desirable employees in any sense, being of a quarrelsome disposition and unstable in their general makeup. The Northern Italians are equal to men of any country. We have few of them, however, this far West.

Deere's wage rates during the first decade and a half of the twentieth century compared favorably with those of other employers in the Moline-Rock Island-Davenport area, as well as with those of competitors in the Chicago labor market. There was some dip in total annual earnings of workers in the sagging market of 1913–14, but the picture for those years was for steadily rising hourly rates and total weekly earnings (the cyclical nature of the business did continue to show in the total employment figures). Appendix exhibit 13 chronicles these figures for the Plow Works; wages in the other Deere factories in the Moline-East Moline area were comparable. While it is always difficult to exactly compare wage rates in different plants and different geographical areas (the job mix generally differs somewhat), Appendix exhibit 14 pictures the Plow Works hourly rates with those of the International Harvester Company's McCormick Works in Chicago and the U.S. manufacturing money wage in the same period, showing Deere's consistently higher rates.

By this time, the company also had refined its concepts of piecework with a sophisticated system, built on the work of the scientific management pioneers, Harrington Emerson and Frederick W. Taylor. "We place particular stress upon fair prices," noted Head in the meeting of 1912. "They must be such as will permit a good workman receiving full return for sufficient effort. With prices so established, the inefficient workman will automatically discharge himself while a good workman will be able to secure earnings commensurate with his greater activity and application. . . . Much has been said relative to the necessity of affording to the workman a SQUARE DEAL. This must not be considered merely in the theoretical sense, but must be made positive in our labor policy. Frequent check-ups are necessary all along the line to eliminate any possibility of deviation from this policy."

The wages, hours worked, and earnings were not nearly the full story; benefits and pensions were generous. For much of its existence, the company had built a strong loyalty among its employees, fostered by an interest in and concern for the living conditions of all of its work force. Some of this loyalty was due to strong attachments to the Deere family, earned over the years by John Deere and Charles. But it continued even when the third generation of management took over after Charles Deere's death. Health and accident benefits had been paid by the company since 1887; in July 1907, shortly after Charles Deere's death (and with his explicit backing), a new pension system was established for the company. It provided for non-contributory pensions after age sixty-five for those with twenty or more years of service, on a sliding scale according to the annual pay for the preceeding ten years, with a minimum pension of eighteen dollars per month. The pension system, and its companion sick benefit and disability programs, while not the first in American industry, certainly were pioneer efforts by Deere.

Deere also experimented with company-built housing during this period. Low-cost housing for unskilled and semiskilled employees had been a problem for a number of years, so in 1909 the company and the Deere estate had joined together to build a section of fifty modest homes in East Moline; in 1912, another 100 were built. Some were sold to employees, others were rented. At first, this venture was only modestly successful. By 1914, sixty-four had been sold, an additional twenty-seven rented, and, on that date, fifty-nine stood vacant. The war-time shortage in housing soon brought a change in fortunes. Thirty-six additional duplexes were built in that year, as well as fifteen additional small homes and a community house. "Every house built has been occupied immediately," George Mixter reported, "and all of the old houses are also occupied." In 1918 additional houses and apartments were constructed in both East Moline and Moline to bring the total to some 259 separate family dwellings. By the peak of the operation, in 1920, some 315 units had been made available.

There were strengths in this employee housing effort. Modestly priced houses were made available, built to reasonably careful standards. The experience prior to the wartime bulge in demand was at best mixed; many of the houses turned over rapidly, hastening deterioration. The picture changed considerably during the war, when the demand for decent housing soon brought interested people into the picture, willing to keep up their properties. The housing projects continued as useful additions to Moline-East Moline housing for many years; most of the homes are still in use today. The question of whether housing is an effective device for holding employees as loyal workers has been debated widely, both in Deere & Company and in other firms that have tried it. The decline of employee housing projects in recent years probably attests to the fact that difficulties outweigh the advantages.[2]

WARTIME DISCONTENT

The conflict in Europe brought tensions across America, and employee relations became much more difficult. George Mixter, in his manufacturing report of October 1914, had still felt optimistic about labor relations: "We are profiting from more efficient men and it is conservative to say that we are getting more for $1.00 per wages than for a number of years." But by late 1915 Mixter had to admit to the board that "things have now begun to change. Labor conditions are not as easy as they were." The year 1916 witnessed the first strike the company had incurred since the very first part of the twentieth century, a two-week strike at the Fort Smith Wagon Company in Arkansas by the International Carriage, Wagon, and Automobile Workers Union, an effort to organize the company. "No concessions of any kind were made," reported Mixter after the strike was over.

General increases in wages were announced in the Chicago area in late 1916. Deere executives were opposed to any plan that was a flat, across-the-board increase, but they decided that wages at the company's various plants should be increased by a figure not less than 10 percent over that in effect the year before, still to be applied by managers' discretion as "best fitted to the individual case of your own plant." In spite of this, the company began to lose good employees to other industries, especially the automobile and munitions-making plants (the Rock Island Arsenal in particular). The board seemed slow to recognize that the wartime demand that increased its profitability also strengthened the bargaining power of workers. The loss of employees to the military further tightened the labor market. Companies with government contracts and orders from abroad competed for personnel so that they could meet their growing commitments. Deere employees became aware of inducements to go elsewhere.

When it did begin to face up to the issue, the board initiated a series of meetings that extended from March 1917 to March 1918. Many key people had been leaving the company, apparently for economic reasons. The company regarded the issue as a diminution in employee loyalty, particularly in management-level ranks. One notion began to dominate the board's thinking—to increase the employees' financial stake in the business, either by direct ownership or by special bonuses. These discussions ranged beyond employee relations issues to a definition, once again, of the values of the institution itself. In the process, the tensions within top management again came to the fore, particularly over the question of employee stock purchases.

When the original employee stock-purchase plans had been introduced in 1911, a sharp distinction had been made between the common stock plan and the preferred stock plan. The latter was designed for broad employee participation, with steady but modest returns; the preferred dividend of 7 percent was to be paid every year if possible, and, if not, it was cumulative. The common stock plan was based on a quite separate rationale. Common stock was to be purchased only by a select group of management, a list developed, name by name, by the board itself. Lists of candidates were to be submitted by the branch houses and factories; the branch and factory managers were to choose people based on "their positions, and their importance to your organization." All were to be sales managers or assistant managers, provided, however, that "a very few of the younger men whose ability is pronounced, and who may be looked upon as logical successors to those now holding positions of great importance and trust" could be added. In their choices of potential recipients, the branch managers were to "list them in order of their importance." They were warned that "the parties whom they have submitted . . . should be held in ignorance" until the executive committee gave final blessing, and that once the employees were notified, "the necessity of secrecy in the matter should be impressed upon them in order to retain harmony among other fellow-workers."

In a scarcely veiled warning, the board's committee for the plan added: "If there should chance to be among those selected certain ones whose conservatism is so marked as that they would elect to acquire 7% Cumulative Preferred Stock," the committee would make this stock available to them. The inescapable implication was that were a person's attitude to be "so marked," it might indicate a tentativeness or excessive caution that would not bode well for rapid rise in management.

When the full matter came forward to the board a few weeks later, a lengthy enabling resolution was promulgated, again stressing that the choice should be "particularly those employees who have shown and may hereafter show unusual ability qualifying them to occupy managerial positions." Specific contracts were authorized at this meeting with eleven members of top management, three of them new board members (Mixter contracted for $250,000, George Peek for $200,000, and Floyd Todd for $100,000; the other eight were for sums between $20,000 and $50,000).

The branch-house list then was laid on the table; there were eighty-four names on it. The executive committee added several people, dropped none, but adjusted a good many of the amounts, both upward and downward. Everyone knew that some employees had more ability and effectiveness, others less, and they were willing to make qualitative judgments on this basis. For example, one individual was "one of the most valuable and competent employees, starting as office boy," and should be given stock "even if it was necessary to scale down others." Interestingly, twenty-one people were allocated preferred rather than common, clearly based on the rubric about conservatism. Seven of these were from Winnipeg, eight from St. Louis. Only six others throughout all the rest of the system opted for preferred. Were Winnipeg and St. Louis less entrepreneurial branches?

The board thus had developed a plan focusing on achievements, with powerful motivational "carrots" built into it. The board members had been willing to make subjective judgments—to look at each member of its managerial group personally, decide who would be the company's best future executives, and reward those people commensurately and selectively.

There was a row about the plan, though, within three years, when a faction of the board, feeling that the existing plan smacked of cronyism, raised the possibility of substantially broadening the numbers of people in it. Butterworth led the advocates, proposing that a number of managers, heads of departments, and foremen "be quietly advised that a certain amount of this stock is available" and that these executives "be permitted to approach employees to whom they would recommend that sale." Mixter was uneasy about this, feeling that "an offering, not universal, but as extensive as proposed, will involve much more unfairness that can justly be charged against the present allotment." George Peek flatly opposed a more general offering: "I think it would be a mistake to undertake to change this condition with the class of men affected." The board finally decided against the additional offering, but the discussion had smoked out the differences in philosophy about executive compensation.

By 1917 widespread dissatisfaction with the common stock plan was apparent. No dividends had yet been paid on any common stock; the book value of the stock had not appreciated in a major way. Complicating the picture was the soaring cost of living that had been fueled by the war. Able middle- and top-management people—the very ones for whom this plan had been developed—were leaving the company in large numbers for more lucrative jobs. "We cannot afford to lose all of our good men," Floyd Todd worried. George Peek agreed: "There is hardly a day goes by that we do not lose some men." Treasurer T.F. Wharton added: "In this day of huge organizations and big business it is not possible for men to go into business for themselves and make the successes and reap the fortunes that were possible a comparatively short time ago. . . . Large organizations must interest their men in the business—to make them partners."

What was the real intention of the plan of 1911, its underlying philosophy? In a general sense, it was to reward and hold loyal employees —just about everyone could agree on this. But the basis for selecting eligible employees in 1911 had been a narrow one, concentrating on key people in upper management. Was a broader approach needed?

Butterworth believed so: "I have never been in favor of picking out one man here and one man there." R.B. Lourie, the Moline branch manager, agreed: "More or less dissatisfaction was created when it became known that certain men were allowed to subscribe for common stock.... I am in favor of paying for loyalty and continued service."

C.C. Webber took issue with this. Not all employees, he reminded the others, had the same ability and motivational drive, particularly in middle and top management: "There is a difference between employees and this was recognized in the selections that were made at the time the stock was contracted for." George Mixter also stoutly defended the incumbent plan: "In looking over the existing common stock contracts . . . generally speaking, they covered men who have continued to grow in the organization . . . there are no apologies to offer." George Peek spoke even more strongly: "We are up against the proposition of finding men to drive this business, not men that will do what we tell them to do or that will merely carry out this, that or the other thing. Men that will push us all.... This business cannot go on unless we can get the drivers

Exhibit 8–2. *Collection of floats in Moline parades; left, Moline Wagon Company, undated; top, Union Malleable Iron Company, ca. 1919; bottom, World War I ambulance wagon, built by Deere. ca. 1918. (Deere Archives)*

interested in the business.... We want men that will crowd all the time."

There was a further complication: Just how much should any stock purchase plan be subsidized? In the plan of 1911 the purchase contracts were for sums that were substantially below the stated book value. Butterworth had been quite apprehensive about this at the time and now returned to his earlier views: "When the stockholders made the contracts with these people they were extremely liberal. They gave it to them at fifty cents on the dollar, which was entirely against the law, on the theory that services rendered were going to pay for the other fifty cents." Obviously, Butterworth felt that this was a gift out of his and others' own pockets, and he had expected that this would motivate a feeling of loyalty. "If a man does not appreciate that, he will never appreciate it. That is the way I feel, and I feel it pretty strongly."

If there was to be a substantial subsidy, it would indeed come in part out of the pockets of the directors themselves, whether existing unissued common stock was used, or the needed common stock was obtained by purchase on the open market. (Small amounts were available from time to time due to deaths of holders; there had been no public sale of common stock at any point, however.) The potential subsidy did not seem to trouble some of the directors with smaller holdings. Frank Silloway, who worked with George Peek in general company sales, stated: "I am willing to sacrifice my own holdings for the good of Deere & Company." Carleton Chase, at this time president and treasurer of the Syracuse Chilled Plow Co., came west for the meeting and seconded Silloway: "I believe in it so thoroughly I am willing to give up any amount of stock that I have bought under this purchase contract...."

But Butterworth and Burton Peek, still caught in their dual roles of executive and trustee, demurred. Peek stated: "Some of our Directors have offered themselves up as a sacrifice. I am not in favor of anybody making a sacrifice. Mr. Butterworth and I both occupy peculiar positions. We certainly want to serve the interests we represent with the utmost fidelity and integrity." Butterworth was honest about his mixed feelings: "I represent about 40% of the stock which is going to be distributed and it amounts to about $1,000,000. And if the stock is worth $60 today it means $600,000 in actual money. That is something that has got to be considered and I want to consider it from that standpoint as well as of the employees and do the best we can for them. I want to take this question up very carefully with those for whom I am responsible and arrive at a conclusion which I hope will be satisfactory not only to the members of the Board but to the stockholders of the Company and to the employees."

(Burton Peek's caution, instinctive from his legal training, sometimes irritated his brother George, just as the latter's "full-speed-ahead" mentality often bothered Burton. For example, in an argument concerning a legal consolidation of the timber companies for tax purposes, George felt

Burton was moving too slowly and wrote his brother: "It is little short of criminal to continually procrastinate when the results are so very vital." Burton fired back: "I am not willing that this misapprehension on your part . . . should pass unanswered," and he proceeded to detail the complex legal ramifications involved in the situation. This was a friendly disagreement between brothers; nevertheless, it was yet another brouha-ha in the complex interaction among Deere board members.)

When the first meeting of 1917 ended inconclusively, George Peek, Mixter, and Todd brought forward what they thought was a compromise —a selective sale of additional common stock to those employees "recently promoted to more important management positions, or [who] have had placed upon them additional duties and greater responsibilities." It provided that stock would only go to employees in managerial positions, and with at least five years of service. Amounts of stock were to be based on multiples of present salary—an explicit productivity linkage, inasmuch as compensation was based on individual merit.

Butterworth was not happy with the new report. "My mind is open and I do not think I should be considered as being a very stubborn individual," he began. "As you know, I have some pretty definite ideas about it and have had since the reorganization and I have not changed these ideas very much." Todd, the presenter of the plan, tried to assure Butterworth: "I am sure this committee does not propose to urge anything . . . in a hasty way or embarrass you in your opportunity to study the plan and reach a well thought-out conclusion." Butterworth called for views from around the table, and it soon became obvious that again the central issue was whether a wide general offering should be made.

Webber continued to plump for selective use—"for the men in high positions." C.W. Mansur, the St. Louis branch manager, agreed, calling up the image of "partners." Morgan, on the other hand, spoke eloquently in favor of broadening: "It is not liberal enough. . . . We want to reach some of these men in the shop. Some of them are foremen, some do not occupy the position of foreman but still they are just as important. My understanding is this proposition will not touch these men at all. . . . It ought to touch salesmen particularly. It is not far reaching enough."

George Mixter disagreed: "If I thought we were going to sell the workmen in the shop . . . I would say that would be utterly wrong. If we handle ourselves judiciously . . . we can place it just where we want to. I am not prepared to say on what basis. I do know we could do it and it would not get away from us."

Butterworth had the last word: "I have been in favor from the first of not limiting the offer to employees. . . . A man in his position, no matter what that position is, who fills it well, is just as important as any other man, at least he is to himself. We could not get along without stenographers, we could not get along without many others such as clerks, etc. who have not been considered in this matter. I have felt right along that we should sell those people. . . . This stock must be distributed fairly and equitably and what I mean by that is it should be distributed not to that person selected, but it should be distributed throughout the organization. I know very well if I were sitting at a desk and doing my work and doing it just as well as I knew how, I should want consideration. We must assume that when a man is being paid a salary by the Company and is retained at that salary the Company must of necessity think that man is worth the money he is getting and therefore he is filling that office just as well as any other man is filling his office. That does not only apply to the office, but I think it applies, as Mr. Morgan has said, to the shop. I do not believe the shop men would be interested but it would have a splendid effect if they know they could get the stock if they liked to. It puts everybody on the same plane."

Feelings were so divided, though, that even the compromise failed to get enough support, and for this reason the board now turned toward consideration of a separate, broad-based profit-sharing concept, not involving stock purchase at all. Just a year before, Leon Clausen had been brought over to Moline from Dain at Ottumwa, where he had been manager, and put in charge of manufacturing while Mixter was on leave in Washington (as a lieutenant colonel in the Signal Corps, working as an inspector of army aircraft procurement). At this point Clausen was given the challenging assignment to develop such a profit-sharing plan.

PROFIT SHARING— A VALID COMPROMISE?

Memoranda and letters flew back and forth in the weeks prior to the announced board meeting of January 25, 1918, scheduled to decide the issue of profit sharing, once and for all. George Peek, too, was now in Washington, as an industry representative on the War Industries Board, and he had to lobby by mail. The final proposal, developed by Burton Peek and Todd, provided that from the net profits of a given year, a sum be deducted amounting to 7 percent of the tangible assets, with the remaining portion of the net profits then split equally between "capital" and "labor" (the deduction had not been in the original Clausen plan, but was added later when a number of board members objected that Clausen had not provided for interest on capital).

Even this modified plan evoked strong criticism, for a number of board members opposed profit-sharing on principle. W.L. Velie, who was one of these, put it most pointedly: "I am irrevocably opposed to any employees' profit sharing plan. . . . Wage earners are now the best paid of all classes, except possibly the farmers. The return journey to normality of wages is going to be a rough one. Why accentuate the dangers? Labor is a commodity in the sense that it is sold to the highest cash bidder. Can we assume that industries in this locality will not be obliged to compete for it? The inevitable result of the operation of the plan submitted by Messrs. Todd and Peek, while worthy from an Humanitarian viewpoint, will be to place all Moline industries, relatively and competitively, in a disadvantageous position. The highest duty of an employer is to see to it that labor is well paid and continuously employed, and that working conditions are excellent. This cannot be done if for long we handicap ourselves in the manner proposed."

Velie was unabashedly in the Webber-Mixter-George Peek camp as far as the use of the common stock plan: "Something real and liberal *must* be done to controvert the present general opinion of our best men that the working-out of our common stock contracts is, to them, unprofitable and sinister, rather than profitable and beneficent, as was conscientiously intended by those of us implicated."

By the time the meeting opened on January 25, 1918, there was open friction among the board members about the very merits of profit sharing. The board had studied several such efforts in other industries and had been particularly impressed with the plan at Procter and Gamble. Burton Peek warned of some dangers, though: "Before they adopted it they called in the best actuaries in the country and it was their judgment as well as the judgment of the management of the company that the nature of their business was such that they could expect the profits which they were then making to continue and increase just as far into the future as soap was used. And that is because they do not know in their business any distinction between bad years and good years. . . . They expected the constant increase and generally speaking they have received it."

Everyone knew in their hearts that the farm-implement business was not steady, but highly cyclical. C.C. Webber cautioned: "This profit-sharing business is surrounded with great danger. I certainly do not think we are ready for it now. We do not know what the future is going to be for us. . . . I do not think we have any cinch on the next five or ten years and I think a profit-sharing plan at this time will be hasty and perhaps very unwise for the Company." Webber's bias may have intruded here, as he commented further: "I remember that some years ago we gave our employees in Minneapolis who drew $100 a month or less a bonus of 10% for several years and we finally found out that it did not do us any good. Nearly all of them were spending it before they got it."

Webber then quoted Willard Van Brunt, who was absent from the meeting, as saying: "I tell you what I think about this labor business. I believe . . . you pay your men well, try and give them steady employment and take an interest in their welfare, go around among them, see that your foreman keeps a little eye on them, if they are sick see what is the matter with them, have somebody help a new man get started."

T.F. Wharton closed the discussion with a view that seemed to sum up most of the members' feelings: "It seems to me that anything that smacks of paternalism will do us harm rather than good. . . . The thing for us to do is to pay our men liberal wages, give them the best working conditions possible, and follow them individually rather than in the mass."

All views now out in the open, the plan came up for vote: there were eight dissenters, only Butterworth, Burton Peek, and Todd supporting it. Profit sharing itself was dead, and along with it the notion of broadening the base of the common stock plan. The minor revisions in the existing contracts were passed; these provided also for additional selective sales. But left intact was the underlying philosophy—that employee common stock was to be used essentially as a managerial motivational device, the "carrot" for the "drivers!"

The debate should not be stereotyped as a corporate "shoot-out at the OK Corral." Both points of view had merit. One does want initiative, achievement, motivation, and business drive; the thrust of the employee common stock plan was much more profound than just monetary reward. Important as money itself was the recognition of individual worth built into the plan. But so, too, was the broad-based bonus concept more than just "reward for service." There were profound values implicit in such statements as Butterworth's, quoted earlier—"A man in his position, no matter what that position is, who fills it well, is just as important as any other man. . . . " Butterworth really meant this, and everyone knew it. A very important piece of the success of Deere & Company in building employee loyalty stemmed from just this kind of leadership exhibited by William Butterworth. In sum, one needs drivers, of course, but pervasive loyalty must be there, too, in order to have an organization worthy of being driven.[3]

THE CLAYTON ACT
TIGHTENS THE TETHER

Public control of marketing was considerably advanced with the passage of the Clayton Anti-Trust Act by the United States Congress in 1914, to be administered by the Federal Trade Commission. The act contained a number of specific prohibitions relating to marketing practices. Price discriminations that "tended to create a monopoly" were outlawed, as were contracts that required a purchaser not to buy or handle products of a seller's competitors. The farm-implement industry was particularly vulnerable to accusations relating to the latter. Most of the larger manufacturers were by this time "full-line" producers, each making available to its own set of dealers a gamut of products intended to take care of all the dealer's needs. In turn, each company pressed hard on its dealers not to stock competing products.

As soon as the Clayton Act was passed, Burton Peek drafted a letter to all the branch houses, spelling out precisely the position of the company in regard to the exclusive dealerships. "As we are advised, none of our subsidiaries are now writing contracts containing an agreement for exclusive representation," Peek began. (Evidently, there still was not enough central Moline control for him to be certain.) "If, however, there were any such contracts in use," he continued, "they should be discontinued immediately." Peek continued, "This does not mean that you should lessen your efforts to secure either full line representation or exclusive representation. Such effort, however, should be directed to convincing the dealer by legitimate persuasion and argument that even though he is not obliged by his contract to do so, it is to his interest to handle the full John Deere line and to handle it exclusively, that in this way he can make more money than by scattering his energies over a variety of competing lines." As for price discrimination, existing Deere discounts based on quantity of the commodity sold were "still quite legitimate."

Pressure for "exclusives" with dealers already had become a central issue in the International Harvester antitrust suit. Prior to 1905, Harvester had required dealers to sign an agreement baldly forcing exclusivity and assessing fines of twenty-five dollars for each grain binder, fifty dollars for each husker and shredder, ten dollars for each mower or reaper, and five dollars for each sweep rake, hay rake, or hay cutter of a competitor's make that the dealer sold. As the antitrust storm began to grow after 1905, Harvester gave up the controversial clause, but the testimony in the antitrust case turned up allegations of widespread Harvester pressure tactics. In the case of Harvester, it was not a simple, straightforward version of exclusivity. Since the company handled several different brands of harvesting equipment, it had made a practice of parceling out dealerships so that a town would have several International Harvester dealers, each handling a different company brand. When the case against Harvester was finally resolved in its consent decree of 1918, Harvester agreed to maintain but one agent in each town.

Frank Silloway was so delighted with this latter ruling that he reported to the board: "It practically eliminates our largest competitor from the competition for the trade of the John Deere dealer." It took only a few more months for Silloway to regret his rash and overly optimistic words, for Harvester quickly repositioned its dealers in an even more effective way.

Deere itself soon had a brief but unsettling brush with the Federal Trade Commission. The Bureau of Corporations of the United States Department of Commerce had turned a harsh light on the farm-machinery industry, with a separate study of farm-machinery trade associations. Its report, in early 1915, alleged that a number of manufacturers were refusing to sell to farmers' cooperatives or to consider them for dealerships. The FTC contacted Deere in March 1915 on complaint of two cooperatives in Pennsylvania who charged they had been refused the right to sell John Deere equipment. Floyd Todd told the investigator: "We analyze a Farmers' Cooperative Association in the same way that we do every other customer and determine our actions by this analysis.... As a rule Farmers' Associations were not very good merchants, although we knew of some exceptions with whom we have done business in the past." Todd elaborated on this: "Farmers buying our goods expect the dealer to expert them and if this was not done satisfactorily, goods were returned and payment was refused.... Our experience has been with many of these Farmers' Associations that they do not have men connected with them of long experience, familiar with all lines of implements who would take care of this expert work in the proper way.... They endeavored to sell farmers upon so close a margin of profit ... and did not figure on doing the expert work necessary and reserved no profit to cover this expense." This apparently satisfied the FTC investigator, for the case was not pursued.[4]

PRICING PRACTICES

When the Federal Trade Commission also began to concern itself with final retail prices, it became ever more important to effect price making in as rational and defensible a way as possible. Marketers in any company want prices low enough to be fully competitive in the field; the production people want transfer prices that provide a healthy margin over all factory costs. Such tensions between production and sales often become exacerbated in business downturns, when hangovers of high raw-material and inventory costs may continue in the face of declining prices in the marketplace. The downturn in the company in 1914 provided a good example of this.

George Mixter and George Peek, so often together on internal company matters, took opposite sides in this argument. As prices for 1914 were being set, Mixter pointed to some large increases in the costs of materials and labor as ample justification for higher prices; he felt that "costs are *permanently* increasing," and advocated that the company "should aim at a permanent increase in price."

Peek argued against this. "Waste in manufacture as a result of incompetent labor and high pressure in the factories" was really the root of the problem. Further, the high production costs had been aggravated by poor management of inventories, frequent revision of manufacturing schedules, and a host of other manufacturing department slippages. Peek was aghast at the price increases suggested by Mixter. The advance, he felt, would result in such reduced volume that many dealers would be forced out of business, particularly in the face of sharp competitive inroads from abroad, especially from the Germans. Finally, Peek added that he feared an adverse public reaction: "We, as well as other newly organized companies, will be subject to criticism in promulgating a general advance, and will be classed with other large concerns now under government observations."

Peek's solution was to make "the strongest effort" to improve purchasing and reduce the cost of production by better scheduling; "if a small advance is necessary, it should be distributed in such a way as to make it least apparent." Mixter, on the other hand, argued persuasively for an across-the-board 3 percent increase for all plows, harrows, and cultivators. He dismissed Peek's selective approach out of hand: "Argument that margin in drills and other high margin articles is now sufficiently high is dangerous ground. The extra return can be had on these lines with certainly no more difficulty than on close margin lines. In general, low margin lines are low for basic reasons, and we cannot hope to squeeze the necessary all from such a poor source."

After considerable argument around the board table, Peek's arguments prevailed, and price increases were voted under a caveat to do it "in such a way as to make it least objectionable to the trade." The percentages agreed to varied from 2 percent on some plow items up to 6 percent on certain harrows.

Peek's criticisms of Mixter's seesaw production patterns were rather gratuitous, for decisions about production schedules and levels of inventory often had been sabotaged by changes of heart from the marketing side. A more rational scheduling program was needed, and at this point a suggestion was put forth to require each branch house to take at least 75 percent of its estimate, the plan to be tried for a year. Such a contingency would certainly make a branch manager more cautious in his estimates, but it still did not get at the real problem, the need for closer coordination between production and sales. After many complaints by the branches, a new, much more formal "system of estimates" was developed a year later; each branch was to submit information to the manufacturing departments by June 1, with a rolling revision each three months (with even shorter time-period revisions if necessary). "We will discontinue the 50 and 75 percent responsibility clauses in the present contracts and make the Branch Houses responsible only in a moral sense for the estimate," the directors finally agreed. This clearly took the heat off the branches, and George Crampton complained: "The branch house manager has all the latest information in hand pertaining to his territory. He should have a better knowledge of the crop condition, tendency of trade toward or away from certain tools. . . . He certainly would resent the idea that someone else could better judge his wants than could he, and would not consent to have his estimates ignored. This being the case, he should make it one of his main duties to keep constantly in touch with the conditions of his estimates and orders. . . . If one or more of the houses neglect to estimate correctly, it throws the whole structure out of line. Then, if the neglectful house should need goods earlier than houses farther north, it becomes a question of filling orders for the delinquent houses and making the others wait, or losing trade." Crampton wanted to increase the responsibility of the branches, up to 85 percent of the final estimate. But the majority felt otherwise, and "moral" suasion remained the only club.

Other events in the 1913–14 period conspired to hasten some already contemplated changes in internal company transfer price equations. The first was the passage of the Clayton Act, with its much more stringent constraints on any form of price discrimination. Before the turn of the century, the prices paid by individual branches for orders from the factories often varied quite substantially. Deals struck by individual branch managers with factory managers were watched over, more or less at arm's length, by Moline central management. Ostensibly, these differences stemmed from differing competitive conditions in various territories, but the divergences were often due to the abilities of strong branch managers to bargain. By the 1910s, branch prices were reasonably uniform (there were freight add-ons, depending upon distance), but certainly not standard. In early 1915, the board learned that International Harvester was planning to set all of its prices F.O.B. the factory, in order to be less vulnerable to Clayton Act accusations. Later that spring, the board voted "that factory prices and terms should be uniform in all Branch Houses.... We realize on the question of terms that different terms have got to be applied to different sections of the country . . . the country should be divided into zones, such zones to be established by the Executive Committee . . . and similar terms applied uniformly to the houses in each zone, in this way perfecting as uniform practice as possible."

George Peek was in Europe at the time of this resolution and when he returned he expressed uneasiness about what he felt was an overly rigid action. To his mind, on-the-spot situations might well dictate modifications in given territories, and he persuaded the board to pass a resolution that "where competitive conditions clearly made it necessary for our factories to depart from the uniform basis of Branch House prices that such variations be permitted." Left unanswered was the question of how the government would react to any such departures from the norm.

THE FEDERAL INCOME TAX
FORCES ORGANIZATIONAL CHANGES

The enactment of the federal income tax in 1913 had a major influence on American business. It seemed obvious that Deere now would be in double jeopardy on its taxation, inasmuch as most of the company factories and branches legally were separate corporations, making their own (hopefully) substantial profits. Thus substantial profits earned by some factories and branches could not be offset by the lesser profits (or perhaps even losses) in other factories and branches. In December 1915, George Peek brought before the board a far-reaching proposal for reorganization. It would consolidate all of the Moline factories, which would then be operated as departments, just as the harvester operation had been from the start. As to the branches, Peek proposed to leave Minneapolis, Omaha, Kansas City, and Dallas without change, but to consolidate a number of the other branches. All remaining branches would thus become sub-branches reporting to the Moline branch. Peek also proposed a reorganization of management; in total there were to be not only income tax and interest savings, but greater efficiencies throughout the organization.

Peek's proposal immediately raised once again the debate over decentralization. The proposed consolidation would inevitably increase the authority of central management and reduce autonomy in the branches and factories. William Butterworth's abiding belief that authority must rest predominantly in the field now once more aroused his opposition to the erosion of this field authority. Butterworth was even willing to pay the extra taxes in order to maintain his longstanding pattern, and his vehement dissent finally resulted in a tabling of the plan.

The problem would not go away, however, and by late 1916 a new approach was suggested by George Peck, his brother Burton, George Mixter, and Floyd Todd. It was for consolidation of the Moline factories only, and this time the resolution passed (with the Union Malleable Iron Company left out of the plan "because of the hardship it might cause that company in securing outside business should the fact become known that it was a subsidiary of Deere & Company"). Two months later, in January 1917, the same process was carried through for the so-called outside factories—Van Brunt, Dain, Syracuse Chilled Plow, Marseilles, and the others. Further, all the existing contracts between branch houses and factories were cancelled and a new arrangement was established.

The central company now made contracts with the branches at Minneapolis, Kansas City, St. Louis, Dallas, Moline, and the Consolidated Wagon & Machine Company (Salt Lake City), whereby the central company would, after buying from the factories, sell to the branches at a "percent discount from the Minimum Moline prices, such as will largely reduce the branch house profit." The drafters of the proposal estimated that this discount would average about 20 percent, but that it would be necessary to vary this in accordance with the varying costs of doing business in the branches. "Such a plan is not in violation of the Clayton Law, for this new method of doing business is not a sale of goods to branch houses, but a handling of goods on consignment and the Clayton Law does not apply. All prices are to be based on the Moline Minimum Dealer's Price, with the proviso that where branch house managers can secure higher prices than these, without material loss in volume, they shall be privileged to do so." The branch house would be entitled to keep this additional margin as branch-house compensation. The central company, in turn, was to buy from the factories at cost plus 10 percent (material labor and indirect factory expense, but not general and sales expense). "This will leave little, if any, profit to these factories," the report's authors frankly stated. After further thought about some of the implications of operating a pricing system so directly tied to cost, the initial 10 percent proposal was altered so that the factories operated on discounts from the Moline minimum dealer's price; these discount percentages varied from as high as 43 percent for the Plow Works, Deere & Mansur, and Van Brunt to the wagon companies' 23 percent.

The thrust of the plan was to remove just about all of the profit from both factory and branch operation, putting it into the "pocket" of the central company. The authors prominently stated in their conclusion "that the factory manager shall be as independent as ever in his field; that is, in making of the best goods in the proper quantities at the lowest possible cost," and further, "that the branch house manager will be as independent as heretofore in his fields; mainly, in the marketing of the greatest amount of goods at the best price obtainable, at minimum expense, and the collection of the money therefore." In essence, the factories were still in charge of production and design of their own individual products (no centralized engineering function existed at this time), and the branches were responsible for all of their selling relationships with dealers; the providing of service, repairs, and parts; and the collection of all of the monies from the dealers (that is, credits and collections were not centralized). Now centralized, though, were all banking functions, as well as pricing decisions, at least for their minimums.

There was considerable disquiet among factory managers and branch managers about this plan. It was so far-reaching in its implications that all concerned realized that the company had gone through a major change. C.C. Webber took the floor at the next meeting of the board, in March, to state "that we wanted every Branch House to know what it was making and wanted it understood that the plan so provided. . . . It was very important that the Branches be run for a profit and that if they can get more money than the minimum Moline Dealer's Prices, they should get it and it should be reflected in their showing." Webber also cautioned that a number of branch personnel were under a profit-sharing plan, and that they should be properly taken care of in adjustments, inasmuch as the profit figures were going to be considerably lower at the branch level. George Peek responded that "there was no thought of lessening the importance of the Branch House Managers . . . but that the General Company desired to attach greater importance to them than has heretofore been done; that the General Company wanted the Branch Houses to be a part of the whole organization and wanted them to run at a profit and not at a loss." Still, there was no doubt in anyone's mind that the company had taken at least one significant step in the direction of centralization.[5]

THE DAIN TRACTOR

The issue of whether the company should build a tractor still remained unsettled. In 1914, an important new step was taken: fellow board member Joseph Dain was himself asked to study the tractor situation and report back to the board.

The instigator of this idea was C.C. Webber, who was an advocate of the tractor, but of a particular kind—a small two- or three-plow tractor "which will sell at about $700." Webber here was articulating a widespread feeling within the industry. Up to about 1914 large tractors—great monsters that weighed sometimes as much as 25,000 pounds or more—had dominated the industry, but they had just not worked out. High cost, spotty serviceability, and excessive repair costs combined to make the farmers real skeptics. Barton W. Currie, in his important book on the tractor, published in 1916, commented on the boom-bust cycle: "Along about the beginning of this century the big gas tractor came in. Western Canada was opening up, the Dakotas, Montana, Western Kansas and the plateaus of the mountain states were calling to the plungers in grain to come in and make a killing. It looked like a golden market for the big gas tractor, and the manufacturers went to it. There was an exhilarating boom and then a bang, followed by a sudden collapse. The big gas tractor had been overexploited and oversold. Numberless excuses were offered and a large variety of causes were carefully dissected. . . . The human factor had been too lightly considered. The big gas tractor had been far from foolproof. Its intricacies demanded the control of experts and there were not enough experts to go round. The automobile had not yet begun to teach mechanics to hundreds of thousands of farmers. There was no permanent employment for high-priced mechanics on the farm. Just as is the case with harvest hands—when they were needed most they were scarcest."

Dain felt that he could produce a tractor close to the Webber specifications, and by early 1915 he had a prototype ready for the board to see. The board voted to continue its development but sent Dain back to test the model in the field. The minutes record the board's ambivalence: "The present was not the time for Deere & Company to decide whether it should go into the tractor business or not; that it might seem wise later and it might not; that the wise thing for the Company to do was to watch the development of this business, and also watch and develop the tractor, in order that the Company might be ready for any emergency."

In a meeting a couple of months later the differences within the board about the tractor were once again laid on the record. R.B. Lourie was worried that "the tractor people are selling plows right on their tractors" and felt that the long-liners with tractors were going to make deep inroads into the wheel-plow trade. Butterworth countered that "we have repeatedly told our bankers that we were not in the tractor business and

Exhibit 8–3. *The Deere All-Wheel-Drive tractor (the Dain tractor):* left, *In parade, July 4, 1919;* right, *An advertising brochure, 1919. (Deere Archives)*

were not going into it." Webber at this point finally chose publicly to differ with Butterworth: "The bankers have very good reasons to be scared about gas tractors, but they have in mind the Rumely, the Emerson, and the Hart-Parr people. They have made a heavy, clumsy machine and have made a failure, and have not made any money. They [the bankers] think it is something we are going to sell on two or three years' time, while we are talking about something that is entirely different.... A little engine is going to be an economical thing for the farmer to buy." George Mixter also must have felt that the moment was right, for a few days later he wrote a lengthy letter to Butterworth, diplomatically advocating the continuation of the tractor project. "Knowing your own feelings in reference to the attitude of Deere & Company toward the whole tractor problem, I am taking this opportunity to briefly state the reasons for my own belief in the necessity of Deere & Company carrying on this development work.... The country is now flooded with attempts at practical small tractors and the extremely wide desire of the farmers to buy such a small tractor cannot be entirely overlooked.... If it be possible to build a small tractor that will really stand up for five or more years' work on the farm, I believe they will be a permanent requirement of the American farmer and especially in view of the plow trade they carry with them, this possibility cannot be overlooked by Deere & Company." Mixter felt so uneasy about bucking Butterworth that he remonstrated: "I do not want you to feel that I am advocating even a serious discussion of any one of these moves at the present time

JOHN DEERE TRACTOR

John Deere Tractor
12—24 H. P.

The All-Wheel-Drive Tractor

THE John Deere Tractor is the result of seven years of investigation and development to find the best in design and materials for tractor work. Its construction accords with the well-known John Deere policy in building farm implements. In all respects, it is a high quality machine, featured by a number of new and exclusive points of merit.

Advantages of the All-Wheel Drive

The John Deere Tractor is an all-wheel-drive, three-wheeled machine, with two wheels in front and one wide wheel in the rear. The front wheels are steering wheels as well as drivers.

Here are the main advantages of this construction:

1. Weight reduction is made possible through using all of the weight for traction. The John Deere weighs only 4,600 pounds considerably less than other tractors of its capacity.

2. Equal distribution of this light weight over the two front wheels, and the wide rear wheel prevents packing the soil and permits work on soft ground where other machines of the round-wheel type could not be used.

3. The front wheels being pullers, it is possible to steer the machine under difficult conditions, an advantage that means much in finishing up lands, plowing round corners and working in soft ground.

4. No differential being used, each wheel has

but am trying to look into the future." Still, Mixter took the opportunity to again counter Butterworth's fears about banker reaction: "It seems to me probably that one or two years from now if we are successful in conducting Deere & Company's business so as to show up well, that our principal banker friends might be consulted as to the wisdom of a small tractor proposition and then at that time it might not look as undesirable as it very rightly has looked to you and to the bankers during the past year."

The Dain prototypes, able to pull three plow bottoms, were tested again in the field over the summer of 1916, and their performance aroused enthusiasm among those who had seen the machines. Costs seemed to indicate a price of somewhere near $1,200, but because the tractor had an all-wheel drive, this added amount seemed saleable to the farmer. By July 1916, the board was told that Dain had already applied for patents on the machine, and George Peek advocated not only moving ahead on a larger scale with the Dain but also exploring the possibility of making a power cultivator, based upon some sketches made by a young engineer, Theo Brown, earlier that year. Brown, a graduate of the Worcester (Massachusetts) Polytechnic Institute in 1901, had come to the company in 1911 to assume the superintendency of the company's Marseilles subsidiary in East Moline; by 1916 his innovativeness had persuaded the Deere management to bring him to the parent company as the head of the experimental department. Brown and Max Sklovsky, the chief engineer, became the Deere mainstays in research and development during this period, aided after 1915 by the latter's nephew, Nathan Lesser. A Sklovsky prototype tractor was also built in 1915, but the project was put aside as wartime demands crowded out most experimentation.

As persuasive as George Peek's arguments appeared both for the power tractor and the power cultivator, Butterworth would have no part of it. Since he had planned to be away from the next board meeting, in September 1916, he wrote a confidential letter to Burton Peek, reiterating his views on the tractor project: "There is one thing I want to ask you to look out for and that is any further action by the Directors relating to the building of a tractor. I am opposed to any step being taken towards the manufacture by any of our factories of a tractor. I have acquiesced in the experimental work which has been done, but I am beginning to feel that we are wasting the stockholders' money in going any further with it." Butterworth spelled out some new misgivings: "Ford's active interest into the tractor business means unlimited capital and resources for marketing. I do not want to use the money of the Deere Estate or my own or that of any other stockholder in an awfully expensive enterprise which will get us nowhere in the end." Once again conflicts of interest had intruded. He continued: "Besides, I think we should be reducing our line rather than expanding it." Butterworth ended the letter with a blunt order to Peek: "I want it plainly understood that I am and will remain opposed to our taking up the manufacture of tractors and will take steps to stop it if an attempt is made to start. . . . If it comes up I want you to stop it."

Burton Peek dutifully reported Butterworth's opposition at the board meeting, but by now he also had become convinced that a Deere-built tractor was a necessity, and so he marshalled his arguments and wrote Butterworth a few weeks later: "I feel that we are making a great mistake if we do not take up the manufacture of the small tractor. It has come to stay beyond any question, with so many of our leading competitors, plow manufacturers and others, making a tractor. I think we will be forced into it for the protection of our plow line if for nothing else." Like Mixter, Peek, too, tried to allay Butterworth's fear of banker negativism: "When I was in St. Louis I attended a luncheon.... All of the St. Louis men were presidents of banks there . . . two of them asked me what we were doing with tractors, and if I read their minds correctly, thought most favorably of the business and its future.... I mention this as showing that the business is not frowned upon."

Both tractor and cultivator experimentation continued over the next year, despite the fact that the company was now deeply immersed in war work. In September 1917, Dain concluded that his version of the tractor was good enough to warrant a small production run, and he came to the board in its meeting of September 12 seeking authorization to build a hundred tractors. The resolution passed unanimously, with no overt opposition from Butterworth.

Two months later, Joseph Dain suddenly died (having caught pneumonia on a field trip to North Dakota) and the whole experimental effort seemed up in the air. At this point, W.L. Velie stepped back into the picture. In one of the more assertive of his many noteworthy letters, written again with separately typed originals to each individual member of the board, he first quoted verbatim the resolution of the meeting of March 5, 1912, "to produce a tractor plow . . . at once." Noting that the resolution at that time was unanimous and "concurred in almost unanimously" he reminded the board that five years and ten months had elapsed since the resolution was passed. "We have produced in the period of five years and ten months about a dozen tractors of various designs. . . . Our expenditure in the process has been $250,000 . . . each tractor has cost us about $21,000." He then reminded the board of the aggressive efforts of the Moline Plow Company, the Rock Island Plow Company, and others and warned: "Our position as either tractor or plow manufacturers is not as strong today as when we started." Apparently he felt that he needed buttress for the economics of his argument, so he continued: "The industrial and economic situation known to intelligent observers seems to preclude the necessity of arguing for the horse as against the tractor for plowing and farm operations of the future. I think it is safe to eliminate the horse, the mule, the bull team, and the woman, so far as generally furnishing motive power is concerned." His ending was blunt: "We cannot profitably make as small a number as 100 tractors, and in the process we become competitors of the independent tractor manufacturers, who have been heretofore our 'allies.'... I cannot refrain from remarking that we should build tractors largely and whole-heartedly, or dismiss the tractor matter as inconsequential and immaterial. Our present course is prejudicial and impotent."[6]

THE VELIE TRACTOR

It was an unexpected reaction from Velie since he had begun to manufacture tractors himself! In 1911, Velie had formed the Velie

Engineering Company to make motor trucks. These turned out to be popular vehicles, and the firm blossomed. In 1916 this company was merged with the automobile company as Velie Motors Corporation, and it began making the Velie Biltwel 12-24, a four-cylinder tractor powered by a Velie-built engine. Its weight was 4,500 pounds, and its price at around $1,750 put it in the more expensive range of tractors. In this sense, it would not have been a direct competitor, at least for the short run, of the proposed $700-machine advocated by C.C. Webber. Over the next months, Deere and Velie joined forces at demonstrations and fairs, a three-bottom Deere plow being pulled by the Biltwel (exhibit 8-4). Proposals for a Deere tractor created a potential conflict of interest for W.L. Velie. Over the previous years Velie's motor and truck manufacturing had been clearly separate from all the Deere lines (though Velie marketed some of his automobile production through Deere branch houses, a pattern not used by Charles Deere in 1906, when as president of the short-lived Deere-Clark Motor Car Co. he sold a few "Deere-Clark" automobiles). It is not at all clear how Velie was able to resolve this new conflict in his own mind. Nevertheless, this written evidence demonstrated that he was one of the prime advocates of a Deere tractor—once again opposing William Butterworth on a key management policy issue.

Exhibit 8–4. *The Velie Biltwel tractor teams with a Deere plow in a field competition, ca. 1918 (Deere Archives)*

The acerbic remarks of Velie in his letter of January 1918 did seem to be the final catalyst for action, and a rapidly evolving set of events ensued. At a meeting on January 25 (with W.L. Velie not present), the board discussed alternatives at length. George Mixter and George Peek were absent, on leave in Washington in their wartime jobs. C.D. Velie opened the discussion, advocating "our getting into the tractor business immediately." Floyd Todd had just returned from North Dakota and while there had talked to a number of dealers. His report was upsetting: "Our situation in the small tool trade—i.e. the horse drawn tool trade, is apparently being jeopardized in the minds of the dealers, particularly by reason of our not being actively engaged in the tractor business." He concluded that he was impressed more than ever with the "real serious-ness of the situation." C.C. Webber followed: "He did not see how we could stay out of the business longer. He had been pretty slow about coming to that conclusion, but it is impairing our business. Mr. Velie has not emphasized it too strongly." W.R. Morgan, the manager of the Harvester Works, was uneasy about the inroads that the Ford Motor Company was making: "I think they will sell thousands of the Ford tractors as soon as they are on the market." Morgan expressed distaste about getting into tractors, but concluded: "If it is coming, and I believe you cannot stop it, we should get into it in some way." Frank Silloway, who now headed sales in George Peek's absence, raised again the question of buying an outside tractor company, rather than generating a tractor from within. Silloway described a promising possibility—he had heard that there was a chance to purchase the tractor plant of the Waterloo Boy, in Waterloo, Iowa. Forthwith, authority was given to Silloway by the board to investigate immediately the Waterloo manufacturer.

DEERE BUYS THE WATERLOO BOY

The Waterloo Gasoline Engine Company was by this time a well-known tractor manufacturer occupying a unique place in early tractor manufacturing. The company was founded in 1895 and had become a substantial manufacturer of stationary gasoline engines before it began to produce its two-cylinder kerosene tractor in 1911.

The precursor of the Waterloo Boy machine was a true breakthrough in tractor history, the famous Froelich tractor of 1892. John Froelich put together an itinerant contract threshing team in 1888, using a J.I. Case straw burner steam tractor and threshing machine. He personally led this firm for about four years, threshing in Iowa and South Dakota, and carrying with him a remarkable knock-down dining and sleeping car for his crew of sixteen men, a precursor of today's modular mobile homes. About 1890 he conceived the notion of using a gasoline engine and purchased a VanDuzen engine, mounting it on a chassis built by an early tractor manufacturer, Robinson Company. By the crop season of 1892 he was ready with this new machine and took it on a fifty-two-day threshing circuit in South Dakota. Some remarkable photographs remain of this field use of the gasoline tractor (exhibit 8-5), considered by the authoritative tractor historian, R.B. Gray, as "probably the first gasoline tractor of record that was an operating success."

Exhibit 8–5. *John Froelich's gas tractor threshing outfit, in its first field trial: "September 30, 1892, Langford, South Dakota at noon . . . on H. Thompson Farm." (Deere Archives).*

Froelich decided to go into full-scale tractor manufacturing, and he joined with a group of Waterloo individuals to form the Waterloo Gasoline Traction Engine Company in early 1893. Four experimental versions of his tractor were built that year, and two of them were sold. Both were returned, and so disappointing was this that the management decided to move into stationary gasoline engines. This endeavor, too, was not particularly successful and the owners sold out to a new group, who then formed the Waterloo Gasoline Engine Company—the company Deere purchased in 1918.

Silloway was back to the board within a few weeks with a comprehensive report on the Waterloo Gasoline Engine Company. By 1918, the firm had a fine manufacturing facility in Waterloo, "filled with up-to-date machinery." The company was building two Waterloo Boy tractors—its model "R," weighing about 5,240 pounds and selling to the farmer for $985, and the model "N," weighing 5,930 pounds and selling for $1,150. The latter differed from the former in the fact that it had two speeds (2⅓ and 3 miles per hour). The production of the company, Silloway reported, had been 4,558 tractors in 1917, up from 2,762 the previous year. (Actual production of tractors in 1917 was 4,007, according to later figures in the Deere & Company manufacturing report of 1921.) In addition to the tractor, the company continued to make its well-known small gasoline engine, also called the Waterloo Boy. The tractors of 1918 were, like their predecessors, kerosene burning, and had a two-cylinder motor. Silloway enumerated the reasons why it had two, rather than four, cylinders:

1st A two cylinder tractor can be built cheaper than a four and price is an important factor, because the tractor is a business machine and must win by its economy.

2nd The tractor, unlike the automobile, must pull hard all the time. The bearing must be adjusted for wear. There are half as many bearings to adjust on a two cylinder tractor and half as many valves to grind.

3rd There are less parts to get out of order and cause delay.

4th The bearings are more accessible on a two cylinder horizontal engine than a four cylinder vertical engine.

5th Two cylinder engines will burn kerosene better than four.

6th Four cylinders are not necessary on tractors. The fact that a tractor is geared 50 to 1 instead of 4 to 1 eliminates all jerky motion. The engine of a tractor can be made heavy and have a heavy fly wheel and can be mounted on a strong rigid frame. Therefore, a two cylinder engine is satisfactory in a tractor and when it is, why go to the four cylinder type.

We must remember Silloway's reasoning, for Deere stayed with a two-cylinder engine until 1960.

There was no doubt about Silloway's enthusiasm: "I believe that, quality and price considered, it is the best commercial tractor on the market today. The only real competitor it has is the I.H.C." Silloway expressed in words what most of the Deere executives apparently felt: "The Waterloo tractor is of a type which the average farmer can buy.... We should have a satisfactory tractor at a popular price, and not a high-priced tractor built for the few." His recommendation was unequivocal: "Here we have an opportunity to, overnight, step into practically first place in the tractor business. . . . I believe that we would be acting wisely if we purchased this plant."

The board still found it hard to be so bold, and decided to hold the matter over for a day, to discuss it again at a second meeting. When Waterloo's president called to say that unless the option Deere held was exercised by that day (March 14), the deal would be off, Silloway moved to buy, "in order that Deere & Company might run no chances of losing the opportunity of purchasing this plant." The resolution passed unanimously. For a sum of $2,350,000 Deere & Company was now the owner of the Waterloo Gasoline Engine Company.

Exhibit 8–6. Left, *Waterloo Boy advertisement published a few weeks before the Deere purchase (*Farm Implement News, *January 10, 1918); right, Waterloo boy tractor at work in threshing, ca. 1919. (Deere Archives).*

The 100 Dain tractors contracted for in 1917 were built in 1919 in East Moline and sent to the Huron, South Dakota, territory. But the Waterloo Boy purchase doomed the Dain tractor, for the latter was higher priced, took considerable time to tool up for manufacture, and, all things considered, was no more advanced than its Waterloo rival. The Waterloo Boy purchase was an enormous step for the company, and initially there were misgivings by some about its wisdom. Though Butterworth voted in favor of the purchase, he remained "just a little bit doubtful about the wisdom," as Silloway put it in a letter to George Mixter a few days after the vote of 1918. Silloway admitted to Mixter that he, too, had not been enthusiastic about getting into tractors, particularly during a wartime economy, until he saw the Waterloo properties. Their quality, and the high acceptability of the Waterloo Boy product, convinced him that the sale was right. "If we did not buy the Waterloo factory we would no doubt continue to spend money on the Dain tractor, and it would be three or four years, perhaps more, before we could get a profitably operating tractor organization together." C.D. Velie tried to reassure Butterworth: "For your own peace of mind, I want to say that the Waterloo business is being looked after very closely by Webber and myself here, and by Mr. Silloway and others at Moline.... I am more than satisfied we have made the best move Deere & Company has ever made, and that it was an extremely fortunate thing we were able to buy this plant. I believe if we handle this proposition right, the Waterloo Boy will be to the tractor trade what the Ford car is to the automobile trade. Of course the Ford tractor will take first place, but if we can take second place that will be good enough for us."[7]

THE SHADOW OF HENRY FORD

Silloway here was expressing the concerns of the entire industry when he referred apprehensively to Henry Ford. Mechanically powered farm vehicles had interested Ford for many years. He had begun as a steam-engine mechanic back in the early 1880s and while on his father's farm even developed a crude self-propelled steam engine for his own use. Soon the gasoline engine began to preoccupy him, but by 1908 he again was toying with tractors, with a notion of adapting his model T Ford for use as a tractor. He even applied for some minor tractor patents in 1910.

The automobile took the lion's share of Ford's interest, though, and while he continued his experimentation with the tractor for several years, it was not until 1915 that he announced his entrance into the tractor field. Ford had been at the Winnipeg plowing trials in 1910, and he had seen the behemoths of that era bog themselves down in the mud. The announcement in 1915 for the new Fordson tractor trumpeted a light tractor to pull a two-plow bottom, to be priced at the incredibly low figure of $200. Indeed, a year later Henry Ford vowed that he would make a Ford car, a Ford truck, and a Fordson tractor and sell all three for $600, adding: "I am going to do it, if I don't croak first." (Henry had had to use the name Fordson for the tractor because a Minneapolis group had already incorporated as the Ford Tractor Company.) A few Fordsons were built in 1917, but it was not until April 1918 that the first domestic production model came off the assembly line. Ford gave it to his old friend, Luther Burbank. At $750, the price was a bit over Ford's original estimate, but the model was nevertheless an instantaneous success. A total of 34,167 was sold in 1918 (with an additional 57,000 in 1919 and 67,000 in 1920).

Deere's plow department and Silloway as head of sales were enthusiastic about the Waterloo Boy addition, for it meant a ready tie-in with plow sales (the existing dealer network was to be used for marketing the Waterloo Boy). Still, only 4,000 or so Waterloo Boys were sold in 1917. (Sales rose in 1918 to 5,634 but declined in 1919 to 4,015). But the Fordson tractor—ah, there was a market for Silloway! If he could get a Deere plow behind even a portion of those tractors, the market potential would be very great indeed. This presupposed that Henry Ford was going to eschew the production of plows themselves (and Ford did make this plain almost from the start).

In early 1918, H.B. Dineen, the manager of John Deere Plow Works, turned a substantial portion of his development work toward the production of a new two-bottom tractor plow, stronger and lighter in weight than previous models, to be made especially for small tractors like the Fordson. (Deere was making a two-bottom tractor plow during this time, but its major emphasis was on three-bottom and larger sizes, the Waterloo Boy taking a three-bottom size). Dineen was optimistic about the possibilities with Ford and wrote George Peek: "We feel that our plows will be so appealing that they may have some influence on the decision of the Ford people as to whether or not they are going to sell plows with their tractors." Threatening news came back from the field all through the early months of 1918, however, that the Fordson tractors being shown at demonstrations were all pulling Oliver plows. Some Oliver dealers were even advertising "Plowing Partner for the Fordson."

In late March, Dineen was successful in getting a personal conference with Henry Ford, who was accompanied by his son Edsel, Charles Sorenson, and other executives. Ford told Dineen that "frankly he does not want to sell implements," that they should be made and sold by the present implement people. Theo Brown was with Dineen, and he commented: "He is a very simple man." Ford told Dineen and Brown of his efforts to help England with its own agricultural problems; he had agreed to send some Fordson tractors there. Ford related that he told Lord Northcliffe: "I don't care a damn about your old war in England but I want to help put English agriculture on its feet." More importantly, Ford appeared impressed with the Deere plow, particularly because it weighed only 410 pounds against the Oliver's 590. "Ford is very keen on lightness," Brown ended.

Out of this meeting came an agreement to send a set of Deere plows to Detroit immediately. Silloway was lyrical: "The chances are we should build and sell fifteen to twenty thousand Ford tractor plows a year. I do not mean by that that we will start off that strong, or go wild or anything like that, but we should sell that many plows, or more." Still, no one was yet quite sure just how the Fordson tractor would perform, and it was not clear whether a retooling effort would be profitable for the company. C.D. Velie questioned whether the Fordson was as powerful as Ford was billing it and wrote Peek: "I do not believe that Ford with the machinery he is building has enough traction to pull plows under difficult conditions— and if he tries to run that tractor of his pulling three plows at 3¹⁄₁₀ miles per hour, I think his traction will prove entirely unsatisfactory.... I hope he is not in that class. If he can do as much work per day pulling two plows and running faster than the rest of us, as we can pulling three bottoms at a lower speed, he will indeed be a dangerous competitor."

Brown and Dineen went back to Dearborn, Michigan, in May and again in June, each time spending substantial time personally with Henry Ford. Ford jokingly threatened that he might build his own tractor factory in Moline, but at the same time he reaffirmed that he had no plans for manufacturing plows himself. It would not be necessary for his distributors to handle implements, Ford continued, but most of them probably would want to and "Ford will not stop him." Brown reported back that the Deere plow had made a hit with Henry Ford; the plow was lighter than the Oliver ("A girl was able to take hold of the rear brace and lift the plow around"), the high grade steel allowed a higher speed, rivets were used almost exclusively ("not true of the Oliver"), and there were only about half as many parts on the Deere plow as on the Oliver. "Mr. Ford likes success, but won't look at a failure.... My impression is that excuses don't go with him."

The National Tractor Demonstrations were coming up at Salina, Kansas, in late July, and Deere had more than eighty people on hand when the show began. Henry Ford had promised to come and Brown and Dineen waited at the train station at the appointed hour. The Ford tractor company brought only a small contingent, who disembarked from the center of the train—but no Henry Ford. Theo Brown rushed down to the end of the train and there was Ford, descending by himself. "I suppose the reason being he wished to avoid as much publicity as possible," Brown wrote. Still, one woman reporter did grab Ford before he had a chance to get to the automobile. Ford only said: "I bet a dollar I know what you want," and then jumped into the Deere car. The Ford and Deere contingents were together most of the time at Salina, even having a great baseball game "with real pitching. We were beaten 7 to 6," Brown admitted. Henry Ford again seemed intensely interested in the design of the new Deere plow and said "he would do anything to the tractor to make it adaptable—add lugs or anything else."

During the summer and fall of 1918 Deere executives continued to debate about whether to sell plows directly through the Ford distributors. Only the Oliver and Grand Detour companies were selling direct; all of the plow companies that also manufactured their own tractors had decided against the link-up with Ford. C.C. Webber admonished George Peek against selling the full plow line through any outside distributor, particularly because of Deere's purchase of Waterloo Boy. Still, "a little tractor plow like the one for the Ford tractor is another question, and should be treated and considered entirely separate from the rest of our engine plows.... If we do not make an arrangement with Ford, it may be that we will lose the sale of a lot of plows without doing our agents much good, because so few of our agents handle the Ford tractors that it might be impossible for them to get much of a plow trade for plows to go behind the Ford Tractors." Still Webber was not wholly convinced of the merits of the Fordson tractor: "I don't know but what this whole Ford proposition is a waste of material. I imagine a lot of small farmers will buy Ford tractors and have no right to own them; a lot of special machinery will be manufactured to go behind them, and I think the country would be just as well off from an economic standpoint, or a whole lot better off, without the Ford tractor than with it. It is going to chew up a lot of material, and the implements that are designed to go behind it are going to chew up a lot of materials, and that material might better be used for other purposes if there is going to be a shortage of material."

The question finally came to the board in September 1918 and, after much further discussion, the directors voted against using outside distributors, Ford included. When Brown visited Dearborn in November,

JOHN DEERE IMPLEMENTS FOR THE FORDSON TRACTOR

JOHN DEERE No. 40 PLOW and FORDSON TRACTOR

Photographed in front of birthplace and boyhood home of Henry Ford, Detroit, Michigan.

The "Business End" of the Outfit

Remember, no tractor plowing outfit is better than its plow, just as no knife is better than its blade. The plow is the "business end" of the outfit. It makes the seed beds—the source of your profits. Start right with your Fordson by getting an especially good plow—the John Deere No. 40.

The JOHN DEERE PLOW CO. of St. Louis

ATLANTA   NASHVILLE   NEW ORLEANS   LITTLE ROCK

Exhibit 8–7. *Henry Ford's Fordson tractor partners with Deere's No. 40 plow, ca. 1921 (Deere Archives)*

he again saw Henry Ford, and Ford reproached him: "We had missed the big opportunity in not selling our plows to Fordson distributors." Almost in the same breath, Ford let Brown and his colleagues in on a surprising development—that Ford was going to dispense with their own tractor distributors, beginning the following August, and would no longer recommend any implements.

In spite of this, Ford continued to push Deere to get back into development of a small plow that would be especially adapted for the Fordson. Ford himself said: "We could build a hundred million of them." With this encouragement, Deere began serious development work on such a plow, and in early 1920 was testing the new Number 40 plow. That fall Ford himself approved of the plow and the company began large-scale production, to be available in the 1921 season. When the new catalog came out, the plow appeared in color and the advertisement prominently stated: "Built Expressly for Use with The Fordson." The explicit recognition of the Fordson stayed in the catalog through 1924; after this, the plow was renamed the 40C and the catalogs dropped the Fordson name, now saying only that it was built "for a small tractor."[8]

DEMISE OF THE EXECUTIVE COMMITTEE

The Waterloo Boy purchase acquisition touched off an unanticipated revolt. On May 20, 1918, W.L. Velie sent a terse, three-sentence letter to William Butterworth: "I am under the impression that I am Chairman of the obsolescent Executive Committee of Deere & Company. In this case, please consider this my resignation of such, and as a member of the Committee as well. I will remain a Director of the Company until I shall have disposed of my holdings therein."

The break had been brewing for years, of course, and could not be attributed solely to the Waterloo Boy events. The real issue was the inherently ambiguous relationship between the executive committee and the board of directors, and especially the relationship between the two chairmen. It had probably been a mistake to have two independent, strong-willed individuals heading two crucial management committees whose reponsibilities had not been precisely defined. In today's business life, it is not uncommon to have a chairman of the board of directors and a separate president of the company—one of whom also carries the title "chief executive officer," a designation that clearly identifies the person in charge. Similarly, the executive committee of companies now generally is composed of operating executives, with the chief executive officer typically as chairman.

These concepts were only incompletely understood by Butterworth, Velie, and the others. Their inconsistent approach to the advisory committee back in the first decade of the century had been repeated in a second unintentional duality in the use of the executive committee after the establishment of the modern company in 1911. If these organizational interrelationships were not themselves enough to breed difficulty and misunderstanding, the incumbents in the two posts—William Butterworth and W.L. Velie—seemed destined to have discordant relationships.

Velie's letter of May 20 was acted upon in the board meeting of June 11, and his resignation was unanimously accepted. James C. Duke, the Dallas branch manager (and board member since 1911), offered a tepid resolution that the board "desires to express its regrets" and "takes this opportunity of recording its appreciation of the important service."

Velie's resignation forced the board to face squarely the question of committee structure. At the meeting of June 11, Floyd Todd offered a lengthy resolution, calling attention to the fact that George Peek and Mixter were away on leave in Washington and noting that "it is necessary that there should be more frequent meetings of some executive body of the business." The resolution then called for a new pattern for the board—weekly meetings on the Tuesday of each week. He conjectured that this idea would probably not be a workable one over any length of time, so Todd's resolution also called for a fundamental re-study of the bylaws themselves.

Interesting behind-the-scenes discussions then ensued. The private letters circulating among several of the board members made clear that no one much regretted the demise of the old executive committee. Several people were quite uneasy, however, over the prospect that Butterworth would draw more power into his own hands. George Mixter wrote Todd: "Yesterday Mr. Butterworth took lunch with me and we discussed somewhat the situation developing from the resignation of the Chairman of the Executive Committee. He, as you probably realize, has very little use for the Executive Committee, and it will require some skillful handling on your part to see that the Committee is perpetuated in the proper way." He continued with his own suggested approach: "What is needed in my mind is this—the By-laws and Rules of Procedure of the Executive Committee as they now exist are predicated on the idea that the Chairman of the Executive Committee should be the really active Executive Head of Deere & Company. How this did not work out you fully understand. I believe that the By-laws and Rules of Procedure should be revised so as to perpetuate the Executive Committee with the full power of the Board of Directors, just as it is today, but that the real power should be granted to the Executive Officer. If you will examine the authority granted to George Peek and myself you will find that we have very little real authority, in fact have operated largely on bluff. I do not recall the other authorities given. I suggest that you go over these matters with the above thoughts in mind. I have talked very briefly with George Peek and he agrees with this point of view."

In another letter to George Peek, Mixter was even blunter: "I am very certain that this matter must be handled wisely, or we will wake up without a real Executive Committee, if the ideas of the President are permitted to carry through." Mixter's ire may have been raised in part by an unrelated issue concerning the terms under which Mixter was to be allowed the purchase of some $250,000 of common stock.

Burton Peek was chairman of the board committee charged with drafting the bylaw changes. When the rewritten version came forward to the board in early September, all references to the executive committee

JOHN DEERE PLOW WORKS
MOLINE, ILLINOIS

General-Purpose Walking Plow

Walking Cultivator

Prairie Breaker Walking Plow

Leverless Riding Cultivator

Stag Sulky Plow

Stag Gang Plow

Balanced Frame Riding Cultivator

Low Wheel Riding Cultivator

New Deere Sulky Plow

New Deere Gang Plow

Two-Way Plow

Automatic Riding Cultivator

Walking Gang Plow

Single Row, Parallel Guide Riding Cultivator

Light Tractor Plow

Pedal Guide Disc Cultivator

Light Tractor Disc Plow

Two-Row Cultivator

Big Engine Plow

Exhibit 8–8. *The Deere product line, as pictured in the annual report of 1918 (Deere Archives)*

DEERE & MANSUR WORKS
MOLINE, ILLINOIS

Single-Row, Crank-Driven Cotton
and Corn Planter

Single-Row, Gear-Driven Cotton
and Corn Planter

Pivoted-Frame Lever-Dodge
Disc Cultivator

Rigid-Frame, Foot-Dodge
Disc Cultivator

Two-Row Riding Cotton
and Corn Planter

Single-Row Riding Cotton
and Corn Planter

Alfalfa Cultivator

Pivoted-Frame, Foot-Dodge
Disc Cultivator

Two-Row Corn Planter with
Single Disc Openers

Two-Row Variable Drop
Corn Planter

Two-Lever Disc Harrow

Four-Row Beet and Bean Cultivator

Beet Lifter

Four-Row Beet and
Bean Planter

Flexible Spring-Pressure
Disc Harrow

Tractor Disc Harrow

DAIN MANUFACTURING COMPANY
OTTUMWA, IOWA

Double-Cylinder Hay Loader

Left-Hand Side-Delivery Rake

Single-Cylinder, Windrow
Hay Loader

Rake-Bar Hay Loader

Truss-Frame, Sweep Rake

Power-Lift Rake

VAN BRUNT MANUFACTURING COMPANY
HORICON, WISCONSIN

Fertilizer Grain Drill

Alfalfa, Grass Seed and Hemp Drill

Low-Down Press Drill

MARSEILLES WORKS
EAST MOLINE, ILLINOIS

Manure Spreader

Portable Grain Elevator

Horse-Power Hay Press

Large Motor-Power Hay Press

Small Motor-Power Hay Press

Automatic Hay Stacker

Double-A Frame Hay Stacker

Large Size Single-Disc Grain Drill

Lime and Fertilizer Sower

Hand Corn Sheller

Power Corn Sheller

Inside Cup Grain
Elevator

SYRACUSE CHILLED PLOW COMPANY
SYRACUSE, NEW YORK

Hillside Plow

Combination Plow

Slat Moldboard Chilled Plow

Sloping Landside Chilled Plow

JOHN DEERE HARVESTER WORKS
EAST MOLINE, ILLINOIS

Vertical Lift Mower

Self-Dump Hay Rake

Corn Binder with Power Carrier

Grain Binder with Quick-Turn Tongue Truck

WATERLOO GASOLINE ENGINE COMPANY
WATERLOO, IOWA

Waterloo Boy Model N Kerosene Tractor
12-25 H. P.

Kerosene Engine

Two-Way Chilled Plow   Three-Lever Disc Harrow   Spring-Tooth Harrow   John Deere Spreader

JOHN DEERE WAGON WORKS
MOLINE, ILLINOIS

John Deere Western Wagon   John Deere Wood Wheel Truck

FORT SMITH WAGON COMPANY
FORT SMITH, ARKANSAS

Fort Smith Farm Wagon   Fort Smith Log and Pipe Wagon

RELIANCE BUGGY COMPANY
ST. LOUIS, MISSOURI

Reliance Auto-Seat Buggy   Reliance Auto-Seat Surrey

had been deleted. The notion of a weekly meeting of the board itself was continued in Burton Peek's plan, with a quorum now set for the board itself of just five members (the same quorum that had been in effect for the weekly board meetings). The "regular" meetings of the Board were still to be four times a year; the weekly meetings, however, "shall possess and may exercise all the powers of the Board" during the interim times. In effect, the weekly board meetings acted as a quasi-executive committee, though not constituted as a separate entity from the board itself.

On their face, these changes in the bylaws might be considered merely the minutiae of corporate life, important only to lawyers and other insiders. In truth, this new set of bylaws put in motion a new management style for the company. No longer was there a divided authority, exacerbated in the recent past by the personal animosity between the two executive heads. Now the board was the sole and single managerial authority; its chairman was to be the president if present at the meeting, the ranking vice president if not (as Peek pointed out, Webber, Mixter, and the two Peeks all had equal seniority). This troubled Peek a bit, as he wrote several board members: "No other practical change has suggested itself, perhaps you can think of one." Mixter's belief that a separate executive committee should be established on a formal basis was eschewed; this clearly left the authority firmly fixed in Butterworth's hands. It remained to be seen how he would handle the increased responsibility.[9]

PERSONNEL LOSSES

The war left a legacy of dislocation and tragedy for the company's work force. A total of 1,611 of the approximately 7,500 employees of the company were active members of the armed forces in the conflict, and 37 of these gave their lives.

For the company itself, some of the most significant fallout from the war came from losses in top management. George Mixter and George Peek had gone to Washington soon after the United States entered the war. After the armistice, neither returned. Peek's resignation came first.

High wartime prices persisted beyond the armistice, but employment in the industrial sector was threatened by a postwar economic slump. The War Industries Board had been czar of the country's productive capacity during the conflict, with Peek as the head of its industrial sector and Bernard Baruch as its chairman. As unemployment rose in early 1919, Secretary of Commerce W.C. Redfield persuaded President Wilson to establish a peacetime version of the board that would work with industry on a voluntary basis to establish lower prices on basic commodities. Its name became the Industrial Board, its head was George Peek.

Peek took the new job with enthusiasm, for he had become a convert to the notion of industry-government collaboration. But the fresh effort turned out to be abortive. The Industrial Board lasted only from February to mid-April. After the government's own Railroad Administration would not cooperate on the pricing of purchased steel rails, Wilson pronounced its death knell. Peek and the other members of the board resigned in early May. The board had lasted less than three months! Peek unleashed a parting blast at the "old railroad guard," and Secretary of the Treasury Carter Glass countered that "there is scarcely one accurate assertion or sane deduction in all of Mr. Peek's intemperate screed." Despite considerable industry support of what was essentially a price-fixing thrust, few people seemed to mourn the Industrial Board, and the whole effort at managed postwar reconversion went astray.

Peek had resigned his position as vice president at Deere & Company to take the job as head of the Industrial Board. After its demise, he returned to Moline, where people assumed that he would come back to Deere. Though Peek had also resigned his directorship, his fellow directors had not filled his post, and it would have been relatively simple to reappoint him. Much to the surprise of a great many people, Peek not only did not return to Deere but chose to join one of the company's great rivals—the Moline Plow Company. John N. Willys, the automobile magnate, had purchased the Moline company by this time, and he was aggressively diversifying it. Peek was brought aboard as president of the expanded firm. At this point Peek sold all of his Deere stock, thus severing completely a relationship that had been very intense both for him and for Deere.

Deere's loss of Peek, serious enough in itself, was followed almost immediately by another. George Mixter tendered his resignation to accept a job as vice president and general manager of the Pierce Arrow Company (he later became president). Mixter, as a lieutenant colonel in the army, had directed aircraft procurement for the government. Late in the war he became embroiled in a conflict-of-interest case—he was holding twenty-five shares in Curtis Wright Corporation, one of the aircraft companies with which he was dealing. Exonerated from the accusation, he received in the process a personal letter of confidence from President Wilson. When Mixter returned to Moline, he was banqueted by the Deere foremen, most of whom hoped he would come back to the company as their head of production. The automobile company outbid Deere, however, and the company lost a second key individual. Mixter did keep his titular position as vice president of the company for several years, as well as his position as director. Nevertheless, the manufacturing operations of the company were no longer under Mixter's strong hand.

In October 1919, Harold Dineen, the manager of Deere's plow factories, also left the company to join the Moline Plow Company. George Mixter commented about it to Theo Brown: "Deere & Company did a rotten job in diplomacy in letting Dineen get away," and to some this seemed to be portent of a wholesale exodus. But fortunately for the company, it was the last personnel loss in top management during this period. A number of new executive positions were created out of these three significant losses. Leon Clausen and Charles Deere Wiman, the nephew of Charles Deere, had been elected to the board in March 1919 (with Clausen now heading all of manufacturing in the position formerly held by Mixter, and Wiman soon after taking a major role at Union Malleable). Other men also moved up the executive ladder, filling positions vacated by the promotions and resignations.

The loss of Peek and Mixter marked the end of a decade of significant change in which each had played an important role. The modern company had been formed out of a complicated and stressful legal and organizational process. Peek and Mixter had been given major roles in this development and had taken strong positions in the discussions of organizational structure, manufacturing, and marketing policy, and the overall financial posture of the firm. Later in the decade, as the philosophy of management was refined under Butterworth's leadership, Peek and Mixter had often joined with C.C. Webber to form a faction dedicated to aggressive marketing and management postures and to innovative and entrepreneurial philosophies of executive development. Since C.C. Webber was not a Moline executive, little was left to counterbalance the caution and containment philosophy of Butterworth and Burton Peek.

It would take strong personalities to follow in the footsteps of Peek and Mixter. One of these now came to the fore. The man was Leon Clausen. The event that brought his strong will into high profile was the Waterloo strike.

YEAR 1922 · THIRD NO. · VOL. XXVII

The FURROW

CHAPTER 9

POSTWAR LABOR STRIFE
AND COMPETITION

What! What's that! How much! Two hundred and thirty dollars!
Well, I'll be . . . What'll we do about it!
Do! Why, damn it all—meet him, of course!
We're going to stay in the tractor business. Yes, cut two hundred
and thirty dollars. Both models—yes, both.
And say, listen, make it good! We'll throw in a plow as well!

Alexander Legge, 1922

◁*Cover from Deere's magazine for farmers,* The Furrow *(Deere Archives)*

In September 1918, with the Allied victory drawing near and the back-home production battles about won, Leon Clausen persuaded his colleagues on the Deere board to pass a ringing resolution restating the company's traditional labor relations policy. Its wording was blunt and self-righteous, signaling a hardening of the company's position. The resolution opened with an avowal: "The Company has demonstrated by many of years of experience in (a) the freedom from strikes and other disturbances, (b) the continuance of old employees in the service, (c) the increased earnings and benefits enjoyed by the employees, (d) the improved financial and living conditions of employees that its policy as to relations with its employees, including the individual contract and the straight piece rate method of compensation, is sound and of mutual advantage to both employees and the Company." War, the resolution continued, has created unusual conditions and numerous disturbances, "resulting in change of policies, the establishment of collective bargaining, the introduction of union conditions, and the reduction of output at various places in the United States," but these were transitory. Though many employees around the country might feel that "the new conditions and policies may become nation wide . . . there is apparently no legal or moral reason for Deere & Company making any change in its labor policy at the present time." The company resolved to stand by "our labor policy as existing previous to the war and as covered by the factory manual of 1912 or instructions modifying the same," and it reaffirmed that "the individual contract covering employment will be consistently maintained, carefully observed and its importance generally recognized." The resolution summed up: "In general, the status quo previous to the war will be maintained in our factories." Clausen's words were unequivocal and moralistic. They defended prewar policy as good for the company, good for the workers, and worth perpetuating. At the center was the commitment to the individual contract as integral to every other labor relations policy of the company—and as a direct rebuff of unionism.

Despite the bravado of this statement, difficulties in employee relations soon became visible in the company's newest factory, Waterloo. Deere's first year of operating the Waterloo Gasoline Engine Company had been promising—indeed, rosy. Sales in 1918 increased to $5.2 million, with profits of more than $1 million—nearly 20 percent of net income. But the high net income obscured some underlying problems. The secretary-treasurer of the predecessor company, the Reverend J.E. Johnson, and its superintendent, L.W. Witry, had been retained as general manager and works manager, respectively, and as Leon Clausen looked over the manufacturing there, he found slippage in their operations. There was a "lack of aggressive purchasing policy and lack of proper records," and in the factory itself "no fixed factory schedule to which production was tied. . . . The operation of the factory seemed to be to build as many tractors and engines as could be made . . . each day making up items which were short the day before. In other words, the factory was running on shortages rather than according to a schedule." The employees, Clausen noted, seemed "very high" class—"an exceptionally fine body of men, and the very best kind of labor supply from which to draw." Unfortunately, "because of the piece rate inequalities and other things, the relations have not been entirely satisfactory. . . ." Clausen felt optimistic about his ability to turn the situation around: "This will be very largely corrected by individual contract . . . discontinuance of the practice of cutting piece rates, and in addition to this the regular Deere & Company policy as to sick benefit, insurance, pension, death and disability benefit. . . . There is no reason why there should be any labor difficulties at Waterloo."

Clausen's rose-colored glasses soon clouded. Labor relations all over the country were in turmoil as the postwar readjustments took effect. The period just before and during World War I had brought militant campaigns and harsh retribution. Joe Hill, a writer of IWW songs, was convicted and executed for a murder for which his believers felt he was not responsible. A Preparedness Day parade in San Francisco in July 1916 was shattered by a bomb explosion that killed nine marchers and spectators, and Thomas J. Mooney and others were convicted, again with evidence that was not completely satisfactory (though Mooney was an avowed radical who had been tried and acquitted for previous dynamitings).

These and other cases led to angry, sometimes hysterical attacks on radical movements, particularly the IWW. After American entry into the war, the IWW was sued under criminal syndicalist statutes in several states and subjected to extralegal harassments. At the end of the war it seemed that the stress would subside, but in April 1919 sixteen packages containing bombs were seized at the New York post office and other bombings around the country soon followed. The campaign against the IWW was renewed with a vengeance, including deportation of its members.

Minneapolis was one of the IWW bastions, and C.C. Webber and C.D. Velie were both upset by it. Velie wrote George Peek in February 1919: "The unions will have to do one of two things, either get rid of the Socialists, Non-Partisans and Bolshevicki . . . or they go down and out. . . . If poisoned by the Bolshevicki . . . the patient will not survive."

It was not just the radical fringe of unionism that was in turmoil. In Seattle a metal-trades strike in January 1919 was augmented a few days later by a sympathy general strike among employees in the area that brought out more than 60,000 employees. There was a general strike in Winnipeg, Canada, in May of that year, a police strike in Boston in September, and a longshoremen's strike in New York City in October. All through this period, too, there was a great uproar in the coal fields (which also resulted in a strike in late 1919). George Peek, in his first public utterance as president of the Moline Plow Company, chose to emphasize the links between all of these, calling them "a conspiracy to substitute internationalism and anarchy for Americanism."

For Deere and its fellow competitors in the farm equipment industry, far and away the most important labor relations story in this period was unfolding at the International Harvester Company. Harvester had adopted a new device as the centerpiece of its labor relations—the "works council."

The concept of an internal works council had been initiated by a few companies shortly after the turn of the century as a way to forestall unionism. It had been popularized by the plan of the Colorado Iron and Fuel Company, launched after its bitter strike in 1913–14. In the wartime period, when the National War Labor Board had used its influence to encourage secret-ballot elections for worker representatives, a number of companies had adopted such shop-committee plans, in one form or another, but almost always without participation by outsiders. The American Federation of Labor supported the concept at first, but as the war ended and the councils appeared more and more to pose a threat to the outside union, the AFL turned against it. The AFL convention of 1919 concluded that "company unions are unqualified to represent the interest of workers . . . a delusion and a snare set up by the companies for the express purpose of deluding the workers."

At International Harvester, the Harvester Industrial Council was promulgated without warning to Harvester employees in 1918. Voting on its adoption was held separately at each plant. A number accepted the plan; the three Chicago plants rejected it, charging that the company manipulated the councils in the plants where they were in use. Councils became one of the central issues in the Harvester strike of July 1919, which involved some 11,500 employees in the Chicago factories. By the end of the strike, in October, the employees had returned to work without an outside contract and the works council stood inviolate, to remain as the rallying point for Harvester labor relations for more than a decade.

Given the bitterness and antagonism in the labor movement throughout the United States, it is not surprising that some rancor spilled over to the towns where Deere had factories, such as Waterloo. Not just one, but a whole group of the major employers of the town were struck. It began on July 28, 1919, when some 450 employees at the Iowa Dairy Separator Company walked out after the company had refused to bargain collectively with the representative of the International Association of Machinists (the international organizer that had come to Waterloo for the purpose of organizing "as many companies as possible"). Wages were at stake, too, but the key issue was union recognition. Over the next several days other companies were struck and finally, on July 31, the Waterloo Gasoline Engine Company employees walked out, the largest group in the strike (some 900 machinists out of a total of 1,300 tractor-factory workers).

Eventually, thirteen separate factories were struck, with more than 2,000 employees involved. Though Waterloo was a good deal smaller than Seattle, events had all the elements of a general strike.

J.E. Johnson was the ostensible spokesman for both the Waterloo Gasoline Engine Company and the Manufacturers Association (he was president of the latter), but internal documentation reveals that Leon Clausen was really calling the shots. On August 4, Clausen sent Johnson detailed "suggestions for handling the immediate situation" and a "suggested policy when employees return to work." Clausen bluntly added, "While we have called these 'suggested policies,' it is our wish that you carry them out as closely as possible."

The wording of these two sets of "suggestions" provides an insight into Clausen's thinking. As to the immediate situation, Clausen stated: "We will be active and aggressive through legal means and otherwise in supporting law and order, and securing protection for such of our employees as want to work, and in their constitutional right to come and go without being molested. . . . We will go to all the necessary legal ends to secure this result. On all matters we will use the policy of passive resistance. . . . We will keep our shop open as long as there are any men to work and who want to work, and when that no longer is the case we will station watchmen and wait until such time as there are men who want to work." Clausen was not in favor of strikebreakers: "We will not try to introduce any men from outside, nor to bring any militia in, or anything of this character for the purpose of protecting such outside men." As to any possible demand for arbitration, Clausen noted: "We will not arbitrate matters which are not properly subject to arbitration—for example, we will not arbitrate whether (a) two and two make four, (b) we live or die in business, (c) we shall change our business policy or not. These matters are not subject to arbitration."

In separate instructions covering returning employees, Clausen demanded "kindly, confidential" interviewing of each person, separately, with each asked to sign an individual contract. He advised: "If they are not in sympathy with the spirit of the contract . . . it is better that we do not hire them. . . . The substance of all this is—we believe it is useless to hire men who are not in harmony with our policy. We had better get along with one-half as many men who are in harmony with our policy than have twice as many with at least half of them who are against us."

There was enormous intimidation implicit in face-to-face interviews between an employee (if he wanted to work) and Clausen or some supervisor who was likely even tougher than Clausen. It seems unlikely that Clausen would have been unaware that these meetings were not completely "kindly"—rather, he was using them as a means of insisting on the individual contract.

At the start of the strike, a majority of the foremen of the tractor company also had walked out. Clausen's remarks covered them as well.

"When the foremen return, I think it would be best to reason with them in a kindly way, and if they cannot see the truth about the industrial situation and they favor the union or belong to the union, we cannot very well use them because they would be opposed to our policy. They cannot serve two masters."

The company truly had hardened its opposition to labor organization, its public rhetoric becoming more combative and uncompromising than in George Mixter's period. In part, it was responding to the growing bitterness of labor relations nationally; newspapers were full of scare stories across the country. In part it was responding to a change in Deere labor policy attributable to Clausen himself. He was a strong-willed, tough negotiator, opinionated about unions and dedicated almost religiously to the open shop.

Operating under Clausen's instructions, Johnson and Witry made public a letter they had just mailed to the employees, alleging that the union was trying to force the company to "abandon a business policy which the Waterloo Gasoline Engine Company has had for more than 27 years, and Deere & Company for more than 80 years." The company was being bludgeoned "into an agreement whereby we will deprive the individual employee of one of his most important constitutional rights . . . the right to make his own contract." Bread-and-butter remarks concluded the statement: "It has always been the policy of this Company to pay the highest wages consistent with good business management. . . . This is a matter that can be handled justly only by dealing with each individual employee."

The strike rapidly turned militant. Picket lines were thrown around plants; soon pushing and shoving began. Both the Waterloo Gasoline Engine Company and the Iowa Dairy Separator Company went to court and both obtained injunctions against the union, barring any future picket line imbroglios. Clausen, however, decided to go further and the Waterloo Gasoline Engine Company appeared in court again within a few days, bringing suit against sixteen different members of the union for their alleged effort to break individual employee contracts. The individual contract, which the union called the "yellow dog" contract, had just been given renewed legal sanction in the case of *Hitchman Coal and Coke Company* v. *Mitchell* (1917), in which the Supreme Court upheld enforcement of individual contracts in the coal fields. The amounts asked in the Waterloo case—$25,000 each (a total of $400,000)—startled everyone, and the *Waterloo Courier* called it "one of the most unique suits in the country." The *Chicago Tribune* had picked up the case by this time and drew comparisons between the Waterloo case and the famous Danbury Hatters case, the U.S. Supreme Court decision of 1908 that put extremely severe constraints on any use of the boycott by labor unions, in the process making unions subject to the Sherman Anti-Trust Act.

After about a week, the manufacturers put out another public statement with a new, pointed threat. "To grant the closed shop would be to sound the death knell of their manufacturing plants in the city within six months," the industrialists claimed; to operate on the closed shop principle would "invite failure, bankruptcy and ultimate loss." They brought up the history of the iron-and-steel manufacturing business in Waterloo over the previous two decades, and averred that "the pathway along the trail of the years is strewn with the wreckage of industrial plants." The failure of the grain crop in the summer in the northwestern states and in Canada was carefully noted, "a reason why under the most favorable circumstances, the factories would have to be cautious in their operating program during the next few months." The message was unmistakably clear—the future of the workers' own jobs was at stake.

The next day, Clausen wrote the Reverend J.E. Johnson, warning the Waterloo group to move more cautiously:

"IN THE SHOP: Passive resistance. Do nothing but what we are now doing . . . i.e., do the little work we have to do with the men who come. Load tractors and prepare for inventory in a small way.
OUTSIDE—In a legal way. Do nothing further than we have done. By this I mean—

(a) Do not press damage suit any further just yet. Hold it in suspense. Do not serve on the International Association of Machinists. I think we can get the same effect by making this damage suit local and holding it in suspense than we could by pressing it just now. We want to keep it so we can go ahead or back up as we feel best—and continue getting evidence.

(b) If there are any direct violations of the injunction, or violation of ordinance, believe we should ask the Chief of Police or Sheriff to make two or three more arrests.

(c) On the whole, sit tight. Do not adopt an aggressive attitude. Adopt the position that our legal activities are protective of our rights and the rights of our employees, that whatever legal activities we have begun were made in self defense to establish a place where the other fellow's rights *leave off, and ours begin.*"

Clausen became increasingly doubtful about the other manufacturers' resolve, fearing defections from their united front: "If we can hold all the manufacturers together, without any break, we can maintain our rights and policies successfully without any material injury to anyone." He proposed to them that they all adopt a common set of labor relations policies—his version.

Despite his harsh rhetoric in the strike, Clausen did affirm the necessity for honest mutual interchange between the individual employee and his employer, with frequent employee evaluation and constant monitoring of weekly earnings "to guarantee him a proper annual income." The path for promotions was to be made clear and open to the employee, and any grievances that the employee had should be promptly addressed. Clausen also proposed a surprising procedural device: an appeal board outside of the individual company. The governing board of the Manufacturers Association would be constituted as the appeal board; the employee could bring a fellow employee with him to witness the presentation of his grievance and after a fair hearing the board would render a decision, to which each employer would be bound by previous agreement. Clausen also proposed that the board should "invite at least three prominent, fairminded, disinterested citizens to sit with them in their deliberations." Though it probably did not even need to be stated, Clausen ended: "There should be no representation of organized labor to have anything to do with the case under any consideration." If all of these policies were followed, Clausen vowed, "there is absolutely no excuse for organized labor in this community and we can have a body of liberty loving, red-blooded, American working men and citizens who will be exercising their own rights instead of being under the dictatorship of a few walking delegates." Unexplained was whether the meeting of an employee with such an employer-dominated board could itself be representative.

Clausen sensed continued timidity among his peers and wrote Johnson the next day: "The more I think over our proposition at Waterloo, the more I feel that the other employers need assistance. They are not at all certain of their course. As I watch them in our meetings, I feel they are more or less inexperienced in handling such matters, and they are in doubt as to just which direction they shall turn. They do want to stand together for the right principles, but they are not sure what move to make next. We can give them help on this matter, and if we handle our part successfully, the entire situation at Waterloo will be cleaned up and put on a real basis of stability and permanence." He decided to forward to Johnson a large batch of the Deere individual contracts, and he exhorted Johnson: "It is up to us more or less, to sell the employers under this proposition."

Clausen wanted to be certain of whom he was dealing with on the union side, and he engaged the Thiel Detective Service Co. to investigate the background of the head organizer sent in by the international union. The detective agency sent back a gossipy, irrelevant report: "_____ is a smooth-tongued organizer. He has a strong personality, is considered a very good hypnotist and practices hypnotism at meetings. . . . He is a radical socialist . . . disliked by all labor leaders because of his socialist connections. He is known to run after women, but is very careful about being caught." There is no evidence that Thiel was used after this.

To further bolster the other manufacturers' resolve, Clausen also sent each one of them a copy of a letter he had written in June of that year to Sen. Medill McCormick, decrying some proposed labor legislation being discussed in Congress at that time. Clausen's rhetoric in this letter was patently anti-union: "Apparently the uplifters, college professors, labor agitators, IWW's, socialists and other professional shouters on the labor question think that we can legislate ourselves a living. They are teaching that two and two make six instead of four, and they apparently seem to believe that we can all sit down and get a living by fiat. After these people have had their turn and the public begins to realize the real truth in the situation, people who know something about the question will have their opportunity.... It is very unfortunate that the present administration has been foremost in the propagation of unsound economic principles of this character, and particularly the forwarding of collective bargaining and other 'isms' which cannot but result in soviet government if they are carried to a logical conclusion. Anyone who has really had some experience with collective bargaining in industry knows that it means gradual assumption of the control and of the profits until there is nothing left to divide."

As the strike dragged on during the weeks of August, violence began to mount. One morning, a group of strikers boarded a streetcar and threw off a number of the employees of the Waterloo Gasoline Engine Company who were going to work, dumping one of them into a creek. Court cases involving assault then began to be processed; in the first of these, the defendant was declared innocent, but there was an unbroken string of guilty verdicts after that. On August 18, the sheriff appointed one thousand additional deputies to maintain order. A few days later the sheriff reported to Johnson "that certain men thought it would be a fine thing to see a bon-fire made of the plants of the Waterloo Gasoline Engine Co. and the Iowa Dairy." Witry wrote Clausen: "It was the judgment of the Sheriff that we should immediately double our night watchmen, that these men should be armed and instructed to shoot any men that were prowling around at night."

Late in August, the strikers asked Gov. W.N. Harding of Iowa to appoint a board of arbitration, under provisions of a state law providing for independent arbitration. The governor promptly complied and requested each of the parties to appoint a representative. The law did not require that any party be forced to participate, and Clausen decided that the Waterloo Gasoline Engine Company would refuse. Witry wrote a long letter to Harding explaining the reasons for the refusal. He first reminded Harding of the depressed condition of the industry, then enumerated the activities of the "professionally paid agitators" that had come to Waterloo "in accordance with a prearranged plan." The demands put forth to the company by the employee group came from "a committee obviously not representing all employees and who were selected apparently from and by a comparatively small portion of the more radical element." Their demands, if they were to be granted, "mean the gradual confiscation of our business." Witry recited again the concept of the individual employee contract and inasmuch as "these men have been induced to break these contracts, we submit that whether our employees have the right to disregard their contract obligations with us does not present a fit subject for arbitration."

Gov. Harding decided to go ahead with the arbitration nonetheless and appointed two public members. Though Iowa law did not include a compulsory provision, the board of arbitration decided to release its findings to the public. They were directed specifically at the Waterloo Gasoline Engine Company. The results were very unsettling to Deere.

The three arbitrators commended the employees appearing before the board as exhibiting "most favorable impressions." The praise continued: "There is manifest in Waterloo no dictatorial spirit, no rule or ruin tendency on the part of the workmen." Further, "it was made clear to the Board that the closed shop is not and has not been an issue in this controversy.... The cause of the strike, from the evidence submitted, seems wholly due to grievances that should have had sympathetic consideration on the part of the employer.... It seems difficult to escape the conclusion that the policy of this employer in the management of its men was adopted in utter disregard of the development of that degree of efficiency and service supposed to be absolutely essential to good results or workable relationship." The local paper added its own "summary" of the testimony—that wages were arbitrarily cut in order to maintain a fixed wage, and that "thru the 'stop watch' system inaugurated when the John Deere people first took over the Waterloo Gas Engine factory, the initiative to turn out a large volume of first class work was denied the skilled workmen." This latter allegation was a particularly galling one to Clausen; in his report to the Deere board for the previous year he had explicitly noted the need to correct a number of past abuses of time-and-motion study techniques. Now Deere itself was being blamed for these earlier misapplications.

Right after the public announcement by the arbitration board, there was a threat that "a bunch of men next week carrying suitcases . . . would apply as employees with the purpose of getting onto the inside of these factories and a little later blowing up certain factories and certain residences in the city." But there was to be no further tumult, nor did the arbitration report have any discernible effect. By early October more than 100 of the Waterloo Gas Engine Company's employees had returned; the number was up to 224 on the last day of the month, to 366 ten days later. The organizers stayed in the area for several more weeks, trying to keep the strike alive, but to no avail. On December 14, Witry noted that "very few meetings have been held at the labor temple owing . . . to the inability to secure coal for heating the building." The strike was over.

After the strike, A.H. Head was sent from Moline by Clausen to become the new works manager. The Waterloo Gasoline Engine Company closed its fiscal year ending October 21, 1919, with total sales of $5.1 million and a net profit of just under $200,000, not nearly as good as the previous year when profits were five times as great, but tolerable for a company that had taken a three-month strike. "A very large demand for tractors" was expected in the upcoming year, and Clausen's report stressed the need for regularized production and upgraded quality standards. (Some slipshod tractors had been sent out into the field from time to time under the previous management.)

With the strike behind him, Clausen decided to publish a pamphlet titled "Americanism in Industry" and to distribute it to all employees. The preface trumpeted that it was "to point out the truth" and Clausen exhorted the employees to "read it carefully." Manufacturing had developed over the previous century "largely due to the mental efforts of a comparatively small number of men with marked ability along inventive and organizing lines," but certain "forces" were at work "to stifle and strangle" the country's companies. "They place barriers in the path of the American boy" in selecting a trade and "strive to suppress individuality . . . kill initiative . . . and hold all men to the level of the poorest." The last section, titled "The Answer," made a ringing case for "free, untrammeled use of ambition" and concluded with a "statement of rights," with the right of individual contract prominent. To make the matter unambiguously clear, the pamphlet contained an appendix with eighteen separately listed reasons why the individual contract was advantageous for the employee. The message was unmistakable.

Clausen's policies coincided with a national campaign for the "American Plan," a concerted effort by manufacturers' associations around the country for the open shop. In October 1920, the Tri-City Manufacturers Association, with William Butterworth chairing the session as president of the association, passed a resolution endorsing it.

The Waterloo strike had been the most serious employee-relations strife Deere had ever experienced, and it resulted in a decline in earnings. Yet the company ended this difficult period with the individual contract uncompromisingly intact as company policy, and with its administration firmly in the hands of Leon Clausen. Though there was little disagreement about these basic policies among the rest of management, there was beginning to be considerable restiveness about the aggressiveness and hardness of Clausen's application of them.[1]

THE FTC INVESTIGATION

On May 4, 1920, the Federal Trade Commission released a long-awaited major study of the farm implement industry. No one had any illusions that there had not been "high prices" all through the economy during 1917 and 1918, when the nation was at war—the ballooning cost of living in that period had threatened to engulf just about everyone's income. It was inevitable that this would bring widespread demands for the government to "do something."

The farmers, for example, felt they were awash in high input prices, especially those of farm implements, and brought pressures for relief. Congress responded in May 1918 by ordering a Federal Trade Commission investigation. The FTC was not only to study prices, but was also directed to "investigate and report the facts relative to the existence of any unfair methods of trade or competition by manufacturers and dealers," who might be banding together in "combination, agreement, or conspiracy to restrict, to depress or control the prices, production or supply of . . . agricultural implements and machinery of every kind and description." The FTC was also to decide whether the farmers were being "prevented from making a fair profit for their labor and money extended toward production." It was an open-ended charge.

The findings of the two-year study—the famous *Report of the Federal Trade Commission on the Causes of High Prices of Farm Implements*— gave the public an unprecedented view of the industry, and in the process it put the spotlight on numerous intercompany relationships that had characterized the industry over the previous decade or so. The commission devoted a full chapter to the International Harvester Company itself, focusing particularly on the dissolution proceedings that had evolved from the court decision of 1918 against the industry's most important firm.

The industry already had had some frustrating experiences with the Federal Trade Commission. The manufacturers had been sharing highly detailed cost information since about 1914, when the National Implement and Vehicle Association established within its framework a "cost bureau." The association had been a major force in pushing for uniform accounting systems that would not only be more useful to the individual manufacturers (some of whom had rather slipshod accounting practices up to this time), but that would also facilitate the sharing of information among all the members of the association.

Yet these same manufacturers who could cooperate on pricing and labor matters were also bitter competitive rivals. Thus they had insisted that an inviolate system of confidential coding be used to keep cost information within the walls of the association, and the latter assiduously maintained these proprietary confidences.

At first, the FTC seemed to countenance such cost comparisons in industry, even putting out a pamphlet on "Fundaments of a Cost System for Manufacturers." But in 1918 the association became increasingly uneasy about the commission's policies and queried it once again. This time the FTC seemed to temporize. When asked point-blank, they allowed that they were not willing "to pass on the legality or illegality" of the studies; it was now to be left to the Department of Justice "whether cost compilation and distribution . . . might be regarded as in any way resulting in an unlawful restraint of trade." Such a lukewarm answer scared the association into dropping the cost sharing. E.W. McCullough, the general manager, wrote Butterworth a few days later: "For now, we cannot even avail ourselves of the Uniform Cost Systems which we have been considering, nor those valuable blanks gotten up for the Wagon Department."

Once the study of prices was initiated, coverage by the implement industry press was quite negative. *Farm Implement News* alluded to an FTC report just done on the shoe and leather industry, accusing the latter of excess profits, and editorially cried: "It would be the irony of fate if the recovery of the trade from its sickly financial status to one of healthy, reasonable earning capacity is made the basis of a charge of profiteering."

But this was exactly what happened. When the report came out in May 1920, the worst fears of the industry were realized. Laid on the public record was an amazingly complete and embarrassing documention of industry practices; prices and costs of individual manufacturers, enumerated for some twenty-three different farm machinery product families, were chronicled. Detailed aggregated figures were also laid on the record on the profits of manufacturers. Extensive sections were devoted to the manufacturers' associations, focusing particularly on the price implications of shared cost data. The Bureau of Corporations report of 1915 on the farm machinery trade associations already had treated harshly the sharing of costs as a price-fixing mechanism: "The meeting of competitors to compare and discuss costs as basis for prices is . . . particularly susceptible of being used as a cloak for conferences to make agreements on price." Now the earlier cost-sharing efforts of the association again were denigrated, resurrecting memories of the flip-flop by the commission just a few months before.

But serious as the charges about the cost data were, they were only the start. The cornerstone of the allegations by the FTC was that manufacturers had worked together in multifarious ways to bring about "concerted price advances and in maintaining prices." The report enumerated a list of activities—there had been price-comparison meetings, cost-comparison meetings, terms meetings, standardization meetings. There had been exchange by mail of price tabulations in parallel columns, letters sharing information on recent advances and contemplated advances, and sellers urging low-price members to increase their prices. Field personnel were accused of spying on their fellow competitors and complaining that they were not "keeping faith." This was a potent litany of slips, imputed both to the National Implement and Vehicle Association and individual manufacturers. The report's documentation made quite persuasive the FTC allegations of concerted activity by the manufacturers in regard to price.

The FTC figures on individual company costs were tantalizing, for they were coded and thus put out of reach any exact knowledge about competitor standings. Not until several years later, when the government brought International Harvester back into court, were lawyers for the government able to subpoena the data from the FTC report and use it as the basis for the famous decision of 1927. The government lawyers admitted that these sensitive figures originally had been given "in camera," but nevertheless they broke the code for many of the tables, especially those relating to harvesting equipment. Deere was able to find out how it had compared, name by name, with the others during the wartime period.

Perspective on just how dominant International Harvester had become in the industry can be obtained from Appendix exhibit 15. The leading five companies held their exact rankings in total sales throughout the period 1913–18, with International Harvester edging up a bit, Deere sagging somewhat, and two of the remaining three modestly increasing their small shares.

Though the FTC authors did not break down these sales figures by product line, a later report of the U.S. Temporary Economic Commission did so, beginning with the year 1921. As expected, International Harvester dominated harvesting equipment, though not overwhelmingly in some products (Appendix exhibit 16). By 1921, International Harvester had purchased Parlin & Orendorff and the Chattanooga Plow Company and commanded a surprising share of the tillage business, though here Deere competed on a more equal footing (Appendix exhibit 17).

But the most interesting figures to the companies were not market share relationships (these were already widely known), but comparative costs. Appendix exhibit 18 shows the dominant cost advantage of International Harvester in 5-foot mower production. Deere's market position in plows was stronger, and its costs were competitive with those of its rivals. Even here, though, their position worsened over the two time periods, 1916 and 1918, used by the FTC for its study (Appendix exhibit 19).

These comparative cost figures must have been unsettling to Deere, murky as they were in 1920, when one could not tell precisely who the others were on the list. It is difficult to generalize from just two years' data on products that were probably not exactly comparable. Still, it seems clear that International Harvester had substantial competitive advantages in buying materials, attributable in part at least to more adept purchasing. Deere was most competitive on direct labor costs even though its wage rates were as high as competitors, for as George Mixter had told the Bureau of Corporations investigators in the latter's investigation in 1910: "Their [Deere's] labor was speeded up and the high rate was due to the effectiveness of the men, shown in turning out a large number of pieces a day." But the company's selling, general, and administrative costs also seemed considerably above those of its arch competitor. In total, the figures gave the Deere management—particularly those in production and sales—considerable pause.

There was an even more startling conclusion from these figures, for they showed that despite the substantial variance in costs, the prices for most of the products were very close. The 5-foot mower prices of the individual companies were almost exactly the same (Deere, Harvester, and Emerson-Brantingham, for example, were selling their mowers at $65, Massey-Harris at $65.50, and the Moline Plow Company at $66, with B.F. Avery the lowest of the regular manufacturers at $62; the Minnesota State Prison made a similar model that sold for $53). Bunchy prices were the norm in most of the implement product families. In Appendix exhibit 20, taken from the FTC report, the wide range of costs for a whole set of products is evident; the bunching of prices is not quite as pronounced, inasmuch as the figure for the "low" was often that of prison-made equipment. (Incidentally, this was a sensitive subject to the industry; many felt that prison directors priced their goods unusually low, subsidized by minimal prison wage rates).

The heart of the FTC report was its minute analysis of the allegations of price fixing among the manufacturers (and to a lesser extent, among the retail dealers). For some 299 pages, the authors of the report detailed, in chapter and verse, an intricate pattern of interrelationships among manufacturers, most through auspices of the National Implement and Vehicle Association. The commission had subpoenaed the records of the association, its constituent departments, the Southern Wagon Manufacturers' Association, and thirteen manufacturers, Deere & Company included. Dozens and dozens of extracts from letters going back and forth among the manufacturers and the executives of the association were spread over the record, Deere's name appearing prominently throughout. The data under the heading of the plow and tillage implement department concentrated on the period 1915–17 and depicted a wide range of cost and price exchanges. Existing and future prices were shared on a wholesale basis and policing was done to "keep prices in line" (the FTC's words). The Moline Plow Company, for example, wrote the J.I. Case Plow Works in 1916: "You will note from the above that our price compares with Deere on soft-center shares. We are both a good deal higher than you on the same. You will also note there is quite a difference on the crucible shares. We called this comparison to the attention of Deere & Co. a few days ago and they are making an investigation." J.I. Case wrote back: "We have investigated the prices on shares of all the leading competitors . . . and conclude that we will raise our prices. . . . The prices that we propose are very closely in line with Deere and other principal competitors, and the only reason why we cannot get closer in line with you is that you are too far out of line with the rest of us." Deere wrote the Oliver Chilled Plow Works in this same year: "On the plows equipped with steel bottoms you will note that our prices are considerably higher than your prices. . . . However, we will undoubtedly have to make some adjustments downward . . . as we consider the difference between us too large. We are loath to do this, especially in view of the materials situations which have been and are still confronting us."

Often the letters were indiscreet, one letter from J.I. Case Plow Works to the LaCrosse Plow Company in 1917 even stating: "We are very glad to have the opportunity of comparing prices with you, and inasmuch as this is all illegal, suggest that you destroy this letter when you are through with it." A number of letters by George Peek in the year 1915 relating to drill prices were included; they discussed the link between Deere and the International Harvester Company. In September he wrote the Moline Plow Company: "You will remember that we were going to go to Chicago and talk over with the International the prices they propose to make on their Superior drill. Would like to know whether you have done anything in the matter, and if not, whether you do not deem it desirable to consider this question with the International?" In this exchange the Moline Plow Company executive developed an interesting concept: "It is not intended by this suggestion to indicate our desire to agree on prices, but to agree that the ratio between various sizes and styles of drills shall be logical and conform measurably to comparative costs." The FTC report's authors were vocally skeptical of this and commented: "The difference between agreeing on prices and agreeing 'that the ratio between various sizes and styles of drills shall be logical and conform measurably to comparative costs' is not explained."

The smaller manufacturers were not keen about this kind of exchange between the two largest companies; F.H. Clausen, the factory manager of the Van Brunt Manufacturing Company, wrote Peek: "Apparently the smaller manufacturers think that the International and Deere have been trying to put one over on them in this matter. The thing to do is to cheer them up as much as possible and indicate to them the advisability of advancing their prices at least as large a percent as others are doing."

Extensive testimony was also introduced on price concert in farm wagons, with E.E. Parsonage, the manager of the John Deere Wagon Company (and also president of the farm wagon department of the association) figuring prominently. The emphasis here was particularly on the need for standardization. Floyd Todd testified to the commission: "The National Association attempted to apply a much-needed remedy. Its efforts were directed to securing the standardization of styles and a proper appreciation of costs. The determination of prices to the trade was not attempted." Parsonage reiterated this belief, being quoted in the report as holding that every manufacturer should "act independently and quickly in order to secure a fair rate on his investment and labors without looking too much at what the other fellow is doing in the matter of prices, terms, etc." Numerous exchanges among tractor manufacturers, ensilage manufacturers, and others were also recorded. In total, the report seemed to document beyond doubt that there was price exchange among the manufacturers.

The findings seemed foreordained, and when the report was made public, the FTC commissioners did indeed find that the farm implement manufacturers and dealers "by concerted action" had advanced prices in 1917 and 1918 by amounts that were "larger than were warranted by the increase in their costs and expenses," with the result of "unusually large profits." Nevertheless, "the farmers were not prevented from making as much profit as before because the prices of farm products increased to an even greater extent." Despite this, the commissioners advocated that judicial proceedings be instituted "against associations who have been active in restraining trade" in the industry. Further, they were not satisfied with the consent decree that the government lawyers had negotiated with International Harvester, and they demanded that the case be reopened in order that a new plan could be developed "that will restore competitive conditions in the harvesting-machine business."

The FTC report was a blockbuster, received with outraged disbelief by the implement trade. Already there had been many fulminations at the start of the inquiry. When Senator Thompson of Kansas proposed the price inquiry, *Farm Implement News* railed: "The sweeping investigations proposed by the Thompson resolution, if done thoroughly and with justice to all concerned, would cost the government millions of dollars and three or four years of work by the Federal Trade Commission. The government has neither money nor time to waste in these days. . . ." Once the report itself was out, it was bitterly challenged by the trade press, and the motives of the commission staff were questioned. *Farm Implement News* quoted E.W. McCullough, one-time secretary of the National Implement and Vehicle Association and later with the Chamber of Commerce of the United States, on "the revelations that could be made of the tactics employed by some of the Commission's agents and examiners who were sent into the field to secure evidence in the investigation. It is hinted that . . . the confidence of certain implement tradesmen was abused by these sleuths. Sufficient for the time being to say that the agents were manifestly imbued in many instances with a feeling that they were detectives on a hot trail and they must 'detect,' come what might."

McCullough further castigated the FTC for the extensive verbatim quotations used in the report: "It was this disguised zeal perhaps that prompted the trade commission's agents to muster as evidence sentences from letters and fragments of correspondence which, when isolated, convey an impression totally at variance with the intent disclosed, if the extracts be considered in their proper environment and with due reference with what preceded and what followed the expressions thus ruthlessly lifted." Some members of the association were upset by the belligerency of McCullough's attack, for he apparently wrote it not as an official of the Chamber of Commerce but as a private citizen. W.H. Stackhouse, the association president, finally was moved to write his executive board: "While I in no wise doubt but that Mr. McCullough was prompted by the most commendable motives, I can readily appreciate the impropriety of any outsider, no matter how well meaning his motives, taking up, without consultation with the officers of this Association, the cudgels in its behalf of attacking the government bureau mentioned." The high profile of the premature McCullough attack had the effect of blunting the association response.

All through the FTC investigation the clever cartoons of editor Charles A. Lukens in *Farm Implement News* had caricatured the agency and assiduously defended industry practice. One of his cover cartoons paraphrased the name of the report as Federal ("Farcical") Trade ("Tortuous") Commission ("Calumnious") Report ("Ridiculous") On ("Officious") Implement ("Intemperate") Prices ("Preposterous") and cartooned the situation bitingly. Another carried a picture of a dour school teacher, "Our Dear Teacher," who was the Federal Trade Commission carrying in her hand a switch, "The Report of the Investigation." One boy, "the Farmer," stands in front of her, saying, "It wasn't him, he didn't hurt me"; the other boy, "the Implement Industry," stands contritely in front of the teacher. The teacher responds: "Well, I thought he had when I started to cut those switches so I am going to use them" (exhibit 9-1).

Probably the most widely quoted response to the FTC report by the industry was the speech made by Deere's Burton Peek to the National Implement and Vehicle Association annual convention in October 1920, shortly after the report came out. The speech was reprinted in full in several trade journals and eventually was printed and bound as a pamphlet for wide distribution, not just among the agricultural machinery manufacturers but among all business leaders who felt threatened by the FTC. Peek first argued that the commission had used the wrong profit figures, not "the irreducible minimum, the Net Income." Thus the commission, in Peek's view, had inflated the profits and deflated the capital accounts of the companies studied. Peek quoted a Haskins & Sells report to the National Implement and Vehicle Association that found the average net profit to capital invested for the years of the war, 1914–18, to be 6.51 percent, which was lower than prewar earnings. Peek struck especially hard at the commission's disclosure of industry cost information efforts. Quoting the report authors' own words that the association's members "were advised to go over their costs carefully in determining their future price policies" and "further action regarding prices was left to the individual judgment of the members," Peek asked: "This is the combination, the conspiracy in restraint of trade, against which the Department of Justice is asked to proceed. Could anything be more absurd?" Peek laid down the gauntlet to the U.S. attorney general: "Upon what theory of the law I should like to inquire would the Attorney General proceed?" Peek needled the commission for their indecision about industry cost-accounting and standardization studies, reminding everyone of the commission's reversal of itself on whether these activi-

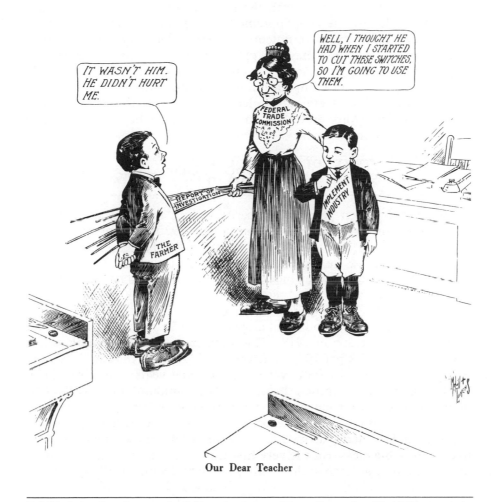

Our Dear Teacher

Exhibit 9–1. *"Our dear teacher" (*Farm Implement News, *September 23, 1920)*

---

ties were proper. Peek averred: "We discontinued, not because we believed in the policies of the succeeding Commission, but because we desired, with a Caesar's-wife rectitude to be above any suspicion of wrongdoing." While Peek maintained that it would be improper for him to make any comment about the International Harvester case, inasmuch as it was still before the courts, he could not resist one parting shot, "however great the breach of propriety." He took issue with the government's efforts to split off International Harvester's two plow companies (Parlin & Orendorff and the Chattanooga Plow Company) into two separate, independent, new competitors for Deere.

Still, despite the report's findings and the ensuing reaction, the industry remained confused about what could and could not be done in discussing costs and prices until the International Harvester Company case was settled by the U.S. Supreme Court in 1927. The court at that time turned away the government case and ruled that "the fact that competitors in business may see proper, in the exercise of their own judgment, to follow the prices of another manufacturer, does not establish any supression of competition, or show any sinister domination." But even this ruling, seemingly a clearcut reversal of the FTC position, was not the last word, prevailing only until 1938, when the FTC again investigated the industry.[2]

THE BUSINESS DEBACLE OF 1920–21

After a half dozen years of prosperity during and immediately after World War I, the economy took a nose dive in 1920. The collapse was so sudden and so severe that thousands of businesses had enormous losses, many being forced into bankruptcy. In agriculture, wholesale prices sagged sharply from the index figure of 148 in 1918 to 88 in 1921(1926=100); the farmers' percent return on total investment, almost 11 percent in 1918, dropped to 2.88 percent in 1920; the farmers' relative share of the national income had dropped to 10.56 percent in 1921 (from more than 21 percent in 1918). The number of farm bankruptcies had skyrocketed to 50.3 per 100,000 farms in 1921 (from 18.8 in 1918), and this trend was accentuated over the next three years, rising to 123 in 1924. All too many farmers had added large amounts of land to their holdings in the wartime period, with expectedly high prices paid all across the country. The rapid deflation after the war, the sag in agricultural prices, and the heavy debt structure of many farmers combined to drive many out of business. For the very first time in the history of the United States, cropping acreage in the country began to decline in 1919. By 1924, 13 million acres had reverted by default to grasslands, scrub brush, and woodland.

The sharpness of the downturn drove many farm implement companies into receivership. After the depression, the National Implement and Vehicle Association compiled a status list of the companies in the industry and found that many well-known company names had disappeared into history. Gone were the Farm Horse Traction Works of Gutenberg, Iowa; the Bulldog Tractor Company of Oshkosh, Wisconsin (also its near-namesake Bull Tractor Company of Minneapolis, Minnesota, and Anderson, Indiana); the Wolverine Tractor Company of Detroit, Michigan. In receivership were the Illinois Tractor Company of Bloomington, Illinois; the Square Turn Tractor Company of Norfolk, Nebraska; the Victory Tractor Company of Greensburg, Indiana; the Four Drive Tractor Company of Big Rapids, Michigan; the Dart Truck and Tractor Corporation of Waterloo, Iowa; and many more. Even the mammoth

General Motors Corporation had lost $33 million on its entrant in the tractor field—the Samson—and had liquidated the entire division. The association's tabulation of the changes in the industry from 1900 listed 60 firms that had sold out or consolidated with other companies, 66 more that had been liquidated, most of them just after World War I, and an additional 22 in receivership—a startling total of 148 firms that had disappeared, and in so short a period of time.

Striking stories in American business history occurred during this period—for example, how Henry Ford weathered the crisis by a ruthless combination of pushing out automobiles on sight-draft to dealers, abruptly cancelling supplier contracts, and laying off both employees and management. It contrasted sharply with the inept efforts of William Durant to resolve this same set of difficulties at the General Motors Corporation. Durant's downfall at General Motors was brought on by a combination of factors, most of them rooted in the lack of centralized coordination and control over the divisions of the corporation. This lack of managerial ability brought the takeover of the General Motors Corporation by outsiders, led by Pierre DuPont and the partners at J.P. Morgan, who then called upon Alfred P. Sloan, Jr., and Donaldson Brown to reconstruct the General Motors management philosophy to its fine-tuned balance between "decentralized operation and coordinated control." Ford's tactics warrant closer examination for they shocked his competitors in the tractor industry, including Deere.

Even as late as April 1920, Frank Silloway was reporting optimistically to the board about the year as being "an extraordinary one . . . sufficiently great so that the capacity of the factories, limited as they will be by the raw material and transportation situations, will be taxed as heavily as their capacity has been taxed this year." A month later, William Butterworth came back from a trip to New York City and interviews with Wall Street bankers with a much more sober view. He reported to the board that "the situation is very extreme." Butterworth "was of the opinion" (his tentativeness here is characteristic) that no additional production of any kind should be contemplated over that already scheduled. A few days later, the board unanimously resolved that the company should not exceed the tonnage produced in the previous year.

In June, and again in September, Butterworth made the same strong representations in board meetings. But it was clear that his exhortations were being ignored by both the branches and the factories. The former had continued to put in additional orders, the latter had continued to purchase raw materials in large quantities and to make these up into whole goods at a pace above that called for by the board. Herbert Copp, the purchasing director (and a company director), reported this again in a November meeting and Butterworth once more exhorted L.H. Clausen and Copp to "give this matter their personal attention and instruct . . . the factories to cancel everything possible in the way of raw material. . . . The factories should take in such material as is absolutely necessary in the operation of the factories on a very conservative basis." But it was just this word, "conservative," that probably put off some of the branch and factory managers. After all, William Butterworth had been conservative on almost every issue over the years.

The orders, purchases, and production continued apace, day after day, and it was not until January 1921 that there was a noticeable pulling back. Lloyd Kennedy, a young financial officer of the company (later the senior financial officer of the the company and the Deere trust), often recounted the apocryphal story of sitting at his window watching railroad car after railroad car filled with steel, stretching from Moline right on back to Chicago—all of them with tags marked "To Deere & Company." The company did have some very large forward commitments for steel from the Republic Steel Company in Chicago, and though Deere was able to halt some of the tail-end orders, much was already in the conduit. When Deere canceled 4,000 tons, Republic then asked the company to share their loss—they had already bought a huge quantity of old rail steel for the Deere order—and Deere did so, paying a substantial penalty.

George Crampton, for one, was outraged by the deliberate intransigence of the factory and branch managers: "This brings up the question who is running this business? Evidently not Mr. Butterworth, who on three different occasions at the most vital period of our history called attention to the situation only to have his ideas ignored. It is also apparent that it is not the Board of Directors, for one of the most important resolutions ever put on the record, that we should not exceed the previous year's tonnage, was violated. It was placed there for the very purpose of preventing a boosting of orders. . . . Yet the Board never had a chance to pass upon the estimates running in excess." Crampton's frustration was manifest: "The answer which has become so frequent of late is the same that was offered in 1914, i.e., that the water had gone over the dam, that it was spilled milk, etc. During this period we have had the opportunity again and again to profit by our experience, but have not done so."

Crampton was second-guessing—the downturn had been so precipitous that everyone had become frightened by its implications and looked for someone to blame. Still, there were profound lessons behind Deere's sluggish managerial process, for once again there was an overriding need for a centralized hand in the situation—the "coordination and control" that Sloan soon built into General Motors. Butterworth's consistent, abiding belief in widely vesting authority in the hands of operating executives had great strengths in building initiative and personal responsibility. Yet, the need for drawing together the multitude of Deere operations was also painfully evident. Losses during the 1920–21 downturn became a stark reminder of the latter.

So, in early 1922, a new committee was once again constituted, this time under the aegis of Butterworth himself, now "very anxious to adopt some plan whereby finished goods inventories may be better controlled and factories operated on a more uniform basis." The plan left in place most of the structure of the previous system—the estimation process, the purchasing policy, and the provision for prompt notification of changes as then occurred all through the crop year. If one gave the report only a cursory look, it seemed just a reaffirmation of the status quo. Yet the 1920–21 experience was so shattering to all concerned that it left a permanent imprint on managerial attitudes, if not immediately on company policies. The unhappy experience of overbuying and overproduction gave new impetus to the need for a more responsive approach by all concerned, though it did not lay to rest all tensions between centralization and decentralization. These issues provide a recurring theme throughout the later years and down to the present time.[3]

DEPRESSION FALLOUT

The effects of the downturn were quickly evident in the company's financial statements. The company had earned $4.6 million in 1920; the downturn caused a loss of $2.8 million in 1921, $2.5 million in 1922. At the annual meeting of October 5, 1921, the directors reduced the dividend on the company's preferred stock from the established rate of 1¾ percent quarterly to ¾ percent quarterly. Though the company made a small profit in 1923 ($1.8 million) and 1924 ($1.9 million), it was not until 1925, when net income rose to $4.5 million, that the directors restored the established dividend and made the first small restitution of the back dividends.

The depression brought significant changes in the company board room. In April 1921, W.L. Velie penned a one-line resignation from the board, stating: "My personal and more important interests under existing conditions will require of me all the thought and effort that I care to expend." Only one Velie was now left in management of the company, Charles Deere Velie, C.C. Webber's colleague in the Minneapolis branch. Dwight Deere Wiman, Charles Wiman's brother, was elected to the board to replace W.L. Velie. Willard Deere Hosford, the eldest son of Schiller Hosford and branch manager at Omaha, was elected to the board in January 1922, and Theo Brown and F.H. Clausen, the manager of Van Brunt, were brought on the board in early 1923. The next year William W. Alexander, the branch manager at St. Louis, and B.J. Kough, the manager of the Plow Works, were also made directors.

Nowhere in the Deere organization, nor in the agricultural machinery industry as a whole, was the effect of the depression more pronounced than in the tractor arena. The future of the Waterloo Boy tractor had appeared bright in 1920, when some 5,045 tractors had been sold. In April the decision had been made to schedule a rate of thirty tractors per day for the last half of the year and forty per day for the first half of 1921. But the heavy capital expenditure for the tractor was just the kind of item a farmer could lay aside in tight times, and this is what happened. Sales fell off by the middle of 1921; production schedules were scaled down to thirty-five per day in July, then twenty-five per day in August, down to twenty per day by September.

On January 27, 1921, Ford made his move in tractors, announcing that his retail factory price of $785 for his stripped Fordson would be cut $165—21 percent. Two small competitors cut their prices immediately, but the rest of the industry hung on, awaiting the March sales figures. When they were announced, it was clear that Ford's action had manhandled the rest of the industry. In early March, International Harvester dropped its tractor prices by 13 to 16⅔ percent to $1,000—still $370 above the Ford price. A week later the rest of the industry followed suit, Deere cutting its prices on March 14. By June a second wave of price reductions came, this time led by other members of the industry— Emerson-Brantingham, Huber, International Harvester. In July the Moline Plow Co. and Deere once again dropped their prices, the latter now selling the Waterloo Boy at $890.

But the irrepressible Ford was not to be outdone. Late in January 1922 he telegraphed every one of his dealers that the factory stripped price of the Fordson was to be a new, low selling price—$395, a full $230 below the already deflated price. Alexander Legge, back at International Harvester as the firm's general manager, exploded: "What? What's that? How much? Two hundred and thirty dollars? Well, I'll be. . . . What'll we do about it? Do? Why, damn it all—meet him, of course! We're going to stay in the tractor business. Yes, cut two hundred and thirty dollars. Both models—yes, both. And say, listen, make it good! We'll throw in a plow as well!" Ford's strategy in his "tractor war" certainly paid off for his company; the production of the Fordsons had a drop in 1921 to just over 35,000 (from 67,000 the previous year), but rose to almost 67,000 in 1922, and hit 101,898 in 1923.

Deere was practically on the ropes. Tractor sales for 1921 had been just 79 tractors, down from 5,045 of the previous year. Orders had plummeted as the spring crop season of 1921 turned sour, and it became necessary not only to lay off employees throughout all the Deere organization, but to cut the salaries of everyone who remained on the rolls (a 10 percent cut for those receiving up to $3,000 a year and additional cuts for those above that salary).

Deere had not changed its tractor for several years; the Model N, the same machine that had been built by the company since the purchase of the Waterloo factory in 1918, now seemed passé. But significant product development had been going on almost from the start, first under L.W. Witry and then others. By 1921 the outlines of a new tractor were in hand.

Exhibit 9–2. *The Model D tractor at work, 1920s (Deere Archives)*

It would be less expensive, selling under $1,000, much closer to those of the main competitors, the International Harvester Company's Titan and the Fordson—"at a price not more than $50 above the Titan and no more per bottom than the Ford."

At this crossroads, Deere faced again the fundamental decision of whether to make a two-cylinder or a four-cylinder tractor. Once more the directors of the parent company came down on the side of the two-cylinder model—it was "simpler, sturdier, and cheaper." But the board must have felt it was "whistling in the dark" just a bit, for the resolution continued: "Having determined upon this policy with relation to the two-cylinder tractor we must adhere to it. . . . We cannot let the rapidly

Exhibit 9–3. *Assembling Model D tractors, August 1924 (Deere Archives)*

changing designs of competitors change us from this course even though they all adopt other types unless field service in the hands of the farmer has actually demonstrated beyond a doubt the superiority of some other type."

The machines were about ready by April 1922, and Leon Clausen came to the board to urge that ten more experimental models of the new tractor needed to be built. Because of the size of the expenditure, he thought it might be wise to discuss again the question of whether the motor should be two- or four-cylinder. C.C. Webber immediately spoke up and argued that the company should continue with the two-cylinder machine "until we have disposed of our present inventory." Webber hardly thought "this was an opportune time to spend any amount of money experimenting with a four-cylinder tractor." Thus the final decision to go ahead with the two-cylinder was made not on technical grounds but on the basis of the short-term embarrassed financial situation.

Sales of the Waterloo tractor factory limped along in 1922, totaling only $780,000 by the end of the year (with losses of more than $430,000). Sales in 1923 were not much better, below $1 million (the loss now down to

$292,000). At this point, a final decision was to be made about phasing out the old Model N and introducing the new tractor, to carry the John Deere name and to be called the Model D. Leon Clausen argued that one thousand of the new tractors should be built in the first year—a very large jump in total production from the three previous years. The tractor price war had continued all through this period, pushed particularly by Henry Ford and joined in by International Harvester. It was a difficult time to take on competition. George Crampton, for one, vehemently opposed the Clausen proposal: "There is great risk in making so many machines the first year, even when tests have been made. Many concerns have gone on the rocks for this reason.... Even if there is a profit, *it is out of all proportion to the risk involved* in putting out so many." Crampton even had reservations about putting out the machine at all: "If a small quantity will not give us now enough for sale then it would perhaps be better not to push the old tractor off the board.... If we had made ten Dain tractors instead of one hundred we would have saved a large sum."

Clausen feared that Crampton's attack could put in jeopardy not just the Model D but the entire tractor operation—there was rampant conservatism on the board at that time—and argued at length for going ahead. "We cannot successfully prosecute our work in the factory unless we know that we have the support of the Board of Directors. We cannot maintain an organization or even a nucleus of an organization of good men unless these men know that they are going to continue in business." He was convinced, he said, that the tractor was "far ahead of anything that has ever been developed for the farmer's use"—it weighed only about two-thirds as much as the Model N but had 40 percent greater drawbar horsepower. It would operate on almost any low-cost fuel (later owners frequently claiming that it would burn "anything that could be poured into its tank"). Parts were simple, repairs could easily be made by the farmer on the spot, its power could pull three 14-inch bottoms in most soils. Further, the machine could be priced competitively with the International Harvester machine of comparable size.

Clausen ended his eloquent plea: "There is a national demand for tractors. We do not have to create it, and when a suitable tractor is built at a reasonable price to the consumer it can be sold.... The farmer can buy a good tractor today for no more than he would pay for a stationary engine of the same horsepower." Clausen personally believed that a company was not really in the tractor business unless it was making from 3,000 to 5,000 tractors. He considered the thousand-tractor goal for the first year as really a minimum.

After heated debate, the board backed Clausen, and the one thousand tractors were built in 1923 and early 1924. The results in the field were almost instantaneous—the machine was a great success from the start. Clausen was vindicated, and the company was in the tractor business for good. There was still a substantial loss in 1924 in the tractor operation,

Exhibit 9–4. *A John Deere dealer's equipment display, ca. late 1920s (Deere Archives)*

but by 1925 it was in the black and the succeeding years saw major growth.

At this point, Leon Clausen left Deere & Company to accept the presidency of the J.I. Case Threshing Machine Company. Clausen had been a strong force with the company, a striking successor to George Mixter, whom he resembled in many ways. Clausen's labor relations policy, however, was heavy-handed and made the company appear dogmatic. William Butterworth and others shared different points of view, and to many people in the company an effort to soften labor relations seemed long overdue. The basic personnel policy of the company had stood it in good stead over the years, and Butterworth now reaffirmed it and signaled a move away from the harshness of the Clausen period.[4]

WERE MACHINERY PRICES TOO HIGH?

One of the results, perhaps an inevitable one, of the decline in the fortunes of the farmer in the early 1920s was a renewed resistance to the prices charged by the agricultural equipment manufacturers. The manufacturers, plagued by high raw material prices, retorted that their prices were realistic and justified. Indeed, a common theme of the manufacturers in the period from 1920 through 1924 was that the farmers were being stirred up by outside agitators to resist prices when prices were in fact quite justified. In 1920, at the beginning of the downturn, Leon Clausen, still head of Deere's manufacturing, wrote to all factory personnel about the "activities of certain socialistic farmers' associations like the Non-Partisan League, or the more or less hysterical press which is searching for headlines." Again in 1923 Deere was quoted in the financial press along the same lines: "The radical politicians of the country continually stir up the farmer and make him feel that he is discriminated against in every way. If it were not for this class of politicians, we believe that the farmers would get into a better frame of mind because they are not as hard up as the politicians try to make us believe." Privately, though, Deere officials were less sanguine about machinery prices, William Butterworth writing Samuel R. McKelvie, the governor of Nebraska, in late 1922: "As you say, the prices of farm products are out of line with prices of other things. . . . Agricultural implements, for instance, are higher than they should be, but prices which are named by the industry are very close and are based on the cost of production."[5]

The trade associations were concerned enough about sales resistance among farmers to mount major publicity campaigns detailing manufacturer costs and profitability. The National Association of Farm Equipment Manufacturers took a series of full-page advertisements in 1924 drawing attention to the ballooning costs of raw materials and labor and highlighting their belief that farmer resistance was breeding a low-volume, high-cost basis of manufacturing (exhibit 9-5).[5]

The First Message of a Series to Dealers, Referring to the Problems of the Farm Equipment Industry

The Glass Distorts the Facts

Exhibit 9–5. *Farm equipment manufacturers' profits—an industry view (National Association of Farm Equipment Manufacturers, December 4, 1924)*

GEORGE PEEK'S MISCALCULATION

One of Deere's old rivals in tractors, its hometown competitor, the Moline Plow Company, had a particularly boom-and-bust experience in this period. George Peek, who had done so much for Deere as the head of sales prior to World War I, now sided with the farmers in the price dispute in a rather strange way, in the process taking the Moline Plow Company off on a dubious marketing sidetrack that led to disaster. At the same time, he became embroiled with Deere in an acrimonious, name-calling exchange that exacerbated already sensitive feelings.

Peek had gone to the Moline Plow Company in 1919 as its chief executive at a salary of $100,000 a year, a fabulous remuneration in those days (particularly for the Moline area). Peek's move to the rival farm machinery company disconcerted Deere management no end, particularly because the "new boy on the street" was literally just down the road from Deere's properties. Frank Silloway, Peek's successor as vice president of marketing, immediately wrote a cautionary memorandum to all factory and branch managers: "You have all known Mr. Peek so well, for so many years, that your own individual feelings at this time can better be expressed by yourselves than us. We shall always remember and meet Mr. Peek as the good friend and companion that he is, but at the same time we must remember now that his identification with this new company makes him, in a business way, our competitor. . . . We suggest that his name be immediately taken off your list of those to whom bulletins are sent."

To Peek's considerable surprise, the Moline Plow Company was in bad financial condition, a fact that he had not known when he came. Peek was ever the marketing man, though, and a thoroughgoing "full-liner." Almost immediately he made evident his desire to expand the company's tractor business. The Moline Plow Company had been making the Universal tractor since about 1918, from an earlier model built in Columbus, Ohio; Peek now wanted new models of the Universal as rapidly as possible and pushed hard on his development engineers and factory managers to get the models into the field forthwith.

From his vantage point as Deere's director of manufacturing, Leon Clausen watched the new tractor being built and later reminisced about the technology of the Universal: "The engine was

Exhibit 9-6. *"Flying Dutchman" trademark of the Moline Plow Company (courtesy of Rock Island County Historical Society)*

mounted high above the ground over the two main drivewheels and the [driver's] offset position was more or less counter-balanced by a concrete weight built into the right-hand wheel. The tractor was very unstable, especially on hillsides and it had a tendency when backing up out of a depression or over a small obstruction to throw the operator over the top of the tractor unless he had a rather heavy implement fastened to the rear end. This actually happened in a number of cases and, of course, accounts for a large measure of the shrinkage in popularity."

Before he had all the "bugs" out of the machine, Peek released the tractor on the market. The poor design gave him rapid feedback—all negative. "Its failure brought repercussions to the entire company from farmers, dealers, and jobbers," Peek's biographer recounted.

Before Peek could remedy the Universal tractor mistake, the depression came, and Peek was in deep trouble. The antagonisms of the dealers over the faulty tractor were compounded by Peek's efforts to push the product out into the field in the face of fast-softening demand. For reasons not entirely clear, Peek introduced a controversial new proposal for marketing—the "Moline Plan."

This time Peek really shook the industry, for his notion struck at the heart of the traditional manufacturer-dealer relationship. He accused the existing full-line companies (and there was no doubt that this included his former employer, Deere & Company) of dominating their dealers by requiring 100 percent exclusivity and thus turning the dealers into agents, not independent merchants. He alleged that the branch-house system had "perpetuated small dealers, small territories, small stocks, and small shipments." Peek's words to describe this were strong: "Debt works, as with the Mexican peon, to keep the dealer 'loaded' with goods and subjugated into agency." All of this, Peek believed, "requires the extravagant armies of the Old Way." Not only was the full-line company degrading its dealers, it was also making the dealer profitless: "It is a cruel, cynical system which spends so great a treasure in the process of reducing its dealers to agency and then destroys their profits by charging this waste to them." The Moline Plan, on the other hand, was going to "restore" retail profit: "It saves the dealer about 10 percent on his purchases." How was this to be done? By selling only for cash and always selling in carload lots. In the process, all "unnecessary expenses due to long terms, bad debts, 'free' service, factory canvassers, high-priced 'experts,' branch house 'help,' etc." would be eliminated.

Peek brazenly laid down the gauntlet to his fellow manufacturers: "The great branch house and selling systems of leading competitors are built on the Old Way. To adopt the Moline Plan, the enormous excess would have to be scrapped, and hordes of dealer dominators turned out of employment." Peek must have been thinking of his recent Deere experience when he continued: "The political situation within their own ranks would prevent it. They would have to suffer a convulsive change in point of view. Few men arrive at middle age doing that. They would have to give up their almost complete domination of the retail business and go out and fight on their merits. It does not lie in human nature."

The influential *Farm Implement News* added fuel to Peek's firestorm by editorializing bluntly about ballooning wholesaling costs. The culprit, it alleged, was the small dealer, buying on a hand-to-mouth basis, and in the process eschewing carload-lot shipments directly from the factory. The periodical cited several anonymous cases, alleging that in some full-line company branches the cost of doing business was double what it was in the pre-war days: "Where in the old days it was considered that a 12 percent overhead was the deadline, branches now cost from 21 to 28 percent of the sales. . . . Another implement manufacturer who jobs many lines quite successfully has overhead at three of his principal branches amounting to 24, 31 and 36 percent." One of the manufacturers' branch houses mentioned in the article actually had overhead exceeding the gross sales of the branch. The editors moralized: "Read that again and consider what it means. The cost of maintaining a branch house organization and a service department has eaten up every cent the branch received from sales this year. Nothing is left for the factory to cover the overhead and the cost of machines sold."

Farm Implement News spoke the truth on the general trend of branch house expenses around the industry—the two depression years of 1921 and 1922 had seen sales sag precipitously, with selling and warehouse expenses not being able to be cut enough to maintain the margins of previous years. Deere's experience was graphic; even C.C. Webber's Minneapolis branch, almost always the company leader in these years, had its expenses balloon. (The company's branch expenses were 14.3 percent of sales in 1915, 22.7 percent in 1922; the Minneapolis branch's were 9.9 percent in the earlier year, 15.5 percent in the latter.)

Part of the problem was attributable to the sharp decreases in sales in the two poor years. Nevertheless, there was reason for concern that the machinery manufacturers' selling and warehousing expenses were indeed rising inordinately. Frank Silloway, acutely conscious of the problem at Deere, constantly exhorted the branch managers about cost cutting, but it was not until 1928 that the percentage of expenses to sales declined to 11.2, once again under the rule-of-thumb of the industry of 12 percent.

But Peek's allegations ran deeper than just caveats about branch-house managers' resolves in holding costs in line. He was challenging the concept of the branch. Was he correct? Was the branch just a parasite, its inflated expenses unnecessary, providing no service to the farmer-buyer? Inasmuch as Peek's assault constituted the most frontal attack on the branch-house system the industry had faced to that time, it is important to chronicle what happened to Peek in this effort, and also to analyze the underlying issue of the validity of the branch house.

There was nothing devious about Peek's approach, once he had decided to go ahead. He began taking large advertisements in regional farmers' trade magazines bluntly criticizing the status quo. One of the first was in the *Utah Farmer*: "TO THE FARMERS OF UTAH: We realize the existing methods of selling and distributing implements and farm machinery are wasteful, extravagant and unnecessarily expensive to the farmers. We hereby announce our new system of selling Moline implements and farm machinery which will save the farmers of Utah $400,000 a year. Our new system eliminates the extravagant, wasteful overhead expenses so common to business and which the farmers pay." In this case, Peek proposed to recognize the Utah Farm State Bureau as a central purchasing agent for the farmers of the state, all to be delivered to the farm bureau through his Salt Lake City warehouse.

Peek's judgment in aggressively courting the farmers' cooperatives was not corroborated by the facts, incidentally. In a significant study at this time of the farmers' cooperative movement, the U.S. Department of Agriculture had reported a new slackening of interest in them on the part of the farmers. *Farm Implement News* faulted the farmer cooperative stores particularly for their lack of service.

Deere management reacted quickly to the Peek challenge, with F.R. Todd sending out a company-wide alert, attached to a copy of the Utah advertisement. Todd felt Peek's approach concealed a booby trap: "Considerable objection . . . will come from their dealers in other states, fearful that this is only the opening chapter in a general arrangement with the Farm Bureaus of other localities." Dismantling an existing dealer organization is always fraught with danger; often many actions taken are irreversible. Peek was to find this out.

With the Moline Plow Company marketing people ranging through the farm regions, trying to persuade farmers to band together as "cooperatives" to put in bulk, carload-lot orders for cash, Deere tried to reassure its own dealer organization. M.J. Healey, the general manager at Kansas City, sent a bulletin to all of his salesmen about the "fanciful concessions" which Peek was making and reminded them particularly of the well-organized service backup that Deere was providing its dealers. The Peek proposition, Healey felt, "might appeal to some gullible dealers." But "most of our customers are good businessmen and if this proposition is presented to them . . . they will not go off half cocked."

R.B. Lourie of the Moline branch also tried to calm his own dealers: "We are satisfied that neither we nor our dealers have anything to fear from it." Still, Lourie wanted quick information about whether "this scheme has been 'put over' in your county or is being considered." C.C. Webber, in his usual blunt style, exhorted the Minnesota dealers: "Do not be deceived . . . as a reliable merchant it is your duty to your customers to not permit them to purchase implements that are not standard because of a savings of a small sum on the purchase price." Webber then made an interesting linkage between farmer and factory, in the process of announcing certain cash discounts and price reductions: "These are not justified by the present cost of production, but as they will result in increased business for our dealers and for ourselves, and THEREBY GIVE EMPLOYMENT TO OUR FACTORY WORKERS, making them larger buyers of the products of the farm, we will all be benefited."

The Deere response soon became more pointed: W.W. Alexander, the St. Louis branch manager, launched a particularly personal attack on Peek and the Moline Plow Company as such. "This concern failed to market their goods successfully in a legitimate way and now it is endeavoring to revive a demoralized business by revolutionary methods, and naturally their 'wild cat' scheme will fail." Peek, needled, immediately wrote back to Alexander: "Your original letter was beneath your own dignity and tone and very erroneous and misleading in statement. We had no plan that failed in 1921. It hardly comports with the courtesy you evoke to say that our goods are unpopular and our business demoralized. It is a queer procedure to call a plan 'wild cat' and 'revolutionary.' Your statement of the 'scheme of the Moline Plow Company' is as untrue in general as it is libelous in particular. While I do not mean to in any way threaten you, I would advise you to ask your lawyer the effect of some of your statements."

A patent dispute between Deere and the Moline Plow Company at this time added to the friction between the two companies. When H.B. Dineen had been at Deere, he had developed a cultivator which the Deere patent department warned its management was infringing on a Moline Plow Company patent. "Notwithstanding that fact and because of the trade demand for the machine we were manufacturing," the board minutes of November 1, 1921, noted, "the factory was permitted to go ahead with their work." After Dineen left Deere for the Moline Plow Company, the latter company brought suit against Deere, and an out-of-court settlement was made for $15,000 and a royalty of $.50 for each cultivator subsequently built by Deere.

Before Peek and his former colleagues at Deere actually could get into a more serious confrontation, events at the Moline Plow Company took the matter out of Peek's hands. Its business had sagged so badly by 1923 that Peek abandoned his attempt to change the marketing structure of the industry as his Moline Plan floundered in a sea of red ink. Preoccupied with saving the company, he turned his attention to pressures from his own board and creditors, who wanted to cut back on the full line of the Moline Plow Company.

Over the vehement objections of Peek, the Moline Plow Company's activities in the tractor, harvester, and drill fields were promptly liquidated, and in May 1924 the Universal tractor plant at Rock Island was put on the market. Within a month Peek had resigned, and later in the year he and two other members of management who had also been caught in the cutback sued the company for $1 million, charging that their five-year management contract had been violated. They won a settlement of $280,000. The company itself came through the reorganization much slimmer and stayed in business beyond Peek's departure.

Deere seriously considered buying the Moline Plow Company properties; the modest profit of the company in 1923 had begun to generate some renewed entrepreneurship among management. William Butterworth and T.F. Wharton assumed the negotiating task, Butterworth noting to himself in his diary, "Horicon and Ottumwa factory products might be made here." The price seemed too high, and the deal fell through.

Shortly after, the plant was sold, and much to the consternation of Deere, the buyer turned out to be the company's archcompetitor, the International Harvester Company, who purchased the entire properties for expansion of its tractor production. The basis for International Harvester's optimism lay in its very successful new general purpose tractor, the Farmall. (The Harvester and Deere experiences with this new type of tractor will be chronicled in the next chapter.)

The nasty exchanges between Peek and the Deere branch managers upset the Deere management, so Frank Silloway, in January 1923, put out a bulletin to all factory and branch managers, cautioning them: "It has been the John Deere policy since the organization of the company, not to talk about competitors. This has proven a good policy and therefore should be followed all the time. We suggest that you instruct your travelers along the above lines so as to refresh their memory in regard to this policy. Of course, when the dealer introduces the subject of the merit of a certain competitor's particular implement or policy, the traveler can explain in a businesslike way the superior merits of ours, but he should confine his remarks to the subject under discussion and get away from it and back to our proposition alone, as soon as possible." The subject so concerned management, however, that at a board meeting a few weeks later a formal resolution was adopted concerning "discussion of competitors." To make the policy unambiguous, the board resolved that "the employees be, and they are hereby advised and instructed that no statement reflecting injuriously on the financial stability of any competitor shall, under any circumstance, be made, and that failure to comply with this instruction will be regarded by this company with grave disfavor." Pointedly, R.B. Lourie, who had been one of the anti-Moline Plow Company writers, voted against the board resolution. A negative vote in Deere's board meetings was a very infrequent event. Was Lourie supporting continuation of "injurious" statements about competitors?

Apparently he was, for he and M.J. Healey mounted further attacks on the Moline Plow Company, now renamed the Moline Implement Company. The denouement came in late 1926, when the latter company brought suit against Deere, alleging slanderous statements by Healey about the solvency of the Moline Implement Company and the quality of its product. Burton Peek rushed a memorandum to all of the company about the issue and reminded them that "all the time the travelers have at their disposal is needed to talk the merits of our own goods and the advantage of the John Deere proposition in general, and they have no time to devote to any conversation about our competitors." The case never came to trial, but the knotty problem of trying to bring strong field personalities into line with general company policy remained to plague the company and the industry.

The hurly-burly of the marketplace was so strongly imbedded, though, that in 1929 the National Association of Farm Equipment Manufacturers finally drafted a formal code of ethics, which exhorted its members to "respect the rights and privileges of competitors and not to interfere with or attempt to have canceled any bona fide orders or contracts taken by a competitor" and "to recognize business courtesies and particular courtesies in the field and not to knock competitors or competitors' goods. If you cannot speak well of them and their products you can at least remain silent." How many did remain silent was a matter of some conjecture.

After the debacle of his ouster, Peek never returned to the industry. Instead, he turned back to his earlier wartime interest in national agricultural policy and his remaining career, a stormy one, found him in and close to government, fighting for his own views of federal farm policy. While in Washington at the end of the war, Peek had come to know Gen. Hugh S. Johnson, and he had brought Johnson with him to the Moline Plow Company. The chemistry between the two was powerful and they had not only jointly run the Moline Plow Company but had collaborated in a remarkable broadside in 1922, titled "Equality for Agriculture." In it was the essence of Peek's philosophy about farm policy that was to endure all through his remaining years. Peek felt that farm imports were fatally damaging American agriculture and he proposed a system that combined a high tariff wall against imports with a federal government-operated system for purchase of domestic surpluses and the dumping of these abroad forthwith. Peek and Johnson propounded the plan at the bellwether National Agricultural Conference, called by Secretary of Agriculture Henry C. Wallace at the direction of President Harding in January 1922. Though the plan itself was treated roughly at the conference, the concept soon surfaced in a bill proposed by Sen. Charles L. McNary of Oregon and Rep. Gilbert N. Haugen of Iowa. This controversial piece of legislation, the so-called "McNary-Haugen Bill," was debated in Congress over several sessions after the National Agricultural Conference, achieving a high profile in the first session of Congress in 1924. The fight for the bill coincided nicely with Peek's abrupt departure from the Moline Plow Company and he then put all of his energies into lobbying for it. The bill eventually lost, but by that time Peek was irrevocably committed to pushing federal legislation via the lobby. His assiduous cultivation of a militant farm lobby soon paid off, for a revived version of the McNary-Haugen bill passed both houses of Congress in early 1928, only to be vetoed by President Coolidge a few weeks later.

This was not the end of George Peek's fight for his views on farm policy. During the early 1930s, he took a major role in Pres. Franklin Roosevelt's early New Deal agricultural efforts, administering the Agricultural Adjustment Act for its first seven months of operation. Peek's orbit had moved away from the agricultural machinery industry by this time, not only in terms of job assignments but, more profoundly, in philosophy. His contributions to Deere & Company were major. During his tenure as the chief marketing officer of the company he had developed clear policies on Deere marketing and followed them with detailed, systematized procedures and operating caveats that gave the sales force a sense of aggressive but ethical behavior that proved over the succeeding years to be one of the most prized of Deere's assets. Yet when he went to the Moline Plow Company he repudiated some of the most basic tenets of agricultural machinery marketing with his attacks on the branch-house system. Though it seemed to be a particular affront to his erstwhile colleagues at Deere, there is no evidence that his friendship with Deere top management (which, of course, included his brother, Burton) suffered in the process. But there is also no doubt about the presence of other animosities—with R.B. Lourie, M.J. Healey, and others. In his subsequent public life as a sometime lobbyist and bureaucrat, Peek turned sharply away from the concepts of free enterprise and competition that he had espoused so eloquently as a Deere executive. In the process, the farm

Exhibit 9–7. Top, *Deere hay press, 1922*; bottom, *Deere binder, 1923. (Deere Archives)*

machinery industry lost one of its most able and thoughtful voices.[6]

Deere had suffered the loss of three strong leaders in its top management group in the first decade as the "modern company"—Peek in sales, Mixter and then Clausen as heads of manufacturing. Peek and Mixter were particularly innovative; both seemed to have had that rare quality of vision—the ability to see trends and, in turn, to be pro-active rather than reactive. Peek seemed to lose this vision, once having departed from Deere—his innovation of the Moline Plan (at the Moline Plow Company) did not match reality in the industry. Clausen was less innovative per se, but he shared the positiveness and entrepreneurial daring so characteristic of the other two.

It was time for the next generation of the company's management to take hold. Frank Silloway was ably filling the shoes of Peek, after coming up through the ranks of the organization without benefit of family ties. Clausen's successor was to be in the same mold—a well-trained, highly respected man who also had come up the ranks through important assignments to become director of manufacturing. He, though, was a family member, the direct lineal descendant of grandfather Charles Deere. His name was Charles Deere Wiman.

DEERE & COMPANY

MOLINE, ILL,

Manufacturers of
PLOWS.

SULKY PLOWS and CULTIVATORS.

*F*ounded by Deere & Company in the 1890s, The Furrow is one of the oldest farm magazines in America. Through the years, it has provided farmers with the latest information on equipment and farming practices. By 1983, it was published worldwide in 37 editions and 13 languages. With its unique combination of editions, languages and circulation, The Furrow is believed to be the world's most widely read farm magazine.

VOL. XVII
NO 3

The FURROW

MOLINE, ILL.

SUMMER
NUMBER
1912

GET
QUALITY
AND
SERVICE
JOHN DEERE
DEALERS
GIVE BOTH

THE name JOHN DEERE has always stood for the highest quality implements. We handle the John Deere Line and give you the best service.

John Deere quality and our service mean satisfaction to you—and satisfaction is what you want to get out of your farm tools above everything else. See us about any implements you need.

KC

YEAR 1916 · THIRD NO. · VOL. XXI

The FURROW

JOHN DEERE QUALITY GOODS
Sold by

GROWTH REGULATORS: breaking the self-control of plants
Now, bunker silos for ear-corn ■ Watch out for stowaway pests
Hideaway for campers

NEW BOOM IN COUNTRY ANTIQUES

SULCO
VERÃO 1982

TUDO AQUILO
QUE SE PODE
EXIGIR DAS SEMENTES
HERBICIDAS NATURAIS
MAIS VITELOS GEMEOS

1876

1912

1936

1937

1950

1956

1968

The leaping deer has appeared in all registered trademarks of Deere & Company since 1876. The strong association of the Deere name with the leaping deer has created one of America's most recognized corporate symbols. At left is the current trademark.

At right are three other variations on the deer theme used by Deere & Company enterprises in the 1880s.

1885

1880

1889

1893

1891

*R*apid growth in the number of John Deere factories and branch houses led to many attempts at separate identities. It was not until the 1960s that the corporate identity was finally reduced to a uniform trademark.

...AND COMPANY,

1884

1907

DEERE & COMPANY

INCORPORATED 1868

TRADE MARK

JOHN DEERE

MOLINE, ILL.

PLOW MANUFACTURERS.

1876

*T*he popular Model "D" tractor (introduced in 1923) is dwarfed in comparison to the awesome 8630, as shown in the 1975 Deere & Company annual report. Improvements in photography, design, and printing transformed annual reports from simple financial disclosures, like those shown at right, into sophisticated "state of the company" presentations.

Annual Report
OF
DEERE & COMPANY
FOR THE
Fiscal Year
ENDED
OCTOBER 31, 1919

1947
Annual Report
FOR THE FISCAL YEAR ENDED OCTOBER 31

DEERE & COMPANY

DEERE & COMPANY
ANNUAL REPORT
1955

FOR THE FISCAL YEAR ENDED
OCTOBER THIRTY-FIRST

*A*nother glimpse into the 1975 annual report reveals further evidence of Deere's long agricultural heritage. The tractor-drawn grain binder (introduced in 1929) was another step towards ending the drudgery of harvesting. Binders like this one could cover 35-40 acres a day, preparing grain for threshing. The 6600 combine (introduced in 1970) could reap and thresh crops in a single operation, frequently harvesting 100 or more acres a day.

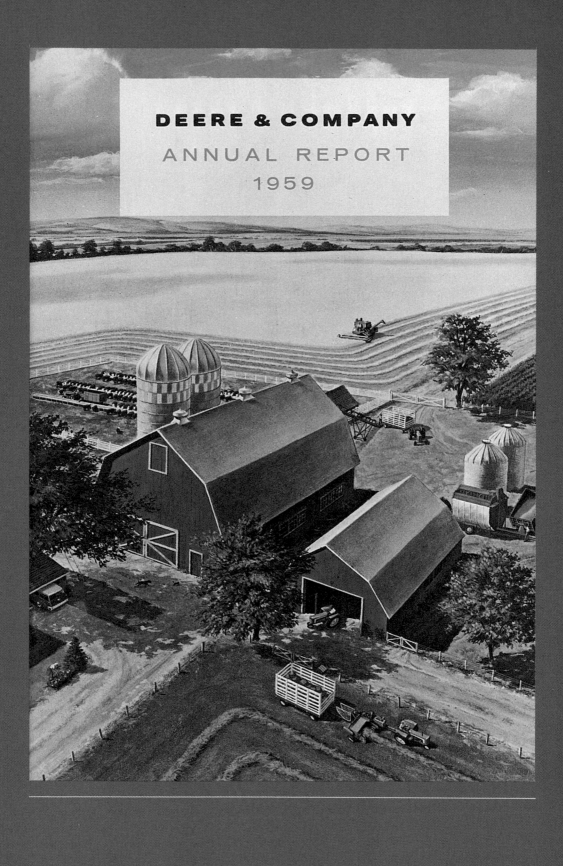

DEERE & COMPANY

ANNUAL REPORT
1959

A portfolio of annual report covers conveys pride in product and visual presentation. The corporate attitude remains much the same as the statement attributed to John Deere: "I will never put my name on a plow which does not have in it the best that is in me."

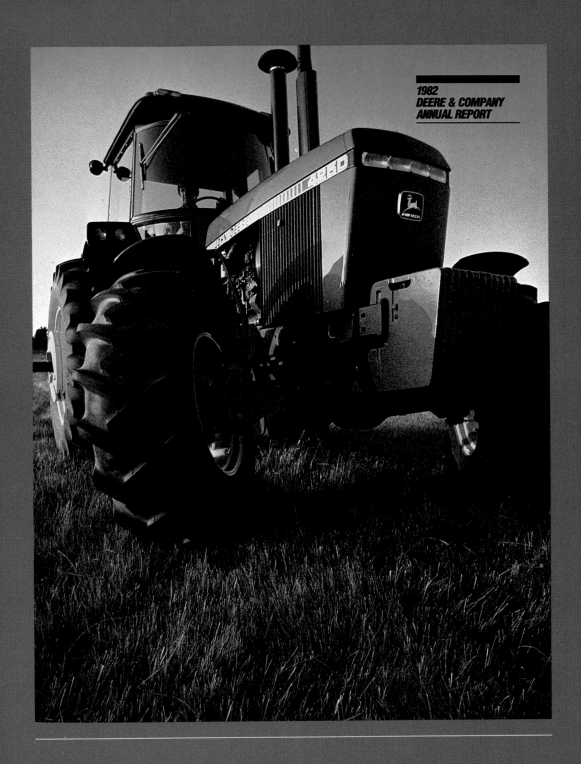

1982
DEERE & COMPANY
ANNUAL REPORT

PART IV

FROM RETRENCHMENT TO EXPANSION:

THE CHARLES WIMAN YEARS (1928–54)

JOHN DEERE

GRAIN & CORN
BINDERS
MOWERS
& RAKES

CHAPTER 10

INNOVATION AND
NEW LEADERSHIP

*Never believed in a two-row cultivator, as a man had all
he could do to run and watch a single row . . . could see the
tractor and planter but not the cultivator . . . the boys
could try it, but did not expect to let them cultivate a whole row
but would have to tell them to take it out . . . had horses
ready to go and do the job. However, the boys cultivated one
row and then another, and then told the boys
to go ahead and cultivate with a three-row . . . frankly
surprised to find out how well the three-row did.*

C. C. Veech, 1927

The early 1920s, especially the depressed years 1920–21, had been very distressing for William Butterworth. At numerous critical junctures in his presidency he had articulated a conservative view of the business—urging caution in taking on a harvester line in the early 1910s when faced with International Harvester's aggressiveness and consistently opposing greater centralization of authority until he was forced to act in the 1920–21 downturn because purchasing and inventory decisions had gotten out of control. He had been faulted often by Willard Velie for dividing his loyalty between the Deere trust and the company; he had repeatedly opposed the entry into tractors, despite the enthusiasm of most of the rest of the board. He seemed less a chief executive than a careful, financially oriented lawyer who felt strongly his fiduciary responsibility to the major shareholders of the company and who believed implicitly that the company should be preserved intact, even if one were to forego some entrepreneurial opportunity. Butterworth's thinking seemed so often to reinforce the status quo.

Butterworth's lack of entrepreneurial spirit was accompanied, however, by an abiding concern for the employees of the company and a view of employee relations that stressed loyalty, trust, and service. The pitched arguments of the World War I period about incentive bonus plans poignantly illustrated this. Butterworth advocated a broad sharing of ownership among all employees, based primarily on length of service, while others, particularly C.C. Webber, George Mixter, and George Peek, adhered to a selective, subjective plan designed to reward management performance.

The 1920–21 downturn heightened, if anything, Butterworth's strongly held views. He warned over and over of the necessity of purchasing carefully—almost hand-to-mouth—and urged the cutting of expense at every turn. In his personal diary are many remarks during the 1920–24 period urging "intelligent saving" and "careful spending of the Company's money." Even after business began to recover in 1923, Butterworth still discouraged building of inventory, writing Charles Wiman from Europe: "Let us not be frightened into buying a lot of high-priced material. . . . I notice our inventory is growing . . . this is a bad sign and should not continue." A roundtable discussion in the board in late 1925 recorded a "spirit of optimism" and a "bright outlook" and C.C. Webber expected "a very large increase in their volume for 1926." Yet Butterworth still raised cautionary caveats about "watching schedules closely," with inventory at a minimum.

Butterworth spent much time with Charles Wiman in the early 1920s, encouraging him and explaining his philosophy of family and company responsibility. In January 1924, Butterworth wrote Wiman about a managers' meeting that Wiman had chaired, complimenting him on "splendid success." He continued: "The fellow we want to keep out of

Exhibit 10–1. Top, *Trolley leaves for Campbell's Island picnic ground on "Deere Picnic Day," ca. 1905, bottom, Deere & Company headquarters, 1919. (Deere Archives)*

our organization is he who says 'it can't be done.' We'll do it or bust and we're not going to 'bust,' is our homely motto." In this letter Butterworth reiterated his view of keeping inventory in control and concluded: "I am writing you somewhat at length, not because I think it is necessary, for I know you have these things in mind, but I'm doing so to emphasize their importance and to indicate to you that the Company officers and directors are thinking along the same lines and that we are all thinking about you and boosting for you."

As business did indeed get better in 1925, Butterworth finally seemed to relax a bit, confiding to his diary: "I feel more comfortable about the future of our Company than I have since its reorganization in 1910. In fact, this is the first time that I really have felt comfortable and contented with our policy and program. We are going ahead now with everybody from top to bottom working for just one thing and that is the success of Deere & Co." At this point, Butterworth decided to share with Wiman, Frank Silloway, and T.F. Wharton a memorandum about his views toward the company that he had written during World War I but had never made public. ("I offer to you the following statements, which I wrote more than seven years ago and which indicates my ideas as to the policies we should pursue.") It is not surprising that he had been reluctant about advancing these views until this moment, feeling that the company was still not stable enough to warrant his being so definitive. The statement again emphasized his concern of employees. "I want to keep in close touch with you and your department and know your successes and your troubles," Butterworth told the three younger men. Each and every employee from the lowest to the highest should have from the management a "real, live, personal interest" and, in turn, each employee should "likewise understand that the Company expects and wants him and her to take and show a real, live interest in the welfare and growth of the Company." The earnings of employees should be watched carefully so as to give "the average man a chance to live comfortably and lay aside something for the rainy day." Thrift was to be encouraged among the employees, with a particular emphasis on purchasing of the company's preferred stock. Young men were to be encouraged to join the business, for which they would be educated "along definite and prescribed lines." College graduates were to be employed, "with preference for the sons of *our men*." (This particular plan, though, met with some resistance. "Not all of the branch houses had been convinced that it was a desirable thing to do," R.B. Lourie reported.) Board meetings should be held weekly, Butterworth continued, to provide a clearinghouse of ideas and to keep all informed, and there should be at least a once-a-year meeting of all branch managers and factory managers with top management, hopefully meeting together. Management should make periodic trips to the factories "to keep our relations close and the shop policies as uniform as possible." He stressed the importance of quality and careful workmanship and reiterated his profound concern for proper management of inventory. Finally, "Watch the expense account, both large and small, keep them at a minimum. A small reduction of each account will help our showing."

This is a document that rings true throughout, epitomizing the benign spirit and cautious ways that Butterworth had brought to the organization and to his personal relations over the previous two decades. Butterworth had become the highly respected—yes, loved—father figure for the whole company. It seems likely that he was now thinking of new leadership for the company, for he had become increasingly active in state and national organizations, particularly the U.S. Chamber of Commerce.

Charles Wiman had moved quickly into a major position in top management after his appointment as director of manufacturing in 1924. As the ranking member of the next generation of the family, it was obviously important for him to prepare for an eventual leadership role in the company. Wiman moved into this role self-assuredly and well, bringing a verve and drive that had been earlier filled in part by George Mixter, George Peek, and Leon Clausen. Wiman had started in the shop in 1915 as a line employee (salary, $.15 an hour); over the ensuing years he had built a strong following among shop employees, engineers, and production supervisors. By 1926 Wiman also had clearly won the respect and cooperation of his older fellow board members; at a board meeting in July of that year, Floyd Todd noted "the excellent feeling and cooperation existing not only in the factory organization but between the branches and the factories as well. This condition . . . was due largely to the efforts of Mr. Wiman."

As business expanded after 1925, it was Wiman who constantly was urging new product development. He seemed to have an instinctive feeling for the larger picture—the needs for coordination, the balancing of units, and so on. The tractor was center stage, he constantly reminded the board, for "it is more important that the tractor factory operate at a uniform pace . . . because it manufactures but one tool, and when they have a given schedule all of the equipment is utilized every day." In effecting this, though, Wiman advocated an aggressive strategy: "We must remember we should be willing to spend considerably more money in promoting tractor sales, either by increasing our field force or through advertising, or both." At one point in the tractor expansion, he even asked the board for a discretionary appropriation of $25,000, to be used for bonus payments to hasten the construction of a building.

Wiman was also willing to move decisively if any manager or employee was not reasonably fulfilling expectations. A few months later, for example, the Waterloo tractor factory foundry and mill room were falling short of quotas and reporting high scrap rates. Wiman relieved the foundry superintendent without delay and sent in two trouble shooters from Moline. "The Waterloo management has had the seriousness of the situation explained to them and has been shown the necessity of correcting the foundry difficulties at the earliest practical date," Wiman told the board. The Waterloo men got the message!

Wiman's influence on product development was particularly felt in two key innovations—the adaptation of the combine to Midwest farming conditions, and the development of the "general-purpose" tractor.[1]

THE COMBINE COMES TO THE MIDWEST

A persistent dream of farmers had been to harvest grain and thresh it in one operation. The first "combine," the machine that could do both jobs in a single operation, antedated even Cyrus McCormick's reaper—a Maine inventor had patented a traveling thresher with a harvesting attachment in 1828. In the early period of commercial development, in the 1870s and '80s, the combined harvesters were commonly known as "travellers." A farmer, asked how he was going to harvest his crop, would either reply "by stationary" (a stationary thresher) or "by traveller" (the combined harvester). After the 1880s the machine was generally known as a "harvester."

Midwest agriculture was unsuited to these early combines, for they would only work well under ideal conditions in which the crop was ripe and dry, which was rare in the Midwest. But the combine was ideal for the great wheat farms of California, which by 1880 had become the number one wheat-growing state of the country. Enormous combines were constructed by competing inventors to harvest for these big spreads —combines that could each harvest as much as fifty acres a day, two thousand acres a season. Many were variations of Hiram Moore's Michigan combine, first perfected in the 1830s, and soon other names were jostling each other for fame—the Shippee, the Berry, and, later, the Holt and the Best. (The Holts had bought out Shippee, and later, in 1925, Holt and Best merged as the Caterpillar Tractor Company to become a prominent producer on the West coast.) By 1910, Massey-Harris had entered the field with its first combine, developed initially for the Australian market.

Australian inventors had experimented with combines as early as the 1850s and South Australia sponsored a major international competition in 1877. The Australian versions were usually smaller, generally being light, horse-drawn, ground-driven machines of the stripper type with an eight-foot cut. The California machines were more often heavy, horse- or power-drawn, motor-driven machines with complete cutting, threshing, separating, and cleaning mechanisms cutting swaths of about twenty-four feet.

The Midwestern wheat farmers knew the cost savings of combining were great. But would the combine work for sections east of those regions where the wheat dried out thoroughly in the head? The year 1924 was the pivotal one in answering this question. In November of that year a bellwether demonstration was made at a Stonington, Illinois, farm of a Massey-Harris combine, in this case harvesting and threshing soybeans. More than two thousand people were there, including farmers, implement dealers, county agents, and experiment station men. A *Farm Implement News* editor attended and reported "entire satisfaction"—the thirty acres of beans had been harvested, threshed, and carried to a granary at a cost of about $.05 a bushel. The Massey-Harris representative running the test averred that the cost of harvesting with a binder, tying in bundles and threshing in the old way, was $.30 a bushel. The editor of *Farm Implement News* made a prophetic statement at the end of his article: "One of the drawbacks to raising soybeans has been the difficulty in harvesting and threshing. It is believed that the success of this demonstration will lead to a big increase in the acreage of soybeans in central Illinois."

Over this same harvest season the combine was also tried with wheat and oats, as well as occasionally on crops of sweet clover, red clover, and timothy. Again the results were most promising. The question remained of just how effective the new machine would be in humid conditions. The crop season of 1925 in Illinois was humid, an ideal condition for tests of the combine. The trade press soon trumpeted its continuing success and touted its potential as a Midwestern harvesting addition. The conditions of 1926 in Illinois and other Midwestern states were not quite as favorable, yet the combine again registered great records in Kansas, Texas, and Oklahoma, as well as in Iowa and Illinois. The U.S. Department of Agriculture also conducted extensive tests during the crop season of 1926. The crop still had to be as dry as possible—users recommended delaying the commencement of harvest from five to nine days later than if headers or binders were used. If the farmer was patient for this time, the results were excellent and the costs remarkably lower. By 1927, *Farm Implement News* was headlining a major editorial, "It's a Combine Year." The demand for combines quickly outstripped the production capacity of the factories, forcing the branch houses of the manufacturers to ration the coveted machines. "The future of the farm equipment trade never looked brighter," commented *Farm Implement News*. There had been just over 3,600 combines produced in 1920; the number for 1927 jumped to 18,307, up over 6,000 from the previous year of 1926.[2]

DEERE BUILDS A COMBINE

Deere had been building harvesting machinery for about fifteen years, the product line consisting of a grain binder and a corn binder, together with several sizes of mowers and rakes. But it was not a leader in the field. Sales of harvest machinery in 1926 were just over $6 million, about one-seventh of the total sales of the company of $47.8 million, and for the first time the harvester division showed a profit.

Deere had shown little interest in entering the thresher field; companies there were well entrenched. The combine business, on the other hand, seemed more promising. But a catalyst was now needed to shake the company out of its lethargy in harvester product development, and it came in the person of Charles Wiman. The Harvester Works was headed by Charles N. Stone, who had succeeded W.R. Morgan after the latter's death in 1923. The Kansas City and Portland branches had already been pressuring Moline to consider combine possibilities; now Wiman and Stone wanted to move ahead fast, and they came to the board with an appropriations request for experimental work. Their memorandum was blunt: "We believe that the combine harvester and thresher will almost completely replace headers . . . and will probably be used almost exclusively in the sections where it can be used."

C.C. Webber was surprisingly negative at the start about the combine, at least as a tool to be sold by the Minnesota branch: "Here is the combination machine. You remember a few years ago that that was talked about everywhere and we did not know but what we would have to make it. Well, we believe it is being demonstrated that the combination machine is useful in a territory where the grain gets dead ripe and it's fit to cut and thresh at the same time, and to use it in any other territory is dangerous. So it seems to me that we have done well to stay out of the combination trade."

The harvesting situation in Minnesota was challenging. There often was an uneven ripening and sometimes a nagging weed problem, so for a long time after other parts of the country turned to combines, many farmers in the Webber territory used windrowers and grain binders. Still, it was incongruous for Webber to be so provincial in this instance, for he generally espoused a broad management perspective.

There was always a tradeoff between new product development and additional product engineering on present products. Webber wanted the latter: "It would be a pioneer work and an uphill job, and it does not seem to the writer that we are in shape at your factory to undertake that kind of a job. Your situation is such that you do not want to take on a machine that you have got to put a lot of money into for several years before it commences to yield any return. . . . I have never been in favor of the undertaking to make a header in the Harvester Works and I have held to that position constantly because I knew you were at work and had to work on a new mower and a new grain binder and that when they had been perfected you would have to equip your factory to make them economically and I felt that you had your hands full, and that all your energy should be devoted to the present line and perfecting that and enabling you to produce it comparatively before you undertake anything else." Given Webber's opposition to the combine, it is all the more remarkable that Charles Wiman stuck to his guns. He got the appropriation.

Next, another dilemma had to be faced. Should some outside machine, already perfected, be purchased or licensed, or should the company itself take on the laborious, expensive process of developing its own product from scratch? Wiman and Stone hedged their bets. There was, indeed, an existing combine available for sale to the company—the Universal, made by a Kansas City company of the same name. Stone and Wiman were uneasy about the company: "The makeup of the Universal Harvester Co. does not inspire confidence. The men of the company have been in bad company, having been with . . . of Savage Harvester Company and the Standing Grain Thresher Company of Wichita, Kansas. Both of these companies had checquered careers and farmers lost money through them after investing as a result of more or less false representation." The Universal machine used a rapidly revolving cylinder with a system of square pin teeth instead of the cutter bar used by most other combines; there were some advantages in terms of simplicity of manufacture, as well as a reputedly high recovery of grain from the field, more than a standard combine. "Statements on this point vary greatly," noted Wiman and Stone, "and some competent observers say that the machine wasted too much grain."

Wiman and Stone finally decided to buy one Universal machine, together with a Massey-Harris machine, and to take these two into the field for testing, along with whatever prototype machine could be developed by Stone's own product development engineers. By the season of 1925, the company had its own prototype ready for tryout, and the three machines were sent for testing near LaCrosse, Kansas. The new Deere machine competed well with the Massey-Harris machine and performed considerably better than the Universal, which was dropped from consideration forthwith.

At the same time that the company was experimenting with the combine, its Harvester Works also had taken on the task of designing and manufacturing a corn picker. Commercially successful pickers had been sold by other companies since before the turn of the century; now Deere decided to develop its own. Twenty-three prototype machines were assembled for the crop season of 1925 and tested in the Minneapolis, Omaha, and Moline branches, again with considerable success "in a wet, difficult picking season."

After both the combine and the corn picker were tested again in the field during the crop season of 1926, the board met in April 1927 to decide what to do about both. The corn picker was a simpler machine and was put right into the product line for the selling season of 1927. As for the combine, the decision was to build forty machines for the crop season of 1927. Stone was blunt about what he felt was needed: "We must act promptly now and move faster in this development than is usually

---

Exhibit 10–2. Top, *Shipping No. 1 and No. 2 combines to Kansas City by rail, 1929;* middle, *Combining, Sioux Falls, S.D., 1930;* bottom, *Mississippi River barge shipment of combines, 1940. (Deere Archives)*

---

necessary in our business . . . but we should not go at it in a way that is too amateurish. It seems likely that real competition in combines will develop shortly and we would be better off not to get into the business at all than to enter it in a half-hearted way." Wiman proposed that they make 500 machines in 1928 and move quickly to 1,500 the following year. "A new building will be needed," Wiman stated, and the directors promptly gave Wiman and Stone the green light.

At this critical juncture, a surprising new development surfaced that sidetracked everyone for a moment. Representations had been made to Deere that a unit of the old Holt Combine Thresher Company in Stockton, California, one of the pioneer companies in the field, was available for purchase. The Holt company had just been merged with the C.L. Best Tractor Company as the Caterpillar Tractor Company, with its corporate headquarters at San Leandro, California (later at Peoria, Illinois). In 1916 Holt had formed a subsidiary, Western Harvester, and it was this entity that was being offered to Deere. The asking price for the Western Harvester organization, however, was $1,256,000; this seemed too steep an entry price, even for a successful member of the combine field, and the board finally rejected the Caterpillar overture.

By 1927, the John Deere No. 2 combine was available to the branches in quantity and a year later the No. 1 was also in the catalog. The No. 2 was available in 12- and 16-foot platforms, the No. 1 with 8-, 10- and 12-foot platforms. (The larger No. 2 had a grain tank of sixty-five bushels, the No. 1 had a forty bushel capacity). Four-cylinder Hercules engines were purchased by the company for the machines. Stone and the others first had felt that the larger No. 2 machine would be the more popular, but the results in the field soon convinced everyone that greater numbers of farmers wanted the smaller machine. The No. 2 was heavier than it should have been and difficult for a Model D tractor to pull in sandy or muddy soil (so it was better adapted for the Minneapolis territory than, say, the Kansas City regions). Further, because Deere had made these first two combines at high quality levels, Stone also wanted a lower-priced machine, somewhat cheaper in construction and lighter in order to meet price competition. By 1929 the No. 1 and No. 2 had been replaced by two new versions, the No. 5, designed as a smaller, lighter-weight, popularly priced combine, and the No. 3, a larger-sized machine similar to the No. 2, but also lighter in weight.

The combine clearly was going to make obsolete the old-fashioned thresher that had served so well over so many years. Despite the pessimistic outlook for the thresher, Deere surprised the industry in 1929 by adding a thresher "in order to complete our line"; so said Frank Silloway in presenting the matter to the board. Silloway and Charles Stone had investigated a nearly defunct company in Minneapolis, the Wagner-Langemo Company, which had been manufacturing the Grain Saver threshing machine. The owners of the faltering concern were

willing to dispose of their patents, dies, tools, patterns, and so forth, as
well as twenty-three complete machines, for a total of $42,500. Stone felt
that these machines could be readily built at the Harvester Works,
without adding any buildings or even very much equipment. Silloway
and Stone anticipated a maximum volume of approximately five hundred
machines a year, not an enormous potential. Nevertheless, the company
voted the purchase and the John Deere Thresher made its debut, albeit
very late in the game! The machine stayed in the line until 1936, selling
only in modest quantities throughout.[3]

THE GENERAL-PURPOSE TRACTOR

There had been one significant shortcoming of all the gasoline tractors
built before 1924—a lack of versatility. They could not be used for many
farm tasks that agriculturalists might wish to convert to tractor power.
Farmers had been using their tractors to prepare seedbeds (plowing,
disking, harrowing) and probably for some harvesting (especially the
cutting of small grains). Tractors were also enormously helpful in driving
other pieces of machinery—in threshing, silo filling, feed grinding, wood
sawing, baling, shelling, shredding. But these tasks were only part of a
farmer's spectrum of horsepower needs, for with all of the row crops—
corn, hay, cotton, kafir, potatoes, tobacco, peas, peanuts, beans, sugar
beets—not only the cultivation but generally the planting was done by
horse. In the way tractors were constructed, it was not very easy to drive
them down a row to plant or cultivate. Similarly, many functions in the
harvest were more readily accomplished by horse—mowing hay, cutting
corn, digging potatoes, etc. One industry executive in 1924 maintained
that the tractors in use replaced on an average only 2.8 horses per tractor
(though he did admit that owners of larger tractors often disposed of six to
eight horses upon purchase of the tractor). A U.S. Department of
Agriculture bulletin of 1925 graphically showed the relatively small part
of the total horsepower need assumed by the gasoline tractor in that
period—only 1.6 billion of 16 billion horsepower hours, work animals
providing 9.7 billion horsepower hours (Appendix exhibit 21).

The incredible potential for the tractor cultivation of row crops was just
waiting for an innovative idea. Indeed, it seemed anomalous that after
more than two decades of gasoline-tractor development, no one had been
able to perfect such a row-crop tractor. But 1924 brought a solution, a very
successful new four-cylinder tractor from the industry leader, International Harvester. Its name ideally described the essence of the need--the
Farmall.

In construction, the Farmall differed radically from other tractors. its
rear axle was built high, with a clearance of thirty inches above the
ground, and the larger rear drive wheels were wide apart (seventy-four
inches between the centers of the wheels); it could clear corn or cotton as

well as the ordinary riding cultivator, and the wheels were wide enough apart to straddle two rows and thus cultivate two rows at a time. The front wheels, some twenty-five inches in diameter, were located close together in order to run between the two rows. A particularly attractive feature to the farmer was the placement of the International Harvester cultivator, out in front of the tractor where the operator could watch the work. The Farmall also filled a real need in planting, being able to plant either two or four rows at a time.

It is difficult to overemphasize the breakthrough in farming technology brought by this one new tractor. The response from the field was instantaneous—the Farmall became an abiding success. It was patently clear to the farmer that the Farmall could do things that the Fordson could not do, that the Deere Model D could not do.

The remarkable dominance of the Fordson tractor in the early 1920s— 70 percent of all gasoline tractors in 1922, 76 percent in 1923, 71 percent in 1924—now began to decline. Though Henry Ford still commanded more than 50 percent of all gasoline tractors produced in 1926, the onrush of the International Harvester Farmall that year soon reversed the figures. By 1928 there were only 12,500 Fordsons produced, and late in that year Henry Ford gave up making Fordsons in the United States (although he did continue to make them in Cork, Ireland, and Dagenham, England). The Fordson was not adaptable to row-crop farming and that must have been one factor, among many, that persuaded Ford to retire from domestic competition in tractors, a surprising decision in retrospect, given his preeminence just a few years earlier. By 1928 International Harvester had moved into a commanding position, building more than 47 percent of all farm tractors that year and almost 60 percent in 1929.

The row-crop tractors did not replace their larger counterparts, of course, and International Harvester continued to make its famous Titan 10-20 tractor and its larger version, the 15-30. Nevertheless, the advent of the Farmall gave International Harvester a competitive edge that brought its dominance in the tractor field to an all-time high. It was an epochal step for the industry.

DEERE'S SEARCH FOR AN ALL-CROP TRACTOR

Deere & Company had entered the tractor field quite late and did so over the grudging opposition of many of its management—William Butterworth, George Crampton, and others. The precipitous decline of the Waterloo Boy right after World War I had been offset by the development at Waterloo of the first commercially viable Deere tractor, the Model D. This machine was an instant market success. Leon Clausen had almost single-handedly ensured that the Model D would be made in enough quantity to give it a good field test; at this point he left the company, thus placing the tractor's future in the hands of Charles Wiman.

Wiman had no doubts about the Model D's viability, and in 1925 he pushed production to more than 3,900 tractors. Further, he quickly committed the company to an all-crop tractor. Theo Brown was given the responsibility in 1925 for designing the machine with the help of a number of Waterloo engineers, particularly H.E. McCray and J.E. Cade, aided by H.B. McKahin, the Planter Works manager.

Right at the start, Brown made an important design decision that was to prove highly controversial—to enable Deere's all-crop tractor to handle a three-row cultivator. McKahin, meanwhile, had gone to Texas to test an International Harvester Farmall that Deere had purchased. He reported back that it could handle both two-row cultivators and four-row versions, and he commented somberly, "A three-row is not going to be popular there as the rows have to be watched to make sure that the old stalks do not drag."

By July 1926, three prototype tractors had been built that could pull a two-bottom plow (both the earlier Waterloo Boy and the Model D were designed for three-bottom plows). There was one especially striking innovation on the tractor—Brown and his colleagues had developed a power lift mechanism that would raise the integral tools of the cultivator or planter by engine power rather than mechanically by operator levers. Thus it had four forms of power—drawbar, belt, power take-off, and power lift. The latter became an "industry first," soon widely adopted in similar forms by competitors.

Within a few weeks the new Deere cultivator arrived to be tested on the all-crop tractor. Brown felt encouraged: "In the afternoon we had the outfit in the field and there is no question but what the outfit followed the ground in fine shape. The swinging frame is fine and is necessary. The lost motion has been taken out of the steering gear, which helps. We had Farmall out too, and in crossing corn we have the advantage of quicker dodge and rather better view ahead. On straight-way Farmall may be a little better, but McCray thinks we are nearly equal and in respect to crossing corn, better. . . . It really seems as though the idea of our cultivator is right and that we are on the right track. It is really encouraging."

By this time the Farmall was in the International Harvester dealers' shops and there was mounting pressure from Deere branches to "get the new tractor into our hands." Wiman feared a misfire by premature release of the prototypes (a la George Peek's Universal tractor fiasco), and he cautioned the board: "Development work of this kind is rather a slow process. . . . This was the best way to proceed, rather than to place the machine on the market before proper field and experimental work had been taken care of."

So further tinkering was done on a number of features of the tractor and it was once more tested early in the crop season of 1927. The test site was Mercedes, Texas, and again the Farmall and the All-Crop competed side by side. Brown reported the tester's reaction: "Hornberg said that he never thought corn could be cultivated with a tractor, but now he thinks it can be, and much faster. However, he is not yet convinced that the three-row idea is right."

The prototypes were also tested by a Decatur, Illinois, farm family, C.C. Veech and his sons. The former put the problem of the three-row cultivator bluntly: "Never believed in a two-row cultivator as a man had all he could do to run and watch a single row . . . could see the tractor and planter but not the cultivator . . . the boys could try it, but did not expect to let them cultivate a whole row but would have to tell them to take it out . . . had horses ready to go and do the job. However, the boys cultivated one row and then another, and then told the boys to go ahead and cultivate with a three-row . . . frankly surprised to find out how well the three-row did . . . would say, as did sons, that the cultivator seemed to be okay."

Wiman agonized over what was obviously a calculated risk—that the concept of three-row cultivation would not be effective. The alternative—to scrap the prototypes and begin afresh—was unpalatable. Wiman warned the board of the opportunity costs of this: "Re-design of the Model 'C' to a so-called little Model 'D' tractor would keep us two years away in point of time from production on such a cheaper two-plow tractor. . . . It seems that our best opportunity, considering everything such as time, economy of manufacture of one model only, supplying to our dealers a reasonably full line of tractors, would dictate that our best procedure now was to manufacture the Model 'C' as a two-plow tractor and should the all-crop feature fail, then proceed to lay out a little Model 'D'."

If the new model was to be built, space would be needed either at Waterloo or elsewhere. If only existing space was used at Waterloo, the 100-tractor-a-day schedule for the Model D would have to be cut back—and just at the point when demand for the D was going up. If the Model D schedules were to be maintained, probably even expanded, then separate additional factory space would be needed for the new model. Wiman estimated the cost of additional space and of its tooling to be more than $3 million, but he pointed out that "even though we should go so far as to abandon the All-Crop idea and go to a small D machine, all of the machinery and tools would be useful, except possibly 10 percent of the original appropriation. . . ." It was the time loss in such an abandonment that would be costly.

After extensive testing over the spring and summer of 1927, considerable questions still remained about whether the three-row cultivator was the right configuration. C.C. Webber wrote from Minnesota: "It worked better than he expected it would work, and you assure us that the men who are running the tractor find it easier than driving a two-row cultivator." Webber then added an upsetting observation: "You have not the power at the present time to pull this three-row cultivator under all of conditions—that we presume you realize."

The question of the tractor's power had made everyone uneasy right from the start, and doubly so when McCray reported in late 1927 about a test on hilly ground. "Straight up on side hills Model C was okay, but sideways not as good as IHC 10-20." Theo Brown confided to his diary: "At meeting in afternoon it was decided to go ahead with Model C, having in mind that it was not equal in power on hills to IHC 10-20. Also, it was decided to design on paper a two-bottom tractor, simply as a plowing job that could be sold for $775 to the farmer. Silloway and Lourie are strong for the General Purpose tractor. Minneapolis wants a two-bottom plowing tractor only."

Frank Silloway, speaking from the sales manager's perspective, argued persuasively for building the full component of the Ds and Cs, and doing it in Waterloo. Others on the board, notably the often conservative George Crampton, argued against it: "I am very much averse to putting any more money in Waterloo for brick and mortar."

C.C. Webber had the final word: "The tractor business is so definitely connected with the other tools in our line that I think we must protect the interests of stockholders and be prepared to supply the demand. We have suffered very much by not having sufficient tractors this year. We must meet the situation and I would favor the program." Wiman, still harboring many personal misgivings about the new tractor, moved that $3.9 million be expended for new buildings at Waterloo and the board passed the measure without further argument. The die had been cast.

Silloway now decided to rename the tractor and at first considered a popularized name—two suggestions were "Powerfarmer" and "Farmrite." He worried about detracting from the Model D, however: "If we were to name either tractor 'Powerfarmer,' we would give that name to our real power farmer tractor, the Model D. . . . We do not care to popularize with a name such as 'Powerfarmer,' the smaller tractor on which we make little profit, as against the Model D which is a profitable tractor for both the dealer and ourselves to sell and the one that most farmers should buy."

Silloway finally decided against a trade name and told the branches why: "Some of the branch houses have objected to Model 'C'. . . . 'D' and 'C' both have the sound of ee. When the dealer orders a tractor over the telephone, it would be very easy for a misunderstanding to arise because of the similarity in sound." Silloway chose the initials "GP," to stand for "general purpose." In the process, the term "all-crop" was discarded.

By October 1928 the production of the GP tractors was up to about twenty-five per day. But at this point Wiman reported to the board about an unsettling development: "For some unknown reason the horsepower had not been up to expectations. It was hoped that the tractor would develop at least 25-horsepower in order to give proper feel of performance but the dynamometer test has indicated that some of the tractors have developed only from 20 to 22 horsepower. The last 300 tractors show on dynamometer tests, 22.6 HP (belt)." Brown was with Wiman in that week and reported: "He is *very blue* because there has been complaint that the GP tractor is short of power. It seems to me this should be rectified as soon as possible. He is discouraged (too easily) and thinks we should build a regular two-plow tractor. All this is disturbing." Wiman even brought the issue to the board, telling them that he had "given some thought to the proposition of making a straight two-plow tractor to be known as the Model B to either replace the GP or be an addition to the line. Such a tractor would have many parts in common with the D but would only pull a two-bottom plow."

Wiman had been the hell-for-leather advocate for the combine, and at that time Webber had demurred. Now the roles seemed reversed. Webber urged the board: "Regardless of the consideration being given to the Model B or two-plow tractor, no efforts should be spared towards completing the job with a GP tractor as this . . . [is] absolutely necessary before going to the two-plow machine." Wiman finally deferred to Webber's judgment.

As if this was not enough, horsepower concerns relating to the Model D now surfaced. The D's horsepower had been improved a bit in 1928 with the addition of a ¼-inch increase in the cylinder bore and an improved carburetor, resulting in an increase in the drawbar horsepower to about twenty-eight, and thirty-six horsepower on the belt. Unfortunately, Wiman reported, "No more horsepower could be built into our present Model D tractor without a pretty thorough redesign throughout . . . this tractor is now up to its limit of strength and stability with the horsepower delivered to the drawbar as at present. . . . If the I.H.C. is able to beat us in the field on field performance . . . we will have to rely on our selling of these machines in volume on the greater simplicity of the Model D tractors, its two-cylinder construction and its reputation as a low-cost machine from an economy standpoint and from the non-use of a large number of repairs."

The horsepower fears were exacerbated when in January 1929 Deere learned that International Harvester had also incorporated a ¼-inch increase in the bore of the cylinder of their 15-30 tractor, which it was rumored would add anywhere from five to twelve horsepower to the machine. This worried Deere not only because of the disappointing horsepower of the GP, but also as a direct assault on the Model D. Inasmuch as the D was the large-production star of the Deere line, any threat to its sales was even more serious. Wiman reported to the board: "It is unfortunate that this vicious circle or race for horsepower has again been started, but it is not strange when you consider the fact that for the last two years we have been able to outperform the International 15-30 machine, that they should increase the speed and power on their machines to equal or better our own. To sell their old 15-30's on the territory, the International Company have cut the price of this machine

$100 and we believe this will have to be cut further yet."

With the renewed threat from the 15-30's increased horsepower, Silloway decided to reemphasize the competitive advantages of the Model D and issued a bulletin headed, "John Deere, a two-cylinder tractor." The memorandum bluntly denied that Deere was thinking of shifting to a four-cylinder tractor. "Why should we?" Silloway wrote, "The John Deere two-cylinder tractors will do plowing and other field work at the lowest possible cost per acre and, after all, that is what the farmer is interested in." Silloway emphasized the light weight that led to fuel economy, the extreme simplicity, with its low cost of upkeep, and the fact that the owner could do his own servicing.

Detractors of the two-cylinder concept often used as their argument the excessive vibration of a two-cylinder motor. But Deere counteracted this attack by sending a Model D tractor to fairs, mounting the machine on four pop bottles, and putting the tractor in operation with the rear wheels turning. There was not enough rhythmic vibration to shake the machine off the mouths of the bottles (exhibit 10-3).

Wiman's skepticism about the GP was soon confirmed by reactions from farmers. To start with, there were a number of breakdowns in operation, requiring rebuilding of some of the tractors in the field. Even more important was the farmer reaction to the three-row cultivating feature. While many farmers in the cornbelt seemed to accept the notion reasonably well, the cotton growers in the South clearly preferred two- and four-row operations. There were also inherent design problems; one was visibility for the driver on the GP. "It seems to me that the view is the real problem now. The Farmall has the best of us there," noted Theo Brown. Wayne H. Worthington, in his definitive study of the agricultural tractor for the Society of Automotive Engineers, succinctly summed up the reputation of the GP: "Unfortunately, the three-row idea failed in its acceptance and the tractor fell far short of Model D performance and durability."

Within a year, Brown and his development team were back at the drawing boards trying to rectify the GP's problems. A crash program soon brought into production a variation of the GP—the GP Wide-Tread. In many respects it was similar to its predecessor except that it had a long rear axle that allowed the machine to straddle two rows and the first John Deere tricycle front to run between two rows, just as the Farmall did. By the crop season of 1929, the GP Wide-Tread was available to buy and its acceptance not only in the South but in the Midwest was more gratifying. In 1931 the GP itself was modified to raise its horsepower ratings to 15.52 drawbar, 24.30 belt-pulley. A year later, in 1932, the GP Wide-Tread was modified to provide a tapered hood to increase the visibility of the driver and to provide changes in the steering apparatus that prevented the tendency of the front wheels to whip on rough ground. With the second model of the GP, and the modifications and additional features, the GP

Pop Bottles Bear Witness to Balance

Look closely under the John Deere Model D and you will notice that the tractor is supported on four pop bottles. What the picture cannot show is that the engine was running and the rear wheels turning, for the gears were in mesh. Thus have various Deere dealers proven the inherent running balance of the engine, for there is not enough rythmic vibration to shake the machine off the mouths of the bottles. This picture was taken at the Dairy Cattle Congress at Waterloo, Oct. 3. Similar demonstrations were made at the Illinois and Iowa State Fairs. P. W. Guyer, Deere traveler, is at the extreme right of the picture.

Exhibit 10–3. "Pop bottles bear witness to balance." (Farm Implement News, *November 21, 1929)*

finally made a respectable showing in the Deere line. Charles Wiman always remembered his experience with the GP, however, as "an outstanding failure" and often mentioned: "Well do I recall how much tractor business was lost by our company due to bad design of the 'GP' line."[4]

RESEARCH AND DEVELOPMENT
IN THE ORGANIZATION

In the process of masterminding the new product developments of the mid-1920s, Charles Wiman came into his own within the company's board of directors. His engineering training at Yale University's Sheffield School had given him the substantive knowledge to understand the complexities of technology all across the spectrum of products, from combines and corn pickers to tractors. Wiman spent a great deal of time with his product engineers during this period, and he was constantly out in the field at the test sites watching performance ("Driving his Stutz back and forth," Theo Brown often reported in his diary).

Driven by a sense of urgency about these new products, he sometimes leaned quite hard on his staff for results. Brown, who as head of the experimental department was himself working on a number of innovations in cultivating tools, seemed sometimes to resent this pressure: "These are busy days and I have to be careful to keep my feet on the ground. There seems to be a tendency for others to want to do redesigning of the cultivator to some extent. Also Charley Wiman is pushing hard to have this new outfit shipped Wednesday. We must do things right and then fast, but right fast." At several points in Brown's diary he railed at Wiman's intrusions into the development process; "all this is very annoying," he commented at several points. Yet Wiman also believed in high standards of quality and, while exhorting his design people for faster and faster work, still was willing to test the products until they were truly ready. "We have had bitter enough experience in the past," Wiman wrote Charles Stone during the high-tension days of the combine development, "in getting into production too soon without a settled, proven-up, practical, from a field standpoint model."

In the early years of the modern company, product development at Deere had been quite decentralized, and this remained the policy during the 1920s. Theo Brown, heading the experimental department, presumably had legitimate interests across all of the product lines. The department had indeed been accorded heightened prestige in the 1920s; its budget had increased markedly throughout this decade (jumping 30 percent in one year alone, in 1923). Yet, the experimental department was never really in charge of a complete product—its engineers were more concerned with new breakthroughs in components, the kind that could be patented. The factory product engineers sometimes sneered at the experimental people as "never having to innovate under budget constraints."

But the product development people in the Harvester Works, in the John Deere Tractor Works, and in the other factories knew where the real power lay—it was right in their own factories, where they made all the new completed machines. And they jealously guarded their prerogatives. When Stone was just beginning the combine push, in 1925, Brown went to the harvester plant to see if he could give some help. "It is a rather delicate task," Brown wrote in his diary, "and so I want to make the right start. . . . Charley Wiman wants me [to] take on gradually the general company job of being a sort of consulting engineer for the various factories in the line of experimental work."

Even Wiman appeared not to be able to force the factories to share their experimental and product development efforts very widely. The factory managers were a strong, independent cadre, brooking no interference from within or without. The 1920s and '30s became an era of long-tenured, dominant personalities in those roles, with the seniors passing reins to equally strong juniors, thus perpetuating the mystique of power. In some of the smaller factories, a single individual could hold sway for many years—Herman Moschel at the Dain plant in Ottumwa from 1919 to 1947, F.H. Clausen heading the Van Brunt plant at Horicon from 1911 to 1943. Virgil Bozeman led the company's Wagon Works from 1924 to 1949, Carl H. Gamble ran the Spreader Works from 1919 to 1947.

It was at the mammoth bread-and-butter factories—plow, planter, harvester, tractor—that the pattern of powerful leaders was most apparent. There a coterie of works managers passed along their tricks of the trade to their handpicked successors, in the process creating legends about the "power of Harvester," the "intransigence of Waterloo," the "tight control at the Planter Works," etc. Charles Stone headed the Harvester Works from 1923 to 1934, going on to become the vice president for all tractor and harvester production. In the process, Stone was probably the closest confidant of Charles Wiman among any of the factory and branch managers. When Stone stepped up to corporate-wide responsibilities in 1934, L.A. Paradise, another able leader, assumed the Harvester Works post for another twelve years. At the Waterloo Tractor Works, A.H. Head held the reins for a full eighteen years (1919–36), during a seminal period when seven basic models of John Deere tractors were spawned. His successor was L.A. "Duke" Rowland, one of the legendary figures among manufacturing men in the company; when Charles Stone relinquished his line assignments in 1944, Rowland then headed all tractor manufacturing. At the Plow Works, where company machines had been built continuously since John Deere brought his shop from Grand Detour in 1848, Benjamin Kough headed the operation from 1919 to 1936, and he, too, was succeeded by a company legend, L.A. "Pat" Murphy, who served until 1942 and then took over responsibility for all implements. Finally, at the Planter Works, H.B. McKahin held the number-one spot from 1917 to 1937; he was succeeded by Harold White, the manager who was consistently the lowest-cost producer (or near to it) all through his tenure. White held his post there until 1949.

Right in this group of people lay great abilities, great prestige and power, and great egos. They guarded every piece of their company "turf" jealously, nowhere more assiduously than in product development. They were secretive about their plans, often even to the board, and certainly to any other factory or branch. This high degree of decentralization in product development had many positive assets—it encouraged responsible engineering, for the factory had to build the dreams of the development engineers. But it often made the factories recalcitrant and unbending when presented with a new product challenge from one of the sales branches. The latter, of course, did not always realize the need of the factories for steady production of long runs.

A further problem began to intrude more and more in factory and branch relations in the 1920s, triggered in particular by the advent of the GP tractor. In the past, an implement factory in the company would assume that it could proceed independently, with little need to check other units—after all, most of the implements would be pulled by a horse, with tractors mostly for plowing. When the general-purpose tractor achieved almost instantaneous success, however, it became considerably more important to coordinate tractor and implement. So, too, with the combine, and indeed with many aspects of so-called "power farming" (the term that became popular in the 1920s). It was a sobering experience for Charles Wiman and his colleagues to realize that the GP tractor was now "driving" many other product developments that had formerly been almost autonomous. Moreover, they saw that the high costs of tractor development and tooling made it imperative that good decisions were made at the start and that everyone involved—implement makers as well—participated in the decisions. This realization led the company to convene all factory managers for the Power Farming Conference of February 1929. Over his years as chief executive officer, Wiman often used simple adages to cut through the maze of detail characteristic of large organizations, and one of his favorites—"Every horse looks fast running by itself"—had particular relevance here. Wiman was blunt in his keynote speech at the conference—he wanted everyone to "thoroughly understand" the need for coordination, and he insisted on the establishment of a "clearing house" of ideas. He stressed the ties between manufacturing and sales, making clear in the process that "sales are made in the designing rooms of the factories.... You gentlemen here are really the force behind the sales force."

The conference still left intact just about all of the personal power of the factory managers—this was not an assault on decentralization. Product development was still a close-to-the-belt decision, held by the individual managers probably to excess. Indeed, it was not until the early 1970s that certain research and development, as well as product engineering decisions and activities, were centralized. Yet the need for greater coordination was clear and the Power Farming Conference made the first halting step in that direction.[5]

DEERE AND INTERNATIONAL HARVESTER PULL AHEAD

The decade of the 1920s was a watershed for the agricultural machinery industry. First, there were major consolidations. In 1928 the Canadian-based Massey-Harris Company took over the J.I. Case Plow Works in Racine, Wisconsin; Massey immediately sold its rights to the "Case" name to the J.I. Case Threshing Machine Company, also in Racine, and kept for itself similar rights to the prestigious Wallis tractor. In turn, the J.I. Case Threshing Machine Company bought the farm implement business of the Emerson-Brantingham Corporation—the old-line Rockford, Illinois, implement manufacturer that had been in continuous operation since 1852—and then changed the combined company's corporate name to J.I. Case Company, Inc. The next year, 1929, saw another new company organized—the Oliver Farm Equipment Company, a merger of the Oliver Chilled Plow Works of South Bend, Indiana; the Hart-Parr Company of Charles City, Iowa; and the American Seeding Machinery Company and the Nichols & Shepard Company of Battle Creek, Michigan. Oliver, continuing to make its own chilled plow (of which it was a pioneer), now added grain separators and farm tractors. In this same year yet another new long-line company came into being, the Minneapolis-Moline Power Implement Company—a consolidation of the Moline Implement Company, the Minneapolis Steel and Machinery Company (builder of the Twin City tractor, the machine that briefly had been sold by Deere in the 1910s), and the Minneapolis Threshing Machine Company (also a builder of tractors). In this same period, Allis-Chalmers Manufacturing Company of Milwaukee, Wisconsin, added to its tractor line by purchasing the business of Monarch Tractors Corporation of Springfield, Illinois, manufacturer of a track-laying tractor, and then becoming a full-line manufacturer with the acquisition in 1931 of the Advance-Rumeley Thresher Co. of LaPorte, Indiana.

In 1921, there had been 186 tractor companies; by 1930, the number had been reduced to 38. Whereas there had been many dozens of tractor companies and many hundreds of implement companies in earlier years, now there were just seven main companies offering full lines—the "long-line" companies were Deere, International Harvester, Case, Oliver, Allis-Chalmers, Minneapolis-Moline, and Massey-Harris.

A second stage of realignment came when every one of these newly combined companies embarked on the quest for its own general-purpose tractor: in 1930 Oliver introduced its new tricycle Row Crop, Massey-Harris came out with a four-wheel-drive general-purpose model, and Allis-Chalmers announced its All Crop general-purpose tractor. The playing field of tractor competition was fast becoming crowded!

Deere, meanwhile, had not only bought two small companies (the potato harvesting equipment of the Hoover Manufacturing Company and a threshing line, purchased from the Wagner-Langemo Company), but had added more than $7.6 million to existing capacity in its factories and branches. By 1930, the company had opened new branches in Fort Wayne, Indiana; Amarillo, Texas; and Edmonton, Alberta, and had also constructed warehouses in Lansing, Michigan; Sidney, Nebraska; Aurora, Illinois; and Swift Current, Saskatchewan—quite a change from Charles Deere's earlier marketing philosophy of a few large branch houses.

The 1920s witnessed major shifts in market position. The long-line companies picked up increasing percentages of the market for most of the key products. Deere and International Harvester were particularly strong; together they dominated most product categories, with Deere moving up faster in many of these. A Federal Trade Commission report made these public (Appendix exhibit 22).

The reasons for dominance by the larger, long-line companies, in the opinion of both industry and outside analysts, lay particularly in the strong marketing structures of these leaders, with the branch house as the linch pin. Warren Shearer's comprehensive study of the industry puts particular emphasis on the 1919–29 period as "the formative decade." Shearer broke down the extensive documentation in the FTC report (cited above) to show that there were indeed sharp differences among the long-line manufacturers in regard to both manufacturing costs and marketing costs, with the latter particularly striking. He used 1929 for comparative purposes, as shown in Appendix exhibit 23.

Shearer's study confirmed the striking strengths of Deere and International Harvester in the 1920s. He concluded, "It has never been charged that IH and Deere had power to restrict production or set limits on the output of their competitors. It is equally true that their pricing policies were not of a sort to discourage competition except in the sense that such competition was unable to meet Deere and IH prices and still make a profit. If we are to discover any control over the market exercised by these two acknowledged leaders it must be found in the distribution system which characterized the industry.... If we neglect the possibility that these two concerns produced a markedly superior product, and it is fair to assume that this was not the case, the great strength of IH and Deere must have been their dealer organizations or the control they exercised over these organizations."

There were technological product breakthroughs for certain products, for example, the general-purpose tractor of International Harvester. Still, Shearer's judgment corroborates the findings of a number of other analysts: it was the large, strong long-line companies that were able to develop comprehensive distribution systems and use the branch-house concept to its fullest, and thus to develop a marketing relationship with both dealers and farmers that gave them greater strength than the smaller long-line companies. Most of the short-line companies were not able to mount extensive dealer networks that included branches (though some were able to maintain their market share by virtue of patent protection).[6]

The strikingly low selling costs of the three industry leaders (Deere, International Harvester, and Allis-Chalmers) shown in Appendix exhibit 23, testify to the substantial economies of scale in the larger branch-house systems. Yet, these three were also serving their dealers, and the latter serving their customers, the farmers, in a more effective way than the other long-line companies. Deere, in particular, never forgot the lesson that John Deere had learned so well—it was the farmer who would be the ultimate arbiter of success for the company. Deere had always been keenly attuned to the needs of the farmer and had been able to inculcate this in its dealers. The company's quality products were assiduously advertised and promoted, always with the customer's need uppermost. Deere had pioneered with a farmers' magazine, *The Furrow*, first published in 1895 and by the 1920s one of the country's preeminent farmers' publications. At the end of the war, its supervision had been assumed by H.M. Railsback (who had joined the company in 1917 to head advertising and publicity). Deere's catalogs were themselves straightforwardly service oriented, chock full of the kinds of information the farmer demanded; several of the company's service manuals themselves became classics (one, *The Operation, Care and Repair of Farm Machinery*, went through twenty-eight editions). All of these printed sales efforts were complemented by a group of sales-force personnel in both the branches and the dealerships, knowledgeable about their products and thoroughly dedicated to the longstanding Deere pride in its close relationship with the farmer.

COMPANY STORES AND PRICE MAINTENANCE

There were tensions between manufacturer and dealer in this period and they focused particularly on two issues—the number of competing dealerships (with the exasperating issue of the company-owned store), and the maintenance of price levels. When the court decree in the International Harvester case in 1920 limited the firm to one dealer per town, it became much more likely that Harvester would exert pressure on its dealers to carry the complete line and give it "adequate" representation. Deere, too, knew it had to limit its own dealerships to one for each town, but Frank Silloway saw no problem; he felt that this would lead to strengthened dealers. International Harvester and Deere (as well as the other long-line companies) did not explicitly require exclusive dealerships, but, as Shearer pointed out: "There can be little question that this injunction was and, to some extent, is ignored by salesmen in efforts to increase their volume in business." The concern by dealers that they were being pressed to accept exclusivity remained high on their agenda of complaints.

Whether there were too many dealers in a locality was another issue that antagonized the dealers. Particularly threatening was the sharp expansion by the manufacturers of the company-owned store. The major long-line companies all had owned retail store properties from time to time; sometimes the only way to get an operation started in a new area was to purchase a property and lease it to an independent dealer. Deere had opened a small number of these before the establishment of the modern company in 1912. (Indeed, Deere was reputed to be the first

Exhibit 10–4. Top, *Road mowers for shipment, Harvester Works, ca. 1929;* bottom, *Twelve farmers ready to drive grain drills from dealer's store, Casselton, N.Dak., ca. 1930. (Deere Archives)*

agricultural machinery manufacturer to use them.)

But what if the manufacturer chose to continue operation of the store itself? The dealers held a simplistic view that they could not compete with a manufacturer's outlet because they themselves had to use local capital, whereas the factory-owned outlet was primarily concerned with volume for the factory and therefore would not worry too much about return on capital invested in the local outlet. Manufacturers were also accused of using excessive trade-in allowances, extended payment dates, and below-market interest rates as devices for maintaining volume, all subsidized by the factory itself. A John Deere dealer in Oklahoma complained: "I believe the implement business with Hi-Power factory salesmen and sales-promotional policies, with excessive trade-ins, extended payments dates and low interest rates will break any independent dealer. I expect to see implements sold through factory-branch stores only in the next few years." Another Deere dealer, in the state of Washington, reiterated the same theme: "If the farmer is smart and plays one [factory-owned outlet] against the other [independent outlet] he can get his machinery for practically his own price. They extend long credit terms to people who do not have any credit standing in the community. I suppose they can do this because of their legal help and collectors they employ in the field."

The manufacturers argued that a few company-owned stores gave them a better feeling for problems at the retail level and provided an excellent training ground for younger executives. It was left unsaid that the potential for opening new stores served as an implied threat to independent concerns that were themselves not too efficient. R.B. Lourie, Deere's Moline branch manager, cleverly put this point across in a speech before an implement dealers' convention in Illinois in 1927. "You dealers have a slogan, 'To the Retail Implement Dealer Belongs the Retail Trade.' I agree in principle with this doctrine, but thinking straight on this subject, does it not predispose that the dealer should be efficient and that he is to give proper service to his customers and to his suppliers?" Lourie hinted, not too subtly, that if the dealers themselves did not prove efficient, the companies would take over for them: "In business there is always a survival of the fittest. The inefficient man is going to be eliminated and the unneeded man is going to be eliminated. The implement jobber, for example, has been very largely eliminated and for reasons that you gentlemen perfectly well know. There are going to be some implement dealers eliminated. The retail implement establishment of the future is going to be one that will have a suitable organization and proper management, so that it will render prompt and efficient service and on a basis that will produce profit for the owners."

By the time of the next Federal Trade Commission investigation of the industry in 1938, the issue of factory-owned stores was a major one. By then, Deere had more than 100 such stores. The company made a formal statement to the FTC about this issue, noting that they had always attempted to put independent dealers in such stores but in cases where they could not find one, "and the community was too important to leave without a dealer representation, Deere & Company, instead of permitting the liquidation of the business, bought it out and continued its operation as a John Deere retail store." Even by this time, though, the company was not enthusiastic about expanding the concept of retail store management and vowed to the FTC: "We are not interested in retail stores and prefer to transact our business through independent local dealers. All these retail stores now owned by us as listed in Section A are for sale as soon as we can find a suitable independent dealer to purchase same."

The dealers also wanted protection from each other when competition seemed too stiff, particularly when price cutting became endemic. The early 1920s, with so much farmer resistance to price, revived price-cutting tactics, and the dealers appealed to the manufacturers for resale price maintenance or, to use the terminology of that day, a "list and discount" method of doing business. The dealers wanted manufacturers to establish a fixed retail price, quoted widely, and then police its maintenance in order that there not be "unfair" competition on the part of dealers shaving the price. The manufacturers, while interested in maintaining retail prices congruent with their own set prices to their branch-house and jobber price lists, were reluctant to see fixed prices on most implements. Only in the tractor market was the list price common (mirroring the approach of the automobile industry).

Both the federal government and the states seemed genuinely ambivalent as to whether to allow or perhaps even support resale price maintenance. One state, New Jersey, had legislation on the books supporting the concept; a number of other states had statutes, usually generally worded, prohibiting price fixing in general terms. At the federal level, as there was no specific legislation relating to resale price maintenance, the law was the product of judicial interpretations under the common law and under the Sherman and Clayton acts and the administrative rulings of the Federal Trade Commission. These administrative rulings of the FTC became the key government constraint. In the 1920s, the FTC promulgated a set of administrative orders against resale price maintenance, based upon an earlier landmark case, a suit between the Great Atlantic & Pacific Tea Company and the Cream of Wheat Company (1915). The FTC views were subsequently modified by the courts, again leaving the issue nebulous. Implement manufacturers were to be able to "request" their dealers not to resell at less than a stated minimum price and were even to be allowed to refuse to sell to a customer if that customer resold on a basis below the requested minimum prices. Further, manufacturers could use "reasonable," though not "cooperative" or "coercive," methods in collecting information about price cutters and in working with them. On the other hand, they could not demand a contract or written agreement about resale prices, nor could they use such methods as group action, licensing, or other cooperative action to coerce dealers. So assiduous persuasion of dealers for price maintenance was countenanced, provided it was not coercive, secret, or involving group sanctions.

Deere now felt in limbo. For years it had been mailing its dealers copies of a retail price schedule, prepared so that dealers could quote such retail prices to farmers who happened to call directly at a branch house. Frank Silloway and the others in the sales organization were careful to point out that these were suggested prices, but not required by the company. Earlier, other manufacturers had not followed such a practice, but when International Harvester decided to do so in 1928, Silloway issued a major memorandum, reiterating Deere's policy: "Of course, according to existing laws we cannot insist upon dealers adhering to any Retail Price Schedule which we make. We, however, can take a fatherly interest in the retail price at which our goods are sold. We believe that from now on all implement manufacturers will take a greater interest in the welfare of the local implement dealers and that in the future we will have cooperation in this endeavor, which for many years we have been obliged to carry on alone. We believe that this cooperative effort will make the retail implement business more profitable, which will have a beneficial and salutary reaction all along the line." The implement business had recovered very markedly by this year, 1928, and many competitive pressures, such as price cutting, were not as pronounced. Thus retail price quotations could be more readily maintained. Later, in the period of the Great Depression, the situation became more difficult again.

The company did have a brush with the government on pricing in 1926, when the Federal Trade Commission brought suit against the National Malleable Castings Association, also involving 100 of its members (all of whom were made defendants in the case). Union Malleable Iron Company was one of these, and its manager, John Simmon, was also made a defendant. The case was to come to trial in September of that year, but a number of the members of the association decided to plead nolo contendere and take fines ranging from $3,000 to $6,000. Burton Peek found no evidence that the subsidiary had participated in any of the alleged price fixing. "If this were a case against the Union Malleable Iron Company alone, I would advise contesting it." As a number of Malleable's sister companies were involved, however, Peek felt that "our situation is affected by our relations to the other defendants" and he advised that Deere also enter such a plea and submit to the fine of $3,000.[7]

A NEW LEADER

In June 1928, Butterworth was elected president of the United States Chamber of Commerce. (He was also mentioned as a possible presidential candidate to succeed Calvin Coolidge, just as he had been mentioned in

1924 as a possible running mate for Coolidge.) The Chamber of Commerce post was to be a demanding one in time and travel, and Butterworth decided to transfer the mantle of operating management to Charles Wiman. In October 1928 Butterworth proposed the creation of a new position of chairman of the board, which he himself would assume. In turn, Charles Deere Wiman was elected the fourth president of the company, thus keeping family leadership intact at Deere & Company. Butterworth told the board that "this would give him an opportunity to work with Mr. Wiman in his position as President, and at the same time get him acquainted with outside work which has to do with the financial side of the business." The bylaws of the company were amended to incorporate the new post; the role of chairman was to be as "ranking officer of the Company" and it was to have "the duty of formulating the policy and of directing the operation of the Company." The president, in turn, was to be "the executive officer of the Company" and was to act for the chairman when the latter was not available. Though the designation "chief executive officer" was not given to either of the two men, it was obvious from that time forward that Charles Wiman was taking the major role in decision making for the company.

The decade had opened for Deere & Company with two years of heavy losses and considerable difficulties in recovering momentum. The decade closed, however, with three years of resounding success—the last year and a half under Wiman. U.S. agriculture as a whole had had an excellent year in 1925, a mild depression in 1926, and then three more excellent years; most of the machinery manufacturers had done well in these years. The net sales at Deere had climbed steadily from just over $28 million in 1923 to more than $76 million in 1929. The years 1927–29 had highly profitable margins, particularly striking in comparison with the rest of the industry; in 1929 Deere had a return on investment of 26.7 percent, with International Harvester at 17.9 percent and the rest of the industry much below (Appendix exhibit 24).

Deere's spectacular figures for 1929 were published in the annual report dated October 31, 1929—just two days after the Tuesday when 16 million shares were traded at the New York Stock Exchange in a frenzied sag in the stock market that was one of the triggers for the Great Depression. Survival during an economic crisis became the challenge facing Charles Wiman, just over a year after he had assumed the presidency of Deere & Company.

CHAPTER 11

DEPRESSION YEARS

*You had a deposit in that bank of about two million dollars
when this trouble occurred, and you had it there for
some time . . . It is this big Deere & Company deposit that
has helped cause this trouble and it has caused our
company a great big loss. It should be stopped and I want to tell
you and Mr. Wharton that fact and you are the men to stop
it and change it and do it just as quickly as you can
and don't let this big balance in that bank ever occur again.*

C.C. Webber, 1931

◁*Kansas farm auction, 1930s (photograph by Grant Heilman)*

If stockbrokers in New York City were indeed jumping out of skyscraper windows, ruined by the "Black Friday" stock market crash, and if small investors all around the country were in shock after losing their "lifetime earnings," farmers and the agricultural machinery industry serving them were in no such disarray as the new decade began. Though tractor production in 1930 dropped about 12 percent from the peak of the previous year (down to 196,297 from the all-time high in 1929 of 223,081), the first year of the business downturn was not particularly threatening to the seven long-line manufacturers and the major short-line companies. Only Massey-Harris among the seven registered a loss that year, and though the very small and very large short-line companies showed small losses as a group, the middle-range short-liners were themselves profitable.

Frank Silloway had reported to the board on October 29, 1929, that "we believe farmers, generally, are feeling better than they have for some time," and he predicted strong sales for the company in the coming year. Record earnings for the past fiscal year were announced in January 1930, and the board declared not only the regular quarterly cash dividends of $1.50 on the common stock and $1.75 on the preferred, but also an extra stock dividend on the common of 1.5 percent. When the board also affected a 5-for-1 split in both the common and preferred stock, the financial community was dazzled. The annual report of the company was "unusually satisfactory," said the *Chicago Tribune*; the *Wall Street Journal* reported on Deere's "good showing last year in the face of low wheat prices." The *Christian Science Monitor* headlined its article, "Deere & Co. has an unusual earnings record since 1924," and *The Economist* reported, "Deere income and outlook unusual," and followed with a surprisingly strong statement for that conservative journal that "favorable marketing conditions enhance attractiveness of common stock" and a prediction of "continued good results." "Prospects for 1930 are bright," corroborated the brokerage house of Jas. H. Oliphant & Co., which continued: "It has been put in splendid condition and methods of accounting are conservative.... The former dividend rate of $6 will doubtless undergo revision upward when payments on new stock begin." Such optimism was not confined to the farm machinery industry, either. Secretary of the Treasury Andrew W. Mellon stated blithely: "I see nothing . . . in the present situation that is either menacing or warrants pessimism."

But such public posturing is notoriously undependable as a predictor of the future. By late in the spring of 1930, Silloway was warning the board of the poor crop in the Northwest and in Canada, the tightness of money in the country areas, and the unfavorable prices that were beginning to show up in farm commodities. Charles Wiman was nudging the factories toward "underrunning rather than overrunning their approved factory schedules." Employment in the company was high, even rising in April to 8,422 employees (though still substantially under the record average in 1929 of 10,820), but by early July Wiman was reporting on the "general slump in business" and some of the factories were temporarily closed. "The factories were told, however," continued Wiman, "that experimental work should go forward without reduction in this account, as it is most important that the design of our goods be kept up to date."

The board mistakenly gauged the situation as temporary. At a round-table discussion at the July 29 meeting, all agreed that "while business is running very much below normal at the present time, prospects seem to be rather bright for a fairly good volume next year." By the end of the fiscal year of 1930, though, the factory pace was very much reduced and employment was down to 4,795 people. When the final results for 1930 were tabulated, total sales had dropped to just over $63 million, down from a record high of $76 million the previous year. There was still a substantial profit for the year—$7.6 million—but this, too, had sagged from the previous year's record of $16 million.

The company was in far better shape to take a downturn than it had been in 1921. Then inventories had been some $36 million, with $14 million owed to banks and $21 million in receivables. At the close of 1930, the inventory was $20 million, there was only $4.9 million in debts owed to the banks, and some $55.9 million in receivables. The surplus account stood in 1930 at $22.9 million, after a conservative board decision to write off the entire good will account of $17.9 million; no back dividends were due, and reserve accounts amounting to $33.4 million were built into the financial statement. "Our debts are low and our receivables are high," noted the comptroller. "These comparisons are given to indicate the splendid financial condition of Deere & Company today, and to show our ability to cope with any situation that may arise."

But the situation over the next three years became far more serious than anyone had anticipated, for the country had entered the Great Depression. Industrial output was almost halved at its lowest point, in March 1933; unemployment mounted in the country to about 12.8 million in that year (the official figure, but likely understated)—at least one-quarter of the civilian force was unemployed. The patterns of idleness embraced every calling and condition, every age and locus of residence. The wholesale price index for all commodities other than farm products fell in 1932 to 70.2 (1926 = 100), and farm prices sagged even further, to 48.2 in that year. Wheat, for example, hit a low of $.32 per bushel. Forced sales of farms due to bankruptcies, foreclosures, and tax delinquencies multiplied all over the country and were exceptionally heavy in the Dakotas and Iowa. Nature also took a hand in worsening the farmers' plight. There was a substantial drought in 1930 and then a disastrous one in 1934 that cut output by about one-third. Withered crops allowed the winds to pulverize the exposed land, and all through the

Midwest great clouds of soil in the air cut visibility, often to less than 700 feet. Soon the term "dust bowl" struck the public consciousness. Oklahoma was a particularly hard-hit state, and the roads were full of dilapidated vehicles carrying "Okie" families to "somewhere" for a more hopeful life.

With agriculture itself almost prostrate, the machinery industry serving it took the full effects of the Great Depression. At Deere, sales plummeted in 1931 to $27.7 million, sagged again to $8.7 million in 1932, and rose only to $9 million in 1933. All three years were loss years—just over $1 million in 1931, $5.7 million in 1931, and $4.3 million in 1933. Critically important events occurring in these three trying years highlighted some company weaknesses and a number of important company strengths.[1]

FINANCING
THE FARMERS

The comptroller's report of 1930 had noted a signal problem that was to haunt the company—those receivables that stood at the end of 1930 at more than $55.9 million. This was a record high total for the company, some 83 percent of sales, compared with 52 percent in 1929, 44 percent in 1928, and a low point of 27 percent in 1919. Indeed, receivables had only risen to 67 percent in the severe year of 1921. The comptroller's report put the proximate reasons succinctly: it was "due to the sales of tractors, combines, etc. on long terms, and poor collections caused by the severe drought, and the drop in prices of farm products."

Back in mid-1929 Frank Silloway had felt that the company was falling behind its competitors, for the latter were taking farmers' paper for direct credit, either through their individual companies or through specially established finance corporations. Silloway recommended that Deere adopt the former practice, and the board enthusiastically agreed. First, the Moline branch was given the privilege experimentally that very month, then the practice was extended to Kansas City and Omaha and later in the year to Minneapolis. Silloway had been optimistic about its potential at that time, predicting: "We would not increase our outstandings thereby . . . it would merely be a different form of doing business."

If the Great Depression had not intruded, Silloway likely would have been right. As it was, the bottom dropped out of farm prices. The farmer now had little or no money to pay off his debts.

The extent of the discrepancy between sales and collections was not fully apparent until the comptroller's report for 1931 was released in January 1932. The total sales for the year of $27.7 million were actually far below the receivables on the books, which now totaled more than $54.6 million, down only $1.3 million from the previous year. The report pinpointed the various debtors:

Farmers' paper taken for direct credit, including Canada...................................	$12,000,000
Dealers' paper for goods sold and secured by collateral, including dealers' current purchases for repairs, etc., which came due from month to month	25,000,000
Dealers' paper for goods on hand, carried over under the terms of our contract	9,000,000
Russia ($1,500,000.00 since paid).....................	3,800,000
Argentina and other foreign countries	2,800,000
General company accounts and notes	2,000,000
Total	$54,600,000

Silloway, extremely disconcerted by the shortfall in collections, issued a special branch-house bulletin: "For the first time since 1911, and perhaps ever, our outstandings at the end of the year exceeded our sales for the year.... Our problem in 1921 was inventory; our problem during this depression is our outstandings."

How was this to be resolved? Credit and collections have always been two of the most subtle, complex marketing issues facing agriculturally based companies. Farmers typically are debtors—it is in the nature of the equation the agriculturalist faces. Seed, fertilizer, equipment all must be amassed ahead of time, and the exigencies of the ensuing crop season then determine whether the debt can be paid. Now that the era of modern "power farming" had dawned, the time line on these debts had been pushed further out into the future—tractors simply could not be paid off with the proceeds of a single crop season. Implicit in Silloway's decision in 1929 to take direct farmer paper was the need to make a longer term agreement with the farmer. In the depths of the depression, with the farmer unable to sell his crop at a price that could even remotely amortize the debt, farmers throughout the country were falling in arrears on their promises.

To many managers, the soundest collection policy in a period like this was to put as much pressure as possible on the farmer to put machinery debts high on his agenda—as the ever-blunt M.J. Healey put it in his instructions to his Kansas City branch collectors, "Farmers should pay us before they pay other creditors." Manufacturers were making "wealth-producing farm equipment . . . absolutely necessary for farmers to have" and, therefore, this was "conclusive evidence that we are entitled to the first payment.... It would not be fair for the farmers to pay for luxuries purchased with the money produced by our implements before they discharge their obligations to us." Yet such heavy-handedness might well be counterproductive in the longer run. Farmers had the reputation of being responsible debtors, and excessive pressure in a period such as this might produce not heightened payments, but only heightened antagonisms. A delicate touch indeed was needed.

The company's decision—though it was actually hundreds of individual decisions in hundreds of individual farmer contracts—was to carry the farmer as long as necessary to amortize the debt. To be sure, certain farmers had simply given up, abandoning their equipment and moving out of farming altogether. These were lost causes, to be written off as bad debts. The reserve for uncollectable accounts rose from $1.9 million in 1931 to more than $2.4 million in 1932 and just under $4 million in 1933. The uncollectables actually charged against the account were considerably less, though, and the comptroller's report of 1933 pointed out that from 1913 through 1932 only $6.6 million had been written off out of a total sales in that period of $803 million—a .009 ratio of uncollectables to sales. The year-by-year percentages during the Great Depression period were naturally much higher—1932 was just under 7 percent, 1933 more than 8 percent, 1934 at 5.5 percent, and 1935 just over 4 percent. Still, despite four years of extremely difficult conditions, almost 99 percent of all the farmers' debts had been paid over the 1913–35 period, a record attributable both to the farmers' sense of responsibility and to Deere's conscious decision to stick with the farmer through both good times and bad. To be sure, the company's strong financial position as it entered the Great Depression aided this policy. Its results proved to be an incalculable asset for the company. The farmers' loyalty to Deere products, always strong, was greatly strengthened during the period of the Great Depression. The company's belief in the farmer was reciprocated by a farmer response that gave Deere a priceless asset for the future.[2]

SOVIET DEBTS ARE PAID

The receivables listed in the comptroller's report for 1931 named two other critically important customers whose accounts were due. The first of these was Russia, a customer in the late 1920s for an astounding amount of Deere equipment. After the Russian Revolution, the newly constituted Union of Soviet Socialist Republics embarked upon extensive agricultural machinery purchases, especially from the United States. The most noteworthy was its interest in the early 1920s in the Fordson tractor. Thousands were shipped into the country, and even one of the early postage stamps of the Soviet Union (in 1923) depicted the Fordson. As early as 1923 some Deere Waterloo Boy tractors were also in the Soviet Union, sent there on behalf of American relief efforts. Frank Silloway, ever conscious of commercial possibilities, noted to the board: "It is our plan to send an expert to see that the machines are properly started in the field. . . . Our representative will also report on the general conditions as far as future prospects of trade are concerned." Deere engineers from Waterloo did indeed go, and they sent back some remarkable photographs of the primitive Soviet farming situation (exhibit 11-1).

Deere first obtained several substantial implement orders in the early 1920s; one order alone, in 1924, called for 500 No.40 plows. This was soon followed by other orders for plows and tractors, the scale of which dumbfounded everyone in Moline. Joseph Stalin's first Five Year Plan had been promulgated in 1928. This rigid, dogmatic document called for the buildup of Russian economic might on a tight, lock-step staging that required particular pieces to fall in place with a hoped-for exactitude. The quantities of output called for by Stalin were stupefying, setting up almost impossible goals. One of the early pieces of this jigsaw puzzle of plans was the heightening of agricultural production. Stalin and his planning coterie had just collectivized much of Soviet farming (in the process killing many thousands of the peasant farmers, the kulaks). The collective farms were presenting a mammoth management problem, and the Soviet experts felt that only through extensive mechanization could the promise of socialist farming be realized. So the country had initiated massive purchases of agricultural machinery—particularly tractors—from abroad. One of the companies to which they turned was Deere.

Another order came for 500 tractor plows; payment terms were 50 percent in cash and the balance over the following two falls. Silloway soon reported, "All accounts have been paid promptly when due. We know that the Russian government is not recognized by the United States and that we are doing business there at our peril.... We believe it advisable to maintain a representation of the John Deere Line in that country, even though at some time we might take a loss." By 1929, the Russians were buying Model D tractors in large volume, too; one order alone in late 1929 called for 1,500 machines. Silloway again had to field questions from a skeptical board about the credit worthiness of the Soviet Union: "There are those who strongly maintain that the present Government in Russia is so securely entrenched in power that it will endure; while on the other hand, we receive reports that the present Government is losing, somewhat, its hold on the people." Silloway countered with an essentially entrepreneurial proposal: "If we believe that the present Government will remain in power until November 1, 1930 and pay the money they will owe us at that time we would be justified in accepting this order." After much discussion, the board concurred and the order was implemented into the factory planning process. A few months later, the Soviets raised the total to 2,000 tractors, to be accompanied by additional purchases of disk tillers. By this time, the Soviet orders on the books were well over $2 million. The realization that domestic orders had just about dried up added an incentive to take chances on a buyer whose credit standing was, if not poor, at least unknown. When the Soviets again came back (through their state trading entity, Amtorg) for an additional 2,000 tractors, Silloway once more recommended acceptance and the board, uneasily, went ahead.

Exhibit 11–1. Top, *Waterloo Boy tractors ready for shipment out of Odessa, Russia, for various colonies, and eighty mechanics, also American personnel in charge of the seven squads;* middle, *Waterloo Boy pulling four implements known as "bookers," used only in Russia;* bottom, *A view of the vast prairies of Russia, and a part of the eighty Waterloo Boy tractors putting the sod back to productivity after ten to twenty years of lying idle;* next page, *Five Waterloo Boys after a day's work in Russia, in their stalls for the night. The American in charge, and his automobile; photographs and captions, taken in March and August 1923. (Deere Archives)*

The John Deere Model Ds were well suited to the Soviet Union—they were simple and dependable—and soon became revered tractors on the Soviet collective farms and in the machine tractor stations. A Russian children's book was written in 1931 about one of these collective farms, in Yeash district, a place according to its author where "counter-revoluntionary views are known . . . and for that reason [it] was chosen to build a collective farm and a machine-tractor station." The station had eighty-six machines—forty Caterpillar track-laying tractors, thirty-seven Model D John Deeres, and a scattering of other makes. The author waxed lyrical: "Racing along, runs a two-cylinder tractor of 'John Deere' make.

He shines with spurs and the noise of his motor carries the echo far into the villages. 'John Deere' showed himself a punctual good worker on a hard service in machine-tractor station. With obstinateness, given honor to American steel, he carries along with steadiness, without being insured of a good technical attention and professional care. Only after a month and a half of unceased labor, the machine began to demand attention. . . . In Fall the wheat Little Ukraine was planted and gave surprising results. The metallic blue of winter crop was no less surprising than the tireless firmness of American 'John Deere'." The author ended his story with a flourish: "The aim of this tale is to show that the tractor 'John Deere' and wheat 'Little Ukraine' are heroes of the success told above."

Fears about the Soviets' punctuality of payment proved to be unfounded. Stalin had pressed ahead with the Five Year Plan despite massive economic dislocations within the country; the tractors, machine tools, and other purchases abroad were being financed in hard currency obtained by selling priceless Russian art on the world market (Andrew Mellon was one of the largest buyers), and even selling quantities of

Soviet wheat abroad, despite a famine that was stalking the Ukraine. Yet the Soviets continued to fulfill every contract they made during this period. Indeed, not only during the time of the Great Depression, but through the succeeding years, the Soviets were known as harsh, devious bargainers who always fulfilled a contract, once it had been reduced to writing.

By early 1931 the Soviets had spent $5.6 million for company goods; all the required payments had been made right on time. All through 1931, with massive domestic nonpayment, the Soviets fulfilled the requirements on each note; the last were due in November 1933 and came into the company's coffers on schedule.

The total Soviet sales were unbelievable. In the three years 1929–31 the Soviets had bought $9.8 million worth of Deere goods. In one year alone, 1930, more than $5.6 million of the company's $63 million in sales had gone just to this one country—almost 10 percent of the total sales of the company. Deere's tractor sales accounted for 20 percent of U.S. tractor exports to the Soviet Union in 1930 and more than 12 percent for the 1927–33 period (exhibit 11-2).

Exhibit 11-2   **Number of Tractors Sold to the Soviet Union, 1927–33 (numbers of machines)**

	U.S. Industry as Whole	Deere & Company
1927	5,105	13
1928	4,588	51
1929	11,364	2,232
1930	20,447	4,181
1931	22,909	1,679
1932	32	31
1933	8	. . .
	64,453	8,187

Source: Deere & Company, "World Wheel Type Tractor Survey, 1927 thru 1944," (December 27, 1945), Deere Archives, 45040.

The end of the outsized Soviet sales came in 1931 (with $2.7 million); in the following year only some $63,000 was spent, with even more miniscule amounts in the following two years. By 1935, the Soviet Union had stopped purchasing Deere equipment and other equipment as well. It had become more or less self-sufficient in tractors. At the end of 1931, the "Russian business" reserve account still stood at something over $1 million. The financial officers transferred this account to a general "Reserve for Uncollectables"—though the Soviets were paying, others were not! The effects of these latter losses were taken in the year 1931. Thus, although the original annual report of 1931 showed a small profit of $409,000, the recast figures put on the permanent record a loss for the year 1931 of just over $1 million. Thus there were losses in three years—1931, 1932, and 1933.[3]

THE ARGENTINE TRADE TURNS SOUR

In contrast to Russia, Argentina had been a major customer for Deere equipment—and other American farm machinery—since well before the turn of the century. Indeed, in 1894, more agricultural implements from the United States were sold to Argentina than to any other country in the world. Deere sold its equipment in South America through an import house, Agar, Cross & Company of Buenos Aires. Relations between Deere and Agar, Cross were close, and sometime in the early 1890s the Buenos Aires company brought out a full-scale catalog of Deere equipment, complete with an unflattering picture of John Deere in its preface. The first and most prominent implement in the catalog was "El Gilpin." Subsequent pages had a number of other Deere plows, some renamed with Argentine words (the Red Jacket became "Le Garibaldino," the Red River breaker became "Le Tucumano"). So important did the Argentine trade become over the next three decades that Frank Silloway told the board in 1923. "I think that the Argentine particularly will always be our most important foreign market." Argentine agricultural prosperity in the mid- and late 1920s did bring large sales, including substantial numbers of tractors; some 2,194 tractors were sold there in just the one year of 1929.

But the Argentine economy quickly took a nose dive after the stock market crash in 1929, just after a very large shipment of Deere tractors was made to Agar, Cross. Sales in Argentina plummeted and Agar, Cross asked for extensions on the Deere notes due early in 1930; these were paid later in the year but a remaining note for more than $1.9 million that was due in early 1931 had to be extended to 1932. Then, in April 1932, the board learned the bad news that "they were unable to pay this amount." Though Agar, Cross did manage to meet the accumulated interest, another extension on the principal had to be made. An Agar, Cross representative came to Moline in that month and reported dolefully that the Argentine company had an inventory worth more than $13 million, with additional receivables amounting to some $6 million. The company's inventory included more than $2 million worth of Deere products, most of them Model D tractors.

When the economy continued to limp badly over the following two years, Agar, Cross extracted an agreement from Deere to take back 900 of the Model D tractors (on the basis of invoice price, with Agar, Cross assuming the freight both ways, but with that figure then credited to their account). Deere also had to take some Argentine treasury notes, to be paid over a fifteen-year period, thus further dragging out the debt. Between the tractors and the notes, about $1 million ended up being credited to the

Agar, Cross account, leaving a balance due of some $750,000. Deere shipments to the Argentine did pick up a bit after 1935, though the modest sales through the remainder of the decade never remotely approached the substantial amount of business done before the crash.

Exhibit 11–3. John Deere-Agar, Cross tractor in Argentina, ca. 1930s (Deere Archives)

Meanwhile, an import house in South Africa—Dunell Edden & Company of Johannesburg—had also been unable to meet its payments to Deere. The amount of business there was not large and the amount overdue not significant, compared with the Russian or Argentine accounts. In late 1930 the obligation stood at some $600,000, including goods on consignment. Dunell Edden reported that it was near bankruptcy and, rather than default altogether, proposed that Deere itself take stock in the company to the amount of some £70,000 South African. An agreement was struck, and Deere acquired one-half interest in the business. The comptroller valued the purchase at $339,500, the stock being paid for in total by the goods that were already in South Africa. Later the firm expanded into manufacturing—in the process putting Deere into the controversial role of being one of the "American companies doing business in South Africa."[4]

JOHN DEERE OF CANADA

Practically no company in the country was expanding or opening plants in 1931 except Deere, at its Welland plant in Canada. The reasons stemmed from unique features of Canadian-American interactions.

The first recorded shipment of John Deere goods to Canada arrived in Winnipeg, Manitoba, in April 1878; probably John Deere plows or harrows had found their way across the border even earlier than that on some grubstaker's wagon. Deere equipment was sold in Manitoba first by a partnership, Wesbrook & Fairchild, and after 1887 with F.A. Fairchild & Company, which acted as the John Deere agency for Canada until 1907. Deere soon opened new branches in Regina and Saskatoon, Saskatchewan, and Calgary and Edmonton, Alberta, as well as keeping the original branch in Winnipeg. Though there have been other sales branches in Canada over the intervening years, these five have remained the key points, the western provinces being the strongest for the company.

In 1907 Deere purchased the partnership and established its own corporation, the John Deere Plow Company, Ltd. Its first resident manager, H.W. Hutchinson, was a Canadian, and over the years Deere has put most of the management responsibility in Canada in the hands of the residents of that country. Sales to these branches were steady—and significant. In the 1910s the amount sold in Canada ranged from 8 percent to 10 percent of total Deere sales; the percentages in the 1920s ranged a bit higher, reaching almost 15 percent in 1928. These branches were treated the same as a domestic branch and were not considered as "export." Yet Canada is across the border from the United States, and thus the important factor of import duties comes into play.

Canada first exacted a tariff on imports of farm equipment far back in 1847, a 10 percent levy. This figure drifted upward over the next several decades, reaching 25 percent in 1879 and 35 percent in 1883 (the highest level ever recorded). These tariffs were instituted primarily to protect Canadian manufacturers, but with a collateral hope by the Canadian government that they would induce American manufacturers to open Canadian production facilities. Not everyone welcomed these tariffs; Canadian farmers particularly opposed them, as they wanted less expensive machinery and American technological superiority. The farmers' views soon held sway, and the forty years from 1890 to 1930 saw a reversal of the upward movement in the implement tariffs. By 1907 import duties on tillage equipment fell below 20 percent, and the rate on harvesting equipment soon followed. By 1924 the rate for harvesting machinery was down to 6 percent; for tillage machinery it was 7.5 percent and for plows 10 percent. No Canadian manufacturer produced small tractors, so these were let in duty free. Large tractors, however, were manufactured in Canada and were protected by a duty set at 17.5 percent.

Prior to the turn of the century, the company had never seriously considered opening a factory in Canada. In the several years surrounding the formation of the Deere modern company in 1911, possibilities for manufacturing in Canada had complicated the picture. The question of what to do about Dain's Welland, Ontario, manufacturing operation loomed. Dain, as an independent company but with close ties to Deere, had purchased the Welland property in 1908 to manufacture mowers and rakes for the Canadian market. When Cyrus McCormick and William Butterworth engaged in their convoluted negotiations in 1910 toward combining operations, one of the McCormick suggestions had been that they act in concert in manufacturing in Canada. The deal fell through, but Dain formally came into the Deere organization in that same year and Deere inherited a Canadian manufacturing plant, not particularly by choice. At this very time, one of the company's "great debates" was taking place—whether to build a harvester to take on International Harvester. There was some discussion about manufacturing the harvester in Canada for import into the United States, but this seemed unrealistic from a United States tariff standpoint, so a decision was taken to open a new harvester plant in East Moline. Meanwhile, production of the Dain line of mowers, hay loaders, side rakes, and other hay tools was continued in the Welland plant, and John Deere spreaders and Van Brunt grain drills were also added to the line. The sum of these activities argued for a plant expansion there, and this was done in 1913.

By the early 1920s, however, the Canadian tariff for most of this equipment was low, and it made sense to serve the Canadian trade, which was primarily for the western provinces, out of the Minneapolis branch. In late 1923 Leon Clausen, in one of his last acts with the company before moving to J.I. Case, recommended the closing of the Welland plant and the moving of the drill and cultivator lines back to Horicon, Wisconsin; the spreader lines back to East Moline; and the hay tools back to Dain's Ottumwa, Iowa, plant. A sales branch had been in operation in Welland at this time; it, too, was to be closed. Though all the machine tools and even some of the office fixtures of the Welland plant were either sold outright or transferred back to other factories in the United States, the company fortunately made a decision to "mothball" the plant building rather than to dispose of it. A few employees were left as a skeleton force to ferret out delinquent accounts from past sales and to look after the plant.

This arrangement continued for six years and might have gone on indefinitely had not a new Conservative government gained power in Canada in 1930. The latter pledged to "test completely the effectiveness of the protective tariff as an offensive weapon to fight the deepest depression in the world's history" and promptly put its campaign rhetoric into reality with a whopping increase in the tariff. Both implement and large-tractor rates were raised immediately to 25 percent (smaller tractors were still left on the free list). Imports of agricultural machinery into Canada, not unexpectedly, dropped precipitously. If Deere wanted to stay competitive in Canadian sales, it would probably have to manufacture in Canada. Should Deere again do so?

Charles Stone took the advocate's role as the board began to debate the notion. He had been manager at Welland briefly after World War I, and so he was uniquely qualified to speak on the situation. After apprising the board of the details of the tariff situation, he warned them that the Canadian government probably would not accept just an assembly plant—to "ship in goods ready to assemble and paint." To qualify as a "manufacturer," it would be necessary to fabricate a significant portion of the parts of the machines. Stone felt that the company should go ahead, advocating that "if the plant is reopened, it should be with the definite idea that it will be operated for all future time, good times or bad times, high tariff or low tariff, or no tariff. Operations would be increased or decreased as conditions might require, but probably never completely discontinued, so that Deere & Company would cease to be a Canadian manufacturer." The board could not reach consensus, so Charles Wiman himself went to Ottawa, Ontario, for a personal conference with Prime Minister R.B. Bennett to, as Wiman put it, "impress the Prime Minister with our desire to comply strictly with the requirements of the Customs Department," but also to extract some concessions for bringing in machinery and machine tools from the United States. The prime minister agreed, and the decision to move ahead as a Canadian manufacturer was made.

The factory was recommissioned in 1931 and equipment installed for the manufacture of disk tillers, grain drills, grain binders, disk harrows, and gang plows. C.R. Carlson, Jr., went to Welland as manager from Deere & Webber in Minneapolis, and there exhibited the energy and enthusiasm that characterized his later tenure as vice president of sales for the entire company. As the Great Depression waned, the Canadian business began to grow again and over the succeeding years the Canadian segment of the company continued to be an important contributor to overall company revenues.[5]

EMPLOYEE TRAUMAS

The period 1930–33—the depth of the Great Depression—wreaked its havoc on the Moline area and the company, just as it did on thousands of other communities and hundreds of thousands of other companies all through the land. The doleful message, "No Orders," made mass layoffs the rule everywhere, throwing breadwinners onto their own resources, painfully little in most cases. When Deere's sales fell from $63 million in 1930 to $8.7 million in 1932, everyone knew that those miniscule purchases would be made mostly out of existing inventory, with little if any new work being required. In mid-1931 massive layoffs had to be made—total factory employment fell to 1,270 from 4,800 the previous year—and even those working shared a reduced-hour schedule. Small wage cuts were made for those factory employees still working; by mid-1932 the average hourly wage at the Plow Works had fallen four cents, from $.57 to $.53. The pattern was essentially the same in the other factories. More substantial cuts were made in salaried employees' wages, with a 5 to 10 percent reduction being made in 1931 (those making more than $2,500 taking the larger cut) and a further 10 percent late in the year.

Then, in mid-1932, a more stringent measure was applied, with those earning more than $3,000 taking a full 25 percent cut, with scaled down amounts for those under this figure.

The greatest challenge was to try to bring the unemployed members of the company through the times without disintegration of their families' living standards. The company's abiding concern for its employees, demonstrated over many years of reciprocal regard, was to be tested under the most trying conditions.

Deere's employee benefit plans aided measurably in this period, particularly the longstanding Thrift Plan. The plan, instituted in the early 1920s, provided two vehicles for employee savings—a conventional savings account, drawing 5 percent from the company, and a mechanism for purchasing savings certificates in fixed denominations, this later to pay 6 percent. By July 1930, more than $1.3 million of the certificates had been purchased and these now functioned as relief measures, George Crampton reporting in that month: "From all quarters we hear of praise and gratification on the part of employees for the accumulated savings to tide over the period of unemployment." Some company benefits had to be put in suspension during these years; for example, vacations with pay were discontinued in 1931 and not reinstituted until 1936. On the other hand, the company continued group insurance for unemployed members of the force and soon was engaging in a wide range of "make work" activities for employees and providing outright relief for others. By 1932, the city of Moline and the state of Illinois began to assume more of the relief burden. Those employees who were renting company houses simply could not pay their rents in many months, and the company made two reductions in the rentals totaling some 17 percent. Temporary reductions were also made in the pension plan, having the effect of reducing the minimum pension from thirty to twenty-five dollars per month, with similar reductions for those retiring with larger amounts.

Deere management clearly suffered less in economic terms, but it shared fully the worries and the disconcerting, unpalatable decisions that had to be made. William Butterworth, while still keeping in touch with the situation as the company's chairman, was several steps removed from the firing line of these decisions. He had been reelected national president of the United States Chamber of Commerce in 1930 and was resident in Washington many days of this period. He often was called for consultation by President Hoover, and he frequently participated in national conferences related to the economic situation. This rarefied perspective seemed to filter the raw facts for Butterworth, who wrote in his diary in July 1932, at the depths of the crisis: "There is very little business, but we are much better off than we were 10 years ago." Inevitably, the burden of day-by-day Deere decision-making fell squarely on Charles Wiman. This was a searing experience for Wiman, one that left permanent marks on the way he viewed the business—and himself.

One incident early in the Great Depression dramatized to Wiman more than any other the wrenching nature of being the final authority, the de facto chief officer. That was the $1,200,000 defalcation at the Peoples Savings Bank in Moline. Peoples had had seventy-four years of uneventful history up to this untimely moment, and all through this period the bank was linked inextricably with Deere & Company. First founded by John Gould, John Deere's old partner, in 1857 as a private bank, it became the First National Bank of Moline in 1863, and John Deere himself was president for one year in 1866. In 1891, a separate bank, the Peoples Savings Bank of Moline, was organized by Charles Deere and others, with Deere himself as president; this entity merged with the First National Bank of Moline in 1905. On Charles Deere's death, William Butterworth had become president, remaining so through the time of the defalcation. George Crampton, the Deere secretary, was also chairman of the board of the bank. Thus, over the years, Deere's name had been synonymous with the Peoples Savings Bank; in 1907, for example, Charles Deere's photograph was featured in the bank's advertising, and the bank was heavily patronized by Deere employees all through its three-quarters of a century of existence.

The swindle was done cleverly, by the cashier and two other inside accomplices. When the full facts became known, the bank examiners found that most of the money had been squandered on real estate investments, none of which would bring the bank much in restitution. The bank's board of directors was faced with not just a scandal, but, given the particular times—in the depths of a depression—the maintenance of the economic lifeline of the town of Moline and the area around it. Butterworth was in Washington and was not available except by telephone, and so it was left to Wiman, Crampton, T.F. Wharton, and Frank Silloway to make an overnight decision about the posture of Deere & Company, in order to forestall closure of the bank the next day by the state bank examiner. The company had maintained an account at the bank of more than $2 million, far beyond its operating necessities; it was in this account that the shortage had been brought about. In essence, the capital, surplus, and undivided profits of the bank were almost entirely wiped out.

Wiman and the other three made the decision that night that Deere would give the bank its check for $1,290,000, for, as Wiman told the Deere board the next morning in a special meeting, "If we do not do this the bank closes. . . . As I view it, there are approximately $7,000,000.00 of savings deposits in this bank, largely made by the wage earners of our factories, and the effects upon them of the closing of the bank, and the resulting consequences to this Company, are beyond calculation." The directors and shareholders of the bank had been contacted and all had agreed to a voluntary assessment of 100 percent upon their own stock, this money to be used as partial repayment to Deere & Company.

Nevertheless, it was clear that the company was going to end up with close to $1 million of notes that might not be paid back for many years, if ever.

The embezzlement became public knowledge the next day and that same day a joint announcement was made to the public by the bank through George Crampton as chairman and Deere & Company through Wiman as president assuring the public that the amount of the defalcation had been fully restored by Deere and by the larger shareholders. A run on the bank was prevented, and though several other banks in the Moline-Rock Island-Davenport area closed in later months due to the depression, the Peoples Savings Bank was able to keep its doors open. The "larger shareholders" were, of course, made up mostly of Deere family interests, and when the state auditor ordered that additional funds were needed for cash reserves, William Butterworth, Charles Wiman, and Dwight Wiman together exchanged their own notes aggregating some $650,000 for notes held by the bank for a like amount. Some were later paid back, but when the final chapter was closed, many years later, the families had taken severe losses.

Other Deere board members from outlying locations rallied to Wiman's side after these decisions were made. Willard Hosford wrote from Omaha about the "favorable notoriety that this action would bring," and S.H. Velie, Jr., penned a sympathetic note from the Kansas City branch. "It came to you like a thunderbolt out of a clear sky and you arose to the emergency and saved the bank and its clientele in a manner that will always be a source of comfort and gratification to yourself and to your kind."

Not so C.C. Webber—he was neither solicitous nor kind to Wiman, writing a stinging letter that rambled a good deal but left no doubt about where he stood. "I have not paid any attention to it of late years, but you had a deposit in that bank of about two million dollars when this trouble occurred, and you had it there for some time. These gentlemen tell me that the thought in having Deere & Company keep this big deposit in this bank was so that it would be as big as its neighbor. That is all nonsense, the size of the bank has nothing to do with its solidity or its worth to the community. Never mind the size, run a good bank and a sound one. It is this big Deere & Company deposit that has helped cause this trouble and it has caused our company a great big loss. It should be stopped and I want to tell you and Mr. Wharton that fact and you are the men to stop it and change it and do it just as quickly as you can and don't let this big balance in that bank ever occur again. . . . It is up to you two gentlemen to realize and change this situation and change it right away. . . . Lord knows, stop it now and correct it, because it is to be the interest of the stockholders of Deere & Company that it be stopped. It has caused them loss enough already."

Wiman wrote a conciliatory, apologetic note back: "I agree thoroughly with you about the carrying of bank balances. It has bothered me in the past and I should have appreciated knowing your attitude in the matter. We want to work out of this bank business just as quickly as possible." Wiman vented his own personal frustration to Webber: "My predilection is for Deere & Company, and not for banking. . . . You have no idea how much trouble this whole affair has caused us." Webber, in his return letter, said he knew that the matter had been distressing but, nevertheless: "I very much hope that you gentlemen will act forthwith to correct the situation as to the size of our bank balance, and that never again will our company be subject to the criticism that can rightly, it seems to me, be laid to it now for carrying a balance in this bank so large as not to be in the interest of Deere & Company."

Webber's acerbic views were dissected by the Moline members of the board over the next few days. Frank Silloway commented: "I think there should be a resolution adopted by this board—perhaps in the next five years—that no director of Deere & Company can be a director in the bank. Within the next five or ten years we want to get out of the banking business and not father it." The board did not follow Silloway's or Webber's advice, though, for in January 1933 a new bank, the Moline National Bank, was organized, with more than 90 percent of the stock held by Deere & Company. The Moline National was put together out of the ashes of the Peoples, which went under at this time. The latter's depositors received only 40 percent of their holdings at first, but by 1941 all the rest had been paid back, due directly to Deere's abiding concern that none of the Peoples' depositors should be left with a loss. The good will generated by this was immense, for the company was seen, correctly, as the savior of the "little people." Hosford was right about the public relations effect of the company's forthright action. (Deere, incidentally, kept its shares in the Moline National until 1958, when it sold them to outside interests.)

Charles Wiman truly had a baptism of fire in this sad case; most of the responsibility had fallen on his shoulders, though William Butterworth did return quickly to Moline to help. The weight of the decisions troubled Wiman so much during this period that he became, at least temporarily, an insomniac, pacing the halls of Overlook, perhaps walking in some of the footsteps that his grandfather, Charles Deere, must have made in the trying times of the proposed combinations and plow trusts at the turn of the century.

Wiman now turned more conservative, harking back to some degree to the same caution preached to him by his uncle, William Butterworth. A poignant exchange between Wiman and Wharton, his now elderly treasurer, illustrates the tension Wiman felt in this period. In July 1931 the Chicago *Journal of Commerce* printed a small article, recounting "a bit of Oriental wisdom . . . a story from old Bagdad" in which a wise man replied to a youngster's question as to how to get value received by saying: "A thing that is bought or sold has no value unless it contains that which cannot be bought or sold. Look for the Priceless Ingredient. . . . The Priceless Ingredient of every product in the market place is the honor and integrity of him who makes it. Consider his name before you buy." Wharton happened to read this little homily, and clipped it for Wiman, attaching his own views: "This applies to John Deere. It is up to us to keep together this organization that puts the quality in John Deere goods, and provides this Priceless Ingredient." Wiman's reply was probably a bit of a surprise to Wharton: "That's true—but the 'Priceless Ingredient' must not cost too much or no one can afford to buy it."

The Webber criticisms of company financial acumen were probably deserved—there had been an overwhelming feeling of pride and proprietorship in the bank, and prudent financial wisdom was undoubtedly submerged in keeping the very large balances in the bank. The ugly incident taught the company's executives a painful lesson; Charles Wiman knew he had made a mistake, and he came out of this situation a financially wiser person.

Wiman's experience with the relief programs of the company had also given him a keen sense of the differences, good and bad, among the Deere employees. He spoke of this at length in a remarkably frank statement to the board in October 1932: "Out of the mass of experience coming from this depression, one thing particularly has been brought forcefully to our attention. When the time comes to increase the force in the various plants of Deere & Company, I am convinced more attention must be given to the character and home life of the people we employ. More and more, employers are assuming responsibility for their employees and society is fixing the responsibility upon them. Social legislation of various sorts is more sure to increase throughout the country. Old age pensions and unemployment insurance are examples. It seems to me in the future it will not be enough to know that a man is a satisfactory workman, we shall have to know something about how he manages his home and his affairs so that he will not become a dependent on the industry immediately after any downward swing in production. In other words, we should maintain about the same record of a family that is now maintained by a good welfare agency. Industry can well afford to help those employees who are helping themselves, but should not be saddled with responsibility for the other type. We can only protect ourselves by more selective employment."

For many years after, Wiman would recount the traumas of the Great Depression and the need for caution and care in the company in order to anticipate such happenings again. In 1946, when there was a small downturn at the end of World War II, Wiman spent the first half hour of a speech to a group of factory and branch managers recounting the various depressions that the company had faced—first the downturns of 1913 and 1921, then the crash of 1929–33, and the smaller downturn after 1937.

This speech was noteworthy also for its positive, optimistic thread and its punch-line ending: "The sky is the limit." The ability of Wiman to preach caution, thrift, and spartan surroundings for offices and factories while also infusing the organization with a sense of purpose and excitement turned out to be the hallmark of his management style after the Great Depression. His charge-ahead personality of the late 1920s had been tempered and chastened by the kinds of decisions he had been forced to make in the downturn. Yet his ebullience, verve, and drive made him an arresting and exciting person with whom to share the work of an organization. *Fortune* magazine, in a breezy but penetrating article about the company in 1936, said of Wiman: "His rapid-fire distinctions between the virtues and costs of four-cylinder, two-cylinder and diesel tractors contrast abruptly with the sententious appraisals of human nature that seem to comprise the day's work of many older officers of Deere.... He is boyish, fast-talking, superstitious. He punctuates his remarks with such period slang as '*Siest du*?' and reminds you of Scott Fitzgerald's post-War Middle West." Max Sklovsky, the Deere experimental engineer and contemporary of Theo Brown, in writing about Wiman in 1946, again emphasized these qualities: "He possesses a combination of realism and vision.... He is a game, at times ruthless, man, but his delightful personality overcomes some of his deficiencies. At times he indicates an alarming frankness and encourages that in others. He ingratiates himself readily. He is no softy at heart but his driving is not always steady."[6]

INNOVATING IN A DEPRESSION

"With everything so quiet it is very hard to get any enthusiasm in work. It is depressing to learn so much about hard times, cutting expenses, etc. An experimental man needs enthusiasm to do good work. And I can see how this depression affects original thinking." Theo Brown, writing downheartedly in his diary in 1931, captured the essence of the dilemma facing a researcher in those darkest days of the Great Depression. How can one feel excited about new ideas when everything around him cries, "Caution! Cut back! Don't do!" Susceptible to depression in this period, Brown confided to his diary his frustration and sense of a loss of purpose.

Several longstanding company experimental endeavors were indeed severely curtailed, including the soil culture department and several experimental farms in the Moline area. The former had been the brainchild of Dr. W.E. Taylor, who had started it for Deere in 1910 and had developed a set of company publications on soil culture that were advanced concepts in the field. Taylor, a prolific speaker, built a strong following among soil scientists around the country. By 1931, he was ready to retire, and it seemed appropriate, given the economic situation, to close the department. Work in soil science continued in the advertising department, though at a slower pace in the 1930s.

But Charles Wiman had no such doubts about basic product research. Of all Wiman's management decisions during the Great Depression, the one that was probably most long lasting in effect was his decision to aggressively continue new product development through the worst days of the downturn. Already the Model D tractor was highly popular with the trade—the company had sold more than 100,000 units by 1930 and would keep the model in the product line twenty-three more years after this date. The GP and its companion, GP-Wide Track, had not done as well, though more than 35,000 would eventually be made before the latter was terminated in 1933, the former in 1935. Still, competition from the other companies constrained one from resting on laurels with one good model and two somewhat limping models. Also, it was becoming increasingly apparent that farmers around the country were avidly looking for many improvements—adjustable tread widths in the rear wheels, less side draft in the tillage instruments, perhaps even smaller versions of existing tractors.

By 1931, Wiman had put Brown and the other engineers to work on new tractor ideas, and a few months later, in April 1932, he sent Brown on a special trip to Dain, Van Brunt, Syracuse, and the Wagon Works to "pep them up somewhat on experimental work." Out of Wiman's constant press for experimental and engineering effort, and his exhortations for fresh ideas, came two new tractors, the Model A (16.22 drawbar horsepower, 23.5 belt-pulley horsepower) and the Model B (9.28 drawbar horsepower, 14.25 belt horsepower). Tested in the Salt River Valley in Arizona in 1933, the Model A was brought into production in the following year; one year later the Model B was introduced.

The two tractors were strikingly successful; both would stay in the product line until 1952, with more than 293,000 of the As sold by that date, more than 309,000 of the Bs. The two tractors rank first and second in popularity over the entire tractor history of the company.

The Model A was the solution to Deere's need for a two-plow tractor. Its adjustable wheel tread answered the farmer's need for moving his wheels outward or inward from the then-typical 42-inch standard row. (There had to be this much room for the farm horse to continue to walk on solid ground for each pass through the field.) The implement hitch for the A, as well as the power shaft, was located on the center line of the tractor, substantially reducing any side draft. An industry first, a hydraulic-power lift system, increased both the efficiency and speed of operation, as well as providing a "cushion" drop of equipment. There were other important features, for example, a one-piece transmission case that allowed high under-axle clearance.

The simple, powerful two-cylinder engine successfully burned distillate, fuel oil, furnace oil, and similar low-cost fuels, as well as kerosene or gasoline. Thus the engine could be started with gas, then switched over to the lower grade fuels. These cheaper substitutes burned more effectively in the big cylinders of the two-cylinder engines than when used in the conventional four- and six-cylinder engines. This was a period of hard times, and an economical design with economical fuel was particularly important. Wayne Worthington, in his definitive study of the tractor, evaluated Deere's decision: "Deere & Company had always taken a contrary position with respect to fuels, and as others turned to the use of Regular gasoline (70 octane) they continued to promote the economies made possible by the use of available low cost distillates. A continuing program of combustion research was followed, which resulted in increasing the compression ratio of their distillate burning engines by some 40%. The resulting fuel economy broke existing records when tested at Nebraska. This served to educate tractor users to the importance of fuel economy even though the price of tractor distillate delivered to the farms was in the order of 8 to 8½ cents per gallon."

The two new tractors were just the right sizes—the Model B was described as "two-thirds the size of the A," and company literature stressed that the A gave the pulling capacity of a six-horse team, the daily work output of from eight to ten horses, with the B having the pulling capacity of a four-horse team and the daily output of six to eight horses. The B was made particularly as a one-plow tractor. It had all the features of the A—the adjustable wheel tread, the clearance, the excellent vision, etc. (and both were available with pneumatic rear tires as alternatives to the regular metal wheels). The B had a hydraulic-power lift and, within a year of their introduction, both were also available with single front wheels (the AN and BN versions). By 1936, there were eleven different versions of the company's three basic tractors—the A, B, and D. Both the A and B were also made with standard tread, there were orchard tractors available (with covered fenders for the rear wheels and no protruding stacks at the top of the tractor), and there were versions of the A and B that had adjustable front-wheel treads, as well as rear-wheel adjustments. As the success of the two new tractors sank in, company literature, such as the catalog of 1936, exultantly extolled the many new features and reaffirmed in aggressive advertising prose the efficacy of the two-cylinder tractor (exhibit 11-4).

Probably no single stage in the entire history of the company's product development was any more important than this one. The appearance of the two new tractors in the depth of the Great Depression was a testimony both to the company's optimism about the future and the farmers' desires for and willingness to buy simple, trouble-free farm tractors. The abiding regard for and love of the two new models—the Model A and the Model B—continued all through the 1930s and '40s up to their final models in 1952 and left a residual of acclaim that made the models collectors' items for tractor buffs down to today.

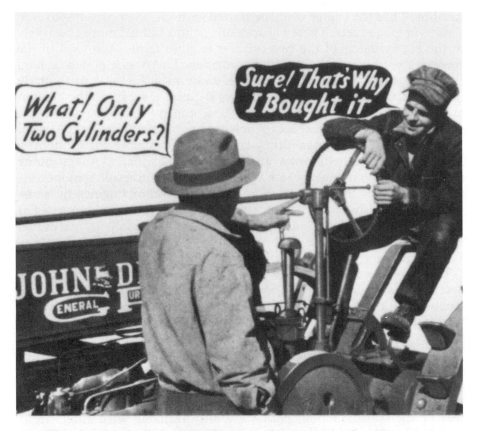

Wise buyers look for simplicity in buying new farming equipment Each farmer's experience with modern farm equipment tells him that the machine with the fewest working parts is the machine that gives the least trouble, and takes the least power to run.

Exhibit 11–4. *"What—Only Two Cylinders!" (Deere & Company general catalog, 1936)*

It is likely that the company would not have taken the steps to initiate these two new models had it not been for Charles Wiman. His longstanding love of both innovation and the engineering to back it up stemmed from his own academic training and his continuing enthusiasm. No armchair philosopher, he was always out in the field observing, and this was seen by everyone to enhance product innovation in the company at a time when it was desperately needed. The expenditures made in that uneasy period were substantial, particularly in light of the cuts in every other expense item in the company, both in factory and branch. It was a gamble by Wiman that was based upon faith and sound judgment, and its payoffs for the company in succeeding years were very great indeed.[7]

THE DEATH OF
WILLIAM BUTTERWORTH

William Butterworth's tenure as president of the United States Chamber of Commerce extended through two reelections and embraced three critical years in the life of the national economy—1929–31. After 1931, he continued as a member of the senior council of the Chamber, maintaining his Washington apartment. He graced the inner council of advisors to President Hoover. Despite his Republican politics, he also was called on not infrequently by Franklin Delano Roosevelt. A member of the board of directors of a number of national business organizations, he continued to be active in conferences and important private gatherings of national business figures.

On Wednesday, May 27, 1936, he was in Chicago to have his picture taken for an upcoming article in *Fortune* magazine, going from there to a board meeting at the Illinois Bell Telephone Company. On the next day, he traveled to New York City for a meeting of the National Industrial Conference Board, leaving that afternoon for Absecon, New Jersey, where meetings were to be held at the "Yama" conference center. He took a walk that afternoon with Gen. Charles G. Dawes and David Sarnoff, president of the Radio Corporation of America. There was golf that day, though Butterworth did not take part. At the conference meeting that evening he was animated and made "quite a speech" on Sunday (according to his friend Silas Strahn). After lunch that day (May 31), he went for a walk with another friend and, as they were laughing and talking, he fell backward and was gone, victim of an acute coronary occlusion.

This was the 99th year for the firm; plans were already underway for the 100th anniversary, scheduled to be celebrated a few months later. Few American companies could boast at that time of 100 years of existence. Even fewer still could point to an unbroken family management—and probably no other company could point to 100 years of existence under just three chief executive officers. William Butterworth was mourned for his leadership, though we have documented a number of weaknesses along with his strengths. He was mourned universally for his personal qualities—he was benign and honest, thoughtful and humane. His deep sense of regard for and care about the employees of Deere & Company made the firm a special, unique Deere "family." It was not just that it was a family-owned corporation—the country had a number of these, not infrequently with less-than-effective managerial climates. The quintessence of the Deere story in those first 100 years was that employer and employee were truly close knit, with progressive policies from the employer and responsible productivity from the employee. Rooted in those first 100 years were cardinal values in being a "Deere employee" (from top management down to the newly hired) that continue to give the company lineaments of human relations and sound personnel interactions that have been the envy of American industry down to today. William Butterworth had a very influential role in this.

MANAGEMENT (AND FAMILY) TRANSITION

Deere & Company was not affected materially by William Butterworth's death, for reasons documented earlier. Top management would miss his counsel, for he had been intimately involved in the company since 1892. In particular, Charles Wiman would mourn the loss of his uncle not only as a revered father figure (William and Katherine Butterworth had had a profound role in raising Charles and his brother, Dwight), but also as an always trusted chairman of the board. Though Charles Wiman was straightforwardly the chief executive officer of the company during the first half of the 1930s, he had drawn upon Butterworth's legal expertise and his wisdom in making the many critical decisions forced upon him during that trying period. Still, the company continued on with scarcely a ripple at William Butterworth's death.

Nor was there any significant change in the pattern of family ownership in the company. At Butterworth's death, he held just over 28,000 shares of common stock and an additional 21,000 of preferred (the total shares outstanding were 1,001,454 for the common and 1,543,000 for the preferred). His shares passed to his heirs in the family but did not much change the basic structure of the family's holdings. These were the owners of the blocs of more than 10,000 shares of the common and the preferred stock in February 1936 (out of a total of 2,401 holders of common, 4,936 of preferred):

	Common	Preferred
William Butterworth	28,636	21,265
Katherine Butterworth	68,172	66,185
Three Charles Deere trusts	259,392	243,205
Charles Deere Wiman	14,654	12,150
Dwight Deere Wiman	10,553	41,000
Pattie Southall Wiman (trust)	. . .	14,650
C. C. Webber family holdings	25,598	37,740
Clarence Nason family holdings	23,157	29,330
John Good family holdings	18,255	. . .
Willard Hosford family holdings	12,446	36,735
Charles K. Velie.	. . .	10,337
George Mixter	. . .	12,000
Three brokerage-firm nominee holdings of common stock for unnamed clients	68,594	. . .
Two other brokerage-firm nominee holdings of preferred stock for unnamed clients	. . .	30,106

Several facts about these figures are important to note. First, both common and preferred stockholders had (equal) voting power for election of the board of directors (the preferred shareholders had been given this right in 1930). Second, the three Charles Deere trusts, so dominant in comparison to all other holdings, were administered (and their shares voted) by the two Wimans and Burton Peek after William Butterworth's death; the proceeds of the trusts went in the main to the Butterworth and Wiman families. Third, though Charles Deere's descendents no longer held an absolute majority of stock (nor did even the entire combination of John Deere descendants and near relatives), the total of the Butterworth-Wiman holdings alone was enough for practical operating control.

Only at infrequent times were the shareholder records put through the laborious process of following each and every family holding (of record and through nominees) to ascertain exactly how much of the company was owned by each of the five direct lineal descendants of John Deere. This research was carefully done in 1948; though it was some dozen years after William Butterworth's death, the patterns were essentially the same as then (remembering that total shares had increased by intervening stock splits):

January 15, 1948

	Common	Preferred
Jeanette Deere Chapman (Hosford, *et al.*)	60,675	42,983
Ellen S. Deere Webber (Webber, Keator, Mixter, Murphy, *et al.*)	57,256	40,460
Charles H. Deere (Butterworth, Wiman, *et al.*).	1,056,500	353,644
Emma C. Deere Velie (Velie, *et al.*)	15,487	17,856
Alice Deere Cady (Cady, *et al.*)	. . .	2,085
Total family, both classes 1,646,946		
Outstanding, both classes 4,547,362		
Percent family holdings 36.22%		

(total number of shareholders: 13,294 of common, 5,994 of preferred)

It was palpably clear that at the death of William Butterworth, Charles Wiman was the dominant figure in both company and family, influenced undoubtedly by Butterworth's gracious and respected widow, Katherine, and by the loyal, longstanding friend and lawyer, Burton Peek. Dwight Wiman was too busy with his burgeoning career as a Broadway producer to have much time for company interests.

Charles Wiman continued in the 1930s a pattern of living that had some outward similarities to that of the life style of William Butterworth in this same period, as Butterworth, having turned his business interests and avocations toward a national focus, spent considerable time both in Chicago and in Washington. In the national capital, Butterworth not only had a comfortable apartment on Dupont Circle, in the same building with Secretary of the Treasury Andrew Mellon, but also a farm near Washington, facing a lake and furnished with antiques to fit the architecture of the house. The presidency of the Chamber of Commerce was just one of many other widespread involvements—he was many years a director of the Playground and Recreation Association of America, a member-at-large of the National Council of the Boy Scouts of America, and so on. William Butterworth finished his productive life as a distinguished participant in public service.

Charles Wiman, on the other hand, was not nearly as involved in activities outside of his presidency of Deere; as *Fortune* put it in the article of 1936, "Charley Wiman sticks to the business of changing the presidency of Deere from the influential sinecure he inherited to a high-tension job of work." Wiman did share one Butterworth pattern, and for Wiman it became a lifetime procedure. Wiman enjoyed Chicago immensely and kept an apartment and office there for the remainder of his life. He also had come to love the family places in Arizona and California, particularly at Santa Barbara, and spent much time there. Charles Wiman became a yachtsman par excellence, maintaining a substantial boat on Lake Michigan and a renowned yacht in California, the *Patolita*, which he raced to Honolulu, Hawaii, in 1949 to a third-place finish in that internationally watched event. As a superficial generalization, one might conclude that Charles Wiman was treating his responsibilities to the business a bit lightly, dabbling in dilettantism. The *Fortune* editors were rather too errant in implying this in their article: "After trying for eight years to think of him as the rightful squire, middle-class Moliners are still a little puzzled by Charley Wiman. They understand that if his job weren't there he probably would not live in Moline, and they class him with his kid brother Dwight, who is a New York theatrical producer and never comes home except for directors' meeting."

Available evidence would surely corroborate *Fortune* in its judgment that Charles Wiman would probably not have chosen to live in Moline if the company had not been there. It is also an established fact that Wiman at least once proposed to the board that the headquarters of the company be moved to Chicago (the board demurred).

But *Fortune* was far off course in implying that Wiman was treating the business a bit cavalierly. Wiman had Deere & Company deep down inside of him, a fierce, aggressive pride about its business and its products. Probably much more than his Uncle Butterworth, he looked upon the company as a producer of a critically needed physical good—agricultural machinery. Butterworth would have used more explicitly financial terms in defining his feeling for the company. The company was an overwhelming, dominating influence on Charles Wiman—and he was an overwhelming, dominating influence on it. It is true that he was able to manage the company with frequent visits away, sending back decisions and advice from afar. There never was any doubt, though, that Charles Wiman was the head man at Deere & Company.[8]

RECOVERY FOR THE FARMER
AND HIS SUPPLIERS

Franklin Delano Roosevelt's New Deal legislation had enormous effect on agriculture. Set in motion in the early and mid-1930s was a system of agricultural support built upon a controversial concept—that the country could resort to planned scarcity to raise agricultural prices and, eventually, the agriculturalists' incomes. The key piece of New Deal farm legislation was the Agricultural Adjustment Act, passed just over three months after Roosevelt took the oath of office in 1933. The act was built on the bedrock concept of subsidy—in return for the farmers voluntarily curtailing acreage and/or livestock, they were to be granted direct cash payments. These benefits were to be paid for by levying excise taxes on primary processors, and there were to be collateral marketing agreements among producers, processors, and distributors for the purposes of raising or maintaining prices. The head of the Agricultural Adjustment Administration in its first months was George Peek. What a way he had come toward collective government action from his days as vice president of sales at Deere & Company!

The first Agricultural Adjustment Act was declared unconstitutional in 1936 because of its processing tax and production control features; it was replaced by another in 1938. Other pieces of New Deal agricultural legislation provided for the use of surpluses for relief measures, for soil conservation, and for rural resettlement and rural credit. In the process, the confidence of the agriculturalists of the country was restored.

The farm machinery companies now began to receive the fruits of the farmers' renewed optimism stemming from the New Deal legislative initiatives. Their sales had totaled over $585 million in 1929; this figure had fallen to $259 million in 1931, and the Department of Commerce did not even develop statistics for 1932 and 1933. The eight long-line companies had accounted for $437 million of the total in 1929; in 1932 their total was just $85 million. By 1936 they had climbed back to $373 million. In the process, though, considerable shifting in market share had occurred (exhibit 11-5).

The erosion of International Harvester's early dominance had become substantial; Deere had taken a chunk out of its arch rival's market share. But the real surprise was Allis-Chalmers. The latter's growth was testimony once again to the fact that gaining additional market share is not an insuperable task when attempted by firms of sufficient size and resources to ensure adequate manufacturing efficiency and marketing

Exhibit 11–5   **Proportion of Sales of Farm Equipment Made By Each
                  Long-line Company as a Percentage of Total Long-line
                  Farm Equipment Sales, 1929 and 1936**

	1929	1936
International Harvester	51.8%	44.7%
Deere	20.6	23.3
Allis-Chalmers	2.9	11.3
Case	7.6	7.8
Oliver	7.6	6.5
Minneapolis-Moline	4.1	3.7
Massey-Harris	3.9	1.8
B.F. Avery[a]	1.7	1.0
	100.0	100.0

[a] *The FTC considered B.F. Avery a long-line company, despite the fact that it did not make tractors (though it did
have a marketing link for its tractor equipment with Allis-Chalmers).*

*Source: Federal Trade Commission, Report on the Agricultural Implement and Machinery Industry, 75th Cong., 3rd
Session, House Document 702 (1938), 626.*

reach. The Allis row-crop tractor became a strong competitor to International Harvester's Farmall almost as soon as it was introduced in 1930. Allis also brought out in 1934 a small-sized 2,800-pound harvester that cut a 5½-foot swath; it was called the All-Crop. A one-man harvester, it was designed especially for family farms of less than 100 acres and was an instant commercial success.

The significant edge of International Harvester and Deere in their selling and administrative costs continued unabated; it was as strong in 1936 as in the earlier periods reported by the Federal Trade Commission. Warren Shearer, in his well researched study of the industry, concluded: "Again, as in the 1916–18 period, the major advantage of Deere and IH lay in their lower costs of distribution."[9]

LABOR RELATIONS IN THE 1930s

After the National Industrial Recovery Act came into being in 1933, the dedication of the federal government to the encouragement of collective bargaining quickly brought a resurgence of labor unions (which had been declining in membership since the early 1920s). When the NIRA was declared unconstitutional in 1935, Congress immediately passed an even stronger piece of legislation, the Wagner Act, which the unions called their "Magna Charta" for collective bargaining. Organizing activities mushroomed all over the country, and the labor movement itself went through profound change, the Committee for Industrial Organization being founded in that same year as an industrial-union alternative to the American Federation of Labor's predominant craft unionism. The CIO established the Steel Workers' Organizing Committee (SWOC) and in March 1937 won a contract with the Carnegie-Illinois

Steel Company, the chief subsidiary of the United States Steel Corporation. There was violence at the Republic Steel Company in 1937, as the SWOC tried also to organize "Little Steel"; the Memorial Day massacre there resulted in deaths on the picket lines, and the smaller steel companies stayed nonunion until 1941.

The CIO's greatest triumph was at the General Motors Corporation; a "sitdown" strike—in effect, a seizure of plants by the employees—first brought more picket-line tension, but soon the capitulation of the company, after intervention in Michigan by Gov. Frank Murphy. Chrysler also signed an agreement in 1937. Ford held out until 1940, signing then with the union involved, the United Automobile Workers (UAW).

In the early NIRA days there were organizing efforts in the Moline-Rock Island area. George Wilson, who handled labor relations for the company, reported to the board in April 1933: "The American Federation is very active both socially and politically, locally and nationally. The communist group, which covers a variety of organizations which have in mind the One Big Union idea, is growing in strength." Left-wing unions had seemed to preoccupy executives in the company for a number of years. Wilson continued: "Our local situation is not particularly bad, although there has been a grouping of organized labor with the various organizations representing Communism, Socialism and the so-called unemployed. It was this Joint Committee that started the hunger march in Springfield. I was waited on by a Committee at home one night last week; rather a tame lot. I think I got more satisfaction out of it than the Committee."

Nothing further happened in Moline that year, but in the summer of 1934 the American Federation of Labor again attempted to organize in that city. The company still had the individual contract as its basic employment policy, and Charles Wiman himself had reinstituted the signing of such contracts earlier that year. The manager at Waterloo, A.H. Head, put out a two-page notice to employees, signed not only by him, but "prepared in collaboration with and jointly subscribed by C.D. Wiman, President Deere & Co." Head alleged that there had been much "misunderstanding and misrepresentation of the facts" connected with the NIRA code—that the code "fully and intentionally protects the individual employee in his right to make his own deal." Head continued: "We have operated an open shop for many years, and in compliance with the Act we shall continue to do so. The mutual welfare of our employees and ourselves is best served by this policy." Through this period of the NIRA, the company vigorously opposed unionization, even contributing money toward employer organizations specifically "to combat unfair propaganda."

When the Wagner Act was enacted in 1935, the company once again interpreted the legislation to embrace the legitimacy of the individual contract. Burton Peek reported to the board in 1937 that Senator Wagner had written the company before the legislation bearing his name had passed that "there is nothing in the bill which prevents employers from dealing individually with their employees, when that has been the basis of satisfactory and peaceful conditions in the past and both the employers and employees desire to continue that arrangement." Peek vowed: "Our existing contracts are valid and in full force and effect, notwithstanding this Act. Until they expire, it is not seen how the Company could engage in collective bargaining. . . ." The company once more opted to issue bulletin board notices, to apprise the employees: "You have the right (but are not required) to bargain collectively. . . . You should know that you have the right to deal as individuals with your employer when you desire. Neither the Wagner Act nor the decision of the Supreme Court denies such right."

Apparently the union movements in both Waterloo and Moline-Rock Island felt they were not strong enough to challenge the company, for the individual contract held sway until 1939. At that time, the National Labor Relations Board (NLRB) ruled on a complaint by the Steel Workers' Organizing Committee (SWOC) against the company, alleging "certain unfair labor practices" at the Killefer Manufacturing Corporation. This small Los Angeles maker of road-grading equipment, subsoil plows, and disk harrows had been purchased by Deere in 1937; most of its sales were in California, with Caterpillar Tractor Company handling its marketing through "Cat" dealers. By this date, Caterpillar and Deere had close links in California and the Killefer acquisition was readily fitted to Deere's and Caterpillar's California sales efforts.

When Deere took over Killefer, it introduced the practice of the individual contract. The company also inherited an incipient union effort from the SWOC and the latter soon alleged that the individual contract was an unfair labor practice under the Wagner Act. The NLRB centered its interest on a particular clause in the written individual contract that asked the employee to agree "not to join in any concerted movement during the life of this contract, for a change in wages, hours or other conditions of this contract," and ruled against the company. Deere was required to "cease and desist" from giving effect to this particular clause. The following year a similar charge was made by the Farm Equipment Workers Organizing Committee (another CIO organizing union) against Deere's Ottumwa and Waterloo factories; again the NLRB ruled against the clause. Though the stipulation did not strike down the individual contract per se, it was the beginning of the end for the practice. Neither union, incidentally, gained a foothold in any factory of the company at that time.

While the company labor policy during the turbulent 1930s was openly anti-union, the general tenor of employee relations was considered by most outsiders to be amicable and effective. The editors of *Fortune*, in their article of 1936, played a bit loose with the facts, but they were right on target about the essence of Deere's labor relations: "Moliners also sense, without understanding, a difference in Deere's labor policies since Charley Wiman took over. Mr. Butterworth, (whose life was threatened more than once by grudge-nursing employees) always liked to find hard working young fellows with the right stuff in them and train them up from the ranks. They do not hear so much about that from Charley Wiman, who used to work in the shops himself, has inaugurated the 40-hour week and vacations with pay, and has had no labor trouble throughout Deere's worst depression." This does some injustice to Butterworth, who had relied heavily on Leon Clausen for his labor policy and the particular use of the individual contract. When Clausen had become too heavy-handed, Butterworth had been instrumental in having Clausen leave the company. Nevertheless, the judgment that the anti-union philosophy of the 1930s was a product of the 1910s and '20s is an accurate assessment.[10]

HENRY DREYFUSS STYLES THE TRACTOR

The farmer loves his tractor, provided, of course, it works well! This machine that had become so important was to him indeed "a thing of beauty." But beauty is in the eyes of the beholder, goes the old adage; the farmer, a practical man, did not worry much about the aesthetics of any of his working life, and his regard for the tractor was rooted in its performance, not its appearance. A few tractor manufacturers had attempted to incorporate aesthetic design features—the Peoria Tractor Company had built a "streamline" version of its tractor in 1920, and one of the Twin City tractors of the Minneapolis Steel and Machinery Company looked a good deal like an automobile racer. But most manufacturers, including all of the major producers, developed strictly utilitarian vehicles never destined to win prizes from outsiders for attractiveness.

Some of Deere's engineers at the Waterloo Tractor Works had the dream, though, of making their tractors more pleasing to the eye, more aesthetically satisfying. By 1937 the notion of good industrial design had been accepted widely among companies, and some well-known designers had achieved prominence in the field. One of these was Henry Dreyfuss, who, with his associates, had formed and nurtured a respected design house based in New York. The engineers pressed Charles Stone, who now headed all of manufacturing, to authorize them to contact Dreyfuss. Stone gruffly allowed that he did not think much of the idea, "but the boys up here want it, so go ahead." One engineer, Elmer McCormick, was delegated to go to New York, unannounced, to engage Dreyfuss. The story, probably apocryphal but often retold, was that McCormick, going to the city in the late fall with a fur coat and a straw hat, so impressed Dreyfuss with the potential for redesigning a tractor, an instrument that

Exhibit 11–6. *Model B tractor, before and after restyling by Henry Dreyfuss (Deere Archives)*

had hardly been touched by industrial design, that the renowned designer got on the train that very night and traveled straight to Waterloo to talk with the group.

Dreyfuss first was given the assignment to look at the aesthetics of the Model A and Model B. A wooden mockup of a streamlined Model B was constructed by the Dreyfuss team, and in November 1937 the model was unveiled to a startled Waterloo group. It incorporated many new design features relating to the grill and louvres, the shroud over the steering shaft, and design of the radiator cowling. Out of this first glimpse of a more "beautiful" Model B soon came a number of design features that improved the physical appearance of both the tractors. By the 1938 model year, the Waterloo engineers and the Dreyfuss design specialists had combined to redesign both the Model A and the Model B in a most striking way. The radiator cowling had been narrowed for better visibility, the louvres had been redesigned as sweeping horizontal slits (the earlier version had been just a standard radiator front), the dash area had been changed both for more ready readability and for good design.

The changes were not only cosmetic, for the basic safety and workability of the tractor had been significantly improved as well. Beyond this, the Waterloo engineers were delighted to find in the Dreyfuss group a view of the manufacturing process itself that frequently gave the engineers new ideas about easier and less expensive ways of manufacturing. For example, the Dreyfuss group also took a look at some of the Deere harrows and suggested that having one of the frames bent from a single piece of tubing, instead of welding four tubes together, was not only more aesthetically pleasing with the rounded corners, but eliminated in the process four distinct welds.

The farmer was not always easy to persuade on these aesthetic changes. One example in this period before World War II will illustrate. The company a number of years back had begun manufacturing the wheels for its plow with spokes of oval design, this having been determined by the engineers to be the strongest structural shape. Soon complaints began coming back from Argentine farmers about the oval wheel spokes, not because of any wheel failures but because the Argentine agriculturalists thought the spokes looked too "light" in appearance. They were used to the heavy round spokes of the European models and felt the American version might not be as sturdy. In truth, the opposite was the case. So design engineers like Henry Dreyfuss had to be able to incorporate both design aesthetics and practicality in order to relate to the eventual customer's reactions.

From this first experience of working with the Model A and Model B, Henry Dreyfuss and his associates formed a lasting association with Deere & Company that has continued to the present, a relationship that has had a major influence on the appearance, safety, and usability of Deere products.[11]

DEERE AND CATERPILLAR JOIN FORCES

Though agriculturalists were overwhelmingly the clientele for Deere tractors, there had been some industrial use of the Model D from about 1926, when Model DI—the John Deere Industrial Tractor—was announced. It was straightforwardly a Model D, with only two required changes. First, hard rubber tires were put on both front and rear steel wheels (pneumatic tires were not used in the industry until 1931; Deere first made them available in 1934). Second, high-speed sprockets and chains were to be exchanged for the standard ones, allowing a road speed of four miles per hour if the sprockets were changed from thirty-eight to twenty-eight teeth, and a full five miles per hour if a twenty-two-tooth sprocket were used. Additional wheel weights could also be put on, as well as an extension wheel in the rear if additional support and traction were required.

The industrial uses of the Model DI were not exploited very well by the company through the remainder of the 1920s and it was not until 1935 that a particularly fortuitous association brought Deere's efforts to a more substantial level. This was the link with Caterpillar.

In the early 1930s, the International Harvester Company had added a crawler-type tractor to its line and at the same time the Allis-Chalmers Manufacturing Company, which had previously made only crawler-type tractors, began making wheel-type tractors. Thus, both companies now offered both types of tractors through their dealers. This was particularly important in one key state, California. Many California agriculturalists farmed on a mammoth scale, and for their big tasks, particularly under certain soil conditions, they demanded track-type machines. At the same time, however, on every farm there still remained a number of utility and smaller cropping efforts that were more readily done by wheel-type tractors. Thus a California implement dealer was not handling a "full line" unless he had both types of vehicles. This lack was painfully evident to both Deere and Caterpillar, neither of whom produced both types of tractors.

The impetus for an accommodation came from Caterpillar in January 1935. Frank Silloway reported unequivocally to the Deere board: "We do not desire to manufacture track-type tractors," but, inasmuch as the Caterpillar industrial dealers wanted a wheel-type tractor, "through this Caterpillar arrangement we will have an opportunity to get into this industrial business in an important way."

One of the most attractive features to Deere in the new arrangement was the opportunity to join Caterpillar abroad. "Cat" already had a significant dealer network in a number of foreign countries; often agriculturalists abroad had the same dual need for track-laying tractors for larger jobs, wheel tractors for smaller ones. In truth, a number of these foreign outlets—for example, in some of the Central and South American

Exhibit 11–7. Top, *No. 35 combine, with Caterpillar tractor, 1941;* bottom, *John Deere DI industrial tractor, pulling Caterpillar Trailer Patrol grader, 1935. (Deere Archives)*

countries—were really too small to fully support a separate Caterpillar or separate Deere dealer network. Joined together, the two companies could have a larger exposure, both of products and of dealer size, which made for better parts service and other backup needs, as well as more initial sales.

There was one uneasy complication to this seemingly amicable relationship—the farmer quite often had a choice as to which tractor would be more effective, and a bit of persuasion could tilt him one way or the other. Would Caterpillar ever persuade him toward a wheel-type tractor, worried the Deere marketing people (an attitude probably shared just as strongly in the opposite direction by the "Cat" men). Frank Silloway decided to bring this issue into the open and wrote the branches: "We told them that we were not thin-skinned in any way, and were willing that they urge these dealers, in the course of their usual sales activity, to push the sale of the track-type tractor. . . . It is our idea that, after all, the farmer is going to be the final court and jury."

Caterpillar also had doubts about the two-cylinder mind set of Deere. They sent forth an equally frank bulletin to their own sales people, first describing the Deere organization and then facing the issue of the two cylinders. "It is most interesting to note," the bulletin's editors began, "that John Deere, the founder of the steel plow industry and Charles H. and Benjamin Holt, founders of the track-type tractor industry, were all natives of Vermont." This homage out of the way, they continued: "The builders of John Deere tractors have been particularly consistent in regard to the design of their engines . . . two-cylinder design is now exclusively a John Deere feature. In selling the John Deere tractor, 'Caterpillar' salesmen may be met with the sales argument that all other tractor manufacturers building two-cylinder tractors have discontinued this feature." But it would be "false reasoning" to assume that the two-cylinder engine was obsolete, inasmuch as "Caterpillar Tractor, recognized the world over as builders of the finest line of engines in existence," included in their line not only two-cylinder but one-cylinder, three-cylinder, four-cylinder, six-cylinder, and eight-cylinder engines. The latest diesel that Caterpillar had just brought out was itself a two-cylinder engine.

Would there be excessive vibration in the John Deere tractor? "Vibration in an engine is not a product of the numbers of cylinders," the bulletin answered, "both the crankshaft and the flywheel of this John Deere tractor are dynamically balanced." The two-cylinder design would give greater simplicity, excellent fuel economy, the ability to burn a number of different fuels, compactness, excellent accessibility, light weight, and better distribution of weight, and many of the above features were exclusive ones. "Inasmuch as the 'Caterpillar' salesman has been trained to sell exclusive features . . . he should welcome these exclusive John Deere features as sales opportunities."

Within a few weeks new literature had been prepared featuring together Deere's Model D and Caterpillar's Trailer Patrol, a pull-type road scraper with an eight-foot blade. Maneuverability of the combination was stressed, as was the ease of operation of the Model D and the rugged construction of the scraper.

Now the Caterpillar-Deere link took a surprising new direction. In 1926 Caterpillar had offered to sell Deere its harvester business—the Western Harvester Company. The offer had been made when Deere was first developing its own combine and shortly after Caterpillar itself had been put together out of the combination of the Holt and Best organizations. The asking price then was more than $1.2 million, too steep a price for Deere. Over the intervening years, Caterpillar had found its niches to be track-laying tractors and road machinery. Its combine business was confined largely to the West coast, the old Holt and Best territories, the total business not being substantial enough to expand efforts into the Midwest. Indeed, it was beginning to dawn on Caterpillar that the combine business was actually getting in the way of their aggressive moves into the industrial construction and road-maintenance areas.

This time the deal was much more favorable to Deere. Caterpillar had been manufacturing two conventional combines and a well-received hillside combine. Deere did not have the latter machine in its line, and this had hurt in the West. Caterpillar's proposal was to discontinue their two models of conventional, level-land combines and to turn over the hillside combine to Deere to manufacture. All the repair parts common to the three machines then would be furnished by Deere; Caterpillar would continue to stock those parts for the other two combines that were not being made by Deere. Deere would also take over Caterpillar's existing inventory of completely fabricated machines at Caterpillar cost. Deere would be given a royalty free, nonexclusive license to the use of all of the Caterpillar combine patents; all of Caterpillar's existing templets, dies, jigs, fixtures, samples, patterns, special flasks, special cutting tools, and equipment were to be delivered to Deere without charge. All of Caterpillar's existing quantity of combine advertising would be turned over to Deere without charge. Caterpillar's tracings, blueprints, bills of materials, production records, cost records, specifications, and stock records would also be given to Deere without charge. Caterpillar was willing to supply Deere with a Caterpillar engine for the combine, though it was not a requirement of the agreement. In sum, Caterpillar had given Deere outright the complete rights to make the hillside combine, and it had backed this with all the necessary engineering and manufacturing expertise Caterpillar had assembled over the years. The arrangement was efficacious for Caterpillar, too, for it extracted the company in a clean way from a product line in which it was no longer interested, yet leaving existing users to be serviced by a responsible organization. Deere gained immensely, for it now had a hillside combine to round out its own combine line—and at essentially no cost.

Now the Deere-Caterpillar combined sales effort needed to be put into high gear, for not only would Caterpillar dealers be selling Deere wheeled tractors and Deere dealers selling some Caterpillar equipment (track-laying tractors, road scrapers, etc.), but now Caterpillar dealers would be phasing out their combines, Deere dealers adding the hillside combine.

There was a price to pay, though, and it came in the effects on Deere and Caterpillar dealers. Frank Silloway again: "If the dealer does not want the agency for the Caterpillar tractor, he need not take it." There were a number of places where track-laying tractors would sell, however, and "we believe that in such a town the John Deere man will be interested in having the dealership . . . and if he is not interested now, he certainly will be when the local dealers of the I.H.C., Allis-Chalmers and Cletrac are selling track-type tractors right out of his town." Silloway wanted to "branch out and make a real bid for this industrial tractor business," so that "the sale of John Deere tractors will not be so completely dependent upon the farmer trade." Caterpillar, in turn, exhorted its dealers that there were a number of places where wheel-type tractors would be needed for "light tasks." Their bulletin continued: "In a lot of cases this work has been done by a Fordson tractor, and in just a lot more cases horses are being used. . . . [While] this possibility can't be classed as a new market, it is just a market for which we have nothing to offer."

For the Deere and Caterpillar dealers over most of the country this was not to be a major new endeavor—one that would require changes in their branch—but just a modest new piece of business that would link two good companies together. There was one place in the country, though, where the wedding had major effects—California.

CALIFORNIA AND THE CATERPILLAR LINK

For years, California's agriculture had been amazingly varied and astoundingly extensive in scope. Individual farms often tended to be very large—by 1935, some 43 percent of California crop land was farmed by only 7 percent of its farmers, in spreads upwards of 500 acres each (with a number of them many thousands of acres). The average value of a California farm at this time was $15,466, the highest of any state in the country (Nebraska, at $11,696, was next; the country's average was $4,823). Deere had operated two branch houses over the years on the West coast, one at Portland, Oregon, the other in San Francisco, California. Neither had been outstanding, nor, in turn, had either been accorded much help from Moline (a constant complaint over the years from the West coast).

In the California branch, the company had been doing business essentially the same as it had in the rest of the country—a quite substantial number of smaller, individual John Deere dealers. In the San Francisco territory at the time of the Caterpillar deal, there were approximately 250 dealers in areas of the state that were to be jointly served by Deere and Caterpillar. Caterpillar's pattern was much different —its dealers tended to be very much larger, much more financially secure, and therefore considerably more independent in relations with the home office, and to serve a wider area. This was a logical pattern, because Caterpillar dealt mostly with large-scale farmers, those who were likely to use the track-laying tractors.

Thus the fit between Deere and Caterpillar dealers, while excellent in the rest of the country, was just not right for California. This fact being self-evident, Deere's San Francisco branch terminated relationships with most of the 250 dealers (who generally then took on competitor brands), and then began selling Deere equipment through the Caterpillar dealers, who totaled only twenty-six at the time of the changeover. By 1940, when Frank Silloway made a major report to the Deere board about California, the John Deere-Caterpillar dealers numbered only eighteen, who had between them thirty-four other branches, for a total of fifty-two towns out of which the combined dealerships operated. In other parts of California, other than the areas of the John Deere-Caterpillar link, there were some ninety-four regular John Deere dealers by 1940, on the same basis as elsewhere in the United States.

The changeover in California to the larger John Deere-Caterpillar dealers brought severe transition problems. The San Francisco branch had to agree with its former dealers to take back stocks of Deere goods and give them credit substantially equal to the cost of such stocks. Unfortunately, much of this stock was shopworn and obsolete and could only be disposed of after reconditioning and at bargain prices. The need for understanding Caterpillar-Deere service and repair concerns required the San Francisco house to invest in a much larger repair department. Further, as the Caterpillar dealers came to the relationship with greater size and financial strength, they were able to buy in carload lots, and Deere had to grant more substantial freight concessions and cash discounts.

So the new John Deere-Caterpillar dealer in California really was an anomaly in the company. The dealerships had a more arm's-length relationship with Deere, and Caterpillar pride and aggressiveness often made the dealer seem to Deere branch-house personnel to be overly caustic and demanding. Benjamin Keator, the branch manager in San Francisco from the time of the Caterpillar link (he had been brought down from the Portland branch, which he had run since 1925), reminisced at the time of his retirement in 1953 about the Caterpillar alliance. Keator concluded that the relationship had been very beneficial to Deere, but also felt that he was "all the time playing second fiddle to the Caterpillar organization, which I can assure you was no fun and would have 'gotten the goat' of most Deere men who had any loyalty in their veins." The feeling grew that Deere was allowing Caterpillar to call the tune in California, and many Moliners felt that Deere should have a larger number of dealers in the joint territory. Frank Silloway was manifestly upset by what he saw as a growing schism and, in a blunt report in 1941, he cited the figures relating to Deere's market share in California (which had risen all through this period). He stated: "You will, therefore, see from all of the above that we do not have much ground for complaint on our John Deere-Caterpillar setup in California. . . . There is too much of an impression in California at the present time that we do not like the Caterpillar dealers and are tolerating them only on account of the John Deere-Caterpillar setup. They feel that our side of the business transaction is influenced by some grudge we bear. Of course, that is not true." Silloway knew there really was a problem and concluded: "We must change our entire attitude and show these dealers that we do appreciate what they are doing for themselves and for us; that we are their friends and are cooperatively with them for a bigger and better business for John Deere in California."

The most effective times for the joint dealerships were those years just before World War II—from 1935 to, roughly, 1941. In this period, the companies had mutual interests in building strong dealerships and interactive sales. The war itself was a dividing line. After Pearl Harbor, Caterpillar sent its equipment all over the world. The Army Corps of Engineers and the Navy's renowned Sea Bees built landing strips, ports, and bridges all over the European and Far Eastern theaters. The Caterpillar tractor (the second word soon not even used, "Caterpillar" becoming almost a generic name) was the chosen instrument for a great amount of this work. The International Harvester crawler was also widely used by the armed forces. By the end of the war, Caterpillar had left its equipment all over the world, with a justly deserved reputation for quality and durability. It had the beginnings of a mammoth, worldwide business, and it made the most of it. Concurrently, many of the domestic joint dealerships were expanding enormously in the sale of new machines and in repairs and parts, with most of this expansion on the Caterpillar side of the aisle. The war had left a residue of need for agricultural equipment, too, but not on the scale of Caterpillar's more industrially based opportunities. In many of the domestic joint dealerships, and widely among the foreign operations, the Caterpillar faction of management now tended to dominate—and probably rightly so.

This raised plenty of hackles all through Deere and seemed to threaten the relationship. R.B. Lourie addressed a joint meeting of branch-house managers and Caterpillar representatives in early 1947 and decided to put the matter frankly to them. He pointed out that though top management in both companies knew and understood the arrangements, some of the people down in each of the organizations were really not completely "sold" on the joint link. (Left unsaid was that a few were even sabotaging it.) As some of the people Lourie was speaking to were these people, Lourie pleaded, "I want to suggest that all of us let by-gones be by-gones' and start fresh as of now to give this Deere-Caterpillar program a real chance to work to our mutual advantage." Lourie had to tiptoe with his own Deere people, and he vowed, "I want to make it very clear right here that we are not interested in cancelling any good, loyal John Deere dealer in order to make room for a Caterpillar distributor or his branch store." But Lourie also wanted to gain a quid pro quo, so he proposed that Deere would consider new dealerships for Caterpillar people if Caterpillar people were, in turn, willing to do so for Deere. The tenor of the meeting was positive, but the undercurrent of combativeness in Lourie's remarks telegraphed the chary feelings of both parties.

It was only a matter of time, though—the relationship was star-crossed. A number of Caterpillar dealers now began to question the validity of diffusing their efforts by also attempting to sell Deere equipment, now not a major part of their business. Finally, more and more dealers were inquiring about the possibility of terminating the joint relationship.

From Deere's side, a severance was not nearly so attractive. To be sure, everyone knew that there was not a full synergy between Deere's and Caterpillar's business, but Deere was not yet ready to develop a competitor track-laying tractor to compete head-on with Caterpillar. (At a later point Deere did decide to move into industrial equipment in a major way and to build a range of machinery in the smaller sizes directly competitive with those of Caterpillar.) Thus the question of the relationship between Deere and Caterpillar was not an inconsequential one for either party. Both knew that there was always the possibility of each moving into the other's product lines.

Over a number of years beginning in the early 1950s and extending into the mid-1960s, the joint dealerships began to split apart (except at certain locations abroad). This left Deere with similar enigmas in regard to dealer choice, except precisely in reverse. Now Deere needed to rebuild a dealer organization, particularly in California, and go through a laborious, sensitive "divorce," moving away from a joint relationship to begin again completely on its own.[12]

PRODUCT DEVELOPMENT IN
THE LATE 1930s

Despite some drift in both the economy and the agricultural machinery industry in 1937 and '38, the late 1930s saw aggressive product development in the industry. The small tractor had been welcomed by the farmer as in no other period before, and there were an estimated 1.6 million tractors in use in the country in 1939—almost double that reported in 1930. Perhaps as many as half of these were general purpose. The United States Department of Agriculture, in a special report in 1940 chronicling the onrush of technology on the farm, estimated that upwards of 60 percent of those farms large enough for motor equipment were using tractors by 1940; they flatly predicted that the number of tractors would increase by 500,000 by 1950. The USDA's authors also reported that what they called the "baby combine," one that cut a swath of five to six feet and could be operated by one man, comprised some 80 percent of the combines sold in 1939.

Deere was nicely positioned in the tractor market, particularly after

Exhibit 11–8. Left, No. 55 combine working a field near Findlay, Ill., ca. 1950; right, No. 55-H sidehill combine in winter wheat, Wenatchee, Wash., 1954. (Deere Archives)

adding the Model A and Model B in 1934–35. A larger version, the Model G, with a 20.7 drawbar horsepower, was marketed beginning in 1937 and a smaller version, the Model H, with a 9.68 drawbar horsepower, joined the line in 1939. The company also added a small utility tractor, the Model L, with a 7.01 drawbar horsepower. The last was built at the John Deere Wagon Works in Moline.

The company was not as strong in the combine market. The hillside combine from Caterpillar had been very effective and the other larger Deere combines were selling well. Mushrooming sales of smaller combines, however, made it necessary to bring out Deere's own versions, and here the company stubbed its collective toe. A six-foot version, the No. 6, was developed in 1936 and tested over the following two years. It was to be Deere's answer to Allis-Chalmers' All Crop. Deere engineers compared the two machines side by side and Theo Brown dolefully reported, "Saw a lot of Allis-Chalmers, all doing well and found #6 John Deere a real lemon." Brown continued a few days later in his diary: "Deere's position in the small combine field is very poor. We must do something soon. . . . It is a tremendous problem." M.J. Healey, the aggressive Kansas City branch manager, was particularly vocal: "It was not a good machine. . . . We are not anywhere up to competition on the small combine." Healey wanted Brown to intrude into the picture but the latter was reluctant, given the continuing decentralization of authority for product development. "I told him my position was that when anything like that was wanted, that I could not butt in but should be asked and wanted." Charles Wiman, sensing the critical nature of the problem with the small combine, stepped into the situation and promptly assigned

Brown to the Harvester Works, once again demonstrating his ability to affect product development from the outside, yet to leave prime responsibility in the hands of the individual organization.

As the demands for smaller combines continued to increase, the company built two new machines, the Nos. 11A and 12A, and put them in the product line in 1939. These were left-hand cut machines, built this way for an interesting reason. During the 1930s there had been a major switch from grain binders to combines. The company branches in the areas of the country where windrowing was the practice felt that if the farmer could not use his binder at all, he would swamp the branch with trade-ins for combines. If a left-hand cut combine were developed, the binders could be converted into windrowers. These two machines were better engineered than the No. 6, and the No. 12A proved to be particularly popular in its thirteen-year life, 116,000 units being built and shipped in that period. There were some problems with these two machines at the start, though, their lightweight construction not holding up in all field conditions, with some of them being returned to the factory for rebuilding.

Thus both the farmers and the farm machinery industry came through the 1930s stronger than any could have imagined at the depths of the Great Depression in 1932. Though the smaller long-line competitors lost market share and relative profitability, the industry seemed characterized at the end of the Depression by more vigorous competition, partly because of the erosion of International Harvester's dominance but particularly because of the aggressive marketing of Allis-Chalmers. Deere, too, was now well positioned for the challenge that lay ahead with the onrushing war.

SINK A SUB FROM YOUR FARM

Bring in Your SCRAP

"Brave Men Shall Not Die Because I Faltered"

ATIu AL   RA   RVEST

CHAPTER 12

WORLD WAR II AND THE POSTWAR DECADE

*I feel this Board must have the vision, sanely—at the
same time boldly—to expand production
facilities. . . . Surely as we are sitting here, if we fail to
provide the necessary facilities, someone else will.
I know we don't want this someone else to be
Ford, General Motors, Curtiss-Wright, Graham-Paige,
or the XYZ Company of New Mexico, nor do we want this
opportunity to be cashed in by IHC, Allis-Chalmers,
Case, Oliver, Minneapolis-Moline or any other company
not now in the business. We must have courage.*

Charles Wiman, 1944

Germany invaded Poland on September 1, 1939; Great Britain and France declared war on Germany and World War II had begun. Though the United States Congress passed a Neutrality Act in that year, by May of the following year extensive aid was being sent to Britain and massive national defense preparedness measures for the United States were underway. When the Office of Production Management was formed in December 1940, the country was already launched on a buildup of military production; a year later, the attack on Pearl Harbor drew the United States into armed conflict.

Incredibly complex questions of priorities faced the country's leaders, and the farm machinery manufacturers were squarely in the middle of some of the most important of them. How were competing needs for food production and war materials to be reconciled? How much new farm equipment and how much replacement and repair equipment would be needed to maintain the necessary level of food production? How much of the farm equipment industry should be shifted into war production and how much of it should continue to make farm machinery? What amount of civilian production was to be allowed?

Who should be able to buy? What of the implementation of these steps—who should work on production (as against going to war), how should they be compensated for their work, what prices should be charged for the products sold both to government and to civilian users, how should critically short supplies of key materials be allocated? Finally, how should the industry reconvert to civilian production after the war?

Just before the United States entered the war, the Office of Production Management issued a "limitation order," holding civilian production of farm equipment for the industry to 80 percent of 1940's production of new machines, 150 percent of 1940's repair and maintenance parts, and 96 percent of 1940's exports as the allowable production for 1942. Vehement protests from both the industry and the farmers soon persuaded the government to relax the restrictions somewhat, but at the same time the industry was chided for not converting enough resources to war production. There was even an implied threat by the Department of Justice that it was considering instituting grand jury proceedings "in an endeavor to obtain an indictment against corporations engaged in the farm machinery industry." In essence, the industry was accused of taking the opportunity to build its inventories for civilian needs, and indeed the farmer did appear to be well taken care of in 1942.

By mid-1942 severe cutbacks in civilian production were demanded by the government. An important limitation order, issued in October of that year, introduced the concept of "concentration" of farm machinery with small- and medium-sized producers, thereby "freeing" the larger manufacturers for mostly war production. This classification scheme had the effect of tilting the farm machinery business in 1942 and '43 toward smaller firms. The manufacture of tractors necessarily had to be left with the major long-line companies, but the amount of civilian business done by International Harvester and Deere in this period was considerably less than it had been before the war. The wartime period gave the smaller long-line companies—Minneapolis-Moline, Oliver, and Massey-Harris—the chance to strengthen their finances and win a much larger market share than they had enjoyed before the outbreak of hostilities. Many farmers were forced by shortages of equipment to purchase new makes; in the process some brand loyalties, built up over many years, were eroded.

Ford-Ferguson, which had been able to put its small, lightweight tractor into production quickly in 1939 and '40, now began to make sharp gains in market share. When the limitation order of 1942 was being debated, the Ford-Ferguson people made a stunning proposal to the War Production Board. Inasmuch as their tractors were lightweight, they argued, why not "exchange the old standard wheel heavy weight, pre-depression made tractors for lightweight tractors of modern design and manufacture." There were almost half a million farm tractors of more than ten years of age, they noted, and if these were turned in and replaced by the lighter Ford tractor, a savings in weight could be made of approximately one ton per machine. By scrapping the old timers, they promised, more than one million tons of steel might be recaptured, enough they said to construct forty-two average battleships. (Underlying this startlingly high figure was an additional assumption that the light tractor would be substituted for the 1942 quota of heavier weight tractors, which they argued then would not need to be built.) Ford-Ferguson would, they proposed, make all the tractors required for the country for this year—100,000 tractors more than Ford was already producing.

Predictably, the rest of the industry was dumbfounded at the idea. In one stroke, Ford wanted to grab the entire market for tractors! The other companies vigorously disputed the claim that a small tractor was inherently better than a large tractor, or that any one tractor would be adequate for all farming conditions. Concentrating repair service in one company also would be devastating for the repair of all the other makes. After much lobbying in both industry and government, the notion was finally shelved.

The industry as a whole now was sensitized to gambits by fellow manufacturers. They did not have long to wait. In early 1944 the government, through the War Food Administration, exhorted farmers in the American wheat belt to increase production by some one billion bushels. Yet large numbers of farmers had been drafted into the armed services, so labor in farm areas was in critically short supply. Massey-Harris sensed a major commercial opportunity. They had just brought out a small, self-propelled combine and now proposed to the War Production Board that they be permitted to produce 500 machines in addition to their regular quota for 1944. These machines would be sold to operators who would agree to harvest, under Massey-Harris supervision, a minimum of 2,000 acres each. Many hundreds of tractors would be released for other work and, in the process, self-propelled combines would supplant a like number of conventional combines. This time the War Production Board agreed to the scheme, and in March 1944 the "Massey-Harris Brigade" was sent south from Canada to begin its well-publicized move up through the harvest areas of the Plains states. It was a signal public relations coup; *Fortune* magazine reported: "The self-propelled carried out an elegant light-armored blitz of the U.S. wheat belt." It was not only great public relations, it carried tremendous commercial implications. Massey-Harris made a technicolor motion picture, *Wonder Harvest*, and by the time the operation was finished Massey had projected its name into the minds of farmers throughout the American farm belt.

The industry continued to protest the concept of concentration and the severity of the limitation orders, and by mid-1943 somewhat more liberal limitation orders were issued. By 1944, as the tide of the war turned toward the Allies, the limitations on civilian production were progressively terminated. By the end of the year the industry was back to virtually unrestricted civilian production.[1]

DEERE'S WORLD WAR II EFFORTS

By mid-1940 Deere's pace had quickened; by December of that year it was making war materiel in the Welland plant, to be delivered to the Canadian government. By March 1941, the company was prime contractor for the fabrication and production of transmissions and final-drive units for the M3 medium tank. The work was done in the Waterloo plant, but under the aegis of a separate company called the Iowa Transmission Company.

After this first large defense contract, the company joined the rest of American industry over the following months of 1941 to gear up for greater defense production. In March 1942 a major new assignment came; Deere was to be a subcontractor to the Cleveland Tractor Company in the manufacture of MG-1 military tractors for the United States armed forces. Heavy tractors (weighing approximately seven tons) with track-type traction, they were intended primarily for use at airports in servicing and pulling aircraft. The Cleveland Tractor Company was one of the important manufacturers of track-laying tractors, under the trade name Cletrac. For some time, Wiman had seemed concerned about how Deere would keep its organization together in the face of war demands (in several previous board meetings he had articulated his own personal worries about this), and now he apparently saw a solution in the Cleveland Tractor link. His idea (as espoused in the board meeting of April 28, 1942) was a merger of the two companies! The notion was debated vigorously in the meeting amid much opposition.

Almost immediately, however, the Cleveland Tractor merger proposal was sidetracked. Charles Wiman's career had built him a wide reputation among government administrators; now he was asked to come to Washington as a colonel in the Ordnance Corps of the United States Army, to work directly in the tank and combat vehicle division. Wiman felt that he had no choice. He resigned as president of Deere & Company and left immediately for Washington. Burton Peek was elected president of the company, to hold responsibility while Wiman was gone. This sudden change in top management doomed the Cleveland Tractor merger proposal, since Wiman had been its chief advocate.

Deere also engaged in a wide range of other defense efforts—contracts for ammunition (75-millimeter and 3-inch shells), subcontracts to provide parts to aircraft manufacturers, and the building of mobile laundry units. Deere assembled the laundry units, which were pulled as semi-trailers by large trucks, to accompany combat troops and thus reduce the age-old problem of war, the vermin that cause so many diseases. The Wagon Works of the company also made various cargo units and just about all of the factories of the company were devoted in a major way to some war production. By the end of the war, more than 4,500 employees had entered military service; even a "John Deere" ordnance battalion had been formed, recruited mainly from employees of factory, branch-house, and dealer organizations, and had served in the European theater of operations.[2]

WIMAN'S WASHINGTON YEARS

Charles Wiman threw himself into the high-tension Washington job in the spring of 1942 with characteristic tenacity and dedication, and later he was awarded the country's Legion of Merit. Then, in January 1944, Donald Nelson, the head of the War Production Board, requested that the Ordnance Department release Wiman so that he could come to the board and assume the directorship of its farm machinery and equipment division.

This job was to be a critically important one, for Nelson and his cohorts were both calibrating the war effort, now coming to a climax in Europe, and planning for the postwar reconversion that was now seen by all as upcoming.

When Wiman arrived at the War Production Board, he found the agency full of tensions and antagonisms concerning reconversion. Throughout industry, manufacturers maneuvered for position and watched over their shoulders the board's policies that would demark civilian from military production. Wiman was on the job no more than three months when he became publicly embroiled in a donnybrook. By this time in the war (early 1944), difficulties on the domestic agricultural front were being aired widely by farmers and their representatives. Farm leaders charged

Exhibit 12–1. *Deere & Company in World War II:* upper left, *Assembling a mobile laundry unit;* lower left, *Eleven Deere factories had a hand in producing the MG-1 military tractor;* upper right, *John Deere Model A armored tractor, Aberdeen Proving Ground, 1941;* lower right, *Assembling a tail wheel for the P47 fighter plane. (Deere Archives)*

Exhibit 12–2. Top left, *Charles Wiman with No. 52 plow, 1936;* bottom left, *Charles Wiman laying the cornerstone at the Deere Tractor Company, Waterloo, November 1946;* right, *The opening of the Atlanta branch house at Chamblee, November 4, 1949;* left to right, *Burton Peek, C.M. Haasl, Bruce Lourie, W.O. Washburn, Charles Wiman. (Deere Archives)*

that shortages in farm machinery were threatening "international disaster" on the food front. They accused the War Production Board of overstating figures about totals of civilian production—that the board was "dishing out glamorized reports." A special Senate committee, the so-called Truman Committee, investigated the national defense program and reported that civilian production was indeed behind schedule, but the committee reminded everyone that farmers were still better equipped than they had been a year earlier. Despite this, the farmers around the country remained vexed. In particular, the so-called quota system was the focus of attack. Production quotas for civilian goods were established on the basis of each firm's production in the immediate prewar period. Many farmers felt that some of the larger manufacturers could not reconvert quickly enough to fulfill their quotas, and that therefore the total amount of goods available for purchase was being kept artificially low. The War Food Administration took the side of the farmers and accused the War Production Board of blocking "prompt and aggressive shifting of quotas" to some of the smaller companies that did not have much production in the prewar period. In early May, Edward O'Neal, president of the American Farm Bureau Federation, appeared before a House committee and bluntly stated: "We simply cannot understand why rigid production quotas are reserved for some manufacturers when they are not able to produce the full amount of their quotas, while other manufacturers who have met their quotas and have the labor and materials to produce far more are not permitted to do so."

At this point, Charles Wiman was dragged into the issue by the press. Rep. Marion Bennett of Missouri charged publicly that the farm machinery division of the War Production Board was "in complete control of representatives of two companies," and named Wiman and the latter's assistant, Harold Boyle of International Harvester, as the two men manipulating the situation. Rep. Fred Crawford of Michigan explicitly blamed the situation on Wiman who, he said, "muscles in and parcels out the business." Crawford introduced a resolution calling for a subcommittee of the House Committee on Agriculture to investigate the situation. Though the House committee did not go further into the matter, Donald Nelson intervened and promptly eliminated most of the quotas that had been in effect.

Wiman was in a very sensitive position as a "dollar-a-year" man, trying to administer programs that affected all of the companies in the industry from which he had come. Inevitably, there were conflicts of interest for him, as there were for many businessmen serving the government during World War II. In order to have the war effort staffed by the people best able to do the job, the government had turned extensively to industry people. In this case, it was natural for the stronger long-line companies— particularly International Harvester and Deere—to desire the perpetuation of the competitive positions that they had earned before the war started. It would not have seemed fair to them to have weak companies bailed out by war contracts and then given market shares at the beginning of the postwar reconversion that were larger than those in effect at the beginning of the war.

But in an imbroglio like this one, politics intrudes in a major way. Allied against the two major long-line companies, Deere and International Harvester, was a potent group of farmers, abetted by the scare tactics of the War Food Administration. This was an unequal match, and it was foreordained that the quotas would fall, with the smaller companies gaining a larger market share in the process. A few weeks later, in June 1944, Wiman suffered a severe attack of pneumonia, and in mid-July he resigned from the War Production Board. Fate had intervened to take him out of an almost untenable situation, after more than two years in Washington.[3]

UNIONS COME TO DEERE

Wartime labor relations policies of the federal government were designed to keep employee effort at top pace, to prevent or settle work stoppages, and, in general, to keep the country's production on as even a keel as possible. Pres. Franklin Roosevelt summoned labor and business leaders to a conference just after the Pearl Harbor attack; out of this came an agreement to foreswear strikes or lockouts for the duration of the war and for the creation of a board to settle all disputes that might result from the suspension of traditional collective bargaining practices. The tripartite National War Labor Board (with membership from management, labor, and the public) enunciated strict wage controls during the war, and labor increasingly chafed under the narrow cost-of-living base. As compensation, the board promulgated a new concept of union security, the "maintenance of membership" clause, that aided unions in holding their membership ranks during the period.

The first unions to be recognized by Deere & Company in its modern period were on the West coast. In November 1937 the Garage Employees (AFL) obtained a contract at the Portland, Oregon, branch, and in August 1938 the San Francisco branch began bargaining with the International Longshoremen's and Warehousemen's Union (the company acting through an employer group, the Distributors Association of Northern California). These unions were only in the branches. Despite considerable organizing activity by competing unions in Ottumwa, Waterloo, and Moline, no factory-line production union had yet been able to organize any Deere plant, including the Killefer operation in Los Angeles, the site of the unfair labor practice case involving the individual contract. Beginning in 1939, a skilled-trades union, the Pattern Makers League (AFL), obtained a contract with the company (at the Plow Works, Harvester Works, and Spreader Works and at Union Malleable), the bargaining unit confined to the skilled journeymen pattern-makers and their apprentices.

Not until 1941, at Ottumwa, was a production-workers union finally able to organize a Deere plant. Inconclusive organizing efforts had been going on there for a number of years; one of several competing unions, the Farm Equipment Workers Organizing Committee, affiliated with the CIO, won a National Labor Relations Board decision in 1939, striking down the same part of the company's individual contract that had been excised in the Los Angeles Killefer plant. In June 1941, that union contested with the International Association of Machinists (AFL) and a nonaffiliated local group, the Independent Farm Implement Workers, in an NLRB certification election. The Independent won but apparently was not up to the task, and a year later, in a second election a newcomer, the United Automobile, Aircraft and Agricultural Implement Workers (UAW), a CIO union, won handily.

At this time, the CIO was allowing, albeit uneasily, competition among its own national unions in representation elections. One of the most tense and acrimonious of all these intra-CIO battles was that between the Farm Equipment Workers and the UAW. Each union was wracked by internecine battles, both attempting to grapple with the left-wing leanings of factions within their leaderships. Critics from not only outside but within the CIO leadership itself were accusing the leftist groups of being Communist-dominated. In the UAW, there were seesaw battles between the "right" and the "left" all through the war, but by 1946

Walter Reuther had succeeded in driving out the left, leaving the UAW a solidly cohesive, strong postwar union, one of the stalwarts of the CIO. In the Farm Equipment Workers, the left held sway, particularly strengthened after 1941 by surprising victories at several key plants of International Harvester, which had been troubled by particularly bitter labor relations all through this period.

The more propitious climate for employee organization nurtured by the War Labor Board soon led to increased organizing activities at other Deere plants. In October 1942 the UAW began organizing workers at the Harvester Works and Spreader Works of the company, as well as at Union Malleable. Meanwhile, the Farm Equipment Workers was attempting to organize the Planter Works (Deere & Mansur). Most people in management did not believe the unions had much of a chance; indeed, most of the bets among the managers were whether the unions could poll a 5 percent favorable vote. To the great consternation and disappointment of most company officials, the UAW won all three of its contests, and the Farm Equipment Workers also was victorious. The tallies were reasonably close at the Spreader Works and Deere & Mansur, but much wider in the other two plants.

The results were a watershed in company labor relations—the first outside union in the company's Moline-area plants. Given the company's long history of benevolent employee relations policies, which had often bordered on being paternalistic, it was no surprise that the presence of the union saddened many people in management. The plant managers felt betrayed—"Yesterday my men were loyal Deere employees, today they are not." Yet their crestfallen view was not rooted in reality. The employees clearly wanted a union at this moment in Deere's history, despite the widespread feeling of good will toward the company, built up over many years, and this had not really been changed by the vote.

The Moline elections were soon followed by similar ones in Waterloo, and again the UAW won (March 1943). At that same time, the Van Brunt workers in the Horicon, Wisconsin, plant voted in an AFL union, a "Federal Labor Union," which was the AFL's answer to the CIO's drive to organize production workers. In May 1943, the company had its first union strikes; the piece-rate workers at the John Deere Spreader Works walked out over the issue of piece-rate price adjustments. A few days later, the employees of Union Malleable went out on strike over piece rates for molders in the plant.

Meanwhile, the company had been notified that the Army-Navy E award was to be given to all 7,000 employees at a mass meeting scheduled for Sunday afternoon, June 20. As the two strikes dragged on nearer and nearer to the date of the award, plans were announced for the celebration. Just two days before the celebration, however, the War Department telegraphed Deere that it was indefinitely postponing the ceremony. Although the War Department did not announce the reasons publicly, the delay was clearly attributable to the strikes, for two provisions required for the coveted award were "avoidance of work stoppage" and "cooperation with the war program." The company put out a bulletin board announcement and press release, bluntly stating these facts and in effect accusing the striking employees of forcing the postponement. The local newspapers sided with the company, one paper headlining its article "Shame! Shame! Shame!" The union retorted that Deere had not followed one other provision, "maintenance of fair labor standards," and that the company's record of accidents, health, and sanitation also were not good. (There was little evidence to support these allegations, though.) The strike was settled shortly thereafter, and the E award belatedly made.

The Farm Equipment Workers registered a further inroad in February 1943 when it won an election at the Plow Works. A month later the company discharged about fifty workers in the plant for allegedly instigating and participating in an unauthorized slowdown. The union cried "lockout," and threatened to press "the government" to "take over" the plant. The issue was settled by the two parties without outside intervention (the employees were rehired), but the episode generated considerable ill will on both sides.

In December 1943 the Farm Equipment Workers gained ground on the UAW by winning the right to bargain for employees at the Moline branch house. A few months later, in May 1944, there was a strike at Deere's Harvester Works that was not even authorized by the leadership of the UAW local. The War Labor Board threatened reprisals, but the Harvester Works employees voted to stay out "until the Company lives up to the contract with the union or the Army takes over the plant." The issue related to vacations. The company had been required to fit its vacation plan to War Labor Board edicts, and it so stated in a bulletin board announcement. The union then implied that the company was attempting to abrogate vacation plans. In effect, the company was caught in the middle between union demands for prewar conditions and War Labor Board requirements for patterns fitting national labor policies. The strike was terminated in June 1944, and later that month the War Labor Board denied the company's more liberal vacation plan, bluntly excoriating the strikers: "This is no time to create the impression that unions violating the no-strike pledge will be rewarded for such conduct."

And so it went during the war—it was a disruptive, acrimonious period for the company and the country, and employee relations were laced with grievances and irritations. Labor relations at Deere during this period were certainly no more troublesome than in most other industrial plants, but compared with the earlier days of industrial peace and direct relations with individual employees, the collective approach of World War II was a change of style that made most company officials uneasy and unhappy. George Wilson, who handled the company's labor relations in the early part of the war, probably summed up the feeling of most of top management when he told the board in October 1944: "The control of labor matters is rapidly passing out of the hands of the employer. There is practically no matter left that cannot be brought before some governmental tribunal for settlement. Bonuses, vacations, merit rating, retrenchment in employment, wages, incentive plans, job evaluation, seniority and even technological improvement are little by little being established as matters for collective bargaining and, therefore, matters on which governmental agencies or arbitrators can make final decisions. Managements' rights as formerly recognized have practically disappeared. Largely your labor costs and your choice of personnel are passing out of your control." The company had existed for 105 years under a philosophy of individual relations with individual employees. Now there was to be a new era, that of collective bargaining.[4]

POSTWAR ANATOMY OF THE COMPANY

Wartime management of companies entails highly centralized decision making. Defense requirements, rather than those of the market, dictate production targets. The price maker is the government; at the same time, the government is also the dominant customer. Tight control from the top—rigid rules from a nation's production "czar"—breeds a similar pattern down into individual organizations. Thus Deere & Company found itself becoming a more centrally managed organization during World War II.

The leadership of the company changed significantly over the war years. In October 1943, T.F. Wharton, long-time comptroller and wartime treasurer of the company, passed away. Coming to Deere at the time of the formation of the modern company in 1911, Wharton had gone on the board in 1918 to become an influential counselor to the company's chief executive officers, first William Butterworth and then Charles Wiman. Lloyd Kennedy became secretary and treasurer of the company, to succeed Wharton as the chief financial officer.

A second death was an even more serious loss to the company. In October 1944, Charles C. Webber died at the age of eighty-five, after an unparalleled sixty-seven years of service with Deere & Company. He had been on the board of directors from early in 1886; thus he had been involved in the general management of the company for more than fifty-eight years. His perspective was always broad, reflecting not only the requirements of the Minneapolis branch but of the entire company as well. His judgment on personnel and on top management organization and interaction was unmatched in the company's history. His blunt frankness was softened by a thoughtfulness and patience that won respect from the rest of top management. It seems almost incredible, given today's retirement ages, that an individual could be fully productive for so many years. From the moment he began work to the last day of his active business life, he was a contributing, integral member of the organization that he saw grow from a small set of loosely knit factories and branches into an integrated company taking an important role in the war. His peers rightly had designated him "the dean of the American implement industry."

In that same month, F.H. Clausen also died. He had been with the Van Brunt organization from 1899 and its president from 1920. In 1923, he became a member of the parent Deere board, and one of its vice presidents in 1941. Clausen was more insular then Webber, and his contributions to the parent were different. Still, a company cannot lose a trusted and capable executive like Clausen without suffering a management gap.

With these losses, the locus of power in top management shifted. Burton Peek clearly viewed himself as a "caretaker" right from the start; everyone sensed that he did not wish to hold the reins of the presidency any longer than was necessary. He was assisted by three other senior members who carried the rank of vice president and who gradually assumed increasing responsibilities: Charles Stone, the Harvester Works manager and Wiman confidant; Frank Silloway, longstanding head of sales, a board member since 1914, a vice president from 1919; and Lawrence "Pat" Murphy, on the Board since 1937 but elevated during the war to a vice presidency. (Murphy was a descendant of the Ellen Webber side of the family, and thus was related to C.C. Webber.)

Murphy was the dynamic leader of a major part of the line organization; he and Stone shared the manufacturing responsibility in the company. Murphy was the dominant representative of his generation for the Webber side of the family. His position was strengthened when Edmund "Budge" Cook joined the company as legal counsel in 1943; Cook was related by marriage to both Pat Murphy and C.C. Webber. As the war wore on, key policy making gravitated toward this smaller group of Silloway, Murphy, Kennedy, Cook, and Stone (with Peek in the chair as a more passive chief executive than Wiman).

In June 1944, while Charles Wiman was in the midst of his final battle at the War Production Board, Charles Stone was shifted out of his direct line role in manufacturing and put in charge of product development. Murphy, in turn, was given responsibility for all of the factories, as well as the engineering department, the testing and research laboratories, and the personnel and industrial relations department. Lloyd Kennedy, who had worked closely with Peek and Wiman in the financial affairs of both the company and the family, was elevated to vice president, responsible for the overall financial policy of the company.

This far-reaching decision was debated over two separate board meetings; at the second, Burton Peek elaborated on its rationale: "War contracts have interfered with the policy of decentralization, which has been an outstanding characteristic of our operations . . . and have created a trend toward centralization. This trend must be reversed.... The purpose is to leave with and restore to the Factories and Branches the maximum feasible operating latitude as in the past."

These announcements of June 1944 had a great effect on the whole organization of the company; for years afterward, the bulletins elaborating these changes were remembered as the singular manifesto that spelled out again the company's basic commitment to decentralization and that restored the power to the branches and the factories. If the war had indeed centralized many functions, now this centralization was to be reversed.

But was it? On the one hand, Frank Silloway had had a thoroughgoing dedication to giving the branch managers "their heads" and had presided over the continuing branch-house decentralization into the hands of such strong leaders as C.C. Webber and Michael Healey. Though Webber and Healey were now gone, there were other new branch-house managers, displaying the same independence—W.D. Hosford in Omaha, R.B. Lourie in Moline, and others. By instinct and longstanding operational style, Silloway was committed to decentralization, and he had developed a relationship with the branch managers over the years that had provided bonds of understanding and communication that gave the system a special Silloway mark. Still, Silloway was in his late sixties, just a few years away from retirement.

Murphy, on the other hand, was in his mid-forties and had been a general company vice president only since 1942. Murphy was quite cognizant of factory prerogatives—he had headed the Plow Works before coming to the general company post. But the consolidation in June 1944 of all general company manufacturing under his responsibility was unprecedented—never before had there been a vice president with this breadth of responsibility for manufacturing. Peek's announcement seemed inconsistent in promoting, on the one hand, the "return" to decentralization, yet at the same time centralizing all manufacturing under one strong vice president, Pat Murphy. The move gave mixed signals to the factories. Murphy needed to be cautious about contradicting his factory managers' decrees (his relationship with "Duke" Rowland, the Waterloo Tractor Works manager, was a particularly prickly one). Yet Murphy's instinct for detail and desire to involve himself in all decision making centralized a substantial amount of authority and power in his hands. Stone's long involvement in the line had ended; as a staff vice president concerned with product development, Stone was now to be more advisory, less directly managerial.

Peek's announcement left no doubt about the sincerity of the board in returning to past ways of managing the company. Still, the messages were not clear—there were mixed meanings in the organizational changes, complex and subtle new roles to work out in new, postwar managerial interactions.

Budge Cook, who had become a director in 1943 and general counsel in 1944, was given the assignment of articulating some of the subtleties in the new moves. In a major speech to the factory managers in July 1944, he exhorted the managers not to leave "your problems" to the general company departments. Cook had been delegated by Murphy to make the speech; surprisingly his remarks seemed to speak directly to Murphy. "Let us suppose that a General Company man is an individual who likes to dominate or suppose there is no one to whom he can refer the situation in which you and he fail to agree; or suppose that he knows that you will be resentful if he does refer the matter to higher authority. If any of these situations persist, the General Company man will strive the harder to force edicts upon you and your people." Cook continued, "I am clear in my own belief that a General Company Department should not be permitted to force that move onto the Tractor Works against its opposition." Cook had moved subtly from a general statement about nuances of policy to a specific example, a carefully chosen one, the Tractor Works. Clearly, stronger, old line factories—the Tractor Works, the Harvester Works, etc.—were to be maintained as almost autonomous units, subject only to general communication and report, after the fact, with corporate headquarters. This was not Murphy's view, for he was a demanding executive who wanted extensive communication with and involvement in his operating department entities. On the other hand, strong factory executives, like Rowland and Harold White of the Planter Works, were not likely to take direction very readily.

Thus, as Pat Murphy, Lloyd Kennedy, and Budge Cook emerged as the next generation of management, subtle differences of opinion had surfaced among them. Kennedy was foremost a representative of the family, only early in the process of becoming the chief financial officer of the company itself. Murphy was a young member of the next generation representing part of the family, a logical person to step into a major role in line management. Cook, though also related by marriage to the Webber side of the family, was a professional; his lawyer's instincts combined with his remarkable philosophical understanding of organization structure to give the company a sophisticated spokesman for the restructuring process, independent of any particular faction within the organization.[5]

CHARLES WIMAN'S "POSTWAR RECONVERSION"

This interplay of responsibility among the three men had to be fitted to an important organization enigma—would Charles Wiman return? Wiman had left abruptly for war as a strong, even dominant chief executive officer of Deere & Company. Wiman had found his assignment with the U.S. Army rewarding; during his illness he had confided to his friend, Edward R. Stettinius, Jr. (just named secretary of state), that he

would like to have gone back to Ordnance "but there was no chance of
my again getting active service.... I could not pass the physicals." His
next assignment, with the War Production Board, had made him once
more privy to the evolving status of the industry. But clearly he had lost
touch with the day-by-day activities of Deere, having attended only a
segment of one board meeting since leaving in mid-1942 (where, incidentally, he had startled everyone by proposing that the company make
airplanes and deep-freeze apparatus after the war). Apparently the challenge of Deere was deep inside him, though, just as it had been all through
his years prior to World War II. After more than a month of serious illness
and an extended convalescence in the fall of 1944, Wiman made his
decision to return to active management in the company.

Wiman's re-entry was tension-filled. The major executive change of the
previous June had thrust Murphy into a pivotal role in the company—in
charge of all manufacturing and engineering. Cook was a new face to
Wiman—Cook's entry into the company had come after Wiman had left
for Washington. Lloyd Kennedy's elevation to a vice presidency was a
change; was he now more independent than in his previous role as the
family's financial counsel?

Charles Wiman had practiced a personal management philosophy of
not giving any one individual in the company such a strong base of
authority. Wiman seemed to have an abiding faith in a constellation of
strong people, with the inevitable tensions among them adding to the
effectiveness of the whole. As Wiman returned and surveyed his top
management relationships, he seemed uncertain as to Murphy's and
Cook's places within the group. Indeed, there is substantial evidence that
the nagging thought had crossed his mind that there was a "barracks
revolt" against him. Deere & Company seldom had been subject to rank
factionalism, erupting into power plays by one group against another (the
only serious instance being the Butterworth-Velie acrimony in the
1910s). On the other hand, what would have been the leadership
succession had Wiman not returned? One of the options would likely
have been the choice of Murphy as president.

Once back on the job, Wiman quickly moved to reassert his leadership
in the company. He was elected to the presidency in a formal board
meeting of October 31, 1944, and at this meeting made a speech that was
vintage Wiman. He praised the monumental job done by the entire
organization during the war, then noted explicitly the restructured
organization stemming from the board decisions of the previous June. He
singled out the Murphy assignment as "a real constructive organization
change" but left no doubt that Murphy only had been put in charge of all
the factories "from the *production-management* standpoint."

"I turn now to the question of my re-entering Deere & Company,"
Wiman continued, "and, as we say in the Army, taking the oath of office,
or as we say in industry, getting on the payroll. This Board made me the

Company's chief executive officer in 1936. I acted in that capacity for 6 years. *If* you want me to come back, my return should be on the same basis."

Wiman then stated his view of the chief executive officer's role with no equivocation: "Mr. Peek and I *privately* (and publicly as far as that is concerned) have agreed that there should be but one chief executive officer. There is nothing in the world that is *worse* than a divided command." There were now to be "local board meetings" held at least once a month during the interim between regular board meetings, but Wiman made it clear that the president would always act as the presiding officer.

Wiman also addressed the new role of Cook. After remarking that Burton Peek had acted as general counsel of the company since the formation of the modern company in 1911, Wiman explicitly suggested that when Peek decided to select his successor, it be Budge Cook. This was a curious tactic, for seldom does a chief executive officer desire to tie his hands on a future appointment. In this case, Wiman seemed to want to acknowledge the contributions made by Cook, at the same time delineating a narrower role for him within the constraints of the legal counsel's portfolio.

Throughout, Wiman exhibited his unique brand of enthusiasm and optimism; he concluded with a ringing call to arms: "I feel this Board must have the vision, sanely—at the same time boldly—to *expand* production facilities. . . . Surely as we are sitting here, if we fail to provide the necessary facilities, *someone else will.* I know we don't want this someone else to be Ford, General Motors, Curtiss-Wright, Graham-Paige, or the XYZ Company of New Mexico, nor do we want this opportunity to be cashed in by IHC, Allis-Chalmers, Case, Oliver, Minneapolis-Moline or any other company not now in the business. We must have *courage,* after due consideration and analysis of the problems to *spend* our money wisely . . . to expand this position and to acquire an even *greater* percentage of the total implement and tractor business than we have had in times past."

The entire speech was a vivid demonstration of Wiman's strong-minded personality and power to persuade. Its effect on the board at that time was great—remembrances are unanimous in characterizing this particular board meeting as the critical one in the postwar reconversion of Deere & Company. The return of Wiman once again reaffirmed the dominance of the Charles Deere side of family ownership and brought back in the process a chief executive officer of uncommon abilities, one who could dramatically energize the management group as no other person within the company at that time could have done. For the health of Deere & Company, it was a crucially important positive step.

Wiman had been back on the job less than three weeks when he made an important change in certain top management assignments. L.A.

"Duke" Rowland had headed the Waterloo tractor factory since 1936 and had been elected a director in the company in 1942. Now Wiman decided to give him an even broader assignment, as general manager of all tractor production (that is, Waterloo and the Moline Tractor Works). The bulletin announcing the change came from Murphy and stated additionally that Rowland "is hereby appointed assistant to this writer." Rowland was a doughty, precise man, born in England, a feisty and independent person who would insist on "running his own show"—the word "assistant" inevitably would have limited meaning as applied to him. Wiman's message was clear—Rowland was going to "head," literally, all tractor production, Murphy to have implements and to continue responsibility for the engineering department, the laboratories, industrial relations, and other staff groups. Murphy's tenure as head of all manufacturing had lasted less than six months. The demarcation was made even more sharply in 1947, when Rowland was elected a vice president, co-equal with Murphy.[6]

DEFINING DECENTRALIZATION, ONCE AGAIN

Though Charles Wiman had laid at rest the issue of executive succession, there was still confusion about where the decentralization policy stood. All the board agreed that too much centralization had been forced by wartime conditions, but just what relation was now to exist between general company vice presidents and constituent factory and branch managers was not well understood.

Wiman had brought many new ways back with him from Washington. He changed the layout of his office, eliminated the prewar pattern of having a secretarial pool next to him, shifted his former private secretary, Maurice Block, to another assignment out of the president's office. Wiman also brought a new person with him when he returned, and the effect of this soon led to more questions about the relationship between central office and field operations.

Wiman had had an assistant at the War Production Board, Harold L. Boyle, in whom Wiman had vested considerable trust. Boyle had been an International Harvester executive for a number of years; when Wiman returned to Deere, he persuaded Boyle to join the company. The titular post for Boyle was purchasing; in reality, Boyle acted more as a personal assistant to Wiman in the first few months of the latter's return to Deere. Boyle seemed for a while to be taking over the role held for a number of years by Charles Stone, that of personal confidant for Wiman. In May 1945 Boyle was elected vice president; the previous month, Boyle had also been elected to the board (along with C.R. Carlson, Jr., a hard-driving executive who had headed the Minneapolis branch after C.C. Webber's death).

Wiman now used Boyle's appointment as purchasing vice president to announce a surprising further decentralization of purchasing functions. Citing again Burton Peek's statement in 1944 that "the trend toward centralization . . . must be reversed," Wiman made it clear that while Boyle would have a major role in company policy making, he was not to be given the central responsibility for the effecting of purchasing decisions. In key respects, Wiman's move here was incongruous—establishing a major officer for purchasing, yet at the same time decentralizing purchasing into the hands of individual factory and branch purchasing officers.

This apparent inconsistency soon triggered much concern. Wiman sensed the unease and apparently felt that the time had come to take on the divisive issue of decentralization in a more organized way. His vehicle was to choose a small group of directors—Frank Silloway, Charles Stone, Pat Murphy, Lloyd Kennedy, Harold Boyle, and Budge Cook—to meet over a number of months and return at the end of the year with firm recommendations that would, he hoped, lay at rest once and for all the tensions concerning lines of authority.

But there were surprisingly deep divisions among even this committee about the philosophy of organization at Deere. Cook and Boyle were particularly in disagreement. Cook espoused a militantly decentralized point of view, Boyle a single-minded concern to enhance the power and authority of the presidency. Cook believed that the various officers should be the "eyes and ears of the Directors," in effect bypassing the president if more direct communication was desired. Boyle vehemently resisted this notion, holding that officers should report to the board "only when requested to do so by the President." Cook stated bluntly that "with rare exceptions of an emergency nature, the president's power to give orders to key people at lower levels will not be exercised." Boyle argued: "No matter what we write in our memo the President will run his job as he sees fit and each of us individually will have to gear our activities to accomplish the end results for which he is striving. He is our boss and he takes full responsibility with the Board of Directors for his activities and ours." Cook had a view of decision making that put complete responsibility in the hands of individuals out in the field (factory managers, branch managers, etc.) and held that officers were "not chargeable with preventing errors . . . not chargeable with the duty to take corrective measures . . . not subject to criticism for lack of action . . . where the subordinate is authorized to finalize decisions." This seemed to Boyle to be excessive autonomy and he retorted: "Important and even isolated mistakes with a key man's field of action should never pass unchallenged. . . . I cannot imagine a ball team making errors and the coach not criticizing the players in an effective and constructive manner. The officers are the coaches on the Deere & Company team and their staffs are the assistant coaches."

The committee continued to meet over a four-month period and produced a remarkable set of minutes. Though the discussions were not acrimonious, so strong was the disagreement on principles that Wiman backed off and decided not to make the committee's report public within the company.

Why this sudden timidity on the part of Wiman, not one of his characteristics in the past? The final minutes of the committee had been frank in stating that there was "unrest, uncertainty and a degree of frustration among key people in the organization. . . . We are in danger of losing or seriously impairing the high degree of morale, loyalty, and efficiency that existed in the past." Wiman knew that if he made definitive judgments at this point, he would bruise some egos. Further, he privately worried that if an attempt was made to codify in writing all of the organization structure this process might not give proper weight to the traditions, habits, and practices that had grown up through the years. It seemed best to Wiman to beat a strategic retreat.

But Wiman was astute enough to know that the fuzzy lines of organization structure would continue to trouble top management until they were more openly resolved. He bided his time, and in October 1947 unilaterally brought the issue of organization structure back to the table for consideration by the officers. This was a period of relative calm—it was at the end of a product and fiscal year that had been quite successful (sales were up to $194 million from the previous year's $131 million, net income had risen to $18 million from the previous year's $12 million). Reconversion problems were largely over; the upcoming year promised to be a good one. It seemed a propitious moment to face up to a controversial issue.

This time Wiman put together the outline of the structure by himself, writing out an organization chart and functional responsibilities in his own hand at home. Once ready, he drew Cook and Charles Stone into his confidence. The three then developed a set of three organization charts. The first, a conventional "line of authority" chart, pictured the organization as it existed at that moment. A second chart showed the same organization, but developed a set of dotted-line relationships among various departments to show advisory and informal linkages.

Stone then suggested an innovative new way of viewing the organization. He likened the lines of communication to lines of travel within a city, observing that the residence of any individual is connected with every other building in the city and with every other building in the United States by a series of highways. These highways were not exclusive, but were for general public use. Stone then suggested the analogy of the streets to the Deere organization—that every key individual in the organization could promptly get onto a highway that would take him to any other part of the organization. Out of this notion, he and Cook developed the third organizational chart, a pictorial effort to show the "highways" of Deere & Company, complete with traffic lights at intersections!

A few simple traffic rules were established—streets and highways were to be used expressly for the purposes of obtaining information and making agreements; orders, directives, and demands were only to issue through the line of authority. Still, information or agreements should be obtained at the nearest practical points, and executives were to go no further or higher than necessary. As each individual used these channels of communication, he was to inform his immediate supervisor of all significant facts obtained and agreements made. Finally, all executives in the entire organization were to apply these concepts, not only in their dealings with the general company, but within their own organizations as such.

With this material in his hand, Wiman made a major decision, to call all branch-house managers and factory managers to Moline to discuss the subject of organization structure at a general meeting, at which the three charts would be used as the points of departure.

The meeting was held on December 12, 1947, amid pregnant anticipation among the executives present. Wiman's opening remarks set the stage: "I wish at this time to pay special tribute to Messrs. C.H. Deere, William Butterworth and C.C. Webber, all of whom carried the policy of decentralization through to the very 'nth' degree. . . . The question is: 'Are we ourselves thoroughly sold on decentralization so that we can practice decentralization in a very efficient way?'" Wiman then discussed the three charts, putting particular focus on the "street chart" (Wiman's words). He spelled out the suggested traffic rules of Cook and Stone and emphasized that traffic was on a two-way street—that the general company officers also were to be free to come into the factories and branches to bring their counsel, advice, and guidance.

The day-long discussion turned up widely different views. On the one hand, Burton Peek spoke vehemently for central control: "I am not one of those who think that there is no necessity for some degree of centralized management. Quite to the contrary. Centralized management must map out and state overall Company policies to the end that so far as that is humanly possible there be no overstepping of bounds and no interference one with another." Pat Murphy took an opposite stance and rejected out of hand any "interference" by central engineering: "There is no Company policy that makes it mandatory to obtain the approval of these departments on any given project. It is the responsibility of these departments to so conduct themselves that the factories and the branches will have confidence in their judgment, and consequently seek their advice." (Murphy must have worried that he had gone too far, for he later requested Wiman's permission to revise his remarks for the formal minutes; he substituted a more innocuous statement that the outside "staff of experts" were to "work with the factories and to keep us informed." The record is mute as to whether this more diplomatic concept of staff was Murphy's own.)

So deep was the division that Wiman ended by asking the entire group to go back to their respective organizations, there to take up to ninety days to give intensive study to all the matters that came forward in the meeting. When each person felt comfortable with his own views, then he was to forward to Wiman suggestions for revision of the charts, together with a statement of what he was doing "toward making fully effective and insuring the continuance of decentralization . . . under your jurisdiction." Wiman also asked each to decide whether it was feasible to publish an organization chart and a general-company bulletin, explicitly stating the organization structure.

The ensuing statements that came to Wiman over the next three months provided remarkable testimony to the interest and concern that the members of top management felt about the principles of Deere organization. Wiman collated all of the comments and, as promised, issued a general-company bulletin to both factory and branch in May 1948, under the title "John Deere Decentralization Policy." It was clear in the bulletin that Wiman still felt it unpolitic to state definitively the organized policy: "While this is being issued in Blue Bulletin form, this method is being used solely as a means of getting the collective opinion and my thoughts into your hands, and I think it would be better if you think of it as a letter rather than a Blue Bulletin outlining a policy."

As to the charts, there was "little doubt as to your general preference for the street (or highway) type of chart, although the line of authority chart did not lack proponents, and at least two replies indicated desire for all three charts." Nevertheless, Wiman stated: "No centralized directive could resolve all your circumstances, nor meet your varying problems on furthering this or any other policy as effectively *as your own initiative and decision*." Again, Wiman had backed off. He concluded: "Your replies leave no doubt as to your intent to maintain and improve John Deere decentralization. . . . They show that you propose to be aggressive leaders, rather than passive followers. They prove that each of you fully plans to apply decentralization in the way he considers best under the particular circumstances in his factory, branch house or department. . . . I am satisfied that a repetition every few years of last December's meeting will keep our tradition alive and effective. . . . Decentralization formally by manual or bulletin at this time would detract from the tradition."

Although this six-month saga did not result in a definitive statement at the end, the sum of all of the efforts was to infuse everyone with the excitement and enthusiasm of continuing to work together as the "Deere family." The concept that there needed to be certain centralized control and coordination, backed by enough authority to make this process stick, was implanted. Not resolved, however, were the many individual rough spots in communication, or the excesses of overly arrogant individual action and the unthinking protection of fiefdoms. After all had been said, the strong factory and branch managers had maintained their personal control more or less untouched. [7]

FINANCING EXPANSION

Deere had not borrowed any money for long-range purposes since it retired the issue in 1921 of $10 million of 7.5 percent "Gold Notes," fully paid off ahead of time in 1925. The board had depended on a conservative combination of short-term bank financing and the plowing of as much of the profits back into the business as was prudent. The effect of the policy of caution, though, was that the company for years had been making only as much equipment as it "could afford," not as much as it could actually sell.

The company's balance sheet on October 31, 1944—the end of that fiscal year—was one that any good conservative executive would be proud of; here in outline is how it stood in that year's annual report:

Current Assets		Current Liabilities	$40.6
Cash	$78.6	Reserves (benefits, price	
Government securities	24.4	declines, war losses,	
Canadian bonds	3.7	contingencies)	36.6
Notes and Accounts		Capital and surplus	
Receivable	18.8	Preferred	31.0
Inventories	38.5	Common	30.0
Property and equipment	21.6	Earned surplus	53.6
Other assets and deferred			
charges	6.2		
	$191.8		$191.8

Charles Wiman had come back from the war enthusiastic enough about postwar prospects to consider a more aggressive policy. Manufacturing capacity for tractors seemed to demand the highest priority. The board already was on record for "producing a low-cost model tractor" and wanted this to be done at a location other than the Tri-City or Waterloo areas (preferably, also on a water route).

A thorough study finally centered on Dubuque, Iowa; the Ordnance Corps of the United States Army wanted Deere to continue manufacturing 75-millimeter shells and offered to share the building of the new factory, part of which could be used also for tractor manufacturing. In January 1945 the board unanimously approved the purchase of land and the immediate construction of the plant. The total cost of the project was estimated to be $9.4 million.

Wiman's postwar ebullience seemed to give him a new perspective about the past financial conservatism of the company; though he did believe that "management had followed the proper course in these years," nevertheless, he now felt that "the freedom of action of management had been restricted" at that time. So, pushed by Wiman's unequivocal commitment to expansion, the board decided to issue new debt instruments. The needs were estimated to be a startling $30 million. A package was put together with Deere's lead Chicago bank, Continental Illinois National Bank and Trust Company, whereby Continental and a group of other banks would subscribe to $10.5 million of serial notes (1.5 percent and 1.75 percent) and the remainder of $19.5 million in twenty-year 2.75 percent debentures that would be offered to the public. The issue sold with no snags, and the company had established the underpinnings of its ambitious postwar financing.

The new debt did raise some eyebrows—many people had taken as immutable Deere's very conservative financial policies. Max Sklovsky, who had retired from his post as the company's chief engineer, wrote Wiman "as a stockholder," questioning the need for the issue and, in the process, gave Wiman an unusually barbed personal criticism, implying too much dominance by him: "It can be assumed normally that the collective wisdom of a Board of Directors transcends that of an individual, yet it is well known that a Board is led by one or two and the rest following saying 'Amen.' It does appear that the results aimed at could be reached in a more simplified manner than that of building factories for complete goods." Wiman seemed stung by the queries of Sklovsky and others, and he drafted a letter outlining the expected uses of the funds. The letter seemed apologetic, ending: "The Directors took into account the obvious truth that they could not read the future with certainty, and recognized that a decision either way could be wrong."

The expansion of plant and equipment moved rapidly over the next two years. The Dubuque plant was completed as scheduled, with housing in such short supply that the company also built some 111 houses, which were first rented and then later sold to employees. By mid-1947 the factory was producing the company's new Model M tractor.

This machine had been in the making since early in World War II (Charles Wiman having insisted that product development continue apace all during the war). The Model M was a general-purpose utility tractor, rated at 14.39 horsepower at the drawbar. It incorporated an innovative hydraulic unit—called the Touch-O-Matic—for attaching and controlling integral equipment. When the tricycle version, the MT, came out in 1949, it had the same hydraulic concept, but with a dual system for independent adjustments of tools working on either side of the tractor.

Dubuque at this point also took on the manufacture of another tractor—the Lindeman crawler tractor—that was the forerunner of a major division of the company. Since 1940, Deere had been supplying to a Yakima, Washington, company, Lindeman Manufacturing, Inc., the Deere Model BO tractor chassis (this was the orchard version of the B, with fenders so that protruding fruit-laden branches would not catch in

Exhibit 12–3. Deere-Lindeman tractor working in an orchard, ca. 1941 (Deere Archives)

the wheels). Lindeman attached its own crawler tracks to the Deere chassis, and the machine was marketed as a "John Deere Lindeman." There was substantial demand for this type of traction among the Pacific Northwest orchard owners; crawler traction was also popular in logging areas—in New England's snow and in the swamps of the Southern timber regions.

In May 1945 Deere purchased Lindeman. When the deal was consummated, nearly two years later, the Lindeman was phased out and the Deere Model MC made in Dubuque but still using tracks made in the newly renamed Yakima Works. The Yakima plant also made some of the Deere tillage and land-leveling equipment. By 1953 it became apparent that the plant's freight costs for shipping back to the Midwest were too high and the Yakima Works was closed. In this year, Dubuque brought out a new larger crawler, the Model 40C, with 15.11 drawbar horsepower; Dubuque began manufacturing the track, too.

Charles Wiman's view of the world, so different after he returned from World War II, continued to expand. In February 1947 he embarked on a three-month trip to South America to visit Peru, Chile, Argentina, and Uruguay. The trip made a profound impression on him, for he sensed great business potential there. Indeed, he cabled back instructions to segregate a significant amount of Deere products for shipment abroad. This was at the height of the shortage of products in the United States,

with farmers clamoring for Deere machines and often expressing irritation over the long waits.

Budge Cook, apparently one of the most expansion-minded members of
top management, wrote Wiman while the latter was in Chile: "My
impression is that many of our people are becoming imbued with a sense
of failure.... Our factory production is at a record peak and yet we are
working in an atmosphere of failure . . . failure to supply an unprecedented demand.... We must create that atmosphere of success, for otherwise
many of our key people will simply wear out and let down under the
strain."

Wiman appeared upset by this and wrote back immediately, "Sense of
failure? No, indeed! We have and are spending all we can." As to the
unnamed people whom Cook felt were "wearing out," Wiman responded:
"I suppose you've certain individuals, or individual in mind—OK, let's
give special treatment . . . but we also don't want a Pollyanna 'what a
good boy am I' feeling to creep in." Still, from this exchange, Wiman
became convinced that additional capacity had to be acquired. When Pat
Murphy proposed to increase the Plow Works production by purchase of a
new plant, Wiman immediately wrote Murphy from South America,
giving his approval for the purchase of a vacant plant in Des Moines, Iowa
(earlier offers of plants at Tulsa, Oklahoma, and Longview, Texas, had
been rejected). This was the former Des Moines Ordnance Plant, at
Ankeny, Iowa, and it was to be bought from the War Assets Administration for $4.15 million. The deal was completed in June 1947; by the end of
the year the plant was in production, making the company's cotton
picker, as well as some cultivating tools.

Significant additions were also made to existing operations in Moline,
Waterloo, and Ottumwa; by October 1947, at the end of that fiscal year,
the depreciated value of the property and equipment of the company had
soared from $21.6 million in 1944 to more than $52 million. This
breathtaking acquisition of bricks and mortar, so exciting when it was in
the formative stage, now began to make Wiman quite uneasy. The
financial ratios had shifted during this three-year period. The ratio of cash
and securities to current liabilities had declined a bit; the notes and
accounts receivable had risen significantly, given the quickened pace of
sales out in the field; and, of course, the property and equipment account
had made the fixed assets side of the ledger much larger. Though there
was certainly nothing in the ratios to trouble a financial expert, Wiman
nevertheless warned the board in January 1948: "Pressures from customers and Government have caused us to place our emphasis very heavily
upon maximum production which, in turn, has involved steps that in
other days would have been looked upon as wasteful if not extravagant."
Plans were already on the drawing board for $30.9 million of capital
expenditures; Wiman now proposed that the sum be slashed by more
than $24 million, and that there be a tightening of spending all through

the organization. He proposed a sharp cutback on further expenditures for facilities and a tightening of the belt throughout the organization.

Later that year, as Wiman reported on the results of fiscal 1948, he was able to say that the company was "closing the finest year" it had ever had. Sales had tripled—rising from $94 million the previous year to $283 million; profits for 1948 were $27.6 million and, after $10.4 million of this was paid in dividends on the common and preferred stock, more than $17 million was retained. The working capital of the firm rose to $147 million from $92 million in 1941 on the eve of the war. The pullback from the earlier expansion plans had put the company in a conservative position. Once again, though, Wiman was ambivalent about his turn toward conservatism, and he ended his statement to the board: "At the same time we must be aware of the business truism that if we stop using money for improvement of our factories and our products, we will cease to progress. We have before us the ceaseless choice between progress on the one hand and financial stability on the other hand.... A major mistake in either direction could be serious to an extreme degree—could be fatal." It seems that Wiman could never truly feel he was off the knife's edge.[8]

POSTWAR LABOR CONFLICTS

As V-J Day approached in the late summer of 1945, industrial relations around the country were in a state of turmoil, as both labor and management prepared to reassert their powers after the tight controls of the War Labor Board were lifted. The period 1945–46 turned out to be strife-ridden. The historic 113-day strike at the General Motors Corporation that began in November 1945 was soon followed by strikes by 100,000 telephone workers, 640,000 steel workers, 75,000 retail clerks, and others. In May 1946 the greatest strike in the history of American railroads took place; it lasted just three days before Pres. Harry Truman went before the Congress to seek the authority to seize the properties and make the walkout illegal. A coal strike at the same time persisted for almost two months; in this case, the government took over the mines and promulgated a settlement. Certainly the two years after World War II vied with the late 1930s as a period of sustained acrimony and overt strike action.

It was not surprising, therefore, that Deere & Company had trouble, too. After the initial signing of contracts with the two CIO unions—the United Automobile Workers and the Farm Equipment Workers—in the early part of World War II, there had been long and inconclusive negotiations for their renewal in 1944. Locals signed extensions, worked without contracts at certain times, then renewed previous extensions. By 1945, with the prospect that negotiations would be freed of governmental restrictions, the unions' aggressiveness grew apace. By late August 1945, employees at the company's Harvester Works and Spreader Works had walked off the job in what seemed, if not a wildcat strike, at least a walkout authorized by a very small segment of the union members (these were UAW locals). The issue primarily centered on wages (the company had offered a 10 percent increase, the unions were demanding 30 percent); there also were issues concerning piece rates and related issues. By early September the tie-up had spread to the Plow Works, where the Farm Equipment Workers local had taken the employees out; again the vote for the strike authorization had been carried through by a very small segment of the union. A week or so later the strike had spread to Union Malleable (UAW) and to the Ottumwa plant (also UAW).

Both the company and the unions had additional agendas beyond the economic issues ostensibly involved in the strikes. Deere officials strongly felt that bargaining should proceed only on a plant-by-plant basis, in keeping with the company's longstanding policy of decentralization. The United Automobile Workers took the opposite position and from the start had pressed the company for multi-plant bargaining, covering all of their jurisdictions as one. The situation was complicated by the fact that another CIO union was involved—the Farm Equipment Workers. At one point early in the strikes of 1945, both unions approached the company about joint negotiations involving all the plants. This suggestion had a short life; not only was the company implacably against such an idea, but the two unions were so competitive that joint action seemed unworkable.

As the strike continued into October, feelings began to run higher, and the two unions decided to band together under the aegis of the Quad-City Industrial Union Council (the overall CIO unit in the area) to jointly promote some mass picketing and demonstrations. Two places were targets. As expected, the first was the Deere main office; the second choice was a shocker—the homes of Burton Peek and Charles Wiman (who lived across the street from each other). Both demonstrations were orderly, though Burton Peek was lustily booed as he drove away from his home shortly after the pickets arrived. The demonstration outside the homes of the two executives seemed to backfire on the unions, for many of the oldtimers were outraged by it, one employee being quoted as saying: "I have always been a union man, and I am still a union man, but I told them bastards that when they picketed a good old s__ of a b__ like Burt Peek, they were going too far."

By early November an ad hoc committee of employees' wives met with the Moline mayor, hoping to persuade him to intervene in the situation, but he did not. The union's strength was waning, though, and a few days later the Harvester Works and Spreader Works strikes were over, settled essentially on the same basis as the initial offer of the company (a 10 percent wage hike being the central feature). The Farm Equipment Workers local at the Plow Works prolonged its strike for about a month

Exhibit 12–4. Top, *Deere employees picketing in front of the Charles Wiman residence during the strike of October 1945;* bottom, *Strikers also visit the Burton Peek residence on that day.*

after the UAW plants had settled, finally agreeing to similar terms, as did the Ottumwa and Waterloo locals.

It had been an inconclusive endeavor for all concerned. The negotiations themselves had not served the process of collective bargaining very well, given the primitive stage of the unions' organizational structures, the competition between the two CIO unions, and the company's difficulties in working out its own role (particularly on the issue of centralized bargaining).

In the industry, meanwhile, industrial relations had become even more acrimonious at several other companies. At International Harvester, the Farm Equipment Workers had taken its locals out on strike in early 1946. Simultaneously, there were prolonged strikes by the UAW at Allis-Chalmers and J.I. Case. In all three of these strikes the major issue was the withdrawal by the companies of wartime union security provisions. (During the war, the War Labor Board had promulgated a maintenance-of-membership clause in these companies' contracts.)

Some very large issues were also being fought out within the UAW itself, where a pitched battle between "right" and "left" factions was coming to a climax. There had been widespread accusations that the leadership of the UAW was Communist-leaning; the left had been particularly in evidence in the violence-ridden 329-day strike at the West Allis, Wisconsin, plant of Allis-Chalmers. There the local leader was alleged to be following the Communist Party line throughout the strike, seemingly prolonging the conflict beyond the time when a settlement had seemed assured. Walter Reuther, the leader of the right-wing faction in the union, had had to go to Wisconsin to bring the situation to a close. Reuther had just won the presidency a few months earlier in the turbulent convention of 1946, one of the most furious gatherings of labor leaders in the modern period of the labor movement. His margin then had been a narrow 104 votes and the membership promptly turned around and gave a majority of the executive board to his opponents (with R.J. Thomas, the former president, reelected as vice president).

In the spring of 1947, the faction led by Thomas proposed that the Farm Equipment Workers be brought into the UAW; inasmuch as the union was also strongly left-leaning, Thomas felt that the votes in the national convention from the small Farm Equipment Workers group would be enough to enable the Thomas faction to recapture control. In Moline, the local Farm Equipment Workers leaders made desperate attempts to persuade the UAW locals to vote favorably on the proposal, but the motion was rejected summarily by members at both the Harvester Works and Union Malleable. Reuther, holding up the West Allis debacle as a warning, engineered the defeat of the merger proposal by a more than two-to-one vote. This breakthrough now allowed Reuther to wrest the leadership from Thomas. The convention of 1947 was much less turbulent than the one the year before, Reuther winning a clearcut victory for the presidency and a majority on the executive board.

Farm machinery negotiations with the UAW in 1947 followed the union's negotiations with the automobile industry, and when the latter bargaining set a pattern, Deere and the UAW agreed to the same terms. They provided for an $.11-an-hour increase and liberalization of vacation pay and night-work bonuses. In separate negotiations, the Farm Equipment Workers quietly concluded the same agreement with the company. Two months later, another quarter was heard from—the International Association of Machinists, who represented the skilled machinists in the company. The walkout lasted three days before a settlement was reached that was essentially the same as that accepted by the UAW.

The lines were now drawn for a full-scale local confrontation between the Farm Equipment Workers and the UAW. The Farm Equipment Workers had also controlled the local at Dubuque, and in the negotiations of 1947 they had rejected the proposed pattern contract and subsequently engaged in mass picketing. The company had petitioned for an injunction to prevent the picketing, and only after some minor picket-line violence was a contract finally consummated there in late June. Apparently there was widespread disenchantment among Deere employees with that union's tactics, and the UAW sensed an opportunity to defeat its rival. In a National Labor Relations Board election in July 1948, the UAW won bargaining rights handily (the Farm Equipment Workers at the last minute even asking that its name be withdrawn from the ballot).

This set the stage for a major battle between the two unions in the Moline area. The UAW sent national organizers in to entice local members of the Farm Equipment Workers at the Deere plants as well as at the International Harvester plant in East Moline. The situation was ripe for violence, and it did not take long in coming. In early February 1949 a bloody battle of fists took place outside International Harvester's plant. The fight began when Farm Equipment Workers members left the day shift and found UAW men lined up outside the gate, passing out handbills. The Farm Equipment Workers then organized a phalanx of its own members behind the gates and, when the gates were suddenly opened, they rushed the UAW men. The latter threw their handbills in the air, and hand-to-hand fighting broke out. The UAW men were forced back along the street to where their cars were parked; by the time the twenty-minute battle had subsided, some twenty-two men were injured, most of them from the UAW faction. "The East Moline battle was a surprise to local authorities," one of the newspapers piously reported; it seems hard to believe, though, that anyone would not have foreseen the potential for violence.

Over the next weeks, the UAW pushed leaflets at Deere's Plow Works, and the Farm Equipment Workers retaliated in kind at the Harvester Works. Bargaining on contracts at the various plants was also going on at the same time, and the negotiations became confused in the face of the internecine union squabble outside the gates of the plants. The Farm Equipment Workers soon began to have internal troubles within its Plow Works local and ten officers were ousted in late March. Finally, an NLRB election was set at the Plow Works, pitting the Farm Equipment Workers against the attacking UAW. When the election was held in late April 1947, it turned out to be a major surprise—by more than a four-to-one margin, the Farm Equipment Workers handily retained bargaining rights.

It was a real setback to the UAW. During the jurisdictional struggle between the unions there were also difficulties on the bargaining front. The UAW called strikes at Des Moines and at one of the locals in Moline, and it threatened to strike at other plants as the contracts expired in May. Within a few weeks, though, after negotiations in the face of these strike threats, an agreement was reached that provided for a wage increase of $.05. But the UAW's demand for a $100-per-month pension for workers at age sixty was not included in the agreement.

As the isolation of the left-wing faction within the UAW was occurring, similar battles between right and left had been taking place within a number of other CIO unions. The CIO itself faced a serious dilemma, for an independent report by the Research Institute of America had listed some eighteen unions, including the very large United Electrical, Radio and Machine Workers of America, as Communist controlled. Several of these unions finally did oust their Communist officers over the period 1945–48. In a landmark decision of the convention of 1949, ten of its affiliated unions were expelled as having "consistently directed their policies and activities toward the achievement of the program or purposes of the Communist Party."

The huge United Electrical Workers was one of those unions; more important to the agricultural machinery industry, the Farm Equipment Workers was another. The latter was a small splinter union by this time, and because of its precarious position it decided to merge with the United Electrical Workers. Thus the Deere & Company contracts at the Plow Works and the Planter Works shifted to the new independent combined union, no longer in the CIO. Now the lines were drawn for an even more vigorous, probably bitter competition at the local level between the UAW and the newly constituted United Electrical Workers/Farm Equipment Workers.

By the time of the negotiations of 1949, Deere had become the first contract renewal for the UAW, so Deere had become the "target" as the union tried to establish an industry pattern. It was the year the UAW sought to bring pension programs into its contracts, hoping in the process to gain joint administration of the plans. Deere already had a very liberal retirement plan and remained unwilling to include the plan in the contract. The final settlement did provide for a reopening after one year for discussion of pensions and insurance and for wage adjustments.

Later, after the Deere agreement of 1949 had been signed, the UAW did obtain pension agreements from the Ford Motor Company, from Chrysler (after a 100-day strike), and finally from General Motors. The last agreement, with the largest company involved with the UAW, was a landmark one. It was a five-year contract, incorporating two types of automatic wage increases during its term. First, an "annual improvement factor" of $.04 an hour per year was to be given to reflect increased productivity. (The contract terminology put it straightforwardly: "A continuing improvement in the standard of living of employees depends upon technological progress, better tools, methods, processes and equipment, and a cooperative attitude . . . to produce more with the same amount of human effort. . . .") In addition, a built-in wage escalator was provided to offset increases in the cost of living. The contract also included a pension and insurance agreement, to be jointly administered by company and union.

As Deere began its "reopener" contract negotiations in June 1950, company officials decided to strive for a similar five-year agreement incorporating the cost-of-living escalator and the annual improvement factor adopted at General Motors. In addition, the company was willing to upgrade its pension program to at least the level of the General Motors plan (but not to have it jointly administered). The company decided its key bargaining demand was to be retention of a tightly worded no-strike clause.

The union, in turn, sought the centralization of bargaining for all seven plants under the UAW contract and the elimination of the no-strike clause that had been in the contract of 1949. In addition, they wanted a central pension board for all plants, to be jointly administered by the union and the company. Pensions by their nature were company-wide in their implications, and Deere industrial relations officials now were forced to modify somewhat their internal organization for bargaining. Local negotiations had been conducted concurrently and at a central location in Moline since 1945; the same pattern was now used again, but the industrial relations director now bargained on the pensions with a company-wide UAW group.

Early in the negotiations, the company decided to "go public" with its proposals, sending a general letter to all employees and releasing statements to the newspapers detailing the company's proposals. By this time, the UAW was already out on strike against International Harvester, and those negotiations complicated the situation at Deere. The UAW rejected Deere's offer (its hand apparently having been forced by the public announcement by the company) and a strike was called for September 1. All seven plants with UAW locals went out on that date, and Deere almost had its first company-wide strike. It soon settled into a harsh battle, with much bitterness on both sides.

As positions hardened, both parties took to the press to win employee and public support. While the Moline area employees seemed to accept the strike as necessary, the company sensed that employees at Waterloo, Des Moines, and Dubuque were less enthusiastic. There had been allegations at Des Moines right from the start that the strike vote had been fraudulent, that the ballot boxes had been depleted of an overwhelming "No" vote and stuffed with a requisite number of fraudulent "Yes" votes. These charges were never definitively proved or disproved, but the press felt it had enough corroboration to print extensive details on them after the strike was over.

In early November the company made a critical decision—to encourage a back-to-work movement at the Waterloo and Des Moines operations. It was a miscalculation. In Des Moines the situation was the most tense. The newspapers had played up the embryonic movement widely through the press, and the union countered with harsh tactics, using flying squadrons of union members (aided by a number of people from outside the area) to terrorize employees thought to be involved in the back-to-work movement. The unidentified groups broke up a fish fry and a skating party, threw bricks through windows of certain employees' homes, and actually assaulted one or two people. At the plant itself, mass picketing was established for the proposed first day's return and there was some scuffling and damage to cars. The picketing subsequently was constrained by local officials, but the situation was so dangerous that few employees seemed willing to risk the picket lines. The events at Waterloo were less violent, but there, too, the back-to-work movement fizzled. Though there was a small increase in returning employees over the succeeding days, in neither plant did the back-to-work movement become substantial.

There was also a violent incident in Moline about the same time. The UAW had struck the Union Malleable plant, and the local negotiations had been quite tense as the strike progressed. In late November, the union added a large number of people to its picket lines and imprisoned two management employees in the factory overnight. No further incidents occurred, but a residue of bitter feelings remained about the imprisonment.

The strike dragged on until December 19. At that point, the union gave up its demands for a master contract and for a central pension board, two of its key goals. In turn, the company altered its position on the no-strike article and agreed to a limited right-to-strike over grievances related to piece work and incentive rates. In handling such grievances, employees had the option of obtaining an outside opinion from independent engineers (a mechanism set up in the contract) or resorting to a strike.

Unfortunately, there were grievances connected with the incentive system, for it had been set up far back in the past as a hodgepodge of individually negotiated rates, with little in the way of comparability among them. Individual factory managers had developed their own incentive systems, and there was an appalling lack of uniformity in the company. Try as they had, the industrial relations group could not persuade factory managers to work out a realistic uniformity, for the managers typically wanted to keep things as they were.

The negotiations of 1950 brought these issues to the forefront again. With the right of the union to have an authorized strike if it disagreed with piece-rate structures now established, it became doubly important to revise the entire incentive structure. Just as soon as the negotiations of 1950 were concluded, Deere began the analytical work necessary to develop some new company-wide form of "standard hour" system. Wisely, they drew the UAW leadership into this process right from the start. As the studies progressed over the period of the five-year contract, the union leadership became as expert as management on the proposed changes in the incentive concepts. Indeed, the union officials probably were more sophisticated and knowledgeable about the system than were many of the people in the factory. This mutual work on the system over the years of this five-year contract proved to be very efficacious as the two parties approached the very important renegotiation of the contract in 1955.

The remaining parts of the contract of 1950 were essentially those proposed by the company at the beginning of negotiations and promulgated in the company's public announcement shortly after the strike started. The contract was for five years and contained the annual improvement factor and cost-of-living escalator adjustments, the pension-plan improvements, and certain hourly rate adjustments. The strike had been monetarily costly to both parties. The 110 day loss of production and wages was very substantial; the union also expended large sums in strike benefits (and found itself with its own internal squabble after paying extra benefits in Waterloo and Des Moines to counter the back-to-work movement). Arlyn John Melcher, in his definitive study of collective bargaining in the agricultural implement industry, concluded about the strike: "The company finally decided to compromise on the key issue and granted the union the right to strike during the contract period. The log jam was broken and in the next two weeks the negotiations for a new contract were completed. . . . The union was firmly in control of the strike and J.D. accepted this condition with as good grace as possible." The strike had been seen as a test of will by both parties, and each came away from the strike feeling that it had established its own independence and resolve. Each party also came out of the long strike with a renewed appreciation of the other, a respect and wariness that pointed to a future of vigorous collective bargaining.[9]

ANTITRUST CHARGES AND DEERE'S DEFENSE

On September 10, 1948, in the U.S. District Court for the district of Minnesota, lawyers for the attorney general of the United States filed a complaint against Deere & Company, International Harvester, and J.I. Case, alleging that the three companies had violated the antitrust statutes of the United States. The government charged that the three were selling farm machinery to dealers on the condition that the dealers refuse to handle competing manufacturers' goods. This, it was alleged, unreasonably limited the market outlets for the farm machinery of the three companies' competitors and therefore was in restraint of commerce under the Sherman Act, as well as a violation of the Clayton Act.

The period right after World War II was one of vigorous antitrust activity by the government, comparable to the prewar crackdown by Thurman Arnold. It seemed particularly preoccupied with corporate concentration. Earlier, Wendell Berge, assistant attorney general, had singled out the farm machinery industry for particular censure, stating to a Wisconsin Farmers' Union convention in 1945: "Unfortunately, monopolies do not expect to continue full production for peace. Their purpose is not to achieve the greatest volume of production and employment, but the maximum profits on the upswing and the minimum losses on what then becomes the inevitable downswing. . . . In farm tractors, for example, four companies control 91% of the production. . . . In the depression, agricultural machinery payrolls were cut nearly 85% but prices were cut less than 15%." Thus the government again raised the specter of large, dominant companies being able to manipulate and control total production of an industry, holding it down for their own purposes—precisely the argument made in the War Production Board flap when Charles Wiman was head of the farm equipment division in 1944.

Deere already had a stated policy, in writing, against pressuring dealers to trade exclusively with the company (so, too, did International Harvester). A number of people in the company felt that the government case was almost frivolous, destined to be easily defeated by the company—just a "political" suit that had no particular consequent. Budge Cook, on whose shoulders as general counsel would fall the greatest burden of the defense, vehemently disagreed, sensing a fundamental threat to existing marketing patterns in the industry. "This is not a money matter, but involves the future functioning of our sales organization. . . . The stake . . . is our ability and our right to market our products."

The government's prayer for relief to the court asked "that the defendant . . . be perpetually enjoined from refusing to sell farm machinery to any dealer because said dealer purchases or sells farm machinery manufactured or sold by another than a defendant." How was this to be interpreted? At the minimum, this might constrain the ability of the company to exhort against sloppy or ineffective practices by dealers; already Cook was getting reports from branch managers in the company that territory managers were becoming timid in their dealings with some of the weaker dealers because of the government suit. If standards of good dealership could not be required by the company, overall dealership productivity would probably slip. There was an even more devastating threat; if the court were to rule that no company had the right to refuse selling their equipment to any dealer who requested it, this truly would mean a revolution in the methods of distribution. No longer would the privilege of being a "dealer" have much meaning—just about anyone could demand to sell machinery.

Given some 4,000 Deere dealers, it was likely that at least a few territory managers (travelers) dealing with them in the field had resorted to heavy-handed methods, despite the company's written policy. Cook explained why in a memorandum to key members of top management: "Nearly 50% of our travelers have never sold goods in a buyer's market. When they come under heavy pressure for sales, their natural tendency will be to reach for the 'big stick' and to force our products rather than to sell them. Even though we are in a position today to defeat the pending suit, still those new travelers carry the possibility of making a case against us in the first year or two of their struggles in a buyer's market." Violations by company travelers might be much the exception, Cook guessed, yet the company would need to prove just how "exceptional" these instances really were.

First there was need to know just how many of Deere's dealers had been handling competing goods in the years in question (the government investigation was to cover the years 1944–48). Such information could be obtained from Deere's territory managers, but such statements would likely be considered by the government to be tainted—and by Deere top management, too, for it would be in a field man's personal interest to gloss over any pressure tactics he might have used in those years. The alternative was to take depositions from some 4,000 separate dealers, a task of quite a different magnitude. Further, the job had to be done by outsiders, not by company personnel; the company finally chose Dun & Bradstreet for the task.

A survey of this ilk was ticklish business—dealers were skittish about discussing their own affairs with any outsider; further, they could not be certain just how Deere really felt about the matter. Some dealers might worry that the company was indirectly threatening a termination. It finally took a number of second visits, coupled with assurances that Deere really wanted to have the full story told, before Dun & Bradstreet got a viable sample. The results were clear-cut—more than 75 percent of the dealers handled at least some competing machinery. This reinforced what Deere marketeers strongly suspected but had not been able to document before. Of course, this was "good" news for the legal case, but it must have given pause to the territory managers and travelers about the obvious competitor inroads. "Why are all these people selling others' goods?"

The company files themselves produced some unexpected benefits. Deere had slipped in efficiency of record keeping in the Wiman period (as contrasted to the Butterworth period, when extensive historical data were maintained). So the company was undeservedly lucky now in finding several key letters of the recent past that documented unequivocally the dedication of the company to the policy of never using pressure for full lines. These letters complemented Burton Peek's blunt bulletin to all factory and branch personnel in 1938, written shortly after the publication of the Federal Trade Commission's report, exhorting all company personnel: "Don't use 'the big stick' in getting business. The use of excessive coercion is unbusinesslike. . . . Sometimes the salesman is inclined to use the 'big stick.' This is not our policy."

The most sensitive issue was that of involuntary termination of dealerships, for one of the first items requested by the government investigators was a list of former dealers, many of whom were to then be interviewed by government field personnel. The total of these terminated dealerships was not inconsequential. In the years just prior to the war, the company had mounted a program to strengthen individual dealers, in the process winnowing out the weaker ones, leaving the remaining ones financially stronger and more effective. There were just under 4,000 Deere dealers in the United States at the time of this case, down from approximately 10,000 in the early 1920s. The very concept itself of being a "dealer" was not nearly as well refined in those earlier periods—many then had seen themselves just as order-takers, with little responsibility for follow-up service.

This incisive winnowing process led to Deere's "key dealer" program, pinpointing those dealers in each particular location in every territory that could be considered as the most effective. The territory managers then were to put particular emphasis on working with the company's most important outlets. The earlier experience with the joint Deere-Caterpillar dealerships in California had been instructive, pointing up the values of having a few large, well-financed independent dealers, rather than a string of smaller, weaker groups.

There were various reasons for terminations: the weakness of too small a scale of operation, personal ethical behavior of the dealer himself, etc. For whatever reason, terminations almost always left hard feelings and recriminations. No one wishes to have a right taken away, whether or not it has been earned by good performance. There also can be unfair terminations, and for this reason several states more recently have enacted legislation constraining the right of companies to unilaterally sever relationships with dealers. The company's interviews of discontinued dealers who also had been interviewed by the government turned up a number who were hostile to Deere. To the surprise of company interviewers, however, a substantial number of them were willing to state frankly that their own failings had led to the terminations, and they were willing to put their views on record for the court. Thus, by the time the company had put together its full list of potential company witnesses, it had found a number of former dealers who would testify on behalf of the company.

Deere top management made an astute decision in the process of conducting this extensive in-company research. Rather than leaving all the legwork to junior personnel within the organization, a deliberate effort was made to involve top-level executives in the field work itself. All through the organization, both leading branch personnel and general-company officers involved themselves in the field interviewing and field research, in the process learning more about the company than probably they ever would have had they stayed back in their own offices.

This introspection and self-examination turned up in the process a number of new ideas that could give the company a more intelligent approach to all of its operations, particularly marketing. Cook wrote Charles Wiman after the case was over: "Branch house personnel have become so acclimated to the problems presented by the lawsuit and actually are doing a more intelligent job today in the field of dealer relationships than was true before the suit was filed." In effect, the case became the venue for an undesignated but nevertheless highly effective executive development program for training of future top management.

THE GOVERNMENT TRIES THE J.I. CASE COMPANY

In April 1950, after an enormous expenditure of time and money on preparation of the case (the direct costs alone were estimated to be more than $1 million), the company was notified by the Department of Justice that Deere was not, after all, to be subjected to trial in the foreseeable future. Rather, the government had decided that the J.I. Case Company would be the first target. All eyes turned to Minnesota, where the Case proceedings were scheduled to come to trial in April 1951 before District Court Judge Gunnar H. Nordbye. The trial lasted most of April and May, and by the end of formal testimony there were some 1,940 pages of documentation on Case's policies and practices. In many respects, Case's practices differed from Deere's; for example, Case did not have an explicit written policy similar to that promulgated by Burton Peek in 1938. The name of Deere & Company did come up from time to time in the trial—it was inevitable that when Leon Clausen, the chairman of Case and former head of all of Deere's manufacturing, was called to the stand, he would be required to answer questions comparing Case with Deere. Clausen did this adroitly, with no prejudicial remarks about Deere itself that would hinder in any substantial way the company's defense, were it also to come to trial later. Each company's situation was different; no one of the three wanted to damage the others' defenses, deliberately or inadvertently—the collective stakes were too high. On the other hand, they really were not in the case "together" and were wary of any overt cooperation, not only for fear of being accused of "conspiring" together, but because each felt that there were sound competitive reasons for keeping a distance from the others.

Deere's day in court never came. Judge Nordbye's decision four months later was a shocker. The entire "case against Case" was unequivocally turned away, all pleas by the government turned aside, the bill dismissed. The judge's decision was a detailed one, extending over a dozen pages. The opinion was considered so uncompromisingly clear that it came to be a "landmark decision" in antitrust suits, soon appearing in texts and law books devoted to pivotal law cases.

Nordbye left no doubt that he thought the government's evidence weak and unconvincing. He stated: "Efforts in salesmanship were used to convince the prospective dealer that his future was more promising if he would devote his efforts to the Case line rather than being occupied principally with other activities, whether they be diversions in selling hardware, automobiles or competing farm machinery. But such a policy, in absense of coercion and pressure, merely reflects sound business judgment and reasonable competitive efforts which do not necessarily constitute competitive restrictions." There were examples of "flagrant attempts to coerce and put pressure on a few dealers, but they sprang up here and there disconnectedly and contrary to the announced policy of the company, and without indicating that there was any pattern. . . ."

More important than the issue of exclusivity was the allegation of restraint of trade, and here Nordbye was equally definitive: "The burden of proof rests upon the Government to establish that defendant has engaged in practices, agreements or understandings, and acts unreasonably restraining commerce . . . and tending substantially to lessen competition and to create a monopoly. . . . This it has failed to do. . . . Here there is no 'potential clog on competition,' which the Supreme Court referred to in the Standard Oil case, and upon which decision the Government principally relies. . . . The bill must therefore be dismissed."

This was a district court decision and could, of course, be appealed to higher courts. The government chose not to do so. At the request of the Department of Justice, the case against Deere was dismissed in April 1952. The court's dismissal was "without prejudice"; the Department of Justice reserved the right to file the same kind of suit at a later date. But it never did.

What judgments can be made about this case? Inasmuch as the government case collapsed completely after Judge Nordbye's decision, one can legitimately infer that the arguments of the Department of Justice lawyers were weak. Moreover, it seems incongruous that the government pursued the industry at this particular time; the pattern of production limitations imposed on the larger farm machinery companies during World War II (particularly the controversial concept of "concentration") gave the smaller companies a remarkable opportunity to increase their market shares and steady their shaky financial statements. The government had depended heavily on market-share statistics to buttress the case that the three big long-line companies were dominating the industry. Judge Nordbye repeated these same figures in his opinion, prefacing them with the following statement: "The evidence reflects that there is healthy competition among all farm machinery manufacturers. The existence of a vigorous growth in the farm machinery business reflecting sound competition seems evident from the following table [exhibit 12-5]."

Exhibit 12–5   **Market Shares of the Seven Full-Line Agricultural Machinery Manufacturers, 1944–48 (percent of total industry sales)**

	1944	1945	1946	1947	1948
J. I. Case	3.7	4.4	3.8	5.3	7.0
International Harvester	15.8	17.6	22.3	23.4	22.8
Deere.	9.6	9.9	15.1	14.1	15.3
Allis-Chalmers.	3.2	4.3	3.5	6.3	6.8
Oliver	2.1	2.9	4.3	3.9	4.2
Minneapolis-Moline.	1.7	1.9	3.1	3.3	3.6
Massey-Harris	1.1	1.3	2.9	2.8	3.8
Full-line companies' share of industry sales	37.2	42.3	55.0	59.1	63.5

Source: United States v. J. I. Case Co., 101 Fed. Sup. 856.

As shown by the figures for 1944, the market shares of the seven long-line companies declined during the war years, due to the limitation orders. By 1948 all seven had made strong recoveries; the four smaller of the seven registered proportionally larger gains from 1944 than did the three large companies that initially were parties to the suit. The two smallest, Massey-Harris and Minneapolis-Moline, had not only more than doubled their 1944 market share, but they had also exceeded their positions in 1936 by substantial margins. International Harvester was the least successful in making a comeback, though it continued to lead the industry. Warren Shearer's definitive study of the industry's competitive relationships, completed just before Judge Nordbye's decision, came to the same conclusions. Shearer commented after lengthy analysis, "The industry was far more evenly balanced than it had been in 1938 and . . . the prospects for continued gain by the smaller of the long-line concerns is excellent. . . . If we draw our conclusions from the present market shares obtained by the leading concerns, it would be necessary to conclude that healthy and effective competition actually prevails." Shearer felt that the stronger financial position of the smaller firms in the industry allowed more resources for investment in research and design, and that "it is this technological battle of which implement executives speak when they talk of 'fierce' competition." Shearer argued that this "design" competition was the key to the industry: "Although IH and Deere remain the leaders, their position is being vigorously contested.

Relative equality of product will prevent many of the abuses which are likely to creep into an oligopolistic situation, as long as that equality is based on legitimate product differentiation. . . . As long as the industry is developing new products or distinctly better products at the rate they have been developed since 1930 there is no danger that the consumer can be made to suffer from price agreements." Shearer concluded, "On economic grounds alone the farm machinery industry meets with fair success the tests we have established for 'workable' competition."[10]

INNOVATIONS IN ENGINE DESIGN

The insatiable demand for agricultural equipment at the end of World War II momentarily gave the manufacturers a booming "sellers market," in which existing models, however obsolete, were snapped up by avid buyers. But fierce competition soon encouraged innovation and change, and the ten-year period from 1945 to 1955 became noteworthy for product improvement. Deere remained in the forefront in yearly, shorter-term product development, but found itself in an increasing dilemma about one crucial longer-term question. How long should Deere stay with the two-cylinder tractor?

During the 1930s the two-cylinder engine uniquely fulfilled some important demands—for low fuel cost, for simple cooling systems, for straight camshafts with no belts or pulleys, and, in general, for an easily understood, farmer-repairable piece of machinery. Distillates could be used as fuel, the "all fuel" concept at that time giving lower costs. Deere had been successful in selling this concept on its fundamentals—that the two-cylinder engine was as good, or better, on its merits than competitor machines for a wide range of farming conditions. For more than two decades company salesmen had vigorously defended the "Popping Johnnies" against competitor sneers; almost yearly, some trade rival would float rumors that "Deere is going to junk the two-cylinders," hoping to panic buyers away from a model threatened by obsolescence. It became an article of faith among Deere marketing men to fight across the board any attack on the two-cylinder concept. The defense worked very well indeed, for the Models D, A, and B continued to sell in large volume.

After World War II the situation began to change. Many thousands of young farm men had gone off to war to drive tanks, jeeps, weapons carriers, and countless other vehicles, almost all of which were either four- or six-cylinder. When they returned to the farm, often to take over from their weary fathers, would they be willing to stay with their two-cylinder "John Deeres"? Further, some of the most potent substantive arguments for the "two" had lost their credence. Distillate fuels, now relatively higher in price, no longer carried a significant cost advantage. Wartime advances in the catalytic cracking process had made heavy fuels sometimes even more expensive than gasoline; moreover, the heavy fuels required lower compression and, thus, less horsepower. Further, the farmer was demanding larger tractors with higher horsepower, and there were upper limits to the size of two-cylinder engines that could be mounted on a tractor. The horizontal-bore configuration and the diameter needed for such power would soon force so large a size that the tractor could not fit on the row of crops it was to work. The slower speed and lower compression of the distillate-burning engine was an advantage in terms of wear, but a disadvantage in gaining higher horsepower. For this reason, right after World War II, the Waterloo tractors were made available in both a distillate "all fuel" version and a higher-compression gasoline-burning model.

Deere lived under a further cloud—it did not have a diesel engine. Rudolph D. Diesel had perfected his engine back in 1892, and adaptations of his design were successfully operating in Germany in 1897 and were sold in the United States before the turn of the century. In these early years, diesels were not so easily adapted to vehicles, for the difficulties in starting the engine made it unpredictable. The first commercial use of a diesel engine in a crawler tractor did not come until Caterpillar's adaptation in 1931. International Harvester followed with a successful wheel tractor version in 1933, and soon many manufacturers were competing with successful models. The diesel had earlier become very popular in Europe, and by the end of World War II a substantial number of the tractors built in the world were diesel-powered.

Thus the Deere dilemma. On the one hand, farmers continued to press for refinements in existing tractors. They wanted better steering control, an independent power takeoff, increased hydraulic power for operating integral equipment (particularly hay balers and forage harvesters), more fuel efficiency, added horsepower for heavier jobs, and, at the same time, more flexible shift-up, throttle-back, fuel-efficient ways of doing lighter work. All of these demanded immediate attention. Competitors were making changes, and if one wanted to stay alive in the marketplace, improvements in existing models had to be constantly provided. This always commanded great amounts of engineering and product planning time.

Yet adaptations to meet competition in the short run always borrowed from longer-term product development. More and more farmers were interested in diesel tractors; if Deere was going to bring out a diesel—say, a two-cylinder version—this would take many months, even years, of hundreds of engineers and designers. If Deere decided to move to a four-cylinder or six-cylinder tractor, or to both, a much longer commitment would be required. Deere manufacturing men had often espoused the rule of thumb that a new model of an older machine generally required about 33 percent new parts; a new line incorporating a major engine change would require new designs for 95 percent of the parts.

The Deere management at both of the tractor factories—Waterloo and

Dubuque—now faced hard choices. A turn in one direction might foreclose all other opportunities. Perhaps the two-cylinder concept could no longer be sold alone on the fundamental argument that two cylinders per se were as good or better than four or six. Rather, the particular values of the Deere versions needed to be stressed—they were so well made, so dependable, and so easy to repair and carried such an excellent reputation with the farmer. On this basis it might be possible to sell those same tractors over many future years; the continued success of the Models A, B, and D held considerable promise for this scenario. There would come a point where this could no longer be the case, but had this point been reached?

By the end of the war, the Deere manufacturing and marketing teams came to believe that the Model D was no longer commercially viable. Though it had been upgraded throughout its product life—mounted on rubber in the early 1930s, restyled in 1939, increased in horsepower in 1940—it was nevertheless becoming inadequate for the wheatland farms, which were growing bigger and demanding a standard tractor with even greater power. The goal now became twofold—to increase power, and to generate that power from a diesel. By 1949 the company was ready with its Model R, the first diesel-powered tractor Deere had ever manufactured. It was also the most powerful, rated 34.27 horsepower at the drawbar, 43.32 at the belt. Charles Stone, by this time the vice president for product development, impressed by the enormity of the new machines, said unequivocally, "We see the limit here to the rubber-tired tractor—after this, it has to be a crawler." (Today wheeled tractors of more than 200 horsepower are not uncommon!)

The Model R had a gasoline-fueled auxiliary starting engine, which eased two problems that had plagued earlier diesels. Most diesel tractors had been started by the operator standing on the ground, manually turning a flywheel; the Model R was started by the operator in his seat, pulling a lever. The earlier diesels had been notoriously difficult to start; the Model R auxiliary starting engine enhanced warm-up, allowing a fast start even in cold weather. To the relief of everyone, the new tractor was greeted with enthusiasm by the trade; Deere was back in the running, with a good diesel engine. It was a two-cylinder engine, though—the company had taken the calculated risk that a two-cylinder diesel could compete with the four- and six-cylinder counterparts in other companies.

With the change in the Model D, the question now came of what to do about Models A and B. These enormously popular tractors had been in the line since the mid-1930s; by 1952, there were more than 600,000 of these two Deere models in operation. But, despite their success, they could not continue to compete forever without change. Once again there was the nagging dilemma—the changes could either be minor (cosmetic or small refinements), or major, or, more basically, they could entail scrapping old models and introducing tractors with more cylinders.

By this time there were strong advocates, including Charles Wiman, for phasing out the two-cylinder tractors. Dubuque engineers had already developed an upright two-cylinder engine for the Model M, and they were experimenting with another upright multiple-cylinder engine for self-propelled harvesters.

Duke Rowland, who still headed all of the company's tractor production, was adamantly reluctant to scrap Waterloo's very successful tractors, however. They were selling well in the field and his organization had its manufacturing on so efficient a basis that the factory was the biggest profit-making unit in the system. Over and over, he told the management in Moline, "We would be run over by our competition if we stopped now to change—we couldn't make the shift within nine months of downtime —we'll go broke, we'd be just like Ford when it changed from the Model T to the A." These arguments worried Wiman, for they called up images of the Great Depression that he had faced early in his career; still, though Wiman was genuinely ambivalent on the timing of the change, he nevertheless advocated making it earlier rather than later.

Once again the authority vested in the factories by the policy of "decentralization" intruded to decide the question. Rowland's conservative posture held sway, and the decision was made to upgrade Models A and B, but to retain the two-cylinder motor. In 1952, two new models were introduced—the Model 50, to replace the B, and the Model 60, to replace the A. Both had many innovations. Each had duplex carburetion (a separate carburetor for each cylinder), which allowed more precise fuel metering and helped increase horsepower (the Model 50 was rated at 20.62 drawbar horsepower and 26.32 belt horsepower). Both were row-crop tractors, like their predecessors, and the 60 was also available in a

Exhibit 12–6. "A Four-Cylinder Engine—Not on Your Life" (John Deere tractor field service bulletin, February 15, 1937)

A FOUR-CYLINDER ENGINE—NOT ON YOUR LIFE

Some of our dealer and tractor owner friends occasionally tell us they have heard that John Deere is coming out with a four-cylinder engine in all John Deere Tractors. Dealers and others who are well informed know that this rumor is false.

We want to assure those who are not so well informed that we are **NOT** coming out with a four-cylinder engine. **THE JOHN DEERE TWO-CYLINDER ENGINE HAS BEEN SO OUTSTANDINGLY SUCCESSFUL THAT THERE IS NO THOUGHT OF A CHANGE.**

JOHN DEERE TRACTOR COMPANY
L. A. Rowland
Vice Pres. and Gen'l Manager

"high-crop" model of particular value to producers of tall, bushy, bedded crops like sugarcane, flowers, etc. These two models were also the first of the Deere tractors available with "live" power shafts, which provided continuous power for operating equipment driven by a power takeoff (PTO). A continuous running or an independent PTO became a necessity for the postwar versions of hay balers and field forage harvesters, for both machines contemplated stopping the forward travel of the tractor from time to time while continuing the PTO for the baler or forage harvester.

An interesting issue surfaced at this time, that of interchangeability. Farmers wanted to be able to use any given power equipment, whatever the make, in whatever combination desired; thus the lack of compatibility of PTOs became an industry-wide problem. Once again, as the industry had done just after World War II with hydraulic control standardization, the Farm Equipment Industry Engineering Advisory Committee set up an industry-wide subcommittee on the PTO to standardize such things as hub and spline dimensions, drawbar hitch and power takeoff location, and drawbar vertical load dimensions. Out of this came a set of standards in 1958 that were uniformly adopted by the industry. Each manufacturer was free to develop his own engineering of the internal mechanisms that would lead to the external PTO, but the couplings themselves would all be standard.

The drive for industry standardization led to an unusual contest between two groups at Deere. Once again it involved Waterloo (and Rowland). The company had fallen behind in the technology of the hitch. One of the most innovative ideas in the Ford-Ferguson tractor, when it was introduced just before the war, was its three-point hitch, which incorporated a hydraulic system that was draft-sensitive, thus making the hitch work for both draft and position. Deere's hitches could not be controlled hydraulically for draft, so several company factories began experimenting, each on its own (decentralization again!). The real push and tug was between the Waterloo Tractor Works and the Plow Works, longstanding rivals in the company. Before the advent of the tractor, the Plow Works had been center stage, the main actor—after all, was not the plow the most important, bread-and-butter product? Pride, a sense of importance was still the legacy there. Similarly, the Tractor Works saw itself in the same light—was not the tractor now the real bread-and-butter product, dominating all others in dollar volume, in profit? Pride and sense of importance were in abundance there, too.

An important step toward bridging the gap between the two touchy groups came in 1949 with the the establishment of the tractor and implement committee, which had high-level representatives from both operating groups, as well as central staff people from the experimental and product planning groups (and was chaired by one of the latter). Still, rivalry and jealousy between the two operating entities persisted and now surfaced once again as each insisted it had the right to develop the definitive version of the hitch. "After all, the hitch is at the end of our tractor," said Waterloo. "No, it's our implement that is to be positioned," said the Plow Works.

Each finally developed its own version, but neither would give ground. The Plow Works prototype was an adaptation of one the Lindeman brothers had developed at the Yakima Works, and there was considerable sentimental feeling that it should be adapted because of this. But sentiment is more often than not a bad decision-making criterion; the hitch was an "add-on" version, not self-contained, and it had enough other disabilities to be dubbed by its detractors "the Stinger." Even this failed to convince the "plow boys," so top management finally decided to hold a field contest between the two. In the ensuing match, the Waterloo version won, hands down. The Plow Works remained unreconciled, predicting "disaster" if the Waterloo hitch was adopted. Only after a compromise was arranged—that the Plow Works could build 1,000 of its hitches, to be stockpiled until the disaster struck—was the conflict settled. The fact that Pat Murphy formerly had been head of the Plow Works had more than a bit to do with this contingency concession. The Waterloo hitches turned out to work very well and soon were adopted for all the company machinery; the 1,000 stockpiled Plow Works hitches were scrapped.

In 1953, the Model 70 arrived in the product line. Originally the model was available with gasoline, "all-fuel," or LP gasoline options but soon was offered with a diesel option, and thus it became the first Deere diesel row-crop tractor. In its Nebraska tractor test, the Model 70 diesel set a new industry fuel economy record, bettering all previously tested row-crop tractors of all manufacturers. By 1954 Deere engineers had perfected another "industry first," an optional factory-installed power-steering system for all three of the new models. It utilized built-in hydraulics to control the steering mechanism, differing from so-called "add-on" systems that used externally mounted motors on the steering shafts or hydraulic cylinders hooked up to tie rods. Deere's power steering was a breakthrough for the industry, soon widely adopted by other manufacturers. Again, though, the engineering time taken to develop it was at the expense of an upright, multiple-cylinder engine.

All of these models were manufactured at Waterloo, with all of the engineering done there. Meanwhile, the Dubuque engineers were equally busy. In 1953 they brought out a new Model 40 in both a standard tractor, a tricycle, and a crawler, replacing the Dubuque-manufactured Models M, MT, and MC. In effect, the Model 40 series was a smaller counterpart of the Model 50, 60, and 70 tractors built in Waterloo. (The 40 tricycle model was rated at 17.16 drawbar horsepower and 21.45 belt horsepower, the crawler was rated at 15.11 drawbar horsepower and 21.45 belt horsepower). In 1955, six years after the introduction of the historic Model R diesel, its own replacement arrived, the Model 80 diesel. This was a gargantuan machine, weighing some 7,850 pounds, and it was quite powerful—57.49 horsepower at the belt, 46.32 at the drawbar. It incorporated many of the most popular features on the other numbered models, such as optional power steering and "live" power shaft, and also included a six-speed transmission. The 80 was capable of pulling a twenty-one-foot disk and working up to 126 acres with it in a single day. A large 32.5 gallon fuel tank allowed the operator to stay in the field many hours before making a refueling stop.

The new models—the 40-50-60-70-80 group—were well received, particularly for the numbers of refinements and innovative new ideas they incorporated. But the handwriting was on the wall about the staying power of any two-cylinder tractor, no matter how good. Waterloo knew this as well as anyone. By this time, Duke Rowland had left his position heading tractor production and Maurice Fraher assumed his post. Both Fraher and Gust Olson, the Waterloo Works manager, were less resistant to change. So a decision was taken, sometime in early 1953. (The exact date is no longer determinable, the whole operation being so secret that no records were kept!) A select group of Waterloo engineers and design men were to be pulled off their regular duties and set to work on the task of developing an upright, multiple-cylinder motor. Their charge: "Start with a blank drawing board." An abandoned building that had housed a grocery store was rented (quickly dubbed by the Deere men "the butcher shop," perhaps an unintended double entendre!), and, amid great security against any communication leaks, the process began.

Right away, there was a serious miscalculation. The marketing managers in the branches had been uneasy about the decision to go ahead: "For 30 years, we've been selling an 'exclusive' . . . you'll have to give us another 'exclusive,' else we will look like we've recanted on all of our claims." So in part to placate them, the first efforts of the "Butcher Shop" group concentrated on a V-4/V-6 notion. The V-design engine had worked well on the automobile, but the idea was flawed for tractors—the narrowness required of the row-crop tractor would not allow the requisite juxtaposition of the pistons. After months of work on the V, the notion was abandoned. In the process, valuable time had been lost. The engineers were forced to turn to vertical positioning, despite the remonstrations of some sales leaders that this was too "conventional." Nevertheless, an irrevocable decision had been made—the company would produce four cylinder engines.

COMBINE AND CULTIVATING PRODUCT DEVELOPMENT

In combines, the new star was the self-propelled combine. The Massey-Harris coup of providing self-propelled combines for the crop season of 1944, the "Harvest Brigade" story recounted earlier in this chapter, alerted all other manufacturers to the need for self-propulsion for their own combines. Massey's version dated back to 1938, when its first models were tested in Argentina. International Harvester also brought out its own successful self-propelled model in 1942 (and made thousands of them during World War II). Deere engineers knew that they had to get into this fray, and by 1947 the company was marketing its No. 55, with a top center-mounted engine and grain tank and using a twelve-foot platform. At first, a canvas platform was utilized, but then the engineers developed a successful auger feed, with retractable fingers at its center; this proved to give a very even feed. Deere's self-propelled combine was an instant success, one of the most widely accepted models of harvesting equipment ever brought out by the company. By the time of its demise, more than twenty-two years later, nearly 84,000 units had been built and sold. The farmers in the windrow areas, particularly in the Northwest, demanded a machine that had the same capacity of the No. 55 but they wanted a pull-type machine because of their large horsepower being idle during the harvest period. This led the company in 1949 to bring out the No. 65, a model similar to the self-propelled. Small combines were also still in demand, but farmers now insisted on more rapid harvesting, so the Deere engineers modified the old No. 12A to accommodate a seven-foot platform, and this was reborn in 1952 as the No. 25. In 1950, the company also brought out its first two-row self-propelled cotton picker, a model that would pick from both sides of a row.

Deere's popular hillside combine, in the line since the purchase from Caterpillar in 1935, had been a pull-behind machine all through the period of the 1930s and '40s. With the great success of the self-propelled combine in the Midwest, several harvester manufacturers began marketing similar models for use on the slopes of the Northwest farms. A problem arose, though. On a hillside combine, the cutter bar necessarily had to follow the ground slope, while the separator stayed level. With a self-propelled machine, the mechanics of this became more difficult. A particular problem was in the required leveling, which had to be done manually on the early machines. A few agriculturalists in the Northwest began experimenting on their own with self-leveling devices, though most of their compatriots ridiculed the idea. Deere saw in these amateur efforts the nucleus of a viable self-propelled, self-leveling machine and purchased some of the farmers' best ideas. The result was the Model 55H, brought out in 1954. It incorporated an automatic lateral leveling device that could keep the separator body level on side slopes of up to forty-five percent—a concept (shared by International Harvester) that revolutionized harvesting in the Pacific Northwest. Not only was the machine more effective—it now could readily be run by one man—but it was a good deal safer.

Probably the most spectacular of Deere's postwar harvesting triumphs was the combine corn head. In 1952, the company brought out its Model

No. 45 combine, a spot-welded machine of more robust construction, especially designed for heavy work in the Midwest corn and soybean areas. Deere engineers had been experimenting with the use of the combine in corn since 1950, at first using modified grain heads to harvest the whole plant. In 1954 they developed the No. 10 two-row corn attachment, especially designed for use with the No. 45. With it, the farmer could pick, shell, and clean up to twenty acres of corn per day in a single operation. Field shelling losses had been reduced as much as 75 percent and the requisite storage space had been cut in half; the corn could be cut while it had as much as 30 percent moisture content, earlier than with other harvesting devices. By 1956, two-row and four-row attachments were also designed to be fitted to the No. 55. All sizes of the corn-head attachment incorporated a unique snapping unit that prevented damage to the ear, thus preventing inadvertent shelling during the snapping operation. The combine corn head was an "industry first" of major importance, one of the most successful of Deere's harvesting innovations.

There were other important implement innovations in this period. In 1947, the first front-mounted, "Quik-Tatch" row-crop cultivators were marketed, and the first planters having remote-control hydraulic cylinders were sold. In 1950 a safety trip standard for moldboard plows was developed, again an industry first. The ten years—1945–55—had been rich ones for product innovation; now to be awaited was the crucial work being done in the "Butcher Shop" on the new "more-cylinder-than two" tractor.[11]

MANUFACTURING ABROAD: THE SCOTLAND PROPOSAL

By 1950, European recovery, buttressed by United States aid under the Marshall Plan, had borne fruit. All through Western Europe the pace of development had hastened agricultural and business recovery, and American business measurably increased its trade with its Western partners. The "Cold War" that began in 1949 did curtail some industrial reconversion, leading to certain restrictions upon civilian production, and this was further complicated by the effects of the Korean War in 1950–53. But despite these hostilities, the first half dozen years after World War II provided great opportunities for American business expansion, now on more of a worldwide basis than it had ever been.

Deere & Company had shared in this postwar expansion of world markets only in a selective way that had telegraphed some disturbing implications. There was a sharp rise in Deere foreign sales (all those outside of the United States and Canada), from only 5.7 percent of total company business in 1946 to 14.7 percent in 1949, but while there were some burgeoning markets, there were also some lagging ones. The imbalance shows graphically in Deere's percentages of total United States machinery sales in five key international areas:

Market	Deere Percentage of U.S. Sales			
	1946	1947	1948	1949
South America	11.8%	16.4%	19.6%	18.4%
Mexico	9.3	11.0	18.4	17.9
Africa	13.2	15.5	19.6	16.8
Europe	5.0	7.5	9.4	9.9
Asia	7.6	4.2	14.2	17.6

The anomaly, obviously, was Europe—Deere's percentage in each of the years from 1946 to 1949 was less than 10 percent of the U.S. agricultural machinery going to European countries.

In March 1950 John Good, second-in-command in the export department, was sent on a long trip through Western Europe—his assignment: to discover why Deere was lagging in Europe, in contrast with the rest of the world. The answer was unsettling. European buyers of agricultural machinery were finding it difficult to obtain hard currency (dollars) to pay for imported machinery and were turning to their own domestic manufacturers, as well as those in contiguous countries, with whom they could finance in local currencies. Several North American companies had already anticipated this and had their own manufacturing plants in Europe. International Harvester and Massey Ferguson were particularly well positioned, serving much of their European market from their own European factories; International Harvester was even expanding its operations in order to make its small tractors in Europe, and Allis-Chalmers had just announced plans to go into England to make its five-foot combine and one of its tractors. It seemed apparent that if Deere wanted to stay alive in European sales, it had to contemplate doing the same.

The notion of manufacturing abroad had not been considered seriously since the early days of the modern company, when the board had summarily rejected George Mixter's quixotic proposal to manufacture in Russia. Export sales were considered as sideline or incidental sales, to be welcomed, of course, but only if they did not interfere with domestic sales, and if most would be paid for in cash and shipped on an irrevocable letter of credit.

When Charles Wiman had plumped in 1946 for an allocation of machinery for Chile and Argentina in the face of domestic shortages and allocations, the sales department had complained loudly. So when he floated the trial balloon in July 1950 of manufacturing abroad, he was greeted with skepticism by a number of board members. But he was not easily discouraged, and he cajoled his colleagues over the remainder of the year and the early months of 1951 to change their minds. Finally, after considerable research, a decision was made to build a plant at East Kilbride, Scotland. The proposal contemplated construction of a plant of approximately 425,000 square feet, to be financed by the British government and rented back to Deere by the Scottish Industrial Estates.

The debates in the board became quite argumentative, for profound differences emerged not only about the project but about the concept of the corporation itself. Was Deere & Company primarily a domestic producer, concerned mostly about the United States and Canada and only peripherally about the rest of the world? Or was the company to turn its sights outward to the rest of the world, becoming in the process a "multinational" corporation?

The amount of capital would dictate the scale of operations abroad. It would be one thing to open a small factory to produce a limited set of tillage implements. Adding perhaps some spreaders, mowers, or even a combine would be yet another scale. But if one contemplated the production of a tractor, including the engine, then the project would entail a very heavy commitment. Where along this continuum did Deere want to buy in?

The minimum price tag seemed to be about $5 million, enough to provide the working capital, including inventory, for a small combine and a spreader, with a few miscellaneous implements. Charles Stone wanted to hold to this scale: "The worst thing would be to start over there with a 12-A combine and spreader, and then find in two or three years that we were not in business unless we make a tractor. . . . I am not saying you should not make a start, but I think if we make a start you want to be very sure not to obligate ourselves to carry this thing on at a very rapid rate. I watched I.H.C. lose $6 million before they broke even . . . pioneering is a hard life." Duke Rowland, still at that time heading Waterloo tractor production, expressed a manufacturing viewpoint, worrying that the small scale of operations might not give production runs of enough size to reach the break-even point. Yet he was not willing to advocate a larger operation. Rowland also worried about where the right men might be found to staff the new factory—"We are spread pretty thin." Pat Murphy was a pivotal person, for he headed all remaining company manufacturing. Murphy had always been domestically oriented, and he now gave only lukewarm backing to even the more modest plans. Murphy worried on the one hand that the operation would eventually require a tractor and that the price tag for producing one would be upwards of $15 million. Indeed, Murphy pointed out: "If we go into France and England, it might be closer to $50 million for plant layout, receivables and inventory. I think we should go into this with our eyes open." Murphy, like Rowland, also was hypersensitive about effects on domestic manufacturing: "If we ever got to the production shown and we were back to normal times, it would take this production away from United States factories and would reduce production in this country." Bruce Lourie, representing sales, worried about how Deere-manufactured goods would be marketed; European jobbers were for the most part undercapitalized, not willing to extend their areas in the face of new opportunities—lukewarm representatives at best. A branch house or houses would probably be needed, and these would raise sensitive questions about when and how to sever relationships with existing jobbers. New dealers would be difficult to find, given the highly competitive nature of the European markets; the best ones were already committed.

The most enthusiastic proponents were, expectedly, from the export department. They were not reconciled to Scotland, however; as late as ten days before the final board vote, they were lobbying for France—and not just for combines and mowers, but for a "single package—25-30 hp tractor, diesel preferred, and five or six integral tools . . . similar to the Ford package."

One thing was clear: Charles Wiman not only wanted to go abroad, but he wanted to go to Britain. Further, he desired to do so on a scale that would ensure that Deere would become a substantial influence. He had made it plain to the British that Deere was contemplating building not just a combine and mower, but other equipment as well. He wanted to keep Deere's options open so that it would be free to make tractors or anything else at a later date. Wiman seemed to have as much fear of too narrow a line as the others did of too wide: "It is important to keep that freedom of action and not get euchred into a short line." He concluded: "If we do not ever start, where will we be in the potential business for the rest of the world? We may have to put a tractor over there, so instead of $10 million it may be around $22 million, but it would increase our business over there, and that might be on the plus side for the long pull. If we wait too long, the parade may go marching by. . . ." Wiman gave the board members a week to contemplate their final decisions.

Given the prevailing sentiment of his colleagues, Wiman finally bowed to the practicalities and decided to bring forward the more modest proposal of an initial expenditure of $5 million to manufacture just the small combines, mowers, and spreaders and a restricted line of tillage tools. When it came to a vote, it passed unanimously, in keeping with the longstanding Deere board tradition of final unanimity, however much there had been prior disagreement or even wrangling. Here, though, Kennedy announced for the record that his vote was a "reluctant yes," and others, particularly Pat Murphy, were equally unenthusiastic.

A small group was to be posted almost immediately to Scotland to begin the planning of the factory, as well as the coordination with the British government. But when the operating departments were approached about potential candidates for these important posts, they seemed very reluctant to give up any of their senior, key personnel. These were manufacturing and engineering units, directly responsible to Pat Murphy, and the latter's insular views about any foreign manufacturing influenced their thinking. As a result, no first-rank senior personnel were assigned to the project, and this proved to be a serious limitation. This same narrow, proprietary stockpiling of subordinate management personnel by factory and branch managers had strongly characterized past personnel policies. Seldom if ever did junior managerial talent have the opportunity to transfer from one factory to another, or from one branch to another. This insular view of executive development was surely a pernicious aspect of the policy of unbridled decentralization.

Many months went by, with extensive efforts by the Deere team on site in Scotland. Then, just after the new year 1952 had begun, an unexpected set of events intruded, stemming from the change in the British government from Labor to Conservative. At the same time an apparently unrelated set of events took place in the company's domestic operations, which proved to have a profound influence on the effort in Scotland.[12]

DEERE'S FERTILIZER VENTURE

In October 1951, just at the time the project in Scotland was being staffed and planned, Charles Wiman visited officials of the U.S. Department of Agriculture in Washington and came away persuaded that fertilizers were, as he put it to the board, the "most attractive" possibility of all projects he had seen. "The production of fertilizer involves a market with which we are familiar and the same facilities and organization capable of producing nitrates for fertilizer can be used as an entree into the broader aspects of the chemical industry, which is one of the newest and most rapidly expanding industries today."

There were some negatives, however, as the study team picked by Wiman soon reported. "A comparison between that industry and our industry makes it obvious that as presently constituted we have very little to contribute in the way of experience, trained personnel or operating methods. Presumably in such a venture we would bring nothing more than a certain amount of capital and willingness to engage in a different business quite unrelated to our normal activities." Further, the chemical industry was characterized by high investment in facilities and low labor cost, and Deere's distribution organization seemed not particularly well adapted to the distribution of fertilizer—a separate organization probably would be needed, both to handle production and distribution. Finally, fertilizer was not really the best kind of diversification, inasmuch as the same economic conditions which lowered the demand for farm machinery would also lower the demand for fertilizer.

All of these caveats by the study team and members of the board did not deter Wiman. Promising the board that he was "not asking for an appropriation, no money with which to build the plant," he persuaded

Exhibit 12–7. *Deere directors at the company's Grand River Chemical Company, Pryor, Okla., October 1963 (Deere Archives)*

the board to allow negotiations to proceed, and he even induced them to "look with favor upon issuance of new securities, either in connection with a merger or construction of a new plant."

From their lukewarm endorsement, Wiman proceeded rapidly. First, he appointed Duke Rowland as the titular head of the project, taking him off his assignment as head of tractor production. Certificates of necessity were needed from the government; these were promptly obtained. By January, he reported back to the board that new personnel had been hired for the project and that a joint venture was being discussed with the Standard Oil Company of Indiana.

But there was now real resistance among the board members, enough so that the minutes of the meeting of January 29, 1952, noted the "concern . . . expressed that embarking upon the synthetic nitrogen project might jeopardize the financial position and the functioning of our farm machinery and tractor business." Wiman ended the meeting by throwing down the gauntlet: "If this Board as a Board is opposed to entering the business and is opposed to giving thoughtful consideration to future requests for appropriations, then it would be well at this time to give the matter extensive consideration and discussion. If there is no such objection, then it seems to me that the program as outlined above can go forward." Few people would want to be considered as in opposition to "thoughtful consideration." No actual vote was taken at this meeting, but neither were there overt efforts to back Wiman.

This still left unanswered the question of financing such a mammoth endeavor. Already the East Kilbride, Scotland, program was calling for capital upwards of $5 million, probably closer to the $20 million that Wiman had estimated. Now this second project was going to demand an additional $20 million. Wiman proposed a public offering to the board and, in July 1952, the company sold 691,276 additional shares of its common stock (at an excellent price of $30.40) and additionally marketed $50 million of 25-year, 3⅛ percent debentures. "Moneymen quickly snapped up the issues," *Forbes* reported. The proceeds to the company from these two sales of securities totaled $69 million.

At this point, Wiman came back to the board, demanding a final commitment to go ahead in the chemical venture; an option on land near the Grand River Dam Authority power plant near Pryor, Oklahoma, already had been obtained by Rowland. There was animated discussion around the table about the disadvantages of the project, particularly the lack of compatibility between the farm machinery business and the chemical business. The capital commitments were very high, too, though the success of the public offering now gave the company considerable new leeway. Finally, Wiman put the issue to vote, and for the first time in many years negative votes were cast. Pat Murphy voted against the project; so, too, did George French. (French was immediately under Murphy, in charge of all implement production; he, Ellwood "Woody" Curtis, and William Hewitt had been brought on the board the previous year.) As if two negative votes were not enough, Charles Stone asked that he be recorded as "not voting."

The die was cast, though—Wiman had singlehandedly persuaded a majority of the board to turn the company in a major new direction. *Forbes* magazine featured the move in a major story, reporting that "entrepreneur Charley Wiman's test tubes will begin to burp, barring delays, early next year." The *Forbes* reporters were not privy to the internal dissension within the board about the venture; their article oozed optimism: "Deere's soundskulled country boys can see a mite beyond the visible horizon. A foothold in synthetic fertilizers will work double dividends, they calculate. In the 13-state midwestern corn and wheat belt which Deere figures to supply from Pryor, nitro-fertilizer demand in 1955 is expected to quadruple 1950's consumption. Corn planters are learning that nitrates increase per-acre yield from 40 to 100 bushels. By thus aiding the farmer (tentative plans call for selling bulk urea, non-trademarked, to fertilizer makers) to more abundant harvests, demand for machinery will become more abundant too."[13]

THE SCOTLAND PROJECT FALLS THROUGH

Just as the chemical company came into being, the project in Scotland was derailed. A change in the British government from Labor to Conservative had brought new views about development, particularly that from outside the country. British officials, while denying that they were terminating the project, nevertheless postponed government financing. The board had three alternatives: Deere could finance construction itself, continue to maintain the company's organization in Scotland and wait out the delay, or disband the Scottish organization. Charles Wiman, preoccupied with the chemical endeavor, had obviously lost some interest in the Scotland venture. This was all it took. With almost a visible sigh of relief, the board unanimously voted to terminate the project. A number of Deere's agents in Europe and elsewhere in the world were upset by the decision; they had envisioned manufacturing in Europe as a potential breakthrough for Deere's products all over the world. V.C. Fischer, the chairman of Agar, Cross, the British trading house (and Deere's Argentine agent), wrote Wiman, expressing unhappiness. Wiman answered: "The fact that we finally reached the decision not to go ahead with the East Kilbride project does not mean that we have made a decision against a foreign manufacturing project as such. We will, of course, continue to study this important subject. . . ." But Wiman also mentioned the fertilizer project to Fischer, further commenting that "increasing nationalism" on the part of various countries in the world was making a decision to manufacture abroad more difficult.

Wiman's shift in focus was sudden, and there is not a ready explanation for his seeming disenchantment with the rest of the world. The Scotland location may have been the wrong place to start. Many board members felt this way; perhaps Wiman was weary of bucking them.

MANAGEMENT SUCCESSION

Sometime in 1954, Charles Wiman learned that he had a fatal illness, one that would give him just a few months to live. One question then to be resolved was his succession at Deere & Company. He had been undisputed head of the company from 1928. The transition would be especially difficult because there had been substantial turnover in the rest of top management in this period of the early 1950s. In the four-year period of 1951–54, the board of directors had lost a cumulative 148 years of actual board service (Dwight Wiman, 31 years; Willard Hosford and Theo Brown, 30 years each; Charles Stone, 27; Harold White, 14; Harold Boyle, 7; Benjamin Keator, 6; Virgil Bozeman, 3. With the exception of Dwight Wiman, these were all operating top management men).

The early Korean War years had given the company excellent financial results—on sales of $337 million in 1950, there was a $42.7 million profit; in 1951 sales rose to $433 million, with profits of $35 million. The next two years' performance gave everyone pause, however. Sales fell in 1952, though profits remained almost level with the previous year, but in 1953 sales again dropped back and profits fell to $24.7 million.

Several predispositions dominated Wiman's thinking at this juncture. Deere & Company had been a family endeavor for its entire 117 years; Deere was known widely as one of the country's preeminent "family companies." But the board had never perceived lineal descent as a sinecure, as a feudal right to leadership. Ineffectual members of the family had held directorships, but their weak ideas had been ignored; a few of these men even had been terminated as directors for poor performance. For senior management posts, the individual family member might have been accorded some marginal preference at the time of selection, but he had to pass muster to continue to hold the job (again, there had been significant instances of demotion, and even severance for low performance). In sum, there was a family ethic of achievement and performance. *Fortune* magazine, in a major article centering on the Wiman transition, elaborated: "Despite Deere's healthy condition, the wrong man could easily have wrecked it. For more than a century, Deere had been characterized by a self-confident operating style that allows managers an extraordinary degree of independence and puts a premium on initiative. By careful choice, more than luck, family leadership had preserved that style over the generations."

Wiman had a keen awareness of this record. If there was an outstanding descendant of the Deere family itself standing ready, this would loom large in selection; if more than one, the best would be picked, whatever the lineal relationship might be. There was inter-family rivalry, some push-and-tug about company matters among the three dominant lines— the descendants of the Deeres, the Webbers, and the Velies. But, contrary to what some thought at the time, there is strong evidence that Wiman would not have let Charles Deere lineal loyalties dominate in any decision. Similarly, if a non-family member of management were clearly the best candidate, he would be picked over any family member. This person would have to be found somewhere within management—it would have been almost inconceivable to Wiman, or to anyone in the Deere group, to have turned to the outside. Harold Boyle, the International Harvester executive brought back to Deere by Wiman at the end of World War II, had been for many years the only top management officer appointed directly. Deere was proud of its proven ability to nurture leaders and confident that it would develop an unending supply of fresh candidates.

As Wiman now surveyed the top management team he knew so well, his initial thinking centered on three people. Two were part of the Deere family—Pat Murphy (from the Webber side of the family) and William Hewitt, Wiman's own son-in-law. The third person was Lloyd Kennedy, a long-time confidant of the family, trustee for both the Charles Deere and William Butterworth estates. None of the extant evidence suggests that Wiman ever considered a fourth person who had been particularly influential in top management in the immediately preceding years, Budge Cook, who was married to Pat Murphy's sister.

Kennedy, at age sixty, had had more than forty-one years of company service, all of it in the financial side of the business. Murphy's service totalled thirty-one years at this point; all had been in the production side of the firm with the exception of a few months as assistant territory manager in the Minneapolis branch. He was fifty-four. Hewitt had just turned forty and had been with Deere & Company for just six years, all of it in the branch side of the firm.

Hewitt was the only college graduate of the three (Kennedy had attended a commercial college for one year, Murphy matriculated at the University of Iowa, staying for a few months). There had been ambivalence in the company over the years about whether a college degree for anyone other than engineers was a plus. Lip service had been paid to "hiring more college graduates," but actual practice seemed to be contrary to this injunction. Wiman, a Yale graduate himself, had tended to value the college degree more than others did in the company, an attitude closer to congruence with the postwar thinking in other major American companies.

Hewitt had worked two years between high school and college as a messenger in a San Francisco bank, then entered the University of California at Berkeley, majoring in economics. "Hewitt blossomed socially in college," the *Fortune* editor commented. "He fell in with one of those groups of young men who strike outsiders as all being destined for success. Among them were Robert S. McNamara; Walter Haas, Jr., now chairman of Levi Strauss; Willard Goodwin, formerly chief urologist at U.C.L.A.; and Stanley Johnson, who became an eminent trial lawyer in San Francisco. It was a close circle." Hewitt, McNamara, and Haas went on to Harvard Business School together. Hewitt had only enough money for one year, and he returned to San Francisco to work first in accounting at Standard Oil of California, then as an advertising copywriter in a men's-wear chain. Joining the Navy shortly after Pearl Harbor, Hewitt rose to the rank of lieutenant commander on the battleship *California*; his cabin mate there was Gabriel Hauge, later chairman of Manufacturers Hanover Bank and from that time a life-long friend and business confidant.

After V-J day, Hewitt returned to his native state to enter the farm machinery business as a territory manager for a Ford-Ferguson distributor. While on this job, he married Wiman's daughter, Patricia. Within a few months, he was asked to join Deere, and after some hesitation, he did so. He began as a territory manager for the San Francisco branch, then was brought in first as assistant branch manager, then branch manager, under Benjamin Keator. The latter was an excellent mentor for Hewitt. He was a Deere family member (from the Webber side) and a judicious and independent person.

Hewitt brought an unusual sense of style to the operation. The *Fortune* editor interviewed branch personnel about his early days with the company: "He conducted himself with grace . . . a good listener . . . did not throw his weight around . . . disarmingly cordial, and acutely sensitive to others . . . a good leader." Hewitt also demonstrated a coolness under pressure, evidenced particularly in the tricky assignment as one of the company investigators in the antitrust suit. After becoming a director in 1950, he was not only coached by his board colleagues on broader, corporation-wide issues, but was also inculcated with the company's special history and traditions. "No man could hope to serve as Deere's chief executive," commented the *Fortune* editor, "without having a deep knowledge of its rather singular character. Deere is a culture as well as a corporation, and the company's officers understand its strengths as reflections of its past."

Still, there was no overt evidence that Hewitt was being uniquely marked. "Contrary to what some of Hewitt's colleagues thought," wrote the *Fortune* editor, "Wiman was not taking any special trouble to help his son-in-law along. . . ." But the onrush of events in 1954 stemming from Wiman's ill health now forced him to bring the question of Hewitt's eventual role into his consciousness.

At this point, Wiman turned to Keator for advice. Keator, always close to Wiman, had just resigned from the board, thus putting himself more at arm's length from the sensitive upcoming decision. Keator immediately wrote Wiman his prescription for the presidency: "We should have a young man—this is most important—who is a leader, who knows the business and has vision for the future of our line, who is cognizant of the problems to be met and how to handle them." Keator felt that Kennedy and Cook were "good in their own fields" but were "getting along in age and also have no sales, field or factory experience." (Cook, at fifty-one, was just a bit younger than Kennedy, at sixty.) Keator felt Pat Murphy too old, too. At fifty-four, Murphy was clearly one of the most respected men in the entire organization, but most observers of this period seem to have agreed with Keator that "while he does know factory operations he has no vision or field experience and lacks progressiveness and enthusiasm." Keator put Murphy as his last choice.

After briefly discussing several other members of the board, Keator turned to Hewitt: "I have felt, of course, that Bill has been pushed along pretty fast but I must say he seems to be able to absorb it in his stride without its affecting his personality or his association with others. He has had enough Branch House experience to know that problem pretty well and he is alert to the requirements in the field. He has youth, he is smart, catches on to things quick and has vision, enthusiasm and courage to get things done . . . he has had a broad field to operate in and had the authority to act. This is important if he is to be able to face up to the task. . . . To be sure, he has had little or no experience in factory operations, which is of course very important in our Company, but couldn't someone be appointed to his staff who could tutor him in these decisions?" Keator concluded, "Bill is a very dignified and personable young man and you would go a long way before you would find his equal for that job."

Wiman wrote back immediately: "I find your comments very keen about the V.P.'s. I had thought a lot of LEK [Kennedy]. I wish I could feel better about Pat Murphy. Your conclusions about Bill H. are what I am now thinking of—I think he'd fill the bill best of all! However, gosh, I wish he were not my son-in-law—for it will look to so many that I am trying to push 'one of the family.' It would be so easy to push for his presidency otherwise—on all counts." Wiman concluded enigmatically: "I will go back to Moline to work on this problem and how it comes out I do not now know."

This worried Keator. Was Wiman going to waiver because of the possible criticism of nepotism? He wrote back immediately: "I can't see why if Bill is the best material and best qualified in every way to take over, both for the present and for the future, as I believe he is, why it should make any difference if he is related or not. After all, everyone concerned should be thinking and wanting to do the best for Deere & Co., both for the present as well as for the future."

Wiman talked further with Burton Peek, but probably with no one else—the subject was too personal. Wiman now was spending most of his time secluded at his Arizona ranch, with only occasional trips to his hospital in New York City; he had been there to chair the annual meeting on April 27, 1954. Finally, in late June he came to Moline from Arizona, having called a special meeting of the board for June 22. With Burton Peek in the chair, Wiman placed in nomination the name of Hewitt for election to the newly created post of executive vice president. The motion carried unanimously, and the die had been cast for management succession.

Hewitt chaired most of the board meetings through the fall and winter of 1954–55, receiving major support from most of the officers. "The prospect of taking over the company at an unexpectedly early time galvanized him," the *Fortune* editor concluded. One of the officers recounted to him: "You could just see him grow after he got to Moline." On May 12, 1955, Charles Deere Wiman died; twelve days later, William Alexander Hewitt was elected the sixth president of Deere & Company.[14]

Though many of Charles Wiman's personal characteristics differed from those of his grandfather, Charles H. Deere, the two men were strikingly similar in their drive to be both successful and innovative. Charles Wiman's legacy to the company could be favorably compared to that of his grandfather for he had inherited some of the same vision that Deere exemplified, as well as the latter's entrepreneurial bent. Wiman often could hardly wait to make changes and move ahead, relishing the challenges; yet sometimes he would turn sharply backward toward caution. The eulogies for Wiman were properly laudatory, but somehow failed to capture this Janus-like quality of his personality—charismatic, enthusiastic, positive, yet sometimes conservative, even pessimistic. His qualities of leadership were outstanding, for he had had a unique ability to fire others to action. He had weaknesses, to be sure—his overemphasis on engineering and development and an unsure grasp of finance. He was not the keen marketing man that both Charles and John Deere had been. His attitudes toward employee relations were progressive, and he enjoyed high respect among management personnel and line employees. He was restless and always searching for something new; as Theo Brown wrote in his diary, "Charlie Wiman said at the table, 'If I wake up in the morning and know where I am I want to take a train and go somewhere else.'" In the last half dozen years of his tenure, this restlessness had almost become idiosyncratic; the sharp shift in interest from the international sphere (the Scotland effort) to the dominating preoccupation with the chemical company was one example among many.

Earlier, in 1946, Max Sklovsky had been writing a book (never published) on the company, in which he emphasized Wiman's "volatile spirit, which some consider a sign of unreliability," and noted that "his driving is not always steady." There was truth to this, a negative on the balance sheet. But the positive qualities overbalanced this: "He possesses a combination of realism and vision," concluded Sklovsky. "Charley Wiman turned into a remarkable executive and became the spark plug of the Company."

PART V

WORLDWIDE CORPORATION:

THE
WILLIAM HEWITT YEARS
(1955–82)

JOHN DEERE

Announcing
a
**NEW
GENERATION**
of
Power

CHAPTER 13

RISE TO INDUSTRY
LEADERSHIP

*All day long the big planes buzzed in and out of Dallas'
Love Field. They carried passengers from New York and New
Dorp (Pa.), from Paris, France and Paris, Ill., from
Seattle and Sewanee (Tenn.). When darkness fell on Monday,
August 29, 1960, more than 6,000 passengers—the
biggest industrial airlift in history—had been safely landed.*

Forbes, 1960

Innovations came rapidly in the first Hewitt decade. Some of them had been initiated by Wiman, in particular the final painful changeover from the two-cylinder to three-cylinder, four-cylinder, and six-cylinder tractors. Other important new directions were initiated by Hewitt himself, notably his ambitious ventures into Europe and Latin America. In addition to this expanded geographical focus, he brought a new set of management philosophies. By the end of Hewitt's first decade, Deere had become a major multinational corporation and the largest agricultural machinery producer in the world.

Hewitt had inherited a sound company from Wiman. Sales for fiscal year 1955 were up markedly from the previous year, as were profits. The company's working capital was at an all-time high, book value of the common stock surpassed all previous years. Prospects appeared excellent; the sound, conservative Deere organization seemed nicely positioned to take advantage of future opportunities.

But was it? A number of small signs in Charles Wiman's last three or four years as president intimated incipient weaknesses within the organization. Benjamin Keator gave a pungent valedictory as a board member in 1953, explicitly asking that his misgivings be put on the record in the board minutes: "I leave the service of the Company with regret and a mixed feeling for the future. . . . Certainly we have efficient management, but we have overlooked some very important things during these 'fat' years that we are going to need awfully badly in the coming lean years. . . ." He particularly urged better sales training programs throughout the organization, "especially of dealers, who C.D. Velie rightly used to say, are the weakest link in our chain." Keator also worried about the design of certain Deere equipment, "where in some cases we are woefully weak and getting pretty badly beaten by our competitors in the field." In a letter to Hewitt at this time, he reiterated the same theme: "All our emphasis for the past few years has been on production and now it is high time we put our emphasis on sales."

Indeed there were weaknesses in the marketing arm of the company, as well as in engineering and product development. Other signals also indicated that the overall organization was not functioning as well as it could. The company's leadership was quite senior in years, and the brand of conservatism that formerly had seemed to serve the company so well apparently was tilting toward excessive caution.

This posed a dilemma for Hewitt. He was a young man, with relatively limited experience in the company—a member of the family, to be sure, but representing the next generation. Though the situation seemed to demand change, organizations tend to have built-in rigidities, making a change agent's role always difficult. Entrenched attitudes in the predominately elderly Deere board made Hewitt's task a formidable one in establishing his credentials as the "chief executive officer" of Deere.

Despite these obstacles, Hewitt did establish his control over the organization quickly and effectively. Within months he had shifted Deere & Company in a major new direction, toward an evolving concept of a "worldwide" corporation. In the process, he made a series of organizational decisions that wrought a fundamental change in the philosophy of the organization.

A first step was a study of the company's organizational structure. Not since the far-reaching, two-year study that Charles Wiman had carried through right after World War II had this been done. Wiman's effort, as well as those preceding it, had been done "within house," by Deere employees themselves. This insular posture had characterized company thinking over the years—a feeling that the company was too closely knit, almost too idiosyncratic for any outsider to truly understand. Perhaps there were features so special and so valuable that they could only be fully appreciated by long-time Deere managers. Hewitt did not believe this to be so and startled the board, less than a month after he had taken office, with a request that the board approve an outside management consultant to analyze both organizational structure and the related problem of executive compensation. The board approved, with scarcely disguised misgivings expressed by a few of the senior board members. The firm of Booz, Allen & Hamilton was engaged, establishing a relationship that extended over two decades.

Hewitt also began to assemble his own personal judgments of the situation. In this he had to keep his own counsel, for while there had been no overt opposition to his election as president, he still was an unproven chief executive. Clearly, a "wait-and-see" attitude characterized the feelings of a number of the board members—some of whom were part of the problem.

Over the fall of 1955, Hewitt put together a frankly written personal document. He first wrote out a set of broad objectives, maintaining that the company should "lead the industry" in six key indices—sales, profit ratios, quality, new designs, safety of operations, and excellence in employee, dealer, stockholder, and public relations. This was a herculean set of goals. Had one queried Deere's then-top management, they most likely would have said, "We're a good No. 2 to International Harvester—let IH innovate." Hewitt challenged this thesis within the first two weeks of his election. In a speech to all the branch-house managers he said: "Yesterday I received a friendly letter from one of our most active competitors, and emblazoned across the bottom of the stationery in splashy red ink was imprinted: 'We are not aiming to be runner up.' Believe me, we in Deere & Company are not aiming to be runner up either—we are aiming to be first in all our business activities." The gauntlet had been laid down: "Pass International Harvester!"

Marketing mistakes and problems dominated Hewitt's thinking. The sales department "is not doing a satisfactory job—weak . . . in many ways the production department is running the sales department." The marketing group made poor presentations at board and committee meetings—indeed, seemed to be "scared" in the way they acted. The advertising department "is too separate in its activities—the sales department guides it and confers with it too seldom." Advertising "is 'written selling'—should be planned more by the sales department, not only by the advertising department." Further, the marketing group should participate more in the basic design decisions. Too often designs were determined unilaterally and privately by the engineering groups in individual factories. Manufacturing design engineers needed to work with product design engineers "after a certain point" to make certain that new machines could be easily manufactured. Hewitt asked himself, "How do we decide to build a machine?" Should marketing be included more directly in such decisions? Were pricing decisions too often dominated by the factories?

Throughout, Hewitt exhorted himself on the need for more effective communication and coordination—better market analysis, more information to the directors, upgraded public relations to the outside, and expansion of foreign-language advertising, service, and parts literature. He wanted a heightening of executive-level training—"men to business

Exhibit 13–1. *Dwight D. Eisenhower, former President of the United States visits the Deere Administrative Center, 1965. Escorting him are William A. Hewitt, left, and Mrs. Patricia Hewitt.*

schools, specific programs of shifting promising young men around." As to internationalization of the company, foreign manufacturing should be entered into "wherever justified."

There were omissions in the document, too; these gave some inkling of Hewitt's potential blind spots. On his entire 8½- by 14-inch page devoted to "finance," there was only a single entry: "Retire preferred stock?" The company did stand in excellent financial shape at this time; nevertheless, net income had dropped in the year 1954, as had working capital and retained earnings. These danger signs carried important financial implications, but they appeared not as important to Hewitt at that moment. Finance was not Hewitt's strong point at the time.

One further item in retrospect turned out to implant a signal Hewitt mark on the entire company: "Build a new office building." Hewitt included two specific views on this. First, the office building should be on "a campus." Second, the engineering department should "handle power houses, foundries, supervision of factory layouts and purchase of machine tools *but not* architecture."

Aside from finance, the document was quite anticipatory; Hewitt had evidenced considerable sophistication about the company, given the rather short period that he had been assigned to the general company. If even a significant portion of the 100-odd items on Hewitt's sheets came true, Deere & Company would be a markedly different company.[1]

EXPLORING OPPORTUNITIES ABROAD

The hallmark of the early Hewitt administration was the company's aggressive extension abroad, in contrast to earlier halfhearted moves. When the Wiman proposal for manufacturing in Scotland aborted in 1952, the board comfortably settled back to a "business-as-usual" emphasis on domestic production and marketing. Left in place, though, was a board committee on "foreign manufacture," chaired by Charles Stone. Stone had been one of the conservatives in the acrimonious discussions about the Scotland venture, and leaving the chairmanship in his hands seemed to imply merely lip service to the notion of foreign manufacturing. But in 1953 Stone, then ready to retire after forty-nine years of service with the company, surprised everyone with his final act. Just before stepping down, he took an extensive trip through Europe, accompanied by one of the senior Waterloo engineers. Reporting to the board on his return, Stone delivered an unsettling message. Deere's export sales were dropping; the foreign exchange problem in most countries was an obstacle to imports and an argument for developing overseas farm machinery manufacturing. "Since we abandoned the Scottish project," Stone continued, "we find ourselves with no definite prescribed course of action and with inadequate information on the subject." Stone's blunt report stirred the board, and he was asked to report back the following month with his recommendation for a next step.

Stone's last act as a company officer was this recommendation, and he did it astutely. Several of the younger members of the board—particularly Hewitt, Ellwood F. Curtis, and George T. French—were interested in the international sphere; there were other new men on the board in 1953, too—Willard D. Hosford, Jr., Frank M. Dickey, Richard Edwards, E.C. English, and Maurice A. Fraher—each of whom might be more receptive to changes than their older counterparts. Fraher was the strong-minded head of tractor manufacturing; a Waterloo executive and provincial in outlook, he had never been out of North America. Nevertheless, Stone now made the seemingly incongruous proposal that Fraher become the head of the committee on foreign manufacture, a "small group of two or three good men," to keep in touch with developments around the world and "apprise the Board of opportunities internationally." Thus Stone had bypassed Pat Murphy, the most vocal opponent of the Scotland project and still the most conservative of the board members who were leery of manufacturing abroad. Fraher had never been global-minded, but he rose to Stone's bait and immediately dispatched a study team to Brazil and Argentina (without him).

In late 1953, another member of the board, Lloyd E. Kennedy, turned up another potential international involvement. Kennedy had gone to Europe in December to investigate a discreet inquiry from a West German banker who asked whether Deere would be interested in purchasing controlling interest in one of the old-line German tractor and implement companies, Heinrich Lanz, located at Mannheim. Lanz had been building farm machinery since 1859, and prior to World War II had been one of the two dominant German tractor manufacturers (at one point claiming more than 40 percent of all German tractor sales, with Deutz taking most of the remaining share). The postwar period, though, had not been kind to Lanz. A very large percentage of its prewar sales had been to the farmers in East Germany, a market that was locked behind the Iron Curtain after the war. Further, the Mannheim factory site had been almost completely leveled by Allied bombing during World War II, and the rebuilding had been helter-skelter, putting the firm back into a weaker manufacturing configuration. Its famous Lanz Bulldog still remained a simple, effective tractor (the name Bulldog had become synonymous in Germany with tractor, similar to Caterpillar's generic association with track-laying tractors). But the company's postwar efforts to upgrade the power of the Bulldog had weakened the machine and led to increasing failures in the field. Compounding the problems of Lanz were other product failures from new, unproven models, prematurely marketed. In sum, though Lanz was a great name in German manufacturing, the company's position in the 1950s was tenuous; it was manifestly going nowhere. Some 30 percent of the shares of Lanz were held by this time by a German bank, which proposed selling its share and securing additional shares so that they could deliver 51 percent of the Lanz stock to Deere. The bank's shares were offered at approximately $2.5 million; Ellwood Curtis analyzed the Lanz financial and operating structures and estimated that a total investment of $13 million would be required over the first five years.

Herein lay the dilemma for Deere. To become established in manufacturing abroad, it essentially had two alternatives. One was to make a "green fields" approach—start a new manufacturing unit from scratch in one or more countries. The other was to purchase an existing agricultural machinery manufacturer. Deere was unprepared to attempt the former; memories were long about the unwillingness of senior executives in the manufacturing, engineering, and marketing groups to depute first-rank subordinates to Scotland. The notion of starting on their own looked increasingly forbidding to the Deere executives, for not only had the price tags for such ventures risen considerably since the Scotland proposal, but Deere did not seem to have the expertise in international efforts that would be required. Perhaps it would be better to buy an existing organization, with manufacturing facilities, personnel, and established marketing channels already in being.

But the Lanz proposal aptly illustrated the difficulties of the alternative approach. Buying an industry leader in a major country for a reasonable price would be ideal, but this was not a realistic prospect. Only the weaker companies were on the market block; moreover, competition had become much more vigorous. Where there had been a few dominant companies in the prewar period, now there were new domestic manufacturers all through the developed countries of Western Europe. In Germany, for example, which had been dominated by Lanz and Deutz, there were more than a dozen tractor and implement manufacturers fighting each other for a larger market share. The situation had degenerated in the early 1950s to aggressive, predatory price cutting and sharp competitive practices. Inevitably, some companies were forging ahead; others, including Lanz, were dropping behind. The Lanz performance in the 1950s was not at all impressive. Yet it was a great name in the agricultural world; perhaps this past reputation could be traded upon to build a new organization that could be infused with Deere methods, products, and esprit de corps.

An extended debate on Kennedy's proposal ensued in a special board meeting on December 23, 1953. Charles Wiman was in the chair; the focus was heavily tilted toward the export implications of North American business. Finally, the vote came: the board turned the proposal down. Compounding the problem, Fraher's study team in South America now reported back and after some initial enthusiasm by some board members about Brazil, the board finally decided that conditions in neither Brazil nor Argentina were favorable at this time for a Deere effort. Once more a Deere initiative abroad had sustained a severe setback.[2]

THE MASSEY-HARRIS-FERGUSON PROPOSAL

In Hewitt's first month of office a startling proposal had come forward to him, on a confidential basis, from a surprising source. James S. Duncan, the president of Massey-Harris-Ferguson, approached Deere about the possibility of merging the two companies. Massey was then in the midst of a complicated (and as later evidence showed, acrimonious) internal squabble growing out of a recent merger. In mid-1953, the worldwide operation of the Massey-Harris Company, Limited, had been merged with the Harry Ferguson Company, with the new organization carrying the name Massey-Harris-Ferguson, Limited. Earlier, Harry Ferguson had broken his relationship with Ford, a bitter severance that had led afterward to a messy lawsuit brought by Ferguson against the Ford organization. The suit finally had been settled in 1952 (in favor of Ferguson), and the future of the Ferguson organization had seemed reasonably bright. But, in truth, its product line had slipped and there were many management tensions, not the least being that Ferguson himself paid less attention to the organization (especially the United States divisions) than others in the group felt necessary. Massey, in turn, brought to the merger of 1953 a set of its own internal problems, not as severe as those of Ferguson, but nevertheless troubling. Though Massey had strong operations in its divisions around the world, and had become one of the first truly multinational corporations in agricultural machinery, its United States operations had lagged, and there were unresolved differences within management about what to do.

The vested interests of managers in each of the Massey-Harris-Ferguson organizations, and the unwillingness of top management to restructure the new firm, soon led to increasing difficulties. The two companies' properties were reasonably compatible, so there was not much duplication of manufacturing facilities. But there was overlap in product lines and further complications in quality control. Exacerbating all of this was the duplication of the distribution systems. Duncan himself had advocated a "two-line policy," whereby there would be some exclusive Massey-Harris dealers, some exclusive Ferguson dealers, and a third set of Massey-Harris-Ferguson dealers. The mixed, often clashing lines of distribution were further complicated by an equally disparate set of products from the two organizations. Over the first two years of the merger, while the overall parent organization was performing reasonably, the North American operations began to sag severely. As if this was not enough, there were tensions among Massey's top managers, with Duncan heading one faction and W.E. Phillips, chairman of the executive committee of the board, leading the other (and backed by an Argus Corporation shareholder bloc).

When Duncan first approached Hewitt, in the spring of 1955, much of this internal dissension was not public knowledge, though Massey's lack of success in the United States was known. Hewitt outlined the pluses of such a merger in a private memorandum to himself: Deere could acquire an already established, large-volume overseas manufacturing and distribution system and thus "avoid 'growing pains' from trial and error type form of expansion." The merger could help solve some of Deere's problems on the West coast of the United States, where it seemed likely that Deere would be severing most of its relationships with Caterpillar in the joint Caterpillar-Deere dealerships. (Deere now made a crawler tractor, directly competitive with Caterpillar.) Massey had strong West coast dealerships. But as Hewitt ticked off the pros and cons of the merger, his list of minuses became much longer. It would not be easy to merge the two groups of officers, directors, engineers, etc. There might be adverse public reaction in Canada if one of its largest industries were taken over by a United States corporation. Important problems loomed in consolidating the tractor and implement product lines, particularly because Massey itself never had been able to solve this problem within its own organization. There would be personnel adjustments, difficulties in meshing the high-quality standards of Deere with the somewhat lower standards at Massey, and there would be some dilution of voting power in the merged corporation.

Most important, there would be enormous difficulty in merging the two distribution systems. Massey already was weakened by conflicts among its own dealers; Deere's dealers would certainly look askance at some of the implications of a Deere-Massey merger. Finally, there was a cloud hanging over the negotiations—antitrust implications. In the United States, Massey was quite strong in combines (stemming in good part from the striking effort in World War II with the Massey "Harvest Brigade," a story recounted earlier). Deere's combines, too, enjoyed a large market share. The total of the two would be a dominating powerhouse in harvesting machinery in the United States. Clearly, the Department of Justice could choose to investigate the merger and might require the merged organization to divest part of its harvesting operations. Such a divestment typically is not on a company's own terms, and Deere might end up having a less strong domestic harvesting business than it did before it went into the merger.

Two meetings were held with the Massey group, after substantial financial analysis by both companies, to project how such an arrangement could be brought about. The negatives were too strong for the Deere group, however. The complexity of the distribution problem alone seemed daunting. The company did not need another antitrust investigation; the experience in the late 1940s had been graphic evidence of the debilitating effects that such an effort brings. Massey also wanted to back off; its divided and bickering management was close to a final break.

(Within a few weeks Duncan's resignation was asked by the Argus group, Phillips took over as the new chief executive officer, and A.A. Thornbrough was confirmed as executive vice president and, later, president.)

A Deere-Massey consummation would have given Deere an instant worldwide operation, with an organization that had strong roots in more countries than any other agricultural machinery manufacturer. Deere might have shortcut what was to be a tortured, difficult road to full-scale multinational status. Yet the disabilities of a merger with Massey seemed to far overbalance the advantages of gaining quick international reach. There was evident relief when Hewitt and his colleagues returned from their last meeting in Toronto, without a foreign operation.[3]

THE ORGANIZATIONAL SHAKEUP

By January 1956 the Booz, Allen & Hamilton report was on Hewitt's desk. It was in two sections—a comprehensive "public" document for all of the board members and top management, and a private document for Hewitt on implementation. In the latter, the Booz, Allen analysts were dispassionately frank as to which executives should retain their incumbent positions, which should move up, and which should be shifted away from their present responsibilities. They were keenly attuned to the sensitive issue of management transition, for the election of Hewitt could have sent two markedly different signals to the organization. It could have been interpreted as an isolated act leaving in place the strong senior management, particularly the powerful triumvirate of Murphy, Kennedy, and Cook. On the other hand, Hewitt's presidency could signal a significant shift in management, bringing into central policy-making roles a new generation of leaders. The Booz, Allen document took the latter course.

The consultants proposed an unusual strategy, the establishment of a new "policy committee" at the top-management level. This group was to be manned by top executives, representing the major divisions of the company —production, sales, and finance. Its members were to spend full time on committee activity and were not to have any direct line of authority. The committee was to report to the president—not to the board—and only the president could issue directions to the line organizations. The committee's primary assignments were to be threefold: to develop objectives, to aid in defining policies, and to conduct special studies. The Booz, Allen consultants also envisioned an additional set of secondary functions: aiding the president in public relations, counseling with the president on administrative affairs, and providing guidance to principal operating executives in the company.

The Booz, Allen analysts avoided any mention of the already existing advisory committee instituted in 1952 by Charles Wiman. The advisory committee had not been effective, perhaps in part because its composition included not only the senior top executives but other lower-level line and staff officers of more limited perspective. The active members of top management had seldom felt it helpful to solicit advice from their older peers, to the evident chagrin of some of the latter. The proposed policy committee was to become a senior advisory group of direct value to the president. The consultants suggested that it initially be composed of four senior executives—Murphy, Kennedy, Cook, and Bruce Lourie. The first three, who had been at the center of the power structure of the organization, would become advisors to the president, rather than senior operating officers. In turn, the suggestion of Lourie recognized Hewitt's desire to make some changes in the operating side of the marketing arm. A further set of personnel moves would fill the line positions that would be vacated by the establishment of the policy committee, bringing younger faces into high-level management positions.

The Booz, Allen analysts put particular emphasis on the concept of decentralization in their public document for the board, in the process paying homage to Deere's longstanding canons of rugged individualism (they even cited the first formation of Deere, Mansur & Company in 1869). But the Booz, Allen authorities had misgivings about how well the concept really was understood; in their view many executives in the company had an overly simplistic view, confusing decentralization with almost complete autonomy. In a private memorandum, Hewitt had intimated similar unease, suggesting that the company "should keep all advantages of decentralization *but* strive for more coordination." (In his first public speech to the organization after assuming the presidency, an address to the branch managers in June 1955, however, he had given no indication of concern about the concept: "My best advice to each one of you is that you keep on doing what you are doing under our decentralized system. . . . The only change I am anticipating right now is that you should expect to be given more responsibility as our Company continues to grow. . . . As more and more authority is delegated to you, it is expected that you will delegate more authority to the men under you.")

The Booz, Allen authors warned of the "limitations of decentralization," noting that there were many groups—stockholders, dealers, farmers, the UAW, the general public—that were not at all interested in a highly fragmented, decentralized operation. "Rather, they demand unity; they require that the Company act with a high degree of uniformity in its relations with each one of them." While the company could readily conduct its operations "with maximum freedom given to the head of each manufacturing and distributing unit," there still was a critical need for "the responsibility of the General Company to provide leadership to the entire enterprise. The decentralized branch houses and factories must be brought together to achieve uniformity."

This was heretical thinking to many of the older generation at the company. While Charles Wiman had sensed the need for additional coordination and control when he instituted the two separate studies of decentralization in 1945 and 1947, in both instances he had pulled back from any decisive elaboration of the relation between the general company and the branches and factories. So the period from that time to the election of Hewitt had remained marked by a high degree of autonomy for branch and factory managers, coupled with a more than occasional unwillingness to coordinate and cooperate with other arms of the company. Now the Booz, Allen report gave Hewitt the opportunity to promulgate a more sophisticated version of decentralization, one that would put the general company more directly into a mode of leadership. This inevitably would mean some loss of autonomy at the branch and factory.

In this same month (January 1956), the Booz, Allen survey of executive compensation also reached the board. The consultants found that Deere's compensation of its top management officers was significantly below that of almost all of its competitors. Booz, Allen recommended significant increases in the base rates for management personnel at the company, so that a somewhat smaller percentage of each executive's total compensation came from year-end bonuses. The report cleared the air for the development of a comprehensive salary structure that put the company's executive compensation in line with that of the rest of the industry. Though the plan has gone through a number of iterations over the years, this report has continued to serve as a basic conceptual structure for Deere's executive compensation planning ever since.

In total, the Booz, Allen reports of January 1956 were seminal ones, far reaching in their changes. Booz, Allen clearly recognized that the company was in a period of critical management transition and needed decisive actions, particularly by Hewitt himself, to establish the new management philosophy of a new generation of Deere managers.

Hewitt's treatment of the Booz, Allen report and his own decisions reveal his evolving management style in this first year of his tenure as chief executive. He moved quickly on the report, and by the annual meeting of April 24, 1956, major organizational changes were announced. Though Hewitt was intrigued with the policy committee notion—even roughed out a hierarchy of assignments for it (including a study of "electronic computers" and a set of overseas visits)—he finally dropped the policy committee suggestion altogether and adopted a more cautious alternative—the appointment of Murphy and Kennedy as the company's first senior vice presidents.

In these new positions, they were to assume policy-oriented roles. The elevation of French to vice president of implement manufacturing and Curtis to vice president, finance division, and treasurer, clearly signaled the transference of line responsibility from Murphy and Kennedy to their successors. This new role was comfortable for Kennedy, not quite so for Murphy. The former had continued his responsibilities as financial advisor to the family, and the new job now freed him of onerous day-by-day financial decisions. Murphy already had evidenced some concern about his relationship with Hewitt and privately had discussed with Hewitt some changes in his own job assignment. At that time he had written Hewitt, "Whether I decide to remain with Deere & Company after April depends on a number of things, primarily whether there is any need for me here anymore, and what standing I will have in the future, etc." Thus Murphy's role as senior vice president was not wholly unambiguous. By nature, he always had immersed himself in operating details, and he now sometimes found it difficult to rise above the day-by-day to assume the policy perspective that the new job implied.

Cook, the other member of the triumvirate, opted for a different direction. He was the most independent and self-assured of the three in personality and by his professional role as a lawyer, which included outside board memberships. Cook had long advocated more rapid upward movement of personnel within the organization and had identified his successor several years before—Lewis D. Wilson. Now Cook chose to retire as general counsel, and at the annual meeting of April 1956 Wilson was elected to that post. In turn, Cook assumed a unique role; the three incumbent members of the advisory committee—Maurice Block, Virgil Bozeman, and J.L. Deffenbaugh—retired from the committee (and the company) and Cook was appointed to it.

The character of the advisory committee now changed. No longer was it a sinecure for senior executives, whether they were directors or not. Rather, it became a one person committee, Cook being its only member for the years 1956–62 (except for a short period when Maurice Fraher took an assignment on it.) In this special role, Cook provided the kind of advisory counsel to Hewitt that the Booz, Allen analysts had envisioned, and he was particularly helpful in one of the most important Hewitt moves in this period, the building of the Deere Administrative Center.

Other important changes were announced at the meeting of April 24, 1956. Burton Peek resigned as chairman of the board of directors at age eighty-four, after an incredible sixty-eight years of service with the company. Peek had always been very supportive of Hewitt but had taken himself out of the mainstream of management decision-making several years before. Apparently this seemed an appropriate moment for his disengagement to be made formal. Another of the "old guard," L.A. "Duke" Rowland, head of Deere's chemical company, also resigned. He did it reluctantly, only with the prodding of Hewitt. One other officer-level appointment was made at this meeting, too—Frank N. Dickey was appointed vice president, industrial relations and personnel.

Thus the management reorganization announced on April 24, 1956, became one of the most important in the company's history. A number of other Booz, Allen & Hamilton recommendations were put into effect, tightening the organizational structure, the communications channels, and the operations policies, particularly in marketing and finance, of the company. There was little doubt in anyone's mind after this critical meeting, just eleven months after Hewitt had assumed the office of chief executive, about "who was in charge." Hewitt had put his mark on the management structure decisively and with sensitivity and aplomb. In September 1957, when he persuaded the dynamic, strong-minded C.R. Carlson to leave the Minneapolis branch and come to the general company as vice president of marketing, Hewitt completed his set of initial moves. Bruce Lourie was appointed vice president of special projects and moved out of direct responsibility for line marketing. At this point Hewitt had his own full management team in place.

Right from the start, one person among these, Ellwood Curtis, had the closest compatibility with Hewitt. The two men were remarkably complementary to each other. Hewitt's strengths in general management, marketing, and public and community relations were balanced by the financial acumen, analytical skill, and realistic perception of projects that Curtis brought to every situation. Hewitt's post as president was an unusually isolated one; most of the people in senior management who ostensibly were to be Hewitt's advisors were candidates for shifting, and yet most of the younger top management people were untried. Only time would determine whether they could successfully assume the key senior management posts of the future.

As subsequent events proved, Hewitt was perceptive in sensing that Curtis was the person he needed to balance his own thinking. Curtis shared Hewitt's enthusiasm about the challenges of building a new, expanded organization, and Curtis was profoundly supportive of Hewitt's thinking. Yet Curtis also brought a leaven of caution and conservatism from his meticulous training as an accountant. The correspondence between these two men in the first years of the Hewitt presidency chronicles a warm and growing mutual respect; one or the other was often in the field, frequently abroad, and these written bonds served both very well. When Lloyd Kennedy retired from the company as senior vice president in the fall of 1959, Hewitt established the position of executive vice president and requested the board to confirm Curtis as its incumbent (in the process moving him ahead of Murphy, the only officer remaining in the senior vice president position).[4]

MOVING INTO MEXICO AND GERMANY

Within days of the collapse of negotiations with Massey-Harris-Ferguson, Hewitt moved to rekindle Deere's international interest. This time he decided that the senior decision makers themselves should do the field work abroad, rather than follow Fraher's pattern of dispatching subordinates. He first urged Fraher himself to go to Europe. Fraher remonstrated that he had never been there, simply had no notion of what to do on such a trip, especially on such short notice. Hewitt replied, "Maurice, go visit with the European representatives of our auditors, go meet with our bankers' European correspondents—just go sit at a sidewalk cafe and observe—but go!" Fraher did. At the same time, Hewitt sent Curtis and three colleagues to Mexico.

Fraher and Curtis reported back in July. An amazing transformation had been wrought in Fraher—he came back an enthusiastic convert, very optimistic about the potentials he saw in Europe and worried about Deere's backwardness in not being there. Indeed, Deere's arch-competitors had been there for years; International Harvester had started a small, experimental manufacturing plant in Sweden back in 1905 and was into substantial production in German and French plants by 1910; Massey had purchased its French operation in the late 1920s. As Hewitt later told a *Forbes* editor, "I'd say our competitors had a 50-year jump on us . . . literally." Fraher now had the litany himself: "If we are to maintain our competitive standing in the industry we *must* have this foreign market. Not to enter it will mean the eventual loss of much of our export business . . . giving up a principal avenue for major growth of the Company." He not only wanted to enter the European market as soon as possible, but to do it on a surprisingly large scale, with the capacity to make sixty to seventy-five tractors a day.

Curtis, too, was positive about the Mexico trip—the Mexican government seemed enthusiastic about a John Deere plant there, either for assembly or for manufacture, "provided its products did not cost substantially more than imported units." Mexico's agricultural needs were substantial; its nearness to the United States might give the company a compatible venue in which to "practice" for further overseas ventures.

New implement companies had already started at several locations in Mexico; the government had promised an umbrella over them by refusing import permits to other manufacturers. Curtis urged early action: "If another company establishes a plant there we probably will lose a substantial part of our participation in that market because of the Mexican government's policy of protecting local industry by import licenses and tariffs." The company's Mexican distributor, Wells Fargo, had not been very assiduous in pushing Deere products, and it was beginning to curtail its operations by closing some of its branches.

Curtis and the Deere territory manager in Central America, Robert A. Hanson, both felt that if Deere wanted to increase its visibility (the company only had about 8 percent of the market at this time), it must set up its own branch in Mexico. If the board were to agree to this, Mexico would have the first sales branch outside of the United States and Canada.

There were some potentially ominous complications, however. The Mexican government had begun to pressure the automotive industry to increase the percentage of "local content"—that is, the proportion of components and parts in the Mexican automobile actually manufactured in Mexico. How would this decree affect tractor manufacturing?

This question did not deter Deere; the board seemed genuinely eager to act, and it immediately implemented the suggestion for a Mexican branch operation. A Venezuelan corporation, John Deere, C.A., was established as a subsidiary to own the Mexican operation and others that might be established abroad.

Harry Pence was appointed executive vice president of the subsidiary and, after a whirlwind investigation, recommended to the board that a plant be built in Monterrey, Mexico. Skilled labor and engineering talent were available there, as well as ready supply lines for the procurement of raw materials. Monterrey was one of the gateways to the agricultural part of Mexico, a logical manufacturing site. By late in the year (1956), the board had appropriated just under $2 million for the purchase of land near the city and for the construction of an assembly plant for some John Deere tractors and a few of the simpler implements used in Mexico—wagons, harrows, and disk plows. The manufacture of parts was to be introduced as soon as it proved economical to do so.

Meanwhile, the Lanz proposal in Germany surfaced again. In July 1956 Hewitt, Kennedy, and Pence returned to Mannheim to negotiate once more with the bank officials holding the block of Lanz stock. Hewitt's sense of urgency soon generated a formal proposal for Deere to purchase a block of 51 percent of Lanz stock for approximately $5.3 million, subject to a Deere audit of both the Lanz financial statements and the actual machinery and equipment in the plants (the tractor works in Mannheim and an operation in Zweibrücken, where harvesting equipment was manufactured). At the ensuing board meeting (on July 31, 1956) Hewitt expressed concern about certain imponderables. Though Deere had been tendered Lanz balance sheets and income statements, "the information they give is considerably less than is customary to publish in this country. . . . It seems to be the European custom to make certain charges against sales before arriving at a gross profit figure. These charges are credited to certain reserves or 'silent assets' which do not appear in published statements. For these reasons, it is difficult to appraise the true financial condition of the European firm."

Lanz receivables and inventories troubled the board, too—both had grown considerably in the two years since Deere had first approached the company. Still, the assets seemed to be somewhat understated—earlier in the year, the company had sold DM 10 million of new stock to purchase machine tools, at the same price that Deere was being offered the stock by the bank. Hewitt was particularly concerned about the outmoded, high-priced Lanz Bulldog: "It is doubtful whether such a tractor can successfully compete with the Ford-Ferguson, International Harvester tractors of modern design." Hewitt proposed that if the company did acquire Lanz, it bring the Dubuque line of diesel tractors to Europe to manufacture in place of the existing Bulldogs. Thus a substantial portion of the Lanz inventory would be subject to shrinkage, so that operating losses for the first few years would be probable. Hewitt estimated that the total investment in Lanz would likely reach a figure of $10–$12 million, not including immediate needs for working capital. The latter would probably balloon the project to a total of some $25 million. Still, with all these reservations, Hewitt strongly supported the purchase.

After lengthy debate, the board acquiesced to the acquisition of the 51 percent block of stock, and the relationship between Deere and Lanz was a fait accompli. Curtis was immediately dispatched to Mannheim to supervise the audit of the financial and physical assets; his preliminary work indicated that the Lanz machine tools were "better than those in our own implement and tractor plants." Curtis placed a value of $15 million on these machine tools, "on a conservative estimate."

Balanced against this were serious disabilities, some of them only incompletely known even at the time of the final commitment. First, preliminary figures on Lanz sales for 1956 showed a figure of $39 million, with a loss of some $2 million—"quite a surprise to some of the German Lanz directors," Lloyd Kennedy reported, "but it includes substantial write-downs of inventory." Kennedy, Pence, and Curtis were further surprised to discover a substantial number of tractor failures in the field and complaints concerning some of the Lanz models. "It had been believed that while the Lanz tractor design was outmoded, it was sturdy and quite acceptable in the areas in which sales were being made. The fact that this is not quite true makes it imperative to change the design," Kennedy admitted. The Lanz inventory of finished goods was quite high, and the study team also worried about relatively high production costs and a shortage of working capital. On the positive side of the ledger, the company appeared to have excellent personnel and still held a fine reputation in Germany and in some of the traditional Lanz export markets.[5]

There were striking similarities in the corporate histories of Lanz and Deere. Heinrich Lanz had founded the German company in 1859, first selling English and American machinery as a distributor. Within a decade he was making his own machinery, concentrating at the start on harvesting equipment. When steam threshing came into prominence in the 1870s, Lanz began making stationary steam engines—Locomobiles— and soon had a substantial hold on the world market. Heinrich Lanz himself was a paternal father figure, a stickler for detail, operating his factory in "absolute strictness" (according to one of his employees). His walks around the plant floor—every day at precisely the same moment— became legendary; for those who were late, he stopped and held a watch under their noses, stating that company employees must start on time. More than once it was reported he sat at the desk of an employee who hadn't arrived yet and took care of his work until the man showed up a

Exhibit 13–2. Top left, *Lanz Bulldog;* bottom left, *Heinrich Lanz factory at Mannheim, Ger., after Allied bombings, 1945;* top right, *Interior of the Mannheim factory, late 1970s;* bottom right, *Factory from the air in the early 1980s (Deere Archives)*

few minutes late. He missed nothing on his factory tours. When he noted any nuts or bolts lying on the floor, he lifted them up quietly and took them over to the foreman, often making a note on his shirt cuff of the incident.

The loyalty of the Lanz employees in this earlier period was also legendary; the company paid well and there was a pride of product and an esprit de corps that made Lanz one of the most respected employers in southern Germany. In 1902 Lanz visited the United States and in the course of his travels met and talked with Charles Deere. (There is no record of where the meeting occurred, however, or whether Lanz visited Moline on the trip.) It is likely that Deere must have seen some similarities between his father, John Deere, and this precise German.

When Lanz died in 1905, the firm remained within the family and was operated by his widow and four children. By 1912 the firm was building agricultural tractors, the first model, the Landbau-Motor, a strange machine with a permanently attached rotary cultivator on the rear. In 1916 the company also expanded its harvesting machinery product line by acquiring an old Zweibrücken firm, founded in 1863 by Christian Wery.

It was the Lanz Bulldog, though, that came to epitomize the Lanz name around the world in the 20th century. In the same year that Lanz had acquired the Wery firm, an engineer named Fritz Huber joined Lanz. Huber developed a single-cylinder, two-stroke engine of extraordinary simplicity and exceptional economy. It was a slow running, low compression engine using low-grade crude oil; the machine had no valves, no camshaft, no carburetor, no water pump. The first commercial model came out in 1921; those earlier versions had an external vaporizing chamber and for ignition used a device on the front called a "glow bulb" (also known as a "hot bulb")—thus a "semi-diesel." The Lanz glow bulb was constructed with ventilation shafts that looked like eyes on the front of the tractor—perhaps the reason that Huber and his colleagues settled on the name "Bulldog." The first production models were 12 horsepower, but the company found that larger versions were becoming so popular for land clearing and other heavy jobs that the firm soon concentrated on the so-called Big Bulldog, in 22 and 28 horsepower. When pneumatic tires from imported American tractors came to Europe in 1929, Lanz adopted these for the Bulldog. By the late 1930s a smaller version had been developed, a Farmer's Bulldog at 15 horsepower that cost only DM 2,750, about $1,100. By World War II, Lanz had produced more than 100,000 tractors out of the Bulldog configuration.

World War II was a disaster for Lanz. More than 80 percent of the Mannheim plant was leveled in a series of Allied bombings in 1944 and 1945. The firm did receive permission from the American Occupation Forces to rebuild, but then the Lanz management made a signal mistake. Rather than razing the whole area and building from scratch, they attempted to reconstruct the damaged buildings piecemeal. The bombings had not left any logical production patterns intact; indeed, as the company rebuilt it compounded its production problems of materials flow, shipping, etc., and left itself with a legacy of scattered, ill-adapted buildings that plagued it through the postwar period. The Bulldogs were still the main product (along with the harvesting machinery from Zweibrücken, the plant there less damaged than the Mannheim operation). Emphasis was still on the old Lanz tradition, and efforts were made to rebuild the worldwide sales organization that had characterized the prewar period.

There had been important links with Australia and several countries in South America. Lanz tractors had also been assembled at a plant in Getafe, Spain, outside Madrid. Lanz Iberica, S.A., had been founded by Ricardo Medem in 1953; Lanz itself owned 8 percent of the manufacturing company. The products were the 28- and 36-horsepower Lanz Bulldogs.

At the heart of the onrush of difficulties that Lanz experienced in the early 1950s was its decision in 1951 to build a new small tractor model called the "Allround Tool Carrier" (later named the "Alldog"). Postwar agriculture in Western Europe encouraged a number of smaller farmers to experiment with mechanized agriculture. The Lanz Bulldog was too large a machine for them; what was needed was a small, general-purpose machine. The Allround/Alldog had a small 13-horsepower gasoline motor mounted above the rear wheels, with a saddle seat for the driver. In front, between the engine and the front wheels, was a long metal frame that allowed various tools to be mounted between its sides. The machine also could be used as a truck-like transport vehicle. In conception, it was innovative and might well have made a major dent in the small-farm market. Unfortunately, Lanz hurried the decision to get into production, deciding to purchase the motor, rather than developing its own. This was a mistake, for the outside contractor made an ineffective engine, resulting in many months of product failure (the frame itself had weaknesses at the early stages, too).

What then had Deere purchased in 1956? First, there was the badly outmoded, failure-prone product line. The Bulldog itself remained a reliable machine, but it was a single-cylinder tractor of limited horsepower that could not be expanded in size without major developmental expenses. By November 1956 the 200,000th Lanz Bulldog had come off the line, certainly testimony to its endurance. Its future, though, appeared limited. The Alldog was a major product disaster, offending a new group of farmers that the company could ill afford to alienate.

The product-line problem was worsened by outmoded methods and heavy personnel costs due to overstaffing and rigid production rules. Financial problems, shortages in working capital, and other miscellaneous difficulties added to the disabilities of the old firm. Though Lanz had very able people throughout the organization, Deere nevertheless was saddled at the start with a management structure that needed considerable honing. An American plant manager, James Wormley, was given the overall responsibility, but only a few able colleagues were sent to him in those first months. Once again, the entrenched managements in many of the Deere factories balked at releasing key personnel that would have eased the transition.

In general, Deere was naive in these first months of the Lanz endeavor. The company was just beginning to learn about the special characteristics of agriculture in the countries in which it was hoping to sell. Many farmers called on their tractors for uses not common to North America—in particular, there was a great deal of over-the-road vehicular use of the tractor. Often the loads were light and the higher-powered diesel engines introduced by Deere frequently were overpowered for such use. Indeed, if a diesel engine is not put under some considerable stress it can develop its own problems from under-utilization—crank case oil dilution by diesel fuels, for example.

Another example of misreading of European conditions was Deere's experience with the dealerships inherited from Lanz. The American marketers made a misguided effort to reconstruct them in the North American tradition of exclusive dealerships carrying a full line of products manufactured by one company. In Western Europe, though, the market was much more fragmented. After World War II large numbers of new, smaller agricultural machinery manufacturers came into being. Most of them were not full-line manufacturers and tilted, if anything, toward relationships with many manufacturers. Massey-Ferguson and International Harvester had been in Western Europe for many years and had been able to develop a cadre of exclusive dealers. But most of the rest of the Western European agricultural equipment dealers were fearful of an exclusive dealership, feeling that there was safety in numbers. They not only wanted to handle several companies' products, they also wanted to carry two competing tractors, two different combines, etc., all lined up together in their yards in a kaleidoscope of company colors. Company marketers persistently pursued the goal of exclusive dealerships, but frequently it was only the weaker dealers who were willing to do so. Thus the dilemma: should the company stay with a strong dealer with only partial Deere loyalty, or go with a weaker one wholly dedicated to Deere? The company was not as sophisticated at the start in making this decision as it was in later years.

Another misjudgment was Deere's attitude toward European cooperatives. The cooperatives in Western Europe historically had been much more important than in the United States, and a great many Deere people had prejudices, growing out of the nineteenth-century experiences with the Grangers, that made it more difficult for them to understand the role of the cooperatives in the European scene.

Overall, the Deere group was very proud of its own name—in North America, it had become synonymous with quality and dependability. They were not used to dealing in an environment in which their company (in this case, Lanz) was losing its reputation and being upbraided for product failures and other slippages. It was a sobering experience for the marketing group out of North America to cope with weak dealers, poor product visibility, product failures, and other irritants.

Was the purchase of Lanz a mistake? In retrospect, it is clear that the company had rushed into the project without full information (albeit such information was not always readily available). Also, its hopes about how quickly it could "turn around the Lanz operation" and become a viable, major producer in Western Europe proved overly optimistic. It was to take almost two decades of very hard work and many disappointments to bring about this turnaround. Thus a short-run assessment would have been premature. But the answer to one important question was clear almost immediately. The Lanz purchase did accomplish in an unequivocal way the basic goal that Hewitt had envisioned from the start—it put the company into the international arena in a way that permitted no turning back. By no stretch of the imagination was the Lanz project just the dangling of a foot in the water—the company was totally immersed in international operations. Perhaps it was a naive new entrant, but it was there, and there to stay.[6]

THE DEERE ADMINISTRATIVE CENTER

Often it happens that a single symbol or achievement comes to stand as a personal mark for a lifetime or an era. Theodore Roosevelt's image as a Rough Rider and Henry Ford's Model T automobile both come to mind as examples. For Hewitt's period of leadership at Deere & Company, the initiation and completion of the new office building—the Deere Administrative Center—epitomizes what he hoped to stand for. Far more than just a new, indeed noteworthy, office building, it sought to define the feeling that Deere & Company employees had about themselves and their organization.

At this point, Deere & Company was 120 years old. Throughout this period, it had employed outside architects only in a limited way in constructing new plants and office buildings. Most of the work was done in-house by the company's own engineering departments. The result was that aesthetics took a back seat to utilitarianism—the buildings and their locations were conventional to a fault. Hewitt now decided to take a different approach, to find a nationally respected architect to mastermind the new building and then to assemble the proper data about that person so that he could persuade the board to authorize the expenditures. Robert McNamara, Hewitt's close friend and classmate at the Harvard Business School, was at this time a top executive at the Ford Motor Company and

Exhibit 13–3. Top left, *William Hewitt and Eero Saarinen discuss the Deere Administrative Center, 1959;* bottom left, *the Center just before its opening, 1964;* top right, *the Center under construction, ca. 1963;* bottom right, *the Deere Administrative Center in 1983.* *(Deere Archives)*

had just overseen the construction of an administration building in Detroit. Hewitt immediately contacted him, and McNamara sent him a packet of some two dozen architects' prospectuses. Henry Dreyfuss, the design consultant who had been so intimately involved with Deere during the Wiman period, suggested that there were two buildings that he (Dreyfuss) felt would be superb models to emulate—the new auditorium at the Massachusetts Institute of Technology and the General Motors Technical Center near Detroit. Hewitt visited each site and while at the latter first met the architect for both buildings—Eero Saarinen. Many years later Hewitt recounted this experience (in the *AIA Journal*). "If you want to work with an architect's architect," Hewitt quoted Dreyfuss, "put Saarinen on your list." Hewitt had found his man. "Then and there I decided Eero Saarinen was the man for the job."

By August 1956 Saarinen was in Moline with Hewitt, quietly looking over possible sites for the new building. One was a piece of land owned by the company along the Mississippi River, a mile or so from the enormous complex of offices and factories that had been the original location of John Deere. This particular property was not very attractive, though. A junkyard faced it from the rear, and it was bordered on one side by railroad tracks. The unsuitability of this river site (the 34th Street property) was quickly apparent to Saarinen and Hewitt. The other possible locations were on properties not then owned by the company. Saarinen observed that "he had never seen a community that offered so many problems in regard to having potential sites marred by the nearness of shacks, trailer camps, cemeteries, cheap commercial buildings and other unattractive blight." After the two had traveled by auto and airplane through the area, they identified a particularly attractive possibility on the edge of the town of East Moline, along a set of bluffs overlooking the Rock River. There were some 120 acres, with enough level land to take care of the necessary properties, yet with trees and attractive views throughout—truly a potential "campus," to use Hewitt's earlier word. Hewitt and Saarinen borrowed a truck from a local utility company with a telescoping tower that allowed them to see out over the smaller trees, in order to envision a multistory building at the location. Both were convinced that this was just the right place.

Now Hewitt had the sensitive task of selling the whole project to his board peers. Hewitt prepared for it carefully. His own verbatim notes remain, and they are revealing in several particulars. A meticulous case was made to reject the company-owned land and to use, instead, the wooded property. It was much too early for any configuration of the building to be discussed, so Hewitt stayed away from the subject. Rather, he concentrated his remarks on the selection of the architect. Saarinen was Hewitt's choice, and he proceeded to build his case, first with a description of a number of the Saarinen buildings around the world, many of them renowned. Then Hewitt posed a question to the board that seems in retrospect to epitomize more than any other single statement or act the direction in which he wanted to take the company. His query: "Is he too 'fancy' for us?" His answer, "No."

Part of the reasoning behind Hewitt's rhetorical question was the expenditure itself. An outside architect of the talent and reputation of Saarinen was not going to be inexpensive. But that was not the real issue, for Hewitt was asking the board to enlarge its concept of the company—to see itself as a major, nationally important entity, on its way to becoming the preeminent firm in the industry. In effect, a statement was to be made by the company, one that Hewitt hoped would reverberate through the organization at all levels and out among the dealers, the customers, and the general public.

It is probably not excessive to say that at this meeting Hewitt turned this insular, Midwestern farm implement company in a new direction, pointing it toward a new role as one of the world's best known multinational corporations. For that is how the Deere Administrative Center did turn out—a superb Saarinen building that came to be known architecturally as one of the finest corporate administrative centers in the world. Most important, though, was its effect on the organization, which would not really be known until well after the completion of the building, all too many years into the future. At this point, it was only an article of faith for Hewitt, who had truly put his personal credibility on the line in a way that was almost irrevocable, once initiated.

The appropriation was authorized by the board in January 1957, with only grudging acceptance from certain board members. Of the senior triumvirate of Kennedy, Murphy, and Cook, only Cook was an enthusiastic booster. Burton Peek already had resigned his post as chairman of the board of directors a few months earlier; Peek had been very supportive of Hewitt ever since the latter had arrived at the general company and he gave a grudging blessing to the new building. Yet Peek could not be truly reconciled to leaving the old offices along the river, where he had gone for so many years. Peek often told a story of a hunting trip he had taken many years earlier in northwestern Nebraska, where Peek's personal hunting companion was Gen. John J. Pershing. During the day of the hunt, Peek and Pershing had come upon a large herd of buffalo in a field on one side of the road, and across the road in another field a single buffalo, "a ruff, mangy, ugly looking old bull." Peek inquired of the local farmer why the single animal was in the field. The farmer replied, "You know, originally when the herd was smaller, the field was smaller and all of it lay on this one-third side. Later, as we increased the herd, we had to increase the field, so we acquired this two-thirds on the other side. We drove the herd over there—all except this one. Try as we would, we couldn't get him to go, we had to leave him where he was, and there he has stayed to this day." Peek now publicly applied this story to the office change: "Someday, if any of you encounter a ruff, mangy ugly looking old buffalo around the present site of Deere & Company's office, please deal with him gently, because he may be Burton F. Peek, reincarnated."

The architectural integrity of the new structure was to be Saarinen's— that much was evident—though Hewitt worked personally with Saarinen (with the help of Nathan Lesser, the head of the engineering department). At the start, Hewitt laid out a comprehensive "letter of intent" for the architect, making clear that the building design "will be in harmony with our functions and additions, and also be indicative of the objectives and progress that we envision for the future." Hewitt characterized the men who had built the company as "rugged, honest, and close to the soil," men who had always put a central emphasis on "quality of product and integrity in relationships with other persons." Inasmuch as "the farmer wants and needs the most efficient and durable tractors and implements," therefore "we also want and need a headquarters building that will utilize the newest and best architectural and engineering concepts." Hewitt concluded, "The several buildings should be thoroughly modern in concept but should not give the effect of being especially sophisticated or glossy. Instead, they should be more 'down to earth' and rugged."

Hewitt spoke here to the concern that several of the more conservative board members had enunciated, that the farmer customers in particular would look upon the building as pretentious and somehow too "urban." Hewitt's instincts were that just the opposite would occur, and he was heartened in this by receiving an articulate anonymous letter from an employee shortly after the building plans were made public. The latter said, in part, "Some persons condemn as foolish the plans as announced; I have heard the opinion advanced that farmers will hold our 'extravagance' against us—raise bitter complaints about prices, etc. Personally, I believe that these farmers will be in a small minority; there would be more danger—more progress to be lost, both for us and our customers—in conforming exactly to the notions these customers might have as to what our Company's character and direction should be. We are in a position where we cannot only manufacture quality equipment—but provide leadership in farming and farmers' thinking." The employee concluded, "There's no longer any reason to hide the fact that we are a large company, alive and virile. . . . Our obvious enthusiasm and faith in the future will tend to attract better personnel to our Company." No one really knew which of these points of view would tend to dominate; only when the building was up and occupied would these subtle nuances of employee and public reaction become clearer.

The design of the new office building and the assignment of offices also concerned the board. These matters were not just part of an inconsequential decision about office layouts and locations of file cabinets, but were seen as clues to the recommendations of the parallel study of the management structure of the company being conducted by the outside consultant. For this reason, the board gave Cook the charge to rationalize the building concept with the management concept, and for most of the remainder of the Deere Administrative Center project, Cook worked closely with Hewitt in fulfilling this assignment. Buildings always take time, though—sometimes more time than the purchasers feel necessary —and the Deere Administrative Center was not to be occupied until more than eight years after Hewitt had first visited Saarinen outside of Detroit in March 1956.[7]

A NEW GENERATION OF PRODUCTS

Innovation burgeoned in the agricultural machinery industry in the 1950s. In tractors, the big news was greater horsepower. "In 1950, few wheel-type tractors exceeded 50 maximum belt horsepower, and most farm tractors were considerably below that size," wrote Lester Larsen in his book on the tractor history of this period. But the year 1950 heralded what was soon to be an all-out "horsepower race" (though few engineers designing tractors at that time would have dreamed that horsepower would reach the levels that today's tractors have achieved).

Exhibit 13–4   **Trend in Field Speeds**
(miles per hour)

Source: Lester Larsen, Farm Tractors, 1950–1975, (St. Joseph, Mich.: American Society of Agricultural Engineers, 1971), p. 4

Tractor field speeds turned up sharply during this period, from about 2.5 to 5.5 miles an hour (exhibit 13-4). Tractor transmissions also were going through a marked change, necessarily so with the heightened motive power of these larger machines. In 1954 International Harvester introduced a torque amplifier (TA), which allowed a regular five-speed transmission to become a ten-speed version (when in TA, the travel speed was reduced about 32 percent and the pulling ability increased about 48 percent). In 1957 J.I. Case introduced a torque converter that replaced the conventional clutch. When it was locked in, the tractor had an exceptionally good ability to start with a heavy load and, after gaining requisite operating speed, the torque converter could be locked out. The converter could be reengaged at any time to provide as much as a 100 percent increase in pull over that of direct drive, thus allowing the tractor to pass more easily through rough spots in the field.

Though distillates had continued to be a popular and economical fuel for many years, by the mid-1950s tractors burning distillate fuels were being phased out (the last distillate tractor tested by the Nebraska Tractor Testing Laboratory was the John Deere 720 All-Fuel tractor, in 1956). The most striking feature of the evolution of fuels, though, was the rapid rise in diesel fuel, a particularly strong trend after 1958. Efforts to provide more operator comfort were also widespread in the 1950s. Somehow, safety considerations had progressed at a slower pace. (Larsen, discussing the experiments with the mercury ignition switch, which would automatically shut off when the tractor reached a certain degree of slope, commented, "Most farmers didn't want to be bothered with such devices, which they termed 'foolishness,' and usually removed them after a short trial period.") It was not until 1966 that the first tractors became available with devices to protect the operator with a roll-over protective structure (ROPS). The pioneer was Deere, with its "Roll-Gard."

Deere's decision to move from the two-cylinder tractor to a four-cylinder model was taken in 1953, after years of arguing within the company, much push-and-tug, and probably a bit too much delay. But it took seven years more for the design engineers, the plant and production engineers, and the many others who had been laboring to bring into being a "New Generation of Power." Meanwhile, the company had to adapt and respond with its existing models to the onrush of new developments that other companies were introducing. Deere's popular 40-50-60-70-80 models that had served the company well in the early 1950s were all upgraded in 1956 to the so-called 20 series. These were successful models, with many refinements in hydraulics, fuel systems, and an engine design that allowed several models to establish new fuel economy records in the ten-hour runs at the Nebraska tractor test course. Operator comfort and convenience had been upgraded, and styling was more attractive (these models being the first to wear two-tone paint on the body, the combination yellow and green that has characterized the recent period). The 30 series that was introduced in 1958 had a number of cosmetic, face-lifting changes, one of which, new fenders for the protection of the operator, added considerable safety margins. Certain of these models were particularly popular, with more than 27,000 of the 720, 50-horsepower, tractor

(PTO) selling in 1956–58 and more than 29,000 of its counterpart 830, 57-horsepower, model in the following three years. Deere also startled the whole industry in 1959 with a four-wheel-drive tractor with more than 200 horsepower, introduced at a John Deere field day in Marshalltown, Iowa. To say that the enormous Model 8010 awed its onlookers is an understatement. It stood some 8 feet 2½ inches tall, was 8 feet wide and more than 19 feet long, and weighed 19,700 pounds (actually, 24,860 pounds with its tires full of ballast). Its twenty-four-volt electrical system provided fast starting in any weather and its articulated power steering and power brakes were regular equipment. It could pull a thirty-one-foot harrow or an eight-bottom plow at speeds up to seven miles an hour, readily lifting the integral plow off the ground for turns at the row ends. Only a few of the machines were built—the market in that particular period was not yet ready for tractors of this size. Within a decade, though, the situation would change, and tractors of this and greater horsepower range would become common.

In harvesting equipment, the company had held its position reasonably well during the 1950s. The combine corn head, first brought out in 1952, had been a great success almost immediately. The self-leveling hillside combine had also been well received. In general, though, Deere's harvesting equipment product development in the 1950s was directed toward minor improvements of existing, successful models. Not until 1963, with the Harvester Works' own "New Generation," did the harvesting machine change very much. Similarly, improvements and minor changes had been made all through the remainder of the company's products—the plowing, cultivating, and haying equipment, cotton pickers, etc.

All thoughts of product development in the company would increasingly turn, though, to the change from the two-cylinder to the four-cylinder tractor, a story that came to a climax in Dallas, Texas, in August 1960. In what *Forbes* magazine called the company's "boldest venture of its 124-year career," Deere introduced its "New Generation" of tractors. The Texas event was a tour de force.

DEERE DAY IN DALLAS

Major model changes, always costly, can sometimes be devastating because of the time spent on conversion. The Ford Motor Company's overlong shift from the Model T to the Model A was a classic example of this. (All Ford's assembly plants, as well as its overseas factories, were completely closed for more than six months, and the company did not resume full-scale production until more than a year had elapsed; in the process Ford had irrevocably lost a startling amount of its market share.) Deere probably had spent too much time in the development stages of the four-cylinder tractor, but the conversion to its production at the Waterloo plant was spectacularly well done. The Waterloo shutdown lasted only

Exhibit 13–5. *"Deere Day in Dallas," August 30, 1960. Top, Entrance to the Dallas Coliseum; bottom, William Hewitt and Stanley Marcus introduce the "New Generation of Tractors" at the Neiman-Marcus store. (Deere Archives)*

about five months and the layoffs were staggered in such a way that as one group of employees was laid off another previously furloughed group would come back. By this time the harmonious results of the 1955–56 contract negotiations with the United Automobile Workers had produced an era of close working relations, and employee-relations tensions during the changeover seemed at a minimum.

Downtime for changeover is typically reflected in production time lost on existing models, and the results of 1960 showed this. Sales dropped from 1959's $577.1 million to $511.7 million in 1960, and the net income took a sharp decline from $50.9 million to $20.3 million. Heavy outlays for the machinery and tooling for the new tractors had pushed total company capital expenditures to approximately $40 million in 1960—the net investment of the company, according to the annual report of 1960, jumped from $98 million in 1959 to almost $120 million in 1960. *Forbes* caught the essence of the situation in its article on the new tractors: "As hindsight proved, Deere could hardly have picked a better year than 1960 to make the changeover.... The shutdown coincided with a marked falloff in domestic farm equipment sales as farmers felt the pinch of lower income in 1959 and early 1960.... Deere did not miss out on a potential bumper year. In fact, its indifferent profit showing was matched last year by competitors who had no such unusual expenses as Deere incurred." In other words, fortunate timing mitigated what might have been a far greater effect. The efficacy of the change still had to be proven by the success in the new models, but it was to this issue that Hewitt and his colleagues now turned with gusto.

"All day long the big planes buzzed in and out of Dallas' Love Field. They carried passengers from New York and New Dorp (Pa.), from Paris, France, and Paris, Ill., from Seattle and Sewanee (Tenn.). When darkness fell on Monday, August 29, 1960, more than 6,000 passengers—the biggest industrial airlift in history—had been safely landed." Thus began the *Forbes* article on "Deere Day in Dallas." The next day's events opened with a preview of the entire line, enthusiastically received by the dealers as the tractors stood in a row in a huge open display area in the parking lot of the Cotton Bowl, near the Coliseum, on the outskirts of the central city. Perhaps the most spectacular single event of that day came at the stroke of noon, in downtown Dallas itself. Inside the prestigious department store, Neiman-Marcus, right next to its exclusive jewelry counter, stood a huge, twenty-foot box. Stanley Marcus, the ebullient impressario and president of the firm, walked up to the box and tugged away its wrappings. *Forbes* described the results: "Its contents: a rakish-looking, grass-green, farm tractor. From its sides myriad diamonds (hastily affixed with Scotch tape by willing [Neiman-Marcus] salespeople) twinkled the name of its maker: John Deere." A diamond coronet was even affixed to the tractor's exhaust pipe. Only slightly less spectacular were the fireworks that evening, the Al Hirt band that had been flown in from New Orleans, the Texas barbecue, and other hoopla. Laced through all of this were hard-sell speeches and informal contacts, with Hewitt himself personally acting as master of ceremonies for the evening events and C.R. Carlson, vice president of marketing, leading the Deere marketing contingent.

The choice of Dallas itself was noteworthy. Previously the unveiling of new tractor models always had been done in Waterloo (or Dubuque, if built there). They were in the "heart of the Midwest," logical places for the farmer customer; Dallas was not. But it was the *dealer* who was involved in the initial viewings, and dealers could be brought from all over the country to anywhere. Dallas was just a dramatic and offbeat enough choice to whet their appetites. (In more recent years, Deere has made extensive use of dealer "fly ins," shuttling them from all over the country to Moline in Deere-owned and commercial-charter aircraft).

The proof had to be the models themselves, and their enthusiastic acceptance was quick in coming. Over the next crop year their field results were excellent, and though a drought slowed down sales during the last half of 1961, the North American agricultural machinery results were up considerably in that year and the total sales for the company rose to $561 million (with income up to $36 million).

There were four models in the new line—the 1010, rated at just under 36 PTO horsepower; the 2010, at 46.6 horsepower; the 3010, at 59 horsepower; and the 4010, at 84 horsepower. The three larger models had Syncro-Range transmission, which provided eight forward and three reverse speeds, with synchronizers in the transmission permitting shifting on the go within a range between forward speeds or shuttle-shifting between forward and reverse. The closed-center hydraulic system of the three larger models provided up to three independent "live" hydraulic circuits to serve a rear rockshaft and one or two remote cylinders. The models were equipped with power steering, and the largest two models had hydraulic power brakes. All four tractors had high ratios of horsepower to weight, allowing operation with equipment loads at higher speeds, reduced lugging strain on the engine, and increased efficiency. All four were available with gasoline, diesel, or LP gasoline engines.

Operator comfort had never been a high priority with tractor manufacturers, but in the new line Deere pioneered, with the help of a perceptive outside consultant, Dr. Janet Travell (a posture specialist who was later White House physician for Pres. John F. Kennedy), the development of an orthopedically sound "comfort" tractor seat. The enclosed Roll-Gard cab was introduced in the early 1970s.

The two largest models were relatively the most successful, some 45,000 of the 3010 being sold in the four years 1960–63 and more than 40,000 of the 4010 in just the three years 1960–62. Their successors, the 3020 (65 PTO horsepower) and the 4020 (91 PTO horsepower), developed in 1963, were even more spectacularly received. In the period 1963–71, more than 86,000 of the former were sold and in the same period some 177,000 of the 4020 were made and sold. The latter was far and away the most widely sold single model of tractor ever built by the company.

Deere had dubbed the new tractors a "New Generation of Power" and *Forbes* thought this "somewhat grandiose." Yet, in terms of the models' eventual success and Hewitt's efforts to establish irrevocably a new company image, the pretentious name for the model group and the hoopla surrounding the Day in Dallas seemed to justify the superlatives. *Forbes* called the new models "symbols of a livelier, more dynamic company" and attributed this in part to Hewitt himself. "He has transformed the eminently successful but rather shy and conservative company," they concluded.

But it is never the chief executive alone. *Forbes* added: "Part of Deere's success, too, unquestionably is due to its long and careful study of the farmer, for the farmer's lot and Deere's are intertwined in a way which broader-based companies are not. Deere men pride themselves on knowing the farmer's wants. Not least of all, they accord him the respect which city dwellers do not always give him." (*Forbes* and other national media often enjoyed stereotyping Deere employees as "country bumpkins," almost as if all of them, top management included, came to work in overalls, pulling the straw out of their hip pockets; they came close to implying that Moline rolled up its sidewalks at night. Such remarks seemed gratuitous to the Deere group, particularly so after the emergence of the company as an international power. "Farmers are no longer hicks, and neither are we," asserted Hewitt to a *Forbes* editor in 1963.)

The company, incidentally, did continue to receive complaints from farmers who were die-hards about the two-cylinder tractor; finally, C.R. Carlson developed a thoughtful, four-page form letter that explained the reasons for the change (probably even this not satisfying some!).

The outstanding success of the New Generation tractors fueled Deere's rise to industry leadership. The company's share of the wheel tractors sold in the United States stood at 23 percent in 1959; by 1964 it was up to 34 percent—more than one-third of all the tractors sold in the country. Even more important, in 1963 Deere passed International Harvester for the first time in history in total sales of farm and light industrial equipment. Deere's $762 million sales exceeded Harvester's $665.4 million. (The net sales of Massey-Ferguson were $636.1 million and of Allis-Chalmers were $543.9 million.) In 1963, Deere was also ahead of its farm machinery competitors in net income per dollar of sales and net income per dollar of total assets (only Caterpillar, mostly in heavy construction, scored above Deere in these two key measures.) Under Hewitt, Deere never relinquished its position as the world's largest producer of farm machinery. Hewitt's euphoric plan to be "No. 1" in the industry had come true; more important, over the next two decades it stayed true.[8]

MISCALCULATIONS IN GERMANY

Euphoria in Moline helped ease memories of depressing results in Europe. James Wormley, appointed president of Heinrich Lanz at the first board meeting in December 1956 and dispatched immediately to Mannheim to head the organization, was the only major top management Deere representative on the scene. Deere had taken a calculated risk to leave in place the entire management structure of the predecessor German organization. The decision could be viewed as naive, as if it had been said, "Let's buy this German company, change the color of the paint, call it John Deere-Lanz, and begin selling tractors in Europe." One could argue, alternatively, that there was wisdom in moving slowly, not uprooting an organization too rapidly. With probably a bit of both of these rationales in mind, Wormley left for Europe. He returned in July 1957 to apprise the Deere board of just what the company had really purchased.

Progress had been made in the months that ensued, though his central message was not reassuring. On January 1, 1957, Lanz had a total of 8,060 employees; by the end of July, total employment had been reduced to approximately 7,400 and Wormley expected year-end employment to be around 6,700. Still, the company was patently overstaffed. The long history of Lanz employee benefits and emoluments had certainly built employee loyalty—the number of second, third, and even fourth generation Lanz employees rivaled that of Deere. Yet there seemed to have been a slackening of employee productivity ever since World War II; Wormley estimated that the output per employee at Lanz was only about DM 18,000 per year; other similar German firms had outputs of DM 25,000 to DM 30,000 per employee for the same period.

The product line, Wormley observed, had been too broad at the time Deere bought the company; Lanz had been producing tractors with 12, 13, 16, 18, 20, 24, 28, 32, 36, 40, 50, and 60 horsepower. Only some of these sold in adequate enough quantities to permit an economic scale of production. Wormley immediately discontinued the 13, 32, and 36 horsepower tractors. All of the remainder, with one exception, were various sizes of the Bulldog—all one-cylinder, two-cycle diesel engines. The exception, an 18-horsepower model, was the Alldog (the forward tool carrier tractor), with a two-cylinder, four-cycle diesel engine (and a purchased motor of dubious distinction, as related earlier). Lanz was also making 4-foot and 6.4-foot pull-type combines and 6.3-foot and 8.5-foot self-propelled types. Wormley immediately discontinued the pull-types because there simply was no market for them. The implement line was composed of fourteen types of machines, including mowers, tedders, hay rakes, side delivery rakes, and potato and sugar-beet diggers. For the moment, Wormley decided to leave those in place.

There were other difficulties, too. For example, there was no central price-making authority; dealers did not know what Lanz would charge them. Indeed, record keeping as a whole was in a shambles. The company even had lent money to employees for personal expenditures without setting up a proper collection system.

Some of the problems hanging over from the earlier Lanz period could be readily ameliorated. There was, for example, a seven-year accumulation of chronic field complaints; to the chagrin of Deere, "previously such complaints were completely ignored" (as Lloyd Kennedy reported after a visit in October 1957). Wormley immediately appointed a new marketing director and insisted that field personnel follow up on all complaints. This paid off—whereas there had been complaints concerning 52 percent of all tractors sold, Wormley was able to reduce them to about 7 percent by April 1958.

The problem of dealerships was more intractable. Lanz's fading reputation in the field had begun to damage the distributorship structure. Many who had formerly sold mostly the Lanz name were still willing to sell the harvesting equipment and the tillage tools, but were less enthusiastic about the Bulldog. In truth, just as Deere tenaciously had held onto the two-cylinder tractor beyond the optimum changeover point, so too had Lanz stayed with a simple, traditional model of tractor at a time when other companies were marketing more attractive, more effective multi-cylinder versions. It seems incongruous that Deere had purchased a company with a single-cylinder engine at just the point when it was going through the lengthy, costly, and disturbing shiftover to the four-cylinder tractor. There were some differences, too—Deere was still able to sell its two-cylinder tractors very effectively in the marketplace, while Lanz was really heading downhill on its sales curve well before the purchase by Deere.

Deere's first three years as majority owner of Lanz were discouraging. The firm sold some $35 million in equipment in 1956, at a loss of $767,000; the sales fell to $33 million in 1957, with a loss of $1.5 million, and similar sales in 1958 produced a loss of $1.2 million. By the end of 1958 the cumulative deficit was $3.5 million. A more rigorous and effective sales program in 1959, while producing only $32.6 million in total sales, did result in a break-even year. By this time, the company had upgraded the outmoded Bulldog product line cosmetically to gain more appeal, at the same time selling the new Deere concept to the dealers and ultimately to the buyers. Henry Dreyfuss had been brought into the picture early, making a visit to the Mannheim plant in 1957, and his simple styling changes added greatly to the appearance of the Bulldog. The Lanz blue paint had been changed to Deere's green and yellow. Even here, though, the Mannheim group designed the paint patterns in a rather complicated, showy fashion; Hewitt wrote Dreyfuss, "The whole darn thing just looks too busy—it looks like a Persian carpet." Dreyfuss immediately suggested new painting combinations and the result was quite striking.

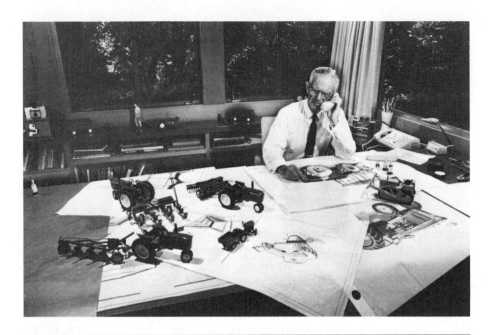

Exhibit 13–6. *Henry Dreyfuss, renowned industrial designer, who was instrumental in the styling and design of Deere equipment for more than three decades, 1966. (Deere Archives)*

Still, it was painfully evident that Lanz needed new, modern tractors; Deere executives had seriously underestimated the sag in the Bulldog's reputation. Faced with a major engineering and manufacturing challenge, the company was forced into a crash program. The effort began in 1957; by late 1959 the models were already in prototype form. In retrospect, this foreshortened development path probably pressured both the North American and German engineers in the company into a set of too-rapid decisions. Compromises were made in attempting to meld American and European field needs. In essence, the Waterloo and Dubuque engineers working on the problem made the decision that the smaller Dubuque tractor was the prototype for Germany, and they proceeded to adapt this model for manufacture in Mannheim (with the engine itself built in Dubuque and shipped to Mannheim for assembly).

There was a serious flaw in this decision, however. The Dubuque tractors were sold in the United States and Canada as utility tractors, not designed in terms of power and ruggedness to serve a multipurpose set of needs. It was true that the German farmer wanted a tractor of this horsepower size, but the uses to which the German farmer put his tractor were strikingly different from those of his North American counterpart. He wanted a tractor that could do heavy plowing and other arduous field work, but also wanted to use it for front loading work, for transport and hauling, even for over-the-road travel. In sum, the German farmer wanted a small tractor, about the size of the utility tractors from Dubuque, but one that was built more ruggedly and with more wide-ranging capacities.

The Waterloo and Dubuque engineers missed the point. Indeed, this is just one example—certainly a serious one—of many misreadings of the European agricultural scene by the American contingent. There was insularity in the Deere views all across the board. Hewitt had sent Maurice Fraher to Europe "to sit at a sidewalk cafe" for just this reason. The learning curve to truly understand and be empathic with another culture is a more upward-sloping line than the Deere people assumed. There was substantial chauvinism, and in the case of the engineers more than a bit of arrogance in dealing with the European. The Lanz engineering group did have rigid ways of structuring itself and dealing with problems, and these seemed to the Americans to be too hidebound. On the other hand, the European engineers were well trained, intelligent, and used to making their own decisions. The fact that the Americans called the shots often irritated and riled the German engineers. Thus there was major difficulty at the start in melding the two engineering groups.

The two-culture problem evidenced itself throughout the organization. Lanz employees had some deeply embedded stereotypes about American business firms and were uneasy about being taken over by one. The German worker believed that "Americans hire and fire without asking" —that American business firms follow boom-and-bust employment patterns. Wormley's necessary reductions in the force had mostly been done by attrition—many employees were leaving Lanz for other employment in the Mannheim area, where there were many excellent jobs available, indeed a labor shortage, at this time. Still, Deere had to get over an initial skepticism by the German workers that Deere's personnel policies were less humane than those of their predecessor. In reality, Deere's policies were, if anything, more employee-oriented than those of the German company—the reputation that had been established by John and Charles Deere in the nineteenth century still held strictly at Deere & Company. This was a fact that could only be fully appreciated over time, though, and at the start Deere-Lanz employee relations were ragged. The infamous "beer strike" was a case in point.

Just about all German companies at this time allowed the sale of beer in their factories, to be quaffed at breaks and at lunchtime. At Lanz, this had been elevated to a science—there were four different locations around the factory where beer trucks would back up each day and deliver fresh kegs; designated employees were then deputed to bring back large mugs of beer. This was done in combination with some rather loose practices relating to the breaks themselves. For example, one of the workers would take fifteen or twenty minutes off to go to the keg for his beer, his assistant standing by. Then, sometimes, the assistant would go to get his beer, and the worker was not fully served. In sum, to the Deere executives

at Mannheim the system seemed woefully loose and potentially dangerous, given the mixing of alcohol and high-speed machinery.

When Harry Pence came to Mannheim to succeed Wormley in 1960, he
decided to tackle this system and in March announced a fixed breaktime,
to be taken by all personnel at the same time and to be precisely fifteen
minutes in length. Concurrently, he announced that only small beer
bottles would be made available at the plant, not the generous steins of
the past. One needs little imagination to guess what happened. Employees instituted a strike and demanded that the workers council take the
matter before the Mannheim labor court for arbitration. The dispute hit
the public press: "Tough Harry . . . would be well advised to pull his
sleeves down," one editorialist vowed. "German workers dislike the
sober and speedy mechanisms of American hustling," said another.
Representatives of the Social Democratic Party at Mannheim quickly
passed a resolution demanding that "American management should
adapt itself to the conditions and laws of the host country." Even the
mayor signed the resolution. Fortunately, the strike lasted only a few
days—it was just at the time when the new tractors that had been
developed out of Dubuque were ready to be manufactured, and a delay at
this point would have been disastrous. Pence was able to tighten the
slippage in the breaks, though his plan for fixed times had to be modified.
Further, the beer remained—and has up to the present. The imbroglio was
a good example of the need to respect cultural differences. Pence started
with an assumption that productivity still lagged at the plant, and that
industrial discipline was badly needed if Lanz was ever to compete with
its aggressive competitors. But taking a man's beer away was too much!

Across the board, Deere's North American management now became
more involved in Lanz. By 1959 Curtis told the board: "Earlier it was
thought that the best policy was to interfere as little as possible with Lanz
management. We have now determined that following this policy was not
fruitful . . . we are now sending more American personnel to assist and
advise Lanz. We shall continue following this policy of increased help in an
effort to inaugurate so far as possible many of the policies and practices
which have proved successful in our North American operations." In the
same year, Deere management persuaded some of the German top managers
to step down from their positions. This created uneasiness among the
employees as they saw colleagues who had been in charge leave without
much of an explanation, but this concern dissipated over time. Subtly over
the period 1959–61 the Lanz organization shifted more into the mode of a
Deere subsidiary, rather than that of an autonomous German company that
just happened to be owned by some Americans. In December 1959, at the
annual shareholders meeting of Lanz, the name of the company was
changed from Heinrich Lanz to John Deere-Lanz A.G.

In January 1960 the two new wholly Deere tractors were ready to be
shown in Germany (prematurely, as we noted above). As the North

American marketers had done before with the changeover from the two-cylinder to the New Generation tractors, the German marketing group now sold out the Bulldog line. The last Bulldog came off the production line in this year; it was number 219,253. The Bulldog had had an unbroken period of production from 1921 to 1960, one of the longest active model runs of any tractor company anywhere in the world. Thus in one year, 1960, Deere said farewell to two historic tractors—the famous North American two-cylinder "Poppin' Johnnie" and the ubiquitous Lanz Bulldog.

The two new John Deere-Lanz tractors were powered by four-cylinder diesel engines—the 300, a 28-horsepower model, and the 500, at 36 horsepower. With Dubuque engines, the remainder of the tractors (including the transmission) was manufactured in Mannheim. Within two years of the introduction of the two basic models, the company also began assembling the model 1010 crawler tractor, with a major portion of its components supplied from Dubuque. A larger model 3010—a 65-horsepower, four-cylinder diesel tractor from the United States—was brought over from Waterloo and assembled in Mannheim, giving Lanz a large-horsepower model to sell in Western Europe.

The exteriors of the two tractors were quite appealing—there were substantial similarities with the North American New Generation line. Most of the basic engineering design was well conceived, too. Still, the tractors had numbers of problems, stemming from the inappropriately wholesale adaptation from the utility tractors made in Dubuque. As horsepower was downgraded from the 40–50 horsepower range, the engineers made compromises that precluded later flexibility (although one always hopes to have a basic engineering design that can be downgraded and upgraded without redesign of certain key dimensions, in this case, many basic dimensions had been locked in). The engines themselves were an older design, the so-called "sleeve and deck" arrangement. This was an outmoded concept, and later the engines had to be changed to a new configuration. There were also transmission and hydraulics problems, along with minor difficulties with the brakes and the fenders. Most of these shortcomings were correctable, though the basic design problem continued to plague the engineers as they both downsized to a two-cylinder, 18-horsepower tractor and upsized to a four-cylinder, 50-horsepower tractor in 1962. The 100-300-500-700 models were certainly a boost for Lanz, for they phased out a Bulldog that had reached the end of its productive career. Still, the new models had serious problems that kept Lanz from putting its best face forward to a market that was extremely competitive in performance and price. Massey-Ferguson and Ford tractors continued to sell at prices below Lanz list prices, and continuing cutthroat competition characterizing the German market in this period made it doubly difficult to sell the more costly Lanz tractors, relatively expensive in their weight-to-horsepower ratio. Deere's German company remained a sick operation.[9]

DEERE MOVES INTO FRANCE

Hard as it was to look above the line of fire in Germany, company personnel could not help but be aware of several major, multi-country efforts occurring in the European environment. The most important, by all odds, was the institution of the European Economic Community (EEC). Its six original members—France, West Germany, Italy, Belgium, the Netherlands, and Luxembourg—had consummated the Treaty of Rome in 1957, and by the early 1960s they had effected an ambitious effort to link their economic policies through the device of a Common Market. Another seminal effort in 1961, the Organization for Economic Cooperation and Development (OECD) brought together the same six Common Market countries with other European countries, as well as the United States and Canada, again with the objectives of expanding trade and economic interrelationships and providing aid to less developed countries. The message to Deere was clear—there was an opportunity, and a need, to get more substantially involved in other European environments, beyond just West Germany. During this period in the late 1950s and early '60s, Western European agriculture had begun to expand; agricultural machinery potentials were attractive indeed. In particular, the use of tractors had accelerated in a major way (exhibit 13-7).

Exhibit 13–7   **Number of Tractors on Farms by EEC and by Country**
1951 and 1962

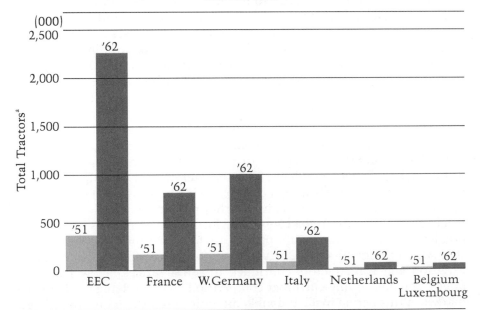

[a]Excludes garden tractors

Source: FAO Production Yearbook, 1963, United Nations, Vol. 17, 1964 Rome.

The formation of the EEC had great portent for companies all through its member countries. In France, three small agricultural machinery companies had become concerned about surviving in the new environment. Remy & Fils manufactured hay tools, disk rakes, cultivating equipment, and forage harvesters in Senoches; Ets. R. Rousseau manufactured low-density balers and threshing machinery at Fleury-les-Aubrais, near Orléans; Thiebaud Bourguignonne also manufactured low-density balers (their smallest version, the "Lady Bug," had achieved great success), as well as grain separators, rakes, and mowers at Arc-les-Gray. All three felt vulnerable because of their small size, lack of anything approaching a "full line," and fears about increased competition from the other EEC countries.

In 1958 the three small French firms formed a fourth company, Compagnie Continentale de Motoculture (CCM), with its central purpose the daunting task of developing a tractor. In effect, the three companies hoped in one fell swoop to jointly become a full-line company. In 1959, almost by chance, Deere made contact with one of the three companies' plants and learned of CCM.

Discussions soon led to Deere joining with CCM; the company would buy a 51 percent controlling interest in CCM and would also purchase small blocks of stock in each of the three companies, somewhere in a 15–20 percent range. A sum of $1 million was appropriated for the interest in CCM, and an additional $1.2 million was to be split three ways to purchase the interests in the three companies. All three companies agreed to adopt the John Deere green and yellow colors; at the start, each manufacturer was to maintain his own trade name. There already were some overlaps among the three companies' products; now Deere was required to further mesh the three sets of products with its own North American products, particularly those from Ottumwa (where Deere's North American mowing equipment, balers, and other related products were made).

The heart of Deere's interest in CCM was the tractor proposal. CCM engineers had already sketched preliminary ideas about how a tractor might be made, but these were far short of what was necessary to make a viable tractor. Deere's agenda was not to build a complete tractor, but, rather, a tractor engine. If this could be accomplished, the engines could be sent across the border to the Lanz factory at Mannheim, replacing imported engines from North America. This notion was especially attractive because the EEC tariff regulations would soon make importation from the United States relatively more costly. Therefore, the initial appropriation of the board for the purchase of CCM, Remy, Rousseau, and Thiebaud stock also included $4.2 million for "establishing or purchasing a tractor plant and providing necessary tools."

Perhaps it was the sobering experience at Lanz in buying a shaky company with multitudes of problems, perhaps it was the fact that there were no readily available engine companies to purchase. At any rate, Deere management assumed right from the start that in this case they would begin with a "green field." A land site was found near Orléans (in its suburb of Saran), and by 1962 a building was underway. When it was finished in 1965, the company began making three- and four-cylinder diesel engines for the German operation.

Two of the three companies in CCM did very well under Deere partnership. Remy in Senoches continued its success in forage harvesters and tillage equipment, while Thiebaud at Arc-les-Gray made all of the French-made balers and prospered with its excellent mower-conditioner, a model more suited to the natural grasses of Europe than the Ottumwa machines (the latter more widely used on legumes). Rousseau had lost its balers to Thiebaud when CCM had been founded; its product line of threshing equipment had not done well and the financial drain from an overly ambitious plant expansion in 1957 had put a severe strain on the company. In 1962 Deere increased its ownership to about 80 percent of the stock of Rousseau; the former managing director resigned and Deere began assembling some of its industrial equipment there, the components coming from Dubuque. (The French requirements for this type of machine were somewhat different than the North American standards, and the equipment had to have special French engineering built into it).[10]

MEXICO: LOCAL CONTENT, LOCAL OWNERSHIP

The Mexican operation had begun as "one of the bright spots in overseas operations," said Curtis in his report to the board in 1959. The new factory building in Monterrey opened early that year; it was given an auspicious, fast start because the company had already been assembling the Model 630, 730, and 830 tractors, together with disk and rotary plows, tool carriers, and harrows in rented quarters. Sales stood at $1.5 million in 1956 and by 1960 they were up to $4.5 million. The Mexican government had promised to protect this new domestic industry by restricting imports from companies outside the country. Costs were higher than in the United States because of smaller production runs and lower employee productivity. Nevertheless, a break-even was expected for the year.

The euphoria of those first four years of operations soon was tempered, as the Mexican government began to reveal, in a rather convoluted way, its long-term plans for the Mexican tractor industry. Its goals appeared to be threefold: (1) to increase the Mexican content of all international companies in the country, (2) to encourage substantial—indeed, majority —participation of Mexican capital in them, and (3) to keep the price of a tractor manufactured in Mexico precisely equal to the cost of an imported tractor, were it to be allowed in the country. At this time (1961), four international companies were selling into Mexico in some quantity—

Deere, International Harvester, Massey-Ferguson, and Ford (only Deere, though, had an assembly operation in Mexico itself). All three of these Mexican goals troubled the international companies. They saw Mexico's tractor market as a limited one, with low-quantity production runs needing to be spread over a wide range of horsepower sizes. Costs would therefore be high. Were there also to be rigid price control at an unrealistic level, profitability would be tenuous indeed. If control of the companies was exercised from within the country, pressures to satisfy short-term stockholder demands at the expense of longer-run growth might be exacerbated.

In the rumor-filled summer of 1961, the companies vied to ascertain the real agenda of the government. There were intimations that only two manufacturers were to be chosen—those with the "best" proposals—and that then the borders would be closed to any further entrants. The first candidates were two English companies, David Brown and Nuffield, but their plans were quickly rejected by the government. Deere, feeling under considerable pressure, finally submitted its own proposal in August 1962, an arrangement that would provide 40 percent local content by the fourth year and 60 percent content by the eighth year, all to be accomplished by a company that would have 40 percent Mexican ownership. Though Deere personnel waited with keen anticipation for an answer, none was forthcoming; they were left in limbo for months, their offer never acted upon by the government.

In November 1963 International Harvester submitted its proposal; whatever the particular chemistry involved, this time the offer was accepted. Once again, Deere submitted its own proposal and now it, too, was approved. Deere proposed to manufacture two models (tractors with 41 and 53 horsepower) and to increase its investment in manufacturing facilities from $1.5 million to $6.1 million (in the process, to add about 500 employees). The local content would reach 60 percent at the end of two years, rather than the eight years previously proposed. In regard to Mexican ownership, 40 percent of the company would be sold "to the Mexican investing public." Just who these investors would be was not clear. Deere pressed the government to reaffirm that the manufacturing program would include only two companies and that importation of all tractors up to 65 horsepower would be prohibited. Finally Deere exhorted the government to set tractor prices at such a level as to permit an adequate return on investment.

The government seemed to have approved these requests, so Deere proceeded to increase the plant size. Rising sales in 1964 and 1965 and modest profits in those two years seemed to justify the decision. Three unsettling developments soon occurred, however. First, imports of tractors by Massey-Ferguson and Ford continued to be allowed. As Deere estimated its unit costs to assemble in Mexico to be about 30 to 50 percent higher than in its United States plants, and as transportation costs were only about 10 percent and duties about 5 percent, the price squeeze was severe. (Deere continued to import its own larger tractors, and the differential worked in its favor there.) Complaints from Deere and International Harvester finally did succeed in shutting off most of the competing products, but the Mexican government more than once surprised them again with special barter arrangements with other international tractor manufacturers that allowed significant importations.

The second problem related to the "Mexicanization" of shareholders. As Deere contemplated ways to sell shares to the general public, it became apparent that the shares had little appeal. Not only were the financial results of the company still quite modest, but also the government required that only Mexican citizens or Mexican-controlled institutions be the purchasers. Sources of considerable capital actually in the country—other foreign nationals living permanently in Mexico, etc.— were excluded by this constraint. Further, the free-wheeling Mexican investing community was skittish of most agricultural projects, given the power of farmers to exert political pressure on the government.

A third problem was even more serious. Just as Deere's manufacturing facilities were nearing completion, the administration of President Lopez Mateos was replaced by that of President Diaz Ordaz. Soon it was known that the latter had no intention of limiting tractor manufacturers to just the two that were already there; in mid-1965 the new administration announced that it was weighing approval of four additional manufacturers. George French, who now headed all overseas manufacturing for the company, pushed the board in mid-1965 to accelerate its efforts to sell shares to local investors: "The new administration does not feel committed to all the agreements of its predecessors. Nevertheless, if 40 percent of the shares were sold at the right time, we expect that the Mexican government would live up to its agreement for not less than two nor more than four years of its administration.... With strong support from Mexican shareowners, it is probable that the present limitation of two manufacturers can be maintained for a long time." Curtis came away from a meeting with one of Deere's local bank officers with much the same feeling: "His real recommendation was that we seriously consider 51 percent because this would go a long way toward buying peace with the Government—not only this Government but succeeding Governments."

Within weeks, though, the Mexican government undercut the French-Curtis thesis by approving, first, a Massey-Ferguson proposal and then a similar Ford offer. Despite this, the government still made it plain that it expected not 40 percent Mexican ownership, but 51 percent. Deere was under the gun—now it simply had to sell 51 percent of its outstanding stock. To its consternation, no investors stepped forward. Finally, 51 percent of the shares were trusted to one of Deere's lead banks there, the Banco Nacional de Mexico, S.A. ("Banamex"), which agreed to use its best efforts to sell at least half to the investing public. Despite the bank's promotional work, only 8 percent was placed and the bank was the trustee for the rest. At least technically, Deere was now "Mexicanized." Given the whimsical actions of the Mexican government, however, all of these developments were most unsettling to company officials. Fortunately, the operations did stay modestly profitable for the rest of the 1960s.[11]

ARGENTINA, SOUTH AFRICA, JAPAN

The old-line British house, Agar, Cross, which had been Deere's distributor in Argentina since the turn of the century, had become overstaffed and debt-ridden by the mid-1950s, with monumental arrears due from Argentine farmers. Yet the Argentine agricultural outlook was quite promising—the country seemed to be entering a period of stable economic growth, its Southern-hemisphere "green belt" one of the great agricultural areas of the world. It seemed a good time to part company with Agar, Cross, and to establish Deere's own bridgehead in the country.

This new Deere initiative included not only marketing but production; in September 1957 the board authorized $3.6 million for construction of a plant to assemble tractors in Rosario, with a capacity to produce 3,000 tractors per year for the Argentine farmer. William Klingberg, Deere's Mexican manager, was brought in to head the Argentine operation. Replicating Mexico, there now began a complex negotiation with the government about the percentage of local content of the manufactured products. Here, though, the definition itself was more complex. First, there were specified levels of local content, separately defined for each manufacturer. Next, there was a further specified list for imported components, some free of import duties, others carrying high tariffs. The Argentine authorities were adamant in insisting on precise explanations of each part's manufacture, an intrusion into the company's internal cost data that Deere officials found upsetting.

The first government decrees in 1959 seemed to allow about 55 percent importation, 45 percent local content. By 1961, the latter was up to 50 percent, a year later to 60 percent, and one year after that to 70 percent. By 1967, the local content required was 90 percent of the total product. A substantial plant addition was required in order to accomplish this; the company put it in place in 1964, and by 1965 Deere did indeed have its local content component up to 90 percent. (Later, in the 1970s, this went to 95 percent.) But there was an even more rigorous requirement: any part that could be made by an Argentine manufacturer was automatically prohibited from importation.

There were further aggravations. The company had had constant problems in clearing imported machine tools through the labyrinthine Argentine customs. Production costs in Argentina were much higher than those in the United States because the large fixed overhead was spread over too small a production run. Further, the company had to pay high prices for locally purchased materials. Finally, the local-content issue remained a central problem. As one of the Deere executives put it in 1966: "Forcing an industry such as ours to a 90 percent or higher local content is not always in the best interests of either the industrial economy or the customer. Undoubtedly, if the local content were reduced to somewhere between 50 and 75 percent, our costs would be greatly reduced and the selling price to the farmer customer would be lower." J.I. Case, a small importer and modest implement manufacturer, pulled out of the country at this time, apparently in part because of the local-content issue. Fiat, the other international company manufacturing in the country, stayed. Its investment was large, and its management was reluctant to jettison a substantial bridgehead, so it too lived with the draconian local-content percentage.

Deere's operation turned unprofitable by the early 1960s—there was considerable labor unrest at the plant, and the optimistic projections of economic stability had faded with renewed political unrest in the country. Deere was third in market share in the country for tractors (after Fiat and Deca S.A.), holding about 14 percent of the tractor business. But the bright promises held about Argentina as a country, and the equally optimistic hopes of Deere about its own operations there, had faded by the mid-1960s.[12]

Deere had been exporting farm machinery to South Africa since well before the turn of the century, but in the early 1960s its market share was still modest. In tractor sales, its 4 percent share was considerably behind those of Massey-Ferguson, International Harvester, and Ford (with only the latter assembling in the country at that time). There had been only a trickle of implement sales—South African duties on such equipment were substantial.

In 1962, a study team was sent out from Moline to look into the possibility of direct manufacture in the country (for both International Harvester and Massey-Ferguson had already decided to do so). Contact was made with a South African implement manufacturer, South African Cultivators (Proprietary) Limited, which had grown from a small farm implement repair shop into a company with an annual volume of about $1 million, making tillage tools and ground-engaging tools, such as disk blades and plow points (some for their own products, some sold as components to other South African manufacturers). The plant was located in Nigel, east of Johannesburg.

The South African company had expanded operations so rapidly that there now were pressing needs for working capital. A proposal was consummated for Deere to buy 75 percent of the stock of the organization, with the founder, Nils Gregerson, to stay as its chief executive. Just over $1 million was appropriated by the Deere board for the purchase.

The new company became known as John Deere-Bobaas (Proprietary) Limited; later in the 1960s its name was changed to John Deere (Proprietary) Limited.

Deere took over the tillage lines, introducing its own products. In addition, some local assembly was done on smaller Deere tractors (the larger sizes still being imported as whole goods). For most of the 1960s the South African company limped along unprofitably, though market share for tractors rose to 6.5 percent in 1966 and 8.2 percent in 1967. The changeover to Deere equipment was not easy. As was often true of equipment placed in a different environment, substantial difficulties were encountered in trying to use American tillage equipment in the South African soils. The harsh, high-silica nature of the latter brought extra wear and some product failures.

Gregerson was a stubborn, production-oriented executive who sometimes overestimated his sales volume and built up too large an inventory. On the other hand, he and his staff had a perceptive ability to deal with South African labor. In the mid-1960s in South Africa the tension between blacks and whites had not yet become as high-profile an issue as it later was. Curtis, in his presentation for the initial purchase, told the Deere board: "It appears unlikely that racial upheavals will occur in the foreseeable future—probably not for at least 10 years. This uncertainty, though important, has not deterred our competitors and major automotive firms from investing." A year later, though, he had increased misgivings and wrote the board: "We believe the racial problems in South Africa have tended to become worse rather than better since we decided to buy the interest in John Deere-Bobaas last July. The possibility of all the other independent nations in Africa banding together with the help of Russia to try to force the 3½ million white people out of South Africa is a definite possibility within the next one or two decades." But another Moline staff member, in a month-long visit in late 1961, played down the issue. "There does not appear to be great concern on the part of the whites that the situation is explosive in nature. They realize they have a problem but are doing something about it."

The nagging question of just what kind of political and social environment really characterized South Africa became more important to Deere in the mid-1960s as the government began to make overtures about encouraging more domestic production. In the past the government had allowed importation of assembled tractors from abroad with only modest duties applied upon entry, and South African agriculture had become increasingly mechanized. Smaller tractors were most popular, owing to the ready availability of inexpensive labor. The initial purpose of the policy to encourage domestic output had apparently been to utilize more local labor. But it soon became clear that the dominant reason was South Africa's increasing preoccupation with self-sufficiency. Pressures from abroad concerning its apartheid policy were mounting by the year; a boycott by other countries that would shut off the flow of materials and products for the country was always a threat. The South African government was quite sophisticated about the implications of pushing "local content" too fast; a forced indigenous industrialization tended very often to result in much-increased prices to the local users, and the ruling officials were keenly attuned to the farmers. The Deere managing director in South Africa wrote Moline in 1967: "This country is determined to become self-sufficient just as quickly as possible for at least two reasons —one, the fear of trouble over South West Africa and the other over the Rhodesian situation. Some months ago, all industry was advised of the need to increase stocks of goods on hand—largely in the spare parts category. Our own Marketing Division was asked to increase their supplies of goods (spares) obtained outside this country and the government even offered to agree to allow the banks to extend lines of credit for their purchase if present lines were exhausted."

Thus, over the remainder of the 1960s, Deere and the other international companies had to grapple with the increasingly insistent proposals of the government to require more manufacturing within the country, with tractors as the central issue. As early as 1963, the government attempted to promulgate a tractor manufacturing protocol for the industry and solicited proposals from the four major international companies. Deere, Massey-Ferguson, and Ford presented a joint proposal in April 1963, after International Harvester had surprised everyone with an offer to manufacture a tractor, including engines, with 70 percent local content within five years. The joint proposal of the three other companies was for 50 percent content, to be balanced by modest tariff and subsidy provisions from the government. In the subsequent bargaining, the government backed off on its effort to pressure the companies, and the tractor manufacturing protocol stayed in suspension. The government raised the matter again in 1967 with a formal "Enquiry into the Tractor Industry," and at this point Deere made a second formal proposal (in March 1968) for local manufacturing, suggesting two alternative options—40 percent and 60 percent local content. Again the proposal was not acceptable to the government and the issue remained a moot one as Deere moved into the 1970s, still searching for a profitable and stable mode in the country.

In 1963 Deere also built a link to Asia through a licensing agreement with Hitachi Ltd., one of Japan's largest manufacturing concerns. Hitachi would produce certain Deere farm and industrial tractors and equipment for the Japanese, South Korean, and Okinawan markets. Deere would furnish technical assistance and would also sell some machines and component parts to Hitachi. The bright promise of the collaboration did not come true. Hitachi had taken on agricultural tractors only at the insistent urging of the Japanese government, which was worried about the lack of mechanization on Japan's predominantly small farms. When pressure from the government eased, Hitachi lost interest—agriculture was not its prime target. Though Hitachi did sell some Deere industrial equipment, it seemed more and more that Hitachi was mostly interested in Deere's technology, not in selling its products. A desultory effort was made in 1969 to put together a new joint venture in industrial equipment, but, as one of the Deere representatives on the scene put it: "There are broad differences in customs and language . . . communication with Hitachi involves the utmost in patience and understanding." Such understanding was not to be, though, and in October 1970 the two companies agreed to go their separate ways.[13]

THE "WORLDWIDE" TRACTOR

In mid-1961 Deere had increased its ownership of Lanz Iberica in Spain to 42.5 percent, at the same time buying a similar percentage of Ricardo Medem's sales company; the latter at first kept 42.5 percent ownership of the manufacturing company and controlling interest in the sales company, but soon sold controlling interest in both to Deere.

Spain was not scheduled to join the EEC for a number of years; meanwhile, the ability to move parts across the border into France and on into Germany was not as propitious as if Spain were already within the EEC. Spain did have high tariff walls and did require substantial local content (90 percent within two years of establishing a company), thus making some of the movement of components and parts from North America and other countries in Western Europe more difficult. In sum, Spain at this particular time was almost the textbook description of a "pocket" market.

With this Spanish addition, the company was now manufacturing in six countries (the others: Germany, France, Argentina, Mexico, South Africa). It was clear that the market for tractors around the world was large, yet a company such as Deere could not produce everywhere or, indeed, satisfy all the special needs of the world's farmers. If the company could achieve some standardization, whereby components manufactured in one location could be utilized by others, it could improve its flexibility and reduce costs.

The initiative for developing a standardized product came during a critically important discussion in September 1960 on the concept of a "worldwide" tractor. A group of thirty-four top executives in the company assembled around the Moline board room table; the group was so large that it had to be divided. Those around the central table were to carry the burden of the conversation and a second group at the outer perimeter was to listen and absorb. Hewitt stated the issue succinctly: "Deere & Company leads competition in the United States; however, competition is ahead of us in the foreign markets. . . . Investments for foreign manufacture will be rewarded if properly planned, and we can contribute to the world welfare by making equipment available. . . . We should evaluate this market, the facilities required, and production capabilities to assess the potential for a worldwide tractor, bearing in mind that farming customs and conditions differ in various countries, and it would be uneconomical and impractical to attempt to design a tractor for each country. Therefore, the final design must represent a composite of world requirements."

Subsequent speakers laid out the market potentials for such a tractor, elaborated on competitor models, and sketched out what such a tractor—"A utility or general-purpose tractor, of low profile"—might look like. A number of suggestions were made about horsepower; the consensus seemed to be that it should be no smaller than 25, nor larger than 50 (PTO). The participants ranged over issues of engineering requirements, interchangeability of components and parts among different countries, provisions for a so-called "basic design," and standardization potentials (including the query of whether the British metric system should now be adopted and concerns about how such a piece of equipment could be tested on a worldwide basis). In total, it was a formidable challenge to the assembled Deere executives; many later recounted the electric feeling that this meeting generated.

Out of these early discussions about the worldwide tractor came detailed plans for two prototypes that would become the heart of the program—the X-21 at 37 horsepower (PTO) and the X-22 at 55 horsepower. As plans progressed in North America on the design of these two tractors, Frank T. McGuire was sent by Curtis on a survey of the European plants, accompanied by Clifford L. Peterson and T.S. Keisling. The rubric laid down by Curtis was that "all Deere factories everywhere in the world were to design their products with the maximum possible standardization." This would allow interchangeability of parts, would ensure the maximum use of design talent, would raise worldwide quality standards, and in the end "should result in a worldwide 'family look'."

McGuire's recommendations took into account manufacturing costs for the two tractors (compared to competition) and the most likely locations for manufacture of various components of the tractors. McGuire felt that Mannheim should make the engines for both tractors, the new Saran factory in France should make the transmissions (the opposite of the original plans for Germany and France). The tractors would be assembled both at Saran and Mannheim. In turn, all of the company's European combine manufacturing would be concentrated at Zweibrücken. (Mannheim had continued to make some combines up to this point.) The Deere operation in Spain, Lanz Iberica, would be licensed to make products specially adapted to the Spanish market, but Spain would not at this time be part of the larger Western European manufacturing complex. McGuire concluded, "The big Deere effort in Europe should be concentrated in France and Germany and devoted to tractors, combines, industrial equipment and balers."

McGuire, too, was preoccupied with the issue of local content, but from the perspective of EEC members. To be sure, a number of the Western

European countries had had substantial tariff barriers. With the advent of the EEC, however, there was now to be a lessening of tariffs and eventually no barriers whatsoever. In other words, there likely would be no "local content" requirement between, say, Germany and France. There might well be subsidies paid by individual countries to their own producers, as was subsequently adopted by several of the "Six" for agricultural products. In terms of manufacturing, though, everyone would be in the same basic situation. The difficulties of meshing Deere's operations in Spain illustrated the implicit height of the borders being put around the EEC.

By the time the X-21 and X-22 models were introduced in 1965, a third model had also been developed. The three prototypes were the 310, a three-cylinder diesel at 32 horsepower (PTO); the 510, also a three-cylinder diesel at 40 horsepower; and the 710, a four-cylinder diesel at 50 horsepower. There had been modifications in McGuire's production planning—the Saran factory was in operation by this time—and it was decided that engines for both French and German tractors were to be made there. In turn, the transmissions and a number of other components were made at Mannheim. Subsequent history proved the efficacy of the switch from the McGuire proposal.

Deere thus took a giant step toward a worldwide manufacturing program, with significant components coming from North America but with major manufacturing shared uniquely by West Germany and France. Deere executives had been overly naive at the beginning of their European venture; indeed, there were some conceptual problems in trying to be a multinational, worldwide corporation even at this point. Nevertheless, the Americans had accomplished a signal victory in realistically bringing the West Germans and the French together in a joint manufacturing venture. Nationalism might have made such a cooperative venture much more difficult had either one of the two countries alone initiated the project. Deere had also thrown an umbrella over the three small French companies and had shown that a large multinational corporation could indeed assuage the fears of smaller firms in Western Europe that were concerned that they were too small to hold their own against evolving competition from the large companies.

Market share for Deere-Lanz now began to climb a bit (Appendix exhibit 25), though Deere's dent in the European market was still modest—only 3.4 percent of all Western European sales. There were to be many more heartaches after the introduction in 1965 of the new models. The European operations were still in a tenuous position, and the following several years would prove even more difficult. One could not have said in 1965 that Deere had "made it" in Europe. What could have been said, though, was that a major conceptual change had been effected in a way that seemed to bridge the gap between the American and European views of management.

Europe was not the "world," the modifier used by that important meeting in September 1960 to discuss the "worldwide" tractor. In 1965, Spain, South Africa, Mexico, and Argentina each remained essentially a "pocket market." The challenge of trying to bring these four country operations more into the mainstream of Deere remained to be met.[14]

HEWITT'S FIRST DECADE IN RETROSPECT

On April 27, 1965, Deere & Company held its quarterly meeting of the board of directors, followed by the annual stockholders' meeting. At the director's meeting, William Hewitt was presented a key to the Deere Administrative Center, to mark his tenth anniversary as chief executive officer of the company. Curtis, in presenting the key, pointed out that it had been especially designed for the occasion by Henry Dreyfuss and "opens all the doors—including the door of the wine cellar." (In truth, wine was served only at state occasions for foreign business visitors; at Deere there was a rigid rule of no alcoholic beverages in any of the United States offices, branches, and factories.)

During Hewitt's first decade of leadership the organization had assumed a new role, a multinational corporation that had "arrived" as the number-one farm machinery manufacturer in the world. Without forgetting its roots in Midwestern conservatism, it had found a new style and verve that gained it widespread national attention. Hewitt now had in place his own management team and had realigned the organizational structure in important ways. After the major shakeup stemming from the Booz, Allen & Hamilton report of 1956, he had tightened the structure more effectively. Factories were consolidated in Moline with the transfer of various assembly operations of the old Wagon Works to other factories in Moline and Des Moines (the Wagon Works as an operating entity was then assigned to oblivion, as had been the wagons it made). In October 1959 an anomaly in the operation of the board itself—interim meetings of the local Moline members of the board of directors in place of an executive committee—was ended. This "local board" had had no official status and had suffered because the quorum requirements for the full board had to be met in order to conduct official business. At the meeting of October 1959 a formal executive committee was reconstituted, with a quorum of five. The new system gave more flexibility and also centered power more strongly in the hands of the Moline members of the board. (Over the years, this sometimes has been a source of irritation on the part of the outlying members.)

In early August 1961, with the death of Pat Murphy, the company lost a loyal and influential executive. He had been ill for a number of months but characteristically had worked until a week before his death. Murphy had been a director of the company for twenty-four years, one of the key leaders of the manufacturing arm of the company for an even longer period. His dedication to the company was unstinting, his leadership qualities significant. His innate conservatism and focused perspective sometimes constrained his willingness to expand his horizons and movement into new areas. Yet an organization must have individuals on all sides of the spectrum, and Pat Murphy's honest and open representation of his point of view served Hewitt and the others on the board very well indeed.

With Murphy gone, George French and C.R. Carlson assumed the key roles as heads, respectively, of manufacturing and marketing (with Curtis as the key financial officer). On the board itself there were also new faces: D.C. Glover, related by marriage to the Wiman side of the family, came on the board in 1955 (but abruptly resigned his management position as industrial sales manager in 1958). Joseph Dain was elected to the board in 1960, himself a third generation link to one of the founding companies. Frank T. McGuire came on the board in 1962, as did Ed W. Ukkelberg, from the marketing side of the business. A.B. Lundahl joined a year later and in April 1964 three additional board members were elected—John H. Gratlund (manufacturing, with a focus on overseas), Clifford L. Peterson (finance), and Comart M. Peterson (marketing).

Hewitt also asked for a significant change in his personal status in the company in April 1964. Explaining to the board that "business people outside the Company feel that 'President' carries more weight than 'Executive Vice President,' even though the responsibility might be the same," he asked that Curtis be appointed president of the company. In turn, Hewitt's title was changed to "chairman." Hewitt made it explicitly clear that this was not synonymous with "chairman of the board"—that he remained the chief executive officer of the company.

There had been persistent problems in organizing for the overseas operation. At the start, only a few American personnel were posted abroad; a number of top-line people who might have profited from an overseas assignment were not sent, their continuing presence jealously guarded by the heads of the domestic operations. As the company learned it needed to become more involved in the foreign operations (particularly as Lanz in Germany and the new French operation continued to have difficulties), more senior management people were deputed abroad.

In 1961, the international group was reorganized. The Venezuelan holding company, John Deere Intercontinental, S.A., was phased out, and a new Canadian company, John Deere Intercontinental, Limited, was formed, not to handle the Canadian operation but to be the rallying point for the rest of the world. Two divisions were set up—a Latin America-Pacific-Far East division under Harry Pence, and a Europe-Africa-Middle East division under Comart Peterson. Still unclear, though, was the way that all of this fitted into the top-management structure at Moline.

Late in this same year, Hewitt asked Booz, Allen & Hamilton to consider the restructuring of the international operations. When the Booz, Allen analysts reported back, they suggested a radical departure. While they felt that the functional basis of organization still made sense on the domestic side of the business (with all manufacturing being centered in one group, all marketing in another), they concluded that a number of factors peculiar to Deere's international operations argued for a different structure there. These factors were the wide variety of ownership situations, the special complexities of international business itself, the development of the "worldwide" tractor concept, and the particular needs for coordination between France and Germany. Their conclusion: the company should be organized abroad in a geographical mode. Two senior vice presidents would be assigned responsibility for managing the two major segments of the business—the North American operations and the international operations, respectively. In turn, the international operation would be divided into two groupings, each to be headed by a vice president. One would embrace all of the European operations, the other everything outside of Europe (*i.e.*, Argentina, Australia, Mexico, and South Africa).

Hewitt adopted most of the report; by early February 1963 a company-wide bulletin announced a "Region I" to include Latin America, Australia, South Africa, and the Far East and a "Region II" to take in all of Europe, North and Central Africa, and the Middle East. In addition, there would be a separate organization for export sales to dealers in countries where no Deere sales branches had previously been established. This concept of dividing the world made eminent sense, and the pattern has stood to the present as Deere's way of operating abroad. (Later there was one modification: as the South African business climate was affected most particularly by patterns in Europe, it was shifted in 1966 to Region II.)

There was one striking modification of the Booz, Allen report, though —the historic functional basis of organization was continued abroad. The strong, sometimes opinionated personalities of the two individuals who were to take the senior vice president positions, C.R. Carlson and George T. French, finally persuaded Hewitt to remain with the functional definition of the company, worldwide. Carlson, as senior vice president of marketing, was given complete charge of marketing throughout the world; the directors of marketing in the two regions reported to a vice president-overseas marketing (Comart Peterson), who was directly under Carlson. In turn, George French, as senior vice president-manufacturing, was given overall supervision of all manufacturing throughout the world, with his vice president-overseas manufacturing, John Graflund, also supervising manufacturing in both of the regions. Hewitt explained his reasoning to the board: "Where previously we had one man in charge of both marketing and manufacturing in each of our various overseas areas, we now have separated the responsibility for marketing from that of management in each of these areas. . . . Carrying this separation of responsibilities up and down the line enables our management people to devote their efforts to their own specialities in which they are well trained. . . . This new organization parallels the proven and successful structure of the John Deere North American organization."

This turned out to be a signal mistake. There had always been an insularity in both the manufacturing arms and the marketing groups in the domestic company. Though this had been an historical source of strength by vesting a high degree of decentralized authority in the hands of, for example, factory managers, it also had been a perennial problem, for this dichotomy of thinking between the two groups of people often made each unresponsive to the other. In the overseas operation the difficulties were compounded—the lines of communication were longer, the differences in each country very striking, and the sophistication and understanding of the Deere personnel about foreign environments much less than that of the domestic operation. For example, if the marketing manager in a foreign operation felt that a product needed to be re-engineered to fit a local condition, he could not make this request directly to the manufacturing man in his country. He had to go through Moline to his own senior vice president of marketing, who then would deal with his counterpart in manufacturing. Obviously there was some communication horizontally between the two functions throughout the organization. Yet the uneasy fact remained that the formal linkages were vertical, and the practical effect of this was to compound insularity. Within three years, the company was forced to change its international organizational structure, turning back to the original Booz, Allen concept.

If there were indeed some organizational difficulties, there was no uncertainty about the overall mission and goal. Hewitt had been able to dramatize and then carry through a wide range of new initiatives. One of his key devices for accomplishing change was a periodic goal-setting process (on an approximate five-year cycle). Each board member participated, developing his own extrapolations of company sales and profitability, as well as his own suggestions for new initiatives. When the process was renewed in February 1964, the evident success of the company over the previous years dominated individual comments. Hewitt had given a ten-point set of his own goals, which focused particularly on the overseas operation and the need for product development and reliability improvement. Permeating Hewitt's own personal presentation and the contributions of each of the directors was a sense of excitement about the challenges and opportunities of the moment. Yet there was a grasp of the future throughout all of the goal-setting process—a realization that short-term growth might not always produce the wisest long-term pattern. A number of years earlier, Frank Silloway had stated this succinctly in one of his most enduring speeches: "We are in business for the long term. Natural human impulses stem from short-term motives. Therefore, resist your natural impulses or, at least, count ten before you yield to them."

In this goal setting of 1964, deep concern about international losses intruded repeatedly into the discussions. The need to look to the longer run was stressed by Frank McGuire in a letter to Hewitt, which was read at the meeting: "For as long as I have been aware of your thinking and observed your leadership, you have emphasized that Deere must seek growth. In this, we may be forced to take short-term losses but will accept these provided the long-term growth will yield satisfactory profit levels. . . . The advantage of this is that no one then could possibly be under any illusion that you are interested in what I describe as 'empty' growth, namely, sales increase with excessive dilution of profits or, worse, a continued lack of profit."

McGuire certainly had nothing to worry about in the ten-year results, 1955–64. Profits more than doubled, reaching nearly $60 million in 1964, and the increase in sales was even greater (exhibit 13-8).

The uses of these funds in the ten-year period give many clues to the increasing strength of the company. Retained earnings were high all

Exhibit 13-8   **Deere Sales and Profits, 1955–64**

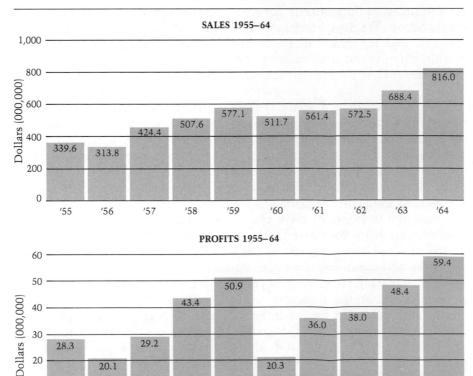

through this period (with the exception of the new-model year of 1960); the average for the last four years (1961–64) was more than 60 percent. After $40 million had been put into capital expenditures in the new-model year of 1960, substantial capital outlays also were made in each of the next four years (reaching $65 million in 1964). Beginning in 1960, the comptroller's report included precise figures on product research and development as a percentage of sales; the figure was well over 4 percent for each of the years from 1960 onward. Thus one of the signal marks of the Hewitt era—the high percentage of company resources invested in new product efforts and new manufacturing facilities—was put in place in this early period. At the same time, organizational changes in marketing found effect in a more aggressive and effective marketing team throughout the Deere organization itself and, especially, among its dealers. The latter group was greatly strengthened during 1955–64.

Perhaps the centerpiece of the first ten years of Hewitt's tenure was the completion of the Deere Administrative Center, which opened in June 1964. Eero Saarinen had died shortly before the construction of the building began; his colleagues, Kevin Roche and John Dinkeloo, finished the architectural planning and oversaw its construction. The concept of the building remained very much that of Saarinen. The site was a beautiful one and it was complemented by a surprising feature that Saarinen incorporated into the building; the exterior was constructed of unpainted steel girders, called "Cor-Ten," intended to weather and rust to blend into the countryside. (Some of the Deere engineers were most alarmed about this: "We've been warning farmers against rust for 120 years, now we are building a big, rusty building.")

The structure, once in place, was indeed striking, and it received dozens of awards. It was one of Saarinen's greatest triumphs, probably his most important administrative building, certainly a worthy companion for many of Saarinen's beautiful public buildings around the world. When articles are written in architectural journals and general-interest publications citing the best of the world's architecture, the Deere Administrative Center is often among those buildings pictured. As an architectural and aesthetic success, the Deere Administrative Center is outstanding.

Beyond this, though, the building was more than just a physical structure to win awards from *Architectural Forum*. It was a statement by the company that it strove for the best in quality, style, and effectiveness. C.R. Carlson, one of the more conservative of the older board members, penned a delighted letter to Hewitt on his first day in the new building. "I have spent the biggest share of my years with Deere working in old buildings. At Welland, as you well know, they were cheap and badly constructed to start with. At Waterloo during the period I spent there we lived in an old wooden second story office that had been built on as a makeshift, and even with water on the roof we cooked all summer long. . . . At Minneapolis, after we put in all new lighting, moved the men's and women's washrooms from right out in front of the sales department offices, and opened the whole office area up, they were comfortable and livable, but of course they were old and nothing like this. I must say that the surroundings are wonderful and the building itself is an excellent one in which to work.... I am sure that it is going to be conducive to better work on the part of all of us who have the privilege of working here."[15]

Carlson's words were a particularly appropriate summary of the first ten years of Hewitt's leadership. The "old guard" had indeed been won over; with considerably more unanimity of purpose than had characterized 1955, the company seemed ready to take on the challenges of the still-sagging international outreach. This key segment of Hewitt's plans had not taken hold.

CHAPTER 14

OBSTACLES ABROAD

Advanced farm equipment and skills have played a positive role in building a modern state farm. It has emancipated people's minds, broadened their vision and made them realize that mechanization is the fundamental way to increase agricultural output. . . . It has battered down management methods that are inappropriate to agricultural mechanization and brought about many changes in farm management.

Guangming Ribao
People's Republic of China, 1979

◁*Balers awaiting shipment at Arc-lés Gray, France, 1978 (JD Journal).*

The year 1964 was "the best ever." Deere's net sales totaled $816 million, its net income more than $60 million (7.3 percent of sales). Yet within this satisfying company-wide performance, difficulties in the foreign operations were a constant source of frustration to management and a drain on company resources. Though the Mexican and Argentine operations each had a small profit, all the rest of the major foreign operations registered unsettlingly substantial losses. Most serious was the German loss of $5.2 million. The French operation dropped more than $1.6 million, Spain was in the red for more than $1 million, and South Africa had a loss of almost $500,000. The pattern continued unmitigated in 1965, 1966, and 1967, with Germany alone losing almost $40 million total in those three years; France lost more than $9 million in this same period; the Argentine operation lost $7.6 million alone in the year 1967.

Not until eight years after that euphoric year of 1964 was the international operation able to turn a profit. It took a full decade for the pivotal German operation to shuck its persistent pattern of losses. A number of problems conspired to produce what turned out to be almost two decades of difficulties in Deere's bold decision to "go multinational." Many new ways of producing and marketing farm machinery in differing environments had to be mastered, and the learning curve for these turned out to be steeper than had been first imagined. In addition, two sets of more fundamental questions about international operations also had to be resolved before the international operation became a balanced component of the business.

First was the problem of structuring the organization itself. Could the domestic operations just be extended intact beyond the shores of North America, as Deere originally thought, or was a totally new structure needed? Further, could Deere go it alone, or was it necessary to join with another strong company, presumably a foreign one, and likely to be European? A second set of questions related to the rampant nationalism in a number of the countries Deere had entered. Could the company live with some of the increasingly stringent demands put upon it by individual countries, particularly relating to import restrictions and local-content restraints? Further, Deere found itself working in, or dealing with, countries whose political and economic philosophies differed sharply from those of the United States. The Eastern bloc and other Socialist countries espoused particular viewpoints that made business arrangements additionally complex; some countries, particularly South Africa, posed complications for Deere outside of the business realm, relating to political ideologies. Finally, questions were being raised about the very appropriateness of Western technology in the developing world. These additional enigmas, beyond the already difficult business situation, made Deere's international outreach a complicated one in the period 1965–80.

REORGANIZING FOREIGN OPERATIONS

To this point, Deere had carried all of its major foreign subsidiaries on its books as equity investments, not consolidated in the company financial statements each year. This had the signal disadvantage that losses could not become offsets in the calculation of United States corporate income taxes for the company. In Germany, there was a further complication that went beyond any narrow financial concern: the German public held a minority of Lanz shares, about 3 percent; under German law this required outside business and labor members on the company's board. All the company's reports and performance instantly became a matter of public information, in a country well known for a relentless business press and a watchful public very keenly interested in business developments. For a fresh, untried competitor, this fish bowl atmosphere was very disconcerting. "Publication . . . has been a detriment of an undeterminable magnitude to our business because of this public knowledge," Frank McGuire told the board in April 1967. McGuire, who was managing director of Region II, which included the European operation, recommended that Lanz revert to a branch operation, similar to a domestic branch. The Deere board concurred and authorized purchase of the minority shares. The offer was a fair one and the outside shareholders sold with alacrity, probably glad to be out of what they perceived to be a star-crossed company.

Unfortunately, the German press reported the sale in unflattering terms. One headed its article (as translated into English), "Heritage Staked and Lost: The Story of an Unsuccessful American Business Venture"; another had a nostalgic article on the long history of Lanz, ending its article, "This name 'Lanz' must not be allowed to be forgotten." Still a third chimed in, "Lanz Stockholders Did Not Wear Mourning." Deere felt the spillover from an inchoate anti-American attitude, and the shift to being a "branch operation" of a foreign company did not help.

Though the branch modus for Germany improved Deere's financial figures, persistent trouble spots remained in the company's handling of foreign operations. It finally was becoming clear that Deere's overall organizational structure was impeding company growth, rather than facilitating it. The greatest difficulties loomed in the international side of the business, where the functional approach and the lack of an on-the-spot management presence had led to substantial confusion. But there were also problems in the North American organizational structure: still too many constraints on marketing's participation in product planning, the failure to resolve questions of overall responsibility for engineering, and uncertainty over the precise role of the rapidly growing industrial equipment division.

Early in 1966, Booz, Allen & Hamilton was summoned again for another organizational study. It turned out to be a major endeavor, extending over seven months and involving five separate progress reports. The Booz, Allen analysts were particularly critical of missteps in the international operations stemming, they believed, from wrong choices in organizational planning back in 1963. They uncovered strong evidence that European design requirements were being given secondary consideration in the North American planning and engineering process. It seemed to take too long to get technical assistance from the United States, and specifications were reportedly changed with little or no advance notification. Further, the unit heads and the regional directors abroad had not exercised the authority inherent in the decentralized concept; this had led to poor performance and excessive turnover in key jobs abroad. There appeared to be a "lack of urgency . . . a lack of leadership" (the consultant's words) in the foreign operations, compounded by confusing signals from senior management in Moline, most of whom evidenced an unsettling degree of myopia about the individual foreign operations. There were especially severe problems in the coordination between France and Germany: "Plant and branch managers and their subordinates are expected to resolve their mutual problems with their counterparts. This has not worked well nor is it likely to when many of the people really do not understand the Deere philosophy, have been in their positions only a short time, often cannot communicate in a common language, and have inadequate written descriptions of responsibilities and procedures. . . ."

Resolution of this apparently widespread mismanagement could be effected, the Booz, Allen analysts maintained, by organizing the international businesses "on a general management concept"—with one senior executive in charge of all manufacturing and marketing abroad. For Europe, the dominant problem area, the consultants urged the appointment of a strong vice president and general manager, to be resident in Europe, with "authority and stature to straighten out the present unsatisfactory situation." The analysts made their point crystal clear: "The Company cannot afford to continue to rely on Deere & Company management resident in Moline to provide this leadership. It has not worked well and the continued financial deterioration in Europe attests to the need for taking drastic action."

For the domestic side, the Booz, Allen analysts were satisfied that the North American farm equipment business should continue to be organized on a functional basis, but they did recommend that the North American industrial equipment business be split off into a separate division "as soon as practical." To strengthen product planning, its executives were to be given a reporting relationship directly to the general-company marketing executive. The domestic factories would continue to have the basic responsibility for product development and design, where the Booz, Allen analysts felt they had done an outstanding job.

This time the board adopted the Booz, Allen recommendations almost in toto. The organization plan, as announced in a major memorandum in late November 1966, provided that George French assume the position of senior vice president, overseas operations, in charge of all manufacturing and marketing abroad. Reporting to French were John H. Graflund as vice president, overseas administration; Francis T. McGuire, managing director, Europe and Africa (Region II); and William R. Klingberg as managing director, Latin America and Australia (Region I). C.R. Carlson retired the following March, and Edgard W. Ukkelberg then became senior vice president, North American operations. French's successor as head of manufacturing and engineering, also at the senior vice president level, was A.B. Lundahl. The rest of the senior officers reporting to Curtis and Hewitt were: Frank M. Dickey as vice president, industrial relations and personnel; Joseph Dain, Jr., vice president, corporate planning; Lewis D. Wilson, vice president and general counsel; and Clifford L. Peterson, vice president, finance.

The most critical ingredient of this plan was sending Frank McGuire to Europe as managing director, the first time that a senior executive of the company had actually been physically stationed overseas. One major exception was taken to the Booz, Allen report—the industrial equipment division was left in place. Robert J. Gerstenberger, who was the director of industrial equipment marketing, reported to Ukkelberg, and the industrial equipment manufacturing was combined with that of tractors under the leadership of H.B. McKahin. By 1969 the industrial equipment division had its own separate marketing organization and in 1970 the original Booz, Allen recommendation that there be a separate division was carried through (George French heading the division for a year before his retirement, Delno W. Brown replacing him at that time).

Domestically the system preserved most of the strong features of decentralization. Some people, though, viewed the reorganization of 1966 as an incipient effort to draw together more authority at the top. Hewitt was concerned enough about any misreading of the plan to comment to the board on the need "of ensuring that the Company's policy of decentralization is in fact being implemented at all levels of the corporate structure. . . . This policy needs constant reiteration so that personnel will not lapse into centralization modes of operation." Hewitt gave practical effect to this by taking this occasion also to remind the board of his strong feeling that personnel should be promoted on the basis of ability, without regard to seniority or age. He stressed particularly the need for "giving promising young employees as much responsibility as they can take as soon as possible. . . . Young people want and need challenges to develop latent abilities."

Hewitt's bulletin to the organization about the new assignments chose not to elaborate on the profound change that had been made in the conceptualization of the overseas structure on a "general management" basis. He warned only that "in many instances they will require substantial changes in familiar habits and relationships." The careful, staged approach of the consulting effort, specified by Hewitt at the start, ensured that everyone concerned had been personally involved in the process, and so there were no surprises at the end. This caution paid off, for the organizational realignment was well received. Deere already was a full-scale multinational corporation; in 1966 for the first time it had the organizational structure to fit that status.

SEEKING A PARTNER: TALKS WITH DEUTZ

The unremitting flow of red ink in the foreign operations persisted through the remainder of the 1960s, despite the reorganization. There had been a short-lived upturn in Germany in 1967 with the arrival of the new Mannheim tractors, the first models designed specifically for the European market. But the agricultural market remained depressed, the old negative Lanz image was exploited by rival firms, and competition continued to be cutthroat, with numerous firms selling tractors below cost. Germany alone lost $19.6 million in 1968, $20.6 million in 1969, and a very unsettling $25.7 million in 1970. The worldwide sales of Deere & Company had risen steadily in the six years 1965–70 and profitability was substantial, though it dropped toward the end of the decade. But serious losses from the overseas operations continued to be heavy (Appendix exhibits 26 and 27).

There were abundant criticisms of the company during this period. Moline management seemed particularly stung (perhaps more than they should have been) by a highly negative article in the German newspaper, *Die Zeit*, in May 1969. The title (translated), "The Gambled Heritage: The History of an American Failure," telegraphed its uncomplimentary message. "Region II is still a weak point. Here the shield animal, the leaping deer, goes lame on the hind legs," the author began. "The new uncles from America came with their pockets full of money" but "their European ambassadors were not good publicity makers. . . . They still do not master the German language . . . they confirmed Jean-Jacques Servan-Schreiber's conclusion that the Americans made more mistakes in Europe than their competitors. At the same time they refuted his opinion that they could well adapt to local conditions."

Deere certainly was not the only American firm to be raked over the coals by the Europeans at this time. The earlier worship of American management superiority, in the late 1940s and early '50s, had long since dissipated; not only had European recovery brought renewed strength in its business sectors (with concommitant pride and chauvinism), but the unpopular American involvement in the Vietnam War negatively affected United States business firms abroad. Still, one cannot gainsay the fact that Deere itself continued to be viewed as an inept newcomer even after fifteen years in Europe. Most of the "bad press" was a direct function of the company's unremitting losses. It was hard for Deere to take, and by the fall of 1970 there was a siege mentality in Moline about the overseas troubles.

At this point, McGuire wrote Hewitt a blunt letter outlining his thoughts on possible alternatives. The most critical issue, he felt, was the Mannheim tractor factory: "Unless we can solve this problem we will continue to have poor performance. It cannot be solved by lower-cost designs alone. We need this, and in addition the very strong benefits to be obtained by economics of scale." McGuire sketched out six possible alternatives: (1) Make all the Dubuque tractors in Mannheim; (2) Form a joint venture with Klockner-Humboldt-Deutz, the Cologne, Germany, truck and tractor company; (3) Consider essentially the same notion with Fiat, the Turin, Italy, conglomerate; (4) Purchase tractors with or without equity involvement from one of the British manufacturers, David Brown or Leyland; (5) Purchase tractors from Japan; (6) Close down and liquidate the Mannheim operation.

Each of the six alternatives had danger signals embedded in it. If all the Dubuque tractors were made in Mannheim, McGuire foresaw a break-even operation, but with serious problems back at Dubuque and Waterloo. Either of the joint ventures had promise, but there would be major difficulties in meshing the product lines and manufacturing facilities, as well as rationalizing the two managements, the marketing structures, etc. Either one of the British proposals, said McGuire, "would be a business of retreat in the eyes of people, but in view of our loss situation it is not totally unpalatable." The Japanese had had little experience with agricultural tractors: "Our experience with Hitachi did not give us a base of experience on which to build." The closing of the Mannheim operation "means simply getting out of the tractor business except perhaps for the pocket markets. . . . We could remain in the pocket markets of Argentina, Mexico, Spain and Australia, and be a short-line implement combine dealer with the EEC." But this had some strong negatives: "Our dealer organization is not strong, but in all probability this action would wreck them and cause chaos for a number of years. . . . It's a solution which is almost impossible to reverse at a later point in time should our successors seek to do so."

A wide divergence of thinking emerged in Moline about these alternatives. Some of the directors did not like any of the six proposals, preferring to continue frontally attacking the market for increased share, just as in the past. But this seemed to others a counsel of despair; the losses, if continued, would eventually erode the strength of the domestic operation. There was some support for exploring a joint venture. At this point, surprisingly without a formal board vote, conversations were initiated with Deutz.

Secret negotiations had been conducted between Deere and Klockner-Humboldt-Deutz AG as early as 1966. At that time the suitor was Deutz, through its chief executive officer, Dr. Karl-Heinz Sonne; Deere's representative was Curtis. Deutz wanted to increase its volume, and Sonne proposed that his firm supply Deere its tractor engines, with Deere providing transmissions for Deutz. In addition, Sonne intimated a possible relationship on combines (Deutz owned the Fahr organization, one of Germany's better-known combine manufacturers). There were also suggestions that Deere might buy Deutz forgings and gray iron castings, Deere to reciprocate with some sourcing for the Deutz Argentine operation through Deere's foundry operation there, a company called Cindelmet. Nothing came of the negotiations, however; Deere had just put its French engine factory at Saran into full operation, and the losses from the German operation were not yet so fearsome as to pressure the company to make a change. Indeed, Deere appeared a bit cavalier in the process of rejecting the overtures.

Four new years of astronomical losses in Germany changed the tune. In 1970 Deere was the aggressor; Curtis and Sonne again were the key negotiators. The two met in Cologne, Germany (the home office of Deutz), in April; once more the negotiations were highly confidential, for fear that premature public notoriety via the always assiduous German press might unduly upset employees, shareholders, bankers, and other interested parties.

The scope of the proposal became much larger. Indeed, Frank McGuire, who handled the on-the-spot contacts, sketched a breathtaking vista in a letter to Hewitt and Curtis in August: "When we were together with Dr. Sonne and his associates, we touched on a full collaboration which in our context would have evolved as an end case into a joint venture up to a full merger." (Sonne, though, did not react as enthusiastically to the notion of a full merger; apparently, he felt that he could not sell it to his stockholders.)

At this point, Deutz was a company of approximately the same size as Deere, with total sales in 1969–70 of just over $800 million; its profit, though, was only about $5.9 million. Deutz also made trucks and buses and was in the seemingly unrelated business of planning and constructing industrial factory buildings.

As the delicate negotiations continued through the fall, both parties envisioned combining all of the tractor production of Deutz and Deere in Europe, as well as combining distribution in many other countries (excluding the United States, Canada, Mexico, Argentina, Spain, or Iran). There were further possibilities, such as a joint venture in Algeria.

At the same time, the hidden agendas of the two wary parties began to surface, exposing three dominant problems. The first was an expected one: how could the two marketing organizations be meshed? Both Deere and Deutz were proud names; neither management group seemed particularly willing to phase out its own colors, let alone face the unpleasant vista of meshing the two dealer organizations in the field. This problem might have been surmounted had not two other contentious issues surfaced: what should be the equity positions of the two parties in the final company, and how would management itself be shared, both at the board level and the operating level? Sonne proposed a fifty-fifty sharing of ownership and voting rights, with Deere taking 70 percent of the profits (the assets Deere would contribute were more than 70 percent of the total); Hewitt felt that the profit sharing was too low for Deere. The second issue was even more sensitive: Sonne did not want any constraints on the ability of the joint venture to eventually sell in the United States and Canada. Deere was not at all interested in subjecting its highly successful North American operations to any intrusive competition from a jointly managed outside entity. On this point, the negotiations began to seriously founder. The "chemistry" between the two management groups had just not been right.

At just about this time, Hewitt happened to meet again an old friend, Giovanni Agnelli, the chairman of Fiat, the huge Italian conglomerate. Agnelli was addressing a symposium in New York City, sponsored by the *Financial Times* of London. His speech held some prophecy for Deere: "Creating Europe's Industrial Giants." When Agnelli suggested that Fiat and Deere explore a joint venture for both agricultural and industrial equipment (but to exclude all United States and Canadian operations), Deere decided to break off the negotiations with Deutz. McGuire notified Sonne in May; the latter's gracious reply preserved the amicable relationship, Sonne even suggesting further talk about the Algerian project. But this never came to fruition and the Deutz-Deere negotiations were irrevocably terminated. Later that summer, the public finally was apprised of the aborted relationship when Sonne, answering a question from the floor at his company's annual meeting, replied that the project "had failed because KHD was not willing to go along with Deere's demand to desist from exporting tractors to North America."[1]

SECOND EFFORT: THE FIAT VENTURE

The Fiat negotiations, begun in December 1971, proceeded with astonishing rapidity. By late January Curtis and McGuire headed a task force of some forty Deere people from both Moline and the German headquarters, "operating under very tight security." Curtis exhorted all the participants that "absolute security is essential" and warned them not to do any trading of their Deere stock "until such time as the project has either been abandoned or been the subject of a public announcement." Harold J. Berry, Deere's outside investment counselor (who by this time was with Merrill, Lynch, Pierce, Fenner & Beane), had been brought into the discussions, as were Deere's bankers in London, its

auditors in Chicago and Milan, and
lawyers from both Chicago and
Washington. Additional counsel in
France and Italy were also employed. By mid-spring, Henry Dreyfuss and his colleagues had been
called in, to be queried about in-
compatibilities in design between
some of the products of the two
companies.

Fiat was the largest industrial
enterprise in Italy, one of the largest companies in Europe. About 88
percent of its overall sales were
automotive (automobiles, trucks);
it was the second most important
automobile producer in Europe,
outranked in sales of units only by
Volkswagen. In addition to its
namesake car, it owned Alpha
Romeo, half of Ferrari, and 30 percent of Citroën, the French auto
producer. The remaining 12 percent of the company's sales were
accounted for by an incredible variety of operations—production of
iron and steel, shipping, trading,
financing and insurance opera-

Exhibit 14–1. *Suggested logos for the proposed joint venture of Deere and Fiat (Deere Archives)*

tions, production of railway rolling stock, marine engines, aircraft,
nuclear energy, engines and turbines, machine tools, domestic applianc-
es, and lubricants.

Most important to Deere, Fiat also made agricultural tractors and
industrial equipment. In wheel tractors, Fiat produced just over double
what Deere was making in Europe in 1969 (Deere at that time had 4.2
percent of the market, Fiat 9 percent). Fiat also produced wheel tractors in
Argentina, where it had 57.3 percent of the market (to Deere's 19.8
percent). Both companies also operated in South Africa; there they were
quite close (Deere's 10.4 percent of the market balancing with Fiat's 13.7
percent). Deere also produced combines, its market share in Europe about
7.2 percent. Fiat was a major producer in Europe of crawler loaders and
dozers (Deere was a very small force there); the joint venture would have
about 35 percent of Europe's market. Fiat was also substantially involved
in wheel loaders, back-hoe loaders, and hydraulic excavators.

One particularly important asset from Fiat was the mechanical front-
wheel drive assist in its 60–90 horsepower sizes. Upwards of 20 percent of

Fiat's sales in Europe were in four-wheel drive vehicles. Curtis wrote Hewitt in early 1971: "We have never produced a four-wheel drive tractor at Mannheim because the standard mechanical four-wheel drive is not a practical possibility due to the design of the transmission of our tractors.... Some two years ago Mannheim was granted a significant appropriation to develop a hydrostatic front-wheel drive patterned after the Waterloo type.... This effort is not yet successful." The lack of this front-wheel drive capability had hurt Deere's European thrust.

Measuring the two companies side by side was difficult—the complex negotiations attempting to meld the two organizations had to grapple with these comparisons in a minute way. Deere's and Fiat's European agricultural and industrial equipment—when combined with the two companies' South African and Argentine operations, together with Fiat's Brazilian operations—added up to be two units of approximately the same size, close enough that a joint-venture could be contemplated without too much adjustment in working capital or other compensations. The Fiat agricultural and industrial enterprises were only a small part of the total Fiat empire, and not one of its most successful, either. The dominant size of the total Fiat operation was especially important because the incredibly complex Fiat operations had a great many merged costs, a complication that plagued the joint-venture discussions from start to finish. Fortunately, from the beginning, Fiat made it clear that it had no intention of eventually pushing the joint-venture company into the North American tractor market, a la Deutz.

The charisma of the Agnelli family was legendary, and its titular head, Giovanni ("Gianni" or "Johnny"), was the most legendary of all. (His brother, Umberto, was managing director of the family enterprise and also an important figure in the story.) In a fascinating article in the magazine *Car and Driver*, just at the time Deere entered negotiations with Fiat, Giovanni was called "the Prince" with an undisguised allusion to Machiavelli. The article spoke of his "multifarious" activities, the author clearly intending an unflattering implication. The writer, perhaps carried away by his own prose, called Agnelli "a beautifully combed and perfumed gray mouse running breathlessly on the inside of a spinning drum as scenes of technicolor utopia are flashed on its mirrored inner surface.... Gianni Agnelli is executive jets, double-breasted shirts, holidays at the world's glamour spots, contacts with hyper-isolated beautiful people." After painting such a broad brush, the article then enumerated the amazing variety of activities that Agnelli presided over and called him "the commander-in-chief of Italian industry." Both *Newsweek* and *Time* had also featured major articles on him at this time; he was even on the cover of *Time*, which called him "the most widely admired and envied Italian industrialist—the *Numero Uno*...." British journalist Anthony Sampson, in *The New Europeans*, commented, "Agnelli has a mythology not unlike President Kennedy's.... Clearly his presence fills some kind of psychological gap."

Superlatives sometimes overstate, but in this case Giovanni Agnelli appeared to be in real life as impressive in stature as were the accounts in the press. It was a heady opportunity for Deere, far and away the most exciting new venture in the post-World War II years. In substance and style, the notion of putting together Fiat and Deere was a compelling proposition; both were major producers, well known for their products, both had outstanding and distinctive managements, particularly at the top. In sum, the combination boded great promise.

Major study committees were formed by the two companies—a manufacturing group, a marketing group, and a financial group, each to report back to a central negotiating body. The latter, in turn, amassed all of the detail and incorporated it into an instrument called the "Heads of Agreement." It ran only thirty-five pages, including two appendixes, and yet in this short space incorporated the essence of the joint venture proposal in such a form that it could be acted upon operationally by the two boards. The new joint entity would include all of Deere's European holdings, as well as those in South Africa, Argentina, Iran, and Turkey; Fiat would contribute its agricultural and industrial equipment operations in Europe, as well as similar operations in Brazil, Argentina, Turkey, and Australia. All of Deere's European wheel tractors and all of Fiat's agricultural wheel tractors would be included, and Fiat would include its agricultural crawler tractors, back-hoe loaders, and crawler dozers. Deere would include certain of its crawler dozers, too. Deere and Fiat were to include their four-wheel drive loaders, Fiat would contribute its hydraulic excavators, and Deere would include certain models of scrapers, graders, and skidders. All of Deere's combines made in Europe would be included, as well as Deere and Fiat balers and forage harvesters. The capital of the joint-venture company would be held 50 percent by each of the parties, with the agreement providing ways of bringing each company's total contributions of working capital, equity, and borrowing to an equal amount. The agreement was to be carried out by July 31, 1971, if possible.

As this document was to be formal authority to proceed apace, the Deere board, when it met on May 17, 1971, knew the meeting had great portent. A number of misgivings surfaced in the many hours of discussion. Hewitt laid out the rationale for bringing the "Heads" agreement to the board: "A public announcement of some sort would be required before completion of these negotiations because too many people in both organizations would be involved in them to permit effective security. Since both parties believe it is unwise to make such an announcement without reasonable assurance that the venture will in fact be consummated, a commitment like the Heads seems a necessary step in the negotiating process. Further, a definition of the broad outlines of the venture . . . will be necessary to support certain discussions with governments, which it is desirable to complete before execution of a definitive agreement." Several members of the board then presented the economic rationale for the project; the "fit" appeared excellent, the case seemed strong.

There were risks: such a step might foreclose all other alternatives, there were knotty details in several important areas, disclosure would itself make the roles of the two companies more complicated. There was significant opposition from at least three of the directors. George French abstained, stating that "while he felt intuitively that the venture should be a useful solution he lacked sufficient information to make a reasonably prudent decision." D.C. Glover not only felt that information was lacking, but argued that the "Heads of Agreement" was a firm commitment that could not be turned around were there to be additional compromising information; he voted against the motion. A third board member, Frank Dickey, abstained, though not putting his misgivings on the record. An overwhelming majority of the board did want to go ahead, and the motion approving the "Heads of Agreement" was passed. Fiat, meanwhile, also had agreed to the proposition.

Now a public announcement of the joint-venture-company proposal was inevitable, and the press coverage (particularly in Europe) was substantial. The journalists commented extensively on the scope of its endeavor, its competitive implications for agricultural machinery in both Western and Eastern Europe, and in general seemed to applaud the move. There were some caveats, though; one influential French magazine asked how a fifty-fifty arrangement could work "by a Latin Expansionist and a Puritan Mid-Westerner." The German press seemed less complimentary to Deere, one paper editorializing: "When such a centralized company strives for a joint solution in an important part of the world market and in doing so allies itself with such a significant partner as Fiat, which is far stronger, then a great deal must have occurred to change the proud minds of the Americans." The Italian press, understandably, concentrated more on Fiat. The agreement did honor to the "enterprising Italian spirit" and would open up new work possibilities and social benefits. One paper alleged that Fiat was "in a state of extreme confusion," and some of the press implied that the venture was a labor relations ploy, that there would be strikes by "Leninist cells." A British correspondent asked whether "the 'new giant' would panic others into 'marriage.'" Much of the press commentary suffered from a lack of details—both Fiat and Deere had much work to do before any further public announcement.

Large teams from the two companies continued to work over the summer and fall of 1971. Agnelli paid a personal visit to Hewitt in Moline, and the latter reciprocated with a visit to Turin, both significant events in that they telegraphed to the organizations the continuing goodwill and desire for agreement on the part of the two chief executives. Cordiality was the hallmark of the meetings for the operating groups, too.

Out of the enormously complex negotiations leading to the many drafts of the "Agreement for Closing," the essential features of the original proposal stayed in place. One Fiat plant (in France) was eliminated, there were complicated questions about Fiat's Argentine operations that had to be answered, there were concerns about timing and about transfer prices for components. Even more difficult to assess were misgivings about the political stability of the project in Italy and in some of the Latin American countries.

Undoubtedly the most difficult problem throughout the negotiations was the projection of costs and profits. Deere was long used to being able to generate precise figures for such proposals; its American accounting practices, established by Curtis and his predecessor, T.F. Wharton, had given the company an analytical financial capability that demanded equally high caliber analysis from other participants. Fiat's accounting practices were truly different from those in the United States. The Fiat accounting and finance system permitted far greater discretion and the Deere executives found it frustrating not to get exact figures comparable to their own.

There was a further problem, unique to Fiat: its many other manufacturing endeavors (particularly those in automobiles and trucks) generated a wide range of common costs and intracompany interchanges that were almost impossible to quantify precisely. From the start, the Fiat projections of the joint-venture-company costs and profitability were quite optimistic, but Deere could not be certain just how realistic they really were. By November, it did appear that some of the projections needed to be downgraded, and the profitability of the joint-venture company seemed less attractive than it did back in May—they were "quite unsatisfactory . . . considerably less optimistic than those contained in the feasibility study," said one top Deere executive. The Fiat negotiators were game, though, and now suggested certain changes—particularly the exclusion of their French manufacturing plant, at Bourbon Lancy, to eliminate some of the overcapacity that had crept into the joint-venture company. In addition, some of the components that were to be supplied by Fiat to the joint-venture company were shifted over to the joint-venture company itself. "We'll guarantee a profit," one Fiat executive promised. The Deere negotiators, however, estimated that only about one-third of the improved financial projections of the new plan represented benefits that would have fairly certain consequences; the remainder represented only a more optimistic assessment of projected economic conditions in the near future.

Fiat at this point began to press Deere for a quick decision. Apparently Fiat felt the pressure of time; they had already spent the previous two years studying a joint venture with Allis-Chalmers, now they had invested another year with Deere. Given Fiat's skittishness, the Deere board decided to meet in an extraordinary session to be conducted over two days, January 11 and 12, 1972. The negotiating team presented all aspects of the proposal, including the new Fiat suggestions. Frank McGuire summarized the conclusion: "The likelihood of profitability which had been demonstrated was insufficient to justify taking the risks and accepting the burdens which are inherent in the joint venture. While it is conceivable that a more thorough probing of Fiat costs, especially for components to be sold to the joint venture, might uncover further possibilities for improvement, such probing could not be completed within the time period for final decisions which Fiat insists on." McGuire cited the further problem of loss of control in a fifty-fifty partnership and commented on the rather unstable political situation in Italy. Finally, the matter was put to a vote; the final decision, to terminate.

Agnelli fortuitously happened to be visiting Henry Ford II in Detroit the following day (Agnelli was in the city to address a meeting of the Society of Automotive Engineers). Hewitt and Curtis, leaving directly from the board meeting, were at the Ford estate for breakfast the following morning. The evident friendship that the two chairmen felt for each other continued to the end. Agnelli asked only one question: "Was it because of our government?" When Hewitt replied in the negative, Agnelli responded, "I have been in your home, and you in mine. Let us continue our friendships that way." The two men shook hands and the Deere-Fiat joint venture had ended.

GOING IT ALONE

As company officials took a retrospective look at the Fiat endeavor, they counted many pluses: "We learned a great deal about ourselves in the process." There is much truth in this assertion; the project forced company personnel to think in a more system-wide perspective, and the company became more "multinational" in the process. Yet there were high costs to the project, too. The salaries and expenses of dozens of people working many months on the project were substantial, particularly for top management. Still, this is a normal expenditure for any alert, growing company. There is little evidence that the out-of-pocket costs of the Fiat project were excessive; profits in 1971 were $63 million—5.3 percent of sales—the second highest profit in the company's history (exceeded only by 1966, at $78 million).

The nonmonetary costs of the negotiations were more substantial. Perhaps no other issue in the post-World War II period had so polarized the board as did the Fiat project. These were serious divisions, going beyond the usual day-by-day differences of opinion. D.C. Glover, at this point no longer in active management, was the most vocal critic, not only of the project but of the management style behind it. Glover abstained in the final vote for termination in the meeting of January 12 but made two suggestions for the record. First, he wanted "management" to present to the board at the following meeting "some suggestions for a solution to our foreign business problems." Second, he advocated that "the Board consider the desirability of bringing in one or more outside Board members with experience in overseas matters." Hewitt agreed that bringing in outside directors should be considered, though he felt that these should not necessarily be limited to persons whose experiences were primarily related to overseas activities. Glover was also exercised about a critical article that had appeared in the *Wall Street Journal* a few days earlier, alleging that the company had incorrectly reported its earnings for the year. (The allegation was patently untrue, and Hewitt adroitly answered the accusation by sending a printed copy of the article, with his marginal comments, to every shareholder.)

George French, too, had been in the "loyal opposition" to the Fiat project; there again the dissent ran deeper than just the Fiat project per se. French had objected to the haste with which negotiations were conducted and to what he felt was inadequate preparation by the Deere team for final board approval. French wrote Hewitt a blunt private letter, advocating "other options" (but did not specify any particulars). Shortly after the Fiat termination, French submitted his request for retirement from his post as senior vice president of the industrial equipment division; he remained a member of the board until 1974.

At the meeting of January 25, Hewitt reminded the board that at the beginning of the Fiat negotiations there had been three alternatives for the company: (1) withdraw from overseas business, (2) find a partner, or (3) go it alone. After a morning of discussion, the dominant opinion clearly favored the third alternative. Hewitt urged each director "to raise a question if he had any misgivings," but none surfaced. The results for 1971 were available at this time; the losses in Germany alone amounted to $26.5 million, the overall losses in the foreign operations were more than $23 million. Was "going it alone" going to continue such a pattern?

When news of the aborted Fiat negotiations became public, there was surprise and consternation among Deere's European dealers. Competitors were quick to exploit the malaise. Some Deere dealers were soon inveigled to defect to competitor products; there had been a particularly skeptical *Forbes* magazine article at the start of the negotiations that seemed to imply that the Fiat effort was a "do or die" hope by the company; one German competitor had the article translated to show to Deere dealers. Neel Hall, by this time director of all the European operations, was worried enough to urge Hewitt personally to attend the company's new product presentations scheduled for Zweibrücken in September. Referring to the *Forbes* article, Hall commented: "Taken out of context, these comments would make some people believe Deere's tenure in Europe would be short. I think that a statement from you to the dealers at this dealer meeting would be very helpful."

Hewitt not only agreed but, when the time came, brought all of the directors of the company with him for a major two-week visit to Germany, France, and Spain. The directors' wives were invited; even Charles Wiman's widow, Patricia, came for part of the sessions. A special meeting of the board was held in Heidelberg on September 11—the first time that a board meeting had ever been conducted outside the United States. Collateral meetings also took place with Pehr G. Gyllenhammar, the president of the Swedish automobile company, Ab Volvo. (Hewitt and Gyllenhammar were discussing a possible collaboration, though this did not later come to fruition.)

An international press conference was held early in the visit, with wide coverage by most of the key European business press. Hewitt took the opportunity not only to emphasize the company's North American strengths and the strong new product lines both in North America and Europe, but made it explicitly clear that Deere intended to stay in Europe. "We are carrying out this lengthy program . . . to make manifest to our employees, dealers, customers and competitors that we view our European operations as an integral and important part of our Company." Reactions from the press were reassuringly positive. *Le Figaro*, the French newspaper, headlined its article, "The American group John Deere takes up the offensive in Europe," and other papers commented on Deere "turning a new leaf" and deciding to "go it alone." An influential British trade paper emphasized "JD's aggressive market tactics." The directors' trip was a resounding success, reminiscent of the euphoric Day in Dallas in 1960; it seemed to defuse competitor inroads and certainly stopped the dealer raiding in its tracks.

Fiat resumed its negotiations with Allis-Chalmers and in 1973 did develop a viable joint venture, but limited in this case to industrial equipment. In 1973 Deere and Fiat once again considered a collaboration, a joint venture for the manufacture of diesel engines. Fiat also hoped to sell its trucks and forklift vehicles in North America. After a brief exchange of ideas, Curtis wrote Fiat that Deere had decided to continue alone in its diesel engine production, but he mentioned again that "the friendship and trust of the Fiat organization are important to us and are a source of satisfaction to us."

The judgment of the board about "going it alone" did indeed prove correct. Few would have predicted that a turnaround would come as quickly as it did, however. The company had put in place a sound organization overseas—the product lines were improved, the manufacturing operations had been realigned and rationalized (at considerable cost), and the dealer organizations were, if not excellent, at least adequate to the job. Further, there was a substantial upturn in European business in the early 1970s, already becoming evident toward the end of the Fiat negotiations. To the evident delight of everyone, the overseas results for 1972 were a net $2.9 million profit (after a $21.5 million loss in 1971).

Australia was still in a start-up position and had lost $1.4 million, Spain had lost $2 million, and the German operation still showed a $9.3 million loss, but the other major operations were profitable enough to compensate. In 1973 the results were even more satisfying—the overseas operation as a whole netted $26.9 million profit. Though the Mannheim factory had still lost $3.7 million, the Zweibrücken factory and the domestic branch were profitable enough for the German operations to show a sizable profit. In 1974 the overseas operation registered a profit of $23.1 million, and this time Germany showed a profit of more than $13 million. The company's decade-and-a-half search for a profitable multinational status had finally been realized.[2]

ECONOMIC NATIONALISM IN MEXICO

In several countries in which Deere manufactured or assembled equipment, the ingredients of a "pocket market" were in place. Usually this term connotes a generally small, local market within a country, insulated from the outside by high tariffs or outright prohibition on imports. The cost of manufacturing and distribution by domestic firms is often higher than it is in the international market because of small production runs, inefficiencies in labor, inadequacies in machinery, etc. Government officials in "pocket market" countries face complex choices about how much international competition the country can take; the strength of indigenous businesses and the economic fortunes of their employees are deeply affected by such competition. This insulation is perpetuated by requirements that foreign companies manufacturing or assembling in the country use considerable proportions of locally made components and parts and that portions of the foreign companies' local operation be owned by nationals. Economic nationalism in countries around the world varies widely from minimal to almost prohibitive. Deere now began to face increasing constraints.

By 1967 the Mexican government had begun to insist on 60 percent local content. With engines and most of the transmissions used by Deere still manufactured in the United States, almost all of the remaining components and parts had to be manufactured or purchased locally. Costs for these were typically higher than in the United States; the bugaboos of small production runs and less efficient manufacturing practices both held sway. But a pervasive populist sentiment, in place since the Mexican Revolution in 1910, made it politically unpopular to penalize farmers by "high" prices of the final product. So price controls were rigidly applied in the tractor sizes manufactured by the company in Mexico (the 60–120 horsepower range); they were particularly onerous during the administration (1970–76) of Pres. Luís Echeverría Álvarez, when politics split the Ministry of Industry and Commerce into two separate groups. Industry lost the function of price control and import permits for machines and parts to Commerce, whose political constituency was the customer. The Ministry of Agriculture also wielded considerable power and seemed always to favor low import prices for farmers. Deere's operation in Mexico did eliminate losses after 1962, and even during the 1970–76 period continued to make modest profits, the $1.7 million figure in 1976 being the largest (it was about 4 percent of its sales). But profitability only became possible because of good margins on imported tractors in the higher horsepower sizes and on imported combines. The Mexican-built tractors were losing money throughout this period.

In 1977, the Mexican government announced a new "Automotive Manufacturing Decree," which for the first time included tractors. Local content was to be reduced from a flat 60 percent to a lower percentage tied to the ability of the manufacturer to export some of its production from Mexico—in effect, a "compensatory exports" credit. Mexican tractor companies generally imported substantial amounts of larger horsepower tractors, and some also imported other expensive specialized machinery, such as combines, which might cost upwards of $50,000 each. Were the tractor companies to be forced to compensate for all of these expensive, specialized imports?

The formula, as eventually evolved by the government, was a complicated one. In essence, Mexican companies were to be required to export the equivalent of 70 percent of all their imports, the latter to be figured at cost price (70 percent of list). In turn, a company could drop its local content from 60 percent to 50 percent and could even further diminish these figures by increasing the actual growth in sales of its Mexican operation (that is, expanding companies were to gain further concessions).

These new requirements were double edged. On the one hand, the drop from 60 percent to 50 percent local content was a major break—some comparatively expensive operations could be eliminated. For example, in the early 1980s Deere was able to import fully assembled engines from the company's European operations, whereas in the past substantial local assembly of motors had had to be utilized. The negatives lay in the rigorous requirements for export. During the recession of the early 1980s it was particularly difficult to fulfill these requirements. Among the Mexican tractor manufacturers Deere came the closest to meeting the compensatory equation; choppers and shredders were shipped from Mexico to other Deere operations abroad, under the aegis of the Ottumwa factory (Ottumwa losing the production in the process). But Deere and the other Mexican manufacturers had increasing problems finding export outlets, for nationalism and protectionism were running rampant around the world and local manufacturers in other countries pressured their governments to protect them from outside competition. Finally, the Mexican authorities realized that they had to be flexible in applying the export requirements, and there was some informal letup in their pressure on the companies.

In 1978, under the government of Pres. José López Portillo, the Ministry of Agriculture and the Rural Credit Bank announced an ambitious expansion program to increase areas under cultivation and to significantly mechanize agriculture. The government in earlier years consistently had been the largest purchaser of tractors; the substantial new government orders were to emphasize large tractors, those particularly built by Deere. Because Mexican manufacturers did not have enough capability to supply such an order as well as the rest of the market, the government initially intimated that substantial imports were going to be necessary. But this brought an outcry of criticism in the public press—why did the country have to import tractors when it had a domestic industry? The foreign companies found themselves in a "Catch-22" situation. If they were allowed to import, there would be intense local reaction; if they expanded domestically in Mexico, the stringent price controls and harsh requirements on local content and compensatory exports made the prospects quite unattractive. This, too, was not what the public wanted to hear.

There was another alternative—the government itself could take care of the increased production needs. By the mid-1970s the pressure for "Mexicanization" already had led both Ford and Massey-Ferguson to suggest the sale of a majority position to the government, and in the early 1980s Ford did consummate such a plan (with Nafinsa, a government bank, taking 60 percent ownership). International Harvester, meanwhile, had sold a majority of its tractor and engine operations to a private Mexican company and had a link with a private Mexican bank for its industrial equipment. Massey-Ferguson sold its entire holdings to a large private conglomerate, the Alfa group of Monterrey; it retained certain licensing and sales agreements in this process.

The private manufacturers were naturally ambivalent about the government involving itself in production. Political pressures on the government by the farmers often forced short-term decisions on price control, etc. On the other hand, a government company often acted as an umbrella over price, particularly if the government operation was somewhat less efficient than a comparable private one.

Deere itself had a further complication: it was under increasing pressure about its own Mexicanization. The earlier attempt to sell shares publicly had aborted, and 26 percent of its shares were still held in trusteeship; by this time, Banco Nacional de México—Banamex—had increased its holdings to about 17 percent, with an additional 8 percent held by other private investors. The government's Foreign Investment Commission now ruled that trusteeship was not true Mexicanization, and this was upheld by the courts. Apparently the government feared that if Deere could successfully use a trusteeship, other foreign manufacturers would immediately attempt the same route; the government felt that this would thwart their own goal of a more nationalistic base for Mexican industry.

Companies in the country that were not majority-owned by Mexicans were not to be allowed to expand in any way. There was a particular threat in this for Deere, for Allis-Chalmers had entered the country to manufacture combines with significant local content. Deere already had some 65 percent of the market with its imported combines; if there were to be further constraints on importation because of the lack of Mexicanization, Deere's market share in combines would shrink.

Several choices were potentially available to Deere. The company could arrange a direct sale of the 26 percent block through private placement, with the buyer either a private group or the government. But such a sale did not provide new financing for expansion and had negative tax implications in the United States. A more desirable approach would be to constitute a new joint venture with a partner and have the latter put enough new capital into the organization to bring the Deere percentage down to 49 percent. Fortunately for Deere, the latter approach became a reality, for Banamex agreed in early 1982 to provide such funding and to join with Deere in increasing the capital structure.[3]

"YO-YO" NATIONALISM IN ARGENTINA AND VENEZUELA

Nationalism was not only strong in Argentina and Venezuela, it was also more unpredictable than it was in Mexico. While Deere may have preferred stability, like most business firms, it encountered in these two countries wide swings in political leadership and sharp changes in economic policies.

Deere's Argentine operation had been on a considerably larger scale than in Mexico, but profitability had been more elusive. (With the exception of 1964, there were continuous losses until 1972.) The decade after the mid-1960s was one of great tension in the country. From 1968, during the regime of Gen. Juan Carlos Onganía, a spate of terrorist atrocities by urban guerrillas subjected Argentina to a reign of terror. The aims of the shadowy groups were dominantly political, but they chose to kidnap (and often kill) industrial leaders, both businessmen and labor leaders. Fiat's managing director had been murdered. Many foreign companies pulled out all of their nationals, and even Argentine nationals in companies were threatened by kidnap, attack, or maiming. The clandestine terror seemed directed particularly at foreign companies, but no operation, Argentine or foreign, was without its fears. One could never be certain whether the union leaders across the bargaining table truly represented their employees; outrage from the left and repression from the right dominated the country. Accompanying this was galloping inflation. The political scene soon took a surprising shift with the return of Gen. Juan Perón to take leadership of the country. Perón died after a year and his demise eventually brought back another military government. The pattern of guerrilla attacks finally tapered off in the late 1970s, but the decade of turmoil had done great damage to the country's business system. In the late 1970s an agricultural depression also hit. Interest rates had been freed from control and had risen enormously—indeed, far over the actual inflation rate, and interest payments combined with greater agricultural taxation to put the farmer into depression. Agricultural machinery sales declined as a result:

	Total	Deere	Deere Market Share
1976	20,674	3,423	16.5%
1977	21,699	3,506	16.1
1978	6,666	1,744	26.1
1979	7,962	1,508	18.9
1980	4,877	1,413	28.9
1981	2,800	821	29.3

During the 1970s, four major manufacturers—Deere, Deutz, Fiat, and Massey-Ferguson—shared roughly one-quarter of the market each. Each of the companies had been forced to develop full-scale manufacturing facilities in Argentina; the government's local-content requirement had risen as high as 95 percent. Deere even had found it necessary to purchase a separate Argentine company, Cindelmet, a manufacturer of rough castings, blocks, heads, machine tools, and windmills. A series of decrees in the late 1970s eased the stringent local-content requirement, but at the same time the barriers on importations were abruptly eased. In the process, the indigenous Argentine tractor companies suddenly found themselves competing with lower-cost imports. This development, combined with the collapse of the market due to the farmers' depression, convinced Deere in 1978 to cease manufacturing in the country. The Argentine legal entity was terminated and the net tax loss of $17.5 million was absorbed in the Deere & Company figures for 1981. Manufacturing virtually ceased at the Rosario plant; the Argentine operation was converted to a branch, with part of the Rosario plant continuing to be used for assembly of components manufactured at other Deere locations in Europe and the United States. Cindelmet, the Argentine subsidiary, was sold.

Thus Argentina lost a tractor factory capable of producing at least 6,000 units per year. Deere emphasized to Argentine authorities that it had no intention of abandoning the Argentine market—it was willing to compete in a market dominated by imports. In a letter to Argentina's minister of economics, José A. Martínez de Hoz in May 1980, Robert Hanson,

Deere's president, did warn, though, that "proliferation of tractor makes in Argentina through indiscriminate importation of units from all over the world cannot work to the farmer's advantage.... Eventually the market will sort out the winners from the losers, but I would suggest that without restricting imports . . . guidelines should require the manufacturer to prove that he has sufficient stock of repair parts, trained personnel and on-site service points reasonably close to the farmer to adequately maintain the operating integrity of the unit he hopes to sell.... Argentina has a great deal to lose by allowing itself to become an uncontrolled dumping ground for farm machinery exporters." With Argentina's great agricultural promise, the world will surely be watching carefully to see what evolves in the 1980s, as Argentina pursues this new path. Meanwhile, the country had lost a significant portion of its domestic agricultural machinery capacity.[4]

Much the same abrupt change of policy occurred in Venezuela in the late 1970s, and Deere again was caught in the middle. Shortly after Carlos Andrés Pérez Rodriguez took office as president of Venezuela in 1974, he invited tractor manufacturers from around the world to submit bids for a project to manufacture (not simply assemble) tractors in Venezuela. These were to be in Venezuela's popular sizes—from 60 to 120 horsepower—and were to have 60 percent or so national content. Venezuela had long suffered from the syndrome of predominantly imported goods; the tractor project was seen as an opportunity to provide critically needed agricultural equipment within the country. The Pérez government did apparently recognize that such a domestic operation, with small production runs, could not compete frontally against low-priced imported tractors, so the government promised a 30–35 percent customs duty protection to overcome any differential.

Twelve different international tractor manufacturers submitted bids for the project. The winner (this word seemed applicable at the time) was Deere & Company. A new company was established, Fabrica Nacional de Tractores Motores, S.A. (Fanatracto); the Venezuelan government held 45 percent ownership (through its Guayana development corporation). Deere took 20 percent, its local distributor took an additional 15 percent, and a financial organization reserved another 20 percent of equity for subsequent sale to other local distributors and groups of retail tractor buyers. The government said it chose Deere because of Deere's excellent reputation, high market penetration in Venezuela, and low cost projections for the project.

Fanatracto was to manufacture diesel engines—some 5,500 per year— and these were to be used not only for the tractors but as marine engines, in construction equipment, and so on. The government stipulated that the plant for the project be located in Ciudad Bolívar, a developing area in the southeast of the country, some 150 miles upstream from the mouth of the Orinoco River. This was not the ideal location for an agricultural machinery factory—the natural markets were far to the north and west—but the government was keen on developing this largely jungle area. Deere projections did show a modest but economically viable market demand for tractors in the country; there were further export possibilities to other Andean Pact countries, particularly Colombia, Ecuador, and Peru. The industrial site in Ciudad Bolívar was also to house a planned Mack-Fiat diesel truck factory.

By mid-1978 Fanatracto had acquired land and begun the construction of a substantial 25,000-square-meter plant. At the same time a pilot plant nearby had been opened for the assembly of a small number of Deere tractors from Waterloo as a part of a major training program for workers who would later be involved in the manufacturing plant. This pilot project soon had tractors rolling off its assembly line; one of them achieved considerable publicity when President Pérez rode it during the presidential election campaign in 1978. Within months, substantial numbers were coming off the assembly line, some 3,200 in total from the pilot plant.

But Fanatracto had enemies, and they began insinuating that the company was somehow cheating on the original agreement—just assembling tractors rather than manufacturing them. The company might have survived these charges had not two unexpected developments occurred. First, there was a substantial economic downturn beginning in 1979, bringing outcries in the farming communities about the high price of the domestic tractor as against what the farmers might pay were foreign tractors to be allowed in the country. The second event was a change in administration, with the election of Pres. Luis Herrera Campins in 1979. Herrera had a substantially different economic philosophy from Pérez— he maintained that domestic demand was large enough to absorb both local tractors and substantial numbers of imported tractors, and he began allowing the latter to come into the country. In turn, Herrera refused to follow through on the customs duty protection promised by the previous administration (the minister of development had approved a 25 percent duty in principle, but it was never implemented). By late 1980, Fanatracto was losing so much money because of high interest charges on the construction project and the substantial losses on each unit of production that it was forced to close the assembly operation. The Herrera cabinet members concluded that the project should be terminated because its high-priced tractors "were not economically justified." When protests were made about the closing, Development Minister Quijada snapped that the only local content in Fanatracto's tractors was "the air in the tires." Other critics pointed out that the awarding of a factory to one company was monopolistic and that high Venezuelan manufacturing costs would never allow the tractor price to be competitive. In truth, the project could have avoided what became a chaotic tractor situation: more than thirty tractor models were imported from all over the world, with practically none backed by service and parts organizations. With Fanatracto's equity arranged so that dealers and groups of tractor users could have had ownership interest in the project, some of the prior difficulties in Venezuela of narrowly based, monopolistic companies might have been avoided.

By 1980, the project was moribund and the assembly operation abandoned. The new factory building, just completed, was put up for sale (with little likelihood that there would be a purchaser). A major article in the influential commercial magazine, *Business Venezuela*, concluded that while the project was "hailed during its short life as one of the most practical and best-planned projects initiated under the government of Pérez . . . it suggests to future investors—both local and foreign—that Venezuelan governments are incapable of recognizing and supporting sound projects inherited from their predecessors, and that a 'firm' commitment made by one group of politicians in power can be meaningless when another group takes office." The Deere executives who put five years of their time in a project that simply disappeared probably would second this judgment.[5]

CONTRASTS: IRAN, TURKEY, BRAZIL, AUSTRALIA

Another victim of political instability was Deere's operation in Iran,

Exhibit 14–2. *Billboard advertising greater productivity with John Deere machinery, Teheran, Iran, 1976 (JD Journal)*

the change in fortune in this case caused by the Iranian hostage crisis of 1979–80. In the late 1960s the Iranian government had launched a major agricultural development effort, and, after trying imported tractors from Romania with poor results, had decided that it wanted its own combine manufacturing plant in the country. Deere was contacted, and subsequent negotiations resulted in a proposal for a factory at the town of Arak (Sultanabad), south and west of Teheran. A joint venture company was formed for the partial manufacture, assembly, and sale of Deere combines, with the intention that tractors and cultivating equipment be added at a later date. Deere's interest was to be 21 percent; a government corporation, the Industrial Development and Renovation Organization (IDRO) took 49 percent, with Deere's distributor in Iran and another private holder taking the remainder.

Arak was a backward area that the government hoped to industrialize; its first step was to erect a massive factory building—a "monument," said one of the Deere executives after seeing it. Though Deere combines did come off the assembly line in small numbers in the early and mid-1970s, the difficulties of manufacture in Arak and the lack of government-promised financing of retail sales resulted in high losses. By 1974 Deere stepped back from major responsibility in management. (Deere had up to this point provided the managing director; now this person was to be furnished by the government.) The company continued to provide components to the operation from its German combine factory at Zweibrücken. The capital of the Iranian company was increased in 1976, and Deere decided to maintain its 21 percent ownership (the government's holdings being 51 percent). When relations worsened between Iran and the United States in the hostage crisis, all Deere business was suspended. The plant continued to be maintained, operating under the aegis of a workers council. After the hostage crisis was resolved, the Iranian company once again became an important customer for combines and combine components.

Internal political upheavals also caused difficulties for Deere in Turkey. From before World War II, one of Deere's most stable Mideast dealers had been the Cukurova group in Turkey, which sold both Deere and Caterpillar equipment. In 1966 the Turkish government threatened to close its borders to imported equipment, so the Cukurova group formed a new company for the assembly of Deere combines (with components shipped out of Zweibrücken); they called this new organization Cukurova Makina Imalat ve Ticaret A.S. (Cumitas). Deere invested $200,000 in the organization, approximately 10.6 percent of the stock. By 1969 the company began assembling combines at a factory in Tarsus. By the early 1970s its production was about 400 units a year; as it was the only combine factory in the country, it commanded an overwhelming market share. In 1975 the Turkish government also authorized domestic assembly of tractors and Cumitas expanded its operation accordingly. The economic and political situation in Turkey in the late 1970s was tenuous and, as no financing was forthcoming through the government, Deere agreed to a substantial loan in 1977. In 1979 the political situation in Turkey forced Deere to sell its shares in Cumitas (at a nominal sum) in order to retain the link with the company through the sale of combine parts from Zweibrücken and tractor parts from Mannheim.[6]

Brazil and Australia stood in contrast to these instances of intrusive nationalism. From the mid-1970s, Deere had been searching for a way to break into the Brazilian tractor market. In 1976 contact was made with a combine manufacturer, Schneider, Logemann & Cia., Ltd., in the southern state of Rio Grande do Sul, for a joint venture for tractor manufacturing. The Logemann family was already manufacturing large numbers of combines, having adopted a number of the Deere features. After discussing tractor possibilities, Deere and Logemann decided to expand the combine operations instead. A new company was formed, with Deere taking 20 percent of the capital stock (for a cash purchase price of about $6.6 million). Deere technology was provided to the new organization, with the quality of the Logemann combines upgraded in the process, and production began with high hopes. By the early 1980s the venture had not yet provided a way for Deere to gain a larger foothold in tractors, however.

The Australian operations of Deere, once viewed as a pocket market venture, suggest the pejorative implications of the term were probably unwarranted for two important reasons. First, though Australia did originally meet one of the criteria for being a "pocket"—it produced higher priced agricultural machinery that could not compete

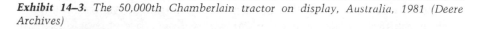

Exhibit 14–3. *The 50,000th Chamberlain tractor on display, Australia, 1981 (Deere Archives)*

internationally—the differential had almost disappeared by the early 1980s. Second, the implication that a pocket market is a small market was becoming patently untrue in Australia. Its natural resources and climate make Australia one of the most important agricultural producers for the rest of the world. For its farm machinery potential, Australia certainly had to be classed in the 1980s as a promising market.

Deere had had a modest distributor network in Australia for many years, with several dealers and a central office in Sydney, but these were combined with one of its vigorous Australian competitors and the only domestically owned tractor manufacturer, Chamberlain Holdings Ltd., in 1970. Out of this came a new company known as Chamberlain-John Deere Pty. Ltd., operated as a wholly owned subsidiary of Chamberlain Holdings Ltd. Deere acquired shares in the latter in a staged arrangement that gave Deere a 49 percent interest by 1976, with the Chamberlain shareholders maintaining a 51 percent holding.

The two lines then needed to be meshed. Deere provided the new company needed expertise in engineering, manufacturing, and marketing, as well as a whole range of Deere products. The larger Deere tractors were imported under Chamberlain aegis, with substantial assembly operations on them being done in Australia from parts shipped from all over the Deere system. Indeed, Australia became perhaps the most apt example of worldwide Deere sourcing—eventually pasture toppers were imported from Mexico; tractors from Mannheim; combines from Zweibrücken and East Moline; balers, mowers, and conditioners from the French operations; engines from Saran; and small tractors from Yanmar, Japan.

In addition, Chamberlain continued to make its own agricultural and industrial tractors, which had become very popular in Australia. Chamberlain maintained its own color—it was yellow, though not quite the shade of Deere's industrial equipment—and its tractor was marketed as a Chamberlain tractor, not as a Deere tractor. Market share in tractors rose to more than 21 percent, making Chamberlain the largest agricultural tractor company in the country (in 1980, Massey-Ferguson had about 15 percent of the market, International Harvester 13 percent, and Ford about 12 percent).

Australia has been an efficacious model for its foreign collaborators—it has pursued a much different approach than have Mexico, Venezuela, and Argentina in encouraging local industry. Rather than establishing tariff barriers, the government chose to use the bounty system. Thus, in 1981, the local automobile industry was given a 57.5 percent bounty, trucks 35 percent, shoes 34 percent, garments generally 51 percent. In the tractor industry the two companies with outside links, Deere and International Harvester, had been given bounties that had begun at higher percentages but had been progressively reduced to 15 percent in 1981 and to 11.8 percent in 1982. Peter Griffiths, the managing director and chief executive officer of Chamberlain, commented on this: "You can see that it is a lightly protected industry, which is another way of saying that it is efficient." In effect, the quality of the Australian operation had improved so measurably over the 1970s that, even with the lower volumes that were still in effect in that country, it was becoming fully competitive with outside machinery. The implications of this for Deere in terms of worldwide sourcing and marketing are very important.[7]

IDEOLOGICAL ENCOUNTERS
IN SOUTH AFRICA

Deere has operated in a few countries whose political and economic philosophies and practices raise issues that go beyond problems of nationalism per se. A country such as South Africa, with its apartheid racial policy, poses difficulties for foreign companies, both in their operations and their public relations. By the early 1970s the presence of American businesses in South Africa was being criticized increasingly in the United States. Ellwood Curtis wrote Frank McGuire in late 1971: "The South African question is getting very hot in the United States right now, particularly since the so-called 'Black Caucus' of all black Congressmen has interested itself in the questions. . . . We do not believe the Black Caucus . . . will be particularly impressed if we say Deere & Company is not involved because we own only 50 percent. . . . We need to be prepared to answer questions and meet accusations."

Deere, not particularly alert to such issues in the 1960s, had allowed its wage rates for unskilled employees to fall below that of the Johannesburg area. In 1971, the top hourly rate in Deere's plant at Nigel—which, because of South African government job restrictions, was used only for white employees—was higher than that at any other of the Deere plants outside of the United States and Canada. At the same time, the top rate for common labor was lower than anywhere in the world except Argentina. (The spread between the common-labor rate and the toolmakers rate in Nigel was 643 percent; the spread in the company's plant in Mexico was 285 percent, in Argentina 178 percent, in Germany 154 percent, and in the United States 148 percent.)

These figures galvanized the Deere board to action, and over the next few years the pattern began to change. By early 1973 McGuire wrote Hewitt: "There is a level of higher paid work referred to as 'European work,' which traditionally was not for the blacks. This has been broken and will continue to be encroached on by steady pressure and without Government approval, but with tolerance if they are not embarrassed by the process." McGuire continued: "We should . . . be at the forefront in our declared policy of equality and fairness equal to all. Wherever we do business around the world we should be out in front. . . . We should not stay out of places where the policies are not today to the level of man's dream of full social justice or run away if a turn backward is experienced.

A presence there is a positive influence, even though small, and an important factor contributing toward achieving the goal of equal opportunity. . . . The force needed is a steady one of encouragement to make more progress."

Realigning South African employee relations practices to fulfill McGuire's goals was not easily carried out, for not only was there government pettifoggery, but the South African employees of the company were reluctant to change. The Moline personnel in charge of employee benefits and wages had isolated a number of discrepancies between practices in the South African operations and the rest of the company. When this was pointed out, the South African managing director wrote back to Moline: "I doubt that there is anyone in South Africa who is familiar enough with Deere & Company wage administration policies and procedures to effectively apply them or make a valid comparison—or adapt them to the peculiarities of the South African labour situation. . . . I question whether there is anyone in Moline sufficiently well acquainted with the current labour situation in South Africa to effectively analyze the current wage policies and procedures as they are applied to our local operation." He was overruled by Moline.

By April 1974 the board in Moline discussed a major policy statement on its South African operations, elaborating on the company's stepped-up efforts for training black employees and calling attention to the uniformity of benefits applied to all employees at the operation. In doing this, the board registered some caveats: "Deere South Africa does not engage in political activity. Its relations with the Government of South Africa consist basically of complying with that country's laws, including the payment of taxes. . . . Deere South Africa is required to observe the laws of that country." The statement concluded: "Deere & Company also believes its presence in South Africa is beneficial to its stockholders and to its employees in South Africa, non-white as well as white. . . . The Company also willingly accepts the social responsibility for being a good citizen wherever it operates, including South Africa."

Deere moved on a wide front over the remainder of the 1970s in bringing up wage rates for black employees in the plant, making promotions available, extending employee benefits, and so forth. By the late 1970s, Deere was paying one of the highest wage rates for black employees in the entire country; however, labor shortages in the skilled occupations (still almost exclusively the domain of the white employee) caused an extremely short supply in that period, and those wages, too, skyrocketed, so that the differential still stood at about two to one. Though government regulations still "required" segregated washrooms and lunchrooms, Deere decided in the late 1970s to eliminate separate facilities. On the Nigel grounds a new facility was constructed for a combination of cafeteria and washroom, the whole to be available to any employee, white or black. The historic unwillingness of the white employees to mix still held firm, however; no white employee used the washroom or lunchroom facilities. Only at major employee functions—service award ceremonies, and so on—were the white employees willing to sit in the same room with the black employees.

The company reevaluated its policy statement on "employment practices in South Africa" in early 1977, and this time the wording was more pointed: "Current racial laws, practices and attitudes in South Africa are in conflict with fundamental views of justice and equality held in this country and in many other nations of the world." The policy statement reaffirmed Deere's belief that "our continued presence in South Africa is constructive and proper." The statement detailed Deere's progress in upgrading wage rates and employee conditions and asserted "that our presence there is helping to improve human conditions for non-whites." While "being present in a country involves, we believe, an obligation for us to obey the law, to be progressive and constructive citizens, and to be sensitive to local institutions," and though the government's constraints "have deep historical roots that have been gradually reinforced by legislation, institutions, customs and time . . . it does not make them more consistent with principles of human dignity or with practices of a fully functioning free market economy. . . . To the extent that South African laws, customs and practices are inconsistent with the principle of equality of opportunity, they are at odds with a fundamental commitment of our Company."

The record in the late 1970s and early '80s documents widely divergent attitudes about the question of foreign investment in South Africa, from both black leaders in South Africa and from representatives of many groups, organizations, and governments outside the country, with the debate particularly acrimonious in the United States. A number of advocacy groups in the United States (particularly various church groups) espoused strong positions, pro and con, on this issue. Some argued for a militant approach, urging American business corporations to close operations in South Africa and leave the country. Others advocated a more evolutionary approach, urging that pressure be put on the South African operations of American companies to upgrade employment conditions and educational and economic opportunities for their employees in South Africa and to become advocates and leaders of social change. A third group opted for a more detached "live and let live" approach—in effect, staying in step with whatever decisions are made by the South African government itself.

Deere became an advocate of the second approach. It decided to stay in South Africa and be a constructive force for change. Deere has always been frank in stating its intention to stay in South Africa; the board documents in 1973 and 1977 made this clear. Thus Deere would not satisfy those who advocated full-scale withdrawal. Deere's advanced employee relations concepts have become widely known in South Africa, however, and no advocacy group pressure has been brought to bear on the company (as it has for so many of Deere's colleague American companies).

This approach by Deere (and a number of other United States companies) has been measurably enhanced since 1977 with the development of the so-called "Sullivan Principles," promulgated by the Rev. Leon Sullivan, minister of the Zion Baptist Church in Philadelphia, Pennsylvania. In 1970 Sullivan had joined the board of directors of the General Motors Corporation, becoming the first black leader to hold such a post in a major American corporation. Sullivan had concluded that those United States corporations that were measurably exerting pressure on the South African government for change should be favorably acknowledged and that those who were standing pat should not be allowed to cover up their position. Sullivan first elaborated a set of principles concerning nonsegregation of the races in eating, comfort, and work facilities; equal and fair employment practices; equal pay for comparable work; training programs to prepare blacks and other non-whites for supervisory and technical jobs; more opportunities for blacks and other non-whites in management and supervision; and improvements in employees' lives outside of the work environment. United States companies were then asked to subscribe publicly to these principles, with Sullivan setting up a monitoring process (using the management consulting firm, Arthur D. Little, Inc.) to ensure that the companies were living up to their rhetoric. By 1979, several dozen United States companies (including Deere) had become "signatory companies," with their results tabulated and made public by the Sullivan group.

The process has not been without problems; the Sullivan group has had difficulty in financing the extensive monitoring that seemed to be required, and a number of black leaders in the United States (as well as in South Africa) have taken exception to the concepts that Sullivan espoused. Other organizations have also carried through similar monitoring efforts; in particular, the Investor Responsibility Research Center (IRRC), a consortium of universities and foundations, has developed its own independent reporting system.

Sullivan ranked Deere in the highest category ("making good progress") after setting up its monitoring system. (There were two other categories, "making acceptable progress" and "needs to become more active.") An IRRC monitoring report of May 1981 affirmed "John Deere's progress to date in establishing generous and equitable pay practices and assisting the local African community" and called the company "one of the more progressive employers in South Africa," all this done "without apparent external pressure." The IRRC corroborated that Deere was paying some of the highest wages of any manufacturer in the country, and it called attention to the company's programs to improve training and advancement opportunities for blacks. (In 1980 Deere had placed a black employee and a coloured employee in the apprenticeship program; the move was only grudgingly accepted by the white employees, who refused to let the two apprentices use the whites' tools, thus forcing the company to purchase tools for them.)

The IRRC also commented on Deere's difficulties in desegregating its facilities. "John Deere has had desegregated facilities in principle, but not in fact. Whites are boycotting the only locker room at the Company as well as the cafeteria set aside for hourly employees." The company had continued to maintain three dining rooms, one in the administration building for its marketing personnel and two cafeterias, one for salaried and one for hourly employees. It was the latter that had been boycotted by the white employees. The IRRC commented, "In South Africa, where most hourly paid workers are black and most salaried employees are white, the companies that have successfully desegregated dining areas are generally those that have built a single cafeteria to serve all employees, both hourly paid and salaried."

In March 1975 the company introduced an African liaison committee, its membership constituted from the black employees. In 1981 a multiracial workers council replaced the previous committee. The subjects discussed by both committees were mostly peripheral issues—bus fares, leave times, and so on. Despite Deere's consistent efforts to make the groups viable entities, the black employees were timid about pushing their views in the face of white employee disapprobation. Consequently, the company decided that it was necessary to conduct a "white-employee reorientation program," and in this the company's principles on the promotion of non-white recognition and integration in the Deere organization have been given special emphasis.

The company also attempted to improve employee conditions outside company environs. A noteworthy contribution was made to the education of black children. Almost all of the Deere employees lived in one area, Duduza, a typical segregated black township, located a few miles outside of the town of Nigel (about a mile from the company plant). The township belied its Zulu name, meaning "Land of Milk and Honey," for most of the homes were small concrete block buildings with metal roofs, few of which had their own indoor plumbing or water supply. Duduza provided schooling only through the eighth grade; the closest high school was in the town of Springs, more than a dozen miles away. Because of this distance, most of the children did not go beyond grade school. Some 180 of the Duduza families had an employee at Deere, a minute fraction of the community's total population, estimated at approximately 25,000. Consequently, the company's options were limited. If it chose to help only its own employees in the town, it would arouse resentment among the others. A suggestion had been made, for example, that Deere provide schoolbooks for children of its own employees, but the company's black employee leaders urged rejection of the idea just for this reason.

After much thought, the company decided in 1980 to build a high school for the township. Through the John Deere Foundation, it contributed $420,000 (R 395, 731), enough to build a fully accredited general and technical high school that could accommodate 700 students. Teachers for the program were to be supplied by the South African Department of Education and Training; Deere itself would also sponsor additional evening adult-education courses. The Urban Foundation, a South African foundation dedicated to improving the quality of life for South Africa's urban blacks, was asked to supervise the completion of the school, to be named the M.O. Sebone Senior Secondary School (in honor of one of Nigel's pioneering black educators). The school opened its doors in early 1981.

Yet, despite improvements in wages and working conditions, the company's black employees see their overall situation in the country as

Exhibit 14–4. *Opening of the M.O. Sebona Senior Secondary School, Duduza, S. Af., 1981 (Deere Archives)*

THE SPRINGS AND BRAKPAN ADVERTISER   Friday, 20th March 1981

An expression of joy from pupils of the new high school, made possible through the concern and generosity of John Deere, the tractor company.

Duduza gets new high school - thanks to John Deere grant

only marginally improved, their housing and living conditions in the township of Duduza as still minimal, their opportunity to participate in the broader economy as very limited. When the black employees talk of their Deere jobs, they express enthusiasm and hope; when they refer to their total lives, they mirror discouragement and bitterness. As one company black employee put it, "We hope for the best—and pray for the worst."

The decade of the 1970s was a propitious one for Deere in South Africa, despite the continuation of racial unrest in the country. By 1980 the company had more than 17 percent of the tractor market in the country; Massey-Ferguson and Ford each had about 22 percent, with Fiat at 20. Thus, four leading companies split most of the South African market. By the late 1970s the South African government again had become concerned about the need for the indigenous manufacture of diesel engines and was able to contract with Perkins Engine and Daimler Benz to allow their engines (the former in sizes up to 125 horsepower, the latter for larger sizes) to be made in a South African-owned factory. The government then mandated that all tractor companies in the country buy from this engine company. Massey-Ferguson's long-time link with the Perkins group made the problem of transition simple for them—they were already using Perkins motors. But Deere, Ford, and Fiat were required to redesign their tractors to adapt to the Perkins configuration. Deere estimated that some 175 parts needed to be redesigned in order to accomplish the changeover; the total cost of this retooling alone was more than $1 million. Once again, the issue of local content had intruded into decision making. Nonetheless, the financial results of Deere's South African operations improved considerably in the 1970s, as a result of a sharp increase in sales. Every year of the decade was profitable except 1979 (Appendix exhibit 28).

This record, while promising, was still well below the company's profitability in the United States over the same period. Many advocacy groups have stereotyped discussions about operating results, implying that United States companies were profiting hugely in South Africa. Deere's figures on relative returns on investment would belie this accusation. It is noteworthy that the company's best performance years have been the most recent ones, after the movement of its black wage rates to the top of the country's scale.[8]

A LITTLE TRADE WITH THE SOVIET UNION

The huge flow of Deere equipment to the Soviet Union in the late 1920s and early '30s under Josef Stalin's first Five Year Plan had dried up—only a trickle of Deere machinery and parts had gone to the Soviets before and after World War II. Not until 1959 was there a substantial new

Exhibit 14–5. *Nikita S. Khrushchev, Premier of the Soviet Union, visits Deere's Des Moines factory, 1959*

contact between Deere and the Soviet Union, and it came in an offbeat way—a visit by Premier Nikita S. Khrushchev to the United States and to Deere. That trip produced many striking images, not the least of which was Khrushchev's trip to Iowa. Khrushchev was "corn-conscious," said the *Wall Street Journal*, for his major experiments in corn production in the Soviet Union had been attacked as ineffective. It was natural that he would visit a corn farm. The hybrid seed-corn operation of Roswell Garst was chosen (Garst having earlier supplied substantial quantities of both seed corn and hybrid technology for the Soviet Union). Of more importance to Deere was Khrushchev's visit to the company's plant in Des Moines.

The company prepared assiduously for the visit, even producing a series of English-Russian publications explaining the company's products. Hewitt himself was on hand to conduct Khrushchev through the factory. "We are competing with you on both farm machinery and corn," Khrushchev told Hewitt. As Khrushchev observed the highly automated Deere factory, he bragged: "We'll beat you, we'll be more automated." The premier's visit was marked by a Soviet order for $100,000 worth of Deere equipment—tractors, combines, harvesters, corn pickers—all in small quantities. The Soviets' intent in purchasing this machinery became clearer when Khrushchev was queried about farm machinery at a major informal dinner in New York City a few days later, when he answered off-the-cuff questions from a number of American executives (including Hewitt). The dinner repartee was reported more or less verbatim in *Izvestia*. The question was put to Khrushchev from the audience: "We are interested in business with you, but why do Soviet organizations purchase only sample machines?" Khrushchev replied, "I will speak to you frankly. If John Dear [sic] wishes to sell us tractors and agricultural equipment, this is not realistic inasmuch as we have our own production of agricultural equipment. We purchase, and may purchase tractors and other agricultural equipment in, for example, ten or one hundred samples. This is done for comparison with our machinery so as to see which is better. But why are you dissatisfied with us? How many tractors or combines do you sell to one farm? Will Garst purchase 1,000 tractors from you? Not a single farmer will buy even a dozen machines. He will buy one or two, and we will possibly buy 100. This dispute about samples is not a realistic thing. I will say frankly that we are not interested in buying tractors, combines, airplanes, or missiles. . . . We are interested in chemical equipment, equipment for machinery building, and oil refining plants. As far as tractors generally, we can sell them to you. If you wish, we will even sell you one tractor."

Khrushchev's testy response underlined the difficulties and frustrations of dealing with the Soviets in farm equipment. On the one hand, the Soviet Union had a burgeoning farm machinery business of its own— indeed, it was the largest producer of tractors in the world. (Even in 1960, it made more units than any other country; by 1975 it was producing about 13 percent more than the combined output of the United States, the United Kingdom, and West Germany, three of the leading producers in the non-Communist world.) In horsepower, though, the lead was far less—the Soviet tractors were lower powered and not as modern in their technology. Thus, as Khrushchev's words indicated, though it was not likely that the Soviets would buy a large amount of production-run United States farm machinery, they were interested in upgrading the quality and horsepower of their own machines, and therefore were potential customers for licensing arrangements, perhaps even co-production efforts.

Little happened between Deere and the Soviets in the 1960s, but in late 1972, shortly after Pres. Richard Nixon's visit with Premier Leonid Brezhnev in the Soviet Union and the development of the protocols for U.S.-Soviet trade, a Deere delegation visited the Soviet Union. The Soviets decided to purchase a small number of several different kinds of equipment, again to "test these machines under their own conditions." Along with this, the Soviets insisted on extensive technological backup.

By this time, Hewitt had become a board member of the US-USSR Trade and Economic Council. Over the remainder of the 1970s, Hewitt made a number of trips to the Soviet Union, with many additional visits by other senior executives of the company. Extended, often convoluted, discussions were carried on—almost a "cat and mouse game," as the Deere executives tried to fathom Soviet intentions. There was extensive testing of cotton-picking machinery, with Soviet promises of licensing arrangements in regard to cotton-harvesting technology. This never materialized. The Soviets were also interested in a high-horsepower, low-weight tractor and persuaded Deere to build a prototype, the XR-50, an adaptation of the 125 PTO horsepower Model 4430 with the weight of the Model 4020. Once again a licensing arrangement was discussed, but not concluded. Thus, total sales to the Soviet Union over the twenty-plus years after the Khrushchev visit were painfully small. Balanced against the amount of management time expended cultivating the Russians, the "cost-benefit" equation tilted heavily to the negative. As one Deere executive put it, "If you take all the gross retail sales to Russia—not just our profit—it wouldn't be enough to cover our total travel and subsistence expenses for all those trips to Moscow."[9]

MAINLAND CHINA: DEERE'S "FRIENDSHIP FARM" EXPERIMENT

The tremendous promise of technology for increasing food output, as well as alleviating the drudgery and inefficiency of small farmers, has accentuated the pace of mechanization in agriculture all over the world. Many observers argue that the only way to stem the exodus from the rural areas of the younger, more innovative people is to provide them with the tools that will enable them to modernize their operations. On the other hand, laboring people have long had a deep-seated, almost primitive fear of being displaced by machines. As a result, there is burgeoning interest around the world in matching the proper pace of development with intermediate-level mechanization—and using what has come to be called "appropriate" technology. There are places in the developing world where higher mechanization has produced rural unemployment; there are also places where the opposite has happened, where mechanization has been labor-enhancing. Firm generalization on this complicated question must be linked to specific case situations.

It is in this context of an evolving debate about the appropriate scale of mechanization in the developing world that Deere efforts with the People's Republic of China take on particular meaning. When Pres. Richard Nixon visited that country in 1972, important protocols resulted that not only greatly eased political tensions between the United States and China but also established the groundwork for economic relations between the two countries. In late 1973 the first fruits of this economic link were realized, with a visit to Mainland China by a high-level business delegation, under the auspices of a newly formed private United

States trade group, the National Council for United States-China Trade. It was a small group of ten, mostly chief executive officers of major United States corporations. The leader was Donald C. Burnham, chairman of the Westinghouse Electric Corporation; he was also chairman of the National Council. Deere's Hewitt was in the party; he was vice chairman of the National Council. Secretary of State Henry Kissinger, in his sendoff to the party, commented: "Your mission is an historic one. It is the first visit to Peking by a broadly represented American business delegation in twenty-four years."

This first contact quickly led to a wide range of initiatives by both countries. China had established its own counterpart organization, the China Council for the Promotion of International Trade (CCPIT). The latter group sent its own senior delegation to the United States in early 1974 for a three-week visit that included Washington, D.C., New York City, Chicago, and Minneapolis, Houston, and San Francisco; there was also a major conference in Washington later that year. In the period 1973–75, China sent ten separate groups to the United States, and there were six United States commercial delegations to China in the same period. The National Council functioned during this period as a catalyst for individual contacts between separate United States companies and appropriate units in China (generally central government ministries).

In June 1975 Hewitt succeeded Burnham as chairman of the National Council for a two-year term. This was a particularly important period for the council, for its earlier emphasis on imports from China now was to be broadened to serve the export focus of the American companies. Information about China was in short supply, and the council served as a central clearinghouse for updated information. But the council could not enmesh itself in individual projects; it had to serve primarily as a backup for initiatives by individual firms. By the end of Hewitt's tenure as council chairman, this important transition had taken place, and the pace and scale of United States-China trade in both directions had heightened significantly.

The People's Republic of China, with its one billion-plus inhabitants, has enormous food needs. Agriculture is a critical sector, its scale necessarily very large indeed. The more than two decades under Chairman Mao Zedong had seen many twists and turns in agricultural policy, as Mao and his opponents debated central planning versus decentralized operation. The interaction between political and economic dogmas was accentuated in agriculture as the country moved through the traumatic land reform period in the late 1940s and '50s and then through the stages of collectivization and evolution of the communes in the mid- and late 1950s.

Through all this period there had been great debates over the extent of mechanization in agriculture, both in manufacture (should tractors, for example, be built in large central factories, or put together in various versions by individual communes?), and in usage (should there, for example, be centralized machine tractor stations, or should the individual tractors be assigned to the communes, perhaps even to production brigades within them?). During the Great Leap Forward (1958–60) there was overwhelming emphasis on "backyard" production in a decentralized mode. Then there was a turn back to centralization in the early 1960s after the failure of the Great Leap Forward, and the machine tractor stations again were utilized on a more centralized basis. This was the period in which Mao's lieutenant, Liu Shaoqi was in the ascendancy, utilizing some of the kinds of Soviet management systems that had been brought to the country in the extensive Soviet-Chinese interchanges. When Mao terminated relations with the Soviets in 1966 and soon began the abortive Cultural Revolution, the pattern of agricultural development and agricultural mechanization again turned away from a centralized frame toward more emphasis on the individual communes. In the mid-1970s, though, in the wake of the wreckage of the Cultural Revolution, there was a shift once more toward a more centrally organized approach to many issues, agricultural mechanization being one. As the United States and the People's Republic of China began their historic new initiative after 1973, China was particularly interested in upgrading the quality and productivity of its agricultural sector, and in the process it became interested in the best of the world's newer technologies in agricultural mechanization. Thus there was a natural interest on the part of Chinese officials in Deere.

Among the Chinese delegations to the United States was one focused on agriculture. This group made an extensive visit to Deere's operations in Moline and Waterloo (as well as a corn and cattle farm in Walcott, Iowa). The company had planned this visit carefully, with all publications printed both in Chinese and English, and with simultaneous translations available at all stages of the visit. The Chinese visitors came away with a broadened understanding of American agriculture, as well as substantial interest in what Deere itself could offer their country. This soon led to one of the most striking projects in China in this period, the "Friendship Farm" collaboration between Deere and China near Jiamusi (Chiamussu), in China's northeast province of Heilongjiang.

Historically, the dominant pattern of Chinese agriculture has been the small farm. Before the Communist revolution these had been privately held plots, with a strong pattern of landlordism. After early land reforms, the plots became state owned, generally run by individual production teams (the smallest administrative unit under the commune). Thus the small farm survived. The famous agricultural operations in the village of Tachai in Shanxi province, where the peasants had literally put together small plot farms with their bare hands from a barren, hostile mountain region, exemplified agriculture in the country under Mao. (He himself coined the pervasive slogan, "In agriculture, learn from Tachai.")

Nevertheless, there were large-scale units in certain parts of the country,

Exhibit 14–6. William Hewitt on an Iowa farm with delegation from the People's Republic of China, 1975 (Deere Archives)

generally organized separately from the communes as "state farms." Most of them were located along the northern and eastern borders of the country, in areas of low population and extensive expanses of undeveloped land. From early in the history of the People's Republic, most state farms were centrally managed (though the production brigade-production team basis of organization still was preserved out in the field). Some of these farms were enormous in size, ranging upward from 60,000 hectares. Clearly, in units of this size, agricultural mechanization of substantial amount was needed. In the early days a number of Soviet tractors were used; later the People's Republic itself developed its own wheeled and crawler tractors, ranging up to about 75 horsepower. A Soviet-designed three-bottom plow was the standard tillage instrument for these larger-sized tractors. Low horsepower and the relative ineffectiveness of a number of these machines made Chinese officials in the mid-1970s particularly interested in upgrading the quality and size of the agricultural equipment for state farms.

They turned to Deere for their first project. There was a 1,000-hectare farm in the northern part of Heilongjiang province, just a few miles below the Soviet border, in an area known as the "Great Northern Wilds," formerly an endless stretch of almost uninhabited wasteland. It was called "Friendship Farm," a name that had been given to it in the early 1960s, when the Soviets and the Chinese were jointly developing this area. This location was now chosen by the Chinese as their key experimental farm for large-scale equipment. For this, they ordered from Deere the whole gamut of

Deere tractors, combines, and tillage equipment. Five tractors were ordered, including two of the largest four-wheel drive versions; the three combines were of the largest size and the planters, plows, and other equipment were all large. These were purchased for hard currency foreign exchange at regular commercial rates.

In effect, the People's Republic had decided that it would test the whole range of advanced agricultural technology: for example, when the Deere executives asked what accessory options the Chinese wanted on tractors, they replied, "All." Thus the big four-wheel drive tractors came all the way to the northern reaches of China equipped with air conditioning and tape decks!

This exciting venture opened up an extensive set of relationships between company personnel and their counterparts in China. Several dozen Deere engineers and agricultural technical experts were deputed to the farm over several years, and handpicked Chinese engineers also visited Deere operations in Moline and Waterloo. At one point in October 1979, Hewitt himself made an official visit to the farm; this was not an inconsequential trip, for transportation was difficult in this part of the country and the demonstration of the company's interest by its chairman's visit put special focus on the importance of the project to the United States.

The experiment was an eminent success and was soon widely reported

Exhibit 14–7. *Local manager of "Friendship Farm," Heilongjiang Province, People's Republic of China, presents ceremonial T-shirts to the William Hewitt family, 1979 (Deere Archives)*

in the Chinese press. There followed a large number of visits to the farm by Chinese agriculturalists from all over the country, and it seemed as if Friendship Farm had truly replaced Tachai as the place "to learn from" (to borrow Mao's phrase).

The project was not without its critics in China. In the influential Beijing publication, *Guangming Ribao*, a reporter praised the results as having "shown that the advanced farm equipment and skills have played a positive role in building a modern state farm. It has emancipated people's minds, broadened their vision and made them realize that mechanization is the fundamental way to increase agricultural output.... It has battered down management methods that are inappropriate to agricultural mechanization and brought about many changes in farm management." But then the reporter continued: "However, we have recently heard some criticism: first, 'there are mistakes in the calculation of labor productivity of the number 2 team'; second, 'importing farm equipment from the United States results in loss of money'; third, 'the equipment drives people away, producing poor results politically.'" The author explored at some length each one of these "discrepancies"; there were contradictions between "specialized production and social cooperation." Further contradictions were alleged in the organizational structure of the units and, perhaps more importantly, there were said to be contradictions among individuals. Tensions between the assistants and the group leaders were noted; there were arguments over the precise way the equipment was to be operated, concerns about the skills of the operators. There had been difficulties at the farm in maintenance and repair, for the Chinese had a fear of working on such complicated machinery. A Deere fieldman reported once, "The central farm shop mechanic 'dared not repair it.' ... When asked who is expected to repair the John Deere machines, the answer was 'John Deere.'" This dependency raised the question of just how long the Deere contingent would need to stay on the scene to make the project effective.

The oblique reference to potentially negative employment efforts pointed up China dilemmas in recalibrating the old forms of rural organization that existed under Mao's regime. On the state farms, located mostly in the vast expanses of the north and northwest, large-equipment mechanization made eminent sense. There would be some employment effects in the process, as a smaller number of higher-skilled operators took over. But population concentrations were low in these areas. As the central government turned in the 1980s to new forms of private enterprise in the rural areas, mechanization in the communes of the rest of the country was again being demanded. But in this case it was often for smaller machines (hand tractors, for example) than characteristically had been used earlier on the communes. One tractor factory in Anhui Province was reported to have shut down because its tractors were "too large." Here again, under this "private enterprise" rubric there were negative employment effects; not everyone in the commune was equally able to take advantage of the new opportunities. The enormous population concentrations in many of these rural areas made for a potentially explosive situation, were there to be substantial unemployment.

The *Guangming Ribao* article ended by again praising the results of the actual mechanization itself and the striking increase in productivity. Still, the article and several others in the same period had hinted at what some Chinese officials felt was an incipient elitism among the employees at Friendship Farm. Perhaps the air-conditioned cabs of the tractors and combines were just too far away from existing Chinese practice to make sense to most of the peasants. (As one Chinese driver put it, "You sit all day in the cab—now you want to go home to your wife?") Nevertheless, the substantive success of the project was unquestioned—modern, large-scale agricultural mechanization made real sense in the larger Chinese operations, particularly the state farms.

This first decade of Chinese-United States economic cooperation also had its problems. The Chinese were meticulous, hard bargainers; the wording of one of the Chinese telegrams to Deere illustrates this very well: "On this occasion we would like to invite your attention to the fact that the price you quoted is too high and is not competitive. In particular, your quotation for lump-sum payment is surprisingly high and with no payment terms at all. . . . However, taking into account the friendly relation between us we are still willing to invite you to China to join in the competition in the hope that you will reduce your price to a great extent so as to win the transaction."

A number of companies spent extensive time and money visiting China, only to find that very little had resulted. On the other hand, the People's Republic had initiated industrialization with too euphoric a view of the nation's capacities to absorb the new. The first problem was money—the foreign currency available from China was just not enough to cover all its plans. Thus, over the latter part of the 1970s a number of previously announced projects were cut back and even terminated.

More was involved than just money, though. The economic philosophy of the country was still not settled enough to assure unanimity on what was needed. Tension continued between the old Maoist groups and the new leadership under Vice Premier Deng Xiaoping. The latter, as de facto head of state, was an advocate of a number of modern Western ideas, even countenancing renewal of some private ownership and individual incentive within the structure.

The organization of agriculture became a central part of this debate; questions were raised about how much consolidation to large-scale agriculture should be part of the new plans. A high level of agricultural mechanization fit well at the larger state farms. But whether some of the smaller plots of the central and southern parts of the country should be consolidated in some way would depend on both the amount of money available for the agricultural sector and the prevailing economic philosophy of agricultural development.

After Deere's successful Friendship Farm endeavor (one that continued with input of Deere personnel into the 1980s), the company entered into extensive negotiations with China about collaborating on a tractor factory. One of the country's older, larger tractor factories was located in Loyang, in Honan province. Originally constructed with Soviet help, it continued to make tractors after relations with the Russians soured. The Chinese wanted to upgrade this factory to produce higher powered, diesel-equipped tractors in the 70–110 horsepower range. The numbers needed were quite substantial—40,000 units as a starter. The Chinese also wanted to make larger 125–175 horsepower tractors in another factory, perhaps 5,000 of these, too. Deere and several other manufacturers competed for this project, and the company prepared elaborate printed brochures on the proposal and visited the country for further negotiations. In the end, China backed off.

After the Loyang project fell through, Deere became involved in a smaller project for the development of grasslands in the northeast of the country near the town of Ganchika, in a remote region in the Inner Mongolian Autonomous Region, just short of the Russian border. Some Deere grasslands equipment was sent there, together with a small cadre of Deere technicians. Unfortunately, no licensing agreements were concluded, though the People's Republic did copy some of Deere's hay tools.

Then, in 1981, a major new joint relationship developed involving combines. Deere technology was licensed for use in China's combine factories at Jiamusi, and Kaifeng in Honan province. Plans included the training of a large contingent of Chinese engineers and technicians at Deere's factory at Zweibrücken and concurrent visits by Deere personnel to the Chinese production units. Investment in the project was small, and Deere was to be reimbursed in part by purchase of Chinese-made components, but the company considered it to be another important step in developing a broad commercial and technological relationship with China. Deere was the first United States corporation to sell agricultural technology; this fit well with China's apparent emphasis on buying technology rather than actual equipment.

Total sales to the People's Republic by the company in this first decade were about $15 million, and the personal relationships and official links between the company and Chinese industry pointed to the possibility of more business in the future.[10]

FOREIGN REPRISE

By the end of the decade of the 1970s, there could have been little doubt in anyone's mind that Deere intended to stay in Europe. Major capital expenditures were made during this period—first, assembly operations were expanded at both Mannheim and Zweibrücken, then a major, multistory administrative center was constructed at Mannheim for the Region II offices. By 1979 a 20 percent addition in capacity was accomplished in Spain and a somewhat smaller expansion at the Saran factory in France. That year was also marked by the decision to build a major new factory at Bruchsal, near Mannheim, particularly for the manufacture of protective cabs and other components. There was also a substantial expansion of parts depots—a 430,000-square-foot building at Bruchsal for German operations (for start-up in 1982), as well as smaller depots in Orléans, France, and Milan, Italy. By 1980 a set of new European tractors came off the assembly lines of Mannheim and Getafe, Spain; these were well received and allowed the company to increase its market share.

Unfortunately, by this time worldwide recession had affected European agricultural equipment sales in a major way. Net income from the international operations continued strongly on the positive side for the years 1974–78, with the $41.3 million of 1976 the high point. (The company as a whole made $242 million that year; the total company had made 7.7 percent on its sales, and overseas had made 5.7 percent.) The European recession in 1979 ended the string of good years. Overseas losses in 1979 were $12.5 million and $54.1 million in 1980. In 1981 the total overseas net income again was positive, just over $1 million.

Exhibit 14–8. *Farm families from Kenya's Masai tribe pose with three of seven John Deere tractors they own, 1979 (JD Journal)*

Though the Zweibrücken operation in Germany remained modestly profitable in these three years, the Mannheim tractor works had large losses. In France, the engine plant at Saran remained modestly profitable, but the other operations lost money. In addition, there were substantial losses in Argentina, England, and Italy, and disturbing losses in Spain. Fortunately, South Africa, Australia, and Mexico remained in the profit columns to help offset some of these major losses. Nevertheless, as Deere moved ahead in the 1980s, the overseas operations were again a source of concern for company officials.

CHAPTER 15

CHALLENGES OF THE 1980s

*Deere has gone around and actually to the detriment of their balance
sheet given support to their dealers. They're the only
people who are going to end up with a healthy dealer network.
10 to 12 percent of the farm machinery dealers in 1982 went
out of business, but the number of Deere dealers that went out of
business was miniscule, and they were immediately replaced
by people with stronger capitalization. So not only are they the low cost
producer, they're going to be the only people around with dealers.*

Wall Street Transcript, 1983

◁*Computer-aided design, John Deere Technical Center, 1983.*

D uring the first three years of the 1980s, the bright promise for agriculture seen by most experts at the beginning of the decade quickly faded. The American farmer had produced bumper crops in 1980 and '81, and the carryover of grains from these years brought severe downward pressures on agricultural prices just as a general recession hit the United States and the world. These events seriously affected the agricultural equipment industry.

WORLD AGRICULTURAL MARKETS

World agriculture went through a profound change in the 1970s. Bad weather—following a diversion of agricultural resources into farm animals—forced the Soviet Union to enter the world grain markets with massive purchases beginning in 1972. Large United States grain exports to that country ensued, and when the crisis in the world's oil markets followed the next year, with its massive transfers of capital and effects on foreign exchange rates, commodities became an even more attractive investment. The resulting upsurge in agricultural prices, with the year 1973 particularly a boom year, enhanced agriculture's prosperity dramatically in a short period of time. It remained strong for most of the rest of the 1970s, to the benefit of the net exporting countries such as the United States. The persistent fear in the 1960s of unwanted surpluses now was replaced by hopes of a long-term balancing of supply and demand. As the 1980s opened, however, the world business downturn that had begun a year or so earlier worsened. Inflationary pressures subsided in the United States in 1981 and 1982, and prices to farmers declined, after bumper crops in those two years. Agriculture was used in a new role as a political weapon by the United States after the Soviet Union invaded Afghanistan in 1980. A grain embargo was imposed, and it had two important results. First, other exporting nations stepped into the breach to fulfill Soviet needs and enter the general world markets more aggressively. Argentina and Brazil, in particular, now became major players in world agriculture. Second, many experts felt that the United States had damaged its credibility as a reliable world supplier and they worried that the United States might be returning to a position of residual supplier.

Projections of world population growth rates in the 1980s, when compared to available food supplies, still appeared to put United States agriculture in a commanding position over the decade. But for this scenario to come true, significant productivity gains would be necessary. These would not come as readily as they had in the past, for several negative factors now intruded:

(1) it would likely cost more for United States agriculturalists to bid additional land and other resources from competing sectors of the economy;

(2) costs of producing would be higher and yields lower on less fertile, fragile land that would be brought into farming;

(3) costs of fertilizer and other inputs, which had been rising rapidly, would likely continue so, adding to the expense of increasing yields;

(4) potential gains in yields from current technologies had already been widely attained, so further gains were estimated to be increasingly expensive; and

(5) greater production might entail increased environmental costs from chemical pollution of rivers and streams and increased soil erosion.

CHANGES IN U.S. AGRICULTURAL PRACTICES

These important developments put pressure on the agricultural machinery manufacturers for heightened productivity in their new models—fuel efficient equipment that could adapt to the many new agronomic practices now demanded by the times. "Conservation farming" seemed destined to be a watchword of the decade—countering erosion threats to topsoil, heightening the regeneration of soil fertility, and monitoring off-farm side effects, such as the depletion of water tables, silting, and chemical runoff from soil erosion. Likely the future would see fewer trips over the field, with more combined operations, reduced tillage, and an overall concern for soil and water conservation practices. Fall tillage would probably be reduced, with rougher surfaces remaining and more residue on top.

Row-crop, monoculture patterns of production potentially could be threatening to soil conservation, though they are often the most financially rewarding. High demand for food had persuaded a great many farmers to move away from traditional rotational practices that included soil-retaining pastures in favor of continuous cropping of corn and other row crops. While American farmers are not likely to turn away from their traditional crops—wheat, corn, and soybeans—renewed sensitivity about soil conservation will bring many back to a more crop-rotating pattern in the future.

Even with single-crop row crops, much can be accomplished by a more sophisticated application of modern reduced tillage practices. Many names are used to describe them—ecofallow, mulch tillage, till planting, less till, minimum tillage, no-till, zero tillage. In essence, all cut down work done to the soil. Rather than conventional tillage—plowing, plus two to five secondary tillage steps, including preplow operations such as disking to knock down weeds and cut crop residues—steps short of full tillage can be practiced. At first, weeds were a perennial bane, but modern herbicides now have mitigated this problem. Selective herbicides, particularly the introduction of 2, 4D in the late 1940s, proved effective on many of the broadleaf weeds found particularly in corn. Since that time, more than 100 other herbicides have been developed, making practical the many variants of reduced tillage. Under "minimum tillage," there

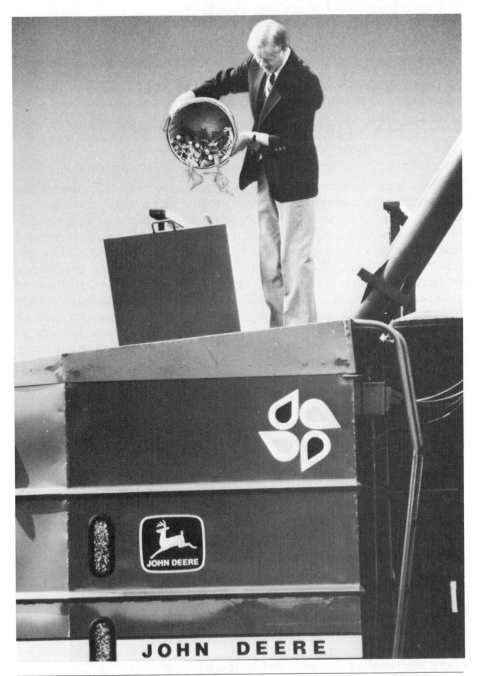

Exhibit 15–1. Pres. Jimmy Carter ceremoniously dumps a basket of corn cobs into Deere's experimental biomass converter during his tour of the company's Moline facilities, 1979 (JD Journal)

might be only one tillage operation before planting; often chisel plowing or mulch tillage would be used in place of a moldboard plow. Zero tillage or no-till involves planting into an essentially unprepared seedbed; no prior tillage would be done except for a narrow strip in front of the planter which might be cut and loosened somewhat by a coulter or some other device at the moment of planting.

The key to the extent of reduced tillage would lie particularly in the draining of the soil. With good drainage, a reduced or no-tillage system could emerge as best; in poorly drained soil, no-tillage methods lowered yield significantly in many cases, as much as 30 percent lower for corn.

The moldboard plow has garnered a particularly bad press in the "reduced tillage" debate. The attack has been considerably more pervasive than in the days when Edward H. Faulkner wrote his little book *Plowman's Folly* in the early 1940s. (He had an unbending antipathy toward the moldboard plow, believing that it carried the surface tilth too far into the ground and that in the process nutrients necessary for that first inch or two of the surface soil were lost.) Now more than one conservation purist imputes to the moldboard most or all of the ills of soil erosion. But this oversimplifies. Today's sophisticated farmers understand the value of the right tool for the right situation. Most continue to purchase moldboards, along with the newer chisels and disks, the former for those times involving a complete turning for weed and pest control and the latter for incorporation of fertilizers and herbicides and for reduced tillage needs. As field speeds have increased, tillage machinery engineers have developed new moldboard configurations and adjustable width bottoms, so that dirt will not be thrown as far (and thus not be so susceptible to wind or water erosion). The farmer has now developed a set of rotation tillage practices in addition to crop rotation patterns, testimony to the vastly increased complexity of today's agronomic decisions on the farm.

Reduced tillage does allow some savings in energy. In the case of no-till, upwards of 75 percent of tillage energy can be eliminated, but part of the savings is cancelled out by the cost of the energy to produce the chemicals for weed and insect control. Further, the energy costs for subsequent operations, including harvesting and drying, are not altered, so the overall savings are modest (perhaps in the neighborhood of 4 percent). Thus the primary rationale for reduced tillage lies particularly in its erosion-prevention potential, the savings from which may be incalculable for the country over the long run.[1]

SHIFTING MARKET SHARES AND RECESSIONARY FALLOUT

The recession of the early 1980s had profound effects on the agricultural machinery industry. In the fast-paced growth of agriculture in the

1970s, farmers took opportunities to leverage themselves with debt for both land and equipment, given what seemed to be a halcyon future. In the process, the farm machinery industry did well. Deere, International Harvester, and Massey-Ferguson continued as giants of the industry, with Allis-Chalmers, Ford, J.I. Case, and New Holland taking significant roles, too. Two companies captured an increasing share in the four-wheel drive tractor market—the Vancouver, B.C., firm of Versatile Manufacturing Company, and the Fargo, North Dakota, firm of Steiger Tractor Company (the latter with a minority holding by International Harvester from 1975). The mid-1970s also brought a new player on the North American scene with the entry from Japan of Kubota, Ltd.

When the farmers' hopes were dashed in the abrupt turnaround, one of the inevitable results was a "make do" mentality on equipment purchases. In the face of a deadly combination of high interest rates and falling farm prices, many potential agricultural machinery purchasers just opted out. The farm equipment industry was left in disarray. Business sagged precipitously, and just about every farm equipment manufacturer, large or small, was faced with cutbacks in schedules, stretchouts in capital spending plans, and, frequently, reductions in staff.

Some manufacturers fared relatively much worse than others. Massey-Ferguson experienced its own set of problems even before the onslaught of the downturn; in 1978 it lost a startling $262 million. After a small profit in 1979, the company again lost heavily in 1980, more than $225 million. The firm was saved from bankruptcy only by a massive financial transaction involving a group of some 250 banks and insurance companies from around the world, together with the Canadian and British governments. Even this $730 million (CDN) rescue package could not stem the tide of red ink for Massey-Ferguson; the company lost $194.8 million in 1981 and losses continued in 1982.

International Harvester had only modest profits in 1976–78, a much better performance in 1979. In 1980 the combination of the business sag, an abortive strike, and certain internal management missteps brought a colossal loss of $397 million. In December of that year Harvester, too, had need for a rescue plan, in this case involving some 200 banks and insurance companies, with a total package of $4.15 billion. 1981 brought a further loss of $393 million; in May 1982 Archie R. McCardell, the chief executive officer from 1977, resigned. The continuing saga of bad news at these two business giants is well known; their difficulties were not just an industry story, for the general press throughout the country widely chronicled the two firms' efforts to forestall bankruptcy.

But there were also many other changes upward and downward in the fortunes of individual companies. Market shares were indeed shifting in a way hardly imaginable in prior years, and some famous names were almost gone altogether from the scene. The White Motor Corporation (the successor combination of Minneapolis-Moline and Oliver) went bankrupt in 1980; its farm equipment division was sold to the TIC Investment Corporation, a Dallas firm. Operations for White continued, but at a low volume with substantial losses. Others, and this included preeminently Deere, picked up market share and relative strength in this period, even while they themselves struggled to maintain equilibrium in the face of very depressing sales outlooks.

Appendix exhibits 29–34 picture in a dramatic way the market share position of Deere in agricultural equipment. Appendix exhibits 29 and 30 graphically show Deere's strong position in the North American market; the first records the company's nearly-30-percent piece of all farm equipment sales, the second eloquently documents its leadership in individual products, where it is the major supplier for six of the ten listed categories.

The company's reach worldwide is pictured in Appendix exhibit 31; its 17 percent market share is the only one in double figures for 1980. Overseas sales are elaborated in Appendix exhibits 32, 33, and 34, both by total sales and country-by-country for the major markets, for both tractors and combines. In overseas sales alone, Massey-Ferguson leads, with Deere second in 1980 (from a third place in 1975, fourth in 1970). The overseas markets are much more fragmented; national boundaries yield major differences, with some countries over-full in numbers of competitors. Deere's overseas success has been greater in combines than in tractors, and there are only a few markets in which the company has a "substantial" market share of 20 percent or more—Spain (tractors, combines), Australia (tractors), and Brazil (combines). Deere's progress has been painfully slow in the two key markets of France and Germany.

Given the desperate condition of some of the larger agricultural machinery manufacturers in the 1980–82 recession, patterns of disruptive "fire-sale" pricing dominated the retail scene, and one could not predict with any certainty how market shares were moving. What had been gradual trends in the 1970s might prove to be more dramatic in the 1980s. It was not beyond the realm of possibility that one or more major companies would either cease manufacturing altogether or at least reduce its product lines, no longer attempting to remain "full line."[2]

DEERE'S NON-AGRICULTURAL DIVISIONS

Deere's strong showing in farm machinery in the 1970s and early '80s must be seen additionally in the context of the entire company; *i.e.*, one must include the two major efforts of manufacturing diversification—industrial and construction equipment, and consumer products. The declining position of the former from 1980 was sobering; the latter's growth was positive, but modest.

The industrial equipment division was a very large endeavor in its own right, reaching almost $1 billion in sales in 1979 (more than 20 percent of

Exhibit 15–2. Top, *John Deere was the official supplier of industrial equipment for the 1980 Olympic Winter Games at Lake Placid, N.Y., 1980;* bottom, *Davenport Works employees with the JD 890 excavator* (JD Journal)

the company total that year). It had cumulated modest profits during the 1970s, with the highest figure some $97 million in 1979 (17.7 percent of Deere's operating profit that year). The recession hit this industry very hard, and sales in 1981 dropped to just over $780 million, with a $38 million loss. Appendix exhibit 35 illustrates the division's market share in its key product lines for 1979–81.

The dominant competitor in industrial and construction equipment sales was Caterpillar, whose dollar volume was about nine times that of Deere's industrial division. Second in the industry was Komatsu, the Japanese producer, with three times the dollar volume of Deere. Third was Case, with about twice that of Deere. Next was the German producer, IBH Holding AG, half again as large as Deere; International Harvester was slightly smaller than Deere. Thus Deere was in fifth place, running considerably behind the industry leader.

In a bit of euphoria in 1978, after its strong showing that year, the industrial equipment division stated its goal to be "number three in the industry by 1990, and number two by 2000." These long-term objectives were scaled down in the strategic plans developed in early 1982, in the light of the sobering statistics of the division in 1981. Lowered profitability had reduced the availability of capital for the planned product expansion into the large-machine arena. A shakeout had been expected in Europe, where there were a number of financially troubled companies. However, IBH, an aggressive company, had been picking up significant numbers of these companies; IBH's approach in this period was to produce as close to capacity as possible and price almost at cost to move what was made. This made for fierce price competition in the European market.

Competition from Japan had also been rigorous. A Boston consulting-group study for Deere in 1980 pointed to a 25–33 percent cost disadvantage in laying goods down in a typical Far Eastern market (the Far Eastern markets representing about 30 percent of industry sales). Komatsu, the key Japanese competitor, had been able to market in the United States at very competitive prices; the American companies had been surprised at the ease with which they established a dealer organization.

A number of positive factors about Deere's efforts mitigated some of the pessimism. The industrial equipment division had excellent manufacturing facilities, having expanded its operations significantly with another large plant in Davenport, Iowa. There was a remarkably close relationship to farm equipment in terms of parts and components commonalities and manufacturing similarities (less of a commonality in marketing). Aggressive company-wide efforts to develop sophisticated manufacturing operations had found application in the division's factories, though the depleted work force at the two key plants at Dubuque and Davenport in 1982 made some of those plans difficult to effect. Plans for new back-hoe models, small crawlers, and a line of excavators were underway. The division continued to exploit its major position as supplier to the forestry industry and in the small and medium segments of the earthmoving markets.

There were still important questions remaining about the extent of the line (by 1983 it had competed only in the small and medium sizes) and about the focus of the division in terms of industries served. Plans called for a more selective approach, both for customers and in terms of geography. Efforts in Europe would be kept at par, a push would be made to reach competitiveness in the Far Eastern markets (perhaps with the help of another Japanese company), and the opportunities in Mexico and several other Latin American countries, in Canada, and in several of the Middle Eastern and African countries (particularly South Africa) would be pursued aggressively.

While there was stark pessimism in the construction industry in the early 1980s, and little optimism in any of the industries using utility vehicles, over the longer term the industrial and construction opportunities seemed quite substantial. Growth rates could likely have been expected to exceed those of the farm equipment business, according to a number of analysts. The long-term position of the industrial equipment division in the total of Deere activities seemed assured.

The consumer products division also was a substantial contributor to the company's revenues, accounting for more than one-third of $1 billion in sales each year in the years 1979–81; it had been profitable over a number of years, accounting for more than 11 percent of the company's operating profit in 1979 (this dropped to below 8 percent for both 1980 and 1981). It was in a different posture than the other two divisions, however. First, the parts commonalities, manufacturing linkages, etc. were far less substantial. Though the division produced the tractors in the lower end of the line, they were lawn and garden tractors, of a much different manufacturing configuration and product characteristic than the larger tractors. The other major consumer products also were unique to this division—snowmobiles, chain saws, etc.

A substantial percentage of the consumer products marketing was done through some 1,000 independent consumer products dealers; other marketing was done through about 2,000 of the John Deere agricultural dealers (sales split about evenly between these two groups). The most substantial growth in the division was in commercial mowing products, the least in snowmobiles. The Horicon, Wisconsin, plant, where the consumer products manufacturing was done, also had been involved at several stages in the development and manufacturing of the compact utility class of tractors. Total market share was more difficult to determine here; by 1982 Deere had about 25 percent of the lawn and garden business, but considerably less than that in snowmobiles.

The closely related John Deere merchandise unit marketed a wide array of consumer products, ranging from a line of ski clothing to high-pressure washers, welding machines, space heaters, outside cooking grills, shop tools, etc. Most were purchased from outside contractors, with marketing through the Deere organization (and again made available not only through consumer products division dealers, but also through agricultural and industrial equipment dealers). Interestingly in light of its venture in bicycles in the 1890s, the company returned again to the bicycle in the mid-1970s, selling a Taiwan-made vehicle under the John Deere trade name. The bicycles were not well enough made to stand as good representatives of the John Deere quality image, and they were discontinued after just a few years of sales.

The verdict was still out about whether diversification in manufacturing had strengthened Deere's balance sheet and profit and loss statement. A simple financial analysis would not tell the whole story, however, for one must look behind raw contribution figures for other less readily identifiable interactions. There had been real synergy between the farm and industrial divisions in the commonalities of parts and manufacturing; though there had not been the same degree of commonality between consumer products and the other two, the widespread involvement of Deere's agricultural dealers in consumer-product marketing gave both divisions some added strength.

Exhibit 15–3. New line of lawn and garden tractors, 1983 (Deere Archives)

One can readily hypothesize that agriculture does not move in lock step with construction, nor with consumer sales. Yet there was little evidence by 1983 to support the notion that either the industrial or consumer products divisions could be a significant contracyclical influence on the agricultural division. Thus Deere's manufacturing diversification efforts had the primary effect of deepening corporate resources, and less that of spreading economic risks for the company.

Deere's "financial services" operating units—the credit and insurance companies—were both profitable in the recession of 1980–82, countering in a significant way the losses in industrial and agricultural equipment. (The retail finance subsidiaries earned $57.7 million in 1981, the insurance companies an additional $27.2 million.) Thus they were a financial offset to the decline in the equipment business. But, the financial service entities were just that—they were not a contracyclical manufacturing balance. Further, both groups were interdependent to a significant degree with equipment and dependent—neither was, in 1983, a fully arm's-length, stand-alone organization. Still, both legitimately could be considered viable efforts at diversification, and, differing with industrial and consumer products, did have the effect of spreading some of the company's risk.

There was no doubt, though, that up to 1983 the agricultural segment of Deere's business was dominant, particularly its North American agricultural sales. There were difficulties from excessively high dealer and farmer receivables, due both to farmer caution and excessive price cutting by some of the financially strapped competitors, but Deere's hold on market share in the North American farm equipment business strengthened markedly in the 1980–82 recession period. This was the area that most outsiders looked to in assessing Deere's strength; the statement of an analyst at the annual review of the industry conducted in 1982 by *The Wall Street Transcript* seemed to mirror the prevailing view about the company: "The rich are going to get richer. That's John Deere. Their Chairman, Bill Hewitt, said it best at their meeting in Moline last summer, when he said that this was the chance that occurs once in every three generations. Deere has one strategic advantage over everyone else. It's called access to capital, and their willingness to use capital for strategic purposes. Their enormous capital investments, their strong dealer network, the fierce brand loyalty among farmers—all suggest that Deere is in a very favored position to sharply increase its market share over the next couple of years."[3]

DEERE INCREASES ITS MARKET SHARE

The first ingredient of "using capital for strategic purposes" is to understand the underlying trends in the market, and Deere seems to have done this very well indeed. A major *New York Times* article comparing

Deere and International Harvester concluded: "Deere correctly saw the post-World War II trend toward fewer and bigger farms. From this came its strategy: continual reinvestment in product and manufacturing innovations, close attention to costs and quality, and lavish support for its dealer network. As a result, Deere is in the enviable position of being the low-cost producer and the high-quality provider."

The forty-five-year-long decline in the number of U.S. farms was reversed in 1981—there were 8,000 net new units in the 1981 farm count for that year. Officials of the U.S. Department of Agriculture (U.S.D.A.) estimated, however, that most of these were in the small-farm, part-time category likely reflected in the movement away from commercial farming.

The commercial potential of American agriculture seems oriented ever more strongly toward the large farm (defined by the U.S.D.A. as those with gross annual sales of $100,000 or more). By 1981, the largest one percent of the farms in the United States was producing about one-fourth of the nation's food; by the year 2000, according to the U.S.D.A., the largest million farms will operate almost all of the nation's farmland. Three-fourths of the farmland will be in the hands of the top 200,000 operations; indeed, the largest 50,000 will produce about two-thirds of all farm output.

Deere analysts consistently emphasized the central importance of this group to the agricultural machinery industry. In the census of agriculture of 1978, those farms with annual sales of $40,000 to $499,999—some 560,000 units—accounted for almost 60 percent of farm products sold and in the process took more than 70 percent of the industry's machinery sales. As the *New York Times* analyst put it, "Deere had the strategy and foresight to see where the market was going . . . and became the market leader in large equipment, which carries the highest margins."[4]

DEERE TRACTOR STRATEGY

By almost any standard, the "large equipment" that is the most important is the tractor. An understanding of Deere's moves on this key product is essential for assessing the company's present strength.

The number of on-farm tractors in the United States had peaked at 4,787,000 in 1965; by 1980 the number had fallen to 4,324,000. Still, throughout this period, the total horsepower continued to rise, with the 248-million-horsepower total of 1980 the highest to that date. Thus there were fewer but larger, higher horsepowered tractors in the country.

Deere responded to this by introducing seven additional tractor sizes above 100 horsepower in the 1970s, giving the company in 1982 a total of thirteen models in 40 horsepower (PTO) and above. The Generation II tractors introduced in 1972 (the 30 series), particularly strengthened the company in the medium-sized (40–150 horsepower) row-crop tractors;

the configurations of the thirteen 40 series tractors introduced in 1977 were essentially the same, but with more internal "guts," as the parallel increase in the width and size of tillage and planting equipment put ever-increasing demands on the tractor.

The number of these medium-sized row-crop tractors sold by Deere was very large. A total of 74,580 of Model 4430, at 126 horsepower (PTO), was sold in 1972–77; the 4440 (at 130 horsepower) sold at the same pace in 1978–80. Their companions in the medium-sized range also sold equally well. By 1981, Deere's market share of United States row-crop tractors was more than 45 percent and in Canada was almost 31 percent.

But it was in the new 50 series, introduced in 1982, that the link between innovation and new field demands became so striking. So important was the breakthrough technology of this new line that the company marketing group chose to rival the historic "Day in Dallas" of 1960, when its first four-cylinder tractors were introduced. Over a week-long period in New Orleans in July 1982, dealers were flown in from all over the world to witness, in the spectacular setting of the Superdome, the unveiling of ten new row-crop tractors. All had increased horsepower (from five to ten horsepower, depending on the model); all were available in mechanical front-wheel drive versions. The most revolutionary new ideas were reserved for the five machines in the 100–190 horsepower range. Each had a new fifteen-speed power shift transmission that gave the operator extremely efficient operation, with an estimated 7 percent increase in fuel economy. Seven of the fifteen forward speeds were in the field working range (with choices of speeds from 3 to 7.5 miles per hour), four more were in the PTO range (below 3), and four were in the faster transport range.

A second feature of these five models—a true innovation, patented by the company—was a clever configuration for the axle of the mechanical front-wheel drive, called CASTER/ACTION. One of the problems in mechanical front-wheel drive adaptations for row-crop tractors had been its increase in the turning radius. When farmers come to the end of a row they demand minimum lost time in the turning swing, before returning to the next row for productive work. With the CASTER/ACTION principle, the front wheels cant as they turn, dipping and giving the effect of turning under a bit, just enough to allow a substantially shortened turning radius. Introduction of the new 50 series tractors was in process in 1983 and field acceptance by farmers remained to be determined. The models' potential seemed outstanding.

Deere's market share in the top-of-the-line four-wheel drive tractors was more modest. The aggressive inroads on this market by the two small companies, Versatile and Steiger (each with horsepower sizes much larger than Deere), coupled with some reliability problems with one of Deere's earlier models (in the early 1970s) resulted in a modest market share for the company. (It had risen to almost 18 percent by 1980, but fell back

Exhibit 15–4. Top, *50 Series tractor, showing the patented CASTER|ACTION principle; bottom, Minimum turning radius of a 50 Series CASTER|ACTION tractor, 1983. (Deere Archives)*

again in 1981 to just over 14 percent.) The eventual success of the 50 series would have much to say on this; the introduction later in the decade of a larger horsepower top-of-the-line four-wheel drive tractor to complement the three members of the 8000 series (the 8450 at 185 PTO horsepower, the 8650 at 235, and the 8850 at 300) would help to determine whether Deere could increase its market share in this behemothian size.

THE SMALL TRACTOR:
THE DEERE-YANMAR COLLABORATION

At the lower end of tractor size, in the utility range, several interesting developments in the 1970s profoundly affected Deere strategy and planning. By the mid-1970s, the issue of the small tractor had become one of the company's most puzzling dilemmas. In 1970 the company was still producing a 30-horsepower tractor. But by 1976, the model line gradually had been shifted upward to the point at which the smallest tractor was the Model 2040 at 40 horsepower. Below this were only the seven lawn and garden tractors, from 7.5 to 14.5 horsepower, manufactured in the Horicon, Wisconsin, plant and marketed through the consumer products division of the company. The lawn and garden tractors were just that—well made, lighter weight machines for the homeowner to take care of his small- or medium-sized yard and garden. In no sense were these machines intended to be full-scale utility service agricultural tractors—their size was too small, their construction not rugged enough for such purposes.

In that gap left between the homeowner and the larger commercial farmer were substantial numbers of people who needed—and would buy—a tractor. Part-time farmers, for example, had increased during the early 1970s—and had done well in income, both in their on- and off-farm efforts. Heretofore, these "sun-downers" (as company marketing people dubbed them) would likely have bought a used, outdated tractor, in the older, lower horsepower sizes (the venerable two-cylinder "Poppin' Johnnies" of the pre-1960 John Deere line being great favorites). Now these people could afford a new tractor, built to the size and specifications they demanded for part-time utility work. These new operators might not necessarily have in mind much commercial farming, as a U.S.D.A. analyst recently pointed out: "To some extent, the small farm comeback may represent the transition of resources out of agriculture, as full-time commercial enterprises are transferred into the hands of others with only secondary interests in farming.... People with fairly sizable non-farm incomes can pay prices for land that mid-size farmers can't match. So they can bid farm resources (such as land) away from all except very well-heeled farmers." Still, whether these people farmed on any substantial scale, they nevertheless represented a potent market for agricultural machinery.

For a while a few American manufacturers continued to make full-scale

Exhibit 15–5. *Three horsepower sizes of the Yanmar-built Deere tractor:* left, *33 horsepower;* center, *27 horsepower;* right, *22 horsepower*

utility tractors in the range of 30 horsepower and below—Ford's 30-horsepower model was one of the most popular—but this intermediate horsepower range (13–30 horsepower) was increasingly coopted by the Japanese. Already the Japanese were the preeminent producers of the two-wheel, walk-behind tractor used all over Asia; now they perfected the four-wheel, under 30-horsepower tractor in many sizes. Moreover, they did this with economy, for the most difficult problem in the smaller horsepower tractor was to keep its comparative price low (its retail price per pound and per horsepower). The numbers of units needed in the range of 20–50 horsepower, worldwide, were large indeed. Deere economists estimated in 1974 that of the total free-world tractor sales in 1975 of approximately 670,000, more than 214,000 would be in that range. Perhaps 40,000 of them would be sold in the United States, substantial numbers in Western Europe, and even greater amounts in Asia, with Japan alone taking some 26,000.

Deere reacted in the early 1970s to the fact that the gap in its line was damaging, and the company began an experimental program at the product engineering center and at the Horicon plant to design a low horsepower tractor (somewhere under 30) that would be competitive with the Japanese machines. By the mid-1970s, the Japanese were selling into the American market in substantial quantities in these utility sizes; by 1977, Japanese shipments into the United States of under 40-horsepower tractors exceeded the numbers sold by all the United States and European manufacturers. Unfortunately, Deere's experimental model—the XR80—turned out to be too expensive for the marketplace. R.W. Boeke, who headed Deere's manufacturing at the time, put the problem succinctly: "Unless we decide to make major capital investments based on marginal returns, it appears likely that we would continue to eliminate lower hp. tractors, and essentially abdicate the smaller hp. sizes on a gradual basis. This could result in direct benefit to Japanese manufacturers." Boeke saw the company's Waterloo plant as making the "large-sized" tractors, the Mannheim plant as the source of "middle-sized" tractors, and the Dubuque plant, which had formerly produced some of the mid-size tractors, turning its production largely to industrial tractors. Spain, Mexico, Argentina, and Australia all likely would remain "pocket markets," none being low-cost manufacturers, and thus they would be able to export competitively only if subsidies were given by their local governments (a step that had been taken only by Spain).

Concurrent with the reduction in production of smaller tractors by the United States producers, the Japanese were aggressively expanding their horsepower sizes from the 15–25 horsepower range up to the 40–50 horsepower range. Several American manufacturers saw opportunities for joining with the Japanese—Ford had a link with Ishi (Ishikawajima-Shibaura), and, later, Massey-Ferguson with Satoh and White with Iseki. Deere had been marketing its Japanese-bound agricultural equipment through Yanmar, a major Japanese diesel engine manufacturer, but earlier had rejected Yanmar's collateral proposal for a possible manufacturing and/or marketing collaboration for small tractors in the North American market.

It seemed wise for Deere to reconsider, for the company now needed a source for tractors in the 20–40 horsepower size (which it did not want to produce itself), and additionally desired a source for the 40–60 horsepower sizes that would be more competitive for the North American market than the company's German-built tractors (the Deutsche mark-dollar exchange rate at that time produced a relatively high dollar figure when German goods were imported).

Deere's fresh start with Yanmar was just in time, too, for Deere soon found out that Yanmar already had been talking with International Harvester. As the Deere-Yanmar sales relationship had been a good one, Yanmar now decided to close out their negotiations with Harvester; the latter then acquired a link with another Japanese company, Kubota. Out of the ensuing discussions between Deere and Yanmar came an important Deere initiative—the introduction of certain sizes of Yanmar-built tractors into the United States as full members of the John Deere line. The tractor would be manufactured in Japan by the Yanmar Diesel Engine

Exhibit 15–6. *Deere-Yanmar "summit meeting" in Japan:* left to right, *Takeo Yoshikawa, executive managing director, Yanmar; Robert Hanson; William Hewitt; Tadao Yamaoka, president, Yanmar. (Deere Archives)*

Company Ltd., the manufacturing arm of the Yanmar group. Yanmar Diesel built industrial and marine diesel engines, outboard engines, fuel injection pumps, construction equipment, and agricultural implements and tractors. There already were seven models of the last in the Yanmar line, from 11 PTO horsepower to just over 26; diesel engines were manufactured in a range from 3 to 3,000 horsepower. Yanmar was the second largest agricultural tractor manufacturer in Japan—in 1975 it produced some 38,000 units to Kubota's 80,000 (of a total production of approximately 204,000).

The Yanmar Agricultural Equipment Company was the marketing organization not only for Deere in Japan, but for all the agricultural equipment manufactured by Yanmar Diesel. Under the new arrangement, this Yanmar arm would still be Deere's distributor in Japan; in turn, certain jointly designed and Yanmar-produced tractors would be sold in North America (and selected countries elsewhere) by Deere—with the Deere name—under a sales agreement with Yanmar. Deere would have no equity ownership in either one of these companies—Yanmar was a family company and did not desire such an arrangement.

Positioned in the middle of all of this as the linchpin was a third entity, a new joint-venture engineering company, owned 50 percent each by Deere and Yanmar, to carry out the development of designs and specifications for agricultural tractors in the range of 22–60 horsepower. Some of the tractors that came out of this effort would be sold under the joint-venture marketing agreement, but both the parent companies also would have the right to use the joint-venture group's designs and specifications that ensued for manufacturing their own tractors. Almost all of the detail design work would be done by Yanmar engineers; Deere would be primarily responsible for setting specifications and for testing the final result. In sum, Deere would elaborate the specifications needed to make a Yanmar tractor under Deere standards, but the joint-venture company would do the design work itself. Initially, the plan contemplated that some Deere engineers would be resident in Japan, working with their Japanese counterparts. In practice, this was not done.

The project was consummated in June 1977, following a moment of unease when the Federal Trade Commission took a look at the project, querying Deere about why it did not build its own vehicles in these sizes. The economics of the situation were clear, though, and the FTC chose not to intrude into the arrangement. This question answered, the project went forward apace. By late 1978, the joint-venture company had produced designs for two new tractors, first a 22 PTO horsepower, then a 27 PTO horsepower. By 1979 the actual tractors were in place in the United States as part of the Deere line (becoming models 850 and 950).

Meanwhile, Yanmar Diesel moved ahead by itself to modify two of its existing models, a 14.5 horsepower and an 18 horsepower, both built to Deere specifications. These, too, entered the Deere line, in this case, though, not under the initial joint-venture marketing arrangement, but in a more arm's-length marketing contract between Deere and Yanmar Diesel. The latter also continued to build its own line of tractors for the United States market, first selling through Yanmar dealers and later in collaboration with Mitsui dealers.

Design and development work by the joint-venture engineering group also went forward immediately for two larger models, at 33 horsepower and 40 horsepower. These models also joined the Deere line. The initial agreement provided that Deere was to be the sole distributor of all Yanmar tractors in the 27–60 horsepower range; two larger sizes, a 50 horsepower and a 60 horsepower, came into the line in 1983, marketed under the joint-venture arrangement.

Were Yanmar Diesel to become interested in building tractors beyond 60 horsepower and marketing them on their own in the rest of the world or even in the United States—a move contemplated by some Japanese tractor manufacturers—they would be free to proceed on their own, for the Deere-Yanmar marketing arrangements did not provide for any relationship beyond 60 horsepower.

By 1983, the Yanmar-made tractors under the Deere name had primarily been marketed in the United States. At the start of the arrangement a complicated territorial agreement was made. Yanmar took most of Asia (its traditional marketing area) but also Brazil and the Soviet Union, as well as the key Middle East countries and several important countries on the northern and western perimeters of Africa. Deere was given North America, the rest of South America, Europe, and Africa, as well as a number of countries in the Middle East, certain countries in South Asia, and Australia and New Zealand.

Deere had to concern itself with a complicated interface in this Yanmar relationship—the Yanmar-made tractors against its own models, manufactured by the company itself. There appeared to be only modest problems at the lower end of the scale—the two smaller tractors, the 14.5 horsepower and the 18 horsepower, sometimes compete with the Horicon lawn and garden tractors for large-lawn and park jobs, but the utility tractors are really quite different from the lawn and garden models. Similarly, in the 18–40 horsepower range, Deere chose not to produce any models itself—the Japanese volume was so dominant that a United States manufacturer was not likely to be able to challenge their unit costs.

At the upper end, though, there were some significant relationships raised by 1983. The joint-venture-designed model 1250, introduced in 1982, is a 40-horsepower version, and the Deere-manufactured model 2040, built in Mannheim, is also a 40-horsepower tractor (though its counterpart, model 2150, introduced in late 1982, is a 45-horsepower model). The rubric was established that the Yanmar model was the "lean and trim" version, the Mannheim a "deluxe." The price of the latter at first was substantially higher than the Japanese tractor, but in the early 1980s the unfavorable Mannheim differential began to narrow as the dollar strengthened against the Deutsche mark, and the Mannheim tractors at the interface of horsepower size could then be landed in the United States at a price much closer to Yanmar than at the start of the latter's relationship with Deere. The Yanmar machines became less "lean" (though presumably equally "trim").

Thus, this interface problem would always be plagued by the bugaboo of exchange fluctuations, among the dollar, the Deutsche mark, and the yen.

The Deere-Yanmar relationship proved to be a promising one. The quality of the design work of the joint venture was outstanding, and the manufacturing capabilities of Yanmar Diesel were certainly close to those of Deere. Through 1981 the Yanmar tractors had not yet been particularly profitable for Deere, given the substantial up-front development costs. The arrangement had the effect of keeping other aggressive Japanese manufacturers (*e.g.*, Kubota) out of Deere dealer lots. But, more than that, the collaboration was one of good will and mutual give-and-take; the relations between the two companies' chief executive officers were a particularly strong force, Hewitt and Tadao Yamaoka (the head of Yanmar) visiting each year for what they came to call fondly "the summit meeting." The choice of Yanmar as a major joint-venture partner has been a felicitous one.

GLOBAL TRACTOR STRATEGY

The Yanmar relationship remained just part of the larger issue of the required global tractor strategy for Deere in the 1980s. Deere's strategic plans that extended out over the decade were proprietary both for competitive relationships with Deere's always aggressive sister companies and also for the sensitive internal changes that would result from them. Factory assignments would be changed, marketing structures would be shifted—the future always has portents for those whose lives are affected. Certain key questions likely will form the basis for Deere's strategy.

For the tractor product lines, how many total models can be successfully sustained? By 1987, the worldwide plans call for some thirty-three separate model numbers across twenty-nine horsepower ratings. Can production runs on each of these models be large enough to exceed break-evens for each, or is this an over-proliferation of models? Product definition appears well structured at the very low and very high ends of the horsepower spectrum; there is less clear production definition in the middle range. Horsepower ratings are close, sometimes identical. Can a strategy of "lean and trim" models (Yanmar) and "deluxe" (European) versions work together? How high in the horsepower range should tractors sourced from outside Deere & Company proper (Yanmar, others) be allowed to go in the Deere line?

For tractor design strategy, how can a tripartite manufacturing responsibility (the Japanese joint-venture company for the lowest horsepower, the low and medium horsepower in Europe, and the high horsepower in the United States) be successfully meshed? What will bring maximum parts commonality and design integrity? Can Deere & Company itself maintain requisite control over major componentry?

In tractor sourcing, how many tractors should come from outside Deere & Company? At what level in outside sourcing does excess capacity appear in Deere factories, and in which ones? Should any whole-goods factories be transformed to componentry operations? What are the longer-run potentials of the factories in Turkey and Iran? What will be the effects of Spain's entry into the Common Market on the sourcing role of Deere's operation there? Are there other countries with promising sourcing potential, for example, the People's Republic of China or Brazil?

For the tractor strategy, two principal markets are envisioned—North America and Europe. Can all other areas of the world be fully served by models developed for one of these two markets? If the market focus in North America is indeed clear-cut, can the same be said for Europe? Can "pocket markets" be sustained over time, with high-cost inefficiencies built in? Overall, how can volatile currency rate fluctuations and political risks of the world best be understood and mitigated?[6]

DILEMMAS IN COMBINES AND TILLAGE AND HAYING EQUIPMENT

The Yanmar relationship particularly focused company attention on the question of worldwide tractor strategy, probably the most important of the questions facing Deere in the 1980s. Nevertheless, tractors are inextricably linked with the other segments of the company's lines—combines, tillage equipment, etc.

The Deere combines were particularly strong competitors in the late 1970s and early '80s; they commanded more than 40 percent of the United States market in 1981. In this case, the company adopted a conservative strategy, continuing with the conventional combine, not building the new "rotary" configuration adopted first by New Holland and then International Harvester in the 1970s. The rotary had some inherent advantages—instead of a reciprocal motion in the conventional configuration, the rotary had a simpler rotary motion. The rotary took more power than did the conventional for a given size, but its construction was more compact. The rotary sometimes did not work well in wet or tough straw and was particularly ineffective when there was a bad season of rain or a heavy weed content. Deere had been testing its own version of a rotary combine since 1958 but at several stages had chosen not to adopt the new concept. In the early 1980s, it was decided that "while John Deere will continue long-term basic research with the goal of achieving a true breakthrough in threshing and separating concepts, our combines will continue to feature our current concepts." The dealers at the New Orleans show in 1982 were explicitly told: "There is no rotary combine on John Deere's horizon." Throughout most of the recent period of the rotary, Deere has picked up market share over its competitors, testimony to the validity of this important decision.

With farmers' demands for combined operations—for example, using a mower, a conditioner, and a windrower in one combination—new, more adaptable tillage and hay-conditioning equipment were obviously needed. Field speed had continued to edge up in the mid- and late 1970s, yet the farmer wanted further gains in total efficiency and productivity and greater savings of his time. This could only be done by wider equipment. Soon there were many eight- and twelve-row, and later twenty-four row, tillage and planting instruments. The soybean crop in the United States more than doubled (in bushels) from 1970 to 1980, and this brought new innovations especially designed for soybean harvesting—for example, the flexible combine platform and the use of a row-crop head (the latter a Deere exclusive in those years).

Especially with planters, the tension for the farmer greatly increased with increased width—it became even more crucial that each of the many rows be working correctly. In the mid-1970s, Deere engineers developed a remarkable new planting concept in the Max-Emerge planter. The engineers began by asking, "What does the seed want?" First, it needs positive contact with firm soil at a precisely set depth. Most planters at this time cut a large trench; before the seed could be placed, much loose dirt fell in the trench and the seed dropped on this loose mass. Further, the seed, once there, germinates best if the soil to fill the trench is firmly packed around the seed, not compacted heavily right over the top. The Max-Emerge planter uses an ingenious combination of a narrow "V" cut and a pair of slanted wheels to drop the seed at a precise depth in the bottom of the V, touching firm soil, then pressing dirt around the seed with the wheels, but not compacting downward. The planting rate of each row is monitored electronically, so that the operator in his cab knows exactly how each row is planting. More recently, concern was put to the issue of not just monitoring the planting itself, but correcting any faults automatically. Deere's Max-Emerge, a patented concept, dominated the field in the early 1980s; the company's planter market share rose as high as 75 percent in one of those years.

Innovations were also made by the industry in baling—the round baler became very popular in the 1970s. The "hydrapush" manure spreader was also well received, particularly in the colder climates, where the more traditional conveyor chain often froze or broke. Deere was a follower for the baler but pioneered with the new spreader.

The broader questions about worldwide strategy applied as well to combines. With combines being made both in East Moline and Zweibrücken and being assembled in several other parts of the world, essentially the same kinds of questions posed earlier about the tractor surfaced once again. Other equipment—hay tools, cotton pickers, tillage instruments—also is made and/or assembled in several locations, and questions of multiple, integrated sourcing apply there, too. The compa-

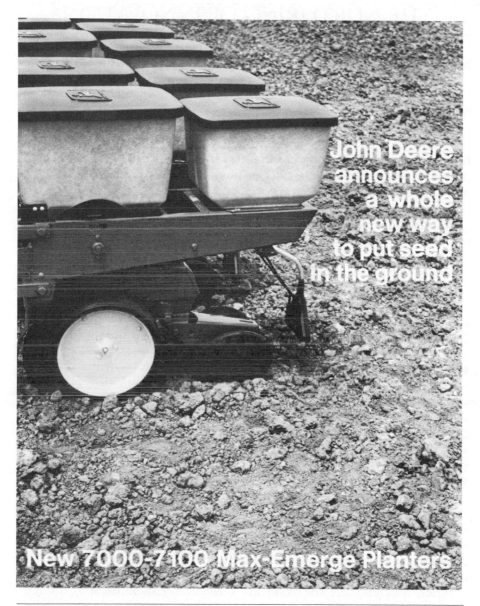

Exhibit 15—7. *Introductory advertisement for the Max-Emerge planter, 1974 (Deere Archives)*

ny's consumer products sourcing was limited in the main to North America, but sales had become international. In construction equipment, major sourcing and marketing questions remained to be resolved, questions of almost as much complexity as those relating to agricultural tractors.

THE NURTURING OF INNOVATION

These puzzles concerning worldwide product strategy relate fundamentally to the company's posture in respect to manufacturing, and the research and development efforts that underlie it. A number of nagging questions had to be resolved in the 1970s for both research and development and production.

Seldom in the history of the company had there ever been any question about the inherent quality of Deere's engineers. Over the years, the very hallmarks of "John Deere" were its sturdily built, well-engineered products. Questions of coordination in engineering did arise, however, particularly in the research and development dimension. At root was that longstanding enigma of the company: how much decentralization?

From the 1910s and the days of Joseph Dain's experimental work with tractors, and later in the 1920s and '30s with Theo Brown's "experimental department," there had been a small amount of centrally coordinated research and development. But most of the key work was done by engineers back at each factory, working on their own particular machines and jealously guarding their "turf." In 1944 Charles Stone shifted his portfolio from vice president of manufacturing to vice president of product development and two central departments—a product research department and a product development department—were established; this placed some of the basic product research at the company level.

In the 1960s, when Frank T. McGuire was made vice president, research, a further move took place: a new engineering research department (incorporating the old product development department) was established, Gordon H. Millar becoming its director of research. These moves signaled to everyone in the company that the research arm was now more centralized, though McGuire still felt it necessary in his memorandum announcing the role of Millar to state: "The role of research is to complement and not compete with our current product engineering efforts which are the responsibility of the factory organization." McGuire described the effort to the Deere board as "non-competitive and compatible with the factory product engineering effort. . . . " The annual research expenditure at this time was budgeted at $1.8 million, representing just 0.3 percent of the approximate $600 million sales level.

When McGuire left the company temporarily in mid-1965, though, there was a malaise in the central engineering research group, further compounded in early 1969 when Millar became assistant general manager at the Waterloo Tractor Works. Shortly after, all of the engineering group responsible for engines and transmissions had also been relocated there. The bulletin explaining this move was frank in stating that "this reorganization represents a basic change from the structure that has had considerable emphasis on our research." Now the function of the "technical center" (as it was renamed) was to explore computer techniques relating to engineering design, to provide a liaison with and appraisal of university experimental work, and to develop "advanced concepts of new products that do not have a direct relationship to our present product line." The technical center work was to be constrained, for the bulletin continued: "By the very nature of our decentralized organization, the engineering activities of the various factory Product Engineering Departments have a tendency to overlap or duplicate engineering work." The message was that such duplication should be eliminated—the factory engineering groups themselves should do the primary development work.

There was considerable unease about this downgrading, and later in that same year the board made a decision that was to have profound effect on the entire research posture of the company. Dr. Fredrick C. Lindvall, a world renowned engineering educator at the California Institute of Technology, was brought to Deere as vice president, engineering. Lindvall, a Moline native, knew a number of the people he was to work with; Hewitt, at this time a Cal Tech board trustee, had become particularly well acquainted with him. Lindvall's charge was to assist especially Deere & Company's principal officers and their staffs in planning "the technological development of the Company."

It took Lindvall only a few months to assess the situation, and in May 1970 he presented a major memorandum to the board. It was blunt in its criticism of the proprietary biases of the individual factory engineering groups. There, he felt: "New product ideas naturally tend to conform to a particular plant's experience and competence. Competitive pressure demands that substantial product engineering effort be concentrated on renovative changes and product line increments which sustain today's business. Cost reduction studies on a large volume item may present a more attractive profit potential than a new item with an uncertain market. Yet such efforts may not assure a longer range future nor anticipate 'the next generation' of demand." The general managers of the major factories had substantial discretionary money involved in this, and extensive engineering and experimental machine testing might have gone on before a "product review" brought the new product development to the attention of the general company officers. "A high level of security can thus be maintained at the factory in the early stages of a development if this appears to be necessary or desirable. However, a lack of communication among product engineers at the several factories may lead to duplication of effort, development of incompatible products, or failure to exploit a good idea which has Company-wide potential." Lindvall felt that the "present informal process through which new products are developed" lacked specific checkpoints and product reviews and that the factory manager, in the absence of clearly expressed views or recommendations from outside his own territory, "is obliged to make his own decision in an atmosphere of uncertainty in which 'silence gives consent.'"

Lindvall recommended "a formal procedure," in which clear statements of objectives would be elaborated, with definite check or review points at which the design or the prototype could be measured against these objectives, all this to be done with good documentation in order that management might later evaluate the development process. Lindvall acknowledged that the particular factories probably had such a procedure already, but that there needed to be "the benefit of inputs and review by personnel of other factories and Deere & Company . . . early enough in the design and evaluation study." Lindvall quoted at length from Patrick Haggerty, the chief executive officer of Texas Instruments, who seemed to be speaking directly to Deere in an article in the magazine *Innovation*. Haggerty pointed out that many companies in the process of developing a high degree of decentralization had found themselves "in danger of becoming no more than the sum total of the decentralized parts, loosely governed at the corporate level, primarily from a financial point of view." Haggerty continued: "At that point, the biggest job the corporation can handle has to be related to the biggest job that one, or at the most a few of the decentralized working units working together can handle. . . . The span of responsibility practically always exceeds the span of authority. Each manager has an authority which extends only to his decentralized unit, but a responsibility which extends across the corporation. Without some countervailing force, even when good innovative managers do develop in a decentralized organization, their innovations are ordinarily restricted to the entity for which they have responsibility or only narrowly and obviously beyond it." Thus, Haggerty felt: "Innovative efforts, even when they exist, tend to come out to fit the size of the decentralized units. . . . There are few or none of what I call breakthrough strategies; that is, strategic and innovative courses of action which, if they succeed, will impact the whole corporation in a major way."

Lindvall's memorandum was a bombshell, for it challenged as no other effort earlier had done the vested interests of the individual factory managers and their engineering groups. The board moved quickly to implement Lindvall's suggestions. In August 1970, two new committees were established: the product engineering council and the product engineering technical committee. The bulletin explaining these two new arms paid homage to the past: "In keeping with the policy of decentralized operations . . . product engineering strategy, problems and staff work . . . have been and continue to be based firmly on the assignment of direct responsibility for product strategy and product engineering activities of each John Deere factory to the general manager of that factory." Then the bulletin continued: "Without either changing or limiting this responsibility, product engineering effectiveness can be strengthened. . . ." Now there were to be "means for corporate coordination" and "means for organized communication."[7]

Lindvall, then at retirement age, stayed with the company only until

August 1972. At this point, Gordon Millar was brought back into the role for which he had originally been hired—vice president, engineering. This time the organizational groundwork was laid for a far more effective effort by general-company research and development work. Frank McGuire had begun a practice of bringing in senior outsiders, engineers on the cutting edge of technological developments around the country; now this was again an accepted pattern (although not always setting well with all of the company's entrenched engineering groups in the factories). The payoff for this move was great; the decade of the 1970s witnessed great strides in Deere & Company research and development efforts, moves that were fundamental to the ability of the company to become so strong in the industry. In the period 1972–76, total expenditures on capital improvements was some $561 million; research and development expenditures added an additional $427 million. Thus the total of the two came to almost $1 billion. In the second half of the decade, 1977–81, the capital improvement amount rose to $1.3 billion, with the research and development expenditure at $951 million, a total for the two well over $2.2 billion.

Each year *Business Week* keeps an "R&D Scoreboard" for the major companies in most of American industry. Deere's expenditures on research and development consistently have been at the top of the agricultural machinery industry, indeed exceeding the others by quite a margin (Appendix exhibit 36).

Such growth indices as the *Business Week* research and development figures are a bit misleading, though, for it matters a great deal just how the mix of these expenditures is being used by a given company. There is a subtle, hard-to-define equation between development work put to existing products as against new products. Particularly for the latter, the question of the degree of innovation sought is also a preoccupation of research and development managers. There is a threat to the profitability of such endeavors if excessive risk is taken or, contrariwise, if not enough risk is taken—a "me too" posture. In exhibit 15–8, both high risk and moderate risk activities are shown with a confidence band that broadens with the increased degree of innovation, or with increasing portions of the research and development budget invested in innovative concepts. Both profit opportunities and exposure to loss of profits increase with an increasing degree of innovation.

Research and development costs are further affected by the degree of vertical integration present in a given organization and by the volumes that can be attained with given product lines within this structure. Too much vertical integration sometimes can diminish profitability because of excessive investment needs in research and development, so that high figures on the *Business Week* tabulations may sometimes be misleading. Similarly, not enough internal vertical integration within a company can reduce profits, even though research and development costs drop signifi-

Exhibit 15–8   **The Relation Between Innovation and Profitability**

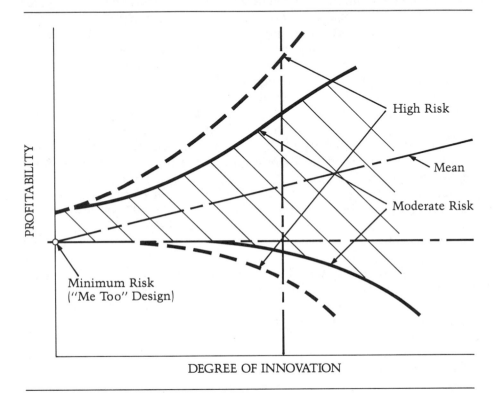

Source: *R.W. Boeke to Robert A. Hanson, August 7, 1980.*

cantly in such a mode. This balancing act can be seen clearly in another
organizational battle that took place in the 1970s at Deere, centering on
the original equipment manufacturing (OEM) group.

SHOULD DEERE SELL ITS TECHNOLOGY TO COMPETITORS?

Deere has often been a supplier to other companies of various pieces of
Deere componentry (engines, hydraulics, transmissions, castings, etc.). If
the company has substantial in-house manufacturing capacity, why not
spread overhead over a larger volume, selling the amounts in excess of
needs to other manufacturers? For some components this notion is quite
straightforward, for others the idea has a threatening dimension. For
example, will the selling of engines give away to competitors important
proprietary technological benefits? Could Deere's research and development costs be recovered under such an arrangement, or would the
company just be "giving the product away?"

Robert J. Carlson, senior vice president for North American farm equipment and consumer products in 1974, put the negative side bluntly, in regard to a proposal for selling a particular pump as an OEM product: "I believe the pump to be more unique than an engine, a Sound Gard body, or a corn head.... Our hydraulic system is the most advanced feature of our tractor line—in short, the area where we have the greatest visible advantage.... The pump is the heart of the system ... the problems inherent with the service of hydraulics are difficult ones. A competitor would help himself greatly if he could point to the industry leader, in this case Deere, and say, 'Ours is the same, don't worry about problems.'"

The key question is whether a technological advantage is being dissipated; in the pump case, Gordon Millar, Deere's vice president of engineering, differed with Carlson: "I don't sense that industry is beating our doors down ... on the basis of the pump's intrinsic capabilities. The real reason people want to buy our pumps is because they are well made and priced competitively. With regard to the pump itself there is nothing intrinsic in its design or manufacture that cannot be copied by competition.... I appreciate the position that Marketing has taken ... but I personally think the risk is greater in not expanding our manufacturing base than it is in giving away technology."

The process works the other way, too. It might well be that for a particular component an outside manufacturer could supply a better and/or less expensive component than Deere itself could make. Each time, though, it erodes some of Deere's traditional vertical integration. Selling one's own machines in the hurly-burly of the competitive world sharpens one's own competitiveness on price and product development. If a company just buys componentry, its internal capability tends to dissipate; as Millar pointed out, "Not going to be in the OEM business does not preclude the requirement for Deere making substantial investment at some future date to remain competitive in the diesel engine marketplace, even if we are our own exclusive customer.... We don't lull ourselves into the trap of thinking that just because we choose not to be in the OEM diesel engine business that this somehow precludes spending sizable sums of money to remain competitive ... not just look at the status quo as keeping us competitive forever."

Collaborative arrangements for selling diesel engines to other manufacturers—in either noncompetitive business, or even for trucks or farm equipment—certainly are possibilities. With the enormous capital costs necessary for redesigning a particular diesel engine (for even the redesign and relocation of production of one series of engines, the 300 series, Deere spent an estimated $175 million), such sales would help to recover some research and development costs. A strong OEM business often has a tendency to drive, rather than follow, internal component manufacturing. A higher degree of standardization is likely needed—for example, more compatible interface connections to other makes. Some special in-house engineering may have to go in the process. A components division of a company can be greatly strengthened by a strong OEM business, however, both by virtue of increased volume and by a more competitively oriented product development.[8]

FURTHER IMPLICATIONS OF CENTRALIZATION

In 1972 and 1973 tractor sales shot up much beyond expectations; forecasts not only predicted higher sales but also indicated rapid increase in the proportion of over-80-horsepower tractors. It seemed incumbent to expand tractor manufacturing facilities.

Engines would be the bottleneck in doing this. Potentials for outside sourcing were considered impractical, so a decision was made to develop a new engine facility and a new foundry. Everyone agreed that the foundry's location should be Waterloo. For the engine factory, however, there was sharp controversy in management about its location. Most of the Waterloo manufacturing group preferred to expand in Waterloo; indeed, Robert J. Carlson, the senior vice president in charge, wanted to have the existing downtown facility expanded by a high-rise building (there being no room to expand horizontally). Others, particularly Delno W. Brown, the senior vice president of the industrial division, advocated moving the engine works away from Waterloo altogether, arguing that the Waterloo organization was getting too large "both as a facility and also in relation to the available labor market."

But this was only part of Brown's argument, for he and others became at this time champions of a far-reaching notion, namely, that the engine decision was the propitious moment to decide upon the establishment of a full-fledged "components division." Brown faulted once again the dominance of the factories (especially Waterloo) in a letter to Hewitt: "The increased interfactory business we are experiencing has exposed a major problem—of priorities in the design and manufacture of interfactory components. A factory manager's success or failure is based on his performance in relation to his own products. This means that components for other factories may be given a lot of 'lip service' but very little priority when there is a conflict with the factory's own product."

The John Deere Engine Works indeed was built, the final decision on location, Waterloo. On a 191-acre site more than one-third of a mile outside of the city's limits, a 21-acre engine manufacturing operation was put under roof. A wholly new electric foundry also began operations in Waterloo in 1972 with a capacity that soon rose to some 90,000 tons annually (with a 1978 addition heightening this capacity to a total of 236,000 tons). In 1975, as the new Engine Works opened at its new site in Waterloo, land was acquired just outside Waterloo at the so-called "Northeast Site" for the construction of a new tractor factory. Over a

Exhibit 15–9. *Interior, Deere's Waterloo Engine Works, 1981 (Deere Archives)*

period of five years, a 2 million-square-foot new factory building was brought into being, opening in May 1981. This was the star in the raiment of Deere's capital expansion program of the 1970s, a remarkable award-winning plant that dramatized more than any other single effort the Deere capital expansion program.

Meanwhile, the notion of a components division was kept alive. The product engineering center became the focal point for some of the tensions between the decentralized factory personnel, particularly at the Waterloo Tractor Works, and those Moliners of a more centralized, coordinating persuasion as advocated a few years earlier by Lindvall. By 1975, when the Engine Works came on line as a separate factory, the product engineering center had developed a separate engine group and the center's reporting relationship was changed to the director of manufacturing, to whom also reported the Tractor Engine Works; this was the first time that the Waterloo Tractor Works did not have its product engineering center unit reporting directly to it. The practical effect of this for the remainder of the 1970s was to concentrate corporate component engineering effort, as well as the design and development of agricultural tractors worldwide, at the Waterloo location. Though some of the overseas operations—Mannheim, Saran, Australia—continued to play a modest role in engineering, the pinnacle was in Waterloo. Similarly, in industrial and construction equipment, the worldwide engineering effort was concentrated at the Dubuque engineering entity. Combine engineering, though, continued to be fully decentralized as in past practice, with the East Moline engineering group taking care of North American combines and the Zweibrücken group designing the European combines. Gordon Millar, the vice president of engineering for the company, worried that the company was not taking advantage of a worldwide product concept for combines: "We have enormous internal difficulties rationalizing a worldwide engineering effort with our concept of decentralization. Breathe the phrase 'central engineering' and you can shoot down in one fell swoop design control, engineering coordination and anything that would relinquish from the factory structure any local control of product design. It may be that we can afford the premium costs and some of the attendant beliefs in our combine engineering effort of the total decentralized approach. . . . I doubt it."

In the summer of 1979, Senior Vice President Robert J. Carlson resigned from Deere to accept a position at United Technologies, Inc. At the same time, the retirements of Senior Vice Presidents A.B. Lundahl and Delno Brown brought the opportunity for appointment of new senior management in these posts. Boyd C. Bartlett became senior vice president of farm equipment and consumer products-United States and Canada. Charles A. Hanson became senior vice president of corporate staff, Joseph Dain became senior vice president of corporate planning and was succeeded, on his retirement a year later, by Thomas A. Gildehaus. L.N. Hall remained senior vice president of the overseas division-farm equipment and consumer products and Clifford L. Peterson continued as senior vice president of the finance division. Robert Boeke, who had been named a senior vice president in 1979, headed the new components division. The major sections of the new components and design manufacturing division initially consisted of two components manufacturing units (the Tractor Works and the Engine Works at Waterloo), as well as the production engineering center, the John Deere foundry, and parts distribution.

The establishment of the components division as an equal in reporting relationship to the other three major operating divisions of the company (agriculture and consumer products, industrial equipment, and overseas) clearly signaled a new dimension of Deere manufacturing strategy. The historic focus of the company on whole-goods design and manufacturing now was to be balanced by a separate concept of worldwide components design and manufacturing.

In the process, the long-sensitive issue of the product engineering center seemed to have been resolved—it was given a reporting relationship directly to the senior vice president of the components division. However, things appear never to be completely settled in the age-old tug-of-war between centralization and decentralization. Late in 1980 operational responsibility for the Tractor Works was taken from components and given back to the farm equipment and consumer products division. Then in August 1982, all two hundred or so of the engineers working on the agricultural tractor vehicles (*i.e.*, everything excluding engines, transmissions, and final drives) were taken away from components, now to report to the general manager of the Tractor Works (they continued to physically reside in the product engineering center, though). How this would work out should components decide to build, for example, an engine that could be sold outside of the company, too, and the tractor division engineers plan a vehicle with special John Deere-only features, remained to be seen.

In 1982 a task force on a "global strategy tractor plan" looked once again at Deere's overall strategy to be the "world's leading manufacturer of agricultural-type tractors" and elaborated explicitly on the component division's mission: "*A componentized product strategy* appears best suited. . . . High production volumes will insure the *lower unit cost* of all critical components. Tractors can then be assembled of extremely cost-effective components, insuring the best cost/price ratios and the *highest profits* in the industry for the total line." The task force identified four specific areas for concentration: (1) providing a family of modular nonstructural power-shift transmissions for all corporate requirements above 90 PTO horsepower; (2) becoming cost effective in the 40 to 80 PTO horsepower tractors by developing a "skinny machine," with a particular focus on volume, rather than a primary emphasis on design of many different special-need products; (3) instituting a feasibility study toward the notion of providing sourcing for tractors in the 80 to 130 horsepower group, from either North American or European sources, with an upward extension of the present utility line in Europe and a downward extension in North America of the row-crop line; and (4) maximizing the commonality between the grounds-care and compact utility tractors in the 10 to 39 PTO horsepower group.[9]

THE "AUTOMATIC FACTORY"

A Deere engineer at a manufacturing strategy conference in 1980, hearing a comment from a fellow participant about a ray of light for Deere's European manufacturing profitability, commented: "That ray of light might turn out to be the headlight of the Japanese Express Train." The preoccupation in American industry with the "Japanese challenge" was pervasive at that time.

These issues really centered on the factory, for it was in manufacturing that the Japanese had acquired such a comparative advantage. (As a matter of fact, there was considerable evidence that American marketers were significantly more adept than their Japanese counterparts, at least at that time.) In the factory, two key components dominated: (1) the configuration of the factory itself, its equipment, logistics, and technical backup and (2) the people who manned it, their work relations, compensation, etc. The new Waterloo Tractor Works was at the cutting edge in regard to both.

The term "automatic factory" was used in a number of write-ups of the Waterloo factory in outside publications. The term tends to conjure up an almost frightening image of an enormous complex of steel and electronics, with robots all over the place at the work stations sending parts here and there and assembling products all automatically, guided by giant

Exhibit 15–10. *Aerial view, Deere's Waterloo Tractor Works, 1982* (The Furrow)

computers in some inaccessible, antiseptic room in the bowels of the plant. While such a Frankensteinian vision of the automatic factory seems overly apocalpytic, there are critical questions at issue in regard to labor's views of the new developments in manufacturing technology at Deere and other companies.

The computer does indeed lie at the heart of the Tractor Works. Even before the factory floor, the computer is critical in the design function; the widely used acronym, CAD-CAM (computer-aided design, computer-aided manufacture) is used as a generic term for a family of sophisticated computer-generated aids to design and manufacturing engineers. In the creation of a particular part, the engineer can use an electronic pen in a geometric modeling system to draw the part directly into the computer, detail it, add dimensional lines, and even reshape it. Three-dimensional visual capability permits the part to be rotated and viewed from any direction on the computer screen. A set of thirty-six standard dimensional descriptions—"round," "hexagonal," etc.—are already in the computer, so that the engineer can instantly call up a particular combination of them to picture a part before his eyes.

The real power of the system, though, is in the next step, for the computer can transform the designer's concept of a part—his mental data set—into an electronic data set that becomes a precise definition of the part, machine-readable in the computer. Thus this data base cumulates past practice; having all of this information in the computer gives the engineer tremendous power to be able to identify whether a part has already been made somewhere in the system before. Instead of engineers at different locations and at different times redesigning the same part, perhaps with slight variations, the process becomes far more standardized. Where perhaps nine or a dozen different variations of a particular part might have been in the system before, now only one or two may be needed.

It is still necessary for design engineers to take advantage of this opportunity for standardization, a process not always easy to accomplish. James F. Lardner, Deere's vice president of manufacturing development, put the dilemma well: "Component planners and design engineers need to develop a constructively skeptical attitude about the degree of uniqueness a component must have for a given end product application, while end product designers must recognize the risk inherent to creating a design for which a unique variant of a standard component must be improvised hurriedly to meet scheduled production dates."

The process of what Deere calls group technology (GT) has already markedly decreased the number of Deere parts in the total system, a remarkable savings when one considers that even in 1983 there were several hundred thousand parts in total in the company (with some 70,000 already in the GT data base).

The cost accounting specialist, incidentally, became a handmaiden in this effort. Formerly, an engineer could redesign a part for a minor savings in material or labor time and get kudos for the presumed lower cost. Yet in the process he was more than likely proliferating the total number of parts, a result far more expensive than the savings that ensued from the "new" part. Thus an ostensible savings of cost by redesign of a new part could only become effective if the part was used in realistic amounts. The Deere accounting group has applied a revised concept of "volume costing," in which the actual volume of a particular part used helps to define its cost. (Standard cost systems are often notoriously insensitive to volume, and sometimes produce "answers" contrary to experience and common sense.)

On the factory floor, too, new concepts (often abetted by the computer) have really come into their own. Of the many Japanese innovations in manufacturing, one of the most potent is their application of the "just in time" concept (what the professional literature calls the Kanban system, named from a Japanese word for a production order card). To put it simply, the theoretical idea would be to have just one part at every work station at the moment that that particular part was needed for machining or assembly. There would never be any downtime because the part was not there in time, nor would there be any excess parts inventory at any prior stage. In practical terms, this concept can never be fully reached—one needs part storage, work-in-process, etc. Yet the potential for savings in inventory in process by tight control of materials management is very important indeed. Conventional wisdom in manufacturing would hold that inasmuch as one should never be caught short of materials, a substantial buffer should be on hand at all times. One management consultant estimated that the Japanese automobile industry was running on $800 million in inventory to produce 11 million cars; the United States companies, he stated, needed $8.5 billion to do the same. Deere needed only to remember its overbuying debate of 1920 to be reminded of the dangers of such thinking.

But concentrating on inventory savings alone misses the real story of Kanban. In truth, the Japanese made these steps primarily to eliminate manufacturing inefficiencies—to take away the artificial cushion of a large parts and inventory backup, a prop for ineffectual managers to "cover their tracks." "The Japanese consider inventories a cover-up for production problems and waste," a Deere executive commented. "They lowered inventories to reveal production deficiencies—once revealed, the problems could be solved." The Japanese coupled this with an innovative use of sequential continuous manufacturing, in which each individual work station is reduced to the ultimate in simplicity but many are linked together in a "cell" arrangement that reduces the time that a part or component stays "in process." (Deere found, for example, that certain components taking only 3½ hours in actual process time were taking five weeks to get through the system; in effect, the components were sitting idle in bins 95 percent of the time.) Such a cell arrangement also cuts down the many jurisdictions that components move through in more conventional systems; the savings in overhead are substantial.

It is in the Waterloo Tractor Works that Deere has progressed farthest in these new manufacturing ideas. The Tractor Works superficially resembles many other manufacturing plants of its type—its conveyors, machine tools, welders, even its programmable controllers, all are familiar and well proven. "Nonetheless," lyrically reported one of the trade journals, "the TW shines as a supernova in the galaxy of today's U.S. manufacturing plants." What makes the Deere factory unique and award-winning is its integrated weaving together of many, many advanced manufacturing concepts. At the heart is the concept of computer-aided manufacturing (CAM). A host computer system gives orders to ten minicomputer systems scattered through the plant; the latter carry most of the burden of managing parts ordering, material flow, storage and retrieval of work-in-process, synchronization, tracking, routing, verification, and logging. Tied to the minicomputers are some 130 computer terminals, so that foremen and production managers can instantly determine where everything is within their systems. An innovative mechanical integration of conveyors, tow lines, monorails, automated storage and retrieval systems, and cranes free the operative for more advanced technical responsibilities.

The potential savings in in-plant transportation and machine usage can be astounding. Deere's president, Robert Hanson, at the annual meeting of the company in 1982, recalled that manufacturing executives had found that whereas the manufacturing of fifty-nine parts had earlier required twenty-three machine tools and twenty-eight different routes through the factory, by the use of another planning concept just being implemented in the company (computer-aided process planning [CAPP], along with the group technology underpinning) these same fifty-nine parts were estimated to be made by only nine machines and fourteen standard routes.

More than a dozen robots were in operation at various Deere factories in the early 1980s, the bulk of them at the Tractor Works, the Dubuque Works, and the Harvester Works. Their uses ranged from the automatic spray painting of individual parts and complete assemblies to loading parts in heat-treat operations and welding. Studies were also underway concerning possible assembly operations by robots. The use of the robot contributed to lower product unit cost through the reduction of a number of labor-intensive jobs. Further, as a company publication noted, "Robots have been found to demonstrate as high as 95–99% uptime and to provide consistently high quality work. In most cases, the robots are doing jobs that can be hazardous or highly repetitive for workers." The report's authors continued: "Justification of some robots is difficult because certain benefits are difficult to quantify (e.g., scrap, repair, quality, consistency, safety, health, etc.). It is almost a 'Catch 22' situation since the robot may need to be in place to gather the data needed to justify the robot."

The acceptance of robotics by Deere's employees has been remarkably good. There is, of course, a primitive, almost instinctive fear of machines taking over from man. As one committeeman in the United Automobile Workers local at the Tractor Works put it, "When people in the plant see these little robots moving down the aisles, they worry about their jobs . . . they think, 'The next robot could take mine.'" Yet, as the president of the Waterloo UAW local put it, "We're concerned, but the UAW has never opposed new technology."

Deere management has been effective in working with employees in planning and understanding the system and in using a participative style of management for group support. A pioneer program at the Waterloo Engine Works for "employee participation" was a significant success, and there were plans to implement it at other plants in the future. The company, incidentally, eschewed such buzz words as "quality circles" in describing its plan and attempted to stay away from Japanese comparisons; as a company report put it, "An encouraging point is that their success is not purely attributable to the Japanese culture.... The Japanese style is working very well in many parts of the world—using Australian, British and American workers."

A United States management consultant visited Deere's Tractor Works and was quoted later in the press as saying: "If you offered the Japanese that plant at a bargain price, they would not take it." (He was particularly critical of the company's high-rise storage units.) But such comments miss the point; as Robert Hanson put it in a keynote speech on Japan before a conference of business leaders in 1982: "The United States is not Japan. Not everything that works there would work here. We're a pluralistic society, not a racially and culturally identical one. Job mobility—a labor force willing and able to move, following new and changing opportunities, is a tradition here; almost the very opposite is the case in Japan. Our unions are generally craft unions, not company-wide unions, and relationships between companies and unions here are at arm's length, unlike the usual situation in Japan. Most companies here have outside directors on their boards, and this is an increasing trend. Few outsiders sit on the boards of Japanese companies. Women have far fewer opportunities in Japanese industry than they do in our own country. And the relationship between large Japanese companies and the Japanese Ministry of International Trade and Industry is a very cozy one. A similar arrangement here might be considered collusion rather than cooperation. So although I think there is much to admire in the Japanese way of doing business and certain areas where we may be able to adapt some of their procedures, I would not suggest that we mimic them."[10]

All of this serves to emphasize that the employee relations implications of the "automatic factory" are critically important to the system's effectiveness.

"GIVE BACKS" IN INDUSTRIAL RELATIONS

Deere, Caterpillar, and International Harvester all had contracts with the United Automobile Workers that were due to terminate in 1979. The situation for these negotiations was complicated first by a set of developments in Caterpillar's UAW local. There a new leadership had gained control, a militant group that soon took Caterpillar out on a strike that was to last some eighty days. The international office of the union had given only desultory support to the calling of the strike and found the acrimonious approach by the local to be counterproductive. This made the situation for the rest of the farm equipment and industrial products companies tenuous and settlements difficult to reach.

At International Harvester, the inflexible approach taken by both its chief executive officer and the UAW complicated an already difficult situation. Harvester's chief executive officer, Archie McCardell, had come to that firm in 1977 with a reputation as a "cost-cutting tiger." He did indeed pare down International Harvester's excess costs, and the corporation showed earnings of $360 million in 1979. It was just at this point that negotiations with the UAW were opening for a new contract, and McCardell took the opportunity to press the union for "give backs" in certain expensive features of the previous contract. The UAW was reputed at that time to have had on hand a $90 million strike fund and, as one commentator put it, "a burning need to prove its virility." The clash between McCardell and the union was traumatic. In the first three months of the strike the company lost some $222 million, at end of the following quarter they had lost another $350 million. By the time the employees got back to work, in mid-1980, they found that the recession had decimated the heavy truck market and International Harvester's sales had plummeted. After that, with high interest rates intruding, things went from bad to worse, leading to the difficulties pictured earlier in the chapter.[11]

Deere, meanwhile, had also taken a strike, but it had lasted only twenty-one days. The final settlement provided for modest wage increases, but also contained provisions for tightening the sick-benefit program.

The key issue in the International Harvester strike, the demand by the company for "give-backs," became a dominating one in American industry during the recessionary period of the early 1980s. What had always been assumed as sacrosanct—union-negotiated gains began to be taken back through negotiation as early as 1977, when the Chrysler Corporation asked its union and nonunion employees to pitch in, along with lenders, suppliers, and dealers, to keep the company going. The pattern of these concessions spread through the automobile industry, with both General Motors and Ford negotiating downward structuring of compensation rates. Worker sacrifices had traditionally accompanied economic recessions, but in the past most of these sacrifices had been in the form of layoffs. Now wage freezes and wage cuts had been advanced as an alternative to such layoffs.

Lurking in the background of this extremely sensitive issue was the bugaboo of Japanese competition. The great promise of the "automatic factory" gave new hope that the apparently vast competitive advantage of the Japanese against comparable American companies might be mitigated. But there was another key competitive imbalance between Japan and the United States, that of employee wage rates. Some unions became skeptical that employers were crying "give backs" like "wolf," alleging noncompetitive wage rates without being willing to back up the comparisons with explicit figures. Nevertheless, there was a widespread belief, from all quarters of American industry, that American wage rates were indeed substantially higher than those in Japan—perhaps by as much as $8.00 per hour.

Precise comparisons are very difficult to make because Japanese industrial relations patterns are quite different from those in the United States. On the one hand, job security in terms of the euphemistic "lifetime employment" of the larger Japanese firms is a plus for their workers. But the smaller firms generally do not have this policy, and the total "safety net" of benefits for the Japanese worker, both in small firms and large, is much below that of the United States. There seems no doubt, though, that when the lower Japanese wage rates are combined with their higher productivity, there is a significant total wage cost advantage for the Japanese, a potent competitive burden for American companies attempting to compete in world markets.

The farm machinery industry, Deere included, initiated its next round of contract negotiations in late 1982, as the three-year contracts of 1979 terminated. With skyrocketing losses at so many companies in the industry, there undoubtedly would be pressure from companies, almost across the board, for wage concessions of one sort or another. It seemed clear from preliminary indications in the public press that the UAW would seek to hold on to, and extend, wage and working-conditions levels in the more successful companies in the industry, knowing that they might face some heavy pressure in the more desperate companies for concessions that may need to be given just to hold on to the companies' jobs. Deere, as one of the more successful companies in the industry at the time, rightfully was concerned that its wage and working-conditions patterns might be thrown comparatively out of line with those of its competitors in the process of the year's bargaining.

FINANCIAL PERFORMANCE

The company has prided itself on its growth and profitability since the 1970s and its financial conservatism in attaining some very attractive performance figures. The overall story is quickly shown in Appendix exhibit 37. The dominance of Deere's profitability in the farm machinery industry, and its second-place position to Caterpillar in the industrial equipment industry, are clearly shown for the same time period in Appendix exhibit 38.

For a number of years, Deere's sales figures put it among the 100 largest industrial companies in the United States (these rankings provided each year by *Fortune* magazine). These firms provide an excellent standard of performance against which Deere can be measured, for they are the companies with which Deere competes for people and capital. It is revealing of Deere's excellent performance in the years 1972–81 and its weak performance in 1982 to look at the company's rankings on some other key indices for these same 100 largest industrials, again provided by *Fortune* (Appendix exhibit 39).

By a number of financial criteria, the agricultural machinery industry is an unusual business. Most of its larger companies are involved not only in manufacturing but in retail financing. Deere's retail finance subsidiaries—John Deere Credit Company in the United States, John Deere Finance Limited in Canada, and John Deere Leasing Company (U.S.)—total well over $2 billion in terms of total assets. Their function is to purchase and finance retail notes from Deere's sales branches and industrial equipment sales regions; these originate from retail installment sales by John Deere dealers of new Deere products and used equipment.

These companies are essentially free-standing entities, not consolidated into the parent company financial statements and carried on the latter's balance sheet as investments, producing income (or losses). The parent company has had an agreement with the credit companies to take any action necessary to maintain the credit companies' ratio of earnings to fixed charges for each of its fiscal years through 1982 at not less than 1.5 to 1 (after 1982, at 1.25 to 1). The Deere & Company annual reports have made it clear that "the agreement is not intended to make Deere & Company responsible for payment of the obligations of John Deere Credit Company." Nevertheless, the link between the parent company and its credit subsidiaries is less than arm's length.

The relationship between the insurance subsidiaries and the parent company is similar to that of the John Deere Credit Company—free-standing in just about all of their operations, yet with certain corporate ties, such as marketing linkages, etc. Plans were afoot in the early 1980s to break this umbilical cord altogether, setting up a multi-line insurance company, completely free-standing, that could be measured not only against Deere corporate goals but against other such insurance companies. A holding company would likely be set up that would consolidate all of the subsidiary boards of directors and bring about a complete separation of the marketing function from the company's equipment marketing. There is no intrinsic reason why the credit companies cannot be managed in at least a quasi-independent mode—indeed, outsiders such as regulatory authorities, customers, and dealers tend to press for this. It would be more complex a process than for insurance, though, given the historically stronger captive relationship and marketing considerations.[12]

Another important financial parameter of the agricultural equipment industry is the presence of long selling terms. Deere, like most of the farm machinery manufacturers, sells to its dealers, not directly to the customer. In other words, the company takes its profits from the dealer. In turn, the company extends terms to these dealers some fifteen or more months out into the future, depending on when the particular product involved is shipped or when it is finally sold to a customer. In effect, goods are shipped on open account, under provisions codified in the Uniform Commercial Code. When the product is sold to a customer, or when the terms expire, the dealer is obligated to pay off 90 percent of the amount due. The remaining 10 percent is then due at the beginning of the second month following the month in which the 90 percent was due. The dealers are not obligated to pay interest during the entire term's period, except on tractors, for which interest is charged after the first nine months.

Often it takes a substantial length of time to sell capital goods such as tractors—a hiatus of many months on the dealer's lot is not uncommon. Some of this is due to the typical seasonal swing in sales, but often a substantial cyclical effect exacerbates this inventory problem. Excessive inventories are a perennial worry of dealers anywhere, in any business; in the case of the farm machinery business, it is equally a worry of the manufacturer, by the nature of this lengthy credit exposure. Thus there is a great need for control of dealer receivables. In some years Deere's receivables at year-end (the key point for measurement) ran as high as 60 percent of the sales for the same year; a "normal" ratio might be around 40 percent, and in the late 1970s the ratio was as low as 35 percent. In 1981, the figure was about 44 percent; in 1982 it had drifted up again to more than 58 percent. (Several of Deere's competitors had much higher inventory percentages in these two years, and this led to much distress selling in the markets as these companies attempted to convert product to cash.)

PREOCCUPATION WITH THE RECESSION

This chronicle concludes at a time of uncertainty—a serious worldwide recession, compounded for a number of industries in the United States by a vigorous foreign challenge. The effects have been felt at Deere in a significant way. Earnings sagged from the excellent profitability records of the period 1972–79. In 1981 indefinite furloughs of several thousand line employees of the company were instituted. The longstanding bonuses paid salaried and managerial employees were temporarily suspended in 1982 and wages were frozen for this group (except for the cost-of-living adjustment). The company's contribution to the employees stock purchase plan was temporarily halted and rigorous cost-control measures were implemented throughout the organization. There is no doubt that the recession of the early 1980s had a significant detrimental effect on the agricultural machinery industry (for example, the crisis situation in Massey-Ferguson and International Harvester); while Deere came through the difficulties in better shape than just about all other members of the industry, it still faced major short-term concerns.

It is this modifier, "short-term," that is the conundrum for American industry and for Deere—and for this book. The reader deserves a realistic view of how seriously the recession has affected Deere, yet the recession is not over, and the nature of "short-term" not yet clear. The following discussion is based primarily upon the situation pictured in the annual report of 1982, when it was determined that the essentially conservative posture of the company had stood it in good stead in the three difficult years of 1980–82. Deere had never chosen to leverage itself with large holdings of debt, a pattern that had been followed by some of the other larger companies of the industry. The percent of short- and long-term borrowings to equity had been in the 40 percent range in 1977 through 1979, had risen sharply to more than 67 percent in 1980, had dropped to about 55 percent in 1981, but had risen again in 1982 to more than 77 percent. Long-term debt, which had been at 31 percent in 1977 and had risen to more than 36 percent in 1978, dropped to just under 28 percent in 1981 but increased to more than 37 percent in 1982. Inventories remained remarkably stable in the three years 1979–81, but decreased by $111 million in 1982.

The short-term debt was a more serious concern. Total current liabilities stood at $1,465 million in 1979, were up to $2,304 million in 1981, and reached $2,395 million in 1982. The shorter-term sales situation was where the real concerns lay. Trade receivables, almost all of which were with Deere's dealers, stood at $1,401 million in 1979, rose sharply in 1980 to $2,093 million, and were up to $2,374 million in 1981 and $2,661 million in 1982. By the end of fiscal 1981, the company's retail finance subsidiaries had an additional $2.3 billion in receivables (after selling some $572 million of their retail notes to financial institutions in 1980, and following this with another sale of $833 million in 1981); an additional $1,035 million was sold in 1982, and the total dropped to just under $2.1 billion. In total, trade receivables and retail finance receivables cumulated to a sobering figure of $4.7 billion at the end of 1981, holding at approximately the same figure held for 1982.

Rapid fluctuations in interest rates complicate this in a major way. The retail notes, for example, can be outstanding for an average of some three years, up to five in some cases. Back three years, prior to 1982, the charges to farmer customers were in the neighborhood of 13–14 percent; in 1982 the company was paying as high as 20–21 percent for its own short-term needs, but this percent had dropped to about 9.47 by the end of 1982.

Clifford L. Peterson, the senior vice president of finance in 1981, commented to a management group about the difficult situation in that year: "We have financed *incremental* assets at an average cost of 17 percent so far this year. For the last 12 months Deere has earned 8.2 percent pretax, preinterest return on assets. This means that we have lost money on every additional asset added so far this year—whether it was dealer inventory, factory inventory, parts inventory or many of our new fixed assets. . . . The 'engine of leverage' is running in reverse."

A significant complication was the influence of waived finance charge programs, instituted by the company through its dealers in 1980, 1981, and 1982 to stimulate retail sales. The concept of "waiving the interest" as a sales incentive device had long historical roots, but generally was applied only in the low-selling season, typically November through March. The pattern in the recent period of year-round waiving—*i.e.*, in-season waiving—was a more troubling development.

The effect of this waiving on the parent company was substantial; the annual report of 1982 explained: "The retail finance subsidiaries received compensation from Deere & Company approximately equal to the normal net finance income on retail notes for periods during which finance charges are waived." Another way of saying this, of course, is that the parent company is subsidizing the credit companies (and therefore the customers), undoubtedly a necessary program to keep dealer strength in the face of a serious situation.

It is not just these waived finance charges that the parent company has had to absorb; in 1981, the company was required to provide a $74 million support payment to the United States retail finance subsidiaries to satisfy the bankers' restrictions on loans. Hewitt explained this in his report at the annual meeting of 1981: "We had to divert $74 million from other projects in order to support our retail finance subsidiary in 1981. But we believe that was good business practice because year after year we depend largely on the same group of loyal customers. We are not in the banking business, but our customers had a special need for credit assistance during this difficult period of high interest rates." Hewitt continued with a description of a new approach to consumer finance: "We are offering a new variable-rate finance plan to help our customers. This plan enables them to avoid being locked into the payment of high interest costs when rates come down in a later period."

Deere's access to the capital markets has been excellent over the past decade. The company's credit rating has moved back and forth between A and AA at various times during this period; in 1982 both the parent company and the credit companies were able to maintain a AA rating. In 1983, however, these ratings were reduced to A due to difficult economic conditions that also affected many other industrial firms' ratings. It seems clear, though, that the capital markets continue to respect Deere's inherent strengths and its longer-term future. Deere's credibility in the equity markets was excellent throughout this period; the longstanding pattern of regular dividends brought some imposing returns for equity owners. For example, 100 shares purchased in 1955 for $3,462 would have grown to 824 shares (through stock dividends and splits) by the end of 1981 (worth $25,995) and $14,771 would have been paid in dividends. Clearly, stockholders have fared well.

As recently as 1981, the company increased its equity position by a public sale through underwriters; in January of that year 4 million shares of common stock were sold, with the company receiving net proceeds of $166 million, the purchasers paying something in excess of $41 per share.

Having noted here a plethora of puzzling financial problems in the recessionary period of 1982, it is well to refer to the quality of the company's products, as attested to by its strong and increasing market share almost across the whole range of products. When the recession subsides, and the farmer returns to the market, Deere's products would seem to be eminently strong. The truly significant amounts of funds that the company has invested in itself—capital improvements of the nature of the Waterloo Tractors Works, sophisticated computer-based analytical underpinnings such as the CAD/CAM system, and research and development—all bode very well indeed for the ability of the company to maintain and improve its already strong line of products. Management itself, at an important transition point in 1983, has been widely recognized as having depth and quality.

Finally, the marketing organization needs always to be remembered. If there is any single arm of the company that has had preeminent historical strength, going back to the very days of John and Charles Deere, it is the marketing structure that came into its own through the sophisticated branch-house system and the development of a corps of John Deere dealers that has had no equal anywhere in the world. As one industry analyst put it in *The Wall Street Transcript* review of the industry in March 1983: "Deere has gone around and actually to the detriment of their balance sheet given support to their dealers. They're the only people who are going to end up with a healthy dealer network. 10 to 12 percent of the farm machinery dealers in 1982 went out of business, but the number of Deere dealers that went out of business was miniscule, and they were immediately replaced by people with stronger capitalization. So not only are they the low cost producer, they're going to be the only people around with dealers."

"John Deere" has always been close to the farmers, with its personnel attuned to the farmers' beliefs and ways and with a keen sense of the need for loyalty from customers. Other companies have built up loyal customers, too, and Deere will not be without competitors. The fact remains, though, that Deere has a superb marketing organization, positioned very well for the longer run.

CONCLUSION

CHAPTER 16

CHARACTER OF A CORPORATION

*[Deere was an exception,] unusual in both the intensity
with which it is connected to the past and for the ability
to turn handsome profits. . . . Deere's sensibilities,
nostalgia and respect for the past make it peculiarly
adept at finding continuities, at making events spring out
of other events, new departures take off from
well-worn paths. . . . It is a company which its executives
are devoted to and dependent on, as a company.
These men are unlike that more modern breed of manager
which, management sociologists tell us, is
"career-oriented", and which considers one company
as useful to him as any other. . . . The Deere men have a
more romantic orientation. They believe in their
company and not, as most salesmen do, out of expediency.
They honestly feel that Deere deserves their
fealty and reverence. The view is not exactly
fashionable these days. But it has stood the test of time.*

Management Today (England), 1973

The era of William Hewitt as chief executive officer ended with his retirement from Deere & Company in August 1982 at the mandatory retirement age he himself established for all management when he first became president in 1955. Hewitt's personal reputation was at its zenith. He had become a key representative of American industry, widely recognized all over the world. When *U.S. News and World Report* published its eighth annual report—"Who Runs America?"—he was included, the only business executive to be listed in the category of agriculture. His services continued to be called upon after retirement. In October 1982, he accepted an appointment as United States ambassador to Jamaica.

Exhibit 16–1. *William A. Hewitt in his office, 1982 (photograph © by Arnold Newman)*

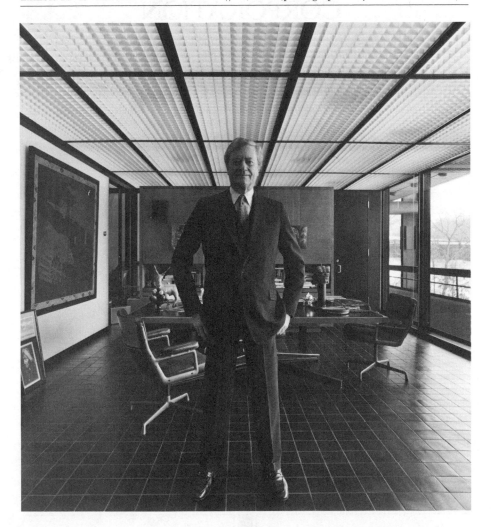

AS SEEN BY OTHERS

In 1982 Deere's reputation was also at a high point, judging from comments appearing in the business and popular press. It had been praised in the early 1980s when American management generally had been faulted for low performance, particularly in the face of challenges from foreign competitors, and for taking too short-run a view. As one analyst wrote in 1982 in the *New York Times*: "The truly great American companies, those most respected and effective offshore as competitors, are not players of funny money games. Rather, enterprises like Caterpillar, John Deere, Procter & Gamble and Eastman Kodak single-mindedly dedicate themselves to deepening their product lines, improving their product delivery and support systems, manufacturing more efficiently and adapting to evolving world market conditions." In the same year, the *Boston Globe* named Procter & Gamble, Caterpillar, and Deere as three of a half dozen examples of organizations "that had kept the corporate eye on the far horizon." The *Los Angeles Times* commented that Deere "has avoided the dominant corporate approach today, which relies on a numbers-oriented portfolio strategy aimed at draining so-called 'cash cows' . . . to provide money for operations promising greater returns."

Despite the pace of the modern business corporation, which sometimes has seemed to obscure the longer-term perspective, Deere's "sense of history" remained intact. A British writer commented: "All large corporations have a history. But in most cases that history is an appendix merely, a footnote. They are dominated and ruled by contemporary ethics and values . . . the successful modern corporation is expedient. . . . Like a chameleon it takes on the coloration of each succeeding era. In business, history *is* bunk usually. . . . Probably the majority that revere their past . . . have a profitless present and anticipate a poor future. They are becalmed. . . . History for them is a substitute for action."

This same analyst had concluded that Deere was an exception, "unusual in both the intensity with which it is connected to the past *and* for the ability to turn handsome profits. . . . Deere's sensibilities, nostalgia and respect for the past make it peculiarly adept at finding continuities, at making events spring out of other events, new departures take off from well-worn paths. . . . It is a company which its executives are devoted to and dependent on, as a company. These men are unlike that more modern breed of manager which, management sociologists tell us, is 'career-oriented,' and which considers one company as useful to him as any other. . . . The Deere men have a more romantic orientation. They *believe* in their company and not, as most salesmen do, out of expediency. They honestly feel that Deere *deserves* their fealty and reverence. The view is not exactly fashionable these days. But it has stood the test of time."

Hewitt, representing the fifth generation of the family, felt strongly this sense of history. Early in his tenure as chief executive officer in 1964 he had inaugurated the "Green Bulletin" series, codifying the key goals and policy statements of the company. In his introduction to the series, cast as a letter to all employees, he first commented on the "rapid changes and increasing complexity of the times." He then continued: "It seems particularly important that we should . . . rededicate ourselves to the store of wisdom—tried, tested and proven—accumulated by the men who built and steered the John Deere organization through these many years. It was their guide and remains as their legacy. It must live in our daily work. . . ." The British writer remarked about Hewitt's predilection: "Time and again in conversation, Hewitt returns to historical touchstones . . . he has much affection for each mosaic of the past. . . . There is in his voice a warmth, a tenderness for the entire accumulation of human time and energy expended within the boundaries of the Company."

Analysts have commented widely on Deere's comparative strength relative to its domestic competitors in the North American agricultural equipment industry. There will be "fallouts and marriages," as International Harvester's chairman, Donald D. Lennox, put it to the *Wall Street Journal* (in February 1983), as companies seek to reduce costs and cut excess capacity. Deere has been seen to be emerging as the dominant company, the "General Motors" of the industry, as the *Washington Post* put it in early 1983. "They really don't have any weaknesses," the *Washington Post* writer concluded. In the annual *Wall Street Transcript* review of the industry in March 1983, analysts cited Deere's unique position as a low-cost producer and pointed to the company's larger-than-average research and development outlays and major capital expenditures over the past decade as portents of increasing market share when recovery of agriculture comes.

The focus on Deere's preeminence in the North American market does obscure difficulties abroad. Deere's ability to source and to sell worldwide will be critical in the upcoming shakeout that the industry is likely to experience. Foreign competitors will be strong in both agricultural machinery and construction equipment and must be challenged on their own grounds and in their own terms. As the previous chapter elaborated, however, Deere's international operations, though they sometimes have had the patina of success, have often reduced the company's profitability. Renewed losses in Europe stemming from the recession of the 1981–82 period have counterbalanced successes in other parts of the world.

Nevertheless, Deere's management does appear to have reason to believe its "good press." Despite the short-term worsening of its financial ratios, its conservative financial policies, long a central tenet of Deere management, have stood it in good stead in the recession of the early 1980s. As one financial analyst put it, "The severe deterioration of the balance sheet of many industry participants will not permit them to compete head on against Deere, which is using capital as a strategic weapon." Deere has three well-run profit centers, its manufacturing entities, the marketing units, and its financial organizations (the credit companies and insurance companies). Thus it has been able to use its capital more effectively; at the same time, its competitors have been forced to withdraw potentially productive assets by out-sourcing, spinoffs of divisions, or outright sales of those assets because of short-term demands for cash.

The dealer organization, always a source of strength at Deere, has survived the ravages of the recession to become even stronger. It is the best financed and most stable in the industry. A marketing group of this quality takes many years to build; it seems highly unlikely that any other competitor, domestic or foreign, can hope to match Deere's dealers, at least over the short run.

Deere's employee relations add a further historical strength. Its bargaining with the United Automobile Workers is in marked contrast to that at International Harvester, Allis-Chalmers, and Caterpillar. Since the watershed 1955–56 negotiations, Deere has had excellent relationships with this union, and the union has been an important barrier to excessive paternalism. In a *Boston Globe* article on the "four companies where quality still counts," a revealing comparison was made between the UAW relationship at Caterpillar and that at Deere. Citing the "long history of difficult labor-management relations at Caterpillar," the *Globe* writer continued: "The Company is a divided society, the salaried workers, who are supposed to have tractor-colored 'yellow blood' on one side, and the hourly union workers on the other." In contrast, at Deere "management speaks a different language," in which "the workers are not divided into white-collar and blue-collar—they just have different responsibilities." Deere has followed a straightforward policy of equal respect for salaried and hourly-paid employees alike. The 1980s will undoubtedly put strains on this relationship, as the company drives to reduce the rate of growth of labor costs in the face of aggressive competition from abroad.

Technological and managerial supremacy must be continually re-earned, and Deere executives know this. Further, few if any organizations have no weaknesses, the *Washington Post* notwithstanding. Some of Deere's most important strengths are at the same time potential sources of weakness. The company's persistent difficulties in sorting out conflicting strands on the concept of decentralization is a case in point.

INSTILLING INITIATIVE

Vesting authority in an individual, who at the same time is made personally responsible for the use of that authority, has proven in practice to be a truly liberating influence on people. Since the days of Alexis de

Tocqueville's *Democracy in America* (1835) and before, Americans have been characterized as individualists striving to carve out their own destinies. The dominance of the frontier mentality, captured so well by Frederick Jackson Turner, colored the development of the West—and at just the time when John and Charles Deere were contributing to the opening of the prairie. Modern social scientists—for example, the pioneers in the field of organizational behavior, such as Rensis Likert, Douglas McGregor, Warren Bennis, Chris Argyris, and others—have reinterpreted de Tocqueville, Turner, and others to emphasize in contemporary terms the great potency of the concepts of participation and individuality in infusing a sense of both contribution and personal worth in organizational environments.

Decentralization of authority and responsibility has been a dominant ingredient of the Deere character, a recurring theme for at least the last 110 of the company's 145 years. (It emerged in the early 1870s with Charles Deere's novel way of organizing the branch houses.) Through all of these years the company has given full effect to this, not only with management and salaried personnel but also with line employees through the use of a truly actuating incentive plan of compensation. One International Harvester executive was quoted in 1982 as saying: "Deere decided they were going to have a truly decentralized management and, believe me, they *are* decentralized. At Deere, you don't make any decisions in the center of the Company except finance, capital-resource allocation and overall strategy. Everything else is done in those operating groups, with super plant managers making the decisions."

This does make the concept sound deceptively simple, but applying it has always required considerable imagination and good sense. Deere's long experience with decentralization has become not only an article of faith but has provided many operational lessons on just how elusive the precise application of the concept can be. These lessons are still not complete, for there will always be new issues that seem to fit individual initiative and that at the same time demand central coordination and control. Recent efforts to set up a worldwide tractor sourcing plan and the decision to set up a corporate-wide components division both seem to imply more "centralization." At the same time, emphasis on worker participation in decisions and the "quality circle" discussions seem to press toward "decentralization." But the former cases do not cut off the potential for vigorous exercise of individual initiative, and the latter cases do not reject the need for realistic authority to ensure coordination and control.

One cannot gainsay the positive effect that the debate over decentralization has had on the company. In training Deere people for leadership, it has probably been the single most important factor. The delegation of authority to the lowest practical level has instilled a sense of initiative in Deere managers, as well as an ability to respond to local conditions and to changing environments. Paired with this has been management's willingness to understand and accept misjudgments. As Hewitt has put it, "Managers have the right to fail, the same way as in baseball the home run king often is the one who strikes out most often in the season. We cannot, of course, tolerate disastrous failures, but we can tolerate reasonable mistakes." He reiterated the same thought in a *Boston Globe* interview: a well-managed company was one "not out to make instant heroes." Deere has been a supportive—and forgiving—institution over the years.

Whether Deere has been able to inculcate a spirit of entrepreneurship in its present management remains a moot question, not yet answerable in this period of cutback and retrenchment. There is no doubt that the current "shakeout" period will have many entrepreneurial potentials, and Deere commands resources that can take advantage of them to make these operational. Personal skills of entrepreneurship must be present, however. These have been there in the past; they must also be in place for the challenging future.[1]

THE SEARCH FOR EXCELLENCE

Deere has always been known for well-engineered products and superb service. Hewitt chose dramatic ways to emphasize the pursuit of excellence embodied in these achievements. His efforts reflected an enduring interest in style, both in design and as a quality permeating the company in its physical aspects, buildings, products, advertising, and literature, as well as the actions of its people. The electric effect on company personnel of the Saarinen-designed Deere Administrative Center has continued to be felt and was enhanced in 1978 when Deere added a new "West Wing" to the center. It proved to be no ordinary addition, for architect Kevin Roche, Eero Saarinen's successor, created an award-winning facility that was not only visually stunning but that enhanced the work environment for the staff. Roche chose to complement the Saarinen masterpiece, connecting it to his wing with a fourth-level corridor-bridge. Featured was an interior atrium through the center of the building, with the offices on all sides overlooking its gardens. The building won a number of awards, including the *Administrative Management* "Office of the Year" citation, just fifteen years after the administrative center had taken the same award.

The company's and Hewitt's continuing concern for architectural and aesthetic excellence has earned widespread recognition. The German magazine *Der Spiegel* commented: "One of the best known patrons of the new glasshouse vogue is William A. Hewitt, an American entrepreneur whose aim has been for 25 years to make outstanding architectural works a sort of trademark for his Company. This has earned him a place among

Exhibit 16–2. *Interior atrium, West Office Building, Deere Administrative Center, Moline, 1978 (JD Journal)*

the ranks of the Medicis and the Bourbons by the American Institute of Architects."

The comparison to the Medicis may be extravagant but it makes an important point. A few corporations have had profound effects on the culture and aesthetic life of communities—Deere in Moline; the Corning Glass Company in Corning, New York; the Cummins Engine Company in Columbus, Indiana. Each has become internationally known for its harmonious relationships to its community, expressed in part by excellent taste in company architecture and art. Critics sometimes have raised the fear of Philistinism in corporate incursions into the arts, but one would be hardpressed to say this about Deere, Corning, and Cummins, all of which seem to have accomplished these efforts with perception and sensitivity. All three are firms that have been family owned, with more than a bit of paternalism, enlightened to be sure, as their past rationale.

In the case of Deere, at least, there is much more to the story than the issue of "corporation as patron." Involvement in the arts was meant to be substance as well as style, as a number of analysts have recognized. An article in *Smithsonian* magazine on architect Kevin Roche featured the Deere Center, "which takes its responsibility to provide a good workplace as seriously as aesthetics." Commenting on Roche's West Wing, the author continued: "Their 1978 addition . . . extends the attempt begun a decade earlier at the Ford Foundation to better the nine-to-five life of office workers. It is an expansion on the idea developed there of combining efficiency and enchantment." A book published by the Yale University Press, *Spaces: Dimensions of the Human Landscape*, remarked on the location of the center: "Deere & Company chose, for consciously formulated symbolic reasons, to build in the Illinois prairie which had brought the company into being. . . . It appears to be a consequence of an unusual and admirable preoccupation not merely with the consumer's image of the company's product but with the self-image of the people who do the producing. . . . When man-made and natural form are combined, consciously or unconsciously, with the symbols that make explicit the culture of the people who use and experience a particular geographical space . . . the sense of place is to the environment what personality is to the person. When a diversity of cultures share a space, environmental forms that unite them create a larger sense of place. . . . Only occasionally do talented people like Saarinen, Sasaki, and Hewitt bring it about all at once. When such designers achieve this, it is not so much because they have the ability to 'create' form as to discover it in the elements that are already there." (Sasaki Associates was the landscape architect for the Center.)

This focus on art and architecture has spilled over to heighten the historic concern for excellence in products, service, and corporate communications. *Fortune* commented: "Hewitt recognized years ago that what Deere needed most of all was an expanded vision of what was possible. His emphasis on perfection and style, symbolized by the Saarinen office building, puzzled many of the Company's older executives, but not a few of them eventually caught on to what he was doing." *Fortune* quoted one of Deere's executives: "Bill made us realize just how good we were . . . before he came along, we were just a bunch of good old country boys. We had a lot of self-respect; we knew we made good farm equipment, but we never really looked at ourselves as in the big league.

We knew we could make it in Moline, but we didn't know that we could make it in New York. Bill showed us we could." *Forbes* reiterated this same thought: Hewitt "helped give Deere people the confidence they needed in order to begin thinking in world terms."

Exhibit 16–3. *Helicopter puts in place Henry Moore's "Hill Arches," Deere Administrative Center, 1974 (Deere Archives)*

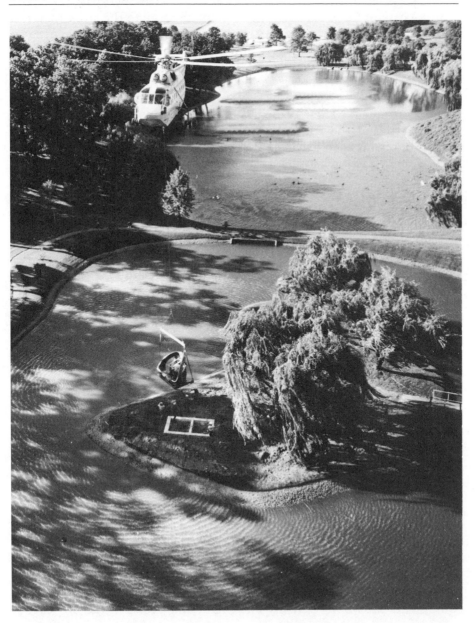

THE TRANSITION IN LEADERSHIP

Hewitt and Curtis had been charting an orderly management succession for several years. The Fiat merger proposal, had it gone through in 1972, would have required the selection of a chief executive officer, and four senior executives were considered—Robert Hanson, Robert Boeke, Delno Brown, and Robert J. Carlson. The proposal fell through, but these four men later became the prime candidates for the next step forward. In early February 1975, Hewitt and Curtis (with the counsel of the outside board members) decided to reinstitute the post of executive vice president. The tension surrounding this anticipated move was substantial. On February 10, 1975, in a meeting attended by all the senior officers of the company, Hewitt announced the choice of Robert A. Hanson for the position (and for a place in the chairman's office). Though it was not automatic that Hanson would later become president, his promotion established the intended line of succession. The decision was not without its disappointments for the others, but it was overwhelmingly popular. The personality of Hanson was compatible with the personalities of his two senior colleagues in the chairman's office. Further, Hanson brought a background of general management experience and breadth that was distinctive within the company.

A potential weakness of any functionally organized company is its tendency toward lifetime compartmentalization of its employees. Deere's tradition of decentralized power had fostered great loyalties and depth of knowledge, but had also tended to breed insularity and parochialism. Many senior managers had risen through promotions in one function, never once having left it. At the time that Hewitt turned the company toward international markets, few of the senior management had ever been abroad for business purposes. Even domestically, it was not typical for a manager from manufacturing to move to marketing at some stage of his career, or vice versa. Indeed, in the early days it was not common for branch personnel to move around among branches.

At the top management level, a company often can use teams of people to achieve the cross-fertilization and interaction necessary for a broad perspective. The long-time relationship between Hewitt and Curtis is an apt example. Hewitt's keen sense of organization, marketing, and external relations blended with the financial acumen and analytical power of Curtis. But many senior management positions require wide-ranging skills and a general management perspective that is not typically developed in a functional system.

One spot in Deere where such perspective is built into the job is the managing directorship of one of the international operations. There are several of these at the middle management level, managing directors of smaller operations, such as South Africa and Mexico. There are major general management posts in Spain, France, and Germany. Finally, the managing directors of the two regions, Region I (Latin America, Australia, and the Far East) and Region II (Europe, Africa, and the Mideast) are called on to exercise broad general management responsibility and perspective.

It was this international career path that shaped Hanson. Boeke, too, had had some international experience. Brown and Carlson largely presided over domestic functions; Brown had headed industrial relations and then taken over industrial equipment, the foundries, and OEM; Carlson worked almost exclusively in marketing.

At the end of the 1970s, several significant senior management appointments were made, each mirroring the importance of general management skills. First, in April 1978, Robert Hanson was elected president of the company, and Curtis moved to the newly created post of vice chairman; Hanson assumed the additional title of chief operating officer in April 1979. A month later, Curtis retired as vice chairman, and Walter Vogel, who had been vice president and managing director of Region II, was given a double-step promotion to the vacant post of executive vice president. This appointment reflected Hewitt's concern that the company think of itself as a truly multinational entity. (Vogel, a West German national, gained almost all of his experience in Europe.) A year later Thomas A. Gildehaus was appointed vice president, and within a few months senior vice president, for the corporate planning portfolio. Gildehaus had come directly to the post from outside the company. He had been an officer in the consulting firm of Temple, Barker, and Sloane, which had worked closely with Deere in long-range planning during the previous seven years. In November 1982 Gildehaus was appointed executive vice president. The appointments of both Vogel and Gildehaus brought strong generalist skills to the top management of the company.

Concern about the dearth of opportunities to move across functional lines has long been matched by concern over recruiting policy. Historically, most managers have been recruited from a small circle. The company selected its new people heavily from plants and branches in the locality. For professional personnel, the colleges and universities in the region have been drawn upon heavily. The company's recruiting power at the Midwestern universities has been impressive, especially for engineers and agriculturally trained personnel. This deliberately local and regional preference in recruiting has given the company enormous strengths stemming from family and friendship ties. Deere became a company with second-, third-, even fourth-generation Deere employees. Deere vice president Robert W. VanSant commented in a *Los Angeles Times* article comparing Deere and International Harvester: "Our customers and our employees talk the same language, share the same commitment to the traditional American work ethic. . . . It's a very nice match from which we derive a lot of strength." An article in *Crain's Chicago Business* in 1982 contrasted International Harvester's downtown Chicago headquarters with Deere's: "One of the good things about Deere is the geographic awareness because most of their executives live on a farm, or near one. . . . Deere's got farm all around it; those guys walk through a history of agriculture before they get to their office. There's a different mentality."

But does this cast too narrow a net? Frank McGuire thought so when he headed engineering in the 1960s. He deliberately plumped for more engineering and technical talent from diverse sources; the Lindvall appointment in the early 1970s epitomized this broader perspective of looking to national figures for talent. Hewitt, right from the start of his assignment as chief executive officer, also stressed this policy: "Hire the best talent from anywhere in the nation—or in the world, for that matter."

It has never been easy for Deere to recruit top personnel, for the small-town atmosphere of Moline and the factory towns of Waterloo, Dubuque, Horicon, and Ottumwa seems provincial and parochial to businessmen who have grown up or worked in large urban centers. The choice of Moline for the technical center and Waterloo for the product engineering center are excellent ones in many ways, but these towns are not strong drawing cards for talent.

Deere has worked hard to make its home office and factory towns more exciting and satisfying places to live. Moline itself has been especially enriched by such cultural efforts as the visiting arts series (exported to most of the other Deere locations, too). The company has made generous contributions to local educational and community efforts, and the John Deere Foundation has supported community projects. Deere also has taken a number of steps to make outsiders aware of the quality of the facilities in Moline, in Waterloo, and in other company areas. Periodically, approximately every third year, the company invites a group of more than 100 financial analysts to a two-day visit in Moline and its environs (generally with a trip to Waterloo, to show the new Tractor Works). The success of these endeavors was chronicled by the Financial Analysts Federation in 1982, which gave Deere an award for excellence in corporate reporting, shared only by thirty other companies in the country.

But there is also a positive side to the small-town environment. *Fortune* magazine commented in an article in 1981 on the family feeling: "Both Corning and Deere have kept their headquarters in small cities, close to some of their plants so executives can visit informally to get a feeling of factory ambience. . . . At both these companies, product people count." Some corporate critics might bristle at this statement, thinking that it suggests an overly paternal top management. Yet Deere seems to have escaped most of the negative features of this close relationship. "Deere is paternalistic, needless to say—perhaps more so than most corporations," commented a British management journal, "but that paternalism may be more benign and less ruthless than is commonly the case."

If the word "paternalism" is taken to mean "a system under which management undertakes to supply needs or regulate conduct of employees in matters affecting them as individuals as well as their interpersonal relations," it does not seem applicable to Deere. As the British quotation states, paternalism was historically often condescending, hierarchical, and all too often ruthless. George Pullman, out of professed benevolence, developed a model town for his employees in the 1880s and '90s, but his Orwellian insistence on total control was a caricature of benevolence, a harsh, authoritarian paternalism run amok. A bitter strike resulted in 1894, one of the landmark cases in American labor relations. This was the time of Charles Deere, and his company, too, had a keen sense of concern and beneficence toward its employees. But paternalism was not its base. Perhaps William Butterworth came closer to the image of a father figure in the company, but again in no sense an authoritarian, intrusive leader. In recent years, Charles Wiman and particularly William Hewitt both exemplified professional managership, a philosophy almost antithetical to paternalism, though they retained a strong attachment to the community.

It is still a fact, though, that many knowledgeable people do not quickly recognize the name "Deere & Company" or know that the company is located in Moline, or even that it is a Midwestern firm. What is recognized much more often are the two words "John Deere." The man, John Deere, is an authentic folk hero of America, and his plow has won an honored place among the country's important artifacts. As Americana, the crowning achievement may have come in the "Peanuts" comic strip reproduced above. The company may well have been unwise in jettisoning the word "John" from the corporate name back in the 1850s. But so long as the company's products carry the well-recognized "John Deere," it's not likely that its sales will be adversely affected.

LOOKING AHEAD

Hanson's accession to the post of president, chairman, and chief executive officer in October 1982 marked the beginning of a new era, which followed a period of unbroken family leadership in the company for 145 years, incredibly with only five chief executive officers. (Burton Peek assumed a stewardship role for two years during World War II, while Charles Wiman was colonel of ordnance in Washington, D.C.) Hewitt had paved the way for guiding the transition to professional corporate leadership. Although a member of the Charles Deere Wiman family (by marriage), he came to the company by an independent route, built on professional management training.

In 1973 the first outside director was appointed; by 1975 there were a total of five out of fifteen. Samuel C. Johnson, chief executive officer of S.C. Johnson & Son, Inc., was Deere's first outside director, elected at the annual meeting of 1973. Later that year, William B. Graham, chief executive officer of Baxter Travenol Laboratories, Inc., joined, and the following year Lloyd B. Smith, chief executive officer of A.O. Smith, Inc., was added. In 1975 two more additions, Edward E. Carlson, chairman of UAL, Inc., and United Airlines, and Robben W. Fleming, president of the University of Michigan, brought the complement of outside board members to five. The total board size stayed at fifteen until 1979, when it was increased to seventeen (the outsiders remaining at five). Robert D. Stuart, Jr., chief executive officer of the Quaker Oats Company, replaced Fleming in 1979. In 1982, Ms. Juanita Kreps, vice president of Duke University, became the sixth outside director, the first woman to hold this post. (There had been one woman corporate officer, during the tenure of Ms. Elizabeth Denkhoff as corporate secretary, 1971–82.) With the addition of the five outsiders, a more general-management atmosphere was slowly inculcated (though some slippage remained because it always is hard for an inside director to "wear two hats").

At the time of the appointment of the first outside director, the "family" owned just over 12 percent of the company's outstanding shares (most of them owned by descendants of the Charles Deere family); the remainder was owned widely by institutions and the general public. Until 1974 these family shares were held in trusteeship and therefore represented a single voting unit, the owners showing only desultory interest in the operation of the company. After the shares were dispersed into individual hands, even the unifying element of trusteeship was lost. There was no lack of pride among the heirs of John Deere, but the company had outgrown the family. Deere & Company was no longer family owned. With the election of outsiders to the board, the remaining vestige of a "closely held" corporation had been eliminated.

Deere & Company thus seems to have been spared most of the disabilities that many family-owned companies suffer after more than one or two generations—idiosyncratic and often fragmented leadership, excessive focus on the past, and difficulties in management succession. Each of the five chief executives surmounted a distinctive set of challenges. John Deere's was survival in a frontier environment. Rapid growth and change characterized Charles Deere's world as the company rose to national prominence by the turn of the century. William Butterworth

Exhibit 16–4. *Robert A. Hanson, chairman and chief executive officer, Deere & Company, 1982*

consolidated the organization, in the process adding several new companies and product lines, including tractors and the combine. Charles
Wiman carried the company through the Great Depression of the 1930s
and World War II, all the time exhorting everyone about the critical role of
product development. Hewitt presided over another era of rapid expansion that encompassed the world. He rebuilt the physical plant, enlarged
the work force, and broadened the company's management to take on the
global challenge, while he preached quality and style. The company
became the largest agricultural machinery producer in the world.

The challenges facing Robert Hanson were daunting, for he began his tenure at a deep trough in the agricultural machinery business cycle. Yet the long-run outlook remained promising. Deere's resources in research and development, its strength in the market, and the quality of its plant and organization should allow the company to come through the recession of the early 1980s poised for growth. Both Charles Wiman and Hewitt often exhorted their colleagues that "Deere's best years are ahead"—and the adage still seems appropriate. Hanson would need to resolve a number of knotty problems. Pressures to cut costs would be very strong—companies would need to be "lean and trim," to paraphrase Deere's slogan for its Yanmar-made tractors, in order to meet "the Japanese challenge" (a term embracing much more than just the actions of Japan itself). Deere's worldwide sourcing issues would be complex in the near future, as would be the related question of the degree of standardization possible in an industry serving a larger clientele with differing needs and geographically dispersed locations. Could the company remain a predominantly single-industry organization, or would further diversification be necessary? A *Los Angeles Times* analyst commented: "Until recently, such devotion to a single industry has been considered a sign of weakness in U.S. corporate circles." But Hewitt pointed out in the same article: "We have zero interest in getting into a business with which we have no familiarity," and he commented on the "growing recognition of the drawbacks of excessive diversification and merger mania." Hanson might have to confront the issue again, however, since research and development and decentralization are persisting concerns.

Deere has a set of enduring qualities that has served it well indeed over a 145-year span. It has been a preeminent example of a well-run family endeavor, and there is no reason why it should not retain some characteristics of a "family company"—the close ties between corporation and community, the employees' sense of identification with the products, and management's concern for the long run. The corporation is now independent of the family, but the "John Deere" legacy is firmly embedded in the organization that "gave to the world the steel plow" and that has provided a model of innovative and responsible American business behavior.

LIST OF APPENDIX EXHIBITS

Exhibit 1
Cost of Manufacture—1869 "Improved Clipper, H.L., A No. 1" (14" Cast Steel Plow)

Exhibit 2
Manufacturing Cost, Dealer Price and Retail List Price, 1869-70

Exhibit 3
Discount Calculations for "Advance" Walking Cultivator (Iron Beam), 1875

Exhibit 4
Sales and Earnings per Implement, 1869-75

Exhibit 5
Two Decades of Corporate Growth Deere & Company, 1868-88

Exhibit 6
Costs of Labor by Hand and by Machine/Hours and Wages by Hand and by Machine

Exhibit 7
Cost of Materials Purchased by Deere & Company, 1869-99

Exhibit 8
Cost of Wood Materials Purchased by Deere & Company, 1869-99

Exhibit 9
Comparative Daily Wage Rates, 1878

Exhibit 10
Comparative Wage Rates of Plow Manufacturers, 1894 (Rate per Day)

Exhibit 11
Deere & Company Performance, 1888-1900

Exhibit 12
Sales and Profits, Deere & Company, 1914-18 ($000)

Exhibit 13
Wages, Hours Worked, and Weekly Earnings, in the John Deere Plow Works, 1901-14

Exhibit 14
Average Hourly Wage Rates—Deere, International Harvester, and U.S. Manufacturing

Exhibit 15
Market Share of Farm Implement Sales for the Five Leading Companies (1913-18)

Exhibit 16
Market Share for Selected Harvesting Implements, 1921

Exhibit 17
Market Share for Selected Tillage Implements, 1921

Exhibit 18
Comparative Manufacturers' Estimated Costs for 5-Foot Mowers, 1918

Exhibit 19
How Deere Ranked with its Competitors on Costs of Producing Plows, 1916 and 1918

Exhibit 20
Implement Manufacturers' Costs, Prices, and Margins, by Product, 1918

APPENDIX EXHIBITS

Cost of Manufacture—1869
"Improved Clipper, H.L., A No. 1"
(14" Cast Steel Plow)

Share (8 lbs. @ 12¢)	96¢	Oval handle brace (1 lb @ 8¢)	8¢
Shinning shave	5	Forging "	1¼
Plating shin	½	Brace rivets	1
Plating share	1⅜	Rod, nuts, and cutting	10
Bending "	1	Clevis	52
Punching "	¾	Bolts for plow	40
Landside and Strip (9¾ @ 12¢)	117	Grinding block and landside	1
Forging	12½	Drilling and punching	25
Punching and straightening	1¼	Grinding plow	25
Planing	1	Polishing	10
Welding share and landside	11	Wear and tear—stone	27
Planing share	1½	Wear and tear—emery	5
Strip for share	6	Borax	3
Standard (6¾ @ 5¼¢)	36	Hardening material	2½
Drawing	1¼	Coal	13
Bracing	5	Breakage	18
Cutting screw	⅜		Total 894.5¢ = $8.945
Back brace (2 @ 6¢)	12		
Bending standard	1	*Finishing*	
Back brace for share (2 @ 6¢)	12	Beam	42
Bending "	1¾	Machining	5
Cast block (6½ @ 6¢)	39	Dressing	5
High landside plate (2¼ @ 12¢)	27	Handles	14
Straightening "	1½	Machining	2
Planing "	1	Bending	2
Cutting plate	2	Dressing	11
Moldboard (15⅓ @ 14¼¢)	220	Rounding	4
Shinning "	4½	Stocking	22½
Strip for "	4	Varnish material	12
Plating shin	½	Varnishing	11
Bending board	4½		Total 130.5¢ = $1.305
Hardening "	2		
Putting on board	7		
Planing board	1½	Total cost, construction,	
Putting up frame	14	and finishing	$10.25

Source: Deere Archives.

Manufacturing Cost, Dealer Price
and Retail List Price, 1869–70

Implement	Manufacturing Cost	Dealer Price @25+20%	Dealer Price @30+10%	Retail List Price
Clipper, A No. 1	$10.25	$16.60	$16.38	$26.00
12-inch Breaker	10.03½	21.00	22.05	35.00
24-inch Breaker	19.70	30.60	32.13	51.00

Source: Deere Archives.

Appendix Exhibit 3	Discount Calculations for "Advance" Walking Cultivator (Iron Beam), 1875

25% =	$21.38
20% + 10% =	20.52
25% + 5% =	20.31
30% =	19.95
20% + 15% =	19.38
25% + 10% =	19.25

Source: Deere Archives.

Appendix Exhibit 4	Sales and Earnings per Implement 1869–75

Fiscal Year (July 1– June 30)	Aggregate Business (Gross Revenue)	Total Earnings (Plants and Branches)	Imple- ments Sold	Average Gross Revenue per Imple- ment	Average Earnings per Imple- ment
1869–70	$ 710,640	$104,944	43,613	$16.29	$2.41
1870–71	548,605	59,406	39,347	13.94	1.51
1871–72	646,305	88,469	42,905	15.06	2.06
1872–73	701,546	28,130	38,954	18.01	.72
1873–74	835,769	93,651	43,533	19.20	2.15
1874–75	1,167,849	127,345	52,100	22.42	2.44

Source: Deere Archives.

Appendix Exhibit 5	**Two Decades of Corporate Growth** **Deere & Company, 1868–88**				
Fiscal Year (July 1–June 30)	Aggregate Business	Total Earnings (Plants and Branches)[a]	Dividend Declared	Ending Net Assets	Plows Sold
1868–69	$ 646,564	$198,237	$ 25,000	$ 423,237	41,133
1869–70	710,640	104,944	50,000	478,181	43,613
1870–71	548,605	59,406	25,000	512,587	39,347
1871–72	646,305	88,469	25,000	576,056	42,905
1872–73	701,546	28,130	50,000	554,186	38,954
1873–74	835,769	93,651	50,000	597,875	43,533
1874–75	1,167,849	127,345	75,000	650,219	52,100
1875–76	1,250,000	139,107	25,000	764,326	60,000
1876–77	1,315,279	162,048	37,500	888,874	66,774
1877–78	1,082,038	139,798	37,500	991,172	66,277
1878–79	1,108,255	180,313	37,500	1,133,985	60,227
1879–80	1,174,846	150,793	37,500	1,247,278	70,223
1880–81	1,312,908	231,192	37,500	1,440,969	86,431
1881–82	1,417,936	221,173	75,000	1,587,142	96,735
1882–83	1,311,317	114,412	850,000[b]	1,601,554	101,739
1883–84	1,222,547	162,094	100,000	1,663,648	82,756
1884–85	1,000,000 (est)	206,064	100,000	1,769,712	66,064
1885–86	1,162,449	276,138	120,000	1,925,849	82,876
1886–87	1,093,500	276,670	200,000	2,002,520	92,722
1887–88	1,162,934	240,675	200,000	2,043,194	75,628

[a]*Includes branch-house dividends, but does not include branch-house retained earnings. Factory earnings are modestly understated—from 1868 to 1890 the factory net-profit figure was calculated on a uniform 10 percent depreciation of all real estate and machinery (the figure was lowered to 4 percent in the years 1890–95, and after that time was depreciated on the basis of "actual wear and deterioration from use").*
[b]*$100,000 cash dividend, $750,000 stock dividend.*

Source: P. C. Simmon, "History of Deere & Company," ca. 1920.

Appendix
Exhibit 6   **Costs of Labor by Hand and by Machine**

Comparison of labor costs (man and animal) for the production of different crops by hand methods (mainly) in early years, and by machine methods in the 1890s. Hours of labor virtually the same in every case (ten a day). In each comparison, the productivity and adaptability of the land is approximately the same (exception for cotton, as indicated).

Crop	Unit of measure	Hand Methods					Machine Methods				
		Date	Daily wage: man ($)	Daily hire: horse, ox, or mule ($)	Labor cost of one unit ($)	Ratio of cost of one unit to daily pay of a man (%)	Date	Daily wage: man ($)	Daily hire: horse, ox, or mule ($)	Labor cost of one unit ($)	Ratio of cost of one unit to daily pay of a man (%)
Wheat: 20 bu. to acre	1 bu.	1830	.50	.12½	.19+	33.34	1896	1.50	.50	.10+	6.75
Corn: 40 bu. to acre: un-shelled, fodder left in field	1 bu.	1855	1.00	.37½	.13−	12.58	1894	1.00	.50	.08+	8.27
Oats: 40 bu. to acre	1 bu.	1830	.50	.12½	.10−	19.35	1893	1.50	.50	.04−	2.67
Hay: loose in barn. 1 ton to acre	1 ton	1850	1.00	.50	1.92−	191.68	1895	1.25	.50	.63	50.51
Hay: baled; 1 ton to acre	1 ton	1860	1.00	.37½	3.19−	318.56	1894	1.25	.50	1.91	132.86
Potatoes: 220 bu. to acre	1 bu.	1866	1.00	.50	.07−	6.59	1895	1.00	.50	.03−	2.99
Cotton: 750 and 1,000 lb. in seed to acre	100 lb.	1841	.50	.25	1.23	246.06	1895	1.00	.50	.94	94.20
Rice: rough; 2,640 lb. to acre	100 lb.	1870	1.00	.50	.27+	27.27	1895	.65	.50	.08−	12.17
Sugar cane: at grinder; 20 tons to acre	1 ton	1855	1.00	.50	1.99−	198.77	1895	.65	.50	.82−	125.91
Tobacco: graded and packed; 1,500 lb. to acre	100 lb.	1853	.75	.37½	1.72+	229.81	1895	1.00	.50	1.87−	156.54

Hours and Wages by Hand and by Machine

Comparison of hours of human labor and wages for the production of one acre each of different crops by hand methods (mainly) and by machine methods (same acres and years as in preceding table).

Crop	Time Worked				Labor Cost	
	Hand		Machine		Hand	Machine
	Hours	Minutes	Hours	Minutes		
Wheat	61	5.0	3	19.2	$ 3.5542	$ .6605
Corn	38	45.0	15	7.8	3.6250	1.5130
Oats	66	15.0	7	5.8	3.7292	1.0732
Hay: loose	21	5.0	3	56.5	1.7501	.4230
Hay: baled	35	30.0	11	34.0	3.0606	1.2894
Potatoes	108	55.0	38	00.0	10.8916	3.8000
Cotton	167	48.0	78	42.0	7.8773	7.8700
Rice: rough	62	5.0	17	2.5	5.6440	1.0071
Sugar cane	351	21.0	191	33.0	31.9409	11.3189
Tobacco	311	23.0	252	54.6	23.3538	25.1160
Total: 10 crops	1,194	12.0	619	15.4	$ 95.4267	$ 54.0711
Total: 27 different crops	9,760	47.7	5,107	52.6	$1,037.7609	$598.1338

Source: Fred A. Shannon, The Farmer's Last Frontier, *(1945), pp. 142-143.*

Appendix Exhibit 7	**Cost of Materials Purchased by Deere & Company, 1869–99**			
	1869	1879	1889	1899
Soft-Center Shares	$13.75	$7.37½	$5.50	$5.00
Cast Steel.	11.75	5.00	3.25	2.75[a]
Bar Iron	3.75	1.80	1.65	1.10
Malleable Steel.	12.00	6.00	3.62½	2.80
Pig Iron	33.50–43.50	22.00–23.50	18.00–21.00	10.50–13.50
Nuts (⅜ inch).	9.50–12.00	3.75–8.00	2.55–4.00	2.00–2.80
Plow Bolts	15.00	11.00	6.00	4.40
White Lead.	13.00	8.00	5.75	5.75
Varnish.	2.25	1.20	1.12½	.70
Green Paint	18.50[b]	9.25	6.62½	6.00
Lard Oil	1.05	.50	.35	.32
Coke (bushel)	.09	7.25	5.04	4.70

[a]1895 [b]1870

Note: Quantities for these prices not specified in company records   *Source: Deere Archives.*

Appendix Exhibit 8	**Cost of Wood Materials Purchased by Deere & Company, 1869–99**				
	Oak	Ash	Hickory	No. 1 Wood Beams	Plow Handles (1½″ × 2½″ × 5′)
1869	$18.00	$25.50	$25.00	$32.50	$5.00
1879	17.00	22.00	20.00	22.00	3.75
1889	22.00	33.50	35.00	27.50	3.00
1899	31.00	30.50[a]	30.00	34.50	3.25

[a]1896   *Source: Deere Archives.*

Appendix Exhibit 9	**Comparative Daily Wage Rates, 1878**						
	Machinist "Extra Good"	Machinist "Ordinary"	Blacksmith "Extra Good"	Blacksmith "Ordinary"	Moulder "Extra Good"	Moulder "Ordinary"	Common Laborer
Moline, Ill.	$2.75	$2.25-2.50	$2.75	$2.00-2.25	$2.50	$2.25	$1.30
Rockford, Ill.	2.50	2.00	2.75	2.00	3.00	2.25	1.40
Plano, Ill.	2.20	2.00	2.20	2.00	2.20	2.00	1.25
Sycamore, Ill.	2.50	1.75	2.25	2.00	2.50	2.00	1.40
Racine, Wisc.	2.37	2.12	2.75	2.25	2.50	N.A.	1.25
Dixon, Ill..	2.75	2.00-2.25	2.50	2.00-2.25	N.A.	N.A.	1.30
Canton, Ohio	2.50	2.00	2.00	1.75	1.90	1.90	1.25-1.50
Hoosic Falls, N.Y...	2.50	1.50-1.75	2.38	1.38-2.00	2.50	1.60	1.30
Auburn, N.Y.	2.25	2.00	2.25	1.50	2.25-2.50	1.75	1.00
Springfield, Ohio . .	2.50	1.75	2.50	1.80	2.75	2.25	.35

Source: Survey by Emerson, Talcott & Company, Rockford, Illinois, 1878.

Appendix
Exhibit 10

Comparative Wage Rates of Plow Manufacturers, 1894
(Rate per Day)

Firm	Common Laborer	Blacksmith 1st Class	Woodworkers	Assembler	Moulder	Painter
Grand Detour Plow Co. Dixon, Ill.	$1.35	$2.25	$1.75	$1.45	$2.20	$1.60
Hoosier Drill Co. Richmond, Ind.	1.50	2.40–2.50	1.60–2.25	1.75–2.00	3.00–4.50[a]	1.50–2.50
David Bradley Mfg. Co. Chicago, Ill.	1.25–1.37½	2.75	2.00	2.00	2.50–3.00	1.75–2.00
Studebaker Bros. Mfg. Co. South Bend, Ind.	1.25	3.00[a]	N.A.	N.A.	N.A.	1.50–3.00
Wm. Deering & Co. Chicago, Ill	1.35	2.40	1.75–2.00	1.50–1.75	2.00–2.50	1.80–2.00
Parlin and Orendorff Co. Canton, Ill.	1.10	2.00	1.40–1.50	1.20	2.50	1.50–2.00
Emerson, Talcott & Co. Rockford, Ill	1.25	1.70–2.00	N.A.	1.40–1.80	2.25[a]	1.30–1.80
Deere & Mansur Co.	1.35	1.75–2.00	1.50–2.50[a]	N.A.	2.75–3.00[a]	1.50–1.75
Deere & Co.	1.35	2.50	1.40–2.25	1.35–1.75	2.50–2.75	1.50–1.75

[a]*Includes piece-work rates.*

Source: Deere Archives.

Appendix
Exhibit 11

Deere & Company Performance,
1888–1900

Fiscal Year (July 1-June 30)	Aggregate Business	Total Earnings (Plants and Branches)	Dividend Declared	Ending Net Assets	Implements Sold
1888-89	$1,151,789	$217,217	$870,000[a]	$1,890,412	91,962
1889-90	1,282,995	324,972	150,000	2,065,335	101,600
1890-91	1,488,535	270,472	150,000	2,185,858	132,518
1891-92	1,911,151	303,179	150,000	2,339,037	146,564
1892-93	1,613,061	272,361	150,000	2,461,399	139,388
1893-94	1,219,118	189,733	150,000	2,501,133	108,956
1894-95	1,223,117	249,493	150,000	2,600,628	114,891
1895-96	1,253,299	284,147	150,000	2,734,775	115,429
1896-97	1,184,318	198,355	150,000	2,783,132	108,398
1897-98	1,765,798	412,004	225,000	2,970,137	140,285
1898-99	1,996,500	511,711	150,000	3,331,849	162,748
1899-1900	2,144,570	495,130	150,000	3,676,980	153,935

[a]*$370,000 cash dividend, $500,000 stock dividend.*

Source: P. C. Simmon, "History of Deere & Company," (ca. 1920)

Appendix   **Sales and Profits, Deere & Company, 1914–18**
Exhibit 12   **($000)**

	Sales	Profits
1914...............................	29,447	2,085
1915...............................	25,562	3,372
1916...............................	26,409	4,806
1917...............................	31,641	4,693
1918...............................	39,910	5,654

Source: Deere & Company Annual Reports (revised).

Appendix   **Wages, Hours Worked, and Weekly Earnings, in the**
Exhibit 13   **John Deere Plow Works, 1901–14**

Fiscal Year	Men Employed	Hours Worked	Hourly Rate	Weekly Earnings
1901–02...........	1016	55.57	$.211	$11.54
1902–03...........	1063	54.50	.221	12.45
1903–04...........	852	53.40	.232	12.39
1904–05...........	949	52.86	.236	12.46
1905–06...........	1101	53.78	.244	13.12
1906–07...........	1210	53.70	.259	13.91
1907–08...........	1055	48.02	.263	12.63
1908–09...........	1109	53.36	.266	14.19
1909–10...........	1559	54.45	.270	14.70
1910–11...........	1872	53.83	.268	14.43
1911–12...........	1465	51.74	.278	14.38
1912–13...........	1980	53.03	.295	15.63
1913–19...........	1399	44.07	.310	13.66

Source: Minutes of Board of Directors, Deere & Company, December 13, 1918.

<table>
<tr><td rowspan="2">Appendix
Exhibit 14</td><td colspan="4">**Average Hourly Wage Rates—Deere, International Harvester, and
United States Manufacturing
(in cents)**</td></tr>
</table>

Year[a]	Deere's Plow Works	International Harvester's McCormick Works	U.S. Manufacturing Money Wage
1902.	21.1	19.4	16.5
1903.	22.1	20.9	17.0
1904.	23.2	22.0	16.9
1905.	23.6	21.8	17.2
1906.	24.4	22.2	18.4
1907.	25.9	21.8	19.1
1908.	26.3	22.0	18.4
1909.	26.6	21.6	18.6
1910.	27.0	22.8	19.8
1911.	26.8	23.8	20.2
1912.	27.8	22.9	20.7
1913.	29.5	25.4	22.1
1914.	31.0	26.2	22.0

[a]*Deere & Company fiscal year, calendar year for the others.*

Source. Deere & Company Board minutes, December 13, 1918; Robert Ozanne, Wages in Practice and Theory:
McCormick and International Harvester, 1860–1960, Madison: University of Wisconsin Press, 1968, Appendix A;
Albert Rees, Real Wages in Manufacturing, 1890–1914. New York: National Bureau of Economic Research, 1961,
tables 10 and 13.

<table>
<tr><td>Appendix
Exhibit 15</td><td colspan="6">**Market Share of Total Farm Implement Sales for
the Five Leading Companies, 1913–18**</td></tr>
</table>

	1913	1914	1915	1916	1917	1918
International Harvester Co.. . . .	56.7	55.8	59.2	59.5	60.8	59.3
Deere & Company	15.1	14.7	13.8	13.0	11.9	12.2
Moline Plow Co..	6.0	6.2	5.5	4.7	4.9	6.0
Emerson-Brantingham Co.	4.6	4.4	4.8	4.0	3.9	3.6
Oliver Chilled Plow Co.	2.2	3.0	2.6	2.9	2.8	3.6

Source: U.S. Federal Trade Commission, Report ...on the Causes of High Prices of Farm Implements (1920), p. 116. For
key to table see U.S. v. International Harvester Co., 274 U.S. 693, Record, p. 607.

Appendix   **Market Share for Selected Harvesting Implements, 1921**
Exhibit 16   **(in percent)**

Implement (with percent of total farm machinery sales)	International Harvester Company	Deere & Company	Massey-Harris Company	Other Manufacturers
Mowers (1.5).	62.4	14.3	2.8	20.3
Grain and rice binders (1.7)	73.2	13.5	3.8	9.5
Sulky dump rakes (0.4)	51.2	14.7	2.9	31.2
Side delivery rakes, combined rakes, and tedders (0.4).	53.3	25.7	8.0	13.0
Hay loaders (0.6).	43.9	26.3	6.5	23.3
Corn binders (0.5).	70.1	17.3	8.0	4.6
Combines (1.1)	85.1	. . .	0.2	14.7

Source: U.S. v. International Harvester Co., 274 U.S. 693, Briefs and Records, p. 20; U.S. Temporary National Economics Committee, Monograph No. 36, pp. 241–242.

Appendix   **Market Share for Selected Tillage Implements, 1921**
Exhibit 17   **(in percent)**

Implement (with percent of total farm machinery sales)	International Harvester Company	Deere & Company
Walking plow two-horse moldboard (0.2).	8.4	10.4
Sulky plow, moldboard (0.8)	13.0	12.2
Tractor plow, moldboard (1.7).	15.8	5.3
Disk harrows, horse and tractor (2.2).	32.2	17.9
Spike-tooth harrows (0.5)	31.5	21.6
Spring-tooth harrows (0.4)	27.1	19.4
Riding cultivators, one-row, two-horse (1.5)	34.8	18.7
Riding cultivators, one-row, horsedrawn (0.6)	23.1	27.1

Source: U.S. Temporary National Economics Committee, Monograph No. 36.

<table>
<tr><td rowspan="2">Appendix
Exhibit 18</td><td colspan="5" align="center">Comparative Manufacturers' Estimated Costs
for 5-Foot Mowers, 1918
(in rank order of total cost)</td></tr>
</table>

Manufacturer	Material Cost	Direct Labor	Overhead, Warehouse, and Shipping	Total Manufacturing Cost	Selling, General, and Administrative	Total Cost of Implement
International Harvester Company...........	$27.37	$4.08	$5.24	$36.69	$ 8.40	$45.09
Moline Plow Company...........	30.40	2.69	5.77	38.86	9.64	48.50
Walter A. Wood Company...........	34.65	3.22	7.90	45.77	6.88	52.65
Deere & Company	38.39	2.80	4.77	45.96	10.07	56.03
Massey-Harris.........	29.67	4.58	7.59	41.84	14.72	56.56
Sears Roebuck and Company	40.47	3.73	5.60	49.80	8.10	57.90
Emerson-Brantingham	34.19	3.47	6.22	43.88	17.32	61.20
Acme Harvester Company...........	42.56	2.01	4.48	49.05	16.30	65.35
Thomas Manufac-turing Company......	39.90	9.38	6.38	55.66	15.23	70.89

Source: U.S. Federal Trade Commission, Report. . . on the Causes of High Prices of Farm Implements *(1920), p. 166.*
For key to table see U.S v International Harvester Co., 274 U.S. 693, Record, p. 494.

<table>
<tr><td rowspan="2">Appendix
Exhibit 19</td><td colspan="12" align="center">How Deere & Company Ranked with its Competitors on
Costs of Producing Plows, 1916 and 1918
(lowest cost producer = 1)</td></tr>
</table>

(No. of Companies Reporting)	Material Cost		Productive Labor		Overhead Warehouse and Shipping		Total Manufacture Cost		Selling General, and Administrative		Cost of Implement Sold	
	1916	1918	1916	1918	1916	1918	1916	1918	1916	1918	1916	1918
Walking Plow 12-inch (3)	2	1	1	1	3	3	1	2	1	1	1	2
Walking Plow 14-inch (8)	4	6	1	3	1	4	1	5	2	4	1	5
Sulky Plow (9)......	1	6	3	6	4	7	2	7	3	6	2	5
Gang Plow 14-inch (8)	4	3	3	7	3	5	2	7	1	4	1	6
Engine Plow 14-inch (8)	8	6	6	8	7	7	5	7	3	5	3	6

Source: U.S. Federal Trade Commission, Report . . . on the Causes of High Prices of Farm Implements *(1920),*
pp.144–150. For key to table, see U.S. v. International Harvester Co., 274 U.S. 693, Record, pp. 608–609.

Appendix
Exhibit 20

**Implement Manufacturers' Costs, Prices,
and Margins, by Product, 1918**

Implement		Number of companies reporting	Cost		Price		Margin	
			High	Low	High	Low	High	Low
Walking plow	14-inch	8	$16.53	$12.39	$22.40	$16.80	$8.80	$1.87
Sulky plow	16-inch	9	53.50	37.61	68.00	55.00	23.41	10.82
Gang plow	14-inch	8	82.67	63.71	107.25	87.50	39.82	14.07
Engine plow, 3-bottom	14-inch	6	125.98	100.96	186.50	180.00	85.54	54.67
Spike-tooth harrow	60-tooth	13	18.65	11.24	22.00	16.73	8.01	.85
Spring-tooth harrow	17-tooth	8	20.31	15.14	27.50	21.98	8.16	4.67
Single-disk harrow	16-disk	6	49.45	33.50	51.50	42.75	12.23	1.55
Double-disk harrow	32-disk, 8 feet	5	91.20	63.00	103.50	94.30	40.50	8.80
Corn planter	2-row	12	52.29	23.96	70.00	30.60	24.34	6.64
Cotton planter	1-row	3	35.96	28.11	41.19	39.00	11.79	3.04
Disk drill	12 by 7	5	98.27	63.04	134.05	74.21	39.31	4.73
Hoe drill	12 by 7	4	91.57	61.56	121.45	69.46	36.81	6.63
Walking cultivator	4-shovel	10	30.39	19.60	37.00	25.15	11.87	3.74[a]
Riding cultivator	6-shovel	12	43.14	26.88	53.00	38.25	14.76	4.89[a]
Mowers	5-foot	9	70.89	45.09	68.75	63.00	19.91	2.89[a]
Dump hayrake	10-foot	7	40.15	24.54	44.00	35.48	13.46	3.57
Side-delivery hayrake		9	79.91	50.27	86.50	73.44	24.73	2.46
Hay loader	8-foot	6	88.31	65.43	100.00	90.00	25.07	6.69
Grain binder	6 and 7 foot	5	164.24	119.77	191.50	175.00	55.23	15.67
Corn binder		5	215.65	112.02	191.00	169.86	62.98	24.65[a]
Manure spreader	70-bushel	3	128.89	124.99	173.00	158.00	48.01	31.72
Farm wagon	3¼-inch skein	5	110.52	78.67	109.20	97.50	27.42	1.32[a]

[a]*A loss (only one company reported a loss).*

Source: U.S. Federal Trade Commission, Report . . . on the Causes of High Prices of Farm Implements *(1920), p. 137.*

Appendix
Exhibit 21

**Estimated Horsepower-Hours
of Power Developed Annually for Farm Operations, 1925**

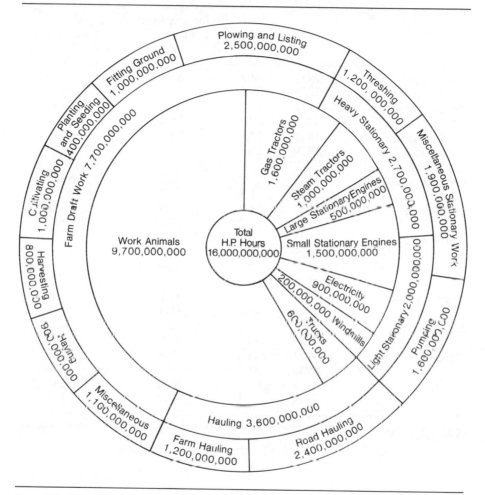

Source: C.D. Kinsman, An Appraisal of Power Used on Farms in the United States. *United States Department of Agriculture, Bulletin 1348, (July, 1925), p. 5.*

Appendix Exhibit 22	**Market Share, Deere and International Harvester 1921 and 1929**			
		Deere %	International Harvester %	Total as per-cent of industry
Mowers (horse or tractor)	1921	14.3	62.4	76.7
	1929	20.7	64.6	85.3
Rakes (sulky, dump)	1921	14.7	51.2	65.9
	1929	20.8	56.2	77.0
Binders (grain and rice)	1921	13.5	73.2	86.7
	1929	25.9	67.9	93.8
Combines.	1921	. . .	85.1	85.1
	1929	6.8	31.8	37.8
Hay loaders	1921	26.3	43.9	70.2
	1929	22.7	53.1	75.8
Corn pickers.	1921	. . .	97.5	97.5
	1929	29.4	48.5	77.9
Sulky plows	1921	12.2	13.0	25.2
	1929	25.2	19.7	44.7
Tractor plows	1921	5.3	15.8	21.1
	1929	26.5	49.1	75.6
Disk harrows	1921	17.9	32.2	50.1
	1929	22.4	41.8	64.2
Corn planters	1921	25.0	32.3	57.3
	1929	41.2	32.0	73.2
Tractors	1921	N.A.	N.A.	N.A.
	1929	21.1	59.9	81.0

Source: Federal Trade Commission, Report on the Agricultural Machinery Industry. *Washington: Government Printing Office, 1938, pp. 150–153.*

Appendix Exhibit 23	Costs per Dollar of Sales, Various Firms, 1929 (in percent)					
	Manu- facturing	Selling	Transfer	Collection	General Administrative	Bad Debts
Deere	57.90	8.52	2.28	0.20	1.76	0.27
International Harvester	69.04	8.35	0.97	1.24	0.87	3.05
Allis-Chalmers	77.51	8.46[a]	N.A.	. . .	2.59	0.46
Case	59.39	23.15	1.07	. . .	1.07	2.42
Oliver	65.25	22.25[a]	N.A.	. . .	2.89	5.07
Minneapolis-Moline	71.38	15.95[b]	. . .	. . .	. . .	5.59
Massey-Harris	76.60	14.61	1.79	1.06	1.79	. . .
B.F. Avery[c]	60.43	18.50[b]	3.86	. . .	10.34	. . .

[a]*Includes collection expense.*
[b]*Segregation of items not made: includes selling, transfer, collection, general administrative, and bad debt expenses.*
[c]*The Federal Trade Commission considered B.F. Avery to be a long-line company, even though it did not make tractors. (It did have a marketing link for its tractor equipment with Allis-Chalmers.)*

Source: Warren Wright Shearer, Competition Through Merger: An Economic Analysis of the Farm Machinery Industry, Ph.D. thesis, (Department of Economics, Harvard University, April 1951), p. 236.

Appendix Exhibit 24	Return on Investment in Farm Machinery Business (After Taxes), Selected Companies, Long- and Short-Line, 1927–29		
	1927 (%)	1928 (%)	1929 (%)
Long-line companies			
Deere & Co.	20.30	24.65	26.67
International Harvester	12.30	17.06	17.92
J. I. Case.	14.22	14.48	7.77
Allis-Chalmers	8.58	9.04	11.90
Oliver Corp.	. . .	. . .	6.63
Minneapolis-Moline	. . .	. . .	7.81
Massey-Harris[a]	.70	2.07[b]	.64
B. F. Avery	6.04	9.83	3.98
Short-line companies			
More than $3,000,000 investment	1.24[b]	5.04	3.40
$1,3,000,000 investment.	9.50	9.99	6.66
$300,000-$1,000,000 investment.	2.59	6.80	5.89
Less than $300,000 investment.	2.65	3.62	3.12

[a]*Includes United States operations only.*
[b]*Loss.*

Source: Warren Wright Shearer, "Competition Through Merger" (1951), p. 233.

Appendix
Exhibit 25

Industry and Deere-Lanz Tractor Sales
(in units)

Country		1955	1960	1965
Western Europe . . .	Industry	299,430	313,520	331,830
	Deere-Lanz	13,528	5,949	11,420
	Percent of Industry	4.5	1.9	3.4
Germany	Industry	98,850	88,680	84,250
	Deere-Lanz	10,848	2,123	4,644
	Percent of Industry	11.0	2.4	5.5
France	Industry	66,190	73,340	71,550
	Deere-Lanz	374	635	2,096
	Percent of Industry	0.6	0.9	2.9
Spain	Industry	5,210	9,760	17,660
	Deere-Lanz	587	2,710	2,630
	Percent of Industry	11.3	27.8	14.9

Source: Market Economics Department, Deere & Company.

Appendix
Exhibit 26

Domestic and Overseas Sales and Income,
Deere & Company, 1965–70
($000,000)

Net Sales

Year	United States and Canada	Overseas	Worldwide
1965	741.6	145.0	886.6
1966	924.7	137.4	1,062.1
1967	935.4	151.0	1,086.4
1968	855.5	175.0	1,030.5
1969	856.2	186.8	1,043.0
1970	939.6	198.1	1,137.7

Net Income

Year	United States and Canada	Overseas Before United States Income Tax Credit	Net	Worldwide
1965	74.2	Not Applicable	(18.4)	55.8
1966	96.1	(20.4)	(17.4)	78.7
1967	82.3	(32.8)	(24.7)	57.6
1968	49.7	(19.9)	(7.1)	42.6
1969	59.2	(18.1)	(5.1)	54.1
1970	59.7	(29.5)	(13.7)	46.0

Source: 1970 Comptroller's Report, Deere & Company.

Appendix Exhibit 27	**Investment in Overseas Subsidiaries October 31, 1970 ($000,000)**		
	Investment in Capital Stock and Surplus or Deficit	Total Investment as Shown on Balance Sheet	Total Investment at Cost
Germany	(60.6)	20.9	123.0
France[a]	26.8	39.6	46.8
Spain[a]	9.8	11.1	15.1
Mexico	9.2	10.1	8.4
Argentina	9.0	24.2	39.3
South Africa	(0.8)	3.6	5.4
Australia	1.6	4.5	4.5
JDIL (Export)	13.8	19.5	5.7
Other	1.5	3.8	6.3
TOTAL	10.4	137.3	254.3

[a]*Includes separate manufacturing and sales companies; totals not congruent because of rounding.*

Source: *Comptroller's Report, Deere & Company (1970).*

Appendix Exhibit 28	**Deere's Operation in South Africa Sales and Profitability, 1964–80**	
	Sales ($000,000)	Net Income ($000,000)
1964	4.9	(0.4)
1965	5.1	(0.0)
1966	5.3	(1.1)
1967	10.6	0.1
1968	11.5	0.1
1969	11.3	(0.2)
1970	15.9	0.7
1971	18.2	1.0
1972	15.9	0.7
1973	24.3	1.6
1974	30.5	1.8
1975	63.0	5.7
1976	51.0	3.8
1977	42.0	2.0
1978	44.0	1.2
1979	33.0	(0.2)
1980	93.0	8.8
1981	139.0	10.1

Source: *Deere & Company Comptroller's Report; sales figures 1975–1981 include Industrial Division shipments from Belgium.*

Appendix Exhibit 29	**Farm Equipment Sales in North America:** **Market Share and Growth Rates, 1970-80**					
Company	Year			Annual Growth Rate		
	1970	1975	1980	1970-75	1975-80	1970-80
Deere	26%	25%	29%	21%	12%	16%
International Harvester . .	18	17	14	21	5	12
Massey-Ferguson	8	8	7	20	7	13
Fiat	NA	. . .	3	NA	NM	NA
Hesston	1	2	NA	34	NM	NM
Sperry-New Holland	4	3	5	16	18	17
Ford	5	4	4	18	9	13
J. I. Case	4	6	6	29	8	18
Allis-Chalmers	6	6	5	22	7	14
Versatile	1	1	2	34	16	24
Steiger	. . .	1	1	91	6	42
Claas	NA	. . .	. . .	NA	NM	NA
Deutz	NA	. . .	1	NA	79	NA
Kubota	NA	NA	NA	NA	NA	NA
Total Industry Sales[a]	$3[b]	$8[b]	$12[b]	22%	9%	15%

NA - Not available; NM - Not meaningful.
[a]*Industry farm equipment dollar sales shown on Exhibits 29, 31, and 32 differ in definition from the U.S. Department of Commerce farm machinery and lawn and garden equiptment sales. Not included in industry sales on the tables are farm dairy machines and equipment; farm poultry equipment; hog equipment; other barn and barnyard equipment; and irrigation systems. These categories have been excluded because the companies shown produce little or no equipment of these types.*
[b]*$000,000,000*

Source: Annual reports, supplemented by Deere & Company estimates.

| Appendix
Exhibit 30 | **North American Market Positions,
1981** | | | | | | | | | |

	Deere	IH	MF	Hesston	New Holland	Ford	Case	AC	Versatile	Steiger
TRACTORS:										
Under 40 HP..............	2	4	5	...	...	2	...	5	...	...
40-89 HP.................	2	3	2	5	...	②	4	5	...	...
Over 90 HP..............	①	2	5	5	...	5	3	4	...	...
4WD....................	2	②	5	...	...	5	3	5	2	2
HARVESTING EQUIPMENT:										
Combines[a]	①	2	2	...	4	...	...	3	...	...
Forage Harvesters	②	3	5	3	2	5	...	...	...	...
Cotton Harvesters..........	①	2	...	...	...	...	...	3	...	...
TILLAGE EQUIPMENT	②	2	5	...	...	5	5	5	...	...
PLANTERS/DRILLERS	①	2	5	...	...	5	...	4	...	...
HAY EQUIPMENT...........	2	3	3	3	②	5	...	...	4	...

	Claas	Deutz	Kubota	White	Yanmar	New Idea	Gehl	Satoh	Vermeer
TRACTORS:									
Under 40 HP..............	...	...	①	5	5	...	...	5	...
40-89 HP.................	...	5	5	5	...	...	...	...	...
Over 90 HP..............	...	5	...	5	...	...	...	...	...
4WD....................	...	...	...	5	...	...	...	...	...
HARVESTING EQUIPMENT:									
Combines[a]	...	...	...	5	...	5	...	...	...
Forage Harvesters	...	...	...	...	...	5	2	...	...
Cotton Harvesters..........									
TILLAGE EQUIPMENT	...	...	...	3	...	...	...	...	...
PLANTERS/DRILLERS				4					
HAY EQUIPMENT...........	...	...	...	5	...	5	5	...	4

KEY: 1 - 30% and over
    2 - 15% - 30%
    3 - 10% - 15%
    4 - 5% - 10%
    5 - 0% - 5%
    ◯ - Major supplier.

[a]*Combines can be split into two categories: conventional and rotary. Deere does not consider a rotary combine to be a distinct product with applications different from a conventional combine.*

Source: Deere & Company estimates.

Appendix
Exhibit 31
Farm Equipment Sales Worldwide:
Market Shares and Growth Rates, 1970–80

Company	Year			Annual Growth Rate		
	1970	1975	1980	1970–75	1975–80	1970–80
Deere	15%	16%	17%	23%	12%	17%
International Harvester . . .	12	14	9	25	4	14
Massey-Ferguson	10	12	9	24	5	14
Fiat	NA	4	5	NA	19	NA
Hesston	1	1	NA	38	NA	NA
Sperry-New Holland	4	3	4	19	14	17
Ford	7	5	4	14	6	10
J.I. Case	2	4	4	32	10	21
Allis-Chalmers	3	3	3	21	7	14
Versatile		1	1	34	20	27
Steiger		1	1	94	8	45
Claas	NA	2	2	NA	11	NA
Deutz	NA	2	2	NA	18	NA
Kubota	NA	4	4	NA	10	NA
Total Industry Sales	$6[a]	$16[a]	$27[a]	21%	12%	16%

NA—Not available
[a]*$000,000,000*

Source: Deere & Company annual reports, estimates.

Appendix
Exhibit 32
Farm Equipment Sales Overseas:
Market Share and Growth Rates, 1970-80

Company	Year			Annual Growth Rate		
	1970	1975	1980	1970-75	1975-80	1970-80
Deere	5%	8%	7%	30%	12%	21%
International Harvester	6	10	6	34	2	17
Massey-Ferguson	12	16	10	26	5	15
Fiat	NA	7	7	NA	13	NA
Hesston	. . .	. . .	NA	97	NA	NA
Sperry-New Holland . .	4	4	3	22	11	16
Ford	8	6	4	13	3	8
J. I. Case	1	2	2	47	15	30
Allis-Chalmers	1	. . .	. . .	9	8	8
Versatile		. . .	. . .	. . .	. . .	NM
Steiger		. . .	. . .	NM	25	NM
Claas	NA	3	3	NA	10	NA
Deutz	NA	3	3	NA	15	NA
Kubota	NA	NA	NA	NA	NA	NA
Total Industry Sales	$3[a]	$8[a]	$15[a]	20%	14%	17%

NA - Not available; NM-1 Not meaningful.
[a]*$000,000,000*

Source: Annual reports supplemented by Deere & Company estimates.

Appendix Exhibit 33	**Deere's Position in Largest Overseas Markets** **Tractor Market Share, 1980 FY** (%)								

Country and Market size[a]	Deere	IH	MF	Fiat	Ford	Deutz	Landini	Other	Other
France (58,719)(units) . .	8	16	13	11	7	7	. . .	Renault 18	. . .
Italy (53,502)	2	2	4	25	4	. . .	8	SAME 18	Lamborghini 7
Germany (46,159)	9	20	6	4	2	17	. . .	Fendt 16	. . .
Spain (25,132)	31	1	b	5	4	3	. . .	EBRO 28	Barreiros 8
U.K. (22,011)	10	12	24	3	25	. . .	. . .	Case 10	Leyland 5
Mexico (18,581)	15	21	30	. . .	33	. . .	. . .	. . .	. . .
South Africa (16,626)	17	5	22	20	22	3	5	. . .	. . .
Australia (14,847)	21	15	14	7	12	4	. . .	Kubota 5	Case 8

[a]*Registrations, retail sales, or sales to dealers.*
[b]*Tractors manufactured by EBRO.*

Source: Deere & Company estimates.

Appendix Exhibit 34	**Deere's Position in Largest Overseas Markets** **Combine Market Share, 1980 FY** (%)								

Country and Market size[a]	Deere	IH	MF	New Holland	Claas	Fahr	Other	Other
Brazil (5,437)(units) . . .	29[b]	. . .	17	33	. . .	. . .	Santa Matilda 9	Ideal 12
France (4,685)	12	13	10	24	20	. . .	Braud 7	Fiat-Someca 10
Germany (4,467)	18	11	6	8	37	19	. . .	. . .
U.K. (2,081)	14	3	24	29	22	. . .	. . .	. . .
Italy (1,981)	8	2	6	19	8	. . .	Laverda 39	Arbos 14
Finland (1,948)	5	. . .	21	5	. . .	21	Sampo 46	. . .
Australia (1,934)	18	32	30	15	. . .	. . .	. . .	. . .
Spain (1,468)	35	1	7	11	16	12	. . .	. . .

[a]*Registrations, retail sales, or sales to dealers.*
[b]*Deere/Schneider-Logemann Corporation collaboration.*

Source: Deere & Company estimates.

Appendix
Exhibit 35

**Position of Deere in the North American Industrial
and Construction Equipment Industry
(Percent of Market Share)**

Product	Calendar Year 1979	Fiscal Year 1980	Fiscal Year 1981
Industrial wheel tractors, all sizes..........................	17.0	20.7	20.0
Wheel log skidders, all sizes.............	31.8	28.6	27.7
Crawler dozers, under 160 NEHP........................	32.3	30.3	30.0
Crawler loaders, total.................	30.0	32.6	29.4
Four-wheel drive loaders, 80 & under 150 NEHP & 250 & under 300 NEHP.................	21.1	20.7	19.1
Elevating scrapers, under 18 cu. yd.	31.8	31.5	36.7
Motor graders, under 200 NEHP........................	24.9	30.4	30.9
Crawler mounted excavators under 40,000 lb. and 85,000 lb.– 100,000 lb.ᵃ........................	32.9	32.5	26.1

ᵃ*All excavator data are shipments.*
NEHP Net estimated horsepower

Source: Comptroller's Annual Report, Deere & Company, 1981.

Appendix
Exhibit 36

**Research and Development Expenses as Percent
of Sales and Dollars Per Employee 1977–81**

Year	Deere % of Sales	Deere $ per Employee	International Harvester % of Sales	International Harvester $ per Employee	Allis-Chalmers % of Sales	Allis-Chalmers $ per Employee	Caterpillar % of Sales	Caterpillar $ per Employee
1977....	3.8	2346	1.9	1230	3.4	1916	3.8	2835
1978....	3.7	2618	1.8	1235	not reported		2.3	1940
1979....	3.8	2877	2.6	2230	3.0	2012	2.5	2131
1980....	4.2	3788	4.0	2930	2.4	1709	2.3	2444
1981....	4.4	3943	3.5	3731	3.2	2431	2.5	2637

Source: "R&D Scoreboard," Business Week.

Appendix
Exhibit 37 **Deere & Company, 1972–82**

	Sales ($000,000)	Net Income ($000,000)	Net Income Per Share ($)	Book Value Per Share ($)
1972	1,500	112	1.91	13.73
1973	2,003	168	2.88	15.91
1974	2,495	164	2.78	17.90
1975	2,955	171	2.89	19.86
1976	3,134	242	4.04	22.86
1977	3,604	256	4.24	25.87
1978	4,155	265	4.38	28.84
1979	4,933	311	5.12	32.34
1980	5,470	228	3.72	34.13
1981	5,447	251	3.79	36.29
1982	4,608	53	.78	35.29

Source: Deere & Company Annual Reports.

Appendix
Exhibit 38   **Deere Profitability Ratios**

A. Net Income as Percent of Net Sales

	Deere	International Harvester	Massey-Ferguson	Allis-Chalmers	Caterpillar
1972	7.5	2.5	3.6	0.9	7.9
1973	8.4	2.5	3.9	1.4	7.8
1974	6.6	2.4	3.8	1.8	5.6
1975	6.1	2.1	3.8	2.0	8.0
1976	7.7	3.2	4.3	3.9	7.6
1977	7.1	3.4	1.2	4.4	7.6
1978	6.4	2.8	(8.8)	4.3	7.8
1979	6.3	4.4	1.2	4.1	6.5
1980	4.2	(6.3)	(7.2)	2.3	6.6
1981	4.6	(5.6)	(7.4)	(1.4)	6.3
1982	1.1	(38.2)	(20.1)	(12.9)	(2.8)

B. Net Income as Percent of Beginning Year Total Assets

	Deere	International Harvester	Massey-Ferguson	Allis-Chalmers	Caterpillar
1972	6.2	2.5	3.1	0.7	11.3
1973	8.9	2.8	4.4	1.3	12.8
1974	8.1	2.9	4.7	1.8	10.2
1975	7.3	2.3	5.1	2.3	13.6
1976	8.4	3.1	5.0	4.3	11.4
1977	7.7	3.4	1.1	4.3	11.4
1978	6.3	2.7	(7.5)	4.3	13.0
1979	7.1	4.8	1.1	3.8	9.8
1980	4.6	(4.1)	(6.3)	3.2	10.5
1981	3.7	(3.8)	(5.5)	(1.2)	9.5
1982	0.7	(16.2)	(12.7)	N.A.	(2.5)

Note: Corporate-wide figures for all companies; finance subsidiary assets consolidated.
N.A. Not available

Source: Deere & Company Comptroller's Annual Reports.

| Appendix Exhibit 39 | **Deere's Rankings Among Fortune Magazine's 100 Largest Industrials, 1972–82** | | | | | |

Year	Sales	Net Income	ROS	ROE	10-Yr. EPS Growth	10-Yr. Total Return
1972	90	45	20	24	20	14
1973	78	40	21	16	16	12
1974	75	47	27	39	49	13
1975	62	38	23	24	17	16
1976	66	37	15	13	21	34
1977	60	36	20	28	6	7
1978	61	41	26	42	3	2
1979	60	51	32	61	10	10
1980	60	64	63	80	28	13
1981	65	62	51	77	41	16
1982	75	85	84	86	84	54

ROS = Net income as percent of sales.
ROE = Net income as percent of stockholders' equity at end of year.
EPS = Earnings per share of common stock.
Total Return = Return to a stockholder, including both common stock appreciation at end of year and dividends.
Assumes dividends reinvested.

Source: Fortune *magazine, "The Fortune 500."*

DEERE FAMILY LINKS IN DEERE & COMPANY*

John Deere
(1804-1886)
(director, 1868-86)
(President, 1869-86)

(1) Demarius Lamb
      (1805-65)

(2) Lucenia Lamb
      (1809-88)

Francis A.
(1828-48)

Frances A.
(1834-51)

Hiram A.
(1842-44)

Unnamed
Child
(stillborn, 1845)

Mary F.
(1851-52)

Jeannette D.-James
(1830-1916) Chapman

Ellen S.-Christopher C.
(1832-98)   Webber

Charles H.-Mary Little
(1837-1907) Dickenson
(director, 1868-1907)
(treasurer, 1871-81,
1883-86)
(vice pres., 1869-86)
(president, 1886-1907)

Emma C.-Stephen H.
(1840-1911) Velie
(1830-95)
(director, 1868-95)
(secretary, 1869-95)

Alice M.-Merton Y.
(1844-1900)   Cady

Schiller Hosford
(1845-1912)
(director, 1900-12)
(asst. treasurer,
1900)
(secretary, 1900-12)

Charles C. Webber
(1859-1944)
(director, 1886-1944)
(vice pres., 1893-1944)

William Butterworth
(1864-1936)
(director, 1893-1936)
(treasurer, 1894-1907)
(president, 1907-28)
(chairman, 1928-36)

Charles D. Velie
(1861-1929)
(director, 1911-29)

(No
descendants
as director
or officers)

Richard S. Hosford
(1885-1922)
(director, 1920-22)
(asst. secretary,
1917-22)

George W. Mixter
(1876-1947)
(director, 1907-42)
(vice pres., 1910-29)

William D. Wiman
(1861-1914)
(director, 1900-14)
(vice pres., 1900-11)

Stephen H. Velie, Jr.
(1862-1933)
(director, 1911-19)

Willard D. Hosford
(1882-1951)
(director, 1922-51)

Benjamin C. Keator
(1885-1968)
(director, 1949-54)

Charles D. Wiman
(1892-1955)
(director, 1919-55)
(asst. secretary, 1922-24)
(vice pres., 1924-28)
(president, 1928-42; 1944-55)

Willard L. Velie
(1866-1928)
(director, 1894-1921)
(secretary, 1895-1900)
(vice pres., 1907-11)

Willard D. Hosford, Jr.
(1912-)
(director, 1952-72)

Edmond M. Cook
(1897-1981)
(director, 1943-67)
(vice pres., 1948-56)
(general counsel, 1944-56)

Dwight D. Wiman
(1895-1951)
(director, 1921-51)
(asst. secretary, 1921-51)

Lawrence A. Murphy
(1900-61)
(director, 1937-61)
(vice pres., 1942-56)
(senior vice pres., 1956-61)

Ben Butterworth
(1904-1969)
(director, 1940-50)

William A. Hewitt
(1914-)
(director, 1951-82)
(executive vice pres., 1954-55)
(president, 1955-64)
(chairman and
chief executive officer, 1964-1982)

D. Coleman Glover, Jr.
(1918-1975)
(director, 1955-75)

*Included are only officers and directors

Five Generations of Deere & Company
chief executive officers, 1837-1982

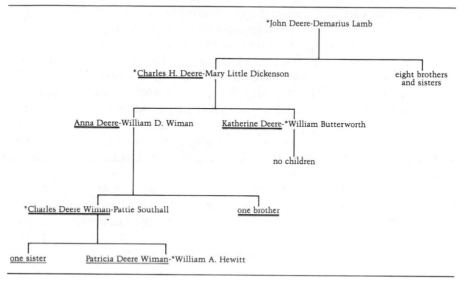

NOTE: Burton F. Peek *was president, 1942-44, when Charles D. Wiman* was in the United States Army.

*-*chief executive officer*
──-*direct descendant of* John Deere

BIBLIOGRAPHIC NOTES

Taken as a whole, the literature of agriculture is extensive, indeed overwhelming. Certain general studies were meaningful for this work, as were general bibliographic efforts that provide additional detail. Writings specifically relating to the agricultural equipment industry vary widely in quality. While the technical literature is comprehensive, even back into the nineteenth century, the economic and social history of the industry is less well documented. A few key theses from young academics—always a fruitful source for bibliographic depth—and important government hearings in the 1910s, 1920, 1938, and 1948 have added extensive documentation of certain aspects of the industry. Still, there have been few significant business histories of individual firms.

The history of Deere & Company is a seminal one in regard to the Westward Movement. John Deere's emigration from Vermont in 1837 and his settlement in Illinois at the time of the opening of the prairie parallel similar efforts by countless thousands of other Americans in the early and mid-nineteenth century. A number of writings on "the frontier," many relating particularly to the Midwest, are pertinent to the Deere story.

Deere & Company records of the nineteenth century are rich for certain times, poor for others. Just scraps remain from the pre-Civil War days of John Deere, though they fortunately document critical points. John Deere himself was not a recordkeeper; his son Charles, on the other hand, kept excellent reports both for the firm and for his own personal use. Charles Deere's diary for 1859–60, for example, reveals many insights, both about the firm and the man. An extensive set of Charles Deere literature for the 1870s and '80s remains, superb material for understanding that hurly-burly period of growth. Records of Deere's efforts to engineer a "plow trust" are extant, as are a number of documents relating to manufacturing that help to build a picture of the technical and labor aspects of the business in that period.

Fortuitously for historians, a trademark court case in the late 1860s—*Henry W. Candee, et al., Appellants* v. *John Deere, et al., Appellees*, Supreme Court of Illinois (1870)—laid on the record a rich panoply of detail about Deere's business, replete with personal statements by many dozens of individuals relating to a wide range of topics. Also, the company has kept meticulous minutes of every one of its directors' meetings since the inception of incorporation in 1868; the earlier years are particularly evocative, with many dozens of the meetings in the first three decades of the twentieth century recorded almost verbatim. Another fascinating, though often undependable, source about the mid-nineteenth century is the diary of Robert Tate, sometime partner of John Deere ("The Life of Robert N. Tate, Written by Himself," Deere Archives). This opinionated but articulate personal view of the firm and its participants is a unique of information about both the company and the town.

In the main, the records of the company in the twentieth century are excellent. William Butterworth, as chief executive officer from 1907 to 1928, left most of his papers intact. Charles Wiman's papers were largely destroyed, but a wide range of collateral documentation allows the Wiman period to come alive. Since the 1950s the company's records have been managed very well indeed; just about everything remains that a serious historian might desire. The company maintains a sophisticated, computerized corporate archives, which is effectively supervised by a professional archivist.

There are several modest books on John Deere and Deere & Company, all of which are cited in the Notes. A number of dissertations at both the master's and doctoral levels have been done; one of the most valuable is William J. Kirkpatrick, "John Deere and His Steel Plow: Their Contribution to the Midwest and the World" (University of Minnesota, 1971). One of the best analytical sources of overall company history was done by P.C. Simmon, the corporate secretary of the first two decades of the twentieth century; his unpublished manuscript is dated 1920. Two company sources relating specifically to tractor history are worth mentioning: the book by Theo Brown, *Deere & Company's Early Tractor Development* (privately printed, 1953) and the promotional brochure "John Deere Tractors, 1918–1976" (1976), by Will McCracken.

Individual business histories of the many other important firms in the industry have been few in number and spotty in quality. Despite the superb raw material available on International Harvester's history—a first-rate archives at the company's headquarters, and additional important McCormick family papers at the State Historical Society of Wisconsin—there had yet to be a full-scale business history of this other giant of the industry by the early 1980s. Cyrus McCormick (the son of the founder), authored an interesting and surprisingly analytical view of the corporation in his *Century of the Reaper, An Account of Cyrus Hall McCormick, the Inventor of the Reaper; of the McCormick Harvesting Company, the Business He Created and of the International Harvester Company, His Heirs and Chief Memorial* (Boston: Houghton Mifflin Company, 1931). A sound biography of the founder himself is William T. Hutchinson, *Cyrus Hall McCormick*, 2 vol. (New York: D. Appleton-Century Company, 1935). Two comprehensive books on International Harvester's employee and labor relations are by Robert Ozanne—*A Century of Labor-Management Relations at McCormick and International Harvester* (1967) and *Wages in Practice and Theory: McCormick and International Harvester, 1860–1960* (1968), both published in Madison, Wis., by the University of Wisconsin Press. Also helpful in understanding International Harvester's role is Helen M. Kramer, "Harvesters and High Finance: Formation of the International Harvester Company," *Business History Review* 38 (1964): 285. There is excellent documentation of International Harvester's early years in Department of Commerce,

Bureau of Corporations, *The International Harvester Company* (Washington: Government Printing Office, 1913) and in the antitrust suits against the company in the 1910s and '20s (*U.S.* v. *International Harvester Co., et al.*, 214 Federal Reports 987 and *U.S.* v. *International Harvester*, 274 U.S. 693). A pictorial history of International Harvester of merit is C.H. Wendel, *150 Years of International Harvester* (Sarasota, Fla.: Crestline Publishing Co., 1981).

For the history of the J.I. Case Company, see Stewart H. Holbrook, *Machines of Plenty* (New York: The Macmillan Company, 1955); for the history of the Oliver Chilled Plow Company, see Joan Romine, *Copshaholm: The Oliver Story* (South Bend, Ind.: Northern Indiana Historical Society, Inc., 1978). For histories of Massey-Ferguson and Massey-Harris, see Edward P. Neufeld, *A Global Corporation: A History of the International Development of Massey-Ferguson Limited* (Toronto: University of Toronto Press, 1969); James S. Duncan, *Not a One-Way Street: The Autobiography of James S. Duncan* (Toronto: Clarke, Irwin and Company, 1971); and Peter Cook, *Massey at the Brink: The Story of Canada's Greatest Multinational and its Struggle to Survive* (Toronto: Collin Publishers, 1981). Several biographical studies that have added significant information on the industry are: Reynold M. Wik, *Henry Ford and Grass Roots America* (Ann Arbor, Mich.: University of Michigan Press, 1972); Gilbert C. Fite, *George M. Peek and the Fight for Farm Parity* (Norman, Okla.: University of Oklahoma Press, 1954); Collin Fraser, *Tractor Pioneer: The Life of Harry Ferguson* (Athens, Ohio: Ohio University Press, 1973); Edith Sklovsky Covich, *Max* (Chicago: Stuart Brent, publishers, 1974). One particularly unique source of information about the companies is the credit correspondence in the R.G. Dun & Company collection in the Baker Library, Harvard Business School; the material on Deere & Company, for example, extends from the 1850s to the late 1880s.

Five doctoral dissertations on the industry are particularly helpful: Michael Conant, "Aspects of Monopoly and Price Policies in the Farm Machinery Industry Since 1902" (University of Chicago, 1949); Warren Wright Shearer, "Competition Through Merger: An Economic Analysis of the Farm Machinery Industry" (Harvard University, 1951); Elvis Luverne Eckles, "The Development of Oligopoly in the Farm Industry" (University of Illinois, 1953); Arlyn John Melcher, "Collective Bargaining in the Agricultural Implement Industry: The Impact of Company and Union Structure in Three Firms" (University of Chicago, 1964); and Harvey Schwartz, "The Changes in the Location of the American Agricultural Implement Industry, 1850 to 1900" (University of Illinois, 1966).

There is a wide range of sources on agricultural machinery. For the British experience, the books by George Edwin Fussell are a useful starting point, especially *The Farmer's Tools, A.D. 1500–1900: A History of British Farm Implements, Tools and Machinery Before the Tractor*

Came (London: Andrew Melrose, 1952). Also excellent is John B. Passamore, *The English Plough* (London: Oxford University Press, Humphrey Milford, 1930). The following four sources are the key pieces for the American experience in agricultural machinery in the nineteenth century: Robert L. Ardrey, *American Agricultural Implements: A Review of Invention and Development in the Agricultural Implement Industry of the United States* (1894; reprinted, Arno Press, Inc., New York, 1972); Leo Rogin, *The Introduction of Farm Machinery in its Relation to the Productivity of Labor in the Agriculture of the United States During the Nineteenth Century* (1931; reprinted, Johnson Reprint Corp., New York, 1966); Clarence H. Danhof, *Change in Agriculture: The Northern United States, 1820–1870* (Cambridge, Mass.: Harvard University Press, 1969); "Report on Trials of Plows," *Transactions of the New York State Agricultural Society*, 1:27 (1867): 385–656 (often reported in the literature as the "Utica Trials"). See the Notes for Chapter 2 for other relevant English and American materials on the nineteenth century.

The American Society of Agricultural Engineers in St. Joseph, Mich., has published important works on the tractor and the harvester: the classic history of the tractor in the twentieth century, R.B. Gray, *The Agricultural Tractor: 1855–1950* (1954); Lester Larson, *Farm Tractors 1950–1975* (1981); and Graeme R. Quick and Lesley F. Buchele, *The Grain Harvesters* (1978). See also C.H. Wendel, *Encyclopedia of American Farm Tractors* (Sarasota, Fla.: Crestline Publishing Company, 1979); Wayne Worthington, *50 Years of Agricultural Tractor Development* (St. Joseph, Mich.: American Society of Agricultural Engineers, 1966); and Robert Kudrle, *Agricultural Tractors: A World Industry Study* (Cambridge, Mass.: Ballinger Publishing Company, 1975). There are a number of books on "vintage farm tools," such as Michael Partridge, *Farm Tools Through the Ages* (Boston: New York Graphic Books, 1973). Similarly, there is substantial coverage of "vintage tractors" in various largely pictorial books, such as Michael Williams, *Farm Tractors in Color* (New York: Macmillan Publishing Company, Inc., 1974) and Philip Wright, *Old Farm Tractors* (London: David & Charles, 1962, reprint, 1974). There is also a burgeoning literature on the steam plow; Reynold M. Wik, *Steam Power on the American Farm* (Philadelphia, Pa.: University of Pennsylvania Press, 1953), is a useful starting point.

From the mid-nineteenth century, certain key monographs, articles, and books seem to sum up agricultural machinery "at the moment." For the period before the Civil War, see the various reports of the commissioner of patents, published as executive documents of the House of Representatives for a given year; J.J. Thomas, "Farm Implements and Machinery," *Report of the Commissioner of Agriculture, U.S. Department of Agriculture Annual Report* (1862), and *Farm Implements and the Principles of Their Construction and Use: An Elementary and Familiar Treatise on Mechanics and on Natural Philosophy Generally, As Applied to the Ordinary Practices of Agriculture* (New York: Harper and Brothers, 1854; later editions titled *Farm Implements and Farm Machinery* in 1869 and 1886, Orrin Judd & Company Publishers). For the second half of the nineteenth century, see Carroll D. Wright, *Thirteenth Annual Report of the Commissioner of Labor, 1898: Hand and Machine Labor,* 2 vol. (Washington: Government Printing Office, 1899); George K. Holmes, *The Course of Prices of Farm Implements and Machinery for a Series of Years,* U.S. Department of Agriculture Miscellaneous Series, bulletin 18 (Washington: Government Printing Office, 1901); H.W. Quaintance, "The Influence of Farm Machinery on Production and Labor," American Economic Society, 3:5 (November 1904): 45. For the first half of the twentieth century, see M.R.D. Owings, "New Methods and New Machines for the Farm: What the Inventor Has Done for Agriculture," *Scientific American* (18 February 1911); Barton Currie, *The Tractor and Its Influence Upon The Agricultural Implement Industry* (Philadelphia, Pa.: Curtis Publishing Company, 1916); Lillian M. Church and H.R. Tolley, "The Manufacture and Sale of Farm Equipment in 1920: A Summary of Reports from 583 Manufacturers," U.S. Department of Agriculture, circular 212 (April 1922); C.D. Kinsman, "An Appraisal of Power Used on Farms in the United States," U.S. Department of Agriculture, departmental bulletin 1348 (1925); Lillian M. Church, "History of the Plow," U.S. Department of Agriculture, Bureau of Agricultural Engineering, Division of Mechanical Equipment, Information Series 48 (October 1935); W.W. Hurst, "New Types of Farm Equipment and Economic Implications," *Journal of Farm Economics* 19 (1937): 483; Harold Barger and Hans W. Landsburg, *American Agriculture, 1899– 1939: A Study of Output, Employment and Productivity* (New York: National Bureau of Economic Research, Inc., 1942); Martin R. Cooper, Glenn T. Barton, and Albert P. Brodell, "Progress of Farm Mechanization," U.S. Department of Agriculture miscellaneous publications 620 (1947). There have been several important hearings and studies of the agricultural machinery industry by the federal government: U.S. Department of Commerce, Bureau of Corporations, "Farm-Machinery Trade Associations" (15 March 1915); Federal Trade Commission, "Report of the Federal Trade Commission on the Causes of High Prices of Farm Implements " (4 May 1920); Federal Trade Commission, "Report on the Agricultural Implement and Machinery Industry," 75th Congress, 3rd session, House Documents 702 (6 June 1938); Temporary National Economic Committee, Investigation of Concentration of Economic Power 36, "Agricultural Implement and Machinery Inquiry" (1940); Federal Trade Commission, "Report of the Federal Trade Commission on Manufacture and Distribution of Farm Implements" (1948).

There have been two important agricultural machinery industry journals, both originating in the late nineteenth century. *Farm Implement News* was founded in 1882 in Chicago, and *Implement and Tractor* was founded in 1876 in Kansas City; the two were merged as *Implement and Tractor* in 1958, published in Overland Park, Kansas. Two professional journals of agricultural history are *Agricultural History*, the quarterly journal of the Agricultural History Society, published by the University of California Press, and *Agricultural History Review*, published by the British Agricultural History Society. *Business History Review*, published by the Harvard Business School, has contained a number of articles relating to the industry. The literature of the trade press in agriculture has been prolific; especially useful are *Country Gentleman*, published from 1853 to 1955 in Philadelphia; *Genesee Farmer*, published from 1840 to 1865 in Rochester, New York; and *Prairie Farmer*, published since 1841 in Chicago. For an excellent review, see *Agricultural Literature: Proud Heritage-Future Promise, A Bicentennial Symposium, September 24, 26, 1975* (Washington: Associates of the National Agricultural Library, Inc., and the Graduate School Press, U.S. Department of Agriculture, 1977).

For general books on agriculture, see Fred Shannon, *The Farmer's Last Frontier, Agriculture 1860–1897* (New York: Reinhart & Company, 1945); a number of the writings of Paul W. Gates, especially *The Farmer's Age: Agriculture 1815–1860* (New York: Holt, Rinehart and Winston, 1960) and *The Illinois Central Railroad and its Colonization Work* (Cambridge, Mass.: Harvard University Press, 1930); and the writings of Wayne D. Rasmussen, especially *Agriculture in the United States: A Documentary History*, 4 vol. (New York: Random House, 1975). Also useful is D. Gale Johnson, ed., *Food and Agricultural Policy for the 1980s* (Washington: American Enterprise Institute for Public Policy Research, 1981). U.S. Department of Agriculture, *Farmers in a Changing World*, Part I (Washington: Government Printing Office, 1940), contains several excellent articles on agricultural history. The agricultural history of New England is well documented in Howard S. Russell, *A Long Deep Furrow: Three Centuries of Farming in New England* (Hanover, N.H.: University Press of New England, 1976). For Midwestern agricultural history, useful starting points are Allan G. Bogue, *From Prairie to Cornbelt: Farming on the Illinois and Iowa Prairies in the Nineteenth Century* (Chicago: University of Chicago Press, 1963) and Percy Wells Bidwell and John I. Falconer, *History of Agriculture in the Northern United States, 1620–1860* (Washington: Carnegie Institution of Washington, 1925). The historical writing on the Westward Movement is prolific. Particularly helpful are: Lewis D. Stilwell, *Migration from Vermont* (Montpelier, Vt.: Vermont Historical Society, 1948); William V. Pooley, "The Settlement of Illinois from 1830 to 1850," *Bulletin of the University of Wisconsin*, History Series I (1908): 207; Malcolm J. Rohrbough, *The Trans-Appalachian Frontier: People, Societies, and Institutions, 1775–1850* (New York: Oxford University Press, 1978); and John D. Unruh, Jr., *The Plains Across: The Overland Immigrants and the Trans-Mississippi*

West, 1840–1860 (Urbana, Ill.: University of Illinois Press, 1979). The manuscript collections of state and county historical societies provide many original documents of the Westward Movement; evocative pieces can be found at the Vermont Historical Society, the Illinois State Historical Society, the State Historical Society of Iowa, the Chicago Historical Society, and the F. Hal Higgins Library of Agricultural Technology, University of California, Davis.

Finally, certain key bibliographic contributions to agriculture should be noted. For the early nineteenth century, see Alan M. Fusonie, ed., *Heritage of American Agriculture: A Bibliography of Pre-1860 Imprints* (Beltsville, Md.: National Agricultural Library, 1975). For a comprehensive bibliography of American agricultural history, see Everett E. Edwards, *A Bibliography of a History of Agriculture in the United States* (Washington: U.S. Department of Agriculture miscellaneous publication No. 84, 1930). The U.S. Department of Agriculture, in cooperation with the Agricultural History Center of the University of California, Davis, has supplemented this basic bibliography with a score of specialized and updated monographs; see, particularly, "A List of References for the History of Agriculture in the Midwest, 1840–1900" (1973); "A List... for the History of Agriculture in California" (1974); "A List... for the History of Agriculture in the Great Plains" (1976); "A List... for the History of Agricultural Technology" (1979); and "A List... for the History of Agricultural Science in America" (1980). See also John T. Schlebecker, *Bibliography of Books and Pamphlets on the History of Agriculture in the U.S., 1607–1967* (Santa Barbara, Calif.: American Bibliographic Center, 1969). For an annotated bibliography of traders' views of Illinois, see Solon Justus Buck, *Travel and Description, 1765–1865*, Illinois Historical Society 9, Bibliographic Sources 2 (Springfield, Ill.: Illinois State Historical Society Library, 1914).

FOOTNOTES

NOTES TO CHAPTER 1: VERMONTERS' WAY WEST

1. Ogle County (Illinois) Circuit Court, September 1843, case no. 918; the plaintiff is John G. Perry, for the use of Jay A. Wright, Deere's former partner in Leicester, Vermont. The particular note in question, which had formed the basis of the Addison County, Vermont, case in 1836, had been dated in Leicester on 9 June 1831. The other notes are also summarized in the Ogle County files.

2. W.B. Irwin, *William and Sarah (Yates) Deere and Some of Their Descendants* (Riverside, Calif.: privately printed, 1964) and Theo Brown, *The Early Life of John Deere in Vermont* (Moline, Ill.: privately printed, ca. 1925), in the Deere Archives (hereafter cited as DA). Both state a family belief that Deere was of Welsh origin. Two genealogical searches by professional organizations, American Historical Society, Inc., *Deere and Allied Families* (New York: 1927) and Debrett's Peerage, Ltd., *The Ancestry of John Deere* (London: 1982) confirm this view. Charles C. Webber, *A Tribute to the Memory of John Deere by His Grandson* (Moline, Ill.: privately printed, 1942), DA, reiterates the belief that Sarah Yates was the daughter of a former captain of British Revolutionary forces who settled in Connecticut after the war; however, *Index to the Vital Records of Connecticut to 1850* notes only one person of this name, born to William Prudence Yates in Salisbury in 1775. See also Mrs. R. Taylor to Mrs. Nellie Rosborough, 12 November 1953, DA, 24091. William Deere is first listed in the United States census of 1800, *Heads of Families-Vermont. Rutland, Rutland County*, p. 124; the spelling there is with an "s" instead of an "e" on the end. American Biographical Publishing Co., *The United States Biographical Dictionary and Portrait Gallery of Eminent and Self-Made Men*, Illinois vol. (Chicago: 1876) states that William and Sarah Deere came to Vermont by way of Canada, but there is no further corroboration of this.

3. There are no official birth records of the children of William and Sarah Yates; the "Family Register" of the Deere family Bible, DA, is the primary source of the birth dates of John Deere and his brothers and sisters. Extant copies of the *Middlebury Mercury* are available at the Sheldon Museum, Middlebury. For the chronicle of the grammar school and Middlebury College, see William Storrs Lee, *Stagecoach North: Being an Account of the First Generation in the State of Vermont* (New York: The Macmillan Co., 1941), pp. 133–134 and 136 ff. The law concerning education passed by the state of Vermont in 1797 is discussed in John C. Huden, *Development of State School Administration in Vermont* (Montpelier: Vermont Historical Society, 1943), pp. 3–34.

4. The original of the William Deere letter of 26 June 1808 is no longer extant; for a photocopy, see DA, 2366. The use of the singular "sister" is of significance because it may explain the mystery of John Deere's sister, Jane, who was born in Rutland but who disappeared without explanation. Since sister Elizabeth lived to old age, one could assume that Jane had died by this date.

5. Samuel Eliot Morison, *Maritime History of Massachusetts, 1783–1860* (Boston: Houghton Mifflin Co., 1941), p. 164, contains some statistics on shipping losses during this embargo period. Frank C. Bowen, *A Century of Atlantic Travel, 1830–1930* (Boston: Little, Brown & Company, 1930), p. 5, describes seizures: "In 1805, the Boston Importing Company started to operate ships between Boston, Liverpool, and London. The first sailing was by the *Sally* which was followed by the *Packet* and the *Romeo*. This service promised well . . . but it was one of the numerous American companies which suffered from the Napoleonic Wars, and when the *Sally* was seized by Napoleon in San Sebastian and the *Packet* at Hamburg, the Company had financial difficulties and had to close down." Morison, *Maritime History of Massachusetts*, p. 164, is the source for the loss of the customs records of Boston. The Middlebury Congregational Church *Catalogue of Members* for 1810 is in the manuscript collection of the Sheldon Museum, Middlebury, Vermont.

6. See, for example, William Deere's advertisement for his school in the Middlebury *National Standard*, 12 November 1821 and 25 March 1823. Benjamin Nixon's advertisement in the same publication is dated 14 March 1820.

7. Enrollment records of Middlebury College are extant from 1820; no Deere appears during this period. More credence can be given the story that John Deere, to help his mother, either quit school or used his free time to work in a tannery; an advertisement appearing in the *National Standard* in 1816 stated that Mrs. Deere had "removed to Ep. Miller's yellow building at the head of Merchants Row." Epaphras Miller was the town's leading tanner. A sample contract for apprenticeship in a blacksmith shop is given in full in Huden, *State School Administration in Vermont*, pp. 28–29, in which the indentured boy is promised "Convenient Meat Drink Washing and Lodging and Physick . . . Two Good Suits of Apparel," as well as instruction to ensure that the apprentice could "Read well in the Bible and write a legable [*sic*] handwriting and Do the Four First Rules of Arithmetick [*sic*]." Information on John Deere's wages is from Webber, *Tribute to the Memory of John Deere*, p. 5. See also *Moline Dispatch*, 12 April 1937, and Yngve P. Magnuson, "John Deere: A Study of an Industrialist on the Illinois Frontier, 1837–1857" (Ph.D. diss., State Teachers College, St. Cloud, Minn., 1956), p. 8. Brown, *Early Life of John Deere*, describes most fully Deere's life as an apprentice and journeyman in Middlebury and Winooski; in the Addenda, p. 26, is his account of Deere's interest in Melissa Lawrence. Numerous photographs and maps place Lawrence's blacksmith shop and old maps show the location of the Allen and Wells shops, while photographs show their homes. The number of blacksmiths is from Zadock Thompson, ed., *A Gazetteer of the State of Vermont: Containing a Brief General View of the State, a Historical and Topographical Description of the Counties, Town, Rivers, &c.* (Montpelier, Vt.: E.P. Walton and the author, 1824), p. 181.

8. Material on Emma Willard is found in many histories of education; Lee, *Stagecoach North*, pp. 136–142 gives an excellent description of her schools in Middlebury and in Waterford and Troy, New York. See also *Harper's Weekly*, 7 May 1870; Margaret Dare ms., DA, 2250. There are no extant enrollment records of her school while in Middlebury; Mrs. Charles H. Dauchy, director of alumnae affairs of the school, stated in a letter dated 29 March 1973: "We can find no listing in the book 'Madam Emma Willard and Her Pupils 1822–1872' for Demarius Lamb, nor in 'Troy Female Seminary Catalogues' . . . or in the earliest Catalogue we have, which is one for 1820 when the School was in Waterford. It may very well be that she attended the School when it was in Middlebury." Irwin, *William and Sarah (Yates) Deere*, is the source for information about Elizabeth and George Deere. Colonel Buel's Winooski mills are described in Henry Perry Smith, ed., *History of Addison County Vermont* (Syracuse, N.Y.: D. Mason and Co., 1886) and in *Records of the Town of Winooski, Land Transfers*. See Thompson, *Gazetteer of the State of Vermont*, p. 168, for the fate of the mills and pp. 181, 241, for figures on the number of blacksmiths. Brown, *Early Life of John Deere*, and Webber, *Tribute to the Memory of John Deere*, have been relied on for the Vergennes story. See *Vermont Aurora* (Vergennes), 4 January 1826, for an advertisement placed by McVene, stating he is prepared to shoe horses and manufacture axes and edge tools "from the best Cast Steel and English Blister." A photograph of his home, the Dudley Gordon House described in H.P. Smith, *History of Addison County Vermont*, p. 684, is included in Brown, *Early Life of John Deere*, p. 11. The quotation about Deere working in a shovel factory is from Max P. Petersen, *Salisbury: From Birth to Bicentennial* (South Burlington: privately printed, 1976), p. 116. Harold F. Wilson, *The Hill Country of Northern New England: Its Social and Economy History, 1790–1930* (New York: Columbia University Press, 1936), p. 57, gives an account of the economic difficulties facing the small artisan at that time. The later life of George Deere is discussed in G.H. Deere, *Autobiography by Rev. George H. Deere, D.D.* (Riverside, Calif.: Press Printing Company, 1980).

9. *Town Records*, Leicester, Vt., contain the deeds of these transactions; photocopies are included in Brown, *Early Life of John Deere*. Walter Derby, a descendant of Apollus Derby, of Leicester, stated that a diary kept by Apollus recounted that his son, Lemuel Derby, distributed implements for John Deere as far as Hoosick, New York, and that Deere hoes, rakes, and shovels were stored in the Derby shed; Margaret Dare ms., DA, 2252. Hope Nash, *Royalton Vermont* (Royalton: South Royalton Woman's Club, Royalton Historical Society, 1975), p. 324, states that: "Amos Bosworth acknowledged receipt of $1.99, Apr. 28, 1836, for freighting the old bell to Boston and bringing back the new one," thus establishing his stage-freighting business and presence in Royalton as late as the spring of 1836, when Deere was considering going west; the quotations about migration and use of metal shares are on p. 26; and Bosworth properties are enumerated on pp. 177–178, 251. Webber, *Tribute to the Memory of John Deere*, suggests that the Bosworth house in Bethel was loaned to Deere. The Deere-Brooks deeds are extant in the *Town Records*, Hancock, Vt., and photocopies are to be found in Brown, *Early Life of John Deere*, together with old maps and photographs that purportedly show the sites of Deere's shops and home at the intersection of the Middlebury and Granville roads. Other sources place the shop across the West Branch River; see, for example, *The Story of Hancock, Vermont, 1780–1964, with Supplement to 1969* (Hancock, Vt.: 1969), p. 26. The quotation about the log chain is from R.J. Flint, "Life As Lived In Olden Time," *Courier* (Bethel, Vt.), 12 April 1928. Webber, *Tribute to the Memory of John Deere*, is the source for the quotations regarding Deere's lack of business acumen and his meticulous craftsmanship.

10. See Luther Goodhue to Enoch Day Woodbridge, 20 July 1833, ms. collection, Sheldon Museum, Middlebury. The newspaper quotation is from *People's Press and Antimasonic Democrat*, 16 May 1837. Excellent material on the sheep-raising frenzy can be found in Percy Wells Bidwell and John I. Falconer, *History of Agriculture in the Northern United States: 1620–1860* (Washington: Carnegie Institution of Washington, Publication 358, 1925), pp. 221–223, 409. See also C. Benton and Samuel F. Barry, eds., *A Statistical View of the Number of Sheep in the Several Towns and Counties in Maine, New Hampshire, Vermont, Massachusetts, Rhode Island, Connecticut, New York, Pennsylvania and Ohio . . . In 1836 and an Account of the Principal Woolen Manufactories in Said States* (Cambridge, Mass.: Folsom, Wells and Thurston, 1837). The governor's remarks were printed in *Vermont Watchman* (Montpelier), 21 October 1842; the warning against selling is in *Vermont Chronicle* (Windsor), 17 October 1834. Lewis D. Stilwell, *Migration from Vermont (1776–1860)* (Montpelier: Vermont Historical Society, 1937), pp. 171–173, remains the classic study of the damage to the Vermont economy by the sheep-raising monoculture. Population figures are from *The Story of Hancock, Vermont*, p. 85. Between 1790 and 1800 Vermont's population grew by 81 percent, but for the next two decades the growth rate dropped first to 41 and then to 8 percent; "After 1810, New England stopped sending settlers into Vermont," stated Huden, *State School Administration in Vermont*, pp. 27–28. The letters on emigration are: Lucy Hurlburt to Charity Bryant, 18 November 1832, and William E. Hale to Joshua P. Champlain, 16 May 1838, both from the ms. collection of the Sheldon Museum.

11. An excellent annotated bibliography of travelers' views of Illinois over the years is contained in Solon Justus Buck, *Travel and Description 1765–1865*, Collections of the Illinois State Historical Library, 9 Bibliographic Series 2 (Springfield, Ill.: Illinois State Historical Library, 1914). Buck's analysis has the advantage of being organized chronologically, allowing ready treatment of separate time periods. For a bibliography of travel and guidebooks for the United States as a whole, see Clarence H. Danhof, *Change in Agriculture: The Northern United States, 1820–1870* (Cambridge, Mass.: Harvard University Press, 1969), pp. 301–304. Illinois farming literature is discussed in Richard Bardolph, *Agricultural Literature and the Early Illinois Farmer* (Urbana, Ill.: University of Illinois Press, 1948). See also *Illinois in 1837 & 8: A Sketch Descriptive of the Situation, Boundaries, Face of the Country, Prominent Districts, Prairies, Rivers, Minerals, Animals, Agricultural Production, Public Lands, Plans of Internal Improvement, Manufactures, & c., of the State of Illinois* (Philadelphia: S. Augustus Mitchell, 1838), p. 20. The quotation regarding "Uncle Sam" comes from D. Stebbens to John Ruddock, 24 June 1838, ms. collection of the author. Evidence of widespread "biliousness" in the Midwest is described in H. Loomis to William Kimball, 6 December 1830, Graff ms. collection, Newberry Library, Chicago, Ill. The anti-emigration sources are John Hayward, *A Gazetteer of New Hampshire* (Boston: J.P. Jewett, 1849), p. 22, and *Vermont Chronicle* (Windsor), 25 February 1836. Well-known travellers contributed their impressions: Charles Dickens in "The Looking-Glass Prairie, Belleville, and Lebanon," in Paul M. Angle, ed., *Prairie State: Impressions of*

Illinois, 1673–1967, by Travelers and Other Observers (Chicago: University of Chicago Press, 1968), p. 210; William Cullen Bryant, *Prose Writings of William Cullen Bryant*, Parke Godwin, ed., vol. 2 (New York: D. Appleton and Co., 1844), p. 16; and Harriet Martineau, *Society in America* (New York: Saunders and Otley, 1837), p. 265. English journals attacked the drain of Englishmen to the new lands, among them the *London Quarterly Review* 27 (1822):91, quoted in the Illinois State Historical Society, *Transactions* 16 (1911):54. The "Nile of America" quotation is from Cornelius Swartout to Robert Swartout, 1 and 9 September 1837; the "milk and honey" quotation is from Cotton Morton to Stephen Longley, 25 October 1842, all in ms. collection, Chicago Historical Society. The comparison with Maine farming is in a letter of an unidentified Princeton, Illinois, settler, 15 October 1853, and the "Grove of Paradise" allusion is in John Garner to Samuel P. Dodds, 22 November 1836, both from ms. collection, Illinois State Historical Library. Monroe's comments of 19 January 1786 are contained in Stanislus Murray Hamilton, ed., *The Writings of James Monroe*, vol. 1 (New York: G.P. Putnam's Sons, 1898), pp. 117–118. John Dean Caton, in a speech read before the Ottawa Academy of Natural Sciences, 30 December 1869, and printed in *Origin of the Prairies* (Chicago: Fergus Printing Company, 1876), p. 52, defends the fire hypothesis of origin. A more complete explanation is found in Robert P. Howard, *Illinois: A History of the Prairie State* (Grand Rapids, Mich.: William B. Eerdmans Publishing Company, 1972), pp. 3–5. The quotation about fires is from Maurice Bostwick to an unnamed uncle, 12 March 1854, ms. collection, Chicago Historical Society. Robert Baird, *View of the Valley of the Mississippi or, The Emigrants and Traveler's Guide to the West* (Philadelphia: H.S. Tanner, 1832), p. 204, makes a direct link between fire and forest: "Whenever the fire is kept out of the prairies, they soon become covered with a dense and rapidly growing forest." For additional discussion of the prairie, see Peter Farb, *Face of North America: The Natural History of a Continent* (New York: Harper & Row, 1963), pp. 206–210; Edith Muriel Poggi, *The Prairie Province of Illinois: A Study of Human Adjustment to the Natural Environment*, Illinois Studies in Social Sciences (Urbana: University of Illinois Press, 1934), pp. 48, 67–70; John Ernest Weaver, *North American Prairie* (Lincoln, Neb.: Johnson Publishing Company, 1954).

12. The reference to properties deteriorating is from Silas McKeen, *The Claims of Vermont: A Sermon Delivered Before the Congregational Convention of Vermont, Bennington, 15 June 1857* (Windsor: The Vermont Chronicle Office, 1857), p. 3. The "simon-pure Vermont settlements" are described in Stilwell, *Migration from Vermont*, pp. 190–191. A detailed description of one of these colonies, at Galesburg, Ill., is contained in Earnest Elmo Calkins, *They Broke the Prairie* (New York: Charles Scribner's Sons, 1937), pp. 45–60. Another is described in E. W. Barber, "The Vermontville Colony," in *Michigan Pioneer Society Collection*, xxviii, 2, pp. 197–265. See also Lois (Kimball) Mathews Rosenberry, *The Expansion of New England: The Spread of New England Settlement and Institutions to the Mississippi River, 1620–1865* (Boston: Houghton Mifflin Company, 1909), pp. 214, 229–230. The "boy settler" quotation can be found in Allan G. Bogue, *From Prairie to Corn Belt: Farming on the Illinois and Iowa Prairies in the Nineteenth Century* (Chicago: University of Chicago Press, 1963), p. 23, and Stilwell's comments on the dominant Yankee qualities are from his *Migrations from Vermont*, p. 193. Thomas Ford, *A History of Illinois, from its Commencement as a State in 1818 to 1847* (Chicago: S.C. Griggs & Co., 1854), pp. 280–281, describes the southern view of the Yankee.

13. The quotation about the lake steamers is from *Chicago Weekly American*, 6 September 1841. William Vipond Pooley, "The Settlement of Illinois from 1830 to 1850," *Bulletin of the University of Wisconsin*, History Series 1 (May 1908): 360–361, gives detailed accounts of costs for migrants. The quotation regarding fares is from Daniel Goodnough to John M. Goodnough, 14 August 1838, ms. collection, Illinois State Historical Library; the quotation for shipment of stock is from *Niles' Register* 58 (1840): 288, the comment about "numbers of men" buying land is from S.B. Percy to E.B. Pendleton, 6 June 1852, Illinois State Historical Library. Inflation is discussed in Sarah Aiken to Julia Keese, 21 September 1835, Illinois State Historical Library. The opportunity for benefiting from land speculation is

lauded by an anonymous minister to the Rev. William Irving, 19 January 1836, ms. collection, Chicago Historical Society. See Daniel Fletcher Webster to Daniel Webster, 3 March 1838, Daniel Webster Papers, Dartmouth College, Hanover, N.H. An excellent book on the emigration from the East to the Midwest is Malcolm J. Rohrbough, *The Trans-Appalachian Frontier: People, Societies, and Institutions, 1775–1850* (New York: Oxford University Press, 1978). This is complemented by another well-documented study of trans-Mississippi emigration, John D. Unruh, Jr., *The Plains Across: The Overland Emigrants and the Trans-Mississippi West, 1840–1860* (Urbana: University of Illinois Press, 1979). A classic study is Frederick Merk, *History of the Westward Movement* (New York: Alfred A. Knopf, 1978). Historians, led by Frederick Jackson Turner, have long debated some of the psychological dimensions of the Westward migration. Turner first advanced his "frontier thesis" at a paper read at the meeting of the American Historical Association in Chicago on 12 July 1893 and reprinted in *Proceedings of the State Historical Society of Wisconsin*, 14 December 1893, and in F.J. Turner, *The Frontier in American History* (New York: Henry Holt & Company, 1920). Four excellent critiques of the thesis are: Richard Hofstadter, *The Progressive Historians: Turner, Beard, Parrington* (New York: Alfred A. Knopf, 1968); Ray Allen Billington, *The Genesis of the Frontier Thesis: A Study in Historical Creativity* (San Marino, Calif.: The Huntington Library, 1971); Lee Benson, *Turner and Beard: American Historical Writing Reconsidered* (Glencoe, Ill.: The Free Press, 1960); Allan G. Bogue, "Social Theory and the Pioneer," in *Agricultural History* 34 (1960): 21–34. *Agricultural History* 32 (1958): 227–261, was devoted to the Turner thesis in 1958, with articles by Gene M. Gressley, Normal J. Simler, and Gilman M. Ostrander. See also George Wilson Pierson, "The Frontier and American Institutions: A Criticism of the Turner Theory," *New England Quarterly* 15 (1942): 224–255; Merle Curti, *Human Nature in American Historical Thought* (Columbia: University of Missouri Press, 1968); James D. Bennett, *Frederick Jackson Turner* (Boston: Twayne Publishers, 1975). For the quotation on "the Prairie man," see Pooley, "The Settlement of Illinois," p. 567.

14. The prospects for mechanics are described by Richard H. Beach, "A Letter from Illinois Written in 1836," *Illinois State Historical Journal* 3 (1910): 96. Royal B. Way, ed., *The Rock River Valley* (Chicago: S.J. Clarke Publishing Co., 1926), pp. 620–621, elaborates the biography of Leonard Andrus; this material is corroborated in Lucius B. Andrus, "A Few Facts About the Andrus Family," (privately printed brochure, 21 October 1936), DA. For a description of the Grand Detour area and the earlier village of Dixon's Ferry, see Charles F. Hoffman, *A Winter in the West* (New York: Harper & Brothers, 1835); the author notes (p. 299) that John Dixon had been "repeatedly driven off by the Indians," but had managed to maintain the settlement over a fifteen-year period. Firsthand information about Andrus' early activities in Grand Detour comes from David Andrews to Leonard Andrus, 17 December 1834 and 26 January 1835, ms. collection, Illinois State Historical Library. The consolidation of claims by Andrus and Willard House is documented in Sarah Hicks, "A Solid Century of Plowmaking" (ca. 1936), DA, which states: "All the claims made by L. Andrus at Grand de Tour on Rock River, the claim made by W.A. House on Pine Creek & his timber-claims, also all the claims of R. Green, Jr. being the southeast qr. of section 2 township 22 r. g." The description of early homes in the area is from the undated remembrances of Miss Florence Bosworth, ca. 1935, DA. Information about the hydraulic company is from Ogle County American Revolution Bicentennial Commission, *Bicentennial History of Ogle County, 1976* (Oregon, Ill.: Ogle County Board, 1976), p. 273. The usual source for information about John Deere's trip to the West is Neil M. Clark, *John Deere: He Gave to the World the Steel Plow* (Moline, Ill.: privately printed, ca. 1937), p. 25.

NOTES TO CHAPTER 2: JOHN DEERE'S STEEL PLOW

1. The account of Deere's financial status is found in J.T. Hamilton, *My recollection of John Deere, inventor of the first steel plow of which we have any record* (privately printed,

November 1916), DA. For an analysis of Deere landholdings in Grand Detour during the period 1842–52, see John Munger, Deere & Company Legal Department file (1957), DA, 1090. For a detailed account of the excavation of the first Deere plow factory and its findings, see Richard Hagen, "John Deere's Buried Plow Factory: An Illustrated Lecture" (ca. 1976), DA, which is also the source for the description of the Deere home that was restored by the John Deere Foundation in 1966–76. The "Oregoner" story is from *Portrait and Biographical Album, Ogle County, Illinois* (Chicago: Chapman Brothers, 1886), p. 864; additional material about Grand Detour's early days may be found in Henry R. Boss, *Sketches of the History of Ogle County, Illinois, and the Early Settlement of the Northwest, Written for the Polo Advertiser* (Polo, Ill.: Henry R. Boss, 1859), pp. 69–70.

2. The question of relative soil fertility between the prairies and the woodlands is discussed in detail in Poggi, *Prairie Province of Illinois*, pp. 54–69. See also Bardolph, *Agricultural Literature*, pp. 112–113. The concept of "strong" soil is noted in Bidwell and Falconer, *History of Agriculture*, pp. 158–159. The quotation on "breaking the turf" is from Cornelius J. Swartwout to Robert Swartwout, 12 July 1837, ms. collection, Chicago Historical Society. The quotation on "arts and sciences" is from R.R. Frisbee, "Ogle County," *Prairie Farmer* 8 (November 1848): 354. The state-of-the-art of chemical analysis of soils is evident in "Chemical Analyses," *Prairie Farmer* 4 (September 1844): 214–215. For a good review of the English experience in preparing the seedbed, see George Edwin Fussell, *The Farmer's Tools A.D. 1500–1900: A History of British Farm Implements, Tools and Machinery Before the Tractor Came* (London: Andrew Melrose, 1952), chap. 2. See also related materials on English plows in note 3, below. The Daniel Webster plow is discussed in "Report on Trials of Plows," *Transactions of the New York State Agricultural Society*, 1:27 (1867): 483–488, often reported in the literature as "Utica Trials." For a discussion of early agricultural literature see Bardolph, *Agricultural Literature*, pp. 121–124. The need for a special set of Midwestern literature was particularly remarked upon in this period; as one farmer wrote in the *Prairie Farmer*: "I looked in vain for the results of well tested and enlightened experiments; and I . . . felt the want of just such a journal as I hope your paper will prove," *Union Agriculturalist and Western Prairie Farmer*, 1 (May 1841): 34–35. The "cutting off . . . at the neck" quote is from *New Genesee Farmer* (August 1846), p. 182, and the "fire fanged" quote is from "Breaking Prairie, Corn, Wheat, & C.," *Prairie Farmer* 3 (April 1843): 90.

3. See Solon Robinson, *Pioneer and Agriculturalist, Selected Writings I*, Herbert Anthony Kellar, ed. (Indianapolis: Indiana Historical Bureau, 1936), p. 287. For costs, see, for example, Bogue, *From Prairie to Corn Belt*, p. 71. At least some settlers were able to shave their costs; one Greene County, Illinois, farmer had 140 acres broken in 1848 at a cost of one dollar per acre (*W.H. Tunnell Journal*, 1847–1852, Illinois State Historical Library). The reference to use of horses is from *Prairie Farmer* 7 (August 1847): 245, while the use of oxen and a heavy plow is reported in *Country Gentleman* 10 (23 July 1857): 57–58. See also "Plowing on the Prairies," *Moore's Rural New Yorker*, 6 (10 November 1855): 358; J. Milton May, "Breaking Prairie," Wisconsin State Agricultural Society, *Transactions* 1 (1851): 243–246; Samuel P. Boardman, "Prairie Breaking," Missouri State Board of Agriculture, *Report* 4 (1868): 39–44. The "work my land" quotation is in a letter to the *Indiana Farmer and Gardener*, 5 April 1845; see also Robinson, *Pioneer and Agriculturalist*, p. 147. The sprouting of "ten-penny nails" is the expression of "T. Hardup," a fictional character used by the *Prairie Farmer* editors in the 1840s; alleged "letters to the editor" from him were published in many issues, and were then responded to by real farmers, often pungently. See, for example, *Prairie Farmer* 4 (January 1844): 24–25. The seminal early writers on the English plow are: Sir Anthony Fitzherbert, *The Boke of Husbandry* (1534; reprinted in Robert Vansittart, ed., *Certain Ancient Tracts Concerning the Management of Landed Property*, C. Bathurst, London, 1767, and in Walter W. Sheat, ed., London: Trubner Co., 1882); Gervase Markham, *Cheape and Good Husbandry* . . . (London: T.S. Nodham for R. Jackson, 1614); and Walter Blith, *The English Improver Improved; or, The Survey of Husbandry Surveyed, Discovering the Improveableness of all Lands* (London: John Wright, 1642). Two of the earlier books have superb plates picturing English plows: Jethro Tull, *The New Horse-Hoeing Husbandry* (Dublin: A. Rhames, 1733) and Thomas Hale, *A Compleat Body of Husbandry* (London: T. Osborne and J.W. Shipton, 1756). Two excellent recent books summarize the English plow and plowing: John B. Passmore, *The English Plough* (London: Oxford University Press, Humphrey Milford, 1930) and Fussell, *Farmer's Tools.* There are four key sources for eighteenth- and nineteenth-century American plows: Robert L. Ardrey, *American Agricultural Implements: A Review of Invention and Development in the Agricultural Implement Industry of the United States* (1894, reprint ed., Arno Press, Inc., 1972); Leo Rogin, *The Introduction of Farm Machinery in its Relation to the Productivity of Labor in the Agriculture of the United States During the Nineteenth Century* (1931, reprint ed., Johnson Reprint Corporation, 1966); Danhof, *Change in Agriculture*; "Report on Trials of Plows," pp. 385–656. Other useful nineteenth-century sources are Cuthbert W. Johnson, *The Farmer's Encyclopedia, and Dictionary of Rural Affairs* (Philadelphia: Carey and Hart, 1844); Henry Stephens, *The Farmer's Guide to Scientific and Practical Agriculture,* two vol. (New York: Leonard Scott & Co., 1851); John J. Thomas, *Farm Implements, and the Principles of Their Construction and Use: An Elementary and Familiar Treatise on Mechanics, and on Natural Philosophy Generally, as Applied to the Ordinary Practices of Agriculture* (New York: Harper & Brothers, 1854), with later editions titled *Farm Implements and Farm Machinery in 1869 and 1886* (Orange Judd and Co.). See also Lillian Church, "History of the Plow," United States Department of Agriculture, Information Series No. 48 (October 1935); Robert H. Gault, *Historical Development of Agricultural Implements* (Chicago: Farm Equipment Institute, 1947). For a classic polemic on who invented the plow, see Frank Gilbert, *Jethro Wood, Inventor of the Modern Plow* (Chicago: Rhodes & McClure, 1882). An excellent summary of plow patents during the late eighteenth and nineteenth centuries is James T. Allen, *Allen's Digest of Plows, with Attachments, Patented in the United States from a.d. 1789 to January 1883* (Washington, D.C.: J. Bart, 1883).

4. An analysis of the early Deere plow was made in Edward C. Kendall, "John Deere's Steel Plow," Contributions from the Museum of History and Technology, United States National Museum, Bulletin 218 (Washington, D.C.: Smithsonian Institution, 1959), pp. 19–20. The traditional version of the origin of Deere's first "scouring" plow comes from the memory of L. Frank Kerns, a close friend of John Deere who must have heard the story from him at least twenty years earlier. The dialogue, as recounted to the editors of the *Moline Dispatch,* 13 January 1902, therefore seems to be Kerns's own memory of how it went, not the actual verbatim words of John Deere (DA, 1128). There are two versions of the Crandall farm trial: Kerns's and one printed in the *Moline Dispatch,* 18 December 1926, quoting an article by Fred Pasley, *Chicago Herald and Examiner,* same date. For the discovery of the John Deere plow of 1838, see *Moline Dispatch,* 11 January 1902. Early commission houses in the marketing of iron and steel, including Naylor & Co., Deere's supplier, are discussed in Glen Porter and Harold C. Livesey, *Merchants and Manufacturers: Studies in the Changing Structure of Nineteenth-Century Marketing* (Baltimore: Johns Hopkins Press, 1971). The construction of the Deere moldboard is discussed in Kendall, "John Deere's Steel Plow," p. 20. For the advertisement for steel, see the *Northwestern Gazette and Galena Advertiser* (Galena, Ill.), 17 July 1841. For the Lyon, Shorb & Company bill dated 24 July 1844, see DA, 1093. The analysis of metal leavings is found in R.J. Christ and A.H. Rauch, "Manufacture of Early John Deere Plows," Report No. 4318, 19 September 1962, and R.J. Christ and O.J. Waters, "Metallic Artifacts from John Deere's Grand Detour Homestead," Report No. 4384, 22 July 1963, Materials Engineering Department, Deere & Company. The quotations on rolling of steel are from James M. Swank, *History of the Manufacture of Iron in All Ages, and Particularly in the United States for Three Hundred Years, from 1585 to 1885* (Philadelphia: James N. Swank, 1884), p. 297. See also the interesting discussion in Louis E. Gruner, *The Manufacture of Steel,* trans. by Lenox Smith (New York: D. Van Nostrand, 1872), pp. 29–36. In *History of Iron and Steel Making in the United States* (New York: The Metallurgical Society, American Institute of Mining, Metallurgical, and Petroleum Engineers, 1961), pp. 9–15, there is an excellent discussion of the Pittsburgh manufacturers in the period up to 1850. Also see Douglas Alan Fisher, *The Epic of Steel* (New York: Harper & Row, 1963), chap. 10. The "polishing" story is from *History of Mercer and Henderson Counties* (Chicago: H.H. Hill & Co., 1882), pp. 769–770. See also Alfred W. Newcombe, "Alson J. Streeter—An Agrarian Liberal," *Illinois State Historical Society Journal* 38 (1945): 418–419.

5. For the "poisoned the land" quotation, see *Transactions of the New York State Agricultural Society*, 1:27 (1867): 448. The quotation about Lane's plow is found in Emma Lane Baird to H.F. Linde, 16 March 1937, DA. Lane's first plow is described in detail in *Farm Implement News*, 17 June 1937. This article notes several references giving Lane credit for this invention, including Holland Thompson, *The Age of Invention: A Chronicle of Mechanical Conquest* (New Haven: Yale University Press, 1921), p. 113; and Waldemar (Bernhard) Kaempffert, *A Popular History of American Invention* (New York: Charles Scribner's Sons, 1924), vol. 2, p. 251. Lane's son, John Lane, Jr., was also a plow manufacturer, later taking out several important patents under the names Lane's Cast Steel Plows, Lockport Clippers, and Sod Breakers. The Lane second prize was described in *Prairie Farmer* 3 (1843): 246–247 and the quotation about the first steel plow is from J.T. Gifford, "History of the Western Plow," *Prairie Farmer* 6 (1846): 42. Production figures for plows, compiled from the original returns of the eighth census of the United States, can be found in *Agriculture of the United States in 1860* (Washington: Government Printing Office, 1864), pp. xix–xx. The first Lyman quotation is from *Sangamo Journal* (Springfield, Ill.), 25 June 1836; the second quotation is from *Peoria Register and North-western Gazeteer* (Peoria, Ill.), 8 April 1837. Burke's comments derive from *Annual Report of the Commissioner of Patents*, House Doc. 52, 29th Congress, 2nd Session (23 January 1847), p. 5, and House Doc. 59, 30th Congress, 2nd Session (28 February 1849). For the purchase of the firm of H.E. Bridge by Benjamin F. Jewett and David M. Hitchcock, consummated on 1 April 1841, and an advertisement, see *Sangamo Journal*, 2 April 1841. The advertisement for the "Jewett's Improved Cary Plow" appeared for almost two years from February 1842 in the *Sangamo Journal* and the *Illinois State Register* (Springfield, Ill.). The Cary Plow antecedents are discussed in Rogin, *Introduction of Farm Machinery*, pp. 8–9. For the John Deere advertisements, see *Rock River Register* (Grand Detour, Ill.), 7 April 1843. The story of May and his plow is from Charles C. Chapman, *History of Knox County, Illinois* (Chicago: Blakely, Brown & Marsh, 1878), pp. 518–519, 692–693. The patent case testimony is from *Henry W. Candee, et al, Appellants* v. *John Deere, et al, Appellees*, Supreme Court of Illinois, Northern Land Division, September 1870, on appeal from Rock Island County, in Chancery (the latter case heard in Rock Island County Circuit Court, May 1867). Harvey H. May did, however, obtain a patent on another type of "prairie" plow on 2 May 1843, and a summary is contained in *Report of the Commissioner of Patents for 1843*, 28th Congress, 1st Session (16 February 1844), doc. no. 451. For the quotation at the cattle show of 1844, see J.A. Wight, "An Address Delivered Before the Union Agricultural Society at its annual cattle show, Plainfield, Illinois, October 17, 1844," *Prairie Farmer* 4 (December 1844): 275–279; for the quotation from the Illinois Supreme Court, see Norman L. Freeman, *Reports of Cases at Law and in Chancery Argued and Determined in the Supreme Court of Illinois*, 54 (Springfield: State of Illinois, 1872), pp. 455–456.

6. Economic conditions in Illinois in the period are described in Walter Buckingham Smith and Arthur Harrison Cole, *Fluctuations in American Business, 1790–1860* (Cambridge: Harvard University Press, 1935), p. 158; Calkins, *They Broke the Prairie*, p. 106. The accounts of business and life in general in Grand Detour are in H.R. Boss, *Sketches of the History of Ogle County*, p. 69; Ogle County Bicentennial Commission, *Bicentennial History of Ogle County*, p. 275; Florence Bosworth ms., DA. The "musick and dancing" quotation is from Charles H. Burton to George N. Burwell, 22 October 1847, ms. collection, Chicago Historical Society. The Fuller quotations are from Sarah Margaret Fuller (Countess Ossoli), *Summer on the Lakes, in 1843* (Boston: Charles C. Little and James Brown, 1844), pp. 35–51, while the diary excerpts are from an anonymous manuscript diary, "Tour West,"

26 September–23 November 1839, ms. collection, Chicago Historical Society. The term "Regulators" is explained in Judge Hall, *Letters from the West* (London: Henry Colburn, 1828), pp. 291–292; Pooley, *The Settlement of Illinois*, pp. 431–432, discusses the Driscoll case, calling the gang "Prairie Pirates." The comments by the Illinois governor are in Ford, *History of Illinois*, pp. 246, 439–440.

7. For the advertisement for the Marshall's sale, see *Rock River Register*, 11 November 1842. The remaining extant information from United States District Court, Office of the Clerk, Chicago, Illinois, concerning the case is contained in Roy H. Johnson, clerk of the court, to John L. Munger of Deere & Company, 4 February 1957, DA, 1090. For Deere's Leicester debt, see Ogle County Circuit Court, September 1843, case no. 918; Justice of the Peace cases from Dockets B and E of Salmon C. Cotton, Grand Detour, 10 April 1841 and 1 November 1846, DA, 19301.

8. The articles of agreement discussed in the text are, respectively, Leonard Andrus and John Deere, 20 March 1843; Leonard Andrus, John Deere, and Horace Paine, 26 October 1844; Leonard Andrus and John Deere, 22 June 1847. Originals in ms. collection, Illinois State Historical Library. Andrus had applied for renewal of his mail route in early 1842; there is an interesting exchange of correspondence between Andrus and Thomas Ford, at that time a justice of the Supreme Court of the state of Illinois and later that year governor-elect of Illinois. Ford wrote friends in Washington petitioning for Andrus to be given the mail route (Thomas Ford to Messrs. John Reynolds, Zadak Casey, R.M. Younger, and I.I. Stuart, 1 April 1842, DA). The Dixon Land Office records are in the Illinois State Archives, covering the period 1836–46; the sales of the four plots of land to, respectively, Major Chamberlin, 10 February 1842; Samuel Wilson, 31 January 1842; Levi Stickney, 13 August 1842; and Peter Newcomer, 21 May 1842 are recorded in the Ogle County courthouse, Oregon, Illinois. For the Case-Deere controversy concerning their respective centennial celebrations, see Frank Everett Stevens correspondence, 1936–37, Illinois State Historical Library. The J.I. Case Company brought out a "centennial plow" in 1937; the company's claims about the 1837 founding date are elaborated in *Farm Implement News*, 10 September 1936. A Congressional bill (H.R. 295, 75th Congress, 1st Session, 25 March 1937) was introduced "to authorize a memorial plaque in the Department of Agriculture commemorating the invention of a steel plow by John Deere in 1837." The bill was not brought out of committee.

9. The Deere-Andrus production figures are noted in a number of places; see, for example, Ardrey, *American Agricultural Implements*, p. 166. (Apparently Ardrey quoted from the interview with John Deere recorded in *Farm Implement News*, March 1886.) For John Gould's quotation, see "Recollections of John Deere," *Moline Dispatch*, 9 January 1911. For Deere's deficiency as a record keeper, as well as his hard-driving attitude, see H.C. Peek, "Reminiscences of John Deere," undated ms., ca. 1911, DA. The quotation on the "real Yankee" is from Charles H. Joiner to Deere & Company, 26 November 1962, DA. (Joiner's grandfather came to Illinois from Vermont at about the same time as John Deere, settling on a farm in Grand Detour.) Tate, in his testimony in the Candee-Swan patent case, was less complimentary about John Deere's personal habits. The comments on Deere's "ordinary" birth are from "Interview with Helen Wood," 31 August 1936, DA, 1114, while the optimism about social rank in Illinois is in M.W. Ross to Francis Edmond, 15 April 1836, ms. collection, Chicago Historical Society.

10. For analysis of the railroad right-of-way decision, see Ogle County Bicentennial Commission, *Bicentennial History of Ogle County*, pp. 104–106, 509–510; further information is in Paul W. Gates, *The Illinois Central Railroad and its Colonization Work* (Cambridge: Harvard University Press, 1934); Carlton J. Corliss, *Main Line of Mid-America: The Story of the Illinois Central* (New York: Creative Age Press, 1950). The Robert N. Tate quotations concerning the dissolving of the Andrus partnership and the offer from Peru, Ill., are from his diary, with notes prepared by Florence M. Bradford (1939), titled "The Life of Robert N. Tate, Written by Himself," DA.

NOTES TO CHAPTER 3: THE MOVE TO MOLINE

1. Information on the Sears dam as well as on the economic development of the area (Davenport, Iowa, and Rock Island and Moline, Illinois) is in numerous books and articles: David B. Sears, "Pioneer in the Development of the Water Power of the Mississippi River," *Illinois State Historical Society Journal* 8 (1915): 300; *Rock Island and Its Surroundings in 1853* (Davenport: Saunders and Davis, 1854), pp. 19–21; *Past and Present of Rock Island County Illinois* (Chicago: H.F. Kett & Co., 1877); and *Rock Island County: Something of Its History and its Peoples from Early Days up to 1885, Selected from Portrait and Biographical Album of Rock Island County* (Chicago: Chapman Brothers, 1885). Copies of the *Rock Island Weekly Advertiser*, the *Davenport Democrat*, the *Rock Island Republican*, the *Davenport Gazette*, and the *Moline Workman* are extant for all or part of the two decades of the 1840s and 1850s.

2. The details of the first days of the new Moline firm come from Tate, "The Life of Robert N. Tate," pp. 75–77b. The details of the partnership with Gould and Gould's role as financial manager are described in John M. Gould, "Recollections of John Deere," DA, 19297. Tate, in his testimony in *Henry W. Candee . . . v. John Deere . . .*, further elaborated on the functional splitting of the work of the firm. For material on partnerships, see Henry Cary, *A Practical Treatise on the Law of Partnership, with Precedents of Copartnership Deeds* (Philadelphia: J.S. Littell, 1834), p. 12. Another study, with notes of American cases by Willard Phillips and Edward Pickering, is John Collyer, *A Practical Treatise on the Law of Partnership* (Springfield, Mass.: G. & C. Merriam, 1834). The literature on the antebellum manufacturing in the East is prolific; see documentation in Alfred D. Chandler, Jr., *The Visible Hand: The Managerial Revolution in American Business* (Cambridge, Mass.: Harvard University Press, 1977), chap. 2. Growth of mills, foundries, and manufacturing on the Midwestern frontier of the 1830s and '40s is less well recorded, see Porter and Livesay, *Merchants and Manufacturers*, chaps. 8 and 9; Thomas C. Cochran and William Miller, *The Age of Enterprise: A Social History of Industrial America* (New York: Macmillan Company, 1942), chap. 3; Rohrbough, *Trans-Appalachian Frontier.*

3. Details of the Andrus-Deere termination agreements are in Tate, "Life of Robert N. Tate," p. 75. The list of agents is in the notebook titled "John Deere's Book" (1851), DA. Further information about the territory, the quotation about plows sold on commission, and the irregularity of the bookkeeping system is from Gould, "Recollections of John Deere." For an interesting description of the general store in antebellum Illinois, see Charles B. Johnson, *Illinois in the Fifties; or A Decade of Development, 1851–1860* (Champaign, Ill.: Flanigan-Pearson Co., 1918), pp. 58–67. Thomas D. Clark, *Pills, Petticoats and Plows: The Southern Country Store* (New York: Bobbs-Merrill Company, 1944), discusses the process of selling plows in the general store. Lewis E. Atherton, *The Frontier Merchant in Mid-America* (Columbia, Mo.: University of Missouri Press, 1971), pp. 76–77, discusses the "drummers" and "borers." The few extant figures on Deere's production in the late 1840s and early 1850s are from Ardrey, *American Agricultural Implements*, p. 166; Danhof, *Change in Agriculture*, p. 197; *Moline Workman*, 21 May 1856; *Country Gentleman*, 10 August 1857; *Farm Implement News*, March 1886; P.C. Simmon, "History of Deere & Company, Including Personnel and Finances of Branch Houses" (Moline: ca. 1921). The census of 1850, Schedule 5, "Products of Industry" for Rock Island County states that Deere made 3,000 plows in the year ending 1 June 1850, with a total value of $74,000.

4. Tate, "Life of Robert Tate," pp. 76–77i and 79a–79b, gives the details of the first year of operation, including production figures, his version of the Atkinson partnership, and the personal references cited in the text. Biographies of Charles Atkinson and Christopher C. Webber are in *Rock Island County*, pp. 215–216 and 645–648. Cost figures are from Tate, "Life of Robert N. Tate," p. 79b, and the quotation about establishing agencies is from Gould, "Recollections of John Deere." For the dealers' refusal to take new plows, the C.C. Alvord quotation, and the Oliver Lester account of "traveling days," see *Henry W. Candee . . . v. John Deere . . . .* Copies of the dealer receipt forms are in DA, 27176. For a useful summary of machinery development and manufacturing practice in the first half of the nineteenth century, see Paul Uselding, "Measuring Techniques and Manufacturing Practice," in Otto Mayr and Robert C. Post, *Yankee Enterprise: The Rise of the American System of Manufactures* (Washington, D.C.: Smithsonian Institution Press, 1981). The classic study on machinery innovation is Abbot Payson Usher, *A History of Mechanical Inventions*, rev. ed. (Cambridge, Mass.: Harvard University Press, Inc., 1954). See also the four books by Robert S. Woodbury, *History of The Gear-Cutting Machine: A Historical Study in Geometry and Machines* (1958), *History of the Grinding Machine: A Historical Study in Tools and Precision Production* (1959), *History of the Milling Machine: A Study in Technical Development* (1960), *History of the Lathe to 1850: A Study in the Growth of a Technical Element of an Industrial Economy* (1961), all published in Cambridge, Mass., by MIT Press.

5. The Gould quotation on use of rivers is in Gould, "Recollections of John Deere." There was much agitation in the early 1850s in Illinois for the development of more plank roads; the *Springfield Daily Record* of 26 February 1851 stated, "There is no portion of the county where plank roads can be built at less expense." The James First quotation is from "Fair Wage of Olden Days 75 Cents; First Tells of Early Experiences," *Moline Dispatch*, 1 January 1914. James First recounted that he had come to Moline in April 1853, starting with John Deere at that point. The company's "Mechanics and Labourers' Handbook" for the years 1853–55 is extant and does not contain First's name. The record begins in August 1853, so if First had begun working with John Deere after the family arrived in April 1853, the work relationship was short-lived; First reports a dispute with John Deere about salary and that he left Deere to work with W.A. Nourse in a new pump and fanning mill, opened a few months before this time. The Deere, Tate and Gould advertisement on Missouri River trade appeared in *Prairie Farmer* (March 1851). The quotation on railroad timetables to Chicago, New York, and the West coast is from *Rock Island Advertiser*, 31 March 1852. The *Effie Afton* story is in Walter Havighurst, *Voices on the River: The Story of the Mississippi Waterways* (New York: Macmillan Co., 1964), p. 121. The role of Abraham Lincoln in the case is discussed in James H. Lemly, "The Mississippi River: St. Louis' Friend or Foe?", *Business History Review* 39 (1965): 7. Transportation efforts in northern Illinois prior to the Civil War are discussed in Judson F. Lee, "Transportation, a Factor in the Development of Northern Illinois to 1860," *Illinois State Historical Society Journal* 10 (1917): 17.

6. Company production figures for 1849–51 and comments on social life are from Tate, "Life of Robert N. Tate," pp. 79a, 81–86. The quotation on "go-a-head men" is from *Prairie Farmer* (April 1851). The original credit ledgers of the Mercantile Agency and its successor, R.G. Dun & Co., ca. 1840–90, are in the R.G. Dun & Company Collection in Baker Library, Harvard Business School. For a history of credit agencies in this period, see James Madison, "The Evolution of Commercial Credit Reporting in Nineteenth Century America," *Business History Review* 48 (1974): 167. For the early history of the agency itself, see Bertram Wyatt-Brown, "God and Dun & Bradstreet, 1841–1851," *Business History Review* 40 (1966): 432. The company's anniversary book is also helpful: Roy A. Foulke, *The Sinews of American Commerce* (New York: Dun & Bradstreet, Inc., 1941). For John Gould's discussion of "wildcat" banking, see his "Recollections of John Deere." The importance of the firm Cook & Sargent to eastern Iowa and western Illinois banking in the 1840s and '50s is described in Erling A. Erickson, "Money and Banking in a 'Bankers' State: Iowa, 1846–1857," *Business History Review* 43 (1969): 171.

7. The extension of the telegraph to Rock Island is discussed in *Rock Island Advertiser*, 11 May 1853. See also the "Deere, Tate, & Gould Journal Blotter C—1850–1851," the account book for 21 November 1850–16 April 1851, DA.

8. For the quotation on "Seymour's grain drill," see *Prairie Farmer* (August 1851). J. Tull, *Horse-Hoeing Husbandry* (1731), discusses drilling. The quotation on "superficial methods" and the Cahoon advertisement are from Rogin, *Introduction of Farm Machinery*, pp. 196 and 201. The Thomas Galt seeder is discussed in Ardrey, *American Agricultural Implements*, p. 192.

9. The development of the Midwestern wholesale houses, such as Lyon, Shorb & Co., is discussed in Atherton, *Frontier Merchant in Mid-America*, chap. 30. Gould's account of the Lyon, Shorb crisis is from his "Recollections of John Deere." Charles Deere's quotation on his childhood is from "Mr. Deere's Own Story of his Early Days and the Beginnings of the Deere Industry," *Moline Review Dispatch*, 8 November 1907, DA, 19815.

10. The reasons for the dissolution of the partnership come largely from Tate, "Life of Robert N. Tate," pp. 92–97 and 100–123, and from Gould, "Recollections of John Deere." For the George Bromley obituary, see *Davenport Democrat*, 23 February 1870. (This newspaper had a number of different names in the nineteenth century, after its founding in 1864; all incorporated the word *Democrat*. Citations that follow uniformly use *Davenport Democrat*.) The Atkinson testimony is from *Henry W. Candee . . . v. John Deere . . .* , pp. 19, 180. The Deere advertisement, "successor to," appeared in *Rock Island Advertiser*, 31 March 1852, and in *Rock Island Republican*, 9 June 1852. The information about Tate's last days with the firm and his new enterprise are from Tate, "Life of Robert N. Tate," pp. 112–137.

11. For advertisements of Deere and Chapman Co., see *Moline Workman*, 1 and 29 November 1854, and *Daily Rock Island Republican*, 5 January 1855. The information about the public schools comes from "Common Schools in Illinois," *Prairie Farmer* (April 1851), and from "Mr. Deere's Own Story," *Moline Review Dispatch*, ca. October 1907, DA. Tate's quotation is from "Life of Robert N. Tate," p. 83. The account of Bell's Commercial College appeared in *Rock Island Weekly Advertiser*, 31 October 1855. The early Charles Deere activity is also in his "Own Story." The Friberg account is from his testimony in *Henry W. Candee . . . v. John Deere . . .* , pp. 276 ff. The hiring of Hemenway appears in "Life of Robert N. Tate," p. 123. For more information about early personnel, see George Vinton to C.C. Webber, 13 May 1908, DA.

12. For plows manufactured, production and work force figures, see as follows: *Rock Island Advertiser*, 25 May 1853; *Rock Island Republican*, 31 December 1853 (4,000) and 10 May 1854 (3,959 for 1853); and for the 8,000 figure, *Rock Islander*, 21 May 1856, and *Moline Workman*, 21 May 1856. For the higher figures for 1855–56, see *Prairie Farmer* (November 1855) (10,000); *Moline Workman*, 7 November 1855; *Country Gentleman*, 20 August 1857 (13,400); and Danhof, *Change in Agriculture*, p. 197. The U.S. census for Rock Island County, Ill., gives annual figures of 3,000 plows for 1850 and 11,000 plows in 1860. Employment figures are found in *Rock Island Republican*, 17 March 1852, "Mechanics and Laborers Time Book," DA, and the U.S. census for Rock Island County, 1850. *Rock Island Argus*, 15 March 1856, reported sixty-eight employees, and *Moline Workman*, 21 May 1856, listed sixty-five men. The information on wages and employment patterns is from "Mechanics and Laborers Time Book," 1852–55. *Rock Island Republican*, 31 December 1853, gave the figure for amount of sales per year as $45,000 to $50,000; *Moline Workman*, 21 May 1856, is the source for the $88,000 figure.

13. The price lists are from the "John Deere Memorandum Book," 1852–55, DA. The flyer included in text is part of the Broadsides Collection, Illinois State Historical Society, ca. 1857. The advertisement concerning "one-third draft" is from *Rock Island and Moline Directory and Advertiser* (Rock Island: Raymond's Book and Printing House, 1855), pp. 16–17. See also *The Cultivator* (September 1859), p. 280. For the "free from flaws" quotation, see *Rock Island Argus*, 27 March 1857. The Andrew Friberg testimony on the Smith controversy is in *Henry W. Candee . . . v. John Deere . . .* , p. 282 ff. The *American Farmer* quotation is from its July 1853 issue. For Deere's claim to "sole rights" for the Michigan plow, see *Rock Island Argus*, 27 March 1857. Quotation on changes in techniques of farming is in Danhof, *Change in Agriculture*, p. 250. For the Deere, Tate and Gould advertisement quoted in the text, see *Northwestern Advertiser*, 26 June 1849. Jethro Wood's interchangeable-part plow (1814) is described in Rogin, *Introduction of Farm Machinery*, pp. 22–24. For an excellent discussion of the development of interchangeability, see Eugene S. Ferguson, "History and Historiography," in Mayr and Post, *Yankee Enterprise*, pp. 1 ff. The extent of interchangeability in agricultural implements is discussed in *Report on the*

Manufactures of the United States at the Tenth Census, June 1, 1880 (Washington: Government Printing Office, 1883), pp. 84–85. For the Friberg testimony on the Ruggles, Nourse copying, see *Henry W. Candee . . . v. John Deere . . .* , pp. 276 ff; for John Gould's story concerning the date of founding, see Gould, "Recollections of John Deere." See also *American Farmer* (July 1853).

14. The results of the First Annual Fair for Rock Island County are noted in *Rock Island Advertiser*, 28 September 1853 and 19 October 1853. The quotation on the Illinois State Fair of 1855 is from *Transactions of the Illinois State Historical Society*, 2 (Springfield: Lampher and Walker, 1857). The "splendid Deere plow" is from *Prairie Farmer*, 25 November 1858. For Deere's victory in the Fairfield, Iowa, fair, see "Report of the Secretary of the Iowa State Agriculture Society," *Proceedings* (Fairfield: Town Centennial Office, 1856); the Muscatine fair is noted in "Report of Third Annual Exhibition of the Iowa State Agriculture Society," *Proceedings* (Muscatine: 1857). The reaction to the *Chicago Tribune* remarks is taken from *Rock Island Advertiser*, 17 October 1855.

15. The English cable system of steam plowing is described in John Haining and Colin Tyler, *Ploughing by Steam: A History of Steam Cultivation Over the Years* (Hemel Hempstead: Model & Allied Publications, Ltd., 1970), chaps. 3, 4; Ronald H. Clark, *The Development of the English Traction Engine* (Norwich, Eng.: Goose & Son Publishers, 1960), chaps. 2, 13; Anthony Beaumont, *Ransomes Steam Engines: An Illustrated History* (Newton Abbot: David & Charles, 1972), introduction. The Obed Hussey steam plow is noted in *American Farmer* (May 1856). The definitive discussion of the Fawkes plow is in Reynold M. Wik, *Steam Power on the American Farm* (Philadelphia: University of Pennsylvania Press, 1953), chap. 4; *Chicago Press* and *Wisconsin Farmer* quotations, ibid., p. 62. For the quotation of John Deere about building a steam engine, see *Prairie Farmer*, 1 April 1858. For the chronicle of the various Fawkes trials, see *Prairie Farmer*, 23 and 30 September 1858; ibid., 21 October 1858; ibid., 18 November 1858; and ibid., 29 September 1859. The Deere involvement in these trials is discussed in F. Hal Higgins to Herman Linde, 16 May 1939, and F. Hal Higgins to Howard Railsback, 11 September 1940, DA. The Abraham Lincoln quotation is from United States Bureau of Agricultural Economics, *Washington, Jefferson, Lincoln and Agriculture* (Washington: Government Printing Office, 1937), pp. 83–84. For the comment on the Vermont State Fair of 1856, see *Moline Workman*, 3 December 1856.

16. For Deere production figures in 1857 and 1858, see *Rock Island Argus*, 7 April 1857; *The Cultivator* (September 1858). The allusion to Napoleon is in *Rock Island Advertiser*, 19 November 1856. The various articles of agreement in the 1857–58 reorganizations are dated 1 July 1857, 5 October 1858, and 17 November 1858, DA. The John Gould quotation on the Naylor & Co. account is from Gould, "Recollections of John Deere." For the Tate quotation on Singer, Hartman, and a discussion of the faulty steel, see "Life of Robert N. Tate," pp. 160–161 and 164. The George Vinton quotation is from G. Vinton to Charles C. Webber, 13 May 1908, DA. The Gould comment about John Deere's involvements is from *Henry W. Candee . . . v. John Deere . . .* , pp. 50 ff. The Stephen H. Velie quotation is from S.H. Velie to Charles Velie, 7 February 1884, DA.

17. For the quotation about political mass meeting, see *Daily Islander and Argus*, 28 September 1858. The formation of the Moline Property Protective Society is noted in *Rock Island Advertiser*, 5 July 1854; its inactivity is commented on in *Moline Workman*, 30 June 1855. Robert Tate's comment on John Deere's robbery is from Tate, "Life of Robert N. Tate," p. 153; the newspaper quotation on it is from *Rock Island Argus*, 27 July 1857. The election figures for 1855 are from *Moline Workman*, 4 April 1855. See the *Daily Islander* for the incident of the runaway buggy, 15 October 1857, the railroad bridge fire, 25 March 1859, and "free love," 1 June 1858.

18. For dissolution of the Union Foundry, see *Rock Island Advertiser*, 17 November 1852. The Charles Deere private memorandum book is in DA.

NOTES TO CHAPTER 4: AFTER THE CIVIL WAR

1. *Davenport Democrat*, 11 January 1860 and 31 May 1860; *Rock Island Argus*, 16 November 1981.

2. *New Genesee Farmer*, August 1861, reported on European agricultural conditions. For an excellent set of papers on the general economic and agricultural situation in the United States during the Civil War period, see David T. Gilchrist and W. David Lewis, *Economic Change in the Civil War Era, Proceedings of a Conference on American Economic Institutional Change, 1850–1873 and the Impact of the Civil War, Held March 12–14, 1964* (Greenville, Del.: Eleutherian Mills-Hagley Foundation, 1965); of particular interest are the remarks of Morton Rothstein (on the international market for agricultural commodities) and Alfred D. Chandler, Jr. (on the organization of manufacturing and transportation). Harry N. Scheiber, "Economic Change in the Civil War Era: An Analysis of Recent Studies," *Civil War History* 11 (1965): 306, reviews the literature on overall economic change during this period. For the agricultural situation in Illinois at the time, see Russell Howard Anderson, "Agriculture in Illinois During the Civil War Period, 1850–1870," (Ph.D. diss., University of Illinois, 1929); Arthur Charles Cole, "The Era of the Civil War, 1848–1870," in Illinois Centennial Commission, *Centennial History of Illinois* (Chicago: A.C. McClurg & Co., 1922). For Iowa agriculture during the Civil War, see Earle D. Ross, *Iowa Agriculture: An Historical Survey* (Iowa City: State Historical Society of Iowa, 1951), chap. 4. For changes in Midwestern agricultural structure, see Paul Wallace Gates, "Large-scale Farming in Illinois, 1850 to 1870," *Agricultural History* 6 (1932): 14–25 (quotation on Sullivant farm from p. 295); see also his discussion of the experience of the Illinois Central Railroad in "The Promotion of Agriculture by the Illinois Central Railroad, 1855–1870," *Agricultural History* 5 (1931): 57–76. On farm costs, see Clarence Danhof, "Farm-making costs and the 'safety valve', 1850–1860," *Journal of Political Economy* 49 (June 1941): 317–359; Robert E. Ankli, "Farming-Making Costs in the 1850's," *Agricultural History* 48 (1974): 51–70; Earle D. Ross, "Retardation in Farm Technology Before the Power Age," *Agricultural History* 30 (1956): 11.

3. See *Rock Island Argus* for formation of the volunteer company, 7 and 23 April 1862; for Chapman's separation, 17 November 1863; for the "general order," 15 December 1863; for the "worthless coote" quotation, 16 April 1863; for the Friberg assault case, 2 and 3 July 1863; for the Chapman resignation, 7 March 1864; and for the election tensions, 4 October 1864 and 10 November 1864. The Stephen H. Velie papers are in DA. For the quotation on Velie's reputation, see *Rock Island Argus*, 14 November 1861. For early Christopher C. Webber advertisement, see *Upper Mississippian*, February 1846. For the quotation about Webber's death, see Tate, "The Life of Robert N. Tate," p. 346.

4. The agreement to again bring John and Charles Deere together is dated 1 July 1864, DA. John Deere's cast steel patents were no. 41203, dated 12 January 1864, and no. 42172, dated 5 April 1864; the plow standard patent was no. 46454, dated 21 February 1865. For discussion of the concept of a "sulky" (cultivator and plow), see Rogin, *Introduction of Farm Machinery*, pp. 36–40, 66–68; Bogue, *From Prairie to Corn Belt*, pp. 151–152. Quotation about "patriotic machine" is from the company's catalog of 1864. Quotation about sulky "for cripples" is from an advertisement for "Pfeil's Champion Sulky Stub and Saw and Sod Plow," *Prairie Farmer*, 26 January 1867.

5. For the first meeting of the "plow makers' society," see *Prairie Farmer*, 23 January 1864.

6. For Candee-Swan citations, see *Henry W. Candee . . . v. John Deere . . . .* Quotation on "pluck" is from *Davenport Democrat*, 11 March 1871.

7. The application to the secretary of state of Illinois was dated 16 July 1868; the certificate of organization was issued on 16 August 1868. The board of directors of the company changed its bylaws on 27 April 1869 and raised the capital stock to $250,000; this was ratified in a stockholders' meeting on 28 April 1869.

8. The grasshopper attacks of 1874 were concentrated in the Dakota Territory, Nebraska, northern Texas, Kansas, and western Missouri. Lesser scourges also occurred in 1875 and

1876. For an excellent description, see Fred Shannon, *The Farmer's Last Frontier, Agriculture, 1860–1897* (New York: Rinehart & Company, 1945), pp. 152–153. Ross, *Iowa Agriculture*, p. 94, discusses the links between the grasshopper attacks and agrarian unrest. The key sources for the overall Grange story are Edward W. Martin (James D. McCabe, Jr.), *The History of the Grange Movement* (Chicago: National Publishing Company, 1874); Solon Justus Buck, *The Granger Movement: A Study of Agricultural Organization and its Political, Economic and Social Manifestations, 1870–1880* (Cambridge, Mass.; Harvard University Press, 1913). For the Midwest efforts, see Oscar E. Anderson, "The Granger Movement in the Middle West," *Iowa Journal of History and Politics* 22 (1924): 3; A.E. Paine, *The Granger Movement in Illinois* (Urbana: University of Illinois Press, 1904). For the farm machinery link, see Arthur H. Hirsch, "Efforts of the Grange in the Middle West to Control Price of Farm Machinery," *Mississippi Valley Historical Review* 15 (1929): 473. See also Solon J. Buck, *The Agrarian Crusade* (New Haven: Yale University Press, 1920); William T. Hutchinson, *Cyrus Hall McCormick*, vol. 2 (New York: D. Appleton-Century Company, 1935), pp. 579–594; Troy J. Canley, *Agriculture in an Industrial Economy: The Agrarian Crisis* (New York: Bookman Associates, 1956); Hallie Farmer, "The Economic Background of Frontier Populism," *Issues in American Economic History: Selected Readings*, Gerald D. Nash, ed. (Boston: D.C. Heath and Co., 1964); Earl W. Hayter, *The Troubled Farmer, 1850–1900: Rural Adjustment to Industrialism* (DeKalb: Northern Illinois University Press, 1968); Benjamin H. Hibbard, *Agricultural Economics* (New York: McGraw-Hill Co., Inc., 1948); and John D. Hicks, *The Populist Revolt: A History of the Farmers' Alliance and the People's Party* (Minneapolis: University of Minnesota Press, 1931). *Prairie Farmer* quotations are from 4 May 1874; 16 and 23 November 1874; 22 March 1873; 4 May 1874. The quotation on the "sick bed" is from *Davenport Democrat*, 19 and 28 January 1874. See also Johanna Johnston, *Mrs. Satan: The Incredible Saga of Victoria C. Woodhull* (New York: G.P. Putnam's Sons, 1967); Arling Emanie Sachs, *The Terrible Siren: Victoria Woodhull* (New York: Arno Press, 1972). Quotation on "fancy rig" is from *Reedsburg Free Press*, Sauk County, Wisconsin, 24 February 1874; quotation about "leech" is from Paine, *The Granger Movement in Illinois*, p. 41. For Cyrus W. McCormick's reaction to the Grangers, see William T. Hutchinson, *Cyrus Hall McCormick*, pp. 581–595. See also *Prairie Farmer*, 8 March 1873, and 2 September 1876; *Chicago Tribune*, 5 and 14 May 1873, and 7 March 1874.

9. The Northwestern Plow Manufacturers Association statement is in its minutes of 2 December 1873, DA. See also *Prairie Farmer*, 29 November 1873 and 20 December 1873. The Charles Deere interview is in *Chicago Tribune*, 17 January 1874; for responses, ibid., 11 and 23 February 1874; *Prairie Farmer*, 28 February 1874; ibid., 14 December 1874; ibid., 17 January 1875; and ibid., 14 March 1875. The quotation on "price wars" is from Shannon, *The Farmer's Last Frontier*, p. 31.

10. For quotation on "shrinkage," see *Prairie Farmer*, 31 March 1877. For discussion of the link between the Granges and the mail order houses, see Hirsch, "Efforts of the Grange in the Middle West," p. 474; *The History and Progress of Montgomery Ward & Company* (Chicago, privately printed, 1925); Boris Emmet and John E. Jeuck, *Catalogues and Counters: A History of Sears, Roebuck and Company* (Chicago: University of Chicago Press, 1950), pp. 19–21.

11. Quotation on "traditional mercantile firm" is from Chandler, *The Visible Hand*, p. 56; his discussion of Singer is from ibid., pp. 402–405. On the marketing revolution see also Porter and Livesay, *Merchants and Manufacturers*, chap. 8. The International Harvester branch-house system is discussed in Cyrus McCormick, *The Century of the Reaper: An Account of Cyrus Hall McCormick, the Inventor of the Reaper; of the McCormick Harvesting Machine Company, the Business He Created and of the International Harvester Company, His Heir and Chief Memorial* (Boston: Houghton Mifflin Company, 1931), chap. 13.

12. These five cities each shared three important factors for growth: (1) geographic locations on major water trade routes contiguous to the vast agricultural lands of the West;

(2) rapid settlement by waves of immigrants after the Civil War; and (3) access to the major railroad lines. In the decade of 1880–90, the population of Omaha increased by 360 percent, that of Minneapolis by 251 percent, and that of Kansas City, Mo., by 138 percent. St. Louis and San Francisco showed more modest rates (25 percent and 28 percent, respectively), but they had already become the largest cities of the West and were by 1890 the fourth and ninth cities of the nation. Value of products demonstrates even more clearly their rising status as commercial centers: in the same decade, Omaha's rose from $4 million to more than $42 million, that of Kansas City from $6 million to $31 million, that of St. Louis from $114 million to $229 million, that of Minneapolis from $29 million to almost $83 million, and that of San Francisco from almost $78 million to more than $135 million. See, United States Census Office, Department of the Interior, *Abstract of Twelfth Census of the United States, 1900* (Washington: Government Printing Office, 1902). The early development of northern Plains agriculture is discussed in Howard W. Ottoson et al., *Land and People in the Northern Plains Transition Area* (Lincoln: University of Nebraska Press, 1966), pp. 25–47; agriculture in Minnesota and the Dakotas is highlighted in Edward Van Dyke Robinson, "Early Economic Conditions and the Development of Agriculture in Minnesota," *University of Minnesota Studies in the Social Sciences* 3 (1915). A book emphasizing the history of upper Midwest agriculture is Hiram M. Drache, *Beyond the Furrow: Some Keys to Successful Farming in the Twentieth Century* (Danville, Ill.: Interstate Printers and Publishers, 1976). See Mildred L. Hartsough, "The Twin Cities as a Metropolitan Market: A Regional Study of the Economic Development of Minneapolis and St. Paul," *Studies in the Social Sciences* 18 (Minneapolis: University of Minnesota, 1925) for the development of Minneapolis. Ira G. Clark, *Then Came the Railroads: The Century from Steam to Diesel in the Southwest*, 1st ed. (Norman: University of Oklahoma Press, 1958) describes in detail the effect of the railroads on Kansas City and other cities in the area; see also Charles S. Gleed's article on Omaha in Lyman P. Powell, ed., *Historic Towns of the Western States, American Historic Towns 4* (New York: G.P. Putnam's Sons, 1901), p. 396; Charles N. Glaab, *Kansas City and the Railroads: Community Policy in the Growth of a Regional Metropolis* (Madison: State Historical Society of Wisconsin, 1962). By the late 1870s, Chicago had replaced St. Louis as the primary trading center in the old Northwest; this struggle for trade supremacy is analyzed in Wyatt W. Belcher, *The Economic Rivalry Between St. Louis and Chicago, 1850–1880* (New York: Columbia University Press, 1947). The development of Omaha is chronicled in John W. Reps, *Cities of the American West: A History of Frontier Urban Planning* (Princeton: Princeton University Press, 1977) and Robert E. Riegel, *America Moves West* (New York: Henry Holt and Co., 1930). The arrival of the Central Pacific Railroad changed San Francisco almost overnight. See, for example, Gunther P. Barth, *Instant Cities: Urbanization and the Rise of San Francisco and Denver* (New York: Oxford University Press, 1975); Glenn C. Quiett, *They Built the West: An Epic of Rails and Cities* (New York: D. Appleton-Century Co., Inc., 1934); Oscar Lewis, *San Francisco: Mission to Metropolis* (Berkeley, Calif.: Howell-North Books, 1966), p. 172. For incorporation of Deere, Mansur & Company on 1 September 1869, see DA, 10782–10784, 10792. For documentation of the correspondence with Smith & Keating on the "Bain" wagon, see DA, 1112. For the first five-year co-partnership at St. Louis on 1 September 1875, see DA, 10783. The corporate record book for Deere & Webber Company is DA, 84. Charles C. Webber's letter books, covering the period 1885–1907, are DA, 20130–20132. The quotation from Ellen Deere Webber and her son's earlier letter to her are documented in DA, 26653. Text quotation from P.C. Simmon is from "History of Deere & Company, including Personnel and Finances of Branch Houses" (Moline: ca. 1921), DA. For additional information on the early days of the Minneapolis branch, see H.A. Anderson to H.M. Railsback, 24 May 1944, DA 26653. Anderson notes that the co-partnership of 1883 operated under the name Deere & Co. of Minneapolis until the formation of the corporation Deere & Webber Co. in 1893. For the original co-partnership of Deere, Wells & Company of Council Bluffs, dated 1 November 1881, see DA, 3374, 3375, 3379, and 12227. The original link in San Francisco was with Marcus C. Hawley & Co.; Simmon dates the first formal jobbing connection as

1875. The San Francisco concern was succeeded in 1882 by Hawley Bros. Hardware Company; the first formal stock company was dated 5 August 1889; see DA, 648, 651, 3303, and 11627. The text quotation is from *California Farmer*, 8 September 1865, DA, 2268; a full front page was devoted to Deere & Company in ibid., 3 December 1874. For the early history of California agriculture, see Paul W. Gates, ed., *California Ranchos and Farms, 1846–1862* (Madison: State Historical Society of Wisconsin, 1967); Howard F. Gregor, *An Agricultural Typology of California* (Budapest: Akadémiai Kiadó, 1974). Reynold M. Wik, "Some Interpretations of the Mechanization of Agriculture in the Far West," in James H. Shideler, ed., *Agriculture in the Development of the Far West* (Washington: Agricultural History Society, 1975), pp. 73–83, suggests that the particular features of California's climate created unique conditions for harvesting and threshing grain crops, thereby enhancing the development of the grain combine. See also Graeme R. Quick and Wesley F. Buchele, *The Grain Harvesters* (St. Joseph, Mich.: American Society of Agricultural Engineers, 1978), pp. 91–112.

13. Development of the multidivisional form of organization structure and the adaptation of the concepts of decentralization is analyzed in Alfred D. Chandler, Jr., *Strategy and Structure: Chapters in the History of the Industrial Enterprise* (Cambridge, Mass.: M.I.T. Press, 1962); for the contributions of Alfred P. Sloan, Jr., at the General Motors Corporation, see ibid., pp. 130–162. Sloan's own words can be found in Alfred D. Chandler, Jr., *Giant Enterprise: Ford, General Motors, and the Automobile Industry; Sources and Readings* (New York: Harcourt, Brace & World, 1964), p. 115 (quoting from "Organization Study," 1920, Du Pont-General Motors Anti-trust Case, Defendants' Trial Exhibit, GM 1).

14. The original Gilpin Moore sulky plow patent was no. 164929, dated 29 June 1875. See also Moore's gang plow patent no. 158859, dated 19 January 1875 and no. 255391, dated 21 March 1882. Robert L. Ardrey, *American Agricultural Implements*, traces the sulky plow back to patents held by F.S. Davenport in 1864. By 1868, according to Ardrey, there were several practical sulkies in operation, and a major sulky trial was held in Des Moines that year. By 1873 there were sixteen different sulky plows in a competition in St. Louis. Thus the Gilpin Moore sulky was a latecomer to the field. Rogin, *Introduction of Farm Machinery*, warns of the confusion between "wheel" and "sulky" and states that the prevailing modern usage for the term "sulky plow" was for the riding implement possessed of a single bottom, the riding implement with more than one bottom being, according to Rogin, a sulky gang plow (p. 37). Simon S. Kuznets, *Secular Movements in Production and Prices: Their Nature and Their Bearing Upon Cyclical Fluctuations* (Boston: Houghton Mifflin Company, 1930), p. 56–57, points to the rapid rise and fall in the number of sulky plow patents, as contrasted to the reasonably stable number of plow patents in the same period. Kuznets explains this as follows: "Evidently because of a narrower field of application, the absolute number of suggested improvements declined much more for the sulky than for the plow." The Gilpin Moore defection is reported in *Davenport Democrat*, 22 November 1874. Charles Deere's purchase of the Gilpin Moore shares is not well documented—an anonymous obituary of Gilpin Moore published by the company at his death mentioned the transfer and the fact that Deere "later traded the shares to an Indiana man for plow handles"; DA. The Rock Island Plow Co. handbill and handwritten comment is in "C.H. Deere Private Scrapbook—1884," DA. For Webber's views, see C.C. Webber to Deere & Co., 24 July 1893; and Webber to Stephen Velie, Sr., 1 April 1889; both in Charles C. Webber papers, DA. For Charles Deere's letter on patent, see Deere & Co. to W.B. Richards, 18 October 1891, in Charles H. Deere papers (R). For Velie quotations, see Stephen Velie, Sr., to Charles H. Deere, 1 July 1889, in Charles H. Deere papers (Sv); Stephen Velie, Sr., to Deere & Co., 17 May 1890, in Webber papers, DA; Stephen Velie, Sr., to Charles H. Deere, 17 March 1892, in Charles H. Deere papers (Sv); ibid., 7 March 1892 and 1 July 1889.

15. For George Fuller on "stiffening" prices, see G. Fuller to Charles Deere, 5 October 1889, DA, 3393. For Lucius Wells's quotation on "street walkers," see 21 January 1893, Charles H. Deere papers (Wel); S.W. Ganz to Charles Deere, 1 December 1887, ibid. The exchanges with Mansur are from Alvah Mansur to Deere & Co., 10 May 1879; ibid., 19 May 1879; ibid.,

21 May 1879; and Stephen H. Velie, Sr., to A. Mansur, 23 May 1879, DA, 3391. For contract between Deere, Mansur and Company and Deere & Company of 1 June 1879, see DA, 3296. Alvah Mansur to Charles H. Deere, 18 January 1883, DA, 3299; ibid., 2 December 1884, DA, 3291; ibid., 19 January 1886, DA, 3293; ibid., 28 May 1888, Charles H. Deere papers (D & M); ibid., 12 December 1888. For Wells's and Webber's quotations on price, see Lucius Wells to Charles H. Deere, 4 March 1888, DA, 12228; Charles C. Webber to Charles H. Deere, 23 January 1889, Deere papers (Web).

16. Alvah Mansur to Deere & Company, 4 August 1885, DA, 32993. For the Pope controversy on shovel attachments, see C.H. Pope to Deere & Co., 16 November 1888; Stephen H. Velie, Sr., to Charles H. Deere, 16 November 1888, in Stephen H. Velie, Sr., papers, DA.

17. Webber papers; George W. Fuller to Deere & Company, 20 October 1885, DA, 3293; Lucius Wells to Deere & Company, 20 October 1885, DA, 3293; ibid., 17 May 1887, DA, 3381; ibid., 16 March 1891, DA, 12228; Charles C. Webber to Charles H. Deere, 5 November 1886, Charles C. Webber letter book. For Velie's views on the Oklahoma Territory, see Velie to Deere, 19 February 1888, Charles H. Deere papers (Sv).

NOTES TO CHAPTER 5: PRODUCTS, PRICES, AND PEOPLE

1. For the quotation on "revolution," see Chandler, *The Visible Hand*, p. 240. Chilled plow development is discussed in John W. Oliver, *History of American Technology* (New York: Ronald Press Company, 1956), pp. 363–364. The check row planter is analyzed in Ardrey, *American Agricultural Implements*, pp. 30–35, 169–172.

2. For the history of the sulky plow, see Rogin, *Introduction of Farm Machinery*; Bogue, *From Prairie to Corn Belt*. The Osage dealer's comment on the Gilpin is from H.H. Bauman to Deere & Company, 15 December 1876, Charles H. Deere Papers (A), DA. The company had won the sulky competition at the Illinois State Fair on 15 September 1874 with its "Ayer's Patent" machine. For the Gilpin competitions in 1875, see Deere Scrapbook No. 2, DA, pp. 84, 91, 101, and 115; Deere Scrapbook No. 3, DA, p. 13. Black's gang was patented by J.S. and W.L. Black, 31 July 1861. See "Paris Exhibition of 1878—Official Trial of Plows," *Scientific American* 39 (14 September 1878): 162–166; the results were in ibid. (21 September 1878); for the United States success overall, see ibid. (12 and 26 October 1878). There were eight grand prizes, of which Deere & Company took one. (The others went to C.H. McCormick's reaping binder, Walter A. Wood's reaping binder, Osborne's reaping binder, Johnston's harvester, Whiteley's mower, Dedrick's hay press, and the Chicago hay press.) "The effect of these victories upon our foreign trade . . . can scarcely be overestimated," the editors stated in ibid. (2 November 1878).

3. Casady's plow is discussed in Ardrey, *American Agricultural Implements*, pp. 17, 20, 202. For the statement on steam tractors, see Rogin, *Introduction of Farm Machinery*, p. 40. See also *Nebraska Farmer* 6 (1882): 129; *Farm Implement News*, 3 and 24 March 1892; ibid., 7 April 1892. The results of the early steam plow trials, such as those in the late 1850s involving Deere, were so discouraging that only two patents for steam-powered plows had been applied for by the 1870s. Most of the men constructing these machines were amateurs with little expertise with engines or with farming and insufficient capital for extensive experimentation. Clark C. Spence, "Experiments in American Steam Cultivation," *Agricultural History* 33 (1959): 116, notes that the steam-engine innovators were forced, for economic reasons, to build their entire apparatus, including the power plant, "from the ground up," rather than to begin with the best engine available. Success with steam-powered threshers, especially on the large-scale farms of the Pacific coast and the plains west of the Mississippi, increased demand for better engines with greater horsepower, encouraging thresher manufacturers to enter the engine production scene. By the late 1870s, the numbers of manufacturers of portable engines had increased substantially, but still needed urgently was a device to create a self-propelled machine. See Wik, *Steam Power on* the American Farm, p. 72. In 1890, 3,000 steam tractors and 2,661 steam threshers were manufactured; by 1905, 7,500 steam traction engines were made by thirty-five different companies, reaching a peak of production in 1913 of 10,000. See also R.B. Gray, The Agricultural Tractor: 1855–1950, rev. ed. (St. Joseph, Mich.: American Society of Agricultural Engineers, 1974). By 1894 with the improvement of gearing, shafting, and wearing parts, more plow manufacturers began to produce multi-bottomed gang plows as attachments. One manufacturer, Holt Manufacturing Company, boasted in 1898 that its traction engines could plow, harrow, and seed from twenty-five to forty acres of land a day. When the big and well-established thresher companies began to redesign their threshers for plowing use, the real era of traction plowing began. In 1904, the J.I. Case Threshing Machine Company put out a steam plowing catalog that included testimonials from farmers stretching from Texas to Canada, indicating the widespread use of the power tractor-plow. High costs of purchase ($1,600–$3,500 for the smaller Eastern plowing machines, $5,000–$6,000 for the much heavier, larger Pacific coast machines), of maintenance, and of operation put the machines out of the ordinary farmer's reach. Most of the plowing in the late 1890s and early twentieth century, in the so-called "heyday" of the steam power machinery, was done by big steam-plow outfits for hire. "Huge steam monsters of as many as 120-horsepower churned across the broad wheatlands of the American and Canadian West, drawing 20 or 30 plows and turning 50 or 75 acres per day," writes C.C. Spence, "Experiments in American Steam Cultivation," p. 116. So many were there of these outfits that in 1908, according to one plowman in Kansas, there was not enough labor to go around to keep the machinery operating; Wik, Steam Power on the American Farm, p. 148. The Steam Age boom lasted only about thirty years. The internal combustion engine appeared on the scene, and the "snorting, puffing giant that men had tried so long to tame" was replaced by a new machine that would be affordable by the average farmer (quotation from Spence, "Experiments in American Steam Cultivation," p. 116). In the summary in Wik, Steam Power on the American Farm, it is claimed that the production of steam engines for agricultural use made a major contribution to agriculture because: (1) they assured the success of large-scale farming; (2) they prepared the farmer psychologically to accept power-farming and the gasoline tractor; and (3) they prepared the way for the shifting of the manufacturers to the production of gasoline tractors. This last was accomplished easily because the manufacturers had already built the large factories needed; the systems of production, distribution, repairs, and sales required; and the engineering staffs and expertise required.

4. The 1879–83 production figures are from DA, 3346. See also Deere & Company Minutes, 17 July 1886, DA.

5. For early planter history, see Ardrey, American Agricultural Implements, p. 30. See also Bidwell and Falconer, History of Agriculture in the Northern United States, pp. 300–301. Danhof, Change in Agriculture, pp. 214–217, discusses planting practices. See also Bogue, From Prairie to Corn Belt, pp. 160–162. See George W. Crampton, "How the Corn Planter Grew Up," The Furrow 34 (1929): 512–513. Quotation on "other men" is from "Notes on the History of the Corn Planter," DA, 3569. The case citation is George W. Brown v. Deere, Mansur & Company and others, Circuit Court, Eastern District Missouri, January 1881, 6 Federal Reporter, pp. 484–493. For the Deere broadside, see Galesburg Republican and Register, 17 January 1881. Quotation on farmers being threatened by patent suits is from Earl W. Hayter, "The Western Farmers and the Drivewell Patent Controversy," Agricultural History 16 (1942): 16–17. Mansur quotation from Charles W. Mansur, "Reminiscences," 10 May 1923, DA, 25600. Quotation on "specialists" is from P.C. Simmon, "History of Deere & Company."

6. For biographical data on James First, see "Fair Wage of Olden Days 75 Cents." For the corporate record book of the Moline Wagon Company, see DA, 108; for Mansur & Tebbetts Implement Company, see DA, 154. For quotation on harness business, see C.C. Webber to Charles H. Deere, 3 September 1903. The "modern safety" bicycle is described in Farm Implement News, 29 October 1891. The Deere bicycle story is chronicled in "John Deere

Bicycles—1894–1900," DA. The C.C. Webber letter to the San Francisco branch is dated 1 June 1893. See also C. C. Webber to Charles Deere, 7 July 1893 and ibid., 2 April 1895. The Deere Road Race is described in *Farm Implement News*, 15 August 1895. Quotation on "fickle taste" is from Arthur S. Dewing, *Corporate Promotions and Reorganizations* (Cambridge, Mass.: Harvard University Press, 1914), p. 249.

7. George K. Holmes, *The Course of Prices of Farm Implements and Machinery for a Series of Years*, U.S. Department of Agriculture Miscellaneous Series, Bulletin 18 (Washington: Government Printing Office, 1901), p. 30; Carroll D. Wright, *Thirteenth Annual Report of the Commissioner of Labor, 1898: Hand and Machine Labor*, 2 vol. (Washington: Government Printing Office, 1899), pp. 20, 24–25, 80–82, 476–479; Shannon, *The Farmer's Last Frontier*, pp. 142–143, 145; H.W. Quaintance, "The Influence of Farm Machinery on Production and Labor," *Publication of the American Economic Society*, third series, 5 (November 1904): 45, 63, 82. For the quotation regarding the cost of plows, see C.D. Wright, *Hand and Machine Labor*, p. 20. Some of the methodology of Wright is disputed in an extensive appendix in Rogin, *Introduction of Farm Machinery*, pp. 213–243.

8. For Kiel quotation, see "Memories of John Kiel," DA, 19094; for report on work simplification, see A.M. Dahl, 20 December 1898, DA, 3354.

9. *Historical Statistics of the United States* (Washington: Government Printing Office, 1976), p. 165; Stanley Lebergott, *Manpower and Economic Growth: The American Record Since 1800* (New York: McGraw-Hill, 1964), pp. 257 ff. For quotation on "lowest class," see *Davenport Democrat*, 9 May 1867; in regard to the saw mill, see ibid., 18 April 1876, for the Deere repair, see ibid., 19 and 22 August 1876; for the company quotation, see ibid., 26 July 1876. "Labor party" quotation is from *Moline Review*, 31 August 1877. Comparative wage survey is DA, 3408. See *Davenport Democrat*, 8 September 1885, for Knights of Labor; in ibid., 24 September 1885, is the listing of all the organizations in the "Trades Union Assembly." See particularly, John R. Commons, ed., *Trade Unionism and Labor Problems* (Boston, New York: Ginn and Co., 1921), Philip Taft, *Organized Labor in American History* (New York: Harper and Row, Publishers, 1964); Leo Wolman, *The Growth of American Trade Unions 1880–1923* (New York: National Bureau of Economic Research, Inc., 1924). For quotation on the grinders' strike, see *Davenport Democrat*, 27 April 1886. For quotation on the Haymarket Riot, see S.H. Velie to C. Deere, 28 April 1886; ibid., 4 May 1886; ibid. 6 May 1886, Stephen H. Velie papers.

10. For quotation on "own guns," see S.H. Velie to C. Deere, 19 February 1888, Charles H. Deere papers (Sv); A. Mansur to C. Deere, 1 May and 7 June 1889, Charles H. Deere papers (D&M); George W. Fuller to C. Deere, 24 May 1889, Charles H. Deere papers (KC 38); G.W. Fuller to C. Deere, 17 June 1889, Charles H. Deere papers (Sv); S.H. Velie, Sr., to G.W. Fuller, 24 June 1889, Stephen H. Velie, Sr., papers; A. Mansur to C. Deere, 9 July 1889, Charles H. Deere papers (D&M); L.B. Tebbetts to C. Deere, 26 October 1889, Charles H. Deere papers (Teb); A. Mansur to C. Deere, 27 December 1889, Charles H. Deere papers (D&C); A. Mansur to C. Deere, 4 January 1892; C. Deere to A. Mansur, 5 January 1892, Charles H. Deere papers (D&C). Many examples of the joint entrepreneurial activities of Charles Deere and Alvah Mansur are found in the Charles H. Deere papers (D&M). The quotation is from A. Mansur to C. Deere, 18 May 1892. See also G.W. Fuller to C. Deere, 17 December 1892, Charles H. Deere papers (KC); John Deere Plow Company of Kansas City, Corporate Record Book 154, and Stock Certificate Book, DA, 60; S.H. Velie to C. Deere, 11 May 1893, Charles H. Deere papers (Sv); Charles C. Webber to Deere & Co., 24 November 1893, Charles C. Webber letter book.

11. For the Hawley story, see Frederick W. Vaughn to C. Deere, 6 November 1889, Charles H. Deere papers (Sf); S.H. Velie, Sr., to C. Deere, 4 January 1890, Stephen H. Velie, Sr., papers. The key Charles H. Deere letters are those of C. Deere to S.H. Velie, Sr., dated 8 February 1890, 12 February 1890, 13 February 1890, 14 February 1890, 15 February 1890 three letters under this date), and 19 February 1890. See also Alvah Mansur to C. Deere, 17 February 1890; the Hawley's counterproposal is in letter to C. Deere, 21 February 1890; also F. Vaughn to C. Deere, 18 April 1890; ibid., 14 December 1892; and ibid., 14 July 1896,

Charles H. Deere papers (Sf); C.C. Webber to C. Deere, 19 August 1896, Charles C. Webber
letter book; ibid., 29 August 1896; ibid., 3 September 1896.
12. H.C. Peek story is in P.C. Simmon, "History of Deere & Company," DA; for Vermont
links, see William T. Ball diary, Nellie Ball Rosborough papers, DA. For thief story, see
Davenport Democrat, 27 January 1868; for accident, see ibid., 23 January 1871; for "hearty
old" quote, see ibid., 18 October 1872; for St. Louis Board of Trade, see ibid., 3 December
1875. The spelling of Lusenia Deere varies in various documents; her own handwriting has
been chosen for verification, DA, 27186 and 35578. For John Deere's election as mayor of
Moline, see *Davenport Democrat*, 16 April 1873; ibid., 13 March 1874; for the temperance
issue, see ibid., 25 May, 5 June, and 25 July 1874; ibid., 30 October 1874. On the crockery
business, see J. Deere to William T. Ball, "February 1886" (no exact date given by Deere),
DA. The tavern story is in Burton F. Peek ms. in P.C. Simmon, "History of Deere
& Company," DA. For spiritualist incident, see Charles H. Deere papers (B), (Dee), (G),
and Wel , DA. Funeral is described in Nellie Ball Rosborough, "I Remember John Deere,"
ca. 1962, DA.
13. For quotations on the will, see *Moline Review Dispatch*, 6 and 11 June 1886. See also
agreement signed by Emma D. Webber, Jeannette D. Chapman, Emma D. Velie, Alice D.
Cady, and Lusenia Deere on 5 July 1886, DA, 35578. The fire-fighting accident was reported
in *Moline Dispatch*, 5 June 1855. The Union League Club suspension is in DA, 25332. The
election results are reported in *Moline Review Dispatch*, 8 April 1881; for quotation from
statement of the twelve manufacturers, see ibid., 28 October 1880. On company activities
for employees, see, for example, *Moline Review Dispatch*, 27 June 1884; ibid., 4 July 1884;
ibid., 19 April 1889. Most of Charles Deere's family papers are in Charles H. Deere papers
(B), DA. For C. Deere's accident, see *Davenport Democrat*, 7 March 1872.

NOTES TO CHAPTER 6: CHALLENGES TO INDEPENDENCE

1. Particularly useful on the consolidation movement in the 1880s and '90s is Dewing,
Corporate Promotions and Reorganizations. Another classic analysis of this period is
William Z. Ripley, ed., *Trusts, Pools and Corporations* (Boston: Ginn and Company, 1905).
See also Hans B. Thorelli, *The Federal Antitrust Policy: Origination of an American
Tradition* (London: G. Allen & Anwin, 1954) and Ralph H. Nelson, *Merger Movements in
American Industry, 1895–1956* (Princeton: Princeton University Press, 1959). For British
capital investments abroad in this period, see Charles K. Hobson, *The Export of Capital*
(London: Constable & Co., Ltd., 1914); Albert H. Imlah, *Economic Elements in the Pax
Britannica: Studies in British Foreign Trade in the Nineteenth Century* (Cambridge, Mass.:
Harvard University Press, 1958); Alexander K. Cairncross, *Home and Foreign Investments*
(Cambridge, Eng.: Cambridge University Press, 1953). See also Brinley Thomas, "The
Historical Record of International Capital Movements to 1913" and Matthew Simon, "The
Patterns of New British Portfolio Foreign Investment, 1865–1914" in John H. Adler, ed.,
*Capital Movements and Economic Development: Proceedings of a Conference held by the
International Economic Association* (New York: St. Martin's Press, 1967) and Leland H.
Jenks, *The Migration of British Capital to 1875* (New York: Alfred A. Knopf, 1927). The
French, Belgians, and Germans also were investing substantially in the United States at this
time. See *Report of the Industrial Commission on Industrial Combinations in Europe* 18
(Washington: Government Printing Office, 1901). Quotation on "good paying prices" from
C.H. Mitchell to Northwestern Plow Association, 3 November 1892, Charles H. Deere
papers (N), DA. In the mid-1880s the organization was called the Northwestern Plow and
Cultivator Association. Velie quotations in S.H. Velie, Sr., to Charles H. Hapgood, 7 October
1887, and S.H. Velie, Sr., to Alvah Mansur, 9 August 1888, in Stephen H. Velie papers, DA;
Charles H. Deere to S.H. Velie, Sr., 2 June 1888, in Charles H. Deere papers (P), DA. See
Chicago Tribune, 5 May 1889, for discussion of "The Big Steel Combine."
2. Documentation of the British syndicate's bid is in the Charles H. Deere papers, as
follows: on capitalization, Stephen H. Velie, Sr., to C. Deere, 26 July 1889 (Sa); on pricing,

Alvah Mansur to C. Deere, 12 September 1889 (Un) and John W. Good to C. Deere, 8 November 1889 (Mol); on Moline Plow Company, F.L. Underwood to Stillman Wheelock, 20 August 1889 (Un); on pricing, F.L. Underwood to C. Deere, 16 August 1889 (Un) and Charles C. Webber to C. Deere, 29 July 1890 (Web); on new promoter's bid, F.L. Underwood to C. Deere, 2 November 1885 (Un); on additional promotions, O.S. Chamberlain to C. Deere, 27 November 1885 (Ch), J.L. Mayer to C. Deere, 20 November 1889 (Ma), William A. Merigold and Co. to C. Deere, 24 October 1889 (Ma), S.D. Loring to C. Deere, 20 January 1890 (Mp), M.I. Ten Eyck to C. Deere, 30 January 1890 (Mn), and A.M. DaCosta to C. Deere, 18 March 1890. The confidentiality of the telegraph (and cable) was carefully maintained by the communications companies; see Chandler, *The Visible Hand*, p. 200. On advice to Moline Plow Company, A.L. Bryant to F.L. Underwood, 5 April, 12 June, and 16 June 1890 (Un); on European reactions, F.L. Underwood to C. Deere, 16 June 1890 (Un) and S.H. Velie, Sr., to C. Deere, 23 June and 15 July 1890 (Su); on Kingman Plow stock, F.L. Underwood to C. Deere, 24 July, 27 July, and 16 August 1890; on Webber misgivings, C.C. Webber to C. Deere, 29 July and 5 August 1890, Charles C. Webber letter book, DA; on Velie warnings, S.H. Velie, Sr., to C.C. Webber, 30 August 1890, Charles H. Deere papers (Un); on Moline Plow Company stock, Thomas F. Nickerson to C. Deere, 26 November 1890, Charles H. Deere papers (Mp). William Wiman to C. Deere, 30 November 1890 (Mp); Erastus Wiman to Charles H. Deere, 1 December 1890 (Mp); Erastus Wiman, "British Capital and American Industries," *North American Review* 150 (1890): 226; Roger V. Clements, "The Farmers' Attitude Toward British Investment in American Industry," *Journal of Economic History* 15 (1955): 151, and the Erastus Wiman quote in 1888 on monopoly in *Boston Herald*, 4 September 1888, relate to Deere's query of Erastus Wiman. For collapse of negotiations, see F.L. Underwood to C. Deere, 30 December 1890; Stephen H. Velie, Sr., to T.F. Nickerson, 11 December 1890; T.F. Nickerson to C. Deere, 20 December 1890, with Charles H. Deere note to Wheelock attached (Mp). The Boston proposal is in F.L. Underwood to C. Deere, 5 and 26 January 1891; C.C. Webber to C. Deere, 24 January 1891, Webber letter book. F.L. Underwood to C. Deere, 20 February 1891; S.H. Velie, Sr., to F.L. Underwood, 27 July 1891; and S.H. Velie, Sr., to C. Deere, 27 February 1891. S.H. Velie, Sr., to C. Deere, 28 February 1891 (Mp) and F.L. Underwood to C. Deere, 7 March 1891, relate to new tactics. *Boston Transcript*, 7 March 1891, contains quotation on "market sags." The close of the negotiations is documented in S.H. Velie, Sr., to G.P. Stevens, 23 March 1891, and S.H. Velie, Sr., to C.C. Webber, 14 March 1891; *Boston Globe*, 3 May 1891; undocumented newspaper clipping from Boston paper in the "Scrapbook" of 11 May 1891 and Charles H. Deere papers (T-110); S.H. Velie, Sr., to C. Deere, 18 April, 22 April, and 20 May 1891 (Mp); Willard R. Green to S.H. Velie, Sr., 3 June 1891 (Mp); F.L. Underwood to C. Deere, 12 August 1891; W.R. Green to C. Deere, 29 June 1892 (Jep); F.L. Underwood to C. Deere, 15 January 1892; Martin Kingman to C. Deere, 20 February 1892 (Mk); A.L. Bryant to W.R. Green, 16 March 1892 (G); S.H. Velie, Jr., to C. Deere, 24 March 1892 (Vj); F.L. Underwood to C. Deere, 6 March 1892 (Un); W.R. Green to C. Deere, 9 April 1892 (G); S.H. Velie, Sr., to C. Deere, 12 April, 13 April, and 5 May 1892 (Su).

3. Two excellent analyses of the 1893–97 downturn are Charles Hoffman, "The Depression of the Nineties," *Journal of Economic History* 16 (1956): 137 and Samuel Rezneck, "Unemployment, Unrest and Relief in the United States During the Depression of 1893–1897," *Journal of Political Economy* 61 (1953): 324. See *Bradstreet's*, 30 December 1893; for L.B. Tebbetts quotation, see *Farm Implement News*, 7 March 1895. For an interesting revisionist view of the farmer in the 1866–96 period, suggesting that his lot was not as negative as pictured by earlier economists, except in the older sections of New England and the South, see Robert William Fogel and Jack Rutner, *The Efficiency Effects of Federal Land Policy, 1850–1900: A Report of Some Provisional Findings*, Report 7027 (Center for Mathematical Studies in Business and Economics, University of Chicago), 1970.

4. For report on the "anarchist," see William Butterworth to Charles H. Deere, 3 October 1893, Charles H. Deere papers (Bu). The Pennsylvania incidents are described in Wayne G. Broehl, Jr., *The Molly Maguires* (Cambridge, Mass.: Harvard University Press, 1964); the

Homestead strike is analyzed in John A. Fitch, *The Steel Workers* (New York: Charities Publication Committee, 1910) and in U.S. House of Representatives, 52nd Congress, 1st Session, misc. Doc. 335 (1892). The Pullman strikes of 1894 were also influential in shaping attitudes toward labor in this period; see Almont Lindsey, *The Pullman Strike* (Chicago: University of Chicago Press, 1942). The Deere correspondence with the Pinkerton National Detective Agency is found in the Charles Deere papers (Hom, Dec), DA. Company wage rates in 1894 are documented in DA, 19329. The grinders' strike is noted in *Moline Dispatch*, 10 September 1895; the story about the dog, Toby, is in ibid., 14 September 1895. The Illinois Board of Arbitration was established in 1895, one year after the notorious Pullman strike, but according to Robert P. Howard, *Illinois: A History of the Prairie State* (Grand Rapids: William B. Eerdmans Publishing Company, 1972), p. 386, it "accomplished little." In the first five years, the board handled only thirty cases, states Edwin E. Witte, *Historical Survey of Labor Arbitration* (Philadelphia: University of Pennsylvania Press, 1952), p. 5. An Illinois Coal Commissioner complaint is recorded in Nicholas P. Gilman, *Methods of Industrial Peace* (Boston and New York: Houghton. Mifflin and Company, 1904), p. 334: "Unless . . . the decrees of the Board can be enforced, they are practically of no value. . . . During the past year (1900) there has not been a single case referred to the State Board of Arbitration." The strike breakers and violence are reported in *Moline Dispatch*, 11 October 1895; ibid., 12 October 1895; ibid., 19 July 1897; and ibid., 3 September 1897. The painters' award is noted in ibid., 14 December 1897; the Gompers visit is reported in ibid., 12 April 1898.

5. *Farm Implement News*, 20 June 1901 and 18 July 1901, discusses the employers' "Declaration of Principles." For the C.H. Deere letter, see *Moline Dispatch*, 3 August 1901; see also DA, 3759, 29 June 1901. The quotation on the National Metal Trades Association is in Philip Taft, *Organized Labor in American History*, p. 191. Clarence E. Bonnett, *Employers Associations in the United States: A Study of Typical Associations* (New York: Macmillan Company, 1922), p. 24, discusses its belligerency.

6. Quotation on "preeminence of Illinois" is from *Twelfth Census of the United States, Taken in the Year 1900*, 10, "Manufactures," part 4 (Washington: United States Census Office, 1902), p. 347. Moline's position is documented in Bureau of the Census, "Manufactures," part 4 (1905); Bureau of the Census, "Manufactures" (1908), p. 134.

7. Quotation on "Skunk Trust" is from *New York Times*, 2 August 1899. For a comprehensive study of the merger movements in the United States after 1895, see Ralph L. Nelson, *Merger Movements in American Industry, 1895–1956* (Princeton, N.J.: Princeton University Press, 1959); merger activity of the farm machinery industry, 1895–1904, is pictured in ibid., table 48, p. 86. Early views on the "Plow Trust" are in *New York Times*, 18 March 1899; ibid., 25 April 1899; ibid., 4 May 1899; *Farm Implement News*, 11 May 1899; *Implement Age*, 15 March 1899; ibid., 1 May 1899; ibid., 15 May 1899. The Charles H. Deere involvement was documented in *Implement Age*, 15 June 1899; *Moline Dispatch*, 5 September 1899; ibid., 15 September 1899; ibid., 26 September 1899; *Farm Implement News*, 25 April 1901; and *Moline Dispatch*, 24 April 1901. See also *Chicago Conference on Trusts: Speeches, Debates, Resolutions, List of the Delegates, Committees, Etc., Held September 13th, 14th, 15th, 16th, 1899* (Chicago: The Civic Federation of Chicago, 1900). For the unsigned Deere statement on attitudes toward consolidation, ca. 1901, see DA, 19302. The headline in the text is from *Farm Implement News*, 16 May 1901. Their opposition to trusts is stated in ibid., 2 and 9 May 1901. The statement by Charles Deere and the reply are in *Moline Dispatch*, 24 and 29 April 1901. For Velie's view on the Grangers, see S.H. Velie, Sr., to C. Deere, 15 July 1890, Stephen H. Velie, Sr., papers, DA. For the progress of the negotiations, see *Farm Implement News*, 9 and 11 May 1901; *Moline Dispatch*, 9 and 24 May 1901. For the increasing doubts, see *Farm Implement News*, 23 May 1901; ibid., 6 June 1901; C.C. Webber to C. Deere, 20 June 1902 (two letters under this date); G.W. Fuller to C. Deere, 20 June 1902; *Moline Dispatch*, 30 August 1901; ibid., 10 September 1901; *Farm Implement News*, 12 September 1901; *Moline Dispatch*, 4 October 1901.

8. Quotation on "exceptional stability" from Harold F. Williamson, *The Growth of the American Economy*, 2nd ed. (New York: Prentice-Hall, 1951), p. 413. For comprehensive coverage of this period, see Everett E. Edwards, "American Agriculture—The First 300 Years," *United States Department of Agriculture, Farmers in a Changing World: The Yearbook of Agriculture, 1940* (Washington: Government Printing Office, 1940), pp. 240 ff. See also Frederick Strauss and Louis H. Bean, *Gross Farm Income and Indices of Farm Production and Prices in the United States, 1869–1937* (Washington: U.S. Department of Agriculture, 1940); Edwin Frikey, *Economic Fluctuations in the United States* (Cambridge, Mass.: Harvard University Press, 1942).

9. For Charles C. Webber's dealer letters, all in Webber papers, DA, see Webber to Brookings Implement Company, Brookings, S.D., 21 February 1903; Webber to J.S. Bresnahan, Grafton, N.D., 14 November 1902; Webber to W.W. Sevright, Hutchinson, Mo., 21 February 1903; Webber to C. Deere, 1 April 1903; Webber to C.W. Mansur, 16 November 1904; Webber to T.A. Conlee, 16 November 1904. For C.C. Webber's views on the St. Louis branch, see Webber to C. Deere, 30 July 1902; ibid., 3 and 31 July 1903; on Dallas, see ibid., 9 August 1902; on Kansas City, see Webber to George F. Peek, 10 May 1904. For his views on Stephen Velie, Jr., see Webber to C. Deere, 23 August 1904; Webber to W.L. Velie, 25 February 1903; Webber to S.H. Velie, Jr., 25 February 1903; Webber to C. Deere, 28 May 1906.

10. For C.C. Webber's views on consolidation, see Webber to T.A. Murphy, 8 April 1902; for his views on the board, see Webber to S.H. Velie, Sr., 5 April 1902; and Webber to W.A. Rosenfield, 10 May 1902, Webber papers, DA. On the advisory committee, see C.C. Webber to C. Deere, 12 July and 12 August 1903; Deere & Company *Minutes*, 19 August 1903; C.C. Webber to Schiller Hosford, 9 November 1903; C.C. Webber to W.L. Velie, 11 November 1903, Webber papers, DA. On the St. Louis branch expansion, see advisory board *Minutes*, 12 January 1905; C.C. Webber to C. Deere, 2 March 1905; C.C. Webber to Deere & Company, 16 March 1905, Webber papers, DA.

11. The history of the first fifteen years of the International Harvester Company is documented in *Report of the Federal Trade Commission on the Causes of High Prices of Farm Implements, May 4, 1920* (Washington, D.C.: Government Printing Office, 1920), chap. 10; Helen M. Kramer, "Harvesters and High Finance: Formation of the International Harvester Company," *Business History Review* 38 (1964): 285. For discussion of the International Harvester Company's dominance on grain binders, see Ripley, *Trusts, Pools and Corporations*, pp. 324–355. The legal attacks on the company are discussed in McCormick, *Century of the Reaper*, chap. 10. Ripley, *Trusts, Pools and Corporations*, p. 326, is the authority quoted for the $43 million profit. The citation for the antitrust case is *U.S. v. International Harvester Co.*, U.S. District Court, 214 Fed. Rep. 987, 12 August 1914. The list of six tactics from the Deere-International Harvester interaction is documented in Ripley, *Trusts, Pools and Corporations*, p. 348. See Charles C. Webber to George G. Mill, 4 April 1903, and C.C. Webber to James Deering, 7 April 1903, Charles C. Webber Letter Books, DA; J. Deering to William Deering, 4 January 1896, *Letterpress*, p. 155, International Harvester Archives; Cyrus H. McCormick to George W. Perkins, 1 December 1902; IHA/M/Bx4/F4, pp. 3, 4, ibid. For Webber's concern about Joseph Dain's defection, see Webber to Dain, 8 October 1903, Webber papers, DA. For conflicting product lines within the company, see Webber to John Deere Plow Company, Portland, Ore., 13 February 1906; Webber to Alvah Mansur, 11 May 1905; Webber to Charles H. Deere, 3 October 1903. Webber to C. Deere, 21 and 22 November 1904, Webber papers, DA, discuss the Acme Harvester proposition. For Webber quotation on "hard canvass," see Webber to C. Deere, 25 March 1904. See also Webber to S.O. Porter (Acme Harvester Company), 23 December 1904. The discussions concerning travelers are in Webber to C.D. Velie, 13 April 1906; Webber to J.W. Anderson, 20 March 1906; Webber to C. Deere, 25 June 1906 and 5 February 1907; Webber to S.H. Velie, Jr., 18 July 1905. The "spending" quotations are from Webber to C. Deere, 28 March 1905; ibid., 10 November 1905; Deere to Butterworth, 11 September 1905, DA, 4169. For Charles Deere's death, see *Moline Dispatch*, 8 November 1907. George Vinton to C.C. Webber, 13 May 1908, DA, contains the "Campbell Island" quotation.

NOTES TO CHAPTER 7: EMERGENCE OF THE MODERN COMPANY

1. Quotations on Charles Deere and on "mail" are from Deere & Company *Minutes,* 26 November 1907. For Butterworth's "lack of experience," see Department of Labor, Bureau of Corporations, *Harvester Investigation,* Report 14, "The Deere Organization," R32897 (26 October 1900), P. 1.

2. George Mixter comments on factory conditions in G. Mixter to William Butterworth, 1 August 1923, DA, 25603. See quotations from Deere & Company *Superintendent's Report, Season 1902–03,* 9 July 1903, DA, 4142; C.C. Webber to C. Deere, 19 October 1903, Webber Letterbooks, DA; George Mixter, "Shop Organization," 1 July 1899, DA, 4169; G. Mixter to W. Butterworth, 15 September 1903; ibid., 4 December 1903; ibid., 7 January 1904; C.C. Webber to G. Mixter, 7 January 1904; ibid., 26 August 1904; ibid., 18 October 1906, Webber papers; W. Butterworth to G. Mixter, 14 April 1906 and reply of same date; G. Mixter to W. Butterworth, 16 January 1907. See also Corporate Record Book, Union Malleable Iron Company, 14 and 28 September 1888; ibid., 7 December 1888; ibid., 19 June 1894; ibid., 16 July 1895, DA. Relations with Union Malleable are documented in G. Mixter to W. Butterworth, 14 December 1905; ibid., 1 July 1906; ibid., 11 July 1906; ibid., 9 August 1906; ibid., 19 January 1907, DA, 4169; C.C. Webber to C.H. Pope, 11 July 1902, Webber papers, DA. Edith Sklovsky Covich, *Max* (Chicago: Stuart Brent, 1974), pp. 66–67, states that Max Sklovsky, one of the engineers working with George Mixter, felt that the latter "was *persona non grata* with Mr. Deere or Mr. Butterworth," and when he needed advice "made a quick trip to Minneapolis to see his uncle. . . ."

3. George Mixter's report on Russia was dated 14 July 1909, DA, 4142. The articles of incorporation of the John Deere Export Co. were dated 18 May 1908, DA, 1025; the articles of agreement between it and Deere & Company were dated 1 July 1908, DA, 9667. The Russian plow order was made in June 1910; see G. Mixter to William Butterworth, 25 June 1910, DA, 4142. See Federal Trade Commission, *Report of the Federal Trade Commission on the Causes of High Prices of Farm Implements* (1920), pp. 58–59, for a discussion of the Lubertzy Works.

4. For J.I. Case proposal, see Deere & Company *Minutes,* 13 July 1909; Burton Peek to William Butterworth, 13 December 1909; George Mixter and Burton Peek to W. Butterworth, 28 December 1909, DA, 103.

5. The International Harvester Company materials concerning amalgamation with Deere are in the former's archives: "Consolidation: Deere Plan 1909–1910," SHSW/MCC/2C/BX33/1HC; and 1 January 1913, BX 38.

6. For development of the "modern company" proposals, see Deere & Company *Minutes of Committee on Reorganization,* 6 January 1910–12 April 1911, DA, 10805, 10807, 10809, 12000–02, 19606, 28696, 28717–19, 28722. The Haskins and Sells analysis of the relation of the companies is in DA, 19606; for the pooling arrangement, see "Deere & Company Pooling Agreement Covering Common Stock Trust Certificates," 1 April 1911, and "Supplement to . . .," 30 May 1914, DA, 2321, 2322. See also Deere & Company *Minutes,* 11 May 1911. For documents relating to the Standard Implement Company and the American Implement Company, see " Complete Record of Meetings of Reorganization Committee," 28 January 1910–17 April 1911, DA, 10804. An ingenious device was used to preserve the name "Deere & Company" itself. First the corporation that had been Deere & Company since 1868 had its name changed legally to the Standard Implement Company. At the same time, a new "paper" company was established, the American Implement Company. The senior lawyer in the firm handling arrangements acted as president; two other lawyer colleagues were the other officers. On the appointed day (10 April 1911) Standard sold most of its assets and good will to American: its officers, acting in their capacity as directors, then changed the name of American to Deere & Company. For a day or so Deere & Company was legally operated by these three lawyers (the realities of management, of course, continuing unchanged under the Deere board members). The three convened an annual shareholders meeting, resolved that its directors be increased from three to seventeen, and formally resigned their officerships and directorships, and Deere & Company voted its regular set of officers and directors. Included was the same set of officers as before, and all of the old directors. There were additions to the latter—several other members of the company and some of the outsiders that had brought their companies into the Deere orbit. Now on the board was Charles Deere Velie, from the Minnesota branch house; C.W. Mansur, from the St. Louis branch house; Floyd R. Todd, from the old Kemp & Burpee organization; George W. Crampton, from Deere & Mansur; Ralph Lourie, a Deere & Mansur sales manager who had come to the parent company to be the manager of the John Deere Plow Company of Moline; and W.D. Wiman, Anna Deere Wiman's husband. Because not all of the property was transferred from the various organizations, the Standard Implement Company remained in existence to house that amount of property not deemed appropriate for the new company—some $700,000 worth of properties in Moline, Kansas City, Minneapolis, and Portland, Oregon. Standard continued as a legal entity for a number of years, with officers, directors, annual meetings, etc., but as an "on paper" holding company for the real estate. The assets of the various constituent companies were first audited by the respected national accounting firm, Haskins & Sells, and physical properties were taken at their true value, as determined by the appraisals, not at their book values. The audit also stated precisely the actual profits made by the entities over the previous five years (three years for the John Deere Plow Company of Winnipeg). New 6-percent cumulative preferred stock in the new company was to be issued to owners of the physical property and real estate; common stock was to be issued for earning capacity and good will in an amount equal to ten times the average annual earnings over 7 percent, as shown by the audit. Each of the constituent companies was to guarantee its accounts and bills receivable at par, less ordinary expenses of collection. Finally, after all of this was accomplished, if the total capital stock of the new company seemed to be overstated, "the same may be reduced by a horizontal reduction of both the Preferred and Common stock of the Holding Company."

7. For Dain history, see "Review of Events Concerning the Founding of the Dain Manufacturing Company, and a Brief Record of its Growth to Present Proportions," ca. 1910, DA, 642. See also DA, 25324–25. For discussions of the executive committee's role, see Floyd R. Todd to Executive Committee, 27 January 1915, DA, 25324. For the Syracuse Chilled Plow Company negotiations, see Deere & Company *Minutes*, 20 December 1910; *Moline Dispatch*, 13 April 1911; *Farm Implement News*, 30 March 1911; ibid., 13 April 1911. George Mixter to W. Butterworth, 1 August 1923, DA, 25603, contains the quotation on the Syracuse Chilled Plow Company negotiations. See also Deere & Company *Minutes*, 11 April 1911; ibid., 11 May 1911. For the Van Brunt Manufacturing Company history, see Allie E. Freeman and Walter R. Bussewitz, *History of Horicon* (Horicon, Wis.: privately printed, 1948); DA, 4155, 11131–33, 19769, 26648. Also helpful in the histories of the constituent companies are the "Reports on the Manufacturing Investment of Deere & Company," prepared each year by George Mixter and his associates, beginning 31 October 1914.

8. For analysis of the new executive committee, see G. Mixter to W. Butterworth, 5 October 1909, DA, 4169; Deere & Company *Minutes*, 4 January 1911. See W. Velie to Burton F. Peek, 6 January 1911; W. Velie to Executive Committee, 23 May 1911; Deere & Company *Minutes*, 1 June 1911. For Wharton appointments, see ibid., 11 May 1911; ibid., 6 June 1911; for central purchasing, see ibid., 29 May 1911; ibid., 19 July 1911; and ibid., 31 August 1911.

9. On the controversy concerning the harvester, see Deere & Company *Minutes*, 10 June 1912; ibid., 12 June 1912; and ibid., 13 June 1912; *Deere & Company Annual Report*, 1912; William Butterworth, "A Statement of the Deere Interests in Reference to the Future Policy of Deere & Company," ca. 10 July 1912, attached to letter of 12 July 1912, in Deere & Company *Minutes* of that date. See also W.L. Velie to Board, 29 May 1912; Deere & Company *Minutes*, 13 June 1912; ibid., 12 July 1912. Records of the meeting of 1 January 1913 at International Harvester are in the latter's archives, SHSW/MCC/2C/Bx 38/IHC:E.

10. The International Harvester antitrust case was first heard by the U.S. District Court for

Minnesota in 1914 (*U.S.* v. *International Harvester Co., et al.*, 214 Federal Reports 987); the consent decree, dated 11 July 1918, was between International Harvester and Attorney General Gregory. *Report of the Federal Trade Commission on the Causes of High Prices of Farm Implements* concluded that the dissolution suit had not reestablished competition and in 1923 the government reopened the case. This led to the definitive Supreme Court case in 1927 (*United States* v. *International Harvester Company*, 274 US 693), upholding the previous consent decree and thus denying the government's case for further relief. For further background on International Harvester's competitive practices, see Department of Commerce, Bureau of Corporations, *The International Harvester Co.* (Washington: Government Printing Office, 1913). See also Elvis Luverne Eckles, "The Development of Oligopoly in the Farm Equipment Industry" (Ph.D. diss., University of Illinois, 1953); Michael Conant, "Aspects of Monopoly and Price Policies in the Farm Machinery Industry Since 1902" (Ph.D. diss., University of Chicago, 1949). The three key antitrust cases were *Northern Securities Co.* v. *U.S.*, 193 U.S. 197; *U.S.* v. *American Tobacco Co.*, 221 U.S. 106; *Standard Oil Co. of New Jersey, et al.* v. *U.S.*, 221 U.S. 1. The reply to the Department of Justice in regard to Deere's testimony in the International Harvester antitrust case is found in the board meetings of 23 November 1911 and 12, 23, and 26 December 1911. The International Harvester request for information about Deere agent contracts is in Deere & Company *Minutes*, 3 October 1912. The William Butterworth testimony in the case was given on 23 November 1912 in Chicago, Illinois; see *Record*, vol. 2, pp. 52–62.

11. The Peek policy manual for branches was titled "For Branch House Managers" and was dated 4 December 1911. The board meeting quoted was that of 2 December 1911. For the branch managers' meeting of 28 February 1912, see G. Peek to W. Butterworth, 12 March 1912, DA, 26996. M.J. Healey to Minneapolis branch, DA, 10976. For quotation on use of automobiles, see Deere & Webber Co. *Minutes*, 27 March 1915, DA.

12. Barton W. Currie, *The Tractor and Its Influence Upon the Agricultural Implement Industry* (Philadelphia: The Curtis Publishing Company, 1916), pp. 14–15.

13. For the early efforts of individual tractor manufacturers, see Charles H. Wendel, *Encyclopedia of American Farm Tractors* (Sarasota, Fla.: Crestline Publishing Co., 1979); Roy B. Gray, *The Agricultural Tractor, 1855–1950* (St. Joseph, Mich.: American Society of Agricultural Engineers, 1954). *Farm Implement News* devoted its entire issue of 27 April 1916 to the tractor industry and included a detailed "Tractor Directory" as of that date. The Winnipeg trial results for the years 1908–12 are listed in Gray, *The Agricultural Tractor*, pp. 19–22. Deere's plow in the meet of 1909 is noted in *Farm Implement News*, 5 August 1909. The Burton Peek correspondence on the proposed purchase of the Gas Traction Company is in Deere & Company *Minutes*, 21 and 28 March 1912 and 14 May 1912. The Hart-Parr relationship is also discussed in the last meeting.

14. For the early sales of agricultural machinery abroad, see *Federal Trade Commission Report on the Agricultural Implement and Machinery Industry*, Part 1, House Doc. 702, 75th Congress, 3rd Session (Washington: Government Printing Office, 1938), pp. 52–61. The George Peek and Burton Peek resolutions in regard to the International Harvester Company are in Deere & Company *Minutes*, 22 June 1911.

15. The Velie resolution is in Deere & Company *Minutes*, 5 March 1912. The history of the Melvin tractor, as well as the later Dain and Sklovsky tractors and the single-row and two-row motor cultivators, is told in Theo Brown, *Deere & Company's Early Tractor Development* (Deere & Company, privately printed, 1953). The White, Weld & Company telegram is in Deere & Company *Minutes*, 9 March 1914; the Butterworth-Peek report on it is in Deere & Company *Minutes*, 18 March 1914. See also Deere & Company *Minutes*, 9, 11, and 17 March 1915; G. Mixter to W. Butterworth, 17 May 1915, DA, 4132.

16. Quotations from Deere & Company *Minutes*, 14 July 1913; ibid., 28 October 1913; ibid., 18 November 1913. For George Peek's views on the executive committee, see "Voting Trustees," 10 October 1913, DA, 4145; for Butterworth's response, see ibid., 3 March 1914. See also G. Mixter to George Peek, 31 December 1914, DA, 35611; W.L. Velie letter (individually sent to each board member) in Deere & Company *Minutes*, 13 February 1915;

T.F. Wharton to W.L. Velie, 14 January 1915, DA, 4146; Deere & Company *Minutes*, 13 February 1915. W. Butterworth to executive committee, 11 January 1915, DA, 4146; Deere & Company *Minutes*, 5 December 1914; ibid., 4–6 January 1915; C.C. Webber to W.L. Velie, 5 December 1914, in Deere & Company *Minutes*, 4 January 1915.

NOTES TO CHAPTER 8: WORLD WAR I AND ITS AFTERMATH

1. The inventory discrepancy is noted in "Report on the Manufacturing Investment of Deere & Company" (1917), Harvester Works, DA, 2205.

2. "Factory Managers Meeting, 1911–1912," DA, 37737–39. The ethnic survey of 1901 was reported in *Farm Implement News*, 5 December 1901. The first pension plan is described in "Pension Plan for the Employees of Deere & Company," 1 January 1908, DA, 2598; George Mixter analyzes the issue in G. Mixter to William Butterworth, 20 June 1907, DA, 4169. The Deere "House Building Operations" are described in the manufacturing reports of 1914–21, DA, 2735. See DA, 19555, for agreement between the company and the Deere estate concerning this housing.

3. For the Fort Smith strike, see G. Mixter's report to the board, Deere & Company *Minutes*, 14 December 1915; manufacturing reports of 1914–21, DA, 2735. The employee common stock plan is discussed in Deere & Company *Minutes*, 20 April 1911, ibid., 19 May 1911; ibid., 6, 13, 18, 19, and 25 July 1911; the modifications of 1914 are discussed in Deere & Company *Minutes*, 5 January 1914; ibid., 18 and 25 February 1914 (the latter containing the quoted passages). Key meetings on employee problems were held on 15 March and 11 September 1917; the meeting of 25 January 1918 completes the story. Todd describes Butterworth's adamancy in his letter to George Peek, 21 December 1917; George Peek's letter to C.D. Velie concerning M.J. Healey's salary is dated 1 January 1918 (both letters in George Peek Papers, University of Missouri). The Willard Van Brunt comment related to the time when his mother, Martha, widow of D.C. Van Brunt, died in 1916 and bequeathed $1,000 to each employee with twenty-five years or more of experience, $800 to those with twenty years or more; despite the fact that Willard felt this did not work well, he made a similar bequest to employees a month before he died in 1935—an enormous gift of some $291,000 to ninety-seven shop employees who had worked with him at the time of his retirement in 1918. No foreman or office employee was included in the will, however; despite threatened suits to contest the will, the shop-only distribution stood. Still, it was a magnificent gift in those Depression days, and Will Rogers wrote of it in the *Milwaukee Journal* of 15 May 1935: "In these days of everybody hollering about the government butting in their business or the labor unions trying to run it, there is plenty of cases in America like this one. An old gentleman, Mr. Van. Brunt who for ?? years ran a factory at Horicon, Wis., and never had one speck of labor trouble. He just gave 89 old time workers and six widows $3,000 apiece. If everybody was Van Brunts, there would be no need for anything. But there is men in business that don't belong in business anymore than the government does and that's why the government has to go in." See Theodore J. Erdman, *The Van Brunt Wood Carving and Family History* (privately printed, 1937), DA, 26649; Freeman and Bussewitz, *History of Horicon*; "Van Brunt Manufacturing Co." (June 1954), DA, 11133; *Farm Implement News*, 23 May 1935.

4. Burton Peek's letter on the Clayton Act is reprinted in Deere & Company *Minutes*, 2 November 1914. Frank Silloway's optimistic words on the provision in the International Harvester consent decree relating to single dealers in a given town are in Deere & Company *Minutes*, 9 April 1920. Floyd Todd's words to the FTC investigator are in Floyd Todd to W.W. Alexander (branch manager at Syracuse), 17 March 1915, DA, 4134.

5. The requirement that branches accept at least 75 percent of their estimates is discussed in Deere & Company *Minutes*, 9 May 1913, and ibid., 9 December 1913; for the revised scheduling plan, see ibid., 9 March 1914. For George Crampton's views, see ibid., 11 March 1914. For Floyd Todd's views on the Clayton Act, see F. Todd to Burton Peek, 13 February

1915, DA, 4146. The board resolutions are in Deere & Company *Minutes,* 1 May 1915, and ibid., 8 June 1915. George Peek's plan for reorganization was first discussed, and William Butterworth's opposition was expressed, in ibid., 15 December 1915. The proposal of George and Burton Peek, George Mixter, and Floyd Todd was presented on 12 February 1916, the enabling resolutions were passed on 22 November 1916 and 12 December 1916; the Union Malleable exception was discussed on 12 December 1916. The final reorganization plan was discussed in the meetings of 25 January 1917 and 28 February 1917, and was agreed to by the board in the latter. C.C. Webber's reservations were expressed in the meeting of 13 March 1917. The final branch-house percentage compensation over the Moline dealer's price was given for each branch in the meeting of 26 January 1918 (revised from preliminary figures adopted on 17 December 1917). Individual factory discounts from the Moline dealer's price were noted in the same meeting.

6. For the quotation on the "gas tractor," see Currie, *The Tractor,* p. 13. For Butterworth's opposition, see W. Butterworth to Burton Peek, 11 September 1916, Burton Peek Papers, DA; for Peek's reply, see B. Peek to W. Butterworth, 10 October 1916. The W.L. Velie letter is reproduced in full in Deere & Company *Minutes,* 25 January 1918.

7. See Wendel, *Encyclopedia of American Farm Tractors,* p. 270, for a description of the Velie tractor; it was also noted in *Farm Implement News,* 12 July 1917. The Velie Engineering Company competed with a Deere plow in the National Power Farming Demonstration at Salina, Kansas, on 29 July–3 August 1918; see *Farm Implement News,* 18 July 1918, and ibid., 8 August 1918. The Deere-Clark Motor Car Co. is described in DA, 6393, 22665, and 25551. The Frank Silloway report on the Waterloo Boy tractor is in Deere & Company *Minutes,* 12 March 1918. See also Frank Silloway to George Mixter, 3 May 1918, and C.D. Velie to William Butterworth, 30 March 1918, both in George Peek Papers, University of Missouri. See Gray, *The Agricultural Tractor,* p. 15. Wayne H. Worthington, "50 Years of Agricultural Tractor Development," Farm, Construction and Industrial Machinery meeting, Society of Automotive Engineers (September 12–15, 1966), states that Froelich "built the first gasoline tractor" and defines it as "the first to incorporate the essential elements of a tractor, viz: internal combustion engine, power train, clutch engaging and disengaging both, a reversing gear, manual steering gear and drawbar." For the early history of John Froelich and his tractor, see L.W. Witry, "Origin and History of the Waterloo Gasoline Traction Engine Company," 5 May 1930, DA, *Farm Implement News,* 8 December 1892, carried a lengthy article on Froelich's machine, heading the article: "This time it is a full grown practical traction." The early photographs of the Froelich tractor in operation in South Dakota are in the F. Hal Higgins Collection, University of California, Davis. A number of gasoline tractors were being built in the early 1890s; R.B. Gray considers the Charter Gas Engine Co. the first, in 1889; six of their machines were built and shipped to farms in the Northwest. For quotations on the Waterloo Boy, see Frank Silloway to G.W. Mixter, 3 May 1918, and C.D. Velie to William Butterworth, 30 March 1918, George Peek Papers.

8. For the Henry Ford quotation, see Reynold M. Wik, *Henry Ford and Grass-roots America* (Ann Arbor: University of Michigan Press, 1972), p. 88. For the Fordson tractor production statistics, see Allan Nevins and Frank Ernest Hill, *Ford: Decline and Rebirth, 1933–1962* (New York: Charles Scribner's Sons, 1962). See also A. Nevins and F.E. Hill, *Ford: Expansion and Challenge, 1915–1933* (New York: Charles Scribner's Sons, 1957); Colin Fraser, *Tractor Pioneer: The Life of Harry Ferguson* (Athens, Ohio: Ohio University Press, 1973), chaps. 6, 7. The Dineen-Brown visits to Dearborn are described in H.B. Dineen to George Peek, 30 March 1918, and ibid., 23 July 1918, George Peek Papers, University of Missouri; in "Report of Conference—F.R. Todd and Theo Brown with Henry Ford and C.E. Sorenson," 6 November 1919, DA, 46548; and "Theo Brown Diaries," Worcester Polytechnic Institute. For the Oliver dealer quotation, see Ford Archives, ACC 38, Box 167, Edison Institute, Dearborn, Mich.; for the Salina quotations, see "Theo Brown Diaries," 29 and 30 July 1918, and ibid., 2 August 1918. For the C.C. Webber quotation, see C.C. Webber to George Peek, 19 July 1918, George Peek Papers. Henry Ford was reported to be contemplating purchasing a controlling interest in Deere & Company in early 1919; see *Farm Implement News*, 13 March 1919.

9. For the demise of the executive committee, see Floyd Todd to G. Mixter, 27 May 1918; G. Mixter to F. Todd, 28 May 1918; G. Mixter to George Peek, 1 June 1918, George Peek Papers. The final change in the bylaws is discussed in Deere & Company *Minutes*, 10 September 1918; Burton Peek elaborates on this thinking regarding these changes in B. Peek to C.C. Webber, Floyd Todd, and Frank Silloway, 3 September 1918.

NOTES TO CHAPTER 9: POSTWAR LABOR STRIFE AND COMPETITION

1. For enunciation of the board's labor relations policy, see Deere & Company *Minutes*, 3 September 1918; see also ibid., 20 August 1918. Leon Clausen to the Rev. J.E. Johnson and L. Clausen to L.W. Witry (at the Waterloo Engine Company), DA, 11855. See also L.W. Witry to L. Clausen, DA, 11836. For strike clippings, see DA, 19864 and 19865. The International Harvester Company works councils are discussed in Robert Ozanne, *A Century of Labor Management Relations At McCormick and International Harvester* (Madison: University of Wisconsin Press, 1967), pp. 116–161. For the Thiel Detective Service Co. report of 16 August 1919, see DA, 11855. The citation for the Hitchman case is *Hitchman Coal and Coke Company* v. *Mitchell*, 245 U.S. 229 (1917); for the Danbury Hatters case, see *Loewe* v. *Lawler*, 208 U.S. 274 (1908). The arbitration award is reprinted in full in *Waterloo Courier*, 18 September 1919; *Waterloo Times-Tribune*, 17 September 1919, comments on "John Deere's 'stop watch' system."

2. For the Federal Trade Commission's position on the National Implement and Vehicle Association cost studies, see *Report by the Federal Trade Commission on the Causes of High Prices of Farm Implements*, pp. 299–307. See also E.W. McCullough to William Butterworth, 8 and 20 June 1918, and ibid., 23 July 1918, DA, 4127. For the quotation regarding the FTC's shoe and leather industry report, see *Farm Implement News*, 14 August 1919. See also the discussion in 1916 between E.W. McCullough and the FTC in the *Report . . . of High Prices*, p. 302. The FTC report (p. 131) elaborated on the slipshod methods used by a number of companies in the industry in ascertaining their costs: "A majority of the companies do not work up estimated costs each year for each implement made, but adjust their previous year's estimates by the anticipated rise or fall in the material and labor markets. In some instances . . . estimated costs were never worked up unless an officer of the company desired the information and then the costs were only compiled in respect to the particular machine in which that officer was interested. The explanation . . . was that the cost of a machine meant nothing to them as they were compelled to fix the price of their machine in conformity with the price fixed by their larger competitors. Another company stated, 'In our plants where a large variety of products are manufactured, the costs were not revised annually . . . the actual costs were figured on a few representative articles and a percentage of increase or decrease as compared with the previous costs was arrived at.' It was by the use of this percentage that the old estimated cost was adjusted. The company then went on to state, 'We have never made up complete costs at the close of the year; we have never kept any record of our costs year by year; and we have never made any effort to prove the correctness of our costs other than as above outlined.'" Exhibit 17 of the same report contains a speech by E.E. Parsonage on the standardization of farm wagons (pp. 274–281); see pp. 178–181 of the report for discussion of the industry refusal to sell to farmers' cooperatives. For quotations from the correspondence among the various farm equipment manufacturers, see *Report . . . of High Prices*, pp. 346–370. For Floyd Todd's testimony on wagon prices, see ibid., p. 470. For the quotation from the Bureau of Corporations study, see *Farm-Machinery Trade Associations* (Washington: Government Printing Office, 1915), p. 55. For quotation on the mounting of the FTC inquiry, see *Farm Implement News*, 16 May 1918; for paraphrase, see ibid., 7 October 1920. For the Lukens cartoons, see ibid., 3 and 24 April 1919; ibid., 24 June 1919; ibid., 23 September 1920; and ibid., 7 October 1920. For the McCullough quote, see ibid., 11 November 1920; for the quotation on profiteering, see ibid., 14 August 1919. See also W.H. Stackhouse to William Black, C.S. Brantingham, George N. Peek, Floyd R. Todd, and H.M. Walter, 2 December 1920, Archives, Farm and Industrial Equipment Institute, Chicago, Ill. See Burton Peek, *A Reply to the Report of the Federal Trade Commission on the Causes of High Prices of Farm Implements*, speech at 27th Annual Convention of National Implement and Vehicle Association, 22 October 1920, DA, 19391. For Federal Trade Commission Investigation of 1938, see *Report on the Agricultural Implement and Machinery Industry*, 75th Congress, 3rd Session, House Doc. 702 (1938).

3. For agricultural implications of the 1920–21 downturn, see National Industrial Conference Board, *The Agricultural Problem in the United States* (New York: Industrial Conference Board, Inc., 1926), chap. 2; U.S. Bureau of the Census, *Historical Statistics of the United States, Colonial Times to 1957* (Washington, D.C.: 1960) pp. 116–117. See United States Department of Agriculture, *Yearbook of Agriculture, 1930*, p. 892, for numbers of horses on farms in the 1920s. Regional patterns of wheat development are discussed in George H. Soule, *Prosperity Decade: From War to Depression, 1917–1929* (New York: Rinehart & Company, Inc., 1947), pp. 235–237. See National Implement and Vehicle Association, "Changes in Farm Implement Industry Since 1900" (20 July 1923), Archives, Farm and Industrial Equipment Institute. The contrast between the approaches used by Henry Ford and William Durant in the 1920–21 business downturn is described in Chandler, *Giant Enterprise*, pp. 71–92. Frank Silloway's optimistic report to the board is in Deere & Company *Minutes*, 9 April 1920; for William Butterworth's visit with the New York bankers, see ibid., 11 May 1920. For continuing Butterworth concern over inventory levels, see ibid., 27 May 1920; ibid., 29 June 1920; and ibid., 21 September 1920; for the Butterworth quotation, see ibid., 9 November 1920. The Frank Silloway-Floyd Todd-Leon Clausen report is reproduced in full in ibid., 22 March 1921; central purchasing is discussed in ibid., 28 March 1922. The Inventory Control, Manufacturing and Sales Program Committee (Silloway, Clausen, R.B. Lourie, and B.J. Kough) added additional detail to this policy in its report to the board, ibid., 23 May 1922. See George Crampton to William Butterworth, ca. 19 September 1922, DA, 19389.

4. For W.L. Velie's resignation, see Deere & Company *Minutes*, 3 May 1921. The Ford Motor Company price war is chronicled in Conant, "Aspects of Monopoly and Price Policies," pp. 63–66. For the Alexander Legge quotation, see Cyrus McCormick, *Century of the Reaper*, p. 197. The optimistic report to the Deere board on Waterloo Boy's prospects is in Deere & Company *Minutes*, 9 April 1920. For Leon Clausen's report on the new Model D, and the reassessment of the two-cylinder engine, see ibid., 25 April 1922; for George Crampton's critical letter, see ibid., 31 December 1923; for Clausen's reply, see ibid., 29 January 1924. The early development of the Model D is discussed in W.A. Young's memorandum of 3 August 1954, DA, 1127.

5. Deere & Company factory bulletin 136A, 18 December 1920; Boston News Bureau release of 31 December 1923, quoting a Deere & Company release; *Farm Implement News*, 13 December 1923; William Butterworth to Gov. Samuel R. McKelvie, 4 December 1922, DA, Scrapbook.

6. For George Peek's move to the Moline Plow Company, see Deere factory and branch bulletins, dated 20 August 1919. Leon Clausen's comments are in L. Clausen, "The Real Story of the Birth and Development of the So-Called Agricultural Support Program," (ca. 1961), DA, 24483. For Peek's quotations on the Moline Plan, see Moline Plow Company brochure dated 1 May 1922, DA, 2483. For quotation on branch houses, see *Farm Implement News*, 15 September 1923. See also, *Eastern Dealer*, 13 April 1922; *Utah Farmer*, 23 April 1921; DA, Scrapbook C; Deere branch bulletin 443, 3 May 1921. The U.S. Department of Agriculture report on the slackening farmers' cooperative movement is reported in *Farm Implement News*, 12 July 1923. See Kansas City branch bulletin of M.J. Healey; 30 July 1920; Moline branch bulletin of R.B. Lourie, 4 October 1921; St. Louis branch bulletin of W.W. Alexander, 14 October 1921; G. Peek to W.W. Alexander, 14 December 1921;

Minneapolis branch bulletin of C.C. Webber, 22 February 1922 (all copies in DA, Scrapbook C). For the advertisement of the Moline Plow Company, see *Farm Implement News*, 8 November 1923. For Peek's dismissal, see ibid., 13 September 1923; ibid., 31 July 1924; and ibid., 27 November 1924. Silloway's memorandum on the denigration of competitors was dated 15 January 1923; for the board resolution on the same subject, see Deere & Company *Minutes*, 30 January 1923. For the quotation on the patent infringement case with the Moline Plow Company, see ibid., 1 November 1921. The code of ethics developed by the National Farm Equipment Manufacturers in 1929 is reprinted in its entirety in branch-house bulletin 659, 2 April 1929. For George Peek's career after his employment at the Moline Plow Company, see Gilbert C. Fite, *George N. Peek and the Fight for Farm Parity* (Norman: University of Oklahoma Press, 1954); Robert D. Cuff, "A 'Dollar-a-Year Man' in Government: George N. Peek and the War Industries Board," *Business History Review* 41 (1967): 404. See George Peek and Hugh S. Johnson, *Equality for Agriculture* (Moline, Ill.: H.W. Harrington, 1922). For a brief review of agricultural legislation in the 1920s, see Chester C. Davis, "The Development of Agricultural Policy Since the End of the World War," in United States Department of Agriculture, *Yearbook of Agriculture, 1940*, pp. 297–326.

NOTES TO CHAPTER 10: INNOVATION AND NEW LEADERSHIP

1. William Butterworth to Charles Wiman, 28 January 1924, DA, 4153; ibid., 21 March 1923, Deere Scrapbook; Butterworth diary, 31 December 1924; Butterworth to Frank Silloway, Charles Wiman, and T.F. Wharton, 1 January 1925, Deere & Company *Minutes*, 3 November 1925. For the Floyd Todd quotation, see ibid., 27 July 1926; for the election of Charles Wiman as president of the company, see ibid., 30 October 1928; for the quotation on evening the production of tractors, see ibid., 28 July 1925; for contractors' bonus, see ibid., 31 July 1928. For William Butterworth's mention as a possible presidential candidate, see *Manufacturers News*, January 1928.

2. For nineteenth-century history of the combine, see Graeme Quick and Wesley Buchele, *The Grain Harvesters* (St. Joseph, Mich.: American Society of Agricultural Engineers, 1978), pp. 86–90. See also Lillian Church, *Partial History of the Development of Grain Harvesting Equipment*, United States Department of Agriculture, Agricultural Research Administration, Bureau of Plant Industry, Soils and Agricultural Engineering, Information Bulletin 72 (October 1947), pp. 45–52; F. Hal Higgins, "The Moore-Hascall Harvester Centennial Approaches," *Michigan History* 14 (1930): 415–437. For the soybean test on the Garwood farm in Stonington, Illinois, see *Farm Implement News*, 13 November 1924; ibid., 12 February 1925; ibid., 23 July 1925. The question of humid-condition constraints on the combine is discussed in ibid., 26 August 1926; ibid., 29 March 1928; and ibid., 18 April 1929. See also ibid., 28 July 1927; ibid., 31 March 1927.

3. The initial Charles Stone memorandum on the harvester project is dated 23 October 1947; see Deere & Company *Minutes*, 28 October 1924. For Stone's memorandum on plans for 1927, see ibid., 26 April 1927. See C.C. Webber to C. Stone, 1 October 1923, and ibid., 11 March 1925, DA, 34818, 34827. Original contact with the Caterpillar Tractor Company had been made in 1925; for rejection of the offer of $1,256,000 by the Deere board, see Deere & Company *Minutes*, 7 June 1927; for Silloway's report on the acquisition of the Wagner-Langemo plant, see ibid., 29 October 1929.

4. For the decline of the Fordson tractor, see Nevins and Hall, *Ford: Expansion and Challenge*; Wik, *Henry Ford and Grass-roots America*, p. 97; A.C. Seyforth, "Tractor History," International Harvester Company, DA, 13864 and 14238. The need for a "general purpose tractor" is discussed by F.A. Wirt in *Farm Implement News*, 17 April 1924; International Harvester's Farmall was introduced in ibid., 29 April 1926; see also ibid., 10 February 1927. For Theo Brown's involvement and McKahin's quotations, see "Theo Brown Diaries," 9 February 1926, and ibid., 2 June 1926, DA. For Wiman's quotations, see Deere & Company *Minutes*, 27 July 1929, ibid., 26 April 1927. For Veech's quotation on trials, see "Theo Brown Diaries," 7 July 1927. See also ibid., 5 July 1927; ibid., 12 and 20 October 1927. For Webber's quotations, see Deere & Company *Minutes*, 20 February 1928; ibid., 26 March 1928; and ibid., 24 April 1928. For Silloway's description of nomenclature, see branch-house bulletin 650, 20 June 1928. For Webber's "absolutely necessary" quotation, see Deere & Company *Minutes*, 30 October 1928; see also "Theo Brown Diaries," 23 October 1928. For the discussion of Model D horsepower, see Deere & Company *Minutes*, 29 January 1929; branch-house bulletin 665, 28 August 1929. Wayne H. Worthington, *50 Years of Agricultural Tractor Development* (Farm, Construction and Industrial Machinery Meeting, Society of Automotive Engineers, September 1966; republished by American Society of Agricultural Engineers: St. Joseph, Mich.). For Wiman's quotation on bad design, see his speech to the Deere Factory Managers Conference, 17 April 1953.

5. Theo Brown quotations are from "Theo Brown Diaries," 28 January 1925; ibid., 30 January 1928; ibid., 12 and 16 March 1928. For quotation on "bitter experience," see C. Wiman to C. Stone, 10 October 1925, DA. The first Power Farming Conference was held on 7–8 February 1929; the Wiman quotations are from its "Proceedings," DA, 663.

6. See Federal Trade Commission, *Report on the Agricultural Implement and Machinery Industry* (1938); Warren Wright Shearer, "Competition through Merger: An Economic Analysis of the Farm Machinery Industry" (Ph.D. diss., Harvard University, 1951), pp. 122–134. The mergers involving Massey-Harris, Allis-Chalmers, Case, Oliver, and Minneapolis Moline are also chronicled in Gray, *The Agricultural Tractor*, pp. 15–21.

7. See Frank Silloway's report on the single dealer per town, Deere & Company *Minutes*, 21 September 1920. International Harvester's retail stores are discussed in *Farm Implement News*, 3 August 1927, and ibid., 14 September 1927. For the quotation on Deere's policy regarding company-owned stores, see Federal Trade Commission, *Report on the Agricultural Implement and Machinery Industry* (1938), p. 120. R.B. Lourie's speech is reported in *Farm Implement News*, 5 December 1927. Retail price maintenance constraints by the federal and state governments are discussed in Ewald T. Grether, *Price Control Under Fair Trade Legislation* (New York: Oxford University Press, 1929), pp. 14–17; A.D. Neale, *The Antitrust Laws of the United States of America* (Cambridge, Eng.: Cambridge University Press, 1970), pp. 272–299. For the "list and discount" suggestion of the National Federation of Implement Dealers Association, see *Farm Implement News*, 5 November 1925; for the vote of the association, see ibid., 20 January 1927. The Frank Silloway memorandum on "retail prices" is dated 24 September 1928, branch bulletin 653. His bulletin 616 of 13 August 1926 discusses the legal parameters of the Federal Trade Commission rulings. See *Great Atlantic and Pacific Tea Company* v. *Cream of Wheat Company*, 224 Fed 556 (1915). For Deere's position in the National Malleable Castings Association case, see Butterworth's remarks in Deere & Company *Minutes*, 25 October 1921; ibid., 16 April 1923. For George Crampton's remarks, see ibid., 25 June 1922; ibid., 25 November 1924. For the C.C. Webber quotation, see ibid., 25 October 1921. See also George Crampton to Frank Silloway, 1 September 1923, DA, Scrapbook.

NOTES TO CHAPTER 11: DEPRESSION YEARS

1. Production statistics on tractors are reported annually by the Bureau of Census; a useful summary of the figures for the 1920s and '30s is in *Implement and Tractor*, 15 May 1948, pp. 60–61. For the quotations on Deere results, see *Chicago Tribune*, 30 January 1930; *Wall Street Journal*, 30 January 1930; *Christian Science Monitor*, 10 May 1930; Jas H. Oliphant & Co. release, 1 February 1930. The Andrew Mellon quotation is from *Commercial and Financial Chronicle*, 4 January 1930. The Deere stock dividend and stock split is noted in Deere & Company *Minutes*, 28 January 1930.

2. For F. Silloway's remarks, see branch bulletin 714, 9 February 1932. See M.J. Healey, "Rules and Instructions for the Guidance of our Collectors," Kansas City branch, 1 March 1935, DA, 28397.

3. The shipment of 1923 on behalf of American relief is noted in Deere & Company *Minutes*, 30 January 1923. For the quotations on Russian credit worthiness, see ibid., 30 October 1928; ibid, 29 July 1930; ibid., 4 August 1930; ibid., 20 and 27 January 1931. For the text of the children's story, written by Boris Kushner and dated 20 January 1931, see DA, 1125. For additional discussion of Russia's purchases of machinery in the 1929–32 period, see Wayne G. Broehl, Jr., *Precision Valley: The Machine Tool Companies of Springfield, Vt.* (New York: Prentice-Hall, 1959), pp. 128–135.

4. For Frank Silloway's remarks on Argentina, see Deere & Company *Minutes*, 31 July 1923; for the Agar, Cross representative's remarks, see ibid., 26 April 1932. The agreement to take back the Model D tractors is first mentioned in ibid., 24 April 1934 (where the number was to be only 500); for the final agreement to take back 900, see ibid., 5 and 31 July 1934. For Deere's purchase of one-half interest in Dunnell Edden, see ibid., 28 October 1930; the comptroller's report of 1932 elaborates on the details.

5. The early history of Deere in Canada is documented in C.A. Carter, "John Deere of Canada" (ca. January 1952), DA, 2300. For Wesbrook & Fairchild, see DA, 19357. For early branch-house history, see DA, 3570. For the Charles Stone memorandum on returning to Canada for manufacturing, see Deere & Company *Minutes*, 27 January 1931; for Charles Wiman's visit to the Canadian prime minister, see ibid., 31 March 1931. For United States-Canadian tariff relations for agricultural machinery, see William G. Phillips, *The Agricultural Implement Industry in Canada: A Study of Competition*, Canadian Studies in Economics, no. 7 (Toronto: University of Toronto Press, 1956), pp. 40–45, 54–61, 68–76.

6. Wage and salary cuts are documented in Deere & Company *Minutes*, 21 April 1931; ibid., 28 July 1931, ibid., 27 October 1931; ibid., 26 April 1932; and ibid., 28 July 1932. For the quotation on the Thrift Plan, see ibid., 29 July 1930; for the decision on suspension of vacations with pay, see ibid., 31 March 1932; for reduction of rents, see ibid., 21 June 1931. The Peoples Bank defalcation is described in ibid., 14 and 15 March 1931; ibid., 21 April 1931; ibid., 25 September 1931, ibid., 27 October 1931. See C.C. Webber to Charles Wiman, 28 and 31 March 1931; C. Wiman to C.C. Webber, 30 March 1931; see also the S.H. Velie, Jr., letter, 21 March 1931, the Willard Hosford letter, 20 March 1931, DA, 1105. For the early history of the bank, see Newton Bateman, ed., *Historical Encyclopedia of Illinois and History of Rock Island County*, vol. 1 (Chicago: Munsell Publishing Company, 1914), p. 749; for the final liquidation in 1941, see DA, 1107, 1108. See clipping from *Chicago Journal of Commerce*, 16 July 1931; for the Wharton and Wiman comments, see DA, 19389. For Wiman's quotation on employees, see Deere & Company *Minutes*, 25 October 1932. See "Deere Plow," *Fortune*, August 1936, p. 73; Max Sklovsky to Charles Wiman, 22 October 1946, DA, Overlook file and attached manuscript, "Excerpts from 'Creators of Deere & Company.'" Charles Wiman's speech to the factory and branch-house managers was at Dubuque, Iowa, on 11 October 1946.

7. See Theo Brown, "Theo Brown Diaries," 13 October 1931; ibid., 29 April 1932. The termination of the soil culture department and Dr. W.E. Taylor's retirement are discussed in William Butterworth to Maurice Block, 19 September 1931, DA. For the decision to terminate the department, see Deere & Company *Minutes*, 27 October 1931. The closing of the experimental farm is discussed in T.F. Wharton to W. Butterworth, 25 June 1931, DA. For Model A and Model B tractor development, see Deere & Company *Minutes*, 25 October 1932; ibid., 25 April 1933; ibid., 30 January 1934. Wayne Worthington, *50 Years of Agricultural Tractor Development*.

8. *Fortune*, August 1936, pp. 155, 159.

9. For index figures, see *Historical Statistics of the United States, Colonial Times to 1970, Bicentennial Edition*, part 1 (Washington, D.C.: 1975), p. 200. For the development of New Deal farm policy, see Edwin G. Nourse, Joseph S. Davis, and John D. Black, *Three Years of the Agricultural Adjustment Administration* (Washington, D.C.: The Brookings Institution, 1934). George Peek's role in the Agricultural Adjustment Administration is described in G. Peek (with Samuel Crowther), *Why Quit Our Own* (New York: D. Van Nostrand Company, Inc., 1936). Shearer, "Competition Through Merger," p. 276.

10. See George Wilson's report to the board in Deere & Company *Minutes*, 25 April 1933; for A.E. Head's notice to foremen and employees, see ibid., 31 July 1934; for the contribution to an unnamed fund by "a number of prominent businessmen in the Midwest States," see ibid., 5 October 1934. For the purchase of the Killefer Manufacturing Corporation, see ibid., 27 April 1937; ibid., 25 May 1937. Burton Peek's testimony in the National Labor Relations Board case involving Killefer and the Steel Workers Organizing Committee is dated 10 May 1938, DA, 10401; the NLRB cease and desist order is dated 10 August 1939, the bulletin board notice on it 5 September 1939, DA, 11482. *Fortune*, August 1936, p. 155.

11. The early design work on the Model A and Model B tractors by Henry Dreyfuss is documented in DA, 2330; see, especially, progress report 2, 24 November 1937. For the story relating to Argentine attitudes on wheel spokes, see H.M. Railsback to Henry Dreyfuss, 2 December 1940, DA, 19765.

12. For Frank Silloway's report on Caterpillar, see Deere & Company *Minutes*, 29 January 1935; see also branch bulletins 773, 774, and 781. Caterpillar's remarks on the Deere two-cylinder engine were first made in a sales meeting, November 1935, and then reprinted in branch bulletin 794. The memorandum of agreement between Caterpillar and Deere is dated 5 March 1935, DA, 19123. For changes in the California branch-house and dealer structure after the Caterpillar cooperative selling arrangement, see "Statement of Facts— Organization and Business of John Deere Plow Company of Moline," ca. 1943, files of Killefer—State of California case, DA. For R.B. Lourie's speech to Deere branch-house and Caterpillar sales representatives on 10 September 1947 in Davenport, Iowa, see DA, 44141. For Frank Silloway's report on California of 28 January 1941, see DA, 19268. See "Brief Outline of B.C. Keator's Service," 26 June 1953, DA, 25589.

NOTES TO CHAPTER 12: WORLD WAR II AND THE POSTWAR DECADE

1. For the history of the War Production Board's efforts in farm machinery, see War Production Board, Policy Analysis and Records Branch, *Farm Machinery and Equipment Policies of the War Production Board and Predecessor Agencies*, Report 13 (10 November 1944). For the threatened Department of Justice action, see ibid., p. 49; for the Ford-Ferguson proposal for building 100,000 lightweight tractors, see ibid., pp. 86–89. For the Massey-Harris harvest brigade, see Merrill Denison, *Harvest Triumphant: The Story of Massey-Harris* (Toronto: McClelland and Steward, 1948), pp. 314–317.

2. For Deere's efforts in World War II, see Neil McCullough Clark, "John Deere War History: An Account of Deere & Company's War Production During World War II," (Moline, 1944), DA. Establishment of the Iowa Transmission Company is discussed in Deere & Company *Minutes*, 29 April 1941. For the Cleveland Tractor Company contract, see ibid., 3 March 1942; for the merger proposal, see ibid., 28 April 1942; for its rejection, see ibid., 28 July 1942.

3. The controversy over the War Production Board statistics for civilian farm machinery production in early 1944 is discussed in War Production Board, *Farm Machinery and Equipment Policies*, pp. 145–153. See *Chicago Tribune*, 15 May 1944, for the quotation regarding "glamorized reports"; see also *Congressional Record*, 78th Congress, 2nd Session, vol. 90 (19 May 1940), p. 4,849; *San Francisco Commercial News*, 13 May 1944.

4. The Killefer case was decided by the National Labor Relations Board on 30 March 1940 (22 NLRB 484), the Dain case on 30 September 1939 (15 NLRB 779). The Farm Equipment Workers (FE) began as the Farm Equipment Division of the Steel Workers Organizing Committee (SWOC); in July 1938 the SWOC authorized the formation of the Farm Equipment Organizing Committee; this group in turn became the United Farm Equipment Workers of America, having been given a separate charter by the CIO as an international union with jurisdiction in the farm equipment industry. For the battle between the United Automobile Workers and the Farm Equipment Workers, see Irving Howe and B.J. Widick, *The UAW and Walter Reuther* (New York: Random House, 1949); Philip Taft, *Organized Labor in American History* (New York: Harper & Row, 1964) devotes chap. 47 to the left-wing issue in the CIO. The definitive book on International Harvester's labor relations is Robert Ozanne, *A Century of Labor-Management Relations at McCormick and International Harvester* (Madison: University of Wisconsin Press, 1967); see also R. Ozanne, *Wages in Practice and Theory: McCormick and International Harvester, 1860–1960* (Madison: University of Wisconsin Press, 1968). The most comprehensive study of labor relations in the agricultural machinery industry is Arlyn John Melcher, "Collective Bargaining in the Agricultural Implement Industry: The Impact of Company and Union Structure in Three Firms" (Ph.D. diss., University of Chicago, 1964). The quoted newspaper headline on the postponement of the Army-Navy E award is from *Davenport Democrat*, 20 June 1943. See L.A. Murphy to Capt. D.C. Hanrahan, 21 June 1943, DA, 19526. George Wilson's remarks are in Deere & Company *Minutes*, 31 October 1944.

5. For quotations on Charles C. Webber's death, see *Minneapolis Morning Tribune*, 22 February 1944; *Minneapolis Daily Times*, 22 February 1944. For the elections of Murphy, Kennedy, Curtis, and Gill, see Deere & Company *Minutes*, 9 and 13 June 1944; Blue Bulletin, 13 June 1944. For Cook's speech to the Factory Managers Meeting, 27–28 July 1944, see DA, 20157.

6. See Charles Wiman to Edward R. Stettinius, Jr., 30 November 1944, DA, Overlook folders. Wiman's suggestions on airplane and deep-freeze production are in Deere & Company *Minutes*, 26 October 1943.

7. Decentralization of purchasing is discussed in Deere & Company *Minutes*, 30 January 1945; branch bulletin 1022, 31 May 1945. See also Edmond Cook's remarks to purchasing agents, ca. April 1945, DA, 20158. For the Cook-Boyle correspondence, see DA, 27000. For the quotation on "unrest," see "Organization Lines and Policies, Memorandum by Edmond M. Cook of Discussions . . . in July 1945 and of Discussions . . . August through December, 1945," 21 December 1945, DA, 27000. Minutes of the Branch and Factory Managers Meeting of 12 December 1947 are in DA, 27000. The first Wiman bulletins on decentralization policy are 562 1/2-A (Factory) and 1085 1/2 (Branch), 12 December 1947; "John Deere Decentralization Policy," bulletins 570-A (Factory) and 1094 (Branch), 20 May 1948. See also "Purchasing Procedures," factory bulletin 564-A, 10 January 1948.

8. See "Report Prepared by Mr. Kennedy. . . ," Deere & Company *Minutes*, 26 October 1937. For the Dubuque plant proposal, see ibid., 30 January 1945; for Wiman's remark on restrictions on the board in earlier years, see ibid., 15 March 1945. The financing proposal is outlined in ibid., 22 March 1945; the Lindeman purchase is in ibid., 1 May 1945. The Tulsa, Oklahoma, proposal is in ibid., 28 January 1947 and 25 February 1947; the Ankeny, Iowa, purchase is in ibid., 19 June 1947. For Wiman's remarks on "business truisms," see ibid., 26 October 1948. For Cook's quotation on the "sense of failure," see Edmond Cook to C. Wiman, 1 April 1947; Wiman's reply is handwritten, on the same letter, DA, Overlook folders. See Max Sklovsky to C. Wiman, 9 April 1945; the Cook memorandum on Wiman's draft letter is dated 28 May 1945.

9. For Deere's attitude toward centralized bargaining, see the confidential memorandum to all factory managers from G.K. Wilson, 29 February 1943, DA, 19-3555. The joint request by locals of the UAW and Farm Equipment Workers to bargain as a group was made in their letter to G.K. Wilson, 20 September 1945; Wilson's rejection came in the meeting with this group on 28 September 1945, "1945 UAW Negotiations," DA, 19-3563. The strike settlements with the UAW locals are elaborated in the 4 November 1945 issues of the Quad City local papers; for the Waterloo settlement, see *Waterloo Courier*, 20 November 1945; for the Plow Works settlement, see the papers of 10 December 1945. The International Harvester negotiations in this period are detailed in Ozanne, *A Century of Labor-Management Relations*. For additional analysis of International Harvester's industrial relations, see U.S. Congress, Joint Committee on Labor-Management Relations, 80th Congress, 2nd session, Senate Report No. 986 (Washington: Government Printing Office, 1948), pp. 118–120; Benjamin M. and Sylvia K. Selekman and Stephen H. Fuller, *Problems in Labor Relations*, 1st ed. (New York: McGraw–Hill, 1950), pp. 606–623; Robert B. McKersie, "Structural Factors and Negotiations in the International Harvester Company," in Arnold R. Webber,

ed., *The Structure of Collective Bargaining; Problems and Perspectives: Proceedings of a Seminar Sponsored by Graduate School of Business, University of Chicago, and the McKinsey Foundation* (New York: Free Press of Glencoe, 1961), pp. 279–303. The Allis-Chalmers strike is described in Melcher, "Collective Bargaining in the Agricultural Implement Industry," pp. 131–139. Leadership battles in the national union of the UAW, and the attempted merger with the Farm Equipment Workers, are described in Howe and Widick, *The UAW and Walter Reuther,* chap 7. For the ouster of the left-wing unions from the CIO, see Philip Taft, *Organized Labor in American History,* chap. 47. See also Melcher, "Collective Bargaining in the Agricultural Implement Industry," pp. 173–174.

10. Wendell Berge, "The Antitrust Program and the Farmers," speech before the Wisconsin Farmers Union Convention, 25 October 1944. For Cook's concern about marketing implications, see his memorandum of 17 September 1948, DA, 2573; Deere & Company *Minutes,* 26 October 1948. For Cook's reference to "elephants," see his memorandum of 15 December 1948. See "Deere & Company Antitrust Suit, Examples of Favorable File Material, EMC Memorandum, 1-12-50 ," Deere & Company *Minutes,* 26 October 1948; branch-house bulletin 873, 8 November 1938; J.M. Burt to H.B. Pence, 25 October 1948, DA, "Dealer Severance" file, 22217. For Leon Clausen testimony on Deere in the J.I. Case Company case, see *United States District Court, District of Minnesota, United States* v. *J.I. Case Company,* trial testimonies, pp. 651–657, DA, 2834; Cook's comment on postponement is in his memorandum of 20 April 1950, DA, 2573. Quotations from the Nordbye decision are in *United States* v. *J.I. Case Company,* 101 F. Sup. 856, 866–867. See Warren Wright Shearer, "Competition Through Merger," pp. 368, 402.

11. For the early history of Rudolph D. Diesel's efforts, see Lyle Cummins, Jr., *Internal Fire* (Lake Oswego, Ore.: Carnot Press, 1976), chap. 14. Caterpillar Tractor and International Harvester diesels are discussed in Gray, *The Agricultural Tractor,* pp. 24 ff.; Wendel, *Encyclopedia of American Farm Tractors,* pp. 69, 159. See also Richard N. Coleman, "Milestones in the Application of Power to Agricultural Machines," in *An Historical Perspective of Farm Machinery* (Warrendale, Penn.: Society of Automotive Engineers, 1980), pp. 76–83. Descriptions of Deere model changes are from Will McCracken, *John Deere Tractors, 1918–1976* (Deere & Company, 1976). The standard-setting process for the PTO is discussed in T.H. Morrell, " The Development of Agricultural Equipment Power Take-Off Mechanism," in *An Historical Perspective of Farm Machinery.* For the development of the self-propelled combine, see Quick and Buchele, *The Grain Harvesters,* pp. 140–141; for the Deere combine corn head, see ibid., pp. 163–164; for the hillside combines, see ibid., chap. 19. See also DA, 1864, 22577, 26692.

12. International sales percentages are from W.R. Klingberg to Charles Wiman, 13 September 1949 and 28 July 1950; see also Deere & Company *Minutes,* 25 April 1950. See H.J. Heinz II to Maurice Block, 30 June 1950. There are no extant copies of John Good's report on Europe of June 1950; there are verbatim minutes of the board discussions of 5 and 8 July 1950, DA, 20034; see also C. Wiman's report in Deere & Company *Minutes,* 25 July 1950. For the possibility of manufacturing in Brazil, see ibid., 13 July 1950; for a verbatim record of the debate of the final proposal and a summary, see ibid., 1 February 1951, DA, 20034. The export department's views are expressed in W.F. Haberer's memorandum, ibid., 20 April 1951. A board "conference" was held 23 April 1951; verbatim minutes are extant in ibid., 23 April 1951. The final proposal is in ibid., 30 April 1951.

13. For the first board discussion of the fertilizer project, see Deere & Company *Minutes,* 10 October 1951; see also ibid., 30 October, 16 November, and 7 December 1951. See *Forbes,* 1 October 1952. C. Wiman's remarks on an independent company are in Deere & Company *Minutes,* 29 January 1952; on working capital, ibid., 29 April 1952. The final vote on the project is recorded in ibid., 16 May 1952.

14. Benjamin Keator to Charles Wiman, 26 May 1954; C. Wiman to B. Keator, 28 May 1954; B. Keator to C. Wiman, ca. 1 June 1954, DA, Overlook file. Max Sklovsky to Charles Wiman, 22 October 1946, and attached ms., "Excerpts from 'Creators of Deere & Company.' " Theo Brown, "Theo Brown's Diaries," 28 October 1952.

NOTES TO CHAPTER 13: RISE TO INDUSTRY LEADERSHIP

1. Benjamin Keator to Charles Wiman, reprinted in Deere & Company *Minutes*, 28 July 1953. B. Keator to William Hewitt, 25 May 1955, DA. The Booz, Allen & Hamilton study was authorized at the board meeting of 20 June 1955; Hewitt's remarks are from Deere & Company *Minutes*. Hewitt's planning document is undated; internal evidence places its completion by December 1955. For Hewitt's speech to the branch-house managers of 8 June 1955, see DA, 46332.

2. For Charles Stone's memorandum to the board on foreign manufacture, see Deere & Company *Minutes*, 4 June 1953; for the recommendation for a new chairman, see ibid., 28 July 1953; for Maurice Fraher's reports on the Brazil and Argentina surveys, see ibid., 27 October 1953, 27 April 1954, 27 July 1954, and 26 October 1954. For Lloyd Kennedy's report on Heinrich Lanz Mannheim A.G., see ibid., 21 December 1953.

3. The best source for the merger discussions between Harry Ferguson and the Massey-Harris group is Colin Fraser, *Harry Ferguson: Inventor and Pioneer* (London: John Murray, 1972). The internal problems of Massey-Harris-Ferguson are documented in Edward P. Neufeld, *A Global Corporation: A History of the International Development of Massey-Ferguson Limited* (Toronto: University of Toronto Press, 1969). The Deere merger negotiations are discussed in ibid., pp. 200–201. James S. Duncan's view of his severance from the company is in J.S. Duncan, *Not a One-Way Street: The Autobiography of James S. Duncan* (Toronto: Clarke, Irwin E. Company, 1971). See also Peter Cook, *Massey at the Brink: The Story of Canada's Greatest Multinational and Its Struggle to Survive* (Toronto: Collins Publishers, 1981). The Hewitt document in preparation for these meetings is in DA, Hewitt ms.

4. The confidential report of Booz, Allen & Hamilton, dated January 1956, is titled "Program for Implementation of the Proposed Plan of Organization," DA, 45515; the overall report, "Top Management Organization Survey," is dated 1 February 1956, DA, 45514; their "Survey of Executive Compensation" is dated January 1956, DA, 45510. See L.A. Murphy to William Hewitt, 30 September 1955, DA, Hewitt ms.; L.A. Rowland to W. Hewitt, 15 February 1956, DA, Hewitt ms. For Cook's explanation of his decision to take early retirement, see Deere & Company *Minutes*, 24 April 1956.

5. Establishment of the Venezuelan subsidiary, John Deere, C.A., was authorized by the board on 26 July 1955; for Curtis' report on Mexico and Fraher's report on Europe, see Deere & Company *Minutes*. For Harry Pence's report on the Monterrey manufacturing proposal, see ibid., 24 February 1956. For Pence's suggestion of Lanz, see ibid., 24 April 1956 and 29 June 1956. For the proposal for purchase of Lanz stock made by Hewitt, see ibid., 31 July 1956; for the appropriation for the Monterrey plant, see ibid., 30 October 1956; for Curtis' remarks on machine tools, see ibid., 30 August 1956. Reconstitution of the Lanz board and concerns about integrating Lanz and Deere dealers were discussed in ibid., 30 October 1956. For the quotation on the lack of sturdiness of Lanz tractors, see ibid., 15 April 1957.

6. For an "official" version of earlier Lanz history, see Paul Neubaur, *Heinrich Lanz, Fünfzig Jahre des Wirkens in Landwirtschaft und Industrie, 1859–1909* (Berlin: Paul Parey, ca. 1910). See also Wolfram Fischer, "Ein Jahrhundert der Landtechnik die Geschichte des Hauses Heinrich Lanz" (1958). There are two company-written histories of Lanz, also covering the recent period: *Geschichte der John Deere Werks Mannheim* (Mannheim, 1979), and *Lanz Und die Land Wirtschaft* (Mannheim, 1960).

7. For Hewitt's first contact about Eero Saarinen, see Henry Dreyfuss to W. Hewitt, 17 January 1956, DA, Hewitt papers. Hewitt first discussed an outside architect in Deere & Company *Minutes*, 15 June 1956. Saarinen's visit to Moline was in August 1956; for the board's authorization of him as architect, see ibid., 29 January 1957. For Burton Peek's buffalo story, see *Moline Dispatch*, 29 October 1953. Saarinen's fees are discussed in E. Saarinen to W. Hewitt, 17 September 1956, and W. Hewitt to E. Saarinen, 5 October 1956, DA, Hewitt papers. For Hewitt's statement of goals for the building, see W. Hewitt to E. Saarinen, 23 August 1957. The anonymous employee letter to Hewitt was dated 21 August

1957; Edmond Cook to Joseph W. Lucy (of the Saarinen organization), 19 April 1957.

8. Lester Larsen, *Farm Tractors, 1952–1975* (St. Joseph, Mich.: American Society of Agricultural Engineers, 1981), p. 2. "Generation Unto Generation," *Forbes,* 1 March 1961, pp. 19–22. The C.R. Carlson form letter explaining the decision to drop the two-cylinder tractor is dated 15 September 1960. For the quotation on "hicks," see *Forbes,* 1 April 1963.

9. For James Wormley's report on Lanz, see Deere & Company *Minutes,* 10 July 1957; for Lloyd Kennedy's report on complaint backlogs, see ibid., 29 October 1957 and 29 April 1958. Report on Deutz-Porsch and Fahr-Guildner relationships is in Curtis' report to the board, ibid., 12 June 1958. Force reduction at Lanz is discussed in W. Hewitt to J. Wormley, 25 March 1957, DA, Hewitt ms. 719. The "beer strike" is discussed in E. Curtis to W. Hewitt, 8 and 11 March 1960, DA, Hewitt ms. 705. See *Der Spiegel,* 16 March 1960; *Badische Volkszeitung,* 15 March 1960; *Bild,* 8 March 1960. For the Henry Dreyfuss involvement in Lanz, see W. Hewitt to H. Dreyfuss, 5 November 1957 and 8 July 1958 (the quotation about "Persian Carpets" from the latter), DA, Hewitt ms. 714. For Curtis' remarks on North American management becoming more involved in Lanz, see Deere & Company *Minutes,* 27 April 1959. The difficulties in changing German officers of Lanz is discussed in E. Curtis to W. Hewitt, 10 June 1960, DA, Hewitt ms. 705. For Harry Pence's report on the slowness of change and low morale at Lanz, see Deere & Company *Minutes,* 27 July 1959. For a discussion of the "semi-diesel" principle and the function of the glow bulb, see Cummins, *Internal Fire,* pp. 267, 277.

10. The Compagnie Continentale de Motoculture was established in November 1958 and was converted to a joint stock company on 22 September 1959 (see "Protocol," 21 July 1959). The Curtis-Lesser-Wilson negotiations are discussed in Deere & Company *Minutes,* 27 July 1959; for the major project proposed by Curtis, see ibid., 17 August 1959. For Deere's investment in the three companies, see ibid., 22 November 1960; for the additional purchase of Rousseau shares, see ibid., 26 June 1962. Difficulties at Rousseau are discussed in E. Curtis to W. Hewitt, 3 October 1961 and 24 March 1962, DA, Hewitt ms. 705.

11. Curtis' remark on Mexico as "a bright spot" is from Deere & Company *Minutes,* 27 January 1959. The local-content issue was first discussed in ibid., 25 April 1961. See also ibid., 30 October 1961. The David Brown and Nuffield proposals are discussed in ibid., 29 January 1962. Deere's proposal that was accepted is dated 30 September 1963; see ibid., 24 March and 27 April 1964. Local participation is discussed in ibid., 27 April and 27 July 1965; George French's quotation is from the latter. See E. Curtis to W. Hewitt, 13 August 1965, DA, Hewitt ms. 705. For a useful summary of the years 1958–66, see "John Deere de Mexico, S.A. de C.V.," Harvard Business School case 9-313-239 (1968). The overall problem facing American industry in regard to percentage of ownership is discussed in "Curbing Yanqui Cash: Mexico's New Regime Increases Restrictions on Foreign Companies," *Wall Street Journal,* 17 June 1965.

12. The best overall description of the Argentine government's decrees on local content is "Una Breve Reseña Sobre la Industria Nacional de Tractores," prepared for Dr. Victorino O. Rodríguez, Secretario del Consejo de la Industria de Tractores (ca. December 1967), DA, 79/17/10. The quotation on local content is from "Problems Pertaining to our Manufacturing Operations in Argentina," 30 June 1966, DA, 79/17/10.

13. The initial feasibility study for South Africa by R.C. Deffenbaugh, O.E. Hintz, and D.M. Willis was dated June 1962, DA, AN/80/43/2. For the proposal to purchase an interest in South African Cultivators (Proprietary) Limited, see Deere & Company *Minutes,* 1 July 1962; see ibid., 13 September 1962, for a modification of the appropriation. The land purchase in Nigel was authorized in ibid., 8 November 1962. For Curtis' remarks on race relations in the project proposal to the board, dated 24 July 1962, Hewitt ms. 705, see ibid., 1 July 1962, and E. Curtis to H.B. Pence and selected board members, 15 May 1963, DA, AN/80/43/2. See J.H. Goddard, "Report of South African Investigation of Cost and Availability of Materials . . ., (29 September 1964), DA. The joint proposal of Deere, Massey-Ferguson, and Ford was "Memorandum to the Board of Trade and Industry, South African Tractor Manufacture" (April 1963), DA. See also Pence memorandum, 8 February

1963; George T. French memorandum, 28 July 1964; "Proposal for the Manufacture of Tractors in the Republic of South Africa" (March 1968), DA. For the quotation on South African government efforts to increase self-sufficiency, see H.I. Martin to G. French, 16 January 1967, DA. The government "Enquiry into the Tractor Industry" was its Report 907 (1967). For Deere's relationships with Hitachi in Japan, see Deere & Company *Minutes*, 27 October 1970.

14. For the situation in West European agricultural machinery in this period, see Cynthia A. Breitenlohner, *Structural Changes in West European Agriculture, 1950–70*, U.S. Department of Agriculture, Foreign Agricultural Economic Report 114 (November 1975); *The Grain-Livestock Economy of the European Economic Community: A Historical Review, 1951–63*, U.S. Department of Agriculture, Foreign Agricultural Economic Report 31 (1966). See also Robert Trow-Smith, *Life from the Land: The Growth of Farming in Western Europe* (London: Longmans, Green & Co., Ltd., 1967); Henri Mendras, *The Vanishing Peasant: Innovation and Change in French Agriculture*, English trans. (Cambridge, Mass.: MIT Press, 1970). The meeting to consider the feasibility of a "worldwide" tractor was held on 9 September 1960, DA, AN/80/10, 4157. The McGuire-Peterson-Kiesling report, "Manufacturing Survey-Europe," is dated 15 December 1961; Curtis' charge to this group of 2 October 1961 is reprinted there.

15. See W. Hewitt to Henry Dreyfuss, 3 May 1965, DA, Hewitt ms., concerning the latter's role in the presentation of the key to Hewitt. Glover's resignation is discussed in D.C. Glover to W. Hewitt, 8 October 1958, DA, Hewitt ms. An excellent discussion of the consolidation of the Wagon Works is in K.W. Anderson to Curtis L. Oheim, 9 August 1956, DA, Hewitt ms. Hewitt's remarks on the reorganization of the international operations in 1963 is in bulletin B-103, 5 February 1963. The Frank Silloway quotation is from DA, 20165. See Frank McGuire to W. Hewitt, 28 January 1964, DA, Hewitt ms. 707; C.R. Carlson to W. Hewitt, 20 April 1964, DA, Hewitt ms. 750.

NOTES TO CHAPTER 14: OBSTACLES ABROAD

1. See Frank McGuire, "Proposal for Qualifying Deere & Company to do Business in Germany," 25 April 1967, DA, AN 80/43/5. The Booz, Allen & Hamilton "Top Organization Study" is in five separate reports: 11 May 1966 (DA, 39247); 27 June 1966 (DA, 39248); 6 September 1966 (DA, 45517); 24 October 1966 (DA, 45518); 4 November 1966 (DA, 39250). Hewitt's remarks on decentralization are in Deere & Company *Minutes*, 31 January 1967. For the analysis of comparative dealer terms in Germany, see Deutz memorandum, "Sales Terms Without Discounts," 27 January 1966, in E. Curtis to C.M. Peterson, 1 June 1966, DA, AN 80/4. For discussions of "under-the-table" practices, see A. Earl Lee to E. Curtis, 24 May 1966, DA. See *Mannheimer Morgen* and *Frankfurter Allgemeine Zeitung* (15 June 1967), and the release of the German Press Agency, Vereinigte Wirtschaftsdienste, for responses to the shareholders' meeting of 14 June 1967. See *Die Zeit*, 2 May 1969, for the quotation concerning "lame deer." See also *Land Technik* 13 (July 1967). McGuire's six alternatives for the German operation are outlined in F. McGuire to W. Hewitt, 22 October 1970, DA, Hewitt ms. 707. The Deutz negotiations are collated in Hewitt ms. 706 and 719 and in DA, AN 80/4. McGuire's remarks on the possible merger are in F. McGuire to W. Hewitt *et al.*, 4 August 1970, DA, Hewitt ms. 706. Comparative information on Deutz and prospects in the marketplace for 1971 are analyzed by Walter Vogel, 7 December 1970, DA, AN 80/4. Positions of the two partners are best seen in the unsigned "Minutes—Deere-Deutz Discussions," 29 October 1970, DA, 719, and Deere & Company *Minutes*, 10 December 1970, Walter Vogel acting as secretary, DA, AN 80/4. McGuire's views on ownership are in his handwritten memorandum to Hewitt and Curtis, ca. December 1970, DA, 719. For McGuire's notification of the impending Fiat negotiations, see F. McGuire to K.-H. Sonne, 18 May 1971; see also Sonne to McGuire, 26 May 1971. Sonne's quotation is from H.J. Schubert to Curtis, 17 August 1971, DA, AN 80/4.

2. For the first formal memorandum on the Fiat project, see Neel Hall to R.W. Boeke, "Notes on a Visit to Fiat, December 15–18, 1970," ca. 20 December 1970, DA, George French ms. See Curtis' memorandum to key personnel on the legal aspects of trading stock, 13 January 1971, DA; his remarks on four-wheel drive capability are in E. Curtis to W. Hewitt, 8 February 1971, DA, Hewitt ms. 706. The involvement of Henry Dreyfuss is discussed in R.J. Gerstenberger to G. French, 22 April 1971, DA. Market share statistics on the two companies are from Joseph Dain to W. Hewitt, 3 May 1971, DA, Hewitt ms., AN 81/37. See Patrick Neville, "The Prince," *Car and Driver*, February 1971; *Time*, 17 January 1969. Hewitt's first meeting with Giovanni Agnelli is briefly documented in DA, Hewitt ms., AN 81/37. The marketing, manufacturing, and finance task force reports were completed in March and April 1971, DA, Hewitt ms. The "Heads of Agreement" is discussed in Deere & Company *Minutes*, 27 April and 17 May 1971 (the full agreement reprinted in the latter). For the D.H. Glover and George French quotations, see ibid.; for press reactions to the "Heads" proposal, see unsigned memorandum, 22 June 1971, DA, Hewitt ms. AN 81/37. For negotiations leading to the final proposal for the "Agreement for Closing" and a Fiat proposal forwarded on 20 December 1971, see DA, Hewitt ms., AN 81/37. George French's misgivings about the project are enumerated in G. French to W. Hewitt, 7 January 1972. Final discussions of the project are in Deere & Company *Minutes*, 11 and 12 January 1972; the press release announcing the termination is dated 19 January 1972. For additional material on the Fiat project, see DA, French ms., AN 80/43; DA, Maguire ms., AN 80/43; DA, Hall ms., AN 80/14, 2176. See *Wall Street Journal*, 29 December 1971; William J. Tagtmeier's report and Hewitt's public reply to shareholders are reprinted in Deere & Company *Minutes*, 13 January 1972. Neel Hall's remarks on competitor dealer raiding are in N. Hall to W. Hewitt, 18 February 1972. See *Forbes*, 1 December 1971. DA, Hewitt ms. 727. See also *Le Figaro*, 20 September 1972. Curtis' remarks on the proposed joint venture with Fiat in 1973 are in E. Curtis to Bruno Beccaria, vice general director of Fiat, 24 July 1973, DA, AN 80/4.

3. For more recent history of Deere's Mexican operation, see Harvard Business School, "John Deere, S.A. (Mexico)," case 4-580-043 (November 1979). The issue of Mexicanization is covered in DA, AN 80/54/2.

4. Tax effects of the Argentine sale are discussed in Deere & Company Annual Report, 1981. See R. Hanson to J.A. Martinez de Hoz, 19 May 1980. The termination of the Argentine subsidiary was voted in the board meeting of 29 July 1980; the sale of Cindelmet was authorized at the meeting of 20 November 1980.

5. For an excellent analysis of the short-lived Venezuelan tractor factory, see Joseph A. Mann, Jr., "Fanatracto: Plowed Under," *Business Venezuela*, November-December 1980.

6. For the proposal for Iran, see Deere & Company *Minutes*, 9 July and 11 October 1976; ibid., 23 February 1977. For the original contact with Iran, see ibid., 30 January 1968; for the project proposal, see ibid., 13 May and 16, 24, and 30 July 1968. The reduction in Deere's ownership is discussed in ibid., 30 January 1973; the impairment of capital in ibid., 9 October 1974; the additional investment of Deere in ibid., 25 February 1976, 19 May 1976, and 17 February 1977; the shift to components in ibid., 25 July 1979. For the early history of the operation in Turkey, see ibid., 17 June 1966 and 5 May 1971. For the loan and swap arrangements with Cumitas, see ibid., 6 July and 26 September 1972. For additional capital investment in the company, see ibid., 12 September 1973 and 9 October 1975. For the tractor manufacturing proposal, see ibid., 6 July 1977; for the sale of Deere shares, see ibid., 3 May 1979.

7. The Brazilian tractor joint-venture proposal is first discussed in Deere & Company *Minutes*, 27 July 1976; the final project is described in David H. Stowe, Jr., to R.A. Hanson and L.N. Hall, 28 November 1977, DA, Hewitt ms. 732. The joint venture is authorized in Deere & Company *Minutes*, 1 December 1977. See also ibid., 14 and 25 July 1978. For the purchase of equity in Chamberlain Holdings Ltd. authorized by the board, see ibid., 18 August 1970; as the purchases were to be made over a six-year period, the amount authorized was specified as a range of $2.2 to $3.4 million. For a discussion of the earlier history of Chamberlain, see J.K. Horwood's remarks in "Dialogue for the Eighties—Presentation to Institutional Investors and Financial Analysts," 21 November 1980, Chamberlain Holdings Ltd.; for the quotation from Peter Griffith's report, see ibid.

8. For the evolving situation in the United States in regard to U.S. business performance in South Africa, see E. Curtis to F. McGuire, 14 October 1971; the wage comparisons in 1971 are from Frank M. Dickey's trip report, 18 November–10 December 1971. McGuire's remarks on "European work" are from F. McGuire to W. Hewitt, E. Curtis, and R.A. Hanson, 23 April 1973. Moline's concern about the application of worldwide employee relations standards is in R. Barry Cronin to Fred N. Gilchrist, 18 October 1974; the managing director's reply is in F.N. Gilchrist to R.B. Cronin, 24 September 1974. See "Summary Report of Deere & Company in South Africa," 30 April 1974, DA, Hewitt ms. 708, and the updated version, "Deere & Company Policy Statement on Employment Practices in South Africa," 4 February 1977, DA, Hewitt ms. 729. There is extensive documentation concerning the "Sullivan Principles" and related efforts in monitoring by the Investor Responsibility Research Center; see particularly DA, Hewitt ms. 729. The Investor Responsibility Research Center report on Deere is dated May 1981; it discusses the workers council, the company's training programs, and its wage and benefit systems. The "white employee reorientation program" is discussed in Gustav A. Pohl to Walter Vogel, 17 April 1979; the issue of giving schoolbooks to Deere employees is in R.L.Anderson to L.N. Hall and R.W. Weeks, 5 September 1979. A succinct description of the township of Duduza can be found in a memorandum of Harry G. Hoyt, Jr., 9 June 1977. The literature on U.S. corporate involvement in South Africa is voluminous; see, for example, Desaix Myers, III, *Business and Labor in South Africa* (Washington: Investor Responsibility Research Center, Inc., May 1979) and *U.S. Business in South Africa: The Economic, Political and Moral Issues* (Bloomington: Indiana University Press, 1980).

9. For Nikita Khrushchev's visit to Deere's Des Moines factory, see *Wall Street Journal*, 23 September 1959. For Khrushchev's quotation from *Izvestia*, see "Vodka and Caviar," privately printed ms., ca. 24 September 1959, DA, Hewitt ms. 714. Comparative tractor statistics are from Earl M. Rubenking, "The Soviet Tractor Industry: Progress and Problems," in Joint Economic Committee, *Soviet Economy in a New Perspective*, 94th Congress, 2nd Session (14 October 1976). For the visit of a Deere delegation to Moscow in 1972, see Deere & Company *Minutes*, 31 October 1972; see also DA, Hewitt ms. 719. The company joined the U.S.-Soviet Trade and Economic Council in 1974. The licensing arrangement for the cotton harvesting technology is discussed in Deere & Company *Minutes*, 9 October 1977 and 8 March 1978; for the tractor licensing, see ibid., 16 May, 5 September, and 20 December 1979 and 22 October 1980. The Russian tractor is discussed in Robert F. Miller, *One Hundred Thousand Tractors: The MTS and the Development of Controls in Soviet Agriculture* (Cambridge, Mass.: Harvard University Press, 1970); Lazar Volin, *A Century of Russian Agriculture: From Alexander II to Khrushchev* (Cambridge, Mass.: Harvard University Press, 1970).

10. For documentation of the early National Council for United States-China Trade, see DA, Hewitt, ms. 716, 727, 730. The formation of the council was widely reported in the press; see, for example, *Business Week*, 31 March 1973. See Henry Kissinger to Donald Burnham, 27 October 1973, DA, Hewitt ms. 727. For a discussion of dilemmas facing the council in its transition period, see Working Paper No. 2, 11 August 1975, DA. For an overall discussion of the development of agricultural mechanization policies in the Mao Zedong period of the People's Republic of China, see Bernard Stavis, *The Politics of Agricultural Mechanization in China* (Ithaca: Cornell University Press, 1978). See *Guangming Ribao*, 29 July 1979; see also "A Test-Case of Farm Mechanization," *China Reconstructs*, December 1979. For the quotations on repairs, see G.R. White to R.A. Thompson, 31 May 1980. For the quotation on the Anhui tractor factory, see *New York Times*, 10 April 1983. For the telegram from the Chinese, dated 23 May 1981, see DA, Hall ms.

NOTES TO CHAPTER 15: CHALLENGES OF THE 1980S

1. For United States agriculture in the 1970s, see J.B. Penn, "Economic Developments in U.S. Agriculture During the 1970s," in D. Gale Johnson, ed., *Food and Agricultural Policy for the 1980s* (Washington: American Enterprise Institute for Public Policy Research, 1981). Recent world population trends are discussed in Rafael M. Salas, *The State of World Population, 1982* (New York: United Nations Fund for Population Activities, June 1982). Negative factors in agricultural productivity are discussed in United States Department of Agriculture, *Farmline*, June 1981; for changes in farm size and structure, see William Lin, George Coffman, and J.B. Penn, *U.S. Farm Numbers, Sizes, and Related Structural Dimensions: Projections to the Year 2000*, Technical Bulletin 1625 (Washington: Department of Agriculture, Economics, Statistics, and Cooperatives Service, July 1980); Luther Tweeten, "Prospective Changes in U.S. Agricultural Structure," in Johnson, ed., *Food and Agricultural Policy for the 1980s*. For the moldboard plow controversy of 1943, see Edward H. Faulkner, *Plowman's Folly* (Norman: University of Oklahoma Press, 1943). The conservation tillage development is discussed in United States Department of Agriculture, Office of Planning and Evaluation, *Minimum Tillage: A Preliminary Technology Assessment* (Washington: Government Printing Office, 1975); Glover B. Triplett, Jr., and David M. Van Doren, Jr., "Agriculture Without Tillage," *Scientific American*, January 1977; Ronald E. Phillips *et al.*, "No-Tillage Agriculture," *Science*, 6 June 1980. For a review of soil erosion problems, see Lester R. Brown, "World Population Growth, Soil Erosion, and Food Security," *Science*, 27 November 1981. Agronomic aspects are discussed in S.H. Phillips and H.M. Young, Jr., *No-Tillage Farming* (Milwaukee: Reiman Associates, 1973). The issue of on-farm energy use compared to food energy produced is analyzed in David Pimental *et al.*, "Food Production and the Energy Crisis," *Science*, 2 November 1973, pp. 443–448; John S. Steinhart and Carol E. Steinhart, "Energy Use in the U.S. Food System," *Science*, 19 April 1974, pp. 307–315.

2. For an analysis of Massey-Ferguson's problems, see Peter Cook, *Massey at the Brink*, pp. 245–273. See also Harvard Business School, "Massey-Ferguson, Ltd.," 4-582-082 (1982). References to International Harvester's travails are extensive; a particularly good summary is "International Harvester's Last Chance," *Fortune*, 19 April 1982. See also "Harvester's Bitter Harvest," *Dun's Business Month*, January 1982; "International Harvester: Can it Survive When the Banks Move in?" *Business Week*, 22 June 1981. White Motor Corporation's difficulties are discussed in "What the Banks Did to White Motor," *Business Week*, 22 June 1981; the sale of its United States operations to the TIC Investment Corp. is reported in *Wall Street Journal*, 21 November 1980; the sale of its Canadian operations to TIC is discussed in *Toronto Globe & Mail*, 6 May 1982.

3. For the industrial equipment division analysis, see "Strategic Plan Update, 1983–1987," March 1982, DA; the Boston consulting group's study is discussed on V: 10–14. See also Brian R. Alm, "A History of the John Deere Industrial Equipment Division," 1982. For consumer products division analyses, see "Strategic Plans, 1983–1987," 26 March 1982, DA. The quotation on the "rich getting richer" is from Eli S. Lustgarten, "Farm Equipment Industry," *The Wall Street Transcript*, 1 February 1982.

4. For Deere's recognition of the "large-farm" trend, see *New York Times*, 22 August 1982. For an analysis of the issue, see Luther Tweeten, "Prospective Changes in U.S. Agricultural Structure," in Johnson, *Food and Agricultural Policy for the 1980s*, pp. 115–116. Some of the inconsistencies of the "Jeffersonian ideal" are elaborated on in William Flinn and Frederick Buttel, "Sociological Aspects of Farm Size," *American Journal of Agricultural Economics* 62 (1980): 946. For "most efficient" farm usage, see Thomas A. Miller, Gordon E. Rodewald, and Robert G. McElroy, *Economies of Size in U.S. Field Crop Farming*, U.S. Department of Agriculture, Agricultural Economic Report 472 (July 1981). Further analysis of farm size is in Harald R. Jensen, Thomas C. Hatch, and David H. Harrington, *Economic Well-Being of Farms: Third Annual Report to Congress on the Status of Family Farms*, U.S. Department of Agriculture, Agricultural Economic Report 469 (July 1981); see also *New York Times*,

2 March 1982. The Deere memorandum on the $40,000-449,000 farm sales group in Roy Harrington, "Farm Equipment Markets Versus Farm Cash Receipts," 18 June 1982, DA.

5. The two Yanmar organizations are described in H. Peter Keller to H.W. Becherer, 25 May 1976, DA, L.N. Hall ms.; the Yanmar agricultural tractor line is analyzed in T.J. Wilkinson to L.N. Hall, 30 July 1976, DA, L.N. Hall ms. An analysis of Deere's XR80 experimental tractor is in R.W. Boeke, "Memo-Planning for Yanmar Visit, June, 1976," 12 May 1976, DA, L.N. Hall ms. For doubts about the profitability of the XR80, see Robert A. Hanson to L.N. Hall, 25 June 1976, DA, L.N. Hall ms.; doubts on the Yanmar tractor's adaptability to Europe are in Walter Vogel to L.N. Hall, 14 July 1976. The joint venture company is described in R.A. Hanson to Susumu Nitta, of Yanmar Diesel, 23 June 1976; the proposal was authorized by the Deere board in its meeting of 11 May 1977. Discussions about the overlap between Yanmar's Model 1250 and Deere's Model 2040 are analyzed in Heinz Laier to L.N. Hall, 29 October 1979, and L.N. Hall to R.W. Boeke, W. Vogel, and B.C. Bartlett, 13 July 1979. For quotation on the Japanese relation to North American agricultural machinery companies, see *Wall Street Journal*, 25 July 1980. For discussion about Yanmar's move into larger models, see H.W. Becherer to L.N. Hall, 12 June and 21 September 1981. Yanmar's Asian sales are discussed in Christopher M. Cowan to H.W. Becherer, 1 February 1978, and in H.W. Becherer to L.N. Hall, 28 April 1978, 4 and 5 May 1978, and 18 October 1970; pricing issues are discussed in H.W. Becherer to L.N. Hall, 6 March 1981.

6. For issues of longer-term, worldwide tractor strategic planning, see R.W. Boeke to L.N. Hall, 30 April 1980; Thomas A. Gildehaus to R.A. Hanson, 2 September 1980; and M.C. Roetvold to B.C. Bartlett (with attached notes of Eugene L. Shotanus), 9 March 1981, DA, Hall ms.

7. For Deere's philosophy of research, see F. McGuire to W. Hewitt, 27 April 1964, DA, Hewitt ms. The redefinition of the research division is described in bulletin B113, the appointment of E.C. Lindvall in B304; the change of name to "technical center" in B290. See the K.W. Anderson memorandum to Lindvall, "Review of Research and Development Activities in Deere & Company General," 17 February 1970; Lindvall's report to Hewitt is dated 13 May 1970, DA, Hewitt ms. 706. The quotations concerning the product engineering council and the product engineering technical committee are from bulletin B338, 28 August 1970. See Lindvall's memorandum to Hewitt and Curtis proposing the committee, 11 June 1970, DA, Hewitt ms. 706.

8. For Robert J. Carlson's remarks on the OEM pump, see R.J. Carlson to W. Hewitt, 12 February 1974; see also Gordon Millar to Joseph Dain, 7 April 1977. The $175 million estimate for the development and relocation of the 300 series engine is in E.R. Curtis to W. Hewitt, 29 March 1979; G. Millar to A.B. Lundahl, 13 February 1974.

9. See Delno W. Brown to William Hewitt, 14 September 1973, DA, Hewitt ms. 706; Gordon H. Millar to Robert A. Hanson, 23 June 1978. The task force report of 1982 is in "Interim Report—Global Strategic Tractor Plan Task Force," 7 May 1982.

10. For the quotation on the "Japanese express train," see "Manufacturing Strategy Conference," vol. 1 (December 1980), p. VII-20. Deere's group technology system is described in "John Deere Group Technology System and Worldwide Information System for Engineering: A Comparative Overview" (August 1981). See also "Implementing CAD CAM Technology in Industry," a speech by James F. Lardner before the Autofact III Conference & Exposition, 9-12 November 1981; "The Computer and John Deere," *American Machinist*, June 1982. Lardner's quotation is from his speech at the Product Engineers' Meeting, 20-21 April 1981. For an excellent description of the "Kanban" system, see Y. Sugimori *et al.*, "Toyota Production System and Kanban System—Materialization of Just-in-Time and Respect-for-Human System," 4th International Conference on Production Research (Tokyo: February 1981). For the quotation comparing Japanese and United States automobile inventory totals, see J. McElroy, "Making Just-In-Time Production Pay Off," *Chilton's Automotive Industries*, February 1982. Similar figures are reported in "Here Comes Kanban," *Ward's Auto World*, June 1982. For Japanese views of inventory as "cover up," see "Industrial Equipment Division Strategic Plan Update, 1983–87," March 1982, DA, V-11.

See also " 'Just in Time' at the Tractor Works," *Materials Handling Engineering*, June 1982. For the quotation on robotics, see "Manufacturing Technology Profile," vol. 1, "Industrial Robots," Manufacturing Engineering Department, Deere & Company (August 1981). For the quotations from UAW committeeman and the local union president, see *Chicago Tribune*, 22 May 1982. For the quotation on Japanese culture, see "Industrial Equipment Division Strategic Plan Update," pp. V–13. For R. Harmon's comment about the Japanese view of the Waterloo Tractor Works, see *Waterloo Courier*, ca. May 1981. Hanson's remarks on Japan are from his speech before the ICED Outlook Conference, Bloomingdale, Ill., 8 June 1982.

11. For the quotations about Archie McArdell and the UAW strike fund at International Harvester, see *Times* (London), 19 April 1981.

12. The Rock River Insurance Company was organized on 22 December 1964; the Fulton Insurance Company, predecessor of the John Deere Insurance Company, was founded in 1929, and its entire assets were purchased by Deere in 1969; the Sierra General Life Insurance Company and the Tahoe Insurance Company were incorporated on 23 July 1973; Security-Gard Holdings, Inc., was incorporated on 9 July 1976. All these companies are wholly-owned subsidiaries of Deere & Company.

NOTES TO CHAPTER 16: CHARACTER OF A CORPORATION

1. "Who Runs America?", *U.S. News and World Report*, 18 May 1981. For the quotation about "funny money games," see John B. Schnapp, "Who for the Pedestal Now?" *New York Times*, 11 July 1982. For the quotation on the "corporate eye on the far horizon," see *Boston Globe*, 3 October 1982; for the quotation on "cash cows," see *Los Angeles Times*, 8 August 1982. For Deere's view of history, see *Management Today* (London), October 1973. For the quotation concerning "fallouts and marriages," see *Wall Street Journal*, 11 February 1983; for the "General Motors of the industry" quotation, see *Washington Post*, 6 March 1983; see also *Wall Street Transcript*, 28 March 1983. For comparison of Deere and Caterpillar labor relations and the comment on "instant heroes," see *Boston Globe*, 3 October 1982. For the quotation on "truly decentralized management," see *Crain's Chicago Business*, 15 November 1982.

2. For the West Wing addition, see *Fortune*, 9 October 1978; the "Office of the Year" citation is from *Administrative Management*, February 1980. For the comment on "the Medicis," see *Der Spiegel*, 17 August 1981. The article on Kevin Roche is in *Smithsonian*, August 1982; for quotation on a "sense of place," see Barrie B. Greenbie, *Spaces: Dimensions of the Human Landscape* (New Haven: Yale University Press, 1981). For the quotation on "big league," see *Fortune*, August 1976; see also, *Forbes*, 21 January 1980. For the "traditional American work ethic" quotation, see *Los Angeles Times*, 8 August 1982; for the comparison of Deere's and International Harvester's offices, see *Crain's Chicago Business*, 17 November 1982. See "Rediscovering the Factory," *Fortune*, 13 July 1981; for the comment on paternalism, see *Management Today* (London), October 1973; for the quotation on single-industry firms, see *Los Angeles Times*, 8 August 1982.

INDEX

Page numbers in italics indicate illustrations.